OZ *Clarke's*
ENCYCLOPEDIA
of WINE

TED SMART

AN A-Z GUIDE TO THE WINES OF THE WORLD

oz *Clarke's*
ENCYCLOPEDIA
of WINE

Gamay is the only grape allowed for red Beaujolais and produces one of the juiciest, most gulpable wines the world has to offer. Beaujolais has that rare quality for a red wine — it is wonderfully thirst-quenching.

The Whitlands vineyards, located at 230m (750ft) high up in the great Dividing Range in Victoria, Australia, provide some of the best grapes for Brown Brothers, the dominant producer in the King Valley.

A LITTLE, BROWN/WEBSTERS BOOK
This edition produced for The Book People Ltd, Hall Wood Avenue, Haydock, St Helens WA11 9UL by Websters International Publishers Limited, Axe and Bottle Court
70 Newcomen Street
London SE1 1YT
www.websters.co.uk
www.ozclarke.com

First published in 1999 by
Little, Brown and Company (UK)
Brettenham House
Lancaster Place
London WC2E 7EN

Copyright © 1999
Websters International Publishers
Text copyright © 1999 Oz Clarke
Maps and artwork copyright © 1999
and Websters International Publishers.

A CIP catalogue for this book is available from the British Library.

ISBN 0-316-85157-4

Colour separations by Technographics, Singapore
Printed and bound in Hong Kong by Dai Nippon Printing

Contributing Editors
Nicolas Belfrage MW, Stephen Brook, Jim Budd, Bob Campbell MW, Anthony Gismondi, James Halliday, Harold Heckle, James Lawther MW, Angela Lloyd, Richard Mayson, Dan McCarthy, Maggie McNie MW, Stuart Pigott, Norm Roby, Victor de la Serna.

Photography Mick Rock/Cephas Picture Library

Editorial Director/Chief Editor Fiona Holman
Art Director/Art Editor Nigel O'Gorman
Deputy Editor Ingrid Karikari
Editors Maggie Ramsay, Anne Lawrance
Assistant Designer Rachana Shah
Editorial Assistant Charlotte Raveney
Maps Andrew Thompson
Desktop Publishing Keith Bambury
Indexer Naomi Good
Production Karen Smith

Page 1: Pinot Noir excels in the Carneros District of California. These vines are at Saintsbury, one of the best wineries in Carneros.

Pages 2–3: New Zealand's Marlborough region has enjoyed spectacular success for quality wines since the 1970s. Inset: Marlborough's snappy, aromatic wines from Sauvignon Blanc brought the region worldwide fame.

CONTENTS

WINE TODAY
6–53

COUNTRY FEATURES

Many wines are aged for a time in oak, either old or new. New oak barriques of 225 litres (50 gallons), such as these in the barrel room at Cloudy Bay in Marlborough, New Zealand, are an integral part of many fashionable wineries. As well as having the same softening effect on wine as old oak, new oak gives its own flavour to the wine. Judging the precise length of new oak aging is a matter of repeated experimentation.

Since the 1950s stainless steel has revolutionized the winemaking process. These fermentation tanks at Vergelegen in South Africa are just the sort on which many a modern winemaker relies.

A-Z OF WINES, WINE REGIONS, PRODUCERS AND GRAPE VARIETIES 54–399

REGIONAL FEATURES

INTRODUCTION

Luscious-looking Shiraz grapes caught in the early morning — still damp with dew but ripe and ready for picking in a few hours' time.

St Peter's crossed keys and an elegant blue and gold flag — simple, unassuming, yet announcing the presence of Ch. Pétrus, one of the world's most famous red wines.

That's about as stony as a soil can get! Ata Rangi produces one of New Zealand's greatest Pinot Noirs from the free-draining soils of Martinborough.

SOMETIMES I STOP and ask myself — when was the last time I had a glass of bad wine? Not wine that is out of condition, or corked wine, or wine that I've left hanging around in the kitchen for too long — but poor, stale, badly made, unattractive wine? And unless I've been extremely unlucky in the previous month or so, I won't be able to remember. The standard of basic winemaking is now so high around the world that a wine-drinker need never taste a wine that is not at very least clean, honest and drinkable. It wasn't like that ten years ago. It certainly wasn't like that a generation past.

And then, I sometimes idly try to work out how many different grape varieties from how many different wine regions of the world I've tried during a typical wine-taster's week. During every week, there will be examples of grapes that I hardly know, from regions and villages that are often still no more than names on a map for me. And it wasn't like that a generation ago either.

OK, let's be specific. Last night at home I picked out a dozen bottles at random from the samples I am sent to taste. Among the more predictable wines like Australian Shiraz and Chilean Chardonnay — yet ten years ago we wouldn't be saying they were predictable and most shops wouldn't be stocking them — was a wild and wonderful bunch that made me marvel at how wide-reaching our world of wine is now. I had a Bonarda from Mendoza in Argentina — a wonderful,

perfumed red. I had a Carignan from Morocco — beefy, but good. I had a Tannat from Uruguay, a Cabernet Franc from California, a Primitivo from southern Italy, a Viognier from southern France — and so it went on. There were also bottles from Bordeaux, Burgundy, Champagne and Chianti — but they didn't hold centre stage, they didn't lord it over the other lesser known wines. Every wine in my random dozen had an equal right to be there, none was thought of as better solely because the name was famous. And if I had to say which I enjoyed the most? It was the Bonarda from Argentina — a virtually unknown grape, from a vast vineyard land that is only now waking up after a century of slumber — and it was the cheapest wine of the lot. And that is the joy of the modern world of wine.

For me, the thrilling thing about this modern world is that we now have choice — endless choice from a vast array of wines that gets bigger every year. And with choice comes excitement, challenge, but also confusion. But that's why this encyclopedia is here: to help you make sense of this cornucopia of flavours and delights that extends from the most famous and expensive wines of Bordeaux and Burgundy — the stuff of dreams rather than reality for most of us — down to the first nervous offerings of virgin vineyards from unsung valleys or the first faltering steps towards modernity from vineyards famous when the Romans stalked the land and preserved in time since then.

We, as wine-drinkers, should take some credit for this transformation. If we were not prepared to try new things, to take a bit of a risk with unknown areas and unknown grapes — winemakers would neither bother to resurrect old areas and plant new ones, nor bother to spread their activities beyond a few universally popular grape varieties. If we weren't prepared to be adventurous, wine companies would simply flood us with a sea of Chardonnay, Sauvignon, Cabernet, Merlot and Shiraz/Syrah, gaudy labels and fantasy names bedecking wines that made no attempt to taste different or individual. And of course, this encyclopedia wouldn't be necessary either.

But it is necessary. We are in the midst of a revolution in wine that is bringing together the best of the new and the old. Traditionalists are realizing that maybe the old ways are not always the best, that they can learn something from the brash young tyros whose conversation is laced with techno-babble, yet whose wines are suffused with a sweet perfumed fruit, the old-timers had never envisaged. And the modernists are quietly laying aside their reliance on cultured yeasts, scientific formulae and refrigerated stainless steel tanks, and listening with respect to the old farmers with their gnarled vines, and their quiet unhurried ways of letting a wine make itself as it will, rather than trying to impose a rigid framework on grapes used to freedom and self-expression.

The result is that the old masters in the heartland of classic wine – France, Germany and northern Italy, in particular – have surreptitiously learned the lessons of the new wave and applied them to their wines. These old classics, seasoned with techniques and attitudes from the New World, have never tasted better.

But what are these New World attitudes? They are the belief that there is never any excuse for incompetent wine-making, that effort and commitment, attention to detail, scrupulous cleanliness and hygiene in the winery, and techniques in the vineyard that have as their objective the best quality of fruit, regardless of what tradition dictates – that these attitudes make it possible to make pleasant wine any-where that the grape will grow. Consultant winemakers fre-quently schooled in the Antipodes, now flood Europe in particular, and their zeal has transformed the wasteland of undrinkable plonk that used to flow from the Mediterranean basin into the European Union's infamous 'Wine Lake'. And these roaming wine wizards have also transformed communities and attitudes. After generations of complacency and neglect, areas like Portugal's Ribatejo and Alentejo, Spain's La Mancha, France's Languedoc-Roussillon and Italy's far south are throbbing with self-belief again. Eastern Europe is being dragged out of vinous chaos and resignation by New World willpower and commitment. Further afield, Mexico, Uruguay, Brazil – even Argentina and Chile – needed these travelling maestros to show them how. And the result for us? More good wine, with more different flavours, from more grape varieties and from more hills and valleys, desert oases and coastal plains, than the world has ever experienced before. It's all there for us to

Tyrrell's Vat 47 Chardonnay from the Show Flat Vineyard in the famous Hunter Valley was the first Australian Chardonnay I tasted. My wine-drinking life would never be the same again.

enjoy as broadly and deeply as we want. And this encyclopedia is here to help you along the way, covering the grapes, the places, the vintages, the people and the flavours in an easy to use A–Z format. There's a massive amount of information in here, but we've made it as easy as can be to access and, I hope, as enjoyable as possible to read.

For help with that, may I thank both my editorial team in London and our various experts around the world who have kept me up to the mark on what's happening in their areas of expertise. Without their input, this undertaking would have been far too arduous for me to do alone. How many wines can a man taste in any one day? How many vintages can he cover in any one year? So I thank my eyes, my ears and my palate in every far flung corner of the world.

THE GLOBAL PICTURE

THE WORLD OF WINE is ever expanding, as the vine has settled happily and productively in regions far from its long-established Mediterranean habitats. The proliferation of wines on the shelves of retailers today may suggest that there is not a country in the world that does not produce wine, but a glance at the map below reveals a very different picture.

For the grape to truly flourish and ripen it needs warmth and water – but not too much of either. Such conditions are found primarily between the latitudes of 30 and 50°N and 30 and 40°S. Winemaking regions also tend to hug coastal areas and river valleys. The reason for this is that water affects the climate in a number of ways. It heats up and cools down more slowly than land, keeping temperatures moderate throughout the year. Some hotter vineyard regions benefit from a cooling sea breeze or coastal fog. Sea currents also affect vine-growing: the Gulf Stream warms the western coast of Europe, while a Pacific current running down from Alaska cools some of California's fine wine regions.

The best wines are made in climates where it is only just warm enough to ripen the grape. Gradual ripening, over a long growing season, allows the grapes to concentrate their flavours in the autumn sun. In an excessively hot climate the grapes will ripen too quickly, and the flavours will be shortlived. But if it is too cold, the grapes will not ripen at all.

In the cooler regions of Europe, growers seek to maximize exposure to the sun by planting their vineyards on the sunniest, south-facing slopes. In the New World, where the sun beats down relentlessly, many vineyards are angled away from the sun to prevent the grapes from baking in the heat. European vineyards are rarely planted more than 300m (1000ft) above sea level because it gets too cool, but some Californian and Australian vineyards are at 600m (2000ft) or more, precisely because the air is cooler.

Riesling vineyards rise steeply above the river Mosel at Bernkastel-Kues, Germany, meeting the sun face on and benefiting from the heat retained by the water.

Sunshine aplenty, but at an altitude of between 400 and 500m (around 1500ft) Australia's Clare Valley produces fine cool-climate wines, including Riesling.

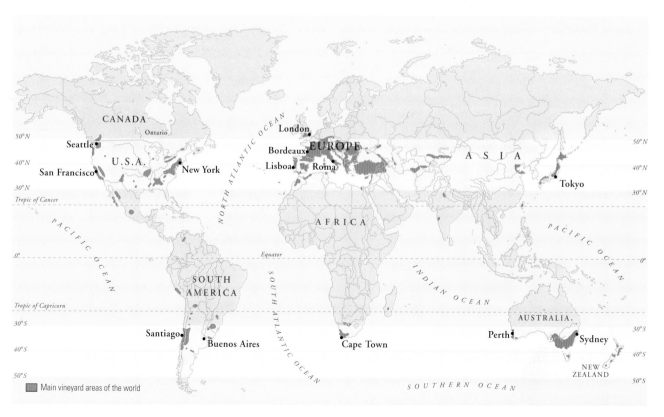

Main vineyard areas of the world

FROM VINE TO WINE

ONCE THE GRAPE'S BASIC climatic demands have been met, a number of other factors affect the flavour of the wine in the bottle you buy. Some are determined by local conditions, others can be controlled or adjusted by the winemaker. The result is an infinite number of variables, which ensure that no two wines, however similar, are absolutely identical.

Grape varieties

The most influential factor determining the flavour of the wine is the variety (or blend of varieties) of grape from which it is made.

When the great surge of interest in fine wine began to build up during the 1970s, and winemakers from all parts of the world looked for models to emulate, the styles which had most appeal were those of Bordeaux and Burgundy, and the sparkling wines of Champagne. So planting the same grape varieties that produced those wines was the first decision the new winemakers took.

In Europe, grape varieties suitable to various locations have gradually evolved over the centuries. Trial and error narrowed down the varieties that best fulfilled the demands of reliability, ability to ripen and economic yield – and these qualities did not always coincide with the best flavoured grapes. The grapes that made it through this empirical selection process were Cabernet Sauvignon, Merlot, Sauvignon Blanc and Sémillon in Bordeaux; Pinot Noir and Chardonnay in Burgundy and Champagne. These are the names that appear on the majority of wines from Australia, California and New Zealand, the new classic wine regions. California was lucky to have ancient plantings of Zinfandel/Primitivo from southern Italy, and Australia benefited from ancient Shiraz/Syrah from France.

When California's Cabernets, Australia's Chardonnays and New Zealand's Sauvignon Blancs began to gain international reputations, their presence soon became too strong to be ignored. They were not the same as the French wines they had tried to emulate – but they were often more approachable, with distinct flavours of the grapes whose names they bore, giving buyers a clear indication of what to expect.

At the same time, forward-looking winemakers, in Tuscany and elsewhere in Europe, began to use Cabernet Sauvignon and other classic grapes in areas where they were excluded from classification under traditional wine laws. Cutting through the restrictions of local regulations and the hierarchy of regional naming, they were able to make better, more internationally appealing wines.

The most famous grape varieties, names seen on the labels of thousands of wines, are the red Cabernet Sauvignon and white Chardonnay, but there are hundreds of others. Some European wines contain blends of several varieties, some of them unique to their area. Many modern winemakers, notably in southern Italy, Portugal and eastern Europe, are beginning to explore the potential of native grapes, and the new and exciting flavours they offer.

Most good winemakers will tell you that the very best they can do is bring out the full potential of the grapes. An attentive winemaker can make decent, fruity wine from unexceptional grapes and a talented one can produce stunning wine from top-quality raw materials – but no-one can make great wine from unhealthy grapes. One of the great advances of the past 30 years has been the research into clonal selection. Growers have been able to develop certain characteristics (early ripening or disease resistance, for example) within a variety. Anyone looking to plant a vineyard can now choose not only the variety but also the clone of that variety most suited to their needs.

Location and soil

The exact valley or hillside where the vines are grown may be sheltered by a forest or warmed by a lake; such local features define the mesoclimate of the vineyard. This definition is the first step in accepting the idea of terroir, the strong sense of place that the traditional winemakers of Europe believe to be the purest expression of character in a wine.

The soil that nourishes the grapes is considered by some producers, particularly in the classic French regions of Bordeaux and Burgundy, to contribute 80 per cent of the quality. Indeed, tasters sometimes claim to detect iron or flint flavours in certain wines. It is true that some grapes prefer slate (Riesling) or gravel (Cabernet Sauvignon), but

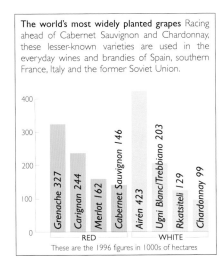

The world's most widely planted grapes Racing ahead of Cabernet Sauvignon and Chardonnay, these lesser-known varieties are used in the everyday wines and brandies of Spain, southern France, Italy and the former Soviet Union.

Grenache 327, Carignan 244, Merlot 162, Cabernet Sauvignon 146 (RED); Airén 423, Ugni Blanc/Trebbiano 203, Rkatsiteli 129, Chardonnay 99 (WHITE). These are the 1996 figures in 1000s of hectares

The terra rossa, or red earth, of Coonawarra, South Australia; this fertile topsoil over free-draining limestone is famous for producing top-quality red wines.

In Burgundy's Côte de Beaune, Pinot Noir vines are traditionally kept low (left); high training with a split canopy (right) exposes the vine to more sunlight, increasing yield.

both are free-draining soils, which supports the alternative, modernist view, that soil is simply a matter of water supply – it either holds water or allows it to drain away. In Europe's cooler, damper regions, a well-drained soil is essential, not only to prevent the vine from becoming waterlogged, but also because a drier soil will be warmer.

Most of the action takes place way below the surface, as the vine sends down deep roots in search of nutrients, but surface characteristics may also affect the ripening of the grapes. Light-coloured soils, such as chalk and limestone, reflect heat back on to the grapes, while slate and other surface stones store heat for chilly autumn evenings.

Despite the best efforts of Australian and Californian winemakers, the classic grape varieties grown in different conditions do not produce fruit with the same flavours. Their vineyards are warmer, their soil more fertile and/or drier. However, when planting their vines they are not tied by tradition: they are able and willing to experiment with a whole new range of viticultural techniques.

Viticulture

Sounds technical, but by this we mean what happens to the grapes in the vineyard. Are they planted close together to conserve heat or far apart, which not only allows cooling winds to fan the vines, but also permits mechanical cultivation? Are the vines grown close to the soil for warmth (but not so low they are vulnerable to frost) or trained high to prevent over-ripening? How hard are they pruned? How are the vineyards fertilized and irrigated (if at all)?

The first decision is whether to aim for a high or low yield. This is a simple trade-off between quantity and quality. Maximizing the number of grape bunches each vine can produce means lots of wine can be made, but lower yields result in grapes with more concentrated flavours. France's quality wine producers rely upon restraint of yield to intensify grape flavour. After careful pruning, the hostility of nature is all that is needed to limit yields in some places, but in warm and fertile valleys controlled irrigation, drainage and shade are the keys to success. A small crop will also ripen faster, so where lack of sun is a problem, yield reduction seems to make sense. But much of the best wine from America and Australia comes from vineyards where heat and sun are in plentiful supply; why restrict yield here? Depending on his or her answer to this question, the winemaker will take appropriate steps in the vineyard.

Over the generations, European producers have developed systems of pruning, trellising and training vines to suit their local conditions. In the hot, arid lands around the Mediterranean, vines are planted fairly far apart – to allow each plant a sip of the meagre water ration – and allowed to develop floppy canopies of foliage to keep the grapes cool and restrict yield. Traditional plantings on such systems in the warm, fertile conditions often found in Australia, California, South America and South Africa usually yield excellent results. However, these warm, fertile conditions would be unlikely to suit the ruthless pruning systems practised in cool, damp areas like Bordeaux and Champagne, because the vines' response would be to throw out ever more shoots and develop jungle-like foliage. The science of canopy management, developed since the 1970s, includes a range of techniques designed to prevent over-vigorous foliage from interfering with ripening.

Canopy management alters the number and position of vine shoots and bunches to maximize exposure of fruit and leaves to the sun. Techniques include winter and summer pruning, shoot thinning and leaf removal, and trellis systems that actually encourage the vine to throw a big crop and lots of foliage. Various methods have been devised to pull the leaves away from the fruit and allow the sun to reach the grapes.

Whereas irrigation is forbidden in the traditional quality vineyards of Europe, in many of the newer wine regions rainfall is in short supply and irrigation is regarded as the ultimate grape growers' tool, controlled by continual fine adjustments judged necessary by the winemaker. All young vines need water, since an overstressed young vine won't develop into a healthy plant. If you plant on a free-draining soil in a hot climate, you have to irrigate because otherwise the vine would lose so much moisture through its leaves that it wouldn't survive. If you plant on heavy fertile soils (unlike those of the great vineyards of Europe), the vines have a better chance of survival when water is in short supply and the crop can be controlled by withholding water. At a certain point in the grapes' ripening, irrigation is cut back to avoid diluting the juice. But if the weather gets very hot the grapes' ripening system will shut down – the vine needs irrigation just to keep it going.

Finally, once the grapes are ripe, the winemaker may decide to harvest at night when temperatures are cooler, so the grapes do not spoil before they get to the winery.

Consultant winemakers, such as Michel Rolland (left), share their knowledge and experience with other wineries; here he is at Casa Lapostolle, Chile.

Training techniques allow optimum ripening conditions. In his Adelaide Hills vineyard, Brian Croser of Petaluma shows the canopy held aloft by catch wires.

One of Australia's hardest-working flying winemakers, Kym Milne MW, assesses some of the wines he has made in southern Italy.

Vintage

The harvest of the grapes each year is known as the vintage. The term vintage is therefore generally used to refer to the year in which the wine was made. Not every bottle of wine declares its vintage. Inexpensive wines may be a blend of wines from different years. Producers of Champagne and other sparkling wines make a standard house style called 'non-vintage' or NV. This is meant to be the same year after year, so the rich wine from a warm year may be added to the lean wine from a colder one to maintain consistency.

Traditionally, the world's most sought-after wines come from places where the grapes are poised on a knife-edge of ripening or failing every year, like Bordeaux, Burgundy, Champagne and Germany's Mosel and Rhine valleys. These are the regions where vintages really matter, because the wines can be so different from one vintage to the next, ranging in quality from triumphant to disastrous. If the grapes are not ripe enough they will lack sugar and flavour; too ripe, and they will lack acidity, freshness and aroma. The winemaker's decision as to when to harvest can be crucial: a few days' wait for the grapes to reach optimum ripeness leaves them vulnerable to being caught in a downpour. In regions with a more predictable climate, the vintage year on the bottle is really no more than an indication of the wine's age.

In the winery

The next significant factor in the character of the wine is the winemaking process. This is the point at which the natural events of fermentation are shaped and controlled with a view to creating a particular end product. The concept of the winemaker as an interventionist who determines the character of the wine is a modern one. Earlier generations simply followed the traditions of their region; wine was more or less left to make itself.

Flying winemakers

Some of the most remarkable examples of winemaker intervention are embodied in the so-called flying winemakers. Often Australian-trained, they jet in to introduce modern regimes and impose higher standards on a winery in some generally underrated part of the wine world, and then jet off to do the same elsewhere. They may seem like gypsies, but the wines of southern France, southern Italy, eastern Europe and many other previously downtrodden regions have been transformed by their work.

THE ORGANIC APPROACH

The organic movement gains momentum every year, supported not only by altruistic environmentalists whose main concern is the future of the planet, but also by growers who are seeing a deterioration in the quality of their soil and consumers who are beginning to make the connection between what they eat and drink and their health. Organic wine, like other organic foodstuffs, is made without synthetic fertilizers, herbicides, fungicides or pesticides, or artificial preservatives. Minute traces of these chemicals, it is argued, have the potential to cause long-term health problems; another theory holds that toxic build-up may contribute to many of the food and drink allergies that are increasingly common.

Over the past 40 years, most crops – including grapes – have been grown with the aid of chemical fertilizers and sprays to encourage a large, disease-free, reliable harvest. Over time, the soil, forced to overproduce, will become weak and dependent on its chemical fix; chemical residues poison the tiniest micro-organisms at the start of the food chain, thus upsetting the natural balance of the ecosystem; certain vineyard pests build up a tolerance to insecticide sprays; and chemicals filter down to pollute the water table. The alternative organic techniques begin with healthy soil, nourished by compost or animal manures. Crop rotation, one of the basic tenets of organic farming, is not an option in the vineyard, but cover crops such as clover both protect the soil and provide it with nitrogen (green manure), while companion planting of vegetables, fruit, flowers and herbs create biological diversity and encourage insects, birds and animals to feed off vineyard pests.

Grape-growers face an additional hazard: their fruit is prone to mildew and black rot. Depending on local organic regulations, they may be permitted to use Bordeaux mixture (a naturally occurring chemical, copper sulphate) to combat the rot, but in practice, organic viticulture is most common in hot dry regions where fungal infections are less of a threat.

The term 'organic' can be used only on wines approved by a recognized certification body, such as the Soil Association in the UK, Terre et Vie in France or Ecovin in Germany. These in turn are co-ordinated by the International Federation of Organic Movements (IFOAM). A far greater number of growers follow broadly organic principles yet find the stringent regulations impracticable; they practise eco-friendly viticulture and recognize the need to reduce chemicals in the wine, but cannot subscribe to an organization that would discredit them for using chemicals in an emergency. Among these are Mas de Daumas Gassac in Languedoc-Roussillon, Domaine de Trévallon in Provence, Dr Loosen in Mosel-Saar-Ruwer, Robert Mondavi in California and Penfolds in Australia.

In theory, organic wines taste different. Healthier vines produce healthier grapes and the lower yield should lead to more intense flavours. Neither the soil nor the resulting wines have been 'standardized' by chemical additives, so organic wines are more honest characters, true to their roots, their region of origin, grape variety and the care in their making. In practice, some organic wines are worthy but dull, others are just plain bad, while some of the greatest wines in the world are a long way from organic.

BIODYNAMICS

Biodynamic winemakers take working with nature one stage further. They are organic, and they also use astronomy and astrology to match the vine and its growth cycles with the natural rhythms of the earth, the moon and the planets. They also practise homeopathy; plant extracts are used in minute doses to replace missing 'energies' in the soil and increase its fertility, and as sprays to protect against pests and diseases. The Demeter Association certifies biodynamic wines internationally.

VEGETARIAN WINES

Wine is made from grape juice, so why isn't it all vegetarian? The process of fining – clearing the wine – can create qualms for vegetarians, since there is no way of knowing whether a wine has been clarified with bentonite (a powdery earth), egg whites, casein or gelatin (derived from animals) or isinglass (from fish). Fining is not always necessary: given the right conditions, wine can fall bright by itself.

RED AND ROSÉ WINES

WINE IS CREATED BY fermentation – yeasts turning grape sugar into alcohol. It's as simple as that, and if you bought a few bunches of ripe grapes, squashed them, put the resulting goo into a bucket and left it somewhere warm like the airing cupboard – well, a wine of sorts would almost certainly be produced. It might taste more like vinegar, but technically it would be wine.

This simple chemical reaction has been refined by hundreds of years of experience and, more recently, by the application of high technology and microbiological know-

how. It is difficult to generalize about winemaking styles and methods in countries and states as diverse as New Zealand and Texas, Argentina and Tasmania. What France or Italy may regard as old hat, the wineries of Brazil or Mexico may barely have begun to think about. At every stage, numerous fine-tunings occur and even the most technocratic winemaker indulges in little personal adjustments – in all but the drabbest corporate winemaker lurks an artist's soul – all of which affect the final character of the wine. But some techniques are standard around the globe.

Crushing

The winemaking process begins when the grapes are brought in from the vineyard. With the exception of Beaujolais and a few other wines using the 'whole bunch' method of fermentation (also called carbonic maceration, see box below), red grapes are put through a crusher to break their skins and release the juice. The crushing machine usually also removes the stems, as these have a tough, tannic taste, but with some grapes, notably Syrah, a proportion is left on to produce a firmer wine. The resulting 'must' – pulpy mush of flesh and juice and skins (which give red and rosé wines their colour) – is pumped into a big vat, ready for fermentation.

Fermentation

Fermentation is caused by the action of yeasts on the sugars in the grape juice. Yeasts are naturally present in the winery, but increasingly, cultivated yeasts are used to ensure a controlled fermentation. At this stage, in the cooler areas of Europe, the addition of sugar is permitted if the sugar content of the grapes is too low, to increase alcoholic strength, a process called chaptalization. Similarly, in very hot regions, a little acid may be added if the grapes are very ripe.

For rosé wines, the fermenting juice is drawn off the skins after a day or so and the

The fermenting juice is continually pumped over the 'cap' of grape skins in order to extract maximum colour and flavour from the skins. In France, this process is known as remontage; this is how it is done at Mas de Daumas Gassac, Languedoc-Roussillon, famous for a rich, Cabernet Sauvignon-based wine.

winemaking process then follows the same path as for white wines (see page 16).

Fermentation lasts from a few days to two weeks, depending on the yeast culture and

cellar temperature. Temperature control is one of the most crucial tools available to the modern winemaker. Excess heat destroys freshness and fruit flavour, and can disrupt the fermentation process itself. Understanding the importance of temperature and the introduction of stainless steel tanks and refrigeration in the 1950s were major breakthroughs in winemaking. Should the winemaker choose a cultured or a wild yeast? European wine regions such as Burgundy have developed populations of beneficial wild yeast strains over the centuries, but newer wine regions have native yeasts that may or may not produce clean-tasting wine.

CARBONIC MACERATION

If you want to make a red wine that can be drunk young, with plenty of easy fruit and very little tannin, you can adopt a technique known as carbonic maceration. The method is widely used in Beaujolais, and involves placing uncrushed grapes inside a container such that the weight crushes the lowest bunches, setting off fermentation and releasing carbon dioxide which blankets the top layer and encourages the uncrushed berries at the top of the container to begin to ferment inside their skins, maximizing flavour and colour, but minimizing tannin extraction. The result is a very fruity, fresh wine for early drinking.

Throughout the process, the grape skins surge upwards, pushed by the stream of carbon dioxide released during fermentation. At the top, they form a thick 'cap' which must be mixed back in continually by punching down or pumping the juice over the cap, so that the wine can extract maximum colour and flavour and avoid air becoming trapped between the skins and the wine. Many red wines, including all those intended for long aging, are left to macerate on the skins for some days or weeks after fermentation is complete, in order to extract all the flavour, colour and tannin from the skins and pips; long maceration also softens the harsh tannins. A full-bodied red wine may macerate for seven to 28 days.

Pressing

When red wine fermentation is finished – all the sugar having been converted to alcohol – the wine is drawn off the vat, and the residue of skins is pressed, to produce a dark, tannic wine called 'press wine'. This may be used for blending purposes and added to the free-run wine to create a deeper, tougher style of wine, or it may be stored apart – it all depends on what the winemaker wants.

Malolactic fermentation

Technically, the wine is now made – but it is pretty raw stuff. To begin with, it probably has a sharp, green-apple acidity. This is reduced through a second fermentation – the 'malolactic' – which converts that tart malic acid into mild lactic acid. Almost all reds undergo this second fermentation, becoming softer and rounder in the process. It occurs naturally when temperatures rise in the spring following the harvest, but is often induced soon after the alcoholic fermentation, by raising the temperature in the cellar and by adding the appropriate bacteria.

Blending

Next the winemaker has the opportunity to alter the wine radically by blending the contents of two or more vats together. That could mean combining different grape varieties to add a whole new dimension of flavour. Some wines use only one variety, but blend grapes from different vineyards. This may be done in order to achieve a consistent style, or to balance the varying characteristics of the grapes.

Maturing

The decision on whether to mature a wine in stainless steel or oak is of enormous stylistic importance. Stainless steel (or concrete) is

Oak barrels add a new dimension to many modern wines – the wood interacts with the maturing wine, creating rich, toasty vanilla flavours. The Wolf Blass winery in Barossa Valley, South Australia, is well known for its oaky red wines, matured in these new oak barriques (small barrels).

inert and amenable to accurate temperature control, which allows the fruit flavours free rein. Small oak barrels allow controlled oxygenation and benign aging of what might otherwise be unduly aggressive wines.

If the wine is to be drunk young it is put in large tanks of stainless steel or concrete to rest a short while before bottling. Almost all rosé is treated in this way. Red wine for aging, however, is stored – often in small oak barrels (barriques) – for anything from six months to over two years. If the barriques are new or only once-used, they impart flavours of spice, herbs, perfume and vanilla as well as adding to the wine's tannic structure.

Racking

During this pre-bottling period, dead yeast cells and other solids fall to the bottom of the tank or barrel. These are separated from the wine by racking – transferring the wine to clean barrels or tanks – which may take place several times before bottling. Racking naturally mixes oxygen with the wine and this usually clears out any sulphuric or yeasty flavours. For cheaper wines, the same effect is achieved through filtration, but here some of the wine's body and flavour is lost as well. Pinot Noir, in particular, reacts badly to filtration.

Fining and filtering

With most top-quality wines, the last stage before bottling is 'fining': removing any particles held in suspension by means of a clarifying agent. The agent – which may be egg white, bentonite, isinglass or gelatin – is spread over the surface and, as it falls down through the wine, it collects all impurities with it. Most other wines are filtered; those for immediate drinking often receive quite a fierce filtration to ensure no deposit forms in the bottle. After fining, some of the best wines are also filtered, but very lightly, as preservation of their personality is all important. Many top red wines are *not* filtered – and a few are neither fined nor filtered – and so develop a harmless deposit in the bottle.

Bottling

For best results, bottling should be cold and sterile, with an inert gas like nitrogen or, for fine wines, carbon dioxide, introduced into the bottle ahead of the wine so that when the cork goes in there is no oxygen in the bottle. Some everyday wines are either 'hot-bottled' or pasteurized. Both treatments involve heating the wine; they ensure its stability but they detract from its personality and make any further development impossible.

Choosing red and rosé wines

ONCE, CHOOSING WINE was a simple matter of selecting what you could afford from the limited range of classic styles that were available outside their region of origin: Bordeaux, Burgundy, Champagne and Rhône from France, Mosel and hock from Germany, Rioja and sherry from Spain and port from Portugal. Today the choice is almost limitless, as winemakers around the world are experimenting with grape varieties, blends and techniques in both vineyard and winery. They may take a classic style or use a classic grape as a starting point, but they often find that the results are very different in their new soil and climate conditions – and this is the springboard for further experiments and diversification. Choosing wine may be trickier these days – but it's far more fun, especially with a few pointers to style and taste.

Red Bordeaux-style/ Cabernet Sauvignon blends

The style may be one of the world's classics, but this example from Catena, one of Argentina's most progressive producers ❶, proves that intense, blackcurranty wines do not necessarily come only from the ancient châteaux of the Médoc. However, the red wines of Bordeaux in France are the originals. These tend to be harshly tannic at first, but they mature over 10–20 years, when the rich blackcurrant fruit is balanced by a heady scent of cedarwood, cigar boxes and pencil shavings.

If you cannot regularly indulge in fine, red Bordeaux, the Cabernet Sauvignon grape, alone or blended with Merlot or other varieties, enjoys worldwide popularity. It is sometimes made to be drinkable young, or it may be aged in oak barrels to add spice and richness. A number of super-Tuscans are based on Cabernet, with a small proportion of Sangiovese. California Cabernets are powerfully flavoursome and well structured; US Bordeaux-style blends are often labelled Meritage. Chilean examples can have intense flavours and gentle tannins; Australia produces ripe-tasting Cabernets; and in New Zealand you will find blackcurrant fruit and often a taste of green leaf. Spain and Portugal both produce a few ripe but densely textured examples. Eastern Europe specializes in simple, budget-priced versions, and the southern French vins de pays made from Cabernet Sauvignon are generally good value.

Red Bordeaux-style/Merlot blends

Merlot is the dominant grape in Bordeaux's Pomerol and St-Émilion wines and appears in most Bordeaux and Bordeaux-style blends. It produces rich, juicy wines with flavours of blackcurrant, plum and mint, and is in demand wherever winemakers want to create a Bordeaux-style wine that can be drunk young. However, at its best, such as this St-Émilion Grand Cru from Ch. Angélus ❷, the wine will become richer after 10–20 years in bottle. Spain blends Tempranillo and Cabernet with good, soft-textured results.

Juicy, fruity reds/Merlot

This Merlot from the Santa Isabel estate of Viña Casablanca in Chile ❸ is typical of the style favoured by modern winemakers and wine drinkers – refreshing, full of vibrant fruit flavours, easy to drink with or without food, and with the gum-drying toughness of tannin kept to a minimum. Hungarian, Bulgarian and Romanian Merlots are simple wines in this style, Italian examples are often even softer, quaffing wines. Some California Merlot is made in this light style, as is some Zinfandel. Australia produces fruity Merlot and similar Grenache for everyday drinking, and Spain lays on the fruit in the Navarra, La Mancha and Valdepeñas regions with both the Garnacha (Spanish for Grenache) and Tempranillo grape varieties. Argentina does a good line in smooth, fruity Tempranillo, ultra-fruity Bonarda and juicy Malbec.

Juicy, fruity reds/Beaujolais

Beaujolais in France, home of the juicy, gulpable Gamay grape with its cherry-sharp fruit flavour, was the original model for this style, but to find it you need to look for a decent producer, such as this Beaujolais-Villages from Gilles Roux ❹. Elsewhere in France, Côtes du Ventoux, some Côtes du Rhône and vins de pays from all over the South fit the juicy, fruity bill, and Gamay de Touraine and Gamay d'Anjou from the Loire Valley are similar to Beaujolais, but cheaper.

Austrian Blauer Zweigelt or St Laurent and Italian Schiava/Vernatsch can be good and juicy. South Africa makes good 'young-vatted' Pinotage, like a smoky Beaujolais. Washington State Lemberger or Grenache is light and tasty.

Red Burgundy/Pinot Noir

In Burgundy the Pinot Noir grape produces some of the world's most superb wines: this one is from the vineyard of les Chaumes in the village of Vosne-Romanée ❺. Good examples are perfumed with strawberry, raspberry or cherry fruit and feel silky in your mouth. The best are frighteningly expensive and after five to ten years the initial strawberry and cherry fruit develops additional aromas of truffles, game and decaying autumn leaves. Sounds peculiar, but one taste and you'll be hooked.

France also has a lighter style in red Sancerre from the Loire Valley. California, particularly the Carneros and Russian River districts, produces Pinot Noir wines with bright, fragrant fruit; lighter styles are a speciality in Oregon. New Zealand is producing ripe, supple, stylish examples and Australia is improving fast. Chile's Pinot Noirs usually have loads of vibrant jellied fruit flavour. South Africa produces a small number of fairly impressive Pinot Noirs, though the fruit is often swamped by the flavour of oak barrels. In Germany the grape is known as Spätburgunder: the best examples, usually from Baden, are fragrant and carefully oaked. However, much commercial Spätburgunder is sweetish and thin. Switzerland's Pinots can be light and perfumed. Romania makes coarse but enjoyable budget versions.

Herby, 'dry' reds/Sangiovese

The most widely planted red grape in Italy, Sangiovese shows all the aromas and flavours typical of Italian wines: herbs, raisins, cherries and a hint of almonds. It is the main grape of Chianti and also of many super-Tuscans such as La Gioia ❻. Deeper and tougher wines come from Brunello di Montalcino and Vino Nobile di Montepulciano, lighter versions from Rosso di Montalcino and Rosso di Montepulciano. What these wines lack in initial fruity appeal is more than made up for by their success as partners for food.

The style is not the sole preserve of the Sangiovese grape: southern Italian reds from Puglia – made with grapes such as Primitivo and Negroamaro – give you the herb and raisin flavours with less aggression. Similar, somewhat fruitier flavours are found in wines made from the Barbera grape, such as Barbera d'Alba, and in top Valpolicella Classico, which uses a blend of grape varieties local to north-eastern Italy. The weird and wonderful Amarone and Recioto della Valpolicella styles made from partially dried grapes are particularly intriguing, with added dollops of chocolate and plum. Nebbiolo is the fierce grape of Piedmont, responsible for the wines of Barolo and Barbaresco. These need at least five years to mature before they reveal their complex flavours: you might find tobacco, chocolate, prunes and rose petals.

The nearest France gets to this style is in Corbières, down towards the Pyrenees. The Sangiovese grown in Argentina bears no more than a passing resemblance to its Tuscan cousins, but the Californian love affair with all things Italian has led to two styles of Sangiovese: an easy-drinking, everyday wine and a sturdier, age-worthy version, sometimes blended with Cabernet Sauvignon.

Spicy reds/Syrah or Shiraz

The grape known as Syrah in France and Shiraz in Australia is loved for its dense, heart-warming, gloriously rich flavours of berries, black pepper and chocolate, ideal for barbecues or winter evenings. Penfolds Grange, a rich Australian Shiraz ❼, is the modern archetype, and you can get good Australian examples at all price levels. The Syrah wines from the northern Rhône Valley in France known as Hermitage, Côte-Rôtie and Cornas are dark, herbal, pungent and smoky; Crozes-Hermitage and St-Joseph are generally lighter and cheaper. In the southern Rhône, where Grenache, Mourvèdre, Cinsaut and Carignan may be included in the blend, the wines of Châteauneuf-du-Pape, Gigondas and Vacqueyras can be excellent. For good value try Côtes du Rhône-Villages, or Syrah Vin de Pays d'Oc, Fitou or Minervois from southern France.

In California the Rhône grapes are high-fashion and often expensive, but Zinfandel made in the powerful style is spicy stuff at a better price. Portugal offers good value with blends of its own grape varieties from the Douro Valley, Alentejo, Ribatejo and Alenquer. In Spain, try wines from Toro and Valdepeñas. Mexico produces Petite Sirah, which is not the same as Syrah, but is made in a similar style. Chile is producing soupy, rich mouthfuls with the Carmenère grape.

Dry rosé

Bright and breezy freshness – a cool drink on a scorching day – is the point of good rosé, rather than any specific flavour. Most countries make a dry rosé, and any red grape will do, but Grenache and Cinsaut make some of the best. Grenache makes beguiling fruity rosés that pack an unexpected alcoholic punch in Lirac, Tavel and Côtes du Lubéron in the southern Rhône Valley. Spain also uses Grenache (called Garnacha here) for some tasty rosado versions of Rioja and Navarra; Gran Feudo ❽ is a good example. Good dry pinks also come from Cabernet Franc in the Loire, and Merlot and Cabernet in Bordeaux, and Pinot Noir does well in Alsace. Southern Italy is well known for fairly gutsy dry rosés, north-east Italy for delicate ones.

Sweetish rosé

California has its 'blush' Zinfandel, which is white with just a hint of pink, but is likely to be rather sweeter than you would expect. One of the best known is Mondavi's Woodbridge White Zinfandel ❾. Elsewhere the Loire Valley and Portugal produce off-dry rosés without much merit.

WHITE WINES

THE CREATION OF ANY wine begins in the vineyard, but the winemaking process proper starts with the annual grape harvest. When it comes to white wines, this involves choices: pick early and make a snappily fresh wine for quick-drinking, or pursue ripeness until the grapes fill with sugar, or, in certain parts of the world, leave the grapes to overripen and hope for an attack of the sweetness-intensifying noble rot.

In the warmer wine regions of the world, the sunshine that has ripened the grapes becomes the grapes' enemy as soon as they have been picked. White grapes are particularly vulnerable to oxidation, which spoils fruit flavours. One of the commonest solutions is to harvest at night or in the early morning when the air is at its coolest. You can then pile your grapes into a refrigerated truck if the winery is a long way away, and you can sprinkle antioxidants such as sulphur dioxide or ascorbic acid over the bunches to keep them in good condition. Some producers crush the grapes immediately and chill the resulting must at the vineyard.

Crushing

Grapes destined for white wines generally need more careful handling than those for reds. The grapes should be crushed without too much force, and may then be left to steep for a while: juice, skin, pulp, pips and all, so that maximum grape flavour can be extracted from the skins where all the varietal flavour and character lie. This 'skin contact' may be as brief as an hour or as long as a day for white wine, and will vary between grape varieties, and also according to what is likely to happen to the wine afterwards: whether it will go into a new oak barrel or a steel tank, for instance.

Pressing

If the juice is not intended to stay in contact with the skins, pressing may form part of the same process as crushing. The best quality juice emerges from the first, very gentle pressing. Further pressing will extract harsher elements from the grape's skin as well as more juice – a bottled wine may be a blend of wines from different stages of pressing, according to the winemaker's requirements.

Chardonnay grapes arriving at the Robert Mondavi Winery in the Napa Valley, California, are moved quickly but gently towards the crusher-destemmer. The juice will be handled with care and kept cool throughout the fermentation process to retain its fresh, fruity flavours in the finished wine.

Fermentation

Once the juice has settled its solids, or been filtered or centrifuged to quicken the process (although filtration will invariably remove some potential flavour as well), it is pumped into a tank – generally of stainless steel, if the objective is to make a young fresh white. A suitable yeast culture is normally added to ensure the fermentation is both efficient and controlled and, in certain cases, to create particular nuances of flavour. Alternatively, wild yeasts may be allowed to work.

The advantage of stainless steel is that it is the easiest material to keep sterile-clean, and the easiest in which to control temperature. The majority of white wines are fermented at cool temperatures to give a fruitier, fresher style, around 15–18°C (60–64°F), with the temperature kept down by running cold water or a coolant through insulated jackets or through coils within the tanks. For the finest white wines, the juice is fermented at up to 25°C (77°F) in an oak barrel, which imparts a rich, mellow flavour even to a dry wine.

Clear juice, free of sediment or any remaining yeast, with a blanket of gas on top, can be kept for some time before fermentation. This enables producers of aromatic white wines to ferment their wines in batches to put on sale at regular intervals, meaning that the wine is always as fresh as possible, and a fragrant Muscat bought a year after the harvest can be as grapy and good as though the grapes came in from the vineyards yesterday.

Malolactic fermentation

After the primary (alcoholic) fermentation, there is a second fermentation, the malolactic, in which green, appley, malic acid is turned into soft, creamy, lactic acid. Most classic whites undergo the malolactic, but as it reduces fresh-fruit character and tangy acidity it is often prevented in modern, fruit-driven whites, by the use of filtration, low temperature or sulphur dioxide.

Maturing

Use of new oak barriques (225-litre barrels) is increasingly common, not just for aging the best wines of Burgundy and Bordeaux, but also for the sturdier styles of white wine, particularly Chardonnay, from all over the

In New Zealand, as almost everywhere in the world that white wine is made, the juice is fermented in large, refrigerated, stainless steel tanks.

world. Marsanne may be aged in oak in the South of France and Australia, Macabeo (Viura) in Spain reacts well to oak, and the great Sauvignon-Sémillon dry whites of Pessac-Léognan, as well as the luscious sweet wines of Sauternes, are generally fermented and aged in oak. New oak gives a toasty, vanilla taste to wine and these days almost every bottle of Australian (or Californian) Chardonnay will have seen some oak during its fermentation and/or maturation. A final blend may consist of batches of wine which have spent time in new, one-year-old and two-year-old oak barrels, as well as some which have stayed in stainless steel. If the barrels are new, or fairly new, they give a strong, creamy or spicy character to the wine. Older barrels merely soften and round out the wine due to the slight contact with oxygen. This maturation can take up to 18 months but, in general, six months is quite long enough for a white wine.

Bottling

A wine for drinking young is generally stored in a stainless steel tank for a short time, racked off its lees if necessary, fined, filtered to produce a star-bright, stable liquid and then bottled – often at only six months old or less – to maximize its fresh, fruity character.

Ideally, the very best wines – having been matured in oak – are hardly filtered at all, since the process also removes a little of the flavour. Sterile conditions are crucial to avoid bacterial spoilage and sulphur dioxide is generally added as an antioxidant.

SULPHUR DIOXIDE

The antiseptic, antioxidant, preservative properties of sulphur dioxide make it invaluable in the winery, but an excess results in an unpleasant smell and taste in the wine, and in some people can cause an allergic reaction – or at least a headache. Before fermentation, sulphur dioxide may be used to kill off wild yeasts and bacteria to allow the flavours of the chosen cultured yeasts to prevail, although the cultured yeasts used by many modern winemakers have reduced the need for sulphur at this stage. If sulphur dioxide is added while the wine is fermenting, again, it will kill yeasts and thus halt fermentation to make a sweet wine. It may also be added at bottling stage to kill any stray organisms and prevent spoilage. Modern winemakers have dramatically reduced the amounts of sulphur used.

MAKING SWEET WINES

White wines achieve a measure of sweetness in various ways. The great sweet wines of Sauternes and the Loire Valley, Alsace's Vendange Tardive and Sélection de Grains Nobles, Germany's Auslese, Beerenauslese and Trockenbeerenauslese, and the late-harvest wines occasionally found in Australia, New Zealand and the United States, are made from grapes that are left on the vine well after the normal harvest, so they are overripe and full of sugar; they also begin to shrivel, which concentrates the sugar.

If conditions are right, they may be attacked by a horrid-looking fungus called 'noble rot' (*Botrytis cinerea*). This sucks out the water, concentrating the sugar even more. During fermentation, the sugar is converted by yeasts into alcohol: the more sugar in the grape juice, the higher the potential alcoholic strength. But yeasts can only work in alcohol levels of up to about 15 per cent (and frequently the winemaker will add a little sulphur dioxide to stop fermentation at around 12–13 per cent). So when the yeasts stop, the rest of the grape sugar remains in the wine as sweetness – full of potential lusciousness. The distinctive flavour of botrytis is much sought after by dessert wine producers; today's winemakers have the technology to create conditions favourable to botrytis, either in the laboratory, or by spraying a fine mist of water in the vineyard.

Hungary's intensely sweet Tokaji is also made from botrytized grapes, which are added to a dry base wine.

Another method of making wine sweet is traditional in parts of Italy (where it is known as *passito* or *recioto*) and in the Jura, France (for *vin de paille*). After picking, the grapes are laid on mats or in shallow trays, or the bunches are hung from rafters. They begin to dry out, losing water, which concentrates all the other constituents, especially the sugars.

By the time the grapes are crushed they are so sweet that even after fermentation to a fair alcoholic degree some sweetness is left. For Moscato di Pantelleria, made on a small island west of Sicily, the grapes are left outdoors in the burning sun for two weeks. For Vin Santo, a speciality of Tuscany, Umbria and Trentino, the grapes may dry out indoors for four or five months.

There are lots of wines which are medium in style, vaguely sweet; for these, fermentation is stopped while there is still some sugar left unconverted to alcohol. Traditionally, this was done by pumping in sulphur dioxide to kill the yeasts, but nowadays it is much more common to remove the yeasts either by chilling the wine right down or by centrifuging it, which eliminates all the solids and leaves a stable wine, sweetness and all. It is also possible to add a little unfermented grape juice after the wine has fermented to dryness. This is the usual method for cheap German-style wines.

Finally, wine can be fortified. The grape juice is partially fermented and then neutral spirit is added which raises the alcohol level to between 16 and 24 per cent. Yeasts cannot operate at more than about 15–16 per cent alcohol, so fermentation stops and the remaining sugar stays in the wine.

Grapes hanging up to dry for Vin Santo in Tuscany. The wine will ferment and then age for several years in the small barrels (caratelli).

Choosing white wines

WHILE RED WINES MAY DISPLAY a fruity 'sweetness', they are nearly always dry. Not so whites, which range from bone dry and neutral accompaniments for seafood, to a whole gamut of perfumed or fruity dry to medium thirst-quenchers and finally to rich, luscious mouthfuls to have with – or instead of – pudding, or to sip when you're in a contemplative mood.

Bone dry, neutral whites

These are the sort of wines you might reach for on a hot day, or to accompany a plate of seafood. They will be served chilled, but it is their crisp apple or lemon acidity that makes them so refreshing and such a good match for shellfish. Neutral flavours in a white wine are an Italian speciality: Pinot Grigio (Pinot Gris) and Pinot Bianco (Pinot Blanc) are generally bone dry and light; Orvieto and Verdicchio are fairly reliable and fuller; Soave and Frascati are often mediocre, but look for Frascati Superiore or Soave Classico for better-made wines – Anselmi's Soave Classico Capitel Foscarino ❶ is one of the best. France offers Muscadet from the Loire Valley and Vin de Pays des Côtes de Gascogne from the South-West. Unoaked wines made from the Viura and Verdejo grapes in northern Spain are generally tart but good, and if you're in Portugal, proper Vinho Verde from the north-west can be neutral with a refreshing light fizz.

Classic white Burgundy

These are the wines that made Chardonnay famous in the first place: rich and succulent whites with subtle nut and oatmeal flavours and a backbone of absolute dryness. If you like this style, you've got a taste for French classics, because the best expression of it is oak-aged Chardonnay in the form of white Burgundy, most famously from the villages of Meursault ❷ and Puligny-Montrachet. The style is sometimes matched in the best examples from California, New York State, New Zealand, Australia and South Africa. Not any old examples, mind you – just the best. Italian producers in Tuscany are having a go, too.

Different flavours, but with a similar subtlety, are found in top-quality oak-aged Pessac-Léognan and Graves from Bordeaux. Here, Sémillon blended with Sauvignon Blanc gives a creamy, nutty wine with a hint of nectarines. Unoaked Semillon from the Hunter Valley in Australia develops surprisingly similar characteristics with time. All of these wines need to be kept for a few years to mature, and they don't come cheap. Less costly alternatives are the Chardonnays from Navarra and Somontano and some white Riojas, all from Spain.

Steely, dry Chardonnay

Unoaked Chablis is the adaptable Chardonnay grape in a dry, minerally style. Many growers from Chablis ❸ (in the north of the Burgundy region) and the Mâconnais (to the south) believe that oak detracts from the fruit flavours of Chardonnay, although there are producers in both regions who choose to age their wines in new oak, which brings them closer to classic white Burgundy. Chardonnay from Austria and Italy's Alto-Adige region are usually similarly dry.

Ripe, spicy Chardonnay

Upfront flavours of peaches, apricots and tropical fruits, spiced up by the vanilla, toast and butterscotch richness of new oak barrels, this is what most people mean when they talk about Chardonnay today. The style was virtually invented in Australia but it is also the hallmark of most Chardonnay in the USA and South America – it's very much a warm-climate style. In California, Au Bon Climat's Talley Vineyard Chardonnay ❹ is lush and beautifully balanced. Australian Semillon is often given a hefty dose of oak and may be blended with Chardonnay. Oaked white Rioja from Spain may be nothing like Chardonnay, but the emphasis is on the vanilla flavour.

Green, tangy Sauvignon

Sharp, grassy, love-them-or-hate-them wines, often with the smell and taste of gooseberries, nettles or asparagus. New Zealand's South Island has these tangy, mouthwatering flavours by the bucketful, as in this Sauvignon from top producer Cloudy Bay ❺. Chile makes similar, slightly softer wines, but South African versions can have real bite, as do examples from Hungary. The original Sauvignon wines are Sancerre and Pouilly-Fumé from the Loire Valley in France. These are crisp and refreshing with lighter fruit flavours

and a minerally or even a smoky edge. Modern Bordeaux Sauvignons from Entre-Deux-Mers are fresh, grassy and inexpensive, as are the vin de pays Sauvignon Blancs from elsewhere in the South of France. Really dry Portuguese Vinho Verde (the style sold in Portugal) is an aggressive alternative with a hint of fizz.

Oak-aged Sauvignons, popular in New Zealand's North Island, California (often under the name Fumé Blanc), South Africa, Australia and the Graves region of Bordeaux, add richness and peachy, apricotty flavours, making a half-way house between ripe, toasty Chardonnay and the more challenging classic Sauvignon style.

Riesling

German Rieslings from the Mosel (in green bottles) and Austrian examples made in the dry, Trocken, style have a fresh green sharpness rather like Sauvignon Blanc, with additional slaty, minerally flavours. French Rieslings from Alsace are similarly austere but with a bit more weight. New Zealand's are delicate and fresh, while Australia's have a delicious lime aroma on top of a heavier style. South Africa produces similarly perfumed styles. All these wines are at their greenest when young and develop a honeyed richness with a strange but delightful petrol aroma after a few years. This example, made in the Clare Valley by Grosset ❻, South Australia's Riesling specialist, will improve in the bottle for ten years.

Perfumy, off-dry whites

This style is the speciality of Alsace in France. Alsace Gewurztraminer wines are spicy and rich with an aroma of lychees and roses; German and Italian Gewürztraminers have a simpler floral character. Alsace Pinot Gris can be richly honeyed; Muscats are more floral with a heady, grapy scent. Aromatic dry Muscats are also made in Australia, South Africa and southern France. Irsai Oliver from Hungary and Torrontés from Argentina have a similar character. German Riesling from the Rhine (in brown bottles) can have this aromatic richness, especially in the Kabinett and Spätlese ❼ styles. France's Rhône Valley grows Viognier for the intensely apricotty and floral wines of Condrieu, and the grape is becoming popular across southern France as well as in California, Australia and South Africa. Müller-Thurgau from New Zealand or Germany provides inexpensive wines in this style.

Golden sweet whites

Many wines fall into this category – I've picked out just a few examples. In France the sweet wines of Bordeaux are at their best in Sauternes and Barsac, where the sweetness of the grapes, mostly Sémillon, is often concentrated by the effect of noble rot. Ch. d'Yquem ❽, one of the world's greatest sweet wines, can improve for 30 years or more. Some good lookalikes come from nearby Cérons and Monbazillac. California and Australia have a few intensely rich, late-harvest Semillon and Riesling wines in the style of Sauternes.

The Loire Valley produces quince-flavoured sweeties with firm acidity from late-harvested Chenin Blanc in Coteaux du Layon and Vouvray. In Alsace, late-harvested grapes become Vendange Tardive wines, while botrytized grapes are used for the more intense Sélection de Grains Nobles.

Germany produces a few rich and delicious wines, usually from Riesling grapes, labelled in ascending order of intensity as Auslese ❾, Beerenauslese and Trockenbeerenauslese, and there's a rarity called Eiswein made from frozen grapes picked in winter which manages a thrilling marriage of fierce acidity and unctuous sweetness. Canada uses the same technique and calls it Icewine. Austria has some excellent sweet wines in the Germanic style.

Hungary's Tokaji ❿ matches acidity and sweetness with a flavour of dried fruits and smoke. Italy's sweet wines are made from dried (*passito*) grapes. Avignonesi's exotically perfumed Vin Santo ⓫ is an outstanding example, and the Veneto region has its gently honeyed, apricotty Recioto di Soave.

The aromatic, grapy Muscat lends itself to sweet wines. Spain's simple, sweet Moscatel de Valencia is incredibly good value, and Greece makes some good Muscats, especially on the island of Samos ⓬. The Muscat *vins doux naturels* from southern France are usually fortified rather than naturally sweet.

❻  ❼  ❽  ❾  ❿  ⓫  ⓬

SPARKLING WINES

THE SECRET TO MAKING SPARKLING WINE is the fact that carbon dioxide is a very soluble gas. Carbon dioxide is given off during fermentation and if the fermenting wine is kept in a pressurized container – either a bottle or tank – the gas is absorbed by the wine – for as long as the pressure remains. That explains why as soon as you open a bottle of sparkling wine there is a whoosh of froth and bubbles as the pressure is released.

All the greatest sparklers are made by inducing a second fermentation in the actual bottle from which the wine will be served. It emerged from the Champagne region of northern France at the end of the seventeenth century and is now practised to great effect worldwide.

There is one major problem – the dead yeast cells form a deposit after they've finished fermenting out the sugar, leaving a nasty sludge in the container. If that container is the bottle itself, removing the sludge is difficult and expensive, but it is crucial to the Champagne method of making a wine sparkle. The natural desire of people to celebrate with fizz, but not pay a massive premium, has led to the development of simpler ways of making a wine sparkle and cleaning out its sediment.

Making the basic wine

The red grapes Pinot Noir and Pinot Meunier are popular for making sparkling wine, and the objective is to press them quickly and gently so that the juice is as pale as possible. These basic wines are then fermented out to dryness, as for white wine. Wines from different grapes and various vineyards are often expertly blended into a single style. These blends are called 'cuvées', even outside France, and many Champagnes have Cuvée in their title, which supposedly denotes the particular blend of the house.

The second fermentation

This is the first of three crucial stages of the Champagne method – creating the bubbles. The still wine is bottled with the addition of a little sugar and yeast to restart the fermentation, tightly sealed, and stored in a cool cellar for anything from a few months to several years. The second fermentation creates carbon dioxide which, since it can't escape, dissolves in the wine. To get good bubbles you want this *prise de mousse*, or 'mousse-taking', to last two or three years, longer if possible.

While this second fermentation has been creating the bubbles, it's also been depositing used-up yeast cells on the side of the bottle. But this yeasty sludge has such an attractive creamy taste that the best sparkling wines will spend a couple of years on their yeast, becoming softer and richer in flavour.

Collecting the sediment

Now, the flavour may be good and the wine may be fizzy – but no-one is going to drink it if it looks cloudy and impenetrable. First, the sludge must be dislodged from the side of the bottle. So the bottles go through a process called riddling, or *remuage* in French: they are gradually transferred from the horizontal to

Here in the Champagne house of Perrier-Jouët in Épernay, bottles of Belle Epoque Rosé vintage Champagne are held at an angle in the traditional pupitres and turned by hand.

Huge, computer-controlled gyropalettes, each holding 2720 bottles, perform the remuage automatically. These are at Domaine Chandon, owned by French Champagne house Moët et Chandon, in California's Napa Valley.

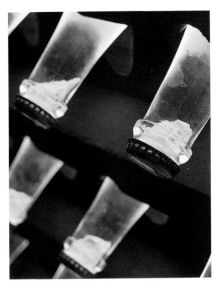

As the bottles are gradually inverted, the sediment of used yeast cells collects on the cap.

the vertical position – but upside-down – as well as being regularly turned and tapped, causing the deposit to slide down inside the glass and collect on the cork.

The process of *remuage*, or shifting the sludge, was invented in the early nineteenth century by Veuve Clicquot, the greatest of the many indomitable widows who have forged the modern Champagne industry. She devised a kind of two-sided desk with holes in it called a *pupitre*. Shove the bottle in the holes, go through the tilt-and-tap routine for three months and you're ready for the next stage in the Champagne method. There are mechanical *pupitres* now, called *gyropalettes* – great big metal palettes of bottles clicking and clunking the sediment on to the cork.

Removing the sediment
The *dégorgement* is literally 'removing' the sludge. It used to require a large number of men with strong wrists and fast reflexes, popping corks and ejecting sediment, but now the neck of the bottle containing the deposit is frozen and the tight, chilled pellet is whipped out on a machine production line.

Adjusting the sweetness
At this stage the wine is still totally dry, since any sugar will have been eaten up by fermentation which is also, of course, what has caused all those bubbles. After the sediment has been removed, the bottle needs to be topped up, usually with a mixture of wine and sugar syrup, the *dosage*. There are very few Champagne houses which don't add some

sugar after disgorging. Even Brut Champagnes, usually the driest a house offers, will have some sugar added back. Good New World sparklers are increasingly made from less ripe grapes, as in Champagne, but simpler, cheaper versions can be made from riper grapes, which give a less acid base wine.

Sealing the bottle
Finally, the special extra-strong Champagne cork is rammed in and secured with a wire cage to keep all those bubbles in the bottle.

Sparkling rosé and red wine
Most sparkling wine is white, but rosé is increasingly popular. This used to be made by fermenting the base wine as a rosé but it was virtually impossible to predict the eventual colour. So nowadays, almost invariably, a little red wine is added to a white sparkling base.

Sparkling red wine is rather an unusual proposition, but Australia has a rich, long-lived style made by a number of producers, using either the traditional method, or the transfer or tank methods (see below). Italy's Lambrusco, usually red, is generally made by the tank method.

Opening sparkling wine
The pressure in the bottle does the work, so all you have to do is control it. If you don't, you'll get a loud pop, a rush of foaming wine and a half-empty bottle of fizz. A cold bottle will open with a less dramatic burst than a warm one.

Tear off the foil to reveal the wire cage, place one thumb over the top of the cork and undo the cage, remembering to point the bottle away from people and breakable objects. Grasp the cork with one hand and hold the bottle firmly with the other. Now turn the bottle slowly while holding the cork in place. The cork will start to ease out under the pressure; it should come free with a sigh rather than a bang. Holding the bottle at an angle of 45 degrees for a few moments should calm the initial rush of foam; then pour it into the waiting glass.

OTHER METHODS AND TERMS

Cuve close or tank method This involves putting wine into a pressurized tank and adding sugar and yeast to start a second fermentation. The wine is then filtered to remove the yeasty sediment and bottled under pressure. Most cheap labour-saving fizz is made this way, but it needn't taste nasty – the Italians make delicious Asti and Prosecco wine using this, or a similar method. It is also called the Charmat method after its French inventor, Eugène Charmat.

Transfer method This is like the Champagne method, without the *remuage*. The second fermentation takes place inside a bottle, but the wine is then filtered and transferred under pressure to its final bottle. The results are greatly superior to the tank method, particularly in the finesse of the bubbles. Indeed, some producers in the United States and Australia are so keen on this method they say they prefer it to the Champagne method – a lot more predictable and similar quality!

Carbonated method This is the most basic method: you simply carbonate the wine by pumping gas into it at the bottling stage. Normally what you get is a pretty vile brew with a very fleeting bubble.

Other methods There are several 'rural methods' employed in France, whereby the first fermentation continues in the bottle or rather starts again. If the sediment is not removed, the wine may be slightly cloudy. These include Blanquette de Limoux from Languedoc-Roussillon and Clairette de Die from the Rhône Valley; many Blanquette producers now use the Champagne method.

Other terms *Mousseux* implies a fully sparkling wine made in France by the *cuve close* method. *Crémant* is used for fully sparkling wine, usually made by the Champagne method, in areas other than Champagne, such as Alsace and Burgundy. *Pétillant* means lightly sparkling – *frizzante* is the Italian equivalent. *Perlant* means very lightly sparkling, less so than *pétillant*.

Choosing sparkling wines

SPARKLING WINES ARE MADE FOR celebrations and these days there are so many well made and inexpensive alternatives to Champagne that the merest excuse suffices to open a bottle of fizz and celebrate. The bubbles alone can create a party mood, especially if you've remembered to chill the bottle down, but good sparkling wine can have some delicious flavours as well.

Champagne styles

Good Champagne has a nutty, bready aroma and fine bubbles. Brut is usually the driest style; only a few very rare brands, often called Brut Zero, Ultra Brut or something similar, are made with no added sugar at all. Extra Dry/Extra Sec is a little gentler than Brut. The majority of Champagne is non-vintage **❶**, in other words it is based on a blend of wines from several years; it improves if you store the bottles for a few months – or even a few years if you want a deeper, nutty taste – before you drink it. Vintage Champagne **❷** is made only in the best years; when mature, with at least eight or ten years in bottle, it is deep, rich and thrilling. Most major Champagne houses produce a prestige or deluxe cuvée as their top wine; this may be either non-vintage or vintage. Moët et Chandon's Dom Pérignon **❸** can be one of the world's finest, but it needs at least ten years in the bottle.

Dry sparkling wines

While other sparkling wines may be referred to colloquially as 'champagne', they are not allowed to use the French region's name on the bottle. Instead, the terms 'classic method' and 'traditional method' (made in the same way as Champagne) and 'fermented in bottle' (made by the transfer method) are seen on labels from Australia, California and New Zealand; winemakers often use traditional Champagne grape varieties such as Chardonnay and Pinot Noir to produce excellent and far less expensive versions. Much of the best is made by subsidiaries of French Champagne producers; Green Point **❹** is an Australian offshoot of Moët et Chandon.

Other good Champagne-method French fizzes include Crémant d'Alsace, Crémant de Bourgogne from Burgundy and Crémant de Loire and the sharper Saumur Mousseux from the Loire Valley. In the south, light, fresh Blanquette de Limoux and grapy Clairette de Die have their own idiosyncratic methods of production and grape varieties.

Italian sparklers made from Chardonnay and Pinot Noir are in the Champagne style, but light and creamy Prosecco is more fun and a lot cheaper. Spanish Cava is pretty good, but tends to be a bit earthy. German sparkling wine is called Sekt: the best – occasionally 100 per cent Riesling – are excellent but the rest are less successful.

Rosé and red dry sparkling wines

Pink sparkling wines, the ultimate in frivolity, can be superb. Rosé Champagne is made in all styles: Laurent-Perrier's Grand Siècle Alexandra Rosé **❺** is a vintage prestige cuvée. Good rosé is generally found wherever traditional-method sparkling wine is made: the Loire Valley, Burgundy, California and Australia.

Australian sparkling red wines made from Merlot, Cabernet Sauvignon or, preferably, Shiraz **❻** are wild things, packed with jammy fruit. You'll either love them or loathe them, but you haven't lived until you've given them a try. Italy's Lambrusco can be either red or white; for a good dry version look for one from a controlled region or DOC.

Medium and sweet sparkling wines

Champagne being a law unto itself, a bottle labelled Sec will be medium-dry; wines then increase in sweetness from Demi-sec (or Riche) to very sweet, but very rare, Doux. Some sparkling Saumur from the Loire Valley is also made in a demi-sec style. Italy's naturally sweet, scented, grapy Asti can be delightful; even better is the frizzante (semi-sparkling) version, Moscato d'Asti **❼**.

FORTIFIED WINES

FORTIFIED WINES ARE WINES TO WHICH extra alcohol in the form of brandy or neutral spirit has been added at some stage during their production. In the case of port, alcohol is added during fermentation while quite a lot of the grape sugar still remains in the warm, bubbling juice. This dose of spirit stops the fermentation and so retains some of the natural sugar. This basic method is also used for Madeira and Moscatel de Setúbal from Portugal, the fortified Grenache and Muscat wines of Spain and southern France, and the Muscats of Australia and South Africa. With sherry the juice is left to ferment until all the sugar is used up. Even sweet sherries start out as dry white wine. Before the spirit is added, this is one of the world's least impressive wines. But the spirit enables it to mature for years in oak barrels – and become one of the world's greatest. Sicily's Marsala is also usually fermented to dryness, then fortified and sweetened with a blend of grape juice and 'cooked' grape syrup.

Making sherry

Fermenting and fortification
Sherry-style wines are made in two basic ways, one of which leads to bone-dry fino-type wines, the other to fuller-bodied, nutty oloroso types. Whatever the ultimate style, the juice is pressed from the skins, left to settle, then fermented right out to make a dry white wine. It is then racked and fortified with grape spirit. Fino-type sherries are fortified to no more than 15.5 per cent alcohol, olorosos up to 18 per cent.

The developing flavour
Finos then develop in a totally different way thanks to an unusual yeast called flor, which occurs naturally in all the areas that make this style of wine. The barrels for all types of sherry are filled just five-sixths full. The surface of the wine in fino barrels then grows a film of squidgy, oatmeal-white flor. While protecting the infant sherry from the air and keeping it pale in colour, flor feeds off the wine and affects its composition and flavour, in particular adding a sharp tang and memorable pungency. The tang is even more pronounced

Palomino Fino grapes, grown in the chalky soil of Jerez in Andalucía, southern Spain, make extremely dull wine, which will be transformed by the sherry process into a superb, world-class drink.

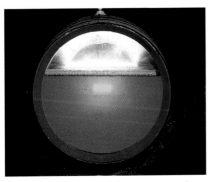
This specially constructed display barrel shows flor yeast growing on the surface of the wine that will become dry fino sherry.

in manzanilla, a fino which is made in the coastal town of Sanlúcar de Barrameda. Flor never grows on oloroso-style wines because it will not tolerate alcohol levels over 16.2 per cent. Olorosos gradually develop in contact with the air, taking on a rich, nutty aroma. Some olorosos are sweetened at this stage.

The third major sherry style, amontillado, develops out of fino. After fino has been in barrel for six years or more, the flor begins to fade and die, and the wine comes in contact with the air, turning amber-coloured and nutty-flavoured while still retaining the pungency and tang of a fino. These are true, fine, dry amontillados. It is a pity that, in the British market especially, amontillado has come to mean nondescript, vaguely sweet sherry. Just as Germany's wine reputation was cheapened by the ubiquitous Liebfraumilch, so sherry's reputation as a great wine style was spoilt by a deluge of mediocre and non-representative amontillado. Similar in style to amontillado are two rare styles of dry wine that fall between fino and oloroso in character: palo cortado and manzanilla pasada.

Aging
All sherries have to be wood-aged for a minimum of three years, but the finest are aged for much longer. During this time, they pass through a solera system, a traditional means of gradual blending. When sherry is needed for bottling, only about one-quarter of the wine from the most mature barrels is run off at a time. Those barrels are then filled from slightly younger ones and so on until the last barrel receives a top-up of the youngest wine. This is vital for fino, as the nutrients in the younger wines keep the flor alive, but amontillado and oloroso sherries also benefit from this continual replenishing of the stock, which helps to prevent oxidation.

Making port

Fermenting and fortification

Port starts life as a dark and toughly tannic red wine, since the skins and pips must continually be mixed with the fermenting juice to extract the maximum amount of colour and tannin in the shortest possible time. Traditionally, this is done by pushing down the 'cap' of floating solids with long poles or by foot-treading in open, shallow tanks called *lagares*. Nowadays, the grapes are often fermented in autovinificators – enclosed tanks in which the pressure of the gases produced by fermentation acts as a natural pump to spray the juice up over the skins.

The wine ferments until it has reached about 8 per cent alcohol, still containing more than half the natural grape sugar, before being fortified with raw grape spirit. This brings the alcohol level up to about 19 per cent, the yeasts die, and the infant port is run off into a clean container, pressed from the skins, and left to settle.

Assessing and blending

Early in the year following the harvest, the young wine is tasted, its quality assessed to

Most of the famous port lodges are in Vila Nova de Gaia, at the mouth of the river Douro; here, various samples are blended to make tawny port.

ensure that the envisaged style is still appropriate, and its consequent method of maturation decided. Wines of similar style and quality are blended together and generally transported to the maturing houses, or

lodges, at Vila Nova de Gaia, where they will be matured in wooden barrels, called pipes.

Racking

The wines are racked – run off any deposit and into a clean cask – about once a year for the first few years, then less frequently.

Aging

The cheapest ports (basic rubies and tawnies) are aged in wood for only about three years, but the finest old tawnies may remain in barrel for up to 40 years. As they age, the wines gradually mellow (though they remain spirity as the level of spirit is kept topped up) and turn from dense, bright red to a lighter tawny colour. Of the wines that started out a finer quality, the best are blended together in the best years to make vintage port, which is aged for just two years in wood, but needs many years in bottle before drinking. It keeps its colour much better in bottle and ends up redder and richer. Wines that are good but not of vintage quality may be kept in wood for four to six years and then sold as Late Bottled Vintage, or LBV.

Making Madeira

Fermenting and fortification

Unlike the port grapes, the different Madeira varieties are kept separate in the wineries. Sercial, Verdelho and Tinta Negra Mole grapes are pressed as for ordinary white wine, and the juice ferments without the skins. With Bual and Malmsey, however, the skins are usually left in the fermenting juice for a couple of days in order to extract more colour, tannin and aroma. The wine ferments at between 18°C and 35°C (64–77°F) in tanks or large wooden vats. Most producers add alcohol to stop the fermentation when the required sweetness level has been reached, sooner for the sweeter styles, later for the drier. Young Madeira is fortified slightly less than port, to around 17 per cent alcohol. But some producers ferment all their wines to dryness, then sweeten them with fortified grape juice.

'Cooking' the wines

Now follows Madeira's unique 'cooking' process, which gives the wines their characteristic caramelly, slightly smoked flavour. The

The aging room in the warm attic of the Madeira Wine Company's old lodge in Funchal, the island's main town.

cheaper wines go into special kettle-tanks called *estufas*, in which coils filled with hot water heat the wine to between 45°C (113°F) and 50°C (122°F) for a legal minimum of 90 days. Fine wines are left in casks for years either in hot attics above the *estufas* or in warehouses heated to 35°C–40°C (77–80°F).

Aging

Even the lowest level of Madeira – confusingly, this is often labelled Finest – must spend a minimum of 18 months in wooden casks after their time in *estufas*. Reserves have to be aged in wood for at least five years, Special Reserves for ten, and Vintages for 20 years.

Choosing fortified wines

FORTIFIED WINES RANGE FROM the very dry to the very sweet; they may be served to stimulate the appetite before a meal or to relax over after dinner. Often known as dessert wines, there is a style to suit every variation of dessert, from a handful of nuts and dried fruits to rich crème brûlée; port is a classic partner for strongly flavoured and mature cheese.

Sweet and warming

Some fortified wines are sweet and warming, tasting of raisins and brown sugar, often densely packed with spicy fruit and other flavours. Port, the rich red fortified wine of Portugal's Douro Valley, is the classic dark sweet wine and no imitator can match the finesse of the best. It is made in a number of styles: the youngest, ruby, should be deliciously fruity, but such wine is hard to find. Vintage-character port is a little older than ruby – again, it should be full of rich fruit but often disappoints. Late Bottled Vintage is produced from a single vintage and bottled, preferably without filtration, after four to six years in cask. Cheap tawny is a thin blend of ruby and white ports; the real thing develops its deep nut and fig flavours after long aging in wood (some may have spent 40 years in a wooden barrel). Vintage port, such as Taylor's **❶**, bottled at two years old, should mature slowly in the bottle for at least 15 years.

Australia and South Africa both make interesting port-style wines. The Portuguese island of Madeira produces some of the most exciting of warming fortified wines, with rich brown smoky flavours and a startling acid bite: Bual and Malmsey are the sweet ones to keep an eye out for.

Cheap sweetened 'brown' sherry is a weak parody of this style. The sweetish wines sold as amontillados are fourth-rate finos darkened and sweetened up with concentrated grape juice. Similarly, creams and pale creams are sweetened-up, low-grade olorosos and finos. The real thing – oloroso dulce – is a rare and beautiful sweet sherry with stunning concentrated flavours.

The South of France and the Rhône Valley produce *vins doux naturels* from the Muscat and Grenache grapes; despite the name these are usually fortified rather than naturally sweet. The most famous is Muscat de Beaumes-de-Venise, though Muscat de Frontignan and Muscat de Rivesaltes **❷** are cheaper alternatives. Australian sweet fortified Muscat from the Rutherglen region **❸** is rich, concentrated and dark, even treacly.

Sicily's Marsala wines, mostly sweet, are often fit only for cooking.

Dry and tangy

Some of the best Marsala, in a style known as Vergine, is unsweetened, and De Bartoli's Vecchio Samperi **❹** is actually an unfortified version, dry, intense and redolent of dates and candied citrus peel. Fortified wines can certainly be bone dry, with startling, stark, sour and nutty flavours – a taste that takes a bit of getting used to but which is well worth acquiring. The originals are the sherries from Jerez in southern Spain. Fino **❺** is pale in colour and unnervingly dry with a thrilling tang. Manzanilla, a type of fino sherry matured by the sea at Sanlúcar de Barrameda, can seem even drier, even leaner, and has a wonderful sour-dough perfume and tingling acidity. Both should be drunk as young and fresh as possible. Traditional amontillado is dark, nutty and dry, not medium-sweet as we often see it. Dry oloroso adds deep, burnt flavours and at best is one of the most haunting, lingering flavours the world of wine can offer. Palo cortado, a sherry with both fino and oloroso characteristics, is rare and dry, with a pungent bite.

Montilla-Moriles is the neighbouring region to Jerez and produces similar wines, but only the very best reach the standard of good sherry. The driest style of Madeira, Sercial **❻**, is tangy, steely and savoury. Verdelho Madeira is that bit fuller and fatter. White port, at its best, is dry and nutty-tasting; most are coarse and alcoholic. Australia and South Africa make excellent sherry-style wines though without the tang of top-class Spanish fino or manzanilla.

KEEPING AND SERVING WINE

WINE IS A LIVING THING – as it lies in its bottle over the months or years, it evolves. Red wines grow paler and develop sediment, whites darken to a honeyed brown. Wines with plenty of acid and tannin become less fierce-tasting and more approachable, and if they have the vital extra ingredient – loads of intense fruit flavour – for the true quality of the wine to be revealed, a few years in the bottle are absolutely crucial, so that the tannins can soften, the acids mellow. Older wine is not always better wine, but if a wine is worth keeping, it's worth making the effort to look after it.

Looking after your wine

Most wine is pretty resilient. A really young bottle can bounce about in the car for days, almost bake to death on the back seat in the sun, then almost freeze to death in the refrigerator and still taste reasonable – not as good as it could, but reasonable. But if the wine is at all special, there's no doubt you have a better chance of enjoying it if you treat it with at least a modicum of consideration. Indeed, if there is a general rule it is that the older a bottle of wine the more you must cherish it and expose it to the minimum amount of stress.

Most of us like to keep a few bottles in the house so we can choose a wine to suit our food or our mood. All an everyday wine requires is to be stored on its side, out of direct sunlight and away from heat sources. For the vast majority of wine the best vintage is the most recent one. Nearly all modern wine is ready to drink the moment it appears on the shop shelf, and with a few exceptions it is a huge mistake to keep any wine too long. Everyday wines simply taste more faded, stale and dull as the aging process goes on. Some bottles have guideline information on the back label, such as 'Best consumed within one year of

WINES TO KEEP

Wines from a good vintage will develop more slowly than those made in a poor year. The vintage tables on pages 400–403 give specific information; what follows are general guidelines.

Reds Cabernet Sauvignon wines are sometimes made for drinking young, but can often improve in bottle for many years. Bordeaux produces a range of Cabernet-based wines of varying aging potential. Basic wines need three years to mature and will last for another couple of years. A Classed Growth château in a good vintage will need ten years to mature, and will last for at least another ten; in a poor vintage it might mature in five years and start to fade in another five. California's Napa Valley has become Cabernet Sauvignon's second home: its wines are as varied as those of Bordeaux, drinkable after three to ten years in bottle, and capable of lasting a further 10–15 years from good producers. Most commercial Australian Cabernet Sauvignon is made to be drunk at three to six years old, although top wines can last up to 25 years.

Bordeaux's very best Merlot-based blends from St-Émilion and Pomerol need 10–15 years to reach maturity; slightly lesser wines will peak at five or six years.

In Burgundy, lesser classifications are best at three to six years; Premiers and Grands Crus will be ready after five to ten years, depending on the vintage, and the best of the lot will last 20 years or more. Elsewhere Pinot Noir should be drunk within three to five years.

Italy's Sangiovese and Nebbiolo wines vary according to the intentions of the winemaker. Some super-Tuscans and modern Barolos may be appreciated three to six years after the vintage, others, especially old-style Barolo, need at least ten years before they are approachable.

Syrah-based wines from the Rhône have good aging potential, up to 20 years in top vintages – only the best Australian Shiraz can compare. In Spain, top Ribera del Duero and Rioja take at least five years to mature, and last up to 15 years. California's Zinfandel, though usually made to drink young, sometimes has the structure to age for five to ten years.

Whites Classic white Burgundy is probably the world's longest-lived Chardonnay: a Grand Cru from Chablis or the Côte d'Or can last 20 years, although it can generally be enjoyed after three to five. Simpler white Burgundies, including those from the south of the region (Mâcon and Côte Chalonnaise), seldom develop for more than a year or two.

Dry, unoaked Chardonnay – whether it comes from Italy, the USA, Australia or elsewhere – should normally be drunk within two or three years of the vintage. Barrel-fermented or oak-aged Chardonnay has the potential to last longer – five or even ten years from exceptional producers.

Sauvignon Blanc generally makes wines to be drunk young, but in Bordeaux it is blended with Sémillon to make the great dry Pessac-Léognan and sweet Sauternes. Lesser Graves should last four years, top châteaux can improve for ten years or more. The finest Sauternes need ten years to mature and can live for decades.

Riesling can be one of the world's longest-lived grapes: a German Kabinett is immediately drinkable but good examples can improve for six to eight years; Spätlese and Auslese (and Alsace Grand Cru Riesling) should last 10–15 years or more; and the great sweet wines, German Beerenauslese, Trockenbeerenauslese and Eiswein, Alsace Vendange Tardive and Sélection de Grains Nobles, should not be drunk for at least ten years and will improve for decades.

The intensely sweet wines from the Loire, and Hungarian Tokaji, if well made, have a lifespan of 50 years or more.

Sparkling wines Non-vintage Champagne improves if kept for a year or two. Vintage Champagnes are sold at around six to eight years old, but are worth keeping for another five years. Australia's sparkling reds can also be kept for five years.

Fortified wines Most fortified wines do not evolve in the bottle, the honourable exception being vintage port, which is not ready to drink until it is about ten years old and reaches perfection after 20–40 years.

purchase' or 'This wine can be cellared for up to five years', but you won't find much of this sort of help on serious-minded wines (the ones that are best suited to long aging).

Longer term storage needs a little more thought. The traditional underground cellar has the ideal combination of even temperature, darkness, humidity and stillness, but few houses have one nowadays, so a disused fireplace, a corner of the garage, or the space under the stairs may have to do. The cooler the place is, within reason, the slower the wines will develop: somewhere between 10°C and 13°C (50°F and 55°F) is ideal. But avoiding sudden changes in temperature is the most important thing. Gradual, gentle aging is the key to bringing fine wines to maturity.

Serving temperatures

The flavour of wine is undoubtedly affected by the temperature at which it is served. It's better to serve wine slightly too cool, because you can always warm the glass in your hand. Don't do anything dramatic to change a wine's temperature like leaving it in front of the fire; sticking it in the freezer should be considered a last resort.

One rule of thumb is the cheaper the wine, the colder it should be served. Sparkling wines should be well chilled to preserve their bubbles. The cheaper the fizz, the closer to freezing! Fino and manzanilla sherry are also much better served chilled than warm.

Reds and rosés Most red wine is best served at room temperature – but that means around 15°C (60°F) or so, which is cooler than many centrally heated houses. Higher temperatures emphasize aromas while minimizing acidity and tannins: full-bodied, tannic and fine wines are therefore best at 15–18°C (60–64°F). No wine tastes at its best above a room temperature of about 20°C (68°F). As long as you don't live in a hothouse, the best way to bring red wine from cellar to room temperature is to stand the bottle in the room in which you intend to serve it a few hours before you open it.

Rosés should always be well chilled, and light, juicy, fruity reds can take a brief chilling, up to an hour, but it's not essential.

Whites Most white wines are probably best at 10–12°C (50–54°F), which they will reach after an hour or two in the refrigerator. If you've left things too late, put the bottle into an ice-bucket, empty in as much ice as you can, then fill it up with water – much more effective than ice alone.

Dry, neutral whites and tangy Sauvignon Blanc wines can take more chilling: up to two or three hours in the refrigerator.

Aromatic wines such as Riesling and Gewürztraminer, and sweet wines, start losing their perfume if you chill them for more than two hours. Chardonnay, especially good Burgundy, and Rhône whites shouldn't have more than about an hour because they begin to lose their attractive nuttiness.

Opening wine

To make this task as smooth as possible, choose a corkscrew with an open spiral and a handle that you find comfortable to use.

First remove the metal foil or plastic seal around the top of the bottle, known as the capsule. Wipe the lip of the bottle with a clean cloth if there is dirt or mould around the top of the cork.

Stand the bottle on a flat surface, press the point of the corkscrew gently into the centre of the cork and turn the screw slowly and steadily, keeping it straight. Try to stop turning before the point emerges at the bottom of the cork. Ease the cork out gently.

To remove a broken cork that is wedged into the bottle neck, drive the corkscrew in at a sharp angle and press the cork fragment against the side of the neck as you work it upwards, maintaining the angle of the corkscrew. If you're having no luck, push the cork down into the wine; it isn't pretty, but the wine will taste no worse for it.

Decanting

There are three reasons for putting wine in a decanter: to separate it from sediment that has formed in the bottle; to let it breathe; to make it look attractive. You don't need a special decanter, a glass jug is just as good.

Simply uncorking the bottle and leaving it to stand is not the same as letting it breathe, as only a tiny surface area is exposed. However, if you pour off half a glass of wine you will expose more wine to the air. Some wines do get softer and rounder after a couple of hours' decanting, and it is a good way to give very tannic red wines a more mature taste. On the other hand, decanting can kill off an old wine if you do it more than a few minutes before serving.

No wine, with the possible exceptions of vintage, single-quinta, crusted and traditional style LBV port, demands decanting. Even an old wine which has thrown a sediment can be poured out successfully from the bottle – do it slowly, avoiding any sudden movements which might make the wine slop about.

To decant, it's best to stand the bottle upright for a day or two to let the sediment settle. An hour or two before you want to drink it, open the bottle, then, with a candle or torch under the neck of the bottle, pour gently in one single motion until you see an arrowhead of sediment arrive at the lip. If you do it carefully you'll waste less than half a glass – and that can go into the gravy.

Glasses

There's one final thing – use nice big glasses which you fill to between one-third and one-half full to allow aromas to build up in the glass. A tulip-shaped glass will help to capture the aromas rather than dissipating them (such a waste!), and the glass should be clear, to show the colour of the wine.

After you've finished with them, hand-wash glasses in very hot water, taking care to rinse away all traces of washing-up liquid.

CORKS

The only requirements for the seal on a bottle of wine are that it should be hygienic, airtight, long-lasting and removable. Cork has stood the test of time, but it is prone to infection and shrinkage. Shrinkage is unlikely to occur if the bottle is kept on its side so the cork stays in contact with the wine and remains moist, but infected corks (sadly, common) will spoil a wine with their musty taste. Modern alternatives can give you a fresher wine. Plastic corks are now common in budget wines and are also used by certain high-quality producers. The best plastics have a soft texture and come in bright colours. To be honest, the humble screwcap is probably as good a closure as any, and keeps wine fresh for years, but an understandable liking for the ritual of cork-pulling restricts its use to cheap wines.

TASTING WINE

TASTING WINE MEANS UNDERSTANDING what you are drinking – and enjoying it more. The ritual observed by professionals is not just showing off: there is a purpose to every stage, and it can help you to get maximum pleasure from a bottle of wine. Wine can be complex stuff, and if you just knock it back you could be missing out on a wonderful sensory experience. Instead, take a few moments to discover a little about a wine's background, appreciate its colour, and savour its scents and range of flavours.

 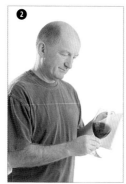   

❶ **Read the label** This tells you a great deal about the wine: its region of origin, age, alcohol level, sometimes its grape variety. The design – traditional or modern – can hint at the intentions of the winemaker. At a blind tasting, you will begin at the next step.

❷ **Look at the wine** Pour the wine into a glass so that it is about one-third full. Tilt the glass against a white background so that you can see the gradations of colour from the rim to the centre. The colour can begin to suggest the taste of the wine, with clues to grape variety, climate and age. A young red wine may have a deep purple tinge, an older one will be lighter, sometimes brick red. A very pale white will be young, fresh or neutral-tasting, a deeper yellow one will be fuller in flavour, sweeter or older (not always a good thing in white wines).

❸ **Smell the wine** Swirl the wine around the glass to release the aromas, then stick your nose into the glass and take a steady, gentle sniff. Register the smell in terms that mean something to you: if it reminds you of herbs, spices, strawberries, wet wool or tar, that is what makes the wine memorable.

❹ **Take a sip** Take a decent mouthful, so that your mouth is about one-third full, and hold the wine in your mouth for a few moments, breathing through your nose. Draw a little air through your lips and suck it through the wine to help the aromas on their way to your nasal cavity. Note any toughness, acidity and sweetness that the tongue detects, then enjoy the personality and flavour of the aromas in your nasal cavity. Now gently 'chew' the wine, letting it coat your tongue, teeth, and gums. Note the first impressions, then the taste that develops after the wine has been in your mouth for a few seconds. You can now swallow the wine or spit it out.

❺ **Spit or swallow** If you have to taste a number of wines in a limited time, spitting is the only way to appreciate the flavours and stay sober. Practise your technique in front of the bathroom mirror. A bucket with sawdust in the bottom makes a practical spittoon.

Assess the wine Now note your impressions. Is the wine well balanced (see box opposite)? Does the flavour linger in your mouth? A long-lasting flavour generally means a better wine.

TASTING WINE IN RESTAURANTS

Translating the above principles to a restaurant situation can save you and your guests from disappointment.

First of all, the waiter should show you the unopened bottle. The label will tell you whether it is the wine you ordered. If it is not, you are entitled to change your order, although in many modern wines the vintage is relatively unimportant. Feel the bottle to check the temperature.

The waiter should then open the bottle within your view and pour a small amount of wine into your glass. Sniff the wine and if all seems fine, take a sip. Take your time. If anything seems wrong about the wine, say so. The restaurant should replace a faulty wine without question. If you prefer to pour the wine yourself, ask the waiter to leave the bottle on the table or in an ice bucket.

Before you taste a wine, a few tell-tale signs might indicate something is wrong. A low level of wine in the bottle or a line of sediment 'baked' onto the side of the bottle suggest that it has not been stored with care. A brownish tinge – to red or white wine – may mean it is oxidized (spoilt by exposure to oxygen), in which case it will smell and taste stale, flat or sherry-like. Pieces of cork floating in the glass have nothing to do with 'corked' wine. Wine that is corked smells distinctively musty and is caused by an infected cork. The vinegary smell of volatile acidity occurs when a wine is infected by acetic bacteria.

Sulphurous wines fall into two categories: a spent-match smell, from excessive use of sulphur dioxide in the winery, will usually dissipate after 30 minutes or so; a wine that smells of rotten eggs should be rejected immediately!

TASTING TERMS

The terms used by wine tasters are a useful shorthand when discussing wines, and are used throughout this and almost every other book on the subject.

Acidity All wines need acidity to be refreshing and capable of aging for any time. Too little acidity makes a wine taste lifeless, although too much makes it taste sharp.

Balance Term used to describe the relationship between the major components of wine: acidity, alcohol, fruit (and tannin in reds). In a well-balanced wine no single element dominates.

Beefy Solid, chunky red wines.

Big A full-bodied wine with lots of everything: fruit flavour, acid, alcohol and tannin.

Body Describes the impression of weight in the mouth. This is what is referred to by the terms light-, medium- and full-bodied.

Buttery Usually refers to the soft, rich, vanilla flavour imparted by new oak barrels.

Chewy Wine with a lot of tannin and strong flavour.

Clean Wine with no bacterial or chemical faults and a simple, direct flavour.

Closed Describes a wine that doesn't have much smell, but gives the impression that it will have more to offer when it matures.

Crisp Refreshing white with good acidity.

Deep A full-flavoured red or white.

Fat A heavy, sometimes clumsy wine, though if made from fully ripe grapes it can imply richness in sweet or dry wine.

Fresh The youthful aromas in a wine, and the combination of good acidity with fruit or floral flavours.

Fruit Term for the fruit element in a wine. It may not taste of grapes, but it will resemble a fruit of some kind (e.g. apple, blackcurrant, cherry) and is crucial to the flavour of most wines. Ripe fruit flavours can be confused with sweetness.

Full A wine with plenty of mouthfilling flavours and alcohol.

Grapy Quite rare flavour of the grape itself in wine. Most common in Muscat, Riesling or Gewürztraminer.

Green Unripe, or tart. This can be attractive and refreshing in light, young wine.

Hard Usually applied to reds which have an excess of tannin. In young reds, this is often necessary to facilitate aging.

Jammy Rather big, 'cooked', seemingly sweetish wines, usually red.

Length The way a good wine's flavours continue to evolve in the mouth even after swallowing.

Nutty Usually applied to dry whites (e.g. a soft Brazil or hazelnut flavour in Chardonnay, a dry richness in medium sherry or Madeira).

Oaky The slightly sweet vanilla flavour imparted by maturation in oak casks. The newer the oak the more forceful its impact on the wine.

Petrolly An attractive smell applied to mature Riesling wines, and sometimes mature Sémillon.

Prickly A wine with slight residual carbon dioxide gas. Usually attractive in light young whites, but in reds it can be a sign of re-fermentation in bottle.

Rich Wine that feels luxurious in the mouth, with sweet fruit flavours, not necessarily a sweet wine.

Ripe Lots of fresh fruit flavour dominates.

Rounded A wine in which the flavour seems satisfyingly complete, with no harshness.

Spicy Exotic fruit and spice flavours in whites, particularly Gewürztraminer, but also a peppery or cinnamon/clove perfume in some reds and whites aged in oak.

Steely Applied to good-quality Rieslings for their very dry, almost metallic flavour.

Sweet Term in dry wines for the elements of ripeness or richness which good quality can often suggest.

Tannin This substance, from the skins and pips of grapes, is what gives most red wines their tough, rather cold-tea, bitter edge. It combines with acidity to give a wine firmness. Too much tannin makes a wine bitter; low tannin makes a wine soft.

Tart Green, unripe wine with excess acidity. Can be desirable in light, dry wines.

Wine and food

Food can have a profound effect on the taste of wine: a well-matched partnership can enhance both food and wine, while an ill-chosen pair can leave a nasty taste in your mouth. The last thing we're going to do is start laying down laws about what you must or must not drink with this or that food. That's up to you. There are, though, certain points worth remembering.

Don't just match the flavour of the wine to the flavour of the food, but also take into account the body or weight of the wine: a heavy, alcoholic or oaky wine such as a spicy red Shiraz will overpower a delicate dish – a Pinot Noir would be a better bet. A rich dish can either be cut through with an acidic wine, or matched with a rich one, but either way the wine should be full in flavour so as not to taste lean and mean. A sauce needs to be considered as part of a dish; acid flavours, like lemon or tomato, need acidity in the wine – try a Sauvignon Blanc or a good Riesling.

Pastry dulls the palate, softening the flavours of the other ingredients with it; go for a more subtle wine than you might otherwise have chosen. Sweet food, including sweetish, fruity sauces, makes dry wine taste unpleasantly lean and acidic.

Red wines are not quite as adaptable as whites and rosés, largely because of their tannin. Tannin makes most fish taste metallic, and becomes more rasping with sweet things, so red wine with dessert doesn't usually work and tannic reds are unlikely to suit meat in fruity or sweet and sour sauces. However, tannin is perfect for cutting through fat, so tough reds are great with the fattier red meats and hearty stews. And the blood present in rare red meat has the knack of smoothing away all but the tougher tannins.

Juicy, Beaujolais-style reds (made from Gamay grapes) and wines based on Pinot Noir grapes have far less tannin and react differently with food. Contrary to the adage that white wine should be served with fish, these red wine grapes can go with certain fish, usually the sturdier-fleshed types such as salmon, monkfish and red mullet.

Red wine is traditionally drunk with cheese, but white is generally better. Blue cheeses, in particular, are unhappy matches for red wines, unless there's an element of sweetness, as in port.

Wine and health

A study published in 1992 highlighted the French paradox – that despite the proven link between the consumption of saturated fat and coronary heart disease, the French, whose consumption of both saturated fat and wine is high, have a significantly lower incidence of heart disease. Since then, many further studies have led most doctors in Western countries to conclude that wine in moderation – a maximum of four 120–150ml glasses a day for men, two glasses for women – can have a wide range of health benefits, particularly in reducing the risk of heart attack and stroke.

FRANCE

NEARLY ALL THE INTERNATIONALLY recognized classic wine types originate in France. All the greatest wine grape varieties are French, with the exception of Riesling. (And there's some of that in Alsace anyway.) All the methods of winemaking now accepted worldwide as the textbook procedures for the production of great wines, red or white, are based on French tradition. Not only that, but French methods of quality control, as laid out in the Appellation d'Origine Contrôlée regulations, have formed the model for such systems all over the world. The French, you see, have had 2000 years of practice at the winemaking game, ever since the Romans landed on the Mediterranean coast and settled at Narbonne, bringing with them their thirst for wine, their winemaking skills, and a tradition of law and order. And however strong the challenges from the rest of the world's vineyards, it's still going to be some time before France's supremacy is shaken.

If there is one thing which exemplifies the French wine style, it is balance – the balance between overripeness and underripeness, too much fruit flavour and not enough. And this is the result of almost 20 centuries of experimentation and refinement which continues today. Generation after generation of winemakers have patiently matched grape varieties with the most suitable soils in the most suitable sites so that appropriate ripening conditions have been found for all the great table wine grapes.

A tour of the regions

The Champagne region, in the far north, is cold and uninviting for most of the year, but in the folds of the Marne Valley and on the neighbouring slopes near the towns of Reims and Épernay, the chalky soil produces the thin acid white which is the perfect base for sparkling wine. Champagne – the world's greatest fizz – only comes from this single area of France.

The eastern frontiers of France are a series of mountain ranges and all of these produce highly individual wines. The Vosges mountains in Alsace slope into the Rhine Valley opposite Germany's Baden region, and the east-facing vineyards, warm and dry long into the golden days of autumn, produce fabulously spicy, perfumed white wines, unlike any other. As well as the dry whites for which it is best known, Alsace also produces luscious sweet wines from late-picked grapes. In the Jura mountains further south they make strange, unforgettably flavoured wines and from Savoie, the old alpine kingdom on the Italian border, come whites which are sharp, tasty and mouth-wateringly good.

Burgundy

Inland from these mountainous redoubts is the great swathe of land which used to make up the Duchy of Burgundy. It has been famous for wine and food since Roman times and it is still the birthplace of some of the most irresistible wine flavours in the world. Burgundy built its reputation on red wines, but several of its most famous wines are white. The northernmost of these is Chablis, a stone-dry white as celebrated as any in France, from a dowdy little town between Paris and Dijon. Red wine production gets into full swing south of Dijon with the Côte d'Or – a narrow but venerated slope of southeast-facing land which produces many of the most famous wines in the world – but in extremely limited quantities. The northern section of the Côte d'Or, the Côte de Nuits, is almost entirely red wine country, while the southern section, the Côte de Beaune, can produce reds and whites of equal splendour.

South of the Côte d'Or is the Côte Chalonnaise – a less spectacular, but extremely good source of Burgundy, reds from the Pinot Noir and whites from the Chardonnay, while the Mâconnais exists primarily as a white wine producer of very varying quality. In nearby Beaujolais the red Gamay grape can perform brilliantly. although it frequently doesn't.

Wines of the south

The Rhône Valley is on the whole a paradise for red wine drinkers, though the white Viognier grape makes startlingly good wine

The vineyards of Ch. Rouquette-sur-Mer overlook the Mediterranean town of Narbonne-Plage in Languedoc-Roussillon, a region that is currently producing some of France's most exciting wines.

at Condrieu. On the steep, cliff-like vineyards of the northern Rhône Valley, the Syrah grape offers fragrance and fiery force with some of France's grandest reds from Côte-Rôtie, Hermitage and Cornas. But the valley spreads out beneath the hill of Hermitage and the flavours soften too as the Grenache blends in with the Syrah, the Carignan and the Cinsaut to produce enormous amounts of easy-fruited Côtes du Rhône and much smaller amounts of concentrated, super-ripe Châteauneuf-du-Pape. In recent years white wines from the Marsanne and Roussanne grapes have started to make their mark.

The whole of the South of France is dominated by red wine – although Provence is more famous for its rosé and there are increasing numbers of fresh, vibrant whites. The AC wines of Languedoc-Roussillon – Corbières, Minervois, Fitou and others – are improving all the time. The Vin de Pays d'Oc, and in particular the *vins de cépages* or varietal wines, continue to make great strides with good-value Chardonnay, Sauvignon Blanc, Syrah, Merlot and Cabernet Sauvignon tempting consumers worldwide.

The South-West, between the Pyrenees and Bordeaux, and along the valleys of the Tarn and Lot rivers, has a very varied geography and range of wines. The Vin de Pays des Côtes de Gascogne uses local grape varieties to produce crisp, fruity dry white wines, while further north in Bergerac, styles merge almost imperceptibly with the lighter wines of Bordeaux. Madiran and Cahors have their own unusual and powerful reds, and Gaillac is best known for its sparklers, made either by a very old rural method or by the traditional method from Champagne.

Wine regions
- Champagne
- Lorraine
- Alsace
- Bourgogne
- Jura
- Savoie
- Rhône Valley
- Provence
- Corse
- Languedoc-Roussillon
- South-West
- Bordeaux
- Loire Valley

Regional Vins de Pays
- Vin de Pays du Jardin de la France
- Vin de Pays du Comté Tolosan
- Vin de Pays d'Oc
- Vin de Pays des Comtés Rhodaniens

Classics from the west

Bordeaux could well lay claim to the title 'red wine capital of the world'. The Merlot grape dominates the clay-rich vineyards of St-Émilion and Pomerol, while the gravelly soils of the Graves and the Haut-Médoc, especially at Margaux, St-Julien, Pauillac and St-Estèphe, provide the perfect conditions for Cabernet Sauvignon to produce a string of stunning wines. Bordeaux produces whites too, using Sémillon and Sauvignon Blanc grapes. Entre-Deux-Mers provides easy-to-drink, fruity but dry whites, while for true greatness, just look at the tangy, intense, dry styles of Pessac-Léognan and Graves. And as for Sauternes and Barsac – their unctuously sweet, rich wines set the standard for sweet

wines throughout the rest of the world, and given the unpredictable nature of their production there has been a generous number of great vintages in the last two decades.

In the Loire Valley the white Sauvignon Blanc, Chenin and Muscadet grapes produce some of France's most distinct wine styles. In the central Loire, Sauvignon creates world classics in the tangy, dry white stakes with Sancerre and Pouilly-Fumé. The ultra-dry, almost smoky green flavour has spawned imitators the world over, and made Sauvignon Blanc a superstar. Sauvignon also thrives in Touraine, but the Chenin then takes over, both at Vouvray, and further west in Anjou. Although difficult to ripen, Chenin can produce good sparkling wines as well as dry,

medium and sweet whites, all depending on the weather and the whim of the winemaker. The Cabernet Franc in a warm year makes thrilling reds at Chinon and Bourgueil. And the Muscadet grape makes – Muscadet, at its best an easy-going light, crisp, fresh dry white. If ever there was an all-purpose white wine, this has to be it.

Between these great classic areas, there are the little backwaters of wine; the byways which usually get forgotten as the big producers surge to the fore. Well, we don't forget them. As well as covering all the major areas, in great detail, the minor areas also get their due. Great and small, famous and unknown, red, white and rosé, together they make up the magical world of France and its wines.

French wine classifications

FRANCE HAS THE MOST COMPLEX and yet the most workable system in the world for controlling the quality and authenticity of its wines, based on the belief that the soil a vine grows in, and the type of grape variety employed, are crucial to the character and quality of the wine. There are three levels above the basic Vin de Table (table wine) level.

At the top is Appellation d'Origine Contrôlée (Controlled Appellation of Origin) usually abbreviated to AOC or AC. All the great French classic wines belong in this group. The second level is Vin Délimité de Qualité Supérieure (Delimited Wine of Superior Quality), usually abbreviated to VDQS. This is a kind of junior or probationary AC.

The third category, Vin de Pays, was created to give a geographical identity and quality yardstick to wines which had previously been sold off for blending. It is a useful category for adventurous winemakers because the regulations usually allow the use of grape varieties which are not traditional to an area and are thus debarred from its AC.

There are three divisions of Vin de Pays: regional (of which there are four, covering large areas of the country – see map on page 31): departmental (each of which covers the vineyards of one *département*, such as Vin de Pays des Pyrénées-Orientales); and zonal (the smallest and most tightly controlled areas, covering a specific locality).

There are seven major areas of control in AC regulations, which are mirrored to a greater or lesser extent in the lower quality levels:

Land The actual vineyard site is obviously at the top of the list. Its aspect to the sun, elevation, drainage – all these crucially influence the grape's ability to ripen. The composition of the soil also affects flavour and ripening.

Grape Different grape varieties ripen at different rates given more or less heat and on different sorts of soil. Over the centuries the best varieties for each area have evolved and only these are permitted so as to preserve each AC's individuality.

Alcoholic degree A minimum degree of alcohol is always specified as this reflects ripeness in the grapes. Ripe grapes give better flavour – and their higher sugar content creates higher eventual alcohol levels.

Vineyard yield Overproduction dilutes flavour and character, so a sensible maximum yield is fixed which is expressed in hectolitres of juice per hectare.

Vineyard practice The number of vines per hectare and the way they are pruned can dramatically affect yield and therefore quality. Maximum density and pruning methods are specified in the regulations.

Winemaking practice The things you can or can't do to the wine – like adding sugar to help fermentation, or removing acidity when the crop is unripe. Each area has its own particular rules.

Testing and tasting The wines must pass a technical test for soundness – and a tasting panel for quality and 'typicality'. Every year a significant number of wines are refused the AC.

Further levels of classification

You may also see words like Grand Cru, Grand Cru Classé or Premier Cru on the label.

Sometimes, as in Alsace and Burgundy, this is part of the AC. But in the Haut-Médoc in Bordeaux, it represents a historic judgment of excellence. In the famous 1855 Classification 60 red wines from the Haut-Médoc – and one from the Graves (now in Pessac-Léognan) – were ranked in five tiers according to the prices they traditionally fetched on the Bordeaux market. In general, the 1855 Classification is still a remarkably accurate guide to the best wines of the Haut-Médoc. Sauternes was also classified in 1855, but Graves had to wait until 1953 for its reds and 1959 for its whites. Pomerol has no classification, though St-Émilion does – it is revised every ten years or so to take account both of improving properties and of declining ones.

These Bordeaux classifications, though obviously influenced by the best vineyard sites, are actually judgments on the performance of a wine over the years – something which is often as much in the hands of the winemaker as inherent in the soil. Alsace and Burgundy have a classification, enshrined in the AC, which delineates the actual site of the vineyards. So the potential for excellence is recognized as either Grand Cru (the top in both areas) or Premier Cru (the second rank, so far only in Burgundy). Ideally, this is the better method, though a bad grower can still make bad wine anywhere.

The 1855 Classification

This was created for the 1855 World Exhibition in Paris by the Bordeaux Chamber of Commerce. It included only red wines from the Haut-Médoc, one red wine from the Graves and the sweet white wines from Sauternes and Barsac. It was revised once in 1973, raising Mouton-Rothschild in Pauillac from Deuxième Cru to Premier Cru status.

Premiers Crus: Lafite-Rothschild (Pauillac); Margaux (Margaux); Latour (Pauillac); Haut-Brion (Pessac-Léognan); Mouton-Rothschild (Pauillac).

Deuxièmes Crus: Rauzan-Ségla (Margaux); Rauzan-Gassies (Margaux); Léoville-Las-Cases (St-Julien); Léoville-Poyferré (St-Julien); Léoville- Barton (St-Julien); Durfort-Vivens (Margaux); Gruaud-Larose (St-Julien); Lascombes (Margaux); Brane-Cantenac (Margaux); Pichon-Longueville (Pauillac); Pichon-Longueville-Comtesse de Lalande (Pauillac); Ducru-Beaucaillou (St-Julien); Cos d'Estournel (St-Estèphe); Montrose (St-Estèphe).

Troisièmes Crus: Kirwan (Margaux); d'Issan (Margaux); Lagrange (St-Julien); Langoa-Barton (St-Julien); Giscours (Margaux); Maléscot-St-Exupéry (Margaux); Boyd-Cantenac (Margaux); Cantenac-Brown (Margaux); Palmer (Margaux); La Lagune (Haut-Médoc); Desmirail (Margaux); Calon-Ségur (St-Estèphe); Ferrière (Margaux); Marquis d'Alesme-Becker (Margaux).

Quatrièmes Crus: St-Pierre (St-Julien); Talbot (St-Julien); Branaire (St-Julien); Duhart-Milon (Pauillac); Pouget (Margaux); la Tour-Carnet (Haut-Médoc); Lafon-Rochet (St-Estèphe); Beychevelle (St-Julien); Prieuré-Lichine (Margaux); Marquis de Terme (Margaux).

Cinquièmes Crus: Pontet-Canet (Pauillac); Batailley (Pauillac); Haut-Batailley (Pauillac); Grand-Puy-Lacoste (Pauillac); Grand-Puy-Ducasse (Pauillac); Lynch-Bages (Pauillac); Lynch-Moussas (Pauillac); Dauzac (Margaux); d'Armailhac (Pauillac); du Tertre (Margaux); Haut-Bages-Libéral (Pauillac); Pedesclaux (Pauillac); Belgrave (Haut-Médoc); Camensac (Haut-Médoc); Cos-Labory (St-Estèphe); Clerc-Milon (Pauillac); Croizet-Bages (Pauillac); Cantemerle (Haut-Médoc).

The 1855 Classification of Barsac and Sauternes

Premier Cru Supérieur: d'Yquem (Sauternes).
Premiers Crus: la Tour Blanche (Sauternes); Lafaurie-Peyraguey (Sauternes); Clos Haut-Peyraguey (Sauternes); Rayne-Vigneau (Sauternes); Suduiraut (Sauternes); Coutet (Barsac); Climens (Barsac); Guiraud (Sauternes); Rieussec (Sauternes); Rabaud-Promis (Sauternes); Sigalas-Rabaud (Sauternes).
Deuxièmes Crus: de Myrat (Barsac); Doisy-Daëne (Barsac); Doisy-Dubroca (Barsac); Doisy-Védrines (Barsac); d'Arche (Sauternes); Filhot (Sauternes); Broustet (Barsac); Nairac (Barsac); Caillou (Barsac); Suau (Barsac); de Malle (Sauternes); Romer du Hayot (Sauternes); Lamothe (Sauternes); Lamothe-Guignard (Sauternes).

The Classification of the Graves (since 1987 Pessac-Léognan)

This classification was carried out in 1953 encompassing only red wines. It was revised in 1959 to include white wines. Ch. Haut-Brion features both in this and the 1855 Classification. The châteaux are listed alphabetically, followed by their commune and whether they are classified for red or white wine.
Bouscaut (Cadaujac) ♥♀; Carbonnieux (Léognan) ♥♀; Domaine de Chevalier (Léognan) ♥♀; Couhins (Villenave-d'Ornon) ♀; Couhins-Lurton (Villenave-d'Ornon) ♀; de Fieuzal (Léognan) ♥; Haut-Bailly (Léognan) ♥; Haut-Brion (Pessac) ♥; Latour-Martillac (Martillac) ♥♀; Laville-Haut-Brion (Talence) ♀; Malartic-Lagravière (Léognan) ♥♀; la Mission-Haut-Brion (Talence) ♥; Olivier (Léognan) ♥♀; Pape Clément (Pessac) ♥; Smith-Haut-Lafitte (Martillac) ♥; la Tour-Haut-Brion (Talence) ♥.

The St-Émilion Classification

St-Émilion Grand Cru is a superior appellation within St-Émilion, and of the several hundred Grand Cru wines a certain number will be classified. The first classification was in 1954, and it was slightly modified in 1969, 1985 and 1996. The possibility of re-grading can help to maintain quality.
Premiers Grands Crus Classés (A): Ausone, Cheval Blanc.
Premiers Grands Crus Classés (B): Angélus, Beau-Séjour Bécot, Beauséjour (Duffau-Lagarosse), Belair, Canon, Clos Fourtet, Figeac, La Gaffelière, Magdelaine, Pavie, Trotteveille.
Grands Crus Classés: l'Arrosée, Balestard-la-Tonnelle, Bellevue, Bergat, Berliquet, Cadet-Bon, Cadet-Piola, Canon-la Gaffelière, Cap de Mourlin, Chauvin, Clos des Jacobins, Clos de

In the vintage bottle cellar at Ch. Latour, a Bordeaux Premier Cru, the cellar master holds a double magnum (equivalent to four standard bottles).

l'Oratoire, Clos St-Martin, la Clotte, la Clusière, Corbin, Corbin-Michotte, la Couspaude, Couvent des Jacobins, Curé-Bon, Dassault, la Dominique, Faurie-de-Souchard, Fonplégade, Fonroque, Franc Mayne, les Grandes Murailles, Grand Mayne, Grand-Pontet, Guadet-St-Julien, Haut Corbin, Haut Sarpe, Lamarzelle, Laniote, Larcis Ducasse, Larmande, Laroque, Laroze, Matras, Moulin du Cadet, Pavie-Decesse, Pavie-Macquin, Petit-Faurie-de-Soutard, le Prieuré, Ripeau, St-Georges (Côte Pavie), la Serre, Soutard, TertreDaugay, la Tour Figeac, la Tour du Pin Figeac (Giraud-Bélivier), la Tour du Pin Figeac (J M Moueix), Troplong-Mondot, Villemaurine, Yon-Figeac.

The Crus Bourgeois of the Médoc

The Cru Bourgeois châteaux were first classified in 1932, listing 444 estates producing wines of regular high quality. The classification was reassessed in 1966 and again in 1978, to finish with 419 estates, which between them represent 50 per cent of the wine produced in the Médoc, as opposed to 24 per cent for the Crus Classés. The following Cru Bourgeois châteaux now produce wines of, or near to, Cru Classé standard: Angludet, Charmail, Chasse-Spleen, Citran, Haut-Marbuzet, Gloria, la Gurgue, Labégorce, Labégorce-Zédé, Lilian Ladouys, Marbuzet, Meyney, Monbrison, de Pez, Phélan-Ségur, Pibran, Potensac, Poujeaux, Siran, Sociando-Mallet, la Tour Haut-Caussan.

Burgundy classifications

There are five levels: regional (Bourgogne); specific regional (e.g. Chablis); village or communal (e.g. Pommard); Premiers Crus; and Grands Crus. Certain vineyards are entitled to the rank Premier Cru: on the label the vineyard name follows the village name (e.g. Gevrey-Chambertin, Combe-aux-Moines). Grands Crus, the top level, are appellations in their own right; and the Grand Cru names can stand alone on the label, without a village name. The following Côte d'Or villages have Grands Crus:

Gevrey-Chambertin: le Chambertin ♥, Chambertin, Clos de Bèze ♥, Chapelle-Chambertin ♥, Charmes-Chambertin ♥ incorporating Mazoyères-Chambertin ♥, Griottes-Chambertin ♥, Latricières-Chambertin ♥, Mazis-Chambertin ♥, Ruchottes-Chambertin ♥

Morey St-Denis: Bonnes-Mares ♥, Clos des Lambrays ♥, Clos de la Roche ♥, Clos St-Denis ♥, Clos de Tart ♥

Chambolle-Musigny: Musigny ♥ ♀, Bonnes-Mares ♥

Vougeot: Clos de Vougeot ♥

Vosne-Romanée: Richebourg ♥, la Romanée-Conti ♥, la Romanée ♥, la Grande-Rue ♥, la Romanée-St-Vivant ♥, Richebourg ♥, la Tâche ♥

Flagey-Échézeaux: Échézeaux ♥, Grands-Échézeaux ♥. These two Grands Crus are often grouped under Vosne-Romanée as all Flagey's other wines are labelled as Vosne-Romanée.

Aloxe-Corton: Corton ♥ ♀ (divided into sub-vineyards or *climats* of which the most important are Bressandes, le Corton, Maréchaudes, Pougets, Clos de Roi, Renardes, and Rognet), Corton-Charlemagne ♀

Ladoix-Serrigny: Corton ♥ ♀, Corton-Charlemagne ♀

Pernand-Vergelesses: Corton-Charlemagne ♀

Puligny-Montrachet: Bâtard-Montrachet ♀, Bienvenues-Bâtard-Montrachet ♀, Chevalier-Montrachet ♀, le Montrachet ♀

Chassagne-Montrachet: Criots-Bâtard-Montrachet ♀, le Montrachet ♀
For the Chablis Grands Crus see pages 120-123.

Alsace Grand Cru

As part of its AC, Alsace has 50 designated Grands Crus (see page 64). Among the best are: Altenberg de Bergheim, Brand, Eichberg, Frankstein, Froehn, Furstentum, Geisberg, Goldert, Hengst, Kaefferkopf, Kastelberg, Kessler, Kirchberg de Barr, Kirchberg de Ribeauvillé, Kitterlé, Mandelberg, Moenchberg, Osterberg, Rangen, Rosacker, Schlossberg, Schoenenbourg, Sporen, Zinnkoepflé, Zotzenberg.

GERMANY

GERMANY IS IN THE THROES of a revolution. It started in earnest only a few years ago, and it has gone from strength to strength. Part of this revolution is a revival of the traditional high-quality grape varieties that used to rule the roost before upstarts like Müller-Thurgau knocked them off their perch. But it is a rebellion as well: many of the country's best growers are rejecting the provisions of the law in order to make and sell their wines with the greatest possible flexibility. During the last five years the question as to whether Germany's top vineyard sites should be legally classified along similar lines to the Grand Cru systems in Alsace and Burgundy has become a political hot potato. Unofficial classifications abound, and are being implemented by leading growers throughout the country. At some point the lawmakers will surely follow suit, but in Germany change of this kind is always slow in coming.

German wine classifications

German wine law dates from 1971, and to wine lovers it is infamous for the confusion it has caused consumers. It grades wines according to the amount of sugar present in the grapes at harvest, on the principle that riper grapes are a sign of quality, and are found only in better vineyards, tended by better growers and in better years.

At the bottom of the ladder there is Tafelwein, or table wine. A notch above this is Landwein, which is the equivalent of the French vin de pays. Anything above this level is quality wine in EU terms. German quality wine falls into two main divisions: quality wine from a designated region, or Qualitätswein bestimmte Anbaugebiete (QbA), and quality wine from a special category, or Qualitätswein mit Prädikat (QmP). The former is Germany's everyday wine, covering everything from Liebfraumilch to the much higher quality basic wines of the finest growers. (A new category, Qualitätswein garantierten Ursprung (QbU), or quality wine of guaranteed origin, indicates that 100 per cent of the grapes come from the area stated on the label.)

Riesling vines in the Würzgarten vineyard above the Mosel at Ürzig. The river both retains and reflects heat, and the slope allows maximum exposure to the sun, helping the grapes to ripen in Germany's cool climate.

Qualitätswein mit Pradikät

It is in the second category, Qualitätswein mit Prädikat, that things get complicated. There are six Prädikat levels, each demanding a progressively higher level of sugar in the grapes. Kabinett is the lightest: Kabinett wines are usually dry or medium-dry, often very delicate and naturally low in alcohol. Spätlese, the next category, means 'late-picked', and these wines are richer and riper, sometimes dry and seldom more than medium-dry. Auslese means 'selected': there may well be some noble rot on these grapes, if the year permits, and you can expect some sweetness. But only with Beerenauslese do the wines become properly sweet. The term means 'berry-selected': noble-rotted grapes are picked individually for these wines, which are rare and expensive. The final category, Trockenbeerenauslese, is also rare: individually picked grapes, shrivelled by noble rot, are all that are allowed in these intensely sweet and long-lived wines. Eiswein ('ice wine') is just as sweet, but there the sweetness is concentrated not by the action of noble rot but by freezing: the grapes are picked on mornings when the temperature is -6°C (23°F) or below, and the water in the grapes is frozen solid. The juice that is then pressed out contains virtually no water, which means that it is very concentrated and sweet.

This is all well and good, but while an Auslese is undoubtedly rarer and more expensive than a Kabinett, it is not necessarily of better quality: much depends on the standards of the grower and the grape variety. A Riesling Kabinett from a fine estate can be streets ahead of an Optima Auslese from the local co-operative.

And this is why the growers are up in arms. A few have opted for making only QmP wines, skipping the QbA category altogether, and selling anything that doesn't make Kabinett level as plain Tafelwein. Some wear Tafelwein as a badge of pride, using the freedom of the lowest of all designations to experiment with the use of new oak barriques for aging their wines (the taste of new oak is frowned upon by the authorities who grant the QbA and QmP designations). Large numbers of growers, too, are doing away with the baffling proliferation of village and vineyard names, and selling their wine simply on their company's name.

Quality wine regions
- Ahr
- Mittelrhein
- Mosel-Saar-Ruwer
- Rheingau
- Nahe
- Rheinhessen
- Pfalz
- Hessische Bergstrasse
- Franken
- Württemberg
- Baden
- Saale-Unstrut
- Sachsen

Quality wine regions

Germany has 13 designated quality wine regions. They are: Ahr, Mittelrhein, Mosel-Saar-Ruwer, Nahe, Rheinhessen, Pfalz, Rheingau, Hessische Bergstrasse, Franken, Baden, Württemberg, Saale-Unstrut and Sachsen, the last two being in what was East Germany. These regions are divided into Bereiche, or sub-regions, which in turn are divided into a total of roughly 150 Grosslagen – a group of vineyard sites. A single vineyard within a Grosslage is called an Einzellage and a wine from an Einzellage should, in theory, be superior to one from a Grosslage. But in Germany most vineyards are divided between more than one producer. Single ownership of a single site, as happens, for example, in Bordeaux, is rare. So standards vary enormously, and while a top vineyard name on a label may be an indication of quality, a far more reliable guarantee is the name of the grower.

Wine styles

The style of the wines varies, too, from one region to another. Partly this is a question of climate and soil, partly a matter of the vines grown, and while there is obviously a change in the climate from north to south, there is a change, too, from west to east. The more easterly regions have an appreciably more continental climate – that is, a climate of extremes – than those in the west. And while the hardy Riesling grape, traditionally Germany's finest, produces supreme elegance and raciness in north-westerly regions like the Mosel, the Rheingau and the Pfalz, in the vineyards of Baden it is the grapes of the Pinot family – Blanc, Gris and Noir – that excel. Here, in the warmer climate of Germany's southerly regions, dry whites and reds can show fuller, softer flavours than we have come to expect from German wines, although Baden's full potential has yet to be realized.

Further east the winters may be too cold even for the Riesling.

The Riesling is still Germany's quality flagship, even though the far inferior Müller-Thurgau beats it in terms of number of hectares planted. The third most popular grape is the Silvaner, with the Kerner close behind. The Kerner is an example of a German phenomenon: the new vine crossing. The famous viticultural research station at Geisenheim in the Rheingau has produced many of these in recent years: they have names like Huxelrebe or Faberrebe and they are designed to produce good yields and to be resistant to cold and frost in the tough German climate. Their quality, in spite of the researchers' best efforts, lags behind the classic varieties, although Scheurebe can be an exception to this rule.

Germany's red wines are made mostly from Spätburgunder (or Pinot Noir), with Blauer Portugieser, Trollinger and Dornfelder also popular. And both red and white wines are year by year, region by region, grower by grower, becoming fuller, better balanced, and drier. Now, how's that for a revolution?

AUSTRIA

AUSTRIA'S VINEYARDS ARE concentrated in the east of the country, and are no respecters of national boundaries: they spill over into Slovakia, Hungary and Slovenia and take their grape varieties with them, just as they did in the days when the Austro-Hungarian Empire covered the whole region. Dry white wines predominate, made from Austria's own Grüner Veltliner and a handful of other varieties, including Riesling, Chardonnay, Sauvignon Blanc and Pinot Blanc, but Austria's great tradition for dessert wines is being revived, and some rich, powerful reds are appearing.

Wine regions

Niederösterreich
1 Wachau
2 Kremstal
3 Kamptal
4 Traisental
5 Donauland
6 Weinviertel
7 Carnuntum
8 Thermenregion

Wien
9 Wien

Burgenland
10 Neusiedlersee
11 Neusiedlersee-Hügelland
12 Mittelburgenland
13 Südburgenland

Steiermark
14 Süd-Oststeiermark
15 Südsteiermark
16 Weststeiermark

Wine regions

Austria has three main wine-producing regions: Niederösterreich (Lower Austria), Burgenland and Steiermark (Styria); the area around Wien (Vienna) is also surrounded by vineyards. While it is principally a white wine country the reds, particularly those from southern Burgenland, are improving all the time. From northern Burgenland come outstanding sweet wines. From just about everywhere these days, since fashion demands it, come first-class dry wines of body and structure and elegance which, thanks to the conservatism of consumers abroad, remain barely known outside their own country. The exceptions are Germans, who think nothing of driving down to Styria to stock up with bone-dry Riesling.

Taste some of the best examples and you can understand why. Dry Austrian whites have the freshness and aromatic style of German wines, but are more full-bodied and harmonious than the dry wines from Austria's northern neighbour. While the Austrians drink them as young as possible they can also

Dürnstein, with its Baroque monastery and ruined fortress, is one of the most famous villages of the Wachau wine region.

age for five, ten or more years in top vintages. During the 1990s there has been a revolution in the dessert wine field with a handful of leading growers starting to produce world class wines. Top producers are also making opulent red wines with aging potential, from native grapes such as Blauer Zweigelt and Blaufränkisch and international varieties like Cabernet Sauvignon and Pinot Noir. However, whether sweet or dry, white or red, top-quality Austrian wines are not cheap.

Austrian wine classifications

Wine quality categories are similar to those in Germany (see page 34), beginning with Tafelwein (table wine) and Landwein (country wine, like the French vin de pays). All Qualitätswein must come from a region specified on the label: this may be one of the 16 main wine-producing regions or a village or vineyard within the region. Like German wines, quality wines may additionally have a special category, but Austrian wine labels give a better idea of the style of the wine: Kabinett is always dry; Spätlese usually dry; Auslese is usually a light dessert wine – although it may be dry (labelled Trocken); Beerenauslese and Trockenbeerenauslese are always sweet, and there is an additional dessert wine category, Ausbruch, between the two styles.

SWITZERLAND

IN SWITZERLAND'S COOL, alpine climate, the vineyards are concentrated around the country's lakes and rivers and are often steep and terraced – the high cost of production is one reason why Swiss wines are expensive. Perhaps surprisingly, nearly half the wines made are red; both reds and whites tend to be delicate and fresh.

Wine regions

Wine regions		
Valais	Bern	Schaffhausen
Vaud	Jura	Thurgau
Geneva	Basel	St Gallen
Neuchâtel	Aargau	Graubünden (Grisons)
Fribourg	Zürich	Ticino

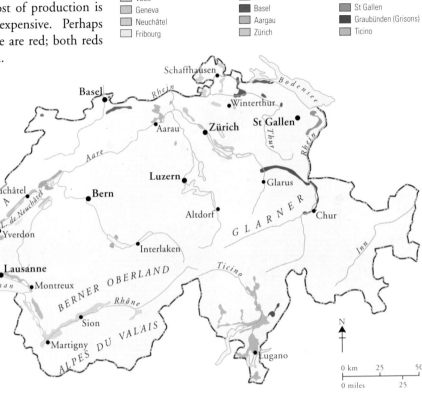

Wine regions

Vaud and Valais, the French-speaking cantons that overlook Lake Geneva (Lac Léman) and the Rhône, are the sources for most of Switzerland's wine; Neuchâtel and Geneva also contribute substantially, while the Fribourg and Jura vineyards are among Switzerland's smallest. The white Chasselas (known as Fendant in Valais, Dorin in Vaud and Perlan in Geneva) is the main variety, making light, neutral, fresh wines; reds come from Pinot Noir and Gamay; rosés, under the stylistic appellation of Oeil de Perdrix ('partridge eye') are also made from Pinot Noir. The German-speaking districts of Basel, Bern, Aargau, Graubünden (Grisons in Italian), St Gallen, Schaffhausen, Thurgau and Zürich make reds and whites from the same grapes (but sometimes under different names – Pinot Noir is also known as Blauburgunder and Clevner), plus Müller-Thurgau (known as Riesling x Sylvaner) and others; the Italian-speaking canton of Ticino makes good ripe Merlot.

Swiss wine classifications

There are three major quality categories: Appellation d'Origine Contrôlée (which is granted to each canton, with the right to regulate appellations within its boundaries; each winemaking village can register its own appellation); generic indication of origin (roughly comparable with the French vins de pays); and wine with no appellation of origin (table wines, labelled 'red' or 'white').

Cantonal regulations vary according to local traditions: some stick to either canton or village appellations, others recognize Crus within the villages, or districts such as Chablais (in Vaud). The appellation also specifies grape variety or style; a well-known light red wine, Dôle du Valais, is a blend of Pinot Noir and Gamay.

These vineyards at Sion, on the right bank of the Rhône, are in the Valais, the most intensively cultivated of Switzerland's winemaking cantons.

A big future for Swiss wine?

Very little Swiss wine is exported: put simply, domestic consumers drink all the wine the country can produce. Another big obstacle to the development of the Swiss wine industry, the nation's protectionist policy to white wine imports, was removed in 1995. During the 1990s some very interesting and innovative dry white and red wines began to be produced in the cantons of Valais, Graubünden and Ticino, which suggest that Switzerland has considerable untapped potential in both these fields. Many of these wines have been made with non-traditional grape varieties such as Chardonnay, which makes sense – cool-climate Chardonnays are often delicious. But would you ever expect to find a Swiss Syrah? And a ripe, fragrant one at that? But the Valais *does* produce Syrah in those sun-traps on the steep mountains. There is Riesling too, which is only logical when you see vertiginous vineyards with stony soils as challenging as any in Germany's Mosel Valley.

Equally interesting are rare and unusual white wines from Switzerland's indigenous vines, Amigne, Petite Arvine and Humagne Blanc. After a long period of protectionism and complacency, Swiss winemakers are beginning to create some Alpine waves.

ITALY

ITALY HAS WINES THAT ARE dry as a bone and wines that are lusciously sweet; wines that are light and dainty, and great strapping monsters; wines that are the essence of subtlety and wines that are outlandishly brash. The country stretches from Austria in the north almost to Africa in the south and houses a vast number of soil types, climates, altitudes and grape varieties, many of them strictly localized. Add to this the thousands of producers making wines in subtly different ways and it's not difficult to see that Italian wines have an almost infinite variety of flavours. And as fast as the authorities tried to classify wines, so producers created wines that didn't fit in. Well, of course, you'd expect nothing less. Creating irresistible chaos out of bureaucratic rule is one of the delights of Italy. Only now is a much improved and flexible legal framework beginning to have an effect. Whether or not the Lords of Misrule reassert their control is another matter.

Italian wine classification

The first classification system, introduced in 1963, didn't do too badly for the first 20 years, the problem is that it has had to last more than 30. Well, 'didn't do too badly' is perhaps being a little kind. From a situation of total mayhem, where almost nothing was as it seemed, a system full of good intentions was put in place. Called DOC (Denominazione di Origine Controllata) it was an Italianization of the French AC system, controlling production zones, grape varieties, yields, alcohol, aging and so on. Criteria were based upon 'local tradition and practice'. If local practices were shoddy and traditional wines dismal, that is what was enshrined. And if laws were blithely disregarded, so long as the prices remained low, no-one seemed to mind too much.

Nevertheless, requests for classification flooded in and there are now around 250, some well known, like Soave, others obscure; some covering just a couple of producers, others embracing vast tracts of land. One has to presume it was an improvement on what had gone before, but clearly if top wines like Brunello di Montalcino and Barolo were being lumped together with industrial Soave and anonymous nonentities of no proven worth, a further classification was needed. And so we got the DOCG, the G standing for 'garantita', or guaranteed. Some 14 areas had the G by mid-1998, including some of Italy's best, but they are by no means all producing top wines. DOC was also too rigid a system to incorporate the hundreds of new, innovative wines Italians were making from atypical grapes or winemaking methods, and there was simply no place for them other than as Vini da Tavola (VdT, or table wine), theoretically the simple, everyday quaffing wine. Hence the term super-Vini da Tavola, to describe these high-priced, often brilliant anomalies.

Now there is a new law which is gradually rolling into action. The basic concept of DOC(G) has been retained but now allows

The rolling hills south of Florence have been famous for their red wine for at least seven centuries. The zone is now known as Chianti Classico DOCG, and continues to produce some of Tuscany's best-known wines.

for a pyramidal structure of increasing quality within areas of decreasing size. This means DOC zones can be broken down into sub-zones, communes, micro-zones, estates and vineyards, with progressively more stringent controls, and can become DOCG at any stage towards the pyramid's tip. And if producers don't make use of a DOC it can cease to exist. There's also a new category, Indicazione Geografica Tipica (IGT), toward the base of the pyramid, between DOC and VdT, which is similar to the French vin de pays.

The above paragraph describes what is possible under the new law. What is actually happening is rather different, and entrenched interests are being used to undermine much of the good it could do. But it *is* doing some good, so let's take one step at a time.

Traditions and innovations

Wine is produced in all of the country's 95 provinces, lying in 20 administrative regions, and often there are no clear divisions between one wine district and the next: changes in style are gradual. So although it is convenient to talk about, say, Tuscan reds or Friuli whites, categorizing wine styles needs a more broad-brush approach.

In broad terms, therefore, the north-east relies for quantity on its reds and quality

DOCG/DOC wine areas and main wines

- Valle d'Aosta
- Piemonte
  1. Gattinara
  2. Barbera d'Asti, Asti, Moscato d'Asti
  3. Roero, Roero Arneis, Barbera d'Alba
  4. Barolo, Barbaresco, Barbera d'Alba, Dolcetto d'Alba
  5. Gavi
- Lombardia
  6. Franciacorta
  7. Valtellina Superiore
- Veneto
  8. Valpolicella Classico, Amarone, Recioto
  9. Soave Classico, Recioto
  10. Breganze

- Trentino-Alto Adige
  11. Teroldego Rotaliano
  12. Alto Adige
- Friuli-Venezia Giulia
  13. Colli Orientali del Friuli, Collio, Friuli Isonzo
- Emilia-Romagna
- Liguria
- Toscana
  14. Carmignano
  15. Chianti Rufina
  16. Vernaccia di San Gimignano
  17. Chianti Classico
  18. Bolgheri
  19. Brunello di Montalcino
  20. Vino Nobile di Montepulciano
- Umbria
  21. Torgiano Riserva
  22. Orvieto
  23. Sagrantino di Montefalco
- Marche
  24. Verdicchio dei Castelli di Jesi
- Abruzzo
  25. Montepulciano d'Abruzzo
- Lazio
  26. Frascati Superiore
- Molise
- Campania
  27. Taurasi
- Basilicata
  28. Aglianico del Vulture
- Puglia
  29. Brindisi
  30. Salice Salentino
- Calabria
  31. Cirò
- Sicilia
  32. Marsala
  33. Moscato di Pantelleria
- Sardegna

comes from the whites, mainly single-variety wines from aromatic grapes, often of French or German origin. Even so, there are some exceptional reds made in Valpolicella and Friuli, as well as some remarkable sweet wines from indigenous varieties. The north-west produces delicate sparkling white wines in Asti, but is celebrated above all for firmly structured red wines. Long aging and serious high quality come from the Nebbiolo grape, younger, zippier wines from Dolcetto, Barbera and others, and there's an overdue renewal of interest in Piedmont's native white varieties. The central Po valley is Lambrusco country. The central-west's grape is red

Sangiovese, its major wine Chianti, but it is more likely to reach its highest expression in Brunello di Montalcino – and innovation is a byword here. There is more Sangiovese across to the east too, which gives way to Montepulciano as you head south. Whites are as important, from the Trebbiano, Albana and Verdicchio varieties. Rome is Frascati, and the whole south is in the process of upheaval, changing from heavy whites and stewy reds to some excitingly promising wines made from local varieties, such as Primitivo (California's Zinfandel), Nero d'Avola, Malvasia Nera and Negroamaro; Puglia leads the way but Sicily is hard on its heels.

Throughout the country there are also new-style wines, often based on the international varieties Cabernet Sauvignon and Chardonnay, but also, in some exciting experiments, on Pinot Noir, Syrah, Sauvignon Blanc and Viognier. There's much use of small, new French oak barriques too. But not everything in Italy's garden is rosy. Some producers use a smart presentation to disguise an average wine; others always sell their 'experimental' wines, whether the experiment has been successful or not. These wines deserve to be buried without trace. For Italy has such tremendous potential, it is criminal not to exploit that potential to its full.

SPAIN AND PORTUGAL

As SEAFARING POWERS, the two nations of the Iberian Peninsula took their wines to the far corners of the globe; the hardiest of these, the great fortified wines of sherry, port and Madeira, survived not only the long journeys but also the test of time – they are as popular today as they have been for more than two centuries. Both countries' fortunes have waxed and waned, but they are now bringing modern versions of their historic wine styles to the world wine party.

Spain

Politically, Spain is divided into 17 autonomous regions, including the Canary and Balearic Islands, with Madrid forming an autonomy of its own, each of which produces wine at all levels. Nearly 50 per cent of the EU's vineyards lie in Spain, but that doesn't mean that Spain makes half the wine: grape yields are only half those of France, although improved viticultural practices have led to a steady increase in yields through the 1990s.

Changes have occurred at such a dizzying pace in the Spanish wine world over the past few years that many clichés no longer hold true. Chances are that the glass of co-operative red you can buy in any local bar will surprise you with a mouthful of clean, fruity wine, as a growing number of those collective wineries are joining the quality bandwagon. Smarter labels are also sprouting up.

One old cliché was that about the paucity of Spain's grape varieties: there was Palomino to make sherry and Tempranillo for all the decent reds – forget about the rest. Now Albariño has emerged as a Viognier-like star in Galicia, soon followed by its neighbour Godello. Rueda's grassy, bitterish Verdejo has made good strides, and Macabeo (Viura) is improving beyond all expectations. Among red varieties, Garnacha and Cariñena have returned to prominence, and new investment indicates that the South-East's ocean of Monastrell vines is in line for improvement. The pungent Graciano's new plantings continue in Rioja and, after Tempranillo, most of what's being planted is – in New World fashion – Cabernet Sauvignon, Merlot and Chardonnay.

Established and rising stars include the fresh, aromatic white wines from Galicia and from Rueda in Castilla-León; the reds of Priorat, Navarra, Rioja and Ribera del Duero; Cava, the DO sparkling wine – usually from Cataluña – and Andalucía's fortified wines: sherry, Montilla and Málaga.

Spanish wine classifications

The general quality wine designation, roughly equivalent to the French AC, is Denominación de Origen (DO); there are now more than 50. In 1991 Rioja was the first region elevated to Denominación de Origen Calificada (DOC), a new supercategory for wines prepared to undergo rigorous scrutiny. Country wines fall into two categories: Vino Comarcal and the increasingly important Vino de la Tierra, which equates to the French vin de pays. Vino de Mesa is the basic table wine level, although, as in Italy, there is an increasing number of non-DO 'super-Spanish'. The presence – or lack – of a DO on the label no longer indicates a given quality level. There are some terrible Riojas and some heavenly Vinos de Mesa. Knowing the producer's name has become much more important than remembering old clichés.

Aging regulations have been standardized throughout Spain. Crianza wines must have a minimum of two years' aging before sale; red Reserva at least three years (of which one must be in oak), white Reserva at least two years (of which six months must be in oak); red Gran Reserva at least two years in oak and three in bottle, and white Gran Reserva four years' aging (of which six months must be in oak).

Portugal

For much of the past 200 years Portugal languished on the sidelines, isolated geographically (and at times politically) from the European mainstream. Globe-trotting grape varieties like Cabernet Sauvignon and Chardonnay have made remarkably few inroads into Portuguese vineyards, and grapes with unfamiliar names like the red Touriga Nacional, Baga and Trincadeira or the white Loureiro and Arinto are still Portugal's own superstars in the making.

At the ultra-modern gravity-fed winery of Abadía Retuerta in Castilla-León, the wine is treated more gently than in most wineries because rather than pumping, the barrels are set up to allow gravity to do the work.

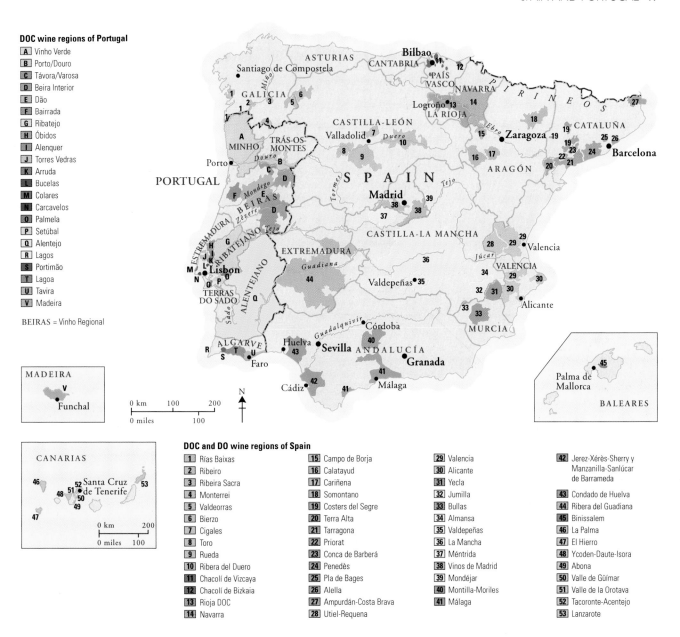

DOC wine regions of Portugal

A Vinho Verde
B Porto/Douro
C Távora/Varosa
D Beira Interior
E Dão
F Bairrada
G Ribatejo
H Óbidos
I Alenquer
J Torres Vedras
K Arruda
L Bucelas
M Colares
N Carcavelos
O Palmela
P Setúbal
Q Alentejo
R Lagos
S Portimão
T Lagoa
U Tavira
V Madeira

BEIRAS = Vinho Regional

MADEIRA

V

Funchal

0 km   100   200
0 miles   100

N

CANARIAS

46   52 Santa Cruz   53
48 51 de Tenerife
      50
47   49

0 km   200
0 miles   100

DOC and DO wine regions of Spain

1 Rías Baixas	15 Campo de Borja	29 Valencia	42 Jerez-Xérès-Sherry y Manzanilla-Sanlúcar de Barrameda
2 Ribeiro	16 Calatayud	30 Alicante	
3 Ribeira Sacra	17 Cariñena	31 Yecla	
4 Monterrei	18 Somontano	32 Jumilla	43 Condado de Huelva
5 Valdeorras	19 Costers del Segre	33 Bullas	44 Ribera del Guadiana
6 Bierzo	20 Terra Alta	34 Almansa	45 Binissalem
7 Cigales	21 Tarragona	35 Valdepeñas	46 La Palma
8 Toro	22 Priorat	36 La Mancha	47 El Hierro
9 Rueda	23 Conca de Barberá	37 Méntrida	48 Ycoden-Daute-Isora
10 Ribera del Duero	24 Penedès	38 Vinos de Madrid	49 Abona
11 Chacolí de Vizcaya	25 Pla de Bages	39 Mondéjar	50 Valle de Güímar
12 Chacolí de Bizkaia	26 Alella	40 Montilla-Moriles	51 Valle de la Orotava
13 Rioja DOC	27 Ampurdán-Costa Brava	41 Málaga	52 Tacoronte-Acentejo
14 Navarra	28 Utiel-Requena		53 Lanzarote

Decades of self-imposed isolation came to an end in 1986 when Portugal joined the European Union. This opened the floodgates for investment in the wine industry and new stainless steel wineries sprung up all over the country. With a number of go-ahead wine-makers (including a handful of Australians), Portugal is now well placed to take advantage of its remarkable viticultural heritage.

Although whites can be good, often dry but slightly musky, it is the reds that should soon propel Portugal into centre stage, fabulously fruity and perfumed, low on tannin and quite unlike any others in the world.

Portugal's wines tend to reflect a varied climate and topography. The Atlantic exerts a strong influence over the coastal wine regions and its moderating effects diminish sharply as you travel inland. As a result, crisp, crackling dry whites like Vinho Verde can be produced in close proximity to hefty reds from the Douro and rich, fortified port.

Portuguese wine classifications

There are four tiers of wine regions. The first tier, Denominação de Origem Controlada (DOC), includes all the established regions in the north of the country like Vinho Verde, Dão, Bairrada as well as the fortified wines port, Madeira and Setúbal. The second tier of small, new regions goes under the rather long-winded heading of Indicação de Proveniencia Regulamentada (IPR). In theory all are candidates for promotion to DOC but many will never make the grade. The third and much more significant tier of wine regions, particularly in the south of the country, is designated Vinho Regional. Rather like the French vins de pays, these cover larger areas and the legislation permits greater flexibility in terms of grape varieties and aging requirements. There are eight regions and a few sub-regions: Alentejano, Ribatejano, Terras do Sado and Estremadura are the Vinhos Regionais most commonly seen on labels. Wines that fall outside the DOC, IPR or Vinho Regional requirements are classified as Vinho de Mesa (table wine).

UNITED STATES AND CANADA

FOR ALL PRACTICAL PURPOSES, American wine is California wine. But wine is everything except practical, and so growers in a dozen other states love to claim that what they grow matters just as much as anything from California, saying it tastes as good or better. California is, and will remain, the superstar, not only because of its remarkable range of soils and climates, but because nearly all of the state is a benign environment for vines. Far from California's sunny disposition, Canada has an icy image, but two areas have thawed out sufficiently to have the makings of a fine wine industry.

United States

Proponents of wine in the USA like to point out that 48 of the 50 American states grow grapes and produce wine; only North Dakota and the District of Columbia have no recorded instances of vine-growing. However, most states grow only native varieties, or minuscule patches of imported types. In any case, they make so little wine that it never appears commercially outside the local area.

The hard fact is that California vineyards yield over 95 per cent of all the grapes used for wine in the United States. New York State is good for just over 2 per cent, Washington State for 1.6 per cent – which doesn't leave much for the other 45 wine-producing states.

California will continue to provide most of the wine America makes and drinks for the foreseeable future because it has both a favourable climate and vast expanses of suitable land. And California alone produces the full range of wine types familiar to drinkers of European wines. However, states other than California have the potential to bring newcomers into the fold with wines that can appeal to local pride, as has happened in Oregon, Washington and New York State. On a smaller scale, Texas and Virginia have recently demonstrated that people who never took any interest in wines from far away can be enticed to try something from just up the road.

The ironic aspect to this is that eastern states, especially New York, once prospered making wine from native grape varieties such as Concord, Isabella or Niagara. However, their flavours are so peculiar and pungent that wine drinkers familiar with European wines turn up their noses. In the south-eastern states, another native vine, the Scuppernong, yields similarly intense and peculiar flavours.

Wines from native grapes came into being after early Americans, Thomas Jefferson among them, failed in their attempts to grow French wine varieties. Native wines began to fall on hard times as soon as a modern generation of growers succeeded with European varieties.

The variables in growing conditions are staggering to contemplate. Washington State has most of its vineyards in what meteorologists call a continental climate. That translates into reliably hot, dry summers, and winters that can be – have been – bitterly cold enough to freeze hundreds of acres of vine roots to their tips. In Virginia, the problem is not freezing winters but muggy summers, favouring every sort of mould and mildew that ever attacked a leaf. New York State has some of each sort of climate.

It is startling, then, that so many states have found some sort of footing so swiftly.

USA and Canada wine regions

- US AVA and other wine areas
- Canada VQA and other wine areas

0 km   500   1000

0 miles   500

While California has grown from 150 wineries in 1960 to 240 in 1970, and today has more than 800, Oregon and Washington between them have gone from three wineries in 1970 to over 200 today. Virginia has progressed from zero to nearly 50 since 1980, and Texas is not far off that pace.

The efforts of growers and winemakers in all of these regions have been bedevilled by a marketplace that until the 1990s has wanted just two types of wine, Chardonnay as a white and Cabernet Sauvignon as a red. A new wine-loving public seems to have settled on those two varietal types as virtually synonymous with white and red. Positive reports from the medical communities about the potential beneficial aspects of wine in general and these wines in particular have created a strong interest in Merlot and more recently in Pinot Noir and Zinfandel.

Growers everywhere in the United States are learning what to grow and how to grow it well enough to make wines that compare favourably with examples from long-established regions – not just California, but France, Germany and Italy too. Unlike Europe, America has no stubborn peasant class clinging to the ways of its fathers and grandfathers. Because Prohibition removed a whole generation from vineyard and cellar, nearly all of the country's grape-growers and winemakers are university-trained.

Vintages

Making judgments about vintages in the United States is a tricky business. In California, climate conditions change so swiftly in the coastal counties that generalizations about vintages are hazardous. The division between North and Central Coast regions is very sharp indeed in some years. This much said, even the worst of years in California yield more adequate to above-average wine than poor stuff.

In most other states, with the possible exception of Oregon and Washington, weather conditions are too variable, the vineyards too far apart and their track records too short to permit even the haziest of guesses. Oregon does face summers so cool and harvests so rainy that little or nothing ripens fully, while other years heap benefits upon the vines.

US wine classifications

During the 1970s the authorities began establishing a system of appellations of origin, using the term AVA, for American Viticultural Area. The system remains in its

Vineyards near Calistoga, in the northern Napa Valley. This valley was the starting point for the modern California wine industry, and is now some of the most valuable vineyard land in the world.

infancy, limited above all by the lack of history within many of the regions it defines.

Where France and Italy, in particular, have appellation systems that specify grape varieties, density of plantings and crop levels, maximum and minimum limits of alcohol, and so on, the American version does none of these things. Still less does it attempt to distinguish shades of quality within a region. This reticence is, for the time being, wise. There remains a great deal of sorting to do before restrictions will pay greater dividends than the current liberty.

For now, all the AVA guarantees is that a minimum of 85 per cent of the wine in the bottle comes from grapes grown in the region named on the label. The use of individual vineyard names on wines is an extension of the AVA idea. Regulations require that 95 per cent of any wine using a vineyard name must be from grapes grown in that vineyard, and from within a recognized AVA.

Canada

Perhaps surprisingly, Canada has been producing wine since the early nineteenth century. Canadian wine has transformed itself over the past quarter century thanks to much improved vineyard practices, more suitable clones and improved technology inside the winery. Instead of native north American

grapes such as Concord, the country's most important grape varieties now hail from the *Vitis vinifera* family and total just under 50 per cent of the area under vine, the balance comprising hardy hybrids. While outstanding Icewine made from Riesling, Vidal, Gewurztraminer and Ehrenfelser has garnered international attention, some of the most exciting new wines are dry table wines.

The bulk of the country's vineyards are located in southern Ontario and British Columbia's southern interior, with a smattering of sites in Nova Scotia and Quebec. In Ontario's Niagara Peninsula and Lake Erie North Shore, Chardonnay, Riesling, Vidal, Pinot Noir, Cabernet Sauvignon and Merlot lead the pack. In British Columbia's Okanagan Valley and on Vancouver Island best bets include Chardonnay, Pinot Blanc, Pinot Gris and Bordeaux-style blends of Cabernet Sauvignon, Cabernet Franc and Merlot. New plantings of Syrah and Viognier have also shown considerable early promise.

Vintners Quality Alliance (VQA) is Canada's classification system, established in Ontario in 1988 and adopted in British Columbia in 1990. Wines are tasted by a professional panel and, if successful, awarded a black or – better – gold VQA seal. There are two categories, the higher of which refers to specific viticultural areas.

SOUTH AMERICA

TROPICAL CLIMATES PRECLUDE much of South America from vine-growing, though planting at cooler, higher altitudes can overcome the problem of excess humidity. The demand for wine for domestic consumption, and for distillation into brandy, means that far more wine is made than is ever seen in world markets, but Argentina and Chile have produced wines of exceptional value for some time, and wines of international standing are now emerging from both countries.

Argentina

Up until recently Argentine wine was only drunk in Argentina. This, despite the fact that Argentina is the world's fourth-largest wine producer (after Spain and pretty much on a par with the United States). The reason is that the Argentinians have traditionally consumed large quantities of wine. When domestic consumption started to drop, under attack from soft drinks and beer, Argentina began to look for export markets. It was at this stage that it discovered what Chile had discovered in the late 1970s, that the world has moved on from old-style oxidized wines. Argentina had a simple choice, continue losing market share or invest heavily to bring standards up to international levels. It opted for the latter in a big way, with much enthusiastic international participation.

Argentina is blessed with conditions that *Vitis vinifera* loves. Almost all of the vineyards are planted well inland where there is next to no ambient humidity, reducing the incidence of fungal diseases to a minimum. Altitudes of 650–1100m (2000–3600ft) above sea level provide vast differences between day–night temperatures, and sunshine, plenty of it, helps. The only downside is precipitation: there is almost none, and what there is tends to come down either in sheets of hailstones (anathema to grapes) or in flash floods that can wipe away entire vineyards. Fortunately, the Incas solved the problem of lack of rainfall a thousand years ago by devising an incredibly intricate irrigation system using snow-melt from the Andes, including a legal framework for equitably dividing water rights, that subsequent generations have gratefully inherited.

The expanse of vineyards planted in Argentina is mind-boggling. From the beautiful Cafayate Valley high up in Salta in the north, down to the sunken and protected Rio Negro Valley in Patagonia to the south, there is a huge surface area dedicated to vines. With over 1000 separate bodegas, or wineries, spread out over three vast growing regions (further subdivided into an array of zones including three DOs), the province of Mendoza is the powerhouse behind Argentine winemaking:

75 per cent of all Argentine wines hail from Mendoza. San Juan, to the north of Mendoza, is another huge producing area. Further north still there is La Rioja – the Argentine province not to be confused with La Rioja in Spain!

Argentine exports are now beginning to reflect the country's enormous production potential. The UK, continental Europe, Scandinavia and Japan are importing ever greater quantities. Although Cabernet Sauvignon and Chardonnay are important, and there are excellent examples of both, Argentina is exciting because of less well-known varieties. Malbec makes sumptuous, perfumed purple-hearted reds. Tempranillo, Barbera and Syrah are good to excellent, and Bonarda is a gorgeous silky red to better Beaujolais. Torrontes is Argentina's indigenous white and has an explosive rose and nutmeg scent and delightful lime acidity. The modern era virtually starts with the 1996 vintage, and every vintage since then, even the poor 1998, has seen a quantum leap in quality.

Brazil

With the eighth-largest economy in the world, Brazil is certainly a place to sell wine. The bravest have decided to make it there as well. This is no easy task, given the conditions. Grapes are natural prey to all kinds of rot in Brazil's climate, even down south, on the Uruguayan border, where the wine region is based. This hasn't stopped market leaders such as Moët et Chandon and Rémy-Martin, nor indeed enterprising winemakers such as Pisano from neighbouring Uruguay, and Aurora, in Bento Gonçalves, from taking up the challenge. At 400m (1300ft) above sea level, Rio Grande do Sul is undoubtedly the best region you could hope to find in Brazil, with its verdant undulating hills. But don't expect miracles – it's pretty humid and unsuitable for grapes, even here, and if it wasn't for the efforts of the occasional flying winemaker and the financial muscle of the European giants, little of interest would appear.

Chile

It's unbelievable how fast Chile has leapt to the fore, in a few short years going from nervous debutante on the world stage to many modern

The Andes form a dramatic backdrop to the exciting new wine region of Tupungato, in Mendoza province, Argentina. The cool, high-altitude vineyards allow the grapes to ripen slowly, concentrating the flavours.

Wine regions
- Venezuela
- Peru
- Bolivia
- Brazil
- Uruguay
- Argentina
- Chile

where else in the world needs to graft the vine onto phylloxera-resistant rootstock.) Ally this to very fertile soils along a north-south line running more than 1000km (600 miles), regular sunshine because the Andes provide a rain shadow, but abundant Andean snow-melt to make up for the lack of rain, and Chile's description as a viticultural paradise is well deserved.

The real heartland for high-quality grapes is Aconcagua, just north of Santiago, spreading west through the Casablanca Valley. Casablanca makes Chile's greatest whites – primarily from Chardonnay and Sauvignon – as well as a few delicious reds. However, the real red core lies south of Santiago, through what is called the Valle Central or Central Valley, from Maipo in the north down through Curicó and Talca and on to the Bío-Bío river 400km (250 miles) south of Santiago. Red grapes dominate in the north and whites become more important as you head south. Every year sees new vineyards planted and further investment from overseas producers, with French and Californian interest the most intense. Chile already makes superb wine. If she stays confident in her own strengths and styles, Chile will be the wine drinkers' darling for a long time yet.

Peru

Peru has a long tradition of winemaking (albeit altar wine), dating back to the time when Spain was the colonial master. Modern winemaking is based principally in the Ica Valley, south of the capital, Lima. Despite warm days and cool nights, varietal character is generally dull. However, Tacama make a reasonable range, including Malbec for red wines and Chenin Blanc for whites.

Uruguay

Uruguay has more rainfall than its neighbour Argentina and temperatures are, on average, higher, so viticulturalists have to work hard to prevent rot and disease attacking the grapes. There is a long-standing tradition for thoughtful innovation that has helped this small, green country overcome such challenges, though. Different training systems, for example, get the most out of the vines. Tannat, a French variety not normally known for its suppleness, has adapted remarkably well here, giving red wines with fruit and substance. Vineyards are spread throughout Uruguay, with a main cluster around Montevideo. Castel Pujol have recently inaugurated an amazing gravity-fed winery, and Juanicó make a good range of wines. Calvinor, further north, have great potential to produce value-for-money wine.

wine drinkers' darling producer. And the reason is fruit. Great big eye-boggling, palate-flooding dollops of rich ripe fruit. And that's the red wines I'm talking about. Just as Australia in the 1980s had taken the world by storm, offering jaundiced wine drinkers the joys of sunshine in bottle, so Chile in the 1990s adopted the same flavour-packed course. What Chile must beware of now is listening to advisers who try to pull her toward a leaner, more tannic red wine style under the pretence that it is more French, and therefore superior. Chile must retain her pride in the sumptuous fruit flavour of her reds and develop her own view of what is superior – and leanness of structure splashed with too much sweet oak is not the way forward.

Chile's reputation was initially built on Cabernet Sauvignon, although Merlot has become at least as important. Pinot Noir is very promising, and the rare Bordeaux grape Carmenère is rapidly assuming considerable importance because virtually all the world's surviving plantings of Carmenère are in Chile. There's a reason for that. After Europe was ravaged by the phylloxera aphid in the second half of the nineteenth century, many grapes like Carmenère were not replanted. But before phylloxera arrived in Bordeaux, cuttings of all the varieties had been shipped to Chile and planted. And phylloxera has never invaded Chile. Desert to the north, the Andes to the east and the Pacific Ocean to the west form barriers phylloxera has not overcome.

Consequently, Chile's vines grow on their own roots. (South Australia is the only other important area to be phylloxera-free; every-

AUSTRALIA

FAR TOO MANY OF US think of Australian wine as a single entity – in fact it's as minutely varied as the wine of any other country. Climate is the major determinant of style in Australia, and while much of the land mass is desert, wholly unsuited to the vine, there are many distinctions to be made between the vineyards that extend for hundreds of miles around the coast. Early settlers found as many areas suitable for making fine wine as there are in France: the Barossa Valley in South Australia is only slightly warmer than Bordeaux, although it's less humid, and the hilltops of Victoria's Yarra Valley are cooler than those in the heart of France's chilliest wine region, Champagne. These cool-climate vineyards can produce complex, subtle wines, but the warmer vineyards hold the trump cards of higher yields, fewer diseases and less expense for the grower, resulting in good-value wines with ripe, mouthfilling fruit and the aroma of new oak.

By 1850 commercial winemaking was under way in Australia and significant markets were established in the United Kingdom. Victoria led the way before being supplanted by South Australia, and the wines had much success in international exhibitions. Even in the enological dark ages of the first half of the twentieth century exports boomed: between 1928 and 1938 inclusive, Australia exported more wine (mostly fortified, sent in barrels) to the United Kingdom than did France. For all that, the industry of today only began to take shape in the mid-1950s, when the first temperature-controlled, stainless steel fermenters were introduced. Following the Californian pattern, Cabernet Sauvignon began to rise from relative obscurity in the early 1960s, Chardonnay in the early 1970s. Now both are staples of British dining tables, due to two main factors: the user-friendly style of wines and their cost-competitiveness. Research carried out for the massive Penfolds Wine Group shows that Australia produces fully packaged wine for significantly less than the United States or France. The principal advantages stem from lower land costs and viticultural efficiencies through mechanization.

What is termed the user-friendly nature of the wines reflects the Australian philosophy of retaining as much as possible of the flavour of the grape in the wine, with structural complexity of secondary importance.

Of course, broad generalizations are precisely that. Australia is a vast continent, with an immense array of climate and terroir. The grape harvest begins in late January in the hot Swan Valley (near Perth, Western Australia) and Hunter Valley (on the other side of the country, in New South Wales), and does not finish until May or even June in the coolest regions such as Tasmania. Thus Chardonnay may be voluptuously peachy/buttery or finely drawn, with intense minerally/citrus flavours; Cabernet Sauvignon may be thick with dark chocolate or as tinged with green leaf as many

Fertile soils, temperate climate and abundant rain in winter and spring ensure high yields in the King Valley, North East Victoria, home to Avalon Vineyard.

a respected Bordeaux – or even as pebbly as a Cabernet Franc from Chinon.

Australia's quasi-indigenous specialities are Semillon, Riesling and Shiraz. The two white wines are made in a uniquely Australian style, and good examples of both develop magnificently in bottle over 20 years or so. Semillon is sometimes aged in oak these days, but even if made without, it slowly develops a nutty toastiness which can lead the most acute judge to taste oak when none is present. Riesling is made crisp and dry, with the lime and passion fruit of youth slowly giving way to the classic whiff-of-petrol and lightly browned toast aromas of age. Shiraz, the Rhône Valley's Syrah, works hard in Australia, making red wines in a variety of styles, culminating in the legendary, thrillingly rich Penfolds Grange from South Australia.

The arrival of Pinot Noir has signalled an immense improvement in the style and quality of sparkling wines, in which it is combined with Chardonnay. There are also a few Pinot Noir red wines of top quality.

Finally, there are those indigenous specialities, the luscious fortified wines of North East Victoria, the so-called Tokay (made from Muscadelle) and Muscat (made from Muscat Blanc à Petits Grains). These magnificent wines overshadow the sherries (from fino to oloroso), tawny and vintage ports, the best to be found outside Spain and Portugal.

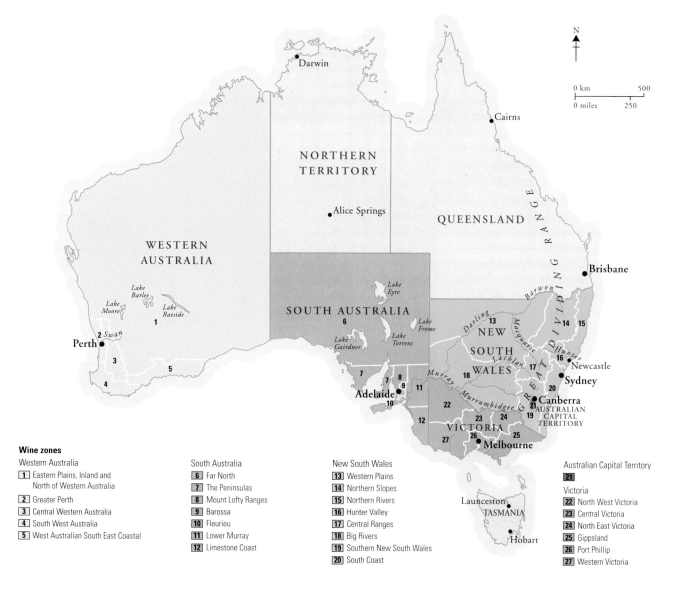

Wine zones

Western Australia
1 Eastern Plains, Inland and
  North of Western Australia
2 Greater Perth
3 Central Western Australia
4 South West Australia
5 West Australian South East Coastal

South Australia
6 Far North
7 The Peninsulas
8 Mount Lofty Ranges
9 Barossa
10 Fleurieu
11 Lower Murray
12 Limestone Coast

New South Wales
13 Western Plains
14 Northern Slopes
15 Northern Rivers
16 Hunter Valley
17 Central Ranges
18 Big Rivers
19 Southern New South Wales
20 South Coast

Australian Capital Territory
21

Victoria
22 North West Victoria
23 Central Victoria
24 North East Victoria
25 Gippsland
26 Port Phillip
27 Western Victoria

Australian wine classifications

In October 1994 Australia put in place the last leg of a legislative framework covering all aspects of wine labelling; most of that framework has been extant since 1963. The 1994 legislation saw the establishment of a committee whose task it was (and is) to oversee the creation of a series of Geographic Indications (GIs) covering the whole of Australia. The first task was to divide each of the states into zones, a task that was expected to be quick (there was no legislative requirement for any identifiable or unifying viticultural or geographical nexus for a zone) but which in fact took almost two years. Each of the main wine-producing states is divided into large chunks: Western Australia has five zones, South Australia seven, Victoria six and New South Wales eight. It is inherently improbable that

zone names will make much of an impact on wine labels, with one exception: the Super Zone of South East Australia, which effectively takes in all of the wine-producing areas of Queensland, New South Wales, Victoria, Tasmania and South Australia.

Of far greater importance will be the 40 or so regions into which those zones will be divided, some of whose names are already familiar. Throughout this book you will find the names of all but a handful of those regions, although not all have been officially declared. One of the best known of all regions, Coonawarra in South Australia, has been the subject of a bitter contest between Petaluma (whose chief executive Brian Croser is a former president of the Winemakers Federation of Australia) and the Coonawarra Vignerons Association. Here the dispute is

over the location of the boundary; in other yet-to-be-formalized regions, a no-less bitter dispute exists over the actual name. Until these debates have been resolved, the mapmakers are being held in limbo. There is also provision within the legislation for sub-regions, and certain of these have already been declared, with many more in contemplation.

Quality, of course, is not defined by lines on maps. A development of the regional classifications has been the concept of Distinguished Vineyard Sites, along the lines of the Bordeaux classifications; this is now widely accepted as authoritative in the wine trade and by investors and drinkers. It has two main classes: Outstanding and the slightly lower Excellent. Classification is only open to wines produced over a period of at least ten years with a record of quality and reliability.

NEW ZEALAND

THE WINES OF NEW ZEALAND and Australia are so different that they tend to complement rather than compete with each other. Australia could never produce a wine that would come close to the pungent and distinctive Marlborough Sauvignon Blanc style, just as it would be futile for New Zealand winemakers to try to produce a wine to challenge a booming Barossa Valley Shiraz. Australia struggles with Pinot Noir; New Zealand makes it superbly. It's very much a matter of climate. New Zealand boasts of being a clean, green land – it has regular sunshine and a cool climate. Australia, on the other hand, with the exception of some vineyard areas on the coast, is arid and parched by the sun.

As you look across the Tasman Sea from Australia to New Zealand, it is as if one is peering through the wrong end of a telescope at a film in fast forward motion. The industry is very much smaller, but the pace of change in New Zealand since 1984 has been frenetic, due in part to government dismantling of protective tariffs, and in part to the same invigorating winds of change as are blowing across Australia and the rest of the New World.

New Zealand is an important market for Australian wine and yet the Australians, somewhat chauvinistically, have only just begun importing New Zealand wine in serious quantity. In 1993 Australia was New Zealand's fifth-largest wine market after the United Kingdom, Sweden, Japan and Canada. Since then exports to Australia have increased seven-fold and Australia is New Zealand's second-largest overseas market.

Wine styles

The driving forces are bracingly crisp and pure Sauvignon Blanc, fine melon-accented Chardonnay, fragrant Riesling, and red berry Merlot from Marlborough at the north end of the South Island; fleshy, fine-grained Cabernet Sauvignon and Merlot, melon and peach Chardonnay from Hawke's Bay on the eastern coast of the North Island; and even more melony and peachier Chardonnay from Gisborne just up the coast.

But, as in Australia, the viticultural map is constantly changing and expanding. Martinborough (also called Wairarapa) at the southern end of the North Island is a small region – even by New Zealand standards – with unlimited quality potential for the 'big five' grape varieties: Chardonnay, Sauvignon Blanc, Cabernet Sauvignon, Merlot and Pinot Noir, and particularly for the last. Nelson, Canterbury and Central Otago on the South Island are flourishing. After a long period of declining vineyard acreage even Auckland is on the ascent as adventurous winemakers discover pockets of land capable of making top wine; Waiheke Island and Matakana are two prime examples. Wine regions appear on labels, but there are currently no further classifications.

New Zealand's greatest strength is in producing white wines of great purity and pungency. Her great leap forward came during the 1990s, when the world was panting for exciting white. Now the pendulum has swung towards red and New Zealand is at a crossroads. She can produce excellent reds, in a restrained, non-ebullient style, but clearly whites are better. Should she plant more red? Just remember, the pendulum always swings back again.

Large stones retain the sun's heat and radiate it back onto the vines at Corbans' Stoneleigh vineyard in Marlborough.

Wine regions

North Island
1 Northland
2 Great Barrier Island
3 Matakana
4 Waiheke Island
5 Kumeu/Huapai/Waimauku
6 Greater Auckland
7 Waikato
8 Bay of Plenty
9 Gisborne
10 Hawke's Bay
11 Wairarapa

South Island
12 Nelson
13 Marlborough
14 Waipara
15 Canterbury
16 Central Otago

SOUTH AFRICA

SOUTH AFRICA IS PROBABLY the only wine industry in the world that can accurately pinpoint its birthday: 2 February 1659, a date remembered thanks to Jan van Riebeek's diary, in which he noted the first pressing of wine from Cape grapes. Carefully recorded subsequent land grants mean there's an on-going celebration of tercentenaries in the Cape winelands. The industry has gone through many ups and downs in the ensuing years. It is only now emerging from the international sanctions imposed during the Apartheid era. New cool-climate areas are being developed and a replanting programme is under way. But most importantly, awareness of international wine styles is at last taking hold.

Producers with international experience, mainly the small independents, have been able to adapt to competing on the world stage. However, around 85 per cent of South Africa's production is still made by the co-operatives, who have not been accustomed to the free market. Although much of their wine shows a modern touch, often with input from UK buyers or flying winemakers, further improvement has not kept pace with price increases. Some have converted to public companies (including KWV), a move they are confident will encourage their shareholders (grape farmers) to focus on quality. It may, in time, but entrenched attitudes are proving slow to change.

A chronic shortage of vine material, mainly rootstock, is holding back the drive to increase planting of premium varieties and the introduction of new ones. South Africa's 'big five' – Cabernet Sauvignon, Merlot, Shiraz, Chardonnay and Sauvignon Blanc – still account for just over 20 per cent of South Africa's nearly 100,000ha (247,000 acres) of vineyards. The locally developed Pinotage, a crossing of Pinot Noir x Cinsaut, is also in short supply, though it makes one of the Cape's most individual, unforgettable red wine styles.

On the upside, there is no shortage of new, quality-oriented wineries opening up and the number of internationally recognized wines is steadily increasing, although it is tough on the small guys who seem to be having to create a positive image for South African wines all by themselves. The lack of a large company leader certainly doesn't help progress.

Wine regions
The majority of the vineyards are concentrated in the Western Cape, stretching 250km (150 miles) north and more like 400km (250 miles) east, with the main Stellenbosch and Paarl regions at the centre. In many ways, this spread offers an ideal climate for grape-growing, although perfectionists would have it a cooler 200km (125 miles) further south, especially the Pinot Noir fanatics. Nevertheless, new quality sites are being earmarked for future development; in particular, the cooler spots around Malmesbury up the west coast and at Hermanus on the south coast.

More international exposure, dedication to quality and, perhaps most important of all, a belief in their own ability, could see South African winemakers realize the country's true potential for great wine in the future, but the future is by no means a done deal yet.

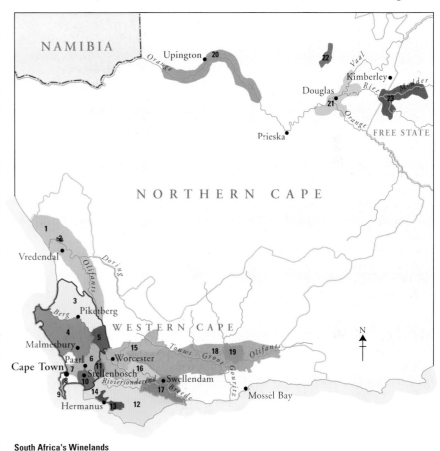

South Africa's Winelands

Western Cape
- Coastal Region
- Breede River Valley
1. Olifants River
2. Lutzville Valley
3. Piketberg
4. Swartland
5. Tulbagh
6. Paarl
7. Durbanville
8. Constantia
9. Cape Point
10. Stellenbosch
11. Franschhoek
12. Overberg
13. Walker Bay
14. Elgin
15. Worcester
16. Robertson
17. Swellendam
18. Klein Karoo
19. Calitzdorp

Northern Cape
20. Lower Orange
21. Douglas
22. Hartswater
23. Riet River FS

0 km 100
0 miles 50

South African wine classification
The Wine of Origin (WO) laws certify a wine's area of origin, grape variety and vintage. Origin is divided into regions, subdivided into districts and wards. As in other New World winemaking countries, there is a strong emphasis on varietal labelling: the wine must contain 75 per cent of the named variety, or 85 per cent for exported wines.

OTHER WINE REGIONS

WHEREVER GRAPES CAN BE GROWN, however inhospitable the climate, there will be a winemaker ready to rise to the challenge of producing something drinkable, pleasant – and preferably saleable. This is not just a modern phenomenon; there have always been people ready to face economic constraints, political upheaval, even war, to make wine. All they needed was someone to drink the wine – and today there are more wine drinkers than ever, ready to give anything a try.

Algeria

French influence lives on in Algeria: there are seven Appellation d'Origine Garantie regions, and the best red wines have a beefy earthiness that is not so very far away from the taste of the Midi, although lack of acidity can be a problem. Western Algeria accounts for 80 per cent of production: Oran is the main area, with the AOG Coteaux de Mascara being probably Algeria's best; Coteaux de Tlemcen can also be attractive. Sixty per cent of the wine is red, 30 per cent white and 10 per cent rosé; Cinsaut is the most widely grown grape for reds and rosés, followed by Grenache, Carignan and Morrastel, all equally suited to hot climates. Farranah and Tizourine are the principal white grapes.

Bulgaria

The central planners of the ex-Comecon region decided that Bulgaria had the potential to supply its wine needs. They were absolutely right. Vast acreages of principally red varietals were planted in easily mechanizable flatlands and well-equipped wineries were set up. In the early to mid-1980s, American investment and expertise gave the Bulgarian wine industry a new focus: Cabernet Sauvignon. This grape, in Bulgaria's warm climate, produced reliably rich, blackcurranty red wines at bargain prices.

As the economic outlook deteriorated, domestic and regional demand fell. The collapse of the Soviet bloc in 1989 and the muddle surrounding privatization led to a morass of uncertainty, and in the early 1990s all the reliable fruit-led pleasure of Bulgarian reds seemed to disappear. It has taken far longer than expected for Bulgaria to recover her quality credentials and even today, the simple, mouthfilling flavours of before are difficult to find. However, some wineries have managed to attract investment and some flying winemakers are stopping by fairly frequently, so things are slowly on the up. Bulgaria does produce white wines, for example from Chardonnay and Sauvignon Blanc, but nearly all the best wines are red, either

Harvesting grapes at Suhindol, one of northern Bulgaria's top wine regions.

from Cabernet and Merlot, or from the local varieties of Mavrud, Gamza and Melnik.

There are four quality categories: Country wines are roughly equivalent to French vins de pays – usually straightforward young wines from a denominated region. Reserve and Special Reserve wines have had longer aging, which is by no means always an advantage. The top category is Controliran wines, whose grapes and vineyards are most closely controlled.

Under Communism, a winery was named after the region in which it was located. Suhindol, Russe, Shumen, Sliven, Svischtov and Iambol are names to look out for, as all have access to good-quality vineyards. As land ownership is resolved we can look forward to improvements in viticulture to match those seen at the wineries, and particular winery names may begin to count for more as some forge ahead of the field.

China

China's vineyards tend to be full of table varieties like Cock's Heart and Dragon's Eye, so anybody contemplating making Western-style wine there has a lot of planting to do. Humid conditions lead to vine disease, but most vines are on their own roots as phylloxera is almost non-existent. The first joint venture, begun in 1980, involved Rémy-Martin, and the site was in the non-tropical north. The Huadong winery produces wines that show promise. Flying winemakers are now widely used.

Croatia

Croatia can offer some good quality, but most of its wine is less impressive than that of neighbouring Slovenia. Sixty four per cent is white, coming from inland Croatia, and tends to be sold in bulk; the better wines are generally red and come from the coastal region, which stretches for 500km (300 miles) along the Adriatic. Cabernet Sauvignon and Merlot are grown, but some of the best reds, with names like Faros, Postup and Peljesac, come from local grapes, notably the Plavac Mali.

Cyprus

This island's wine industry is in desperate need of modernization, and while this has for years seemed just around the corner, it has never yet happened. On the plus side there is a government scheme to uproot the worst, hottest, coastal vineyards, and the unfriendly, tannic, fruitless red Mavron grape may no longer be planted. On the minus side grapes still sit in the hot sun for hours before being processed in old-fashioned wineries; the wines that emerge are generally the opposite of the fresh, fruity wines that the export market craves. However, regional wineries are being constructed near or in the vineyards, a move supported by the government, and this should help. The government-run model winery is doing the best job, and a few private growers are taking quality initiatives. The best-known exports are the sherry-style wines and the dessert wine Commandaria, which is seldom, alas, exciting nowadays.

The Czech Republic

The 'velvet divorce' left this part of the former Czechoslovakia with two regions, Bohemia and Moravia, both of which produce wine. Most of the wines, since this is a of smaller companies who have striven strongly for quality, standards have risen dramatically and fresher wines are replacing the tired, dusty ones of a decade or two ago.

Retsina (resinated, piney-tasting white wine) is still widely available, but so, increasingly, are reds from Xynomavro, Agiorgitiko, Cabernet Sauvignon and Merlot, and whites from Assyrtiko, Robola, Chardonnay and Muscat. Native grape varieties are being blended with international ones to produce some superlative wines in a number of areas. Appellations to look out for include Naoussa and Nemea, but many of Greece's most exciting wines are being made in non-appellation areas by small producers who have planted their own land and chosen their own vines.

Hungary

Western investment here, particularly at estates like Neszmély and Gyöngyös, is producing snappy, crisp but fruity Sauvignon Blancs and Chardonnays made in a crowd-pleasing style. Hungary's other winner is its sweet wines from the Tokaji vineyards: now that private ownership is increasingly important, quality is improving, and this unique wine has a chance to regain its reputation. Otherwise the demise of Communism in Hungary has revealed a rather bleak picture: lots of potential, good grapes, but absolutely no money and no sign of any, except what can be attracted from abroad. There are vineyards everywhere except in the extreme south-east, but more than half are on the flat, windswept Great Plain, where most of the wine is white and somewhat characterless. Only about 30 per cent of Hungary's wine is red, and it is mostly light: the south of Hungary is the main area for red wine. The local taste in white is sweetish and spicy, and the main grape is the Olasz Rizling; other whites are made from Ezerjó, Furmint, Hárslevelü, Leányka, Muscat Ottonel, Tramini (or Traminer) and others; red wine grapes include Kadarka, Kékfrankos, Merlot and Pinot Noir. The work of flying winemakers in the Lake Balaton region and Neszmély and Gyöngyös in the north, plus more concentrated red wines from regions such as Villany, all show great potential.

India

There are plenty of vineyards in India, many of them encouraged under the Raj, but most of the grapes are not used for wine; most Indian wine, anyway, is sweet and rather thick. The most successful Indian wines are

England's largest vineyard, Denbies, is planted on the rolling North Downs of Surrey. With modern winemaking and attention to detail, the estate is looking to conquer export markets.

distinctly chilly climate, are white, from such varieties as Pinot Blanc, Müller-Thurgau, Silvaner, Riesling, Laski Rizling, Traminer, Sauvignon Blanc and the native Irsay Oliver, but the reds, when they are good, can be very attractive, made from Frankovka (alias Germany's Limberger), St Laurent and Pinot Noir. The quality under Communism was pretty dire, but Western investment is producing pockets of excellence. The march of privatization means that there will soon be lots of new wines, from new companies, appearing abroad.

England

Anyone who hasn't tasted an English wine for a few years is way out of touch. Quality is improving all the time, and there is an English trademark taste developing: a delicate, hedgerow floweriness and fruit. Oddly enough this often comes from vine crossings that were developed in Germany and seldom succeeded in producing high quality there: grapes like Müller-Thurgau (England's most widely planted variety), Huxelrebe, Optima and Reichensteiner, as well as the hybrid Seyval Blanc. The term English wine includes Welsh wine as well, but the main

counties of production are Kent and Sussex, with Oxfordshire, Dorset, Berkshire, Surrey and Somerset also yielding some good bottles and reliable growers. The least reliable factor is the weather. A most interesting development has been sparkling wine, which would appear to have a great future.

Georgia

The Georgians don't want their wines fresh; they like them well aged in wood, preferably tannic and certainly sweet – and that's only the whites. They've evolved some curious winemaking techniques to help them achieve these ends: leaving the (white or red) skins in contact with the new wine for three to five months is one of them. Not surprisingly, not much is exported to the West.

Greece

The earliest fine winemaking area recorded in history, Greece lost its long-standing reputation under the Ottoman Empire, and winemaking dwindled into a village industry. Today, however, the position is very different. Led by four major exporting companies, Achaia-Clauss, Boutari, Kourtakis and Tsantalis, and supported by a large number those of entrepreneur Sham Chougule, the best known of which is the Champagne-method Omar Khayyam and its demi-sec cousin Marquise de Pompadour.

Israel

There are big improvements coming out of Israel. The Golan Heights winery led the way in the 1980s with clean, fresh, varietal wines that were also kosher; now the country's biggest producer, Carmel, has been pushed by competition into modernizing its wine-making. There's no reason why kosher wine shouldn't taste nice as well; it's just that, with a captive market, it was able to get away with old-fashioned techniques others would have jettisoned years ago.

Japan

Japan's wine laws allow foreign grapes, must or wine to be imported and (usually, but not always) mixed with Japanese wine to be re-labelled as Japanese. Suntory, however, make the real thing, as does Chateau Lumiere.

Lebanon

One would be forgiven for thinking some-times that Chateau Musar is Lebanon's only wine producer. There are others, but none that approaches Musar on quality. It's a land that is most suited to red grape varieties like Cabernet Sauvignon, Cinsaut and Carignan; white grapes include Muscat, Ugni Blanc, Sauvignon Blanc and Chardonnay. Another major producer is Kefraya, whose fruity, well-made wines – red, white and rosé – are attracting considerable attention.

Luxembourg

Not all Mosel wine is German. Luxem-bourg's vineyards are based along the upper Mosel (or Moselle) and like Germany's, they produce only white wine. Unlike Germany's Mosel, the main grape varieties are Rivaner, Elbling, Riesling, Auxerrois, Gewürz-traminer, Pinot Blanc and Pinot Gris. Much is made into sparkling wine, and most of the rest is on the lean side, though Riesling, Rivaner and Auxerrois can be good.

Mexico

Only about 6 per cent of Mexico's grape harvest ends up as wine, the rest being served up as table grapes, raisins or brandy. The Sierra Madre, 1500m (5000ft) above sea level in the north-east, Baja California, in the north-west and Guadalajara to the south, provide the backdrop for winemaking in

Vineyards at Dealul Vei in the Dealul Mare region of Romania, in the foothills of the Carpathian Mountains. The region is known above all for its red wines, from Merlot, Pinot Noir and Cabernet Sauvignon.

Mexico. Although Mexico's wine industry can be traced back to colonial times, L A Cetto has brought stainless steel hygiene, cold fermentation, fresh and vibrant fruit and an excellent reputation to Mexican wines. Nebbiolo and Petite Sirah have been notable successes. Other modern wineries such as Pedro Domecq (from Spain), Casa Madero, Santo Tomás and Monte Zenic give Mexican winemaking a diversity that is evi-dent in the varieties used. You can find red wines from Cabernet Sauvignon through Barbera to Pinot Noir and Zinfandel, whites from Chardonnay to Viognier.

Moldova

Moldova is the best of the former Soviet states in wine terms: it has the largest quan-tities of Western grape varieties, some pretty good wineries and stocks of well-aged reds that resemble old-fashioned red Bordeaux, at some old-fashioned prices. It also has a lot of international activity; both Penfolds and Hugh Ryman have been involved at the Hincesti winery. Moldova's vineyards extend over most of the country; they are planted with, among others, Cabernet Sauvignon, Merlot, Pinot Noir and the native Saperavi for red wines, Chardonnay, Sauvignon Blanc, Aligoté and the native Rkatsiteli for

whites. The most important local grapes are the white Feteasca Alba and Feteasca Regala from neighbouring Romania.

Morocco

North Africa's best reds come from here. Well over half the vines produce table grapes, but winemaking is reasonably up to date, and the reds are muscular and rich. The whites are best avoided. There are 12 Appellations d'Origine Garantie regions, of which most are found in the region of Meknès and Fez. Toulal Guerrouane is a rich, earthy red; Gris de Boulaouane is the most famous rosé.

Romania

Climatically Romania has many regions that suit the grape vine perfectly. Phylloxera played havoc with Romania's native grape varieties but led to the introduction, at the end of the nineteenth century, of grapes such as Cabernet Sauvignon, Merlot and Pinot Noir. Fortunately, many delightful native varietals survived: Feteasca Regala, Feteasca Alba and Tamaîioasa Româneasca make pow-erfully scented white wine; Feteasca Neagra is a red variety of great potential.

The Ceausêscu regime, committed to maximum agricultural output in terms of foodstuffs, consigned many vineyards to the less mechanizable hilltops, that is, to the spots that vines love best, but the country has nonetheless been held back by lack of foreign investment in modern technology, and domestic tastes are not those that might attract international palates. There is a tendency to retain residual sugars and leave wines to age for extended periods to allow the sugars to dry out. This leads to some pretty extraordinary white wines and to some interesting but less-than-commercial reds. The establishment in 1991 of Vinexport (with British, German, Dutch and Danish capital) allowed Romanian producers access to outside investment, know-how and markets. Since then Romanian wine has experienced an important change for the better.

Pinot Noir has made an impression outside the country because it has a faint whiff of Burgundian character, at a fraction of the price. What is even more interesting is that Romania has more Merlot than anywhere else except France, and we are beginning to see the benefits that modern winemaking can bring to this variety in the shape of some very attractive wines. The Sahateni winery makes fine examples.

Regions to look out for include Dealul Mare, in the valleys of the Carpathian Mountains, where good-value Pinot Noir and surprisingly good Merlot can be found. Murfatlar, on the Black Sea coast, is known for its sweet white wines, but also has Cabernet Sauvignon and some oak-aged Chardonnays that can be worthwhile. Whites predominate in Tirnave, Transylvania, but there is also some good Merlot. Iasi, on the lowlands towards the north-eastern border, specializes in native grape varietals, especially luscious and lingering Tamaîioasa dessert wines.

Russia

The republics of the former USSR grow progressively more native grape varieties and progressively fewer Western ones the further east one travels along the Black Sea coast. Russia grows such grapes as Muscatel, Silvaner, Cabernet Sauvignon, Riesling, Aligoté, Pinot Gris and Pinot Noir, but also Rkatsiteli, Pukhjovsky and Tsimlyansky. Sparkling and still whites come from the north and west, reds from other areas.

Slovakia

Since its split with the Czech Republic in the early 1990s, Slovakia has had something of a bonus in wine terms – two-thirds of the vineyards of the former Czechoslovakia, plus a corner of the Tokaji vineyards, most of which are in Hungary. In fact Hungary used to lease this extra bit from Czechoslovakia in exchange for beer, but now that that deal has come to an end we should begin to see Slovakian Tokaji as well as Hungarian.

The wines of the rest of Slovakia, though, are similar to those of the Czech Republic: mostly white, from Pinot Blanc, Müller-Thurgau, Roter and Grüner Veltliner, Silvaner, Traminer, Rhine Riesling, Laski Rizling, Sauvignon Blanc and Irsay Oliver, with Frankovka, St Laurent and Pinot Noir for the reds. The reds tend to be light, since Slovakia is well to the north and the climate is cool, but when they are good they can be very attractive, and Frankova can be very concentrated. The wines of Austria and Hungary are the nearest comparison for style. Western investment and advice is busy turning the rather tired local style of wine into something fresh, fruity and gauged to international tastes, particularly at the Nitra winery.

Slovenia

Slovenia produced only 6 per cent of the wine of the old Yugoslavia, but the quality was good, and if the Slovenians are able to export it at a reasonable price we should begin to see some ripe, fresh, clean Laski Rizling, Sauvignon Blanc, Pinot Blanc, Merlot and others. And yes, fresh and clean are the operative words. The Yugoslav Laski Rizling so far exported is not a wine one would necessarily associate with that description, but the Slovenians can do a great deal better than that.

There are three wine regions: the Primorski or Littoral region, which borders Italy's Collio; the Podravski or Drava Valley, which borders Austria's Styria, and the Posavski or Sava Valley, in the south-east and east. Overall about half the wine is red and half white, and while many of the better winemakers curse their inability to afford the latest equipment, the standard of some of their wines indicates that they are doing their best in spite of their handicaps. As for the slovenly winemakers – well, as elsewhere, they'll have to change their ways or go under.

Turkey

Turkish wine is highly taxed and no wine is imported. The wines that are made seldom seem appealing to Western palates, since what were clearly originally fruity wines have been left in cask for far too long. Only 2 to 3 per cent of Turkey's vast grape production is turned into wine, and while there are officially some 1250 grape varieties, only 50 or 60 of them are grown on a commercial scale. Still, that's a fair number, and a few impart some earthy, spicy tastes to the wine. Western varieties tend to be grown most in the west of the country. Diren is one company trying harder than most, but stick to the reds.

Ukraine

The Ukraine has three main winemaking areas: Crimea is the most important, and there are also vineyards around Odessa on the Black Sea coast and in the Kherson and Nikolayev regions on either side of the Dnipro river. Red and white wines are made from a wide range of grape varieties, some internationally famous, some strictly local, and both Odessa and Crimea produce reasonable sparkling wines. The dessert wines from the Massandra winery in the south of the Crimea have traditionally imitated the great dessert wines of the West, with 'port', 'Tokay', 'Marsala' and 'Madeira'. They can live 100 years or more; after a large sale at Sotheby's, London, in 1990, it is still occasionally possible to find them on wine merchants' lists in various countries.

Yugoslavia

The republics of the former Yugoslavia are all capable of producing wine, but at the time of going to press, war renders discussion academic. Traditionally, most wine made in the western Balkans is red, except in the north Serbian region of Vojvodina and the now-independent republics of Bosnia Herzegovina, where white is in the majority, and in Macedonia, where the split is pretty equal.

Zimbabwe

One would imagine there's not much incentive to make wine in Zimbabwe, its summer rainfall being a hindrance during the December/January harvest, not to mention political uncertainty. Nonetheless, vineyards were planted in the 1960s, the mix very much reflecting the influence of neighbouring South Africa, with Colombard, Chenin Blanc and Cabernet Sauvignon, as well as Sauvignon Blanc, Pinotage and Merlot. Much progress has been made in the 1990s, and a flying winemaker, New Zealander Clive Hartnell, is now a regular visitor at Stapleford, one of Zimbabwe's two wine producers. Mukuyu is the other. Both produce wines of varying quality, but the best are well made.

A–Z OF WINES,
WINE REGIONS,
PRODUCERS
AND
GRAPE VARIETIES

The A–Z section from page 56 to page 399 covers entries on wines, wine regions, producers and grape varieties from all over the world.

The wine, wine region and producer entries follow the same format: the heading contains information on the country, region, appellation and local classification where relevant. The grape varieties listed in these entries are divided into the colour of wine they make, indicated by a glass symbol. The symbols stand for red ♥, rosé ♥ and white ♀ wines. Where a grape variety has a local name, this appears in brackets. There are also boxed features on the world's most important grape varieties.

Many large companies, especially in the New World, have vineyards and winemaking facilities in as many as a dozen places. Because of limited space, most producers have been given only one address; the main text makes it clear what the company does and where.

If you cannot find the wine or producer you want in the A–Z, it may be described under a wine region or grape entry, so try the Index on page 407.

To help you find your way around the A–Z, wines, wine regions and producers that have their own entries elsewhere are indicated in the text by SMALL CAPITALS.

The A–Z section includes special two-page features on the world's most important wine regions, including maps and lists of related entries to be found elsewhere in the A–Z. These regional features appear alphabetically within the A–Z by local name.

Mountain ranges form a dramatic backdrop to many of the Cape vineyards in South Africa. These immaculate vineyards belong to the Plaisir de Merle estate, a showpiece winery stretching up the Paarl side of the Simonsberg range.

ABADÍA RETUERTA

SPAIN, Castilla-León, Vino de Mesa de Castilla y León

❦ *Tempranillo, Cabernet Sauvignon, Merlot, Petit Verdot, Syrah, Grenache Noir (Garnacha Tinta)*

This 700-ha (1730-acre) estate on the Duero river, immediately west of the RIBERA DEL DUERO boundary, had an 800-year legacy in winemaking, but all the vines had been removed by the late 1970s. When the huge Swiss firm Novartis acquired it in 1988, it set about replanting 205ha (507 acres) with Tempranillo and French varieties and then built a futuristic gravity-driven winery with more than 80 stainless steel fermenting vats to vinify the grapes separately. Since 1996 winemaking consultant Pascal Delbeck (from ST-ÉMILION's Ch. BELAIR) and enologist Ángel Anocíbar have made a number of highly individual, concentrated wines that have stunned international critics. The single-vineyard Pago Negralada (Tempranillo) and Pago Valdebellón (Cabernet Sauvignon) are the top wines and all the wines are certain to improve as the vineyards mature. Best years: 1998, '97, '96.

ABRUZZO

ITALY

This region of Italy is gloriously beautiful, poorly known and might be positively obscure had the name not been included in its two major wines: Trebbiano d'Abruzzo and MONTEPULCIANO D'ABRUZZO. Those who complain that you can't produce good wines in southern Italy because it is too hot forget its saving grace – a mountainous backbone. Here the Apennines are at their highest, and there is little flat land. Winemaking practices here sometimes verge on the eccentric, but most production is in the hands of co-operatives such as the exemplary Casal Thaulero and Tollo. The major grapes are white Trebbiano and the superb red Montepulciano, some of which is made into a rosé or lightish red called Cerasuolo. Too many of the vines are currently planted on the high-yielding *tendone* system. But nowhere is perfect.

ACACIA WINERY

USA, California, Napa County, Carneros AVA

❦ *Pinot Noir, Zinfandel*

♀ *Chardonnay, Viognier*

Faltering after a brilliant beginning, Acacia was acquired by the CHALONE Group in 1986. Since then, it has been a steady producer of CARNEROS Chardonnay and Pinot Noir

ACACIA WINERY
Acacia has been a leading producer of Pinot Noir and Chardonnay from the Carneros region for more than 20 years. The St-Clair Vineyard Pinot is deep and velvety.

despite supply problems created by phylloxera. In the 1990s as its many growers were replanting vineyards, Acacia reduced its roster to a regular and Reserve bottling of Chardonnay and also of Pinot Noir.

It is currently offering single-vineyard Pinot Noir from Iund, St-Clair and Beckstoffer Vineyards. As vineyards return to production, the winery will expand its range. Though the vineyard wines capture wonderful bright fruit, it is the Reserve Pinot that stands out with ripe black-cherry fruit, deeper flavours, and a rich, velvety texture. Best years: 1997, '96, '95, '94, '93, '92, '91. Old Vine Zinfandel, Viognier and a Brut sparkling wine aged *en tirage* for over four years are regularly offered as well.

ACKERMAN-LAURANCE

FRANCE, Loire, Anjou-Saumur, Saumur AC

❦ *Cabernet Franc*

♀ *Chinon Blanc, Chardonnay*

This is the oldest sparkling SAUMUR company, established in 1811. Until recently Ackerman, with its associated company Rémy Pannier, was a by-word for very poor, often undrinkable wines. Fortunately there has been a marked change of policy and Ackerman has recognized that the future lies less in the traditional *négociant*'s role of wine doctor, trying to rescue other people's mistakes, but more in making their own wine from either bought-in grapes or must. A large modern winery has been built at le Puy Notre Dame and there are projects elsewhere in the LOIRE working directly with domaines to improve their winemaking. Jacques Lurton, the flying winemaker from BORDEAUX, is involved in a number of these projects. Wines sold as Vin de Pays du Jardin de la France now account for a quarter of production. Chardonnay, Chenin Blanc and Cabernet Franc are the principal varieties used. In the whites, both single varietals and blends have been successful. All these wines are for drinking young.

TIM ADAMS

AUSTRALIA, South Australia, Mount Lofty Ranges Zone, Clare Valley

❦ *Syrah (Shiraz), Cabernet Sauvignon, Grenache*

♀ *Semillon, Chardonnay, Riesling*

CLARE VALLEY youthful veteran Tim Adams makes memorable wines that combine modern knowledge with sensitivity to traditional Clare Valley style. The richly fruity and sweetly oaked Aberfeldy Shiraz and Fergus Grenache are outstanding reds, while Semillon and Riesling are high quality and long-lived. Best years: (reds) 1997, '96, '95, '94, '92, '91, '90, '89, '88.

ADELAIDE HILLS

AUSTRALIA, South Australia, Mount Lofty Ranges Zone

Intense political pressure as well as climatic and geographic factors has meant the Adelaide Hills wine region is now part of the Mount Lofty Ranges Zone. The redrawn Adelaide Hills, with the Piccadilly Valley in the south and extending to Kersbrook and Mount Crawford in the north, is a more homogenous region, but there is still tremendous variation in climate: north and north-east-facing slopes are far warmer (and usually much better) than south and south-west-facing slopes. Powerful, dark, plummy Pinot Noir, apple, pear and citrus-tinged Chardonnay, Riesling and crisply delicate Sauvignon Blanc dominate plantings in the south, but even here some exceptional Shiraz can be found. In the north, fullish Semillon, some exhilarating spice and cherry Shiraz, Cabernet Sauvignon and Chardonnay do well. Best producers: Ashton Hills, Barratt, Bridgewater Mill, Chain of Ponds, LENSWOOD Vineyards, Nepenthe Vineyards, PETALUMA, SHAW & SMITH, Geoff WEAVER. Best years: 1998, '97, '94, '93, '91, '90, '88.

ADELSHEIM VINEYARD

USA, Oregon, Yamhill County, Willamette Valley AVA

❦ *Pinot Noir*

♀ *Pinot Gris, Chardonnay, Riesling, Pinot Blanc*

David Adelsheim's winery in the Portland suburbs reliably produces one of OREGON's more stylish Pinot Noirs, capitalizing on the region's powerful fruit perfumes, especially the improving richer Reserve wine. The Pinot Gris offers subtler, more complex flavours along with the usual crisp acidity. The Chardonnays show dramatic improvements and the Rieslings are reliable. Best years: (Pinot Gris, Pinot Blanc, Riesling) 1998; (Chardonnay) 1996; (Pinot Noir) 1996, '94.

AGE

SPAIN, La Rioja, Rioja DOC

♟ *Tempranillo, Grenache Noir (Garnacha Tinta), Carignan (Cariñena, Mazuelo), Graciano*

♀ *Macabeo (Viura)*

AGE Bodegas Unidas, just outside the little RIOJA village of Fuenmayor, has built a new vinification centre right across the road from the original bodega, and the young red wine is now bursting with cherry, damson and almond flavour. The 'united bodegas' of the company's name came together in 1967. AGE was an acronym of the initials of the three founding families and it is now part of Spain's largest wine group, BODEGAS Y BEBIDAS. It's fair to describe a majority of the AGE wines as adequate rather than exciting. Their oak-aged white, aspiring to the intense style of the white from MARQUÉS DE MURRIETA, is worth noting as one of the few remaining oaky white Riojas. Best years: 1995, '94, '91, '87, '86, '85.

AGLIANICO

Among the dozen or so red grapes clamouring for attention in the south of Italy, Aglianico has historically claimed top billing, although several other red varieties are now making a determined challenge. Aglianico is wholly responsible for two of the most distinguished southern reds, Taurasi (from Campania) and Aglianico del Vulture (from Basilicata), and has a good stake in a third, Falerno (from Campania).

It produces surprisingly intense and elegant wines of medium colour, firm tannin and moderate alcohol, capable of long aging. Like Nebbiolo, it has sufficient complexity to stand alone, and is ideally suited to the long growing season imposed by the mesoclimate of its classic homelands. Were the general standard of winemaking higher it might have maintained a greater supremacy over its rivals, but its exponents are all too often inclined to emphasize structure over charm. Grown mainly in Campania and Basilicata, there are also some plantings in Molise and Puglia.

AGLIANICO DEL VULTURE DOC

ITALY, Basilicata

♟ *Aglianico*

Monte Vulture is an extinct volcano 1326m (4350ft) high, in the north of BASILICATA. The vineyards are on the east-facing (coolish) slopes, from 200m (660ft) to about half way up. Good Aglianico del Vulture is an intense, earthy wine that, with time, softens and develops complexity, especially if from a good vintage like 1998, '97 or '90. From such vintages the wines may be released as Riservas, with at least five years' aging.

Growers are mostly small part-timers, selling their grapes to co-operatives or *commercianti* who make the wine, increasingly resorting to barrique-maturation. The best-known producer is Fratelli d'Angelo, whose DOC and IGT Aglianicos (Riserva and the cru Canneto) exemplify the *botte*-aged and barrique-matured styles respectively.

LA AGRÍCOLA

ARGENTINA, Mendoza

♟ *Cabernet Sauvignon, Malbec, Tempranillo, Bonarda, Merlot, Pinot Noir*

♀ *Chardonnay, Chenin Blanc, Viognier, Torrontés*

Under José Alberto Zuccardi, La Agrícola has gone from being an experimental bodega set up to help sell the high-tech irrigation equipment his father designs to being Argentina's most successful exporter. Everything is here, all the latest equipment, expertly kept vineyards, clear ideas as to where to go, an ability to absorb new ideas and a willingness to move ahead fearlessly. Argentina's first barrique-aged Tempranillo is on the market now. It spearheads a new range of exciting wines called simply Q (for quality). Other wines are sold under the Santa Julia label. Watch out for recent vintages of the oak-aged Chardonnay, the Malbec Oak, and the excellent 'most recent vintage' juicy reds from a range of varietals. La Agrícola's vineyards are split into two groups: 360ha (890 acres) in Santa Rosa and 170ha (420 acres) in Maipú. The future looks bright for all the wines: 1999 wines are the best yet, and '98 was reasonable, though lacking the vibrancy of the '99s due its being the wettest harvest in Mendoza for 50 years.

AHR

GERMANY

The river Ahr flows into the Rhine just south of Bonn, and the region to which it gives its name was the most northerly of all German wine regions until the two regions of the former Democratic Republic, SAALE-UNSTRUT and SACHSEN, joined the party. Ahr is also very small, with just 510ha (1260 acres) of vines, 75 per cent of which are planted with red grapes. Pinot Noir (Spätburgunder) is the main variety and makes the best reds; the Riesling would surely be better if there were more interest in white wines here.

But reds are the region's acknowledged speciality, and so the Ahr goes on ignoring the logic of its northerly climate. The reds that result are mostly pallid, although there is a move to deep-coloured, more tannic wines led by growers such as J J Adenauer, Deutzerhof and Meyer-Näkel. The soil is slaty, and the best Rieslings can reflect this with a steeliness to their flavour, plus a certain earthiness; but they seldom compete with the finest from the top German wine regions like the RHEINGAU or the MOSEL. Average vineyard holdings in the Ahr are small; most producers take their grapes to the local co-operative. Just one Bereich – Walporzheim-Ahrtal – covers the whole region; there is also only one Grosslage, Klosterberg. Best producer: Meyer-Näkel.

AIGLE

SWITZERLAND, Vaud, Chablais

This village in the CHABLAIS region of the VAUD overlooks the river Rhône close to where it flows into Lake Geneva and is principally a white wine area. The Chasselas grape usually doesn't produce wines with much character, but here, where it's called the Dorin, they can be tangy and crisp. The Pinot Noir can be attractive and is fashionable in Switzerland. Best producer: Henri Badoux.

DOMAINE DE L'AIGLE

FRANCE, Languedoc-Roussillon, Limoux AC

♟ *Pinot Noir*

♀ *Chardonnay, Mauzac and others*

Jean-Louis Denois is one of the new breed of producers revolutionizing ideas in the Midi region of France. Originally from CHAMPAGNE, Denois settled in Limoux in 1989 convinced that the cooler climate of this hilly region offered the potential to cultivate his native Chardonnay and Pinot Noir. He was proved correct and now produces an exciting range of still and sparkling wines. In Limoux AC, the Classique is made from Chardonnay and Mauzac, and les Aigles from barrel-fermented Chardonnay. Both are ripe and fruity with a refreshing zip of acidity. The red Vin de Pays Pinot Noir Terres

Rouges has Burgundian cherry fruit aromas but is softer and riper. Among the sparkling wines the non-AC Cuvée Tradition Brut, produced from 70 per cent Pinot Noir and 30 per cent Chardonnay, spends three years on its lees and is full, biscuity and a bargain. His attempts to make Riesling and Gewürztraminer have run into problems with the authorities. Best years: (whites) 1997, '96, '95, '94, '93, '92; (reds) 1997.

AIRÉN

This simple-flavoured white grape covers nearly one-third of Spain's vineyards, making it the world's most planted variety. The Airén lake would be even vaster were it not for the fact that most of the vineyards are on the hot central plains of La MANCHA, where yields are tiny. Nevertheless this grape can produce fresh, decent whites. All new Airén plantings are currently banned in Castilla-la Mancha.

AJACCIO AC

FRANCE, Corsica

♥ ♟ *Sciacarello*

♀ *Vermentino, Ugni Blanc*

From the west of the island around Ajaccio and with 230ha (568 acres) under vine, this is one of the best Corsican ACs. With the shining exception of Comte Peraldi, whose excellent white shows real class in both oak-aged and non-oaked versions, the whites are still all potential and little realization, as are the distinctly orange-hued rosés. However, the reds from Sciacarello can show a bit of form even if the rather sour edge of acidity still intrudes more than it should into the fairly plummy fruit. Comte Peraldi and Clos d'Alzeto are in a different league from the others, though there are rather rustic but tasty efforts from Clos Capitoro and Domaine Martini. The reds often need two to three years in bottle to show at their best. Best years: (reds) 1998, '97, '96, '95, '94.

ALBANA DI ROMAGNA DOCG

ITALY, Emilia-Romagna

♀ *Albana*

Produced over a large area between Bologna and Rimini, this, in 1987, was the first white wine to be 'promoted' to DOCG status, much to the astonishment and dismay of those who thought, perhaps naively, that Italy's highest denomination surely ought to be awarded on the basis of quality rather than on that of political clout! The sweet and *passito* versions, admittedly, are capable of considerable complexity and interest, notably in the form of

ZERBINA
This luscious passito wine with a deft touch of new oak is from one of the leading estates in the Albana di Romagna DOCG.

ZERBINA's Scacco Matto. Other good producers: Celli, Umberto Cesari, Leone Conti, Fattoria Paradiso, Tre Monti, Tenuta Uccellina. Drink dry Albana young.

ALBARIÑO

Albariño is the top-quality white grape of GALICIA, the green and fertile region in Spain's far north-west (and just over the border around Monção in Portugal's VINHO VERDE country where it is called Alvarinho). When it's well made, Albariño wine can have complex fruity flavours of apricot, peach, grapefruit and even grape. Though the vines are very productive, the grapes are extremely thick-skinned and pippy, producing relatively little juice. Because of this, the grapes fetch high prices – and the wines are among Spain's most expensive whites. Newer styles (oak-fermented, late-harvest) are progressively joining the ranks of new-wave Albariño.

ALBET I NOYA

SPAIN, Cataluña, Penedès DO, Cava DO

♥ *Tempranillo, Cabernet Sauvignon, Merlot, Syrah*

♟ *Pinot Noir, Merlot*

♀ *Macabeo, Xarel-lo, Parellada, Chardonnay*

Josep Maria Albet i Noya is a pioneer of ecological viticulture and natural winemaking in Spain, as well as a remarkable self-made man. The scion of a modest family of *rabassers* (the Catalan equivalent of the French *métayers* – farmers who till land owned by someone else), he was an orphan at 15 and had to care for his whole family. He later succeeded in acquiring the land he tilled. He now owns 40ha (99 acres) around the village of Subirats, where he makes a wide range of still wines and some CAVA. Outstanding fruit purity is an estate hallmark. The top wine is the red Reserva Martí, named after his son: a structured, complex blend of Tempranillo, Cabernet Sauvignon, Merlot and Syrah. There are also age-worthy, oak-fermented whites. Best years: 1997, '96, '95, '94, '91.

ALCAMO DOC

ITALY, Sicily

♀ *Catarratto, Damaschino, Grecanico, Trebbiano Toscano*

Take the road west from Palermo and round the Gulf of Castellammare, turn inland past Alcamo and you drive through such dense hills you can rarely see more than a few hundred yards in any direction. But every single slope of every hill is dark green with vines, mainly of the Catarratto family (though all too few of these are of the superior Catarratto Bianco Lucido sub-variety as distinct from the prolific Catarratto Bianco Comune). It is sobering to note that Catarratto in its two types is Italy's second most-grown grape, after Trebbiano which also thrives here. Small wonder, then, that Alcamo is almost invariably a neutral and stretched wine, especially as overproduction is endemic. Only those producers whose vineyards are at an highish altitude and who severely limit production achieve a wine of real interest, and you can count them on the fingers of a single hand.

Nonetheless, Alcamo remains one of SICILY's few DOCs, though the producers do not make a great play of it. For example, the label of the lively, crisp, appley and almondy white Rapitalà, from Alcamo's best estate, looks the same as the Rapitalà red and rosé, which are VINO DA TAVOLA. Other respectable producers include I.VI.COR., M.I.D., Spadafora. Drink the wines young.

ALEATICO

The Italian grape Aleatico is such an odd combination of Muscat-like aroma, style and longevity that some reckon it is a Muscat mutation. The wines are dark red, usually richly sweet, tasting of wild strawberries, redcurrants and other berry fruits. They are rounded, often alcoholic, and absolutely delicious but scarce. Aleatico is found mainly in PUGLIA, though there are outcrops by Lake Bolsena in LAZIO, Tuscany, UMBRIA and even on Elba. Best producers: AVIGNONESI (Tuscany), Candido (Aleatico di Puglia).

ALELLA DO

SPAIN, Cataluña

♥ ♟ *Grenache Noir (Garnacha Tinta), Tempranillo (Ull de Llebre), Merlot, Cabernet Sauvignon, Pansá Rosáda, Garnacha Peluda*

♀ *Xarel-lo (Pansá Blanca), Grenache Blanc (Garnacha Blanca)*

This is one of Spain's smallest DOs, making mostly whites, the best of them light and fresh. Over the last two decades, vineyards have rapidly been giving way to villas. The first plots to go were the prettiest, high up in the rolling hills north of Barcelona, and these, sadly, were also the coolest and best vineyard sites. Alella's inland vineyards grow mainly Pansá Blanca (the Xarel-lo of the PENEDÈS) while the slopes that face east, seawards, grow Garnacha Blanca in the more Mediterranean climate. The co-operative produces 60 per cent of the region's wine, with unimpressive results, and most of the rest comes from the reliable firm of Parxet (Marqués de Alella), which has varieties new to the region, such as Parellada, Macabeo, Cabernet Sauvignon and Chardonnay.

ALENQUER DOC
PORTUGAL, Estremadura
♥ *Camarate, Periquita, Mortagua, Preto Martinho, Tinta Miuda*
♀ *Arinto, Fernão Pires, Jampal, Vital*

Vineyards set in rolling country around the small whitewashed town of Alenquer produce the best wines in Portugal's ESTREMADURA. Sheltered from the Atlantic westerlies by the Serra de Montejunto, it lies close to Lisbon north-west of the river Tagus (Tejo). Reds (mostly based on the Periquita grape) tend to be better than whites although Quinta D Carlos makes a delightful varietal Arinto. The leading properties are Quinta de Abrigada and Quinta de Pancas (where the owner has some Cabernet Sauvignon and Chardonnay vines in addition to the indigenous varieties). Reds are capable of aging for five years or so. Whites should be drunk as young as possible.

ALENTEJO DOC
PORTUGAL
♥ *Tempranillo (Aragonez), Moreto, Periquita, Trincadeira and others*
♀ *Arinto, Antão Vaz, Diagalves, Mantuedo, Roupeiro*

The Alentejo is a huge rolling plain that takes up much of Portugal south of the river Tagus (Tejo) stretching inland from the Atlantic east to the frontier with Spain. Vineyards are not all that evident in this expansive landscape where fields of flowing corn often stretch as far as the eye can see. Until as recently as the 1980s, the Alentejo's main link with the wine world was through cork. Over half the world's cork comes from Portugal, mostly from the Alentejo.

Vines tend to be found around the outskirts of bright whitewashed towns and villages which form wine enclaves in their own right. Borba, Évora, Granja-Amareleja,

The Australian winemaker David Baverstock has done much to revitalize the Alentejo region through his work at the huge Esporão estate.

Redondo, Moura, Portalegre, Redondo, REGUENGOS and Vidigueira are all new sub-DOCs of the new Alentejo DOC. But the Alentejo is all about the big picture and the whole region is now classified as a Vinho Regional under the name of Alentejano. Most producers tend to opt for the latter designation which allows more flexibility in terms of grape varieties and in enabling them to blend wines from grapes sourced from over a wide area.

Alentejo wines were once the butt of frequent jokes. But, with the help of investment from the EU, the region's wines have undergone such a transformation that the locals are now having the last laugh. Gleaming stainless steel wineries have been springing up all over the region and there is now an insatiable demand for Alentejano wines from the increasingly demanding hordes of supermarket buyers in Lisbon and Oporto.

In this climate, it is not surprising that most of the Alentejo's reputation is based on red wines. Apart from Arinto, few white grape varieties can stand up to the sweltering daytime heat and the wines tend to lack acidity. Nevertheless white grapes still predominate around Vidigueira (perhaps the hottest part of the entire region) and the ESPORÃO estate near Reguengos makes some fresh, subtropical dry whites. Red grapes like Trincadeira and Aragonez (alias Tempranillo) are much better adapted to the Alentejo scene. Carignan and Alicante Bouschet (still much derided in France) lend ballast to

many of the region's finest wines. Mouchão made by Herdade de Mouchão is perhaps the best example of a resolutely Alentejano red made from this eclectic mix of grapes.

Other leading producers are widely spread throughout the province. In the north around Portalegre, where the climate is somewhat more temperate, Tapada do Chaves and d'Avillez (the latter belonging to José Maria da FONSECA) make outstanding reds. In the central belt around Évora, Borba, Redondo and Reguengos, Quinta do Carmo, Cartuxa (Fundação Eugenio de Almeida), Esporão and José de Sousa (also belonging to José Maria da Fonseca) are the leading estates. J P VINHOS sources wines throughout the Alentejo and makes their leathery Tinto da Anfora red at Arraiolos. The dynamic João Portugal Ramos also makes a smooth, spicy oak-aged red near Estremoz and the nearby town of Borba boasts a well-run co-operative. In the deep south of the region, Portugal's largest winemakers SOGRAPE has an estate at Vidigueira where they make the fleshy red Vinha do Monte. The Danish-owned Cortes de Cima is a welcome new producer to this rapidly expanding region.

ALEXANDER VALLEY AVA
USA, California, Sonoma County

The Alexander Valley AVA is centred on the Russian River as it cuts a long, broad swathe from SONOMA COUNTY's northerly limit at Cloverdale south to Healdsburg. It is fairly warm here with only patchy summer fog and there is a sharp contrast between vines from the valley floor vineyards and those from the low hills that frame it where the vines are often lower yielding.

Chardonnay unquestionably leads the white wines; the finest examples set understated varietal flavours against firmness of texture. Sauvignon Blanc can be formidably grassy, but Cabernet Sauvignon can be juicy and soft-textured; the heartily ripe Merlots are the valley's most intriguing reds. Zinfandel, made from pre-Prohibition

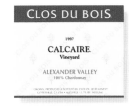
CLOS DU BOIS
One of the largest producers in Sonoma, Clos du Bois makes a speciality of Chardonnay. This barrel-fermented Chardonnay comes from the Calcaire vineyard.

vineyards, can be exceptional here. Best years: 1998 (reds only), '97, '95, '94. Of the 20 or so wineries, GEYSER PEAK and SIMI are the oldest wineries. JORDAN and Alexander Valley Vineyards are younger but established; MURPHY-GOODE and De Lorimer show promise. The larger CLOS DU BOIS and Chateau Souverain draw grapes from inside the valley and outside, but contribute much to its reputation. Other good producers: Estancia, Field Stone, Sausal, Scherrer, Seghesio, SILVER OAK, Trentadue.

ALGARVE VINHO REGIONAL
PORTUGAL
🍷 *Bastardo, Moreto, Negra Mole, Periquita*
🥂 *Arinto, Diagalves, Perrum, Rabo de Ovelha, Tamarez*

Portugal's holiday coast has a captive market among the droves of sun-worshippers who bask on the region's beaches each summer. They don't tend to bring much of the local hooch home with them though because the wines are fairly dire. The lion's share of the region's wine is red. It's pretty feeble stuff: high in alcohol and low in colour and flavour. The Algarve is sub-divided into four separate DOCs: Lagoa, Lagos, Portimão and Tavira, each based on the local co-operative. Of these, wines from the Lagoa co-operative are the best. But if you go there on holiday my advice is to drink the wines from the ALENTEJO province immediately to the north of the Algarve or stick to the rasping but refreshing VINHO VERDE.

ALIANÇA
PORTUGAL, Bairrada DOC, Dão DOC, Douro DOC, Vinho Verde DOC, Palmela IPR, Alentejo Vinho Regional
🍷 *Baga, Aragonês (Tempranillo), Trincadeira, Periquita*
🥂 *Bical, Fernão Pires (Maria Gomes)*

The family-run Caves Aliança is one of Portugal's leading wine companies. It is based

ALIANÇA
Caves Aliança is leading the way in the Bairrada region, making soft, approachable red wines for early drinking instead of the traditional hard, tannic reds.

in the BAIRRADA region but buys in wines from all the main DOC regions of northern Portugal. It has also made a foray into the ALENTEJO where two heady red wines are made – Alabastro and Borba-Monte da Terrugem. Caves Aliança is a forward-looking organization and the company's red Bairradas are approachable and easy to drink whereas others require longer aging.

Aliança's whites are fresh and aromatic, especially the varietal Bical which is one of Portugal's most promising white grapes. Cabernet Sauvignon, a grape which performs well in the Bairrada region, and Chardonnay have also joined Bical in the range of Aliança's varietal wines under the Galeria label. Elsewhere in Portugal, Aliança's most successful wines are well-made reds from PALMELA (south of Lisbon) and the Alentejo. Best years: (Bairrada) 1995, '94, '92.

ALICANTE DO
SPAIN, Valencia
🍷🥂 *Mourvèdre (Monastrell), Grenache Noir (Garnacha Tinta), Bobal, Tempranillo, Merlot, Cabernet Sauvignon, Syrah, Pinot Noir*
🥂 *Merseguera, Muscat (Moscatel), Verdil, Riesling, Chardonnay*

Down in the hot, dry south-east corner of Spain, the Alicante DO makes mostly red wines, traditionally very dark and heavy with alcohol. Recently, with investment in both vineyards and wineries, there have been improvements, though most whites (dry, medium and sweet) are still dull, alcoholic and best avoided. The exception is attractive Moscatel from the Muscat of Alexandria grape made by the producer GUTIÉRREZ DE LA VEGA, in the ideally situated Marina Alta sub-region near Denia right on the Mediterranean amid the orange groves.

The region's finest wine – and a local curiosity well worth seeking out for tourists becoming weary of the beach – is Fondillón, a dry fortified wine from the Monastrell grape with a minimum of 16 per cent alcohol, which is aged in a solera for at least eight years before being bottled. Unique to Alicante, it's one of Spain's best *rancio* wines with rich, nutty, toffee flavours similar to a tawny PORT.

Few of Alicante's vineyards actually reach down to the Mediterranean as most of them are located on the cooler slopes way inland in the hills of the Vinalopó around the town of Villena near the border with MURCIA. The Salvador Poveda firm makes a characterful,

strong, herby red Viña Vermeta Tinto and a strong, quite tannic, oaky-herby-plummy red called Viña Vermeta Reserva. Best years: 1995, '90, '87. Best producers: (Fondillón) Bodegas Alfonso, Bodegas Brotons, Salvador Poveda, Primitivo Quiles; (Moscatel) Felipe Gutiérrez de la Vega; (table wines) Enrique Mendoza.

ALIGOTÉ
This French white grape – almost certainly of Burgundian origin – has a lemony tartness, with a smell when ripe rather like buttermilk soap, and sometimes a whiff of pine and eucalyptus. It gives immeasurably better wine from old vines, and many of the best Aligoté wines in Burgundy come from vines more than 50 years old. In warm years the wine can resemble a Chardonnay, especially if a little new oak is used in the winemaking.

The best known area for Aligoté is Bouzeron in the Côte Chalonnaise where the wine has its own AC (Bourgogne-Aligoté de Bouzeron) and yields are limited to 45 hectolitres per hectare, compared to 60 hectolitres elsewhere in Burgundy. However, several other Côte d'Or villages produce equally fine Aligoté from old vines, though these are only allowed to use the Bourgogne-Aligoté AC. Pernand-Vergelesses makes particularly good examples. As well as the Côte d'Or and the Côte Chalonnaise there is some Aligoté in the Hautes-Côtes, in the Mâconnais, and in the Yonne at St-Bris-le-Vineux and Chitry-le-Fort. Virtually every single one of the 1276ha (3153 acres) of French Aligoté is planted in Burgundy, except for a few vines in the Rhône's Châtillon-en-Diois appellation – where the wine is rather nutty and not half bad.

Aligoté is also found in Eastern Europe – in Romania, Bulgaria and the Black Sea coast, especially in Moldova.

ALKOOMI

AUSTRALIA, Western Australia, South West Australia Zone, Margaret River

♥ *Cabernet Sauvignon, Shiraz, Malbec, Merlot and others*

♀ *Riesling, Chardonnay, Sauvignon Blanc and others*

The supposed tyranny of distance has never impacted on Merv and Judy Lange, who have steadily built the Alkoomi empire upon the bedrock of consistently excellent and moderately priced wines made from 100 per cent estate-grown grapes. A refusal to expand more rapidly than their means allow has surely helped too. Razor sharp varietal definition is the hallmark of all the wines. Best years: 1997, '96, '95, '94, '90, '88, '87, '86, '84, '83.

ALLEGRINI

ITALY, Veneto, Valpolicella DOC

♥ *Corvina, Molinara, Rondinella*

One of the earliest pioneers of quality VALPOLICELLA was Giovanni Allegrini, who a few years prior to his premature death in 1983 purchased the Grola hill in Sant'Ambrogio for the purpose of producing fine cru wines with new methods of planting and vinification. His modernist principles have been continued and adapted by his children, who now run the company.

All their wines are from grapes grown in their own 70ha (170 acres) of vineyard. They include La Poja, from Corvina vines planted at the top of the Grola hill, probably the single greatest table wine (i.e. unaided by semi-dried grapes) ever to come out of Valpolicella; La Grola, a single-vineyard Classico Superiore aged in French oak *fusti*; Palazzo della Torre, a wine made according to a VENETO version of Tuscany's *governo*; an outstanding AMARONE of the modern, relatively light type; and an intensely fruity RECIOTO named, appropriately, Giovanni Allegrini. Allegrini will remain for the foreseeable future leader of the modernist school in Valpolicella. Best years: (La Poja) 1995, '94, '93, '92, '90.

ALLEGRINI
La Grola is a stylish and elegant single-vineyard Valpolicella Classico from the usual Valpolicella blend of Corvina, Molinara and Rondinella.

ALLENDE

SPAIN, La Rioja, Rioja DOC

♥ *Tempranillo, Graciano, Grenache Noir (Garnacha Tinta), Mazuelo*

Miguel Angel de Gregorio had a fledgling estate of his own ready when he left his job as Bodegas Bretón's winemaker in 1997. The son of MARQUÉS DE MURRIETA's longtime vineyard manager, de Gregorio is a devotee of old vines, and his Finca Allende is actually a collection of small plots around the village of Briones, long reputed as having one of the best terroirs in RIOJA ALTA. They total 18ha (44 acres) of mostly 50-year-old Tempranillo, with a small number of other RIOJA varieties in the field blend. The bodega itself is a very modest, even basic facility.

De Gregorio's Murrieta roots are also reflected in his affection for carbonic maceration, which he uses for a percentage of each of his wines, in the old style of the classic Logroño bodega. He favours big, concentrated, uncompromising wines that place him near the top of the new-wave Rioja producers. He makes a basic Allende wine and a top-end Aurus, which includes a good dollop of the rare Graciano in the blend. French oak is favoured here. Best years: 1996, '95.

ALOXE-CORTON AC

FRANCE, Burgundy, Côte de Beaune

♥ *Pinot Noir*

♀ *Chardonnay*

This important village nestling beneath the south-east side of the hill of CORTON at the northern end of the CÔTE DE BEAUNE produces mostly red wines. Aloxe-Corton has the largest amount of Grand Cru land anywhere in the CÔTE D'OR and its reputation is based on the two Grands Crus, Corton (mainly red wine) and CORTON-CHARLEMAGNE (white wine only) which it shares with the villages of Ladoix-Serrigny and PERNAND-VERGELESSES. The vines flow across the slopes of the hill of Corton from east to almost due west, with the highest vines nuzzling the forest-covered brow.

The large Corton vineyard is the Côte de Beaune's only red Grand Cru. It is also the Côte d'Or's least expensive red Grand Cru – and the most variable. The vineyards further down on the flatter land qualify for the village AC only and used to offer some of Burgundy's tastiest village wine at a fair price; nowadays the reds rarely exhibit their characteristically delicious blend of ripe fruit and appetizing savoury dryness. Although there are a number of Premier Cru vineyards, these

TOLLOT-BEAUT & FILS
This top-quality company makes excellent village Aloxe-Corton wine with succulent fruit and a good black cherry flavour.

are hardly ever named on the label, but 'Premier Cru', denoting a blend of several Premier Cru wines, is quite common.

Almost all of the white wine of Aloxe-Corton is now sold as Grand Cru (both Corton and Corton-Charlemagne); straight Aloxe-Corton Blanc is very rare. The best can show remarkable richness of flavour and character for a fully dry white. Best years: 1997, '96, '95, '93, '90, '89, '88, '85; (whites) 1997, '96, '95, '92, '90, '89, '88. Best producers: Ambroise, Bize, CHANDON DE BRIAILLES, Chapuis, Delarche, DROUHIN, Dubreuil-Fontaine, FAIVELEY, Guyon, JADOT, LATOUR, LEROY, Maillard Père et Fils, Senard, TOLLOT-BEAUT, Voarick.

DOMAINE ALQUIER

FRANCE, Languedoc-Roussillon, Faugères AC

♥♀ *Grenache, Syrah, Carignan, Mourvèdre*

♀ *Roussanne, Viognier, Marsanne, Grenache Blanc*

Domaine Alquier was founded in 1870 and, unlike many other properties in the Midi, this is no recent convert to quality; the Alquier wines have been good for some time. Gilbert Alquier planted Grenache in the 1950s, followed by Syrah (which does particularly well in FAUGÈRES) in the '60s. His sons, Jean-Michel and Frédéric, added Mourvèdre when they took over the reins of this immaculately kept 30-ha (74-acre) domaine in the 1970s.

The wines are dense, ripe but elegantly structured, produced from hand-picked grapes that achieve optimum maturity. Grapes from vines under 12 years old are used for the rosé wine. The two top cuvées are both aged in oak barriques – Maison Jaune is Grenache-dominated while les Bastides has a high percentage of Syrah, spends 12–15 months in mainly new oak and requires a minimum of five years' aging. There is also a white Vin de Pays d'Oc Roussanne-Marsanne and a Viognier-Marsanne. Best years: (reds) 1997, '96, '95, '94, '93, '90, '89.

ALSACE France

SOME OF THE MOST DELICIOUSLY individual white wines in France come from Alsace yet, at first sight rather than taste, you might well mistake them for German. Alsace bottles are tall, slender and green – just like the bottles from the Mosel region of Germany. The name of the producer is almost certain to be Germanic, and also, in many cases, the name of the wine – Riesling, Sylvaner, Gewürztraminer… Despite the German influence Alsace is proudly, independently, French. Many of the grapes may be the same but Alsace winemakers create completely different flavours – drier, yet riper, with fuller alcohol, yet unnervingly scented.

The key to producing wine so far north lies in the Vosges mountains – rising high to the west, they draw off the moisture from the westerly winds, leaving an east-facing slope to enjoy the second-driest climate in France. Only Pinot Noir, Alsace's lone red, has difficulty ripening here, needing exceptional summers to make red rather than rosé.

Although we now see bottles labelled according to grape type from all over the world, Alsace was the first area of France to enshrine this practice in its own wine laws. A single AC was created for the whole region – Alsace AC – and apart from the blends, called Edelzwicker, most table wines are called by the grape name used. Usually this is the

The steep Schoenenbourg Grand Cru vineyard towers over the beautiful village of Riquewihr, a major centre of the Alsace wine trade. Riesling and Muscat have traditionally done best here, especially as late-harvested wines.

only description of wine type on the label but the best 50 vineyards have now been designated Grand Cru. Only wines made from Riesling, Pinot Gris, Gewürztraminer and Muscat are entitled to be labelled Grand Cru.

Alsace usually benefits from long, sunny autumns, so in most years it is possible to leave parcels of grapes to overripen on the vine. The resulting Vendange Tardive (late-harvested) wines tend to be very rich and intense, with a little residual sugar to balance the powerful fruit and high alcohol. Less common are the wines labelled Sélection de Grains Nobles, which are produced from even riper grapes, usually concentrated by botrytis (noble rot). These wines are rare and extremely expensive.

At the opposite end of the taste spectrum are the lively sparkling wines called Crémant d'Alsace. These are usually made from varieties with high natural acidity such as Pinot Blanc, Auxerrois and Riesling, which are picked long before they reach the high ripeness levels that would make them less well suited to the production of fresh, zesty sparkling wine.

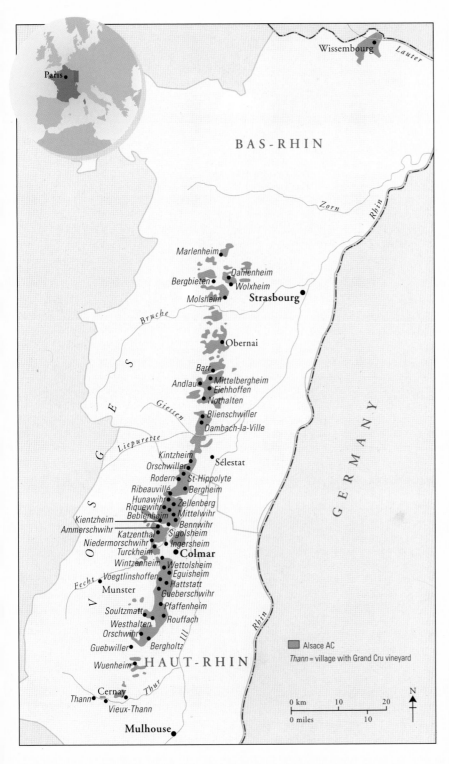

DOMAINE SCHOFFIT
The Clos St-Théobald wines from the fabulous Rangen Grand Cru vineyard are full bodied and very rich.

SCHLUMBERGER
Cuvée Christine, a Vendange Tardive equivalent, is one of the top wines from this large, family-owned domaine.

RENÉ MURÉ
From the superb terraced vineyard of Clos St-Landelin comes this seductive, fruity Muscat with heavenly perfume.

DOMAINE WEINBACH
This famous domaine's top wine, from the Schlossberg Grand Cru, blends the austerity of Riesling with depth, complexity and seductive aromas.

ZIND-HUMBRECHT
The leading Alsace estate produces a long list of brilliant wines, including many at Vendange Tardive level.

ERNEST BURN
The Clos St-Imer is a small terraced vineyard on the upper slopes of the Goldert Grand Cru and is wholly owned by the Burn family. It is one of the few Alsace domaines specialising in Muscat.

HUGEL ET FILS
Hugel's rich, ripe spicy Vendange Tardive wines are usually capable of lasting for 20 years or more.

ALBERT MANN
Gewurztraminer is the most voluptuous of all Alsace wines and the Sélection de Grains Nobles wines from the Furstentum Grand Cru can be astonishingly rich and concentrated.

REGIONAL ENTRIES
Alsace Edelzwicker, Alsace Gewurztraminer, Alsace Grand Cru, Alsace Muscat, Alsace Pinot Blanc, Alsace Pinot Gris (Tokay), Alsace Pinot Noir, Alsace Riesling, Alsace Sylvaner, Alsace Vendange Tardive, Crémant d'Alsace.

PRODUCER ENTRIES
Beyer, Blanck, Bott-Geyl, Deiss, Hugel et Fils, Kreydenweiss, Kuentz-Bas, Schlumberger, Trimbach, Cave Vinicole de Turckheim, Weinbach, Zind-Humbrecht.

ALSACE EDELZWICKER

FRANCE, Alsace, Alsace AC

♀ *Chasselas, Sylvaner, Pinot Blanc and others*

In the mid-nineteenth century Edelzwicker was very highly regarded (*edel* means 'noble'), being a blend of the best grape varieties – Riesling, Gewurztraminer and Pinot Gris. Since ALSACE gained its AC in 1962, the tendency has been towards all the best grape varieties being vinified separately, so now Edelzwicker is generally a blend of Chasselas, Sylvaner and Pinot Blanc, beefed up with a splash or two of Gewurztraminer or Riesling. Never expensive, it can be very good value and is for drinking young. The name Edelzwicker is also giving way to wines labelled simply Alsace or Vin d'Alsace. Some producers use proprietary names for their blended wines rather than the debased Edelzwicker name, for example, HUGEL's Gentil. Best producers: Dopff & Irion, Éguisheim co-operative, Ehrhart, Klipfel, Rolly Gassmann, Schoech.

ALSACE GEWURZTRAMINER

FRANCE, Alsace, Alsace AC

♀ *Gewurztraminer*

Gewurztraminer's problem is that it is absurdly easy to enjoy. Our rather Puritan ethic of wine appreciation can't stand its willingness to be enjoyed with no pain and no recrimination. Well, that's too bad, because Gewurztraminer must be wallowed in to get the best out of it.

Given that Alsace wines are renowned for their flowery spice, the 'Gewürz' (as it is often called – appropriately, since Gewürz is German for 'spice') is the most Alsatian of flavours because the smell is an explosion of roses, grapes, lychees, mangoes and peaches and the flavour is often thick with the richness of oriental fruit. Sometimes there's just not enough acidity to cope, but the effect is so luscious, you often don't mind.

It's worth emphasizing that these wines are almost always dry. The flavours are most evident in late-picked wines from hot years, but even cheap Gewurztraminer from a co-operative will be flowery, aromatic, exotic and unmistakable. Despite their low acidity, Gewurztraminer wines can be very long-lived, though they are always approachable young. Best years: 1998, '97, '95, '93, '92, '90, '89, '88, '85, '83, '76, '71. Best producers: J-B Adam, Becker, BEYER, BLANCK, Cattin, Dopff & Irion, Ginglinger, Hertz, HUGEL, Josmeyer, Kientzler, Koehly, KREYDENWEISS, KUENTZ-BAS, Lorentz,

TRIMBACH

This Trimbach wine is a gloriously dry, full-bodied, rich and spicy example of the pink-skinned Gewurztraminer grape which is at its best in Alsace.

Mann, Ostertag, Rolly Gassmann, Schleret, SCHLUMBERGER, Schoech, Sparr, Turckheim co-operative, TRIMBACH, WEINBACH, Willm, ZIND-HUMBRECHT.

ALSACE GRAND CRU AC

FRANCE, Alsace

♀ *Riesling, Gewurztraminer, Pinot Gris or Muscat*

This appellation is an attempt, beginning with the 1985 vintage, to classify the best vineyards in ALSACE. It is fiercely resisted by some merchants, who argue that a blend from several vineyards always makes the best wines, but this just isn't so. It is the same now-discredited argument used for generations by the merchants of Burgundy who, anxious to keep tight control over their profitable share of the market, would deny a grower the right to say, 'This slope has always been special and I can show you why by offering you my version of its wine – unblended and undiluted.' At the same time, no-one would dispute that the houses that have refused to use this appellation system – notably HUGEL, BEYER and TRIMBACH – make some wines of outstanding quality. Part of their objection to the system is that too many Grands Crus were created, largely at the behest of growers with a vested interest in their existence, and that their borders were too broadly confirmed.

Nonetheless, the system is clearly here to stay and, for all its deficiencies, does help identify some of the region's most remarkable sites. The Grand Cru vineyards vary in size from 3ha (7½ acres) to 80ha (200 acres) and are defined by broad geological principles.

At the moment 50 vineyards are classified, mostly in the southern Haut-Rhin section, though there are other sites under consideration. Only Gewurztraminer, Riesling, Pinot Gris and Muscat grapes qualify for Grand Cru status and the grape varieties must be unblended. Things look promising, especially since the minimum natural alcohol level for

Grand Cru is much higher (10 degrees for Muscat and Riesling, 12 degrees for Gewurztraminer and Pinot Gris) and the yield allowed is 65 hectolitres per hectare (soon to come down to 60), as against 100 hectolitres for AC wine. This alone can dramatically improve quality. However, despite a series of excellent vintages there are still a disturbing number of inconsequential Grand Cru wines. Best years: 1998, '97, '96, '95, '94, '93, '92, '90, '89, '88. See also page 33.

ALSACE MUSCAT

FRANCE, Alsace, Alsace AC

♀ *Muscat (Muscat Ottonel, Muscat à Petits Grains)*

Alsace Muscat can be sheer heaven. Few wines have any taste of grape at all, but this one can seem like the purest essence of fresh grape – and yet be totally dry. It is a magical combination – the heady hothouse smell of a vine in late summer, the feel in your mouth delicate and light, yet the gentle fruit as perfumed and refreshing as the juice crunched from a fistful of Muscatel grapes. A slight muskiness, like fresh coffee, adds to the pleasure.

The Muscat à Petits Grains variety used to predominate, but its susceptibility to rot meant that producers turned increasingly to Muscat Ottonel. Now, luckily, growers are once more turning to the higher quality Muscat à Petits Grains, with good results. The two varieties cover less than 3 per cent of the vineyard area in ALSACE, because they are prone to disease and often only ripen well one year in two. If you see one – snap it up, chill it for an hour, and serve it either as the perfect apéritif or after dinner drink – the Muscat flavour in a light, dry wine is far more reviving than a bumper of port or brandy. Drink young. Best producers: Albrecht, Becker, Burn, Cattin, Dirler, Dopff & Irion, Ginglinger, Gisselbrecht, Klipfel, KREYDENWEISS, Kuehn, KUENTZ-BAS, Mader, Muré, Rolly Gassmann, Schoffit, Sorg, TRIMBACH, ZIND-HUMBRECHT.

ALSACE PINOT BLANC

FRANCE, Alsace, Alsace AC

♀ *Pinot Blanc, Auxerrois Blanc*

For an apparently simple wine, a Pinot Blanc can have an awfully complicated make-up. Usually it is a blend of Pinot Blanc and the similar, but unrelated, Auxerrois and is a soft dry white, appley, slightly creamy – the perfect wine-bar drink.

However, Pinot Blanc wine can also be made from three other grape varieties: white wine from the red Pinot Noir is called Pinot

Blanc and can be delicious, full and creamy; Pinot Gris wine can be called Pinot Blanc too and is sometimes used to beef up a weaker pure Pinot Blanc; and there is a little Chardonnay planted which is also called Pinot Blanc! The wines all share a fresh, soft, easy-drinking style and are excellent young, but sometimes also capable of aging well. Klevner or Clevner, the Alsace name for Pinot Blanc, seldom appears on a label – if it does, it generally applies to a Pinot Blanc-Auxerrois blend. Best producers: J-B Adam, Bechtold, Becker, BEYER, BLANCK, Cattin, DEISS, Gisselbrecht, HUGEL, Josmeyer, KREYDENWEISS, Mann, Rolly Gassmann, Schleret, Schoffit, Sipp, TRIMBACH, TURCKHEIM co-operative, ZIND-HUMBRECHT.

ALSACE PINOT GRIS

FRANCE, Alsace, Alsace AC
♀ *Pinot Gris*

Top-line Pinot Gris wines are frequently the greatest wines in ALSACE and even the basic ones have a lovely lick of honey to soften and deepen their attractive peachy fruit. The wines used to be called Tokay d'Alsace and you may see a few labels saying 'Tokay-Pinot Gris'. Once a minor player in Alsace, Pinot Gris is now firmly in fashion and its share of the vineyards is on the increase.

The legend is that an Alsatian soldier, de Schwendi, attacked the Hungarian fortress of Tokaj in 1565, captured 4000 vats of their Tokay wine and liked it so much that he sent his servant to fetch some Tokay vine cuttings. Now, Hungarian Tokaji (as the wine is called today) is made from Furmint grapes; yet the servant brought back Pinot Gris, already well known in much more hospitable and less distant Burgundy. So perhaps he really sneaked off there, and only pretended to go to Hungary. Anyway, the name Tokay stuck, but the wine is always made from Pinot Gris; and nowadays the label is supposed to say

Pinot Gris in order to avoid confusion with the Hungarian Tokaji.

This golden wine's acidity is low, but that doesn't stop the wine aging brilliantly, blending a treacle, honey and raisin richness with flavours like the essence from the skins of peaches and apricots, and a slight smokiness. And, again, in Alsace this is almost always a dry wine! The Vendange Tardive styles are particularly exciting but even at the basic level you should glimpse these flavours. The wine can be drunk immediately or aged for some years. Best years: 1998, '97, '96, '95, '94, '93, '92, '90, '89, '88, '85, '83, '81, '78, '76. Best producers: J-B Adam, Albrecht, BEYER, BLANCK, Boxler, Burn, Cattin, Dopff & Irion, Frick, Gisselbrecht, HUGEL, Josmeyer, Koehly, KREYDENWEISS, KUENTZ-BAS, Mader, Muré, Ostertag, Rolly Gassmann, Schaller, Schleret, SCHLUMBERGER, Sparr, TRIMBACH, WEINBACH, ZIND-HUMBRECHT; Eguisheim, Gueberschwihr, Pfaffenheim and TURCKHEIM co-operatives.

ALSACE PINOT NOIR

FRANCE, Alsace, Alsace AC
♥♀ *Pinot Noir*

It's bad luck on ALSACE that, although the region boasts one of the greatest cuisines in France, it can't produce the great red wines many of the dishes cry out for. You have to go south to Burgundy or the RHÔNE for that. The only red grape they manage to ripen in Alsace is the Pinot Noir – and then only in the warmer years. Frankly, it hardly ever achieves much colour or much weight, although in years like 1996 and '90 some quite impressive specimens were made.

But, even if it is closer to pink than red, Alsace Pinot Noir often reveals a hauntingly spring-like perfume rare in a red wine, and a gentle soothing strawberry flavour that slips down pretty easily (chilling it for an hour isn't a bad idea). A growing number of producers are now aging the wine in small oak barrels with often a sizeable proportion of new oak, which is stretching things a bit since these wines rarely have the guts to cope with oak-barrel aging. In any case, the wines should be drunk for their bright, cherry-red fruit and that's the first thing to disappear if you leave the wine in an oak barrel for six months or if you leave it in the bottle for too long. Best years: 1997, '96, '95, '93, '92, '90. Best producers: Cattin, DEISS, Hertz, HUGEL, KUENTZ-BAS, Mann, Muré, Rolly Gassmann, Wolfberger; Bennwihr, Éguisheim and TURCKHEIM co-operatives.

ALSACE RIESLING

FRANCE, Alsace, Alsace AC
♀ *Riesling*

Among ALSACE winemakers Riesling is the most revered grape variety. Although it is the great grape of Germany they take positively provocative pleasure in asserting that their totally dry, yet full-bodied style is superior to Germany's lighter, sweeter product. And although Germany is now making dry (*trocken*) styles, few of these wines are a patch on Alsace Rieslings.

About 23 per cent of the region is planted with Riesling and this is increasing. When the wines are young they should have a steely streak of acidity, cold like shining metal splashed with lemon and rubbed with an unripe apple. As they age, sometimes after two years but sometimes not until ten years or more, a pure, strangely unindulgent honey builds up, a nutty weight balancing the acid which itself slowly turns to the zest of limes and the unmistakable wafting pungency of petrol fumes. Alsace Riesling is not as easily liked as Muscat or Gewurztraminer, but it certainly is highly individual. Vendange Tardive and special Sélection de Grains Nobles wines are mostly likely to show this style. There is a growing tendency to leave some residual sugar in the wines, which rounds them out and gives them instant appeal, but also obscures the exciting mineral steeliness of Alsace Riesling at its best. Ordinary blends can be a bit bland, particularly since many Riesling growers over produce. Best years: 1998, '97, '95, '93, '90, '89, '88, '85, '83, '81, '79, '76. Best producers: Adam, Albrecht, Becker, Bennwihr co-operative, BEYER, BLANCK, Boxler, Cattin, DEISS, Dirler, Dopff au Moulin, Ehrhart, Ginglinger, Gisselbrecht, Gressert, Josmeyer, Kientzler, KREYDENWEISS, KUENTZ-BAS, Lorentz, Mader, Mittnacht-Klack, Ostertag, Ribeauvillé co-operative, Rolly Gassmann, Martin Schaetzel, SCHLUMBERGER, Schoffit, Sick-Dreyer, Sparr, TRIMBACH, WEINBACH, ZIND-HUMBRECHT.

ALSACE SYLVANER

FRANCE, Alsace, Alsace AC
♀ *Sylvaner*

Sylvaner used to be the most widely planted of ALSACE's grapes but now accounts for only 17 per cent of the vineyard area. It is gradually being supplanted by Pinot Blanc and Riesling, both superior non-aromatic varieties (Gewurztraminer, Pinot Gris and Muscat are the 'aromatics'). It has quite good

ZIND-HUMBRECHT
The Pinot Gris from the Clos Windsbuhl site in Hunawihr is a fabulously rich and concentrated wine from this top estate.

acidity and ripens well in the vineyards of the northern Alsace *département* of the Bas-Rhin, and down on the plain. From a good producer, young Sylvaner wine can acquire an earth and honey fullness, streaked with green apple acidity, though it often brings along a whiff of tomato too – which is not really what you expect in a white wine. Best years: 1998, '97, '95, '92, '90, '89. Best producers: Boeckel, Dopff au Moulin, Kientzler, Landmann, Ostertag, Pfaffenheim co-operative, Rolly Gassmann, Schoffit, Seltz, TRIMBACH, ZIND-HUMBRECHT.

ALSACE VENDANGE TARDIVE AC
FRANCE, Alsace
♀ Riesling, Muscat, Pinot Gris, Gewurztraminer
Vendange tardive means 'late-harvest'. The grapes are picked almost overripe, giving much higher sugar levels and therefore much more intense, exciting flavours. The wine must be made from one variety, and only from one of Alsace's four noble varieties – Riesling, Muscat, Gewurztraminer or Pinot Gris. The minimum natural alcohol strength is 12.6 degrees for Riesling and Muscat and 14 degrees for Gewurztraminer and Pinot Gris. Fourteen degrees is quite a mouthful, and given the aromatic personality of ALSACE wines, there are some exceptional late-picked wines to be had from warm years such as 1997 and '90.

Most wines are totally dry, but usually rich and mouthfilling, and often need five years or more to show their personality. They can be disappointingly 'shut in' at two to three years old, but then superb five years later. A growing number of Vendange Tardive wines now contain some residual sugar, which is fine if the wine is balanced. Unfortunately there is nothing on the label to indicate the style of the wine.

There is a further subcategory of special Alsace wines. This is the Sélection de Grains Nobles wines, from very late-picked grapes affected by botrytis or noble rot (the same fungus which creates the sweetness in SAUTERNES). The minimum natural alcohol here is 14.6 degrees for Riesling and Muscat and 16 degrees for Gewurztraminer and Pinot Gris. In the years 1994, '90, '83 and '76 the actual sugar levels were often much higher. Since the yeasts cannot ferment the wines much beyond 15 degrees, they are often sweet and incredibly concentrated, able to age for decades. Very little is made, and it is always wildly expensive. Best years: (Vendange Tardive and Sélection de Grains Nobles)

1998, '97, '96, '95, '94, '90, '89, '88, '85, '83, '76. Best producers: BEYER, Boxler, DEISS, Dirler, HUGEL, KREYDENWEISS, KUENTZ-BAS, Mann, Muré, Ostertag, SCHLUMBERGER, TRIMBACH, WEINBACH, ZIND-HUMBRECHT.

ELIO ALTARE
ITALY, Piedmont, Barolo DOCG
♦ Nebbiolo, Barbera, Dolcetto, Cabernet Sauvignon
Scion of a Nebbiolo-producing family of La Morra, Elio, influenced by his trips to Burgundy, began in 1978 the process of bunch-thinning in pursuit of top-quality BAROLO, much to the horror and disbelief of his father. This insanity resulted in his temporary expulsion from the 1948-founded Cascina Nuova family estate. He later returned, introduced French oak barriques (in 1983, one of the first in Barolo) and took to horrifying just about everybody with maceration periods for Nebbiolo so abbreviated that the pulp had scarcely the time to introduce itself to the skins before it was racked away into small barrels to finish the fermentation and do the malolactic. His aim was, and is, to produce Burgundy-like wines, svelte in youth yet capable of aging; wines that can be drunk with pleasure at any time.

His Nebbiolo wines include a Barolo *normale* as well as a much sought-after Barolo Cru, Vigneto Arborina and an even more sought-after Langhe Arborina which is aged exclusively in barrique (his Barolos are allowed a whiff of large old wooden *botte*). His famous barrique-aged Langhe Larigi, from Barbera is a veritable emblem of the revolution that Italian wines in general and Piedmontese wines in particular have undergone in the past 25 years or so.

Altare's is the most cogent and radical voice of the modernist Barolo school, of which he may be considered the grand guru. Others of his ilk – sometimes referred to as the 'Barolo Boys', include Domenico Clerico, Mauro Molino, Luciano SANDRONE, Enrico Scavino. The old guard consider the methods of these young turks insane, but no-one can deny that their

ALTARE
Elio Altare crafts some of the most stunning wines of the Alba region. His Barolo Cru Vigneto Arborina is intense and long-lived.

wines are delicious, even if they are neither traditional nor typical. Best years: 1995, '94, '93, '90, '89, '88, '86, '85.

ALTO ADIGE DOC
ITALY, Alto Adige
♦ Cabernet Franc, Cabernet Sauvignon, Lagrein, Malvasia (Malvasier), Merlot, Pinot Noir (Pinot Nero, Blauburgunder), Schiava (Vernatsch) and others
♦ Lagrein, Moscato Rosa (Rosenmuskateller)
♀ Chardonnay, Moscato Giallo (Goldmuskateller), Müller-Thurgau, Pinot Blanc (Pinot Bianco, Weissburgunder), Pinot Gris (Pinot Grigio, Ruländer), Welschriesling (Riesling Italico), Riesling (Riesling Renano, Rheinriesling), Sauvignon, Sylvaner, Gewürztraminer (Traminer Aromatico) and others
Alto Adige, or Südtirol as it is called by the German-speaking majority, is the part of Italy north of Trentino that is almost in Austria (indeed it was until 1919), and enjoys official Italian/German bilingualism. Vines grow on the steep slopes of the mountains that tumble down to the Adige river (Etsch in German) and its tributary, the Isarco (Eisack), and sometimes on the narrow valley floor too.

The range of altitudes afforded by the mountains gives winemakers an unparalleled opportunity to grow a wide variety of grape types. Of the many grapes used to make varietal wines, some have their origins in Germany, some in France, a few in Italy. Red varieties, such as Lagrein, Schiava and Cabernet, grow lowest down. French whites, such as Chardonnay, Pinot Grigio and Pinot Bianco, are planted a little higher and German ones, such as Riesling, Müller-Thurgau and Sylvaner, are found on the highest slopes. The pergola *trentina* – high trunk with an upward-angled branch – is the classic training method, but is giving way gradually to the lower *spalliera* – guyot or cordon spur – especially for quality red grapes.

Alto Adige is an historic wine region, going back some 3000 years or more. The growing area is centred on the city of Bolzano, which stands at the crux of a Y-shaped system of valleys of which the upper right-hand branch, in the direction of Bressanone (Brixen), is constituted by the Eisack river, while the Adige descends from upper left (direction Merano/Meran) and, meeting the Eisack at Bolzano, continues on down to Salorno (Salurn) below which it enters the province of Trento. A clue to Alto Adige's success as a quality growing area is the fact that Bolzano, Italy's northernmost provincial capital, occasionally in summer records the highest temperatures in the land, beating even Palermo and Cagliari.

Alto Adige's combination of climate, altitude and slope allows in its wines a wonderfully pure expression of varietal character. Although Chardonnay is seen more and more, it is Pinot Bianco (which it much resembles) that makes the French-style white that connoisseurs rate highest, while German grapes, like Riesling, Müller-Thurgau and Sylvaner can be piercingly clean and pure-tasting. All Alto Adige wines are usually drunk young, although from the best producers they will improve for two or three years and sometimes much longer.

Pale Schiava is Alto Adige's predominant red wine, while Lagrein is its best. There is also some very good sparkling wine made from Chardonnay and Pinots Bianco, Grigio and Nero. The best, using the CHAMPAGNE method or *metodo classico*, is Vivaldi. Other leading producers are Giorgio Grai, Franz HAAS, Hofstätter, LAGEDER and TIEFENBRUNNER.

ÁLVAREZ Y DÍEZ

SPAIN, Castilla-León, Rueda DO
♀ *Verdejo, Sauvignon Blanc, Macabeo (Viura)*

Álvarez y Díez, the biggest private wine company in RUEDA, have stainless steel galore for fermentation and more wooden barrels than the rest of the region put together. Besides making flor-affected, sherry-like wines, they still use barrels to age the best of their light wines, too. Álvarez y Díez also pride themselves in being absolutely organic.

Their Mantel Pálido and Mantel Dorado are the best of the region's sherry-style wines, but most interesting are the light, crisp whites for which Rueda is fast making its name. Álvarez y Díez use much more of the high-quality, flavourful Verdejo than most producers in the region, to produce soft, nutty Mantel Blanco Rueda Superior and as a component in the finer, freshly acidic, Mantel Blanco Sauvignon Blanc. Drink the whites within two to three years.

LEO ALZINGER

AUSTRIA, Niederösterreich, Wachau, Loiben
♀ *Riesling, Grüner Veltliner, Chardonnay (Feinburgunder)*

Although he may be a man of few words, the tall, silver-haired Leo Alzinger makes some of the sleekest and most pristine dry Rieslings and Grüner Veltliners in Austria. His best wines are the Rieslings from the Loibenberg and Steinertal sites in the village of Loiben,

which are extremely elegant considering they have 13 degrees or more of natural alcohol. For some reason Austrian wine drinkers have never got quite as excited about these wines as those from some other top WACHAU growers, so these wines are easier to get hold of. Best years: 1998, '97, '95, '94, '93, '90.

CASTELLO DI AMA

ITALY, Tuscany, Chianti Classico DOCG
♀ *Sangiovese, Merlot, Pinot Noir (Pinot Nero)*
♀ *Chardonnay*

This sizeable estate, purchased in 1977 by a group of Romans, is managed today by the daughter of one of them, Laura Sebasti, and her viticulturist/winemaker husband Marco Pallanti. Since the mid-1980s Castello di Ama has produced some of Tuscany's best CHIANTI CLASSICO and SUPER-TUSCAN wines. Pallanti has been responsible for identifying the merits of particular sections, or *vigneti,* of the estate (81ha/200 acres under vine with a further 10ha/25 acres to come) and for re-grafting or re-planting them according to their optimum potential.

Today the estate is best known for its Chianti Classico crus, Bellavista (with a small percentage of Malvasia Nera) and Casuccia (with Merlot), and especially for the super-Tuscan Vigna l'Apparita, from Merlot vines grafted in the early 1980s on to Canaiolo and Malvasia Bianca in a clay-rich 4-ha (10-acre) section of the Bellavista vineyard and trained, unusually, on the open lyre formation. L'Apparita, indeed, has become almost as famous in its genre as SASSICAIA became among Cabernet Sauvignons of the world in the 1970s, and its tremendous fruit, its power combined with elegance, has brought it glory in numerous tastings and competitions. Other super-Tuscans include a Pinot Nero (Il Chiuso) and a Chardonnay (Al Poggio).

In future, however, now that the vineyards are mature and things are running smoothly, the plan is to pour maximum resources and effort into making outstanding Chianti Classico which can be produced in a far larger quantity. Certainly, the Chianti Classico, 100 per cent barrique-aged (25 per cent new) is many cuts above your run-of-the mill stuff, having very sleek tannins, subtle fruit and a finely balanced elegance that few others can rival. Whether any of the wines can justify what are becoming extraordinarily elevated prices is, however, a question that will only be answered by the market over the coming years. Best years: 1995, '94, '93, '91, '90, '88, '86, '85.

AMARONE DELLA VALPOLICELLA DOC

ITALY, Veneto, Valpolicella DOC
♀ *Corvina, Corvinone, Rondinella, Molinara and others*

Amarone is the dry version of ancient Recioto (*Acinaticum*, as it was called in the early 'Dark Ages' by Cassiodorus of the Longobards). It is not, as some would have it, that Amarone is a recent development, nor that it was an aberration from the classic sweet wine; rather it is that this dry style has only recently come into fashion.

Amarone is made from early-picked, high-quality VALPOLICELLA grapes that are left on shallow racks in a cool, airy place after the harvest to dry for up to four months. The resulting shrivelled, concentrated *passito* bunches are then fermented to dryness – except that the wine never seems absolutely dry, and often exceeds its supposed maximum of eight grams per litre of residual sugar. Even the aromas seem to promise a wine of power and richness, while on the palate there is the sweetness of fruit and alcohol, with the promised bitterness cutting in at the end to provide a dry finish. Indeed, even the bitterness is chocolaty, with, in the best examples, a wealth of the cherry-fruit aromas that is so characteristic of the wines of Valpolicella.

At its best Amarone is not just one of the great wines of Italy but a world classic. The quality is improving every year as more and more producers join the quality-first bandwagon and the prices rise inexorably, making the whole labour-intensive exercise increasingly worthwhile. The recent construction of a huge purpose-built centre in the Valpolicella commune of Fumane, complete with automatically triggered wind-producing machines to prevent any botrytis during the drying period, is a testament to the success of Amarone. Best years: 1997, '95, '93, '90, '88, '86, '85, '83. Best producers: Accordini, ALLEGRINI, Bertani, Brigaldara, Brunelli, Bussola, Corte Sant'Alda, DAL FORNO, MASI, Mazzi, QUINTARELLI, Le Ragose, Serègo Alighieri, Speri, Tedeschi, Zenato.

ANDALUCÍA Spain

ANDALUCÍA, A VAST SPREAD of eight provinces stretching right across the sunbaked south of Spain, welcomes millions of tourists each year. But relatively few of them ever stray far from the Costa del Sol. Those who do discover a land quite different from the rest of the Iberian peninsula as this was the part of Spain longest occupied by the Moors – the words 'la Frontera' tacked onto many local place names, including that of Jerez, reflects how for a full hundred years these towns were on the frontier between Christian and Moorish Spain. Whitewashed walls, cool courtyards and roof terraces on the oldest houses testify to eight centuries of Arab dominion, as do the place names, local crafts and even the inevitable flamenco dancing. Solitary farmhouses are a feature of the countryside, set in the eastern provinces among landscapes of olive trees or cereals, irrigated fruit trees or early vegetables, and in the west among fields of sunflowers, cereals and vines.

Andalucía overflows with vines, but there are far more in the west than the east. All four of Andalucía's DOs (Jerez y Manzanilla, Montilla-Moriles, Málaga and Condado de Huelva) lie to the west of Granada, and the DOs themselves account for over half Andalucía's vineyards. But it seems strange that the famous wines made in such a hot

climate should all be fortified – until you taste the unfortified wines. It is hard to get excited by any of the bland, flavourless whites, and those are the good ones. The bad are horrific. Thank goodness the Andalucíans evolved a way to turn their basic table wines into nectar to accompany the incessant socializing and lengthy meals. For this is a part of Spain where lunch never starts before three in the afternoon, and you consider yourself lucky if you sit down to dinner by midnight, after delicious hours of tapas – copious nibbles of olives, anchovies, fried peppers, salted almonds, squid – and glass after glass of chilled fino.

In Jerez the tulip-shaped *copita* glass would contain fino sherry, in Sanlúcar de Barrameda, manzanilla, in inland Córdoba it might be Montilla, and in Málaga, down by the coast, a stiff tot of the 'mountain' wine so loved by the Victorians.

Despite the relentless, glaring heat, the sherry region, in particular, is well suited to vines. The best soil – finely grained, dazzlingly white *albariza* which sweeps right across the central growing area – contains between 60 and

The magnificent La Concha or 'Seashell' bodega in Jerez belongs to González Byass. Its revolutionary circular design was the work of the French engineer, Alexandre Gustave Eiffel who later went on to design the Eiffel Tower in Paris.

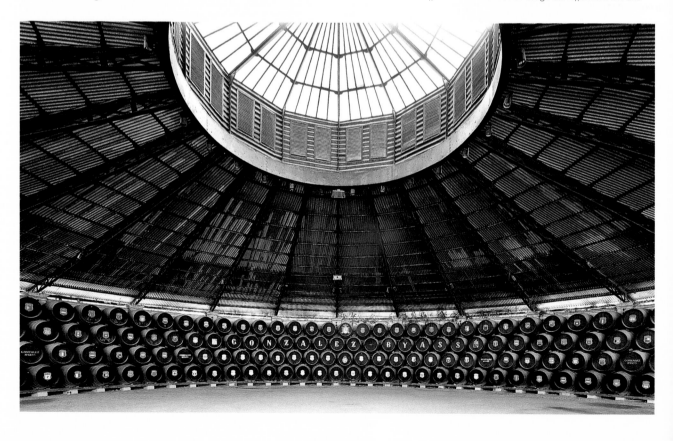

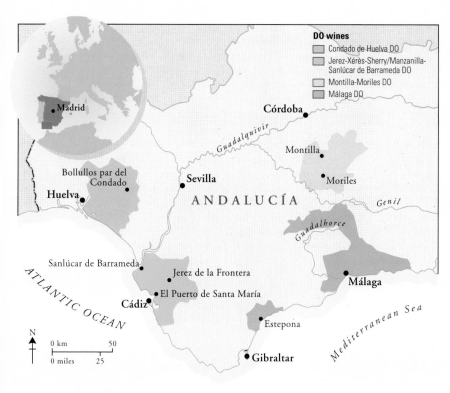

DO wines
- Condado de Huelva DO
- Jerez-Xérès-Sherry/Manzanilla-Sanlúcar de Barrameda DO
- Montilla-Moriles DO
- Málaga DO

EMILIO LUSTAU
Based in Jerez, Lustau is renowned for its Almacenista range of very individual, dry, single-batch sherries from small private producers.

BARBADILLO
From the coastal town of Sanlúcar de Barrameda, this crisp, fresh salty young manzanilla is a perfect accompaniment to food.

HIDALGO
With its intense salty aroma, Hidalgo's Manzanilla La Gitana is deservedly the bestselling manzanilla in Spain.

GONZÁLEZ BYASS
Superb old sherries are the speciality of the González Byass firm – Amontillado del Duque is dry and powerful with magnificent flavour and length.

80 per cent chalk and acts as a sponge, soaking up and storing the ample winter rainfall until the vines crave it in the height of midsummer. Accordingly, yields are high, for the vineyards of Jerez, all trained on wires, are among the most modern in Spain, and the Palomino Fino – the main grape for sherry – is always a generous bearer.

But the wine not turned into sherry often finds a buyer who will distil and age it to make the rich, dark brandies for which Andalucía is also famous.

REGIONAL ENTRIES
Jerez y Manzanilla, Málaga, Montilla-Moriles.

PRODUCER ENTRIES
Barbadillo, Caballero, Díez-Mérito, Domecq, Garvey, González Byass, Harveys, Hidalgo, Lustau, Osborne, Toro Albalá, Valdespino.

VALDESPINO
This very old-fashioned, very high-quality family business makes a range of top-class, dry sherries including the stylish, elegant Inocente Fino with its pungent, flor-influenced aromas.

ALVEAR
The Pedro Ximénez grape, which can stand up to the withering heat of the Montilla-Moriles area, is used to make this powerful, dense, sweet fortified wine.

PEDRO DOMECQ
Palo Cortado is a rare, dry style of sherry and this example from Domecq, a leading sherry house, has a superb, refined, complex aroma of nuts and ripe fruits with good richness.

OSBORNE
From the sherry arm of Osborne, Spain's biggest drinks company, at Puerto de Santa María, comes Bailén Oloroso, a dry, rich and powerful fortified wine with a fine, nutty character.

ANDERSON VALLEY AVA

USA, California, Mendocino County

Almost overnight this small valley has acquired cachet as a source of CHAMPAGNE-method sparklers. In the late 1960s these hills, a few miles inland from the Pacific Ocean, had been earmarked for Gewurztraminer, Chardonnay and Pinot Noir. Then, in 1985, the famous Champagne house ROEDERER elected to locate its US operation in the valley because the weather is almost as foul as Champagne's own, or so said one of the decision-makers in the deal. The indications are that it was an excellent decision. NAPA's DUCKHORN VINEYARDS have established Golden Eye, a winery focusing on Pinot Noir. Other producers include Edmeades, Greenwood Ridge, Handley Cellars, Husch, Lazy Creek, Navarro Vineyards and Pacific Echo (formerly Scharffenberger). Best years: (reds) 1997, '96, '95, '94; (whites) 1998, '97, '96.

HANDLEY CELLARS
Handley is one of the rising stars of California and in the cool Anderson Valley region makes a range of excellent sparkling wines.

ANDREW WILL WINERY

USA, Washington State

Merlot, Cabernet Sauvignon, Sangiovese

Chardonnay, Chenin Blanc

Andrew Will Winery is owned and operated by Chris Camarda who makes complex and textured reds that rank with the USA's finest. The BORDEAUX-style blend 'Sorella' reveals the deftness of his winemaking, balancing ripe berry fruit, oak and glycerin in perfect proportions. Andrew Will specializes in single-vineyard bottlings of Merlot that express the regional differences of four of the state's best vineyards – Klipsin, Pepper Bridge, Ciel du Cheval and Seven Hills. Small amounts of dry Chenin Blanc and OREGON Chardonnay are sold under the Cuvée LuLu label. Best years: (reds) 1998, '97, '95, '94; (whites) 1998, '97, '96.

CH. ANGÉLUS

FRANCE, Bordeaux, St-Émilion Grand Cru AC, Premier Grand Cru Classé

Merlot, Cabernet Franc, Cabernet Sauvignon

Judging by the price of the wine, you would expect Ch. Angélus to be a leading Premier Grand Cru Classé – and the rich, warm, mouthfilling flavour would confirm this. Yet it was only classified as Premier Grand Cru Classé in the 1996 revision of the ST-ÉMILION classification. This shows how the influence of an energetic owner, a talented winemaker, or investment in the winery can upgrade the quality of a vineyard's wine – just as laziness, incompetence and penny-pinching can dilute it. Angélus is well placed on the lower part of the *côtes* (slopes) to the west of the town of St-Émilion, and the soil is rather heavy. Until 1979 this resulted in fruity, though slightly bland wine. But in the 1980s lower yields, severe selection and new oak-barrel aging were introduced, adding a sturdy backbone and a richer concentration of fruit. The wines of 1997, '96, '95, '94, '93, '92, '90, '89 and '88 showed glorious fruit and richness but also a gratifying firmness that will allow them to age beautifully.

MARQUIS D'ANGERVILLE

FRANCE, Burgundy, Côte de Beaune, Volnay AC

Pinot Noir

In the 1930s the d'Angervilles were among the first owners to bottle wines under their own name, and today, the Marquis d'Angerville remains in the top tier of VOLNAY's first-rate producers. The present Marquis is elderly, so there have been a few inconsistencies in some recent vintages, but overall these wines are fully representative of the elegance and persistence of Volnay at its best. The Premiers Crus from d'Angerville include Taillepieds and Champans, and the exclusively owned Clos des Ducs, which is often the estate's top wine. There is also some POMMARD and the BOURGOGNE Rouge can be good value. Best years: 1997, '96, '95, '93, '91, '90, '89, '88, '85.

CH. D'ANGLUDET

FRANCE, Bordeaux, Haut-Médoc, Margaux AC, Cru Bourgeois

Cabernet Sauvignon, Merlot, Cabernet Franc, Petit Verdot

The wine from this English-owned property has a delicious, approachable burst of blackcurrant-and-blackberry fruit that makes you want to drink it immediately – yet it ages superbly for up to a decade or more. Its price-quality ratio is one of the best in BORDEAUX since the wine is always of Classed Growth standard but the price is well below it – if you want to buy to lay down start with Angludet. Best years: 1997, '96, '95, '94, '93, '90, '89, '88, '86, '85, '83, '82.

ANJOU AC

FRANCE, Loire, Anjou-Saumur

Cabernet Franc, Cabernet Sauvignon, Pineau d'Aunis or Gamay

Chenin Blanc, Chardonnay, Sauvignon Blanc

This catch-all AC covers the whole Maine-et-Loire *département*, as well as bits of Deux-Sèvres and Vienne. The Anjou region is best known for its rosé wine (ROSÉ D'ANJOU), but increasingly the leading winemakers are turning their hand to reds with considerable success, particularly with Gamay or Cabernet Franc grapes. Gamay is the BEAUJOLAIS grape and using the Beaujolais method of vinification – carbonic maceration – the results for Anjou Rouge can be similar, if a bit rougher. Best years: 1998, '97, '96, '95. Best producers: (reds and rosés) Angeli, Cailleau, Cochard, Daviau, Richou, Touche Noire.

During the 1990s Chenin's potential as the Loire's greatest white grape has been increasingly recognized. Up to 20 per cent Chardonnay or Sauvignon can be added to Anjou Blanc but increasingly producers prefer to use only Chenin. Using modern cool-fermentation methods and in the hands of the best producers, Anjou Blanc is being transformed from its mediocre former self. There are some medium-dry wines too and these are increasingly attractive – fresh, slightly honeyed and good value. Unfortunately Anjou Blanc still has an identity crisis: it is not one style but several, and still too much is poorly made and sold very cheaply. This poses problems for producers intent on making more concentrated, 'serious' versions, some of which may have been fermented and aged in oak. Anjou Blanc is now increasingly a source of good straight French whites, dry or semisweet; some of the better ones come from the Anjou Coteaux de la Loire sub-region. The production of sparkling dry or off-dry Anjou Mousseux remains limited, with just over 250,000 bottles a year being made. Best years: 1998, '97, '96, '95, '94. Best producers: (whites) Angeli, Dom. de la Bergerie, Bidet, Cady, Cailleau, J-Y Lebreton, Musset-Rouiller, Ogereau, Ch. Pierre-Bise, Renou, Richou.

ANJOU-VILLAGES AC

FRANCE, Loire, Anjou-Saumur

Cabernet Franc, Cabernet Sauvignon

Since the ANJOU AC is such a blanket term – and one with a fairly poor reputation and price tag to boot – the better producers of red wines have lobbied for years to get their wines upgraded. From the 1985 vintage they managed it and 46 villages in Anjou can now use the Anjou-Villages AC for red wine from Cabernet Franc and Cabernet Sauvignon grapes. Some extremely attractive, dry but fruity reds are beginning to surface, with better aging potential than straight Anjou Rouge.

Although some producers still make a very light Anjou-Villages which makes it difficult to distinguish it from their plain Anjou, serious ones ensure that their Villages wine has more concentration and structure. Producers are also paying attention to ripeness and being careful not to extract too much tannin, so that their wines are more approachable and not overlaid with a lot of harsh tannins. There is a sub-appellation, Anjou-Villages Brissac, for the area around the town of Brissac-Quincé, which has a reputation for producing the best reds. Best years: 1998, '97, '96, '95, '93, 90, '89. Best producers: Bidet, Closel, Daviau, Pascal Delaunay, J-Y Lebreton, Ogereau, Ch. Pierre-Bise, Richou, Touche Noire.

ROBERTO ANSELMI

ITALY, Veneto, Soave DOC
♥ *Cabernet Sauvignon*
♀ *Garganega, Trebbiano di Soave*

The man behind the world-famous name of Anselmi is the cigar-smoking, fast-driving, expansive Roberto Anselmi who is rightly credited with being one of the two major forces behind the revival of SOAVE, an ancient but industrially degraded wine. From the moment he entered the business in 1974, he began making improvements. In the vineyard, he was the first to introduce French-style viticulture and to plant a French grape, Chardonnay. He also brought in staggered picking (ensuring ripe, healthy fruit) and bunch-thinning. For the winery he purchased the newest technology and, most significantly, introduced barriques (probably the first in Italy for whites) in which to ferment and mature certain of his wines.

These policies began paying off and Anselmi became known worldwide for the quality of their wines, sold at significantly higher (though still reasonable) prices than they ever had before. Today, Anselmi the pioneer is almost establishment, but the dynamism continues and the enthusiasm lives. Perhaps his most renowned wine is the barrique-aged Recioto I Capitelli; other successes include the Soave Classico Capitel Foscarino and the revolutionary barrique-fermented Soave Classico Capitel Croce. Almost as revolutionary was his introduction – to this white wine region – of Cabernet Sauvignon, from which he makes a sleek Bordeaux-style wine called Realdà. Best years: (Soave Classico) 1997, '96, '95, '94, '93.

ANTINORI

ITALY, Tuscany, Florence; Umbria, Orvieto DOC
♥ *Sangiovese, Cabernet Sauvignon, Merlot, Canaiolo*
♀ *Chardonnay, Grechetto, Trebbiano*

The Antinori family are proud of the fact that they have been in the wine business for over 600 years, covering 26 generations. Arguably, however, it is during the present generation, under Marchese Piero Antinori's leadership, that the company has had the greatest influence – on the wines of Tuscany first and foremost, on those of middle Italy (they have a major estate near Orvieto in UMBRIA called Castello della Sala, where they make one of Italy's finest white wines, Cervaro della Sala), on those of Italy generally (they have owned the important Piedmontese firm of PRUNOTTO for several years), and indeed on those of the world (they were pioneers with Sangiovese at ATLAS PEAK VINEYARDS in the NAPA VALLEY, and have also invested in a Hungarian estate called Bataapati).

Their principal stronghold, however, is Tuscany. Antinori were among the first to refuse to accept the now outmoded DOC system for CHIANTI and to experiment with Sangiovese-Cabernet blends, their two flagship SUPER-TUSCAN wines, Tignanello and its mirror-image Solaia, being the two prototypes of this increasingly important genre. In so far as they have kept faith with CHIANTI CLASSICO they have done it outside the Consorzio Gallo Nero and in their own way with single-estate wines like Peppoli and Badia a Passignano (both 90 per cent Sangiovese/10 per cent Merlot), the blend-of-estates Riserva called Tenute Marchese Antinori (10 per cent Cabernet Sauvignon) and the traditional blended Villa Antinori (10 per cent Canaiolo).

Antinori have also invested in estates in three of the most important Tuscan quality zones outside Chianti Classico: VINO NOBILE

ANTINORI
The success of Tignanello (80 per cent Sangiovese, 20 per cent Cabernet Sauvignon) in the 1970s sparked off the super-Tuscan movement outside DOC regulations that has produced many of Italy's most exciting wines.

DI MONTEPULCIANO (La Braccesca – Vino Nobile and Merlot IGT); BOLGHERI (Tenuta Belvedere – Guado al Tasso, a 60-40 Cabernet Sauvignon-Merlot blend); and BRUNELLO DI MONTALCINO (Pian delle Vigne). As he approaches retirement age Piero Antinori has handed over power increasingly to his three daughters, Albiera, currently managing director of Prunotto, Allegra who handles international public relations and Alessia, a qualified enologist who helps on the technical side which is under the overall control of Renzo Cotarella. Best years: (Solaia) 1995, '94, '93, '91, '90, '88, '86, '85; (Cervaro della Sala) 1996, '95, '94, '93, '92, '91, '90.

ANTONOPULOUS

GREECE, Peloponnese, Patras AO
♥ *Aghiorghitiko, Cabernet Sauvignon, Cabernet Franc and others*
♀ *Lagorthi, Moscophilero, Chardonnay and others*

This very high-quality 5-ha (11-acre) estate was founded by Constantine Antonopulous, who was sadly killed in a road accident in 1994. Both Greek and international grape varieties are planted on the estate. The fine wines include a white Mantinia from the aromatic Moscophilero grape, excellent oaky Chardonnay, and some stunning reds such as Nea Dris from Cabernets Sauvignon and Franc. Best years: (reds) 1996; (whites) 1997.

ARAGÓN

SPAIN

Isolated from maritime influences by mountain ranges on three sides, Aragón's high plateaux are the epitome of the harsh and dry continental climate of most of inland Spain. Its wines have also been typical: heavy, alcoholic, often oxidized and, as a result, the ancient reputation of its wines plummeted and bulk production became the norm. Progressively, the implantation of DO regions and the installation of better equipment has begun turning the tide.

Improvement came first to the northern SOMONTANO DO, in the foothills of the Pyrenees, with massive new investment including the planting of international grape varieties. Then, more slowly, in the other DOs: CAMPO DE BORJA (which actually adjoins the RIOJA Baja and NAVARRA vineyards), CALATAYUD and CARIÑENA. This is overwhelmingly red wine country from the Garnacha grape, with the white Macabeo grape a distant second. Tempranillo, Cabernet Sauvignon and Merlot, however, are being planted at a brisk pace.

ARBOIS AC

FRANCE, Jura

Trousseau, Pinot Noir, Poulsard

Chardonnay, Savagnin

This is the largest of the specific ACs in the JURA region of eastern France, centred on the busy town of Arbois. There are now 937ha (2315 acres) of vines with an annual production of just over 4 million bottles, all unified by the death-defying Savagnin grape. This is the local white grape, though there is an increasing amount of very good light Chardonnay. The Savagnin manages, uniquely and disconcertingly, to infect the amiable qualities of mountain vineyard dry white wine with the palate-numbing, sweet-sour properties of a really dry fino sherry. In an ordinary Arbois white wine this effect is to make you question whether the wine is 'off'.

However, there is a type of white Arbois called *vin jaune* (yellow wine), made from Savagnin, which actually develops a flor yeast growth on its surface similar to that of fino sherry. *Vin jaune* is also made in other Jura ACs, at its best in CHÂTEAU-CHALON. The wine is left in barrel with the flor for six years, during which time it oxidizes, develops an arresting damp sourness like the dark reek of old floorboards, and yet also keeps a full fruit, albeit somewhat decayed. There is also a rare and expensive sweet *vin de paille* (straw wine) – from grapes supposedly dried on straw mats. Best producers: (whites) Arlay, Bourdy, Henri Maire, Domaine de la Pinte, Rolet; Arbois, Pupillin and Tissot co-operatives.

You don't see much red Arbois outside France: the chief red grape, Trousseau, usually gives hefty, thick-edged wines, though modern winemaking is toning things down a bit. The Poulsard grape can produce quite pleasant light reds and good, smoky rosés. Pinot Noir gives pale but tasty, perfumed reds. Some of the best wines come from Pupillin. Best producers: (reds) Bourdy, Désiré, Henri Maire, Rolet; Aubin, Pupillin and Tissot co-operatives.

ARCHERY SUMMIT WINERY

USA, Oregon, Yamhill County, Willamette Valley AVA

Pinot Noir

Pinot Gris, Pinot Blanc, Chardonnay

Production at this relatively new winery in the Dundee Hills region of WILLAMETTE VALLEY is mainly focused on Pinot Noir. The Andrus family of NAPA VALLEY's PINE RIDGE WINERY owns the modern facility and four vineyards totalling 28ha (70 acres). Very dark, very intense Pinot Noir is made using lots of new oak. Two estate Pinot Noirs, Arcus Estate and Red Hills Estate, lead the range. A small amount of white wine, a blend of Pinot Gris, Pinot Blanc and Chardonnay called Vireton, is also produced. Best years: (Red Hills Estate) 1998, '96, '95, '94; (Vireton) 1998.

ARGIOLAS

ITALY, Sardinia

Grenache (Cannonau), Monica, Carignano, Bovale Sardo, Malvasia Nera and others

Cannonau, Monica, Carignano and others

Vermentino, Nuragus, Nasco, Malvasia and others

Sardinia may be conceived by some as being stuck somewhere in the past, but there is nothing archaic about this fully modernized company making top-quality wine from 200ha (494 acres) of vineyards. Brothers Franco and Guiseppe Argiolas are third-generation growers who had the sagacity years ago to call in the services of Italy's greatest winemaker, Giacomo Tachis.

They have been rewarded with a series of wines which regularly figure not only among the best of the island, but among the best of Italy. Top billing goes to Turriga, a grandiose, multi-prize-winner of a red wine mainly from Cannonau (the Sardinian name for Grenache) which requires at least five years' aging. The dessert wine Angialis, from the Nasco and Malvasia varieties, is also outstanding, while white table wines Costamolino (Vermentino) and Argiolas (a blend of grapes) and reds Costera (Cannonau) and Perdera (Monica) are always well made and excellent value. Best years: 1997, '95, '93, '92, '91, '90.

ARGIOLAS
Angialis is a sweet wine with a light golden colour, elegant bouquet and rich, smooth flavours with a hint of oak. An after-dinner wine, it is also perfect with biscuits.

ARGYLE (DUNDEE WINE CO.)

USA, Oregon, Yamhill County, Willamette Valley AVA

Pinot Noir

Chardonnay, Pinot Gris, Riesling

Argyle makes a relatively large quantity of excellent CHAMPAGNE-method sparkling wine – nearly 192,000 bottles a year. OREGON's cool climate is perfect for harvesting the high-acid Pinot Noir and Chardonnay needed for quality sparklers. Working with yeast strains from the Champagne firm of BOLLINGER, winemaker Rollin Soles crafts crisp, yeasty vintage Brut that is arguably one of America's best. Rich Chardonnay from new Dijon clones, a dry Riesling style and a spicy Pinot Gris are the still whites produced. Regular and Reserve Pinot Noirs are consistently good. Best years: (Pinot Noir) 1998, '96, '94; (Pinot Gris, Riesling) 1998, '96.

ARINTO

This is one of Portugal's most promising white grapes, which succeeds in hanging on to its natural acidity whatever the weather, even in the scorching heat of the ALENTEJO. It is most at home in the tiny DOC region of BUCELAS (and in neighbouring ALENQUER) where it is sometimes blended with the even more fiercely acidic Esgana Cão (Dog Strangler). Allowed to blossom on its own, Arinto makes fresh, fragrant grassy dry white wines which last quite well in bottle. It is also planted extensively in the much cooler VINHO VERDE region, where it goes under the name of Pedernã, but due to its overbearing acidity it is rarely used to make varietal wine.

DOMAINE DE L'ARLOT

FRANCE, Burgundy, Côte de Nuits, Nuits-St-Georges AC

Pinot Noir

Chardonnay, Pinot Gris

Jean-Pierre de Smet is that rarity in Burgundy, a newcomer to the region. Supported by the French insurance company AXA, he based himself at an estate in the southern part of NUITS-ST-GEORGES, a property that included the large monopole vineyard Clos de l'Arlot. Assisted by Jacques Seysses of Domaine DUJAC, another newcomer, de Smet made his first vintage here in 1987. Like Jacques Seysses, de Smet seeks elegance rather than maximum extraction. The wines are often light in colour, but rarely lack flavour, and often age surprisingly well. Although aged in 50 per cent new oak, they are rarely dominated by oak and tannin. The domaine also produces a small quantity of Romanée-St-Vivant and BEAUNE Grèves.

One curiosity here is a white made from old vines in the Clos de l'Arlot, which include Pinot Gris as well as Chardonnay. It is aged in 20 per cent new oak. However, the vines are now being replanted and it will be some years before this wine is back on the market. Best years: 1997, '96, '95, '93, '90, '89.

DOMAINE COMTE ARMAND

FRANCE, Burgundy, Côte de Beaune, Pommard AC
🍷 *Pinot Noir*

Tasting at this leading POMMARD domaine does not take very long, since the principal wine comes from a single monopole vineyard, the 4.6ha (11½ acres) Clos des Epeneaux, an enclave within the Premier Cru Epenots. In 1995 some new wines were introduced: a VOLNAY Fremiets and white wines from MEURSAULT and AUXEY-DURESSES. Except when adverse weather conditions make it near-impossible, the vineyards are organically cultivated. This is quintessential Pommard: rich, dark, brooding, complex, and requiring quite a few years in bottle to show at its sumptuous best. The wines have been made since 1985 by a Canadian, Pascal Marchand, who neither fines nor filters them. Best years: 1997, '96, '95, '93, '92, '90, '89, '88.

ARNEIS

Arneis can be one of Italy's best white grape varieties, subtly intricate, releasing a fascinating array of perfumes – peaches and pears, nuts and licorice, and revealing hidden depths of complexity of flavour. Though known for hundreds of years under various names, by the early 1970s it was almost extinct. Now it is making a strong comeback in Piedmont's ROERO zone, where it makes Roero Arneis; and to a lesser extent on the opposite – right – bank of the Tanaro river, around Alba. Styles vary from light and delicate and ephemeral to (occasionally) rich and powerful, sometimes oaked (usually to excess), sometimes *passito*. The potential of Arneis remains exciting, especially in a region like Piedmont where red wines dominate.

CH. L'ARROSÉE

FRANCE, Bordeaux, St-Émilion Grand Cru AC, Grand Cru Classé
🍷 *Merlot, Cabernet Sauvignon, Cabernet Franc*

This is one of those unknown properties that swept to international prominence so quickly you had to keep checking your tasting notes to see you hadn't got the name wrong. But this small estate, situated on a good slope just south-west of the town of ST-ÉMILION, really is exciting: it makes a rich, chewy and wonderfully luscious wine, with a comparatively high proportion (35 per cent) of Cabernet Sauvignon in the blend. This is a real hedonist's wine, especially in the big, broad years of 1995, '90, and '85. Best years: 1997, '96, '95, '94, '93, '90, '89, '88, '86, '85, '83, '82.

The Arruda dos Vinhos co-operative is one of many rural co-operatives in Portugal to have improved in enormous strides in recent years.

ARROWOOD VINEYARDS & WINERY

USA, California, Sonoma County, Sonoma Valley AVA
🍷 *Cabernet Sauvignon, Merlot*
♀ *Chardonnay, Viognier, Riesling*

CHATEAU ST JEAN's chief winemaker for 13 years until 1985, Dick Arrowood became well known for Chardonnays and a series of late-harvest white wines, as well as familiar with a host of vineyards scattered throughout SONOMA. At Chateau St Jean he made a habit of bottling wines from single-vineyard sites. But for his own wines, Arrowood prefers to use grapes selected from several sources to obtain balance and complexity. The Chardonnay is an appealing balancing act, a little less succulent than its brilliant Reserve. Recent Cabernets and Merlots have much impressed with their richness and polish. Best years: 1998, '97, '95, '94, '92, '91, '90.

ISMAEL ARROYO

SPAIN, Castilla-León, Ribera del Duero DO
🍷♀ *Tempranillo (Tinto del País), Albillo*

This is exactly the kind of bodega that shows why the reds from RIBERA DEL DUERO are so fashionable and, unfortunately, shooting up in price. Rich reds and good fresh rosés are made by Ismael Arroyo, a medium-sized family business in Sotillo de la Ribera. There are 6ha (15 acres) of vineyards planted almost exclusively with Tinto del País, and they also buy in some grapes from neighbours. The aged reds are impressive wines – Val Sotillo Reserva is fat and super-ripe, Val Sotillo Crianza more ele-

gant and balanced, but all the wines show the virtues of modern fermentation and careful (not overdone) oak maturation. Best years: 1996, '95, '94, '91, '90, '89.

ARRUDA DOC

PORTUGAL, Estremadura
🍷 *Camarate, Periquita, Tinta Miuda*
♀ *Fernão Pires, Jampal, Vital*

Crowned by abandoned windmills, the hills that surround the town of Arruda dos Vinhos, 40km (25 miles) north of Lisbon, are some of the most intensively cultivated in the whole of Portugal, with high-yielding vines producing copious quantities of wine. The reds are simple, fruity and destined for early drinking but, despite improvements in vinification, the whites are usually rather bland and uninspiring. Production is mainly in the hands of the local co-operative, which is one of the more competent ones. Peter BRIGHT frequently sources wine in the area.

ARTADI

SPAIN, País Vasco, Rioja DOC
🍷 *Tempranillo, Graciano, Mazuelo, Grenache Noir (Garnacha Tinta), Viura*
♀ *Viura, Malvasía Riojana*

In just 15 years, this erstwhile co-operative in Laguardia (whose official name, Cosecheros Alaveses, has been totally obscured by its brand name) has moved from making fresh, fruity, clean *cosechero* (unoaked) wines to producing some of the most ambitious, striking and acclaimed wines in the fast-changing RIOJA scene.

The founding partners brought with them about 70ha (173 acres) with a large proportion of old vines. Winery manager Juan Carlos López de la Calle and enologist Benjamín Romeo mapped out a shrewd course, building on the young wines' success to introduce ever more ambitious oak-aged cuvées. Long macerations producing intense, fruit-dominated wines are characteristic of Artadi. The Viñas de Gain, a Tempranillo varietal from younger hillside vineyards that's aged for 18 months in barrel, is the bodega's impressive war horse. Pagos Viejos, Viña El Pisón and Grandes Añadas are its stars. Best years: 1996, '95, '94, '92, '91.

ASTI DOCG

ITALY, Piedmont
♀ *Muscat (Moscato Bianco)*

Asti, for long an 'industrial' wine subject to multiple ingenious frauds lowering both its price and its prestige, has recently had its socks pulled up by the Asti Consortium, which has taken over the work of policing production and commercial practices. At its best it is delicious stuff, light, effervescent, delicate, grapy and refreshingly sweet but not cloyingly so, with good balancing acidity to give it a clean finish. It is pretty low in alcohol too (between 7 and 9 degrees).

It is also worth remembering that traditional Asti (which, until its promotion to DOCG, was called Asti Spumante) is produced by the most natural way ever of making sparkling wine. Part way through its transformation, in large pressurized tanks called *autoclavi*, the fermentation is stopped by lowering the temperature to around 0°C (32°F), so that there is plenty of natural grape sweetness left. The bubbles are natural too, being trapped in the pressurized tanks, and since it's bottled under pressure, following very tight filtration to ensure stability, they stay in the wine until it is poured.

Many of Turin's big sparkling wine and vermouth houses (such as Cinzano, Gancia, Martini & Rossi and Riccadonna) make reliable Asti. Better still are the wines from Araldica Vini Piemontesi, Arione, Bera, Caudrina, Duca d'Asti, Fontanafredda, Vallebelbo and Vignaioli di Santo Stefano. Asti is not a wine for keeping – the fresher it is, the better.

ATLAS PEAK AVA

USA, California, Napa County

Tucked away in the south-east corner of NAPA VALLEY, this hillside appellation is named after the tallest point in the nearby mountains. Approved as an AVA in 1992, it includes 243ha (600 acres) of vineyards. The leading varieties are Cabernet Sauvignon, Chardonnay and Sangiovese. William Hill revived the area in the 1970s and developed its reputation for Cabernet Sauvignon. International attention came in the 1980s when ATLAS PEAK VINEYARDS, BOLLINGER and others selected it as an ideal spot for Sangiovese. Best years: 1997, '96, '95, '94.

ATLAS PEAK VINEYARDS

USA, California, Napa County, Atlas Peak AVA

❦ Cabernet Sauvignon, Merlot, Sangiovese

❦ Chardonnay

Once Piero Antinori of ANTINORI moved from minority partner to sole vineyard owner, Atlas Peak steadied itself and began to live up to its early expectations as a Sangiovese leader. With 162ha (400 acres) of vineyards, including one of the largest plantings of Sangiovese

ATLAS PEAK VINEYARDS
California producers like Atlas Peak are now working some of their magic on the Sangiovese grape, making both easy-drinking and sturdier ageworthy versions.

in California, Atlas Peak focuses on Sangiovese in several guises – a straight version, a Reserve and a Cabernet Sauvignon-Sangiovese blend named Consenso. After a few uneven vintages, the winery has concentrated more on Sangiovese's bright fruit and less on oak character to improve all three versions. However, it has also been offering impressive Cabernet Sauvignon and promising Chardonnay from its now fully mature mountainside vineyards in the ATLAS PEAK AVA. Best years: (reds) 1997, '96, '95, '94.

AU BON CLIMAT

USA, California, Santa Barbara County, Santa Maria Valley AVA

❦ Pinot Noir

❦ Chardonnay, Pinot Blanc

Winemaker Jim Clendenen and co-founder Adam Tolmach are true believers in the Burgundian emphasis on *climat* or vineyard site. As sole proprietor today, Clendenen works with Pinot Noir and Chardonnay from a variety of vineyard sites within fog-cooled SANTA BARBARA, and sometimes SAN LUIS OBISPO COUNTY, and takes the high-risk, anti-technological approach. In most vintages, the results have dazzled. The Chardonnays from Bien Nacido and other vineyards offer a succulent richness of fruit with warm insidious spice from new oak. A similar sweet core of (red) fruit, with floral and cherry perfume, is found in the Bien Nacido and Sanford & Benedict Pinot Noirs. Best years: 1997, '96, '95, '94, '93, '92, '91, '90, '89. Il Podere dell Olivos is Clendenen's label for exciting wines from Italian varieties.

AUCKLAND REGION

NEW ZEALAND, North Island

Vineyards in this region have shrunk from 32 per cent to 4 per cent of New Zealand's total, yet the region remains important, encompassing four districts: Greater Auckland, including Henderson and South Auckland, WAIHEKE ISLAND, Kumeu/Huapai/Waimauku and Matakana. The last two are increasingly exciting areas for Cabernet Sauvignon and Merlot. The development of Waiheke Island and Matakana, in particular, has arrested the declining acreage in Auckland which is now experiencing a modest expansion. Best years: 1998, '97, '96, '94, '93, '91, '89, '87. Best producers: BABICH, COLLARDS, COOPERS CREEK, Fenton Twin Bays, Goldwater Estate, Heron's Flight, KUMEU RIVER, MATUA VALLEY, NOBILO, Peninsula, Providence, SELAKS, STONYRIDGE, Te Motu, VILLA MARIA.

AUDE

FRANCE, Languedoc-Roussillon

A large *département* which stretches inland from Narbonne on the Mediterranean, up the Aude valley to Carcassonne and the Limoux hills, and south-west into the mountain wilderness of the CORBIÈRES. This area tended to be dismissed with a derogatory remark about wine lakes and oceans of cheap wine, but recently it has emerged as one of the most exciting areas in France. The predominance of mountainous land, particularly in the vast ACs of Corbières and MINERVOIS, and the smaller ones of FITOU, Limoux and BLANQUETTE DE LIMOUX, means that the potential is enormous, and each vintage brings a new crop of exciting wines. Yet apart from Limoux, Blanquette de Limoux and the sweet Muscat de St-Jean-de-Minervois, they are almost without exception red.

There is a lot of VIN DE PAYS activity in the Aude – on average 150 million bottles are made a year, the majority red or rosé. About two-thirds go under the Vin de Pays de l'Aude title, but there are 20 vins de pays de zones, which include Coteaux de Peyriac with an enormous 35 million bottles, the Val de Cesse and the Vallée du Paradis. Local co-operatives and big companies such as Chantovent, Nicolas and Skalli/FORTANT DE FRANCE have imaginatively pioneered Merlot, Cabernet Sauvignon, Chardonnay, Sauvignon Blanc, Sémillon, Chenin Blanc and Viognier alongside the more common varieties. The first results show fruity reds and clean, fresh whites of pure varietal character as well as stunning barrel-fermented Chardonnays. Drink the wines as young as possible.

AUSBRUCH

AUSTRIA

Today in Austria Ausbruch is a Prädikat for dessert wines between Beerenauslese and Trockenbeerenauslese in body. However, in the town of RUST on the bank of Lake Neusiedl in BURGENLAND, it is a distinct wine style whose origins go back to the early seventeenth century. For the town's leading growers it remains that: a dessert wine fermented until it has the high alcoholic content of a SAUTERNES, then aged in wooden cask. Best producers: FEILER-ARTINGER, Peter Schandl, Heidi Schröck, Robert WENZEL.

CH. AUSONE
FRANCE, Bordeaux, St-Émilion Grand Cru AC, Premier Grand Cru Classé
❧ *Merlot, Cabernet Franc*
This beautiful, tiny property (only 7ha/ 17 acres), situated on what are arguably the best slopes in the ST-ÉMILION AC, has had a troubled history. Traditionally thought of as being on a par with St-Émilion's other great property, Ch. CHEVAL BLANC, few wines between the end of World War Two and the 1980s had shown much personality, certainly not First Growth personality. However, a new, young winemaker, Pascal Delbeck, arrived in 1975 and during the 1980s he made a series of impressive wines that once more had the influential wine critics dancing attendance. Yet, despite a restored reputation, family quarrels and financial problems never entirely disappeared and the owner Alain Vauthier has basically made the wines since 1996, with the local wine star Michel Rolland as his consultant winemaker. The change of style is dramatic – more power, less elegance. But is it better? Best years: 1997, '96, '95, '94, '93, '90, '89, '88, '85, '83, '82.

AUXEY-DURESSES AC
FRANCE, Burgundy, Côte de Beaune
❧ *Pinot Noir*
♀ *Chardonnay, Pinot Blanc*
Auxey-Duresses is rather a backwater village up in the hills behind the world-famous MEURSAULT. In times of inflated prices, it can be a crucial source of supply for those who want to drink good white Burgundy yet are damned if they'll pay a loony sum. It makes it all the more incomprehensible that the standard of Auxey-Duresses varies so dramatically. At its best – from producers such as the Duc de Magenta or Roulot – the white is dry, soft, nutty and hinting at the kind of creaminess which should make a good Meursault. Too often, though, the wines end up rather flabby and flat. The whites make up about 25 per cent of the annual production and it's best to drink them between three and five years old. Best years: (whites) 1997, '96, '95. Best

producers: (whites) Ampeau, Creusefond, Diconne, Duc de Magenta, LEROY, M Prunier, P Prunier, Roulot. The cherry-and-strawberry-fruited reds are rather lean but often recently these wines have seemed dilute or coarse. They can soften up after a few years in a bottle. Best years: (reds) 1997, '96, '93, '90, '89, '88. Best producers: (reds) COCHE-DURY, Diconne, Duc de Magenta, LEROY, M Prunier, P Prunier, Roland, Thévenin.

AVIGNONESI
ITALY, Tuscany, Vino Nobile di Montepulciano DOCG
❧ ♀ *Sangiovese, Canaiolo, Merlot, Pinot Noir (Pinot Nero) and others*
♀ *Chardonnay, Sauvignon Blanc, Trebbiano, Malvasia*
Owned by the brothers Falvo, one of whom married into the Avignonesi family in the 1970s, this firm is often credited with bringing respectability back to the ancient wine area of VINO NOBILE DI MONTEPULCIANO in southern Tuscany. They produce wine from 100ha (247 acres) of vineyards spread over three farms, two (Le Capezzine and I Poggetti) in the Montepulciano zone and the third (La Selva) near Cortona.

The vineyards are gradually being replanted to superior clones and varieties. Innovative wines come from La Selva: the barrique-fermented Chardonnay Il Marzocco and Sauvignon Il Vignola, two of the earliest and still most successful of their type from central Italy, as well as the varietal Merlot and Pinot Nero. On the other hand, nobody produces the classic Tuscan *passito* wines – VIN SANTO (from Tuscan white grapes dried up to six months and aged in *caratelli* as long as nine years) and Occhio di Pernice (similarly made but from Sangiovese) – in a more traditional manner, and for nobody else's Vin Santo is the market so desperate to obtain just a handful of very expensive half-bottles.

Also on the traditional side, but with obvious modern touches such as the elimination of white grapes, is the range of Sangiovese-based wines, featuring mainly the

AVIGNONESI
First made in the early 1980s, Grifi is a barrique-aged super-Tuscan Sangiovese and Cabernet Sauvignon blend with intense fruit character and considerable structure.

hierarchy of Vino Nobiles – straight, Riserva and Riserva Grandi Annate, the latter made only in outstanding vintages. In respect of these, Avignonesi's style is surprisingly austere, eschewing easy options like the addition of French grapes and the use of small French barriques and sticking to the formula of 80 per cent Sangiovese topped up with Canaiolo and Mammolo, with aging in large oak barrels. Best years: 1995, '94, '93, '91, '90, '88.

AYL
GERMANY, Mosel-Saar-Ruwer
One of the top villages in the Saar, Ayl produces thrilling, racy Rieslings that in a decent year are as good as anything Germany can offer. Its main vineyard is the Kupp, which provides some very steep slopes that make the business of making great wine as uncomfortable as possible for the growers. The weather does the rest, refusing, in really poor years, to ripen the grapes at all and needing a really long, warm autumn to show that fine Saar wine is more than a pipe dream. Best producers: Bischöflicher Konvikt, Peter Lauer, Dr Heinz WAGNER.

BABCOCK VINEYARDS
USA, California, Santa Barbara County, Santa Ynez Valley AVA
❧ *Pinot Noir, Syrah, Sangiovese*
♀ *Chardonnay, Sauvignon Blanc, Gewurztraminer, Riesling, Pinot Gris*
Making bold, dramatic wines is the goal of Bryan Babcock, whose family-owned Santa Ynez Valley vineyard provides him with intensely flavoured fruit. A fanatic when it comes to cluster-thinning his vines for low yields, Babcock proves his point with Reserve Chardonnays and massive Eleven Oaks Sauvignon Blancs which lean towards the ripe melon style. Best years for both: 1998, '97, '95, '94, '92, '91. Highly perfumed barrel-fermented Gewurztraminer and exotic, floral Riesling, both firmly textured, are indeed high drama. Though the Pinot Noir captures the region's typical cherry character, the amount of oak can be overly dramatic. Best years: 1998, '97, '95, '94, '92, '90, '91. The Cuvée Lestat Syrah is one of the region's most concentrated versions.

BABICH
NEW ZEALAND, North Island, Henderson
❧ *Cabernet Sauvignon, Merlot and others*
♀ *Chardonnay, Sauvignon Blanc and others*
A family winery, Babich ranks among New Zealand's top ten producers. The majority of

fruit for its wide range of wines is drawn from GISBORNE, MARLBOROUGH and HAWKE'S BAY, with some from Babich's own Henderson vineyard. Joe Babich and chief winemaker Neill Culley produce an impressive, elegant Chardonnay (a prolific trophy winner) and classic, powerful Cabernet-Merlot blend under the Irongate label, both built for aging. Top-of-the-range wines are The Patriarch Chardonnay and Cabernet Sauvignon from the exciting Gimblett Road district in Hawke's Bay. The Mara Estate range includes Merlot and Cabernet Sauvignon; there's also a light, sweet-fruited Pinot Noir and pungent Sauvignon Blanc, full of opulent gooseberry fruit and great balance. Best years: 1998, '96, '94, '91, '90, '89.

BACHARACH
GERMANY, Mittelrhein

This small medieval town at the southern tip of the MITTELRHEIN is the source for many of the region's best wines. Here Riesling reigns supreme, growing on precipitously steep slopes with a slate soil rather like that of the MOSEL Valley. The climate is warmer here though, so while the wines bear a family resemblance to those of the Mosel they are fuller, with more forthright fruit aromas. Best producers: Fritz Bastian, Toni JOST, Dr Randolf Kauer, Helmut Mades, Ratzenberger.

BACKSBERG
SOUTH AFRICA, Western Cape, Paarl WO
🍷 *Cabernet Sauvignon, Pinotage, Syrah (Shiraz)*
🍾 *Chardonnay, Chenin Blanc, Sauvignon Blanc and others*

Many outstanding results are quietly achieved on this PAARL property. The Back family have always fostered worker empowerment; the Freedom Road label, launched in 1998, is the culmination of a partnership venture between Backsberg workers and management, which will lead to workers being able to acquire capital to buy their own homes away from the farm. A ground-

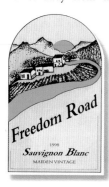

BACKSBERG
The Freedom Road label is a new range of wines launched by this well-established Paarl estate.

breaking Sauvignon Blanc, Simunye (Zulu for 'We are one'), is the first wine in a joint-vineyard venture in which Michael and Jill Back have teamed up with Californian husband and wife team, Zelma Long and Phil Freese. Freese also consults here and his substantial viticultural changes have seen improved fruit quality in reds particularly. The supple, limy Chardonnay is the mainstay white. Best years: (Chardonnay) 1997, '96, '95, '94, '93, '92, '91.

BAD KREUZNACH
GERMANY, Nahe

Bad Kreuznach is a busy spa town on the banks of the NAHE, and home to many well-known cellars, as well as the traditional site for the region's wine auctions. But until 1994 Kreuznach was also the name of a whole Bereich, covering 1000ha (2470 acres) of vineyards from the town itself north to the confluence of the Nahe and Rhine at Bingen. A wine from an individual vineyard at Bad Kreuznach is a very different proposition from one labelled Bereich Kreuznach.

The town itself has 22 individual vineyard sites, most of which are planted with Riesling, which is now the biggest single grape variety in the Nahe region. The Kahlenberg and Brückes sites, both of which face south, often produce the best wines. The Steinweg and Krötenpfuhl vineyards are almost as good, and Riesling also does well in Forst,

Kauzenberg, Steinberg and Narrenkappe. Best producers: Anton Finkenauer, Carl Finkenauer, von Plettenberg.

BADEN
GERMANY

Baden, being the most southerly of Germany's wine regions, is also the warmest; so you would expect it to grow different grape varieties from the chillier north, and it does; or at least a different balance of varieties. But Baden is so huge that it cannot easily be summed up. It covers about 15,850ha (39,165 acres) of vines and stretches over 400km (250 miles) from one end to the other, and the best wines are often not Riesling at all but come from the Pinot family – Blanc (Weissburgunder), Gris (Grauburgunder) and Noir (Spätburgunder). Fully one-quarter of the wine is red.

Many of the Baden vineyards lie along the Rhine. In the north is the district of Tauberfranken or Badisches Frankenland, which in all aspects except that of political administration is part of Franconia; its wines are dry and earthy. To the south comes Badische Bergstrasse/Kraichgau with Müller-Thurgau, Ruländer and Weissburgunder making attractive, medium-weight white wines. The Ortenau, south of Baden-Baden, is one of Baden's most famous districts: the wines are complex and distinctive, from Spätburgunder and Riesling (here called

Baden wines owe their full-bodied dry style to the region's warm, sunny climate. Perched high above the excellent Schlossberg vineyard in the Ortenau, Schloss Ortenberg has been a wine research centre since 1950.

Klingelberger); its neighbouring district, Breisgau, can be good, but grows a lot of Müller-Thurgau as well as the Pinot siblings Grauburgunder and Weissburgunder. Then comes Kaiserstuhl-Tuniberg. Kaiserstuhl is a long-dead volcano, and the wines here can be among Baden's best: dry, rich and powerful. Markgräflerland and Bodensee are other Bereichs.

Baden likes to promote its wines for their dryness and vinosity, and the extra ripeness that comes from being in the south. Some of the most remarkable Baden wines are the Spätburgunders. The Baden version of Pinot Noir is undergoing a rapid transformation from the sweet jammy style once common to so many German reds, to a more oaky, dry, well-structured style. Good co-operatives abound, since Baden is above all co-operative country; most make wine to a high standard, and the enormous Badische Winzerkeller, which acts as a central co-operative, is more than reliable.

BADIA A COLTIBUONO
ITALY, Tuscany, Chianti Classico DOCG
♥ *Sangiovese, Canaiolo*
♀ *Chardonnay*

Current owner Piero Stucchi Prinetti's ancestor, Florentine banker Guido Giuntini, purchased this superb thousand-year-old abbey (*badia*) at Gaiole in the middle of the nineteenth century, and it has been known since then as one of the foremost CHIANTI CLASSICO estates. The 50ha (124 acres) of vineyards are planted entirely to Tuscan varieties. There was a time, years ago, when the wines of Badia, one of the zone's earliest estate-bottlers, represented the 'old' CHIANTI style – strongly tannic from over-macerating and excessive barrel-aging, with aromas that reminded one more of meat stew than of fresh fruit. The wines today are fresh and bright with the accent on fruit and ripe tannins and quality oak.

The SUPER-TUSCAN Sangioveto is the star performer and made only in the best years. With a pronounced oaky style, the wine nevertheless has good fruit depth, and needs six to ten years' aging in order to harmonize its parts and put flesh on its bones. Coltibuono is a new Chianti Classico from Sangiovese grapes, not necessarily all from their own vineyards, and is bright and nicely balanced, with hints of quality oak (it gets just five months in barrel). The straight Chianti Classico and Riserva are 90 per cent Sangiovese and 10 per cent Canaiolo, and

both have something of the structure we have come to expect from Badia without sacrificing fruit. For more immediate consumption there is also a range of unoaked wines – Chianti Classico, Sangiovese, Rosato and Bianco. Best years: (Sangioveto) 1995, '94, '90, '88, '85.

BAGA
This Portuguese grape is rich in colour and tannins, giving dense red wines that can be bitterly astringent; it takes modern techniques to bring out its piercing blackcurrant fruit and make the wines approachable, but it can be done. BAIRRADA is its principal habitat but it also grows in substantial quantities in neighbouring DÃO and the RIBATEJO. Well-made Baga wines from Bairrada have the capacity to age for decades.

BAILEYS
AUSTRALIA, Victoria, North East Victoria Zone, Rutherglen
♥ *Cabernet Sauvignon, Syrah (Shiraz)*
♀ *Muscat, Muscadelle, Chardonnay*

This is one of the great names of the fortified wines of North East Victoria, making Muscat and Muscadelle (labelled Tokay in Australia) in an inimitably rich, almost treacly style. These wines come in two grades: Founders and at the top, Winemakers Selection and you get substantially more than you pay for. The unfortified reds are impressive, the whites pleasant but unremarkable. Baileys is now part of the MILDARA Blass group.

BAILEYS
Winemaker's Selection is the top level of luscious fortified wines from this old, very traditional winery at Glenrowan in North-East Victoria.

BAIRRADA DOC
PORTUGAL, Beira Litoral
♥ *Baga, Periquita, Tinta Pinheira*
♀ *Bical, Fernão Pires (Maria Gomes), Rabo de Ovelha*

Bairrada achieved demarcation only in 1979, though its red wines, principally from the red Baga grape, have been used for years to make some of Portugal's most impressive Garrafeiras. These wines, with startlingly rich

wild-berry aromas and flavours, are often marred by excessively hard tannins which take decades to soften. Much of the region's wine is made in co-operatives who, with the benefit of newly installed stainless steel, are making ever more approachable wines, often bottled under the local Vinho Regional designation of BEIRAS. Caves ALIANÇA and SOGRAPE, two of the largest private winemakers in Bairrada, and an Australian, Peter BRIGHT, have also been toying with the production of softer, earlier-maturing red wine.

The traditionalists (although most are by no means as traditional as they used to be) are the single-estate producers like Luís PATO, Casa de Saima and Caves SÃO JOÃO. All three make extremely impressive wines with the capacity to develop well in bottle for about 20 years. They count among Portugal's finest reds. White wines from Bairrada are much less interesting than the reds and should generally be drunk young, although, on its own, the Bical grape is capable of producing some elegant dry wines which age well. Much of the region's white ends up in the local sparkling wine industry. Best years: (reds) 1995, '94, '92, '90, '85.

BALEARES (BALEARIC ISLANDS)
SPAIN
The tourist trade happily guzzles down most of the wine produced in the Balearic Islands. Practically all of the 1400ha (3458 acres) under vine are on the largest island, Mallorca, which has one DO, Binissalem, in the centre, on an undulating plain. The native Manto Negro and Callet grapes, plus Tempranillo, Monastrell (Mourvèdre) and Cabernet Sauvignon dominate among red varieties and the wines are usually rather alcoholic but pale. There is some dull white, from the native Moll (Prensal Blanc) as well as Macabeo, Parellada, Moscatel Romano and Chardonnay. There is a larger wine area to the east and south around the towns of Felanitx and Petra, which uses the Vinos de la Tierra Pla i Llevant name. The local market is willing to pay rather high prices and commercial success seems to have thwarted serious winemaking progress. Best producers: Miguel Oliver, Franja Roje.

CH. BALESTARD-LA-TONNELLE
FRANCE, Bordeaux, St-Émilion Grand Cru AC, Grand Cru Classé
♥ *Merlot, Cabernet Franc, Cabernet Sauvignon, Malbec*

This is satisfyingly reliable wine and rightly popular. It is full of strong, chewy fruit and is reasonably priced. Once again this property demonstrates ST-ÉMILION's ability to produce numerous wines below the top rank of Premier Grand Cru Classé that are still immensely enjoyable and able to age well for 10–20 years. Obviously it has been popular for a fair old while, because the label reprints a poem which François Villon wrote back in the fifteenth century that describes Balestard as 'this divine nectar'. There is nothing like an unsolicited testimonial. Vintages in the 1990s have been less consistent. Best years: 1996, '95, '90, '89, '88, '86, '85, '83, '82.

BANDOL AC

FRANCE, Provence

🍷 Mourvèdre, Grenache, Cinsaut, Syrah
🍾 Clairette, Ugni Blanc, Sauvignon Blanc, Bourboulenc

There's no doubt that Bandol is a lovely resort town and fishing port, and that many of the vineyards are spectacular, cut high into the cliffs and slopes which tumble down to the Mediterranean beaches. Not only this, but it still ranks as Provence's top red wine.

The Mourvèdre grape, grown on terraced vineyards, is the grape that gives Bandol its character (the blend must include a minimum of 50 per cent) – gentle raisin and honey softness with a slight, tannic, plum-skins nip and a tobaccoey, herby fragrance. Other grapes, in particular Grenache, Cinsaut and occasionally Syrah, make up the blend. The reds spend at least 18 months in wood. They happily age for ten years, but can be very good at three to four. The rosés, delicious and spicy but often too pricy, should be drunk as young as possible. Best years: (reds) 1997, '96, '95, '94, '93, '91, '90, '89, '88, '85, '83, '82. Best producers: (reds and rosés) Bastide Blanche, l'Hermitage, Mas de la Rouvière, PIBARNON, Pradeaux, Ray-Jane, Roche Redonne, Ste-Anne, Tempier, la Tour de Bon, Vannières.

Bandol's reputation rests heavily on its ability to make quality reds, and the neutral, vaguely nutty whites (consisting of Clairette, Ugni Blanc and Bourboulenc) scarcely pose a challenge. Growers are now permitted to add Sauvignon Blanc to the blend, and there has been a considerable improvement in the freshness of the wines which use it, a green appley fruit balancing a vaguely aniseed perfume. The wines should be drunk as young as possible, but the excessive price tag no longer hurts quite so much. Best producers: (whites) Bastide Blanche, Mas de la Rouvière, Pibarnon, Roche Redonne, Ste-Anne, la Tour de Bon, Vannières.

CASTELLO BANFI

ITALY, Tuscany, Brunello di Montalcino DOCG

🍷 Sangiovese (Brunello), Cabernet Sauvignon, Syrah, Merlot and others
🍾 Muscat, Chardonnay, Sauvignon Blanc and others

When contemplating this gigantic, American-owned, Italian-run operation, 'the largest continuous wine estate in Europe' runs the blurb, 'covering some 2800ha (6919 acres) in all, of which about one-third is planted to vines', the numbers are so great as to be almost meaningless. Two men, apart from owners John and Harry Mariani, are behind the success of this huge operation: winemaker Pablo Harri, a young Swiss who seems to be able to handle all those different grapes and wines with amazing equanimity, as well as talent; and, principally, Ezio Rivella, a man whose CV reads almost like a history of Italian wine development over the past 30 years.

Considering the numbers he is working with, it is impressive how much fruit Harri manages to get into the ROSSO and BRUNELLO DI MONTALCINO (especially the cru Poggio all'Oro) without losing seriousness; his use of oak, too, is finely judged – something one can only say when the vanilla or woodsmoke add a dimension rather than knocking out the essential fruit. But the two masterpieces are blends – Summus is an unlikely mix of Sangiovese, Cabernet and Syrah with rich coal-tar and black-fruit aromas, sweet complex fruit on the palate and creamy texture, balanced by bright acidity. Better still is Excelsus, one of Italy's finest Bordeaux-style blends. Best years: (Poggio all'Oro) 1993, '91, '90, '88, '86, '85.

BANNOCKBURN

AUSTRALIA, Victoria, Port Phillip Zone, Geelong

🍷 Pinot Noir, Cabernet Sauvignon, Syrah (Shiraz), Merlot
🍾 Chardonnay

From low-yielding vineyards, this small winery makes one of Australia's best Pinot Noirs,

enormously rich Chardonnay, good Cabernet Sauvignon and idiosyncratic Shiraz. The winemaker Gary Farr has worked harvests at MOREY-ST-DENIS since 1983 and is wholly committed to Burgundian practices. He creates wine of concentration, power and structure, with unmistakable varietal character. The Pinot Noirs are outstanding and are still improving in bottle but, despite using Burgundian techniques, their flavour is far more muscular and rich than any Burgundy you're likely to come across. Best years: 1997, '95, '94, '91, '88, '86, '85.

BANYULS AC

FRANCE, Languedoc-Roussillon

🍷 Grenache, Cinsaut, Syrah and others

This is one of those strange, rather heavy, fortified wines – *vins doux naturels* – which the French like well enough but which seldom have the style and character of the fortified wines from Spain (sherry, MONTILLA, MÁLAGA) and Portugal (PORT, MADEIRA). The wine, either red or tawny, must contain at least 50 per cent Grenache Noir.

It is sometimes made fairly dry, but its strong plum and raisin flavour tastes best in a sweet version and when bottled young. Older tawny styles can be excellent too. BANYULS Grand Cru is at least 75 per cent Grenache, has 30 months' wood-aging and is a bit richer as a consequence. *Rancio* means that the wine has been intentionally oxidized and will have a tawny colour. Best stick to the red. Best producers: CELLIER DES TEMPLIERS, Clos des Paulilles, l'Étoile, MAS BLANC, la RECTORIE, la Tour Vieille.

BARBADILLO

SPAIN, Andalucía, Jerez y Manzanilla DO

🍾 Palomino Fino, Pedro Ximénez

Antonio Barbadillo is the largest of the sherry companies based in Sanlúcar de

Barrameda, the cool, breezy seaside home of manzanilla. It makes a huge range of sherries in a tasty, salty style. Among the best are the Manzanilla de Sanlúcar, delicate and saltily tangy, the Manzanilla Pasada Solear, lean and almost herbaceous, and Principe, a manzanilla amontillado, rich but soft, fleshy and elegant, with the nutty, toffee character of amontillado. There is also a dry still white, Castillo de San Diego, pleasant enough in a neutral sort of way when sitting in front of a plate of fried fish in one of Sanlúcar's seafront restaurants, but unimpressive when removed to cooler northern climes.

BARBARESCO DOCG

ITALY, Piedmont

♟ *Nebbiolo*

People talk about 'BAROLO and Barbaresco', never the other way round, but there are advantages to being number two. You can tend your grapes and make your wine in comparative peace. The wine is a little lighter than Barolo, so there is more chance of getting some feminine elegance into a notoriously masculine style. Barbaresco benefits from a lower minimum alcohol level (12.5 per cent) and a less stringent aging requirement of just 21 months (45 for the Riserva category), of which only nine months need be in wood. The weight of Barbaresco will depend a great deal on who makes it, but the fascinating taste of the Nebbiolo grape with its flavours of violets and raspberries, prunes and chocolates, truffles and licorice, its acidity, and its firm tannin, should always be present.

The principal communes of within the Barbaresco zone are Barbaresco itself, Neive and Treiso. Sites considered among the best include GAJA's San Lorenzo and Sorì Tildon, Cisa Asinari's Gaiun and Camp Gros, PRODUTTORI DEL BARBARESCO's Montestefano, Ovello and Rio Sordo, GIACOSA's Santo Stefano and Ceretto's Asili.

You may need to take out a second mortgage to try the wines of Gaja, but there is a rising number of excellent producers whose bottles shouldn't constitute such a drain on the finances, including: Cigliuti, Cisa Asinari, Gastaldi, Bruno Giacosa, Moccagatta, Nada, I Paglieri, Pasquero, Pelissero, Produttori del Barbaresco, Albino Rocca and Bruno Rocca. Also worth a try, too, are some of the Barbaresco wines from predominantly Barolo producers (Barale, Ceretto, Pio Cesare, Michele Chiarlo, PRUNOTTO, Rinaldi, Scarpa, Vietti). Best years: 1998, '97, '96, '95, '93, '90, '89, '88, '85, '82.

BARBERA

Barbera crops up all over the place in Italy; in Lombardy, Emilia-Romagna, Puglia, Campania, Sicily and elsewhere, but its homeland is Piedmont, particularly around Alba, Asti and the district of Monferrato. In recent years there has been far too much Barbera available, so the heights of ingenuity have been employed to use up the surplus. This has resulted in light Barbera, white Barbera, even fizzy Barbera. Good straight Barbera, though, is great stuff: vividly coloured, plum-skins sweet-sour, fruit-packed, with enlivening high acidity, a low tannin level and a bone-dry, astringent finish. With carbonic maceration or in a lighter style it is at its liveliest when young; traditionally vinified with sensibly low yields, it shines when two to six years old. It also has a great affinity for barrique-aging, gaining both tannin and meaty roundness.

Mexico and Argentina also make considerable use of Barbera, but mostly as a high-acid blender. This makes sense, because much of the wine industry, particularly in Argentina, was established by Italian immigrants who would have used Barbera to freshen up blends in Italy. Argentina is now producing some excellent Barbera as a single varietal, both oaked and unoaked. California has lots of Barbera and is just now beginning to appreciate its qualities and even Australia has a couple of varietal examples.

BARBERA D'ALBA DOC, BARBERA D'ASTI DOC, BARBERA DEL MONFERRATO DOC

ITALY, Piedmont

♟ *Barbera*

In whichever Barbera-producing part of Piedmont one happens to find oneself, producers are always firmly convinced that theirs is the best zone, theirs the archetype. Jovial self-aggrandizement apart, there really is no such thing as a 'best' Barbera area. There are only style differences prompted by different aspects and mesoclimates. Those who go for

extract and concentration, and get enthused by smokiness highlighting redcurrant fruit and balancing acidity, will choose Barbera from Alba, where top-class BAROLO and BARBARESCO producers know just how to create a wine that makes one sit up and take notice. Best producers: ALTARE, Boglietti, Clerico, Aldo CONTERNO, Giacomo CONTERNO, Conterno-Fantino, Matteo Coreggia, Corino, GAJA, Elio Grasso, Bartolo Mascarello, Giuseppe MASCARELLO, Pio Cesare, PRUNOTTO, SANDRONE, Vajra, Vietti.

If, on the other hand, the preference is for the young, lively, gulpably light, sometimes *frizzante* style of Barbera, the Monferrato hills, south-east of Asti, are the place to look. Avoid the aged Superiore which apes, not always successfully, the firmer styles of Alba, be ready for a good bite of acidity (or drink it to cut a vibrant swathe through salami, cheese and other rich foods) and search out the freshest samples you can find from estates such as the exemplary Bricco Mondalino.

Barbera d'Asti stands in between Alba's weighty style and Monferrato's more frolicsome one. It can be fine drunk young or aged a couple of years, great unoaked or resplendent after aging in barrique. The grapes can even be successfully semi-dried first, as Maruccia Borio of Cascina Castlèt's *passito* wine, Passum, shows. Other top producers include Araldica Vini Piemontesi (especially Ceppi Storici), Bricco Mondalino, Coppo (especially Pomorosso), Duca d'Asti, Rivetti, Scarpa, Viticoltori dell'Acquese (Bricco) and the late Giacomo Bologna's remarkable BRAIDA, whose crus Bricco dell'Uccellone, Ai Suma, La Monella and Bricco della Bigotta are Asti's banner-wavers.

BARDOLINO DOC

ITALY, Veneto

♟ ♟ *Corvina, Rondinella, Molinara and others*

Bardolino is one of the three famous names of the Veneto (with SOAVE and VALPOLICELLA). It can be good but, sadly, often isn't, perhaps because the light, fresh, summery style of red too easily pleases the tourists who flock to the banks of Lake Garda in the hot months. The overall standard, however, is improving. Bardolino at its best has a vibrant, ripe-cherries-and-slightly-bitter-almonds character that is usually better the younger, cheerier and less serious the wine is. However, in the hands of quality producers like Cavalchina, Corte

Gardoni, Guerrieri-Rizzardi, Le Vigne di San Pietro and Zeni, more serious, weightier Bardolino can work well. Bardolino Chiaretto or rosé is obtained by giving the Bardolino grapes just a few hours' contact with the skins. It has the crispness and freshness of a white, but with the ripe cherry-like fruit you would only ever normally find in a red.

BAROLO DOCG
ITALY, Piedmont
♥ *Nebbiolo*

Barolo may be a very acquired taste, but once acquired it can become an obsession. Tough, tannic and astringent the wine may be, but there is a wonderful nugget of fruit that seems to flow round the more abrasive elements to make a remarkably alluring whole. Barolo can be as exhilarating as a summer pudding of raspberries and other berried fruits. It can be as ethereal as the scent of violets. It can be earthy, truffly, smoky, deep and mysterious. It can be pruny, chocolaty, rich and seductive. Or it may be any combination of these. True, only the great Barolos can inspire the muse. And if it is a cheap example, it may well be enjoyable but it won't be revelatory.

Barolo's homeland is in the steep, angular Langhe hills of southern Piedmont. More and more producers are extracting full benefit from the diversity of sites and making single-vineyard wines. In the last ten years or so, a new breed of winemakers has grown up, led by Elio ALTARE, who introduced drastically reduced maceration times and maturation in small oak in order to get more obvious fruit in his wines. The wines of the so-called 'Barolo Boys', Altare's acolytes, are a revelation to those unmoved by the wonders of traditional Barolo – the fruit fairly leaps out of the glass. Traditionalists, committed to protracted maceration and avoidance of waftings of oak, which tend to mask the subtle aromas of the Nebbiolo grape, still maintain that this new wine is not Barolo – good though it may be as international-style red wine. I disagree.

But there's room in Barolo for all these styles: basic and magical, cru and non-cru. There is room for vintages like 1993 and '91, which are ready to drink in five years; and for the brilliant '97 and '90 which need up to ten years at least. Best years: 1998, '97, '96, '95, '93, '90, '89, '88, '85, '82. Producers capable of excellence are almost too numerous to mention, but include (apart from Altare) Gianfranco Alessandria, Azelia, Enzo Boglietti, Clerico, Aldo CONTERNO, Giacomo CONTERNO, Conterno Fantino, Corino, GAJA

(Sperss), Bruno GIACOSA, Elio Grasso, Silvio Grasso, Bartolo Mascarello, Giuseppe MASCARELLO, Mauro Molino, Pira, Principiano, PRUNOTTO, Ratti, SANDRONE, Scavino, Vajra, Vietti, Gianni Voerzio, Roberto Voerzio.

BARÓN DE LEY
SPAIN, Navarra, Rioja DOC
♥ *Tempranillo, Cabernet Sauvignon*
♥ *Grenache Noir (Garnacha Tinta), Tempranillo*
♀ *Macabeo (Viura)*

This is one of the new breed of RIOJA estates that intends to make all the red wine sold under its label from its own grapes, starting with the 1987 pure Tempranillo, grown in 90ha (222 acres) of vineyards at Mendavia in the Rioja Baja. Over half the bodega's 4000 barrels are of French Limousin oak, which the owners believe will give a more refined style of red wine. Barón de Ley white and rosé wines are made from bought-in grapes. They have also been growing some Cabernet Sauvignon on an experimental scale. This is currently not permitted for Rioja wines, although Cabernet Sauvignon is encouraged in the neighbouring DO of NAVARRA. Best years: 1995, '94, '91, '87.

BARÓN DE LEY
Barón de Ley is regarded as the leading bodega in the Rioja Baja region. The Reserva Rioja shows good balance between berried fruit and vanilla oak.

BAROSSA VALLEY
AUSTRALIA, South Australia, Barossa Zone

It was German, principally Silesian, settlers who were largely responsible for founding the South Australian wine industry here between 1840 and 1880. German place-names are more numerous than English, and brass bands and Lederhosen frequently displace rock groups and jeans.

The Barossa Valley is home to many of Australia's biggest wine companies, but due to a predominance of low-yielding, dry-farmed vineyards most fruit comes from other, lower-cost areas, and the grape tonnage is of declining importance. However, a new wave of young 'old-timers' is working at putting Barossa's reputation back on the map

and home-grown wines include generous Riesling, mouthfilling Shiraz and intensely fruity Cabernet Sauvignon. Best years: 1998, '97, '96, '94, '93, '91, '90, '88, '86, '82, '80, '76, '73, '70. Best big producers: Wolf BLASS, Leo BURING, KRONDORF, Peter LEHMANN, ORLANDO, Penfolds, Saltram, SEPPELT, Tollana and YALUMBA. Best small producers: BASEDOW, Grant BURGE, Elderton, Charles MELTON, Rockford, St HALLETT.

BARROS ALMEIDA
PORTUGAL, Port DOC, Douro DOC
♥ *Tinta Roriz, Tinta Barroca, Tinto Cão, Touriga Nacional, Touriga Francesa and others*
♀ *Gouveio, Viosinho, Rabigato, Malvasia Fina and others*

One of the larger but less well known PORT shippers, the Barros group is still family owned and is made up of a number of companies, among them Feuerheerd, Fiest, Hutcheson and Kopke. Kopke itself is the oldest port shipper still in existence, having been founded in 1638. The bulk of the company's production is young ruby and tawny destined for the continental European market, but Barros maintain substantial stocks of sublime old tawnies and colheitas. Kopke has also declared some impressive vintages (particularly 1970). Red and white DOURO wines are bottled respectively under the Vilar da Galeira and Enxodreiro labels. Best years (vintage ports): 1995, '94, '91, '70.

BARSAC AC
FRANCE, Bordeaux
♀ *Sémillon, Sauvignon Blanc, Muscadelle*

Barsac has the dubious distinction of being the only AC in Bordeaux to have suffered the ignominy of having one of its Classed Growths rip up the vines and go back to sheep grazing – within its very boundaries. That's what Ch. de Myrat did in 1976 after the owner gave up the struggle of trying to make ends meet – although after his death his heirs replanted in 1988 and the wines are now pretty good again. It is the largest of the five communes entitled to the SAUTERNES AC and comprises about 620ha (1532 acres) out of a total for Sauternes of 2255ha (5572 acres). The sweet wines of Barsac can also call themselves Barsac AC if they want – and most of the top properties do this. Some even label themselves Sauternes-Barsac.

Barsac lies close to the Garonne in the north of the Sauternes AC. Along its eastern boundary runs the diminutive river Ciron – source of the humid autumn mists crucial to the development of noble rot, which intensifies the sweetness in the grapes and without which you can't make truly sweet wine. The important grapes are Sémillon, which can produce syrupy, viscous wines in the best years, and Sauvignon Blanc, which adds fruit and acid balance. There is a little Muscadelle, which is particularly useful for its honeyed spice in less good years.

In general, Barsac wines are a little less luscious, less gooily indulgent than other Sauternes, but from good properties they should still be marvellously heady, full of the taste of peaches and apricots and creamy nuts. Unfortunately, they're expensive, especially from the Classed Growths, of which there are nine in Barsac. Best years: 1998, '97, '96, '95, '90, '89, '88, '86, '83, '76, '75. Best producers: (Classed Growths) BROUSTET, CLIMENS, COUTET, DOISY-DAËNE, Doisy-Dubroca, DOISY-VÉDRINES, NAIRAC; (non-classed estates) Cantegril, Cru Barréjats, Gravas, Liot, Ménota, Piada.

BARTHOD-NOËLLAT
FRANCE, Burgundy, Côte de Nuits, Chambolle-Musigny AC
♥ *Pinot Noir*

Some years ago Gaston Barthod handed over the running of this excellent estate to his daughter Ghislaine. Quality, which has always been high, has, if anything, improved under her stewardship. The estate is fortunate in possessing a number of Premiers Crus – les Cras, Beaux Bruns, Charmes and Varoilles – and tastings from any vintage reveal subtle differences between the four. The wines are rarely powerful or earthy; instead, they typify the ethereal beauty of CHAMBOLLE at its best. Their aroma can be pure raspberry, with the violet tones that are a hallmark of the village, and on the palate they are subtle, elegant and complex. Aged in about one-third new oak, they are best enjoyed during their first ten years. The BOURGOGNE Rouge can be delicious. Best years: 1997, '96, '95, '93, '92, '90, '89, '88, '85.

BASEDOW
AUSTRALIA, South Australia, Barossa Zone, Barossa Valley
♥ *Cabernet Sauvignon, Syrah (Shiraz), Grenache*
♀ *Riesling, Semillon, Chardonnay, Muscat (Frontignan)*

This winery, formerly part of the Peter LEHMANN group of wineries, consistently produces wines that rise above their station in personality and flavour and yet remain relentlessly reasonable in price. Indeed, the continued presence of Basedow quality and price on export markets during the 1980s did much to ensure BAROSSA's enduring reputation when it was trendy to dismiss the area as irrelevant to modern trends in wine. The Wood Matured Semillon, with its creamy, vanilla fruit and oak, is best, but fleshy Chardonnay and smooth, moderately rich Cabernet Sauvignon and Shiraz also show the BAROSSA VALLEY's traditional drinkability. Best years: 1997, '96, '94, '93, '91, '90, '88.

BASILICATA
ITALY

Basilicata is in the instep of Italy, a smallish region sandwiched between CAMPANIA, CALABRIA and PUGLIA. It is Italy's poorest region and the second lowest in population. The march of progress has been slow. Even the *autostrada* didn't arrive until the beginning of the 1980s. It is hilly and mountainous, surprisingly bleak and cold in winter. On the other hand, the beaches along the Ionian (instep) and the fragment of Tyrrhenian (west) coasts are not to be sneezed at. Folk are friendly and it is peaceful and unspoilt. There's not a great deal of wine, and most of this comes from the historic Aglianico grape (AGLIANICO DEL VULTURE is the region's only DOC).

BASS PHILLIP
AUSTRALIA, Victoria, Gippsland Zone
♥ *Pinot Noir and others*
♀ *Chardonnay*

Winemaker Phillip Jones produces tiny quantities (less than 1000 cases per year) of Australia's most eagerly sought and stylish Pinot Noirs under the Reserve, Premium and varietal labels, together with a hatful of Gamay and Chardonnay for home consumption. The flavour is elegant yet penetrating and incredibly long-lasting, rapidly taking on the forest undergrowth character of high-class red Burgundy. Best years: 1997, '96, '94, '92, '91, '89, '85, '80.

DR VON BASSERMANN-JORDAN
GERMANY, Pfalz, Deidesheim
♀ *Riesling, Pinot Blanc (Weissburgunder)*

This PFALZ estate has a long history of making top-quality wines. The 42ha (104 acres) of vineyards, practically all Riesling, cover most of the best sites in the Mittelhaardt, including Jesuitengarten, Kirchenstück, Ungeheuer in FORST, and the Grainhübel and Hohenmangen of DEIDESHEIM among others. Since Margrit von Bassermann took control following her husband's death in 1995 and appointed Ulrich Mell winemaker, the estate has shot back to the finest rank of Pfalz producers. Best years: 1998, '97, '96, '90, '89, '88, '86.

CH. BASTOR-LAMONTAGNE
FRANCE, Bordeaux, Sauternes AC, Cru Bourgeois
♀ *Sémillon, Sauvignon Blanc, Muscadelle*

There's no such thing as a good, cheap SAUTERNES. Good Sauternes is fiendishly expensive to make, the vineyard yield is low and the incidence of sweetness-inducing noble rot erratic and unpredictable. There is one shining exception – Ch. Bastor-Lamontagne. This 50-ha (124-acre) Sauternes property is on a good site in the commune of Preignac, just north of the great Ch. SUDUIRAUT. Year after year it produces luscious, honeyed wine at a price which allows you to wallow in the delights of high-class Sauternes without taking out a second mortgage (just). Best years: 1997, '96, '95, '94, '90, '89, '88, '86, '85, '83.

CH. BASTOR-LAMONTAGNE
Year after year this large Sauternes estate produces luscious, honeyed wine typically showing fine botrytis character and ripe apricot fruit at a reasonable price.

CH. BATAILLEY
FRANCE, Bordeaux, Haut-Médoc, Pauillac AC, 5ème Cru Classé
♥ *Cabernet Sauvignon, Merlot, Cabernet Franc, Petit Verdot*

A byword for value-for-money – which, in the rarefied world of PAUILLAC Classed Growths, is an infrequent accolade indeed. Made in the plummier, broader Pauillac style, Ch. Batailley should be a byword for reliability too, because every year since the mid-1970s the wine has been good; marked by a full, obvious blackcurrant fruit (even when very young), not too much tannin, and a luscious overlay of good, creamy, oak-barrel vanilla. As is to be expected from a good Pauillac red, this wine is sturdy enough to age well for 15 years, yet lovely to drink at only five years old. Best years: 1997, '96, '95, '94, '90, '89, '88, '86, '85, '83, '82.

BÂTARD-MONTRACHET AC, BIENVENUES-BÂTARD-MONTRACHET AC, CRIOTS-BÂTARD-MONTRACHET AC

FRANCE, Burgundy, Côte de Beaune, Grands Crus
♀ *Chardonnay*

Bâtard-Montrachet is a superb Grand Cru white Burgundy. Straddling the communal border between PULIGNY-MONTRACHET and CHASSAGNE-MONTRACHET, the vineyard produces wines of enormous richness and grandeur. They fill your mouth with flavours of freshly roasted coffee, toasted bread still hot from the stove, brazil nuts and spice – and honey, which after six to eight years becomes so strong it seems to coat your mouth. Yet despite all this, Bâtard-Montrachet is a fully dry wine; there is not the slightest hint of sugar. The richness is simply the alchemy of a great vineyard, a great grape variety – Chardonnay – and the careful, loving vinification and aging in good oak, that has given Grand Cru white Burgundy its reputation as the world's greatest dry white wine.

There are two other parts of the Bâtard Grand Cru: 3.7ha (9.1 acres) of Bienvenues-Bâtard-Montrachet just to the north (*bien venues* means 'welcome') and 1.6ha (4 acres) of the less opulent Criots-Bâtard-Montrachet, directly to the south and entirely within Chassagne-Montrachet. These are also great white wines, flavoursome and rich, although they are generally a little less overwhelming than Bâtard-Montrachet. Best years: 1997, '96, '95, '92, '90, '89, '88, '86, '85. Best producers: Blain-Gagnard, DROUHIN, J-N GAGNARD, Gagnard-Delagrange, Louis JADOT, Domaine LEFLAIVE, Pierre Morey, RAMONET, Sauzet, Verget.

LES BAUX-DE-PROVENCE AC

FRANCE, Provence
🍷♀ *Grenache, Syrah, Cabernet Sauvignon*
♀ *Ugni Blanc, Clairette, Grenache Blanc, Sauvignon Blanc*

This exciting AC in the south of France is showing how organic farming methods can produce spectacular results. It's a weird place, though – a desolate moonscape of tumbled rocks and gaunt, skull-like cliffs, dominating the scenery between Cavaillon and Arles in the foothills of the Alpilles in the Bouches-du-Rhône *département*.

Still, the welcome is in the wines. Fruit is what marks them out, and an incredible softness for wines that are well-structured, full and balanced, and suited to aging for several years; yet even when young they seem to soothe your palate and calm your thoughts. The most important grape is the Syrah, which here gets into its joyous, fruit-first mood. The one-time leading estate, Domaine de TRÉVALLON, is the chief exponent of the Cabernet-Syrah blend, but has been barred from the AC for exceeding the limits set for Cabernet Sauvignon. Virtually all of the wine so far is red, but both the quality of the fruit and the inspiration displayed in the winemaking is so good in this region, that we are sure to see some good whites soon. Estates like Mas de Gourgonnier, using 40 per cent Sauvignon Blanc in its fresh, snappy white, and Terres Blanches are among those leading the way. Best producers: Hauvette, Mas de la Dame, Mas de Gourgonnier, Mas Ste-Berthe, Terres Blanches. Best years: (reds) 1998, '97, '96, '95, '94, '93, '90.

CH. BEAU-SÉJOUR BÉCOT

FRANCE, Bordeaux, St-Émilion Grand Cru AC, Premier Grand Cru Classé
🍷 *Merlot, Cabernet Franc, Cabernet Sauvignon*

There was a hue and cry when Beau-Séjour Bécot was demoted from the ranks of ST-ÉMILION's Premiers Grands Crus Classés in 1985. Luckily, brothers Gérard and Dominique Bécot wasted little time dwelling on the problem and the estate was reinstated in 1996, the domaine much improved and the wine back to its very best. Beau-Séjour Bécot's 16.6-ha (41-acre) vineyard is situated on St-Émilion's limestone plateau and *côtes* and is planted with 70 per cent Merlot, 24 per cent Cabernet Franc and 6 per cent Cabernet Sauvignon. The wines are classically vigorous with a fine tannic structure and elegant oakiness. They improve with long aging, from which they gain both in aroma and complexity. Best years: 1998, '97, '96, '95, '94, '93, '90, '89, '88, '86, '85.

CH. DE BEAUCASTEL

FRANCE, Southern Rhône, Châteauneuf-du-Pape AC
🍷 *Grenache, Syrah, Mourvèdre, Counoise and others*
♀ *Roussanne, Grenache, Bourboulenc*

In terms of consistency as well as quality, Beaucastel is arguably the finest estate in CHÂTEAUNEUF-DU-PAPE. Other estates may occasionally surpass Beaucastel in individual vintages, but no other estate performs so steadily, even making drinkable wines in the poorest of years. Beaucastel, which is owned by the Perrin family, takes a very traditional approach to the red wine, growing all 13 permitted varieties of the appellation organically and vinifying them without recourse to new oak or other modish techniques. One peculiarity here is the high proportion of Mourvèdre, a grape that does not ripen easily here. But when it does it gives a density and structure to the wine that probably helps account for its remarkable ability to age. In

In the north-east of the Châteauneuf-du-Pape AC, Ch. de Beaucastel's vineyards have a high proportion of the famous Châteauneuf stones or galets roulés which store daytime heat as well as retaining valuable moisture.

exceptional vintages, when the Perrins are dazzled by the quality of the Mourvèdre, they bottle a small quantity of a very expensive cuvée called Homage à Jacques Perrin.

The white wines are equally remarkable: one is produced mostly from Roussanne and partly barrel fermented, while the Vieilles Vignes bottling is made only from Roussanne and is immensely concentrated. Both wines can be enjoyed young or kept for at least ten years. Prices of these excellent wines have risen in recent years, but the Perrins also produce a fine CÔTES DU RHÔNE called Cru de Coudoulet from vineyards just outside the appellation, which can give you a hint of the Beaucastel experience for half the price. Best years: (reds) 1997, '96, '95, '94, '93, '90, '89, '88, '85, '83, '81, '78. Best years: (whites) 1997, '96, '95, '94, '93.

BEAUJOLAIS AC, BEAUJOLAIS SUPÉRIEUR AC

FRANCE, Burgundy, Beaujolais
 Gamay
 Chardonnay

About one-third of the Beaujolais drunk nowadays goes under the label BEAUJOLAIS NOUVEAU or Beaujolais Primeur. That's a pretty big proportion and exactly how it should be. The word Nouveau (new) or Primeur (first) on the label shows that the wine is as young as it can be, and youthful effervescence is precisely what makes Beaujolais such fun. It gushes from the bottle into the glass and down your throat with a whoosh of flavours – banana, peach and pepper fruit – typical of the Gamay grape.

This gluggable quality is usually obtained by a vinification method known as carbonic maceration. The grapes aren't pressed before fermentation; instead, they are piled into the vat in whole bunches. The skins of the grapes at the bottom of the vat gradually burst and the juice released begins to ferment. As the vat heats up during fermentation, the grapes on top ferment inside their skins, where the perfume and colour are concentrated. The result is loads of bright colour and orchard fruit, with minimal tannins and acids from the outside of the grape skins.

The Beaujolais AC is the basic appellation covering 22,000ha (54,000 acres) of vineyards between MÂCON and Lyon. Almost all the wine is red, though there is some rosé and a little white. In the south, towards Lyon, the wide carpet of vines produces simple AC Beaujolais, an easy-going light red wine to be drunk within months of the vintage. In the

north, towards Mâcon, most of the reds qualify either as BEAUJOLAIS-VILLAGES or as a single cru. These ten crus, or villages, definitely do produce superior – and more expensive – wine: BROUILLY, CHÉNAS, CHIROUBLES, CÔTE DE BROUILLY, FLEURIE, JULIÉNAS, MORGON, MOULIN-À-VENT, REGNIÉ and ST-AMOUR.

The Beaujolais Supérieur AC denotes a wine with a minimum alcoholic strength one degree higher than straight Beaujolais. Since freshness is everything, extra strength isn't really the point. Best years: 1998, '97, '96, '95, '94. Best producers: (reds) Bernardin, Carron, Chaffanion, Charmet, DUBOEUF, Garlon, Didier Germain, Jambon, Labruyère, de la Plume, Terres Dorées, Texier; (whites) Charmet, Dalissieux, Duboeuf.

BEAUJOLAIS NOUVEAU

FRANCE, Burgundy, Beaujolais, Beaujolais AC
 Gamay

This is the first release of bouncy, fruity BEAUJOLAIS wine on the third Thursday of November after the harvest. The wine will normally be between seven and nine weeks old, depending on the date of the vintage – the earlier the better. The quality is usually reasonable, despite what all the killjoy critics say, since much of the best Beaujolais AC is used for Nouveau. The wine usually improves by the New Year and good ones are perfect for the first picnics of summer. Best producers: Cellier des Samsons, la Chevalière, DROUHIN, DUBOEUF, Ferraud, Gauthier, Jaffelin, Loron, Sapin, Sarrau.

BEAUJOLAIS-VILLAGES AC

FRANCE, Burgundy, Beaujolais
 Gamay

This AC covers a grouping of just over 40 communes with supposedly superior vineyard sites in the north of the BEAUJOLAIS region. When carefully made from ripe grapes, Beaujolais-Villages can represent all the excitement of the Gamay at its best. Some Villages wine is made into Nouveau and is worth keeping for six months.

Many Beaujolais-Villages are now bottled under a 'domaine' name, the label indicating the name of the village. However, the larger merchants usually make up a blend from several villages. Best villages: Beaujeu, Lancié, Lantignié, Leynes, Marchampt, Quincié, St-Étienne-des-Ouillières, St-Jean d'Ardières. Best years: 1998, '97, '96, '95, '94. Best producers: Aucoeur, Depagneux, Depardon, DUBOEUF, de Flammerécourt, Jaffre, Large, Loron, Miolane, Pivot, Tissier, Verger.

BEAULIEU VINEYARD
The Private Reserve Cabernet is the flagship wine from this historic Napa estate. In the best vintages it continues to be beautifully balanced and refined.

BEAULIEU VINEYARD

USA, California, Napa County, Napa Valley AVA
 Cabernet Sauvignon, Pinot Noir, Merlot and others
 Chardonnay, Sauvignon Blanc and others

Much of the NAPA VALLEY's early fame for Cabernet Sauvignon rested upon the wines made at Beaulieu by Georges de Latour between 1900 and 1919, and by André Tchelistcheff between 1937 and 1970. The style of BV's premier Cabernet, Georges de Latour Private Reserve, is one of the most distinctive in CALIFORNIA, owing to its extra-ripe grapes and three to four years in American oak barrels. Best years (recent): 1996, '95, '94, '92, '91, '90, '87, '86.

BV's second, less costly Cabernet, Rutherford, is lighter and ages faster. A red Meritage, Tapestry, has a hefty proportion of Merlot for instant accessibility. Beaulieu also makes a reasonable Sauvignon Blanc. Its CARNEROS Chardonnay and Carneros Pinot Noir are at last beginning to merit attention, and future improvements are likely once all recently replanted vineyards reach maturity.

BEAUNE AC

FRANCE, Burgundy, Côte de Beaune
 Pinot Noir
 Chardonnay, Aligoté

Beaune is the capital of the CÔTE D'OR and one of Burgundy's most important wine towns. Almost all the wines are red, with a delicious, soft red-fruits ripeness, no great tannin, and not much obvious acidity, plus a slight minerally element which is unique and very enjoyable. The wines age well, gaining a savoury yet toffee-rich flavour over five to ten years, but they are also among the easiest of Burgundies to drink young. There are no Grands Crus but many excellent Premiers Crus, especially Boucherottes, Bressandes, Cent Vignes, Clos des Mouches, Clos du Roi, Grèves, Marconnets, Teurons and Vignes

Franches. These Premiers Crus account for about two-thirds of the vineyards. Best years: (reds) 1997, '96, '95, '93, '90, '89, '88, '85. Merchants dominate the vineyard holdings but in general seem to make a reasonable effort to produce typical wines. But there are some independent owners – such as Besancenot-Mathouillet, Jacques Germain, Lafarge, Morot, Mussy and TOLLOT-BEAUT. Best merchants: BOUCHARD PÈRE ET FILS, Chanson, DROUHIN, Camille Giroud, JADOT, Jaffelin, Labouré-Roi, LEROY, Thomas-Moillard.

Although most people think of Beaune as a red wine AC, 5 per cent of the 538ha (1329 acres) of vines are planted with white varieties. Drouhin makes Clos des Mouches, an outstandingly good, creamy, nutty wine. Beaune whites age well, particularly the oaky Clos des Mouches, but are also delicious at only two years old. Best years: (whites) 1996, '95, '93, '92, '90, '89.

BEAUX FRÈRES
USA, Oregon, Yamhill County, Willamette Valley AVA
♥ *Pinot Noir*

Noted wine authority, Robert M Parker, Jr. is a partner in this WILLAMETTE VALLEY winery, a controversial issue early on, that quickly faded after a few intense, full-bodied Pinot Noirs were released. Winemaker Michael Etzel is Parker's brother-in-law, hence the name Beaux Frères. The wine shows tremendous blackberry fruit and new oak flavours. A second wine is produced under the Belles Soeurs label. Best years: 1998, '96, '94.

BEIRAS VINHO REGIONAL
PORTUGAL, Beira Alta, Beira Baixa, Beira Litoral
♥ *Baga, Bastardo, Jaen, Periquita, Touriga Nacional and others*
♀ *Arinto, Bical, Cercial, Maria Gomes, Rabo de Ovelha and others*

Covering most of central Portugal, Beiras is a diverse region which stretches from the fertile coastal plain to the Serra de Estrela, Portugal's highest mountain range. It embraces both BAIRRADA and DÃO and much of the wine bottled under the Beiras label is declassified from these two well-known DOCs. Many different grapes are permitted, including foreign ones like Chardonnay and Cabernet Sauvignon which are not allowed under the more restrictive DOC legislation. Cabernet performs well in Bairrada and is increasingly blended with the local Baga grape. The wines are generally for early-drinking. Best producers: Caves ALIANÇA, Sociedade Agricola de Beiras, BRIGHT BROS, José Neiva, Quinta de Foz de Arouce.

CH. BELAIR
FRANCE, Bordeaux, St-Émilion Grand Cru AC, Premier Grand Cru Classé
♥ *Merlot, Cabernet Franc*

Belair is Ch. AUSONE's neighbour on the steep, south- and south-east-facing clay limestone slopes just below the town of ST-ÉMILION. The fortunes of the estate were revived in the late 1970s with the arrival of winemaker Pascal Delbeck, until 1996 also responsible for the winemaking at Ausone. The wines are always meticulously crafted, lighter in style than Ausone, but refined and elegant with good aging potential. Recent vintages have shown greater depth and density. Best years: 1998, '97, '96, '95, '94, '93, '90, '89, '88, '86, '85, '83, '82.

CH. BELAIR
From the limestone slopes just outside the town of St-Émilion, this estate produces some of the most elegant wines in the appellation which mature relatively quickly.

BELLET AC
FRANCE, Provence
♥♀ *Folle Noire, Braquet, Cinsaut, Grenache Noir*
♀ *Rolle, Chardonnay*

Bellet is a tiny area – only 50ha (124 acres) of mainly white Rolle and red Braquet and Folle Noir vines in the hills behind Nice – whose existence was so precarious that the authorities almost withdrew its AC in 1947. Most whites are dominated by Rolle, but Ch. de Crémat includes some Chardonnay, which makes a difference. However, Bellet has Nice as its home market, and after a day on the beach people don't seem to care much what their wine tastes like so long as it is supposedly rare and overpriced. In the chic eateries you're better off ordering a pastis or a gin and tonic. Best producers: Ch. de Bellet, Ch. de Crémat. Best years: (reds) 1998, '97, '96, '95, '94; (whites) 1998, '97, '96, '95.

BENDIGO
AUSTRALIA, Victoria, Central Victoria Zone

Bendigo was the focus of the Victoria gold rush, from which much of the Victorian wine trade grew: today's 21 Bendigo wineries compare with over 100 in 1880. But this region is superb for reds, with the Heathcote subregion justifiably regarded as one of Australia's greatest producers of rich, structured, dark cherry-flavoured Shiraz which lives for decades. Best years: 1998, '97, '96, '94, '93, '92, '91, '89, '88, '87, '86, '84, '82, '75. Best producers: Balgownie, JASPER HILL, Mount Ida, Passing Clouds, Water Wheel.

BENZIGER FAMILY VINEYARDS
USA, California, Sonoma County, Sonoma Valley AVA
♥ *Cabernet Sauvignon, Merlot, Pinot Noir, Syrah, Zinfandel*
♀ *Chardonnay, Sauvignon Blanc, Viognier*

Led by patriarch and marketing whizz Bruno Benziger, this family launched a popular-price line of wines under the Glen Ellen Winery name. It quickly became a driving force during the White Zinfandel and low-budget Chardonnay era, and Glen Ellen went on to become one of the success stories of the 1980s. After Bruno's death, the family attempted to work on an upgraded line of Sonoma varietals labelled Benziger Family, but by 1993 they sensed a need to disassociate themselves from the volume-oriented Glen Ellen giant and sold it to Heublein.

With the family now able to concentrate on the Benziger Family wines, they have been on an upward quality course, offering sound wines from SONOMA COUNTY and better ones from their estate vineyard in the SONOMA MOUNTAIN AVA. Their Sonoma Chardonnay, Merlot and Zinfandel are good value and the Reserve Carneros Chardonnay, various Reserve Cabernet Sauvignons and Sonoma Mountain Meritage wines named Tribute are among the best. Best years: 1997, '96, '95, '94. Also of considerable interest is an eclectic group of esoteric and overlooked varietals (Cabernet Franc, Malbec, Aligote and others) under the Imagery Series.

BERCHER
GERMANY, Baden, Burkheim
♥ *Pinot Noir (Spätburgunder)*
♀ *Pinot Gris (Grauburgunder), Pinot Blanc (Weissburgunder), Riesling, Muscat (Muskateller)*

Located in the KAISERSTUHL area of BADEN, the Bercher Brothers, Rainer the winemaker and Eckhardt the vine grower, are jovial perfectionists making wine for pleasure rather than analytical dissection. The Grauburgunders and Weissburgunders are rich and fleshy Kaiserstuhl wines, but cleaner and better balanced than these wines usually are.

Their Spätburgunder reds are deeply coloured and have plenty of soft tannin. The 'Selektion' bottlings of all three, which are cautiously barrique-aged, are superb. They also make the best dry Muscat and Riesling in the Kaiserstuhl, which thankfully see no oak at all. Best years: 1998, '97, '96, '94, '93, '92, '90.

BERGDOLT

GERMANY, Pfalz, Neustadt-Duttweiler

❦ Pinot Noir (Spätburgunder)

♀ Riesling, Pinot Blanc (Weissburgunder), Silvaner and others

Rainer Bergdolt, the owner of this 19-ha (46-acre) estate, aims for freshness and fruit in his wines and achieves it in bucketfuls. The powerful dry Weissburgunders, among the best wines made from this grape anywhere, are much in demand in Germany. There is also some experimental Chardonnay and recently also good Spätburgunder reds. Wines made in stainless steel are sold with a vineyard designation on the label (the best is Kirrweiler Mandelberg); the barrique-aged wines are sold without such a designation. Best years: 1998, '97, '96, '94, '93, '92, '90.

BERGERAC AC, BERGERAC SEC AC, CÔTES DE BERGERAC AC, CÔTES DE BERGERAC MOELLEUX AC

FRANCE, South-West

❦ ♀ Cabernet Sauvignon, Cabernet Franc, Merlot

♀ Sémillon, Sauvignon Blanc, Muscadelle and others

Bergerac is the main town of the Dordogne and the overall AC for this underrated area east of Bordeaux; the region might consider itself unlucky to be denied the more prestigious BORDEAUX AC, since its vineyards abut those of Bordeaux's BORDEAUX-CÔTES DE FRANCS and CÔTES DE CASTILLON ACs, and the grape varieties are mostly the same. Indeed, for centuries Bergerac wines were sold as Bordeaux. Production is pretty sizeable – 15 million bottles a year, of which about half is red, and the rest rosé and white.

The red is like a light, fresh Bordeaux-style wine, a bit grassy but with a good raw blackcurrant fruit. A few producers make a more substantial version under the Côtes de Bergerac AC, which stipulates a higher minimum alcohol level. Bergerac rosés can be exciting too. In general drink the most recent vintage, though a few estate reds can age for three to five years. Best years: 1996, '95, '94, '93, '90, '89. Best producers: (reds) le Barradis, Court-les-Mûts, de Gouyat, la Jaubertie, Lestignac, la Rayre, TOUR DES GENDRES, La Tour des Verdots, Treuil-de-Nailhac.

Production of white Bergerac Sec is dominated by the fairly efficient local co-operative, whose wines are generally clean and slightly grassy. However, good dry white Bergerac, made under the Côtes de Bergerac regulations, can have a very tasty, strong nettles and green-grass tang to it, with a little more weight than an equivalent Bordeaux Blanc. Around one quarter of the white wines are sweet; the Côtes de Bergerac Moelleux AC covers sweet wines from the whole region and these should be pleasant, fruity, easily sweet, yet not exactly rich. The tiny Saussignac AC makes Sémillon-based sweet wines. Best years: 1996, '95, '93, '91, '90, '89. Best producers: (whites) Belingard, Clos d'Yvigue, Court-les-Mûts, Eyssard, Gouyat, la Jaubertie, Panisseau, TOUR DES GENDRES.

THE BERGKELDER

SOUTH AFRICA, Western Cape

❦ Cabernet Sauvignon, Merlot, Pinotage, Syrah (Shiraz) and others

♀ Sauvignon Blanc, Chardonnay, Chenin Blanc, Cruchen Blanc (South African/Cape Riesling)

The Bergkelder is the wine arm of Distillers Corporation and one of the biggest wine companies in South Africa. It is both merchant and winemaker of its own wines. In the early 1980s, the then cellar master, Dr Julius Laszlo, promoted the use of new, small oak barrels. As with other producers, this oak aging often overpowered the anyway slender wines. More recently, the best wines have achieved better balance. Like STELLENBOSCH FARMERS' WINERY, this producer has the clout to help establish the country's international reputation instead of leaving this mammoth task to the small independent producers, but it seems to hold on to an inward-looking approach.

Hopefully, this will change after 1999, when a large new winery in Durbanville, concentrating on grapes from that region, comes on line. Another new project is a dedicated sparkling wine cellar for the J C le Roux brand in STELLENBOSCH's Devon Valley. The ripe, yeasty Pongracz is one of the Cap Classique labels produced by this brand. Of the other own labels, Fleur du Cap represents value for money for everyday drinking, Stellenryck is slightly better quality. Under the new SA Wine Cellars umbrella, it provides aging and marketing facilities for 12 estates; among the best and most famous are MEERLUST and La Motte, while the wholly owned Le Bonheur also produces good quality. Best years: (reds) 1995, '94, '93, '92, '91, '90; (whites) 1998, '97, '96, '95, '94, '93, '92, '91.

BERINGER VINEYARDS

USA, California, Napa County, Napa Valley AVA

❦ Cabernet Sauvignon, Zinfandel, Gamay, Merlot

♀ Chardonnay, Sauvignon Blanc, Gewurztraminer, Chenin Blanc

With a long history of winemaking, Beringer is one of California's leading producers. Of its 1214ha (3000 acres) of vines in NAPA and SONOMA's Knights Valley, almost 243ha (600 acres) are Chardonnay in the southern NAPA VALLEY. This is the source of Beringer's best-known white wine, the Private Reserve Chardonnay – big, richly ripe and oaky. Best years: 1998, '97, '96, '95, '94, '93, '92, '91. The Napa Valley Chardonnay can be just as impressive. Dark, tannic, sometimes perfumy, often cedary, the Private Reserve Cabernet Sauvignon, from four small vineyard sites, is one of Napa's best Cabernets. Best years: 1996, '95, '94, '93, '92, '91, '90, '87, '86, '85. The Knights Valley Cabernet is fruitier and suppler. The stylish Oakville Gewurztraminer, HOWELL MOUNTAIN Merlot, Meritage White and Napa Valley Fumé Blanc are all wines with considerable personality and flavour.

BERNARDUS WINERY

USA, California, Monterey County, Carmel Valley AVA

❦ Cabernet Sauvignon, Merlot, Pinot Noir

♀ Chardonnay, Sauvignon Blanc

European industrialist and former race driver for Porsche, Ben Pon carved out an estate vineyard along the gentle slopes within the Carmel Valley, a sheltered corner of MONTEREY that has demonstrated fine potential for Cabernet Sauvignon. After planting 20ha (49 acres) to Cabernet with small patches of Merlot and Cabernet Franc for blending purposes, he is now busy carving out an international reputation. The top wine is Marinus, a polished, well-structured estate red. Receiving three years of oak aging, it has the depth to age for a decade in the bottle. Best years: 1997, '96, '95,

'94. There is also tasty Pinot Noir from Bien Nacido Vineyard in SANTA BARBARA and a brisk, gooseberry-tinged Sauvignon Blanc from Monterey County.

BERNKASTEL

GERMANY, Mosel-Saar-Ruwer

This village on the Mosel is home to some superb vineyards. Rising 200m (656ft) above the town, and almost squeezing the houses into the river, they include the world famous Doctor vineyard. The Riesling vines here, and in the neighbouring Graben and Lay sites, make some of the best wines that Germany has to offer.

But Bernkastel also gives its name to a Bereich and two Grosslagen, Kurfurstlay and Badstube, far larger areas that include much less distinguished vineyards. The small Badstube Grosslage covers the five best vineyards, so the wines should be of high standard, but avoid the others which are invariably inferior. Best producers: Dr LOOSEN, Molitor, Dr PAULY-BERGWEILER, J J PRÜM, SELBACH-OSTER, Dr H THANISCH, WEGELER.

BEST'S

AUSTRALIA, Victoria, Western Victoria Zone, Grampians

🍷 *Cabernet Sauvignon, Syrah (Shiraz)*

🍷 *Chardonnay, Riesling*

This small winery was established in 1866, and is the last survivor, along with SEPPELT, of the wineries established in the region to slake the thirst of a society crazed by gold. Its priceless old vineyards are some of the few historic plantings left in the area, and contribute, in particular, to the wonderful, silky smooth, cherry and mint Shiraz (especially in the Thomson Family Shiraz from 130-year-old wines) which is deceptively long-lived. The full, honeyed Chardonnay and the well-balanced, blackcurranty Cabernet Sauvignon are also pretty good. Best years: 1997, '96, '94, '92, '91, '90, '88, '87, '84, '80, '76.

CH. BEYCHEVELLE

FRANCE, Bordeaux, Haut-Médoc, St-Julien AC, 4ème Cru Classé

🍷 *Cabernet Sauvignon, Merlot, Cabernet Franc, Petit Verdot*

This beautiful château overlooking the Gironde graciously announces your arrival in ST-JULIEN – the most concentrated stretch of top-quality vineyards in all BORDEAUX, with 85 per cent of the land occupied by great Classed Growths. Although it is ranked only as a Fourth Growth, its quality is usually

Talented Ernst Loosen, in charge at the Dr Loosen estate based in Bernkastel, is one of Germany's leading organic winemakers.

Second. The wine has a beautiful softness even when very young, but takes at least a decade to mature into the fragrant cedar-wood-and-blackcurrant flavour for which St-Julien is famous. When this occurs, Beychevelle is a sublime wine, always expensive, frequently worth the price. Second wine: Réserve de l'Amiral. Best years: 1997, '96, '95, '94, '93, '90, '89, '86, '85, '83, '82.

BEYER

FRANCE, Alsace, Alsace AC

🍷 *Pinot Noir*

🍷 *Riesling, Gewurztraminer, Pinot Gris, Pinot Blanc, Muscat*

Léon Beyer was founded in the 1860s and is a fairly large company, releasing about 800,000 bottles annually. Although Beyer has holdings in the Eguisheim Grands Crus, it is firmly opposed to the Grand Cru system for Alsace, and bottles its finest Riesling, Pinot Gris and Gewurztraminer under the brand names of Cuvée des Comtes d'Eguisheim. These are classic, rich but dry wines and all but the most basic bottlings benefit from bottle aging. The Vendange Tardive and rare Sélection de Grains Nobles can be outstanding. Best years: 1997, '96, '95, '94, '93, '90, '89, '88, '85, '83.

BIANCO DI CUSTOZA DOC

ITALY, Veneto

🍷 *Trebbiano Toscano, Garganega, Tocai and others*

The existence in the south-eastern corner of Lake Garda of quality white wines from a mixed bag of varieties (no less than eight are

allowed) has been documented as far back as the seventeenth century. Today the wine is named after the central commune of Custoza, the zone overlapping with part of the BARDOLINO area. Best producers: Arvedi d'Emilei, Cavalchina (Amedeo), Corte Gardoni, Lazise, Montresor (cru Monte Fiera), Sparici Landini, Le Tende (Oro), Le Vigne di San Pietro (San Pietro), Zeni. Drink most wines as young as possible.

BICAL

This white Portuguese grape variety is known in the DÃO region as Borrado das Moscas ('fly droppings') because of its mottled skin. It is actually very good, full of subtle and intriguing flavours of marzipan, butter, mushroom and spice. BAIRRADA is its main home, where it is capable of producing wines which develop well in bottle with age.

BIDDENDEN

ENGLAND, Kent

🍷 *Dornfelder, Gamay*

🍷 *Ortega, Müller-Thurgau, Reichensteiner and others*

One of England's best and most reliable wine estates, Biddenden has 9ha (22 acres) of vineyards. The land is undulating rather than hilly and is planted almost entirely with Germanic grape varieties. Of these, the Ortega is usually the best, full of slightly sweet, elderflower and apricot fruit, but the basic Müller-Thurgau is also good. The red wine (a blend of Dornfelder and Gamay) is light and attractive, with good cherryish fruit. Most vintages since 1990 have been very difficult.

JOSEF BIFFAR

GERMANY, Pfalz, Deidesheim

🍷 *Riesling, Pinot Blanc (Weissburgunder)*

Throughout the 1990s this medium-sized PFALZ estate made some of the most thrilling Rieslings in the region. Whether dry, off-dry or frankly sweet they were expressive and crystal clear. It remains to be seen if the new winemaker Dirk Roth can live up to the achievements of his predecessor Ulrich Mell. Best years: 1997, '94, '93, '92, '91, '90.

BILBAINAS

SPAIN, La Rioja, Rioja DOC

🍷 *Tempranillo, Grenache Noir (Garnacha Tinta), Graciano, Carignan (Cariñena, Mazuelo)*

🍷 *Macabeo (Viura), Malvasía, Grenache Blanc (Garnacha Blanca)*

Bodegas Bilbainas is an ultra-traditional wine producer that's been changing fast since its acquisition by the giant CODORNÍU group. Now, fashion has forced Bilbainas to abandon its oak-aged whites in favour of modern wines, cool-fermented in stainless steel tanks. The company owns over 243ha (600 acres) of vineyard. After two decades of constantly slipping standards, the hiring of winemaker José Hidalgo (one of the creators of new-age Albariño in GALICIA) in the mid-1990s, plus Codorníu's management savvy, started a dramatic turnaround, best exemplified by its elegant new La Vicalana cuvée. There is also a pleasantly appley CAVA, Royal Carlton. Best years: 1995, '94, '92.

BILLECART-SALMON
FRANCE, Champagne, Champagne AC
🍷 🍷 *Pinot Noir, Chardonnay, Pinot Meunier*
If you want elegance, balance, a gently insistent creaming mousse rather than a spring tide of foam – and a character that is enjoyable young, but thrilling with a few more years' age – Billecart-Salmon is the CHAMPAGNE producer to go for.

This is a small family-owned company, based at Mareuil-sur-Ay, making just over half a million bottles a year. The rosé and various vintage wines are justly famous, but it is Billecart's rare ability to produce totally consistent, totally satisfying, elegant non-vintage Champagne, year in year out, that is Billecart's most important achievement. The finest vintage wines are the stylish Blanc de Blancs, Rosé Cuvée Elisabeth Salmon and the rich, complex Cuvée N.F. Billecart. Best years: 1990, '89, '88, '86, '85, '82.

BIONDI-SANTI
ITALY, Tuscany, Brunello di Montalcino DOCG
🍷 *Sangiovese*
This is the estate that 'invented' BRUNELLO DI MONTALCINO towards the latter part of the nineteenth century. The policy of holding bottles back from certain vintages has enabled Biondi-Santi to put themselves forward as the producers of Italy's longest lasting wine – a card which Franco Biondi-Santi has astutely played throughout his life to command prices which many contend are far too high for the quality. The charge may be true for most vintages, but no-one who has tasted the Riservas of 1891, 1945, '55, '75, '83, '90 and especially of 1964 could deny that they are indeed capable of great longevity, even if they never quite seem to arrive at the point of being a pleasure to drink. The Riservas are made only in top years and only from vines at least 25 years old.

In the 1990s a classic father versus son struggle developed between Franco and his son Jacopo, the latter taking himself off to the estate of Poggio Salvi to do his own thing. The wines he made there included an increasingly well-received varietal Sangiovese called Sassoalloro and a Cabernet/Sangiovese/Merlot blend called Schidione, both easier-drinking wines than those from the paternal estate.

With the dispute now amicably settled and with the help of enologist Vittorio Fiore, Jacopo should be able in the years ahead to bring Biondi-Santi back into the modern world, although the doughty few who can cope with the old style might question whether this is desirable, maintaining that Biondi-Santi's strength lies in its archtraditionalist approach. Best years: 1990, '88, '85, '83, '82, '75, '71.

BISCHÖFLICHE WEINGÜTER
GERMANY, Mosel-Saar-Ruwer, Trier
🍷 *Riesling*
In Mosel terms this is a huge estate, with 97ha (240 acres) of vineyards, and like all big ships it has a large turning circle. However, there is no doubting that with the vintages of the late 1990s it has succeeded in turning. After a period of decline in the '80s, the great majority of the wines once again have the racy, elegant style and clearly defined personalities that they had during the 1960s and '70s when the estate was in the top rank. This improvement is the work of the new assistant director Gernot Kollmann and young cellar master Johannes Becker and it is now an estate to watch. Best years: 1998, '97, '95, '90, '89.

BLAGNY AC
FRANCE, Burgundy, Côte de Beaune
🍷 *Pinot Noir*
🍷 *Chardonnay*
Blagny is a tiny hamlet in the Côte de Beaune straddling the boundary of the more famous communes of PULIGNY-MONTRACHET and MEURSAULT. Its red wine, sold as Blagny, can be fair value if you like a rough, rustic Burgundy. Matrot is the best producer in this style. Olivier LEFLAIVE, on the Puligny side, produces a lighter, more typically fragrant wine. The white wine, characteristically high in acidity, is sold as either Puligny-Montrachet, Meursault Premier Cru or Meursault-Blagny. Best years: (reds) 1997, '96, '95, '93, '92, '90; (whites) 1997, '96, '95, '92, '90.

PAUL BLANCK
FRANCE, Alsace, Alsace AC
🍷 *Pinot Noir*
🍷 *Pinot Gris, Gewurztraminer, Riesling, Pinot Blanc, Muscat, Sylvaner*
The Blanck family of Kientzheim are passionate about their wines. Tasting here can be an exhausting experience, so many and varied are the wines. In addition to the Grand Cru bottlings, there may be other wines from individual vineyards, as well as different bottlings for old vines. Riesling is probably the best wine made, especially from the Grands Crus of Furstentum and Schlossberg, but the Pinot Gris (especially Furstentum) and Gewurztraminer can be spectacular too. The Blancks revel in Vendange Tardive and Sélection de Grains Nobles styles when vintage conditions are appropriate. Best years: 1997, '96, '95, '94, '93, '90, '89, '88, '85, '83.

PAUL BLANCK
This excellent estate makes a wide range of fine wines, including Riesling Vieilles Vignes from the Furstentum Grand Cru, an opulent, concentrated Alsace classic.

BLANQUETTE DE LIMOUX AC
FRANCE, Languedoc-Roussillon
🍷 *Mauzac, Clairette, Chenin Blanc, Chardonnay*
The publicity people for Blanquette de Limoux have made great play of the claim that their product is the oldest sparkling wine in the world and that Dom Pérignon and his chums, who are supposed to have 'invented' CHAMPAGNE in northern France, pinched the idea on their way back from a pilgrimage to Spain. These wine legends are good fun, impossible to prove or disprove, and totally irrelevant to the quality of the drink, which in this case is pretty high.

Blanquette de Limoux is from a hilly region in the AUDE *département*, a surprising place to find a sharp, refreshing sparkling wine, since most southern whites are traditionally flat and dull. The secret lies in the Mauzac grape, which makes up a minimum 90 per cent of the wine and gives it its striking 'green apple skin' flavour. The Champagne method of re-fermentation in the bottle is used to create the sparkle, although the more rustic *méthode rurale*, finishing off the original fermentation inside the bottle, is also used. For some time this very dry, lemon and apple-flavoured wine was accorded second place after Champagne among France's sparkling wines, but the improved quality of the CRÉMANT wines from the Loire, Burgundy and Alsace means this position is now hotly disputed. A certain amount of Chardonnay, Clairette and Chenin Blanc have been planted to give a rounder, deeper, if less individual flavour. Best years: 1996, '95, '94, '93, '92. Best producers: Collin, Delmas, Guinot, Laurens, Martinolles, SIEUR D'ARQUES co-operative (making the bulk of the 6 million bottles produced annually), Terres Blanches.

WOLF BLASS

AUSTRALIA, South Australia, Barossa Zone, Barossa Valley
♦ *Cabernet Sauvignon, Syrah (Shiraz)*
♀ *Riesling, Chardonnay, Colombard*

The 1991 merger with MILDARA has brought significant changes in the Wolf Blass wines: during the '90s Wolf Blass has emerged as the outstanding producer of mid-priced, lime juice Riesling, with a stream of trophies and gold medals reminiscent of the success of Black Label Cabernet Sauvignon in its heyday. Classic White and Chardonnay are both pleasant wines, the sparkling wines are similarly enjoyable. After tinkering around the edges of the red wines, the old adage 'if it ain't broke, don't fix it' has been applied, and the reds continue to have abundant lashings of vanilla-scented American oak. Black Label is the top label for reds. Best years: 1997, '96, '94, '92, '91, '90, '88, '86, '82.

BLUE MOUNTAIN

CANADA, British Columbia, Okanagan Valley VQA
♦ *Pinot Noir, Gamay*
♀ *Chardonnay, Pinot Gris and others*

From the moment they opened in 1992, owners Ian and Jane Mavety met with success, establishing Blue Mountain as the quintessential British Columbia estate winery. Situated on 25ha (62 acres) of rolling vineyard, Blue Mountain has focused on a handful of vinifera grapes led by Pinot Noir and Chardonnay. Other varietals include Pinot Blanc, Gamay Noir and one of the OKANAGAN's best Pinot Gris. Three CHAMPAGNE-method sparklers complete the range of outstanding wines. Despite its emphasis on quality wine the winery remains outside the umbrella of the Vintners Quality Alliance (VQA) organization. Best years: 1998, '95, '94.

BODEGAS Y BEBIDAS

SPAIN

This is Spain's largest wine company. It owns good wine producers such as AGE, CAMPO VIEJO and Marqués del Puerto in RIOJA, Vinícola Navarra in NAVARRA, Casa de la Viña in VALDEPEÑAS and Bodegas y Bebidas in JUMILLA. Away from the top-quality wine scene for years, Bodegas y Bebidas is planning to make up lost ground with a new, independent winery in Rioja, devoted to upscale wines.

JEAN-CLAUDE BOISSET

FRANCE, Burgundy, Nuits-St-Georges
♦ *Pinot Noir, Gamay*
♀ *Chardonnay*

In just over 30 years, Jean-Claude Boisset has expanded this *négociant* company into a vast business. In 1989 colossal cellars were built on the outskirts of NUITS-ST-GEORGES, but Boisset is a major proprietor of other, formerly independent *négociant* businesses throughout France. Within Burgundy itself, well-known names such as Ropiteau, Pierre Ponnelle, Delaunay, Thevenin, Moreau, and Charles Viénot, not to mention Mommessin and Cellier des Samsons in BEAUJOLAIS, are now Boisset brands. The quality of the wines can be mediocre, but two of Boisset's other acquisitions, Bouchard Aîné and Jaffelin, are producing wines of good quality at sensible prices. Boisset's sheer size – about 5 per cent of all Burgundy grapes and wines are purchased by the house – has given it immense influence, which has caused Boisset to be viewed with deep suspicion, and more than a touch of envy, by other Burgundian producers. Best years: 1997, '96, '95, '93, '90.

BOLGHERI DOC

ITALY, Tuscany
♦ ♀ *Cabernet Sauvignon, Cabernet Franc, Merlot, Sangiovese*
♀ *Vermentino, Trebbiano Toscano, Sauvignon Blanc*

Just inland from the Tyrrhenian coast, nestling under the coastal hills, Bolgheri is an improbably picturesque little artists' town, which traditionally has had little to do with wine but which just so happens to be the nearest village to the SASSICAIA estate of Marchese Incisa della Rocchetta. All this is land which, not so long ago, belonged to the Gherardesca family whose various branches – ANTINORIs, Incisas, Zileris, latter-day Gherardescas themselves – have all now climbed upon the Sassicaia bandwagon, leaving just enough space for the odd peasant or personality to squeeze in. The reputation of the Bolgheri DOC rests almost entirely on

LE MACCHIOLE
Vermentino is the traditional grape for the white wines from the Tuscan coast such as Bolgheri Bianco. Now that Sauvignon Blanc and Chardonnay are beginning to dominate the white plantings in the region, wines like this are set to disappear.

Cabernet and Merlot, although Sangiovese does well on its own here – Michele Satta is the only producer to use Sangiovese on its own, since the BORDEAUX blend, with or without some token Sangiovese, sells for much more with a lot less effort. The whites are based traditionally on Vermentino and Trebbiano but now include Sauvignon and Chardonnay. Best producers: Belvedere (Guado al Tasso), Grattamacco, Le Macchiole, ORNELLAIA, SASSICAIA, Michele Satta. Best years: 1998, '97, '93, '90, '88, '85.

BOLLINGER

FRANCE, Champagne, Champagne AC
♦ ♀ *Pinot Noir, Chardonnay, Pinot Meunier*

Far too much Bollinger gets drunk in the wrong way. It has long been the preferred tipple of the English upper classes baying for the sound of broken glass, and their more recent imitations, financial whizz-kids with more money than manners. Which is very unfair on poor old Bollinger, just about the most serious CHAMPAGNE company imaginable.

The non-vintage (called Special Cuvée) is the best-known wine, but the company also produces a range of vintage wines (called Grande Année) which are made in a full, rich style. (Unusually Bollinger ferments its base wine in barrels.) As well as a normal vintage release, it does a Vintage RD. RD stands for *récemment dégorgé* – recently disgorged – showing that the wine has been left in the cellars lying in bottle on its yeast for longer than usual before disgorging, picking up loads of flavour on the way. It also produces Vintage Année Rare – an RD which has spent even longer on its lees, and Vieilles Vignes Françaises Blanc de Noirs – from a single vineyard of incredibly ancient, ungrafted vines in Ay. Impressive stuff. Problems of inconsistency noted in the early 1990s have been resolved and the wines are extremely reliable across the range. Best years: 1990, '89, '88, '85, '82, '79, '75, '70.

BONARDA

You won't often see this red grape outside Italy – and within Italy you'll be lucky to see it far outside the OLTREPÒ PAVESE in LOMBARDY and the COLLI PIACENTINI in EMILIA-ROMAGNA. It makes gulpable red wine full of plums and cherries, lively and scrumptious. It's also known as Croatina, but Bonarda Piemontese is a different variety. New research in Argentina means that clones of Barbera there are now being relabelled as Bonarda. Keep a look out for it.

HENRI BONNEAU

FRANCE, Southern Rhône, Châteauneuf-du-Pape AC
♥ *Grenache, Syrah, Mourvèdre, Cinsaut, Counoise, Vaccarèse*
♀ *Clairette*

Henri Bonneau has become a cult figure in CHÂTEAUNEUF-DU-PAPE, although he himself is almost reclusive. A traditionalist, his Grenache-dominated wines are bold and immensely powerful expressions of the local wine. His 6ha (15 acres) include a substantial proportion of old vines, which helps explain why his wines are so dense. In a ripe vintage he doesn't destem, so the wines tend to be tannic as well as rich, and even after prolonged cask aging they usually need quite a few years in bottle. The wines that make his admirers swoon are the Réserve des Célestins and the only marginally less rich Cuvée Marie Beurrier. Best years: 1997, '96, '95, '94, '92, '90, '89, '88, '86, '85, '83, '81, '79, '78.

DOMAINE BONNEAU DU MARTRAY

FRANCE, Burgundy, Côte de Beaune, Pernand-Vergelesses AC
♥ *Pinot Noir*
♀ *Chardonnay*

Anyone wishing to understand why CORTON-CHARLEMAGNE is such a special and distinctive white Burgundy only need reach for a bottle from Bonneau du Martray, which in most vintages encapsulates the enthralling combination of power and richness that makes this such a celebrated wine. Comte Jean le Bault de la Morinière took over the reins at the family estate in 1994 and has thrown himself into the task with great enthusiasm. The quality of the wine derives from the 11ha (27 acres) of vineyards, which are among the largest holdings within the appellation, rather than from extravagant winemaking techniques. Only about one-third new oak is used, but the wine certainly doesn't lack complexity. These wines are among the most long-lived from an appella-tion that provides many of the grander old Burgundies. The red wines are less exciting, but Le CORTON in particular has been improving in recent years. Best years: (reds) 1997, '96, '95. Best years: (whites) 1997, '96, '95, '94, '92, '90, '88, '86, '85, '83.

BONNES-MARES AC

FRANCE, Burgundy, Côte de Nuits, Grand Cru
♥ *Pinot Noir*

A Grand Cru of 15ha (37 acres), of which 88 per cent is in the commune of CHAMBOLLE-MUSIGNY and the rest is in MOREY-ST-DENIS. This is one of the few Burgundian great names to maintain its consistency during the turmoil of the past few decades – the introduction of strict AC laws for the export trade, the see-saw of the American market, changing fashions in vineyard and cellar – which produced inconsistencies in much top Burgundy. Bonnes-Mares managed to keep its deep, ripe, smoky plum fruit, which starts rich and chewy and matures over 10–20 years into a flavour full of chocolate, smoke again, and pruny depth. Best years: 1997, '96, '95, '93, '90, '89, '88, '85, '78. Best producers: DROUHIN, DUJAC, Groffier, JADOT, G Lignier, ROUMIER, de VOGÜÉ.

BONNEZEAUX AC

FRANCE, Loire, Anjou-Saumur, Grand Cru
♀ *Chenin Blanc*

A wise and prudent few are at last taking an interest in the great sweet whites of the Loire. After a gradual decline after World War Two, there are now 110ha (272 acres) planted out of a possible 130 (321) in Bonnezeaux. The whole Layon Valley, which extends south-east from the Loire near Angers, makes sweet wines (see COTEAUX DU LAYON), but Bonnezeaux and QUARTS DE CHAUME, the other Grand Cru, are potentially the best. However, much of the recent drive to improve the quality of sweet wines in the Layon has come from outside these two Grand Cru areas, which have been slightly inclined to live on their reputation. They have the lowest yields – Bonnezeaux is allowed just 25 hectolitres per hectare and often achieves only 15 hectolitres – and because they can request a higher price than their neighbours, the growers generally wait for noble rot to affect their grapes in late October, or even November, and then pick only the most shrivelled, raisiny grapes.

This is the same winemaking method as in SAUTERNES, but the flavours are different. In the Layon Valley only Chenin Blanc grapes are used, with their very high natural acidity. Consequently Bonnezeaux can seem surprisingly dry at first, because the acidity is masking the sweetness. But give it 10, 20 or even 40 years and the colour deepens to an orange gold, and the sweetness builds to an intense, yet always acid-freshened, peach and apricots richness. Never quite as luscious as Sauternes, it is nonetheless unique, best drunk by itself, or perhaps with some of those peaches and apricots. It's also good with blue cheeses and rich paté, in particular *foie gras*. Best years: 1997, '96, '95, '94, '93, '90, '89, '88, '85, '83, '79, '76, '70, '64, '59, '47. Best producers: Angeli, de FESLES, Petit Val, Petite Croix, Renou.

BONNY DOON

USA, California, Santa Cruz County, Santa Cruz Mountains AVA
♥ *Grenache, Mourvedre, Syrah and others*
♀ *Mourvedre, Grenache*
♀ *Marsanne, Roussanne, Chardonnay and others*

Randall Grahm started out as a Francophile with a special itch to show CALIFORNIA what grape varieties from France's RHÔNE VALLEY can do. His main red, Le Cigare Volant, is Grenache-based, but uses a varying roster of other grapes to achieve its deep, raspberryish flavours. Old Telegram is Grahm's paean to CHÂTEAUNEUF-DU-PAPE's Domaine du VIEUX TÉLÉGRAPHE, and now made entirely from Mourvedre. Both are husky and heady in emulation of the wines that inspired them. Mourvedre is also used for a fine dry rosé, Vin Gris de Mourvedre. His main white, Le Sophiste, began by blending Marsanne and Roussanne, but he favours Roussanne much more today. Syrah, Zinfandel and Riesling remain among his favourites. Grahm's imagination is now being applied to grappa, fruit brandies, and a host of Italian varieties and blends. Best years: (Le Cigare Volant) 1997, '96, '95, '94, '93, '92, '91, '90, '87; (Old Telegram) 1997, '96, '95, '94, '93, '92, '91, '90, '87, '86.

BONNY DOON
Randall Grahm is one of California's most innovative winemakers and Le Cigare Volant is his homage to France's famous red wine from Châteauneuf-du-Pape.

BORDEAUX France

BORDEAUX CARRIES A HEAVY RESPONSIBILITY, because just about every wine book describes it as the greatest wine region in the world. Is it? Well, yes, and no. It has produced many of the world's most famous red wines over the last 150 years – the great Classed Growths of Pauillac and Margaux, the sumptuous St-Émilions and exotic Pomerols. It has produced many of the greatest sweet wines of the world from the villages of Sauternes and Barsac. More recently it has produced a string of world-class, barrel-fermented dry whites from Pessac-Léognan. And indeed there is probably more fine wine being made in Bordeaux now than ever before, while worldwide, each year produces a veritable flood of wines based on the principles of winemaking in Bordeaux. Based on the red Cabernet Sauvignon, Cabernet Franc, Merlot and Pinot Verdot grapes; based on the white Sémillon and Sauvignon Blanc; based on trying to recreate the almost inexpressible beauty of fruit that is ripe, but not too ripe, oak that is sweet, but not too sweet, tannins that are firm, but fond, perfumes that beguile, but do not overpower, memories that linger in the brain more than the heart, satisfaction expressed with a sigh of intellectual contentment rather than a gourmand's bellowed shout for more.

This is the Bordeaux of legend – and reality. But this reality is only a small proportion of the whole Bordeaux. This reality is based upon the miracle of perfectly sited vineyards on the Médoc's gravel banks, on the limestone slopes of St-Émilion, on the sticky clays of Pomerol, on the banks of the tiny river Ciron in Sauternes. Here nature conspires with a cool, damp and unpredictable climate to allow grapes to creep to a mellow ripeness as the autumn fades to winter, the harvest almost never being complete before the storm clouds hurtle in from the Bay of Biscay. On the knife-edge between ripening and failing to ripen, these top wines achieve a balance and a beauty that wines from the warmer, more reliable conditions of California's Napa Valley, Australia's Coonawarra, Chile's Maipo or South Africa's Stellenbosch seldom achieve.

But these are the top wines. Most of Bordeaux is not on gravel – it's on the various heavy clays laid down over the millennia by the Dordogne and Garonne rivers. Most of the vineyards do not have special aspects towards the sun, special protected mesoclimates hiding them from wind and rain. Most of Bordeaux, in truth, is pleasant but ordinary, it's wine unexceptional, often dull, often lacking ripeness and definition. Indeed, although Bordeaux is thought of above all as a red wine Nirvana, red grapes ripen with difficulty in the lesser vineyards which would in any case be more suited to producing rosé or white. But the world wants to drink red Bordeaux. History tells 'twas ever thus.

Although the vineyards were initially established by the Romans in St-Émilion, it was the period between 1152 and 1453, when Bordeaux belonged to the English, that laid the foundation for today. Benefiting from direct access to the sea, its wines – almost all red – were enthusiastically drunk all over northern Europe, and consequently a taste for red Bordeaux – or claret as the English called it – was taken with their traders to all the other continents, in particular North America.

As a result, Bordeaux became immensely wealthy and the vineyards became dominated by large estates – called châteaux – and a powerful merchant trading elite. This system still holds today, though the prices that top Bordeaux properties can demand are now so high that many properties are now owned by commercial conglomerates rather than by the families who built their reputations. And, alongside these ritzy superstars, are the rest of the 10,000 growers who struggle to grow the remainder of the 500 million bottles produced annually.

Ch. Pichon-Longueville-Comtesse-de-Lalande is Bordeaux's leading 'Super-Second' wine. With vineyards on excellent land, the estate has been run since 1978 by the inspirational figure of Madame de Lencquesaing.

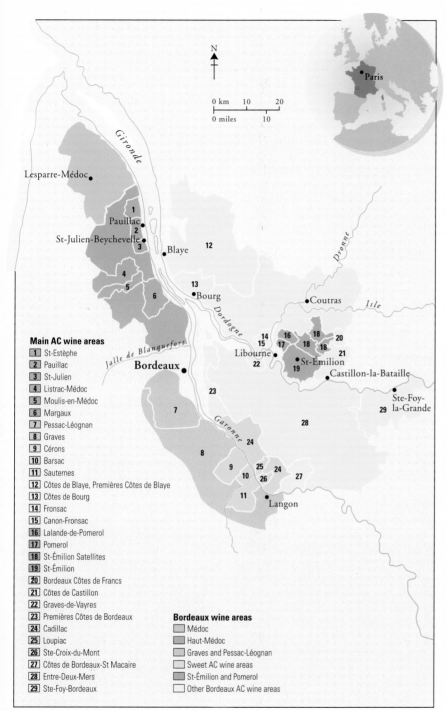

Main AC wine areas

1. St-Estèphe
2. Pauillac
3. St-Julien
4. Listrac-Médoc
5. Moulis-en-Médoc
6. Margaux
7. Pessac-Léognan
8. Graves
9. Cérons
10. Barsac
11. Sauternes
12. Côtes de Blaye, Premières Côtes de Blaye
13. Côtes de Bourg
14. Fronsac
15. Canon-Fronsac
16. Lalande-de-Pomerol
17. Pomerol
18. St-Émilion Satellites
19. St-Émilion
20. Bordeaux Côtes de Francs
21. Côtes de Castillon
22. Graves-de-Vayres
23. Premières Côtes de Bordeaux
24. Cadillac
25. Loupiac
26. Ste-Croix-du-Mont
27. Côtes de Bordeaux-St Macaire
28. Entre-Deux-Mers
29. Ste-Foy-Bordeaux

Bordeaux wine areas

- Médoc
- Haut-Médoc
- Graves and Pessac-Léognan
- Sweet AC wine areas
- St-Émilion and Pomerol
- Other Bordeaux AC wine areas

AC ENTRIES

Barsac, Bordeaux, Bordeaux Clairet, Bordeaux-Côtes de Francs, Bordeaux Supérieur, Cadillac, Canon-Fronsac, Cérons, Côtes de Blaye, Côtes de Bourg, Côtes de Castillon, Entre-Deux-Mers, Fronsac, Graves, Haut-Médoc, Lalande-de-Pomerol, Listrac-Médoc, Loupiac, Margaux, Médoc, Moulis, Pauillac, Pessac-Léognan, Pomerol, Premières Côtes de Blaye, Premières Côtes de Bordeaux, St-Émilion, St-Émilion Grand Cru Classé, St-Émilion Premier Grand Cru Classé, St-Émilion Satellites, St-Estèphe, St-Julien, Ste-Croix-du-Mont, Sauternes.

SEE ALSO

Graves & Pessac-Léognan, pages 190–191, Médoc, pages 242–243, St-Émilion & Pomerol, pages 326–327, and Sauternes, pages 336–337.

CH. PÉTRUS

This rich, exotic, succulent wine, from almost 100 per cent Merlot, is one of the world's most expensive red wines, and often one of the greatest too, as a result of the caring genius of the Moueix family, Pétrus' co-owners since 1962.

CH. MOUTON-ROTHSCHILD

The most magnificently rich and indulgent of the great Bordeaux reds when young, , the wine takes 15–20 years to open up fully to its brilliant blackcurrant and cigar box best.

CH. REYNON

This stylish white wine, from a blend of Sémillon and Sauvignon Blanc, is made by the brilliant enology professor, Denis Dubourdieu.

CH. CITRAN

This large Cru Bourgeois estate produces a wine that is usually big, plump and richly extracted with a very ripe blackcurrant and new oak bouquet.

CH. ROQUEFORT

Straight red Bordeaux wine such as this one should have a bone-dry grassy fruit and an attractive earthy edge.

CH. MARGAUX

This is the most consistently excellent and fragrantly perfumed of the great Médoc wines.

CH. D'YQUEM

At its best this sublime wine is undoubtedly one of the best sweet wines in the world.

BORDEAUX AC

FRANCE, Bordeaux

🍷 🍷 *Cabernet Sauvignon, Merlot, Cabernet Franc, Petit Verdot, Malbec*

🍷 *Sémillon, Sauvignon Blanc, Muscadelle and others*
See also Bordeaux, pages 90–91

The simple Bordeaux AC is one of the most important ACs in France and, at the same time, one of the most abused. Its importance lies in the fact that it can apply to the red as well as to the dry, medium and sweet white wines of the entire Gironde *département*, the largest fine wine area in the world. Most of the best wines are allowed more specific geographical ACs, such as SAUTERNES or MARGAUX, yet a vast amount of unambitious but potentially enjoyable wine is sold as Bordeaux AC. Indeed, straight red Bordeaux – frequently known as 'claret' in Britain – is one of the most recognizable of all 'generic' wines. It often has a fresh, grassy fruit and an attractive, earthy edge. But standards vary: much Bordeaux Rouge is pretty raw.

Bordeaux Blanc, on the other hand, had until recently become a byword for flabby, fruitless, over-sulphured brews. But quality has picked up, and there are now very many pleasant, clean wines, frequently under a merchant's rather than a château label, which make refreshing drinking. Cool fermentation in stainless steel tanks to preserve the fruit aromas of the grapes, and occasional steeping of the juice and grape skins together after crushing but before fermentation (a process which dramatically increases fruit flavours) are the keys to improved quality. Whites with less than 4 grams of sugar per litre are labelled Bordeaux Sec or Vin Sec de Bordeaux. Since many of these are 100 per cent Sauvignon wines, the grape name may also be used on the label.

The Bordeaux AC also applies to wines made in superior appellations, but in the wrong style. White wine made in the red wine ACs of the MÉDOC can only be AC Bordeaux, and red, rosé or dry white wines made in the sweet wine ACs of Sauternes and BARSAC are also only allowed the Bordeaux AC (or BORDEAUX SUPÉRIEUR for reds). With rare exceptions (like Ygrec from Ch. d'YQUEM, and Pavillon Blanc from Ch. MARGAUX), all AC Bordeaux Blanc wines should be drunk as young as possible; good Bordeaux Rouge may cope with a year or so of aging. Best years: (reds) 1998, '96, '95, '90, '89. Best producers: (reds) Arromans, Bonnet, de Roques, Sichel, Terrefort, Thieuley, Tour de Mirambeau; (whites) Carsin, DOISY-DAËNE, Reynon, de Sours, Thieuley, Tour de Mirambeau.

BORDEAUX CLAIRET AC

FRANCE, Bordeaux

🍷 *Cabernet Sauvignon, Cabernet Franc, Merlot*

A pale red wine, almost rosé in fact, which can be an excellent way to use red grapes that aren't quite ripe. The name 'claret', which is applied to any red wine from BORDEAUX, derives from *clairet*. What this means is that a few hundred years ago all Bordeaux reds were made in a light, early-drinking style. As winemaking knowledge improved, the reds became darker and stronger, and Bordeaux Clairet almost faded away. Interestingly, a few ritzy Classed Growth properties in the MÉDOC still make a little to have with lunch.

BORDEAUX–CÔTES DE FRANCS AC

FRANCE, Bordeaux

🍷 *Merlot, Cabernet Sauvignon, Cabernet Franc, Malbec*

🍷 *Sémillon, Sauvignon Blanc, Muscadelle*

Bordeaux-Côtes de Francs, a tiny area on the eastern fringe of ST-ÉMILION with good clay and limestone soil, has the warmest and driest mesoclimate in BORDEAUX. Its potential for wine is immense – at the best properties, closely controlled yields plus the use of new oak barrels give the wines a remarkable concentration of fruit, deep plum and blackberry flavours, strengthened by tannin and oak spice. The Thienpont family, owners of Puygueraud and other estates, have long been the driving forces in the AC. Investment from other St-Émilion winemaking families has also given the region a boost. As the vineyards mature, we can expect great things in the future. Best years: 1998, '97, '96, '95, '94, '90, '89, '88, '86, '85. Best producers: (reds) Charmes-Godard, de Francs, Laclaverie, Marsau, Moulin la Pitié, la Prade, Puygueraud.

About 10 per cent of the million or so bottles produced a year is white. Most of it is dry, though sweet wine is permitted under the Côtes de Francs Liquoreux AC. Quality from the top estates is fairly good.

CH. PUYGUERAUD
The flagship estate for the tiny Côtes de Francs AC makes tannic, robust and complex wines with good potential for aging.

BORDEAUX SUPÉRIEUR AC

FRANCE, Bordeaux

🍷 🍷 *Cabernet Sauvignon, Cabernet Franc, Merlot, Petit Verdot, Malbec*

This appellation covers the whole of the Bordeaux region, as does the BORDEAUX AC. The difference is that Supérieur must have an extra half a degree of alcohol for red and rosé, a lower yield from the vines, and is not allowed on the market until the September following the vintage, eliciting a longer period of maturation. This makes a considerable difference to the quality, the wines generally being more concentrated and structured, sometimes with an added note of vanilla from aging in new oak barrels. Statistically, 75 per cent of the production is bottled at the property, the reverse of Bordeaux AC. Almost all the *petits châteaux* which represent affordable drinking in Bordeaux will be Bordeaux Supérieur. Best producers: Abbaye de St-Ferme, Barreyre, de Bouillerot, de Courteillac, Grand Verdus, Jonqueyres, Méaume, de Parenchère, Penin, Reignac, de Seguin, Trocard. Best years: 1998, '96, '95, '90, '89.

BORGO DEL TIGLIO

ITALY, Friuli-Venezia Giulia, Collio DOC

🍷 *Merlot, Cabernet Sauvignon*

🍷 *Tocai Friulano, Chardonnay, Malvasia Istriana, Sauvignon Blanc, Riesling Renano, Verduzzo*

Nicola Manferrari comes from a long line of viticulturalists. On his 9ha (22 acres) or so spread over three vineyards he makes reds and whites varietally or blended (the blends changing constantly). Although most of his grapes are white, from which he produces some impressive barrel-fermented wines, he is perhaps most respected for his Rosso della Centa. This is a barrique-aged varietal Merlot and shows the potential of this grape in the Collio region. Best years: (Rosso della Centa) 1994, '93, '90.

PODERI BOSCARELLI

ITALY, Tuscany, Vino Nobile di Montepulciano DOCG

🍷 *Sangiovese, Cabernet Sauvignon and others*

This estate, situated in the Cervognano subzone which some consider the best in the VINO NOBILE DI MONTEPULCIANO DOCG, has proceeded by stages since its purchase in 1962 by Egidio Corradi to its present position as challenger for pre-eminence among all Vino Nobile growers. The tragic loss by the current owner Paola Corradi of her husband Ippolito De Ferrari in 1983 pushed her to take on consulting enologist Maurizio Castelli and to instil in her sons Luca and Niccolò, who today share the responsibilities of the estate, her passion and commitment to high quality.

Today the 13ha (32 acres) of vineyard, principally of Sangiovese, with small amounts of Cabernet Sauvignon, Merlot and Syrah among red varieties, are being gradually replanted to superior clones at higher densities and the *cantina* re-equipped to facilitate optimum extraction from the carefully cultivated fruit. The Sangiovese-based wines are all marked by concentration of flavour and charm of aroma allied to a great finesse. Indeed the higher crus – Vino Nobile Vigna del Nocio and the SUPER-TUSCAN Boscarelli – are endowed with a structure which, while allowing for relatively early drinkability, will also enable lengthy aging. Best years: 1995, '94, '93, '90, '88, '86, '85.

DOMAINE BOTT-GEYL

FRANCE, Alsace, Alsace AC
♀ *Pinot Gris, Gewurztraminer, Riesling, Pinot Blanc, Sylvaner, Muscat*

This estate, based in Beblenheim just north of Colmar, is a relative newcomer to Alsace, having been founded in 1947. It has substantial holdings in Grand Cru Sonnenglanz and smaller parcels in three other Grands Crus, Mandelberg, Furstentum and Schoenenbourg. Until the early 1990s the reputation of this house was middling but the arrival of the new generation in the form of Jean-Christophe Bott has seen a considerable improvement in quality. The best wines are usually the Gewurztraminer and the Pinot Gris from Sonnenglanz, but the Muscat can be excellent too. Best years: 1997, '96, '95, '94, '93, '92, '90.

BOUCHARD FINLAYSON

SOUTH AFRICA, Western Cape, Walker Bay
♂ *Pinot Noir, Sangiovese, Nebbiolo, Merlot*
♀ *Chardonnay, Sauvignon Blanc and others*

Peter Finlayson's fascination with Pinot Noir began when he was winemaker at HAMILTON

BOUCHARD FINLAYSON
The powerful, firm Galpin Peak Pinot Noir from cool-climate Walker Bay has elevated Cape Pinot wines to a new level of excitement.

RUSSELL but the realization of the quality really possible in the southern reaches of the Hemel-en-Aarde valley came when he established vineyards next door in the late 1980s. He was joined in this venture by Burgundy's Paul Bouchard, who wanted a foreign interest but not to follow where all his fellow countrymen had gone. Burgundian clones and viticultural methods provide wines with a good concentration of colour, fruit and tannin. Galpin Peak, as the home-grown Pinot is called, makes a forceful argument for grappling with this difficult variety in the Cape, which is normally too warm. Chardonnay is drawn from home vineyards and also from much higher spots, some close to the snow line. Whether barrel-fermented or unoaked, these wines are well-layered and elegant. Finlayson is an inveterate experimentalist; he also produces a varying number of unoaked Sauvignon Blancs and has 'invented' an original blend of Sangiovese, Nebbiolo and Pinot Noir; only one vintage so far, made in tiny, non-commercial quantities. Best years: (Pinot Noir) 1997, '96, '95, '94, '93, '92, '91.

BOUCHARD PÈRE ET FILS

FRANCE, Burgundy, Beaune
♂ *Pinot Noir*
♀ *Chardonnay*

Bouchard have always had one great claim to fame: the ownership of 71ha (175 acres) of Premier and Grand Cru sites in the Côte d'Or, along with their 24ha (60 acres) of village wines. The company is based in old buildings close to Beaune's town walls, and the vast Bouchard cellars are dug beneath the medieval bastions. The firm prided itself on being able to supply older vintages of its numerous wines. In addition to their domaine wines, Bouchard purchased grapes.

However, since the 1970s, if not before, quality had been deeply disappointing. With trembling hand, one raised a glass of MONTRACHET or Chevalier-Montrachet and, tasting it, realized it was scarcely worth its reputation, let alone price. The reds were usually marginally better than the whites. In the mid-1980s the company invested heavily in new cellars, but even this did not seem to raise the quality level significantly. Implication in a wine scandal in the 1980s certainly didn't help and seems to have demoralized the Bouchards. In 1995 the last of the Bouchards, Jean-François, sold the company to Joseph Henriot, hitherto known as a CHAMPAGNE producer. Henriot lost no time in improving the quality. He began by throwing out or

BOUCHARD PÈRE ET FILS
One of the outstanding wines from this important merchant and vineyard owner is the deep, plummy red Corton which needs eight to ten years of aging.

declassifying many thousands of bottles, including quite a few from the most prestigious appellations that he felt, rightly, were unworthy of the name. Quality improved overnight, or to be exact from the 1995 vintage, and from now on Bouchard Père et Fils, with its fabulous vineyards and resources, will be a force to be reckoned with. Henriot does not like his acquisition to be thought of as a *négociant*, preferring to present it as a great domaine that also buys in grapes. Best years: (reds) 1997, '96, '95, '93, '90, '89, '85; (whites) 1997, '96, '95, '92, '90, '89, '86.

HENRI BOURGEOIS

FRANCE, Central Loire, Sancerre AC
♂ *Pinot Noir*
♀ *Sauvignon Blanc*

This well-run grower and *négociant* business in the little village of Chavignol is both one of the largest concerns and one of the top producers in this part of the LOIRE Valley. Commitment and quality are hallmarks of the Bourgeois operation, despite its size. The company is now run by Jean-Marie Bourgeois in tandem with his son, Arnaud, and Jean-Christophe, a cousin and the winemaker. Bought-in grapes and must represent 40 per cent of their production with the rest coming from their own vineyards; the Bourgeois work closely with their suppliers, who all have long-term contracts.

The wide range of wines, ranging from Sauvignon Vin de Pays du Jardin de la France to the top non-wooded cuvée, la Bourgeoise, are always well made. Étienne Henri is vinified in oak and le MD comes from vineyards on the Côte des Monts Damnés, the very steep slopes that overlook Chavignol. Most of these slopes were abandoned after phylloxera and the Bourgeois have been instrumental in their replanting over the past 20 years. La Demoiselle de Bourgeois is the name of their POUILLY-FUMÉ wine. Best years: 1998, '97, '96, '95, '93, '90, '89.

BOURGOGNE (Burgundy) France

THE NAME BOURGOGNE (Burgundy in English) always seems to be more suitable for red wine than white. It sort of booms: it's a rich, weighty sound, purple rather than pale, haunches of venison and flagons of plum-ripe red rather than a half-dozen oysters and Chablis.

Yet white Burgundy is nowadays at least as important as red Burgundy, possibly more so. The term Burgundy applies to a large swathe of eastern France which at one time was the Grand Duchy reaching right up to the North Sea, way down to beyond Lyon and across to the mountains guarding Switzerland and Italy. What is now left of this grandeur is some inspiring architecture – and a tradition of eating and drinking which still makes gourmets describe it greedily as the 'belly' of France. Modern Burgundy starts at Chablis in the north, stretching down through the Côte d'Or south of Dijon, the Côte Chalonnaise and on to the Mâconnais and Beaujolais. In all of these areas, except Beaujolais, white wine is of crucial importance and in two – Chablis and the Mâconnais – red wine is almost irrelevant.

The two most important grapes are the white Chardonnay and the red Pinot Noir. Chardonnay is the grape of Chablis, of the great white wine villages of the Côte d'Or, the Côte Chalonnaise and the Mâconnais to the south. In each region it makes marvellously individual wines that have been copied the world over. Pinot Noir is most important in the great red wine villages of the Côte d'Or, and also in the Côte Chalonnaise. Aligoté plays a significant though second-fiddle role in the Côte Chalonnaise and Gamay is largely derided except in the Beaujolais where it excels.

Between Dijon and Chagny lies the thin sliver of land called the Côte d'Or – the Golden Slope. The northern section, the Côte de Nuits, is almost entirely red wine country with villages such as Gevrey-Chambertin, Morey-St-Denis Chambolle-Musigny, Vougeot and Vosne-Romanée producing compellingly powerful wines. The Côte de Beaune, as well as red, produces fabulously rich white wines from the villages of Aloxe-Corton, Meursault, Puligny-Montrachet and Chassagne-Montrachet.

Côte Chalonnaise whites used to be mostly made into sparkling wine, but Rully, Mercurey and Montagny are now showing they can produce lovely whites and reds without the help of bubbles. Mâconnais wines are mostly simple and refreshing, but in Pouilly-Fuissé and St-Véran a few producers are creating excellent whites. Beaujolais, a large area that tumbles up and down the granite hills between the Mâconnais and Lyon is regarded as part of Burgundy, but the style of wine is completely different, being a bright breezy gluggable red made from Gamay.

Harvesting Pinot Noir at Auxey-Duresses in the Côte de Beaune. For quality wines in Burgundy hand-picking is still the normal method used, especially for Pinot Noir grapes which are very difficult to detach from their stalks.

The various top Burgundy villages along the Côte d'Or have a great deal in common: the subsoil is limestone and most of the vineyards face east or south-east. Yet what makes great Burgundy such a fascinating wine is the subtle nuances that distinguish one fine wine from another. In the Côte de Beaune, Volnay and Pommard are neighbouring villages but the wines are extremely different, Volnay being delicate and elegant, while Pommard is richer and more rustic. These nuances are conserved in the cru system which ranks all Burgundy's vineyards into a hierarchy based, supposedly, on quality. A Grand Cru wine should be the finest (and most costly), followed by Premier Cru and Village wines. At the bottom of the scale are simple Bourgogne wines, which are usually from vines planted outside the boundaries of the best-known villages. Grands Crus are only encountered on the Côte d'Or and in Chablis. In practice, however, the reputation and track record of individual producers counts for as much, if not more, than the status of the vineyard.

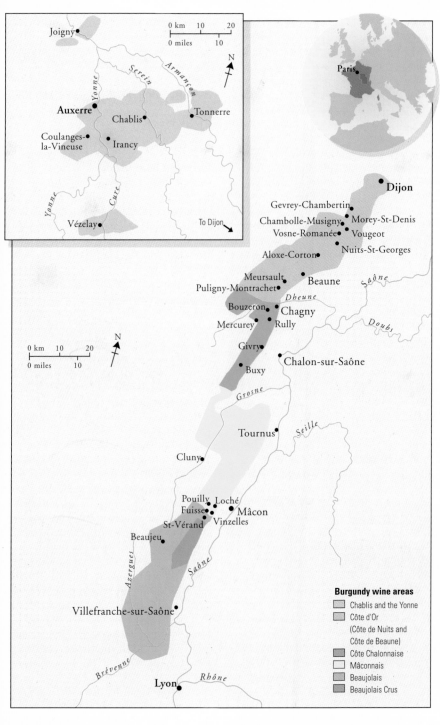

Burgundy wine areas
- Chablis and the Yonne
- Côte d'Or
  (Côte de Nuits and
  Côte de Beaune)
- Côte Chalonnaise
- Mâconnais
- Beaujolais
- Beaujolais Crus

LOUIS MICHEL & FILS

This unoaked Chablis has an array of delicate stone-fruit flavours and honey and increases in richness with age.

LOUIS JADOT

From one of Beaune's top merchants, this wine is often thought of as being Grand Cru quality.

DOMAINE ANNE GROS

Anne Gros makes one of the best wines from Clos Vougeot – dark-coloured, sweetly oaky, yet very fine and elegant.

BOUCHARD PÈRE & FILS

The Corton-Charlemagne Grand Cru at the top of the famous Corton hill produces some of Burgundy's top whites.

JOSEPH DROUHIN

The Beaune Clos des Mouches wines, both red and white, are some of the best Drouhin wines.

CH. FUISSÉ

Jean-Jacques Vincent is the leading grower in Pouilly-Fuissé, producing rich, ripe concentrated Chardonnay.

GEORGES DUBOEUF

Duboeuf's top Beaujolais wines are those he bottles for small growers, including la Tour du Bief in Moulin-à-Vent.

REGIONAL ENTRIES

Aloxe-Corton, Auxey-Duresses, Bâtard-Montrachet, Beaujolais, Beaujolais Nouveau, Beaujolais-Villages, Beaune, Blagny, Bonnes-Mares, Bourgogne, Bourgogne-Côte Chalonnaise, Bourgogne Grand Ordinaire, Bourgogne-Hautes Côtes de Beaune, Bourgogne-Hautes Côtes de Nuits, Bourgogne-Passe-Tout-Grains, Brouilly, Chablis, Chablis Grand Cru, Chablis Premier Cru, Chambertin, Chambolle-Musigny, Chassagne-Montrachet, Chénas, Chiroubles, Chorey-lès-Beaune, Clos de la Roche, Clos de Vougeot, Corton, Corton-Charlemagne, Côte de Beaune, Côte de Brouilly, Côte de Nuits-Villages, Coteaux du Lyonnais, Crémant de Bourgogne, Échézeaux, Fixin, Fleurie, Gevrey-Chambertin, Givry, Irancy, Juliénas, Ladoix, Mâcon, Maranges, Marsannay, Mercurey, Meursault, Montagny, Monthélie, le Montrachet, Morey-St-Denis, Morgon, Moulin-à-Vent, Musigny, Nuits-St-Georges, Pernand-Vergelesses, Pommard, Pouilly-Fuissé, Pouilly-Loché, Puligny-Montrachet, Régnié, Richebourg, la Romanée, Rully, St-Amour, St-Aubin, St-Romain, St-Véran, Santenay, Savigny-lès-Beaune, la Tâche, Volnay, Vosne-Romanée, Vougeot.

SEE ALSO

Chablis, pages 120–121, and Côte d'Or, pages 146–147.

BOURGOGNE AC

FRANCE, Burgundy

🍷 🍷 *Pinot Noir, Gamay*

🍷 *Chardonnay, Pinot Blanc, Pinot Gris (Pinot Beurot), Aligoté*

See also Bourgogne, pages 94–95

BOURGOGNE is the French name we have anglicized as 'Burgundy'. As a generic appellation, from CHABLIS in the north way down to BEAUJOLAIS some 290km (180 miles) to the south, it mops up all the wine with no specific AC of its own. There are massive differences in style and quality.

Pinot Noir is the red Burgundy grape, and is used for most Bourgogne Rouge. Yet around Chablis the local varieties César and Tressot occur (albeit rarely), and Gamay in the Mâconnais and Beaujolais. As for quality, well, some of the less reputable merchants buy wine from any source so long as the price is low. On the other hand, some unlucky but dedicated growers possess land only entitled to the simple Bourgogne AC yet lavish on it the same devotion as on a Grand Cru.

Red Bourgogne is usually light, overtly fruity in a breezy, upfront, strawberry and cherry way, but if the perfume is there, no-one minds if the flavour is a bit simple. It should be drunk young – two to three years' aging is enough – and it shouldn't be fussed over too much; just enjoy it. The better merchants' blends usually come into this category. Sometimes, however, it can be much more than this, the cherry and strawberry fruit deeper, thickened into a plummy richness, and perhaps with the creamy softness of some oak-barrel aging added in. Made from Pinot Noir, Bourgogne Rosé can be a pleasant pink wine but very little is produced.

Bourgogne Blanc may be either an elegant, classy, dry white of marvellous, nutty character or an overpriced washout, depending on how the appellation has been interpreted. In general, Chardonnay is used, but there is some Pinot Blanc and Pinot Beurot, as Pinot Gris is known here, thrown in for good measure. Usually Bourgogne Blanc will be a bone-dry wine from vineyards not considered quite good enough for a classier appellation, but vaguely in the same style. So a Bourgogne Blanc from the Yonne region will usually be light, slightly tart and refreshing, one from the Côte d'Or might have some of the nutty fullness of nearby MEURSAULT, while one from the Mâconnais will probably be fatter and rather appley.

If the wine is from a grower the flavours will follow regional style. However, if the address on the label is of a Côte d'Or merchant, the wine could be from anywhere in Burgundy. The best wines usually come from a single grower who has declassified some of the wine from his top label, either because it lacked the necessary concentration, or because the vines are outside the appellation boundaries. Best years: (reds) 1997, '96, '95, '93, '90. Best producers: (reds, growers) BARTHOD-NOËLLAT, BURGUET, COCHE-DURY, Germain, d'Heuilly-Huberdeau, Lafarge, MÉO-CAMUZET, Morey, Parent, Patrice Rion, Rossignol; (reds, merchants) DROUHIN, FAIVELEY, JADOT, Labouré-Roi, LEROY, Vallet; (co-operatives) BUXY and Hautes-Côtes. Most Bourgogne Blanc should be drunk within two years, but those matured in oak can age well. Best years: (whites) 1997, '96, '95, '92. Best producers: (whites, growers) Boisson-Morey, Boisson-Vadot, Boyer-Martenot, Henri Clerc, Coche-Dury, Javillier, C & R Jobard, F Jobard, René Manuel, Roulot; (whites, merchants) Drouhin, Faiveley, Jadot, Labouré-Roi, Olivier LEFLAIVE; Buxy co-operative.

A ET P DE VILLAINE
The Bourgogne-Côte Chalonnaise AC is rapidly gaining a good reputation and there are some excellent producers making both red and white wines.

BOURGOGNE-CÔTE CHALONNAISE AC

FRANCE, Burgundy, Côte Chalonnaise

🍷 *Pinot Noir, Gamay*

🍷 *Chardonnay, Aligoté*

Compared to its northerly neighbour, the CÔTE DE BEAUNE, the Côte Chalonnaise is a more traditionally rural world where the vine is merely one part of the texture of rustic life. As a result, it is the least known of all the Burgundy regions. The area was given its own generic appellation in 1990, created to cover 240ha (593 acres) of vines in the Saône-et-Loire *département* around the villages of Bouzeron, RULLY, MERCUREY, GIVRY and MONTAGNY, which all have their own ACs. The Côte Chalonnaise vineyards could almost be thought of as an extension of the CÔTE D'OR, since they are directly to the south, but they are far less cohesive. Despite the lack of renown, the area has gained enormously in importance in the last few years,

particularly as a result of the spiralling price of white Burgundy. Best years: 1997, '96, '95, '94, '93, '92, '90. Best producers: Besson, BUXY co-operative, Goubard, de Villaine.

BOURGOGNE GRAND ORDINAIRE AC

FRANCE, Burgundy

🍷 🍷 *Gamay, Pinot Noir, César, Tressot*

🍷 *Chardonnay, Aligoté, Pinot Blanc and others*

This is the only French AC to admit in its name that the wine may actually be pretty duff stuff but you hardly ever see it. Chardonnay (though anyone who uses this for 'BGO' – as the locals call it – must be nuts), Aligoté, Pinot Blanc, Pinot Beurot, Sacy and Melon de Bourgogne (the MUSCADET grape which was supposedly banished from Burgundy generations ago for being too boring) can be used for whites, and Gamay, Pinot Noir, César and Tressot for the reds. It's mostly sold as quaffing wine for the local bars – for which it can be perfectly suitable, especially if you add a splash of cassis.

BOURGOGNE-HAUTES CÔTES DE BEAUNE AC

FRANCE, Burgundy, Côte d'Or

🍷 *Pinot Noir*

🍷 *Chardonnay, Pinot Blanc*

These wines come from vineyards set back in the hills behind the great CÔTE DE BEAUNE slopes. If scenery could influence what went into the bottle, this lost little region of twisting country lanes, ancient trees and purest sylvan peace would surely produce ecstatic wines. However, in this higgledy-piggledy landscape, the aspect of the sun is rarely ideal and the altitude, at 350–400m (1150–1300ft), is also a handicap; all the best vineyard sites on the Côte de Beaune itself are below 300m (1000ft). So don't expect wines with very ripe flavours. If the price of decent red Burgundy had not been pushed through the roof during the 1970s, we probably wouldn't be hearing too much of the AC at all. This forced merchants to replant derelict vineyards.

Now, the area is reasonably prosperous and the wines are fairly good. Only in exceptional years like 1990 and '96 will they attain the quality of Côte de Beaune, but in their light, raspberry-fresh way, they often give a purer view of what Pinot Noir should taste like than many supposedly classier offerings. Best years: (reds) 1997, '96, '95, '93, '90.

There's some white wine too, and the 20 villages entitled to the AC can produce pleasant, slightly sharp Chardonnay and, under the Bourgogne-Aligoté AC, some good, ultra-dry Aligoté. In really hot years the Chardonnay can even take on a dry, but discernibly nutty, taste after a couple of years in bottle, which ever so slightly might remind you of a wispy CHASSAGNE-MONTRACHET. Best years: (whites) 1997, '96, '95, '94, '93, '92. Best producers: Carré, Caves des Hautes-Côtes, C Cornu, L Jacob, Joliot, Marcilly, Ch. de Mercey, Naudin-Ferrand, M Serveau.

BOURGOGNE-HAUTES CÔTES DE NUITS AC

FRANCE, Burgundy, Côte d'Or
♦ *Pinot Noir*
♀ *Chardonnay*

The relatively compact Hautes Côtes de Nuits vineyards belong to 18 villages directly behind the Côte de Nuits, and there are just over 500ha (1235 acres) planted, mostly with red grapes. Inevitably, altitude, averaging 400m (1300ft), is a problem and frequently the land over this height is just scrub. So ripening of the grapes, above all of Pinot Noir, is by no means guaranteed. The granting of AC to the Hautes Côtes de Nuits and BOURGOGNE-HAUTES CÔTES DE BEAUNE in 1961 acted as a spur, and several growers, in particular Hudelot and Thévenot, planted large estates. They were followed by the merchant houses, and the establishment of the Caves des Hautes-Côtes co-operative in 1968 gave cohesion to the area.

The wines are never weighty and are, if anything, a little leaner to start with than the Hautes Côtes de Beaune, but they do have an attractive cherry and plum flavour, sometimes with a pleasing bitter finish. Best years: (reds) 1997, '96, '95, '93, '90. Best producers: Caves des Hautes-Côtes, C Cornu, Delauney, Dufouleur, Michel Gros, Hudelot, Jayer-Gilles, Thévenot-le-Brun, Verdet. The whites from Chardonnay and Aligoté (under the Bourgogne-Aligoté AC) tend to be rather dry and flinty. In general drink young, although they will age. Best years: (whites) 1997, '96, '95, '94, '93, '92. Best producers: Caves des Hautes-Côtes, Chaley, Dufouleur, Hudelot, Jayer-Gilles, Thévenot-le-Brun, Verdet.

BOURGOGNE PASSE-TOUT-GRAINS AC

FRANCE, Burgundy
♦ ♀ *Gamay, Pinot Noir*

Almost always red (with just a little rosé) this appellation is for a mixture of Gamay with not less than one-third Pinot Noir in the blend. In recent years in the Côte Chalonnaise and CÔTE D'OR, as vineyards are replanted, the percentage of Pinot Noir has increased, yielding wines of better quality. These wines should now show a good, sturdy, cherry fruit when very young, offset by a raspingly attractive, herby acidity from the Gamay, but softening over three to four years to a gentle, round-edged wine. Best producers: (growers) Bersan, Chaley, C Cornu, Rion; (merchants): Chanson, LEROY. Best years: 1997, '95, '93.

BOURGUEIL AC

FRANCE, Loire, Touraine
♦ ♀ *Cabernet Franc, Cabernet Sauvignon*

Bourgueil is a village just north of the river Loire between Angers and Tours. The area is unusually dry for the LOIRE Valley, favouring the ripening of red grape varieties, which explains why, in a region known for its white wines, Bourgueil is famous for red. Cabernet Franc is the main grape, topped up with a little Cabernet Sauvignon, and in hot years the results can be superb.

Although the wines can be rather peppery and vegetal at first, if you give them time – at least five years of aging and preferably ten – they develop a wonderful fragrance which is like essences of blackcurrant and raspberry combined, with just enough earthiness to keep their feet firmly on the ground. Best years: 1997, '96, '95, '93, '90, '89, '88, '86, '85, '83, '82. Best producers: Yannick Amirault (Domaine de la Coudraye), Audebert (estate wines), Breton, Caslot-Galbrun, Caslot-Jamet, Druet, Lamé-Delille-Boucard, des Raguenières.

CASLOT-GALBRUN
The Bourgueil AC makes some of the Loire Valley's best red wines and in hot years the best examples, such as this one, have a good depth of blackcurrant fruit.

BOUZY

FRANCE, Champagne, Coteaux Champenois AC
♦ *Pinot Noir*

This leading CHAMPAGNE village on the Montagne de Reims grows the region's best Pinot Noir, which is usually made into white Champagne. However, in outstanding years, a little still red wine is made from Pinot Noir. It is light, high in acid and often with a cutting, herby edge. But now and then, a waif-like perfume of raspberry and strawberry is just strong enough to provide a fleeting pleasure before the chalky tannins take over again. Don't age it on purpose, although it can keep for several years. Best years: 1996, '95, '93, '90, '89, '85. Best producers: Bara, Clouet, Georges Vesselle, Jean Vesselle.

LOUIS BOVARD

SWITZERLAND, Vaud, Cully
♦ *Syrah, Merlot, Pinot Noir (Blauburgunder)*
♀ *Chasselas*

If you think that Chasselas can only produce thin, neutral whites that need Alpine views in order to be enjoyable, then you should taste Louis-Philippe Bovard's DÉZELAY Médinette, from terraced vineyards which soar to the sky from the northern bank of Lake Geneva. They need a couple of years of bottle age to give their best, then are as minerally as any CHABLIS, with a supple, savoury character style. Almost as good are the firm Epesses Terre à Boire and the more elegant Aigle Cuvée Noe. Best years: 1998, '97, '95, '93.

BOWEN ESTATE

AUSTRALIA, South Australia, Limestone Coast Zone, Coonawarra
♦ *Cabernet Sauvignon, Syrah (Shiraz), Merlot*
♀ *Riesling, Chardonnay*

Doug Bowen is one of the most highly regarded red winemakers among the small COONAWARRA wineries. As part of his winemaking studies he prepared a report on Coonawarra's potential way back in the early 1970s, before the area was fashionable, and immediately put his money where his mouth was by setting up a vineyard and winery in 1972. His 7000-case annual production is largely given over to a wonderfully peppery, spicy Shiraz and an elegant, discreetly herbaceous Cabernet Sauvignon, with, recently, a dash of Merlot. Best years: 1996, '94, '91, '90, '88, '86, '84, '80, '79.

BRACHETTO D'ACQUI DOCG

ITALY, Piedmont
♦ *Brachetto*

It's not always the most revered wine that gives the most delight. Brachetto d'Acqui is one such. Light red, with a bit of fizz, its aromas are reminiscent of Muscat with a suggestion of strawberries. The taste is light, delicate and sweet although the odd dry version exists. Drink young. Best producers: BANFI, Bersano, BRAIDA, Viticoltori dell'Acquese.

BRAIDA

ITALY, Piedmont, Barbera d'Asti DOC
❢ *Barbera, Pinot Noir (Pinot Nero)*
♀ *Chardonnay, Riesling and others*

If anyone put Barbera on the map as a potentially great wine-grape it was the late Giacomo Bologna, whose family now run this winery. A rotund, jovial man, Bologna was one of a band of enthusiastic enologists who, in the 1970s, began visiting France to study the ways of the great French winemakers. The most important lessons he learned were the need, especially with the hyperacidic Barbera, to complete the malolactic fermentation expeditiously and that the barrique was primarily a marvellous tool for rounding out the sharp and rough edges of an otherwise all-too-rustic wine.

Bologna's most renowned creation is Bricco dell'Uccellone, today recognized as one of Italy's classic wines. Another barrique-aged Barbera is the cru Bricco della Bigottà. Ai Suma is a rich, concentrated wine made from late-harvested grapes, while La Monella is a light-hearted quaffer brightened by a touch of that fizz which the Piedmontese have always appreciated in their Barbera wines. Best years: (reds) 1995, '94, '93, '92, '91, '90.

DOMAINE BRANA

FRANCE, South-West, Irouléguy AC
❢ *Cabernet Franc, Cabernet Sauvignon, Tannat*
♀ *Courbu, Gros Manseng, Petit Manseng*

Étienne Brana will be chiefly remembered for his contribution to the revival of the IROULÉGUY AC in the heart of the Pays Basque. He created a spectacularly steep vineyard on the flanks of the Aradoy mountain in 1986 but did not live to see the results of his labour. His son Jean, however, has continued the good work, producing a deep-coloured, robust but refined red Irouléguy aged in oak barriques and a full but lively dry white made from a blend of Courbu and Gros and Petit Manseng with a tiny percentage vinified in oak. The domaine now covers some 34ha (84 acres). Second wine: Harri Gorri. Best years: (reds) 1997, '96, '95, '94.

BRAND'S LAIRA

AUSTRALIA, South Australia, Limestone Coast Zone, Coonawarra
❢ *Cabernet Sauvignon, Merlot, Syrah (Shiraz), Malbec*
♀ *Chardonnay, Riesling*

Brand's Laira is now owned by the McWILLIAMS winery, which has helped broaden the range and make quality consistent across the board. The accent is still on red wines, aided by excellent vineyards which include a precious patch of Shiraz planted in 1896, which provides the super-premium Stentiford Shiraz. All the reds are full flavoured and supremely honest with abundant fruit – the Cabernet at its best can epitomize the COONAWARRA mulberry flavours – while the white wines have improved out of all recognition. Best years: (reds) 1997, '96, '94, '93, '91, '90, '88, '87.

CH. BRANE-CANTENAC

FRANCE, Bordeaux, Haut-Médoc, Margaux AC, 2ème Cru Classé
❢ *Cabernet Sauvignon, Merlot, Cabernet Franc*

Brane-Cantenac has been in the Lurton family hands since the 1920s and is now owned and managed by Henri Lurton, a qualified enologist. The estate's sprawling 86-ha (212-acre) vineyard is located principally on the Cantenac plateau, the 70 per cent Cabernet Sauvignon vines planted on poor, fine gravelly soils. Despite the location Brane-Cantenac has not always lived up to its Second Growth status, the wines often lacking depth and consistency. However, change does seem to be in the air, the 1997 and '96 showing definite signs of improvement with more weight and concentration but still the MARGAUX charm and finesse. Best years: 1997, '96, '95, '90, '89, '88, '86, '85.

CH. BRANE-CANTENAC
Recent vintages at this large estate have seen a definite improvement in quality and the wine shows some of the Margaux AC's delicacy and finesse.

BRAUNEBERG

GERMANY, Mosel-Saar-Ruwer

Just upstream from BERNKASTEL lies the small village of Brauneberg, facing its precipitously steep Juffer and Juffer-Sonnenuhr vineyards on the opposite side of the river Mosel. The latter is unquestionably one of the most favourable sites in the entire MOSEL Valley. In the nineteenth century these vineyards were reckoned the best in all the Mosel, but fashion has changed: the heavy soils of Juffer and Juffer-Sonnenuhr produce heavier, fuller wines with great complexity, yet too much weight for today's conception of Mosel as something light and delicate. But they are splendid wines, so to hell with fashion. Best producers: Bastgen, Fritz HAAG, Willi Haag, Max Ferdinand RICHTER.

BREAKY BOTTOM

ENGLAND, East Sussex
♀ *Seyval Blanc, Müller-Thurgau*

Peter Hall is one of England's strongest defenders (and best producers) of the EU despised Seyval Blanc grape which, being a hybrid variety, is banned from the EU-approved Quality Wine scheme. He proves Seyval Blanc wine can age in bottle for three or four years and become ever creamier, richer and more honeyed. His Müller-Thurgau also exhibits far more hedgerow pungency and perfume than most of his rivals. He has 2ha (6 acres) of vineyards on the South Downs near Lewes. Best years: (Seyval Blanc) 1995.

BREGANZE DOC

ITALY, Veneto
❢ *Cabernet Franc, Cabernet Sauvignon, Merlot, Pinot Noir (Pinot Nero)*
♀ *Pinot Blanc (Pinot Bianco), Pinot Gris (Pinot Grigio), Tocai, Vespaiolo*

Breganze is a small wine zone east of Verona in Veneto's province of Vicenza. The gently hilly countryside is scattered with the superb Palladian villas of Venice's tycoons, and there is a tranquillity and a stateliness about the ambiance which seems curiously un-Italian.

Wine production goes back a long time, but today the only significant historic grape is Vespaiolo, beloved of wasps (*vespe*), increasingly used for the making of Breganze's most famous wine, indeed one of Italy's finest stickies, Torcolato. Total production of Breganze DOC wine is modest – around 2.7 million bottles a year – at least half of which is devoted to Breganze Rosso, based primarily on Merlot, and Bianco, a dry white based on Tocai Friulano. These are supplemented by a wide range of varietals, including sometimes intense Cabernet and dry Vespaiolo. Quality production is dominated by MACULAN, and Beato Bartolomeo da Breganze is an efficient co-operative.

GEORG BREUER

GERMANY, Rheingau, Rüdesheim
♀ *Riesling, Pinot Gris (Grauburgunder), Pinot Blanc (Weissburgunder)*

Bernhard Breuer has gone from being one of the champions of dry German wines to an apostle of vineyard classification. His 'Premiers Crus' – 'Erster Gewächs' in German – are powerful, concentrated, dry Rieslings from the Berg Schlossberg of RÜDESHEIM and the Nonnenberg of RAUENTHAL. The Nonnenberg is spicy, fleshy and quite quick to develop, while the Berg Schlossberg is always slow to develop; reserved in its youth but becoming a siren-like beauty when mature after four to ten years. Montosa is a blend of wines not quite good enough for 'Erster Gewächs'.

The standard dry wines are sold under the village names of Rüdesheim and Rauenthal. There is also excellent fizz and barrique-aged Grauburgunder. Breuer is now one of the top RHEINGAU names. Best years: 1998, '97, '96, '94, '93, '92, '90, '86, '83.

BRIGHT BROS.

PORTUGAL, Ribatejo
🍷 *Baga, Cabernet Sauvignon, Merlot, Touriga Francesa, Touriga Naçional*
🍷 *Fernão Pires, Chardonnay, Sauvignon Blanc and others*

The Australian Peter Bright is the driving force behind much of Portugal's modernization. He made his name as the winemaker for J P VINHOS until he set up his own firm. Still based in Portugal, where he has interests in the RIBATEJO, ESTREMADURA and the DOURO, he now roves the world in search of grapes for his own-label wines, most of which are varietal. The Fiúza-Bright operation is located in the small town of Almeirim in the Ribatejo and the Fiúza family vineyards supply Bright with grapes from foreign varieties like Chardonnay, Sauvignon Blanc, Cabernet and Merlot. Despite having no vineyards of his own, he makes wines as far afield as Sicily, Spain and Argentina. With the exception of a new Duoro red called TFN (a blend of Touriga Francesa and Touriga Naçional), most of his wines are for early drinking.

BROKENWOOD

AUSTRALIA, New South Wales, Hunter Valley Zone, Hunter
🍷 *Cabernet Sauvignon, Syrah (Shiraz)*
🍷 *Chardonnay, Semillon, Sauvignon Blanc, Verdelho*

Until 1982 only reds were produced here, but since that time Brokenwood's success has allowed it to spread its wings in many directions. It produces classically delicate, unoaked HUNTER VALLEY Semillon (with a Reserve version), a grassy, subtly oaked regional blend Semillon Sauvignon Blanc and, more recently, a Verdelho sourced from COWRA vineyards

Here at the Fiúza winery at Almeirim in the Ribatejo Peter Bright makes beautifully focused, keenly priced wines from French grape varieties.

in which it has an interest. The appropriately dark and brooding Graveyard Shiraz is one of the top half dozen Shiraz wines in Australia, but it also produces a single-vineyard (McLAREN VALE) and regionally blended Shiraz. Powerful Cabernet Sauvignon is another wine in the armoury.

Finally, Brokenwood has acquired Seville Estate in the YARRA VALLEY, where winemaker Iain Riggs adds supple Pinot Noir to his large repertoire, and also Chardonnay, Shiraz and Cabernet Sauvignon in very different style from that of the Hunter Valley – far more restrained and less extractive. Best years: 1997, '96, '94, '93, '91, '89, '87, '86, '85, '83.

CASTELLO DI BROLIO

ITALY, Tuscany, Chianti Classico DOCG
🍷 *Sangiovese, Merlot, Cabernet Sauvignon*
🍷 *Chardonnay*

Despite the fame of the Ricasoli name in CHIANTI CLASSICO circles, this large estate in Gaiole underwent a comprehensive down-marketing over a 20-year period up until the early 1990s, when the winery was leased out to a succession of Brits and Aussies who knew not what they were doing. Rescue came in the form of young Baron Francesco Ricasoli, along with help and advice from successful, quality-minded people such as FONTERUTOLI's Filippo Mazzei and the now almost legendary enologist Carlo Ferrini. The new broom swept clean the cobwebs, and the pile of debts, and before anyone

knew it they were putting out world-class wines like the SUPER-TUSCAN Sangiovese Casalferro, as well as some very handsome and impressive Chianti Classicos and Riservas. The cheaper Barone Ricasoli label is excellent value for money. Best years: (Reds) 1995, '94, '93, '90.

BROOKFIELDS

NEW ZEALAND, North Island, Hawke's Bay
🍷 *Cabernet Sauvignon, Merlot*
🍷 *Sauvignon Blanc, Chardonnay, Gewurztraminer*

Peter Robertson acquired Brookfields in 1977 and began the process of converting it from an ailing producer of fortified wine into the highly regarded winery it is today. The 1983 Cabernet Sauvignon and Cabernet-Merlot wines put the winery on the map. As well as his own small (5-ha/13-acre) estate, Robertson sources fruit from local HAWKE'S BAY growers; the Gewurztraminer is well made, flavoursome and spicy; the Sauvignon Blanc and Chardonnay are restrained, the former grassy and herbal, the latter having light, honey and peach fruit and smoky, nutty oak. Best years: 1998, '96, '94, '93.

BROUILLY AC

FRANCE, Burgundy, Beaujolais, Beaujolais cru
🍷 *Gamay*

'A bottle of Brooey' doesn't sound quite serious, does it? Well, why should it? Brouilly is the largest of the ten BEAUJOLAIS crus (the top-ranking Beaujolais villages in the northern part of the region which are allowed to use their name on the label). But it's still Beaujolais: it's still made from the juicy-fruity Gamay grape; it's still supposed to make you laugh and smile – not get serious; and you're still supposed to drink it in draughts, not dainty sips.

What makes Brouilly special is that it is the closest of the crus to the BEAUJOLAIS-VILLAGES style (a lot of growers make both wines). It is the most southerly of the crus and comes from vineyards around the hill of Brouilly, whereas CÔTE DE BROUILLY is the cru covering vineyards on the hill itself. South of Brouilly the 'Villages' and the simple 'Beaujolais' vineyards stretch away towards Lyon. The wine is very fruity and can make a delicious Nouveau. One or two growers have started using oak barrels to make an age-worthy example, but there does not seem much point in aging it. Best years: 1998, '97, '96, '95, '94. Best producers: la Chaize, DUBOEUF (Combillaty, Garanches), Fouilloux, Hospices de Beaujeu (especially Pisseuieille Cuvée), Michaud, Pierreux, Rolland, Ruet, Thivin, des Tours.

CH. BROUSTET
FRANCE, Bordeaux, Barsac AC, 2ème Cru Classé
♀ *Sémillon, Sauvignon Blanc, Muscadelle*

This Second Growth BARSAC is now owned by the Laulan family, locals of the region. Production at the 16-ha (40-acre) estate is limited to 2000 cases per year. The wine, which is vinified in stainless steel tanks and aged in oak barrels, doesn't have great fruit but does have thick, lanolin-like richness coating your mouth, which is pretty satisfying. Best years: 1997, '96, '95, '90, '89, '88, '86, '85, '83, '81, '80, '75.

BROWN BROTHERS
AUSTRALIA, Victoria, North East Victoria Zone, Rutherglen
♥ *Cabernet Sauvignon, Syrah (Shiraz), Tarrango, Graciano and others*
♀ *Chardonnay, Riesling and others*

This is a remarkable century-old, family company with the three sons of John Brown each involved in selling over half a million cases of wine per year. Brown Brothers draws on fruit from a number of vineyards in Victoria, in both warm and cooler, upland sites, and uses both familiar and unusual grapes to produce a wide choice of styles, including fortified sweet Tokay and sparkling wine. Perhaps partly due to the kindergarten winery, a 35,000 case 'winery within a winery', Brown Brothers has produced a considerable number of trophy and gold medal winning wines in recent years, supplementing its more down-to-earth commercial range. Best years: (reds) 1997, '96, '94, '93, '92, '91, '90, '88, '86.

BROWN BROTHERS
Late-harvested Noble Riesling is a golden, richly botrytized meld of honey, spice, mixed peel and vanilla from King Valley grapes.

BRÜNDLMAYER
AUSTRIA, Niederösterreich, Kamptal, Langenlois
♥ *Pinot Noir, Merlot, Cabernet Sauvignon*
♀ *Riesling, Grüner Veltliner, Chardonnay, Pinot Gris (Grauburgunder), Pinot Blanc (Weissburgunder)*

Willi Bründlmayer is Austria's most versatile winemaker. It was with his barrique-aged

Chardonnay that he first attracted attention more than a decade ago, then his classic style dry Rieslings and Grüner Veltliners shot to the top of the Austrian class at the beginning of the 1990s. Anyone who doubts that Austria can produce world-class dry whites should experience his Riesling Alte Reben from the Heiligenstein vineyard and his Grüner Veltliner from the Ried Lamm; magnificently concentrated, sophisticated wines. Bründlmayer has also mastered the art of sparkling winemaking as no other in the German-speaking world, and in recent years his red wines have also gained in depth and sophistication. The finest of these is the fragrant, Burgundian-style Pinot Noir Cuvée Cecile. Since 1996 Bründlmayer has also been the winemaker for the nearby Schloss Goeblsburg estate which concentrates on dry Grüner Veltiner and Riesling, which means that he now works with grapes from almost 81ha (200 acres) of vines. Best years: (reds) 1998, '97, '96, '95, '94, '93, '92, '91.

BRUNELLO DI MONTALCINO DOCG
ITALY, Tuscany
♥ *Sangiovese*

Driving south from Florence through CHIANTI CLASSICO, one passes Siena. Suddenly the previously ubiquitous vineyards disappear and not a vine is seen for miles. The surroundings seem drier, and the atmosphere gets noticeably warmer, as if you have crossed an invisible climate barrier. After about half an hour a huge hill looms on the horizon with a castle on the top. This is the town of Montalcino. Ascending the hill, entering the castle, one looks out from its ramparts to see, in one direction, an undulating blue-grey moonscape. Yet in the other direction the land is as green and vine-clad as one might expect. It then becomes clear what a unique enclave Montalcino is.

Brunello di Montalcino is often referred to as simply 'Brunello', although this is (or was) the name of the grape, a clone of Sangiovese which got its name from the brownish hue it has when ripe. It should be a long-lived, big, rich, powerful wine with all the firm, peppery-spicy, tea-and-cinnamon, figgy character of the grape. The biggest, richest wines come from the sunbaked south-west of the area (Case Basse, Col d'Orcia, Lisini, Poggio Antico, Il POGGIONE, Talenti); the most elegant from the hill's north-eastern-facing scarp slope (Altesino, Caparzo); the firmest from the sheltered

south-eastern slopes (BIONDI-SANTI, Cerbaiona, Costanti). These producers show what Brunello is all about. Other producers capable of excellence are almost too numerous to list, but include Argiano, BANFI, Capanna, Casanova di Neri, CASTELGIOCONDO, Ciacci Piccolomini, Col d'Orcia, Fattoria dei Barbi, Fuligni, Mastrojanni, PIERE S RESTITUTA, Siro Pacenti, Salvioni la Cerbaiola, and Val di Suga. The wines still have to age four years from the first of January following the vintage, but at least the minimum time in wood, until recently three years has now been reduced to two years, at the behest of producers concerned that such treatment in a lesser vintage was excessive. A separate DOC, ROSSO DI MONTALCINO, produces an increasing number of very good fruit-dominated – and more affordable – reds. Best years: 1998, '97, '95, '94, '93, '91, '90, '88, '85, '83, '82, '78.

BUÇACO PALACE HOTEL
PORTUGAL, Beira Litoral
♥ *Baga, Tinta Pinheira, Bastardo, Touriga Naçional and others*
♀ *Bical (Borrado das Moscas), Maria Gomes (Fernão Pires), Muscat (Moscatel), Rabo de Ovelha and others*

Some of Portugal's finest traditional wines, both red and white, are made at this large and extravagantly ornate hotel – set amid gardens and a magnificent forest above the spa town of Luso. Wine has been made here since 1917, both from the hotel's own vineyard and from grapes bought in from nearby producers in BAIRRADA and DÃO. Traditional methods prevail. After fermentation the whites spend 12–18 months in old wood, the reds about three years. When released for sale (only to guests at the hotel and at other establishments belonging to the Alexandre d'Almeida hotel group), both red and white are rich, well-balanced, complex wines with an elusive pine and eucalyptus-like scent.

BUCELAS DOC
PORTUGAL, Estremadura
♀ *Arinto, Esgana Cão and others*

On the outskirts of Lisbon, the historic wine enclave of Bucelas nearly disappeared in the 1980s but has recently undergone a small revival. The DOC applies to dry white wines made mainly from the Arinto grape, which has the capacity to retain naturally high levels of acidity despite the warm maritime climate. Its partner (alias MADEIRA's Sercial grape) is so acidic that it is known locally as

Esgana Cão ('Dog Strangler'). Caves Velhas has been the mainstay of Bucelas for many years but it has now been joined by three estates: Quinta do Avelar, Quinta da Murta and Quinta da Romeira. Drink young, within two or three years.

BUENA VISTA WINERY

USA, California, Sonoma County, Carneros AVA

🍷 *Cabernet Sauvignon, Pinot Noir, Merlot, Zinfandel*

🍷 *Chardonnay, Sauvignon Blanc, Gewurztraminer and others*

Northern CALIFORNIA's oldest winery began under the ownership of Agoston Haraszthy in 1857. Sometimes called the Father of California Wine, he took his winery to exhilarating peaks and gloomy depths before he eventually went off to South America and was supposedly eaten by alligators. Today, Buena Vista's winery sits amid 445ha (1100 acres) of vineyards on slopes facing San Francisco Bay in CARNEROS. Now German-owned, it is a solid performer. The Chardonnays are vibrant with a refreshing grapefruit streak of acid from the Carneros fruit. Best years: (whites) 1998, '97, '95, '94, '92, '91. The Pinot Noirs are unnecessarily lean, but the Reserves are richer.

VIN DU BUGEY VDQS

FRANCE, Savoie

🍷 *Gamay, Pinot Noir, Mondeuse, Poulsard*

🍷 *Jacquère, Chardonnay, Altesse, Aligoté and others*

A few years ago these straggly little vineyards covering 300ha (741 acres) halfway between Savoie and Lyon in the *département* of Ain, made thin, lifeless whites from the Savoie grapes Altesse and Jacquère, sometimes hindered even further by Aligoté. Red varieties rarely ripen and have a distinct flavour of damp vineyards and vegetable patches. But remarkably the Chardonnay from here has become one of the trendiest quaffing wines in France. It is light, wonderfully creamy and fresh as mountain pasture. Rumour has it they make a decent fizz too. All these wines are for drinking young. Best producers: Bolliet, Cellier de Bel-Air, Crussy, Monin, Caveau du Mont July, Peillot.

REICHSRAT VON BUHL

GERMANY, Pfalz, Deidesheim

🍷 *Riesling, Rieslaner, Scheurebe, Pinot Blanc (Weissburgunder)*

These are top-class, assertive PFALZ wines from a historic estate that is now leased to the Japanese Sanyo group, with lots of stainless steel for fermentation. Von Buhl can boast vineyards in most of the region's top sites, like

FORSTer Jesuitengarten and RUPPERTSBERGer Reiterpfad; more straightforward wines are sold under the company name. Best years: 1997, '96, '95, '94, '90, '89.

BUITENVERWACHTING

SOUTH AFRICA, Western Cape, Constantia WO

🍷 *Cabernet Sauvignon, Merlot, Pinot Noir and others*

🍷 *Sauvignon Blanc, Chardonnay, Riesling (Rhine/Weisser Riesling)*

The name is probably the most difficult thing to get to grips with at this property, and the wines have undoubtedly lived up to their name (meaning 'Beyond Expectations') since the first vintage in 1985. Although part of the original CONSTANTIA wine farm, the vineyards have been totally replanted. A consistently excellent Sauvignon Blanc underscores the region's talent for this grape and the Chardonnay is immediately delicious but can improve for a couple of years. Winemaker and MOSEL-enthusiast Hermann Kirschbaum focuses on producing a light-bodied, lively Riesling with some success. Undoubtedly, the most talked-about wine is the BORDEAUX blend, Christine. Its fine tannins, seamless fruit and complementary barrel-maturation make this a Cape classic. Best years: (reds) 1994, '93, '92, '91, '90, '89; (whites) 1998, '97, '96, '95, '94, '93, '92, '91.

BUITENVERWACHTUNG
From this leading estate in Constantia, Christine is an elegant red wine from the classic Bordeaux blend of Cabernet Sauvignon and Merlot.

BULL'S BLOOD

HUNGARY, Eger

🍷 *Blaufränkisch (Kékfrankos), Cabernet Sauvignon, Merlot and others, including the original grape, Kadarka*

A great name and a great marketing exercise: there are umpteen legends (of varying age and, no doubt, authenticity) involving the Hungarians getting the better of the invading Turks because they drank Bull's Blood (which they would have called Egri Bikavér) – a bit like Popeye and his spinach. These days it's a blend of the rather inferior Kékfrankos grape and others, and would instil fear only into those Turks unaccus-

tomed to anything made from grape or grain. The wine is generally adequate and most comes from Hungarovin, owned by German sparkling wine producer, Henkell.

BERNARD BURGAUD

FRANCE, Northern Rhône, Côte-Rôtie AC

🍷 *Syrah*

One look at Bernard Burgaud and you can see this is a man who entertains few doubts. Although still quite a young man, he defined his style some years ago and has stuck to it. He owns 4ha (10 acres) of vines in various locations and vinifies them separately. He likes to obtain good extraction and colour, and practises destemming, punching down the cap, and ages the wine in about 20 per cent new oak. In Burgaud's view, this is not innovation but a return to how the wines would have been made two centuries earlier. He opposes the addition of Viognier to the wine, believing that it was added to provide alcohol, whereas his own wines never lack sufficient alcohol. The powerful fruit always absorbs the oak influence without problem, and one would not describe these wines as oaky so much as extracted, concentrated, and elegant. Burgaud recommends drinking them very young for their superb fruit or keeping them at least eight years. Best years: 1996, '95, '94, '91, '90, '89, '88.

GRANT BURGE

AUSTRALIA, South Australia, Barossa Zone, Barossa Valley

🍷 *Syrah (Shiraz), Merlot, Cabernet Sauvignon, Grenache, Mourvedre*

🍷 *Riesling, Sauvignon Blanc, Chardonnay*

Time flies; from one of the brightest of the bright young boys of the early 1970s, Grant Burge is now a highly mature senior citizen, with an extremely successful business based on the most extensive vineyard holdings in BAROSSA under single family ownership, and marketing techniques reminiscent of the best of Wolf BLASS. Generously flavoured wines are the order of the day, with heaps of American oak ladled in at every stage of winemaking. Would less be better? In the view of some at least, yes. Best years: (reds) 1997, '96, '94, '92, '91, '90.

BURGENLAND

AUSTRIA

One of Austria's three principal wine regions, Burgenland makes most styles of wine, but its speciality is the rich, sweet botrytized wines from the NEUSIEDLERSEE and NEUSIEDLERSEE-

HÜGELLAND. Further south the rather flat Mittelburgenland area makes mostly reds, from the Blaufränkisch grape. In recent years the wines have become drier, and are often blended with Cabernet Sauvignon. Good, attractive reds and mostly dry whites come from Südburgenland. Best producers: (Neusiedlersee) Haider, HEINRICH, JURIS, KRACHER, NITTNAUS, OPITZ, UMATHUM, VELICH; (Neusiedlersee-Hügelland) FEILER-ARTINGER, KOLLWENTZ, Schandl, Schröck, TRIEBAUMER, WENZEL; (Mittelburgenland) GESSELLMANN; (Südburgenland) Krutzer.

ALAIN BURGUET

FRANCE, Burgundy, Côte de Nuits, Gevrey-Chambertin AC
♥ *Pinot Noir*

In the mid to late 1980s Alain Burguet, operating out of modest cellars in the centre of GEVREY-CHAMBERTIN, was an insider's secret. Although he owned only a few hectares of village-level vineyards, he managed to craft, even in modest vintages, impressive and complex wines, especially from the parcel bottled as Vieilles Vignes. In 1988 he finally acquired some Premier Cru vines in Champeaux. Today he owns almost 5ha (12½ acres). By this time word had spread about the quality of his wines, and his prices began to rise. Nonetheless, this is an impeccable source of Gevrey-Chambertin. Best years: 1997, '96, '95, '93, '91, '90, '89, '88, '87, '85.

LEO BURING

AUSTRALIA, South Australia, Barossa Zone, Barossa Valley
♥ *Syrah (Shiraz), Cabernet Sauvignon*
♀ *Riesling, Semillon, Chardonnay*

Owned by Southcorp, Leo Buring was once unchallenged as Australia's finest producer of Riesling, notably from the EDEN and CLARE VALLEYS, though many newer wineries are now snapping at its heels. These wines mature magnificently, peaking at 10–20 years. Those from the Eden Valley retain a lime juice character and flavour all their life, while those from Clare have an added touch of toast. Changing of the guard with brand managers has led to a changing of the guard with labels, further confusing an already confused situation. If you see the word 'Leonay' on the new split-label design, you know this is a special bottling (either from Eden Valley or Watervale in the Clare Valley), which is the equivalent of the old Reserve Bin series. Best years: (classic Rieslings) 1997, '94, '93, '91, '90, '87, '86, '84, '79, '75, '73, '72.

DR BÜRKLIN-WOLF

GERMANY, Pfalz, Wachenheim
♥ *Pinot Noir (Spätburgunder)*
♀ *Riesling, Weissburgunder, Chardonnay, Scheurebe, Muscat (Muskateller), Gewürztraminer*

Since Christian von Guradze took over here at the beginning of the 1990s he has transformed a sleeping giant into one of Germany's most dynamic wine producers. His most revolutionary step was to introduce a stringent internal classification of the estate's wines based upon the Royal Bavarian surveyor's classification of the PFALZ vineyards from 1832. The Rieslings from the top sites are now labelled only with the vineyard name, like Burgundian Grands Crus, and are only vinified dry. Rich, weighty and succulent, they are closer in style to top ALSACE or Austrian wines than typical German wines.

The finest of these is the wine from the Kirchenstück vineyard of FORST. The simpler Riesling wines are all sold under village names, but now even these are of very good quality. The estate's Riesling Auslese and higher Prädikat dessert wines remain among the greatest from the RHEIN. Weissburgunder is normally a supple, medium-bodied dry wine for early drinking. All the other grapes are only grown in small quantities and normally vinified dry. Best years: 1998, '97, '96, '95, '94, '90, '89, '83, '76, '71.

BURMESTER

PORTUGAL Douro, Douro DOC, Port DOC
♥ *Tinta Roriz (Tempranillo), Tinta Barroca, Tinto Cão, Touriga Naçional, Touriga Francesa and others*
♀ *Gouveio, Viosinho, Rabigato, Malvasia Fina and others*

The Burmester family arrived from Germany in the eighteenth century and established a PORT dynasty which continues to this day. Now effectively Portuguese, this relatively small family company ships a wide range of ports, including some supremely refined old tawnies and colheitas. Vintage ports have improved considerably since Burmester acquired its own DOURO vineyard, Quinta Nova da Nossa Senhora do Carmo, in 1991. Unfortified Douro wines are bottled under the Casa Burmester label. Best years: (vintage ports) 1994, '92, '91, '85, '77, '70, '63.

BURROWING OWL

CANADA, British Columbia, Okanagan Valley VQA
♥ *Merlot, Cabernet Sauvignon*
♀ *Chardonnay, Pinot Gris*

The Burrowing Owl winery opened in 1998 on an 11-ha (28-acre) piece of land in the heart of the Burrowing Owl vineyard in the southern part of the OKANAGAN VALLEY. The winery intends to concentrate on Cabernet Sauvignon, Merlot, Chardonnay and Pinot Gris. Californian Bill Dyer, who also consults at CALIFORNIA's Marimar TORRES winery, makes the wine. The winery boasts the Okanagan Valley's first underground cellars for fermentation and barrel aging. Burrowing Owl's debut release, featuring two 1997 barrel-fermented whites, Chardonnay and Pinot Gris, was met with wide enthusiasm. Best years: 1998, '97.

BURROWING OWL
Some of Canada's best Chardonnay, including this wine from the new Burrowing Owl winery, comes from the southern end of the Okanagan Valley.

CAVE CO-OPÉRATIVE DE BUXY

FRANCE, Burgundy, Côte Chalonnaise
♥ *Pinot Noir*
♀ *Chardonnay, Aligoté*

This co-operative, dominating the Côte Chalonnaise far to the south of Burgundy's CÔTE D'OR, is a shining example of how the modern co-operative movement can transform a region, its reputation, and its profitability – if the will is there. The will is provided by Roger Rageot, director at Buxy since 1963. When he arrived there, he found a demoralized, impoverished vineyard region with no identity and no self-confidence. Yet the soils were mostly excellent limestone and chalk, and the vines planted were mostly high-quality Chardonnay and Pinot Noir. Using the great wine of the neighbouring Côte d'Or as his models over the next 30 years, by relentless pursuit of acceptable modernization and technological improvements, improved vineyard techniques, and, since 1984, the increased employment of oak barrels to ferment and mature the wines, he has made Buxy wines a byword for consistency and affordable quality. Without Buxy's efforts, the AC MONTAGNY, of which Buxy controls 65 per cent, would never have achieved its current reputation for quality and value for money. And, almost certainly, the new BOURGOGNE-CÔTE CHALONNAISE AC would never have been created without Buxy's influence for good on the region. Also keep an eye out for single-vineyard BOURGOGNE, Clos de Chenôves, from a hamlet close to Buxy. Best years: 1997, '96, '95, '93, '92.

BUZET AC

FRANCE, South-West

♦♀ *Cabernet Sauvignon, Cabernet Franc, Merlot, Malbec*

♀ *Sémillon, Sauvignon Blanc, Muscadelle*

From being an obscure appellation squashed into the edge of the Armagnac region, south of the river Garonne, Buzet has achieved fame simply by offering the public what it wants. The vineyards were planted with the BORDEAUX mix of grapes, and as the prices of Bordeaux wines rose in the early 1980s, Buzet produced a string of delicious, grassy-fresh, blackcurranty reds – sharp enough to be reviving, soft enough to drink as soon as they were released – and at a lower price than Bordeaux. This kind of move into a market vacuum was facilitated by the fact that 95 per cent of the production is controlled by the co-operative which, luckily, knows what it is doing. Its red Cuvée Napoléon, aged in oak, is extremely good to drink at five to ten years. There is very little rosé. Whites, so far, lag behind the reds and are a little too earthy. Best producers: Les Vignerons de Buzet co-operative, Daniel Tissot. Best years: 1996, '95.

CA' DEL BOSCO

ITALY, Lombardy, Franciacorta DOCG and DOC

♦ *Pinot Noir (Pinot Nero), Cabernet Sauvignon, Merlot and others*

♀ *Chardonnay, Pinot Blanc (Pinot Bianco), Sauvignon Blanc*

Since the early 1970s, when Maurizio Zanella first began producing Italian versions of the classic French wines, he has poured money and passion into his impressive winery. He even purchases the wood for his barriques in France, leaving it there to season for up to three years before having the barrels built by French craftsmen. To such an extent, indeed, has he travelled the road of spare-no-expense that he was obliged in 1994 to sell a 60 per cent share to Santa Margherita, the VENETO producer that made Pinot Grigio famous in the 1960s. Ca' del Bosco owns nearly 100ha (247 acres) of vineyard in various parts of the zone, feeding an annual production of some 900,000 bottles, of which just under half is sparkling wine.

The outstanding sparkling wines include Franciacorta Brut, a non-vintage blend, and Annamaria Clementi, the top wine, which after six months in barrique spends five years in bottle on the yeasts, developing in the process an amazing complexity and tremendous wealth of flavour. The still wines include good Terre di Franciacorta Rosso and Pinero (Pinot Noir) and startlingly good Chardonnay and a Bordeaux blend, Maurizio Zanella (best years: 1995, '93, '91, '90, '88, '86). The best vintages of both the reds and whites are ready at between five and ten years.

CABALLERO

SPAIN, Andalucía, Jerez y Manzanilla DO

♀ *Palomino Fino, Pedro Ximénez, Moscatel*

Caballero, the sixth-largest sherry producer, owns four bodegas in the seaside town of El Puerto de Santa María as well as the famous castle, Castillo San Marcos, from which Christopher Columbus set forth to discover America. The wines are still made in a fairly traditional way but the quality is nevertheless very good. It is also one of only two producers (the other is BARBADILLO) who have started to put their fino sherry back into casks for a couple of months – under the yeast-film of flor – after filtering it (when most firms bottle it) and before bottling. This keeps the fino fresher and tangier. You can recognize this style by Puerto Fino on the label.

Caballero bought the firms of José de la Cuesta and Burdon in the 1930s, and still sells some sherry under these brand names. Puerto Fino Dom Luis Amontillado is a gentle, yeasty amontillado and Burdon's Heavenly Cream Rich Old Oloroso is delicious, sweet, raisiny, nutty wine. The latest and most prestigious acquisition has been that of Emilio LUSTAU.

CABERNET D'ANJOU AC

FRANCE, Loire, Anjou-Saumur

♦ *Cabernet Franc, Cabernet Sauvignon*

This semi-sweet rosé from Cabernet is higher in alcohol and sweeter than ROSÉ D'ANJOU. It is customary to stop the fermentation to leave some residual sugar and the wine is now quite fashionable in France. Drink this modern style young. It used to be made in a sweeter style from riper grapes and aged remarkably well, gaining in complexity. If you ever come across examples from the 1940s or '50s from the Domaine de Bablut, they are well worth trying.

CABERNET FRANC

It's extraordinary how our judgment of grapes and wines is affected by what goes on in the Médoc region of Bordeaux. There, where the Cabernet Sauvignon is king, its cousin the Cabernet Franc isn't even in line for the throne: it's lucky to take up 20 per cent of a vineyard and its soft but grassy flavour does no more than calm the aggression of the Cabernet Sauvignon. Because of this we tend to think of Cabernet Franc as being an unimportant, uninteresting grape variety; yet cross the Gironde into St-Émilion and Pomerol and suddenly it takes a starring role. Many properties here have 30 per cent Cabernet Franc and two of the greatest châteaux, Ausone and Cheval Blanc, use 50 per cent and 60 per cent respectively, blending it with Merlot to add toughness and backbone to the luscious, fat Merlot fruit.

Then there's the Loire Valley. It is in cooler areas like this, or in areas where the soil is damper and heavier and where Cabernet Sauvignon cannot ripen properly, that Cabernet Franc comes into its own. The finest Anjou, Saumur and Touraine reds and rosés are likely to be Cabernet Franc: tops for reds are Saumur-Champigny, Bourgueil and Chinon, where, in a hot vintage, the wines are full of sharp, juicy, raspberry and blackcurrant fruit, and delicious.

In its other main home, the north-east of Italy, it has been a mainstay of production for well over a century, although these days there is a strong belief that what has always been called Cabernet Franc (or plain Cabernet) in Alto Adige, Trentino, Veneto and Friuli is in fact an entirely different ancient Bordeaux variety called Carmenère. Cabernet Franc is grown as far south as Puglia and Sicily, where it can yield soft, fragrant wines.

Cabernet Franc's use in the New World is limited, because Cabernet Sauvignon generally ripens easily in these vineyards, but Australia, California and even Canada do produce a few rather good examples.

CABERNET SAUVIGNON

This grape is deservedly the world's most famous red wine grape, and is responsible for an astonishing number of the world's best red wines. It's also the grape behind an annual world-wide flood of tasty, mid-priced red wines, because it's a very easy traveller, easy to grow, easy to make into wine. Whether at the top end of the scale – the Médoc, the Napa Valley in California, Australia's Coonawarra, New Zealand's Hawke's Bay, Chile's Maipo, certain estates in Tuscany and Spain, or at the value-for-money end in all these countries as well as Eastern Europe and southern France, Cabernet Sauvignon always tastes of itself. But it is still Bordeaux that is the benchmark for Cabernet Sauvignon – curiously, perhaps, since it is always blended with other grapes there. The great clarets of the Médoc, Cabernet's heartland, are, however, usually based on at least 60 per cent, and often up to 85 per cent, Cabernet Sauvignon, and it's here that the grape shows its full glory of blackcurrant, cigar boxes, black cherries, plums and cedar, producing wines that may be firmly tannic when young, but which mellow with age – perhaps for 20 years in the greatest wines – into glorious complex harmonies.

It is such wines that many of the world's other great producers are trying to emulate. They may equal top Bordeaux in quality, but the wine's character is rarely the same. California's Napa tries hardest, and achieves wines of splendid depth and structure, with delicious flavours of black olive, black cherry and herbs. Sonoma, next door, is equally successful in a juicier, lusher way, while Washington State produces wines of power and intense blackcurrant fruit. New York State and Canadian Cabernets are usually on the green side.

In South America, Cabernet Sauvignon was responsible for the high reputation of Chilean reds and still makes many of Chile's best, pulsating with fruit and minty perfume, but capable of aging well. Argentina is rapidly acquiring the Cabernet knack but is still some way behind Chile.

Australian Cabernet Sauvignon is famous – whether it be the lean but densely structured wines of Western Australia's Margaret River, the blackcurrant, minty wines of South Australia's Coonawarra or the richer, plummier versions from the warm irrigated vineyards of the Murray Valley. New Zealand, however, has found it difficult to ripen this grape, but recent warm vintages and the development of suitable sites in Hawke's Bay and Waiheke Island, both on the North Island, are beginning to produce exciting results.

South Africa has had Cabernet planted for generations, but until recently the grapes were generally picked not entirely ripe – this was due to virus infection in the vineyards, and a liking for high acid reds among the wine fraternity. Since the end of Apartheid, South African vineyards have been extensively replanted and wines made with a more acceptable international character – but they are still truly South African. Stellenbosch and Paarl now ripen Cabernet well but the wines retain an austere yet attractive style.

Greece has pockets of quality like Chateau Carras, Israel has the Gamla Cabernet Sauvignon from the Golan Heights, Lebanon has Chateau Musar and Eastern European countries all grow it, with Bulgaria, followed by Hungary, the most consistent. There is no reason not to assume that all around the southern and eastern Mediterranean and Eastern Europe, especially in countries with no real wine traditions, the easy-to-grow, easy-to-make, easy-to-sell Cabernet will become the most important quality grape.

But it is where the grape has been planted in the wine regions of western Europe, with their own established traditions, that it has caused the most controversy.

Cabernet Sauvignon in Spain, Italy, southern France and even Germany and Austria has become a bone of contention because, being the good traveller it is, it brings its own style and flavours and in so doing can all too easily overpower the local character of the region into which it has been introduced. In southern France, Cabernet has been the most important red variety in the Vin de Pays movement that has transformed the quality of basic wine in France's Languedoc-Roussillon. Its success has inspired many growers to make greater efforts with the local varieties – so, even as they complain about the international interloper, they clamber up the quality trail revealed by Cabernet's success. It has been a 'tolerated', 'experimental' variety in Rioja in the 1990s. It covers a quarter of the vineyards in Vega Sicilia, Spain's finest red wine, and the best Penedès reds are totally or principally Cabernet. The Portuguese, with their own impressive range of indigenous grapes, have proved less amenable to Cabernet than most European countries.

Cabernet Sauvignon is traditional in north-east Italy, where it makes grassy wines, and is increasingly planted in Piedmont. In Tuscany it may be made as a varietal, or used to add an international flavour to the native Sangiovese. Such wines are frequently delicious and high-quality, and that's what matters, but the debate as to whether or not such an international grape should be planted there will run for a long time yet.

CADILLAC AC

FRANCE, Bordeaux

♀ *Sémillon, Sauvignon Blanc, Muscadelle*

This rather amorphous sweet white AC, created in 1973, is situated along the northern bank of the Garonne, in the southern part of the PREMIÈRES CÔTES DE BORDEAUX AC. The area under vine varies depending on whether the producers declare their wines as Cadillac or Premières Côtes de Bordeaux, but now averages around 253ha (625 acres).

The quality of Cadillac was for many years extremely mediocre due to high yields, lack of investment and a slump in the market for sweet wines. But in the 1990s, neighbouring SAUTERNES began to regain popularity and consequent high prices with a string of good vintages, and Cadillac, though still regarded as something of a poor relation, was given the incentive – and the stuff of good vintages – to persuade growers that a bit more effort would be worthwhile.

Yields have been reduced and selective harvesting and barrel-aging have become more widespread. There is even a lobby for a 'Grains Nobles' status for more concentrated cuvées. Cadillac vineyards do get affected by the botrytis or noble rot fungus, but styles vary from fresh, semi-sweet to richly botrytized with prices varying accordingly. Best years: 1998, '97, '96, '95, '90. Best producers: Berbec, Carsin, Cayla, Juge, Manos, Mémoires, Renon, Ste-Cathérine.

CAHORS AC
FRANCE, South-West

♥ *Malbec (Auxerrois), Merlot, Tannat*

After BORDEAUX, Cahors, along with MADIRAN, is the leading red wine of France's South-West, if only because it makes no attempt to ape Bordeaux and its flavours. But then, why should it? Cahors has been famous since Roman times, and was often used by Bordeaux winemakers to add colour and fruit to their wines which, two centuries ago, were nearer Bordeaux rosé than red in style.

The Cahors vineyards are on both sides of the river Lot in the Lot *département* and the whole region is about as far from hustle-bustle as can be. Only red wine is produced, with Auxerrois as the main grape (70 per cent). This is called Malbec in Bordeaux, where they don't think much of it, but in Cahors it produces dark, tannic wine which has an unforgettable flavour of plummy richness, streaked with fresh acidity. With age it takes on a gorgeous tangle of tastes, dominated superbly by tobacco spice, blackberry and sweet prunes. The vineyards are on slopes, where the toughest wines originate, but also on the valley floor, which produces lighter, more mainstream flavours. Best years: 1996, '95, '94, '92, '90, '89, '88, '86, '85. Best producers: Cayrou, du Cèdre, CLOS TRIGUEDINA, la Coutale, de Gamot, Gaudou, Gautoul, Haute-Serre, Lagrezette, Lamartine, Pineraie.

CAKEBREAD CELLARS
USA, California, Napa County, Napa Valley AVA

♥ *Cabernet Sauvignon, Merlot, Pinot Noir, Syrah, Zinfandel*

♀ *Chardonnay, Sauvignon Blanc*

A former wine country photographer, founder Jack Cakebread revived an old RUTHERFORD vineyard and made a name for his winery with enormously fruity, barrel-fermented Sauvignon Blancs and hulking reds. Run today by his children, the winery was among the first to redevelop phylloxera-plagued vineyards in the early 1990s.

It re-emerged with a new emphasis on Cabernet Sauvignon, with both a Rutherford Reserve and a Napa Valley Cabernet from vineyards within the prized Rutherford and Oakville AVAs. Growers in CARNEROS and similar cool sites supply the winery with Chardonnay and Pinot Noir, while its Zinfandel is drawn from low-yielding hillside and mountain sites. Merlot from various vineyards, a knockout Reserve Chardonnay, and Syrah complete the revamped roster. Although the reds are far less tannic and rustic than those of a decade ago, Cakebread wines, including the Chardonnay and the still rich and juicy Sauvignon Blanc, tend to be big and assertive. Best years: 1997, '96, '95, '94, '92, '91.

CALABRIA
ITALY

Calabria, Italy's toe, is basically two very long coastlines sandwiching the southern continental section of the Apennine ridge which runs through it from top to bottom like a giant backbone. It's pretty easy to get lost in those mountains, which make it ideal bandit and mafia country. The coasts could be beautiful were it not for the tens of thousands of partially built houses – it seems every time a Calabrian in Argentina or Australia manages to save a few more dollars he sends them home to have a few more reinforced concrete pillars added to what he hopes will one day be his retirement home back in the old country.

Winewise, Calabria produces little of note considering her size and potential, and in all that vast territory there is only one significant DOC – CIRÒ Classico – and with only one principal producer – LIBRANDI. The main red grape is Gaglioppo, a Nebbiolo lookalike in respect of its colour and tannins, capable of making wines of considerable character and intensity. Calabria also has its own version of the white Greco, which reaches its apogee in the sweet whites of the town of Bianco (Greco di Bianco). Producers like Librandi and Odoardi are also experimenting with various international varieties.

CALATAYUD DO
SPAIN, Aragón

♥ *Grenache Noir (Garnacha Tinta), Carignan (Cariñena, Mazuelo), Tempranillo, Monastrell*

♀ *Macabeo, Malvasía, Moscatel Blanco, Grenache Blanc (Garnacha Blanca)*

Calatayud is known for peaches, pears, apples and cherries but not, till now, for wine. Most of the vineyards lie up little valleys whose streams feed the Jalón river. It is attractive countryside with mountains sheltering the region to the north, east and south, but there seemed little to justify Calatayud's promotion, in 1990, to DO status. However, increasing amounts of modern, fruitier wine are beginning to emerge from a lake of old-fashioned cheap wine. The Garnacha is the main grape, made into reds and rosés, and there are some dull whites. The Maluenda co-operative and visiting international winemakers are leading the way.

CÁLEM
PORTUGAL, Douro, Port DOC

♥ *Tinta Roriz (Tempranillo), Tinta Barroca, Tinto Cão, Touriga Nacional, Touriga Francesa and others*

♀ *Gouveio, Viosinho, Rabigato, Malvasia Fina and others*

Until 1998 Cálem was owned by the family that founded it in 1859. The company ran into financial difficulties in the mid-1990s and was bought by a local consortium led by Rógerio Silva (ex-Rozes Port) and Manuel Saraiva. The firm's quintas, Foz and Sagrado, in the heart of the DOURO where the river Pinhão flows into the Douro have remained with the Cálem family.

Aged tawnies (from 10 to 40 years old) and colheitas are a speciality of Cálem. The colheita wines are wonderful and vintage ports, particularly those from the 1960s and '70s, can be a match for the big PORT names. However, in the 1980s and '90s Cálem's vintage ports have been disappointing and it is up to the new regime to put things right. Cálem's biggest market is Portugal itself. Best years: (vintage ports) 1994, '92, '91, '75, '66.

CÁLEM
Known as Old Friends in English, Velhotes Tawny is Cálem's best-selling port and one of the leading brands in Portugal and France.

CALERA WINE CO.
USA, California, San Benito County, Mt Harlan AVA

♥♥ *Pinot Noir*

♀ *Chardonnay, Viognier*

After Yale and Oxford, Josh Jensen continued his education in the cellars of Burgundy and in the northern RHÔNE. Learning there that legendary Pinot Noirs originate from limestone-rich slopes, on his return to the USA he searched out similar conditions in CALIFORNIA. In the early 1970s Jensen laid out three vineyards to Pinot Noir – Reed, Selleck and Jensen – and added a fourth, Mills, a decade later. Chardonnays, added to help pay the bills, evolved into serious contenders that have been overshadowed only by the rich, creamy Viogniers. The Pinots, beset only by low yields, can be sensational overall, each unique to its vineyard site. Best years: 1997, '96, '95, '92, '91, '90, '88, '87, '86, '85.

CALIFORNIA USA

CALIFORNIA SHOULD BE INTENSELY PROUD of the fact that she was the catalyst and then the locomotive for change that finally prised open the ancient European winelands' rigid grip on the hierarchy of quality wine and led the way in proving that there are hundreds if not thousands of places around the world where good to great wine can be made. If other countries and regions have now caught up with California, and in some cases overtaken her, we should nonetheless remember that until the exploits of California's modern pioneers of the 1960s and '70s, no-one had ever before challenged the right of Europe's, and in particular, France's vineyards, to be regarded as the only source of great wine in the world.

These pioneers were men like Robert Mondavi, Warren Winiarski, Joe Heitz and others who caught hold of what was a tenuous thread of quality tradition in California, and determinedly wove their thread into the mighty hawser that is California today. But California wine very nearly did not survive into the late twentieth century. Although founded by Franciscan missionaries in the 1770s, and although making wines of some renown by the late nineteenth century, the vine louse phylloxera had destroyed all the *Vitis vinifera* vines (the only ones suitable for fine wine production) by 1900. Attempts to recreate the vineyards to grow quality wine were then beset by Prohibition, the Great Depression and World War II, and by the 1950s, generations of Americans had grown up with no understanding of fine wine.

Although California has conditions suitable for growing almost every kind of wine, from pale, limpid Rieslings to sturdy vintage 'port', her great strength has always been the self-confident determination of her inhabitants. This is more than ever evident today as more and more vineyards are established away from the traditional areas, and grapes other than the ubiquitous Chardonnay and Cabernet Sauvignon are planted with increasing success. A second attack by the phylloxera louse during the 1990s has meant that there has been a tremendous opportunity dramatically to improve vineyard practices and to plant varieties genuinely suitable to each mesoclimate.

The bulk of California's wine comes from the inland Central Valley. Hot and dependent on irrigation, most of the wine is dull and could be much improved upon. Napa Valley is the most famous quality area – a 50-km (30-mile) valley covered with vines – but most of its best wines come from the cooler southern half, or from mountainside sites to the east and west of the valley. Sonoma County, to the west, is less famous but at least as fine in quality.

North of these, there are good vineyards in Mendocino and Lake counties, but much of the most exciting wine comes from south of San Francisco Bay. The Santa Cruz and Gavilan mountains both produce small amounts of delicious wines. Monterey and Paso Robles, in San Luis Obispo County, after a shaky start, are producing fine wine, and the areas of Santa Maria and Santa Ynez, in Santa Barbara County, have produced some of California's finest wine to date.

Currently California has over 800 wineries and 160,000ha (400,000 acres) of vineyards. Although phylloxera has forced growers to replant over 12,000ha (30,000 acres) in the North and Central Coast regions, the total land under vine in Napa and Sonoma has remained about the same. Most of the vineyard expansions in the 1990s has taken place in the Lodi region of the Central Valley and to a lesser degree, in Central Coast Counties.

The springtime flowering of wild mustard, here at Rutherford in the Napa Valley, is one of the loveliest sights in California wine country. The mustard is deep-rooted and encourages the vine to be likewise which improves its nutrition.

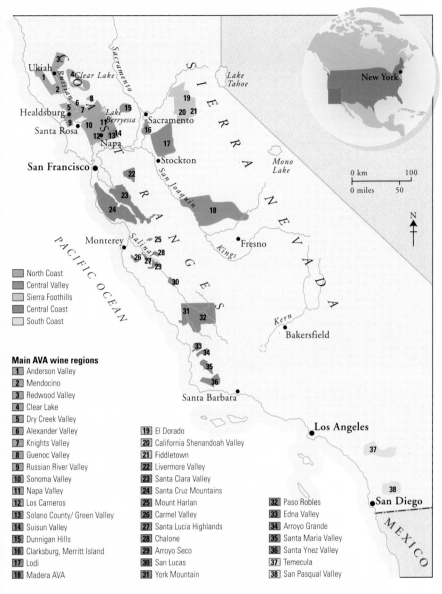

North Coast
Central Valley
Sierra Foothills
Central Coast
South Coast

Main AVA wine regions

1	Anderson Valley
2	Mendocino
3	Redwood Valley
4	Clear Lake
5	Dry Creek Valley
6	Alexander Valley
7	Knights Valley
8	Guenoc Valley
9	Russian River Valley
10	Sonoma Valley
11	Napa Valley
12	Los Carneros
13	Solano County/ Green Valley
14	Suisun Valley
15	Dunnigan Hills
16	Clarksburg, Merritt Island
17	Lodi
18	Madera AVA

19	El Dorado
20	California Shenandoah Valley
21	Fiddletown
22	Livermore Valley
23	Santa Clara Valley
24	Santa Cruz Mountains
25	Mount Harlan
26	Carmel Valley
27	Santa Lucia Highlands
28	Chalone
29	Arroyo Seco
30	San Lucas
31	York Mountain

32	Paso Robles
33	Edna Valley
34	Arroyo Grande
35	Santa Maria Valley
36	Santa Ynez Valley
37	Temecula
38	San Pasqual Valley

ROBERT MONDAVI
From its first vintage in 1966 Mondavi has always been associated with Cabernet Sauvignon. The Reserve wine is enormously concentrated and complex with tremendous depth.

RIDGE VINEYARDS
This dark, concentrated blackcurrant- and oak-dominated wine from the Monte Bello Vineyard is regularly one of California's top Cabernets.

MATANZAS CREEK WINERY
During the 1990s top-quality Merlot rapidly became the most sought-after wine in California. This Sonoma Valley wine is rich and elegant with concentrated blackberry and cassis fruit.

SAINTSBURY
The Reserve Chardonnay from this top winery is heavily oaked but still keeps its rich peach fruit and bright lemon acid.

A RAFANELLI
For classic Zinfandel from old vines, long-established wineries like this one are the places to go.

REGIONAL ENTRIES
Alexander Valley, Anderson Valley, Atlas Peak, Carneros, Central Valley, Dry Creek Valley, Edna Valley, Howell Mountain, Livermore Valley, Mendocino County, Monterey County, Napa Valley, Paso Robles, Russian River Valley, Rutherford District, San Luis Obispo County, Santa Barbara County, Sonoma County, Sonoma Mountain, Sonoma Valley, Spring Mountain District, Stags Leap District.

PRODUCER ENTRIES
Acacia Winery, Arrowood Winery & Vineyards, Atlas Peak Vineyards, Au Bon Climat, Babcock Vineyards, Beaulieu Vineyard, Benziger Family Vineyards, Beringer Vineyards, Bernardus Winery, Bonny Doon, Buena Vista Winery, Cakebread Cellars, Calera Wine Co., Carmenet Vineyard, Caymus Vineyards, Chalone Vineyard, Chateau
Montelena, Chateau St Jean, Cline Cellars, Clos du Bois, Clos du Val, Clos Pegase, Cuvaison, Dalle Valle, Dehlinger Winery, Diamond Creek Vineyards, Domaine Carneros, Domaine Chandon, Dominus Estate, Duckhorn Vineyards, Dunn Vineyards, Edna Valley Vineyard, Far Niente Winery, Ferrari-Carano Vineyards, Fetzer Vineyards, Firestone Vineyard, Franciscan Vineyards, Frog's Leap Winery, E & J Gallo Winery, Geyser Peak Winery, Grgich Hills Cellar, Hanzell Vineyards, Heitz Cellars, The Hess Collection, Iron Horse Vineyards, Jordan Vineyard, Kendall-Jackson, Kenwood Vineyards, Kistler Vineyards, Kunde Estate Winery, La Crema, Laurel Glen Vineyards, Marcassin Winery, Louis M Martini, Matanzas Creek Winery, Meridian Vineyards, Peter Michael Winery, Robert Mondavi Winery, Mumm Napa, Murphy-Goode Winery, Newton Vineyards, Niebaum Coppola Winery,
Opus One, Pahlmeyer Winery, Paradigm Winery, Fess Parker Winery, Joseph Phelps, Pine Ridge Winery, Quivira Vineyards, Qupé Winery, A Rafanelli, Kent Rasmussen, Ridge Vineyards, J Rochioli Vineyards, Roederer Estate, St Francis Winery, Saintsbury, Sanford Winery, Schramsberg Vineyards, Shafer Winery, Silver Oak Cellars, Silverado Vineyards, Simi Winery, Sonoma-Cutrer, Spottswoode, Staglin Family Vineyards, Stag's Leap Wine Cellars, Steele Wines, Sterling Vineyards, Stonestreet Winery, Sutter Home Winery, Swanson Vineyards, Lane Tanner, Marimar Torres, Turley Cellars, Viader Vineyards, Villa Mt. Eden, Wente Vineyards, Williams Selyems Winery, ZD Wines.

SEE ALSO
Napa, pages 264–265.

CH. CALON-SÉGUR

FRANCE, Bordeaux, Médoc, St-Estèphe AC, 3ème Cru Classé

Cabernet Sauvignon, Cabernet Franc, Merlot

This is the most northerly of all the MÉDOC's Classed Growths and the lowest in altitude, averaging less than 10m (30ft) above sea level. What gives Calon-Ségur Classed Growth quality is a spur of chalky, gravelly soil – usually found on higher ground in the Médoc. None of the neighbouring properties – struggling along on heavier clay soils – can produce wine that remotely matches Calon-Ségur.

Until the 1960s, Calon-Ségur used to be thought of as ST-ESTÈPHE's leading château, but has now been clearly surpassed by MONTROSE and COS D'ESTOURNEL. In the mid-1980s Calon-Ségur's problem was that its wine, though quite good, was ever so slightly dull and, at the high prices demanded by Médoc Classed Growths, dullness isn't really on. Reduced yields, more rigorous fruit selection and an increase in the percentage of new oak for aging helped produce notable wines in '95 and '96 but the estate still lacks consistency. Second wine: Marquis de Ségur. Best years: 1996, '95, '94, '90, '89, '86, '82.

CAMERON WINERY

USA, Oregon, Yamhill County, Willamette Valley AVA

Pinot Noir

Chardonnay, Pinot Blanc

Years before Burgundy's Robert Drouhin established an OREGON outpost, Cameron's winemaker John Paul was applying every known Burgundian method and trick of the trade to WILLAMETTE VALLEY fruit. After brief stints working in Burgundy, California and New Zealand, Paul had settled on the Red Hills of Dundee as his destiny. Using grapes from Abbey Ridge vineyard, he has created a reputation for highly individualistic, sometimes wonderfully eccentric Pinot Noir, as well as impressively quirky Chardonnay. Best years: 1998, '96, '95.

CAMERON

Cameron's jovial winemaker, John Paul, uses lots of very ripe fruit and new oak to embellish his Chardonnay and Pinot Noir with thrillingly whacky flavours.

CAMPANIA

ITALY

This is the region centred on Naples: bustling, chaotic, where black is the colour of the economy and theft is raised to an art form. It's the region of Sorrento, Amalfi, Ravello, Capri – 'a little piece of heaven fallen on earth' as holiday brochures smugly quote. Campania is a geologically unstable region, where earthquakes and other terrestrial fluctuations are frequent occurrences. And it is the region of wines such as FALERNO, FIANO DI AVELLINO, Greco di Tufo, Solopaca, TAURASI and others, some of them reaching cult status, some still little known, as well as home to the overrated LACRYMA CHRISTI DEL VESUVIO.

Every region has at least one grape that it can proudly claim as its own. Campania boasts a whole slew of them. The whites Falanghina, Fiano and Coda di Volpe, as well as the red Piedirosso, are virtually exclusive to the region, as are Ischia's Forastera and Biancolella. Best known are the white Greco di Tufo and the red Aglianico, which may be found elsewhere in the southern mainland but are principally associated with Campania. There is also the weird Asprinio, which produces acidic, spritzy whites from vines trained up trees to a height of 20–30m (65–100ft): an ancient Etruscan would feel quite at home. Nor should one forget the international varieties – Cabernet Sauvignon and Merlot blend with Aglianico in a Campanian vino da tavola called Montevetrano from the Montevetrano estate near Salerno that has become world-famous.

All in all, in this land of Vesuvius and the Campi Flegrei, there is considerable activity under way, with more producers of real quality arising all the time to realize the potential of a very considerable patrimony.

CAMPILLO

SPAIN, País Vasco, Rioja DOC

Tempranillo, Cabernet Sauvignon, Graciano

Macabeo (Viura)

This top-class bodega just outside Laguardia makes elegant but concentrated fruity red wines from pure Tempranillo. There is also a small amount of goodish oak-aged white Crianza, and some forgettable rosé. Campillo used to be a subsidiary label belonging to Faustino Martínez, but now has its own, very positive identity. The beautiful bodega is an extremely popular destination for visitors from all over the Basque country, who buy more than half the production. Best years: 1995, '94, '90, '89, '87, '86, '85, '82, '81.

CAMPO DE BORJA DO

SPAIN, Aragón

Grenache Noir (Garnacha Tinta), Macabeo, Tempranillo, Carignan (Mazuelo, Cariñena), Cabernet Sauvignon

Macabeo, Moscatel Romano

A bottle of headache pills is no longer needed if you venture south of RIOJA and NAVARRA down on to the undulating plains of Campo de Borja. Most of the wines are being turned out younger, fruitier, less astringent and somewhat less alcoholic, but 13 per cent is still considered the lightest of light. Wood aging was traditional here, but many wines are now being sold with none (and are the better and fruitier for it). Experiments with Tempranillo, Cabernet Sauvignon and Mazuelo for blending with Garnacha have produced some more appetizing results. White wines have also been included in the DO since 1989 and these, commendably, can be made with as little as 10.5 per cent alcohol. Best producers: Co-operativa Agricola de Borja, Bordejé. Best years: 1995, '92, '91.

CAMPO VIEJO

SPAIN, La Rioja, Rioja DOC

Tempranillo, Carignan (Cariñena, Mazuelo), Grenache Noir (Garnacha Tinta), Graciano

Macabeo (Viura)

Campo Viejo, the main company in BODEGAS Y BEBIDAS, Spain's largest wine group, is huge – easily the largest producer of RIOJA. But the wines are, mostly, good. The basic Rioja and Crianza are fairly forgettable but, at Reserva and Gran Reserva level, it is unusual to be disappointed.

Albor is one of the best examples of modern white Rioja, clean, appley and perfumed; the 100 per cent Tempranillo, red Viña Alcorta Reserva is even better, lean and stylish, with lively, raspberry and wild strawberry fruit. The basic Campo Viejo Gran Reservas are good, but the Marqués de Villamagna Gran Reservas are excellent, with lovely, aromatic, wild strawberry fragrance and elegant fruit. Best years: (reds) 1995, '94, '91, '90, '89, '87, '85, '83, '82.

CAN FEIXES

SPAIN, Cataluña, Penedès DO, Cava DO

Tempranillo, Cabernet Sauvignon

Parellada, Macabeo, Chardonnay, Pinot Noir

Josep Maria Huguet's family has owned the historic Can Feixes estate, with its 70ha (173 acres) of vineyards, for a century. This is the farthest PENEDÈS vineyard from the Mediterranean Sea, near the region's northern boundary, beneath the Montserrat mountains. It is 400m (1300ft) above sea level, so temperature variations are more marked than in lower-sited vineyards. This is conducive to highly perfumed white wines, both still and bubbly, which is not frequent in Penedès. The Blanc Selecció, an unusual blend of Parellada, Macabeo, Chardonnay and Pinot Noir, and the Huguet Gran Reserva Brut Nature CAVA are the bodega's star wines.

Huguet, in addition, has been improving his red wine range constantly, getting a character, a vigour and a concentration that are not all that common in the area. He makes a Can Feixes Negre and a Can Feixes Negre Selecció Reserva, both of them blends of Tempranillo and Cabernet Sauvignon. Best years: 1996, '94, '93, '91.

CAN RÀFOLS DELS CAUS
SPAIN, Cataluña, Penedès DO, Cava DO
♥ *Merlot, Cabernet Franc, Cabernet Sauvignon, Tempranillo*
♥ *Merlot, Syrah, Tempranillo*
♀ *Xarel-lo, Macabeo, Chardonnay, Chenin Blanc, Parellada and others*

The Esteva family acquired this 350-year-old, 450-ha (1110-acre) agricultural estate in the 1930s. Only one-tenth of the surface is devoted to vineyards; the rest includes almond and olive trees and Carlos Esteva makes a stupendous extra virgin olive oil. However, wine is certainly more important to him and he makes some of the best reds in PENEDÈS in his small, modern winery installed in the old stables and adjoining buildings of the ancient hilltop farmhouse.

Esteva favours BORDEAUX grape varieties for his reds and intriguing blends of Catalan varieties with Chardonnay and Chenin Blanc for his whites. He is the leading Spanish proponent of Merlot, and his Caus Lubís red cuvée may be Iberia's best Merlot varietal. Merlot is also the sole grape of Gran

CAN RÀFOLS DELS CAUS
Some of the most exciting and ambitious Penedès reds, and deliciously fruity rosés, are produced under this estate's Gran Caus label.

Caus rosado. Gran Caus red, on the other hand, is the lone Cabernet Franc-dominated wine in all of Spain – that is, if it isn't finally proven that the Bierzo DO's own Mencía grape is actually Cabernet Franc under a different name! There is, at any rate, none of the thinness and austerity usually associated with Penedès reds in these full-blown wines. Best years: 1995, '94, '91.

CANARIAS (CANARY ISLANDS)
SPAIN
From the times of the legendary Canary Sack of Elizabethan England, the exotic sweet wines made in the Spanish archipelago off the western African coast had notable fame, which dwindled through the years as their MADEIRA neighbours displaced them in the British market. Wine remained an important local product in the Canary Islands, where there are still more than 11,000ha (27,170 acres) of vineyards, particularly on Tenerife, Lanzarote and La Palma islands, often on precipitous slopes. Here, as in the BALEARES, tourists consume most of the production and pay high prices for it. But here, the seemingly disproportionate creation of new DOs has been reflected in real quality improvement.

There are no fewer than five DOs on Tenerife island alone: Abona in the southern half, and Tacoronte-Acentejo, Ycoden-Daute-Isora, Valle de la Orotava and Valle de Güímar further north. This is dry table wine country, with Negramoll the prevalent red grape variety, followed by Listán Negro, and Listán Blanco the main white one. Wines from Viña Norte, El Lomo, Monje and Viñátigo are very original – intensely fruity and minerally at the same time.

La Palma and the volcanic Lanzarote island have their own DOs, in which the rediscovered sweet Malvasía wines can reach real distinction. El Hierro DO and the Vinos de la Tierra areas of Gran Canaria and Gomera hold much less interest.

CANBERRA DISTRICT
AUSTRALIA, New South Wales, Southern New South Wales Zone
This area is currently home to 15 wineries, clustered just outside the Australian Capital Territory and the capital city, Canberra. Some seem to have a tenuous hold on the realities of life and the need for consistency; while others possess the commitment to succeed. The winters, and nights, are cold, the summer days hot and dry: virtually every grape variety is grown here, and the wine

styles are extremely diverse. The arrival of BRL HARDY, albeit on a modest scale, has given the area a boost – ironically only a short period before a devastating frost in October 1998. Best years: 1997, '96, '95, '92, '90. Best producers: Brindabella Hills, Doonkuna, Helm's, Lark Hill, Madew.

CANEPA
CHILE, Maipo Valley
♥ *Cabernet Sauvignon, Merlot*
♀ *Sauvignon Blanc, Chardonnay*

Viña Canepa was among the first bodegas in Chile to modernize, establishing one of South America's most advanced wineries in 1982. Recent investments have seen 220ha (550 acres) of vineyards added as well as the construction of a new winery in Colchagua, to complement Canepa's traditional base in Maipo and the Cabernet Sauvignon vineyards in Curicó. Canepa also buys grapes from growers based in many of Chile's best grape-growing valleys, including Cachapoal, San Fernando and Lontué. The Magnificum Cabernet Sauvignon and Private Merlot Reserve are impressive wines and the Private Reserve Chardonnay from Cachapoal is also worth looking at. Best years: (reds) 1998, '96, '95.

CH. CANON
Historically Ch. Canon has long been recognized as one of the top Premiers Grands Crus Classés of St-Émilion and following a change of owners the late 1990s should see a welcome return to form.

CH. CANON
FRANCE, Bordeaux, St-Émilion Grand Cru AC, Premier Grand Cru Classé
♥ *Merlot, Cabernet Franc, Cabernet Sauvignon*

Canon used to make some of the most perfect, most recognizable, most reliably rich ST-ÉMILION – reeking of that toffee-butter-and-raisins mellow ripeness which only Merlot can impart. The wine was deep, with a rich plummy fruit, and in good vintages was impressively tannic at the outset. Unfortunately, recent vintages have not lived up to this ideal, but in 1996 Canon was bought by French fashion and perfume company Chanel, owner also of Ch. RAUZAN-SÉGLA, which is pulling out all the stops to get things right. So expect a return to the good old days somewhere in the near future.

The vineyard is just west of the town of St-Émilion and completely surrounded by other First Growths. Second wine: Clos J Kanor. Best years: 1998, '90, '89, '88, '86, '85, '83, '82, '81, '79, '78.

CANON-FRONSAC AC

FRANCE, Bordeaux

♀ *Merlot, Cabernet Franc, Cabernet Sauvignon, Malbec*

This AC is the heart of the FRONSAC region, covering 305ha (755 acres) of hilly vineyards between the villages of Fronsac and St-Michel de Fronsac. As in the neighbouring Fronsac AC, great strides have been made to curb the rustic tannic element once inherent in the wines. The best ones are now deeply coloured, richly textured and with a firm but refined tannic structure. They age well and, after going through a rather gamy period at a few years old, usually emerge at ten years plus with a lovely, soft, Merlot-dominated flavour and a good mineral tang. Best producers: Barrabaque, Canon, Canon-de-Brem, Cassagne-Haut Canon (La Truffière), La Fleur Cailleau, Grand Renouil, Moulin-Pey-Labrie, Vrai-Canon-Bouché, Vrai-Canon-Boyer. Best years: 1998, '97, '96, '95, '94, '90, '89, '88, '85, '83, '82, '79, '78.

CH. CANTEMERLE

FRANCE, Bordeaux, Haut-Médoc AC, 5ème Cru Classé

♀ *Cabernet Sauvignon, Merlot, Cabernet Franc, Petit Verdot*

You head out of BORDEAUX on the D2, through suburbs, shrubland, damp meadows, and the occasional vineyard, and you begin to wonder if you're on the wrong road for the great wine land of the MÉDOC. Then the forests fall away and suddenly the land is thick with rows of neatly trained vines. There, on the right, is Ch. la LAGUNE then, on the left, Ch. Cantemerle, a jewel set inside its own little woodland glade. Drive up the long avenue shrouded over with age-old trees and stand in front of the turretted castle. Silence. Stillness. Fairyland? Not far off.

Cantemerle was ranked last in the 1855 Classification of Bordeaux wines but when the merchant house Cordier took over in 1980, quality greatly improved for a decade. In general, the wine is relatively delicate, but the 1983 and '90 are whoppers – rich, concentrated and dark, yet already showing an exotic fragrance. Apart from the '83 and '90, which will benefit from 15 or more years' aging, you don't have to age Cantemerle for more than seven to ten years. Consistency at the estate is variable and in general vintages of the early 1990s were disappointing. Second wine: Villeneuve de Cantemerle. Best years: 1997, '96, '95, '94, '90, '89, '83, '82.

CANTERBURY

NEW ZEALAND, South Island

This region's cool-climate viticulture is taken to extremes by the spring and autumn frosts and this means that most of the plantings are white – in particular Riesling, Chardonnay, Gewurztraminer and Pinot Blanc. But the most famous wines have been Pinot Noir, and the Waipara district is proving to be excellent for red and white. Best years: 1998, '94, '91, '89. Best producers: GIESEN, Pegasus Bay, Mark Rattray, St Helena, Waipara Springs.

CAPE MENTELLE

AUSTRALIA, Western Australia, South West Australia Zone, Margaret River

♀ *Cabernet Sauvignon, Syrah (Shiraz), Zinfandel*

♀ *Semillon, Sauvignon Blanc, Chardonnay*

The rammed-earth walls and local timber of one of MARGARET RIVER's leading wineries blend perfectly into the landscape, with its exotic native plants and a tiny rivulet meandering by. Founder David Hohnen crafts his wines with intense care and sensitivity. He works hard to invest his Cabernet Sauvignon with the right amount of tannin to balance its full, dark fruit, but his exuberant, spicy, cherry-flavoured Zinfandel and spicy Shiraz sometimes steal the show. Recent vintages of Semillon-Sauvignon Blanc and Chardonnay have been excellent. Cape Mentelle is co-owned, along with New Zealand's CLOUDY BAY, by French CHAMPAGNE house VEUVE CLICQUOT. Best years: 1996, '93, '92, '91, '90, '88, '86, '83, '82, '78.

CAPEL VALE

AUSTRALIA, Western Australia, South West Australia Zone, Geographe

♀ *Syrah (Shiraz), Cabernet Sauvignon, Merlot*

♀ *Chardonnay, Sauvignon Blanc, Riesling, Verdelho, Chenin Blanc*

The far-flung empire of Capel Vale, driven by the indefatigable owner Dr Peter Pratten, continues to flourish, drawing grapes from Capel, Mount Barker (in the GREAT SOUTHERN) and Donnybrook (like Capel, in the new GEOGRAPHE region, but cooler), and finally from MARGARET RIVER. Elegant, tangy

New oak barrels are expensive but Cape Mentelle, in the Margaret River, carefully marries fine French oak with top-quality fruit.

Riesling, Sauvignon Blanc and Chardonnay all reflect relatively cool climates, the red wines (including the deluxe Kinnaird Shiraz and Howecroft Cabernet Sauvignon Merlot) skilfully marry opulent fruit with opulent oak and age well. Best years: 1997, '96, '95, '94, '93.

CAREMA DOC
ITALY, Piedmont
❡ *Nebbiolo*

Carema, north PIEDMONT's best wine, is produced almost entirely by the weekend pottering of local commuters, who part with their prized grapes to the co-operative (Cantina Produttori) or to a private producer such as the assiduous Luigi Ferrando. It is not easy work. Viticulture is only possible because the Dora Baltea river flows swiftly through the area and keeps the air moving, therefore bringing sun to a narrow strip surrounded by cloud. Nebbiolo grown in such marginal conditions gives Carema a rare, elegant, violet-like style. Try Ferrando's Black Label, only made in the best years, like 1997, '96, '95, '93, '90, '89, '85: his normal label is white. Or try the co-operative's reserve wine, Carema Carema.

CARIGNAN

Carignan is supposed to have originated in Spain, where it is still grown in CATALUÑA, under the name of Cariñena; as Mazuelo or Mazuela, it used to be important in RIOJA. It's the dominant red grape in the South of France and forms the backbone of most anonymous French vin de table, but can produce excellent juicy wines when modern methods are used on low-yield fruit from old vines.

It also pops up in Sardinia, called Carignano, and in North Africa, South Africa, California and Chile. What it likes best are hot, dry conditions where it can produce deep-coloured, astringent wines that, lacking richness, aroma and flavour, are nevertheless useful in blending. However, there is potential for delicious spicy fruit there as well, especially when the BEAUJOLAIS method of carbonic maceration is used to make the wine.

LOUIS CARILLON & FILS
FRANCE, Burgundy, Côte de Beaune, Puligny-Montrachet AC
♀ *Chardonnay*
❡ *Pinot Noir*

This is a large estate, with some 22ha (55 acres) under vine, and not all the wine is bottled by the Carillons, who also sell some of their production to *négociants*. Louis Carillon is now assisted by his sons Jacques and François. Their

best wines are usually the brilliant PULIGNY-MONTRACHET Premiers Crus – Perrières, Champ Canet and Referts – and the Bienvenues-Bâtard-Montrachet. The Premiers Crus are aged in 25 per cent new oak. Carillon also produce sound red wines from CHASSAGNE-MONTRACHET and ST-AUBIN. Best years: 1997, '96, '95, '93, '92, '90, '89, '88, '86, '85.

CARIÑENA DO
SPAIN, Aragón
❡ *Grenache Noir (Garnacha Tinta), Carignan (Cariñena), Tempranillo, Cabernet Sauvignon, Merlot and others*
♀ *Macabeo (Viura), Moscatel Romano, Grenache Blanc (Garnacha Blanca)*

This DO exemplifies the astonishing changes taking place in Spain. Where about half of the wine was once sold in bulk, the figure is now less than 2 per cent. Bottled wines still tend to be basic and alcoholic, but better harvesting and winemaking practices are reflected in an increasing amount of seriously fruity reds and fresher whites from the dominant co-operatives and the slowly growing number of private bodegas (now about two dozen). Vineyard diversification, with Tempranillo, Cabernet Sauvignon and Merlot acreage on the upswing, is certainly helping. Best-equipped among the co-operatives is the huge Bodegas San Valero, which makes young, fresh, spicy reds and rosés under the Don Mendo label, and pretty good, oak-aged Gran Reserva Monte Ducay reds. But the new innovator is the private Solar de Urbezo winery, whose reds are based on Tempranillo, Cabernet Sauvignon, Merlot and some experimental Syrah rather than on Garnacha Tinta. Best years: 1996, '93, '92, '91.

CARMEN
CHILE, Maipo Valley
❡ *Cabernet Sauvignon, Petite Sirah, Carmenère, Merlot, Pinot Noir and others*
♀ *Sauvignon Blanc, Chardonnay*

Carmen's great advantage lies in an exceptionally talented winemaker, Alvaro Espinoza, who is developing 4ha (10 acres) of organic vineyards, within Carmen's larger vineyard holding, that promise great things. Although owned by the giant SANTA RITA, Carmen acts independently and Espinoza is always experimenting, most recently with Pinot Noir and Syrah. His Wine Maker's Reserve is a full-blown blend of Cabernet Sauvignon, Petite Sirah, Carmenère and Merlot in a seductive combination, only outdone by the Gold Reserve. Best years: 1998, '97, '96.

CARMENET VINEYARD
Carmenet's Dynamite label is for early-maturing, accessible, California-style Cabernet Sauvignon and Merlot wines.

CARMENET VINEYARD
USA, California, Sonoma County, Sonoma Valley AVA
❡ *Cabernet Sauvignon, Merlot and others*
♀ *Sauvignon, Semillon, Chardonnay*

Situated on a hillside a short distance from Louis MARTINI's famous Monte Rosso Cabernet vineyard, Carmenet was created by its parent company, CHALONE Inc., to serve as the BORDEAUX-style standard bearer in its portfolio. So far, Carmenet's reds and whites are brilliantly, yet not slavishly Bordeaux in style, the red all blackcurrant and cedar, the white superbly grassy yet subtly oaky too. Carmenet relies on its 22-ha (55-acre) estate. Among the first to establish its own underground aging *caves*, it almost seems to follow old-time Bordeaux winemaking traditions to a fault, but modern know-how and old-time traditions are a potent combination. Best years: 1997, '95, '94, '93, '92, '91, '90, '89, '87, '85.

CARMIGNANO DOCG AND DOC
ITALY, Tuscany
❡ ♀ *Sangiovese, Cabernet Franc, Cabernet Sauvignon, Merlot, Canaiolo and others*

Carmignano, west of Florence, has an impeccable pedigree, from wine pots found in Etruscan tombs to citations in the 1300s. Yet it took tireless work by Conte Ugo Contini Bonacossi of Villa di Capezzana to get Carmignano accepted, first as DOC, now as DOCG. One stumbling block was the use of

VILLA DI CAPEZZANA
This very long-lived wine develops great complexity and elegance with age and comes from Carmignano's main producer, Villa di Capezzana.

Cabernet, Bonacossi's argument centring on its traditional presence in the times of the Medici. Capezzana's wine is elegant, classy, restrained and lasts well up to ten years, although 1931 is still legendary. The area also produces a young-drinking version, called Barco Reale (now DOC), a lovely rosé called Vinruspo and a VIN SANTO, also now DOC.

Other good producers: Ambra, Artimino, Bacchereto, Il Poggiolo and the Villa di Trefiano of Ugo Contini Bonacossi's son, Vittorio. Best years: 1998, '97, '95, '94, '93, '90, '88, '85. Capezzana's individual contribution to the area's renown also includes the SUPER-TUSCAN Ghiaie Della Furba, a BORDEAUX-style blend of Cabernets Sauvignon and Franc plus Merlot. It is mellow, blackcurranty, with plenty of weight and staying power, yet retaining a lightness of touch that gives refinement.

CARNEROS AVA
USA, California, Napa and Sonoma Counties
The grassy knolls of windy Los Carneros (meaning 'the rams' in Spanish because of the sheep farms that once reigned here) are draped like a rumpled old lion skin across the San Francisco Bay ends of both the NAPA and SONOMA VALLEYs. Much of the district is right in the path of those same wind-driven sea-fogs that chill summer tourists at Fisherman's Wharf, and they roll over these low, barren hills to cool the climate to un-CALIFORNIA-like levels. But these fogs were recognized as crucial in creating the cool climate necessary to yield fragrant Pinot Noir, finely balanced Chardonnay, lush, fruit-filled Merlot and intense, dramatic Syrah.

The weather and poor, scrubby soils combine to produce good Chardonnays (ACACIA, Bouchaine, MacRostie, Rasmussen, SAINTSBURY, Truchard) and exciting Pinot Noirs (Acacia, Carneros Creek, Rasmussen, Saintsbury). And while good Chardonnay is being made elsewhere in California, the regions that have proved themselves suitable for Pinot Noir, the most difficult and temperamental red, are far fewer. Best years: (reds) 1998, '97, '96, '95; (Chardonnay) 1997, '96, '95.

BEAULIEU VINEYARD, CLOS DU VAL, CUVAISON, DOMAINE CARNEROS, Charles Krug, Robert MONDAVI and STERLING VINEYARDS are wineries with major vineyards here and many other big Napa wineries use CARNEROS fruit for their Chardonnays and Pinot Noirs. The district is also important for excellent CHAMPAGNE-method sparkling

The combination of hot sun and clammy fogs in the low-lying Carneros region at the northern end of San Francisco Bay means that grapes grown here enjoy a very long, cool ripening period.

wine: CODORNÍU, Domaine Carneros, DOMAINE CHANDON, Gloria Ferrer and MUMM NAPA have vineyards or wineries here.

CARR TAYLOR
ENGLAND, East Sussex
♀ *Reichensteiner, Gutenborner, Schönburger*
David Carr Taylor is one of the most enterprising names in English wine. He has 16ha (40 acres) of vineyard near Hastings in Sussex, and also makes wine on a contract basis for other growers in the area. His own sparkling wine, made by the CHAMPAGNE method by a visiting French winemaker, is from grapes grown on south-facing chalk soils and improves year by year. The vineyards have been planted since 1971 and Carr Taylor has invested huge efforts in discovering the right grape varieties to withstand the English climate. Best years: 1998, '97.

CASA LAPOSTOLLE
CHILE, Rapel Valley
♀ *Cabernet Sauvignon, Merlot*
♀ *Sauvignon Blanc, Chardonnay*
Casa Lapostolle, based in the Rapel Valley, is the newest venture of the Marnier Lapostolle family, owners of Grand Marnier. Their philosophy is to use French varietals and a Gallic outlook to make high-quality wines in Chile. Michel Rolland, the international star winemaker from BORDEAUX, is responsible for the

towering quality of the wines, particularly the Merlot Cuvée Alexandre, which is beginning to show that the Merlot grape may be Chile's trump card. The no-expense-spared winery also makes intense Sauvignon Blanc, rich, buttery Chardonnay and blackcurranty Cabernet Sauvignon, the latter two also available in the sought-after Cuvée Alexandre range. Best years: 1998, '97, '96, '95.

CASABLANCA VALLEY
CHILE, Aconcagua Valley
North-west of Santiago, within the Aconcagua Valley, lies one of the newer additions to the growing list of Chilean wine regions, the Casablanca Valley. Initially it was seen as a bit of a gimmick, an expansion on to new soil because there was nowhere else to go, but when the first Sauvignon Blanc wines started to emerge this rumour was firmly quashed. Benefiting from the coastal fog that rolls off the nearby Pacific, Casablanca is cooler than the traditional vineyard areas in the VALLE CENTRAL. It is clearly fine winemaking terroir, and as the vines mature we are bound to see some exciting wines. The best Chilean Sauvignon Blanc grapes hail from here as well as excellent Chardonnay and a small amount of remarkable Merlot and Cabernet. Best producers: Caliterra, CARMEN, CONCHA Y TORO, CONO SUR, ERRÁZURIZ, SANTA RITA, Veramonte, Villard, VIÑA CASABLANCA.

CASSIS

FRANCE, Provence

🍷 *Grenache, Cinsaut, Mourvèdre*

♀ *Ugni Blanc, Clairette, Marsanne and others*

Cassis is really a white wine town. Rosé and reds don't figure much on the quality stakes, although they represent almost half the production. The red wine is dull at best; the rosé can be lovely and can age for a surprisingly long time – but only from a single estate such as Clos Ste-Magdeleine or Mas Calendal. White Cassis, based on Ugni Blanc and Clairette, sometimes with Marsanne, Sauvignon Blanc and Bourboulenc to help out, is the most well-known and most overpriced white wine of the French Riviera. Could the stunning views of the vineyards rising up towards the steep cliffs, the port's daily catch of the Mediterranean's freshest fish, and the array of quayside restaurants crushed tight with trendies from nearby Marseille and Toulouse have something to do with it? The wine can be fair enough if it's fresh. Best producers: Clos Ste-Magdeleine, Ferme Blanche, Fontblanche, Fontcreuse. Best years: 1998, '97, '96.

CASTEL DEL MONTE DOC

ITALY, Puglia

🍷 *Uva di Troia, Bombino Nero, Montepulciano, Sangiovese and others*

🍷 *Bombino Nero, Uva di Troia, Montepulciano*

♀ *Pampanuto, Trebbiano, Bombino Bianco, Palumbo*

An arid, hilly zone inland from Bari, Castel del Monte provides the ideal habitat for the Uva di Troia grape, a gutsy, high-quality variety which can make long-lasting wine. In the hands of a top producer, Castel del Monte red can be a fragrant glassful reminiscent of rich strawberry jam, with a bitter-dry finish and fine at around three years old. Bombino Nero, on the other hand, develops less alcohol, retains good acidity and yields extract and colour quickly during fermentation, making it a natural for rosés; Castel del Monte Rosato has long been among Italy's leading rosés. New varietal reds and rosés are

now appearing from Aglianico and Pinot Noir (Pinot Nero).

The vaguely earthy whites, however, are undistinguished, but increasing amounts of varietal Chardonnay, Sauvignon Blanc and Pinot Blanc (Pinot Bianco) are being made.

The producer RIVERA has cornered the quality market, especially with its red Riserva Il Falcone, an excellent, full-blooded southern red, with a bumped-up level of Montepulciano. Il Falcone is a well-structured, 'serious', earthy, minerally, licorice-like wine with a ten-year aging potential. Best years: (Il Falcone) 1997, '96, '94, '93, '92, '91, '90, '85.

TENUTA DI CASTELGIOCONDO/ LUCE DELLA VITE

ITALY, Tuscany, Brunello di Montalcino DOCG

🍷 *Sangiovese, Merlot*

In 1989 the family of the Marchesi FRESCOBALDI purchased a large vineyard in Montalcino called Castel Giocondo with well over 200ha (500 acres) of vines. From these vines they produce a classic, well-structured but barrique-influenced Brunello (called Castelgiocondo) and a relatively insubstantial but early-drinking Rosso di Montalcino (called Campo ai Sassi), plus Lamaione, one of the best of the ever-increasing range of pure Tuscan Merlots.

In 1995 the Frescobaldis formed a joint venture with the MONDAVI family of NAPA, called Luce della Vite, and since 1993 (from existing wines) and more significantly since 1995 (from grapes of both Castel Giocondo and the joint venture vineyards) created a seriously high-image, high-priced blend called Luce, from half Sangiovese half Merlot. The style is unashamedly 'international', rich in flavour and texture with tannins smoothed down and fruit interweaving with fine oak. A second wine from this venture is Lucente, 85 per cent Sangiovese, 15 per cent Merlot from various vineyards belonging to the Frescobaldis, barrique-refined (of course), which from its second

vintage, 1996, has shown increasing promise. Best years: 1996, '94, '93, '92, '91, '90, '88.

CASTELLBLANCH

SPAIN, Cataluña, Cava DO

🍷 *Monastrell, Tempranillo (Ull de Llebre)*

♀ *Macabeo, Xarel-lo, Parellada*

Castellblanch – with a large, unattractive, modern bodega in San Sadurní de Noya – is one of the world's largest CHAMPAGNE-method sparkling wine companies. It is now a subsidiary of another CAVA giant, FREIXENET, and also makes Cava sold under the Conde de Caralt label. Castellblanch owns some vineyards, but mostly buys in grapes and wine from elsewhere. The wines, under the brand names Brut Zero (which has no sweetening) and Cristal Seco, are rather better than the uninspired surroundings might suggest, and Conde de Caralt, in particular, can be good. The rosé is pleasant too.

CASTILLA-LA MANCHA

SPAIN

More than half of Spain's vineyard surface, or 608,000ha (1,502,350 acres), lies in the interminable, dry, high plains of the Castilla-La Mancha autonomous region, where most of the production is distilled into grape alcohol. Better times are on the horizon as the so-called European 'wine lake' has evaporated, the EU no longer demands that any vineyards be scrapped and the legalization of irrigation makes it possible to move away from the hardy, boring white Airén variety and bring in better-quality northern Spanish and international varietals.

In addition to the huge La MANCHA DO, there's also Méntrida south of Madrid (reds from Garnacha Tinta/Grenache Noir that are currently mediocre), VALDEPEÑAS (light red blends that are slowly improving as the amount of Cencibel/Tempranillo increases), Almansa (solid reds from Monastrell/Mourvèdre and Cencibel) and the new Mondéjar DO which vies with Méntrida for the dubious distinction of being last in Spain's quality rankings.

But curiously the most progressive bodegas of the region lie outside any DO boundaries and their wines are sold as Vinos de Mesa. These are MARQUÉS DE GRIÑÓN in Toledo province, Dehesa del Carrizal in Ciudad Real, Manuel Manzaneque in Albacete and Calzadilla in Cuenca. These small properties make some of Spain's best Cabernet Sauvignon-based wines.

CASTILLA-LEÓN Spain

The Viña Alta vineyard in Ribera del Duero belongs to Alejandro Fernández who discovered that the region's high altitude meant that the Tinto Fino grape grew thin-skinned with high levels of acidity, resulting in rich, aromatic reds.

MANY CENTURIES BEFORE RIOJA surprised the world with delicate Bordeaux-style wines, and many centuries before La Mancha became an immense vineyard, the kingdoms of Castile and León were covered with vines as the Christian kings started reconquering the Iberian peninsula, almost entirely occupied by Arab and Berber invaders since the early eighth century. Planting vines and raising hogs were two hallmarks of advancing Christiandom, and the fortress monasteries which dotted the severe Castilian landscape in the mid-twelfth century, often run by French monastic orders, were responsible for both activities.

Good strong wines from Peñafiel, Toro or Medina del Campo became famous and were an enduring source of wealth. But the Mediterranean regions, followed by Jerez, by La Mancha, and finally by Rioja, progressively took over the markets. The nineteenth-century nationalization of the Catholic Church's assets was as much of a death blow as phylloxera was. After the louse struck, thousands of acres were replanted with the hardy but mediocre Palomino and Garnacha Tintorera grapes, and quality native varieties became almost extinct. Nothing but the supplying of cheap bulk wines seemed to remain on the horizon for Castilla-León, and vines were pulled by the million.

As recently as 1980 beetroot was the main crop in Ribera del Duero, and no wine book in the world mentioned the two old kingdoms (now part of the modern Castilla-León autonomous region) as anything like a quality wine region. Yet an old isolated estate and some enterprising people from Rioja were getting ready to rekindle the flame. The Vega Sicilia estate had steadfastly proven, since the 1860s, that Ribera grapes could produce an astonishing wine if properly vinified, and by the 1970s some neighbours, led by toolmaker Alejandro Fernández, had taken their cue and were following Vega's lead, making deep, dense, powerful wines from these high-altitude vineyards.

Meanwhile, the historic Rioja Alavesa firm of Marqués de Riscal had decided not to make white wines in its home region any longer, but instead to replant the native Verdejo (and later to introduce Sauvignon Blanc) on the high plateau of Rueda, where both varieties succeed now in producing aromatic, zippy modern whites. These were the sparkplugs to the revival. Success in Ribera and Rueda became the story

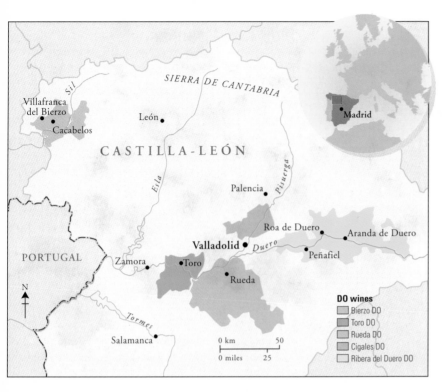

TEÓFILO REYES
From its first acclaimed vintage in 1994 this wine has shown a ripe, spicy, tobacco-influenced fruit character with excellent depth and concentration.

ISMAEL ARROYO
This tiny bodega run by the Arroyo family in Ribera del Duero is known for its long-lived, tannic Val Sotillo Gran Reservas that blossom into long-lasting reds of opulent yet refined beauty.

ABADÍA RETUERTA
From a new vineyard on a historic site renowned for fine wine since the twelfth century, the lightly oaked Rivola wine is an aromatic blend of Tempranillo and Cabernet Sauvignon.

ANTAÑO
Wines labelled Rueda Superior must contain at least 85 per cent of the local Verdejo grape variety. Rueda is now Spain's top inland wine region for white wines.

of the 1990s, and by the closing of the century the other DOs in the region (Toro, Cigales and Bierzo) were starting to join, albeit timidly, the bandwagon. High altitude means a harsh continental climate here, but the valleys (particularly that of the Duero) bring just enough humidity to create some superior mesoclimates for grape-growing. The vineyard surface is again above 70,000ha (172,970 acres), and overwhelmingly, the main varieties are native ones, though French cultivars now occupy sizeable surfaces.

REGIONAL ENTRIES
Cigales, Ribera del Duero, Rueda, Toro.

PRODUCER ENTRIES
Abadía Retuerta, Álvarez y Díez, Arroyo, Fernández-Tinto Pesquera, Marqués de Riscal, Mauro, Peñalba López, Hermanos Pérez Pascuas-Viña Pedrosa, Dominio de Pingus, Protos, Reyes, Vega Sicilia.

VEGA SICILIA
From mainly Tempranillo with some Cabernet Sauvignon, the slow-maturing Unico is the top wine from Spain's most hallowed winery.

ALEJANDRO FERNÁNDEZ-TINTO PESQUERA
Unlike the wines from neighbouring Vega Sicilia, the Pesquera wines are made entirely from Tempranillo. The Gran Reserva is made only in the best years.

MARQUÉS DE RISCAL
Sauvignon Blanc has adapted well to the Rueda region and these whites almost single-handedly caused the renaissance of the region in the late 1970s.

CATALUÑA Spain

CATALUÑA IS ALMOST ANOTHER COUNTRY. It has a separate language, Catalan, an immensely cultured capital, Barcelona – and a thriving separatist movement. It also has the reputation of being the hardest-working and most efficient of Spain's autonomous regions. Wine, and especially sparkling wine, has also been a major source of prosperity.

The production of both sparkling wine and much of Cataluña's quality still wine is centred on the DO region of Penedès, between Barcelona and Tarragona. Here, wine producers turn out palatable to excellent wines around every corner. Practically every other DO region in Cataluña also has its star property or properties testifying to the potential of the vines. And the backwoods co-operatives and lacklustre companies without the equipment and the know-how to make good wine are now mostly a thing of the past – witness the extraordinary quality reached by the Capçanes co-operative in the Tarragona DO.

With nine still wine DOs plus a large area overlapping these which also qualifies for the Cava DO, Cataluña scores more DOs than any other autonomous region, and 90 per cent of Catalan wine is sold with a DO. Four of these DO wine areas are quite recent creations: Terra Alta, declared in 1985, Costers del Segre in 1988, Conca de Barberá in 1989 and Pla de Bages in 1995. None of these initially deserved the title, though inland Costers del Segre makes some good reds and whites notably at the important estate of Raimat, and neighbouring Conca de Barberá grows Torres's stunning Milmanda Chardonnay. But all of them have subsequently earned their spurs. However, it is the oldest of them all, Priorat, that has made the most spectacular strides, recovering an international lustre it last enjoyed long ago during the Middle Ages and Renaissance. The new boutique wineries in Priorat have revolutionized the map of Spain's quality wine regions which in turn has energized some smaller producers in the other southern DOs of Tarragona and Terra Alta. Most of the DO regions fan out from the dusty plain of Tarragona, into the gentle slopes of Penedès, the hills of Terra Alta, Conca de Barberá and Priorat. Dotted elsewhere are only tiny Alella on the Costa Dorada above Barcelona, verdant Ampurdán-Costa Brava up between the rocky northern coast and the French border with an easy local tourist market lapping up whatever is made, and the small, scattered patches of Costers del Segre bordering Aragón.

Some of Cataluña's most exciting new wine is emerging from the Priorat region. The landscape here is dramatic too and rugged mountains tower over small vineyards buried deep in the valleys and interspersed with almond and olive trees.

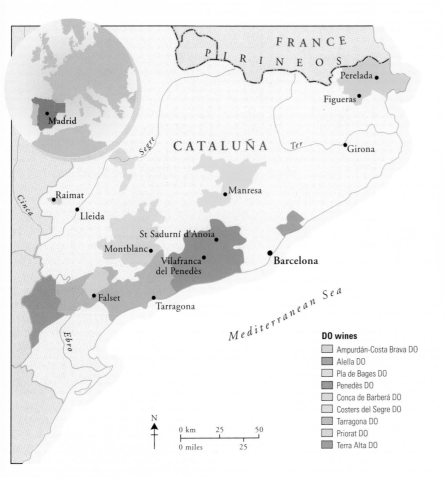

TORRES

Milmanda Chardonnay is the superstar white from Torres and Spain's first and still her best coolish-climate Chardonnay.

CAN RÀFOLS DELS CAUS

Some of the most exciting Penedès reds are produced from this estate. Caus Lubis is a Merlot wine and an unusual success in Spain for this variety.

COSTERS DEL SIURANA

Carles Pastrana makes stylish structured red wines, particularly Clos de l'Obac, a super-ripe Garnacha/Cabernet Sauvignon-based wine.

ALVARO PALACIOS

Alvaro Palacios is one of the leading producers in Priorat and Finca Dofì is an amazingly perfumed wine with a concentrated complex tannic structure.

CLOS MOGADOR

This estate helped pioneer the rebirth of Priorat in the late 1980s. The wines are high in alcohol, tannic and with natural acidity – brooding monsters built to last forever.

It's all tremendously encouraging, even though the final flowering of Cataluña has been an awful long time coming since Miguel Torres first set Spanish winemaking on its head in the 1970s. But the new Cataluña really does feel like a new country to a visitor who's been away for a while. A new country deserves new wines – and it's getting them.

REGIONAL ENTRIES
Alella, Cava, Conca de Barberá, Costers del Segre, Penedès, Priorat, Tarragona.

PRODUCER ENTRIES
Albet i Noya, Can Feixes, Can Ràfols del Caus, Castellblanch, Clos Mogador, Codorníu, Costers del Siurana, Freixenet, Juvé y Camps, León, Marqués de Monistrol, Mas Martinet, Alvaro Palacios, Raimat, Torres.

MARQUÉS DE MONISTROL
This fresh and fruity Cava with increasing quality comes from the Marqués de Monistrol winery at Sant' Sadurní d'Anoia.

CODORNÍU
Codorníu is now the biggest Champagne-method sparkling wine company in the world and Jaume Codorníu Brut is one of Spain's best made Cavas.

JUVÉ Y CAMPS
Juvé y Camps is well-respected, ultra-traditional – and expensive. Unusually for a Catalan company, most of the grapes come from its own vineyards.

CATENA

ARGENTINA, Mendoza

♟ *Malbec, Cabernet Sauvignon, Merlot*

♀ *Chardonnay*

Owning a quarter of Argentina's plantings of the top international grape varieties and situated in the upper reaches of MENDOZA with its temperate climate, it is not surprising that Dr Nicolás Catena produces some of Argentina's best wines. Under the banner name of Catena he produces wines at a number of locations, almost all in Mendoza. Bodega Esmeralda produces Catena and the top-of-the-range Catena Alta wines of Chardonnay, Cabernet Sauvignon and Malbec, which are definitely world class. Alamos Ridge is a decent budget brace of Chardonnay and Cabernet. La Rural produces a range of rather more variable varietal wines; the Merlot sold under the Rutini label is particularly worth trying. Bodega Escorihuela makes very reasonable and less expensive wines. Best years: 1997, '96.

CATENA

Nicolás Catena has invested hugely in his top-of the range wines, sold under the new Alta label; these are wines with enormous aging potential.

DOMAINE CAUHAPÉ

FRANCE, South-West, Jurançon AC

♀ *Gros Manseng, Petit Manseng*

Henri Ramonteu is synonymous with the revival in quality of the dry and sweet white wines of JURANÇON and he makes a range of astonishing wines at the 31-ha (77-acre) Domaine Cauhapé at Monein in the western Pyrenees. The dry wines, from Gros Manseng, include the fruity, aromatic Chant des Vignes and fuller, firmer Sève d'Automne. In exceptional years a dry Noblesse du Temps is made from Petit Manseng, the variety used for Jurançon's sweet wines. These are aged in new and one-year-old oak barriques and are gloriously rich and unctuous. The Symphonie de Novembre is made from late-harvested grapes picked during the first *tris* or selection and Noblesse du Temps from the second *tris*. A tiny amount of barrel-fermented Quintessence is made from extremely late-harvested grapes, often picked in January. Best years: 1997, '96, '95, '94, '93.

CAVA DO

SPAIN

♟ *Parellada, Macabeo, Xarel-lo, Grenache Noir (Garnacha Tinta), Monastrell, Pinot Noir*

♀ *Parellada, Macabeo, Xarel-lo and others*

Cava differs from the rest of Spain's wine DOs in that it's not confined to one geographical area. The word Cava is Catalan for 'cellar', and came to be applied to the CHAMPAGNE-method sparkling wines of CATALUÑA. Since all but a tiny proportion of Spain's Champagne-method fizz comes from Cataluña, the Catalan name was adopted for these sparkling wines throughout Spain.

There was a problem, however. The EU wine authorities insisted that any newly created DO should have specific geographical qualifications as well as rules relating to how the wine should be made and out of which grapes. So the Cava DO rules, declared in 1986, specified 159 villages across Spain where the grapes were authorized for Cava production. Most of them are in Cataluña, with a scattering of individual villages in the still wine regions of RIOJA, CAMPO DE BORJA, CARIÑENA, CALATAYUD, NAVARRA, Utiel-Requena, Ribera del Guadiana, COSTERS DEL SEGRE, Ampurdán-Costa Brava and TARRAGONA. These villages gained the right to the Cava DO simply because they had a long tradition of making Champagne-method wines – generally using the same grapes as their still wine neighbours. Quality didn't come into it. Indeed, many of the Cava DO villages turn out mediocre wines, while a strong contender for top spot on the quality scale doesn't even qualify: Castilla La Vieja in RUEDA simply hadn't been at it for long enough. Several villages that would have qualified failed to send their applications to Madrid by the prescribed date, so they can't call their fizzy wine Cava either. They have to use the appetizing term *vino espumoso natural método tradicional*.

Unfortunately, very few brands of Cava have particularly fruity, interesting flavours, DO or not. The grape varieties traditionally used are either dull or bland, and they don't age well, despite the fact that the Cava regulations insist upon a minimum of nine months' aging. The majority of Spanish fizz, from Cataluña, is made from Macabeo, Parellada and Xarel-lo; so, ironically, the best, fruitiest buys are the youngest and therefore cheapest wines. The few fizzes from Rioja are boring, too, made from Viura, alias Macabeo.

Some good Cavas made with the traditional grapes come from the firms of MARQUÉS DE MONISTROL, Mont Marçal, Cavas Hill and DOMAINE CHANDON in Penedès, and Parxet in Alella (both regions of Cataluña). But look out especially for Cava made from the Chardonnay grape by CODORNÍU or RAIMAT and a few others now springing up with Chardonnay on the label. Spanish Chardonnay fizz can have lovely fruit and flowery-buttery flavours, and a softer character than Champagne – and it *can* benefit from a bit of aging.

CAVE SPRING CELLARS

CANADA, Ontario, Niagara Peninsula VQA

♟ *Pinot Noir*

♀ *Chardonnay, Riesling*

Cave Spring Cellars was founded in 1986 and is situated some 20km (12 miles) west of Niagara Falls. Its vineyards occupy a narrow shelf of land known as the Beamsville Bench in the heart of the NIAGARA PENINSULA. Planting began in 1978 and today over 50 per cent of the winery's annual grape requirements are met by estate vineyards.

Winemaker Angelo Pavan is the man behind Cave Spring's wines, which include a series of concentrated Rieslings made in three styles: dry, late harvest (Indian Summer) and Icewine. The Chardonnay is another wine that sets the tone for the cool-climate, fruit-driven style that is the defining style at Cave Spring Cellars. Best years: 1998, '95, '94.

CAYMUS VINEYARDS

USA, California, Napa County, Napa Valley AVA

♟ *Cabernet Sauvignon*

♀ *Chardonnay, Sauvignon Blanc and others*

Owner Charlie Wagner is not a man to rush into anything, so when Caymus picks a style for a wine, one has the comfort of knowing it will be around for years. The two varietal Cabernets are dark, a bit fleshy, but always built on a solid frame of tannins and – in youth – strongly flavoured by new American oak. With age they achieve a synthesis of rich fruit flavour and nicely integrated oak. Best years: 1997, '95, '94, '92, '91, '90, '87, '86, '85, '84, '80, '78, '76, '75.

Conundrum, an exotic, fleshy, delicious combination of white varieties, has developed its own fan club. Best years: 1998, '97, '96, '95, '92. There is also a pleasant Sauvignon Blanc, softened up with a dollop of Chardonnay. A long search for a Chardonnay site ended in MONTEREY COUNTY where the Wagners are making full-bore Chardonnay under the Mer & Soleil label. Best years: 1997, '96, '95.

DOMAINE CAZES

FRANCE, Languedoc-Roussillon, Rivesaltes AC
♥♟ *Grenache, Carignan, Syrah, Mourvèdre,
Cabernet Sauvignon, Merlot and others*
♀ *Muscat, Macabeo, Chardonnay, Rolle*

The Cazes brothers, André and Bernard, are
a real powerhouse in the Roussillon. Not
content with producing a superb range of
RIVESALTES (Vintage, Ambré, Tuilé, Aimé
Cazes) and a consistently fresh and aromatic
MUSCAT DE RIVESALTES, they also produce a
wide range of red and white CÔTES DU
ROUSSILLON or Vin de Pays des Côtes
Catalanes table wines at their extensive
160-ha (395-acre) domaine. The red Canon
du Maréchal is a fruity wine of simple pleasure made by carbonic maceration while the
white Canon is an exotically perfumed dry
Muscat. The Côtes du Roussillon-Villages is
a more serious wine made from Grenache,
Syrah and Mourvèdre, which requires three
to four years' bottle age. The latest addition
to the range is the international-styled Le
Credo, a Cabernet-Merlot blend aged in new
oak casks (first vintage: 1993). Best years:
(reds) 1996, '95, '94, '93.

CELLIER DES TEMPLIERS

FRANCE, Languedoc-Roussillon, Banyuls AC
♥ *Grenache, Carignan, Syrah, Mourvèdre*
♀ *Grenache Blanc*

The Cellier des Templiers is a serious-minded
co-operative close to the Spanish border that
produces an astonishing range of COLLIOURE
and BANYULS. All told there are 18 Banyuls
and 9 Collioures on offer, ranging in quality,
style and price according to the method of
production and length of aging. The vintage
or *rimage* Banyuls is a supple fruit-driven
wine for early drinking. Among the prestige
cuvées of Grand Cru Banyuls (which receive
longer aging in large wooden barrels), the
Viviane Le Roy, Henri Caris, Amiral Vilarem
and Président Henri Vidal vary from dry to
sweet in style. A number of the Collioures,
which are made from a varying blend of
Grenache, Carignan, Syrah and Mourvèdre,
come from individual estates. These include
the Abbaye de Valbonne, Ch. des Abelles and
Domaine du Roumani.

CENTRAL OTAGO

NEW ZEALAND, South Island

Central Otago boasts New Zealand's only
truly continental climate, with cold winters
that bring a high degree of frost risk and, in
the critical late summer/early autumn ripening period, hot days with cool nights to

accentuate fruit flavours. It is now New
Zealand's fastest growing wine region with
over 240ha (590 acres) of vineyards. Pinot
Noir is the most planted variety and certainly the most successful wine. Chardonnay
ranks in second place, making fine, zesty,
Chablis-style wine that often has a mineral
influence. Both varieties support a small but
burgeoning sparkling wine production.
Riesling, Pinot Gris and Sauvignon Blanc
can all come up trumps in a good vintage but
may fail to gain full ripeness in a cooler than
normal year. Gewurztraminer is a minor variety but produces some of the country's very
best examples of the style. Best years: 1998,
'96, '94, '91. Best producers: Black Ridge,
Chard Farm, Felton Road, Gibbston Valley,
Rippon Vineyards.

CENTRAL VALLEY

USA, California

The actual 'Big Valley' practically runs the
entire length of California, consisting of the
Sacramento and San Joaquin Valleys. The
Central Valley is home to over 50 per cent of
California's total planted grape acreage,
which, due to high yields, supplies close to
70 per cent of the state's wines and 99 per
cent of its brandy and fresh table grapes. The
French Colombard, Chenin Blanc, Barbera
and Zinfandel are widely planted and provide the liquid content for almost all
low-priced table wines and White Zinfandel
which is more familiarly known as 'Blush',
due to its pinkish hue. Better northerly
plantings in the Lodi region have upgraded
quality and now supply such brands as R H
Phillips, Sebastiani Vineyards, Sutter Home
and Woodbridge (MONDAVI).

WOODBRIDGE
*After reviving the Lodi-Woodbridge region, Napa's
Robert Mondavi Winery is now showing the way
towards tasty, everyday berry-flavoured Zinfandel.*

CENTRAL VICTORIA HIGH COUNTRY

AUSTRALIA, Victoria, Central Victoria Zone

Central Victoria High Country appears likely to be the name of a region previously best
known as the Strathbogie Ranges. While covering a relatively large area, it is unified by its

elevation and by the hilly topography. Most
of the vineyards are planted at between 300
and 500m (950 and 1650ft). Between 1992
and 1997 plantings increased by 300 per
cent. The major players are Mount Helen,
Plunkett Wines, DELATITE, DOMAINE
CHANDON and Murrindindi.

CÉRONS AC

FRANCE, Bordeaux
♀ *Sémillon, Sauvignon Blanc, Muscadelle*

Cérons is an enclave in the GRAVES region of
Bordeaux. The AC is for white wine, both dry
and sweet. Throughout the 1960s and '70s
interest in sweet white wine waned and hard
times hit Cérons and SAUTERNES alike. The
only solution was to use the grapes to make
dry wine and these, with Graves AC or Cérons
Sec on the label, are now more important here
than the gently sweet, mildly honeyed wines.
Best years: 1998, '97, '96, '95, '88, '86, '83.
Best producers: de Cérons, Grand Enclos du
Château de Cérons, de Chantegrive, Seuil.

L A CETTO

MEXICO, Baja California
♥ *Cabernet Sauvignon, Nebbiolo, Petite Sirah,
Zinfandel*
♀ *Sauvignon Blanc, Chardonnay*

The L A Cetto winery at Tlanepantia in Baja
California brought modern winemaking right
up-to-date in Mexico with the use of stainless
steel, temperature-controlled technology. The
grapes come from the relatively cool
Guadalupe Valley, about 80km (50 miles)
south of the US border, and can develop reasonably good aromatic flavours. Cetto has
established a reputation for dark, full-
flavoured varietal reds, especially for Nebbiolo
and Petite Sirah. There is also a range of white
wines. Drink the wines young.

CHABLAIS

SWITZERLAND, Vaud
♥♟ *Pinot Noir*
♀ *Dorin*

The name Chablais is not a misprint for
CHABLIS but a Swiss wine region: a sub-
division of the VAUD, south-east of Lake
Geneva, which specializes in white wine from
the Chasselas grape, here called the Dorin. In
the best villages like AIGLE, Yvorne and Bex,
where the grapes are grown on steeper hills
than is common, even in Switzerland, it can
be attractively tangy. The Pinot Noir, as well as
making red, also makes a very good pink Oeil
de Perdrix. Best producers: Henri Badoux,
Delarze, Grognuz, J & P Testuz.

CHABLIS France, Burgundy

CHABLIS HAS MANAGED TO MAKE A VIRTUE out of the fact that in most years it barely manages to ripen its grapes, and the resulting wines have long been a byword for green, ultra-dry whites of no discernible richness and little discernible fruit. Yet that just shows how easy it is for a reputation to linger on long after it bears little resemblance to the truth. Chablis is certainly dry, but it is very rarely green or raw nowadays, and although it doesn't have the almost tropical fruit ripeness of some white wines from further south in Burgundy, it does have a gentleness and a light unassertive fruit which can make for delicious, undemanding drinking.

Also, Chablis does come from one small decidedly marginal area in the frost-prone, autumn-cool valley of the river Serein between Dijon and Paris – and from there alone. Sadly for Chablis, non-French winemakers and marketing men found the name beguiling to the eye, and extremely easy to pronounce and remember. Consequently all over the world the name Chablis has been adapted to local wines. Today, California, Australia and many other regions produce 'Chablis' versions – which are limited by one thing only – not the grape type, not by the wine style, but by the fact that they are cheap wines.

True Chablis comes only from the Chardonnay grape, comes only from the French AC region, and is always white and dry. And it is never cheap. It cannot be cheap because the vineyards are at the northern limit for fully ripening Chardonnay grapes. The Champagne region is a mere 30km (19 miles) to the north, and you only have to taste a still white Coteaux Champenois to realize how tart and thin unripe Chardonnay can be. The best Chablis vineyards – the seven Grands Crus – are tightly packed together into one south-west-facing stretch of sloping suntrap next to the town of Chablis. The best Premiers Crus are similarly angled south- to south-west to pick up every possible ray of sun and protected from cold winds by the twists and turns of the little valleys. Also the harvest is notoriously unreliable due to the risk of spring frosts, the likelihood of bad weather when the vines flower, and the probability of early winters.

You might wonder if it is worth the effort. Well, it is. New methods of frost protection are cancelling out the worst effects of a spring-time relapse into winter. A better

The Chablis Grands Crus cover a magnificent south-west-facing slope above the river Serein. Les Grenouilles is in the foreground with Valmur and les Clos beyond. The famous Chablis Kimmeridgian limestone soil can be clearly seen.

Map

Ligny-le-Châtel

Paris

Maligny

Villy

Lignorelles

Bougros
les Preuses
Vaudésir
les Grenouilles
Valmur
les Clos
Blanchots

la Chapelle-
Vaupelteigne

Fontenay-
près-Chablis

la Fourchaume

Montée de Tonnerre

Mont de Milieu

Beauroy

Fyé

les Fourneaux

Beine

Poinchy

Milly

Chablis

Fleys

Serein

Béru

Côte de Léchet
Vaudevey

Vaucoupin

Chichée

Vaillons
Mélinots
Montmains

Courgis

Vaucoupin

Vosgros

Chemilly-sur-Serein

Préhy

Chablis AC
- Chablis Grand Cru
- Chablis Premier Cru
- Chablis and Petit Chablis

Vosgros = main vineyard

0 km — 5
0 miles — 3

N

RENÉ ET VINCENT DAUVISSAT
This is one of Chablis' top domaines, specializing in concentrated, oak-aged wines.

JEAN-PAUL DROIN
The best wines here are ripe, buttery Premiers and Grands Crus which are fermented and/or aged in oak barrels.

DOMAINE LAROCHE
One of Chablis' larger négociants, Laroche produces wines that are generally light, fresh and fruity.

WILLIAM FÈVRE
William Fèvre is one of the most enthusiastic users of new oak and owns vines in all seven Grands Crus.

LOUIS MICHEL & FILS
The prime exponents of unoaked Chablis. The wines are intensely flavoured, minerally and long-lived.

JEAN-MARIE RAVENEAU
This small, traditional estate produces beautifully nuanced wines using both oak and stainless steel fermentation.

ETIENNE ET DANIEL DEFAIX
Released later than most Chablis, these wines have a concentrated, classically austere character.

LA CHABLISIENNE
The Cuvée Vieilles Vignes is one of the best wines from this important and reliable co-operative.

JOSEPH DROUHIN
From substantial vineyard holdings in Chablis, this Beaune merchant offers good-value Chablis with a lively ripe fruit character.

---

understanding of the malolactic fermentation (which converts tart malic acid into softer, creamier lactic acid) means that very few wines are now harsh and green, though some may be a touch dull. And, despite Chablis' 'bone-dry' reputation, an increasing number of producers are experimenting with oak aging – resulting in full, toasty, positively rich dry whites.

In the late 1980s many producers jumped on the new-oak bandwagon, producing wines of considerable richness, but often they lacked Chablis character and at the same time never quite achieved the mellow richness of a Meursault. Today such over-oaked wines have become rare and growers use small oak barrels more judiciously, reserving them for their best Crus. The majority of producers opt for aging their wines in small oak barrels that have been used several times and lost all their vanilla spice – or in stainless steel.

REGIONAL ENTRIES
Chablis, Chablis Grand Cru, Chablis Premier Cru.

PRODUCER ENTRIES
Dauvissat, Laroche, Michel et Fils, Raveneau.

CHABLIS AC, PETIT CHABLIS AC
FRANCE, Burgundy
♀ *Chardonnay*

The Chablis AC covers 4400ha (10,880 acres) of land around the little town of Chablis between Dijon and Paris but only 2800ha (6900 acres) are actually planted with vines. It is Burgundy's northernmost outpost, and only the Chardonnay grape is used to create the wine, which is refined, expensive and bone dry.

Chablis' trouble is that it has become synonymous in many parts of the world with cheap, dry-to-medium, white-to-off-white wine from any available grape. Real Chablis couldn't be more different. It is always white and dry, often bone dry, so green-edged, so flinty that the taste reminds one of the click of dry stones knocked together. More often nowadays the dryness opens out into a broader taste, nutty, honeyed even, yet never rich, a Puritan's view of honey spice, rather than a Cavalier's.

The Chardonnay only ripens with difficulty in the Serein Valley, and there is a dreadful record of devastation by frost. Consequently the price of the wine is high. Too high, given the amount of good ripe Chardonnay now being produced elsewhere in the world and selling for less money. In general, straight Chablis AC is drunk at one to two years old, but the better producers often produce wine that can improve for three to five years. Best years: 1997, '96, '95, '92, '90. Best producers: Billaud-Simon, P Bouchard, Brocard, la CHABLISIENNE, Collet, Dampt, D-E Defaix, Droin, DROUHIN, Durup, Fèvre, Laroche, Legland, Long-Depaquit, Malandes, Michel, Pinson, Régnard, Simonnet-Febvre, Tribut, Vocoret.

Petit Chablis means little Chablis – and that name fits the bill exactly. The Petit Chablis AC covers uninspired, rather green, unripe Chardonnay wine from the least good nooks and crannies of the Chablis region. And since the authorities have cynically 're-scheduled' most 'Petit Chablis' vineyards as 'proper' Chablis you can imagine how feeble what's left must be. The la Chablisienne co-operative is the best bet for an adequate light Petit Chablis – but it's not even a bargain any more, so why bother?

CHABLIS GRAND CRU AC
FRANCE, Burgundy
♀ *Chardonnay*

This is the heart of Chablis: the vineyards of Blanchots, Bougros, Les Clos, Grenouilles, Preuses, Valmur and Vaudésir and which comprise a single swathe of vines rising steeply above the little river Serein, facing serenely towards the south-west and able to lap up every last ray of the warm afternoon sun. It is only because of the perfect exposure, the steep elevation and the unique Kimmeridgian limestone that the Chardonnay grapes can fully ripen and gain the fatness and strength which should mark out a Grand Cru.

Grand Cru growers, in general, have been making exceptional wines during the 1980s and '90s, especially those who have used oak to mature their wines, adding a rich warmth to the taut flavours of the wine. Fèvre and Droin are the most enthusiastic users of new oak, although both producers have learnt to use oak more judiciously over the past decade. Prices for Chablis Grand Cru wines are high, naturally, because supplies are very limited – especially since the Grands Crus suffer more than the other vineyards from the late frosts which can decimate Chablis' crop in the spring.

There is much argument between those who use new oak to age their wines and those who don't. The anti-new oak brigade do make *le vrai* Chablis – if you're after a wine which always keeps a firm grip on that lean streak of self-denial which, even after ten years, stops a Grand Cru ever wallowing in its own deliciousness. If you use new oak barrels, the wine gains a rich, almost tropical, apricotty fruit, nuts and cream flavour, and the spicy butter of the oak completes a picture of high-quality indulgent white. And then, just when you're about to say 'this is as sumptuous as Montrachet' you find that reserved, minerally restraint clambering back to centre stage, admonishing you at the last gasp for forgetting the prim self-restraint that is the key to Chablis' character.

Never drink Grand Cru too young – it's a total waste of money. Five to ten years are needed before you begin to see why you spent so much. Best years: 1997, '96, '96, '95, '93, '92, '90, '89, '88, '85, '83. Best producers: P Bouchard, la CHABLISIENNE, Collet, Dauvissat, D-E Defaix, Droin, DROUHIN, Fèvre, LAROCHE, Long-Depaquit, Malandes, Michel, Pinson, RAVENEAU, Régnard, Robin, Servin, Simonnet-Febvre, Vocoret.

CHABLIS PREMIER CRU AC
FRANCE, Burgundy
♀ *Chardonnay*

Just over a quarter of Chablis' vineyards are designated Premier Cru or First Growth, one level below Grand Cru (Great Growth) in the

DANIEL-ÉTIENNE DEFAIX
The Defaix wines are known for their rich, buttery yeast character, the result of spending 18 months in vat on their lees, which are stirred up for nourishment.

Burgundian pecking order. There's no doubt that some of these Premiers Crus are on splendid slopes, but Chablis has been the scene of much contentious politicking over the years as 'interested' parties (those owning the relevant vineyards) have sought to upgrade Petit Chablis land to CHABLIS AC, and much straight Chablis land to the superior AC, Chablis Premier Cru. There is little evidence yet that the 'new' Premiers Crus are doing anything except lessening the expectations of the consumer when confronted by a Premier Cru label. Of those 759ha (1850 acres) of Premier Cru vineyards, 200ha (494 acres) date from recent promotion.

So what of the good Premiers Crus? The best ones are Montée de Tonnerre, Vaillons and Monts de Milieu, just south of the Grand Cru slopes, Fourchaume, and some parts of Côte de Léchet and Montmains, both south-east-facing slopes to the west of the town of Chablis. The flavours are still dry, and are often nutty, fairly full, with a pronounced mineral streak. Whereas straight Chablis, from vines mostly grown on flatter land, is steely without any pronounced terroir flavours, a Premier Cru should show that mineral raciness which is a hallmark of fine Chablis, giving the wine a long, lingering, rangy finish. A Premier Cru should also be bigger and more intense, and if the winemaker has used wood rather than stainless steel to make his wine, it probably will have these characteristics.

But at these prices, satisfaction, unfortunately, is not guaranteed, and the sincerity of the producer is actually more important than the vineyard site. A good Premier Cru may take five to ten years of aging to show its full potential. Best years: 1997, '96, '95, '93, '92, '90, '89, '88. Best producers: Billaud-Simon, P Bouchard, la CHABLISIENNE, Dampt, Dauvissat, D-E Defaix, Droin, DROUHIN, Durup, Fèvre, LAROCHE, Malandes, Michel, Pinson, RAVENEAU, Régnard, Servin, Simonnet-Febvre, Testut, Tremblay, Vocoret.

CHALONE VINEYARD

USA, California, Monterey County, Chalone AVA
🍷 *Pinot Noir, Cabernet Sauvignon*
🍇 *Chardonnay, Pinot Blanc, Chenin Blanc*

Chalone Vineyard has enjoyed near-cult status for at least three decades now. Despite the death in 1998 of founder Richard Graff in a plane crash, this benchmark winery is likely to remain a successful producer of full-blown but slow-developing Chardonnay and concentrated Pinot Noir. The winery and vineyard occupy an AVA all of their own on a gentle slope just below a sheer rock face called the Pinnacles and high above MONTEREY's Salinas Valley to the west.

The Chardonnays tend to be marked by a strong note of charred wood from being fermented and aged in mostly new French barrels and have a mineral scent that may take several years to marry in. They are tart to start with, but durable. Best years: 1997, '96, '95, '94, '93, '92, '91, '90. The Pinot Blancs show somewhat less of the charred wood notes and more fruit; even so, they are, if anything, a bit firmer and more tart on the palate. Chalone Chenin Blanc is made in the same style. The Pinot Noirs, from 1984 on, have been darker than most of their kin, and a good deal more tannic; they age eccentrically but superbly in the manner of a Burgundian CÔTE DE NUITS.

Chalone Inc. also owns all or part of EDNA VALLEY VINEYARD in SAN LUIS OBISPO COUNTY, ACACIA in the CARNEROS district of NAPA, and CARMENET, high up in hills framing the east side of SONOMA VALLEY. It is also part owner of WASHINGTON STATE's Canoe Ridge, an increasingly good producer of finely structured reds. Mid-priced Central Coast varietals are labelled Echelon.

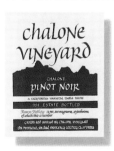

CHALONE VINEYARD
The limestone vineyards on the arid eastern slope of Monterey's Coastal Range have an ideal cooler mesoclimate for the slow, balanced ripening required for quality Pinot Noir.

CHAMBERS

AUSTRALIA, Victoria, North East Victoria Zone, Rutherglen
🍷 *Cabernet Sauvignon, Cinsaut, Alicante Bouschet*
🍇 *Muscat, Muscadelle, Riesling, Gouais*

Bill Chambers is one of Australia's most experienced wine show judges and knows a good wine when he sees one. So it must be through

sheer perversity that he produces a range of mediocre but cheap table wines. But his Muscat and Tokay (Muscadelle), each available in three grades, are another thing altogether. The top Old Liqueur range is unmatched for its elegant intensity. Whenever someone has the temerity to buy some, Chambers puts the price up. The taste is almost impossible to describe: intensely honeyed, raisiny fruit, yet drying off on a perfumed finish which lingers and lingers. The other grades understandably are not quite so intense and luscious, but the style is similar.

CHAMBERTIN AC, CHAMBERTIN CLOS-DE-BÈZE AC

FRANCE, Burgundy, Côte de Nuits, Grands Crus
🍷 *Pinot Noir*

The village of GEVREY-CHAMBERTIN has no fewer than eight Grands Crus, which between them can produce some of Burgundy's greatest and most intense red wine, with remarkable flavours that develop as the wine ages. Chambertin and Chambertin Clos-de-Bèze, the best Grands Crus, are neighbours on the stretch of slope at just below 300m (1000ft), running from Gevrey-Chambertin south to VOSNE-ROMANÉE, the village which produces the most sublime reds in Burgundy. The wines are basically the same, and Clos-de-Bèze can simply call itself 'Chambertin' if it wants to. 'Chambertin, King of Wines' is how the old-timers described this powerful wine and 'Emperor of Wines' might have been more apt since this was Napoleon's favourite tipple. They say he drank it wherever he went – Russia, Egypt, Italy … Waterloo? Perhaps 1815 was a bad vintage? Well, maybe, but this can be a hell of a wine, the biggest, most brooding of all.

In a good year the wine starts off positively rasping with power, the fruit all chewy damson skins and tarry tannin. But give it time, five years, maybe ten, or even 20, and Chambertin transforms itself. The scent is exotic and rich, fleetingly floral, but more likely to envelop you with the powerful warmth of

DOMAINE BRUNO CLAIR
Bruno Clair's top wine is his Chambertin Clos-de-Bèze – dense and concentrated, it has new oak, black cherries and wild floral notes in the bouquet.

choice damsons and plums so ripe they would long have fallen from the tree – add to this the strange brilliance of black chocolate, prunes, and the delicious decay of well-hung game – and you have one of the most remarkable flavours red wine can create. Both Grands Crus are popular and overproduction is a recurrent problem; there are many Chambertins simply not worth the high price demanded for them, but the best wines can be so good it is worth persevering. The top wines can age for a decade or more. Latricières-Chambertin, Mazis-Chambertin, Griotte-Chambertin and Ruchottes-Chambertin also produce rich, long-lived wines, while the remaining Grands Crus, Chapelle-Chambertin and Charmes-Chambertin, tend to be lighter in style. Best years: 1996, '95, '93, '91, '90, '89, '88, '87, '85, '83, '80. Best producers: D Bachelet, Clair, Damoy, DROUHIN, Claude Dugat, Bernard Dugat-Py, FAIVELEY, JADOT, Leroy, Mugneret, Perrot-Minot, Ponsot, Rebourseau, Rémy, Rossignol-Trapet, Roty, Roumier, Rousseau, Jean Taupenot, Tortochot, Trapet.

CHAMBOLLE-MUSIGNY AC

FRANCE, Burgundy, Côte de Nuits
🍷 *Pinot Noir*

Chambolle-Musigny is supposed to produce the most fragrant, perfumed red wines in all Burgundy. Well, yes and no. Some bottles from the Grands Crus of BONNES-MARES or Le MUSIGNY can really set the heart fluttering and from some growers the Premier Cru Les Amoureuses can be of comparable quality. The names of Premiers Crus such as Les Amoureuses and Les Charmes, both leading sites, suggest coy, flirtatious femininity – all rustling silks and fans – and is what many writers claim as the character of Chambolle-Musigny wines. The fact that 'Charmes' probably derives from the French for 'straw' or 'hornbeam' takes away some of the romance and the fact that most modern Chambolle-Musigny suffers from the Burgundian disease of over-cropping and over-sugaring the grape juice doesn't help much either. But the potential for beautiful wines from these well-sited vineyards, just south of MOREY-ST-DENIS, and located between 250 and 300m (800 and 1000ft) up the Côte de Nuits slope, is unquestionably there. Best years: 1997, '96, '95, '93, '91, '90, '89, '88, '87, '85, '78. Best producers: Amiot, BARTHOD-NOËLLAT, Christian Clerget, DROUHIN, DUJAC, GRIVOT, Groffier, Hudelot-Noëllat, JADOT, LEROY, MUGNIER, ROUMIER, Bernard Serveau, de VOGÜÉ.

CHAMPAGNE France

THE CHAMPAGNE REGION OF FRANCE has given its name to the whole concept of sparkling wine. Fizz is thought of and described as 'Champagne' even when it's made thousands of miles away from this chilly, windswept northern area. And although the hordes of imitations throughout the world relentlessly pursue a style as close as possible to that of true Champagne, they never achieve it – for one simple reason. No-one in their right mind in a country like Spain, Italy, Australia, the United States or Argentina – where sunshine to ripen the grapes is taken for granted – would ever risk planting vines in such an unfriendly, hostile environment as the stark chalklands of France's far north. It's a region where it never gets warm enough for a grape to ripen totally, where the acidity stays toothachingly high and where the thin, meagre flavour of the young still wine makes it virtually undrinkable on its own.

But this is a description of the perfect base wine for great sparkling wine. If you make sure this workhouse gruel of a wine is made from top-quality grape varieties like the white Chardonnay and the black Pinot Noir and Pinot Meunier (rosé Champagne is usually made by blending a little red wine with the white), then you can hardly go wrong – as long as you use the *méthode champenoise* (Champagne method) of winemaking to create the bubbles by a second fermentation in the bottle. It's a good thing, though, that the Romans decided to plant grapes here. It must have been warmer then, and it's unlikely that anyone would think to do it now.

'La Champagne' – the only place in the world real Champagne can come from – is mostly a charmless bitingly cold prairie land to the east of Paris. Yet centred on Reims and Épernay, and stretching down towards the northern tip of Burgundy, there are five areas where the combination of chalk soil and well-drained, protected mesoclimates allows the grapes to ripen. The Montagne de Reims is a low, wide hill curving south of Reims where Pinot Noir excels. The Côte des Blancs is a long east-facing slope, south of Épernay, almost exclusively planted with Chardonnay. This has become Champagne's most prestigious region. Although

The Premier Cru vineyards surrounding the village of Villedommange are some of the best in the Petite Montagne, an area just south-west of Reims at the western end of the Montagne de Reims.

highly regarded producers such as Krug and Bollinger use a lot of black grapes, many houses, and consumers, relish the incomparably elegant and Chardonnay-dominated wines from the Côte des Blancs. The Vallée de la Marne runs through Épernay and grows good Pinot Meunier and Pinot Noir. There are two other areas – the Aube and the Côte de Sézanne. There are very few red and white still wines made in the region, labelled Coteaux Champenois.

POL ROGER
Known for marvellously consistent and long-lived elegant wines, Pol Roger was Winston's Churchill's favourite Champagne house.

KRUG
Krug's top Champagne is a rare and expensive Blanc de Blancs from the Clos du Mesnil vineyard in the Côte des Blancs.

ALFRED GRATIEN
Gratien's vintage Champagne is deliciously ripe and toasty when released but can age for a further ten years. Rare nowadays, Gratien still makes its wine in wooden casks.

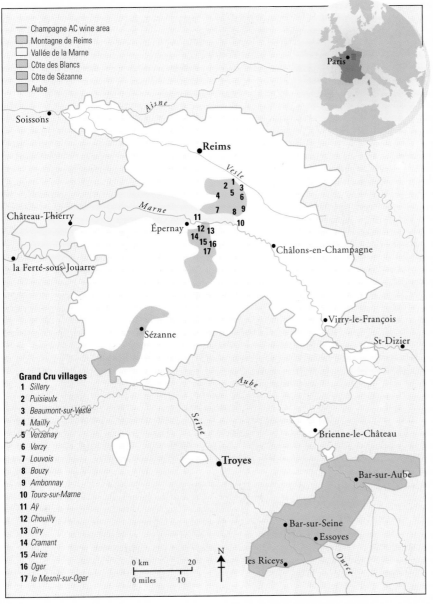

Grand Cru villages

1 Sillery
2 Puisieulx
3 Beaumont-sur-Vesle
4 Mailly
5 Verzenay
6 Verzy
7 Louvois
8 Bouzy
9 Ambonnay
10 Tours-sur-Marne
11 Aÿ
12 Chouilly
13 Oiry
14 Cramant
15 Avize
16 Oger
17 le Mesnil-sur-Oger

- Champagne AC wine area
- Montagne de Reims
- Vallée de la Marne
- Côte des Blancs
- Côte de Sézanne
- Aube

LOUIS ROEDERER
This is elegant, sophisticated Champagne of incomparable finesse, and consistent too.

VEUVE CLICQUOT PONSARDIN
Veuve Clicquot's full-bodied, toasty, non-vintage has a distinctive orange label.

LAURENT-PERRIER
This delicious vintage wine is one of a consistently good range of Champagnes from this large, family-owned house.

BILLECART-SALMON
The top Champagne from this excellent, family-owned house is the elegant Cuvée Nicolas-François, a gentle, yet richly satisfying nutty vintage wine.

MOËT ET CHANDON
Dom Pérignon is Moët's prestige Champagne. It can be one of the greatest Champagnes of all but needs aging for at least 10 years from the vintage date before reaching its potential.

JACQUES SELOSSE
This fine Champagne is the result of partial use of barrel fermentation and religiously tended vineyards in the best bits of the Côte des Blancs.

TAITTINGER
Taittinger's prestige Blanc de Blancs Champagne has a creamy, refined elegance with a real richness after about ten years' aging.

REGIONAL ENTRIES
Bouzy, Champagne, Coteaux Champenois, Rosé des Riceys.

PRODUCER ENTRIES
Billecart-Salmon, Bollinger, Deutz, Gosset, Alfred Gratien, Charles Heidsieck, Krug, Lanson, Laurent-Perrier, Moët et Chandon, G H Mumm, Perrier-Jouët, Pol Roger, Pommery, Louis Roederer, Ruinart, Salon, Taittinger, Veuve Clicquot.

CHARLES HEIDSIECK
Under the ownership of Rémy Martin a lot of effort has gone into improving quality and it is now one of the most reliable and satisfying of all Champagnes.

BOLLINGER
This great Champagne house makes wines in a full, rich, rather old-fashioned style. The Grande Année vintage, from two-thirds Pinot Noir, is best at 10 to 15 years.

CHAMPAGNE AC

FRANCE, Champagne

♀ ♈ *Pinot Noir, Chardonnay, Pinot Meunier*

The renown of Champagne is such that it is the only appellation contrôlée wine that does not have to bear the words Appellation Contrôlée on its label. Yet Champagne is an AC and one more tightly controlled than most because of the insatiable thirst of the world for this most exciting of sparkling wines. Champagne is thought of as a general term for sparkling wine but in fact the AC applies only to sparkling wines (mostly white but also rosé) which have gained their bubbles by undergoing a second fermentation in the bottle from which they will eventually be served (called the Champagne method) and which come from one precise geographical location, centred on Épernay and Reims, to the east of Paris. Nothing else can be true Champagne.

Grapes rarely ripen fully this far north, and the result is a light wine of very high acid, which is perfect for making sparkling wine, so long as the wine comes from good grape varieties. In Champagne it does. The Chardonnay is one of the world's greatest white grapes and here produces lovely, fragrant wines which become surprisingly creamy with a little maturity. Pinot Noir and Pinot Meunier are both high-quality red grapes, but in this northerly region their skins never develop much colour and with careful pressing the juice can be removed with virtually no coloration.

Some Champagne is made only from a single grape variety – Blanc de Blancs from Chardonnay, or Blanc de Noirs from Pinot Noir – but most is the result of blending the three grape varieties. Blending between the different villages is also crucial, and most Champagnes will be a blend of wines from perhaps a dozen villages from throughout the region. The villages are classified according to quality. There are 17 Grand Cru villages at the top, followed by 38 Premier Cru villages.

An increasing amount of Champagne is now made by grape growers themselves – this is usually unblended, and can be exciting when it comes from a Premier Cru or Grand Cru village. This will be clearly marked on the label. However, most Champagne is made by large merchant houses. It comes in sweet, medium, medium dry, very dry (brut) and very, very dry (ultra-brut) styles. It is ideally a blend of two or more years, labelled 'non-vintage', but when the vintage is good, a 'vintage' cuvée is released of wine from a single year's harvest. There are also 'de luxe' cuvées, normally vintage and supposedly the crème de la crème of Champagne.

The Côte des Blancs, where the chalky subsoil often breaks through to the surface, provides most of the finest Chardonnay grapes for the Champagne blend.

Frequently, they are more remarkable for the weirdness of their bottle shapes and high prices, than for the perfection of their flavours. Good pink Champagne has a delicious fragrance of cherries and raspberries to go with the foaming froth and should be drunk as young as possible, though a few wines, like POMMERY and TAITTINGER, age well. Best years: 1998, '96, '95, '90, '89, '88, '86, '85, '83, '82, '81, '79, '76, '75. Best producers: BILLECART-SALMON, BOLLINGER, DEUTZ, Duval-Leroy, Gosset, Alfred GRATIEN, Henriot, Charles HEIDSIECK, Jacquesson, KRUG, LANSON, LAURENT-PERRIER, MOËT ET CHANDON, PERRIER-JOUËT, POL ROGER, Pommery, ROEDERER, SALON, Taittinger, VEUVE CLICQUOT; (rosés) Billecart-Salmon, Krug, Laurent-Perrier, Moët et Chandon, Pommery, Roederer, Taittinger Comtes de Champagne.

DOMAINE CHANDON DE BRIAILLES

FRANCE, Burgundy, Côte de Beaune, Savigny-lès-Beaune AC

♈ *Pinot Noir*

♀ *Chardonnay*

This is one of the rare domaines in Burgundy, or indeed in France, run by women: the Comtesse de Nicolay, and her daughter Claude, who has married into the DROUHIN family. A beautiful mansion in SAVIGNY is the headquarters of a 13-ha (32-acre) estate with vineyards, more or less organically cultivated, in PERNAND-VERGELESSES and CORTON as well as Savigny itself. With the possible exception of Corton Clos du Roi and Corton

Bressandes, these vineyards are not known for powerful dense wines, and the Chandon de Briailles style is one of exceptional charm, subtlety and finesse. Pernand-Vergelesses lacks the renown of Corton or even Savigny, but Chandon de Briailles makes some of the very best wines from the appellation, especially the Premier Cru Île de Vergelesses. Best years: 1997, '96, '95, '93, '91, '90, '89, '85.

CHAPEL HILL

AUSTRALIA, South Australia, Fleurieu Zone, McLaren Vale

♈ *Cabernet Sauvignon, Syrah (Shiraz), Pinot Noir and others*

♀ *Chardonnay, Riesling*

This is one of the fastest rising stars in Australia, with wealthy investor owners and Pam Dunsford as winemaker. The Reserve Shiraz, crammed with juicy red berry fruit, opulent oak and balanced tannins, is a prolific winner of major show trophies. The Reserve Chardonnay, similarly opulent, and deeply flavoured Cabernet Sauvignon are only a whisker behind. There is also a CHAMPAGNE-method fizz made from the classic blend of mainly Chardonnay with some Pinot Meunier and Pinot Noir, and a Riesling. Best years: 1996, '94, '93, '92, '91, '90, '89.

LA CHAPELLE LENCLOS

FRANCE, South-West, Madiran AC

♈ *Tannat, Cabernet Franc, Cabernet Sauvignon*

♀ *Petit Manseng, Courbu*

Patrick Ducournau is one of the leading names in the MADIRAN AC. Following in the footsteps of Ch. MONTUS he produces rich, concentrated wines with a rounded tannic structure from aging in oak barrels. He has also acquired a reputation for his patented sytem of controlled oxygenation, known as *microbullage*, which softens the potentially hard tannins of the Tannat grape during maturation. Two wines are produced from the 18-ha (44-acre) vineyard, la Chapelle Lenclos and Domaine Mouréou. The former is a firmer, longer-aging wine, but both need a minimum five years' bottle age. There is also a small amount of sweet white PACHERENC DU VIC BILH. Best years: (reds) 1997, '96, '95, '94.

CHAPOUTIER

FRANCE, Northern and Southern Rhône, Provence

♈ *Syrah, Grenache, Cinsaut and others*

♀ *Marsanne, Roussanne, Viognier and others*

Until the late 1980s Chapoutier was a deeply old-fashioned merchant house based in Tain l'Hermitage. The wines were fairly priced, but often uneven in quality. In 1988 Michel and Marc Chapoutier took over the firm and turned the place inside out. In the vineyards yields were reduced drastically, and by the mid-1990s their own vineyards were being cultivated biodynamically, and in the cellar good-quality French oak replaced ancient chestnut casks. The brothers were zealous in spreading the word about the changes they were making, but the wines have proved to be their best ambassadors. To the standard range of RHÔNE wines, they added costly single-vineyard wines such as HERMITAGE (Pavillon), CÔTE-RÔTIE (Mordorée), CROZES-HERMITAGE (Varonniers), and CHÂTEAUNEUF-DU-PAPE (Barbe-Rac). They also acquired properties in PROVENCE's COTEAUX D'AIX and in ROUSSILLON's BANYULS, as well as land in Australia. Despite fears that the Chapoutiers might be over-extending themselves, quality has remained extremely high. Best years: (Northern Rhône reds) 1997, '96, '95, '94, '90, '89; (whites) 1997, '96, '95, '94, '93, '92 .

CHARDONNAY

Is there no end to the Chardonnay bandwagon? Few growers who aspire to international standing can afford to be without it, and only in the most traditional non-Chardonnay areas – Bordeaux, for example – will you find winemakers happy in its absence.

There are several simple reasons. First, Chardonnay sells. That magic word on the label can make bottles walk off the shelves. Next, it's extremely versatile. Grown in cool climates, and with no oak aging, it will reveal the character of its region beneath its lemony, nutty fruit; in warmer spots it will be rich and complex, and take to new oak barrels like a duck to water, soaking up flavours of spice and cream. Last, it blends superbly with all manner of other grape varieties. In Australia some goes into partnership with Semillon; in the Loire Valley winemakers use it to soften the Chenin Blanc. And in the South of France, where it appears on its own in the vins de pays and the recently created Limoux AC, a splash or two can also be used to perk up an otherwise dull blend of other varieties.

Chardonnay's other main incarnation is in Champagne and its lookalikes, when its tart, thin, still, cool-climate wines become graceful, complex and fascinating when made into bubbly by the Champagne method.

It's just as well it is so versatile, because there's an awful lot of it about. California alone has some 36,000ha (90,000 acres) of Chardonnay; Australia has 10,550ha (21,060 acres) and Burgundy, which in its very top vineyards can produce the sort of Chardonnays that push all the others into second place, has 10,400ha (25,700 acres). For it is here on the Côte d'Or, and further north in Chablis, that still Chardonnay wine can be better than just about anywhere else in the world. In Chablis it is chalk-dry and nutty, though often these wines are oaked as well; and from the top Côte d'Or vineyards it can reach extraordinary heights of complexity and elegance.

Further south it makes traditionally light and delicate, but increasingly full-bodied, discreetly oaked wines in Italy's Alto Adige, Trentino and Friuli, where the age-long confusion between Chardonnay and Pinot Blanc (Pinot Bianco) has been sorted out, with the result that there is apparently more Chardonnay and less Pinot Bianco there than anyone suspected 20 years ago. Bigger, richer, oakier and more international styles come from Tuscany, and it has invaded Soave as well, where it is now accepted officially as an optional part of the blend. In fact, Chardonnay has invaded the whole of Italy, with impressive versions coming from Piedmont (Gaja, Coppo) right down to Sicily (Regaleali, Planeta); and of course it is an essential ingredient of Italy's growing prestige *metodo classico* or Champagne-method sparkling wine industry, the zenith of which is represented by the Franciacorta DOCG in Lombardy. Chardonnay has crept into Portugal and seems to do well in the central-south of the country in the Ribatejo, Terras do Sado and Estremadura. In Austria both oaked and unoaked styles are made, a common synonym for the grape being Morillon. In Germany the area planted with the grape remains small, but some good examples come from Baden and the Pfalz.

The best Chardonnays from eastern Europe are those made in Hungary, where local winemakers were quick to learn the tricks of the trade from visiting flying winemakers. Slovakia, Bulgaria and Romania all have the potential for excellent Chardonnay but progress is slow.

California's Chardonnays have the reputation of being the biggest, beefiest and richest of the lot, and to some extent that is still true, though greater elegance and finesse have been appearing for some years now. There was even a time a few years ago when the attractive richness was being strangled, as winemakers unwisely tried to re-create lean, cool flavours from their lush, fragrant grapes. Nowadays, California's cool areas like Carneros and Russian River get the balance just right. The grape is grown in all of the USA's wine grape-growing states, but only Washington State, with a wide range of interesting styles, Oregon, with generally leaner, tarter versions, New York State – especially Long Island – Virginia and Texas produce consistent results. Canada's best Chardonnay comes from the southern Okanagan close to the Washington border and selected sites on the Niagara bench in Ontario. The style is generally bright and fruit-driven, with good supporting acid. A mix-up with imported vine material in the early 1980s saw South Africa plant large quantities of Auxerrois instead of Chardonnay. The real thing took off only in the mid-'80s but is now well represented in all the major wine areas. Time has brought more balance to the wines, which in the early days tended to be over-oaked, but few have yet achieved real complexity. Australia produces just about everything from understated complexity in a few top wines to brilliantly commercial oaky styles that sell at come-and-get-me value-for-money prices. The biggest wines here tend to come from the Hunter Valley, McLaren Vale and Barossa Valley, the leanest from cooler regions like the Adelaide Hills and Tasmania.

New Zealand's Chardonnays vary from the light and lean to the rich and tropically fruity; Gisborne, Marlborough and Hawke's Bay are the main regions. South American countries also grow Chardonnay in considerable quantities; Chile, in particular, has developed its own soft, fruity style.

CHASSAGNE-MONTRACHET AC

FRANCE, Burgundy, Côte de Beaune

♦ *Pinot Noir*

♀ *Chardonnay*

This is the least fashionable of the great CÔTE DE BEAUNE white wine villages. One explanation might be that over half the production of this supposedly white wine commune was, until quite recently, red – although the whites are better. Another explanation is that Chassagne has no restaurant, no café – not even a bar. You have to walk across the dangerously busy Route Nationale 6 into PULIGNY-MONTRACHET to find somewhere to relax.

Well, that can be turned to our advantage, because the general price level in Chassagne is lower than in Puligny or MEURSAULT and the quality of the whites right now is increasingly good. This is one of the larger communes of the Côte d'Or: there are 356ha (880 acres) of vines in this AC, situated between Puligny and SANTENAY at the southern end of the Côte de Beaune. The commune includes some of Burgundy's greatest white wine vineyards – 3.5ha (8.6 acres) of the great MONTRACHET Grand Cru as well as 6ha (15 acres) of BÂTARD-MONTRACHET and the entire 1.6ha (4.4 acres) of the smallest white Grand Cru – Criots-Bâtard-Montrachet.

There are around 160ha (400 acres) of Premier Cru vineyards, and 70 per cent of the Premier Cru is white. The Premiers Crus are not well known, but can offer big, nutty, toasty white wines. Les Caillerets, les Ruchottes, la Romanée, Morgeot, les Vergers and les Embrazées can be exciting wines – especially if aged for four to eight years. Ordinary white Chassagne-Montrachet may lack the complexity of the Premier Cru, but is usually a thoroughly enjoyable high-quality Burgundy. Best years: (whites) 1997, '96, '95, '93, '92, '90, '89, '88, '86. Best producers: (whites) Bachelet-Ramonet, Blain-Gagnard, Marc Colin, Duc de Magenta, Fontaine-Gagnard, GAGNARD, Albert Morey, Marc Morey, J-M Pillot, RAMONET.

Red Chassagne is always a little earthy, peppery and plummy, and can be enjoyable, though hardly a bargain. The top wines can age for over a decade. Look out for the following Premiers Crus: Clos de la Boudriotte, Clos St-Jean and Clos de la Chapelle. Best years: (reds) 1997, '96, '95, '93, '92, '90, '89, '88, '85. Best producers: (reds) J-C Bachelet, Carillon, Patrick Clerget, Duc de Magenta, GAGNARD, Gagnard-Delagrange, Lequin-Roussot, Albert Morey, RAMONET.

Ornate architecture and beautiful gardens seem in keeping with Chateau St Jean's Japanese ownership. This Sonoma Valley winery, long famous for its rich Chardonnays, has now added impressive reds to the range.

CHASSELAS

One of the world's most neutral white grapes, this is the Gutedel of Germany and the Fendant, Dorin or Perlan of Switzerland. In France it is on the way out; there is a little in Savoie, and at Pouilly on the LOIRE, where it makes the AC Pouilly-sur-Loire in the same area as the better, Sauvignon-based wine, POUILLY-FUMÉ. Most French Chasselas, though, is found in ALSACE, where it makes simple jug wine or is blended into ALSACE EDELZWICKER.

CH. CHASSE-SPLEEN

FRANCE, Bordeaux, Haut-Médoc, Moulis AC, Cru Bourgeois

♦ *Cabernet Sauvignon, Merlot, Cabernet Franc, Petit Verdot*

All owners of lesser BORDEAUX properties who gaze wistfully at the Classed Growths and sulk in silent envy at the prices they can charge should look at the example of Chasse-Spleen. Since the mid-1970s, this property has backed up vigorous quality control with an astute marketing strategy. The result is that this rich, round, grandly textured wine is now more expensive than many of the lesser Classed Growths, and yet everyone thinks it is splendid value for money. Second wine: l'Ermitage de Chasse-Spleen. Best years: 1996, '95, '94, '93, '90, '89, '88, '87, '86, '82.

CH. CHASSE-SPLEEN
This tremendously consistent wine from the Moulis AC is right at the top of Bordeaux's Cru Bourgeois hierarchy.

CHÂTEAU-CHALON AC

FRANCE, Jura

♀ *Savagnin*

This tiny AC, covering 45ha (111 acres) in the centre of the mountainous JURA vineyards, applies only to one of the most daunting wine types yet invented, *vin jaune* or yellow wine, which offers the same kind of experience as pot-holing, hang-gliding or taking an afternoon nap on a bed of nails. Yet for a brave few, the eventual pleasures far outweigh the initial torments. Only the Savagnin grape is used to make *vin jaune*. It produces a fierce, farmyardy white, blending oily thickness with a raw volatile acidity and a strong whiff of damp straw. It can develop a raging, sour, woody brilliance that only the very best sherries ever get.

There is nothing like it in the world of wine. Its nearest equivalent would be an old fino sherry – and the reason they both grow a flor yeast on their surface is because they age endlessly in barrel, which imparts this strange sweet/sour intensity. *Vin jaune* lies in barrel for six years; during this time the wine evaporates by perhaps one-third, but is protected from oxidation by the flor. The painfully concentrated liquid is put in dumpy 62cl *clavelin* bottles, and you can age it for, well, certainly up to 100 years. Best producers: Jean Baud, Jean Bourdy, J-M Courbet, Durand-Perron, Fruitière Vinicole de Voiteur, Macle.

CHATEAU DES CHARMES
CANADA, Ontario, Niagara Peninsula VQA
♦ Pinot Noir
♀ Chardonnay, Gewürztraminer, Riesling

Chateau des Charmes' owner Paul Bosc is a pioneer of the new Ontario wine industry. Bosc planted the winery's original 25ha (62 acres) Estate Vineyard back in 1983. He has since added the 50-ha (124-acre) Paul Bosc Estate Vineyard and the 35-ha (86-acre) St David's Bench Vineyard, making Chateau des Charmes the largest estate winery on the NIAGARA PENINSULA.

An impressive new, château-style winery opened in 1994, leaving Chateau des Charmes with all the tools required to be a regional leader. Top labels here include the St David's Vineyard Chardonnay, a Gewürztraminer, late-harvest Riesling and a superb Riesling Icewine, one of Ontario's finest. Best years: 1998, '96, '95, '94.

CHÂTEAU-GRILLET AC
FRANCE, Northern Rhône
♀ Viognier

This single estate of 3ha (7 acres) which, although within the CONDRIEU AC, is renowned as having its own AC, one of the smallest in France. This rare, exciting RHÔNE white from the village of Vérin, south of Vienne, can be remarkable stuff. The Viognier, the only permitted grape variety, produces a most exciting dry wine – all apricots and slightly soured cream, spring blossom floating on the wind and honey tinged with tangerine spice.

Château-Grillet is very expensive – but then there's very little of it. Is it worth the price? No, for less than half as much you can buy a bottle of Condrieu – same grape, same taste and no uneasy feeling that perhaps you're being taken for a bit of a ride. However, there have been signs of improvement since the 1995 vintage. Best years: 1997, '96, '95, '93, '91, '90.

CHATEAU LUMIERE
JAPAN, Honshu, Yamanashi
♦ Cabernet Sauvignon, Cabernet Franc, Merlot
♀ Semillon, Sauvignon Blanc

Japanese wine law is remarkably lax about allowing imported wines to be blended and labelled as Japanese: however, Chateau Lumiere is a rarity in that its wine genuinely is Japanese. The family of Toshihiko Tsukamoto owns Chateau Lumiere, and its vineyards are planted with red vine cuttings brought from Ch. MARGAUX in BORDEAUX. The white wines, in another top-drawer copycat exercise, are in sweet botrytized style. The standard of both red and white wines is quite high. Drink these wines young.

CHATEAU MONTELENA
USA, California, Napa County, Napa Valley AVA
♦ Cabernet Sauvignon
♀ Chardonnay, Riesling

For years Montelena has had to live down the fact that its Chardonnay was judged best in the famous Paris tasting in 1976. Its owners had intended Cabernet Sauvignon from the estate vineyard to be Montelena's pathway to fame, but it was not until the appearance of the 1979 and '82 wines that they could argue their case for Cabernet. Never lacking in bravado, and packed with ripe fruit and generous new oak, Montelena Cabernets are genuine keepers. Best recent years: 1996, '95, '94, '93, '92, '91, '90, '89. Still at the head of the pack, NAPA VALLEY Chardonnay has plenty of spiced apple fruit and oak. Best years: 1997, '96, '95, '94, '93, '92, '91, '90.

CHATEAU MUSAR
LEBANON, Ghazir
♦ ♦ Cabernet Sauvignon, Cinsaut, Syrah
♀ Chardonnay, Semillon

This winery can provide more hair-raising tales than any other: Serge Hochar made wine right through the Lebanese civil war. His vineyards are in the Beka'a Valley and the winery is at Ghazir, and in some years long detours had to be made between the two to avoid the front line; in 1984 they couldn't get there at all; in 1989 the winery was shelled and in 1991 it was one of the safest places to be, and the locals sheltered there. Yet, with the exception of 1984 and '76, wine has been made successfully every year. And very fine it is, too.

In some years the red is something like a MÉDOC, in others a fine northern RHÔNE, but it is never quite like either: there is always something smoky and spicy and indefinably

exotic about Musar. Hochar maintains it should not be drunk until it is 15 years old, and will last until it is 30; few Musar lovers have that much patience. A white and rosé wine are now being made as well as the red. Best years: 1994, '91, '90, '89, '87, '85, '83, '81, '77, '72, '70, '69, '64.

CHATEAU MUSAR
From an unlikely blend of Cabernet Sauvignon, Cinsaut and Syrah, Serge Hochar makes a spicy, gutsy red that will live for 30 years or so.

CHATEAU REYNELLA
AUSTRALIA, South Australia, Fleurieu Zone, McLaren Vale
♦ Shiraz (Syrah), Merlot, Cabernet Sauvignon

The National Trust-classified and beautiful buildings of Chateau Reynella house the corporate headquarters of BRL HARDY. A limited range of Basket Pressed Shiraz, Basket Pressed Merlot and Basket Pressed Cabernet Sauvignon are released under the Reynell label, all exhibiting awesome power, concentration and depth of blackberry/blackcurrant fruit, and all enjoying great success in Australian wine shows. Best years: 1998, '96, '94, '92, '91, '90.

CHATEAU ST JEAN
USA, California, Sonoma County, Sonoma Valley AVA
♦ Cabernet Sauvignon, Merlot, Pinot Noir
♀ Chardonnay, Pinot Blanc, Sauvignon Blanc and others

Chateau St Jean was once known for single-vineyard Chardonnay and botrytis-affected sweet wines, mostly Riesling and Gewürztraminer. The hallmark of the dry whites, especially the Chardonnays, is a rich texture and an attractive fillip of bitterness at the finish, and Robert Young Vineyard has shown the way, with Belle Terre and others hard on its heels. But things have changed and the red wines (Merlot, Cabernet Sauvignon and Cinq Cepages – a delicious, soft Meritage) are now in the spotlight. Limited volume Reserve Cabernet and Reserve Merlot display refined fruit and classic structure. Best years: 1997, '96, '95, '94, '93, '92.

CHATEAU STE MICHELLE

USA, Washington State, Columbia Valley AVA
🍷 *Cabernet Sauvignon, Merlot*
🍷 *Chardonnay, Sauvignon Blanc, Semillon and others*

WASHINGTON STATE's largest and oldest winery has carried the name of the state further and wider than any other. All the wines are soundly made. The most impressive carry reserve labels or individual vineyard names. Chardonnay, Merlot and Cabernet from Cold Creek and Canoe Ridge are particularly good. Best years: 1998, '97, '96, '95, '94. Intensely varietal Semillons and Sauvignons have been impressive, and late-harvest White Rieslings are among the USA's best. There is a sister line of varietals under the Columbia Crest label, of which the whites have been consistently attractive. The reds are led by a formidable Merlot and sturdy Cabernet.

CHATEAU TAHBILK

AUSTRALIA, Victoria, Central Victoria Zone, Goulburn Valley
🍷 *Syrah (Shiraz), Cabernet Sauvignon*
🍷 *Marsanne, Riesling, Semillon, Chardonnay*

The Tahbilk winery is one of the gems of the wine industry in Australia. Largely unaltered since its construction in the 1870s, and still possessing a block of Shiraz vines planted in 1864, Tahbilk's reds are reminders of another era in Australian wine, while the white Marsanne – a rarity in itself – was served to the young Queen Elizabeth in 1953. It often develops a delightful honeysuckle aroma. The Shiraz and Cabernets are wines with mouth-ripping tannin but enough flesh and fruit to persuade you that the 20- to 30-year wait will be worthwhile. Best years: 1996, '94, '91, '90, '88, '86, '84, '81, '79, '78, '76, '71, '64, '62.

CHÂTEAUNEUF-DU-PAPE AC

FRANCE, Southern Rhône
🍷 *Grenache, Syrah, Mourvèdre and others*
🍷 *Grenache Blanc, Clairette, Bourboulenc and others*

Châteauneuf-du-Pape is a famous name, but how many of us have ever tried a good bottle? It isn't that the wine is scarce: this large vineyard area, between Orange and Avignon, covers 3200ha (7900 acres) and produces about one million cases every year – 97 per cent of them red. It's just that Châteauneuf-du-Pape ('the pope's new castle') used to be one of the most abused of all wine names: low-priced bottles appeared on every wine list, tasting thick, muddy and coarse. It's different now. Much Châteauneuf comes from single estates – it's no longer cheap, and deservedly ranks as one of France's top wines.

CH. LA NERTHE
From one of the grand estates of Châteauneuf-du-Pape, Cuvée des Cadettes is a blend of mainly old Grenache and Mourvèdre, which spends a year in new oak.

Châteauneuf now has very strict AC regulations – which is apt, because it was here, in 1923, that Baron le Roy of Ch. Fortia formulated the rules which became the basis of all French AC laws. A remarkable 13 grape varieties are permitted for the red wine – eight red and five white – though most growers only use half-a-dozen or so. Five per cent of the crop must be left on the vine at harvest – thus reducing the use of poor grapes. And the minimum alcohol level is the highest in France – 12.5 degrees.

There are two styles of red Châteauneuf: a light BEAUJOLAIS-type which has a delicious dusty warmth, juicy spice and raspberry fruit; and a more traditional style, which may need aging for five years or more and can last for 20. It is fat, weighty and piled high with fruit – raspberry, blackcurrant, plums – plus a chocolate- coffee-cinnamon richness and the tang of southern herbs. Acidity is low, tannin usually overwhelmed by fruit and the whole effect is a richly satisfying red. It is always worth buying an estate wine which is distinguished by a coat of arms embossed on the bottle above the label. Best years: (reds) 1998, '97, '95, '94, '90, '89, '88, '86, '85, '83, '81, '78. Best producers: BEAUCASTEL, BONNEAU, Bosquet des Papes, les Cailloux, Chante-Cigale, Chante-Perdrix, Clefs d'Or, CLOS DU MONT OLIVET, CLOS DES PAPES, Font du Loup, Font de Michelle, Fortia, La Gardine, Grand Tinel, la Janasse, Marcoux, La Nerthe, Pégau, Quiot, RAYAS, Sabon, VIEUX TÉLÉGRAPHE; also good, Guigal, JABOULET.

The rare white Châteauneuf, when made with modern cool-fermentation methods, can be brilliant – licorice and peach fruit, freshened up with mountain herbs and the snappy acidity of lime. The wines are good between one and two years old, although the top wines will age for five years or more. Best years: (whites) the most recent. Best producers: Beaucastel, Clos des Papes, Font de Michelle, Mont-Redon, Nalys, la Nerthe, Vieux Télégraphe.

CHAVE

FRANCE, Northern Rhône, Hermitage AC
🍷 *Syrah*
🍷 *Marsanne, Roussanne*

It's not easy to assume the mantle of a world-famous father, but Jean-Louis Chave has managed it. His father Gérard made some of France's greatest reds and whites from eight different parcels of land the family owns on the hill of HERMITAGE, and Jean-Louis has continued the brilliant succession of vintages without missing a beat. He vinifies all the parcels separately, rarely destems the reds, and ages them in old barrels of various sizes before blending and bottling. The whites also age in old barrels and age as well as the reds; indeed, they rarely show well until they are ten years old, when they gradually begin to unfold and show a complex bouquet of dried peaches, nuts and butter.

The red Hermitage gives some indication of why this appellation was so highly regarded by the nineteenth-century merchants of BORDEAUX, as a tip-top blender! It's dark, brooding and dense, but always has a core of rich black fruits which gradually take on more prominence as the wine ages and sheds its tannins.

In complete contrast, Chave produces a small quantity of ST-JOSEPH which is intended to be drunk young, and is in any case usually too delicious to keep. In great vintages such as 1990, Chave produces a barrique-aged Hermitage called Cuvée Cathelin, and also a very rare, intensely sweet *vin de paille*. Both these wines, unlike his regular Hermitages, are extravagantly priced. Best years: (reds) 1997, '96, '95, '94, '91, '90, '89, '88, '85, '83, '82, '79, '78, '72. Best years: (whites) 1997, '96, '95, '94, '93, '92, '91, '90, '89, '88, '83.

CHÉNAS AC

FRANCE, Burgundy, Beaujolais, Beaujolais cru
🍷 *Gamay*

Chénas is the smallest of the BEAUJOLAIS crus and its wines, usually quite tough when young, benefit enormously from two years or so aging. They only rarely have the gorgeous juicy fruit of young Beaujolais, but can make up for this with a deep, gently Burgundian flavour when mature – less peaches and red-currants, more chocolate and strawberries, with a lean, dry streak of earthy reserve. Best producers: Guy Braillon, Louis Champagnon, Ch. de Chénas, Lapierre, Perrachon, Daniel Robin. Best years: 1997, '96, '95, '94, '93, '91, '90.

CHENIN BLANC

Chenin Blanc is really too versatile for its own good; as a result we don't always know what to expect, which isn't helped by the tendency of producers in its native Loire to give no indication on the label as to whether the wine is dry or medium. It can also be sparkling or sweetly honeyed and concentrated by botrytis, though these wines' distinctive flavours of lime and pear and quince can come as a surprise to those reared on the more familiar flavours of Sémillon. At a decade or two old or more they are complex and fascinating, but until then they can be closed and rather dull. Anjou, Vouvray and Montlouis are the places to look for sweet Chenin Blanc. In Anjou try Coteaux du Layon (including Quarts de Chaume and Bonnezeaux) and Coteaux de l'Aubance.

Chenin Blanc is more familiar in its dry or sparkling incarnations. In the Loire Valley the most acidic, least ripe grapes go into the fizz, and although some of it is full of apples flecked with honey, the unripeness of the fruit means much is green and raw.

During the 1990s there has been a revolution in quality in the still wines. First the sweet wines were improved by reducing the vineyard yields and picking selectively. More recently the spotlight in Anjou-Saumur has turned to dry Chenin, and a number of growers now make very good wines. Dry Chenin, particularly in hot years, can be difficult to make because as the grape ripens sugar levels rise very rapidly. Dry Vouvray and Jasnières

can be marvellously nutty – if you allow them the five or ten years they need to soften. The medium-sweet versions from Anjou and Vouvray are probably the most underrated of the lot; unfashionable because of their style, their balanced angelica and quince fruit makes them perfect apéritifs.

Apart from some in the Aude at Limoux and in the Bouches-du-Rhône at the huge Listel winery, you need to cross the Atlantic or the whole of Africa to find Chenin Blanc in any quantities elsewhere.

Chenin Blanc is the most widely planted variety in South Africa. Called Steen prior to the country's re-admittance to international markets, it is now more frequently called by its French name. Its main drawcard has been versatility, making anything from sherry styles, through sparkling wines to fortified desserts, although to be honest, its suitability for distillation explains its vast acreage in the Cape. The botrytis-affected sweet wines are often among the best South African interpretations.

The same spectrum applies in California. The best-balanced dry wines can come from the North Coast, and a few producers in Sonoma concentrate on quality. Washington State has done remarkably well with off-dry wines from the Yakima Valley and the occasional ice wine. South America grows a fair amount but without distinction. Chenin Blanc grows very well in the Mendoza region of Argentina but is rarely made very proficiently. Much better are the rare but very attractive Chenins from New Zealand and the exciting quince and herb examples from Western Australia.

CH. CHEVAL BLANC

FRANCE, Bordeaux, St-Émilion Grand Cru AC, Premier Grand Cru Classé

♥ *Cabernet Franc, Merlot*

Although AUSONE (since 1978) and, to a lesser extent, FIGEAC contest the position, Cheval Blanc is the leading property in ST-ÉMILION, and likely to remain so for the foreseeable future. It is a large property, right on the border of POMEROL, at the end of a

billowing row of gravel humps which run north from Figeac. Cheval Blanc derives much of its backbone, which allows it to mature for longer than most St-Émilions, from this gravelly land; but up by the Pomerol border there are rich veins of clay, mixed with sand and iron, which give the wine its phenomenal richness and sumptuous fruit. Strangely for St-Émilion, Merlot is the minor grape, only 40 per cent of the blend, with

60 per cent Cabernet Franc. You might expect the wine therefore to lack some of the luscious Merlot fruit, but on the contrary, Cheval-Blanc is one of the grandest, most voluptuous, perfumed St-Émilions. Even lesser years like 1980 and '87 can be a successes. Best years: 1998, '97, '96, '95, '94, '93, '90, '89, '88, '86, '85, '83, '82, '81, '75, '70, '66, '64, '61, '59, '47.

DOMAINE DE CHEVALIER

FRANCE, Bordeaux, Pessac-Léognan AC, Cru Classé de Graves

♥ *Cabernet Sauvignon, Merlot, Cabernet Franc*

♀ *Sauvignon Blanc, Sémillon*

Domaine de Chevalier white is frequently one of the best dry whites in BORDEAUX. The red faces stiffer competition, but usually ends up at least in the winning frame. Yet there's no elegant château, just a low, white homestead and modern cellar block surrounded by vines. From this homely source flows a series of red wines which always start out rather dry and reserved, but over 10–20 years gain that piercing, fragrant cedar, tobacco and blackcurrant flavour which can leave you breathless with pleasure. Best years: (reds) 1998, '96, '95, '94, '93, '90, '89, '88, '85, '83, '82, '81, '75.

The white grapes produce at best 9600 bottles a year as against 60,000 bottles of red. The wine is both fermented and aged in oak barrels. At first the Sauvignon greenness is very marked, but after three to four years this fades and an increasingly creamy, nutty warmth takes over, building at ten years old to a deep, honeyed, smoky richness, just touched with resin. Second wine: (red and white) l'Esprit de Chevalier. Best years: (whites) 1998, '96, '95, '94, '93, '92, '90, '89, '88, '86, '85, '83, '82, '81, '79, '78, '75.

CHEVERNY AC

FRANCE, Loire, Touraine

♥ ♥ *Gamay, Cabernet Franc, Cabernet Sauvignon, Pinot Noir and others*

♀ *Sauvignon Blanc, Romorantin, Chenin Blanc, Chardonnay*

Cheverny is a little-known area south of Blois covering 400ha (1000 acres) of vineyards. Although Gamay, Cabernet Franc, Cabernet Sauvignon and Pinot Noir are the main red varieties, the wines never perform as well here as they do in warmer areas. They can smell rather good – sharp and distinct – but they usually taste raw and acid, better suited to marinating meat than accompanying it. The rosés are a slight improvement.

Cheverny whites are more of a mixed bag, depending on the vines used. Grape varieties like the Romorantin (with its own new AC, Cour Cheverny) presumably survive simply because of the local producers' stubbornness in preserving their traditions – it can't be because of the nice flavour of the wine. The Romorantin grows only in Cheverny and gives an unremittingly harsh wine, bone dry, almost bitter in its acidity, and smelling like a farmyard in need of a good hose down. Cheverny can make very attractive, light, nutty Chardonnay and the CHAMPAGNE-method sparkling wine is sharp, clean and bracing. Best years: 1997, '96, '95. Best producers: Cazin, Cheverny co-operative, Courtioux, Gendrier, Gueritte, Puzelat, Tessier, Tué Boeuf.

ROBERT CHEVILLON

FRANCE, Burgundy, Côte de Nuits, Nuits-St-Georges AC

♥ Pinot Noir
♀ Chardonnay

All of Chevillon's 13ha (32 acres) of vines are in NUITS-ST-GEORGES, and his range of Premiers Crus – les Cailles, les Perrières, les St-Georges, les Roncières and Vaucrains – are exemplary expressions of these varied sites. Les St-Georges is often the best and most complex wine. Chevillon likes about one-third new oak, so that the difference between the crus is not obscured. The wines are very consistent, and even in modest vintages can be of excellent quality. In style they are both muscular and vigorous, just as good Nuits-St-Georges should be. A small quantity of white Nuits is also produced. Best years: 1997, '96, '95, '93, '91, '90, '89, '88, '85.

CHIANTI DOCG, CHIANTI COLLI ARETINI DOCG, CHIANTI COLLI FIORENTINI DOCG, CHIANTI COLLI SENESI DOCG, CHIANTI COLLINE PISANE DOCG, CHIANTI MONTALBANO DOCG

ITALY, Tuscany

♥ Sangiovese and others

Chianti is an enormous region, producing practically a million hectolitres of wine, covering much of central Tuscany, most of which is divided into seven sub-districts. If a wine doesn't come solely from a sub-district, or if its producer so opts, it will have no more glorious title than Chianti, plain and simple. The denomination is often seen on the own-label Chiantis that flourish as the basic wines of the major brands. The advantages are two-fold: first, producers can buy grapes from wherever

Aging top-quality red wines in barriques is an important part of the Tuscan wine scene today. This is Fattoria di Felsina, a leading Chianti Classico estate.

in the region suits them for consistency of quality and style; second, even if the wine is from just one of the sub-districts, labels are kept simple. Most wine sold as plain Chianti is red-purple, youthful, tasting of tea and not-quite-ripe plums with a twist of bitterness on the after-taste. It can start tiring after as little as 18 months, though usually lasts a good bit longer. Sangiovese makes up from 75 to 90 per cent of the blend. 'Others' can include Cabernet, up to 10 per cent. Although the traditional straw-covered *fiasco* bottle is not seen much any more, it almost always contains basic Chianti – a fact which makes a mockery of the DOCG system.

Five of the seven Chianti sub-districts get lumped together here because, for one reason or another (often because Chianti is a second or even third wine in these zones after the likes of BRUNELLO DI MONTALCINO, VINO NOBILE DI MONTEPULCIANO or CARMIGNANO), the wines are generally unremarkable. Colli Aretini is scattered in various parcels between the east of the CHIANTI CLASSICO zone and Arezzo. Invigorating acidity is the wines' hallmark. Best producer: Villa Cilnia.

Colli Fiorentini is partly sandwiched between Florence and the northern limit of the Chianti Classico zone, which it also partly envelops. Light, young quaffers and more serious, aged wines are produced here. At its best it is indistinguishable from refined Classico, at its worst very easily distinguishable indeed. Best known producers: Fattoria di Lucignano,

Fattoria Montellori, Castello di Poppiano, Pasolini dall'Onda Borghese, Fattoria la Querce, Fattoria di Sammontana, San Vito in Flor di Selva, Fattoria dell'Ugo.

Colli Senesi is the largest sub-district, scattered extensively south of the Classico zone, and around Montalcino and Montepulciano. The distinguishing features of the wines are rich body and high alcohol and the most distinctive wines usually come from those producers who also make good BRUNELLO or VINO NOBILE. Best producers: Amorosa, Castello di Farnetella, Castello di Monteriggioni, Pacina, Pietraserena.

Colline Pisane is in the west of the region, south of Pisa and behind Livorno. The textbooks say its wines are light and soft but a new wave of winemakers, led by the doggedly determined, inspired and forward-looking Bruno Moos, are turning out some terrific, vibrant, powerful, punchy examples.

The slopes of Montalbano, west of Florence, between Pistoia and Empoli, lie cheek by jowl with those of Carmignano and thanks to Carmignano's winemakers some pretty attractive, if light, easy-drinking wines are produced. Best producers: Artimino, Villa di Capezzana. Best years: 1997, '95, '94, '93, '90.

CHIANTI CLASSICO DOCG

ITALY, Tuscany

♥ Sangiovese and others

The CHIANTI hills, that central area between Florence and Siena that was first delineated in 1716 and whose territory was last defined, a little more extensively, in 1932, is where the now world-famous name originated from. The original communes were Castellina, Gaiole and Radda, all in the province of Siena, to which have been added, over the centuries, parts of Castelnuovo Berardenga and Poggibonsi (Siena) plus the whole of Greve and parts of Barberino Val d'Elsa, San Casciano and Tavarnelle Val di Pesa (Florence).

Chianti Classico is the heart of Tuscan development, experiment and innovation. While the basic grape variety (at 75–100 per cent) remains Sangiovese, traditional blending varieties like Canaiolo, Malvasia Bianca and Trebbiano have given way to international ones like Cabernet Sauvignon and, increasingly, Merlot. SUPER-TUSCANS are rife in the region: practically every estate has at least one high-priced 'fashionable' cru, in the making of which barrique-aging features heavily. In the late 1980s the Consorzio Chianti Classico launched investigations into which clones, planting densities and training systems were suitable for high-quality production in the twenty-first century, at the dawn of which wholesale replanting is becoming necessary. Known as Chianti Classico 2000, these experiments are now bearing fruit.

Top years like 1997, '95, '93, '90, '88 and '85 bring forth superb Classico wines and brilliant Riservas usually best at 5–10 years. The so-called *normali* or straight wines should be drunk sooner. Fine producers are myriad – price, for once, being generally a fair guide to quality. Best producers: Castello di AMA, ANTINORI, BADIA A COLTIBUONO, Castello di BROLIO, Castello di Cacchiano, Carobbio, Carpineto, Casa Emma, Castellare, Castell'in Villa, Fattoria di FELSINA, Castello di FONTERUTOLI, FONTODI, ISOLE E OLENA, La Massa, Monsanto, Monte Bernardi, MONTEVERTINE, Fattoria di Nozzole, Podere Il Palazzino, QUERCIABELLA, Castello dei RAMPOLLA, Riecine, SAN FELICE, San Giusto a Rentennano, Terrabianca, Vecchie Terre di Montefili, Villa Cafaggio, Castello di Vicchiomaggio, Vignamaggio, Castello di VOLPAIA.

CHIANTI RUFINA DOCG

ITALY, Tuscany

🍷 *Sangiovese and others*

Rufina (pronounced 'Roo-fi-na' and not to be confused with the huge producer RUFFINO who has cellars there) has sound claims to be considered second only in the CHIANTI stakes to CHIANTI CLASSICO. It is the smallest Chianti sub-district and lies east of Florence, in the foothills of the Apennine mountains. The soils are like those of the central Classico but most vineyards are higher and the mesoclimate is cooler, giving higher tannin and acid levels. Hence the wines age better – vintages like 1977, '75, '68 (stupendous), '65, '58 and even '47, if found, can still provide memorable drinking. Good wines have emerged, too, from recent vintages (1997, '95, '93, '90). Best producers: Basciano, Bossi, FRESCOBALDI (Montesodi and Castello di Nipozzano), Grignano, Travignoli, Villa di Vetrice. SELVAPIANA probably tops them all.

FATTORIA SELVAPIANA
This estate has always produced excellent, refined wines typical of the Chianti Rufina zone, and is now ranked as one of the top Tuscan estates.

CHINON AC

FRANCE, Loire, Touraine

🍷🍷 *Cabernet Franc, Cabernet Sauvignon*

🍷 *Chenin Blanc*

This is the best LOIRE red wine. The growers of BOURGUEIL, on the opposite, northern banks of the river Loire, might dispute that, but the wonderful thing about Chinon is that it is so good so young, yet can improve for five, ten, 15, even 20 years to a fragrant, ethereal shadow of the great châteaux of the MÉDOC, and as such is a rare and precious delight. Good Chinon is doubly precious because the Cabernet Franc, which normally makes up all, or almost all, of the wine achieves a pure, startling intensity of fruit – the piercing acid/sweetness of blackcurrant juice pressed straight from the bush, sweetened and perfumed with a few drops of juice from ripe raspberries and an earthiness like fields after summer rain. White wines only account for about 1 per cent of Chinon production.

There are three types of soil that give three different wines. Sandy soils, especially close to the confluence of the Loire and Vienne rivers, give light wines ready to drink young; gravel soils, along by the Vienne, give wines with more structure but still ready to drink fairly young; and, finally, limestone makes the most structured and long-lived wines. Best years: 1998, '97, '96, '95, '93, '90, '89, '88, '85, '83, '82, '78, '76, '64. It's always worth buying a single-estate wine. Best producers: Alliet, B Baudry, C Baudry, Colombier, COULY-DUTHEIL, Joguet, Noblaie, Olga and Jean-Maurice Raffault.

CHINOOK WINES

USA, Washington State, Yakima Valley AVA

🍷 *Merlot, Cabernet Sauvignon, Cabernet Franc*

🍷 *Chardonnay, Sauvignon Blanc, Semillon*

The winemaking team of Kay Simon and Clay Mackay combines the enological and viticultural talents of experienced specialists. Chardonnay and Sauvignon Blanc are consistently good. Merlot is stylish and sweetly balanced. The Cabernet Sauvignon is given additional bottle age before release and is one of WASHINGTON's top reds. A tiny amount of Cabernet Franc is well crafted. Best years: (reds) 1998, '96, '94, '93; (whites) 1997, '96.

CHIROUBLES AC

FRANCE, Burgundy, Beaujolais, Beaujolais cru

🍷 *Gamay*

This is the lightest, most delicately fragrant of the ten BEAUJOLAIS crus, often little more than deep pink in colour with a perfume full of strawberries and flowers with just a whisper of cherries. There are only two things wrong with Chiroubles; there isn't much of it and it costs too much. At 395ha (976 acres) it is one of the smallest crus. It's expensive because the Parisians go batty about it; restaurants queue up for it, and allow their customers to pay too much for what is often only a marginally superior BEAUJOLAIS-VILLAGES. But fashions for wines always change; Chiroubles lost its chic during the '90s and has only now begun to recover its fans. Best years: 1998, '97, '96, '95, '94. Best producers: DUBOEUF, Domaine de la Grosse Pierre, Javernand, Maison des Vignerons.

CHIVITE

SPAIN, Navarra, Navarra DO

🍷 *Tempranillo, Grenache Noir (Garnacha Tinta), Merlot, Cabernet Sauvignon*

🍷 *Grenache Noir (Garnacha Tinta)*

🍷 *Macabeo (Viura), Moscatel de Grano Menudo (Muscat Blanc à Petits Grains), Chardonnay*

You couldn't get much more family run than Bodegas Julián Chivite, NAVARRA's largest wine producer, which in 1997 mourned the death of its patriarch, Julián Chivite. His children, Julián junior (export), Fernando (winemaker), Carlos (finance) and Mercedes (public relations) are all actively involved. The bodega started out as a coaching inn on the main road through Cintruénigo. The Chivite family began to make their own wine to sell to thirsty clients, and gradually the wine edged out the inn-keeping. In 1989 they completely overhauled the outdated winery equipment, installing new grape presses and stainless steel, temperature-controlled fermentation tanks. A new barrel-aging cellar, bottling line and 5000 new oak barrels completed the renovations. The 125-ha (310-acre) Señorío de Arínzano vineyard was planted in the early 1990s.

The basic Gran Fuedo line of wines is reliable enough, but the Collección 125 represents the very best of the new improved Chivite – a red Reserva made with Tempranillo and Merlot, a barrel-fermented Chardonnay and a late-harvested, barrel-fermented Moscatel de Grano Menudo (Muscat Blanc à Petits Grains). Best years: (reds) 1995, '94, '92, '91, '90, '89; (whites) 1996, '95.

CHOREY-LÈS-BEAUNE AC

FRANCE, Burgundy, Côte de Beaune

🍷 *Pinot Noir*

This is one of those tiny, almost forgotten Burgundian villages we should be thankful for, because they mean that we can still experience the flavour of good, if not great, Burgundy, without having to take out a second mortgage. The wine should not by rights be very special, as the village, with its 120ha (297 acres) of vineyards, is almost entirely on the flat valley land, just north of BEAUNE and east of the main N74 road. The general rule in the CÔTE D'OR is that decent wine only grows west of the N74, but Chorey is lucky in having several very committed property owners based there, who, although they also own much more classic land elsewhere, use their considerable skills on their local wine. Without them, Chorey-lès-Beaune wine would merely be sold as Côte de Beaune-Villages and never heard of again – which would be a pity. The wines can age for five to eight years, being at their best soft with a wispy strawberry fragrance. Best years: 1997, '96, '95, '93, '90, '89, '85. Best producers: DROUHIN, Germain, Goud de Beaupuis, Maillard, TOLLOT-BEAUT.

JOH. JOS. CHRISTOFFEL

GERMANY, Mosel-Saar-Ruwer, Ürzig
♀ *Riesling*

He may seem very cautious and reserved, but when it comes to wine quality Hans-Leo Christoffel does not hesitate. At his tiny estate housed in a lovingly restored seventeenth-century, half-timbered house, he makes some of the finest wines from the vineyards of ÜRZIG and ERDEN. Christoffel is a master of the MOSEL winemakers' art of balancing natural sweetness and vibrant acidity, and the hallmark of his wines is a jewel-like brilliance. His Rieslings from the Würzgarten vineyard of Ürzig are fuller and more aromatic, while those from the Treppchen of Erden are sleeker, taut and muscular. All will age well for five years and more. Best years: 1998, '97, '95, '94, '93, '92, '90, '88, '85.

CHURCHILL

PORTUGAL, Douro, Port DOC
♂ *Tinta Roriz (Tempranillo), Tinta Barroca, Tinto Cão, Touriga Naçional, Touriga Francesa and others*
♀ *Gouveio, Viosinho, Rabigato, Malvasia Fina and others*

The Grahams are synonymous with PORT but when their family company fell on hard times in 1970 it was taken over by the Symingtons (who also own DOW and WARRE). In 1981 Johnny Graham re-established his own port house, using his wife's patriotic-sounding maiden name (the company's full title is Churchill Graham). It was the first port

business to start up from scratch in 50 years. Until recently the company owned no vineyards and sourced their wines from a number of A-grade vineyards in the heart of the Douro. Since 1983 Quinta da Agua Alta has been released as a single-quinta vintage port and is one of the finest in its class.

The remainder of the wines, ranging from rich, complex crusting port and LBV to a stylish vintage, go simply by the name of Churchill. With Johnny Graham's experience in the trade, it goes without saying that all are skilfully made. The white port is especially good, aged in wood until it is golden and nutty in style. Best years: (vintage ports) 1994, '91, '87, '85.

CHURCHILL

Single-quinta vintage ports such as the excellent Agua Alta are usually made in the 'non-declared' years; the quality can be as good as a vintage year.

CIGALES DO

SPAIN, Castilla-León
♂ *Tempranillo (Tinto del País), Grenache Noir (Garnacha Tinta)*
♀ *Tempranillo (Tinto del País), Grenache Noir (Garnacha Tinta), Albillo, Verdejo*

Despite its elevation to DO status in 1991, Cigales has quite a way to go before toppling NAVARRA from its position as producer of Spain's best rosados. But rosés are the strong point of Cigales: light, aromatic wines made mainly from the Tinto del País. Growers in Cigales are being encouraged to concentrate on rosés and to grow more Tinto del País. Some red wine is made, but it's nowhere near the standard of neighbouring RIBERA DEL DUERO. However, the high, flat conditions just north of Valladolid have combined with vastly improved winemaking to make Cigales a worthy new DO.

CINSAUT

A useful rather than exciting red grape, the Cinsaut (also spelled Cinsault) grows all over the South of France and appears too in North and South Africa (where it was famously crossed with Pinot Noir to produce Pinotage). The colour is often light, the fruit

rather neutral and the acidity high, which makes it an ideal blending partner for Grenache, which is pretty much the opposite.

CIRÒ DOC

ITALY, Calabria
♂♀ *Gaglioppo, Trebbiano Toscano, Greco Bianco*
♀ *Greco Bianco, Trebbiano Toscano*

CALABRIA's best-known wine, Cirò has been around since the time of Ancient Greece when it was known as Cremissa and, so the story goes, was the wine given to the original Olympic champions to toast their success. To retain the tradition, the modern Italian Olympic team still gets Cirò rations.

Cirò Rosso is the standard bearer, and the best chance to appreciate Gaglioppo, Calabria's most important red grape. Red Cirò has potentially excellent structure, weight and concentration of fruit, plus touches of spice and chocolate, qualities best noted in the top cru of the leading producer LIBRANDI. The warm rosé, too, has good fruit and balance, and the white, based on Calabria's version of the Greco grape, is no longer the dull, flabby thing of the past but can have a lively, almost citrus character. The reds can age well, the whites and rosés should be drunk young. Best producers: Caparra & Siciliani, Ippolitu, Librandi, San Francesco.

CH. CISSAC

FRANCE, Bordeaux, Haut-Médoc AC, Cru Bourgeois
♂ *Cabernet Sauvignon, Merlot, Petit Verdot*

Sometimes, tasting Cissac, you feel as if you are in a time warp. The tannin is uncompromising, the fruit dark and stubbornly withheld for many years, the flavour of wood more like the rough, resinous edge of hand-hewn pine than the soothing vanilla creaminess now fashionable. Well, it is something of an anachronism. Although not included in the 1855 BORDEAUX Classification, it nonetheless doggedly refuses to accept the situation, and makes high-quality wines for the long haul by proudly traditional methods: old vines, lots of wood everywhere and meticulous exclusion of below-par wine from the final blend. The wines are deeply coloured and slow to mature. Best years: 1996, '95, '94, '90, '89, '88, '86, '85, '83, '82, '78.

DOMAINE BRUNO CLAIR

FRANCE, Burgundy, Côte de Nuits, Marsannay AC
♂ *Pinot Noir*
♀ *Chardonnay, Pinot Blanc*

Although based in MARSANNAY, the 21-ha (52-acre) Bruno Clair vineyards are dispersed throughout the CÔTE DE NUITS. This is not to say that his Marsannays should be neglected in favour of more prestigious wines, since half of the estate's production is released under this appellation. He produces a number of cuvées of red Marsannay, of which Longeroies is often outstanding. Marsannay used to be best known for its rosé, and the Bruno Clair bottling shows how enjoyable this style can be. The white can be good too, and contains about 20 per cent Pinot Blanc. There are excellent, solidly structured wines from CHAMBERTIN Clos-de-Bèze (two-thirds of the Clair holdings date from 1912) and GEVREY-CHAMBERTIN les Cazetiers, and an outstanding Premier Cru from SAVIGNY, les Daminodes, parts of which were planted in 1902. In 1993 the estate leased vines in CORTON-CHARLEMAGNE. Clair's winemaker since 1986 has been Philippe Brun, and the wines show every sign of going from strength to strength. Brun has a light hand with the oak, and even the weightier wines are never aged in more than 40 per cent new oak. Best years: 1997, '96, '95, '93, '92, '90, '89, '88, '87.

DOMAINE BRUNO CLAIR
The Gevrey-Chambertin Premier Cru les Cazetiers is one of the top wines from this excellent producer in the village of Marsannay.

CLAIRETTE

This rather low-acid white grape has done a fair amount of travelling from its base in southern France: it's found in Israel, South Africa, Zimbabwe and North Africa, in all of which it makes rather dull, flabby wine that needs careful handling and is best drunk extremely young.

The wine for which it is most famous, the central Rhône's CLAIRETTE DE DIE, in fact gains most of its attraction from variously sized additions of Muscat Blanc à Petits Grains in the blend; Clairette de Die Tradition is made from at least half Muscat. Clairette's more usual role in southern French white ACs, though, is as a blending partner to Grenache Blanc, Ugni Blanc and Terret. One fine example of almost unique Clairette is the Ch. SIMONE white in the PALETTE AC.

CLAIRETTE DE DIE AC

FRANCE, Central Rhône
Muscat Blanc à Petits Grains, Clairette

The thinking man's ASTI, this can be one of the most deliciously enjoyable sparkling wines in the world. The best is made from at least 50 per cent Muscat grapes mixed in with Clairette, and the result is a relatively dry or off-dry, light wine with a lovely creamy bubble and the most wonderful orchard-fresh fragrance of ripe grapes and springtime flowers.

East of the Rhône, Die is one of those lost areas of France on the road to nowhere and ringed round with hills. It's a very relaxing place to visit, with the river Drôme meandering through its centre. Clairette de Die wine is made to sparkle by the *méthode Dioise*. This involves fermentation in bottle, but the process (unlike in CHAMPAGNE) is arrested before all the grape sugar has been used up, and the wine is then filtered and re-bottled under pressure. As a result, the wine retains the flavour of the grape sugars as well as that heavenly Muscat scent. There is a Crémant de Die Brut (not Tradition) from 100 per cent Clairette grapes and made by the Champagne method – but it isn't nearly as good. Drink young. Best producers: Achard-Vincent, Andrieux, Buffardel, Clairette de Die co-operative, Raspail.

AUGUSTE CLAPE

FRANCE, Northern Rhône, Cornas AC
Syrah
Marsanne

Some growers in this appellation are fighting the stereotype of CORNAS as a dense wine that can't even be broached until it has been in bottle for eight years, but Auguste Clape remains staunchly traditionalist.

His dark wines can be very dense in their youth, but after a few years the full, complex, smoky succulence of the Syrah grape comes to the fore. Clape's wines even manage to succeed in tough years, though they will be initially coated in tannin. The grapes are not destemmed, and all parcels are vinified separately, so as to give Auguste and his son Pierre-Marie as many blending components as possible. Using their vineyard resources, they are able to draw on vines planted immediately post-phylloxera in the 1890s. The wines are aged in large old casks before being bottled. There are also small quantities of ST-PÉRAY and an inexpensive pure Syrah CÔTES DU RHÔNE whose fruit is usually mostly from young Cornas vines. Best years: 1997, '96, '95, '94, '91, '90, '89, '88, '86, '85, '83, '78.

CLARE VALLEY

AUSTRALIA, South Australia, Mount Lofty Ranges Zone

Together with the EDEN VALLEY, Clare produces Australia's finest Riesling, grapefruity and reserved when young, then blooming with four or more years of bottle age to show flavours of lime, passionfruit and more toast. There is also first-class Semillon, concentrated Cabernet Sauvignon (sometimes teamed with Malbec), and rich Shiraz. Best years: 1998, '97, '96, '94, '93, '91, '90, '87. Best producers: Tim ADAMS, Jim Barry, GROSSET, KNAPPSTEIN, LEASINGHAM, Mitchell, PETALUMA, Pikes, QUELLTALER, Sevenhill, Taylor's, WENDOUREE, Wilson Vineyard.

CLARENDON HILLS

AUSTRALIA, South Australia, Fleurieu Zone, McLaren Vale
Pinot Noir, Grenache, Syrah (Shiraz), Merlot
Chardonnay

Roman Bratasiuk, a larger-than-life figure, makes similar wines, charged with almost unimaginable amounts of flavour, extract and tannin. The most controversial is the flagship Astralis Shiraz, which rides a technical roller-coaster, seducing some and infuriating others. Best years: 1996, '93, '92, '91, '90.

CH. CLARKE

FRANCE, Bordeaux, Haut-Médoc, Listrac-Médoc AC, Cru Bourgeois
Cabernet Sauvignon, Merlot, Cabernet Franc, Petit Verdot

Twenty-five years ago Ch. Clarke was just a wistful Anglo-Saxon footnote in the more scholarly books on BORDEAUX, and the vineyard looked more like a bomb site. Then in 1973 one of the numerous Rothschilds (the late Baron Edmond) decided to recreate from scratch this derelict has-been. He spent millions on it, totally redoing the vineyards and their drainage, and building imposing new installations. It is a stunning sight – sparkling new masonry, gleaming steel and reassuring piles of new oak barrels. It reeks of money and commitment, which since the 1983 vintage has shown in the wines. These have a delicious blackcurrant fruit and a warm, oaky richness not found elsewhere in LISTRAC-MÉDOC, though they still don't match the best of neighbouring MOULIS. Since 1992 a white wine, le Merle Blanc, has also been made. Michel Rolland has been the consultant enologist since the 1998 vintage. Second wine: les Granges des Domaines Edmond de Rothschild. Best years: 1996, '95, '90, '89, '88, '86, '85.

CLEARVIEW ESTATE

NEW ZEALAND, North Island, Hawke's Bay

♀ *Cabernet Sauvignon, Merlot, Cabernet Franc*

♀ *Chardonnay, Sauvignon Blanc*

Follow the scenic coastal road north out of Napier for about ten minutes and you will reach the small community of Te Awanga and the enormously successful Clearview winery. Owner Tim Turvey battled to establish his vines and olive trees in the arid conditions without the aid of irrigation by hand-watering his vines. His efforts have paid off. Clearview is one of HAWKE'S BAY's superstar wineries with perhaps New Zealand's biggest and most concentrated Chardonnay, powerful, ripe Reserve Merlot and a Basket Press Cabernet Sauvignon that could double as writing ink and will last so long that it will probably be regarded as immortal. Rich, ripe and concentrated Sauvignon Blanc also impresses, with an oak-aged version that is even better. High demand and small production severely limits the availability of most wines, which are seldom exported. Best years: 1998, '96, '95, '94.

CH. CLIMENS

FRANCE, Bordeaux, Barsac AC, Premier Cru Classé

♀ *Sémillon, Sauvignon Blanc*

This is BARSAC's leading property. The 30-ha (74-acre) vineyard lies on the highest ground in the AC to the south-west of the village of Barsac, its vines coming to rather an abrupt end when they meet the A62 autoroute that runs between Bordeaux and Toulouse. This height gives Climens a particularly well-drained vineyard and helps to account for its reputation as the most elegant and refined of all Barsac properties.

The wines are rich, luscious and exotic. They may not burst with the peach and pineapple fruit of some 'sweeties', but they make up for this with an exciting syrupy sweetness, a most appetizing, toasty, nutty, dry edge and a light, lemony acidity that keeps the wine fresh. They are easy to drink at five years old, and a good vintage will be richer and more satisfying after ten to 15 years. There's a lovely second wine called les Cyprès. Best years: 1997, '96, '95, '90, '89, '88, '86, '83, '81, '80, '76, '75.

CLINE CELLARS

USA, California, Sonoma County, Carneros AVA

♀ *Mourvèdre, Syrah, Zinfandel and others*

♀ *Marsanne, Roussanne, Viognier*

One of California's original 'Rhône Rangers', Fred Cline began as a grower overseeing an old vineyard in Contra Costa County which contained Zinfandel and another variety eventually identified as Mourvèdre. Armed with one of the most prized RHÔNE red varieties, he led the charge with varietal Mourvèdre and also with blended wines labelled Oakley Cuvée, which contained Mourvèdre and other Rhône varieties. This early success enabled the Cline family to move to CARNEROS to build a winery and develop adjacent vineyards with Syrah, Viognier, Marsanne and Roussanne. Best years: (Rhônes) 1997, '96, '95, '94. Zinfandels under a half-dozen guises appear each year, with the annual favourites being old vineyards such as Bridehead and Big Break, and a Reserve-style Zinfandel labelled Jacuzzi, honouring the famous spa manufacturer and great-grandfather of the Clines. Best years: 1997, '96, '95, '94, '93.

CLOS DU BOIS

USA, California, Sonoma County, Alexander Valley AVA

♀ *Merlot, Cabernet Sauvignon, Pinot Noir*

♀ *Chardonnay, Sauvignon Blanc, Gewurztraminer*

Founded in 1974 by Frank Woods (hence the quirkily translated Clos du Bois) and now owned by the Wine Alliance, a division of Allied Lyons Inc, this winery has made a speciality of Chardonnay, which it offers in three or four versions. All the Chardonnays have a distinct note of French oak and are barrel-fermented. Best years: 1997, '95, '94, '93, '92, '91, '90. The melony Sauvignon Blanc is worth a close look, too.

The Cabernets have the distinctive herbaceous, blackcurrant ALEXANDER VALLEY note, enriched by aging in American oak. Marlstone is a full-flavoured Cabernet-Merlot blend and Briarcrest a classy varietal Cabernet Sauvignon; both are single-vineyard wines. Best years: 1996, '95, '94, '92, '91, '90, '87, '86. Zinfandel, offering straightforward berry fruit, and a concentrated, lovely Reserve Chardonnay are new and welcome additions to the range.

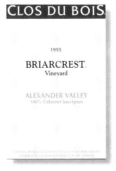

CLOS DU BOIS *From the Alexander Valley AVA, the rich, strong Briarcrest Cabernet Sauvignon has an earthy, herbal and blackcurrant fruit bouquet.*

CLOS CENTEILLES

FRANCE, Languedoc-Roussillon, Minervois AC

♀ *Cinsaut, Syrah, Carignan, Mourvèdre, Pinot Noir, Grenache and others*

Daniel Domergue and his wife Patricia produce a range of eclectic wines at their 13-ha (32-acre) domaine in the Cévennes foothills. Fervent believers in the regional grape varieties, they produce Carignanissime, a soft, spicy wine from 100 per cent Carignan, and Capitelle de Centeilles, a big, ripe, warm-hearted wine made from 100 per cent Cinsaut that can age five years or more. Other good wines include Campagne de Centeilles, another Cinsaut-dominated wine, this time with a splash of Syrah, Clos Centeilles, a classic Syrah-Mourvèdre-Grenache blend, and Guiniers, made, unusually for the Midi, from Pinot Noir. Best years: 1997, '96, '95, '94, '93.

CLOS MOGADOR

SPAIN, Cataluña, Priorat DO

♀ *Grenache Noir (Garnacha Tinta), Cabernet Sauvignon, Syrah, Pinot Noir*

René Barbier Ferrer is the bearded, genial vinegrower-turned-winemaker who led the rebirth of PRIORAT by attracting a bunch of young friends to the then-forgotten region in southern CATALUÑA in the 1980s. In 1997 he made a big decision and changed the name of his winery from René Barbier Fill (meaning son, in Catalan) to Clos Mogador, which had been the name of his wine. He hoped to end confusions with the René Barbier firm of PENEDÈS, now a mass-market brand of the giant FREIXENET group. That bodega had been sold by his family, and there was no longer any connection between the two.

It was Léon Barbier who had first bought land in Priorat, back in 1870, and thus sown the seeds of his great-grandson's rediscovery. Unlike his colleagues in the area, René, his wife and his young son (also named René) make a single wine from their 20ha (50 acres) of old-vine Grenache and younger-vine French varieties on hilly schist soils. His style is one of great ripeness, almost overripeness, with great extraction and a marked *sauvage* character. They are regularly among the best in Priorat. Best years: 1996, '95, '94, '92, '90.

CLOS DU MONT-OLIVET

FRANCE, Southern Rhône, Châteauneuf-du-Pape

♀ *Grenache, Mourvèdre, Syrah, Muscardin, Cinsaut*

♀ *Clairette, Bourboulenc, Grenache Blanc, Roussanne*

Mont-Olivet is a classic example of a highly traditional CHÂTEAUNEUF estate. The 25ha (62 acres) of vineyards are in various locations, and about 75 per cent of them are planted with Grenache, many of the vines being very old. The wine is strong, dark and rich, and in good vintages can age for a very long time. The wines are aged in large old casks – no new wood here – and bottled without fining. There is also a wine made from 100-year-old vines called Cuvée Papet. Although the Châteauneuf from Mont-Olivet can be among the finest of the appellation, there is one drawback. The Sabon brothers, who own the estate, tend to bottle the wine on demand, so some wines, especially from lesser vintages for which demand is low, can be aged for up to six years in cask, which doesn't do them any favours. Although older vintages are always for sale, it is probably better for this reason to stick to more recent years. The white Châteauneuf here is of less interest than the red. Best years: (reds) 1997, '96, '95, '94, '90, '89, '88, '85, '83, '81, '78.

CLOS DES PAPES

FRANCE, Southern Rhône, Châteauneuf-du-Pape AC
♟ *Grenache, Mourvèdre, Syrah, Vaccarèse, Muscardin, Counoise*
♀ *Clairette, Roussanne, Bourboulenc, Grenache Blanc, Picpoul*

The Avril family can trace their origins back 250 years in the town where they still have their cellars, but there is nothing antiquarian about their winemaking. Paul Avril, now joined by his son Vincent, has achieved a fine balance between traditional styles and a careful re-evaluation of practices in vineyard and winery that will best express their terroir. Thus Clos des Papes now contains more Mourvèdre than before, and yields are firmly kept in check. The red wines have a kiss of new oak, more because of the need to replace aged casks from time to time than because the Avrils want oaky flavours in the wine. The wines are robust and age extremely well. The white is one of the appellation's best, and although it is usually drunk young so that its lovely fruit can be enjoyed to the full, it can age beautifully. Best years: (reds) 1997, '96, '95, '94, '90, '89, '88, '86, '85; (whites) 1997, '96, '93, '91, '90, '88, '87, '86.

CLOS PEGASE

USA, California, Napa County, Napa Valley AVA
♟ *Cabernet Sauvignon, Cabernet Franc, Merlot*
♀ *Chardonnay*

Art collector Jacob Shram explains that he set out to fuse wine and art by building a winery which is a temple to wine, and by making his

One of the Napa Valley's most striking winery buildings is Clos Pegase at Calistoga at the northern end of the valley.

winery also an art gallery, displaying his world-famous collection. In addition to vineyards near his winery in Calistoga, Shram developed 120ha (297 acres) in the CARNEROS district, and Merlot and Chardonnay dominate the plantings. In the vintages of the early 1990s, the quality of the wine finally caught up with the quality of the facility. Today's roster features Merlot, Cabernet, and a red Meritage, Hommage. Best years: (reds) 1997, '96, '95, '94, '92. Chardonnay is divided between one from Mitsuko's Vineyard and a Reserve. Best years: (whites) 1998, '97, '95, '94.

CLOS RENÉ

FRANCE, Bordeaux, Pomerol AC
♟ *Merlot, Cabernet Franc, Malbec*

Clos René is the ideal wine to convert a white-wine drinker to red BORDEAUX. This 11-ha (27-acre) estate is on sandy soil in the less fashionable western side of the POMEROL AC. The result is wonderfully plummy, juicy, fleshy wine – fleshy like the flesh of peaches or pears or lychees – oozing fruit, and slipping down hardly touching the sides. You think it's almost sweet, and as it ages it acquires a kind of chocolaty, creamy consistency. It is sometimes sold under the label Moulinet-Lasserre. You can drink Clos René young but it also ages well for at least ten years. Best years: 1998, '97, '96, '95, '94, '90, '89, '88, '85, '83, '82, '81.

CLOS DE LA ROCHE AC, CLOS DE TART AC, CLOS DES LAMBRAYS AC, CLOS ST-DENIS AC

FRANCE, Burgundy, Côte de Nuits, Grands Crus
♟ *Pinot Noir*

It is strange that the little-known village of MOREY-ST-DENIS has five Grands Crus (the four named here and a sliver of BONNES-MARES) when far better-known villages like NUITS-ST-GEORGES don't have any at all. Clos de la Roche is the best and biggest. The wine has a lovely, bright red-fruits flavour when young which, from a grower like DUJAC or Ponsot, may get chocolaty or gamy as it ages. Clos de Tart is unusual in that it is entirely owned by one firm – Mommessin, of BEAUJOLAIS fame. The wine, light and dry at first, can develop an unexpected but delicious savoury richness. Clos des Lambrays, also under single ownership, was made a Grand Cru only in 1981. New owners took it over and began renovating it in 1979, and in 1996 it was sold again to an ambitious German proprietor, Gunther Freund. Clos St-Denis is well made by producers like G Lignier and Dujac – red fruit browning gracefully with age – but is rarely seen. Best years: 1997, '96, '95, '93, '91, '90, '89, '88, '85, '78. Best producers: Castagnier-Vadey, Dujac, G Lignier, H Lignier, Magnien, Mommessin, Perrot-Minot, Ponsot, Armand ROUSSEAU.

CLOS ROUGEARD

FRANCE, Loire, Anjou-Saumur, Saumur-Champigny AC
♟ *Cabernet Franc*
♀ *Chenin Blanc*

This tiny domaine has had an influence out of all proportion to its size of 9ha (22 acres). Ten years ago the Frères Foucault, Charly and Nadi, were viewed locally as rather bizarre curiosities. Now that there is a growing interest in making serious red SAUMUR, the Foucaults are treated with the respect they fully deserve.

They have always aged their SAUMUR-CHAMPIGNY in young oak barrels – this is not a question of fashion but rather one of tradition – growers during the 1930s always ordered a few new oak barrels every year. The Foucaults use a mixture of new and second-hand barrels, the second-hand ones coming only from top properties such as Ch. MARGAUX, PÉTRUS and Domaine de la ROMANÉE-CONTI. Yields at the Foucaults are always low – never more than 40–45 hectolitres per hectare and often lower. This means that the wines have sufficient concentration to benefit from being matured in oak.

The brothers are best known for their Saumur-Champigny – le Bourg is the 'basic' cuvée, while les Poyeaux is from old vines. In good vintages they make a little sweet COTEAUX DE SAUMUR, which, like the red, is capable of aging for a very long time. Since 1995 they have made a white Saumur from a parcel of old Chenin vines that the owner was no longer interested in using. This wine shows what an extraordinary potential dry Chenin can have when it is treated seriously. Best years: (reds) 1998, '97, '96, '95, '90, '89, '85, '83, '76, '59, '47, '37, '21 (whites only).

CLOS TRIGUEDINA
FRANCE, South-West, Cahors AC
♥ *Malbec (Auxerrois), Merlot, Tannat*
♀ *Viognier, Chardonnay*

One of the best-known domaines in the CAHORS AC, Clos Triguedina was established by the Baldès family in 1830 and is today managed by Jean-Luc Baldès, the eighth generation. The wines at the 57-ha (1401-acre) domaine continue to be powerful and age-worthy, dominated by the Auxerrois grape which represents 70 per cent of the plantings. The prestige cuvée, Prince Probus, is produced from 100 per cent Auxerrois and aged mainly in new oak barriques. There is also a small amount of white VIN DE PAYS produced from a blend of Viognier and Chardonnay. Best years: (reds) 1997, '96, '95, '94.

CLOS UROULAT
FRANCE, South-West, Jurançon AC
♀ *Petit Manseng, Gros Manseng*

Charles Hours has made this one of the best addresses in JURANÇON, both for dry and sweet wines. Unfortunately, quantities from the small 7.5-ha (18½-acre) domaine are limited to around 35,000 bottles a year and demand far outstrips supply. The dry Jurançon Sec Cuvée Marie is fermented and aged in oak barriques, providing a little more elegance, weight and structure to the fruit. The sweet wine, made from Petit Manseng, is rich but perfectly balanced with a deliciously long, lingering finish. Best years: 1997, '96, '95, '94, '93.

CLOS UROULAT
Charles Hours makes exceptionally elegant dry Jurançon which is vinified in oak and becomes gently honeyed with age.

CLOS DU VAL
USA, California, Napa County, Napa Valley AVA
♥ *Cabernet Sauvignon, Merlot, Pinot Noir, Sangiovese, Zinfandel*
♀ *Chardonnay, Semillon*

When Bernard Portet, a Frenchman from the MÉDOC, came to the NAPA VALLEY in 1972, he wanted to make Cabernet Sauvignon that was different from the heartily ripe, wooded style then in vogue in CALIFORNIA. What he sought, he said, was wine that started out with the texture of rough velvet and the flavour of fruit, then matured with the feel of silk and a fine, floral perfume. Despite these excellent intentions, the wines could be bolder and the fruit more in evidence. Portet is now moving towards a softer, fruit-driven California style. The BORDEAUX influence often gives wines that never really lose their austerity. Best years: 1997, '96, '94 ,'92, '91, '89, '87, '86, '85.

His Merlot echoes the Cabernet though with a little more obvious fruit, not enough, but a little more. His Zinfandel is richer and weightier, though still polished smoother than seems necessary for such a gutsy grape variety. Best years: 1997, '96, '95, '94, '92, '91, '90, '89, '87, '86, '85. The Semillon has all the hallmark suppleness and wonderfully subtle flavours of a good Bordeaux example. Best years: 1997, '96, '95, '94, '93, '92, '89.

CLOS DE VOUGEOT AC
FRANCE, Burgundy, Côte de Nuits, Grand Cru
♥ *Pinot Noir*

Clos in Burgundy means a vineyard enclosed by a wall, hence Clos de Vougeot is the 'walled vineyard in the village of Vougeot'. Founded by Cistercian monks in the fourteenth century, it had reached 50ha (124 acres) by the time they put a wall round it with due proprietorial pride and for more than 600 years this original boundary has stayed intact.

But the French Revolution put paid to single ownership. The vineyard was confiscated and sold, gradually becoming fragmented until it now has over 80 owners. This multiplicity of ownership has turned it into one of the most unreliable Grand Cru Burgundies. And there's another reason. The Clos runs from the top of the CÔTE D'OR slope, next to the Grands Crus of GRANDS-ÉCHÉZEAUX and MUSIGNY, right down to the flat, clay soil on the N74 road – only two cars' width away from dead-end land relegated to the basic appellation BOURGOGNE. Yet it is all Grand Cru. A good owner should be able to make great wine on the upper slopes, but these heavy, muddy lower vineyards can never

produce wine of the fragrance and beauty a Grand Cru label demands.

However, when it's good it is wonderfully soft, fleshy wine, the fruit like perfumed plums backed up by a smoky chocolate richness, turning dark and exotic with age. Best years: 1997, '96, '95, '93, '92, '91, '90, '89, '88, '85, '80, '78. Best producers: Arnoux, Confuron, DROUHIN, ENGEL, GRIVOT, Jean Gros, Haegelen-Jayer, Hudelot-Noëllat, Jayer, Lamarche, LEROY, MÉO-CAMUZET, MORTET, ROUMIER, Ch. de la Tour.

CLOUDY BAY
NEW ZEALAND, South Island, Marlborough
♥ *Cabernet Sauvignon, Merlot, Pinot Noir*
♀ *Sauvignon Blanc, Chardonnay, Semillon*

The evocative Cloudy Bay label announces a wine that is now an international brand. A complex, structured, melon, peach and oak Chardonnay and a fabulous fizz – Pelorus – are also stars, with Pinot Noir in the wings, but the real Cloudy Bay is the superlative Sauvignon Blanc. A touch of smoky oak, a twitch of Semillon, stringent grape selection combined with skilful winemaking produce a mouth-tingling, smoky, gooseberry-flavoured wine, the taste of which goes on forever. Recent vintages have been softer, milder. Hopefully this is a temporary aberration. Best years: (Sauvignon Blanc) 1997, '96, '94, '91.

J-F COCHE-DURY
FRANCE, Burgundy, Côte de Beaune, Meursault AC
♥ *Pinot Noir*
♀ *Chardonnay*

The wines of Jean-François Coche-Dury have become legendary, in part because they are so difficult to obtain. For many this is the quintessence of MEURSAULT, bold rich wines, subtly oaked and bottled without filtration. The estate is small, with 7ha (17 acres) of vines, so production of some of the most celebrated wines, such as the magnificent Meursault les Perrières and CORTON-CHARLEMAGNE, is minuscule. The less acclaimed, but still very good, red wines are from VOLNAY and MONTHÉLIE. Best years: 1997, '96, '95, '94, '93, '92, '90, '89, '88, '86, '85, '83.

COCKBURN-SMITHES
PORTUGAL, Douro, Port DOC
♥ *Tinta Roriz (Tempranillo), Tinta Barroca, Tinto Cão, Touriga Nacional and others*
♀ *Gouveio, Viosinho, Rabigato, Malvasia Fina and others*

Cockburn, one of the best known of all PORT shippers, sells more port in the UK than any other company. Its fortunes are largely based on Special Reserve, a rich, approachable premium ruby. Cockburn has some of the most enviable quintas in the DOURO, among them the huge Vilariça vineyard way upstream in the Douro Superior and Quinta dos Canais which faces TAYLOR's Quinta de Vargellas. The fact that they have control of so much of their production makes Cockburn's Special Reserve such a consistent wine.

Cockburn's more up-market ports have a slightly more patchy reputation. Although the vintage ports tend to be dense and rich in style a number of Cockburn declarations in the 1980s were not up to scratch. You have to go back to the 1970s to find a Cockburn vintage port in the classic mould. The 10- and 20-year-old tawnies are top-notch and the Anno LBV is on the light side but soft and raisiny. Cockburn's also produces an excellent red Douro wine known as Tuella.

Cockburn-Smithes, as it is known in full, is part of drinks multinational Allied Domecq. Best years: (vintage ports) 1994, '91, '70, '67, '63.

CODORNÍU

SPAIN, Cataluña, Cava DO
♂ Monastrell, Parellada
♀ Macabeo, Parellada, Xarel-lo, Chardonnay

This family-owned PENEDÈS giant is the largest CHAMPAGNE-method sparkling wine company in the world. It occupies a spectacular estate in San Sadurní de Noya, 60km (37 miles) south-west of Barcelona, complete with nineteenth-century Art Nouveau buildings which are national monuments. Codorníu Chardonnay is the best CAVA on the market – reasonably fruity, with honeyed, tropical fruit flavours. The big brand, Codorníu Brut, is also good in its class, clean, fresh and lively.

Codorníu also owns the improving Penedès still wine company of Masía Bach, the exciting RAIMAT estate in COSTERS DEL SEGRE, Rondel, another huge Cava company, the traditional and revamped Bodegas BILBAÍNAS in RIOJA, California's Codorníu Napa and Agro 2001, which supplies many of Spain's best quality, clonally selected vines to much of the Spanish wine industry.

COLARES DOC

PORTUGAL, Estremadura
♂ Ramisco
♀ Malvasia, Arinto, Jampal, Galego Dourado

The tiny coastal wine enclave of Colares, north-west of Lisbon, produces one of

PAULO DA SILVA
Almost black in colour, this Colares wine starts out exceedingly tannic but are said to soften with age. Drink with at least ten years' aging..

Portugal's most historic wines. The vineyards are planted on a sandy cliff-top plateau among windswept pine groves, thickets of bamboo and scattered holiday villas. The sand, a metre or more in depth, helped to protect the roots of the vines against phylloxera in the nineteenth century and the vineyards that have survived the commercial pressures of the twentieth century are still ungrafted. A clear distinction is therefore made between the wines from the Chão de Areia (sandy soil) and those from the Chão Rijo (hard ground).

The reputation of Colares has suffered due to some heavy-handed winemaking by the local co-operative, which held a monopoly of the region's wine production until the early 1990s. Red wines tended to be hard and astringent and whites were made in an old-fashioned oxidative manner. A number of private producers have tried to rescue Colares in recent years but so far no-one has arrested the region's decline. Judging by some of the ethereal old wines from the 1940s and '50s, Colares is clearly a region worth saving.

COLDSTREAM HILLS

AUSTRALIA, Victoria, Port Phillip Zone, Yarra Valley
♂ Pinot Noir, Cabernet Sauvignon, Merlot, Cabernet Franc, Syrah (Shiraz)
♀ Chardonnay, Pinot Gris, Sauvignon Blanc

James Halliday, our Australian contributor and consultant, founded Coldstream Hills in 1985. In 1996 it was acquired by Southcorp, but Halliday remains responsible for winemaking. Plummy, tobacco and strawberry Pinot Noir has been the great success, hotly pursued by fine, crisp and long-flavoured Chardonnay. Merlot and Shiraz join the roster as single-variety wines as from 1997, but a Cabernet, Merlot and Cabernet Sauvignon remain. The very limited production Reserve range of Chardonnay, Pinot Noir, Merlot and Cabernet Sauvignon are especially complex, all relying on fruit rather than oak to do the talking. Best years: 1997, '96, '94, '92, '91, '88.

COLLARDS

NEW ZEALAND, North Island, Henderson
♂ Cabernet Sauvignon, Merlot, Pinot Noir
♀ Chardonnay, Sauvignon Blanc, Riesling, Gewurztraminer, Semillon, Chenin Blanc and others

Family-owned since the outset, Collards did not emerge as a significant quality wine producer until the 1970s. Grapes come from various sources: vineyards at Henderson and Waimauku (Rothesay Vineyard) are supplemented by GISBORNE, HAWKE'S BAY and MARLBOROUGH. The Chardonnays are the flagship wines; quality shines through in the positive, yet not overblown, oaking of the Hawke's Bay and Rothesay wines. The Sauvignon can be excellent, though less immediately compelling than many New Zealand styles, and a lush, lightly oaked, tropical fruit salad Chenin Blanc is the other speciality. Best years: 1998, '96, '94, '91, '90, '89.

COLLI BERICI DOC, COLLI EUGANEI DOC

ITALY, Veneto
♂ Cabernet Franc, Cabernet Sauvignon, Merlot, Tocai Rosso
♀ Garganega, Pinot Blanc (Pinot Bianco), Sauvignon Blanc, Tocai Bianco

Colli Berici, south of Vicenza, was venerated as a wine region until the arrival of the phylloxera bug almost a century ago, which destroyed many of the vineyards. Growers replanted on the easier-to-cultivate flat land down in the valleys and the zone's illustrious history ground swiftly to a halt. Only at the Lazzarini's Villa dal Ferro did they laboriously bring topsoil back up to the hills and plant on these difficult, but rewarding, steep slopes. Another good producer is Cavazza.

Across to the west, towards Padua, rises another range of hills, the Colli Euganei. The producers Vignalta, with excellent Cabernet- and Merlot-based wines, and Ca' Lustra have highlighted the potential here.

COLLI BOLOGNESI DOC

ITALY, Emilia-Romagna
♂ Barbera, Cabernet Sauvignon, Merlot
♀ Pignoletto, Pinot Blanc (Pinot Bianco), Welschriesling (Riesling Italico), Sauvignon Blanc

Most of the landscape of EMILIA-ROMAGNA is flat as a pancake, so the odd outcrops of hills bring great relief. The Colli Bolognesi, overlooking Bologna, may not be the highest range of hills in the world, but 100m (330ft) or so helps enormously, especially when the slopes are so conveniently angled for growing vines. The first estate to aim for quality was

Enrico Vallania's Terre Rosse, with 20ha (49 acres) of vineyard planted to various international grapes such as Cabernet Sauvignon, Chardonnay and Pinot Blanc (Pinot Bianco), as well as Sauvignon Blanc, Riesling and Malvasia. Tenuta Bonzara now leads a growing pack of quality-minded producers, including Gaggioli, Isola and Vallona.

COLLI ORIENTALI DEL FRIULI DOC

ITALY, Friuli-Venezia Giulia

♟ *Cabernet Franc, Cabernet Sauvignon, Merlot, Pinot Noir (Pinot Nero), Refosco, Schioppettino*

♟ *Merlot*

♀ *Chardonnay, Malvasia Istriana, Picolit, Pinot Blanc (Pinot Bianco), Pinot Gris (Pinot Grigio), Ribolla, Riesling (Riesling Renano), Sauvignon Blanc, Tocai, Traminer Aromatico, Verduzzo*

Viticulturally, the southern part of Colli Orientali or the 'Eastern Hills' is practically identical to the adjacent zone of COLLIO; only towards the north does quality tail off a little. Even so, only wine from vineyards on hilly terrain is permitted the Colli Orientali denomination. Colli Orientali's aromatic, restrained, elegantly youthful, single-varietal whites are its forte, especially Pinot Bianco, Pinot Grigio, lemony native Ribolla, Tocai Friulano and perfumed Sauvignon and Riesling, all made with balance, rather than power, in mind. The reds, with the brambly Schioppettino leading the way for native varieties and Cabernet Franc for the internationals, are improving dramatically, often offering a spicy, herbaceous tang, and good potential for aging. Best years: 1998, '97, '96, '94, '93, '90.

The sweet wines are exciting, most notably from Verduzzo in its sub-zone, Ramandolo, and delicate Picolit making subtle, floral, honeyed wines. And since the vine suffers from a distressing-sounding affliction, floral abortion, which prevents it flowering properly, production is tiny. Best producers: Abbazia di Rosazzo, Ca' Ronesca, Dario Coos, Danieli, Dorigo, Dri, FELLUGA, Gigante, Meroi, Miani, Rocca Bernarda, Rodaro, Ronchi di Cialla, Ronchi di Manzano, Ronco dei Roseti-Zamò, Ronco del Betulle, Ronco del Gnemiz, Specogna, Torre Rosazzo, La Viarte, Vigne dal Leon, Volpe Pasini, Zamò & Zamò.

COLLI PIACENTINI DOC

ITALY, Emilia-Romagna

♟ *Barbera, Bonarda, Pinot Noir (Pinot Nero)*

♀ *Malvasia, Ortrugo, Pinot Gris (Pinot Grigio), Sauvignon Blanc*

A quirk of the regional arrangement means the boundary between Emilia and LOMBARDY

The medieval town of Castell'Arquato is in the Colli Piacentini DOC, a hilly area of Emilia in the Apennine foothills and more or less an extension of Lombardy's Oltrepò Pavese DOC. The wines are also very similar.

comes plumb through a prime viticultural area. The result is one district with two names: Colli Piacentini (Emilia) and OLTREPÒ PAVESE (Lombardy). Miles away (literally as well as figuratively) from the typically Emilian Lambrusco, Colli Piacentini is an umbrella DOC, covering various sub-denominations and varietal wines, sometimes a touch *frizzante*. The jewel is Gutturnio, a brilliant, raspberry, truffly, mocha blend of Bonarda with Barbera, and Ortrugo is the local oddity, a bitter-finishing white. Best producers: Fugazza, Molinelli, Mossi, Romagnoli, La Stoppa, La Tosa.

COLLIO DOC

ITALY, Friuli-Venezia Giulia

♟ *Cabernet Franc, Cabernet Sauvignon, Merlot, Pinot Noir (Pinot Nero)*

♀ *Chardonnay, Malvasia Istriana, Müller-Thurgau, Picolit, Pinot Blanc (Pinot Bianco), Pinot Gris (Pinot Grigio), Ribolla, Riesling (Riesling Renano), Welschriesling (Riesling Italico), Sauvignon Blanc, Tocai, Traminer Aromatico*

The COLLIO zone is an arc of hills squeezed up along the Slovenian border. The nearby Adriatic has a beneficial effect on the climate, keeping the area warm but well ventilated, bringing forward the growing season. Collio Goriziano (so-called after the nearby city of Gorizia) has been hailed as the cradle of the Italian white wine revolution, and while there is an element of overstatement in this, there is

also an element of truth. It is certainly true that, from the 1960s and '70s on, producers like Mario SCHIOPETTO, Vittorio Puiatti, Livio FELLUGA and Silvio JERMANN have been turning out finely crafted whites from the wealth of varieties available in the zone – whites of grace and subtlety rather than of power, concentrating on pure varietal aromas in the early days, at least, rather than on those of oak. No Italian zone had ever previously managed fine white wine on such a scale.

It is also true, however, that this district, which owes as much to Austrian, French and Slavic influences as it does to Italian ones, has a strong international feel about it, and could hardly be said to be 'typical' of Italy as could, for example, the SOAVE zone, or the Castelli Romani zone around Rome, or indeed the Castelli di Iesi zone in the MARCHE which today is challenging for the mantle of top white wine zone in the land. Collio's answer has been to diversify. In the white department, while still turning out pristine varietals, producers are turning more and more to ingenious blends – mixes of BORDEAUX (Sauvignon), Burgundy (Pinot Blanc or Chardonnay) and, say, ALSACE (Gewurztraminer) such as no-one in France, or anywhere else, for that matter, would contemplate.

The other area of expansion in Collio of late has been into red wines. Cabernet and Merlot have been produced here for well over a century, but it is only in the last few years that Collio has been able to put flesh on the bones of its traditionally rather meagre, metallic reds while retaining the hallmark of cool understatement and restraint which the more flamboyant Tuscan reds, for example, cannot boast. Best years: 1998, '97, '96, '95, '93, '90. Serious producers, apart from the above-mentioned, include Borgo Conventi, Borgo del Tiglio, La Castellada, Ca' Ronesca, Dal Fari, Marco Felluga, GRAVNER, Edi Kante, Edi Keber, Primosic, Princic, Radikon, Ronco dei Tassi, RUSSIZ SUPERIORE, Subida di Monte, Tercic, Venica & Venica, Villa Russiz.

COLLIOURE AC

FRANCE, Languedoc-Roussillon
♦ *Grenache, Mourvèdre, Carignan and others*
This tiny and beautiful coastal AC is tucked away in the Pyrenean foothills on the border between France and Spain. The wine, based on ripe Grenache and Mourvèdre, with some Carignan and Cinsaut, is throat-warming, head-spinning stuff but hardly seen elsewhere. It's capable of aging for a decade but marvellously aggressive when young. Best producers: CELLIER DES TEMPLIERS, Clos des Paulilles, MAS BLANC, la RECTORIE, la Tour Vieille. Best years: 1998, '97, '96, '95, '94, '93, '90.

JEAN-LUC COLOMBO

FRANCE, Northern Rhône, Cornas AC
♦ *Syrah*
The northern RHÔNE, until the late 1980s, was a deeply conservative place, and when it came to growing grapes and making wine little seems to have altered since the nineteenth century. Then along came Jean-Luc Colombo and changed all that. Colombo was an enologist, and thoroughly acquainted with the whole world of wine. CORNAS, in his view, was falling behind, producing backward wines that had a small band of ardent followers but no wider recognition. Colombo simply applied his knowledge and skill to the local vineyards, persuading some of the growers for whom he acted as a consultant to destem their grapes and to age them in barriques, even in a proportion of new oak. Soon he purchased some vineyards of his own, which he farms organically, and began turning out a string of wines that may sometimes have lacked what most people think of as Cornas typicity, but which were extremely good in their own right.

His best wine is called les Ruchets (from old vines and aged in 80 per cent new oak), and there are other bottlings named Terres Brûlées and la Louvée (70-year-old vines, aged in 100 per cent new oak). In the early 1990s Colombo put a few noses out of joint by charging considerably more for his wines than the other growers, but it certainly helped this sleepy appellation to gain the attention it needed. Colombo also runs a *négociant* business – his whites from the southern Rhône can be delicious – and acts as a consultant for many wineries, such as the Cave de Cairanne. Best years: 1997, '96, '95, '94, '91, '90.

COLUMBIA WINERY

USA, Washington State, Columbia Valley AVA
♦ *Cabernet Sauvignon, Merlot, Pinot Noir, Syrah and others*
♀ *Chardonnay, Riesling, Pinot Gris*
British Master of Wine David Lake has been making wine at Columbia Winery, in WASHINGTON STATE's YAKIMA VALLEY, since 1979. The grape flavours in all his wines are understated, allowing the winemaking to show through. This is particularly true of the Chardonnay. Best years: 1996, '95, '94. Other whites made here include the first Pinot Gris made in Washington. The red wines are led by his single-vineyard, age-worthy Cabernets – especially from Red Willow Vineyard and Otis Vineyard – and fruity Pinot Noir, as well as Merlot and Syrah. Best years (reds): 1995, '94, '92, '91, '90.

COLUMBIA WINERY
The white wines from this large but still high-quality winery are fresh and elegant. Columbia makes a stylish Pinot Gris, a grape variety which is rare in Washington.

COMMANDARIA

CYPRUS, Troodos Mountains
♦ *Mavro*
♀ *Xynisteri*
This intensely sweet dessert wine never seems to be as good as its hype says it is. It comes from the lower slopes of the Troodos mountains, from 14 designated villages, and is made by sun-drying white Xynisteri and/or red Mavro grapes on mats for about ten days, and then fermenting them. No fortifying alcohol is added. Some is made as a simple commercial wine, sometimes used as altar

wine, and only very little is made with the legendary concentration. Even then, one feels it should be better. The best wines are made from Xynisteri grapes only and are aged in a solera system. They are very different and more expensive than the basic wines.

VIN DE PAYS DU COMTÉ TOLOSAN

FRANCE, South-West
♦ ♀ *Cabernet Sauvignon, Merlot, Duras, Tannat, Fer Servadou, Cabernet Franc, Syrah and others*
♀ *Chardonnay, Sauvignon Blanc, Colombard, Sémillon and others*
One of France's four regional VINS DE PAYS, the Comté Tolosan covers the South-West of France, from south of BORDEAUX to the Pyrenees and east into the Aveyron and Tarn *départements*. The range of varietal wines uses international varieties such as Chardonnay and Cabernet Sauvignon as well as blends with local varieties like Duras, Tannat and Fer Servadou. The reds and rosés are of most interest but decent whites are produced by the PLAIMONT co-operative. Best producers: Cave de Crouseilles, Labastide-de-Levis co-operative, Producteurs Plaimont, de Ribonnet.

CONCA DE BARBERÁ DO

SPAIN, Cataluña
♦ ♀ *Grenache Noir (Garnacha Tinta), Trepat, Tempranillo (Ull de Llebre), Cabernet Sauvignon, Merlot*
♀ *Macabeo, Parellada*
This small, promising DO, created only in 1989, is the highest region in Cataluña, therefore cooler, and capable in theory of making really fresh, aromatic wines. This is one of the CAVA DO regions, but little fizzy wine is actually made here. As much as 80 per cent of Conca de Barberá's grapes, juice and wine is sold to the Cava firms of PENEDÈS. White grapes now account for nearly three-quarters of production and the white wines can be fresh, fruity and lemony. Concavins and the small Sanstravé winery have demonstrated the exciting potential of the region's reds. Star of the region is the TORRES estate of Milmanda and its spectacular Chardonnay.

CONCHA Y TORO

CHILE, Maipo Valley
♦ *Cabernet Sauvignon, Merlot*
♀ *Semillon, Riesling, Sauvignon Blanc, Chardonnay and others*
Concha y Toro has been supplying some of Chile's most reliable exported wines for quite a time now, with a reputation for ripe,

fruity red wines. The Don Melchor, Marqués de Casa Concha and Casillero del Diablo (especially the barrel-fermented and -aged Sauvignon Blanc) are highlights of the main range, with the Trio label offering a tasty budget line. In an effort to improve quality even further, an intriguing partnership has arisen with Ch. MOUTON-ROTHSCHILD, to make a range of wines called Almaviva. Best years: 1998, '97, '96.

CONCHA Y TORO

The renaissance of Concha y Toro continues and the Marqués de Casa Concha label offers excellent Cabernet, Merlot and Chardonnay at keen prices.

CONDRIEU AC

FRANCE, Northern Rhône

♀ *Viognier*

The ugly modern village of Condrieu is the unlikely birthplace of one of the world's great white wines. To the west of Condrieu, stark, forbidding cliffs rear towards the clouds; from the road you can see rows of ancient vineyard terraces. Although the AC covers a protected 200ha (494 acres), fewer than 60ha (148 acres) of vineyard cling to the daunting rockface. In recent years, because of the great demand for this wonderful, fragrant wine, there have been new plantings on the plateau behind which will increase, though certainly not improve, production. But we should be grateful that Condrieu has been rescued from near extinction. In 1971 a trifling 12ha (30 acres) were being cultivated.

But what a wine those original straggly patches of struggling vines produce. The Viognier is a disease-prone, shy-yielding vine found only here, at neighbouring CHÂTEAU-GRILLET, at CÔTE-RÔTIE (where it can be mixed with the red Syrah), and, in increasing amounts, in the southern RHÔNE and LANGUEDOC and the New World. A pathetic yield – rarely more than 20 hectolitres per hectare – and a propensity to rot and floral abortion (when no grapes develop from the flowers) are the reasons for this scarcity: an entire vintage has been known to produce only 19 hectolitres.

But the flavour... A fragrance of ripe apricots and juicy Williams pears, freshened by spicy flower perfumes. Yet the wine is dry. Full in your mouth, yes, almost thick and viscous – juicy apricot skins and ripe golden peaches, coated with a perilous richness like double cream about to turn sour. These remarkable wines fade with age, and are horrifyingly expensive – but at one to three years old they are a sensation everyone should try just once. Best years: 1998, '97, '96, '95. Best producers: Gilles Barge, CUILLERON, Delas, Dézormeaux, Dumazet, Gaillard, Gérin, GUIGAL, Jurie des Camiers, Perret, Niéro Pinchon, ROSTAING, Ch. du Rozay, VERNAY.

CONO SUR

CHILE, Rapel Valley

♟ *Cabernet Sauvignon, Merlot, Pinot Noir*

♀ *Sauvignon Blanc, Chardonnay*

After the pioneering work done in Chile by Miguel TORRES, Cono Sur was one of the first Chilean wineries to adapt itself to truly modern winemaking standards. When Ed Flaherty, the Californian enologist (now with ERRÁZURIZ) credited with dragging much of Chile's winemaking into the modern age, kicking and screaming, first arrived, there wasn't even a suitable water supply. Now Cono Sur, owned by CONCHA Y TORO, produces very reliable wines under the Cono Sur and Isla Negra labels. CASABLANCA VALLEY provides its best fruit, and Pinot Noir makes a creditable appearance under the Cono Sur label. Best years: 1998, '97, '96.

CONSTANTIA WO

SOUTH AFRICA, Western Cape

Along with STELLENBOSCH, Constantia is probably South Africa's best-known wine region and is the historic heart of the country's wine industry. It certainly was back in the eighteenth century, when Constantia dessert wine was famous throughout Europe. Today, it is recognized for modern, New World styles. Sauvignon Blanc has proved particularly successful on all five properties, which line the slopes running down the spine of the Cape peninsula. In the main, these face south-east, so benefit from the full effect of the breezes blowing off False Bay. The soils are deep and well-drained. Virtually the only downsides are susceptibility to botrytis and, in the case of the BUITENVERWACHTING, GROOT and KLEIN CONSTANTIA estates, the early disappearance of the sun behind Table Mountain. Later-ripening red varieties thus struggle to reach optimum sugar levels.

These three farms cover most of the land originally granted to Simon van der Stel in 1685 and which was divided into three on his death. A little apart, to the south, historic Steenberg and Uitsig have lighter soils and longer sunlight. As well as elegantly intense Sauvignon Blanc and, interestingly, Semillon among the white wines, Merlot in particular is showing some exciting results for red varieties in the valley. Best years: (whites) 1998, '97, '96. Best producers: Buitenverwachting, Constantia-Uitsig, Groot Constantia, Klein Constantia, Steenberg.

ALDO CONTERNO

ITALY, Piedmont, Barolo DOCG

♟ *Nebbiolo, Barbera, Dolcetto*

♀ *Chardonnay*

Aldo Conterno is an open, friendly man, revered as a guru by numerous younger members of the BAROLO-producing fraternity. Yet although he broke with his traditionalist brother, Giovanni, in 1969 (see entry below), Aldo could not really be accused of being a modernist. His Barolos, generally recognized as some of the absolute greatest, could perhaps best be described as of classic style without the defects, packing as he does into his finest bottles just about every nuance of which great Barolo is capable. Aldo's top cru, only produced in the best vintages, is Granbussia, a blend of vineyards on the Bussia slope which in very good years are also made separately, to wit Vigna Cicala and Vigna Colonello. Bussia Soprana is his mainstay Barolo, produced in every year except bad ones, and it can be particularly fine in lesser years, when it contains all the best grapes.

Aldo is against the use of French barriques for aging Barolo but he does use them for his LANGHE Nebbiolo, from young vines, called Il Favot. He refers to this as his sons' wine – his three boys, Franco, Stefano and Giacomo, all having followed him into the business, Stefano taking on the crucial role of winemaker. He is also in favour of barriques for Barbera and he was, indeed, one of the earliest practitioners of that felicitous style. And his Chardonnay Bussiador is unmistakably oak-fermented and matured in the best Burgundian tradition. Best years: (Barolo) 1993, '90, '89, '88, '85, '82.

GIACOMO CONTERNO

ITALY, Piedmont., Barolo DOCG

♟ *Nebbiolo, Barbera, Dolcetto, Freisa*

The elder brother referred to in the above entry (his name is actually Giovanni, Giacomo having been their father), Giovanni Conterno could not be more different in character from his extrovert sibling, Aldo.

Signor Conterno (one would not call him Giovanni, nor use the familiar 'tu', although his son Roberto, now taking over, is a lot less formidable) is marginally less of a traditionalist than he was when the fraternal disputes were taking place in the 1960s, especially in respect of length of wood-aging, but he still turns out BAROLOs of heroic structure, capable of lasting a human lifetime. His top cru, Monfortino, is sought by wine collectors the world over, and even his Barolo Cascina Francia is sold out virtually before it hits the market.

The difference between these two wines lies entirely in the vinification, since only top quality grapes from the 16-ha (40-acre) property of Cascina Francia in Serralunga are used for both. Whereas the straight Barolo is macerated for three to four weeks maximum at controlled temperature, Monfortino will get a good five weeks on the skins with no attempt to keep down the temperature. Best years: 1993, '90, '89, '88, '87, '86, '85, '82.

CONTINO
SPAIN, La Rioja, Rioja DOC
♂ *Tempranillo, Grenache Noir (Garnacha Tinta), Carignan (Cariñena, Mazuelo) and others*
Contino is one of the few wines made in RIOJA from the grapes of a single estate, and a testimony to the advantages of a good site – in this case, a 45-ha (110-acre), west-sloping vineyard in the heart of the Rioja Alavesa. The majority of the wine is made from Tempranillo, with some Graciano and Mazuelo, and all the fermentation is in stainless steel tanks. The bodega entirely skipped the 1992 and '93 vintages as it rebuilt its cellars to solve a problem of barrel mustiness. It later introduced an interesting Graciano varietal. With staggeringly rich, blackberry fruit, the wines will improve for at least five years. Best years: 1996, '95, '94, '91, '90, '89, '88, '87, '85, '82.

COONAWARRA
AUSTRALIA, South Australia, Limestone Coast Zone
The name, an Aboriginal word meaning honeysuckle, is the most romantic feature of Coonawarra. It is a flat, featureless dot in a flat, featureless plain in the middle of nowhere, which just happens to be Australia's best wine region for velvety rich and smooth Cabernet Sauvignon, of high-quality Shiraz (Syrah) tasting of cherry, mint and a dusting of spice, and good Chardonnay, Riesling and Sauvignon Blanc.

The magic lies in a narrow strip of land which has a layer of reddish soil – terra rossa

– over a limestone base, and also in the cool climate. The best red wines are opulent and intense and will live for 30 years or more while the whites have a real intensity of cool-climate fruit when properly made. Best years: 1998, '96, '94, '93, '91, '90, '88, '86, '84, '82, '80. Best producers: Balnaves, BOWEN ESTATE, BRAND'S LAIRA, HOLLICK, KATNOOK ESTATE, Leconfield, LINDEMANS, Majella, MILDARA, ORLANDO, Parker, PENLEY ESTATE, PETALUMA, ROSEMOUNT, WYNNS, Zema Estate.

COOPERS CREEK
NEW ZEALAND, North Island, Huapai
♂ *Cabernet Sauvignon, Merlot*
♀ *Chardonnay, Sauvignon Blanc, Chenin Blanc and others*
For a relatively small winery, Coopers Creek has always had a high profile, thanks in part to accusations of mislabelling, but most importantly to the quality of its wines. Both GISBORNE and HAWKE'S BAY Chardonnay are outstanding and concentrated wines, with classic peach and fig flavours surrounded by nutty, spicy oak; Coopers Dry is an arresting pungent blend of grassy Sauvignon Blanc, Semillon and Chenin Blanc, while the Sauvignon Blanc shows wonderfully opulent gooseberry fruit and the Riesling is delicate but fragrant. Best years: 1998, '96, '94, '91.

CORBANS
NEW ZEALAND, North Island, Henderson
♂ *Cabernet Sauvignon, Merlot, Pinot Noir*
♀ *Chardonnay, Sauvignon Blanc, Muller-Thurgau, Riesling, Gewurztraminer, Semillon*
Corbans is owned by a brewery, the publicly listed DB Group, and is comfortably the second-largest New Zealand winemaker. Chardonnays come under various labels; the buttery, malty Cooks Private Bin and the Longridge (made from HAWKE'S BAY grapes) as well as Stoneleigh and Robard & Butler (both from MARLBOROUGH grapes). Best of

CORBANS
The sweet and concentrated Noble Rhine Riesling is one of several excellent wines made by this enormous company selling wines under a wide range of labels.

the reds are the succulent, rich, chocolaty Corbans Merlots and Cabernet-Merlots (sourced from Marlborough and Hawke's Bay) but the overall performance of the Cooks label in particular is still patchy. Best years: 1998, '96, '94, '91, '90.

CORBIÈRES AC
FRANCE, Languedoc-Roussillon
♂♀ *Carignan, Cinsaut, Grenache, Syrah, Mourvèdre*
♀ *Bourboulenc, Clairette, Grenache Blanc, Macabeo, Marsanne, Rousanne, Rolle, Muscat and others*
The Corbières region south of Narbonne is one of the most captivating in France. It is a wild, windswept, sun-drenched marvel of stubborn hills and delving valleys and it's hardly surprising that consistency was never the watchword in the wines.

Carbonic maceration is on the increase in the region, used with discretion to produce big beefy reds, made mainly from Carignan, dusty to the taste but roaring with a sturdy juicy fruit, a whiff of spice and a slap of herbs. These are wines of excellent quality at an excellent price to drink young. The old-style Corbières, heavy, thick and cloddish, is less and less seen. Some producers are aging wines in wood and these can be worth keeping for a few years. Best years: (reds) 1997, '96, '95, '94, '93, '90. Best producers: Baillat, Caraguilhes, Étang des Colombes, Fontsainte, Grand Crès, Grand Moulin, Lastours, Mansenoble, les Palais, St-Auriol, VOULTE-GASPARETS; also numerous co-operatives, especially Camplong d'Aude, Mont Tauch, les Vignerons d'Octaviana.

White Corbières is very much the minor partner, with only about seven million bottles produced annually. Few of these are more than adequate as most producers concentrate on their gutsy reds. However, the use of modern winemaking techniques – temperature control, skin contact and aging in new oak barrels along with the wide range of grape varieties available – means that some interesting aromatic whites have evolved, usually for drinking young. Best producers: Baronne, Étang des Colombes, Grand Moulin, Lastours, Mennier St-Louis, St-Auriol, Voulte-Gasparets.

CORNAS AC
FRANCE, Northern Rhône
♂ *Syrah*
Cornas is the northern RHÔNE's up-and-coming star. Fifteen years ago the region didn't really have any star, though HERMITAGE and CÔTE-RÔTIE were both making splendid wine. But the spiralling prices of red Burgundy and BORDEAUX encouraged wine-lovers to look

elsewhere for excellence. Both Côte-Rôtie and Hermitage are now very expensive, so the spotlight turned to the very south of the northern Rhône, where the valley spreads out at Valence.

Cornas is the last roar from the great Syrah grape. The thin terraces clinging doggedly to these granite cliffs can make the most massive of all Rhône reds. The colour when young is a thick, impenetrable red, almost black in the ripest years. It is tough and chunky, pummelling your mouth with tannin and sheer force of personality. So you wait, five years at least – more like ten. The colour is still deep, but tingling with life; the smell is rich and opulent, blackcurrants and raspberries, heady and exotic; the taste is almost sweet, with the fruit bursting through its tannic chains; and there's the roar – pure, sensuous fruit, coating your mouth, tannin too, and herbs, and deep chocolaty warmth to sear the flavour into your memory. Prices have inevitably risen in recent years, but then so has the quality. Best years: 1997, '96, '95, '94, '91, '90, '89, '88, '85, '83, '78. Best producers: Allemand, de Barjac, CLAPE, COLOMBO, Delas, Dumien-Serrette, JABOULET, Marcel Juge, Lionnet, Robert Michel, VERSET, Voge.

1994
LES RUCHETS
CORNAS

JEAN-LUC COLOMBO
Les Ruchets is Jean-Luc Colombo's top wine. Made in a modern, balanced style, it has obvious new oak but is still hugely fruity, deep and rich with ripe tannin.

VIN DE CORSE AC
FRANCE, Corsica
🍷🍾 Nielluccio, Sciacarello, Cinsaut, Carignan, Grenache and others
🍾 Vermentino, Ugni Blanc and others

Corsica has been slower than mainland southern France to catch on to new wine technology. The problems lie in the dogged traditionalism of most of the owners of the best-sited vineyards, and the carpet-bagging mentality of many of the grape-growers from French North Africa who re-settled on the island's flat eastern plains during the 1960s. AC wines represent only 15 per cent of production, while the bulk is still labelled as vin de table.

However, on this heavenly island which effortlessly lives up to its title Île de Beauté

(the name of its VIN DE PAYS too), there are many fine hillside vineyards, producing good fruit – primarily the local red Nielluccio and Sciacarello varieties. White Vermentino has possibilities too. What is lacking is good winemaking. Most reds are volatile and oxidized, most rosés and whites flabby and dull.

Things are slowly improving – largely due to the quality leadership of Comte Peraldi in AJACCIO and the increased activities of Skalli/FORTANT DE FRANCE and the UVAL co-operatives. The five superior sub-regions – Calvi, Cap Corse, Figari, Porto Vecchio, Sartène – are allowed to add their name to Vin de Corse, while Ajaccio and PATRIMONIO have their own ACs. Most of the white Corsica ACs employ Ugni Blanc and Vermentino (the best wines are 100 per cent Vermentino). Interesting results are extremely rare, but Coteaux du Cap Corse and Calvi, both in the north, can produce fair stuff. And if you're there, try the sweet Muscats – especially from Cap Corse and Patrimonio – they're deep, rich, grapy wines, and at long last have been awarded an AC. Best producers: Couvent d'Alzipratu, Clos Culombu, Clos Landry, Clos Nicrosi, Clos Reginu, Piretti, Sica UVAL, Skalli, Torraccia.

CORTON AC
FRANCE, Burgundy, Côte de Beaune, Grand Cru
🍷 Pinot Noir
🍾 Chardonnay, Pinot Blanc, Pinot Gris

The vineyards occupying the sections of the Corton hill mostly facing south and east on red, iron-rich soil are the only red Grand Cru in the CÔTE DE BEAUNE. In a typically quirky example of Burgundy's appellation intricacies, there is an AC for white Grand Cru Corton too, but whereas red Corton is the greatest red wine from this hillside, white Corton is not – the CORTON-CHARLEMAGNE Grand Cru has that distinction. Corton now has 21 sub-divisions spanning the villages of Ladoix-Serrigny to the east, ALOXE-CORTON to the south (the most important section) and PERNAND-VERGELESSES to the west; all can label their red wine Corton. Ideally, the wine has the burliness and savoury power of the top Côte de Nuits wines, combined with the more seductive perfumed fruit of the Côte de Beaune. Red Corton should take ten years to mature but many modern examples never make it. Best years: 1997, '96, '95, '93, '91, '90, '89, '88, '85. Best producers: Ambroise, BONNEAU DU MARTRAY, CHANDON DE BRIAILLES, CHEVALIER, Dubreuil-Fontaine, FAIVELEY, JADOT, LATOUR, Thomas-Moillard, Rapet, Senard, TOLLOT-BEAUT, Voarick.

Very little white Corton is produced – some comes from Aloxe-Corton but more from Ladoix-Serrigny, at the north-east end of the hill. The best example is from the Vergennes vineyard. The Domaine CHANDON DE BRIAILLES also makes white Corton in its Bressandes vineyard (a tip-top red site) from half-and-half Chardonnay and Pinot Blanc.

CORTON-CHARLEMAGNE AC
FRANCE, Burgundy, Côte de Beaune, Grand Cru
🍾 Chardonnay

Corton-Charlemagne, a wide strip of vineyard at the top of the hill of CORTON, part south-facing in the commune of ALOXE-CORTON, but veering round to the west in PERNAND-VERGELESSES, is the largest of the Burgundy white Grands Crus with an annual production of about 150,000 bottles. The name really does stem from the Emperor Charlemagne whose favourite vineyard this was – though in those days the wine was red, which left an awful mess on his flowing white beard. After a fair bit of nagging from his wife, he ripped up the red vines and planted white instead – the inferior Aligoté, though, not the delicious Chardonnay.

Nowadays, the vineyard is all Chardonnay and can produce the most impressive of all white Burgundies – rich, buttery, nutty, a blast of splendid golden flavours, not as perfumed as MONTRACHET – more a kind of super-MEURSAULT. Yet it is more than that, because if it does only show its true minerally splendour after ten years or so, that slow revelation of unsuspected depths and nuances is the mark of a great wine. Best years: 1997, '96, '95, '93, '92, '90, '89, '88, '87, '86, '85, '83. Best producers: BONNEAU DU MARTRAY, COCHE-DURY, Dubreuil-Fontaine, FAIVELEY, JADOT, Laleure-Piot, LATOUR, Rapet, TOLLOT-BEAUT.

CH. COS D'ESTOURNEL
FRANCE, Bordeaux, Haut-Médoc, St-Estèphe AC, 2ème Cru Classé
🍷 Cabernet Sauvignon, Merlot

Cos d'Estournel bears more than a passing resemblance to a Chinese temple complete with pagodas and bells. Indeed Monsieur d'Estournel was a horse dealer in the early nineteenth century who traded extensively with the Far East, and discovered his wine improved enormously if he took it on the journey with him. So he went 'oriental' in a grand manner as a way of promoting his wine. Cos d'Estournel is now one of BORDEAUX's leading châteaux and the top name in ST-ESTÈPHE. In 1998 it was sold by the Prats family to the

Taillan group, owners of Ch. CHASSE-SPLEEN and GRUAUD-LAROSE. Although St-Estèphe wines are generally less perfumed than those of neighbouring PAUILLAC, because of the heavier clay soil, Cos d'Estournel makes up for this by using just under 40 per cent Merlot and through extensive use of new oak barrels. The former second wine, Ch. de Marbuzet, is now a cru in its own right. Second wine (since 1994): les Pagodes de Cos. Best years: 1997, '96, '95, '94, '93, '92, '90, '89, '88, '86, '85, '83, '82, '81, '79, '78.

COSTERS DEL SEGRE DO

SPAIN, Cataluña

♥ Grenache Noir (Garnacha Tinta), Tempranillo, Cabernet Sauvignon, Merlot, Pinot Noir, Syrah

♀ Macabeo, Parellada, Xarel-lo, Chardonnay

The winemakers of the 'banks of the Segre', at the western limits of CATALUÑA, can thank the powerful CAVA firm of CODORNÍU for their elevation to DO status in 1988. Few of the region's wines used to be worth a second sip, except, that is, for the excellent wines of the RAIMAT estate, subsidiary of Codorníu. So the grapes permitted in the DO have been influenced by the international varieties cultivated in Raimat's immaculate irrigated vineyards. Now such smaller bodegas as Castell del Remei and L'Olivera have reached Raimat's quality level. Costers del Segre consists of four smallish separate zones, mostly in the dry, slightly undulating province of Lleida. This was traditionally white wine country and, in general, any vineyard land that has not sunk into decline still produces dull whites and the odd tough red, thankfully, rarely seen outside the area. Best years: (reds) 1996, '95, '93, '92, '91.

COSTERS DEL SIURANA

SPAIN, Cataluña, Priorat DO

♥ Grenache Noir (Garnacha Tinta), Cabernet Sauvignon, Carignan (Cariñena), Tempranillo, Merlot, Syrah

♀ Grenache Blanc (Garnacha Blanca)

Carles Pastrana, now the idiosyncratic mayor of the village of Gratallops at the heart of PRIORAT, was one of the pioneers who relaunched the region by adding some French varieties to the old Garnacha and Cariñena vines and bringing in modern winemaking practices. His estate has grown to 33ha (82 acres) and is one of the largest of the newer ones. He is the only grower with Tempranillo vines: the RIOJA grape is as much a foreigner in the region as Cabernet Sauvignon. This goes into his second wine, Miserere. There is also a basic Usatges red and a barrel-fermented Usat-

ges white. The *grand vin*, Clos de l'Obac, is perhaps the best known of the new-wave Priorat wines in international markets and has progressively developed a somewhat lighter, high-toned personality in relation to other Priorats. Best years: 1995, '94, '90.

COSTIÈRES DE NÎMES AC

FRANCE, Languedoc-Roussillon

♥ ♀ Carignan, Grenache, Syrah and others

♀ Clairette, Bourboulenc, Grenache Blanc and others

This large AC of around 3600ha (8896 acres) lies between Nîmes and the Rhône delta in the GARD *département*. Carignan is still the major red variety, but an increasing number of small domaines are using Syrah and Grenache instead to make soft, spicy, early-drinking reds. The rosés can be fresh and fruity when young.

There are 25 million bottles produced annually; only one million are white, although the trend is increasing and at best, from careful, cool fermentation, they are light, appley wines. Grenache Blanc, which can add an attractive aniseed freshness, is being widely planted, and, increasingly, also Marsanne, Roussanne, Macabeo and Rolle, which are also permitted in the AC, so personality will increase. Best years: 1998, '97, '96, '95, '94, '93, '90. Best producers: L'Amarine, Paul Blanc, Mourgues du Grès, de Nages, Roubaud, de la Tuilerie.

CÔTE DE BEAUNE AC, CÔTE DE BEAUNE-VILLAGES AC

FRANCE, Burgundy, Côte de Beaune

♥ Pinot Noir

The Côte de Beaune AC covers a couple of late-ripening vineyards around the town of Beaune and is very rare. The wine is usually very dry to start, but has a good lean fruit which can be delicious at two to three years old. Best producers: BOUCHARD PÈRE & FILS, DROUHIN, Jolliette, Labouré-Roi.

Côte de Beaune-Villages is the general appellation covering wine from 16 villages in the Côte de Beaune. These villages have the right to use their own names, but, since some of them are not well known, merchants may prefer to blend several wines together to sell under the Côte de Beaune-Villages label. This used to be one of the commonest Burgundy appellations in the export market, but, nowadays, even villages like PERNAND-VERGELESSES and AUXEY-DURESSES sell wine under their own name and what's left over for Côte de Beaune-Villages often tastes as though they really had to scrape the bottom of the barrel. Best years: (reds) 1997, '96, '95, '93, '90.

CÔTE DE BROUILLY AC

FRANCE, Burgundy, Beaujolais, Beaujolais cru

♥ Gamay

We don't see much of this BEAUJOLAIS cru – perhaps because we see a great deal of BROUILLY. Well, that's a pity; the Côte de Brouilly is a volcanic mound rising to 500m (1650ft) in the middle of the Brouilly AC at the southern end of the Beaujolais crus and, on its steep slopes, the sun ripens the grapes more fully than on the flatter vineyards.

This extra ripeness is reflected by the fact that the minimum alcohol requirement for Côte de Brouilly is higher than for any other Beaujolais cru. And that extra sun produces a full, juicy, strawberry-and-peach ripeness – a sort of 'super-Brouilly' which is good young, but can age well for several years. Best years: 1997, '96, '95, '94, '93, '91, '89, '88. Best producers: Conroy, DUBOEUF, Large, Ravier, Thivin, Verger.

CÔTE DE NUITS-VILLAGES AC

FRANCE, Burgundy, Côte de Nuits

♥ Pinot Noir

♀ Chardonnay, Pinot Blanc

Unlike CÔTE DE BEAUNE, Côte de Nuits as such is not an AC. It is simply a geographical description of the northern part of Burgundy's great CÔTE D'OR. Côte de Nuits-Villages, however, is an appellation specific to the villages of Corgoloin, Comblanchien and Prissey in the south of the Côte de Nuits, and Brochon and FIXIN in the north. Fixin wines may also be sold under their own name. The 300ha (750 acres) of vines in the appellation are overwhelmingly red. The wines are often good, not very deep, but with a good cherry fruit, and an attractive resin-bitter edge which can go smooth and chocolaty with age. Best years: 1997, '96, '95, '93, '90, '89, '88, '85, '83, '80, '78. Best producers: (reds) ARLOT, Durand, Jayer-Gilles, Daniel Rion, Rossignol. There is only a tiny amount of white produced, and, as so often in the Côte de Nuits, the rather lean, fruitless, minerally style makes you realize why the vineyards are overwhelmingly red.

DANIEL RION ET FILS
This domaine, based in Prémeaux-Prissey, makes a wide range of excellent wines, including Côte de Nuits-Villages with impressive cherry fruit.

CÔTE D'OR France, Burgundy

THE CÔTE D'OR is Europe's northernmost great red wine area as well as one of its greatest white wine producers. The name, meaning 'Golden Slope', refers to one single stretch of vines in Burgundy, starting just south of Dijon, and fading out 48km (30 miles) later west of Chagny. It is divided into two sections. The Côte de Nuits in the north encompasses little more than 1400ha (3460 acres) of vines, since the slope is often only a few hundred yards wide. It is almost entirely devoted to red wine.

The Côte de Beaune is the southern section, beginning in the north at the famous hill of Corton. Beaune is the main town, and as the Côte progresses southwards past Volnay, white takes over from red as the most exciting wine style, until red briefly reasserts itself at Santenay where the long north-south slope of the Côte de Beaune comes to an end. The less abrupt slopes of the Côte de Beaune possess 3000ha (7410 acres) of vines.

The soil in the Côte d'Or is a mix of clay, marl and limestone. Where the marl is dominant, red wines are produced from Pinot Noir; where the limestone takes over white wines from Chardonnay are best. In the Côte de Nuits where the marl is more prevalent, the slopes are steepest, so the rich-

ness of the soil is offset by particularly efficient drainage. Further south in the Côte de Beaune the slopes are more gently inclined and more south-facing, but easy-draining limestone is much in evidence.

Over the centuries grapes growing on the best sites have consistently ripened earlier than those too high up the slope or on flatter ground at the bottom. So a minutely accurate system of vineyard classification has evolved. Top of the hierarchy are the Grands Crus or Great Growths, which are allowed to use only the vineyard name on the label without the village name. These are almost always situated at between 250 and 300m (800 and 1000ft) in elevation, and facing between south and east. With the exception of Corton in the Côte de Beaune all the red Grands Crus are situated in the Côte de Nuits. Slightly less well-situated vineyards are accorded Premier Cru or First Growth status. Their wines should still be excellent. Wines produced from vineyards with no special reputation on the bottom of the slope will usually carry just the village name.

The medieval belltower at Chambolle-Musigny, one of the most unspoilt villages in the Côte d'Or, can be clearly seen rising above the vines. More producers are now bottling their own wines here with an increase in quality generally.

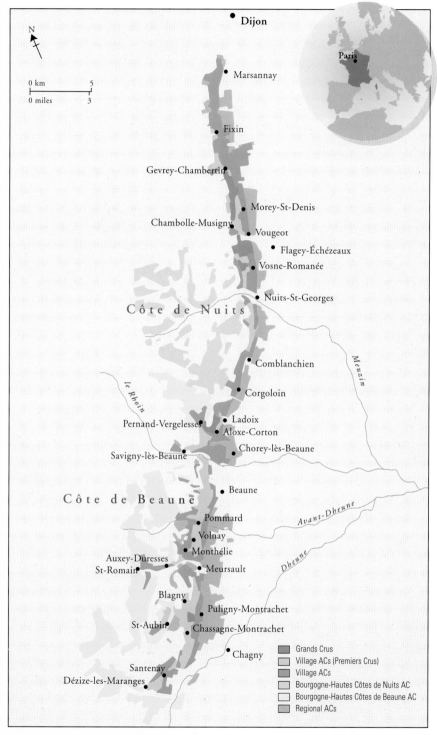

DOMAINE DENIS MORTET
Denis Mortet is one of the rising stars in Gevrey-Chambertin, making impressive wines.

DOMAINE MÉO-CAMUZET
New oak barrels and luscious, rich fruit are the hallmarks of this quality estate based in Vosne-Romanée.

DOMAINE DE LA ROMANÉE-CONTI
La Tâche is one of the greatest red Burgundies and is wholly owned by this world-famous estate.

DOMAINE ROBERT CHEVILLON
Old vines and meticulous winemaking go hand in hand at this distinguished domaine.

BONNEAU DU MARTRAY
The Corton-Charlemagne from this historic estate is a stylish, powerful white Burgundy needing more than a decade of aging.

DOMAINE DES COMTES LAFON
Dominique Lafon is the leading producer in Meursault and one of Burgundy's best winemakers.

DOMAINE LEFLAIVE
The most famous white Burgundy estate of all has extensive holdings in some of the world's greatest vineyards.

DOMAINE ARMAND ROUSSEAU
Clos de la Roche is the best and biggest of the five Grands Crus in Morey-St-Denis.

REGIONAL ENTRIES
Aloxe-Corton, Auxey-Duresses, Bâtard-Montrachet, Beaune, Blagny, Bonnes-Mares, Bourgogne-Hautes Côtes de Beaune, Bourgogne-Hautes Côtes de Nuits, Chambertin, Chambolle-Musigny, Chassagne-Montrachet, Chorey-lès-Beaune, Clos de la Roche , Clos de Vougeot, Corton, Corton-Charlemagne, Côte de Beaune, Côte de Nuits-Villages, Échézeaux, Fixin, Gevrey-Chambertin, Ladoix, Maranges, Marsannay, Meursault, Monthélie, le Montrachet, Morey-St-Denis, Musigny, Nuits-St-Georges, Pernand-Vergelesses, Pommard, Puligny-Montrachet, Richebourg, la Romanée, St-Aubin, St-Romain, Santenay, Savigny-lès-Beaune, la Tâche, Volnay, Vosne-Romanée, Vougeot.

PRODUCER ENTRIES
l'Arlot, Armand, Bonneau de Martray, Bouchard Père et Fils, Burguet, Carillon et Fils, Chandon de Briailles, Chevillon, Clair, Coche-Dury, Drouhin, Dujac, Engel, Faiveley, Gagnard, Gouges, Grivot, Hospices de Beaune, Jadot, Lafon, Louis Latour, Laurent, Leflaive, Olivier Leflaive, Leroy, Méo-Camuzet, de Montille, Mortet, Mugnier, Pousse d'Or, Ramonet, de la Romanée-Conti, Roumier, Rousseau, Tollot-Beaut & Fils, de Voguë.

CÔTE-RÔTIE AC

FRANCE, Northern Rhône

🍷 *Syrah, Viognier*

Côte-Rôtie – the 'roasted slope' – is the most northern vineyard area in the RHÔNE Valley, and definitely one of the oldest – there have been vines planted on these slopes for 24 centuries. Yet it is only very recently that wine drinkers have become aware that this is one of France's greatest wines. The red grape of the Rhône, Syrah, bakes itself to super-ripeness on these steep, south-east-facing slopes.

What marks Côte-Rôtie out from the heftier Rhône reds like HERMITAGE is its exotic fragrance, quite unexpected in a red wine. This is because a little of the heavenly scented white Viognier grape is allowed in the vineyard (up to 20 per cent, though five to ten per cent is more likely). The result is damson-juicy, raspberry-sweet, sometimes with a hint of apricot skins and pepper. Lovely young, it is better aged for ten years. The two best slopes are called Côte Brune and Côte Blonde; they are usually blended together but some growers vinify and label them separately. There are also prestigious single vineyards such as La Landonne. Best years: 1998, '97, '96, '95, '94, '91, '90, '89, '88, '85, '83, '78. Best producers: Barge, BURGAUD, Champet, CHAPOUTIER, Clusel-Roch, CUILLERON, DELAS, Gaillard, Gerin, GUIGAL, Jaboulet, JAMET, Jasmin, ROSTAING, VERNAY, Vidal-Fleury.

COTEAUX D'AIX-EN-PROVENCE AC

FRANCE, Provence

🍷🍷 *Grenache, Cabernet Sauvignon, Syrah and others*

🍷 *Ugni Blanc, Grenache Blanc, Sémillon, Sauvignon Blanc*

The Coteaux d'Aix-en-Provence region, covering a large area around Aix-en-Provence in the Bouches-du-Rhône *département*, was awarded its long-overdue AC in 1985. Prejudice against Cabernet Sauvignon was the cause of the delay; 95 per cent of the AC's production of 20 million bottles is red or rosé and it was the first southern French area to acknowledge that Cabernet can enhance the local varieties of Grenache, Cinsaut, Mourvèdre and Carignan.

Some quite good fresh rosé is made, but the best wines are red, and they are allowed a maximum of 60 per cent Cabernet Sauvignon in the blend. The wines are good but should do better, because some enterprising estates from neighbouring CÔTES DE PROVENCE and, in particular, from Les BAUX-DE-PROVENCE, achieve richer, more succulent fruit flavours. The wines can age, but they're better young.

Traditional whites, based on Ugni Blanc, are pretty flabby mouthfuls. But cool fermentation in stainless steel tanks, early bottling and an increased use of Grenache Blanc, Sémillon and Sauvignon Blanc are now producing some pleasant, but hardly riveting, dry whites – to knock back sharpish. Best years: (reds) 1998, '97, '96, '95, '94, '93, '90. Best producers: (reds) Bas, Béates, de Beaupré, Calissanne, Fonscolombe, Salen, du Seuil, Vignelaure; (whites) Bas, de Beaupré, Calissanne, Fonscolombe, du Seuil.

COTEAUX CHAMPENOIS AC

FRANCE, Champagne

🍷 *Pinot Noir, Pinot Meunier*

🍷 *Chardonnay*

This AC covers still wines from the whole CHAMPAGNE area. White Coteaux Champenois is pale gold, but shockingly dry, with that chalky austerity like the lick of a cat's tongue on your cheek. Made from red grapes, Coteaux Champenois can either be red or rosé, but usually pretends to be red. The trouble is, even when fully ripe, these Champagne grapes don't have a lot of colour or sugar, so with few exceptions (usually from the villages of BOUZY or Ay) the wine is pale and rather harsh, though it often has a fresh strawberry or cherry scent. No wonder they turn 99 per cent of the region's wine into fizz. The wines tend to be over-priced. Best years: 1998, '97, '95, '90, '89, '88, '86, '85, '83, '82. Best producers: Bara, BOLLINGER, LAURENT-PERRIER, S Mathieu, Joseph Perrier, Ch. de Saran (MOËT ET CHANDON), G Vesselle.

COTEAUX DU LANGUEDOC AC

FRANCE, Languedoc-Roussillon

🍷🍷 *Carignan, Cinsaut, Grenache, Syrah, Mourvèdre*

🍷 *Grenache Blanc, Bourboulenc, Clairette and others*

This increasingly successful, large AC runs approximately from Montpellier to Narbonne, with 121 villages producing over 50 million bottles of red and rosé. Although the wines used to have, at best, a rather solid, sturdy kind of fruit, things are now on the move, and this is one of the areas in the South of France which has become the French Australia of the 1990s, with a flood of fresh, fruity, well-made wines. Prices remain in the affordable bracket, except for certain highly priced special cuvées. In an 'incentive and reward' approach to improving quality, 11 leading villages can add their own names to the AC name. Best of these are La Clape, Montpeyroux and Pic St-Loup. Some of these villages now use oak barrels to mature the best reds,

MAS JULLIEN
Working with traditional Midi varieties, Olivier Jullien makes exciting wines and is always experimenting with new blends. Les Depierre is a dense red wine with a striking fruit character.

and these can age for several years. In general, drink the wines young, but there is sufficient fruit in a growing number of the reds to take aging. A relatively small production of white also exists. Grenache Blanc, Bourboulenc and Clairette are the principal varieties, with the better estates increasing plantings of Roussanne and Marsanne. Generally these are for drinking within two to three years. Best years: (reds) 1998, '96, '95, '94, '93, '91. Best producers: Abbaye de Valmagne, de l'Aiguelière, d'Aupilhac, Bruguière, Calage, Cazeneuve, Clavel, la Coste, HORTUS, des Jougla, Lascaux, Mas des Chimères, MAS JULLIEN, Pech Céleyran, Pech Redon, Peyre Rose, PRIEURÉ ST-JEAN DE BÉBIAN, Roquette-sur-Mer.

COTEAUX DU LAYON AC, COTEAUX DU LAYON-VILLAGES AC

FRANCE, Loire, Anjou-Saumur

🍷 *Chenin Blanc*

It's a mixed blessing being a winemaker in one of those rare locations where the noble rot fungus, *Botrytis cinerea*, strikes. If the rot claims all your vines and you carefully pick only the most syrupy, mushy grapes, then you have the chance of making great, intensely sweet, luscious white wines. The Layon Valley does get noble rot most years – and the Chenin grape reacts well to it. But it is incredibly risky to wait into the late autumn for the fungus to develop. If you get SAUTERNES' prices, maybe it's worth it, but, except for its two Grands Crus – QUARTS DE CHAUME and BONNEZEAUX – no-one does here.

Over the past ten years, there has been a quality revolution in the Coteaux du Layon and neighbouring Coteaux de l'Aubance as an increasing number of producers have striven to make even better wine. The secret lies in low yields and selective picking. A few producers such as Patrick Baudouin and Jo Pithon have pushed ripeness to extremes. In 1997 Pithon made a tiny amount of Cuvée Ambroisie from individually picked grapes and there was an astonishing 32° of potential alcohol. All the best producers now make a series of cuvées in ascending sweetness and levels of botrytis.

Seven villages can use the Coteaux du Layon-Villages AC and put their own name on their labels. To qualify the wines must have at least one degree more alcohol than straight Coteaux du Layon. These wines are definitely underpriced for the quality and the village of Chaume is one of the best. Best years: 1998, '97, '96, '95, '94, '93, '90, '89, '88, '85, '83, '76, '75. Best producers: Baudouin, Bidet, de Breuil, Clos de Ste-Cathérine, Delesvaux, Fresne, Guimonière, Jolivet, la Motte, Ogereau, Ch. de Pierre-Bise, Pithon, Joseph Renou, Robineau, la Roulerie, Sauveroy, Sorin, Soucherie, Yves Soulez, Touche Noire.

COTEAUX DU LYONNAIS AC
FRANCE, Burgundy
♦ ♦ *Gamay*
♀ *Chardonnay, Aligoté, Melon de Bourgogne*

These are good, light BEAUJOLAIS-style reds with a few whites and rosés. The area became an AC in 1984 and produces only a million or so bottles annually. The red is generally light, quite fruity and very pleasant drunk young and chilled. In what is a rather sad comment on the quality of much present Beaujolais, the simple charm of a Coteaux du Lyonnais wine is often preferable to the insipid hollowness of much supposedly superior Beaujolais. There's a little white wine, mostly fresh and snappy and to be drunk at six months old. Best producers: Régis Descotes, DUBOEUF, Fayolle.

COTEAUX DU TRICASTIN AC
FRANCE, Northern Rhône
♦ ♦ *Grenache, Syrah, Cinsaut and others*
♀ *Marsanne, Bourboulenc*

This large and fast-growing vineyard area was only created in the 1960s to cater for a flood of displaced grape-growers fleeing from North Africa after Morocco, Tunisia and Algeria gained independence from France. The available area for the AC is pretty spread out in the southern part of the Drôme – between Montélimar, the nougat capital of France, and Bollène. The zone became VDQS in 1964 and AC in 1974.

Right from the start the wines have been good because the new settlers introduced modern methods – formulated to cope with the desert conditions in Africa – on to good virgin vineyard land. Reds and rosés are often quite light, but very fresh, having an attractive juicy fruit livened up with some peppery spice – and rarely marred by excess of tannin or acid. Only a tiny amount of white is made, but it's worth trying for a fairly good, nutty, but fresh drink,

ideally to consume within the year. Best years: 1998, '97, '96, '95. Best producers: de Grangeneuve, Lônes, Tour d'Elyssas.

COTEAUX VAROIS AC
FRANCE, Provence
♦ ♦ *Grenache, Cinsaut, Mourvèdre, Syrah, Cabernet Sauvignon and others*
♀ *Grenache Blanc, Ugni Blanc, Clairette and others*

A large area of some 1600ha (3954 acres) to the north of Toulon, and nudging CÔTES DE PROVENCE to the east, Coteaux Varois in the Var *département* was promoted to AC in 1993. This was largely because a lot of growers were making great efforts, especially with new plantings of classic grapes such as Cabernet Sauvignon and Syrah, to upgrade quality. Good for them. Otherwise the grapes are much the same as for CÔTES DE PROVENCE: Grenache, Cinsaut and Mourvèdre. A splash of Malvoisie helps make the whites more interesting. Best years: (reds) 1998, '97, '96, '95, '94. Best producers: Deffends, Routas, St-Estève, St-Jean-de-Villecroze.

CÔTES DE BLAYE AC
FRANCE, Bordeaux
♀ *Sémillon, Sauvignon Blanc, Colombard*

This AC covers dry or sweet whites from vineyards on the right bank of the Gironde. Almost all of the best whites are now dry. A few sweetish wines remain, none very good, and these may be seen under the Premières Côtes de Blaye label. The most interesting wines include a fair percentage of the Colombard grape, which has far more character here than Sauvignon and Sémillon, and which reacts well to modern winemaking. Drink the wines young. Best producers: Marcillac co-operative, Marinier.

CÔTES DE BOURG AC
FRANCE, Bordeaux
♦ *Merlot, Cabernet Franc, Cabernet Sauvignon, Malbec*
♀ *Sémillon, Sauvignon Blanc, Muscadelle and others*

Ch. MARGAUX, Ch. PALMER, and all the other luminaries of the MÉDOC big-time are just a tantalizing mile or two away on the other side of the Gironde, yet Bourg shares none of their glory. These seemingly perfectly placed vineyard slopes are one of BORDEAUX's forgotten areas, struggling to regain the place in the sun they used to enjoy. After all, the Romans planted vineyards in Bourg when the Médoc was merely a swamp.

Côtes de Bourg is very much a red wine district, an enclave inside the larger Blaye area; its sloping vineyards are mostly clay, but there is

enough gravel to suit the Cabernet Sauvignon, and the good local co-operative at Tauriac and leading properties are now using new oak as they strive to upgrade their wine. They deserve to succeed as affordable good Bordeaux is difficult to find. The red wines are quite full, fairly dry, but with an attractive blackcurrant fruit which ensures the earthy quality doesn't dominate; when they are splashed with the spice of new oak, they can age to a pleasant maturity at six to ten years old. Best years: (reds) 1998, '97, '96, '95, '94, '90, '89, '88, '85, '83, '82. Best producers: de Barbe, Bousquet, Brulescaille, Bujan, Falfas, Guerry, Haut-Guiraud, Haut-Macô, Mercier, Nodoz, Roc de Cambes, Rousset, Tauriac co-operative, Tayac.

Only a tiny amount of Côtes de Bourg production is white. Mostly made from Sémillon with a little Sauvignon Blanc, the wines are bone dry, rather lifeless and flat.

ROC DE CAMBES
This ripe, concentrated wine, aged in 50 per cent new oak barrels, lifts the Côte de Bourg appellation on to an altogether higher plane.

CÔTES DE CASTILLON AC
FRANCE, Bordeaux
♦ *Cabernet Sauvignon, Cabernet Franc, Merlot, Malbec*

East of ST-ÉMILION on the river Dordogne is the little town of Castillon-la-Bataille, where defeat at a crucial battle in 1453 lost the English control of Aquitaine – and their supply of BORDEAUX wine. We didn't hear much about Castillon after that until the 1980s, when the prices of decent red Bordeaux became so loony that we began searching for a few understudies able to produce decent flavours at a fair price. Côtes de Castillon manages to be more special than simple Bordeaux Rouge because the vineyards impart flavours of mint, blackcurrant and cedar to the wine – in miniature maybe, but these are the flavours which made the MÉDOC famous. They use a high proportion of Merlot and some estates now use new oak barrels to age the wine, which is pretty tasty at three to ten years old. Best years: 1998, '97, '96, '95, '94, '90, '89, '88, '86, '85, '83, '82. Best producers: l'Aiguilhe, de Belcier, Cap de Faugères, la Clarière Laithwaite, Côte-Monpezat, Lapeyronie, de Pitray, Poupille, Robin, Vieux-Château-Champs de Mars.

CÔTES DE DURAS AC

FRANCE, South-West

🍷 *Cabernet Franc, Cabernet Sauvignon, Merlot, Malbec*

🍷 *Sauvignon Blanc, Sémillon, Muscadelle*

Côtes de Duras, in the Lot-et-Garonne *département*, has spawned a very active co-operative movement, which offers good, fresh, grassy reds and whites from traditional BORDEAUX grapes, at distinctly lower prices. The skills of roving winemaker, Hugh Ryman are producing exciting results here, particularly in whites. There is some sweet white but it is the dry wine, often labelled Sauvignon Blanc, which is now far more important – it has a strong, grassy green fruit, but a surprisingly soft, gentle texture. Drink the wines young. There are signs of the use of oak barrels down here, too. Best years: (reds) 1998, '97, '96, '95, '90. Best producers: (reds) Conti, Cours, Ferrant, Laulan, Duras and Landerrouat co-operatives; (whites) Duras and Landerrouat co-operatives.

CÔTES DU FRONTONNAIS AC

FRANCE, South-West

🍷 *Négrette, Cabernet Sauvignon, Cabernet Franc and others*

This is one of the most original red wine flavours in south-west France. The vineyard area isn't very big, clustered round Toulouse on dry, sun-soaked slopes. Négrette is the chief grape and the wine can be superb, positively silky in texture – very rare in a red wine – and combining a juicy fruit like raspberry or strawberry, coated in cream, with a lick of aniseed. They drink almost all of it in Toulouse but a little is exported and is well worth seeking out. It can age, but it's best drunk in its full flush of youth. There's a little rosé – good but not so good. Best years: 1998, '97, '96, '95, '94. Best producers: de Baudare, Bellevue-la-Forêt, la Colombière, Ferran, Flotis, Laurou, Montauriol, la Palme, le Roc, St-Louis.

VIN DE PAYS DES CÔTES DE GASCOGNE

FRANCE, South-West

🍷 *Colombard, Ugni Blanc, Listan (Palomino) and others*

🍷 *Tannat, Cabernet Sauvignon and others*

Vin de Pays des Côtes de Gascogne is the zonal used principally for VIN DE PAYS, dry white wines produced in the north of the Gers *département*. This is Armagnac country and following the decline in demand for the brandy in the 1980s a large number of producers converted their vineyards to the production of Côtes de Gascogne, a saving grace for the

region. Temperature-controlled vinification has provided the wherewithal to produce crisp, tangy, fruity wines from local grape varieties. The PLAIMONT co-operative, which accounts for over 1200ha (2965 acres) of vines, has been a particularly innovative and motivating force in recent years. Best producers: des Cassegnoles, Yves GRASSA (du Tariquet), de Joy, Producteurs Plaimont, Hugh Ryman.

CÔTES DU JURA AC

FRANCE, Jura

🍷 *Poulsard, Trousseau, Pinot Noir*

🍷 *Chardonnay, Savagnin, Pinot Blanc*

The regional AC for JURA covers a wide variety of wines, including sparkling and still dry whites, reds, rosés, *vins jaunes* and *vins de paille*. Most of the vineyards lie in the south of the region between Poligny and Lons-le-Saunier, where they spread up the mountain sides or nuzzle into thickly forested slopes. The area is wonderfully relaxing, often hemmed in by trees, always shadowed by the Jura mountain range, and sometimes affording spectacular vistas across the Saône Valley to Burgundy. But sadly the flavours of the wines, especially the whites, aren't of the delicate sylvan sort at all. The reason for this is the white Savagnin grape – a strange, sour creature – which admittedly does come into its own with the dark yellow, sherry-like *vin jaune*.

However, there is respite in the friendly form of Chardonnay and, more rarely, the Pinot Blanc, which both perform well here. Some unblended Chardonnay is now coming on to the market. It can still be infected with the strange, resiny Savagnin character, particularly when not vinified in a separate cellar; but at its best, especially from the vineyards between Poligny and Arbois, it is a particularly thirst-quenching, mountain-fresh Chardonnay. Drink at one to two years old, although the Chardonnay can age.

It would be nice to report that such a mountain paradise had nectar-like red wines too, but both reds and rosés are rarely special

– and often aggressively weird. The southern part of the region can produce some lighter reds and rosés from the Trousseau and Poulsard grapes which are not too savage, while the Pinot Noir can yield rather good, light, perfumed reds. Poulsard also produces a very pale pink, *vin gris*. Only 20 per cent of Côtes du Jura AC is red or rosé. Best producers: (reds) d'Arlay, Bourdy, Gréa, Morel-Thibault, Pirou; (whites) d'Arlay, Bourdy, Chalanard, Gréa, Morel-Thibault, Pupillin co-operative.

CÔTES DU LUBÉRON AC

FRANCE, Southern Rhône

🍷 *Grenache, Syrah, Cinsaut and others*

🍷 *Ugni Blanc, Clairette, Bourboulenc*

This lovely lost area to the east of Avignon and north of Aix, running along the Durance Valley and sharing the land with asparagus crops, was promoted to AC in 1988. The landscape is dominated by the Montagne du Lubéron and the region's wine production is dominated by co-operatives. The vines are mostly spread along the north banks of the Durance in the Vaucluse *département* and yield light, easy wines for early drinking. They are not exactly long on complexity and perfume, but between six and nine months old they are bright, refreshing and very enjoyable. The one exception to this rule is Ch. Val Joanis – a vast new plantation wrested from the wild scrubland whose white, though still at its best within the year, can develop a full, soft peachy warmth, spiced with a hint of aniseed if you leave it for longer, and whose best rosés are deliciously fruity. Reds have been more variable but the best are delicious for drinking young. Best producers: des Blancs, Canorgue, Ch. de l'Isolette, Mille, la Tour-d'Aigues co-operative, Val Joanis.

CÔTES DU MARMANDAIS AC

FRANCE, South-West

🍷 *Abouriou, Fer, Cabernet Sauvignon, Merlot, Syrah and others*

🍷 *Sémillon, Sauvignon Blanc, Muscadelle, Ugni Blanc*

This region in the Lot-et-Garonne *département* actually adjoins the ENTRE-DEUX-MERS and Marmandais producers have always set out to make red BORDEAUX lookalikes – with a fair amount of success. However, the potential is there for a red with a local flavour, because Bordeaux varieties make up only half or less of the grape mix. Ninety-five per cent of the wine comes from two co-operatives, of which the Cocumont examples are the better.

You need to have the nose of a bloodhound to track down white Marmandais –

there is very little of it. The wine ought to be a cheaper version of Bordeaux Blanc as it's produced a little way up the Garonne from Entre-Deux-Mers. But it is hampered by including the feeble Ugni Blanc in the brew. Best years: (reds) 1998, '97, '96, '95. Best producer: Cocumont co-operative.

CÔTES DE PROVENCE AC

FRANCE, Provence
🍷 🍷 *Mourvèdre, Grenache, Syrah, Cabernet Sauvignon and others*
🍷 *Ugni Blanc, Rolle, Sémillon, Clairette*

Provence is such a hauntingly beautiful region and happily an increasing number of growers are rediscovering the magic in the soil. Rosés are becoming fruitier, and reds are emerging which, along with the powerful pine, thyme and rosemary perfumes of the rugged sun-soaked hillsides, are now displaying other scents (myrtle is one) as well as the one component previously lacking – fruit.

New plantations of Cabernet Sauvignon, Syrah and Mourvèdre are primarily responsible, as are cooler fermentations and restricted yields. This is good news because, though the wines from this large 18,000-ha (45,000-acre) vineyard area have never been cheap, Provence's romantic overtones have seduced people into buying them. There are three main vineyard areas: the coastal strip between Ste-Maxime and Toulon, providing most of the quaffing wine for the fashionable watering holes of the Riviera; the coastal vineyards between Toulon and Marseille, where most of the best sites qualify for the BANDOL or CASSIS ACs; and the vast sprawl north of the Massif des Maures, where quality is rarely considered.

Nearly 80 per cent of the enormous production is rosé, 15 per cent red, and most of the whites suffer from the usual southern French grape varieties of Ugni Blanc and Clairette, though these can be improved by Sémillon or, unofficially, by Sauvignon Blanc. Domaine Gavoty is creating waves by using the Rolle grape to make a delicious fruity wine – and a few producers are following suit. Drink the wines very young.

Best years: (reds) 1998, '97, '96, '95, '94, '93, '90. Best producers: (reds) la Bernarde, Commanderie de Peyrassol, Domaine de la COURTADE, Gavoty d'Esclans, les Maîtres Vignerons de St-Tropez, Minuty, Ott, Rabiega, Réal Martin, Richeaume, Rimauresq, St-André de Figuière, Ste-Roseline; (whites) Commanderie de Peyrassol, la Courtade, Gavoty, les Maîtres Vignerons de St-Tropez, Richeaume, Rimauresq.

CÔTES DU RHÔNE AC

FRANCE, Southern Rhône
🍷 🍷 *Grenache, Cinsaut, Syrah and others*
🍷 *Clairette, Roussanne, Marsanne and others*

Although this general AC covers the whole viticultural RHÔNE Valley, most of the wine comes from the broad southern section between Montélimar and Avignon. The chief red grape is Grenache, followed by Cinsaut, Syrah, Carignan and Mourvèdre; the last three in particular have lots of warm spicy southern personality to offer to the rich, heady flavours of Grenache. The reds used to be marked by a rather heavy, jammy fruit and a rough, herby perfume. Modern techniques – temperature control, stainless steel installations, some carbonic maceration – have revolutionized the style, and the wines should be juicy, spicy, raspberry-fruited, very easy to drink, ideally within two years of the harvest. Single-estate wines can age considerably longer. Best years: 1998, '97, '95, '94, '93, '91, '90, '89. Best producers: (reds) Aussellons, BEAUCASTEL, Cantharide, CLAPE, DUBOEUF, Fonsalette, les GOUBERT, Grand Moulas, Guigal, JABOULET, Mont-Redon, Mousset, Pascal, de Ruth, Ste-Anne, St-Estève d'Uchaux, Tardieu-Laurent.

Some of the best whites come, incongruously, from a BEAUJOLAIS producer, Georges Duboeuf, who created his 'Rhône-Mâcon Villages' flavour by fermenting early-picked grapes really cool in stainless steel tanks. The result? Fresh, appley, dry whites, lovely to quaff young, and, yes, distinctly Burgundian. Other producers' whites are generally a little flatter and nuttier. Best producers: (whites) Cabasse, Chambovet, Duboeuf, Fonsalette, l'ORATOIRE ST-MARTIN, Pelaquié, Rabasse-Charavin, Ste-Anne; and Chusclan and Laudun co-operatives.

CÔTES DU RHÔNE-VILLAGES AC

FRANCE, Southern Rhône
🍷 *Grenache, Cinsaut, Syrah, Mourvèdre, and others*
🍷 *Clairette, Roussanne, Marsanne, Bourboulenc and others*

The Côtes du Rhône-Villages AC is distinguished from the CÔTES DU RHÔNE appellation by requiring a higher minimum alcohol content (12.5 per cent as opposed to 11 per cent) and a lower yield. It only applies to 17 villages, which are often named on the label; if no village name is identified, then it's probable that the wine is a blend from two or more villages. These villages are dispersed among three *départements*, the Vaucluse, the Drôme and the GARD. Almost all the best wines are red, exhibiting a marvellously spicy

flavour, a reasonable amount of tannin, and a capacity to improve in bottle for up to ten years. Only Chusclan and Laudun have much of a reputation for white wines.

Inevitably, some villages have a better reputation than others. Cairanne has long been identified as a likely candidate for promotion to AC status, a promotion previously granted to GIGONDAS and VACQUEYRAS. Other excellent villages include Beaumes-de-Venise, RASTEAU, Sablet, Séguret, Valréas and Visan. Best years: 1998, '97, '95, '94, '93, '90, '89, '88. Best producers: l'Amandine, Armeillaud, Beaumes-de-Venise co-operative, Boisson, Brusset, Cabasse, Cave de Cairanne, Combe, Deurre, GOUBERT, Grangeneuve, l'ORATOIRE-ST-MARTIN, Pélaquié, Piaugier, Présidente, Rabasse-Charavin, Richaud, St-Antoine, Ste-Anne, Trignon, Verquière.

DOMAINE STE-ANNE
The Cuvée Notre Dame des Cellettes is a full-bodied red Côtes-du-Rhône-Villages with intense, spicy, peppery and berry fruit aromas.

CÔTES DU ROUSSILLON AC, CÔTES DU ROUSSILLON-VILLAGES AC

FRANCE, Languedoc-Roussillon
🍷 🍷 *Carignan, Cinsaut, Grenache, Syrah and others*
🍷 *Macabeo, Malvoisie, Grenache Blanc and others*

Roussillon is the frontier area where France melts imperceptibly into CATALUÑA and Spain, somewhere high among the Pyrenean peaks. The wine you drink here is Côtes du Roussillon – red, dusty as a mountain track, but juicy as fresh orchard fruit – based on the Carignan, but increasingly helped by Cinsaut, Grenache, Syrah and Mourvèdre.

Roussillon was one of the first areas of France where the co-operative movement geared itself towards quality, and although this has stamped the wines with a certain uniformity, it is a small price to pay for consistency and an immediately attractive wine style. As usual in the far South of France, the Côtes du Roussillon AC – which spreads south of Perpignan to the foothills of the Pyrenees, as well as taking in a good deal of the flatter land to the north along the Agly river valley, and the most suitable vineyard sites to the west – is primarily red wine land.

The winemakers emphasize the carbonic maceration method, which draws out the juicy flavours of red grapes and is crucial when the potentially rough Carignan makes up the majority of the blend. The finer blends have a higher percentage of Grenache and Syrah. Average annual production for both ACs is now 30 million bottles, 95 per cent of it red or rosé. The price is never high and so long as the wine is young, both red and rosé provide some of southern France's best-value drinking. Best producers: (reds) ALQUIER, Cave de Baixas, Casenove, CAZES, Celliers Trouillas de Jau, Mas Crémat, Mas Rous, Piquemal, Sarda-Malet, Vignerons Catalans.

Out of the millions of bottles of Côtes du Roussillon produced annually, only about 5 per cent are white. These come mainly from the unmemorable Macabeo grape but – in the hands of the modern co-operatives – if picked very early or almost unripe and fermented at low temperature, it makes bone-dry, lemon and aniseed-scented white wine for very early drinking, which isn't half bad at less than a year old. More adventurous producers are using Grenache Blanc, Rolle and Roussanne and both fermenting and aging in oak barrels. Best producers: (whites) CAZES, des Chênes, GAUBY, Mas Crémat, Sarda-Malet, Vignerons Catalans.

The Côtes du Roussillon-Villages AC covers the best sites around the river Agly in the northern part of the AC where the PYRÉNÉES-ORIENTALES *département* meets the Aude. The wine, especially from the villages of Caramany, Latour-de-France and Tautavel, which can add their names to the AC, is full, ripe, wonderfully juicy when young but also capable of maturing for several years. Quite a few private estates are now making their mark, with some impressive wines aged in new oak. Best years: (reds) 1998, '96, '95, '94, '93. Best producers: Cazes, des Chênes, Fontanel, Forca-Réal, Gardiès, Gauby, de Jau, Piquemal, des Schistes.

CÔTES DE ST-MONT VDQS

FRANCE, South-West

🍷 🍷 *Tannat, Cabernet Sauvignon, Cabernet Franc, Merlot*

♀ *Arrufiac, Courbu and others*

This is an increasingly good VDQS, thanks to the go-ahead PLAIMONT co-operative, producing quite sharp but intensely fruity reds and some fair rosé, from a hilly region just south of Armagnac bordering MADIRAN. Small amounts of dry white are also made. Best producer: Producteurs Plaimont.

Harvesting Grenache at Tautavel in the Côtes du Roussillon-Villages AC. Increasing use of Grenache and other superior grape varieties in many of Languedoc-Roussillon's red wine blends is bringing positive results.

CÔTES DU VENTOUX AC

FRANCE, Southern Rhône

🍷 🍷 *Grenache, Syrah, Cinsaut, Carignan, Mourvèdre*

♀ *Clairette, Bourboulenc, Grenache Blanc, Ugni Blanc*

Côtes du Ventoux, away to the east of CHÂTEAUNEUF-DU-PAPE, is one of those ACs that has still not found its own identity. These lovely vineyards, which tumble down the sides of the magnificent 1830m (6000ft) Mont Ventoux, towering above the eastern side of the RHÔNE Valley, have enjoyed their own AC since 1974. With the exception of a couple of single estates making good reds, the wines are usually thought of as a kind of innocuous Rhône substitute. The local co-operatives make 80 per cent of the 18 million bottles produced annually, which are then sold off anonymously to merchants. A good deal of rosé is also produced.

When well-made from a single estate, the reds have a lovely fresh juicy fruit – tasting of raspberry and spice – which is bright and breezy and undemanding. There are some fuller reds now made, especially from serious merchants like JABOULET, but the best still keep this lovely simple flavour – they just have a bit more of it per bottle! The white production is insignificant but, interestingly, the area was making fresh, breezy whites before Big Brother CÔTES DU RHÔNE cottoned on to the fact. Best producers: Anges, Crillon, JABOULET, Pascal, Valcombe, la Vieille Ferme.

CÔTES DU VIVARAIS VDQS

FRANCE, Southern Rhône

🍷 🍷 *Grenache, Syrah, Mourvèdre and others*

♀ *Clairette, Marsanne, Bourboulenc and others*

Spread along the west bank of the RHÔNE where the river Ardèche joins it at Pont-St-Esprit, this is predominantly a red wine zone. When the wines use the typical southern Rhône varieties – Grenache, Cinsaut, Carignan – the result is light, fresh red and rosé, for drinking young. But plantings of grapes such as Cabernet Sauvignon and Syrah are producing exciting, rich, fruity wines at irresistible prices. Hopefully, the whites can start on the same upward path and there are signs of classier ones such as Sauvignon Blanc and Chardonnay creeping in. Best years: 1998, '97, '96, '95. Best producers: Gallety, Orgnac l'Aven co-operative, Domaine de Vigier.

COTNARI

ROMANIA, Moldavia

♀ *Grasa de Cotnari, Tamîîoasa Romaneasca, Fetească Albă*

There was a time during the 'roaring '20s' when Cotnari, an intense, sweet dessert wine with an exceptional, lingering finish, was the toast of Parisian café society. The key to the wine is the combination of grapes, all of which are well suited to making rich but well-balanced sweet wines with some aging potential. Today it is rarely seen outside Romania.

QUINTA DO CÔTTO

PORTUGAL, Douro, Douro DOC, Port DOC
🍷 *Tinta Roriz (Tempranillo), Touriga Francesa, Touriga Naçional and others*
🍷 *Avesso, Malvasia Fina, Rei*

The Champalimaud family are controversial. They own a vineyard in VINHO VERDE country (Paço de Teixeiró) as well as Quinta do Côtto, an estate nearby in the westerly reaches of the DOURO. Miguel Champalimaud holds forth that his C/D grade PORT vineyards deserve to be just as highly rated as those further upstream, but it is his unfortified Douro wines that have really made him a name. There are two levels of red wine: the straightforward and much improved Quinta do Côtto and, in the best years, Quinta do Côtto Grande Escolha. The latter wine can seem rather unwieldy and oaky when young, but develops delicious flavours with a few years in bottle. Quinta do Côtto continues to make a small quantity of fine but rather quirky port which is fortified to a lower strength than wines from the mainstream shippers. Best years: (Douro wines) 1995, '94, '92, '90, '87, '85.

COULY-DUTHEIL

FRANCE, Loire, Touraine, Chinon AC
🍷 *Cabernet Franc*
🍷 *Chenin Blanc*

This family firm, run by Pierre and Jacques Couly with Pierre's son, Bertrand, in charge of winemaking, is the leading grower and *négociant* in CHINON. Couly-Dutheil's top two properties are the Clos de l'Écho, the most famous vineyard in the region and once owned by the author Rabelais' family, and the Clos de l'Olive. There are a number of other cuvées, including les Gravières, the lightest of their Chinons, and Baronnie Madeleine, which is mainly a blend of the best parcels of bought wine. Les Chanteaux is an attractively floral white Chinon. Couly-Dutheil's wines are always reliable and the top cuvées are among the best from the appellation. They age extremely well: the 1964 Clos de l'Écho remains a revelation! Best years: 1998, '97, '96, '95, '93, '90, '89, '85, '82, '79, '78, '64.

DOMAINE DE LA COURTADE

FRANCE, Provence, Côtes de Provence AC
🍷🍷 *Mourvèdre, Syrah, Grenache*
🍷 *Rolle*

Established in the 1980s on the Mediterranean island of Porquerolles, across from Hyères, la Courtade, owned by Henri Vidal, has the originality of an island haven, maritime climate and schistous soils. There are now some 27ha (67 acres) of vineyards and

with the vines acquiring a respectable age the wines have gained in depth and intensity. The red is made mainly from Mourvèdre with a small amount of Grenache and Syrah and is finely textured and flavoured. The white is aromatic but with extra flesh and complexity added by barrel fermentation. The rosé is full-bodied and fruity. Second wine: (red, white and rosé) Alycastre. Best years: (reds) 1996, '95, '94, '93; (whites) 1996, '95, '94, '93.

COUSIÑO MACUL

CHILE, Maipo Valley
🍷 *Cabernet Sauvignon, Merlot*
🍷 *Semillon, Sauvignon Blanc, Riesling, Chardonnay*

Cousiño Macul is Chile's most traditional wine estate and for a long time it was regarded as Chile's leading one almost as if by right. In the relatively recent days when few people cared where Chile was or what she produced, Cousiño Macul made a string of marvellous deep reds, packed with blackcurrant fruit and infused with smoke. Times have changed and Cousiño Macul is now in danger of being left behind in terms of style, quality and reputation as younger companies jostle with each other for the title of top dog. It shows how healthy progress is in Chile, but at Cousiño Macul a radical rethink is necessary for future success. Best years: 1998, '97, '96, '95.

COUSIÑO MACUL
Smoky but driven by blackcurrant fruit, Antiguas Reservas Cabernet Sauvignon continues to be the top wine at Chile's most traditional winery.

CH. COUTET

FRANCE, Bordeaux, Barsac AC, Premier Cru Classé
🍷 *Sémillon, Sauvignon Blanc, Muscadelle*

This is BARSAC's largest Classed Growth property, with 38.5ha (95 acres) under vine. Traditionally a close second to Barsac's other First Growth, Ch. CLIMENS, Coutet has been disappointing throughout the 1980s and early '90s. Luckily, recent vintages have shown a return to form with wines of excellent balance and concentration. Coutet blends up to 20 per cent Sauvignon with the Sémillon, producing a wine more delicate

than powerful. Even so, the wines are aromatic and complex with notes of tropical fruits, honey and spicy oak. In exceptional years, a minuscule quantity of specially selected Cuvée Madame is produced – a wine that has few rivals when it comes to aroma and intensity and which can age for 15 years or more. Best years: 1997, '96, '95, '90, '89, '88, '86, '83.

COWRA

AUSTRALIA, New South Wales, Central Ranges Zone

This is an increasingly important area situated in central western New South Wales, which specializes in high-quality, honey-lush Chardonnay. Arrowfield, BROKENWOOD, Charles Sturt University, Cowra Estate, Hungerford Hill, Richmond Grove, ROTHBURY ESTATE and Windowrie all produce wines under the Cowra label, but only Cowra Estate and Windowrie are 100 per cent regional producers. Best years: 1998, '96, '95, '94, '91, '90, '89, '87, '86.

QUINTA DO CRASTO

PORTUGAL, Douro, Douro DOC, Port DOC
🍷 *Tinta Roriz (Tempranillo), Touriga Francesa, Touriga Naçional and others*

The Roquettes have quickly established their family property as one of the leading quintas in the DOURO. Situated midway between Régua and Pinhão in the heart of the region, Crasto produces both PORT and unfortified red Douro wine from grapes grown on the estate. The Douro wines, produced with the help of an Australian winemaker, have become better known than the ports and Quinta do Crasto Reserva is a wonderfully supple red, softened by short aging in new oak. Depending on the year, the property also releases the occasional varietal wine made from Tinta Roriz (Tempranillo) or Touriga Naçional. When it comes to port, Crasto confines itself to a traditional LBV or a vintage port, with 1994 being the most successful year to date. Both are foot-trodden in stone *lagares* in the traditional way, a practice which is very rare. Best years: (vintage ports) 1994; (Douro wines) 1997, '95, '94.

CRÉMANT D'ALSACE AC

FRANCE, Alsace
🍷 *Pinot Blanc, Auxerrois, Riesling and others*

This CHAMPAGNE-method sparkling wine shot to fame when the price of Champagne rocketed in the early 1980s. Enthusiasm has since waned for this pretty tasty sparkler – usually made from Pinot Blanc – but, paradoxically, the quality is better now that the opportunists have departed the fray, and annual production has increased from half a million bottles to more than 13 million in the last ten years. The only trouble is that the price is much higher than it was. Best years: 1996, '95, '94, '93, '92, '90. Best producers: Cattin, Dopff au Moulin, Dopff & Irion, Ginglinger, Gisselbrecht, KUENTZ-BAS, Muré, Ostertag, Staffenheim co-operative, Willm, Wolfberger.

CRÉMANT DE BOURGOGNE AC

FRANCE, Burgundy

♀ ♂ *Chardonnay, Aligoté, Pinot Blanc, Pinot Noir*

Not so long ago Crémant de Bourgogne was dismissed as raw and reedy fizz, but in the mid-1980s things took a dramatic turn for the better. Most Burgundian Crémant is white and contains Chardonnay – sometimes up to 100 per cent – and in many vintages the full, soft, almost honeyed flavour of ripe Chardonnay grapes makes far more attractive drinking than the green, tart, bargain-basement CHAMPAGNE produced further north. Cheap Champagne is improving, but Bourgogne from a producer like the Lugny co-operative is still a better – and less expensive – wine. It ages well for two to three years, but is usually good to drink when released.

There is a growing amount of pink wine being made in response to the fad for pink fizz which Champagne has enjoyed. The best rosé is made in the CHABLIS and Auxerre regions, where wines of considerable class and fruit are possible. Best years: 1996, '95, '93, '90. Best producers: Delorme, Lucius-Grégoire, Simonnet-Febvre; co-operatives at Bailly, Lugny, St-Gengoux-de-Scissé and Viré.

CRÉMANT DU JURA AC

FRANCE, Jura

♀ ♂ *Poulsard, Pinot Gris, Pinot Noir, Trousseau, Chardonnay, Savagnin*

This new appellation was created in 1995 and has the same strict regulations as the other Crémant ACs, such as Alsace and Bourgogne. It covers the whole of the CÔTES DU JURA and can be either white or rosé, although most is white and now replaces the ACs for Arbois Mousseux and sparkling L'ÉTOILE and Côtes du Jura. Best producers: Cave des Byards, Cabellier, Ch. de l'Étoile, Fruitière Vinicole d'Arbois, Fruitière Vinicole de Voiteur, Rolet.

CRÉMANT DE LIMOUX AC

FRANCE, South-West

♀ *Chardonnay, Chenin Blanc, Mauzac*

This CHAMPAGNE-method sparkling wine AC was introduced in Limoux in 1990. The wines must have a minimum of 30 per cent Chardonnay and/or Chenin Blanc, but no more than 20 per cent of each. The rest comes from the local Mauzac grape. The wines are aged on lees for a year and generally have more complexity than BLANQUETTE DE LIMOUX, but should be drunk young. Best producers: L'AIGLE, Antech, Guinot, Laurens, Martinolles, SIEUR D'ARQUES co-operative, Valent.

CRÉMANT DE LOIRE AC

FRANCE, Loire

♂ *Cabernet Franc, Cabernet Sauvignon, Menu Pineau, Pineau d'Aunis, Pinot Noir and others*

♀ *Chenin Blanc, Chardonnay, Cabernet Franc*

If there is a way forward for sparkling LOIRE wines, Crémant de Loire should provide it. The problem with most Loire sparklers, and especially SAUMUR MOUSSEUX, is a rasping, rather fruitless acidity and an explosive bubble. The Crémant de Loire AC was created in 1975 in an effort to improve the quality of Loire sparkling wines by lowering yields – 50 hectolitres per hectare instead of the 60 allowed for Saumur – and requiring that 150kg (331lb) of grapes are used to produce one hectolitre of juice rather than the 130kg (287lb) allowed for Saumur. Crémant de Loire is always made by the CHAMPAGNE method.

The wines now are much more attractive, with more fruit, more yeast character and a more caressing mousse. But although Crémant often outclasses sparkling Saumur and VOUVRAY, the designation hasn't fully taken off. It is generally a softer wine than Saumur and is usually good to drink as soon as it is released. Best producers: ACKERMAN-LAURANCE, Berger, Gabillière, Vincent Girault, Gratien & Meyer, Liards, Michaud, Oisly-et-Thésée co-operative, Passavant.

BERGER

With a period of bottle age to develop flavour, this non-vintage Crémant de Loire is soft, round and mouthfilling. The wine is ready to drink on release.

CRÉPY AC

FRANCE, Savoie

♀ *Chasselas*

Covering 80ha (198 acres) of hillside just south of Lake Geneva, Crépy is definitely a front-runner for the title of 'white AC with the least discernible taste'. The problem is its grape, the Chasselas, which is fine for eating but produces wines which are water-white and water-light. It has a low alcoholic strength – only 9 degrees – with a relatively noticeable acidity of the 'neutral lemon' sort. The only examples with any zip are those bottled off their own lees (*sur lie*, like the best MUSCADETs). This traps a little carbon dioxide in the wine and may leave the slightest hint of yeast. The wines are best drunk as young as possible. Best producers: Goy, Mercier.

CRIMEA

UKRAINE

The Black Sea peninsula of Crimea is part of the Ukraine, and winewise alternates effortlessly between two extremes: sparkling wine inland, and sweet dessert wines along the coast. The coastal vineyards, for which the main winery is MASSANDRA, benefit from the Black Sea and the mountains have a more temperate climate; inland the winters can be very cold and the summers hot.

The first fizz made in Russia came from the Crimea in 1799 and today the Crimea attempts to meet the seemingly insatiable demand in the former Soviet Union countries for sparkling wine. Much of it is exported further afield, too, particularly to Germany, and it's generally fair quality for what it is – which is definitely not imitation CHAMPAGNE. Some is made by the Champagne method but most is made by the tank method or the Russian Continuous, which involves pumping base wine and yeast into a series of tanks, and bottling what emerges at the other end. Sparkling Krim is made in various styles, from brut to sweet, including a sweetish red.

CROFT

PORTUGAL, Douro, Port DOC

♂ *Tinta Roriz (Tempranillo), Tinta Barroca, Tinto Cão, Touriga Nacional, Touriga Francesca and others*

♀ *Gouveio, Viosinho, Rabigato, Malvasia Fina and others*

Croft is one of the oldest British PORT firms, having been founded in the late 1600s as Phayre & Bradley – the first Croft joined the firm in 1736. It now belongs to UDV, a division of drinks multinational, Diageo. The large and beautiful Quinta da Roêda has belonged to Croft since the end of the nineteenth century and forms the backbone of Croft vintage ports. Wine from Roêda is sold as a single-quinta wine in between vintage declarations. Croft had a high reputation for its vintage port in the 1960s and '70s but the wines suffered a

This is Croft's beautiful Quinta da Roêda in the Cima Corgo sub-region of the Douro Valley. Sweeping over the slope in the foreground are the new-style patamares terraces, designed to allow limited mechanization.

nose-dive in the 1980s. Recent vintages, made by Australian-trained Nick DELAFORCE, seem to be firmly back on track. Keep an eye open for the exceptionally fine Twenty-Year-Old Tawny. Best years: (vintage ports) 1994, '91, '77, '70, '66, '63.

CROZES-HERMITAGE AC
FRANCE, Northern Rhône
♣ *Syrah*
♀ *Marsanne, Roussanne*

Crozes-Hermitage is the largest of the northern RHÔNE ACs, with 1200ha (2965 acres) of vines spreading over the hillocks and plains behind the great hill of HERMITAGE. The last few years of Rhône wine history have been notable for the succession of rising stars, particularly in this small but high-quality northern section. Hermitage, CÔTE-RÔTIE, CORNAS and ST-JOSEPH have all been getting the showbiz treatment, but with the finite amounts of wine available from the terraced hill slopes of these ACs, and the prices they can command, people are suddenly discovering that red Crozes-Hermitage is rather better than they thought.

Ideally, it should have a full red colour, a rich blackcurrants, raspberries and earth smell, and a strong, meaty but rich flavour. As so often with Syrah, the delicious fruit flavours have to mingle in with strange tastes

of vegetables, damped-out bonfires, well-hung meat and herbs. You can drink it young, especially if the grapes were grown on flat land, but in ripe years, from a hillside site, it improves greatly for three to six years. Since the 1988 vintage the quality of Crozes from almost every quarter has leapt. Best years: 1998, '97, '96, '95, '94, '91, '90, '89, '88, '85, '83, '82. Best producers: (reds) Bégot, Belle, CHAPOUTIER, Caves des Clairmonts, Domaine Combier, DELAS, Desmeure, Fayolle, GRAILLOT, JABOULET (Thalabert), Robert Michelas, Pochon, Tain co-operative.

The white wines are almost never as exciting as Hermitage whites, even though the same grapes are used (Marsanne and Roussanne). This is because, except on the hilly slopes at Mercurol, most of the wine is grown on fairly flat, productive land and so the fruit lacks the astonishing concentration which marks out Hermitage. There is another reason – modern winemaking techniques. While much white Hermitage is still produced in the traditional manner, resulting in thick, gluey wines which may take ten years to open out properly, Crozes-Hermitage is now almost always made by cool fermentation to draw out the fruit and perfume. Although Desmeure still makes a highly successful old-style white Crozes – thick with the flavour of buttered almonds and bruised apples – the

best modern Crozes is now extremely fresh, with the flavour of raw nuts and apple blossom. In general, drink white Crozes young, before the floral perfume disappears. Best years: 1998, '97, '96, '95, '94, '93, '91, '90. Best producers: (whites) Desmeure, Fayolle, Graillot, Jaboulet, du Pavillon, Pochon, Pradelle.

CRUSIUS
GERMANY, Nahe, Traisen
♀ *Riesling, Müller-Thurgau, Pinot Blanc (Weissburgunder)*

Now run by Dr Peter Crusius, this is one of the most famous wine estates of the NAHE, and has some of the best vineyards of the region at its disposal, including the legendary Traiser Bastei, a south-facing 2.5ha (6 acres) of vines at the foot of the gigantic Rotenfels cliff, a natural sun-trap that yields rich, ripe wines of great pungency, and the Schloss-böckelheimer Felsenberg where the soil is rich, volcanic melaphyry that imparts intense spiciness to the wines. This is what Crusius is famous for: wines with a clarity and depth of flavour, strongly marked by the soil and preserved by careful, traditional winemaking. Big old oak casks are the norm here and many of the wines are *trocken* in style. Best years: 1998, '97, '96, '95, '94, '89, '88, '86.

YVES CUILLERON
FRANCE, Northern Rhône, Condrieu AC
♣ *Syrah*
♀ *Viognier*

Yves Cuilleron took over the family estate in CONDRIEU in the early 1990s and soon made quite an impression. He was one of the first growers to produce a barrel-fermented Condrieu in a Vendange Tardive style; called les Eguets and labelled Récolte Tardive to avoid confusion with the Vendange Tardive wines of ALSACE, the wine was a remarkable and gorgeously aromatic wine. Cuilleron insists this is no trendy innovation, but a return to a style that was popular two centuries ago in Condrieu. His top cuvée is les Chaillets Vieilles Vignes.

Although the largest single proprietor in Condrieu, with 8ha (20 acres) of vineyards, Cuilleron soon expanded his operations by producing small quantities of excellent ST-JOSEPH and CÔTE-RÔTIE. There are two white St-Joseph wines, Izeras and le Bois Lombard, the latter being produced mostly from old vines. The red Cuvée Prestige is also made from old St-Joseph vines and is aged in 25 per cent new oak. Best years: (reds) 1997, '96, '95, '94, '92; (whites) 1997, '96, '95, '94.

CULLEN WINES

AUSTRALIA, Western Australia, South West Australia Zone, Margaret River

🍷 *Cabernet Sauvignon, Merlot*

🍷 *Chardonnay, Sauvignon Blanc, Semillon*

This is one of the leaders of the MARGARET RIVER region, run by mother Diana and daughter Vanya Cullen, and making marvellously idiosyncratic wines. Its complex, structured Cabernet-Merlot lays significant claim to be Australia's best, joined by a very complex, fairly oaky but long-lived Chardonnay and an oaked, or, as Australians say, Fumé-style blend of Sauvignon Blanc and Semillon which sometimes soars like an eagle. Best years: 1996, '95, '94, '93, '92, '91, '90, '86, '84, '82.

CUVAISON

USA, California, Napa County, Napa Valley AVA

🍷 *Merlot, Cabernet Sauvignon, Zinfandel, Pinot Noir*

🍷 *Chardonnay*

This Calistoga winery made a name for itself during the 1970s with a string of deep, brooding reds, of fascinating quality potential yet little commerciality. Then a Zurich banker named Schmidheiny bought it, began planting 160ha (395 acres) of vineyards in CARNEROS and installed John Thacher as winemaker. Thacher has made Chardonnay his particular speciality and the wines are stylish without really setting the pulse racing. However, in better vintages the Carneros Reserve is splendid in a bold style. Best years: 1997, '96, '95, '94, '92, '90. Carneros is also the source of Merlot and Pinot Noir, both varying widely in quality. The Cabernet, in a big, slow-aging style with plenty of tannin, becomes quite enjoyable with ten years' aging. Best years: (reds) 1997, '96, '95, '94, '92, '91, '88.

CVNE

SPAIN, La Rioja, Rioja DOC

🍷 *Tempranillo, Grenache Noir (Garnacha Tinta), Carignan (Cariñena, Mazuelo) and others*

🍷 *Grenache Noir (Garnacha Tinta)*

🍷 *Macabeo (Viura), Grenache Blanc (Garnacha Blanca), Malvasía*

'The biggest of the smaller bodegas' is how the Compañia Vinicola del Norte de España (CVNE, pronounced 'coonay', for short) describes itself. 'And one of the best of the lot' it might justifiably add. Quality at this RIOJA bodega is extremely high. Where CVNE is among the region's big boys is in its vineyard holdings – 470ha (1161 acres), which provide over two-thirds of the red grapes needed and one-third of the white. As well as the elegant, plummy Viña Real wines, Crianza, Reserva

Didier Dagueneau, a much-needed quality fanatic in the Pouilly-Fumé AC, takes a sample of Pur Sang, one of his barrel-fermented Sauvignon Blanc wines.

and Gran Reserva, there's a lovely, young, light, plummy CVNE Tinto. A prestige red called Imperial is made in the best years, sometimes Reserva, sometimes Gran Reserva, aged for at least a year in tank, three in oak, and three in bottle before release. CVNE is one of the few Riojan companies to make really good, old-style, wood-aged whites. Monopole (made from Viura with 20 per cent Malvasía) is fresh with nice oak from 13 months in barrel. Best years: (reds) 1996, '95, '94, '91, '90, '89, '87, '86, '85, '82, '81, '78, '76.

DIDIER DAGUENEAU

FRANCE, Central Loire, Pouilly-Fumé AC

🍷 *Sauvignon Blanc*

A rebel by nature, the mercurial Didier Dagueneau makes some of the most remarkable dry Sauvignon Blanc in the world. He preaches high density plantings, low yields and organic viticulture. Dagueneau's plain speaking (he is often critical of standards in Pouilly) and his good relations with the media have not endeared him to his neighbours in POUILLY-FUMÉ. Dagueneau's winery, built in 1989, is one of the most striking in the region. It operates by gravity, which means that the must and the wine can be moved around the winery in the most natural way possible. He makes a number of cuvées, which include the approachable En Chailloux, the single-vineyard Buisson Menard and the barrel-fermented Pur Sang. His most famous wine is Silex, made from old vines in the flinty soil that is characteristic of part of the Pouilly vineyards. This is also fermented and aged in young barrels. Best years: 1998, '97, '96, '95, '93, '90, '89.

ROMANO DAL FORNO

ITALY, Veneto, Valpolicella DOC

🍷 *Corvina, Rondinella, Croatina and others*

🍷 *Garganega, Trebbiano Toscano, Turbiana*

On his small estate at Illasi, outside the VALPOLICELLA Classico area, Romano Dal Forno makes wines that were already being hailed as among the best in Valpolicella before he started introducing new French oak in 1990. Today there are those who consider Romano Dal Forno the quality king of Valpolicella, combining as he does, in his AMARONE Monte Lodoletta, a mighty structure with a concentration of flavours and perfumes scarcely paralleled anywhere in Italy. The Valpolicella Vigneto di Monte Lodoletta, too, can be quite stunning. Nor is the RECIOTO Monte Lodoletta any less of a liquid bombshell. To Dal Forno must go credit for proving conclusively that great Valpolicella can be made outside the Classico area and for demonstrating how modern winemaking can be used to enhance an ancient wine without in any way compromising typicity. Best years: (Amarone) 1990, '89, '88, '86, '85.

DALLA VALLE

USA, California, Napa County, Napa Valley AVA

🍷 *Cabernet Sauvignon, Cabernet Franc, Sangiovese*

Founded by the late Gustav Dalla Valle, this beautiful hillside winery was a little slow in starting, but is now running neck and neck with NAPA's finest. On a slope overlooking the Silverado Trail, Dalla Valle developed a 10-ha (25-acre) vineyard which supplies all of the winery's needs. In addition to its Cabernet Sauvignon, which hit full stride in 1990, there is Maya, a magnificent Cabernet Sauvignon and Cabernet Franc blend. Both will smooth out beautifully after ten years. There is also the Sangiovese, Pietre Rosse, that was impressive from its first vintage and seems destined to enjoy the cult status presently conferred on Maya and the Cabernet Sauvignon. Best years: 1997, '96, '95, '94, '93, '92, '90.

DALWHINNIE

AUSTRALIA, Victoria, Western Victoria Zone, Pyrenees

🍷 *Pinot Noir, Syrah (Shiraz), Cabernet Sauvignon*

🍷 *Chardonnay*

Dalwhinnie is consistently the best producer in the Pyrenees, drawing upon 20-year-old, low-yielding, unirrigated estate vineyards which are immaculately maintained. The quality of the grapes shines through in the carefully made wines: complex, melon and grapefruit-accented Chardonnay, almost as substantial in its way as the black cherry, berry

DALWHINNIE
Lovingly tended vines and low yields are the keys to the powerful, long-living Shiraz and other wines from Dalwhinnie, the best producer in the Pyrenees region.

and mint Shiraz and the sweet, cassis and chocolate Cabernet Sauvignon. A couple of startling Pinot Noirs contract-made by Rick Kinzbrunner have also made their appearance in minute quantities. Best years: 1997, '96, '95, '94, '92, '91, '90, '88, '86.

DÃO DOC
PORTUGAL, Beira Alta
♥ Alfrocheiro Preto, Bastardo, Jaen, Touriga Naçional and others
♀ Encruzado, Assario Branco, Bical (Borrado dos Moscas) and others
In central Portugal, Dão has all that it takes to produce some of the country's best reds. Mountains shelter the region from the Atlantic and yet there is sufficient rain for vines to flourish in the poor granite soils. The problem has been in the winemaking and for decades the co-operatives continued to churn out hard, over-extracted reds and oxidized whites. During these dark times, only Caves SÃO JOÃO kept the flame alight to remind everyone just how good traditional red Dão could be. Fortunately the co-operatives lost their stranglehold after Portugal joined the EU in 1986 and Dão has been on the way up ever since.

Portugal's largest wine producer, SOGRAPE, led the way, building a new winery in the heart of the region. Grão Vasco, the best-selling brand of Dão wine, has improved immeasurably since. Sogrape has since been joined by a new wave of single quintas, many of whom used to supply co-operatives but now have the wherewithal to make and market their own wines. Quinta das Maias, Quinta dos Roques and Quinta de Saes are now making some seriously good reds alongside Sogrape's two premium wines (called Duque de Viseu and Quinta dos Carvalhais) and Fonte do Ouro made by Boas Quintas. The redoubtable Caves São João's Porta dos Cavaleiros Dão red is just as good as ever. Whites, though much improved on the days of yore, will never be Dão's forte. Drink the whites young. Best years: (reds) 1998, '97, '96, '95, '94, '92.

D'ARENBERG
AUSTRALIA, South Australia, Fleurieu Zone, McLaren Vale
♥ Shiraz (Syrah), Grenache, Cabernet Sauvignon
♀ Riesling, Chardonnay
This winery first sprang to prominence in the second half of the 1960s, with a 1967 Burgundy (composed largely of Grenache) which won seven trophies and 25 gold medals, an astonishing record by the standards of the time, followed up by a 1968 Cabernet Sauvignon which won the coveted Jimmy Watson Trophy in 1969. Things then settled down until the 1990s when Chester Osborn took over from father d'Arry, and with the help of savvy marketing (e.g. wines called The Dead Arm Shiraz, The Footbolt Old Vine Shiraz, Ironstone Pressings, D'Arry's Original Shiraz Grenache) has proceeded to make exceptionally lush cherry, currant, berry, spice and plum-filled wines with an appropriate lick of new oak. Best years: 1997, '96, '94, '91, '90.

RENÉ ET VINCENT DAUVISSAT
FRANCE, Burgundy, Chablis AC
♀ Chardonnay
There are many CHABLIS estates with the Dauvissat name, but the most distinguished is that run by Vincent Dauvissat. Almost all the wines here are either Premier Cru (Forêt, Séchet, Vaillons) or Grand Cru (Preuses, les Clos). The winemaking is without frills: the must is fermented in tanks and barrels, very little new oak is used, no more than is required to replace worn-out barrels. The wines usually go through malolactic fermentation before being aged in Burgundian barrels as well as the traditional small barrels peculiar to Chablis and known as *feuillettes*. These are classic Chablis with a great purity of fruit and a strong mineral presence. Best years: 1997, '96, '95, '94, '92, '90, '89, '88, '85.

DEALUL MARE
ROMANIA, Transylvania
Few places can be as evocative as picturesque Transylvania. The image of Germanic-style, turreted castles nestling atop hillsides overlooking pretty little villages is all true. What is equally appealing is that the wine there is improving by the vintage. Pinot Noirs from valleys that fan down the Carpathian Mountains, such as Valea Calugareasca (Valley of the Monks), have reasonably focused Burgundian character, but it is the Merlots, especially some young vatted wines, that are currently worth chasing. Talented young Romanian enologists are linking up with Aus-

tralian winemakers in a bid to attract attention, and they surely will. Romanian oak is being used to great effect in some of the finer wines, and, when new and clean, it is giving surprising results. The Prahova winery is making the most interesting Merlot and new investment in Sahateni is beginning to yield good results.

MARCO DE BARTOLI
ITALY, Sicily
♀ Grillo, Inzolia and others
In the early 1980s Marco De Bartoli almost single-handedly restored the credibility of MARSALA as a high-class wine with his Marsala Vergine-like wine called Vecchio Samperi, even though it did not qualify for the Marsala DOC because he refused to fortify it up to the minimum 18 per cent alcohol. Nonetheless, the wine showed the splendours of which Marsala is capable, and laid down the gauntlet to those still producing industrialized rubbish. Vecchio Samperi comes in three versions, 10-, 20- and 30-Year-Old, and is bone dry. The predominant grape variety is Grillo, the best Marsala grape, and the wine is aged in wooden barrels, successively blended with small quantities of much older wines in the time-honoured solera system also used for sherry.

De Bartoli also produces kosher Marsala, a discreetly sweetened Superiore and a Superiore Oro called Vigna la Miccia, and these again are probably the best of their genre. De Bartoli is also particularly strong in Pantelleria, where he makes a delicious sweet MOSCATO DI PANTELLERIA Bukkuram from sun-dried Zibibbo (Muscat of Alexandria) grapes as well as a delicious dry Muscat called Pietranera. Everything he does is top-notch, so it is ironic, if not surprising considering the long knives that came out for him when he started denouncing Marsala's industrialization and deliberate self-degradation, that he remains embroiled in a bureaucratic mess over documentation which has dragged on for years now, blocking him from selling wines of superb quality which remain sealed in his barrels.

DE BORTOLI
AUSTRALIA, New South Wales, Big Rivers Zone, Riverina and Victoria, Port Phillip Zone, Yarra Valley
♥ Merlot, Cabernet Sauvignon, Pinot Noir, Syrah (Shiraz)
♀ Semillon, Chardonnay, Riesling, Gewurztraminer
This winery owes its worldwide reputation to a single wine which was first made in 1982 and then largely fortuitously. What is more, the wine – a magnificent, luscious botrytis

Semillon called Noble One – that even upstaged Ch. d'YQUEM in some tastings – represents less than 3 per cent of De Bortoli's production. De Bortoli now also owns an extremely smart winery in the YARRA VALLEY. The other RIVERINA wines are adequate, good value and user-friendly; the Yarra ones are increasingly classy. Best years: (botrytis Semillon) 1996, '94, '93, '92, '91, '90, '88, '87, '85, '84, '82.

DEHLINGER WINERY

USA, California, Sonoma County, Russian River Valley AVA

❦ *Pinot Noir, Cabernet Sauvignon, Syrah*
♀ *Chardonnay*

The overall quality of Dehlinger wines took a quantum leap in 1985, which was the year when winemaker Tom Dehlinger became the sole proprietor. A perfectionist to the extreme, Dehlinger has quietly turned out a series of surprisingly deep Pinot Noirs from his estate, as well as mouthwatering Syrah and Chardonnays. The Pinots from the low-yielding, coolish site age particularly well, while the Chardonnays are best drunk young. The Syrah has the depth and structure to give a good HERMITAGE a run for its money. Best years: 1997, '96, '95, '94, '93, '92, '91, '90, '89, '88, '87, '85.

DEIDESHEIM

GERMANY, Pfalz

This village, along with FORST and WACHENHEIM, forms the centre of the Mittelhaardt, that part of the PFALZ with the greatest concentration of quality vineyards. Anything labelled with the Grosslage name Deidesheimer Hofstück, may have come from one of the neighbouring villages. The best vineyards in Deidesheim itself are Grainhübel, Hohenmorgen, Kalkofen and Leinhöhle. Best producers: BASSERMANN-JORDAN, von BUHL, BÜRKLIN-WOLF, WOLF.

DEISS

FRANCE, Alsace, Alsace AC

❦ *Pinot Noir*
♀ *Riesling, Gewurztraminer, Pinot Gris, Pinot Blanc, Muscat, Sylvaner*

No grower in Alsace is quite as fanatical about the notion of terroir as Jean-Michel Deiss. In some vintages he will bottle six or more different versions of Riesling alone. Deiss can explain the precise soil structure and meso-climatic conditions for each location, and the wines are indeed different from each other. All his wines have exemplary intensity and

vigour, but the greatest Rieslings usually come from the Grands Crus Altenberg in Bergheim and Schoenenbourg in Riquewihr. Deiss claims not to be terribly interested in Pinot Gris but manages to produce sensational wines each year, nonetheless. Indeed, it is hard to think of a weak line in the Deiss range of wines. The Vendange Tardive and Sélection de Grains Nobles wines are stunning. Prices are high, but for once they are justified by quality. Best years: 1997, '96, '95, '94, '93, '92, '90, '89, '88, '85.

DELAFORCE

PORTUGAL, Douro, Port DOC

❦ *Tinta Roriz (Tempranillo), Tinta Barroca, Tinto Cão, Touriga Nacional, Touriga Francesa and others*
♀ *Gouveio, Viosinho, Rabigato, Malvasia Fina and others*

Though Delaforce has joined CROFT (and is therefore part of the Diageo group), it is still run quite separately. The company itself owns no vineyards but has exclusive arrangements with the fabulous Quinta da Corte in the Torto Valley which is sold as a single-quinta vintage port in between major declarations. Like Croft, Deleforce vintages suffered in the 1980s, but with Nick Delaforce having taken on the role of winemaker for both firms, recent vintage ports are much improved. His Eminence's Choice is a well-nurtured ten-year-old tawny. Best years: (vintage ports) 1994, '85, '70, '66, '63.

DELAS

FRANCE, Northern Rhône

❦ *Syrah, Grenache*
♀ *Marsanne, Roussanne, Viognier*

This long-established *négociant* house happens to own some of the very finest sites in the northern RHÔNE, especially within HER-MITAGE, yet the wines were often lacklustre, although there have been some excellent CONDRIEU and CÔTE-RÔTIE wines. All that began to change in 1997, after Delas was purchased by the CHAMPAGNE house of DEUTZ. A new director, Jacques Grange, who had

previously worked with CHAPOUTIER and COLOMBO, didn't take long to work out what was wrong at Delas. He reorganized the cellars and discarded many of the older barrels. It is too early to see how successful these improvements will be, but it is reasonable to assume that within a few years Delas, like Chapoutier, will be experiencing a renaissance in quality and renown. Best years: 1997, '96, '95, '90, '89, '88, '85, '83.

DELATITE

AUSTRALIA, Victoria, Central Victoria Zone, Central Victorian High Country

❦ *Pinot Noir, Cabernet Sauvignon, Merlot, Syrah (Shiraz)*
♀ *Riesling, Gewurztraminer, Chardonnay*

Here in the lee of the Australian Alps is a climate so cool that in some years the grapes do not ripen fully. As a result the Delatite style, particularly in the red wines, is unmistakable. The whites have extreme finesse and subtlety, the fine acid and sherbet-like tingle softening slightly with age to reveal fruit of pristine purity. The red wines all have an essence-of-mint taste, a cross between peppermint and eucalyptus, which divides critics between those who love it – especially in the Devil's River Cabernet-Merlot – and those who find it disturbing in the gentler Pinot Noir. I'm a fan. Best years: 1997, '94, '93, '92, '91, '90, '88, '87, '86, '82.

DELEGATS

NEW ZEALAND, North Island, Henderson

❦ *Cabernet Sauvignon, Merlot*
♀ *Sauvignon Blanc, Chardonnay*

New Zealand's brother and sister team, Jim and Rose Delegat, specializes in Chardonnay, Cabernet-Merlot and Sauvignon Blanc, and quality is improving all the time. The winery uses fruit from its own vineyards and contract growers in HAWKE'S BAY and MARLBOROUGH. Top of the range is the Reserve Chardonnay – with its ripe, peachy, apricot fruit and a light oak touch – and Sauvignon Blanc. The Marlborough Chardonnay and Sauvignon wines are sold under the Oyster Bay label. Best years: 1998, '96, '94, '92, '91.

DELILLE CELLARS

USA, Washington State, Woodinville

❦ *Merlot, Cabernet Sauvignon, Cabernet Franc*
♀ *Sauvignon Blanc, Semillon*

Winemaker Chris Upchurch crafts heady, oaky, cherry-filled reds that appeal to many palates. Using fruit from a variety of YAKIMA VALLEY vineyards, he selects his best grapes for a BORDEAUX-style blend called Chaleur Estate. A second wine, D2, is a selection of lighter barrels of Cabernet and Merlot that is appealing early. Chaleur Estate Blanc is an oaky Semillon-Sauvignon Blanc blend, emulating a white Bordeaux that is best drunk young. Best years: 1998, '97, '95, '94.

DENBIES
ENGLAND, Surrey
♥ *Pinot Noir, Dornfelder*
♀ *Bacchus, Reichensteiner, Pinot Gris and others*

This is England's most ambitious vineyard project yet, with 111ha (274 acres) of vines on the chalky North Downs near Dorking. There are some 20 varieties in the vineyard and intelligent blending has resulted in a range of consistently good dry and medium-dry wines. There is also a CHAMPAGNE-method fizz and a botrytized dessert wine. Marvellous Riesling, Chardonnay and Pinot Gris have been produced in tiny quantities. Drink at two to three years old.

DEUTZ
FRANCE, Champagne, Champagne AC
♀ ♥ *Chardonnay, Pinot Noir, Pinot Meunier*

By the late 1980s, the once distinguished house of Deutz had seen its reputation in decline, so there was probably a collective sigh of relief when in 1993 it was bought by one of the most quality-conscious producers in the region, Louis ROEDERER. No doubt believing that part of Deutz's problems lay in its divided attention between French and New World operations, Roederer wound down the Californian sparkling wine facility, but maintained its winery in New Zealand.

Almost a million bottles of CHAMPAGNE are produced annually. The mainstay of the range is the Brut, made in equal proportions from the three Champagne grape varieties. There is a range of full-bodied vintage wines too, including the Blanc de Blancs, the Pinot Noir-dominated Cuvée William Deutz and the outstanding William Deutz Rosé. Best years: 1990, '89, '88, '85, '82.

DEVIL'S LAIR
AUSTRALIA. Western Australia, South West Australia Zone, Margaret River
♥ *Cabernet Sauvignon*
♀ *Chardonnay, Semillon, Sauvignon Blanc*

Phil Sexton is a master brewer who made a considerable sum out of two boutique beer brands acquired by Fosters, promptly invested the gains in establishing the beautiful Devil's Lair vineyard and winery with its

enormous lake, and parlayed that into even more money when Southcorp, Australia's largest wine company, acquired Devil's Lair in late 1996. James Halliday has group wine-making responsibility for Devil's Lair as well as COLDSTREAM HILLS and the HUNTER VALLEY brands of Southcorp, but the style of Devil's Lair has not changed markedly (nor will it).

The accent is on concentrated, structured, barrel-fermented Chardonnay and an equally concentrated red, simply called Devil's Lair, but with a BORDEAUX-blend composition. The high volume flyers are the Fifth Leg White (Semillon, Sauvignon Blanc, Chardonnay) and Fifth Leg Red (Merlot-dominant, but with other bits and pieces) which are from MARGARET RIVER grapes but not necessarily estate-sourced. Best years: 1996, '95, '94, '92, '91, '90.

DEVIL'S LAIR
Based in the chic Margaret River region, this is an exciting, rapidly rising quality producer of opulent Chardonnay and other wines.

DE WETSHOF
SOUTH AFRICA, Western Cape, Robertson WO
♥ *Pinot Noir*
♀ *Chardonnay, Sauvignon Blanc, Riesling (Rhine/Weisser Riesling), Muscat à Petits Grains (Muscat de Frontignan/Muscadel), Gewurztraminer*

German-trained Danie de Wet was one of the Chardonnay pioneers in ROBERTSON and, like many others, found he had unwittingly planted Auxerrois rather than Chardonnay. The real thing he now has a-plenty in his vineyards; from it he crafts a number of different styles, both wooded and unwooded. Gewürztraminer and Rhine Riesling reflect his German wine education, while the fortified Muscat de Frontignan Blanc confirms his local roots. The estate's first red grapes will come from a newly planted 4-ha (10-acre) vineyard of Pinot Noir, being established with the help of Californian viticulturist, Phil Freese. It may be coincidental, but de Wet's increased activity within the industry (among many other responsibilities, he's a KWV director) seems to be reflected in a recent loss of momentum in the range. Best years: 1998, '97, '96, '95, '94, '93, '92, '91.

DÉZALEY
SWITZERLAND, Vaud

The wines of this Swiss village are, with those of its cousin Dézaley-Marsens, the tastiest of the Lake Geneva region; they come from between Lausanne and Montreux, the best of a stretch of vineyards in the VAUD that produces some of Switzerland's most appealing whites. The wines come from the Chasselas grape, which here goes under the name of Dorin, and have their own appellation to take account of their distinctive, almost pungent style. Unlike most Chasselas wines, Dézaley improves with up to five years of bottle aging. Best producers: Louis BOVARD, Dubois Fils, les Frères Dubois, J D Fonjallaz (l'Arbalète), Gerard Pinget, Testuz.

DIAMOND CREEK VINEYARDS
USA, California, Napa County, Napa Valley AVA
♥ *Cabernet Sauvignon*

On Diamond Mountain in northern NAPA, three separate vineyard blocks give their names to intense, individualistic Cabernet Sauvignon bottlings. This trio – Volcanic Hill, Red Rock Terrace and Gravelly Meadow – have always been among the most expensive and talked-about CALIFORNIA Cabernets. Early vintages were tannin-laden, but vintages since the 1980s have displayed a restraint that works well with the core of rich fruit. Best years: 1997, '96, '95, '94, '92, '87, '86, '85, '84, '81, '80.

SCHLOSSGUT DIEL
GERMANY, Nahe, Burg Layen
♥ *Pinot Noir (Spätburgunder)*
♀ *Riesling, Pinot Gris (Grauburgunder), Pinot Blanc (Weissburgunder)*

Wine writer, restaurant critic, television personality, campaigner for vineyard classification and who knows what else, Armin Diel is rightly nicknamed 'the big Diel'. After a period of stylistic oscillation, Diel came down firmly in favour of classic style Rieslings with the 1989 and '90 vintages, since which time the estate has been one of the quality leaders in the NAHE. Although it is Diel's Eiswein that hits the headlines, achieving record prices at auction, it is the Spätlese and Auslese wines from the rocky slopes of DORSHEIM's excellent Burgberg, Goldloch and Pittermännchen sites that are the estate's signature wines. While those from the Pittermännchen can easily be mistaken for top-class MOSEL wines, the wines from the Burgberg are juicy with a minerally acidity and the Goldloch Rieslings are the most noble, with a bouquet of ripe apricots.

Diel also produces barrique-aged wines from the Pinot family. These days the oak in them is much milder than it was when he began experimenting with the style 15 years ago. This, together with lower yields, has made the wines richer and silkier. Victor is the top wine of this range, a blend of Grauburgunder and Weissburgunder and capable of aging for five years and more. Best years: 1998, '97, '96, '95, '93, '92, '90, '89, '88.

SCHLOSSGUT DIEL
The very full-bodied and sweet Riesling Eisweins from this estate, one of the best in the Nahe region, are world-famous for their thrilling intensity.

DÍEZ-MÉRITO
SPAIN, Andalucía, Jerez y Manzanilla DO
♀ *Palomino Fino, Pedro Ximénez, Moscatel*

Díez-Mérito wines are among the biggest sellers in JEREZ, yet no wine is made these days in the Díez-Mérito winery. In 1987 the Díez-Mérito wines moved out of their old-fashioned Ali-Baba jars (*tinajas*) and into new, super-modern, temperature-controlled stainless steel at Bodegas Internacionales – now Jerez's biggest bodega. The best wines of all are selected for the expensive Fino Imperial and the deliciously nutty, concentrated Victoria Regina Oloroso (brands of Díez Hermanos, the original name of Díez-Mérito). The second quality, still excellent, goes to the Don Zoilo range.

CH. DOISY-DAËNE
FRANCE, Bordeaux, Sauternes AC, 2ème Cru Classé
♀ *Sémillon, Sauvignon Blanc, Muscadelle*

This is a consistently good BARSAC estate, though it uses the SAUTERNES AC, and is made almost exclusively from Sémillon. Since 1989, the wines from this 15-ha (37-acre) estate, which is neighbour to the great Ch. CLIMENS, have been stunning – rich, powerful and bursting with tropical fruit flavours. Owner Pierre Dubourdieu's recipe for success has been low yields, successive selective picking, and vinification and aging in oak barrels. The wines are

beautiful to drink young, but will age ten years or more. In 1990 and '96 an infinitesimally small amount of super-rich Sauternes from individually picked botrytized grapes was produced under the label Extravagant. Best years: (sweet) 1998, '97, '96, '95, '94, '90, '89, '88, '86, '83, '82, '80, '79.

There is also a highly successful dry perfumed white called Doisy-Daëne Sec, made essentially from Sauvignon Blanc and sold under the BORDEAUX AC. As with the sweet wines, the grapes are hand harvested and the wine then vinified and aged in oak barrels with *bâtonnage* (lees stirring) for 11 months. The wine is full-bodied, aromatic and subtly oaked. Drink the dry wine young. Best years: (dry) 1998, '96, '95, '94, '90, '89, '88.

CH. DOISY-VÉDRINES
FRANCE, Bordeaux, Sauternes AC, 2ème Cru Classé
♀ *Sémillon, Sauvignon Blanc, Muscadelle*

Next door to DOISY-DAËNE in the BARSAC AC, this is the larger of the Doisy estates. Unlike most of its Barsac neighbours, Doisy-Védrines produces a wine with more of the richness and weight of SAUTERNES (it even uses the Sauternes AC label) from extremely low-yielding vines. Fermented and aged in barrel, the wines are fat and powerful, marked by new oak when young, and need five or six years' bottle age to be at their best. Best years: 1998, '97, '96, '95, '94, '90, '89, '88, '86, '85, '83, '82, '80, '76, '75.

DOLCETTO

Dolcetto is an unmistakably Italian red grape whose name, translated, means 'little sweet one' – reputedly because the grape is particularly sweet at vintage time. The wine, however, while intensely fruity, is invariably dry, usually with the easy fruit of BEAUJOLAIS, but with an edge of bitterness.

The zone of Acqui Terme, in southeastern Piedmont, is said to be the grape's historic home, so that, among the region's numerous Dolcetto DOCs, it is Dolcetto d'Acqui which is perhaps the most typical, generally light and fruity and not overly serious. Dolcetto d'Asti is similar in style (best producers: Alasia/Araldica Vini Piemontesi). Dolcetto di Dogliani is thought to represent the best quality and, in fact, has been grown on the west-facing slopes bordering the river Tanaro for hundreds of years (best producers: M & E Abbona, Boschis, Chionetti, Einaudi, Gillardi, Manfredi, Pecchenino, Pira, San Fereolo, San Romano), even though it is Dolcetto d'Alba that boasts the greatest number

of high-class producers. This is not so surprising when you consider that although many Albese producers make BAROLO and/or BARBARESCO for a business, and often BARBERA too, it's actually Dolcetto they drink at practically every meal. (For good producers refer to Barolo, Barbaresco and Barbera d'Alba.) Dolcetto di Diano d'Alba, just south of Alba, is just beginning to become known as a high-quality zone (Claudio Alario and Bricco Maiolica are good producers). LANGHE Dolcetto tends to be a second choice, supermarket level wine.

Some Dolcetto is found outside Piedmont: in neighbouring LIGURIA for example, where it goes under the name of Ormeasco; and further afield in Australia, where Garry Crittenden at DROMANA ESTATE in VICTORIA's MORNINGTON PENINSULA region, for one, has carried out some interesting experiments; and also in California and in Argentina.

DÔLE
SWITZERLAND, Valais
♟ *Pinot Noir, Gamay*

The best-known wine of the VALAIS, this is a light red blend of at least 51 per cent Pinot Noir with Gamay. The darker, richer versions with 100 per cent Pinot Noir may call themselves Pinot Noir, and anything too light for Dôle is classified as Goron, a more basic blend of these varieties. Best producers: G Clavier, M Clavier, J Germanier, Gilliard, Caves IMESCH, Mathier, Mathier-Kuchler, Maye, Orsat, Raymond, Roduit, A Schmid, Zufferey.

DOMAINE CARNEROS
USA, California, Napa County, Carneros AVA
♟ *Pinot Noir*
♀ *Chardonnay, Pinot Blanc*

A joint venture between the CHAMPAGNE house of TAITTINGER and Kobrand, its marketing agent, Domaine Carneros is an imposing, château-like structure presiding over green rolling hills in the centre of the CARNEROS AVA. With all eyes watching every move of this prestigious Taittinger project, Domaine Carneros has developed slowly and cautiously to an impressive quality level.

Under the guidance of winemaker Eileen Crane, it has earned high marks for its Blanc de Blancs and the Brut, both displaying Taittinger's signature of elegance and finesse. New to the act is an ultra-charming vintage deluxe cuvée called Le Reve. A small amount of still Pinot Noir with typical Carneros fruit and youthful charm is also made. Best years: (sparkling wine) 1995, '93, '92.

DOMAINE CHANDON

AUSTRALIA, Victoria, Port Phillip Zone, Yarra Valley

♟ *Pinot Noir*

♟ *Chardonnay*

'Anything you can do, I can do better' might well be the song sung by this Domaine Chandon to the CHAMPAGNE house MOËT ET CHANDON's other overseas subsidiaries, and in particular to the NAPA VALLEY. In a little over ten years it has established itself as one of Australia's top three sparkling wine producers, along with SEPPELT and SEAVIEW, succeeding handsomely both in the domestic and export trade (in the latter being known as Green Point). Its five different sparkling wines are united by their finesse and elegance, typically with a gentle creamy texture and flavours of citrus and ripe pear. Its table wine Chardonnay and Pinot Noir aren't bad either. Best years: 1997, '96, '94, '93, '92, '90, '88.

DOMAINE CHANDON
Moët et Chandon's highly successful Australian off-shoot, Domaine Chandon, uses the name Green Point on the export market..

DOMAINE CHANDON

USA, California, Napa County, Napa Valley AVA

♟♟ *Chardonnay, Pinot Noir, Pinot Meunier, Pinot Blanc*

MOËT ET CHANDON's Domaine Chandon is the grandaddy of the CHAMPAGNE-owned sparkling wine houses in CALIFORNIA, located since 1975 in its own ultra-modern facility in the heart of the NAPA VALLEY. It is also the biggest, with more than 405 ha (1000 acres) of vines, mostly in CARNEROS. It buys grapes from elsewhere in California to feed its second label, Shadow Creek, which is exported.

The traditional Champagne grapes of Chardonnay and Pinot Noir are the basic grape varieties used, with Pinot Blanc and Pinot Meunier added occasionally. Chandon Brut is well enough made but usually too ripe-tasting; Blanc de Noirs is smoother, with a faint copper hue. The Reserve, kept for longer on its yeasts, is fuller and toastier. Étoile is an aged de luxe wine, showing better and better with each new release, and an elegant Étoile Rosé is also produced that is simply charming. With rare exceptions, most of the wines are not vintage dated.

DOMAINE DROUHIN

USA, Oregon, Yamhill County, Willamette Valley AVA

♟ *Pinot Noir*

♟ *Chardonnay*

After tasting OREGON Pinot Noir competitively with red Burgundies, the well-known French *négociant* Robert DROUHIN liked its potential and in 1987 he purchased 73ha (180 acres) in the WILLAMETTE VALLEY. His daughter, Véronique Drouhin, travels to Oregon to oversee the winemaking and her talent has placed the wines among the best in Oregon. Her Pinot Noir exhibits texture and refinement that few Oregon Pinot Noirs possess. In 1996 a Chardonnay from new Dijon clones was released. Best years: 1998, '96, '94, '93.

DOMECQ

SPAIN, Andalucía, Jerez y Manzanilla DO and País Vasco, Rioja DOC

♟ *Rioja: Tempranillo, Carignan (Cariñena, Mazuelo), Graciano, Macabeo (Viura)*

♟ *Grenache Noir (Garnacha Tinta)*

♟ *Jerez: Palomino Fino, Pedro Ximénez; Macabeo (Viura)*

Pedro Domecq is the world's biggest brandy producer and the oldest and largest of the sherry companies. Big certainly isn't bad in this case: La Iña, fresh and yeasty-tangy, is one of the best of all fino sherries and one of the lightest in alcohol. It is the second bestseller in the world, and accounts for one-third of Domecq's sherry production. Rio Viejo, a medium-bodied dry oloroso, and especially the elegant, dry, austere Botaina Amontillado Viejo are worth a try. But best of all is Domecq's top range: Amontillado 51-1A, a gloriously drinkable dry amontillado, with tangy, salty concentration to the fore and toffee and hazelnut in the background; Sibarita Palo Cortado, richer, sweeter, but still with a streak of lean, iodiny concentration; and Venerable Pedro Ximénez, an alcoholic, liquid version of raisin toffee.

Domecq has invested heavily in RIOJA since the early 1970s and is now by far the biggest vineyard owner in the region. Most of the wines are red: Viña Arienzo is a lightish, fruity, reliable wine. The Marqués de Arienzo Gran Reserva is even better. Best years: (Rioja) 1995, '94, '91, '90, '89, '87, '85, '82, '81.

DOMINUS ESTATE

USA, California, Napa County, Napa Valley AVA

♟ *Cabernet Sauvignon, Merlot, Cabernet Franc*

Christian Moueix of Ch. PÉTRUS has played a key role in Dominus since co-founding the winery in 1984. After a few controversial vintages, he became the sole owner in the 1990s and he has brought stability and admirable quality standards to the winery. Relying on Cabernet Sauvignon, Merlot and Cabernet Franc from the historic (planted in the 1880s) Napanook Vineyard in Yountville, Moueix has managed to create an estate red with a high percentage of Cabernet Sauvignon that resembles the fine POMEROL wines made by the Moueix firm which rely more on Merlot.

After a bumpy run in the 1980s, followed by a succession of winemakers, Moueix had Dominus operating at a high level in the late 1990s. Concentrated, with tremendous ripe fruit and lavish oak, Dominus ages well for at least a decade and its better vintages will easily develop for two decades. Best years: 1996, '95, '94, '92, '91, '90.

DONAULAND AND CARNUNTUM

AUSTRIA, Niederösterreich

The Donauland-Carnuntum region has now been divided into two parts – Donauland now covers the section west of Vienna. It is best known for white wines and the region's most famous wine estate, Klosterneuburg, is the largest vineyard owner in Austria. The quality of its wine tends to lag behind, however. Carnuntum, named after a Roman city, is the eastern section and now a wine region in its own right. Its wines are similar to those of Donauland. Best producers: (Donauland) Fritsch, Fritz, Leth, Hans Pitnauer, Wimmer-Czerny; (Carnuntum) Markowitsch.

H DÖNNHOFF

GERMANY, Nahe, Oberhausen

♟ *Riesling, Pinot Blanc (Weissburgunder), Pinot Gris (Grauburgunder)*

Helmut Dönnhoff is one of Germany's greatest winemakers and obsessed with the subtle differences between wines from neighbouring vineyard sites. During the 1990s he has steadily expanded his holdings in almost all the top vineyards of the Middle NAHE Valley. Dönnhoff's most complex and refined wines come from old Riesling vines in the NIEDERHÄUSer Hermannshöhle site; the Kupfergrube of SCHLOSSBÖCKELHEIM gives the most racy and piquant wines, while the Felsenberg site makes more lavish wines with an apricotty character. From the Oberhäuser Brücke site he regularly makes some of Germany's most exciting Eisweins. Although he makes some fine dry wines, his first love is the Spätlese and Auslese wines with natural sweetness – these have extraordinary finesse and will age at least a decade, often longer. Best years: 1998, '97, '96, '95, '94, '93, '90, '89, '88, '86, '83, '79, '76, '75, '71.

DOURO Portugal

AFTER THE TAGUS (TEJO), THE DOURO is the most important river in Portugal (and its importance continues over the border into Spain, where it becomes known as the Duero). It is not surprising, then, that the wine region takes its name from the river, as, without this waterway, Douro wines might never have reached the outside world. The Douro is a wild and beautiful part of Portugal. Its very poverty of natural resources has driven the inhabitants to ingenious extremes in order to wrest a living from what can only just be called soil. The part of the Douro where port can be made has the poorest soil – slate-like schist that must be broken up by digging or even dynamiting before vines can be planted. Where the slate gives way to granite, the permission to make port is withheld, limiting production to Douro table wine.

Mankind's hand is evident everywhere in the Douro landscape. In order to plant vines on the steep slopes plunging down to the Douro and its tributaries, terraces have been carved out of the slate rock. Traditional terraces are narrow, and supported by dry stone walls (one of the few ways of disposing of large boulders before the advent of proper roads and tractors). More recent planting has been undertaken with limited mechanization in mind. Some growers favour *vinha ao alta* (up and down) vineyards but the majority have opted for *patamares* or contour terraces without supporting walls.

The river has changed, too, and it is no longer a fast-flowing waterway where every journey taking wine down to Oporto (Porto) was an exciting adventure. A series of dams constructed along the river from the late 1960s has tamed the Douro's roar to a placid gurgle. The port trade is divided between the farmers who grow the grapes and the shippers who buy either grapes or young wine, though most also own some vineyards themselves. In the spring after the harvest the wine is usually taken from the wineries in the Douro Valley to Vila Nova de Gaia, facing Oporto at the mouth of the river where it is left to mature in the shippers' cellars or lodges. No pipes of port still make the traditional journey by boat to the lodges; instead, large tankers make the twisting road between Oporto and the Douro region hell for other motorists.

The climate in the Douro becomes hotter as you travel inland from west to east. The wet coastal climate that envelops Oporto never penetrates as far as the Douro wine region, stopped by the 1400-m (4600-ft) peaks of the Serra do Marão mountains. But there is more rainfall between Mesão Frio and Régua (the Baixa Corgo) than is good for really high-quality port, and not enough in the very hot, eastern Douro Superior, stretching 50km (30 miles) in from the Spanish border. The prime port zone is the Cima Corgo, centred on Pinhão, an area where many of the famous port houses have their quintas (estates).

Port is one of the most tightly controlled wines in the world and the production area was demarcated in 1756. Nowadays every one of the 85,000 vineyards is given a rating (from A to F); not all the Douro's grapes qualify to be made into port – a quota is established every year (using the *benefício* system) and the rest of the grapes are made into table wines under the Douro DOC. Nearly all the best ones are red and some of them are now among Portugal's most exciting new red wines. In the 1990s red Douro wines established a reputation in their own right and some now

Quinta do Crasto, enjoying a superb location overlooking the Douro river between Pinhão and Régua, is one of the new sensations of the region. Wine previously sold in bulk is now made into delicious, stylish ports and red table wines.

FERREIRA
First made in the 1950s, and only in outstanding years, Barca Velha was for many years until the 1980s the one great traditional Douro red table wine.

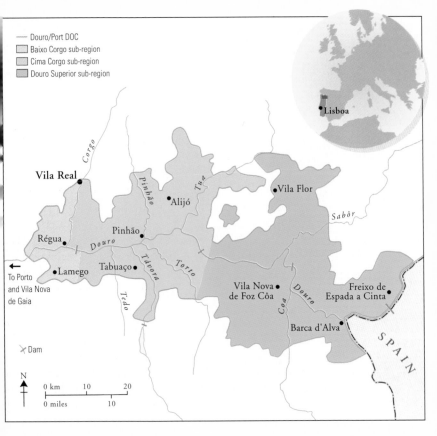

Legend:
- Douro/Port DOC
- Baixo Corgo sub-region
- Cima Corgo sub-region
- Douro Superior sub-region

QUINTA DO CRASTO
Australian David Baverstock is the inspired winemaker here, producing scented, fruit-drenched red wines as well as excellent vintage port.

RAMOS PINTO
This innovative port company now owned by Roederer, the Champagne house, makes marvellous aged tawnies, particularly Quinta do Bom-Retiro.

CHURCHILL
New port company established only in 1981 makes an excellent range across the board, including single-quinta Agua Alta.

command retail prices equivalent to LBV port. As a result, some producers are allocating high-quality grapes (that would have once been used to make port) for unfortified Douro wines. White grapes on the other hand have tended to lack the incisive natural acidity, although both Niepoort and Quinta do Côtto have succeeded in producing attractive, balanced, dry white wines.

REGIONAL ENTRIES
Douro, Port.

PRODUCER ENTRIES
Barros Almeida, Bright Bros., Burmester, Cálem, Churchill, Cockburn-Smithes, Quinta do Côtto, Quinta do Crasto, Croft, Delaforce, Dow, Ferreira, Fonseca Guimaraens, Graham, Martinez Gassiot, Niepoort, Quinta do Noval, Ramos Pinto, Quinta de la Rosa, Smith Woodhouse, Sogrape, Taylor, Fladgate & Yeatman, Quinta do Vesúvio, Warre.

QUINTA DO NOVAL
Long famous for its extraordinary Nacional port from ungrafted vines, Quinta do Noval has recently improved the rest of its port range including the vintage.

TAYLOR, FLADGATE & YEATMAN
This is the aristocrat of vintage ports, and also one of the longest-lived and highest priced, from a company over 300 years old and still going strong.

FONSECA
Owned by the same group as Taylor's, Fonseca makes ports in a rich, densely plummy style. 20-Year-Old Tawny is one of the best in the Fonseca range.

WARRE
Warre's aromatic figgy vintage port is consistently one of the best produced and is made for keeping.

DOURO DOC

PORTUGAL, Douro

♀ *Touriga Nacional, Touriga Francesa, Tinto Roriz (Tempranillo), Tinta Barroca, Tinto Cão and others*

♀ *Gouveio, Viosinho, Rabigato, Malvasia Fina, Donzelinho and others*

See also Douro, pages 162–163.

Although most people still think of the Douro region only in terms of PORT, it is being increasingly identified with unfortified wine which has its own DOC. Until recently, much of Douro's red wine was seen merely as a by-product of port (made from leftover grapes after the official authorization had been used up) but unfortified wines are now being made in their own right.

Following the outstanding success of FERREIRA's Barca Velha, along with relative newcomers like Quinta do CÔTTO, Quinta de la ROSA and NIEPOORT's Redoma, even some of the most die-hard port producers are now dabbling with reds. The grape varieties are the same as those used for port and, partly as a result of some rather heavy-handed winemaking in the past, many Douro wines used to be excessively tough and tannic. The younger generation of winemakers in the Douro (including some Australians) seems to have circumvented this problem and the recent trend has been towards full, fruit-driven reds, softened with a touch of new oak. The list of successful producers grows apace and, apart from the wines mentioned above, includes Quinta do CRASTO, Quinta de Gaivosa, Vinha do Fojo and Vallado. It can't be long before some of the other big port names join in alongside BARROS ALMEIDA, BURMESTER, COCKBURN, NOVAL and SOGRAPE. Best years: 1997, '96, '95, '94, '92, '91.

DOW

PORTUGAL, Douro, Port DOC

♀ *Tinta Roriz (Tempranillo), Tinta Barroca, Tinto Cão, Touriga Nacional, Touriga Francesa and others*

♀ *Gouveio, Viosinho, Rabigato, Malvasia Fina and others*

Dow is the brand name of Silva & Cosens, one of a number of PORT shippers belonging to the Symington family. The Symingtons are careful to maintain a separate identity for each of their firms and Dow's wines are based on the vineyards at Quinta do Bomfim near Pinhão. They tend to be slightly drier in style than those of either WARRE or GRAHAM (the other two main companies in the Symington fold) and Dow's vintages (which start out austerely tannic) have a reputation for their extraordinary longevity. This was proved by a tasting spanning over a century of Dow's ports, which was staged to commemorate the company's bicentenary in 1998. Since 1978, Quinta do Bomfim has been released as a single-quinta wine in years when a Dow vintage is not declared. Dow also produces a good premium ruby known as Trademark, a fine range of aged tawnies and a crusted port which is notable for its richness and intensity. Best years: (vintage ports) 1994, '91, '85, '83, '80, '77, '70, '66, '63.

DROMANA ESTATE

AUSTRALIA, Victoria, Port Phillip Zone, Mornington Peninsula

♀ *Cabernet Sauvignon, Merlot, Pinot Noir, Nebbiolo, Sangiovese, Barbera, Dolcetto*

♀ *Chardonnay*

The ever-restless Garry Crittenden, who started this model winery in 1982, is a unique combination of viticulturist, winemaker and marketer extraordinaire. He makes the more or less estate-based, high-priced Dromana Estate range; the mid-priced Schinus range (previously called Schinus Molle, the botanical name for pepper tree); and more recently and emphatically, the Garry Crittenden 'i' range, resplendent in Italy's national colours and offering four of the major Italian red grape varieties. The Schinus and 'i' ranges use grapes from here, there and everywhere, but not from the MORNINGTON PENINSULA. Best years: 1998, '97, '94, '92, '91, '90.

DROMANA ESTATE
Garry Crittenden uses the latest techniques at this model vineyard in Mornington Peninsula to make squeaky-clean, modern wines.

JOSEPH DROUHIN

FRANCE, Burgundy, Beaune

♀ *Pinot Noir, Gamay*

♀ *Chardonnay, Aligoté*

This is one of the most important Burgundy *négociant* houses, not only because of volume – usually about 330,000 cases a year, but also because, even in the darker times for quality in Burgundy, Drouhin wines maintained an integrity and personality, at, it must be said, a pretty high price.

Part of this is due to Drouhin's considerable holdings – 64ha (158 acres) in CHABLIS and CÔTE D'OR Premier and Grand Cru sites – and also because the current owner Robert Drouhin rightly saw that in a small region renowned like Burgundy, there will always be customers somewhere in the world who will be prepared to pay a premium, so long as the quality of the wine is guaranteed. The style is fairly elegant rather than exalted and powerful. BEAUNE Clos des Mouches, MONTRACHET and the Côte de Nuits Grands Crus are particularly good, but Drouhin wines from large appellations like RULLY, ST-AUBIN and straight Chablis are also very fine. Drouhin also owns DOMAINE DROUHIN in Oregon, USA. Best years: (reds) 1997, '96, '95, '93, '91, '90, '89, '88, '85, '83; (whites) 1996, '95, '93, '92, '90, '89, '88, '86, '85.

DRY CREEK VALLEY AVA

USA, California, Sonoma County

Almost all Dry Creek's narrow valley floor is vineyard, and hillside plantings continue to expand. Red grapes have dominated since the 1870s, and Zinfandel still leads. The major white variety is Sauvignon Blanc. Dry Creek Vineyards revived the area in the 1970s and is one of the best white producers there. Best producers: Dry Creek Vineyards, Duxoup, FERRARI-CARANO, Frick, GALLO, Lake Sonoma, Michel-Schlumberger, Nalle, Pedroncelli, Preston, QUIVIRA, RAFANELLI. Best years: 1997, '96, '95, '94, '92, '91.

GEORGES DUBOEUF

FRANCE, Burgundy, Beaujolais

♀♀ *Gamay*

♀ *Chardonnay*

Easily the most important of the BEAUJOLAIS merchants, Duboeuf was responsible more than any of the others for the worldwide popularization of Beaujolais during the 1970s and '80s. His marketing flair made BEAUJOLAIS NOUVEAU a chic wine, and his winemaking and wine selection skills kept its quality high even during periods when world demand outstripped supply. Often called the 'King' of Beaujolais, Georges Duboeuf controls about 12 per cent of the region's output, and is impressive at the top and bottom ends of the market. Particular successes are Duboeuf's Beaujolais cru wines, MOULIN-À-VENT, FLEURIE, JULIÉNAS and BROUILLY. Best years: 1998, '97, '96, '95, '94, '93, '91.

Georges Duboeuf comes from a family of white wine growers in the Mâconnais and, once again, in a period when Mâconnais

GEORGES DUBOEUF
Famous for his Beaujolais wines, Georges Duboeuf also specializes in excellent Mâconnais, including crisp, attractive St-Véran.

quality has largely veered between dubious and dull, Duboeuf wines have been consistently good. He has begun to produce RHÔNE wines too, with considerable success. Best years: 1997, '96, '95, '94, '93.

DUCKHORN VINEYARDS
USA, California, Napa County, Napa Valley AVA
♥ *Cabernet Sauvignon, Merlot*
♀ *Sauvignon Blanc*

Rather than try to make a name for himself in the crowded Cabernet Sauvignon market, Dan Duckhorn had the good sense to cast his lot with Merlot when he opened up shop in the late 1970s. His first Merlots – Three Palms and NAPA VALLEY – were pricy but captured richness and sufficient suppleness to provide welcome relief for jaded Cabernet fans. By today's standards these flavour-packed Merlots are more robust than subtle and often need about ten years' aging to soften. A HOWELL MOUNTAIN Merlot has joined the team. Quite brash when released, it too needs time for the wild berry and cherry fruit to shine through. A more approachable personality has surfaced in the Napa Valley Merlot. Best years: 1997, '96, '95, '94, '93, '92, '91. Duckhorn's Cabernets, brooding and intense when young, often develop faster, and sometimes more successfully than the Merlots. Best years: 1996, '95, '94, '93, '92, '90, '87, '86.

CH. DUCRU-BEAUCAILLOU
FRANCE, Bordeaux, Haut-Médoc, St-Julien AC, 2ème Cru Classé
♥ *Cabernet Sauvignon, Merlot, Cabernet Franc, Petit Verdot*

You really do get a feeling of quiet confidence as you gaze at this imposing nineteenth-century château owned by the Borie family. If this image also conjures up reliability, then this has been its reputation for many years. Until the late 1980s there hadn't been a single bad wine in more than 20 years, and in the 1970s this fact was recognized when the wine

consistently sold for higher prices than any other Second Growth. Ducru-Beaucaillou was one of the best Second Growths – and though the more showy, extrovert COS D'ESTOURNEL, LÉOVILLE-LAS-CASES and PICHON-LONGUEVILLE-COMTESSE DE LALANDE wines were also as good, many people preferred the fragrant cedar perfume, the soft, gently black-curranty fruit and the satisfying round sensation of Ducru-Beaucaillou. Since 1994 Ducru has once again been back on form. If you want to seek out the epitome of ST-JULIEN, mixing charm and austerity, fruit and firmness, this is where you'll find it. Second wine: Ch. la Croix-Beaucaillou. Best years: 1998, '97, '96, '95, '94, '86, '85, '83, '82, '81, '78, '75, '70, '66, '62, '61.

DOMAINE DUJAC
FRANCE, Burgundy, Côte de Nuits, Morey-St-Denis AC
♥ *Pinot Noir*
♀ *Chardonnay*

In the late 1960s the young Jacques Seysses gave up a business career to devote himself to wine. He bought a small estate in MOREY-ST-DENIS, which has been gradually expanded over the years. The holdings are impressive, with Grands Crus such as CLOS DE LA ROCHE, CLOS ST-DENIS, BONNES-MARES, Charmes-Chambertin and ÉCHÉZEAUX, as well as Premiers Crus in CHAMBOLLE-MUSIGNY and GEVREY-CHAMBERTIN.

Seysses and his long-term vineyard manager, Christophe Morin, are increasingly preoccupied with the vineyards, even to the extent, in a hail-damaged vineyard, of removing affected grapes with tweezers to prevent the spread of rot. During the 1980s, when most Burgundian winemakers were seeking ever greater extraction and colour, Seysses was going in the opposite direction. He has never been one to accept conventional wisdom. To this day, he retains stems during fermentation, arguing that this does not, as is often thought, increase tannins, but can help reduce them. Although almost all his wines are aged entirely in new oak, which is air-dried to his specifications, he does not look for oaky flavours in his wines and thus specifies a light toast. The wines are bottled without filtration. They are deceptively light in colour, but do not lack flavour or structure and can age very well. There are few Burgundies that more perfectly capture the charm and complexity of Pinot Noir at its most elegant. Seysses also makes a small quantity of white Morey-St-Denis. Best years: 1997, '96, '95, '93, '92, '90, '89, '88, '87, '85, '83, '82.

DUNN VINEYARDS
USA, California, Napa County, Howell Mountain AVA
♥ *Cabernet Sauvignon*

Whether he planned it or not, Randy Dunn thrives on the mystique surrounding the HOWELL MOUNTAIN appellation and himself as a winemaker. Dunn made CAYMUS's wines between 1975 and 1985, and then retreated to Howell Mountain on the eastern side of NAPA VALLEY to work with a small Cabernet vineyard and produce his famous, perfumed but brawny Howell Mountain wine.

Grapes from the Napa Valley floor make up a somewhat softer and more accessible Napa Valley bottling which is also rich and aggressive, but which captures a fragrance rare for Napa Valley. Dark, concentrated in black-currant and plum fruit, his wines develop very slowly, but that hasn't stopped them achieving cult status. Best years: 1996, '95, '94, '93, '92, '91, '90, '88, '87, '86, '85, '84.

DURBACH
GERMANY, Baden

In contrast to many of Germany's wine regions, BADEN is usually thought of as being wine co-operative country, with many small growers and few lordly estates, but the village of Durbach, in the Ortenau district south of Baden-Baden, is practically wall-to-wall aristocrats. Between them they make a lot of red wine, which is not so unusual for Baden, but the village also claims to have more Traminer or Pinot Blanc planted than any other village in Germany – and to confuse the issue they call the Traminer grape here 'Clevner'.

Durbach is known for its Riesling, too, unlike the rest of Baden, only here it is called Klingelberger. The poor granitic soil and steep inclines suit the Riesling just fine; accordingly, it flings plenty of spice and structure into its wines. Best producers: Andreas Laible, Heinrich Männle, von Neveu, Schloss Staufenberg, Wolff-Metternich.

DÜRNSTEIN
AUSTRIA, Niederösterreich, Wachau

This picturesque small town on the Danube still has the extensive medieval defences built with the ransom money extracted for the return of Richard the Lionheart, King Of England, in 1192. Today it occupies itself with the more peaceful businesses of tourism and wine. Not only does the town boast two of the region's finest vineyard estates in the Kellerberg and Schütt, it is also home to the producer Schmidl and the remarkable co-operative, the Freie Weingärtner WACHAU.

ÉCHÉZEAUX AC, GRANDS-ÉCHÉZEAUX AC

FRANCE, Burgundy, Côte de Nuits, Grands Crus
🍷 *Pinot Noir*

Of all the Grands Crus in the CÔTE DE NUITS, Échézeaux is the one with the least reputation. However, it can be a subtly powerful wine, developing a seductive raspberry and chocolate perfume as it ages. The smaller and more prestigious Grand Cru of Grands-Échézeaux (so-called apparently because the rows of vines here are longer) gives deeper, richer wine, still showing a core of raspberry and chocolate fruit, but smokier in flavour, more plum-rich. It can age to a marvellous gamy, chocolaty welter of flavours over ten to 15 years. Best years: 1997, '96, '95, '93, '91, '90, '89, '88, '85, '78. Best producers: Clerget, DROUHIN, DUJAC, ENGEL, GRIVOT, JAYER, Mongeard-Mugneret, Domaine de la ROMANÉE-CONTI, Sirugue.

EDEN VALLEY

AUSTRALIA, South Australia, Barossa Zone

After a 20-year tug of war between the ADELAIDE HILLS and the BAROSSA VALLEY, tradition and history have prevailed over geography and climate, and the Eden Valley has been joined with the Barossa Valley in the Barossa Zone, and excised from the Mount Lofty Ranges Zone. And so what? The fact is this undulating, windswept region produces some of Australia's best, racy, steely Riesling and is home to the country's most famous single-vineyard Shiraz, HENSCHKE Hill of Grace. Wine style and quality are significantly affected by altitude and by site orientation; virtually any combination can be found. Best years: 1998, '97, '96, '94, '93, '92, '91, '90. Best producers: Heggies, Henschke, Hill-Smith Estate, MOUNTADAM, Pewsey Vale.

EDNA VALLEY AVA

USA, California, San Luis Obispo County

One of the coolest regions within CALIFORNIA's Central Coast, Edna Valley is a small coastal area south-east of San Luis Obispo town. Cooling ocean breezes make much of the area ideal for Chardonnay, the most widely planted variety, but more protected pockets have proved suitable for Pinot Noir as well as for Viognier and other RHÔNE grapes. EDNA VALLEY VINEYARD is the largest producer and its partner, Paragon Vineyards, with 240ha (600 acres), is the biggest single vineyard. Best producers: Alban, Corbett Canyon, Edna Valley Vineyard, MERIDIAN, Talley. Best years: 1997, '96, '95, '94, '92.

EDNA VALLEY VINEYARD

USA, California, San Luis Obispo County, Edna Valley AVA
🍷 *Pinot Noir*
🍷 *Chardonnay*

The winery is a joint venture of CHALONE, which provides the winemaking skills, and Paragon Vineyards, which contributes the grapes. In its relatively short history (since 1980), Edna Valley Vineyard has earned a substantial reputation for Chardonnays patterned directly on those of its winemaking parent, with richly toasty to outright buttery flavours coupled with attractively Burgundian, lean-limbed textures. Best years: 1997, '96, '95, '94, '92, '91, '90, '88, '87. The Pinot Noirs, marked by the vegetative regional flavours in the early vintages, are now attractive in a light style.

NEIL ELLIS

SOUTH AFRICA, Western Cape, Stellenbosch WO
🍷 *Cabernet Sauvignon, Merlot, Pinotage and others*
🍷 *Sauvignon Blanc, Chardonnay, Rhine Riesling (Rhine/Weisser Riesling) and others*

Neil Ellis is one of South Africa's top winemakers, and like other serious producers from that country, his wines are making an impact abroad. His goal has always been to reflect site specificity and to this end he sources grapes from far and wide. The cool, apple-orchard heights of Elgin provide him with a penetrating Sauvignon Blanc, elegant Chardonnay and, more recently, a silky, well-oaked Pinot Noir. A weightier, succulent Sauvignon Blanc comes from Groenkloof on the West Coast, while the warmer STELLENBOSCH area yields more Chardonnay as well as Cabernet, Merlot, Pinotage and the latest attraction, Shiraz. All the reds are balanced and sensitively oaked. The whole winemaking operation is now carried out under one Stellenbosch roof in the picturesque Jonkershoek Valley. The attractive, modernized cellar boasts a unique cooling feature in the barrel maturation area; a waterfall and stream running through it. Best years: (reds) 1996, '95, '94, '93, '92, '91, '90; (whites) 1998, '97, '96, '95, '94, '93, '92, '91.

NEIL ELLIS
This intense Cabernet Sauvignon, with deep, spicy blackcurrant perfume and warm ripe flavour, comes from warmer Stellenbosch vineyards.

ELTVILLE

GERMANY, Rheingau

This RHEINGAU town on the banks of the Rhine west of Wiesbaden doesn't have quite the reputation of some of its illustrious neighbours. Eltville's vineyards tend to be sloping rather than precipitous but it is home to a number of good producers, among them Becker, Fischer, Hans Hulbert and the Staatsweingut Eltville.

EMILIA-ROMAGNA

ITALY

Despite their political unity, there is a good case for considering Emilia and Romagna separately, so diverse are their wines. The vast plains of Emilia are home to the LAMBRUSCO grape, which flourishes on its ubiquitous high trellises in Emilia around Modena and Reggio Emilia and further afield. The flatlands of Romagna also bring forth grapes in equally astonishing abundance, this time in the form of Sangiovese and Trebbiano.

In the foothills of the Apennines, however, from COLLI PIACENTINI in the west via the COLLI BOLOGNESI in the centre almost down to the Adriatic in the east there is viticulture of real and increasing worth, with quality Sangiovese rubbing shoulders with the likes of Cabernet and Chardonnay, not to mention the indigenous Albana (see ALBANA DI ROMAGNA) and Pagadebit white grapes and red Barbarossa and Cagnina.

EMRICH-SCHÖNLEBER

GERMANY, Nahe, Monzingen
🍷 *Riesling, Pinot Gris (Grauburgunder), Müller-Thurgau (Rivaner)*

Werner Schönleber is the leading winemaker of the Upper NAHE, making Rieslings with a crystalline clarity and intense peach and currant aromas. His top site is the Halenberg of Monzingen which has a slate soil similar to that of the MOSEL, and produces similar, if slightly bigger wines. The Frühlingsplätzchen wines are softer and more juicy. There is good dry Grauburgunder and Rivaner, too. Best years: 1998, '97, '95, '94, '93, '92, '90.

ENATE

SPAIN, Aragón, Somontano DO
🍷 *Tempranillo, Cabernet Sauvignon, Merlot*
🍷 *Cabernet Sauvignon*
🍷 *Chardonnay, Gewürztraminer*

This visually stunning new winery, isolated in the foothills of the Pyrénées, is aiming to become the quality leader in the reborn region of SOMONTANO, despite its large size

Much of the wine from the Entre-Deux-Mers region comes from large co-operatives, but the quality has improved dramatically in recent years. However, new oak barrels for fermenting the wine are still a rarity.

(300ha/740 acres under vines and 120,000 cases produced in an average year). Enologist Jesús Artajona, who gained prestige during a prior stint with TORRES, is one of the main reasons why Viñedos y Crianzas del Alto Aragón (Enate's official full name) has made such vast strides since its first vintage in 1992. The winery specializes in fruit-laden Chardonnays and refined, consumer-friendly reds led by the Reserva Chillida, a Merlot-Cabernet Sauvignon blend. The young, aromatic Gewürztraminer has been an unexpected hit in Spain. Best years: 1995, '94, '93.

RENÉ ENGEL
FRANCE, Burgundy, Côte de Nuits, Vosne-Romanée AC
🍷 *Pinot Noir*
When Philippe Engel took over the family estate in the mid-1980s, he knew it was in serious need of improvements. These he has brought about, and Engel is once again one of the leading domaines in this prized corner of the Côte de Nuits. His clutch of Grands Crus includes CLOS VOUGEOT, ÉCHÉZEAUX and Grands-Échézeaux, and there is also the exceptional VOSNE-ROMANÉE Cru, Les Brûlées. Philippe Engel has introduced greater grape selection at harvest and more punching down of the cap during fermentation, and has almost eliminated filtration. He likes to use a good deal of new oak, especially for the robust Grands Crus. Best years: 1997, '96, '95, '93, '90, '89, '88, '87, '85.

ENTRE-DEUX-MERS AC
FRANCE, Bordeaux
🍷 *Sémillon, Sauvignon Blanc, Muscadelle*
The phoenix has risen from the ashes. Thirty years ago Entre-Deux-Mers was a byword for boring, fruitless, vaguely sweet white wines of the sort that could put you off drinking for life. But in the 1980s there was a dramatic about-turn, and Entre-Deux-Mers now produces some of the freshest, brightest, snappiest dry white wine in the whole of France. The AC only covers dry white wines, on average 18 million bottles annually. Red wines are produced extensively in the region but they can only use the BORDEAUX Rouge or BORDEAUX SUPÉRIEUR AC.

The wine flavours are totally dry, grassy, appley, sometimes citrus, often with a little more weight than straight Bordeaux Blanc AC. A few properties use new oak barrels for aging, rarely for fermenting, and this adds a creamy, apricotty flavour to the wine, which can be delicious. In general, drink the wine of the latest vintage, though the better wines will last a year or two, particularly when aged or fermented in barrel. The sweet wines are sold under the following appellations: PREMIÈRES CÔTES DE BORDEAUX, Côtes de Bordeaux-St-Macaire, LOUPIAC and STE-CROIX-DU-MONT.

Much of the wine is made by modern co-operatives, but there are some excellent private producers too. Best producers: Arromans, Bonnet, Canet, Castelneau, Castenet-Greffier, de Fontenille, Moulin-de-Launay, Nardique la Gravière, Rauzan-Despagne, Ste-Marie, Thieuley, Tour de Mirambeau, Toutigeac, Turcaud.

ERBACH
GERMANY, Rheingau
This village in the heart of the RHEINGAU produces firm, racy and weighty wines. Some of the biggest and fullest in the region come from the Marcobrunn vineyard, a piece of land which the passer-by would probably dismiss as being obviously unsuitable for fine wine – it's at the foot of the hill, right down by the river, it's far too low, the soil too rich, it looks like a frost-trap and it probably turns to a quagmire after rain. But you would be wrong on all counts. The deep, marl soil is very well-drained and the vineyard is a suntrap rather than a frost-trap. Part of it lies within the boundaries of the neighbouring village of HATTENHEIM, but good Erbach growers include Freiherr zu Knyphausen and SCHLOSS REINHARTSHAUSEN.

ERBALUCE DI CALUSO DOC, CALUSO PASSITO DOC
ITALY, Piedmont
🍷 *Erbaluce*
North of Turin, around the Olivetti town of Ivrea, is a strip of vineyards cultivated with Erbaluce. Its lean, flinty dry white wines and occasional sparklers, both called Erbaluce di Caluso, aren't bad, if not exactly earth shattering. But when the grapes are laid out to partially dry for up to six months before slowly fermenting, followed by aging for at least five years, a rich, sweet, citrus, creamy wine called Caluso Passito emerges, which just might make the earth quiver a bit. Best producers: Cieck, Orsolani, Luigi Ferrando. Drink the dry wines young.

ERDEN
GERMANY, Mosel-Saar-Ruwer
The slopes behind the village of Erden are broad and gentle and planted largely with Müller-Thurgau rather than with the superior Riesling. Although they can give pleasant wines, they are nowhere near being the MOSEL's finest. For top Riesling, full of fire and breeding, you must swim the river and scale the slope just where it suddenly becomes steeper opposite the village: this is the brilliant Prälat vineyard. Just above it and to the east is the Treppchen vineyard, another steep Riesling site, and not to be confused with the identically-named Treppchen vineyard at PIESPORT (also, confusingly, in the

Mosel). Best producers: Joh. Jos. CHRISTOF-FEL, Dr LOOSEN, Meulenhof, Mönchhof, Peter Nicolay, Dr PAULY-BERGWEILER.

ERRÁZURIZ
CHILE, Aconcagua Valley
🍷 *Cabernet Sauvignon, Merlot*
🍷 *Sauvignon Blanc, Chardonnay*

There can be no doubt that Errázuriz is one of Chile's towering wine establishments. The combination of Ed Flaherty (formerly of CONO SUR) as winemaker and Pedro Izquierdo, viticulturist, is a red-hot one. The bodega's prime location, on the Panquehue slopes in the Aconcagua Valley, allows it to grow some of the best Cabernet Sauvignon in Chile. Its Merlot and Wild Ferment Chardonnay are two of Chile's trailblazers. A new joint venture with Robert MONDAVI has produced a BORDEAUX-blend, Sena, now one of Chile's most expensive red wines. Best years: 1998, '97, '96, '95.

ESPORÃO
PORTUGAL, Alentejo, Reguengos DOC
🍷 *Aragonés (Tempranillo), Cabernet Sauvignon, Periquita, Trincadeira, Moreto and others*
🍷 *Arinto, Antão Vaz, Roupeiro, Perrum and others*

After a chequered start in the 1970s, Herdade do Esporão has emerged as one of the ALEN-TEJO's leading producers. Much of its success is due to the visionary businessman, José Roquette, and the winemaker, Australian David Baverstock. Extending to around 500ha (1235 acres), Esporão, boasts the largest single vineyard in Portugal. A modern winery produces a number of different red and white wines, from Esporão, through the middle-ranking Monte Velho to the young, fruity Alandra. All are meticulously well-made. Some of the best wines are varietals from Aragonês and Trincadeira, illustrating the huge potential of Portugal's indigenous grapes. Best years: (reds) 1997, '95, '94.

ESPORÃO
This firm yet supple red wine is typical of the many good-quality wines now coming from the Alentejo region of Portugal.

EST! EST!! EST!!! DI MONTEFIASCONE DOC
ITALY, Lazio
🍷 *Trebbiano Toscano, Malvasia Bianca, Trebbiano Giallo*

This wine, from a zone in the north of LAZIO on the UMBRIAn border, no doubt owes such fame as it enjoys more to the apocryphal and ridiculous story about how it was discovered by some bibulous bishop in the twelfth century than to its quality, which, seeing as it is principally made from the hopelessly boring Trebbiano, will never be anything more than simple and refreshing. The producers Falesco and Mazziotti are making the greatest efforts to defeat the odds against them.

CH. DES ESTANILLES
FRANCE, Languedoc-Roussillon, Faugères AC
🍷 *Syrah, Mourvèdre, Grenache and others*
🍷 *Marsanne, Roussanne, Viognier*

Michel Louison has single-handedly turned this estate into one of the top domaines in the LANGUEDOC-ROUSSILLON. Arriving from TOURAINE via Switzerland in 1976, he steadily planted Syrah, Mourvèdre and Grenache and now has 25ha (62 acres) of vines. Syrah, though, is his preferred variety and is used on its own in his top wine, Cuvée Syrah, a spicy, oaky, blackcurranty wine that needs a minimum five years' age. The Cuvée Prestige is a well-balanced blend of Syrah, Cinsaut, Grenache and Mourvèdre and there is also a fruity, aromatic white COTEAUX DU LANGUE-DOC that is partially barrel-fermented. Best years: (reds) 1997, '96, '95, '94, '90.

ESTREMADURA VINHO REGIONAL
PORTUGAL
🍷 *Alfrocheiro Preto, Cabernet Sauvignon, Camarate, Periquita, Tinta Miuda and others*
🍷 *Arinto, Chardonnay, Esgana Cão, Fernão Pires, Jampal, Malvasia Rei, Tamarez, Vital and others*

The rolling country on the Atlantic coast north of Lisbon is among the most productive in Portugal. For many years it was the preserve of huge co-operatives, which churned out large quantities of bland red and white wine for consumption in the nearby capital. Although Estremadura remains as Portugal's largest single wine-producing region in terms of volume, quality has improved such that it is now an excellent source of value-for-money wines. As in much of Portugal, red tends to be better than white. Brands like Ramada, Alta Mesa and Orla Maritima all come from the same co-operative vat and proffer character at a modest price. Much of the transformation is

down to the roving, locally trained wine-maker José Neiva. His best wines are undoubtedly those from the Companhia das Vinhas de São Domingos, masquerading under the names of Espiga, Palha Canas and Quinta de Setencostas. The Australian wine-maker Peter BRIGHT has also been making some good, spicy reds in conjunction with a co-operative in the region and there are two excellent single quintas, Abrigada and Pancas, both near the town of Alenquer. Pancas has made headway with both Cabernet Sauvignon and Chardonnay. All the wines from this region are for drinking young.

ETCHART
ARGENTINA, Salta and Mendoza
🍷 *Cabernet Sauvignon, Malbec*
🍷 *Chardonnay, Torrontés*

Bodegas Etchart have two main centres, one in MENDOZA and another in Cafayate, SALTA. The best wines come from Salta and enologist José Luis Mounier is striving to improve the range even further. The Torrontés is Argentina's most delicate and accessible (go for the latest vintage) white wine. Through immaculate vineyard care and site selection he has also achieved good flavour extraction from high-altitude vines, (Salta may have the world's highest commercial vineyards), especially Cabernet Sauvignon and Malbec. The blockbuster Arnaldo B Etchart Reserva blend can be deep and mature, but has been susceptible to bad storage. For that reason it is best to choose a 1997 or later, although if you find a 1993, buy it just in case. It can be glorious.

ETNA DOC
ITALY, Sicily
🍷🍷 *Nerello Mascalese, Nerello Cappuccio and others*
🍷 *Carricante, Catarratto, Trebbiano, Minella Bianca*

Etna's fruit in general is greatly prized – the flavour of its apricots, plums, lemons and so on is famous – but its wines remain stubbornly lacklustre, no doubt in part because of the generally unremarkable grape varieties grown here (nor has the introduction of Cabernet helped much). The vineyards grow on the sides of the volcano, facing east only, forming a long, narrow crescent at an altitude of 500–1000m (1640–3280ft), much chillier than down on the coast. Traditional red Etna, a harsh, tannic, acidic assault on the senses, has almost disappeared, together with the earthy, flat white. Wines of more direct appeal are coming from Benanti, Tenuta di Castiglione, Barone Scamacca and Barone di

Villagrande – perhaps the most interesting thing here is the sight of a huge 250-year-old chestnut barrel, still in use.

L'ÉTOILE AC
FRANCE, Jura
♀ *Savagnin, Chardonnay, Poulsard*

L'Étoile – the star – is a lovely name for a tiny little area in the centre of the CÔTES DU JURA which has its own AC for white wines and *vin jaune* only. The local Savagnin grape is much in evidence, though less so than further north in the region, and there is a good deal of Chardonnay, either unblended – when it is light and fresh, but creamy – or blended with Savagnin, when it succeeds in soothing the savage character of the grape. The red Poulsard variety can also be part of the white wine blend.

In general the wines are cleaner and fruitier than most Côtes du Jura or ARBOIS whites, and the CHAMPAGNE-method fizz, l'Étoile Mousseux (now called CRÉMANT DU JURA), can be as good as that of Pupillin in ARBOIS. There is also the daunting *vin jaune*, a sherry-like 'yellow' wine made from Savagnin, and even the very rare sweet *vin de paille*. Best producers: Ch. de l'Étoile, l'Étoile co-operative, Domaine de Montbourgeau.

CH. L'EVANGILE
FRANCE, Bordeaux, Pomerol AC
♂ *Merlot, Cabernet Franc*

A neighbour to PÉTRUS and CHEVAL BLANC, l'Evangile is undoubtedly one of the top Pomerols and, of course, has a price tag to match. The Merlot-dominated wines from this 14-ha (35-acre) estate are big, rich and powerful, with layers of exotic fruit and spicy complexity. They need a minimum ten years' bottle age but good vintages will mature for 20 years or more. Since being acquired by the Rothschilds of Ch. LAFITE-ROTHSCHILD in 1990, l'Evangile has produced a string of vintages that even the great Pétrus would find hard to rival for quality and consistency. Best years: 1998, '97, '96, '95, '94, '93, '90, '89, '88, '86, '85, '83, '82.

EVANS & TATE
AUSTRALIA, Western Australia, South West Australia Zone, Margaret River
♂ *Syrah (Shiraz), Merlot, Cabernet Sauvignon*
♀ *Semillon, Sauvignon Blanc, Chardonnay*

Having started life in the SWAN Valley with its Gnangara Shiraz-Cabernet, transforming the then-prevalent disdain for the Swan Valley, Evans & Tate has now moved its operations to the MARGARET RIVER, where it has grown at

EVANS & TATE
Aromatic and stylish Semillon is one of an impressive range of wines from this important Western Australian winery which relocated to the Margaret River region in 1997.

an exponential rate. Fine, gently herbaceous, subtly oaked Semillon; Classic Dry White with sweetness and acidity as cleverly counterplayed as salt and pepper by a three-star chef; svelte, midweight, tangy Chardonnay; and increasingly complex and powerful Shiraz, Merlot and Cabernet Sauvignon make an impressive roster. Best years: 1997, '96, '95, '94, '93, '92, '91.

ÉVENTAIL DES VIGNERONS PRODUCTEURS
FRANCE, Burgundy, Beaujolais, Beaujolais AC
♂ *Gamay*

This group of leading BEAUJOLAIS producers collaborates on such matters as bottling, storage and distribution. But each producer vinifies his own wine, so that the differences in origin and style between each grower remain intact. In general, membership of the Éventail guarantees sound quality; the top domaines in the group include Pelletier in JULIÉNAS, Georges Passot in CHIROUBLES and Louis Desvignes in MORGON. Best years: 1998, '97, '96, '95, '94.

EXTREMADURA
SPAIN

Since 1997 a single DO, Ribera del Guadiana, has encompassed the large surface (87,000ha/ 214,890 acres) which vineyards occupy on the vast plains of Extremadura – near the Spanish-Portuguese border – in competition with cork trees and pastures for black-hooved Iberian pigs, Merino sheep and Retinto cattle. There is no geographic or climatic unity of 'origin' in such a large region and this is clearly one of those 'political' macro-appellations which are sprouting up in Europe to counteract the market advantages which New World exporters, who are not saddled with stringent EU regulations, have enjoyed. The newcomers

are led by such established bodegas as Inviosa, whose Lar de Barros wines sell well both in Spain and abroad. Investment is leading to fast winery modernization and vineyard improvement. Modern winemaking is bringing out unexpected quality from such indigenous varieties as the white Cayetana and Pardina but the DO recognizes many cultivars – local, northern Spanish and French.

THE EYRIE VINEYARDS
USA, Oregon, Yamhill County, Willamette Valley AVA
♂ *Pinot Noir, Pinot Meunier*
♀ *Chardonnay, Pinot Gris*

Owner David Lett was one of the pioneers of OREGON winemaking, planting vines in 1966, and still has lessons to teach about finesse and restraint. His was a make-do operation to begin with – housed in an old turkey-processing plant, and equipped with cast-off tanks from dairies. It is still in the same building, but today the equipment is a little more up to date.

His style of winemaking is spare; even by Oregon standards his Pinot Noirs are a shade pale, lean in texture, with understated – sometimes too understated – varietal aromas. A reserve Pinot Noir made from the South Block parcel of the original vineyard is seldom seen, but can be worth the hunt. Pinot Gris and Chardonnay are individualistic wines – but David Lett came to Oregon to avoid the mainstream, so that's what you should expect. Best years: (Pinot Noir and Chardonnay) 1996, '95, '94, '92, '91, '90, '85.

FABRE MONTMAYOU
ARGENTINA, Mendoza
♂ *Malbec*
♀ *Chardonnay*

What happens when you blend French *savoir faire* with perfectly toned Argentine brawn? Fabre Montmayou, more commonly known as Domaine Vistalba (or Temporada – the name given to some of the wines) is a result of just this sort of marriage. The outcome? Due to the perfect location of the vineyards at 850m (2790ft) above sea level in Luján de Cuyo, this pretty little bodega makes enjoyable Malbec. Chardonnay is another strong point. Domaine Vistalba is the more up-market brand, but for all its humble appearance, Temporada Malbec is one of the unoaked stars of the Malbec firmament. Winemaker Armand Meillan has a delicate touch with wood (an important skill to possess as too much oak can easily coarsen Malbec's brilliant perfumed fruit), which is particularly visible in the Grand Vin range. Best years: 1997, '96.

FAIRVIEW

SOUTH AFRICA, Western Cape, Paarl WO

♟ *Cabernet Sauvignon, Syrah (Shiraz), Merlot, Pinotage and others*

♀ *Chardonnay, Chenin Blanc, Semillon and others*

Charles Back would undoubtedly be proud of his namesake and grandson, who now runs this farm with enormous energy and success, using new varieties and unconventional styles or blends which are seriously good value for money. The warm, south-west-facing vineyards favour full-bodied reds such as Shiraz, Pinotage, Cabernet Sauvignon and Merlot but the unusual Zinfandel-Cinsaut blend is invariably the richest of the lot. Charles Back coaxes a delicious fruity balance in these wines by throwing a percentage of whole bunches in the fermentation vat, a sort of mini carbonic maceration.

Among the white wines, Chardonnay and Semillon, a Back favourite, are consistently notable, but the maiden vintage of Viognier, a South African first too, stole the show in 1998 with its rich texture and peachy/honeysuckle aromas. A farm in the Swartland has now extended the scope, especially for whites. It is here, also, that The Spice Route Wine Company, Back's venture with his co-directors, THELEMA's Gyles Webb, well-known wine writer John Platter, and wine marketing man Jabulani Ntshangase, is based. Best years: (reds) 1998, '97, '96, '95, '94, '93, '92, '91; (whites) 1998, '97, '96, '95, '94, '93, '92, '91.

JOSEPH FAIVELEY

FRANCE, Burgundy, Nuits-St-Georges

♟ *Pinot Noir*

♀ *Chardonnay*

François Faiveley, who has been running this *négociant* business for over two decades, often has a worried look. It's hard to know why, since the quality here has long been outstanding. Like many other Burgundy *négociants*, Faiveley is also the owner of some magnificent Grand Cru vineyards, invariably the source of his greatest wines: Clos de Bèze, Mazis-Chambertin, CLOS VOUGEOT and CORTON Clos des Cortons.

Faiveley takes enormous pains to ensure his wines are of the highest quality the vintage will permit. He was one of the first to introduce a *tapis de triage*, a moving belt on which grapes can be sorted on reception at the winery, and most of his top wines are bottled

The ruins of the medieval Ch. de Fargues loom over the vineyards owned by the Lur-Saluces family, who were until recently also owners of Ch. d'Yquem.

without filtration direct from the barrel. Some wines are aged entirely in new oak, and need several years to lose their youthful tannic grip. Faiveley also owns substantial vineyards in MERCUREY and has an infectious enthusiasm for this often under-valued region. Usually his Mercurey bottlings, which include many single vineyards, have the robustness without the coarseness that can mar wines from this village. Other superb wines include a powerful CORTON-CHARLE-MAGNE, and a rich red from the exclusively owned Premier Cru, NUITS-ST-GEORGES Clos de la Maréchale. Best years: 1997, '96, '95, '93, '91, '90, '89, '88, '85, '82.

FALERNO DEL MASSICO DOC

ITALY, Campania

♟ *Aglianico, Primitivo, Piedirosso*

♀ *Falanghina*

The most fabled wine of the ancient Romans was Falernum. The nearest we can get to it is Falerno, recreated after years of patient ploughing through ancient texts by the Avallone family, whose Villa Matilde estate is now synonymous with the wine.

White Falerno is a creamy wine with perfumes of roses and raspberries and an underlying herbiness. The cru version, Vigna Caracci, is richer and more complex.

Red Falerno is a delicious mix of slightly sour-tinged red fruits, cinnamon and a touch of earthiness. Even better, spicier and gutsier is Cecubo, made mainly from Piedirosso, and Villa Matilde's reincarnation of another Roman gem, Caecubum. Vigna Camarato is a punchy, long-lived cru from Aglianico and made only in the best vintages. All the reds are improving in quality and aging capability from year to year. Best years: 1998, '97, '96, '95, '93.

FAR NIENTE WINERY

USA, California, Napa County, Napa Valley AVA

♟ *Cabernet Sauvignon*

♀ *Chardonnay*

Proprietor Gil Nickel arrived in CALIFORNIA from Oklahoma and made his presence felt quickly. The impressive collection of Bentleys and the vast maze of aging cellars make their points. Far Niente's Cabernets, with a dollop of Merlot and Cabernet Franc, are for collectors with a long life expectancy. Their Chardonnays have always been rich, opulent, broad-flavoured wines – even when such wines have been out of vogue in California – but the high price they sell for show that there are still a lot of people prepared to pay for flavour rather than fashion. Best years: 1997, '96, '95, '94, '92, '91, '90, '87, '86, '85.

CH. DE FARGUES

FRANCE, Bordeaux, Sauternes AC, Cru Bourgeois

♀ *Sémillon, Sauvignon Blanc*

The most remarkable thing about Ch. de Fargues is that, even though it is a mere Bour-

geois Growth, it regularly sells for more than any other wine in the AC save the great Ch. d'YQUEM. It is owned by the Lur-Saluces family, formerly of Yquem. The vineyard – 15ha (37 acres) on the edge of the SAUTERNES AC in the village of Fargues – is by no means ideal, and the quality of the wine is more a tribute to the commitment of the Lur-Saluces family than to the inherent quality of the estate. The vines ripen around ten days later than at Yquem, and the selection of grapes is so strict that each vine only yields two-thirds of a glass of wine. The result is that the total production rarely exceeds 10,000 bottles of rich, reasonably exotic wine, very honeyed, indeed almost syrupy, with something of the taste of pineapples and peaches, and a viscous feel, like lanolin, which coats your mouth. This is fine, rich wine but there are several Classed Growths which are better, and less expensive. Best years: 1998, '97, '96, '95, '94, '90, '89, '88, '86, '83, '81, '80, '76, '75.

FAUGÈRES AC

FRANCE, Languedoc-Roussillon
♦ *Carignan, Grenache, Cinsaut, Syrah*
♀ *Clairette, Bourboulenc, Grenache Blanc, Marsanne*

Faugères was the first of the communes in the LANGUEDOC area to create a reputation of its own. For a year or two at the beginning of the 1980s it was the new buzz wine of the Paris bistros, and duly received its AC status in 1982. Luckily the wine is good and well deserves its AC. It's almost entirely red, and comes from hilly vineyards in seven little villages just north of Béziers. Annual production is about seven million bottles. What marks it out from other Languedoc reds is its ripe, soft, rather plummy flavour, and though it's a little more expensive than neighbouring wines, the extra money is well worth it.

Faugères has the terrain to make good white wine too, but so far production is relatively insignificant. Of course, if your only white grape is the dullish Clairette there's not an awful lot you can do and the best results until recently have come from winemakers who have picked the grapes early, fermented the juice cold and then sold the wines for drinking as young as possible. One or two more progressive growers have planted Bourboulenc, Grenache Blanc, Marsanne, Roussanne and Rolle, which is beginning to produce wines with a lot more character. Best years: 1998, '96, '95, '94, '93, '90, '89. Best producers: ALQUIER, ESTANILLES, Faugères co-operative, du Fraisse, Grézan, Haut-Fabrègues, la Liquière, St-Antonin.

FAUSTINO MARTÍNEZ

SPAIN, País Vasco and Rioja, Rioja DOC, Cava DO
♦ ♀ *Grenache Noir (Garnacha Tinta), Carignan (Cariñena, Mazuelo), Graciano*
♀ *Macabeo (Viura)*

Excellent Reservas and Gran Reservas are the specialities of this large, family-owned RIOJA bodega, though all its wines are good. The reds start with a delicious, fresh Viña Joven or Viña Faustina, made by fermenting the grapes uncrushed, BEAUJOLAIS-style. The strawberry-scented Faustino V Reserva and deep, rich, spicy Faustino I Gran Reserva rate among Rioja's best. The whites are fair, the CAVAS pleasant, simple and honeyed. Faustino Martínez also owns Bodegas Vitorianas, makers of Don Darias and Don Hugo – oaky, Rioja-like table wines, sold to enthusiastic hordes at ultra-keen prices. Best years: (reds) 1995, '94, '92, '91, '90, '89, '87, '85, '82.

FAUSTINO MARTÍNEZ
This family-owned Rioja company makes good, traditional, scented, oak-dominated Reserva and rich, powerful Gran Reserva red Riojas as well as other wines.

FEILER-ARTINGER

AUSTRIA, Burgenland, Neusiedlersee-Hügelland, Rust
♦ *Blaufränkisch, Blauer Zweigelt, Cabernet Sauvignon, Merlot, Pinot Noir (Blauburgunder)*
♀ *Pinot Blanc (Weissburgunder), Pinot Gris (Grauburgunder), Chardonnay, Sauvignon Blanc, Welschriesling, Neuburger*

Hans Feiler and his son Kurt make the finest AUSBRUCH dessert wines in RUST. Ten years ago they began switching from large neutral wooden casks to French oak barriques for the fermentation and maturation of these, and with the 1993 vintage they mastered this new style. The 'Pinot Cuvée' Ausbruch made from a blend of Weissburgunder, Grauburgunder and Neuburger is already famous beyond Austria's borders, having already won many prizes and blind tastings. You could mistake it for a top SAUTERNES were the acidity not so fresh and animating. The whole range of Ausbruch wines from the 1995 vintage is superb. The Feilers' red wines get better and better with each

vintage, Cuvée Solitaire, a medium-bodied, not too tannic Cabernet-Merlot-Blaufränkisch blend probably being the best. While the dry whites are good they are all clean, fruity wines for drinking when fresh. Best years: (sweet) 1998, '96, '95, '94, '93, '91; (dry whites and reds) 1997, '94, '93, '92.

LIVIO FELLUGA

ITALY, Friuli-Venezia Giulia, Colli Orientali del Friuli DOC
♦ *Merlot, Cabernet Sauvignon, Refosco*
♀ *Pinot Gris (Pinot Grigio), Tocai, Pinot Blanc (Pinot Bianco), Sauvignon Blanc, Pinot Gris (Pinot Grigio)*

The octogenarian Livio Felluga was a pioneer of the now fashionable FRIULI blended white wine and his estate is now run mainly by his sons, Andrea and Maurizio. One of the largest vineyard owners in eastern Friuli, with some 135ha (334 acres) mostly in the COLLI ORIENTALI zone at Rosazzo, Felluga has for decades now been considered at the top of the quality tree not only for its white varietals (perhaps somewhat less so for its reds) but especially for Terre Alte, an unoaked blend of Tocai, Chardonnay and Sauvignon, which year after year (though it's not produced in poor vintages) receives the highest praise. Not that Felluga has anything against wood – it uses both barriques and barrels for maturing the reds, and ferments its new blend of Chardonnay and Pinot Grigio, called Esperto, in barrel. But the accent, for Terre Alte, is on ripe fruit and sumptuousness of palate. And as the production is large the price is not outrageous. Best years: 1997, '96, '95, '94, '93, '91, '90.

FATTORIA DI FELSINA

ITALY, Tuscany, Chianti Classico DOCG
♦ *Sangiovese, Cabernet Sauvignon*
♀ *Trebbiano Toscano, Chardonnay, Sauvignon Blanc*

The best thing Giuseppe Mazzocolin ever did was to fall in love with Gloria Poggiali, not only because she is a lady of exceptional quality but also because her father just happened to have acquired, in the mid-1960s, this large and wonderfully endowed wine estate at Castelnuovo Berardenga in the extreme south-east corner of the CHIANTI CLASSICO zone. Schoolteacher Giuseppe fell in love all over again, this time with wine, departed the classroom and has devoted himself heart and soul ever since, with the expert guidance of consultant Franco Bernabei, to making this one of the greatest wine estates in Italy.

While producing one of Italy's finest Cabernet Sauvignons in Maestro Raro, as well as one of the better Chardonnays in I Sistri, it is into his Sangiovese wines that Giuseppe pours the lion's share of his considerable enthusiasm. Felsina's straight Chianti Classico, put together by master-taster and blender Bernabei and displaying the firmness yet fruitiness conferred by the various subzones at his disposal (now substantially increased by the purchase of the neighbouring Pagliarese estate), is better than many estates' Riserva wine. The 100 per cent Sangiovese Fontalloro, considered by many Felsina's best wine, is a veritable Classed Growth in disguise, for breeding combined with power. Finally, the single-vineyard Chianti Classico Riserva Vigneto Rancia is one of the greatest Sangiovese wines, especially in a fine vintage – very concentrated with impressive fruit depth and marked tannin, and rich and harmonious after several years' bottle age. Best years: 1997, '96, '95, '94, '93, '91, '90, '88, '85.

ALEJANDRO FERNANDEZ-TINTO PESQUERA

SPAIN, Castilla-León, Ribera del Duero DO
❦ *Tempranillo (Tinto del País)*

In the mid-1980s, few people outside RIBERA DEL DUERO had ever heard of the Viña Pesquera wines of Alejandro Fernández. Enter an American merchant and some influential American wine writers, one of whom compared Viña Pesquera to one of the world's finest reds, Ch. PÉTRUS. It doesn't really taste like Pétrus, but for sheer power and perfume, there is a similarity. Now these richly coloured, firm, fragrant plummy-tobaccoey reds are among the most famous and most expensive wines in Spain.

Until 1972 Alejandro Fernández ran the village smithy as well as his own agricultural machinery business. With the proceeds, he gradually built up his own vineyard holding, and constructed his own winery – even making his own vats. To supplement his vineyards in the village of Pesquera, Fernández bought a further 100ha (248 acres) of vineyard and built a second bodega in the neighbouring village of Roa, which is rapidly becoming the new wine capital of the region. Oak-aging is important here – the cellar is full of American and French oak barrels, many renewed each year. The wines are 100 per cent Tinto del País (Tempranillo). They are sold as Reserva and Gran Reserva in the best years, otherwise as Crianza. A further 100ha (248 acres) of Tempranillo have been planted on a newly acquired estate near Zamora, outside the DO. Best years: (reds) 1996, '95, '94, '93, '92, '91, '90, '89, '86.

FERRARI

ITALY, Trentino, Trentino DOC
❦ *Pinot Noir (Pinot Nero), Cabernet Franc, Cabernet Sauvignon, Merlot*
♀ *Chardonnay, Sauvignon Blanc*

One of the cornerstones of high-quality fizz in Italy is the Trento-based firm of Ferrari (no relation, although it makes the most of the perceived connection with the motor-car – apparently Ferrari is the third commonest name in Italy). The founder of the firm was Giulio Ferrari, who in 1902, when TRENTINO was still part of the Hapsburg empire, decided on the basis of experiences in CHAMPAGNE and GEISENHEIM that the Trentino region would be an ideal location for growing Chardonnay and Pinot for sparkling wines. Now known as Ferrari Fratelli Lunelli, the company has nine million bottles in stock at any given time and annual sales of three million.

Grapes for the non-vintage wines are bought in from about 150 growers, many of whom have been with the firm for many decades, the cuvées being 95 per cent Chardonnay, with a touch of Pinot Nero – and more than a touch for the rosé. Minimum time on yeasts is 24 months for the Brut and rosé, rising to 30 for the Maximum Brut and 36 for the vintage Perlé, a 100 per cent Chardonnay from the firm's own vineyards, of which they have 70ha (173 acres) at highish altitudes. Top of the range is the renowned pure Chardonnay Riserva del Fondatore Giulio Ferrari. The grapes come from vineyards more than 15 years old and the wine receives between seven and eight years on the lees, like a grand old *récemment dégorgé* Champagne.

FERRARI
The elegant Riserva del Fondatore is one of Italy's best Champagne-method sparkling wines: it has a yeasty, toasty fragrance and deep, complex flavours.

FERRARI-CARANO VINEYARDS

USA, California, Sonoma County, Dry Creek Valley AVA
❦ *Cabernet Sauvignon, Merlot, Sangiovese*
♀ *Chardonnay, Sauvignon Blanc*

Developing 182ha (450 acres) of vineyards spread between 12 SONOMA COUNTY sites, hotelier Don Carano started slowly as a wine producer, but he is in it for the long haul. His showcase winery in DRY CREEK VALLEY contains a vast aging cellar and an Italian villa with magnificent gardens.

The first vintages of Chardonnay gained a phenomenal amount of attention and certainly did have a ripeness and concentration all too rare in modern CALIFORNIA. After a dip in quality, this winery is now back on top; the whites include a perky, stylish Fumé Blanc, and the reds, Merlot, Cabernet Sauvignon, Tresor (red Meritage) and Siena (a SUPER-TUSCAN blend of Cabernet Sauvignon and Sangiovese). The reserve Chardonnay has now regained its former rich concentration. Best years: 1996, '95, '94 ,'92, '91, '88, '87.

FERREIRA

PORTUGAL, Douro, Port DOC, Douro DOC
❦ *Tinta Roriz (Tempranillo), Tinta Baroca, Tinto Cão, Touriga Nacional, Touriga Francesa and others*
♀ *Gouveio, Viosinho, Rabigato, Malvasia Fina and others*

Owned by SOGRAPE, Ferreira is the best-known PORT shipper in Portugal and deserves greater recognition elsewhere. With two prime vineyards at Quinta do Seixo and Quinta do Porto just downstream from Pinhão and another in the DOURO Superior, Ferreira makes a complete range of ports, although it is the aged tawnies (the 10-Year-Old Quinta do Porto and 20-Year-Old Duque de Bragança) which justly earn most of the accolades. Vintage ports, though elegant in style, tend to be on the light side and relatively early maturing, although the unfiltered LBV is as rich and solid as any.

Ferreira is just as well known for unfortified Douro reds as for port. Barca Velha, devised in the 1950s, is Portugal's uncrowned 'First Growth'. Originally made at Quinta do Vale de Meao, high in the Douro Superior, production has now transferred to nearby Quinta da Leda, although the philosophy remains the same. It is made from top-quality fruit and aged for about 18 months in new oak (formerly Portuguese, now French). Rather like a vintage port, the wine is only released as Barca Velha in truly exceptional years. Good interim years are sold under the name Reserva Ferreirinha. Ferreira also produces a third Douro red, Vinha Grande, which is distinctly cheaper than Barca Velha or Reserva Ferreirinha (both of which command high prices). The relatively lightweight Esteva underpins the range. Best years: (vintage ports) 1994, '91, '87, '85, '83.

CH. DE FESLES

FRANCE, Loire, Anjou-Saumur, Bonnezeaux AC
♥ *Cabernet Franc*
♀ *Chenin Blanc*

Fesles has long been the leading property in BONNEZEAUX. The château is built on one of the highest spots in the area and the vineyards face south, overlooking the river Layon. Made by Jean Boivin, the 1947 wine remains a living legend. His son Jacques subsequently took over the estate and it remained in the family until it was sold in 1991 to Gaston Lenôtre, the Parisian chef and noted *pâtissier*. Soon after, Lenôtre also bought Ch. de la Guimonière and Domaine de la Roulerie (in nearby Chaume). Unfortunately, although Lenôtre was initially highly enthusiastic, he did not fully appreciate the need to take risks to make a top-quality sweet LOIRE wine and quality started to suffer. Having renovated the château and the *chai* at considerable expense, Lenôtre also started to run out of money.

In 1996 he sold out to Bordeaux *négociant* Bernard Germain and since then there has been an immediate improvement, with the 1996 wine being noticeably superior to the '95. Germain also acquired vines in nearby SAVENNIÈRES, the 1996 was light and attractively easy, while the '97 is altogether more concentrated and complex. Germain now owns 100ha (247 acres) of vines in the region, including the excellent Domaine des Roches Neuves (SAUMUR and SAUMUR-CHAMPIGNY) run by Germain's son, Thierry. Best years: (Bonnezeaux) 1998, '97, '96, '90, '89, '76, '59, '47.

FETZER VINEYARDS

USA, California, Mendocino County
♥ *Cabernet Sauvignon, Zinfandel, Merlot, Pinot Noir*
♥ *Zinfandel*
♀ *Chardonnay, Gewurztraminer, Sauvignon Blanc*

Barney Fetzer had nine children when he launched a small winery in MENDOCINO COUNTY's Redwood Valley in 1968. Eight of them were fully involved in the business when their father died in 1981; they built the enterprise from fewer than 20,000 cases a year to more than 1.3 million. In general the increase in volume has been matched by an impressive consistency of style. In 1992, the Fetzer winery was purchased by Brown-Forman, which has expanded the winery and pushed annual production close to three million cases.

Fetzer comes at three price levels: regular, Barrel Select (good varietal flavours) and Reserve (bigger, oakier, and more limited in volume). Look for Chardonnay, Cabernet

FETZER VINEYARDS
Well known for its drinkable, good-value wines, Fetzer makes wines from organically grown grapes under the Bonterra label, including toasty Chardonnay.

Sauvignon and Zinfandel. A second label, Bel Arbors, is slightly cheaper than the regular bottlings. Wines made from organic grapes are labelled Bonterra. Overall, Fetzer continues to give good value for money. Best years: (reds) 1997, '95, '94, '92; (whites) 1997, '96, '95.

FIANO DI AVELLINO DOC

ITALY, Campania
♀ *Fiano, Greco, Coda di Volpe, Trebbiano Toscano*

People either go completely crazy about Fiano or they fail to see what all the fuss is about. It may be of little more than passing interest when young; but by a couple of years old it can be fabulous, with its restrained charms and subtle, but concentrated, peachy-nutty-creaminess. The classic production zone is in the Apennine hills east of Naples, around the town of Avellino. MASTROBERARDINO, which makes no fewer than three Crus, has long been the main producer but it, increasingly, is being challenged by up-and-coming newcomers like Colli di Lapio, Feudi di San Gregorio, Struzziero, Terre Dora di Paolo, Vadiaperti, Vega and Vignadora.

CH. DE FIEUZAL

FRANCE, Bordeaux, Pessac-Léognan AC, Cru Classé de Graves (reds only)
♥ *Cabernet Sauvignon, Merlot, Petit Verdot, Cabernet Franc*
♀ *Sauvignon Blanc, Sémillon*

This is a delightful estate, with a reputation for both its red and white wines. Investment during the 1980s in the 45-ha (111-acre) estate, just south of DOMAINE DE CHEVALIER near Léognan, has made it one of the most up-to-date properties in the region, but ownership changes now put its reputation in question.

The white wine is fermented and aged in new oak barrels and is rich, dense, balanced – and outstandingly good, whether drunk young, or aged. The red used to be equally impressive, succulent, rich and perfumed, but recent vintages seem to have lost their sensuous heart. I long for its return. Both wines are

drinkable almost as soon as they're drawn from the barrel, but both should age for a decade or more. Second wine: (red and white) l'Abeille de Fieuzal. Best years: (reds) 1998, '97, '96, '95, '90, '89, '88, '87, '86, '85, '83, '82, '78; (whites) 1998, '97, '96, '95, '94, '90, '89, '88, '87, '86, '85.

CH. FIGEAC

FRANCE, Bordeaux, St-Émilion Grand Cru AC, Premier Grand Cru Classé
♥ *Cabernet Sauvignon, Cabernet Franc, Merlot*

You have hardly finished shaking hands with Thierry Manoncourt, the delightful though zealous owner of Ch. Figeac, before he has marched you over into the vineyards, and pointed accusingly to the north. Half-a-mile away sit the small, whitewashed buildings of CHEVAL BLANC, acknowledged as ST-ÉMILION's greatest wine. This small area, at the western end of the appellation, is called 'Graves' St-Émilion because of the high proportion of gravel soil which gives the wine its special quality. Yet who has the most gravel? Not Cheval Blanc, but Figeac. Indeed you quickly learn that Cheval Blanc used to be part of Figeac, was only sold as 'Vin de Figeac', and derives its name (meaning 'white horse') from the fact that it was there that Figeac had its stables.

Well, it's true, but Manoncourt shouldn't fret so much because Figeac's own wine is superb, but in a different way from Cheval Blanc. Figeac uses 35 per cent Cabernet Sauvignon (rare for St-Émilion) and 35 per cent Cabernet Franc – both are grape varieties which love gravel – and only 30 per cent of St-Émilion's main variety, Merlot.

The result is wine of marvellous, minty, blackcurranty perfume, with some of the cedar and cigar-smoke spice of the great MÉDOCs, and a caressing gentleness of texture. It is often more 'beautiful' than Cheval Blanc and in a smoother, more voluptuous style, though it is rarely so grand. It is lovely young yet ideally should age for ten to 20 years. Second wine: la Grangeneuve de Figeac. Best years: 1998, '97, '96, '95, '94, '93, '90, '89, '87, '86, '85, '83, '82, '78, '76, '75.

FINCA FLICHMAN

ARGENTINA, Mendoza
♥ *Cabernet Sauvignon, Malbec, Syrah and others*
♀ *Chardonnay, Chenin Blanc*

For its first overseas venture, SOGRAPE, the Portuguese company famous for giving the world Mateus rosé, recently acquired Finca Flichman, a large, single-estate winery in

MENDOZA. Flichman had two things to recommend such a purchase: good vineyards in Mendoza planted on an interesting mixture of soils, and a winery with spanking new stainless steel, rare in Argentina. Wines originally aimed at the lower end of the market will doubtlessly begin to ascend the quality scale. At the moment most of the wines, sold either under Flichman, the premium Caballero de la Cepa or the Aberdeen Angus labels, exhibit all the symptoms of transitional wine, neither one thing nor the other, but first sightings of the difficult 1998 vintage showed that they're heading in the right direction.

FINCA FLICHMAN
The Caballero de la Cepa label is the premium range from this Argentinian winery now belonging to Portugal's largest wine company, Sogrape.

FIRESTONE VINEYARD

USA, California, Santa Barbara County, Santa Ynez Valley AVA

♥ *Merlot, Cabernet Sauvignon, Cabernet Franc, Pinot Noir, Syrah*

♀ *Chardonnay, Riesling, Gewurztraminer, Sauvignon Blanc, Viognier*

The improbable alliance of an American tyre-making family and a Japanese distiller (Suntory) has been a leader in SANTA BARBARA COUNTY since its first vintage in 1975. Now owned entirely by the Firestone family, the winery showed the way by producing pleasing Merlot which is supple and polished and avoids the vegetative streak that is often detected from this region. The Cabernet Sauvignon has rich blackcurrant fruit, sometimes a little high-toned. Cabernet Franc has also performed well as a key player in the winery's Meritage Reserve Red. Best years: (reds) 1997, '96, '95, '94, '93.

With experience Firestone has been able to craft Chardonnay with balance and complexity. Good Riesling is rare in CALIFORNIA, but from the beginning, its Johannisberg Riesling won a strong following, and is best enjoyed young. Known for its fair pricing policy, this winery is maintaining that image as it adds Viognier and Syrah to its line-up.

FITOU AC

FRANCE, Languedoc-Roussillon

♥ *Carignan, Grenache Noir, Cinsaut and others*

The main Fitou area is a pocket of land around the lagoon of Salses, on the coast between Perpignan and Narbonne, but there are also some villages where much better, more interesting wine is made, in the heart of the CORBIÈRES hinterland, of which Tuchan is the most important. Fitou's strong, burly character comes from the Carignan grape, which makes a pretty stern basic brew, so there is a minimum aging requirement of 18 months in wood. The wine then ages well for five to six years at least. Best years: 1996, '95, '94, '93. Best producers: Bertrand-Bergé, l'Espigne, Lerys, Mont Tauch co-operative, des Nouvelles, Rochelière, Dom. de Rolland.

FIXIN AC

FRANCE, Burgundy, Côte de Nuits

♥ *Pinot Noir*

♀ *Pinot Blanc*

Fixin would love to be talked of in the same breath as the great villages of the CÔTE D'OR. There it sits, looking down indulgently on its great neighbour, GEVREY-CHAMBERTIN, confident in the knowledge that the Grand Dukes of Burgundy used to spend their summers here. But the wines never manage to scale the heights. They are worthy and tannic enough to last well, but the perfume, fragrance, the mysterious mix of flavour and fantasy that marks out the greatest red Burgundies is hardly ever there. Only one-third of the vineyards within the commune are entitled to be labelled as Fixin; the rest must be sold as CÔTE DE NUITS-VILLAGES. Best years: 1997, '96, '95, '93, '92, '90, '89, '88, '85. Best producers: Berthaut, Bruno CLAIR, Gelin, Joliet.

FLEURIE AC

FRANCE, Burgundy, Beaujolais, Beaujolais cru

♥ *Gamay*

At its best Fleurie, the third-largest but best-known BEAUJOLAIS cru, reveals the happy, care-free flavours of the Gamay grape at their most delightful, plus heady perfumes and a lovely juicy sweetness. Luckily, there's a fair amount of wine to go round but, not surprisingly, demand has meant that some of the wines are now woefully overpriced and ordinary. Best years: 1998, '97, '96, '95. Best producers: Bernard, Berrod, Louis Champagnon, Gérard Charvet, Chignard, DUBOEUF, Fleurie co-operative, la Grande Cour, Montgénas, Quatre Vents, Fernand Verpoix.

FONSECA GUIMARAENS

PORTUGAL, Douro, Port DOC

♥ *Tinta Roriz (Tempranillo), Tinta Barroca, Tinto Cão, Touriga Nacional, Touriga Francesa and others*

♀ *Gouveio, Viosinho, Rabigato, Malvasia Fina and others*

Fonseca is held in the highest regard and even earns sneaking respect from many competing PORT shippers. The firm was founded in 1822 and the winemaking remains the responsibility of the Guimaraens family, even though Fonseca has been owned, since 1948, by another highly regarded shipper, TAYLOR, FLADGATE AND YEATMAN.

Fonseca's mainstay is Bin No 27, a ripe, opulent premium ruby, but the firm reigns supreme with some outstandingly fine aged tawnies and vintage ports. In great years like 1994, '85, '77 and '66, Fonseca manages to combine sheer power with glorious finesse although the '83 and '80 vintages were somewhat out-of-sorts. Wines from good non-declared years (like '95) use the Guimaraens label but frequently outscore fully declared wines from other shippers. Best years: (vintage ports) 1994, '92, '85, '77, '70, '66, '63.

JOSÉ MARIA DA FONSECA SUCCESSORES

PORTUGAL, Terras do Sado, Setúbal DOC, Palmela IPR, Arrábida IPR, Terras do Sado Vinho Regional

♥ *Periquita (Castelão Francês) Alfrocheiro, Espadeiro, Touriga Nacional and others*

♀ *Arinto, Fernão Pires, Rabo de Ovelha; Setúbal: Moscatel de Setúbal, Moscatel Roxo, Tamarez, Arinto, Fernão Pires*

Family owned and run, José Maria da Fonseca Successores is one of the most traditional yet innovative wine companies in Portugal. Based at Azeitão on the SETÚBAL peninsula, it is the largest producer of the sweet, fortified Setúbal wine, made mainly from Moscatel grapes. The company is best known for its brand of Periquita red, the wine that gave the nickname to the Castelão Francês grape. Quinta de Camarate is the flagship vineyard and this produces a ripe, plummy red from Periquita (the grape) and Espadeiro, together with a small amount of Cabernet Sauvignon.

Garrafeira wines, mysteriously coded as 'T E', 'R A' and so on, are supple and gamy. José Maria da Fonseca also has interests in the DÃO region, where it produces Terras Altas, and in the ALENTEJO. In 1986 the company bought the José de Sousa estate in Reguengos de Monsaraz, which makes a rich, warm-country red known as Tinto Velho.

Wine from another family-owned estate in the northern Alentejo near Portalegre is bottled under the d'Avillez label.

José Maria da Fonseca has recently bought a sister company formerly known as J M da Fonseca Internaçional, which was hived off in the 1970s to produce Lancers Rosé and Espumante (sparkling wine).

TENIMENTI DI FONTANAFREDDA

ITALY, Piedmont, Barolo DOCG

♥ *Nebbiolo, Barbera, Doletto, Freisa, Grignolino*

♀ *Moscato, Pinot Noir (Pinot Nero), Chardonnay*

Once the property of King Vittorio Emanuele's bastard son, Emanuele Guerrieri di Mirafiori, this estate is in the heart of BAROLO's Serralunga d'Alba commune. It has been owned since 1931 by the Monte dei Paschi bank of Siena. A relatively enormous operation – 70ha (173 acres) of prime vineyards, grapes bought in from over 600 growers of Piedmont and beyond, plus an annual production of over six million bottles of which some 750,000 are Barolo and nearly four million are ASTI – Fontanafredda is one of the few giants in a land of smallholders. Biggest Barolo production by far is of the ubiquitous *normale*, rarely very inspired since Fontanafredda started making crus commercially in the early 1970s. But the traditionally crafted, single-vineyard wines – La Rosa, La Delizia, La Villa, Gattinera and Lazzarito, to name a few — can be impressive. As well as Asti, other sparkling wine production covers CHAMPAGNE-method fizz, including the good vintage brut Contessa Rosa. Best years: (Barolo) 1998, '97, '96, '95, '93, '90, '89, '88, '85.

CASTELLO DI FONTERUTOLI

ITALY, Tuscany, Chianti Classico DOCG

♥ *Sangiovese, Cabernet Sauvignon*

The Mazzei family, father Lapo, sons Filippo and Francesco, supported by one of Tuscany's outstanding enological consultants Carlo Ferrini, wanted to celebrate the 600th anniversary of the original Ser Lapo Mazzei's earliest inscription of the word 'Chianti', in 1398, with a bang.

In a bold gesture to show that Fonterutoli has sufficient faith in the revival of the historic CHIANTI denomination, a new wine, CHIANTI CLASSICO Riserva, has replaced two well-established ones, Concerto (a fine SUPER-TUSCAN from Sangiovese and Cabernet) and Riserva Ser Lapo. And, indeed, the first vintages of the new wine are stunning. The amount of Cabernet Sauvignon in the

In the late autumn, nylon netting prevents birds from eating the Riesling grapes as they become shrivelled by botrytis, the noble rot fungus, in the Ungeheuer vineyard at Forst.

new Riserva is only 10 per cent so as to retain more Tuscan typicity without losing power. The grapes come from the high-quality Siepi vineyard at 260m (850 ft) altitude and the Fonterutoli vineyard at 450m (1750ft). Deep coloured, with a wealth of berry fruit, dark-chocolate and coffee aromas, it has a hefty structure which will ensure considerable aging, despite the ripeness of the tannins. The highly sought-after Sangiovese-Merlot super-Tuscan called Siepi is still being made. Best years: (Riserva) 1996, '95.

FONTODI

ITALY, Tuscany, Chianti Classico DOCG

♥ *Sangiovese, Cabernet Sauvignon*

♀ *Pinot Blanc (Pinot Bianco), Sauvignon Blanc*

Indisputably one of Italy's high flyers, this stunningly situated estate has 60ha (148 acres) of vineyard covering the slopes south of Panzano in the heart of CHIANTI CLASSICO. In 1968 the Manetti family, terracotta manufacturers of Florence, took control of the estate and Fontodi's modern era began. Anyone looking for a model operation illustrating all that's dynamic and forward-looking in Chianti Classico today need look no further. Sangiovese, not surprisingly, is the hub of the wheel, and Fontodi has been among the leaders in Tuscany experimenting with clones and planting methods; nor is Giovanni Manetti one of those who snubs the Consorzio, playing instead an active role.

The exemplary SUPER-TUSCAN Flaccianello della Pieve is from a single vineyard of old Sangiovese vines and there is a consistent, reliably polished Chianti Classico *normale*. The Riserva Vigna del Sorbo, a single-vineyard wine (using organic methods), brings some high-quality Cabernet into the equation at the limit of what is allowed under the Chianti regulations. There are also two more unusual varietal wines under the newer Case Vie label – Pinot Nero and Syrah. Best years: (Flaccianello) 1995, '94, '93, '91, '90, '88, '86, '85.

FORST

GERMANY, Pfalz

The attractive small village of Forst has a single street, a clutch of top-quality vineyards and a reputation for high quality. It can boast a list of top growers as good as any Rhineland village and vineyards of the calibre of Jesuitengarten (refinement and elegance), Kirchenstück (balance and nobility), Pechstein (racy drive) and Ungeheuer (powerful and earthy).

There is an outcrop of black basalt above the village which for years has been quarried and used in the vineyards to aid heat-retention and enrichment of the potassium-rich soil, unique in the region. Best producers: BASSERMANN-JORDAN, von BUHL, BÜRKLIN-WOLF, Georg MOBACHER, J WEGELER, J-L WOLF.

FORTANT DE FRANCE

FRANCE, Languedoc-Roussillon, Vin de Pays d'Oc

🍷🍷 *Cabernet Sauvignon, Merlot, Syrah, Grenache*

🍷 *Chardonnay, Sauvignon Blanc, Grenache Blanc*

This is the trade name for the wines of Robert Skalli, who is the most important wine producer in the South of France, and who is also credited with transforming the Midi from the much-derided spring of the European wine lake into one of the world's most exciting wine regions.

Skalli has done this by using New World methods of winemaking, by cajoling the local French growers to modernize their wineries and to plant international grape varieties – and by labelling his wines with the grape variety under the catch-all Vin de Pays d'Oc label. There are three basic Fortant de France ranges – an unoaked range that concentrates on pure fruit flavours, a subtly oaked range of varietals and a top-of-the-line 'collection' range, initially baptized Réserve F, but now changed to Fortant F. Drink the white wines young, the reds with two to five years' aging.

FRANCIACORTA DOCG, TERRE DI FRANCIACORTA DOC

ITALY, Lombardy

🍷 *Cabernet Franc, Barbera, Nebbiolo, Merlot*

🍷 *Pinot Blanc (Pinot Bianco), Chardonnay*

The Franciacorta DOCG, between Bergamo and Brescia in the centre of LOMBARDY, is known mainly for CHAMPAGNE-method sparkling wine, which at its best has an elegance and creamy, grassy classiness that is hard to upstage. It is best kept a couple of years before broaching. CA' DEL BOSCO tends to be the benchmark, especially their Cuvée Annamaria Clementi, but the Vittorio Moretti Riserva Extra Brut from Bellavista is also superb. Cavalleri, Lorenzo Faccoli, Ferghettina, Gatti and Uberti are all good producers for various styles of fizz, including in some cases a *crémant* or low-pressure fizz referred to hereabouts as Satèn; and a rosé version, which generally gets its colour from a little Pinot Noir juice in the blend.

In order to avoid confusion with the sparklers, the still wines of the zone are today grouped under the Terre di Franciacorta DOC. The reds have an unusual grape mixture that, in the right hands, is very good. From PIEDMONT, to Franciacorta's west, come Barbera, giving zest and acidity, and Nebbiolo, giving grip and backbone. From FRIULI, to Franciacorta's east, come Cabernet Franc, giving stylishness and grassiness, and Merlot, giving roundness and suppleness.

The white is less idiosyncratic, although one never quite knows whether it is pure Chardonnay or a blend. Best producers: Bellavista (Uccellanda, Convento dell'Annunciata), Cà del Bosco, Cavalleri (Seradina).

FRANCISCAN VINEYARDS

USA, California, Napa County, Napa Valley AVA

🍷 *Cabernet Sauvignon, Merlot, Zinfandel*

🍷 *Chardonnay, Sauvignon Blanc*

Of all NAPA's boom-era wineries, Franciscan got off to one of the most wayward starts, and it is only since 1985 that the outfit has gained a sense of direction. The wines generally have a good fruit and attractive oak perfume and are beginning to show balance, restrained fruit and skilful winemaking. Those labelled Franciscan come from estate grapes in the Napa Valley, and those called Estancia come from SONOMA and MONTEREY. Cuvée Sauvage is a stunning, limited release Chardonnay. The Merlot offers generous plum fruit and appealing richness. Best years: 1997, '96, '95, '94, '93, '92, '91, '90, '87, '85.

Franciscan also owns Mount Veeder Winery, which is gaining a good record for Cabernet Sauvignon and Reserve Red. Quintessa, a single-vineyard red Meritage, is a new wine growing in importance. In 1999 the winery was sold to Canandaigua, the USA's second largest wine group.

FRANCISCAN VINEYARDS
Magnificat, Franciscan's Meritage or Bordeaux blend, is a highly successful, long-lived wine with great concentration of flavour.

FRANKEN

GERMANY

It is climate that is the essential difference between Franken and Germany's other wine regions such as the RHEINGAU. The summers are hotter and the winters colder here, and the growing season is distinctly on the short side. Silvaner is the classic grape, producing understated, sturdy wines with a touch of earthiness. More recently, however, Müller-Thurgau has taken over as the principal grape in Franken. What is less good news is the

fondness of Franconian growers for new, frost-resistant crosses like Bacchus and Kerner, with their over-assertive aromas; subtlety is one of the great virtues of Franken wine, and it's not often found in Bacchus or Kerner. Rieslaner, however, a cross between Riesling and Silvaner, is more promising. The wines are bottled in the distinctive flagon-shaped Bocksbeutel and are mostly dry. WÜRZBURG, the capital, is in the Bereich Maindreieck (it is the river Main that weaves its way unsteadily through the Franken vineyards) – this is the heart of Franken, as far as wine is concerned. The other two Bereichs are Mainviereck for the region towards Frankfurt, and Steigerwald for the eastern part, where the climate is most extreme and vines are only grown in scattered warm spots, on south-facing slopes.

FRASCATI DOC

ITALY, Lazio

🍷 *Trebbiano Toscano, Malvasia di Candia, Malvasia del Lazio, Greco*

Frascati is one of the few Italian wines that most people have tried at some time or another. When drunk in and around Rome, its homeland, it goes down well enough and is drunk with anything, even with what we would consider red wine foods. It is when one broaches Frascati in the cold grey light of home that one realizes just how dull most of it is, although there are now an increasing number that are perfectly OK to going on good, and one or two which are outstanding.

Best when young, Frascati should taste soft, creamy and nutty. The wine can be made from just Trebbiano – great for neutral background vinous swill but not much else; or just Malvasia – too prone to oxidation if not handled properly, but peachy, nutty, flavoursome and characterful. To make matters worse, of the two Malvasia varieties permitted, use of the better one (del Lazio) is restricted, the less good one (di Candia) can be used as much as the winemaker likes. The decent companies mix Trebbiano and Malvasia in varying proportions. A few ignore the law and bump up the Malvasia del Lazio, others go further and use mainly Viognier.

Castel de Paolis' Vigna Adriana is probably the best Frascati money can buy but Colli di Catone also have good, cru wines – Colle Gaio and Casal Pilozzo. Fontana Candida, a reliable producer, also has a single-vineyard wine called Santa Teresa. Casale Marchese, Costantini (Villa Simone), Pallavicini and Conte Zandotti can also be good.

Marino, Montecompatri, Velletri, Zagarolo and Castelli Romani are all neighbouring DOCs which, in their white versions, approximate the far more famous Frascati. Paolo di Mauro's Colle di Picchioni is undoubtedly the best of the Marino wines; Tenuta le Quinte makes good Montecompatri.

FREIXENET
SPAIN, Cataluña, Cava DO
♟ Macabeo, Parellada, Xarel-lo, Tempranillo (Ull de Llebre)
♀ Macabeo, Parellada, Xarel-lo

When you take into account Freixenet's two sparkling wine subsidiaries, Castellblanch and Segura Viudas, the Freixenet group is the biggest CHAMPAGNE-method producer, not just in Spain, but in the world. Quality here is sound, but most of the wines suffer from the inherent defects of Catalan CAVA – lack of true personality and an unappetizing earthiness because of the grapes used and the lengthy aging. However, the Brut Nature is fresh and lemony, if slightly earthy, and the Cordon Negro Brut can be clean and relatively attractive.

Freixenet also owns Conde de Caralt (Cava and still wines), Castellblanch (Cava), Segura Viudas (Cava and still wines), René Barbier (still wines), Canals & Nubiola (Cava), the Gloria Ferrer winery in CARNEROS, Henri Abelé in Champagne and Sala Vivé in Mexico.

MARCHESI DE' FRESCOBALDI
ITALY, Tuscany, Florence
♟ Sangiovese, Canaiolo, Merlot and others
♀ Trebbiano, Malvasia, Chardonnay and others

Frescobaldi rests its reputation on two impressive pillars: its 700-year, 30-generation experience as growers and winemakers, the present hierarchy consisting of brothers Vittorio (President), Ferdinando and Leonardo (Vice-Presidents), with several younger Frescobaldis already involved in the business; and the fact that, with what will soon be over 800ha (1977 acres) of vines planted in various parts of Tuscany, it is probably the largest family-owned producers of quality wines in Europe. The strengths do not end there, however, having in Lamberto Frescobaldi and Nicolò d'Aflitto, star Italian wine consultant, a pair of highly talented enologo-agronomists of Tuscan origin but with wide international experience.

Perhaps the most representative property is Castello di Nipozzano, in the DOCG zone of CHIANTI RUFINA, where some 180ha

MARCHESI DE' FRESCOBALDI
Of real structure and depth, this Chianti Rufina has complex, oak-influenced flavour and is elegant and long.

(445 acres) are planted principally to the Tuscan varieties of Sangiovese, Malvasia Nera, Canaiolo and Colorino; and to Cabernets Sauvignon and Franc, with some Merlot. From this property the principal wines are Castello di Nipozzano, a traditional Chianti Rufina Riserva of some considerable aging ability; Mormoreto, 100 per cent Cabernet Sauvignon, barrique-aged (50 per cent new) for 18 months, a wine whose complexity and harmony have come on apace since d'Aflitto took over here in 1995; also what is probably the greatest of all Frescobaldi wines, despite the chi-chi surrounding others, Montesodi, a pure Sangiovese of exceptional refinement and breeding.

The wines of Castello di Pomino are of an entirely different ilk, being grown at between 500 and 700m (1640 and 2300ft) and consisting of two-thirds whites. Best known wines are the Chardonnay-Pinot Grigio-Pinot Bianco blends of POMINO Bianco (today one of the best-value Tuscan whites around) and Pomino Benefizio, a single-vineyard wine benefiting, to a larger extent than the Bianco, from discreet barrique-aging. Best years: (reds) 1998, '97, '96, '95, '94, '93, '91, '90, '88, '86, '85, '82.

FRIEDRICH-WILHELM-GYMNASIUM
GERMANY, Mosel-Saar-Ruwer, Trier
♀ Riesling, Müller-Thurgau, Kerner

The Jesuits founded this large TRIER estate in 1563; later on Karl Marx was educated at the school from which it takes its name. Neither of these facts, though, has much bearing on the style of wines it produces, which are now light and elegant, typical of the MOSEL and Saar regions.

Cellar techniques are extremely careful and pretty traditional, with extensive use of old wooden barrels. The wines are often approachable quite young, although they can also age well. After a disappointing run at the beginning of the 1990s, there was a return to form in 1995. Best years: 1997, '95.

FRIULI AQUILEIA DOC, FRIULI GRAVE DOC, FRIULI LATISANA DOC
ITALY, Friuli-Venezia Giulia
♟ Cabernet Franc, Cabernet Sauvignon, Merlot, Pinot Noir (Pinot Nero), Refosco dal Peduncolo Rosso
♀ Chardonnay, Pinot Blanc (Pinot Bianco), Pinot Gris (Pinot Grigio), Riesling Renano, Tocai Friulano, Traminer Aromatico, Verduzzo Friulano

These flatland zones constitute the engine-room of high productivity in FRIULI. Best known and largest is what until recently was known as Grave del Friuli, followed by Aquileia and Latisana, to which has been added the obscure Friuli Annia. The grape varieties are a mix of the Gallic and the Germanic, with a smattering of the indigenous. The wines tend more towards the workmanlike than the exciting. Good producers in Aquileia include Zonin at Cà Bolani, Tenuta Beltrame and Mulino delle Tolle. In Grave there is di Lenardo, Plozner and Villa Chiopris and in Latisana there's, er – well, there must be somebody.

FRIULI ISONZO DOC
ITALY, Friuli-Venezia Giulia
♟ Cabernet Franc, Cabernet Sauvignon, Merlot, Franconia, Pinot Noir (Pinot Nero), Refosco dal Peduncolo Rosso, Schioppettino
♀ Chardonnay, Malvasia, Moscato Giallo, Pinot Blanc (Pinot Bianco), Pinot Gris (Pinot Grigio), Riesling Renano, Sauvignon, Tocai Friulano, Traminer Aromatico, Verduzzo Friulano

Isonzo is one of the most recent, and most surprising, of the star zones of Italian viniculture, given that 20 years ago it was virtually unknown and yet today is turning out possibly the finest white wines in Italy.

The surprise comes from the fact that Isonzo, like the other FRIULI zones of Grave, Aquileia and Latisana, is perfectly flat, yet the Sauvignon Blancs from here come redolent of perfume, the Chardonnays full of body and concentrated of taste, the Pinot Grigios creamy and intense, and even some of the reds are beginning to show signs of real distinction. Isonzo's rich topsoil with a pebbly subsoil, combined with a constant cooling breeze from the hills of nearby Slovenia, seems to be the secret.

The outstanding producer is Gianfranco Gallo of Vie di Romans, whose Sauvignon Blanc wines, Vieris and Piere, are benchmark wines. Other best producers are Lis Neris-Pecorari, Pierpaolo Pecorari and Giorgio Badin at Ronco del Gelso. Best years: 1998, '97, '96, '95.

FRIULI-VENEZIA GIULIA Italy

THE REGION OF FRIULI-VENEZIA GIULIA, often called just Friuli for short, is the true Italian north-east. Bordered by Slovenia to the east and Austria to the north, and suffering down the centuries from innumerable wars, situated as it is on one of Europe's historic crossroads, Friuli has become a meeting place of three cultures: Slavic, Teutonic and Venetian (from the west). The atmosphere in its scattered villages and sedate towns is of diligence and collaborative dedication, yet still the region remains undeniably Italian.

The wine zones of Friuli cover much of its southern half, most of which is a flat gravel plain – the zone of Friuli Grave DOC. Quality here basically depends on the soil: the pebbly gravel gives such rapid drainage that the vines are water-stressed most of the summer, holding down yields. Even so, Friuli Grave is still responsible for its fair share of basic wine, much of it still issuing forth in large

bottles declaring 'Tocai' (white) or 'Merlot' (red). The Friuli Aquileia, Friuli Latisana and Carso DOC zones are of lesser importance, all being coastal areas where growers battle for quality on alluvial, unstable terrain. The high reputation the Friuli wines enjoy hinges on three small wine districts next to the Slovenian border: Collio, Colli Orientali del Friuli and Friuli Isonzo. The first two are historic rivals, despite which there is not a great deal to choose between them, the dividing line being a provincial boundary rather than soil or climate differences. Their historic pre-eminence over other Friuli DOCs is due to their situation on hill terrain. So much importance is placed on this aspect that only wines from proper hill slopes are allowed to use these highly regarded names. As for Friuli Isonzo, it is only in the last decade of the twentieth century that this plain-land has shot to prominence, thanks to the efforts of a clutch of enthusiastic young growers sometimes referred to as the 'Isonzo Boys'.

There is a wide range of grape varieties grown in Friuli, a mix of local, French and German, each traditionally vinified and bottled separately. A count in 1998 revealed over 150 different combinations of zone, grape and wine style for DOC wines alone and the number continues to grow. The essence of the Friuli style has always been varietal purity, but subtly; in other words, the understated approach. When it works, as it frequently does, the wines have an elegance and a classiness that are hard to beat. Most grape varieties are white: Germanic Traminer and Riesling rub shoulders with French Sauvignon Blanc and Chardonnay as well as with the local Ribolla, Verduzzo and Malvasia, the widely grown Pinot Grigio and Tocai, and the underrated Pinot Bianco, to name just a few.

In recent years, however, the blended white wine has become fashionable. The trend began with growers like Jermann putting together grapes as disparate as Sauvignon Blanc, Chardonnay, Ribolla, Malvasia and Picolit in the now cult wine, Vintage Tunina. Livio Felluga's Terre Alte and Josko Gravner's oak-aged Breg are two other famous examples of a style now spreading rapidly.

Red wines have traditionally trailed behind whites in the Friuli region in terms of market recognition. They, too, have been largely varietal, although here again blended wines are becoming more important, especially the ones made in a Bordeaux-style. But among these super premium styles that flirt with the over-oaked international flavours

The vineyards of Giacomo Dri are in the alpine foothills above Nimis at the northern end of the Colli Orientali del Friuli zone. Here, around the village of Ramandolo, the native Verduzzo grape produces rich, well-balanced sweet wines.

ABBAZIA DI ROSAZZO
This historic abbey has been noted for wine since the eleventh century. Pignolo is a naturally low-yielding red grape local to Friuli.

LIVIO FELLUGA
This classy Merlot Reserva Sossò comes from the Felluga estate which is a substantial producer by Friuli standards and effortlessly combines quality with quantity.

VILLA RUSSIZ
Named after Villa Russiz's French founder, Conte de la Tour, who is credited with introducing Bordeaux grapes to Friuli in the 1870s, this high-class Merlot-Cabernet blend is the flagship wine from this prestigious estate.

JOSKO GRAVNER
Based in Collio, almost on the Slovenian border, Josko Gravner concentrates on making wood-aged white wines.

that can be found worldwide, we shouldn't forget that Friuli makes wonderfully refreshing simple grassy Merlots and Cabernets with no oak at all as well as a chunky but enjoyable oddity called Refosco, for when you want an oddball winter red.

SCHIOPETTO
Mario Schiopetto was a pioneer in Italy of high-quality, intensely concentrated whites, including impressive Pinot Bianco.

REGIONAL ENTRIES
Colli Orientali del Friuli, Collio, Friuli Aquileia, Friuli Isonzo.

PRODUCER ENTRIES
Borgo del Tiglio, Felluga, Gravner, Jermann, Russiz Superiore, Schiopetto.

BORGO DEL TIGLIO
Nicola Manferrari continues to keep this estate in the vanguard of Collio producers. Both whites and reds are consistently good and characterful wine.

PUIATTI
This Collio producer is noted for white wines made without oak. The Archétipi range is reserved for the top wines that will develop with age.

JERMANN
Silvio Jermann is one of several producers who brought a whole new image to Friulian wine. Vintage Tunina is based on late-harvested Sauvignon and Chardonnay.

FROG'S LEAP WINERY

USA, California, Napa County, Napa Valley AVA
♥ *Cabernet Sauvignon, Zinfandel, Merlot*
♀ *Chardonnay, Sauvignon Blanc*

John Williams may have split with former partner Larry Turley and moved to the Red Barn Winery but he continues to earn high grades for his Sauvignon Blanc. Only hinting of oak, the Sauvignons offer subtle melon flavours and pleasing tanginess. Williams views Zinfandel as a class act and brings out its blackberry, spicy fragrance, berry and chocolate flavours, held together by firming sweet oak and tannin, while the Cabernets keep a grassy tang to enliven their full black cherry and blackcurrant fruit. Merlot, made in a lush fruit style, is another success. Best years: 1997, '96, '95, '94, '93, '92, '91, '90, '89, '87.

FROMM WINERY

NEW ZEALAND, South Island, Marlborough
♥ *Cabernet Sauvignon, Merlot, Pinot Noir, Syrah*
♀ *Chardonnay*

Owner George Fromm, who also owns a winery in Switzerland, believes that MARLBOROUGH offers huge potential for reds if the vines are grown under an organic regime and more time is spent in the vineyard. Fromm claims to invest more man-hours in the vineyard than the regional average by around 150 per cent. Most of his grapes come from a north-facing hillside vineyard called Clayvin Estate.

Results have been impressive, with an outstanding Reserve Pinot Noir, good Merlot, and a surprisingly pleasing Syrah that shows concentration and ripeness considering its cool-climate location. Chardonnay is the only white wine. The reds all have good aging potential while the Chardonnay is also capable of developing well in the bottle for more than five years. Best years: 1998, '96, '94.

FRONSAC AC

FRANCE, Bordeaux
♥ *Cabernet Franc, Cabernet Sauvignon, Merlot, Malbec*

For 20 years now people have been saying that Fronsac wines would soon be the next star in the BORDEAUX constellation but we're still waiting. Yet there has been significant progress in recent years, particularly since 1994, with Fronsac's 'rustic' tannins more firmly under control and the wines generally richer and riper. The area does have some good properties, and tucked in next to POMEROL it also has good vineyard sites. But the area still hasn't

taken off. Perhaps with the present drive for quality and relatively attractive prices Fronsac's time has now come? Best years: 1998, '97, '96, '95, '94, '90, '89, '88, '86, '85, '83. Best producers: Dalem, Fontenil, la Grave, Haut Carles, Mayne-Vieil, Moulin Haut-Laroque, la Rivière, Tour du Moulin, Les Trois Croix, LA VIEILLE CURE, Villars.

CH. FUISSÉ

FRANCE,, Burgundy, Mâconnais, Pouilly-Fuissé AC
♥ *Gamay*
♀ *Chardonnay*

The Vincent family are the unquestioned stars of this much maligned appellation. In a region where the wines generally seem overpriced and overhyped, the cuvées of Ch. Fuissé are usually of exceptional quality. For once, the prices demanded do not seem too much out of line with the quality in the bottle. Although the standard bottling is very good, the best wines are Le Clos and the Cuvée Vieilles Vignes, which is rich and full-bodied, and can be very long-lived. It is matured in about one-third new oak. Other wines made by the domaine include an excellent and inexpensive ST-VÉRAN and a few BEAUJOLAIS crus. Best years: 1997, '96, '95, '94, '93, '92, '90, '89, '88, '86.

RUDOLF FÜRST

GERMANY, Franken, Bürgstadt
♥ *Pinot Noir (Spätburgunder), Frühburgunder, Domina*
♀ *Riesling, Pinot Blanc (Weissburgunder), Silvaner, Müller-Thurgau*

Though not nearly as well known as the wine estates owned by the big charitable foundations of WÜRZBURG, Paul Fürst makes some of the very best wines in FRANKEN. Almost none is typical for the region though, with red wine his speciality in a white wine region. This works because Bürgstadt is the warmest place in the entire region, making deeply coloured, silky reds that have enough power to take some new oak. The best of these are Fürst's pure Spätburgunders, which age much better than most German reds. Simpler, but also impressive, is Parzival, a blend of Pinot Noir and the local Domina, which has no sado-masochistic tendencies and is full of blackberry fruit. The barrique-aged Weissburgunder has a Chardonnay-like nuttiness and in good vintages is a big heady wine. The dry Rieslings are sleeker, but unusually aromatic for a region whose whites are usually rustic and earthy. Best years: (reds) 1997, '96, '94, '93, '90; (whites) 1998, '97, '94, '93, '92, '90.

JEAN-NOËL GAGNARD

FRANCE, Burgundy, Côte de Beaune, Chassagne-Montrachet AC
♥ *Pinot Noir*
♀ *Chardonnay*

Monsieur Gagnard is a reticent man, clearly more happy among his vines and barrels than in the tasting room. But his wines are regularly among the finest in a village that can now boast a fair number of excellent domaines. His most sought-after wine is BÂTARD-MONTRACHET, but his numerous Premiers Crus from CHASSAGNE-MONTRACHET are also of the highest standard. The whites are deservedly the best known, but there is also a good range of reds, not surprisingly, given that half the vineyards in Chassagne are planted with Pinot Noir. Gagnard's white wines are characterized by elegant ripe fruit with an underlying base of fine acidity. Best years: 1997, '96, '95, '93, '92, '90, '89, '88, '86, '85, '83.

GAILLAC AC

FRANCE, South-West
♥♥ *Duras, Fer, Gamay and others*
♀ *Mauzac Blanc, L'En de l'El, Ondenc and others*

About seven million bottles of wine are produced annually from vineyards scattered between Albi and St-Sulpice in the Tarn *département*, and about half of these are white. The Mauzac, with its sharp, but attractive, green apple bite, is the main white grape, abetted by the local l'En de l'El (which seems to mean 'out of sight' in the dialect), Ondenc, Muscadelle, Sauvignon and Sémillon. Mauzac has a very 'direct' line of taste, so even the best whites are rather stern, but from a decent grower there is a sharp apple and licorice fruit which is extremely refreshing.

The star of GAILLAC, however, is the fizz – made by either the CHAMPAGNE method or the *méthode rurale* in which the fermentation is arrested, then finished off in bottle, to create the bubbles. This Gaillac Mousseux AC can be fabulous – full of apricots and apples, honey and peaches and a sting of tobacco and pepper too. The local co-operatives make a *pétillant* (a sort of demi-semi-sparkler), Gaillac Perlé AC, which is not the same thing at all. Drink all the wines as young as possible.

Little of the red and rosé wine has any great character (although the Tecou co-operative isn't bad). However, there are now a few wines from single producers and these can be exciting – sharp, peppery, tangy. Drink young. Best producers: Albert, Boissel-Rhodes, Bosc Long, Jean Cros, Cuasses-Marines, Labarthe, Labastide de Lévis co-operative, Larroze, Mas Dignon, PLAGEOLES, Rotier, Tecou co-operative.

ANGELO GAJA

ITALY, Piedmont, Barbaresco DOCG

♥ Nebbiolo, Cabernet Sauvignon
♀ Chardonnay

A legend in his own lifetime, Angelo Gaja deserves, and receives, much of the credit for dragging the wines of BARBARESCO (and of Italy) to the top of the world wine tree. He began in the family business – already the major vineyard-owner of Barbaresco – in the early 1960s, and after trips to France to study the techniques of the great winemakers, and various stormy disputes with his father began to implement his radical ideas. He introduced severe *diradamento* (thinning to reduce yields), or pruning, thermo-controllable fermentation equipment, malolactic fermentation, French barriques, French grape varieties, single-vineyard production and grand cru prices.

Having shocked the old guard, he then proceeded to rock the establishment further by planting Cabernet Sauvignon in a prime Nebbiolo site in Barbaresco in the late 1970s. Then, having for 25 years worked solely with the grapes of his own estate, in the 1980s he started buying or leasing property in other blue-chip zones of Italy, starting with BAROLO, then BRUNELLO DI MONTALCINO, and most recently in BOLGHERI.

GAJA

Angelo Gaja is recognized as one of the world's leading winemakers. His Barolo Sperss is an outstanding wine, with tremendous depth of fruit.

His principal Barbarescos are the crus Sorì Tildin, Sorì San Lorenzo and Costa Russi, plus one which could be described as *normale* except that there's nothing normal where Angelo Gaja is concerned.

In Barolo, since 1989, he has produced the Sperss cru (dialect for 'nostalgia', indicating the longing that Gaja had felt to return to the making of Barolo after so long) from a 12-ha (30-acre) site at Marenca e Rivette in Serralunga. More recently he has taken on production at a property called Gromis in La Morra, with its cru Conteisa Cerequio. He also makes a barrique-aged Nebbiolo-based VINO DA TAVOLA of distinction called Sito Moresco. His Cabernet Sauvignon vino da tavola, Darmagi, is probably the best of its type in Italy, as is his Chardonnay Gaia & Rey. Best years: (Barbaresco) 1998, '97, '96, '95, '93, '90, '89, '88, '85, '82, '79, '78, '71.

GALICIA

SPAIN

When phylloxera struck Spain in 1901, few wine regions were as badly hit as verdant, mountainous Galicia, in the north-western corner of the Iberian Peninsula, directly north of Portugal. And what was to come was almost as bad: most of the vineyards were replanted with 'foreign', low-quality, high-yield grape varieties, particularly Palomino (locally called Jerez or País) and Garnacha Tintorera. This condemned the region to utter obscurity for decades.

Only in the 1970s, under the leadership of a few pioneers led by retired engineer Santiago Ruiz, were native varieties gradually recovered and the interlopers axed. The seaside DO of RÍAS BAIXAS led the way. By 1998, 96 per cent of its 2100ha (5187 acres) under vine was occupied by the fragrant Albariño, Spain's best white cultivar.

There are now four other Galician DOs: the historic RIBEIRO, plus Monterrei, VALDEORRAS and Ribeira Sacra. The last two specialize in aromatic young red wines made with the Mencía grape, but all the regions are strong, and improving, in whites. The dominant white varieties are Treixadura and Torrontés in Ribeiro, the appley Godello in Valdeorras and Dona Branca in Monterrei. The wines are now vinified in a modern, fresh style in well-equipped, clean wineries. The point most in their favour is perfume. Spain's whites are largely made from neutral grape varieties, yet in Galicia these native varieties are all capable of sensuous perfume and mouth-watering fruit.

E & J GALLO WINERY

Gallo Sonoma is the much publicized Sonoma operation set up to give the Gallo image a new quality sheen. The acclaimed new wines include estate Chardonnay.

E & J GALLO WINERY

USA, California, San Joaquin Valley

♥ Cabernet Sauvignon, Zinfandel and others
♀ Grenache
♀ Chardonnay, Sauvignon Blanc, French Colombard and others

E & J Gallo, founded in 1933, was for many years a two brothers act. Ernest was the businessman and Julio, until his death in 1993, the winemaker. But Gallo has always been bigger than any other similar act in the history of wine. Its experimental vineyard – let alone its regular plantings – is upwards of 405ha (1000 acres); the winery's cellar of oak tanks exceeds the area of three football pitches; its main blending tank holds 50,000 hectolitres (1.1 million gallons); it has its own glass factory and annual sales are somewhere between 50 and 60 million cases. For years the bulk table wine production focused on off-dry generics – 'Chablis', 'Hearty Burgundy' and their kin. In these, Gallo remains virtually untouchable in American terms, though the wines don't rate so well against international competition.

New Gallo Sonoma and premium estate-bottled wines, however, are in a different league. Gallo Sonoma quickly evolved into a separate brand featuring varietal wines from Gallo's extensive vineyards (809ha/ 2000 acres) in the RUSSIAN RIVER VALLEY, DRY CREEK VALLEY and ALEXANDER VALLEY within SONOMA COUNTY. Leading the way are the high-priced Estate Chardonnay and Estate Cabernet Sauvignon, but there are also many good to excellent varietal wines. Tops among them are Zinfandel, Chardonnay and Merlot from Dry Creek Valley, Cabernet Sauvignon and Barbera from Alexander Valley, and Chardonnay from Russian River Valley. Single-vineyard Chardonnays (Laguna and Stefani) are also fine. Ongoing vineyard acquisitions and vineyard development programmes indicate we are seeing just the first fruits of a new Gallo.

GAMAY

In most of the world, the Gamay grape is considered a common kind of creature. In general, its wine is rather rough-edged, quite high in raspy acidity – and a bit raw of fruit. But on the granite outcrops of Beaujolais, Gamay has one glorious fling, producing juicy peach and strawberry-and-cherry happy juice, which at its breeziest is Beaujolais Nouveau and at its most heady and exciting is a single-domaine wine from Fleurie, Morgon or Moulin-à-Vent. Good examples can age to a very attractive, slightly farmyardy, gentle Pinot Noir imitation – toffee and chocolate and plums. Elsewhere in France, the Mâconnais has a lot of Gamay grapes, the Côte d'Or has the odd plot, while both Touraine and Anjou make rather dry, occasionally pleasant, light reds and rosés. Gamay is found, too, in the South and South-West.

For years California grew two varieties, the Napa Gamay and the Gamay Beaujolais. Then it was decided that the Napa Gamay was the real Gamay, the Gamay Noir à Jus Blanc, while the other was merely a weak strain of Pinot Noir. Recent studies have demonstrated that most of what was thought to be Napa Gamay is really another variety, Valdiguié. Those few wineries offering wine from the grape have begun using the Valdiguié name, and the style ranges from light and simple to dark coloured and robust. As a result of lengthy discussions with French officials, California wineries have agreed to prohibit the use of the terms Gamay and Gamay Beaujolais by the year 2007.

MARTA & DANIEL GANTENBEIN
SWITZERLAND, Graubünden, Fläsch
♥ Pinot Noir (Blauburgunder)
♀ Pinot Blanc (Weissburgunder), Chardonnay, Müller-Thurgau, Riesling

The wines made by this husband-and-wife team prove that it is not only in the French- or Italian-speaking parts of Switzerland that innovative winemakers are at work. Here in the Upper Rhine valley is a pocket of viticulture with a much more favourable climate than you would imagine when you see the snow-capped peaks on all sides. The Pinot Noir reds for which the Gantenbeins are best known have improved in leaps and bounds since the early 1990s when they began barrique-aging the entire production. Good vintages have the perfume, rich black cherry fruit and elegant tannins that make you think of Burgundy. The Gantenbein's Chardonnays are no oak-and-alcohol monsters, having a Chablis-like sleekness and a strong minerally character. They age well too. Successful experiments with Riesling have persuaded the Gantenbeins to plant this variety too. Best years: (red) 1997, '95, '94; (white) 1998, '97, '96, '95, '94.

GARD
FRANCE, Languedoc-Roussillon
The Gard could consider itself a bit unlucky, because of all the southern French *départements* it has the shortest coastline and what it has is merely a sliver of unprepossessing marshland just east of Montpellier – better known as the Camargue. It's a little unlucky in its wines, too, because although there is a decent-sized chunk of the CÔTES DU RHÔNE AC in the Gard, with TAVEL and LIRAC also inside its borders, for real Rhône fireworks one must travel east or north.

To the south and west of the Gard, the Languedoc has taken off as a wine producer, with increasing amounts of exciting gutsy wines that are causing a stir the world over – and yet the Gard can't quite get in on that act either. Its reds have a rather meaty, earthy style and, Lirac apart, its only white AC of any renown is the flat, dull Clairette de Bellegarde, although some fresh whites and fruity reds are now being made by good, young, COSTIÈRES DE NÎMES producers. Otherwise, there are bright signs in the experimental plots of Chardonnay and Sauvignon Blanc and the occasional Grenache Blanc.

GARDA DOC
ITALY, Veneto
♥ Cabernet Sauvignon, Cabernet Franc, Merlot, Pinot Nero, Groppello, Marzemino, Corvina, Barbera
♀ Garganega, Pinot Bianc (Pinot Bianco), Pinot Gris (Pinot Grigio), Chardonnay, Tocai Friulano, Riesling Renano, Cortese, Sauvignon

Created in 1997, this is a catch-all DOC for wines which previously would have been classed as VINO DA TAVOLA. It's a pretty large zone in the province of Verona, stretching from Lake Garda east to the farthest reaches of SOAVE via BARDOLINO and VALPOLICELLA, and taking in those parts of LOMBARDY which abut on to the lake on the west and south, in the provinces of Brescia and Montova respectively.

Its purpose is to allow producers in those zones to do pretty well what they feel like and still remain within the DOC system, and it grew up, not as a revolutionary throwing open of the gates but as a belated official reaction to an existing system (i.e. the wine producers were already doing what they felt like).

All the above-mentioned grapes can be made into varietal wines using a minimum of 85 per cent of the variety mentioned. The DOC also allows a red blend, a white blend and a chiaretto (rosé); these latter, together with Groppello and Groppello Riserva, having the right to add the subtitle 'Classico' should they so desire. Being a recent creation, major producers have yet to emerge.

GARGANEGA
The prolific Garganega, Italy's fifth most-planted white variety, can be found in various parts of north-east Italy, but its historic home is the western Veneto in the provinces of Verona and Vicenza. It is a very vigorous grape which, like its mate Corvina, requires training on a long arm. Maturity occurs between the last third of September through to the middle of October, depending on altitude and the degree of ripeness desired by the producer.

The first mention of this grape in literature comes in the early fourteenth century, when in Pier de' Crescenzi's *Trattato dell'Agricultura* we find reference to 'Garganica'. That Garganega has a long tradition of high quality may come as a surprise to those who associate its wines, notably SOAVE, with industrial table wine, but grown on the slopes where yields are self-regulating Garganega can bring forth a wine of great delicacy and finesse, not to mention versatility and durability.

Garganega is probably related to that Grecanico of presumed Greek origin so diffuse today in Sicily, from where it might have travelled to other parts of Italy and found a home in the hills of Verona. The theory is based on a great resemblance between the respective bunch, berry and leaf shapes, together with a similarity of aromas and wine styles. It would also explain the curious name of Garganega with its accent on the third-from-last syllable (Gar-ga-ne-ga; cf. Gre-ca-ni-co).

GARVEY

SPAIN, Andalucía, Jerez y Manzanilla DO

Palomino Fino, Pedro Ximénez, Moscatel

Garvey's San Patricio is one of the finest finos available, as well as one of the leading dry sherries with a slightly lower level of alcohol. Other favourites are the rich, nutty Garvey Palo Cortado, and a wonderfully treacly Pedro Ximénez. Other brands include Tio Guillermo old Amontillado, Ochavico nutty old Oloroso, Long Life Oloroso (medium sweet) and Flor de Jerez Cream. Garvey still uses its beautiful old bodegas in the town of Jerez and owns 500ha (1235 acres) of top-quality vineyards in the region.

GATTINARA DOCG, GHEMME DOCG

ITALY, Piedmont

Nebbiolo (Spanna), Bonarda di Gattinara, Vespolina

Gattinara lies in northern PIEDMONT, in the province of Vercelli, in the vineyard area called Coste della Sesia, where the Nebbiolo grape tends to a softer, plummier style than in BAROLO or BARBARESCO. At its best, Gattinara can be full-bodied and fairly powerful yet with distinct floral aromas, displaying a touch of spice and a lightly bitter finish, and drinking well from five to 15 years old or more. It can also be as tough as Barolo, and it can be mediocre in quality, tending to oxidize rather rapidly. Best years: 1998, '97, '96, '95, '90, '88, '85. Best producers: Antoniolo, Nervi, Travaglini.

Other DOC zones on the right bank of the Sesia river are Bramaterra and Lessona, whose stars have slipped considerably farther into obscurity even than that of Gattinara. On the opposite, left bank of the Sesia, in the Novara vine-land today called Colline Novaresi, the dominant if nonetheless tiny production zone is that of Ghemme, whose wine has characteristics similar to those of Gattinara while being tauter, more delicate, less earthy. The only producer of note is the Antichi Vigneti di Cantalupo (crus Collis Breclemae and Collis Carellae). Other production zones in this area are Boca, Sizzano and Faro, all DOCs of little distinction.

DOMAINE GAUBY

FRANCE, Languedoc-Roussillon, Côtes du Roussillon AC

Carignan, Grenache, Syrah, Mourvèdre and others

Muscat, Grenache Blanc, Macabeo, Viognier

A leading figure for the younger generation in the Roussillon, Gérard Gauby has always pro-duced impressively powerful, concentrated wines but has now added a little finesse as well. Highlights from this 40-ha (99-acre) domaine include the firm, rich, cassis-laden CÔTES DU ROUSSILLON-Villages Vieilles Vignes and the suave, spicy la Muntada, made almost exclusively from Syrah aged in oak barriques. The whites include the imposing Cuvée Centenaire, produced from 80-year-old Grenache Blanc, a VIN DE PAYS Viognier and a late-harvested Grenache Blanc that tastes of figs and crème brûlée. Best years: (reds) 1997, '96, '95, '94, '93.

GAVI DOCG

ITALY, Piedmont

Cortese

This white wine of southern PIEDMONT, so often dismissed as an overpriced nonentity, can sometimes rise to the occasion. It develops a subtle but engaging, delicate, steely, toasty, lemony-fruited character that impresses more and more, especially at one to two years after the vintage. Too often, though, it is drunk too young, when its acidity is still searing and seemingly ill-integrated with the wine.

Usually the wine is just called Gavi; to make it seem even more important the idea was hatched of calling it Gavi di Gavi. The only estates permitted to do so are those with vineyards in the commune of Gavi, but since that is most of them the cachet is somewhat devalued. Best producers: La Battistina, Bergaglio, Broglia, Castellari Bergaglio, La Chiara, Michele Chiarlo, La Giustiniana, Martinetti, San Pietro, Santa Seraffa, La Scolca, Castello di Tassarolo, Villa Sparina.

CH. GAZIN

FRANCE, Bordeaux, Pomerol AC

Merlot, Cabernet Franc, Cabernet Sauvignon

One of the largest châteaux in POMEROL with 24ha (59 acres), Gazin is situated on the eastern plateau next to Ch. PÉTRUS and l'ÉVANGILE. Despite the prime location on Pomerol's clay-limestone soils and with the vines in a single block, the wine from Gazin was remarkably inconsistent in the 1960s, '70s and early '80s and only really hit top form from 1988. The estate is owned by Nicolas de Bailliencourt while J-P Moueix handles sales. It is now one of the most improved Pomerol properties and the Merlot-dominated wines show a truly rich, ripe, unctuous character with finely woven tannins, making them delicious young but capable of long aging. Best years: 1996, '95, '94, '93, '90, '89, '88.

GEELONG

AUSTRALIA, Victoria, Port Phillip Zone

Geelong was almost as famous as the YARRA VALLEY in the nineteenth century, but fell prey to the fatal vine infestation phylloxera, with every vineyard compulsorily destroyed by government order in 1881. The measure was intended to stop phylloxera spreading, but failed. The region is windswept, cool and at times hostile to the grape-grower, but Pinot Noir can be terrific, all plums, truffles, spices and violets, while Idyll makes an idiosyncratic, woody and long-lived Cabernet/Shiraz blend and a spicy, tannic Gewürztraminer which seems to wish it were a red. Best producers: BANNOCKBURN, now pursued (in a softer style) by SCOTCHMANS HILL. Best years: 1998, '97, '95, '94, '91, '90, '88.

SCOTCHMANS HILL

This exciting Geelong producer has established a fine reputation in a relatively short period. The Pinot Noir is silky with beautifully focused, meaty, strawberry fruit.

GEISENHEIM

GERMANY, Rheingau

The name Geisenheim is famous on two counts. First, as a wine village with excellent vineyards, notably the Rothenberg, Kläuserweg and Mäuerchen sites. The Rothenberg is named after the vineyard's iron-rich, red soils which produce rich, earthy wines. Best producers: Forschunganstalt Geisenheim, A Freimuth, Prinz von Hessen, JOHANNISHOF, J WEGELER, Freiherr von Zwierlein.

The second reason is Geisenheim's wine school, founded in 1872, where aspiring winemakers come to study, and the research institute which is the source of all those new vine-crossings that have helped or bedevilled (depending on your point of view) German wine over the past few decades.

Vines like Optima, Kerner, Reichensteiner and Bacchus were all born here, generally as part of the search for vines that will withstand the harsher aspects of Germany's climate and still give wine with flavour and style. There are open days several times a year and a walk through the institute's experimental vineyards could give a sneak preview of German viticulture in the next century.

GEOGRAPHE

AUSTRALIA, Western Australia, South West Australia Zone

This is a newly created wine region, effectively representing the southern half of the previously much larger Southwest Coastal Plain region, and extending from Bunbury in the north to Capel in the south, and inland to the east of Dardenup. It presently has seven wineries, three in the coastal area and four around Dardenup.

Geographe's coastal climate is very similar to that of northern MARGARET RIVER, but that of the interior is quite different: this is (or was) apple and stonefruit country. Grapefruit-accented Chardonnay, tangy Semillon and Sauvignon Blanc, and highly aromatic Riesling lead the white wines. Shiraz, varying from light to full-bodied, and berryish Cabernet Sauvignon are the main red styles. Best producers: CAPEL VALE, Fergusson Falls Estate, Killerby.

GESELLMANN

AUSTRIA, Mittelburgenland, Deutschkreutz

♦ *Blaufränkisch, Blauer Zweigelt, St Laurent, Pinot Noir (Blauburgunder), Cabernet Sauvignon, Merlot*
♀ *Welschriesling, Pinot Blanc (Weissburgunder), Scheurebe*

Albert Gesellmann's winemaking inspiration comes from time spent working in CALIFORNIA and South Africa, and what he learnt there enabled him to improve the colour, depth and balance of the already interesting range of red wines which his father had developed during the 1980s. Bella Rex, a rich Cabernet-Merlot blend in an almost Californian style is the best, followed by Opus Eximum, a blend of French and local grapes whose composition varies from vintage to vintage, but like Bella Rex also gets a dose of new oak. Best years: (reds) 1997, '95, '93, '92.

GETARIAKO TXAKOLINA DO (CHACOLÍ DE GUETARIA DO)

SPAIN, País Vasco

♦ *Hondarribi Beltza*
♀ *Hondarribi Zuri*

Almost all the wine from this DO (also known as Chacolí de Guetaria in Spanish) gets drunk near where it is made, in the coastal Basque country. Only 34ha (89 acres) of vines are currently in production, and vineyards are tiny – some not even measuring 0.5ha (1.2 acres). Since 1994 there has also been a DO for nearby Bizkaiko Txakolina (Chacolí de Vizcaya in Spanish). The wine is called Chacolí in Spanish, Txakoli in Basque.

The Hondarribi Zuri white grapes that constitute 90 per cent of the plantings also have optional spellings. The wine is high in acidity, with a strong fruity flavour, a refreshing, natural prickle of gas and lowish alcohol, usually 9.5 to 10 per cent, sometimes as high as 11 per cent (the minimum is 9.5). A little red Chacolí is also made.

GEVREY-CHAMBERTIN AC

FRANCE, Burgundy, Côte de Nuits

♦ *Pinot Noir*

Gevrey-Chambertin is an infuriating village. With its Grands Crus CHAMBERTIN and Chambertin Clos-de-Bèze, it is capable of making the most startling, intoxicatingly delicious red wines of Burgundy, yet maddeningly liable to produce a limp succession of pale, lifeless semi-reds which really don't deserve the AC at all. It's the old Burgundian problem of supply and demand. With its world-famous top vineyard, Chambertin, leading the way, all the wines – Grand Cru, Premier Cru and the village wines – are keenly sought-after. Production increases – Gevrey-Chambertin already has easily the biggest production on the CÔTE D'OR – less suitable land is planted (some of the Gevrey-Chambertin AC is on the plains side of the N74 road, which is generally seen as the boundary below which good wine cannot be made), and standards slip. So straightforward Gevrey-Chambertin village wine should be approached with circumspection. On the other hand, top growers such as BURGUET, Dugat-Py and Denis MORTET make powerful and exciting wines from village parcels.

But good examples are proud, big-tasting Burgundy at its best, usually a bit chewy, jammy even, when young, but gradually getting a fascinating flavour of perfumed plums and dark, smoky chocolates after six to ten years' aging. The finest of the 26 Premiers Crus, such as Clos St-Jacques and Combe aux Moines, come close to rivalling the Grands Crus in terms of power and longevity. And as a new generation takes over, we are seeing the gradual demise of the cynicism that bedevilled the 1970s and '80s and the return of a certain muscular 'don't mess with me' pride. Best years: 1997, '96, '95, '93, '91, '90, '89, '88, '87, '85, '83, '80, '78. Best producers: D Bachelet, L Boillot, Burguet, CLAIR, Damoy, DROUHIN, Dugat, Dugat-Py, DUJAC, Michel Esmonin, FAIVELEY, JADOT, Phillipe Leclerc, Denis Mortet, RODET, Rossignol, Rossignol-Trapet, Roty, ROUSSEAU, Trapet, Varoilles.

GEWÜRZTRAMINER

Are Gewürztraminer and Traminer synonyms for the same grape or are they two different grapes? In France's Alsace, where the grape achieves its highest quality and its greatest fame, there's no problem. It's Gewurztraminer and that's that. In Italy, where it grows in Friuli, as far south as Calabria, and as far north as the Südtirol or Alto Adige (which is the region of the village of Tramin from which the grape takes its name) it may be either Traminer or Traminer Aromatico (alias Gewürztraminer). Sometimes it depends on the degree of spicy flavour in the wine, the prefix 'Gewürz' meaning spice in German; there has, in times past, been some confusion with the less aromatic Rotertraminer. Or the name Traminer may just be a convenient local shorthand. In Germany it is mostly known as Traminer, and grows (albeit in small quantities) mostly in Baden and the Pfalz; the Austrians go overboard and call it Gewürztraminer, Traminer, Roter (red) Traminer or Gelber (yellow) Traminer. Australia tends to be pretty relaxed about which name it uses.

Even the less spicy sort should have something of the rose petals, tropical fruit and musk perfume that has brought fame and fortune to the Alsace versions, though some wines from Austria's Steiermark region and Italy's Südtirol can be very pared down. But that's not really what Gewürztraminer is for. It's about opulence and intensity – for which it needs good balancing acidity if it is not to turn flabby.

Most New World producers content themselves with making off-dry wines for quick drinking. Some California growers, however, are doing better things, particularly in Mendocino's Anderson Valley and Sonoma's Russian River Valley. Oregon, Texas and New York State, especially Long Island, also show promise. Chile's cooler areas can produce pale, beautifully fragrant wines. Australia's are usually a little fat, but New Zealand's can equal Alsace at their best.

GEYSER PEAK WINERY

USA, California, Sonoma County, Alexander Valley AVA

🍷 *Cabernet Sauvignon, Merlot, Shiraz (Syrah), Zinfandel, Sangiovese*

🍷 *Chardonnay, Sauvignon Blanc, Riesling*

After several ownership changes, Geyser Peak was heading nowhere fast until it was rescued in 1982 by Henry Trione, well-known SONOMA COUNTY resident. Bringing 405ha (1000 acres) into the fold, Trione put the winery back on an even keel, and a sharp upturn in quality occurred after the arrival of winemaker Daryl Groom of Australia. Sent to Geyser Peak during a short-lived partnership with PENFOLDS, Groom stayed on to improve quality by working with growers and by making dramatic changes in the winery and its approach to winemaking. Both the fruit-driven regular and succulent, nicely oaked Reserve Chardonnay are charming, as is the effusive, vibrant Sauvignon Blanc.

But the real story here revolves around the reds. The current stars are a massive, beautifully crafted Reserve Cabernet Sauvignon and handsome, wildly flavourful Reserve Shiraz. Reserve Alexandre is the winery's enticing red Meritage. With lush, plummy fruit, Merlot is soft and delicious. Sangiovese in several guises, and single-vineyard Chardonnay and Cabernet Sauvignon are sold under the Venezia name. Canyon Road is another brand used for low- to mid-priced varietals, including an always interesting Semillon. Best years: (reds) 1997, '96, '95, '94, '92.

GIACONDA

AUSTRALIA, Victoria, North East Victoria Zone, Ovens Valley

🍷 *Pinot Noir*

🍷 *Chardonnay*

One suspects to his absolute dismay, the shy, quietly spoken Rick Kinzbrunner has achieved vinous rock-star status since establishing his tiny Giaconda winery in north-east VICTORIA in 1985. Part of the hysteria may be due to a total annual production of less than 1000 cases, but it is hard to say whether his Burgundian lookalike, tight yet complex Chardonnay or his silky, slippery, sappy, foresty Pinot Noir is the most highly regarded wine. The wild yeast, no-filtration winemaking regime also helps Kinzbrunner's image of 'aw shucks' achievement, so I'm afraid he's just going to have to grin and bear it. Best years: 1997, '96, '95, '92, '91, '90, '88, '86, '85.

Giesen is Canterbury's largest winery and makes outstanding botrytized and dry Rieslings from its sunny but wind-battered vineyards.

BRUNO GIACOSA

ITALY, Piedmont, Barbaresco DOCG

🍷 *Nebbiolo, Barbera, Dolcetto and others*

🍷 *Arneis*

The Giacosa tradition is that of the *commerciante* or merchant on the highest level. Bruno and his father before him have always bought grapes from growers with whom they have enjoyed life-long relationships, growers having some of the finest vineyards in Italy. Today, with the rise and rise of the grower-bottler the company is beginning to acquire its own vineyards, starting with Falletto in the commune of Serralunga in BAROLO and Asili in BARBARESCO.

The winemaking philosophy could be best described as updated-traditional: the grapes are still macerated for up to 30 days on the skins, but no longer for more than 50 as previously; large oak *botti* are still used for aging, but the oak is now French, not Slavonian. Giacosa is contemptuous of people who reduce maceration time to a few days and who dose their wines with Cabernet or Merlot or wood aromas. He is very strict about what he deems suitable to be bottled under his label: his cru Barolos and Barbarescos were all sold in bulk in 1991, '92 and '94.

Apart from Falletto, Giacosa also produces Barolo cru Collina Rionda (Serralunga) and Villero and Rocche (Castiglione Falletto). In Barbaresco his most famous wine is Santo Stefano di Neive. He also makes a traditional *botte*-aged version of NEBBIOLO D'ALBA from Valmaggiore di Vezza d'Alba and excellent CHAMPAGNE-method Extra Brut from Pinot Noir. Best years: 1997, '96, '95, '93, '90, '89, '88, '85, '82, '78, '71.

GIESEN

NEW ZEALAND, South Island, Canterbury

🍷 *Cabernet Sauvignon, Pinot Noir*

🍷 *Riesling, Sauvignon Blanc, Chardonnay and others*

The Giesen family moved from the Rhine Valley in Germany in 1980, to establish this substantial (50,000-case) and still growing winery, choosing a cool and windy climate with which they were familiar. Not surprisingly, they have succeeded best (and at times brilliantly) with non-wooded aromatic wine styles, both dry and lusciously sweet (through botrytis). The botrytized Rieslings can rightly lay claim to being some of the finest in the southern hemisphere. Best years: 1998, '97, '96, '95, '94, '91.

GIGONDAS AC

FRANCE, Southern Rhône

🍷🍷 *Grenache, Syrah, Mourvèdre, Cinsaut*

Gigondas is a large village below the craggy slopes of the Dentelles de Montmirail on the east of the RHÔNE VALLEY near Orange, with 1250ha (3089 acres) of vines. The wines certainly have personality, with a tougher, chewier, jam-rich fruit than those from nearby CHÂTEAUNEUF-DU-PAPE; they take longer to soften and never quite set the heart so aflutter. Best years: 1998, '97, '95, '94, '93, '90, '89, '88, '86, '85. Best producers: Cayron, Clos des Cazaux, Roger Combe, Font-Sane, la Garrigue, les GOUBERT, Grapillon d'Or, GUIGAL, JABOULET, les Pallières, Pascal, de Piaugier, RASPAIL-AY, St-Gayan, Santa-Duc, Tardieu-Laurent.

CH. GILETTE

FRANCE, Bordeaux, Sauternes AC

🍷 *Sémillon, Sauvignon Blanc, Muscadelle*

This extraordinary wine unusually avoids oak barriques like the plague. Instead it is fermented in stainless steel and then aged for 12–14 years in concrete vats. Just to round things off it is then bottled and stored in the Gilette cellars for a further three to five years before being finally released to the consumer (as Crème de Tête) a minimum of 15 years after the harvest. This method significantly reduces the oxygen contact and preserves the lively fruit character in the wines. These have a deep golden colour, sumptuous bouquet of raisined fruits, orange zest, coffee and vanilla and a rich unctuousness on the palate with an interminable finish. The volume of wine produced from the tiny 5-ha (12-acre) vineyard is, of course, minimal and the price tag is consequently high. Best years: 1978, '76, '75, '70, '67, '61, '59, '55, '53, '49.

GIPPSLAND

AUSTRALIA, Victoria

This fairly cool, sprawling zone, extending for 200km (125 miles) south-east of Melbourne, is principally noted for Chardonnay and Pinot Noir. Some of the flavours so far produced match anything in Australia for power and intensity. Best years: 1998, '97, '95, '94, '91, '90, '88, '87. Best producers: BASS PHILLIP, Nicholson River.

GISBORNE

NEW ZEALAND, North Island

The Gisborne or Poverty Bay area was once a largely anonymous provider of low cost, pleasantly fruity grapes to keep the pumps flowing for bag-in-the-box wines. The area has moved up-market (much of NZ's bag-in-the-box wine is now imported from Australia, Chile and Spain) and labels itself 'the Chardonnay capital of NZ'. Improved vineyard sites and lower crop levels have done much to raise Gisborne's image. Best performers are MATAWHERO and Millton, together with premium Gisborne-branded wines from some of the major players, in particular Chardonnay from MONTANA's Ormond Estate, Matua Judd's Estate and NOBILO's Dixon Vineyard. Best years: 1998, '96, '95, '94.

CH. GISCOURS

FRANCE, Bordeaux, Haut-Médoc, Margaux AC, 3ème Cru Classé

♥ *Cabernet Sauvignon, Merlot, Cabernet Franc, Petit Verdot*

Ch. Giscours made a number of fabulous wines in the 1960s and '70s. They started off with a rather solid, almost tarry quality but also had a heavenly perfume, just asking for a few years' maturity, and a fruit that was blackberries, blackcurrants and cherries all at once.

Things tailed off disappointingly in the 1980s to a rather more typically dilute MARGAUX style of wine, and recently infighting among the owners and a scandal in 1998 concerning a vat of HAUT-MÉDOC wine that found its way into Giscours' second wine, la Sirène de Giscours, has surely halted progress. One can only hope that Giscours will be back on the rails soon, as the potential is definitely there. Best years: 1996, '95, '90, '86, '83, '82, '81, '80, '79.

GIV (GRUPPO ITALIANO VINI)

ITALY

With production cellars in ten separate locations throughout northern and central Italy,

Father and son, Walter and David Finlayson of Glen Carlou tasting a barrel sample of their acclaimed Chardonnay, which can mature for four or five years, longer than most other South African Chardonnays.

from northern LOMBARDY to Rome, and a total vineyard area in excess of 800ha (1976 acres), GIV describes itself as 'Italian and European leader in the quality wine market'. Despite its massive size, GIV's wines are always of a good standard, at least, and sometimes of a remarkably high one.

Run by Emilio Pedron, GIV's administrative seat is at Calmasino in the VENETO region where it also controls two wineries, Lamberti at Pastrengo and Santi at Illasi. Both wineries make the entire gamut of Veronese wines, plus others, Lamberti concentrating on supermarket products while Santi is somewhat more up-market, turning out also a range of TRENTINO wines from Mezzocorona.

Nino Negri, GIV's cantina in VALTELLINA, in northern Lombardy, is the leading winery in the area and the Sfursat Cinque Stelle is rich and full-bodied with complex flavours. Elsewhere in the north, GIV controls Conti Formentini in FRIULI and Cà Bianca in PIEDMONT. In TUSCANY GIV controls the house of Machiavelli/Conti Serristori in San Casciano (top wines: CHIANTI CLASSICO Fontalle and Ser Niccolò Solatio del Tani/Cabernet Sauvignon) and Melini in Poggibonsi (top wine: Chianti Classico La Selvanella).

In UMBRIA GIV owns Bigi, whose cru Orvieto, Vigneto Torricella, and barrique-fermented Grechetto Marrano are among the best of their type. In Rome, GIV is the proprietor of the giant Fontana Candida company, whose cru Santa Teresa is one of the best Frascati wines.

GIVRY AC

FRANCE, Burgundy, Côte Chalonnaise

♥ *Pinot Noir*

♀ *Chardonnay*

This is an important Côte Chalonnaise wine village with 120ha (297 acres) of vineyards, west of Chalon-sur-Saône. The red wines are generally good, not that heavy, and with a full, ripe strawberry perfume and a gently plummy flavour.

Whites wines from Givry are much rarer – only about 140,000 bottles out of an annual production of one million – and they often used to veer towards the sharp and neutral (not at all like Chardonnay should be in southern Burgundy). But in recent years the wines seem to be a little fuller and nuttier – which is much more attractive. In the 1990s about 25 vineyards were elevated to Premier Cru status. Best years: (reds) 1997, '96, '95, '93, '90, '89, '88, '86, '85, '83, '82. Best producers: Chofflet-Valdenaire (reds), Derain, Joblot, F Lumpp, Ragot, Sarrazin, Thénard.

GLEN CARLOU

SOUTH AFRICA, Western Cape, Paarl WO

♥ *Cabernet Sauvignon, Merlot, Cabernet Franc, Pinot Noir and others*

♀ *Chardonnay, Chenin Blanc*

Over the years, Walter Finlayson has attracted a loyal following, initially for his red wines, but since his move to this PAARL farm he has also gained recognition for excellent Chardonnay. His career started in STELLENBOSCH, on the family farm, Hartenberg (then known as Montagne); he then helped to put the Blaauwklippen estate on the map. Ten years ago, he moved to his own property, GLEN CARLOU on the Paarl slopes of the Simonsberg, where he has specialized in two loves, BORDEAUX and Burgundy. Son David is now following capably in his father's footsteps and has reinforced the farm's already fine reputation for bold, complex Chardonnay. A good air-flow down the valley helps Pinot Noir here to turn in a surprisingly good performance on these north-facing slopes; although lightish, it has inviting ripe black cherry and raspberry flavours.

These classically styled, quality wines attracted Donald Hess of California's HESS COLLECTION. His partnership has brought renewed impetus and growth to this leading Cape producer. Best years: (reds) 1996, '95, '94, '93, '92, '91, '90; (Chardonnay) 1998, '97, '96, '95, '94.

GLENORA WINE CELLARS
USA, New York State, Dundee, Finger Lakes AVA
♀ *Chardonnay, Riesling, Seyval Blanc*
Sparkling Brut Reserve

Glenora Wine Cellars is a top-quality, large-scale producer of vinifera wines in the Finger Lakes AVA. Its yeasty, complex sparkling wines, including a light and refreshing vintage Blanc de Blancs, are very good and a fine Riesling and attractive barrel-fermented Chardonnay are the best still wines. Best years: 1997, '95, '94.

GOLAN HEIGHTS WINERY
ISRAEL, Golan Heights
♥ *Cabernet Sauvignon, Merlot, Pinot Noir*
♥ *Cabernet Sauvignon*
♀ *Sauvignon Blanc, Chardonnay, Semillon, Emerald Riesling*

This is the winery setting the pace for all others in Israel. Its actual name is Hatzor, but it's known as Golan Heights because that's where it is located. The Golan Heights vineyards are planted up to 1100m (3600ft), and this altitude and the cool nights are the winery's secret weapons. Using night harvesting for the white grapes and winemaking equipment and techniques derived from California, the winery produces surprisingly light, fresh wines that are a world away from what used to be thought of as kosher wines.

All the Golan Heights wines are kosher, but since the vineyards are outside the Biblical Old Kingdom, the rule that says that the vineyards must lie fallow every seventh year need not be observed. However, the most

GOLAN HEIGHTS
Israel's leading quality wine producer combines the latest Californian techniques with kosher strictures. Yarden is the label used for the top wines.

scrupulous orthodox drinkers avoided the 1987 for this reason. The Yarden range is the best, followed by Gamla and Golan. Drink the wines young.

GONZÁLEZ BYASS
SPAIN, Andalucía, Jerez y Manzanilla DO; La Rioja, Rioja DOC; Cataluña, Cava DO
♀ *Palomino Fino, Pedro Ximénez, Moscatel*

Tio Pepe, González Byass' fino, is the top-selling sherry in the world. Unusually for such a big brand, it's also one of the very best. González Byass owns 2000ha (5000 acres) of prime vineyards and also has long-term contracts with grape-growers from a further 1000ha (2470 acres). Unlike many JEREZ firms, it never buys in grape juice or ready-made wines, preferring to put all the raw material of the grapes through its own quality-oriented plant.

Amontillado del Duque is a fine, dry, austere, pungent and nutty wine, one of the world's great wines for a very fair price. Matusalem is a sweetened old oloroso, big, deep and pruny, majestically rich. And Apostoles Oloroso Viejo is medium-dry, nutty and grapy. The next step down, Alfonso Dry Oloroso, is also very good. As well as Tio Pepe, there's a cheaper fino sold under the brand name Elegante and, typically sweetened for the UK market, La Concha Amontillado, San Domingo Pale Cream and Caballero Amontillado. González Byass also owns Castell de Villarnau, a CAVA producer in PENEDÈS, and the fine Bodegas Beronia in RIOJA.

GOSSET
FRANCE, Champagne, Champagne AC
♀ ♥ *Chardonnay, Pinot Noir, Pinot Meunier*

There have been dramatic changes at this venerable house. Promoted to *grande marque* status in 1992, it was then bought by the Cointreau family of Cognac. However, the new owners have retained the former wine-making team and show no signs of increasing annual production to more than the current

500,000 bottles. Of Gosset's two non-vintage Champagnes, the outstanding one is the Grande Réserve Brut, a rich, sumptuous wine, composed mostly of Chardonnay. The vintage Grand Millésime has a higher Chardonnay content, and there is also a fine vintage rosé. Overall, these are big, bold Champagnes which may not be appreciated by those who value freshness and delicacy above all else. Best years: 1990, '89, '88, '85, '82.

DOMAINE LES GOUBERT
FRANCE, Southern Rhône, Gigondas AC
♥ *Grenache, Syrah, Cinsaut, Mourvèdre*
♀ *Clairette, Bourboulenc, Viognier*

Jean-Pierre Cartier began making the wines at his 23-ha (57-acre) family estate in GIGONDAS in 1974. When he and his wife took themselves off to enology and wine-tasting courses at a French university, their neighbours thought they were mad. Indeed, Jean-Pierre's spirit of inquiry and willingness to innovate still sets him apart from his more parochial neighbours; moreover, in the poor 1992 vintage he had the courage to bottle not one drop of red wine.

His reds, whether a simple CÔTES DU RHÔNE or a more complex Beaumes-de-Venise or Gigondas, are always rich and deep, imposing yet lovely wines that can age very well. In the mid-1980s he enraged traditionalists by aging a special cuvée of Gigondas in barriques, largely new. Cuvée Florence went down well with his American followers, but within Europe it proved more controversial.

In the 1990s Cartier turned his attention to making white wines as well as reds, and he is now fermenting much of his white Sablet in oak; there is also a barrel-fermented Côtes du Rhône wine made entirely from Viognier.

Les Goubert no longer stands out within the Gigondas appellation now that other estates are matching its high standards, but it still remains an impeccable source of delicious, well-structured, classic southern RHÔNE wines. Best years: 1997, '95, '94, '93, '90, '89, '88, '86, '85.

DOMAINE LES GOUBERT
Jean-Pierre Cartier makes a good range of wines at his Gigondas estate. Cuvée Florence, his top wine, spends 18 months in oak and is unfiltered.

HENRI GOUGES

FRANCE, Burgundy, Côte de Nuits, Nuits-St-Georges AC

Pinot Noir

Pinot Noir [sic]

Henri Gouges was one of the pioneers of fine, unadulterated Burgundies in the 1920s and '30s. But by the late '70s the estate seemed to be in decline. Fortunately, the present generation, Christian and Pierre, have made the wines once again among the very best of the appellation. Indeed, so they should be, given the excellent vineyards belonging to the family. Of the 14.5ha (36 acres) of vines, at least 10ha (25 acres) are Premiers Crus, of which the finest are St-Georges and Vaucrains. Two fascinating whites are produced from Clos des Porrets and les Perrières; they are made from a long-established mutation of Pinot Noir, and although white in colour and aroma, they have the body and substance of a red wine. Best years: 1997, '96, '95, '93, '90, '89, '88, '85.

GOULBURN VALLEY

AUSTRALIA, Victoria, Central Victoria Zone

Goulburn Valley is located north of the Great Dividing Range, where it becomes drier and warmer. At the southern end of the valley, CHATEAU TAHBILK makes monumental, tannic reds, from ancient vines, while MITCHELTON produces modern, oaky wines. Here the Goulburn River creates billabongs (or backwaters) lined with white-trunked eucalyptus trees and inhabited by an amazing variety of bird life. In the flatter and less picturesque north, where the Goulburn joins the Murray River, irrigated white and red varietals of good quality and modest price are produced by four wineries. Best producers: Chateau Tahbilk, Mitchelton, Osicka. Best years: 1998, '97, '96, '95, '94, '92, '91, '88, '86, '85, '81, '75, '71.

GOUNDREY WINES

AUSTRALIA, Western Australia, West Australian South East Coastal Zone, Great Southern

Cabernet Sauvignon, Syrah (Shiraz), Pinot Noir

Riesling, Chardonnay, Sauvignon Blanc

The acquisition of this estate by American-born former media magnate Jack Bendat has seen a massive inflow of capital and the expansion of both vineyards and winery. Tight, steely Riesling that unfolds into lime and passion fruit in four or five years, crisp, melon-and-grapefruit Chardonnay with a smoky, spicy oak character, lean yet spicy Shiraz and Cabernet Sauvignon showing just a hint of its vast potential at three years old, are all high quality. Best years: 1996, '95, '94, '91, '90, '88, '87, '85, '82, '77.

GRAACH

GERMANY, Mosel-Saar-Ruwer

With the village of Graach we are in the heart of the MOSEL region. The soil is deep slate, fine slivers of grey rock that hold the heat and impart a once-tasted-never-forgotten whiff of smoke to the Rieslings it supports. On richer soils like these, the wines are full, honeyed, yet intense. The vineyards' south-west exposure to the sun is ideal, and there's plenty of it: the vineyards rise almost vertically from near river level to 200m (660ft). The vineyard names to look for are intensely minerally Domprobst, the more floral Himmelreich and spicy Josephshöfer; anything from one of these Graach Einzellagen should be a treat. Best producers: von KESSELSTATT, Dr LOOSEN, J J PRÜM, S A PRÜM, Willi SCHAEFER, WEGELER.

GRAHAM

PORTUGAL, Douro, Port DOC

Tinta Roriz (Tempranillo), Tinta Barroca, Tinto Cão, Touriga Nacional, Touriga Francesa and others

Gouveio, Malvasia Fina, Rabigato and others

One of the main PORT shippers belonging to the Symington family, Graham has a house style that is usually sweeter and more florally scented than those of the other Symington companies. This is best reflected in its outstanding vintage port based on Quinta dos Malvedos, just west of the river Tua and its confluence with the Douro. Recently declared vintages like 1994 and '91 are ports in the classic mould, with intensely sweet fruit offset by beguilingly firm, broad tannins. In good interim years wine from Malvedos is bottled as a single-quinta vintage port.

Graham also produces some fine, aged tawnies and large quantities of LBV (filtered, unfortunately, to remove the need for decanting) which is consistently among the best in its category. Six Grapes is the brand name for Graham's rich, satisfying premium ruby. Best years: (vintage ports) 1994, '91, '85, '83, '80, '77, '70, '66, '63.

ALAIN GRAILLOT

FRANCE, Northern Rhône, Crozes-Hermitage AC

Syrah

Marsanne and others

Alain Graillot has a background as an agro-chemist and first decided to make wine in 1985, buying in grapes for the purpose. By that time he had gained some experience by working in Burgundy at various wineries, and adopted some Burgundian techniques such as giving the red grapes a cold soak before fermentation and aging a proportion of the wine

in used barriques he purchases from his friends in the CÔTE D'OR. The wines, both red and white, have been outstanding from the outset, with a suppleness and richness rarely encountered in CROZES-HERMITAGE. The top red Crozes is la Guiraude, which can age as well as JABOULET's more celebrated Thalabert. The white is made mostly from Marsanne and is partly fermented in older barrels. In the mid-1990s Graillot was able to acquire a small parcel of vines in HERMITAGE, and he also makes a little ST-JOSEPH. Best years: 1998, '97, '96, '95, '94, '91, '90, '89.

GRAMPIANS

AUSTRALIA, Victoria, Western Victoria Zone

Great Western is the name by which this area has been better known, but almost 70 years of legal skirmishing between BEST's and SEPPELT over its use made the adoption of Grampians the only sensible solution. Syrah (Shiraz) is the great grape of the region, forming a symbiotic but subtly different relationship with the winemakers at Best's, MOUNT LANGI GHIRAN and Seppelt, ranging from cherry and mint to more spicy savoury flavours. Best years: 1998, '97, '95, '94, '93, '91. Best producers: Best's, Garden Gully Vineyards, Mount Langi Ghiran, Seppelt Great Western.

SEPPELT
From its 70-year-old St Peters Vineyard in Grampians, Seppelt produces a benchmark red fizz, Show Sparkling Shiraz, with sweet ripe fruit and deep, spicy flavour.

CH. GRAND-PUY-LACOSTE

FRANCE, Bordeaux, Haut-Médoc, Pauillac AC, 5ème Cru Classé

Cabernet Sauvignon, Merlot, Cabernet Franc

Don't be fooled by this wine only being a Fifth Growth. Because PAUILLAC dominated the awards of First Growths in the 1855 BORDEAUX Classification, one sometimes gets the feeling that several very exciting properties were rather unceremoniously dumped in the Fifth Growths for appearance's sake.

However, this 50-ha (125-acre) estate owned by the Borie family of Ch. DUCRU-BEAUCAILLOU makes a classic Pauillac. It isn't as weighty and grand as better-known Pauillac wines like Ch. LATOUR and MOUTON-ROTHSCHILD, but the purity of its flavour

CH. GRAND-PUY-LACOSTE
This is classic Pauillac with lots of blackcurrant and cigar-box perfume. As the wine ages and develops, the flavours mingle with the soft sweetness of new oak.

marks it out as special. Although it begins in a fairly dense way, that's just how a Pauillac should start out; as the years pass the fruit becomes the most piercingly pure blackcurrant and the perfume mingles cedar with lead pencils and the softening sweetness of new oak. Recent wines have been splendid. Best years: 1998, '97, '96, '95, '94, '93, '90, '89, '88, '86, '85, '83, '82, '81, '79, '78.

GRANGEHURST
SOUTH AFRICA, Western Cape, Stellenbosch WO
There is no flashy over-capitalization at this boutique winery. The owner, Jeremy Walker, vinified his early harvests in a converted squash court on his late parents' Helderberg farm. Success and increased production (eventually topping at 9000 cases) has demanded two subsequent expansions, which have incorporated innovations such as fermentation tanks with detachable floating lids; but the squash court remains an identifying and used feature.

Despite being surrounded by vineyards, Walker owns none, preferring to draw from specific growers in various quality STELLENBOSCH areas. Thus individuality is highlighted in his two-wine range – the Cabernet-Merlot enjoys the New World's bright fruit and the Old's structured dryness. His elegantly modern Pinotage is one of the Cape's most sought after. Oaking is always generous but never unbalanced; a portion of American barrels adds to the wines' succulent richness and power. Best years: 1997, '96, '95, '94, '93, '92.

GRANITE BELT
AUSTRALIA, Queensland
Situated on the western side of the Great Dividing Range, the 21 wineries of the Granite Belt constitute the epicentre of winemaking in QUEENSLAND, notwithstanding the rash of wineries forming a ring around Brisbane and which have sprung up in the latter part of the 1990s. Winemaking in the Granite Belt originated with the local

Italian fruit growers who used table grapes to make rough and ready jug wine, the first *Vitis vinifera* (Syrah/Shiraz) appearing in 1965. Shiraz has proved to be the best red grape, followed by Cabernet Sauvignon, while Semillon, Chardonnay and Sauvignon Blanc have provided the best white wines. It has to be said that these are relative judgments; the principal market is the none-too-critical tourist passing through on holidays. Best years: 1996, '95, '94, '93, '90. Best producers: Bald Mountain, Ballandean Estate, Kominos, Mountview Wines, Robinson Family Vineyards, Stone Ridge, Violet Cane.

GRANS-FASSIAN
GERMANY, Mosel-Saar-Ruwer, Leiwen
♀ Riesling and others
This MOSEL estate is not yet terrifically well known but is fast building a reputation for stylish, fragrant wines. There is a willingness to experiment which is reflected in the un-Germanic use of barriques for some of the wines. Gerhard Grans' best wines come from TRITTENHEIMer Apotheke, a superb, steep vineyard site for Riesling. Best years: 1998, '97, '95, '94, '93, '92, '90, '89.

YVES GRASSA
FRANCE, South-West, Vin de Pays des Côtes de Gascogne
♀ Colombard, Ugni Blanc, Gros Manseng, Chardonnay, Sauvignon Blanc
♟ Merlot, Tannat, Cabernet Franc
Pierre Grassa was one of the pioneers of crisp, snappy, fruity, dry white CÔTES DE GASCOGNE. His son Yves and daughter Maïté now carry on the charge, producing a range of white wines at eight different domaines, including the 80-ha (200-acre) Domaine du Tariquet. The different cuvées include a Colombard-Ugni Blanc blend, the Cuvée Bois for a similar blend aged in oak, a barrel-fermented Chardonnay and a late-harvested sweet white produced from Gros Manseng labelled Premières Grives. Not content with producing this excellent range of whites, the Grassas have now equipped themselves with oak vats and barrels and a system for *micro-bullage* in order to produce some top-flight reds under the Domaine du Mage label. There are also some good Armagnacs.

ALFRED GRATIEN
FRANCE, Champagne, Champagne AC
♀ ♟ Chardonnay, Pinot Noir, Pinot Meunier
For CHAMPAGNE, this isn't a big company, producing only 200,000 bottles a year in its

backstreet cellars in Épernay (the giant MOËT ET CHANDON, for instance, produces over 26 million a year) but whoever said you had to be big to be good? In the modern world of Champagne, where many companies are more obsessed with brand image than they are about the quality of their wines, Gratien declares its image to be the quality of the wines and absolutely nothing else.

The Champagnes are fermented in wooden casks, which is very rare nowadays, moved only by gravity since pumping is thought to bruise the wine, kept on their lees under a real cork – most other houses use crown corks similar to those on a Coca-Cola bottle – and stored appreciably longer than usual before release. The non-vintage blend is usually four years old when released for sale – many other companies sell their wine aged for little more than two years. The vintage wine is deliciously ripe and toasty when released but can age for another ten to 15 years, and is usually in the slightly less fizzy, *crémant* style. There is also a non-vintage Cuvée Paradis, usually made from Chardonnay and Pinot Meunier, and aged about ten years on release. Best years: 1990, '88, '87, '85, '82, '79.

ALFRED GRATIEN
Only tiny amounts of the pricy Cuvée Paradis are made. Both this and the rosé version are non-vintage but wonderfully individual.

GRAUBÜNDEN
SWITZERLAND
Although there are only 350ha (865 acres) of vineyards between the towns of Vaduz and Chur in the Upper Rhine Valley in eastern Switzerland, they are the source for many of Switzerland's best Pinot Noirs (called Blauburgunder here). This is the result of a combination of poor slate soils and the warm Föhn winds which come over the Alps from Italy, making this one of the warmest spots in the entire country. Improved winemaking during the 1990s has given many of the wines more depth and tannin. Best producers: Donatsch, GANTENBEIN.

GRAVES & PESSAC-LÉOGNAN France, Bordeaux

IT IS NOW OVER TEN YEARS since the world of Graves was thrown into turmoil in 1987 when the northern part of the area, closest to the city of Bordeaux, and containing all the most famous properties, declared independence, and announced that from henceforth it would be called Pessac-Léognan, after its two leading communes. So now, although the whole region is still known as the Graves, it has two ACs: Pessac-Léognan for the area closest to Bordeaux, and Graves for the rest, primarily to the south down to Langon and encircling the sweet white wine areas of Cérons, Sauternes and Barsac. The 16 Crus Classés of the Graves are all located in Pessac-Léognan and although the original feeling was that the exit of the Pessac-Léognan aristocrats would be bad news for the Graves producers, it seems, in fact, to have acted more as a kick up the backside.

The name 'Graves' means gravel, and the vineyards which now make up the new Pessac-Léognan appellation are notable for their gravelly soil. Gravelly soil is heat-retaining and quick-draining, and this, allied to a warmer climate than that of the Médoc further north, and a close proximity to the city of Bordeaux, meant that the 'Graves', as the area became known, was for a long time the leading Bordeaux wine area. At one time the bulk of the wine made was white. However,

most of this was extremely poor white wine, so it is hardly surprising that almost two-thirds of the wine now is red. However, the white wines that are now produced must be counted among France's classics. A revolution has taken place which has seen the reintroduction of hand harvesting, grape selection, gentle pressing, skin contact and fermentation and aging in new oak barrels, creating one of France's most exciting white wine regions. The major grapes are Sémillon and Sauvignon Blanc for whites and Cabernet Sauvignon and Merlot for reds.

Pessac-Léognan encompasses ten communes and has roughly 1300ha (3250 acres) under production. The gravelly soil tends to favour red wines over the rest of the Graves, and in fact this appellation is home to the only Bordeaux red outside the Médoc to be awarded First Growth status in 1855 – Ch. Haut-Brion. Still, white grapes can be grown successfully on the sandier, and less well-exposed areas of the Graves AC further south towards Langon. The best estates use new oak barrels to make wines with rich, apricotty fruit and creamy vanilla spice. The Graves reds

Ch. Haut-Brion was the only property outside the Médoc to be included in the great 1855 Bordeaux Classification. These barriques in the first-year chai illustrate the enormous investment required to remain in the first rank today.

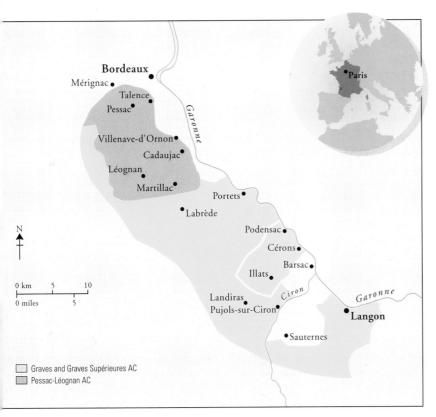

CH. HAUT-BRION

In the 1990s the red wine from this famous estate has nearly always fully justified its exalted status.

DOMAINE DE CHEVALIER

The red has a superb balance of fruit and oak and with 10–20 years' aging it gains wonderful fragrant cedar, tobacco and blackcurrant flavours.

CH. SMITH-HAUT-LAFITTE

This is the leader of modern-style Pessac-Léognan white. From 100 per cent Sauvignon Blanc, the wine ages beautifully, losing some of its more pungent Sauvignon aromas.

CH. DE FIEUZAL

This is one of the most up-to-date estates in Pessac-Léognan and the ripe, oaky wines sell at a high price. The white wine, intensely oaky and with ripe, fruity perfume, is a leader among Bordeaux's new wave whites.

CH. COUHINS-LURTON

Run by André Lurton, this is one of the few estates in the Graves to make its white wine solely from Sauvignon Blanc. Since 1982 it has been barrel-fermented in new oak, which has improved the quality considerably.

CH. LATOUR-MARTILLAC

This is now one of the most improved estates in Pessac-Léognan, for both red and white wine.

CH. MALARTIC-LAGRAVIÈRE

This is one of the few Pessac-Léognan Crus Classés whose reputation is for its white wine (made entirely from Sauvignon Blanc), not for its red.

have also improved, with a greater percentage of Merlot now being used in the blend.

The Graves AC only applies to reds and dry whites, but there is the little-known Graves Supérieures AC, which can be applied to sweet whites, and which sometimes comes up with super, sweet wines at a very low price. However, if the Graves is to produce world-class wine, we mustn't try to force the price too low – or it won't be worth their while.

AC ENTRIES
Graves, Pessac-Léognan.

CHÂTEAUX ENTRIES
de Chevalier, de Fieuzal, Haut-Bailly, Haut-Brion, Laville Haut-Brion, la Louvière, Malartic-Lagravière, la Mission-Haut-Brion, Pape Clément, Smith-Haut-Lafitte.

CH. LA LOUVIÈRE

This is one of Pessac-Léognan's unclassified stars and its fine reputation is almost entirely due to André Lurton who has revitalized the estate over the last 30 years.

CLOS FLORIDÈNE

This white Graves is the equal of many Pessac-Léognan Crus Classés. From mainly Sémillon, it is barrique-fermented and aged on lees to provide added complexity.

GRAVES AC, GRAVES SUPÉRIEURES AC

FRANCE, Bordeaux

🍷 *Cabernet Sauvignon, Merlot, Cabernet Franc*

🍇 *Sémillon, Sauvignon Blanc*

See also Graves and Pessac-Léognan, pages 190–191.

The Graves has always relied for its good reputation on the efforts of a small number of famous properties situated just south-west of the city of Bordeaux. Here, the soil is extremely gravelly – which is how the area came to be called 'Graves' – and the climate is slightly warmer than the MÉDOC to the north – excellent conditions for producing high-quality wine. Well, it can't rely on this any longer, because in 1987 the villages in the north of the Graves formed their own AC – PESSAC-LÉOGNAN – to emphasize what they see, rightly, as their historic superiority. So, although the Graves region extends for about 60km (37 miles) from the very gates of Bordeaux to south of Langon, the AC is now used mainly for wine from the less-favoured southern section. This weakened its red wine hall of fame more than the white, because much exciting white was already being created outside Pessac-Léognan, particularly in Portets, Arbanats and Illats.

For too long Graves, apart from the Classed Growths, was a byword for murky-tasting wine of no style whatsoever. However, there is a new wave of winemaking sweeping through the region. An increasing amount of bone-dry white, with lots of snappy freshness and a lovely apricotty flavour, as well as some richer, barrel-fermented and aged white is being made. Add to this an increase in Merlot for the reds to produce juicier wines and a touch of spice from new oak barrels, and the Graves AC doesn't really have any reason to be sorry for itself at all. Best years: (reds) 1998, '96, '95, '94, '90, '89, '88, '86, '85, '83, '82; (dry whites) 1998, '96, '95, '94, '90, '89, '88, '87, '86. Best producers: Archambeau, d'Ardennes, Bonnat, Brondelle, Chantegrive, Clos Floridène, Grave, Magence, Magneau, Rahoul, Respide-Médeville, Roquetaillade-la-Grange, St-Robert, Vieux Ch.-Gaubert, Villa Bel-Air.

The Graves Supérieures AC is for white Graves, dry, medium or sweet, with a minimum alcohol level of 12 degrees as opposed to 11 degrees for Graves. The sweet wines can, in good years, make decent substitutes for the more expensive SAUTERNES. Best years: (sweet) 1997, '96, '95, '90, '89, '88, '86. Best producer: (sweet) Clos St-Georges.

JOSKO GRAVNER

ITALY, Friuli-Venezia Giulia, Collio DOC

🍷 *Cabernet Sauvignon, Cabernet Franc, Merlot*

🍇 *Chardonnay, Sauvignon Blanc, Pinot Gris (Pinot Grigio), Riesling and others*

Gravner is the epitome of the moody genius, getting on with his own thing whether others approve or not. His thing, these days, is making blended whites for long aging, and while some of the journalists he despises dismiss them as being totally unbalanced, there are others who consider his dense, rich, concentrated Breg (a blend of Chardonnay, Sauvignon Blanc, Pinot Grigio, Riesling, Ribolla, Malvasia and the obscure Blera), involving months of oak-aging, epitomizes the best of Friulian white wines.

Certainly for weight, complexity and longevity, Breg is a remarkable wine. And there are others around the border village of Oslavia, principally Stanislao Radikon (Slatnik) and the brothers Bensa of La Castellada (Bianco della Castellada) who make similar wines. But these are wines which aim to compensate in opulence and complexity for what they lack in elegance and freshness. They are not afraid of the tannins or the element of oxidation derived from extensive oak treatment. Followers of the New World style may hate them, but they must admit one thing: they are wines of tremendous character and, indeed, courage which deserve to be taken seriously for all their sins against contemporary thinking. Best years: 1998, '97, '96, '95, '94, '93.

GRAVNER

As well as some of Friuli's most interesting white wines, Gravner makes a red called Rujno from a blend of Merlot and Cabernet Sauvignon.

GREAT SOUTHERN

AUSTRALIA, Western Australia, South West Australia Zone

This is a vast, wide-flung area which includes Frankland River, Albany and Mount Barker. The scenery is at times spectacular, with rounded granite boulders rising from tens to hundreds of feet high. Traditionally a producer of steely Riesling and firm Cabernet Sauvignon, Mount Barker has more recently produced some high-quality Chardonnay, Sauvignon Blanc and Pinot Noir. Attention is now beginning to focus on the northern (cooler) parts. Best years: 1997, '96, '95, '94, '93, '91, '89, '87. Best producers: ALKOOMI, Forest Hill, GOUNDREY, HOWARD PARK, PLANTAGENET, Wignall's King River.

GRECO, GRECHETTO

Around 2500 years ago the Greeks were responsible for importing various grape varieties into Italy, often via the port of Naples but also directly into parts of Magna Grecia – the southern mainland. These often ended up carrying a general epithet of origin – such as Greco (Greek), Grechetto (little Greek) or Aglianico (Hellenic) – rather than more precise names, even if there was little or no connection between them. Hence the confusion we have fallen into today, with two white 'Grecos', if not three, still prevalent in southern Italy, not to mention the Grechetto of Umbria, the latter being a white grape increasingly used varietally and in blends, most famous of which is ANTINORI's Cervaro della Sala (Chardonnay topped up with 10 per cent of Grechetto).

Best known of the 'Grecos' is Greco di Tufo, found in the uplands of CAMPANIA on the tufa soil around the village of Tufo, near Avellino. Most of the grapes used to find their way into producer MASTROBERARDINO's cellars and its cru Vignadangelo, flavoursome, smoky and minerally, is still the benchmark wine. An increasing number of Mastroberardino's erstwhile grape-growers, today, are taking a punt at making their own wine. The results are still wobbly and some are operating on a very small scale but it's clear that before too long we're going to get a much better idea of Greco di Tufo's real capabilities.

Then there is the Greco of Bianco, a small village in the extreme south of CALABRIA where the grape is grown on low, east-facing terraces overlooking the sea. Greco di Bianco is a *passito* wine, with a minimum 14 per cent alcohol and another 3 per cent worth in sweetness and a distinct citrus/orange tang which one will seek in vain in Greco di Tufo.

Further north up the same, eastern coast of Calabria is the Greco of CIRÒ, which local growers do not consider to be related to the variety at Bianco; one excellent reason for thinking this being that it tends to be rather weak in grape sugar, which Greco di Bianco certainly is not.

GRENACHE NOIR

Grenache revels in hot, dry conditions. It can produce dull, pallid, insipid wine just about anywhere, if it's allowed to overcrop, but in the southern Rhône, where it is the most important of the 13 varieties allowed in the Châteauneuf-du-Pape blend, it brings high alcohol and rich, spicy fruit to blend with the tannin and backbone of some of the other grapes. Grenache is important, in fact, throughout the South of France and Corsica. The best southern rosés, from Tavel, Lirac and Côtes de Provence in particular, are based on Grenache, usually blended with Cinsaut. In Rasteau (Côtes-du-Rhône) and Languedoc-Roussillon (especially Rivesaltes, Maury and Banyuls) it also makes thick, sweet, fortified reds. In the Languedoc it now often teams up with Syrah and Mourvèdre to make some of the more exciting red wines.

In Spain, where it is known as Garnacha Tinta, it is found almost everywhere: from Rioja to Penedès and La Mancha. At its best it is blended with less blowsy varieties, like Tempranillo. Only the richest and best of Garnachas, notably in Priorat, stand up to much aging. Grenache also flourishes in Sardinia, where it is called Cannonau and makes every possible style, from light to massive, dry, sweet or fortified, oaked or thoroughly stainless steel in outlook.

Grenache's other success story is in California, where Randall Grahm of Bonny Doon and other winemakers have a passion for the Rhône grape varieties. In Australia, it has undergone a remarkable renaissance, with the century-old, dry grown, bush-pruned vines in the Barossa Valley and McLaren Vale producing grapes that are in great demand for blending with Shiraz (and perhaps Mourvèdre) to make rich, Rhônish dry red wines.

There is also a white version, Garnacha Blanca in Spain, where it makes big, dull wines with little flavour, and Grenache Blanc in France, which can be good when drunk very young.

GRGICH HILLS CELLAR

USA, California, Napa County, Napa Valley AVA

♥ *Cabernet Sauvignon, Zinfandel*

♀ *Chardonnay, Sauvignon Blanc, Riesling*

Winemaker Miljenko (Mike) Grgich and grower Austin Hills began their collaboration in 1977, hard on the heels of a Grgich-made Chardonnay from CHATEAU MONTELENA winning first place in a famous Franco-American tasting in Paris. Grgich's Chardonnay style has evolved since then, but he is still in favour of rich textures and bold flavours. Best years: 1997, '96, '95, '94, '93, '92, '91, '90, '87, '86, '85. The Cabernet Sauvignons, similarly, are sturdily built and full of flavour, as are the Zinfandels. Best years: (reds) 1997, '96, '95, '94, '92, '91, '90, '87, '86, '85.

JEAN GRIVOT

FRANCE, Burgundy, Côte de Nuits, Vosne-Romanée AC

♥ *Pinot Noir*

In the 1970s, Jean Grivot established this domaine, with its numerous excellent Premiers Crus in VOSNE-ROMANÉE and NUITS-ST-GEORGES, as a very reliable source of stylish and full-bodied red Burgundies. In the early 1980s, Jean's son, Étienne, began to take over the winemaking, and the wines seemed as good as ever. Then in 1987 the enologist Guy Accad was hired as a consultant, and the wines changed profoundly. Accad believed in a prolonged cold maceration before fermentation to extract as much colour and richness as possible from the grapes. The wines were impressive, but they certainly didn't seem Burgundian. By the mid-1990s Étienne had seen the error of his ways, and returned to more traditional winemaking practices. There was an immediate transformation, and today the Grivot wines are truly splendid, showing both the finesse one expects from Pinot Noir at its best and the richness and power one looks for from these appellations. The domaine also owns some parcels of CLOS VOUGEOT and RICHEBOURG. Best years: 1997, '96, '95, '90, '85.

GROOT CONSTANTIA

SOUTH AFRICA, Western Cape, Constantia WO

♥ *Cabernet Sauvignon, Syrah (Shiraz), Pinotage, Merlot and others*

♀ *Chardonnay, Sauvignon Blanc, Riesling (Rhine/Weisser Riesling), Gewurztraminer and others*

Groot Constantia is one of the three historic CONSTANTIA estates, just south of Cape Town, which represent the beginnings of South Africa's wine industry. Founded in 1685, its fame was greatest in the eighteenth and early nineteenth centuries when the dessert Muscat, called Constantia received much acclaim. Napoleon drank it; so did Frederick the Great and Jane Austen wrote about it. Today, there are moves to re-create this great wine. In the meantime, white wines such as Sauvignon Blanc, Weisser Riesling, Chardonnay and Gewurztraminer benefit from this cooler area. Reds have some catching up to do. As might be expected from one of Cape Town's most popular tourist attractions, many of the wines are unashamedly commercial. Best years: (Gouverneurs Reserve a red BORDEAUX-style blend) 1996, '95, '94, '93, '92, '91, '90, '89; (whites) 1998, '97, '96, '95, '94, '93, '92, '91.

GROS PLANT DU PAYS NANTAIS VDQS

FRANCE, Loire, Pays Nantais

♀ *Gros Plant*

Traditionally Gros Plant is searing stuff – one of the grape's other names is Picpoul, which roughly translates as 'lip-stinger' – and, as well as in the Gros Plant vineyards around Nantes, it is also grown in the Cognac and Armagnac regions (under the name Folle Blanche or Picpoul) because its searingly high acid wine is perfect for distilling. Yet strangely, if you have a great plateful of seafood plonked down in front of you – wreathed in seaweed and still heaving with the motion of the ocean and the crunching of Atlantic rollers against the battered Brittany coast – you'll find the barefaced, eye-watering tartness of Gros Plant is surprisingly well-suited as a quaffer to cope with oysters, mussels, crab and the rest. Since they eat seafood by the bucketful around Nantes this probably explains its survival as the local white. But generally you'd be better off paying a few francs more and drinking the other equally dry, and – in comparison – positively sumptuous local wine: MUSCADET. Drink as young as possible. Best years: 1998, '97, '96. Best producers: Bois-Bruley, Clos des Rosiers, Cuvée du Marquisat, Guindon, Hallereau, Herbauges.

ALOIS GROSS

AUSTRIA, Steiermark, Südsteiermark, Ratsch

♀ *Sauvignon Blanc, Chardonnay (Morillon), Pinot Blanc (Weissburgunder), Pinot Gris (Grauburgunder), Riesling, Muscat (Gelber Muskateller)*

Alois Gross's wines are some of the most consistently impressive wines in Südsteiermark or southern Styria. They divide into two groups: Steirische Klassik, which are vinified entirely in stainless steel for fresh fruit and crispness; and the wines with vineyard designations that have all seen some wood, and in the case of Grauburgunder and Morillon new wood. Perhaps the best wines in this range are the extremely clean and aromatic Muskateller and the rich, nutty-buttery Grauburgunder. Best years: 1998, '97, '95, '93, '92.

GROSSET

AUSTRALIA, South Australia, Mount Lofty Ranges Zone, Clare Valley

♥ Pinot Noir, Cabernet Sauvignon, Merlot
♀ Riesling, Semillon, Sauvignon Blanc, Chardonnay

If democratic elections were held for the position of King of Riesling in Australia, Jeffrey Grosset would likely emerge as the winner. The crystal clarity of the Polish Hill Riesling, with fragrant whispers of herb and spice, and the fractionally richer Watervale Riesling, with a vibrant twist of lime, evolve with shimmering beauty over a ten-year period. Gaia, a Cabernet-dominant BORDEAUX blend, redolent with blackberry and sweet cassis fruit, somehow introduces finesse into a region more famous for blockbusters. His ADELAIDE HILLS trio of Semillon-Sauvignon Blanc, Piccadilly Chardonnay and Reserve Pinot Noir are as scarce as hen's teeth, but decidedly more useful if you can put your hands on them. Best years: 1998, '97, '95, '94, '93, '90.

CH. GRUAUD-LAROSE

FRANCE, Bordeaux, Haut-Médoc, St-Julien AC, 2ème Cru Classé

♥ Cabernet Sauvignon, Merlot, Cabernet Franc, Petit Verdot

Of all the MÉDOC's great wines, Gruaud-Larose blows its own trumpet most *sotto voce*; it just quietly goes about the business of making brilliant wine at a reasonable price. At 82ha (203 acres) of vines, Gruaud is one of the largest ST-JULIEN estates. With vineyards set a little back from the Gironde estuary, Gruaud used to exhibit a softer, more honeyed style when young than, say, the trio of LÉOVILLE estates whose vineyards slope down to the Gironde. This didn't stop the wine aging superbly and gaining a piercing, dry, blackcurrant and cedarwood aroma over 20 years or so. The vintages of the 1980s and '90s have been made darker, deeper, thick with the flavours of blackberry and plums, sweetened with wood, toughened with tannin. Robust and powerful by nature, these wines still have a long aging potential. Second wine: Sarget de Gruaud-Larose. Best years: 1998, '97, '96, '95, '94, '93, '90, '89, '88, '86, '85, '83, '82, '81, '79, '78, '75.

Marcel Guigal is among the most famous names in the Rhône Valley, owning important vineyards in Côte-Rôtie as well as being a leading négociant.

GRÜNER VELTLINER

If you happen to be sitting in a café in Austria and order a quarter litre of white wine, there's a fair chance it'll be made from the Grüner Veltliner grape: fresh, cold and straight from the most recent vintage. Very nice it will be, too: slightly appley, slightly peppery, slightly smoky. There's masses of it in the country. It is at its best in NIEDERÖSTERREICH, where it can give powerful, concentrated dry wines with great aging potential. There's also a bit in the Czech Republic and Slovakia.

GUELBENZU

SPAIN, Navarra, Navarra DO

♥ Cabernet Sauvignon, Tempranillo, Merlot, Grenache Noir (Garnacha Tinta)

The Queiles Valley in southern NAVARRA is cooled by imposing mountains, but this is resolutely a red wine region with a warm Mediterranean influence. In the 1980s the Guelbenzu family resurrected their bodega, abandoned for a century or so. The 38ha (94 acres) of vineyards satisfy the bodega's needs. The speciality here is powerful, no-holds-barred, oak-aged reds: Guelbenzu, which is a Cabernet Sauvignon-Tempranillo-Merlot blend, and the complex, Cabernet Sauvignon-dominated Guelbenzu Evo. Small batches of an unoaked Garnacha red, Guelbenzu El Jardín, are also produced. A luxury cuvée based on old-vine Garnacha and Merlot, called Lautus, was first made in 1995. Best years: 1996, '95, '94, '93, '91, '89.

GUIGAL

FRANCE, Northern Rhône, Côte-Rôtie AC

♥ Syrah, Grenache and others
♀ Marsanne, Roussanne, Viognier and others

If one man is venerated above all others in the northern RHÔNE, it is Marcel Guigal. Justifiably too, since it was he who dragged the region into the late twentieth century. Guigal is both a major owner in the CÔTE-RÔTIE appellation and a leading *négociant* for wines from both the northern and southern Rhône. His strength is that he is able to excel on both fronts, producing brilliant wines from his own vineyards and assembling remarkably satisfying blends from other regions. His standard CÔTES DU RHÔNE, with its high proportion of Syrah, is always one of the top generic wines of the region. But his reputation rightly rests on the trio of single-vineyard Côte-Rôties: la Landonne, la Mouline and la Turque. In 1978 he began aging these wines in 100 per cent new oak for over three years, and despite all the warnings of sceptics, the wines have aged superbly, have retained their typicity, and in repeated vintages have demonstrated the terroir of each site. More recently, Guigal has extended his magic touch to CONDRIEU, where he produces two bottlings – la Doriane, the special cuvée showing a hefty whack of new oak without sacrificing typicity.

With renown has come prosperity, and the once-unassuming Guigal, rarely seen without his cloth cap, is now the owner of the magnificent Ch. d'Ampuis, a name he has adopted for another top Côte-Rôtie wine. Guigal has also absorbed another local *négociant*, Vidal-Fleury, but the two companies operate independently. Best years: 1997, '96, '95, '94, '91, '90, '89, '88, '85, '83, '82, '78.

CH. GUIRAUD

FRANCE, Bordeaux, Sauternes AC, Premier Cru Classé

♀ Sémillon, Sauvignon Blanc, Muscadelle

In 1981 Guiraud was bought by a quality-obsessed Canadian, Frank Narby, who, with his son Hamilton, was bent on making great SAUTERNES. They've managed it. The 1983 was exceptional, the '86 was stunningly rich right from the start and the '90, '96 and '97 even more so. The winemaker and manager, Xavier Planty, ruthlessly selects only the best grapes, uses at least 50 per cent new oak each year to ferment and age the wine, and charges justifiably a very high price. The wine needs at least ten years to reach its peak – and good years may need 15–20. Best years: 1998, '97, '96, '95, '90, '89, '88, '86, '83, '82, '81.

GUMPOLDSKIRCHEN

AUSTRIA, Niederösterreich, Thermenregion

This town in the THERMENREGION was the source of one of Austria's most famous wines. Then came the Austrian wine scandal of 1985, and the sort of sweet wines made here went out of fashion. Some growers turned to dry whites; others persevered with the traditional style, and there are signs that the latter might be beginning to find favour again. The traditional wine is a blend of two white grapes, Zierfandler and Rotgipfler, and with time acquires a spicy apricot character. Josef Weiss makes wines in the old style, as do Friedrich Hofer and Franz Kurz. Best producers: Biegler, Gotfried Schellman.

GUNDERLOCH

GERMANY, Rheinhessen, Nackenheim

Riesling, Silvaner, Pinot Gris (Grauburgunder), Müller-Thurgau (Rivaner)

During the 1990s, Fritz and Agnes Hasselbach's Rieslings from the great NACKENHEIMer Rothenberg vineyard have continually extended the possibilities of what the RHEINHESSEN can produce. These are now some of the most concentrated dry and sweet white wines you'll find anywhere in Germany. This quality and their growing reputation has rapidly pushed prices for their Beerenauslese and Trockenbeerenauslese dessert wines to stratospheric heights.

However, the Spätlese and Auslese wines, which ripple with exotic and grapefruit aromas and have a stunningly tense interplay of fruit, minerals and piercing acidity, will not break the bank. The Jean Baptiste Riesling Kabinett, which is a blend of grapes from the Rothenberg and the best vineyards of NIERSTEIN, offers some of the best value for money in top-class German wines. Grauburgunder and Rivaner are two Gunderloch specialities, both coming from old vines, the former vinified like a late-harvest ALSACE wine, the latter fermented dry. Best years: 1998, '97, '96, '95, '94, '93, '92, '90, '89.

GUNDERLOCH

The Beerenauslese and Trockenbeerenauslese wines from the great Nackenheimer Rothenberg site on the Rhine are some of Germany's top sweet wines.

GUTIÉRREZ DE LA VEGA

SPAIN, Valencia, Alicante DO

Merlot, Cabernet Sauvignon, Grenache Noir (Garnacha Tinta)

Muscat of Alexandria (Moscatel Romano)

Felipe Gutiérrez de la Vega has been showing for over 20 years that seaside vineyards in touristy ALICANTE province have the potential to produce world-class sweet Muscat wines. He owns 10ha (25 acres) of vines on terraces that, legend says, go back to Greco-Roman times, overlooking the Mediterranean in the Marina Alta sub-region. Some of the vines are grafted to red varieties, giving ample, pleasant reds and rosés. But the various Moscatel Romano-based wines are the speciality, including dry and semi-sweet fizzy ones. The star is the Casta Diva cuvée, a golden, full-bodied, honeyed, modern sweet wine. It is fermented in new oak and bottled within six months of the harvest. Drink young.

GYÖNGYÖS ESTATE

HUNGARY, Gyöngyös

Pinot Noir

Sauvignon Blanc, Chardonnay

This was the first of Hungary's wineries to show that the country could, with a kick start, produce exactly the sort of crisp, fruity wines the world is thirsty for, and at affordable prices, too. Englishman Hugh Ryman was the man responsible. After the frosts of 1991 had decimated his vineyards in his stamping ground of south-west France, Ryman looked around for a new source of grapes to make up the shortfall. When he decided on Hungary, he promptly installed his own winemaker, revolutionized the winemaking and put his fingerprint on nearly all the Sauvignon Blanc there is in this part of northern Hungary. The Chardonnay is good, too, and plenty of good Pinot Noir is promised. The winery was bought in 1995 by the German firm of St-Ursula and Ryman is no longer involved. Drink the current vintage.

FRITZ HAAG

GERMANY, Mosel-Saar-Ruwer, Brauneberg

Riesling

Wilhelm Haag of the Weingut Fritz Haag is a winemaker of supreme quality, with just a handful of hectares of Riesling in some of the MOSEL's top vineyard sites, particularly BRAUNEBERGer Juffer and Brauneberger Juffer-Sonnenuhr. The Juffer-Sonnenuhr is the smaller site, and has the edge in stylishness, but all Haag's wines are terrifically elegant and concentrated. In youth they are difficult to taste, with high levels of acidity, despite an impressive overall level of ripeness that warn the drinker not to commit infanticide; with maturity they display all the fire and race of the best of the Mosel, but that maturity can take 10–20 years. Winemaking is traditional, in old oak barrels, and is meticulous. Best years: 1998, '97, '95, '94, '93, '92, '91, '90, '89, '88, '85, '83, '79.

REINHOLD HAART

GERMANY, Mosel-Saar-Ruwer, Piesport

Riesling, Weissburgunder (Pinot Blanc)

In good years the Riesling wines from the great amphitheatre of vines that is the Piesporter Goldtröpfchen vineyard tend to Baroque extravagance, often losing the delicacy typical of MOSEL wines. Theo Haart is the first winemaker to succeed in giving these wines real elegance without in any way diminishing their power. The result is some of the finest and most expressive wines in the entire Mosel region. Their blackcurrant, peach and citrus aromas and crisp acidity make them easy to enjoy young, and they age magnificently as examples such as the 1971 and '75 Auslese show. Since 1991 he has also made fine wines from the great, but overlooked, Wintricher Ohligsberg site. Best years: 1998, '96, '95, '94, '93, '91, '90, '89, '88, '83, '76, '75, '71.

HALLAU

SWITZERLAND, Schaffhausen

This is one of the best wine communes in the German-speaking Swiss canton of Schaffhausen, situated between the river Rhine and the JURA mountains. This is mainly red wine country, from Blauburgunder (Pinot Noir), and the wines are light in flavour and heavy in price; the best, though, can be good. Hallau's top vineyard is the Im Hintere Waatelebuck. Best producer: Hans Schlatter.

HAMILTON RUSSELL VINEYARDS

SOUTH AFRICA, Western Cape, Walker Bay WO

Pinot Noir

Chardonnay, Sauvignon Blanc

It is mainly thanks to Tim Hamilton-Russell that South Africa has shown so much progress with Burgundy's Pinot Noir grape. When, in 1974, he found what he considered the ideal spot for this grape, and Chardonnay too, the land in Hemel-en-Aarde Valley, near the coastal town of Hermanus, had no official quota from the KWV to grow vines. This did not deter him from his quest to make Pinot Noir and Chardonnay to international standards. Today his determination has been vindicated. Now under the ownership of his son, Anthony Hamilton-Russell, HRV, as it is affectionately known, is still among the leading Pinot producers but, more importantly, has encouraged others to follow. Perfectionist winemaker, Kevin Grant, and a broader selection of vine material has seen shifts in style, but, after a slight hiccup with the maiden vintage, the all new-clone Ashbourne Pinot Noir should show what the Cape is capable of producing from this fickle grape. The toasty, fruitily concentrated Chardonnays are among only a few local examples which have proved they can mature over four to five years. Best years: (Pinot Noir) 1997, '96, '95, '94, '93, '92, '91; (Chardonnay) 1998, '97, '96, '95, '94, '93, '92, '91.

HAMILTON RUSSELL VINEYARDS
South Africa's first great Pinot Noir came from Hamilton Russell and the wine is still one of the best in the country, despite stiff competition.

HANZELL VINEYARDS
USA, California, Sonoma County, Sonoma Valley AVA
♥ *Pinot Noir*
♀ *Chardonnay*

Hanzell has an unchallenged place in CALIFORNIA wine history. It was here, in the 1950s, that the importance of aging wines in new oak barrels was first realized, and Hanzell's Chardonnays stunned consumers with their richness and balance, the 1957 lingering in top form for a good 20 years. Now owned by the Estate of Londoner Barbara de Brye, Hanzell has managed to stay in the upper crust, but not quite in the first rank. The estate Chardonnays are of the big, slightly heady, buttery school. The Pinot Noirs seem closer to southern RHÔNES than to red Burgundies, very satisfying if taken in that frame of mind. Best years: 1997, '95, '94, '93, '91, '90.

HARDYS
AUSTRALIA, South Australia, Fleurieu Zone, McLaren Vale
♥ *Cabernet Sauvignon, Syrah (Shiraz), Merlot, Malbec, Grenache*
♀ *Riesling , Chardonnay, Sauvignon Blanc, Sémillon*

BRL Hardy (formed when twin RIVERLAND co-operatives Berri Estates and Renmano took over the then family-owned Thomas Hardy) is now the second-largest wine company in Australia. The group now includes the Berri, Renmano, Hardy, HOUGHTON, CHATEAU REYNELLA and LEASINGHAM brands. It has gone from strength to strength since the merger and now has fine quality across the board, thanks to a dedicated and skilled winemaking team.

The greatest of the Hardy wines are the Eileen Hardy Shiraz (made from basket-pressed MCLAREN VALE and PADTHAWAY grapes), Eileen Hardy Chardonnay (the ultimate, grapefruit-with-melon Padthaway style), some superb 'Beerenauslese' sweet wines from Riesling, and the 'vintage port' – probably Australia's best PORT-style wine. Some outstanding 'old-fashioned', burly but intensely ripe and sweet-oaked Shiraz and Cabernet is released under the Chateau Reynella Basket Press label. Vibrant ADELAIDE HILLS Sauvignon Blanc heads up a new series of regional varietals made in small lots. The Collection Series and the Nottage Hill range are both high-quality, keenly priced and tasty varietal wines. New life is being breathed into the sparkling wines. Best years: (Eileen Hardy Shiraz) 1995, '93, '91, '90, '88, '87, '81, '79, '70.

HARGRAVE VINEYARD
USA, New York State, North Fork of Long Island AVA
♥ *Merlot, Cabernet Franc, Pinot Noir*
♀ *Chardonnay*

Alex Hargrave was one of the early pioneers of winemaking on Long Island, fostering the planting of vinifera varietals there in the early 1970s. Chardonnay is consistently very good but the thrill comes from the red wines – excellent Cabernet Franc, remarkable Merlot and inspired, velvety Pinot Noir. Best years: 1997, '95, '94, '93.

HARVEYS
SPAIN, Andalucía, Jerez y Manzanilla DO
♀ *Palomino Fino, Palomino de Jerez, Pedro Ximénez*

Harveys is the biggest, through certainly not the greatest, sherry producer. For 174 years, Harveys did not have its own bodega or vineyards in JEREZ but bought the wine which went into its sherries. However, on being taken over by Allied Lyons (now the vast Allied Domecq drinks empire), Harveys bought bodegas in Jerez, set up joint vineyard ventures on a massive scale with two other sherry producers, BARBADILLO and Garvey, and built a super-modern vinification plant.

The best Harveys wines are the 1796 up-market range, the name based on the date of establishment of the original Bristol Cellars. The range includes oloroso-style, full, dry, soft, nutty-savoury Palo Cortado and a slightly sweetened, curranty-nutty Fine Old Amontillado. Fino Tio Mateo (Palomino y Vergara) is also good, light and tangy. Harveys Bristol Cream is more glitzy packaging than memorable wine.

HASTINGS RIVER
AUSTRALIA, New South Wales, Northern Rivers Zone

The Hastings River region is the only Australian region to have been established in the last 15 or so years without irrigation being deemed necessary. The climate is relatively warm, very humid and with high summer rainfall. This means that the French hybrid Chambourcin, with its resistance to rot, is the most widely planted red grape. The region is dominated by one winery: Cassegrain. The Chardonnay is rich, generous and fruitily sweet in a peach/tropical fruit spectrum. The vivid purple of Chambourcin immediately sets it apart, suggesting that it should be drunk young while the black cherry and plum primary fruit characters are at their most expressive. Best years: 1998, '97, '95, '93, '91.

HATTENHEIM
GERMANY, Rheingau

This is one of the best RHEINGAU villages for Riesling. It lies on the banks of the Rhine between Oestrich and ERBACH, with its vineyards in the hills behind, including the world-famous Steinberg and part of the famous Marcobrunn, which today carries the name of Erbach. Nussbrunnen, Wissellbrunnen, Engelmannsberg, Mannberg, Hassel and Schützenhaus are the other top vineyards.

Hattenheim is also the home of Kloster Eberbach, the medieval Cistercian monastery that is nowadays the site of some singularly unmonastic feasting: the German Wine Academy is based here, and runs courses for wine enthusiasts, and it is also the centre of the Rheingau's annual autumn festival, Glorreiche Rheingau Tage, a wine auction that involves hours of tasting and some gargantuan meals. Best producers: August Eser, Hans Lang, SCHLOSS REINHARTSHAUSEN, SCHLOSS SCHÖNBORN, Langwerth von Simmern.

CH. HAUT-BAGES-LIBÉRAL
FRANCE, Bordeaux, Haut-Médoc, Pauillac AC, 5ème Cru Classé
♥ *Cabernet Sauvignon, Merlot, Petit Verdot*

This obscure property doesn't make the most classic PAUILLAC – but the wine has big, unbridled bucketfuls of delicious plum and blackcurrant fruit. Vintages in the 1990s have a little more depth and structure and the wine is taking on greater depth as the vines mature. The wines will age, but are already deliciously drinkable at five years. Since 1980 the property has been part of the Taillan group, owners also of COS D'ESTOURNEL, GRUAUD-LAROSE, CHASSE-SPLEEN and Ferrière. Best years: 1998, '97, '96, '95, '94, '90, '89, '88, '86, '85, '83, '82.

CH. HAUT-BAILLY

FRANCE, Bordeaux, Pessac-Léognan AC, Cru Classé de Graves

♥ *Cabernet Sauvignon, Merlot, Cabernet Franc*

Haut-Bailly makes the softest and most invitingly charming wines among the GRAVES Classed Growths. The 28ha (69 acres) of vines are on gravelly soil with rather more sand than usual, just to the east of the village of Léognan, and this contributes to Haut-Bailly becoming agreeably ready to drink very early. However, the wines do age fairly well and what is ready to drink at ten years old often seems magically unchanged at 20. Until 1970 the wines were consistently fine, but there was then a gap until 1979, when the property returned to the top level. Vintages in the 1990s were splendid. Second wine: la Parde-de-Haut-Bailly. Best years: 1998, '97, '96, '95, '94, '93, '90, '89, '88, '86, '85, '82, '81, '79.

CH. HAUT-BATAILLEY

FRANCE, Bordeaux, Haut-Médoc, Pauillac AC, 5ème Cru Classé

♥ *Cabernet Sauvignon, Merlot, Cabernet Franc*

They call this estate the 'ST-JULIEN' of PAUILLAC. It's a small property of 20ha (50 acres) of vines set back from the melting pot of brilliant wines close to the Gironde estuary, and is owned by one of St-Julien's greatest wine families – the Bories of Ch. DUCRU-BEAUCAILLOU.

Haut-Batailley gets its 'St-Julien' tag because it lacks the concentrated power of a true Classed Growth Pauillac. This lack of oomph wouldn't matter if the wines had the perfume and cedary excitement of St-Julien, but they rarely do; they're pleasant, a little spicy, but rarely memorable. Recent vintages have improved, though, and 1997 and '96 show a marked improvement, with greater depth and structure and a return to some of the beautiful wines made in the 1970s. The wines can be drunk relatively young. Best years: 1997, '96, '95, '94, '90, '89, '88, '85, '83, '82.

CH. HAUT-BRION

FRANCE, Bordeaux, Pessac-Léognan AC, Premier Cru Classé de Graves

♥ *Cabernet Sauvignon, Merlot, Cabernet Franc*

♀ *Sémillon, Sauvignon Blanc*

Haut-Brion was the first BORDEAUX property to get a write-up in the British press. In 1663, Samuel Pepys wrote that during a session at the Royal Oak Tavern he 'drank a sort of French wine called Ho Bryan; that hath a good and most particular taste that I never met with'. It was a good 50 years before other Bordeaux wines began to be known by their own château name.

One reason for this is that the excellent gravel-based vineyard which constitutes Haut-Brion is actually in the suburbs of the city of Bordeaux and so was readily accessible to visiting merchants. Haut-Brion's continued popularity is shown by the fact that when the local merchants decided to classify the top red wines of Bordeaux in 1855 all the wines they chose were from the MÉDOC – except one, Haut-Brion from the GRAVES (now PESSAC-LÉOGNAN), which was accorded First Growth status.

There's no doubt the wine deserves its lofty position. It has all the potential longevity and weight of the Médoc First Growths, and starts out tasting very like them because of the vineyard's deep gravel soil. Yet after a few years the flavour changes course; the tough tannins fade away more quickly, a gentle creamy-edged fruit takes their place and a few years' more maturity brings out all the fruit of plums and blackcurrants mingled with a heady scent of unsmoked Havana tobacco. Second wine: Bahans-Haut-Brion. Best years: (reds) 1998, '97, '96, '95, '94, '93, '90, '89, '88, '86, '85, '83.

The white wine can be inconsistent, but at its best, Haut-Brion Blanc is fabulous wine, which after five to ten years blossoms out into a wonderfully lush flavour of nuts and spice, cream and a hint of apricots. Best years: (whites) 1998, '97, '96, '95, '94, '90, '89, '88, '87, '86, '85, '83, '82, '81, '79, '76.

CH. HAUT-MARBUZET

FRANCE, Bordeaux, Haut-Médoc, St-Estèphe AC, Cru Bourgeois

♥ *Cabernet Sauvignon, Merlot, Cabernet Franc*

Haut-Marbuzet's 50-ha (124-acre) vineyard is sited between its more illustrious neighbours, MONTROSE and COS D'ESTOURNEL. The energetic Monsieur Duboscq treats his wine like a top Classed Growth – right up to using 100 per cent new oak for maturing it – and

CH. HAUT-MARBUZET
Exotic, opulent and powerful, this St-Estèphe wine stands out both when it is young and with as much as 20 years of aging.

the great, rich, mouthfilling blast of flavour with lots of new oak certainly isn't subtle, but certainly is impressive. The wine also ages extremely well, shaking off its cloak of oak to reveal a complex spectrum of aromas and flavours. Best years: 1998, '97, '96, '95, '94, '93, '90, '89, '88, '86, '85, '83, '82, '81, '78.

HAUT-MÉDOC AC

FRANCE, Bordeaux

♥ *Cabernet Sauvignon, Merlot, Cabernet Franc and others*

The Haut-Médoc is the southern half of the MÉDOC peninsula, stretching from Blanquefort, in the suburbs of the city of Bordeaux, north to St-Seurin-de-Cadourne. All the Médoc's finest gravelly soil is situated in this southern half, and there are six separate village ACs: MARGAUX, LISTRAC, MOULIS, ST-JULIEN, PAUILLAC and ST-ESTÈPHE. The Haut-Médoc AC covers all the parts of this geographical area not included in one of the specific village appellations. There are five Classed Growths within the AC, including the excellent Ch. la LAGUNE and CANTEMERLE in the south, but otherwise the wines vary widely in quality and style. They are inclined to lack a little fruit but age well in a slightly austere way. The most intense and concentrated can be cellared for ten, even 15 years. Best years: 1998, '96, '95, '94, '90, '89, '88, '85, '83, '82. Best producers: Beaumont, Belgrave, Camensac, Cantemerle, Charmail, CISSAC, Citran, Coufran, la Lagune, Lamarque, Lanessan, Liversan, Malescasse, Maucamps, Ramage-la-Batisse, SOCIANDO-MALLET, la Tour-Carnet, la Tour-du-Haut-Moulin.

HAUT-POITOU AC

FRANCE, Loire, Touraine

♥♀ *Gamay, Cabernet Franc, Cabernet Sauvignon*

♀ *Sauvignon Blanc, Chardonnay, Chenin Blanc*

This little island of vineyards is near Poitiers, well on the way south to BORDEAUX. You've got to relish crisp, zingy acidity to like Haut-Poitou whites, because they are austere, squeaky clean demonstrations of the varietal flavour of each grape. Not surprisingly, with this high acid but characterful style they're having a go at sparkling wine, and the CHAMPAGNE-method Diane de Poitiers is a great success. Red Haut-Poitou, normally made from Gamay, is light and dry, veering towards the raw except in warm years. The rosé, usually Cabernet-based, is also very dry, but can be good and refreshing, marked by a nice grassy tang when young. There are also some Cabernet reds, which, in good years like 1997 and '96, repay keeping for a couple of years. The Neuville co-operative completely dominates production and the wines are now marketed by DUBOEUF.

HAWKE'S BAY

NEW ZEALAND, North Island

Hawke's Bay is traditionally regarded as New Zealand's greatest red wine region, but it is only the best mesoclimates and soils that really deliver – much of the valley floor land is too heavy. The finest vineyards can be found on the gravelly river terraces of the Tuki Tuki and Ngaruroro rivers and on the foothill edges of the plains of Fernhill, Ngatarawa, Taradale, Haumoana, Havelock North and the Esk Valley. The climate is warm and sunny with high ultraviolet penetration, yet not so hot as to bake out the true flavour of Cabernet Sauvignon, Merlot, Cabernet Franc and Chardonnay. Even Syrah grows here, and only Sauvignon Blanc lives in the shadow of the MARLBOROUGH region. Best years: 1999, '98, '96, '94, '91, '89, '86, '85, '83, '82. Best producers: Alpha Domus, BROOKFIELDS, CLEARVIEW, Esk Valley, The McDonald Winery, Mission (Jewelstone), NGATARAWA, C J Pask, Sacred Hill, Stonecroft, Te Awa Farm, TE MATA, TRINITY HILL, Unison, Vidal, VILLA MARIA.

HEDGES CELLARS

USA, Washington State, Columbia Valley AVA
❢ *Cabernet Sauvignon, Merlot*
♀ *Sauvignon Blanc, Chardonnay*

Hedges Cellars earned a reputation in the late 1980s with an affordable Cabernet-Merlot blend that was an international success. While red wines are the main emphasis, including the Three Vineyard Cabernet Sauvignon and oaky Red Mountain Reserve, increasing amounts of an unusual blend of Sauvignon Blanc and Chardonnay called Fumé-Chardonnay are being made. The Sauvignon Blanc adds spice and crispness to the fruity, young Chardonnay. Best years: 1998, '96, '95, '94.

The Ngatarawa winery is one of Hawke's Bay's top estates and the viticulture is organic, with Chardonnay and botrytized Riesling producing the best results to date.

HEEMSKERK

AUSTRALIA, Tasmania, Pipers River
❢ *Pinot Noir*
♀ *Chardonnay, Riesling*

Changes have run fast and furious at Heemskerk. After never really fulfilling its potential, it was acquired by PIPERS BROOK VINEYARDS in 1998, and its flagship sparkling Jansz was sold by Pipers Brook to YALUMBA (the Champagne house of ROEDERER has long since ceased to be a joint venturer in Jansz). This leaves Heemskerk with a nutty, buttery Chardonnay, elegant Riesling and (in some years) delicious strawberry/plum Pinot Noir. Best years: 1998, '97, '95, '94, '92, '91.

DR HEGER

GERMANY, Baden, Ihringen
❢ *Pinot Noir (Spätburgunder)*
♀ *Riesling, Pinot Gris (Grauburgunder), Pinot Blanc (Weissburgunder), Muskateller, Scheurebe*

Joachim Heger makes some of the finest dry Weissburgunder and Grauburgunder in Germany. Each variety makes two styles of wine: the barrique-aged one with '***' on the label and a sleeker version which only uses stainless steel during the winemaking stages.

In recent years he has also attracted attention with his red wines, which are international in style and some of the best Spätburgunders that BADEN has to offer. His yields are low, which is part of the story – just 30–45 hectolitres per hectare. He looks for tannin, and accordingly gives the more expensive wines a 28-day

maceration; the rest get about a week. And they are made in standard Burgundian style, on the skins, without the aid of thermovinification or pressurized tanks, which some Baden growers use for their reds. He is ambitious for his wines to succeed, so look out for them on export markets. Second label: Weinhaus Joachim Heger. Best years: (reds) 1998, '97, '96, '93, '90; (whites) 1998, '97, '96, '94, '93, '90.

CHARLES HEIDSIECK

FRANCE, Champagne, Champagne AC
♀❢ *Chardonnay, Pinot Noir, Pinot Meunier*

Under the direction of the brilliant winemaker Daniel Thibault, Charles Heidsieck went through a revolution in the 1980s. Thibault had built up stocks of reserve wines, which he blended into the revamped non-vintage Brut, renamed Brut Réserve. With 40 per cent of reserve wines in the blend, it was a terrific wine and met with well-deserved success. Another, but more controversial innovation, was the release of Mis en Cave Champagnes in the late 1990s. These carried dates, but were non-vintage wines; the dates referred to when the wine was bottled to begin its aging process. These are excellent CHAMPAGNES and far from cheap and though the consumer might be confused into thinking they were vintage wines, they shouldn't worry because the quality *is* vintage.

The outstanding wine in the Heidsieck range is the vintage Blanc de Blancs called

Cuvée des Millénaires, which is wonderfully rich and biscuity. Despite a total annual production of over two million bottles, quality here is high. Best years: 1990, '89, '88, '85.

GERNOT HEINRICH

AUSTRIA, Burgenland, Neusiedlersee, Gols
❦ *Blaufränkisch, Blauer Zweigelt, Cabernet Sauvignon*
♀ *Pinot Blanc (Weissburgunder), Pinot Gris (Grauburgunder), Chardonnay, Muscat (Muskat Ottonel), Neuburger*

Gernot Heinrich is one of the first winemakers in Austria to play the 'dynamic young winemaker' role successfully in the national media, but he is also genuinely talented in the cellar. The 'regular' whites only see stainless steel and are very fresh and zingy. In contrast, the white Pannobile is a barrique-aged blend of Chardonnay, Weissburgunder, Grauburgunder and Neuburger which packs quite a punch. The best of the 'regular' reds is the straight Blaufränkisch, a fleshy, blackberry and plum wine with loads of soft tannins. These also play an important role in the top red Gabarinza, a blend of Cabernet and local grapes which is rich and velvety. Best years: (reds) 1997, '96, '94, '93, '92; (whites) 1998, '97, '95.

HEITZ CELLARS

USA, California, Napa County, Napa Valley AVA
❦ *Cabernet Sauvignon, Grignolino, Pinot Noir*
❦ *Grignolino*
♀ *Chardonnay*

In an era when the mob is chasing after Merlot and other grapes to temper Cabernet Sauvignon, outspoken Joe Heitz sticks to the old CALIFORNIA idea of the pure item, picked as ripe as possible and aged upwards of three years in oak. While others use only wood from this forest or that cooper, Heitz uses a bit of everything.

He and his winemaker son, David, make three Cabernets – Martha's Vineyard from Oakville, Bella Oaks from RUTHERFORD and NAPA VALLEY. Until the 1985 vintage all three are powerfully aromatic, sturdy wines with a complex array of subtleties that last and last, but since then apparent problems in the winery seemed to be taking the gloss off this old-timer. These problems now appear to have been dealt with, but times move on, and their Cabernets are no longer at the top of the rankings, although they remain in the picture. Vineyard replanting disrupted the production of the Martha's Vineyard Cabernet from 1993 to 1996. The rosé is fairly dry, with a good bite. Best years: 1995, '94, '92, '91, '90, '87, '86, '84, '83, '81, '80, '79, '78.

HENRIQUES & HENRIQUES

PORTUGAL, Madeira, Madeira DOC
❦ *Tinta Negra Mole*
♀ *Sercial, Verdelho, Bual, Malvasia (Malmsey) and others*

Henriques & Henriques is the second-largest MADEIRA wine producer, after the MADEIRA WINE COMPANY, and owns the largest vineyard on the island. Managed by John Cossart, the wines have improved greatly in the 1990s and are now of exemplary quality.

The range begins with a young, dry apéritif Madeira known as Monte Seco, based on Tinta Negra Mole, and continues through 3-Year-Old, 5-Year-Old and 10-Year-Old wines to a good range of venerable vintage wines. The four Henriques & Henriques 10-Year-Olds are probably the best in their class. Made according to sweetness from the four 'noble' Madeira grapes, Sercial, Verdelho, Bual and Malvasia, they have the clean, incisive, high-toned character of well-aged Madeira and at a reasonable price. Best years: (vintage Madeira) 1957 (Bual), '54 (Bual and Malmsey), '44 (Sercial), '34 (Verdelho).

HENRY OF PELHAM

CANADA, Ontario, Niagara Peninsula VQA
❦ *Cabernet Sauvignon, Merlot*
♀ *Chardonnay, Riesling*

Henry of Pelham is a small winery with a big reputation for producing top-flight wines. Winemaker Ron Giesbrecht and his assistant Sandrine Epp work with some 31ha (77 acres) of vines on the sloping hills of the Niagara Bench. The vineyard strategy is to work with low yields that translate into concentrated wines. The best efforts are labelled Reserve Chardonnay, Proprietor's Reserve Riesling, Riesling Icewine and, in warm years, Cabernet-Merlot. Current production remains at just under 4000 cases annually but is expected to rise as new plantings begin to bear grapes in 2001. Best years: 1998, '97, '95.

HENRY OF PELHAM
The Proprietor's Reserve Riesling has intense, floral fruit flavours and is one of the top wines from this quality producer in the Niagara region.

HENSCHKE

AUSTRALIA, South Australia, Barossa Zone, Eden Valley
❦ *Syrah (Shiraz), Cabernet Sauvignon, Malbec*
♀ *Riesling, Semillon, Chardonnay*

The already high reputation of Henschke has been lifted to another plane over the past decade. Hill of Grace (from a single plot of Shiraz) is now even scarcer than PENFOLDS Grange, and comes second only to Grange in the Australian price hierarchy. Cyril Henschke Cabernet Sauvignon and Mount Edelstone Shiraz have followed in the slipstream of Hill of Grace, with ever-rising prices reflecting ever-growing world demand. The various reds reflect to the fullest the very old (up to 120 years) vines still yielding at Henschke, with their deep colour, dark cherry and blackcurrant chewy fruit and lingering tannins, but in the Australian style they also taste wonderful on release, yet are worth waiting for too.

The Henschke portfolio has been significantly expanded by the establishment of its substantial Lenswood vineyards in the ADELAIDE HILLS. Here, Chardonnay, Pinot Noir, Riesling, Cabernet Sauvignon and Merlot all flourish, the style being generally lighter and more fragrant than that produced by the old vineyards in the EDEN VALLEY. Best years: (Eden Valley Shiraz) 1996, '94, '92, '91, '90, '88, '86, '84, '82, '80, '78, '72.

HÉRAULT

FRANCE, Languedoc-Roussillon

The Hérault *département* was once the fountainhead of France's infamous contribution to the European wine lake. It is used to produce a positive deluge of rock-bottom rot-gut every year. However, this is now the heart of the Brave New World of winemaking, which has transformed the Midi into a high-tech, Australian-style provider of cheap, attractive, everyday table wines. This weather-beaten and ancient land, centred on Béziers and Montpellier, is the most densely planted *département* in France – and until the 1980s had the fewest ACs. Fortunately, politicians realized you can't protect sub-standard producers for ever, and during the 1980s in Hérault and the neighbouring *département* of AUDE, over 30,000ha (74,000 acres) of vines were uprooted. There is now a good deal of interesting wine coming from the hills, most of it red, but as methods of cool fermentation in stainless steel take hold, and as new grape varieties come into production, the whites are improving too.

Until the 1980s, the Hérault only had one table wine AC – the dull and insipid white

Clairette du Languedoc. Since then FAUGÈRES, ST-CHINIAN and the widespread COTEAUX DU LANGUEDOC (where several villages, notably La Clape and Pinet, now have a good reputation for white as well as red) have joined the AC list. But it is the VIN DE PAYS de l'Hérault – France's most elephantine vin de pays at a giant 200 million bottles annually – that is doing sterling work in improving the quality of wine throughout the region. Here plantings are heavily loaded in favour of red Carignan. The resulting wine can be coarse and tough but, when made by carbonic maceration, can be pleasant and fruity. Plantings of Syrah, Mourvèdre, Cabernet Sauvignon and Merlot are increasing yearly. There is one superstar property, MAS DE DAUMAS GASSAC, whose fans liken the wine to Classed Growth BORDEAUX. The company of Skalli, at Sète, is showing in its FORTANT DE FRANCE range that wines can be produced in bulk without sacrificing quality.

LANGUEDOC-ROUSSILLON's leading fortified Muscat is made at Frontignan, on the coast near Sète, and the 27 Vins de Pays de Zone in the Hérault are encouraging wine merchants to be innovative and to demand quality. Chardonnay, Sauvignon Blanc, Sémillon and Marsanne varietal wines have appeared, as well as attractively aromatic versions of Grenache Blanc, Bourboulenc, Macabeo and dry Muscat. Best producers: (Vin de Pays de l'Hérault) du Bosc/Chante Cigale, Ch. Capion, la Fadèze, la Granges des Pères, Jany, Lenthéric, Limbardie, Mas de Daumas Gassac.

HERMITAGE AC
FRANCE, Northern Rhône

🍷 *Syrah*
🍷 *Marsanne, Roussanne*

There was a time, a century or more ago, when Hermitage was regarded by many as the greatest red wine in France. And there was a time, amid the BORDEAUX and Burgundy fever of the early 1980s, when it was dismissed by almost all as merely a rough-and-tumble RHÔNE red. And now once again Hermitage is revered – rare, rich red wine, expensive, memorable, classic. But these words are too cold to describe the turbulent excitements of a great Hermitage. The boiling cauldron of flavours – savage pepper, herbs, tar and coalsmoke biting at your tongue, fruit of intense blackcurrant-raspberry-and-bramble sweetness – is intoxicatingly delicious, and, as the wine ages, a strange, warm softness of cream and licorice and well-worn leather blends in to create one of the greatest red-wine taste experiences.

PAUL JABOULET AÎNÉ
Jaboulet's Hermitage La Chapelle was the wine that finally brought the great red wines of the northern Rhône back into the limelight with the 1978 vintage.

Now, not all Hermitage achieves this eccentric but exciting blend of flavours, because the vineyard – flowing down the slopes of this bullish mound above the little town of Tain l'Hermitage on the banks of the Rhône – only covers 150ha (371 acres) and a lot of merchants will take any grapes just to have Hermitage on their list. But the best growers – using the red Syrah, with sometimes a little white Marsanne and Roussanne, and carefully blending the wines from different parts of the hill (which do give very different flavours) – can make superbly original wine, needing five to ten years' aging even in a light year; but for the full-blown roar of flavours which a hot, ripe vintage brings, then 15 years is hardly enough for the tip-top wines. Best producers: Belle, CHAPOUTIER, CHAVE, DELAS, Desmeure, Faurie, Fayolle, Ferraton, GRAILLOT, Grippat, GUIGAL, JABOULET, Sorrel, Tardieu-Laurent.

White Hermitage is rather less famous than the red – but the best can actually outlive the reds. Some winemakers, like Jaboulet, are making modern, fruity, fragrant whites – with an exciting floral, lemon peel, licorice and apple flavour. These are lovely as young as one to two years old. But there are others – from grizzly-minded traditionalists who won't be swayed by fashion and the chance of an easy sale. They've been growing the Marsanne and Roussanne grapes on the dizzy slopes of the giant hill of Hermitage for generations, and they don't care if their wine then takes generations to mature so long as it is the 'real thing'.

The flavour of white Hermitage from producers like Chave, Grippat or Chapoutier will seem fat and oily at first, reeking of bruised apples, soured peaches and unswept farmyard rubbish; but if you give it ten years, 20, maybe twice as long, then a remarkable and welcome transformation will take place – apples and pears blend with fresh-roasted nuts, toffee, licorice, pine resin, herbs from the wild Rhône hills, mint and peaches and cream.

From such sullen beginnings the glory of white Hermitage finally blazes forth. About 26 per cent of the vineyard is white, producing some 200,000 bottles a year. Best years: (reds and whites) 1998, '97, '96, '95, '94, '91, '90, '89, '88, '85, '83, '82, '78. Best producers: Belle, Chapoutier, Chave, Desmeure, Grippat, Guigal, Jaboulet, Sorrel.

THE HESS COLLECTION
USA, California, Napa County, Mount Veeder AVA

🍷 *Cabernet Sauvignon and others*
🍷 *Chardonnay*

The steep mountainous slopes of Mount Veeder, in the south-western corner of the NAPA VALLEY, were becoming notorious for rough-hewn, tannic reds until Hess started releasing its Cabernet Sauvignons. Despite owning 110ha (275 acres) of vines, Swiss-born art collector Donald Hess chose to ease slowly into winemaking and his winery is only now hitting full stride.

From 1985 the Hess Collection Cabernets, assisted by Merlot and the other BORDEAUX varieties, began to serve notice of what these mountainous vineyards can produce. They have that typical mountain-infused flavour of earth and tobacco, but are richly fleshed out with sweet blackcurrant fruit and toasty oak. The Cabernet Reserve is often a brilliant success, with great depth and complexity. Hess says his objective is to 'tame the mountain'. He's not been as successful in this aim with his Chardonnay, and today's primary bottling blends mountain and valley floor Chardonnay grapes. Best years: (reds) 1997, '96, '95, '94, '93, '92, '91, '90, '89, '87, '86.

HESSISCHE BERGSTRASSE
GERMANY

The best place to taste the wines of Hessische Bergstrasse is in the region itself. You're unlikely to find them anywhere else, for the simple reason that there aren't many of them: 455ha (1124 acres) of vines, divided between over 1000 different growers. It is impossible, with such a small, little-known region, not to view its wines in the light of those of other regions. If Hessische Bergstrasse's Rieslings are like lesser RHEINGAUs, its Müller-Thurgaus are like lesser Müller-Thurgaus from BADEN, without the richness and finesse that the best of the latter can have, even though Hessische Bergstrasse is geographically a northerly continuation of Baden. And its Silvaners are like lesser FRANKEN Silvaners, without quite the same firmness and depth.

Even so, the best wines of the region can surpass these levels: there are powerful, well-structured wines to be had, particularly the Eisweins. Best producers: Bergsträsser Gebiets-Winzergenossenschaft, Staatsweingut Bergstrasse (Domaine Bensheim).

HEURIGER

AUSTRIA

Heuriger is the new wine of the year in Austria, and a Heurige is the family-owned premises on which it is drunk: in Vienna, a number of Austrian winemakers run a Heurige, serving only homemade food. Even the pigs (and the food relies heavily on pig) have to be home-reared.

Outside Vienna the taverns are more properly called Buschenschanken, but the principle, and the atmosphere, are the same. Sometimes the wines of Austria's top growers can be sampled like this: a bit like dropping into Ch. LAFITE for a quick glass. The wines served may be the full range produced by the grower, but the Viennese Heuriger wine itself is traditionally a mix of varieties that relies on freshness for its attractiveness.

HEYL ZU HERRNSHEIM

GERMANY, Rheinhessen, Nierstein
♀ *Riesling, Silvaner, Müller-Thurgau, Pinot Blanc (Weissburgunder)*

One of the finest estates in the RHEINHESSEN, Heyl zu Herrnsheim has a prime position in NIERSTEIN, right in the middle of the Rhein Terrasse. Its vines ascend steeply into the red slate Pettenthal vineyard, the Hipping, the Ölberg and the little Brudersberg vineyard, which the company owns in its entirety. Raw materials like these would give any winemaker a good head start; Heyl zu Herrnsheim capitalizes on them with meticulous winemaking and rigorous selection.

The estate has recently been taken over by Markus Ahr, who is undertaking a modest expansion with new vines in the NACKEN-HEIM Rothenberg. Best years: 1998, '97, '96, '94, '93, '92, '90, '89, '88.

HEYL ZU HERRNSHEIM
This top Rheinhessen estate practises organic viticulture to produce fine wines, especially from the wholly owned Brudersberg site in Nierstein.

HEYMANN-LÖWENSTEIN

GERMANY, Mosel-Saar-Ruwer, Winningen
♀ *Riesling, Pinot Blanc (Weissburgunder)*

Before Reinhard Löwenstein began building his estate up from scratch in 1980 there was not much going on in the Lower MOSEL, an area he recently succeeded in getting renamed the 'Terrassen Mosel'. From his steep terraced vineyards in the Röttgen and Uhlen sites of WINNINGEN he produces by far the best dry Rieslings in the entire Mosel. The Röttgen wines have a ripe pineapple character, the Uhlen wines are peachy and minerally with excellent aging potential. Since 1993 he has also produced some impressive Auslese and higher Prädikat dessert wines in a no-holds-barred blockbuster style. Best years: 1998, '97, '96, '95, '94, '93, '92.

HIDALGO

SPAIN, Andalucía, Jerez y Manzanilla DO
♀ *Palomino Fino, Pedro Ximénez*

The three Hidalgo cousins who run this small 200-year-old company specialize with great success in manzanilla, and make all their wines from their own and other family vineyards. Besides Manzanilla La Gitana (Spain's best-selling manzanilla), they also make a good range named Mariscal, excellent Fino Especial and Miraflores, Amontillado Napoleón, Pedro Ximénez Viejo, Oloroso Viejo and a dry Jerez Cortado.

HILLTOPS

AUSTRALIA, New South Wales, Southern New South Wales Zone

After a brief but successful period of viticulture towards the end of the nineteenth century, the vines disappeared until 1975, when the late Peter Robertson decided to plant some on his large farming property. Barwang, as it was called, was acquired by MCWILLIAM'S in 1989, and since that time plantings have grown from a token 13ha (32 acres) to many hundreds of hectares, with little end to the expansion in sight. All the vineyards are planted above the 450m (1480ft) contour line, and the dry summers and autumns provide excellent ripening conditions.

The principal wines here are stony/minerally Chardonnay, moderately spicy Syrah (Shiraz) with a range of chocolate, mint, black cherry and more briary characters, and Cabernet Sauvignon, predominantly cassis/blackcurrant but balanced with some more earthy/chocolate undertones. Best years: 1998, '97, '94, '93, '92, '91, '90. Best producer: McWilliam's Barwang.

FRANZ HIRTZBERGER

AUSTRIA, Niederösterreich, Wachau, Spitz
♀ *Grüner Veltliner, Riesling, Pinot Gris (Grauburgunder), Pinot Blanc (Weissburgunder), Chardonnay (Feinburgunder), Muscat (Gelber Muskateller)*

Franz Hirtzberger's natural charm and political skills have made him an excellent president of the WACHAU winegrowers' association, Vinea Wachau, under whom the region has taken a great stride forward. As a winemaker he has repeatedly demonstrated the elegance and aromatic refinement of which the region's wines are capable, even with natural alcohol contents far above 13 degrees. His finest wines are the concentrated and exotic Riesling Smaragd from the Singer-riedel site of Spitz and the creamy spicy Grüner Veltliner Smaragd from the next-door Honivogl vineyard. Easier to experience, because the demand is not quite so extreme, are the lavish, succulent Riesling Smaragd from the Hochrain and the muscular Grüner Veltliner Smaragd from the Rotes Tor. Best years: 1998, '97, '95, '94, '93, '92, '90, '88.

HOCHHEIM

GERMANY, Rheingau

This RHEINGAU village is best known for lending its name to the generic name in the UK for all Rhine wine: English attempts at pronouncing Hochheimer led to 'hockamore' and from there to 'hock' was but a short step for the abbreviating English tongue.

Hochheim's other main claim to fame is Queen Victoria's rather feeble joke, 'A glass of hock keeps away the doc', and all this embellishment can obscure the fact that Hochheim does indeed make some very good wine. It's archetypal Rheingau; firm, earthy and long-lived, with the accent on the earthy. These are not wines to take too lightly or too young: they are long-lived, and mature beautifully. The best vineyards are the Domdechaney, the Hölle, the Kirchenstück and the Königin Victoriaberg, named after Queen Victoria, of course. Best producers: Aschrott, Franz KÜNSTLER, Balthasar RESS, SCHLOSS SCHÖN-BORN, Staatsweingut Eltville, WERNER.

THE HOGUE CELLARS

USA, Washington State, Yakima Valley AVA
♂ *Cabernet Sauvignon, Merlot*
♀ *Chenin Blanc, Riesling, Chardonnay, Sauvignon Blanc*

Long-time farmers in the dry YAKIMA VALLEY, the Hogue family jumped into grapes early in the 1970s when WASHINGTON STATE was getting started, and quickly hit a stride that now has them near the 200,000-case level. The Hogues maintain a style of fresh, lively flavours, with cautious oak for Chardonnay and both reds. Chenin Blanc and White Riesling are impeccable off-dry fresh-fruities to drink within the year. The Chardonnay, subtle in flavour but sturdy in texture, is meant to last for a few years. Both the Reserve Cabernet Sauvignon and Merlot are candidates for long aging. Best years: 1996, '95, '94, '92, '91, '90, '89.

FÜRST ZU HOHENLOHE-ÖHRINGEN

GERMANY, Württemberg, Öhringen im Schloss
🍷 *Lemberger, Pinot Noir (Spätburgunder)*
🍸 *Riesling, Müller-Thurgau and others*

This princely estate dates back to the fourteenth century. There is a lot of old wood in its seventeenth-century cellars, and some new in the form of the fashionable barriques: some Riesling and Chardonnay find their way into them. To have so much Riesling in the red-wine region of WÜRTTEMBERG is unusual and here it is made fashionably dry, even austere; the warm Württemberg climate means, however, that the wine has plenty of the ripeness it needs to balance the dryness. At some 20ha (49 acres) this is a large estate for Württemberg, and includes sole ownership of the Verrenberger Verrenberg vineyard site. Best years: (reds) 1997, '96, '95, '93, '92; (whites) 1998, '97, '96, '95, '93, '92.

HOLLICK

AUSTRALIA, South Australia, Limestone Coast Zone, Coonawarra
🍷 *Cabernet Sauvignon, Merlot, Syrah (Shiraz), Pinot Noir*
🍸 *Riesling, Chardonnay*

Ian and Wendy Hollick have been joined in partnership by former Tollana winemaker Pat Tocaciu, and are producing well-crafted wines, ranging from CHAMPAGNE-method sparklers through to perfumed Rieslings and deep, ripe-textured Chardonnays. However, reds are the traditional Hollick strength. Top-of-the-range Ravenswood Shiraz can be exciting, but the supple and fragrant Cabernet Sauvignon and Cabernet-Merlot have stood out as the archetypal COONAWARRA styles for a number of years. Best years: 1996, '94, '93, '91, '90, '88.

DOMAINE DE L'HORTUS

FRANCE, Languedoc-Roussillon, Coteaux du Langue-doc–Pic St-Loup AC
🍷 *Syrah, Mourvèdre, Grenache*
🍸 *Chardonnay, Viognier*

Jean Orliac of the Domaine de l'Hortus spotted the potential of the Pic St-Loup, a

sub-region of the COTEAUX DU LANGUEDOC, while rock climbing in the area in the 1970s. Through the 1980s he planted Syrah, Mourvèdre and Grenache, producing his first wine in 1990 in shared cellars with Jean-Benoit Cavalier of Ch. de Lascaux. He now has his own wooden cellars and 32ha (79 acres) of vineyard. The Cuvée Classique is a fruity, early-drinking wine matured in stainless steel vats whereas the Grande Cuvée has a higher percentage of Mourvèdre in the blend, is aged 15 months in oak, mainly new barriques, and is a more structured, elegant wine that can age five years or more. There is also a buttery, peachy, barrel-fermented white VIN DE PAYS made from Chardonnay and Viognier. Best years: (reds) 1998, '97, '96, '95, '94.

HOSPICES DE BEAUNE

FRANCE, Burgundy, Beaune
🍷 *Pinot Noir*
🍸 *Chardonnay*

When in 1443 Nicolas Rolin founded the charitable hospital in Beaune now known as the Hospices, he could never have imagined that over five centuries later it would still be thriving. Over the decades bequests have made the Hospices a major landowner in Burgundy, and the profits from the sale of the wines made from these mostly outstanding vineyards have sustained the Hospices financially.

Almost all the 58ha (143 acres) of vineyards owned by the Hospices are in the CÔTE DE BEAUNE. Before they are sold at the highly theatrical auction at the November weekend known as the Trois Glorieuses, the wines are vinified in new oak by the Hospices' winemaker, from 1977 to 1987 the legendary André Porcheret, who returned to this post in 1994. After the auction the barrels are nurtured and bottled by the purchasers. Although there are some outstanding wines from the Hospices holdings, clearly any negligence during the barrel-aging process will result in an indifferent bottle. However, most purchasers tend to be *négociants* who know what they are doing, so the Hospices label is

HOSPICES DE BEAUNE
The different cuvées of Hospices de Beaune wines are named after the individuals who bequeathed the vineyard sites.

often a sign of excellent quality. Inevitably, since the auction is for charity the prices paid for the wines tend to be higher than they might otherwise be. Best years: (reds) 1997, '96, '95, '94, '93, '90, '89, '85, '83, '78; (whites) 1997, '95, '94, '92, '90.

HOUGHTON

AUSTRALIA, Western Australia, Greater Perth Zone, Swan District
🍷 *Cabernet Sauvignon, Syrah (Shiraz)*
🍸 *Chenin Blanc, Muscadelle, Chardonnay, Verdelho, Riesling*

HWG, sold outside the EU as Houghton 'White Burgundy', is one of Australia's leading bottled white table wines. It is a modestly priced blend of Chardonnay, Chenin Blanc and Muscadelle and made in huge quantities. Older vintages, though, can be remarkable, and these and other wines are released under a Show Reserve label, which is well worth the search and certainly worth the money.

As part of the giant BRL HARDY group, Houghton has large vineyard holdings in the Frankland River sub-region of the GREAT SOUTHERN, and takes significant quantities of grapes from the Pemberton region and from MARGARET RIVER. Supplemented by its Moondah Brook vineyard (and brand) it produces a kaleidoscopic array of wines ranging from the monumental show reds called Jack Mann (in memory of the great Houghton winemaker) through to fine, subtly oaked Semillon-Sauvignon Blanc and Chardonnay, together with some startling grapefruit- and passionfruit-accented Riesling. Best years: 1998, '96, '95, '94, '93, '91.

VON HÖVEL

GERMANY, Mosel-Saar-Ruwer, Konz-Oberemmel
🍸 *Riesling, Pinot Blanc (Weissburgunder)*

Ebullient Eherhard von Kunov makes elegant, well-structured wines from steep vineyards in and around the village of Konz-Oberemmel on the Saar. The wines are matured in cask and have the steely acidity typical of the region, as well as, in less than ripe years, the typical distinct green apple taste. Nearly 200 years old, the estate has twelfth-century cellars, and vineyards in some of the Saar's best vineyard sites.

Notable are the Scharzhofberg – in good years, this can be a superb wine – and the Hütte vineyard in Oberemmel, of which von Hövel is the sole owner, and which yields some of its best wines. Since 1993 the quality has been superb. Best years: 1997, '96, '95, '94, '93, '92, '90, '89, '88, '85.

HOWARD PARK

AUSTRALIA, Western Australia, South West Australia Zone, Great Southern
🍷 *Cabernet Sauvignon, Merlot, Cabernet Franc*
🍇 *Riesling, Chardonnay*

After leaving an indelible mark as the maker of WYNNS' first John Riddoch Cabernet Sauvignon (in 1982) John Wade moved to WESTERN AUSTRALIA, setting up an immensely successful career as a contract winemaker and consultant to others while simultaneously establishing his Howard Park label, and ultimately the second label, Madfish Bay. His two signature wines are the rapier-like Riesling and Cabernet-Merlot, which in years such as 1994 is nothing short of sublime; cedar, blackcurrant, olive and spice running through the finest imaginable tannins. The Chardonnay is very nearly as impressive, and Madfish Bay white and red are darlings of the smart brasserie set. Best years: 1998, '97, '94, '92, '91, '90.

HOWELL MOUNTAIN AVA

USA, California, Napa County

Both an appellation and a state of mind, Howell Mountain is a small region in NAPA's north-eastern hillsides made famous in the 1980s by DUNN VINEYARDS' massive Cabernet Sauvignon. At elevations of 500–670m (1600–2200ft) above the fog zone, it has rocky, well-drained volcanic soil that is suitable for Merlot, Zinfandel, and several RHÔNE varieties, as well as Cabernet Sauvignon. Vineyard plantings have slowly grown to 240ha (593 acres). Best producers: BERINGER, DUCKHORN, Dunn, La Jota, Lamborn, Liparita, PINE RIDGE. Best years: 1997, '95, '94, '92, '91, '90.

HUADONG WINERY

CHINA, Shandong Province
🍷 *Syrah (Shiraz), Pinot Noir, Gamay and others*
🍇 *Chardonnay, Welschriesling (Laski Rizling), Chenin Blanc and others*

This joint venture of the Chinese authorities and Allied Domecq aims to make the best dry white wine in China – though anyone who has tasted any others might not think there is much competition. There are 12ha (30 acres) of vineyards in the Shandong Peninsula planted with European grape varieties, and new winemaking equipment, including French oak barriques, has been installed.

The wines are sold under the Tsingtao label and the style is emerging as light and crisp. Massive investment, however, cannot change the climate and excessive moisture from the summer rainy season can cause

Astute marketing around the world by Jean Hugel has meant that Hugel has been one of the best known Alsace wine names for many years.

problems in the vineyard. It is also proving difficult to convince the local growers of the importance of ripening the grapes properly.

BERNHARD HUBER

GERMANY, Baden, Malterdingen
🍷 *Pinot Noir (Spätburgunder)*
🍇 *Chardonnay, Pinot Blanc (Weissburgunder), Pinot Gris (Grauburgunder)*

Since going solo from the huge Badische Winzerkeller co-operative in 1987, Bernhard Huber has become the rising star of BADEN. Single-handedly he has proven the enormous potential which the Breisgau area of Baden has for the Spätburgunder grape with the most powerful Pinot Noirs produced anywhere in the country (look for the 'R' or Reserve bottlings). An accident of history has also given Huber what could be Germany's only old Chardonnay vineyard, from which he makes an unashamedly Burgundian-style wine. This and his best dry Weissburgunder and Grauburgunder also see new wood. Best years: (reds) 1997, '96, '95, '93, '92; (whites) 1998, '97, '96, '95, '93.

HUET

FRANCE, Loire, Touraine, Vouvray AC
🍇 *Chenin Blanc*

The present high reputation of Maison Huet was established by Gaston Huet, now well into his 80s. His first vintage was 1929 and Huet was always uncompromising in his insistence

on quality. Demi-sec and *moelleux* wines, for instance, are never made here unless there is sufficient natural sweetness. For the last 20 years, the estate has been run by Noël Pinguet, Huet's son-in-law, although Gaston remains active. The 35-ha (86-acre) estate is run along biodynamic lines – one of the largest in France to wholly use this labour-intensive method. There are three vineyards, le Haut-Lieu, le Mont and the Clos du Bourg, all of which are sited on some of the best land in VOUVRAY.

The wines, particularly the dry styles, can be austere when they are young but they develop a honeyed complexity as they age. Even quite modest vintages will last for at least 30 years and great vintages, such as 1959 and '47, can last for a century. There are still wines from the nineteenth century in the Huet cellars that remain in good condition. Best years: 1997, '96, '95, '93, '90, '89, '85, '76, '59, '47.

HUGEL ET FILS

FRANCE, Alsace, Alsace AC
🍷 *Pinot Noir*
🍇 *Riesling, Pinot Gris, Gewurztraminer, Pinot Blanc, Muscat, Sylvaner*

Jean Hugel is the best-known ambassador for the wines of ALSACE, although he has now delegated the daily running of his winery to the next generation, the twelfth since the firm started to make wines in Riquewihr in 1637. Lovers of sweet wines have Hugel to thank for the creation of the Vendange Tardive and Sélection de Grains Nobles styles which are now one of the glories of Alsace. At the top level (Cuvée Tradition, Jubilee and Vendange Tardive), Hugel wines remain of the highest quality, but the regular bottlings are dependable rather than exciting.

There are some house specialities. In very ripe years such as 1990, the Pinot Noir here can survive, and benefit from, barrique-aging, and in 1992 Hugel revived its Edelzwicker, Gentil, a blend of Sylvaner and just about everything else. Although Hugel owns some outstanding sites, it never uses the words Grand Cru on the label, and prefers to remain free to make up the blends as it sees fit. Best years: 1997, '96, '95, '94, '93, '92, '90, '89, '88, '85, '83, '76.

HUNTER'S

NEW ZEALAND, South Island, Marlborough
🍷 *Cabernet Sauvignon, Pinot Noir, Merlot*
🍇 *Sauvignon Blanc, Chardonnay, Gewurztraminer, Riesling, Semillon*

The death of Ernie Hunter in 1987 deprived New Zealand of one of its most flamboyant characters, but, headed by the charismatic Jane Hunter OBE, it has not stopped the progress of the winery to all-star status. It is a matter of argument whether the Sauvignon Blanc or the Chardonnay is the better wine; both are the personification of the intense, thrilling fruit flavours that have made MARLBOROUGH famous. Sauvignon Blanc has certainly earned the company a greater share of medals in the past decade. A tasty sparkling wine, Miru Miru, was released in 1998.

The reds so far don't achieve the same quality as the whites, though there are occasional hopeful signs with the Pinot Noir. But for the true glory of Hunter's, you have to try the Sauvignon Blanc – as sharp, as tangy, as shockingly intense as any Sauvignon in the world. The spicy, oak-aged Sauvignon Blanc is good, but takes several years of bottle-aging to come together. Best years: 1998, '97, '96, '94, '91, '89.

HUNTER VALLEY

AUSTRALIA, New South Wales

The Hunter Valley is an infuriating and frustrating place which defies all logic; it would never have survived, let alone prospered, as a wine region were it not for its proximity to Sydney (only 1¾ hours' drive). The soils are largely hopeless, the meagre annual rainfall has a disconcerting habit of falling in the middle of the harvest and the climate is ridiculously warm for quality grape-growing.

Yet despite all this both the Upper and Lower Hunter Valleys regularly produce Semillon of a quality, longevity and style to be found nowhere else in the world; Chardonnay of a peachy lusciousness which propelled the valley to stardom first in Australia and then with equal panache in Europe; and Syrah (Shiraz) which has a freakish ability to age with extreme grace over 30 years or more.

Cabernet Sauvignon, Merlot, Pinot Noir and Verdelho are also grown in the Hunter; the reds develop a regional style with age, an amalgam of tarry, velvety, earthy, farmyardy tastes which may sound an awkward mix but often makes a strangely appealing combination, so long as the fruit is strong enough to achieve dominance over the sweat and the leather. The premium vineyards are mainly in the Lower Hunter, although ROSEMOUNT's exceptional white vineyards are in the Upper Hunter. Best years: 1998, '96, '94, '91, '87, '86, '83, '79, '75. Best producers: Allandale, BROKENWOOD, Evans Family, LAKE'S FOLLY, LINDEMANS, MCWILLIAMS, Petersons, Rosemount, ROTHBURY ESTATE, TYRRELL'S.

HUNTINGTON ESTATE

AUSTRALIA, New South Wales, Central Ranges Zone, Mudgee

🍷 *Cabernet Sauvignon, Syrah (Shiraz), Merlot*
🍷 *Semillon, Chardonnay*

Mudgee is most successful as a red wine region, and Huntington, established in 1969, is a red wine specialist, producing robust, long-lived wines variously fashioned from Shiraz, Cabernet-Shiraz, Cabernet Sauvignon and Cabernet-Merlot. These are dark, blood red and angular in their youth, and may seem a little too coarse-textured to promise real style, but they turn to brick red with age as they soften and fill out, and they always seem to retain a core of velvety sweet fruit in a cocoon of soft tannins. Best years: 1997, '96, '94, '93, '91, '88, '86, '84, '83.

HUNTINGTON ESTATE
This exemplary Mudgee producer draws on its own substantial vineyards for its excellent red wines, including rich and chocolaty Shiraz.

IASI

ROMANIA

Iasi is an important university town in north-eastern Romania. Spread out around the city are well-maintained vineyards that supply a clutch of reasonably modern wineries with good-quality fruit, much of it indigenous Romanian varietals. Tămîioasă Românească and Grasă de Cotnari are the most notable. Tămîioasa is a white variety that makes some lavish, florally aromatic, penetrating dessert wines that seem capable of eternal aging. Feteascǎ Neagrǎ is a red grape that offers refined aromas and good structure although haphazard winemaking often spoils its potential.

IDAHO

USA

Along with OREGON and WASHINGTON, Idaho is part of Pacific Northwest wine country, with some of the USA's highest vineyards. Though much smaller in acreage, at 283ha (700 acres), and with only a handful of wineries compared to Oregon and Washington,

Idaho has produced some impressive wines during its short history. Ste Chapelle is Idaho's one major vineyard and cellar and uses much of the state's grapes, as well as buying in from Washington State, to create sound whites, especially Chardonnay and Riesling.

IHRINGEN

GERMANY, Baden

This is the most important wine town of the Kaiserstuhl region in BADEN. The best wines come from the volcanic soil of the great Winklerberg site whose massive terraces look southwest across the Rhine plain to ALSACE and enjoy the warmest conditions of any German vineyard. The 'Burgunder' grapes – Weissburgunder (Pinot Blanc), Grauburgunder (Pinot Gris) and, increasingly, Spätburgunder (Pinot Noir) – rule here, giving big, powerful wines. Best producers: Dr HEGER, Stigler.

CAVES IMESCH

SWITZERLAND, Valais, Sierre

🍷 *Pinot Noir, Gamay*
🍷 *Chasselas (Fendant), Petite Arvine*

Since 1989 Yvon Roduit has been turning this 200-year-old company into one of the VALAIS' most dynamic wine producers. Even the Fendant has a body and substance that you rarely find in the wines from this – the Chasselas – grape. Perhaps his best wines are those from the Nobles Cépages range such as the Petite Arvine, a big, spicy, dry white with some aging potential. Best years: 1997, '95, '94, '93.

INNISKILLIN WINES

CANADA, Ontario, Niagara Peninsula VQA

🍷 *Pinot Noir*
🍷 *Chardonnay, Riesling, Vidal*

Credited with pioneering the estate winery movement in Canada, Inniskillin co-founders Donald Ziraldo and Karl Kaiser established Canada's first estate winery in 1975. Today, Inniskillin churns out 140,000 cases of wine a year, an amazing 13,000 of which comprise assorted Icewines. The Inniskillin Vidal Icewine is admired worldwide by dessert wine *aficionados*.

On the drier side, winemaker Karl Kaiser continues to work extensively with Pinot Noir and Chardonnay, bottling regular, single-vineyard and reserve editions of each variety. All the grapes used at Inniskillin come from the winery's 49ha (120 acres) or are purchased from a handful of specially selected growers spread about the NIAGARA PENINSULA. Best years: 1998, '95, '94.

IPHOFEN

GERMANY, Franken

This is the most important commune in the Steigerwald, right in the east of the FRANKEN region. Here, the heavy gypsum marl soils and the excellent exposure of the Julius-Echter-Berg site give the most massive, earthy, dry Rieslings and Silvaners in the entire region; these are not wines for the faint-hearted! Best producers: Johann Ruck, WIRSCHING.

IRANCY AC

FRANCE, Burgundy

🍷 🍷 *Pinot Noir, César, Tressot*

This northern outpost of vineyards, just south-west of CHABLIS, is an unlikely champion of the clear, pure flavours of Pinot Noir. In the compact south-facing amphitheatre of 63ha (156 acres) of vineyards, the sun gives just enough encouragement to the vines to produce a delicate, clean red wine that is lightly touched by the ripeness of plums and strawberries. The wines will also age reasonably well, especially if they include some César and Tressot, two local grape varieties of diminishing importance. César, in particular, adds colour and body to the wine. There is a little rosé which can also give a fleeting glimpse of Pinot Noir fruit.

Two other local reds are BOURGOGNE-Coulanges-la-Vineuse – rougher than Irancy, with a disconcerting rooty taste – and Bourgogne-Épineuil – frail, rare, but a delightful summer red. There are also Bourgogne-Chitry and Bourgogne-St Bris. Best years: 1997, '96, '95, '93, '92, '90. Best producers: Bienvenu, Brocard, Cantin, Colinot, Delaloge, Fort, Michaut, Simonnet-Febvre.

IRON HORSE VINEYARDS

USA, California, Sonoma County, Sonoma-Green Valley AVA

🍷 *Pinot Noir, Cabernet Sauvignon*

🍷 *Chardonnay, Sauvignon Blanc*

When Forrest Tancer and Barry and Audrey Sterling began their partnership in 1978, the emphasis was on still Chardonnay and Pinot Noir; CHAMPAGNE-method sparklers were an amusing sideline. The latter have since become the tail that wags the dog, enormously successful for their delicacy and freshness of texture and flavour. The Brut is primarily Chardonnay, the Blanc de Noirs nearly all Pinot Noir. Still wines include Chardonnay, Pinot Noir, a rich, ripe Sauvignon Blanc, a plummy but green-streaked Cabernet Sauvignon blend labelled Cabernets, and an exotic, full-flavoured Viognier. Best years: (sparkling wines) 1994, '92, '91, '90, '88.

IROULÉGUY AC

FRANCE, South-West

🍷 🍷 *Tannat, Cabernet Franc, Cabernet Sauvignon*

🍷 *Petit Manseng, Gros Manseng, Courbu and others*

Tucked away up in the Pyrenean mountain valleys, this is probably one of the most obscure French ACs. The wines are not as good as the scenery but the red has improved greatly over the years, with more body and structure, due to greater ripeness and oak aging being added in the 1990s. The rosé is, well, rosé. Rare whites come from Étienne BRANA and the local co-operative. Drink these wines young – preferably with your picnic in the meadows by the winery at St-Étienne-de-Baigorry, just below the snow line. The co-operative dominates production from the appellation's 170ha (420 acres) of vineyards. Best producers: Arretxea, Brana, Etxegaraya, Ilarria, Irouléguy co-operative. Best years: 1998, '97, '95 ,'94.

ISOLE E OLENA

ITALY, Tuscany, Chianti Classico DOCG

🍷 *Sangiovese, Canaiolo, Syrah, Cabernet Sauvignon*

🍷 *Chardonnay, Malvasia, Trebbiano*

This estate of 40ha (99 acres) has become almost an emblem of modern-style, high-quality CHIANTI CLASSICO, but has also been as innovative, indeed iconoclastic as any other Tuscan producer in experimenting with non-Tuscan varieties like Syrah, Cabernet Sauvignon and Chardonnay. Paolo de Marchi, whose Piedmontese family bought the estate in the 1960s, took charge in the mid-1970s. Since then he has spared no effort to improve every aspect of his production, despite a quasi-permanent shortage of funds.

His standard-bearer is the straight Chianti Classico, always approachable while maintaining a serious side and an uncompromising individuality. To maintain the quality of this wine he will, in lesser vintages, sacrifice his famous cru, the barrique-aged 100 per cent Sangiovese Cepparello, effectively his Riserva wine, for which he can command a considerably higher price.

One of Paolo's innovations was the introduction of the RHÔNE'S Syrah grape into Tuscan viticulture, which he will sprinkle into the Chianti Classico blend if need be. In good years he makes a varietal wine called l'Eremo in the so-called Collezione De Marchi range, which also includes excellent Cabernet Sauvignon and Chardonnay. His VIN SANTO, too, is special and one of the finest of the modern fruit-driven style. Paolo de Marchi, with his fluent, accented English, has become

ISOLE E OLENA

Cepparello is Paolo de Marchi's top wine. From 100 per cent Sangiovese, it is an austere yet beautiful rendering of Tuscany's classic red grape.

one of the greatest ambassadors of Chianti Classico abroad. Best years: 1998, '97, '96, '95, '94, '93, '91, '90, '88, '86, '85.

CH. D'ISSAN

FRANCE, Bordeaux, Haut-Médoc, Margaux AC, 3ème Cru Classé

🍷 *Cabernet Sauvignon, Merlot*

We didn't see much of d'Issan during the 1970s, and during the '80s and early '90s the wines frequently promised much from the barrel, but disappointed in the bottle. They lacked a certain weight and density, and the heavenly scent that made the wines so irresistible when young never seemed to survive the bottling. However, it does look as though the owners have begun to address these problems in the later '90s. The property is a reasonable size at 32ha (79 acres) and is unusual for not having any Cabernet Franc in the vineyard, plantings being 75 per cent Cabernet Sauvignon and 25 per cent Merlot. Second wine: le Blazon d'Issan. Best years: 1998, '97, '96, '95, '90, '89, '85, '83, '82, '81, '78.

PAUL JABOULET

FRANCE, Northern Rhône, Hermitage AC

🍷 *Syrah, Grenache*

🍷 *Marsanne, Roussanne*

For decades Jaboulet has been one of the most consistent of RHÔNE merchant houses, the overall quality of its wines no doubt boosted by the ownership of 91ha (225 acres) of vineyards. Almost all the wines originate from northern Rhône sites, the most prized one being HERMITAGE. Jaboulet's Hermitage La Chapelle is one of the Rhône's great classics, an elegant, beautifully structured and very long-lived wine, the quintessence of Syrah in top vintages. There was an unsatisfying period in the early to mid-1980s, but the wine is now back on form. So is the white Hermitage (Chevalier de Stérimberg), which spends a few months in new oak. Until very recently Jaboulet's top CROZES-HERMITAGE, Thalabert, was always the appellation's top wine; it remains excellent and ages very well, but today there is more competition from other growers. Crozes-Hermitage les Jalets is designed for earlier drinking, and there is a rich white Crozes called Mule Blanche. The range is completed with two wines from CORNAS (including the superb Domaine de St-Pierre), a fine ST-JOSEPH, a dependable CÔTES DU RHÔNE called Parallèle 45, and a cheap and cheerful CÔTES DU VENTOUX. Best years: 1997, '96, '95, '94, '91, '90, '89, '88, '78.

CH. DES JACQUES
FRANCE, Burgundy, Beaujolais, Romanèche-Thorins
🍷 *Gamay*
🍷 *Chardonnay*

This 36-ha (89-acre) BEAUJOLAIS estate has been owned since 1996 by Louis JADOT of BEAUNE; the property includes 9ha (22 acres) planted with Chardonnay. Although white BEAUJOLAIS-VILLAGES and white MÂCON-VILLAGES are produced, the mainstay of the domaine is the MOULIN-À-VENT, which is partially aged in barrels for about ten months. The vineyards are divided into five Clos, which are usually bottled separately. There is also a high-priced Réserve de Vieilles Vignes bottling from old vines. Jadot has retained the traditional winemaking style, with destemming of most of the bunches, and the wines are as expressive of their appellation as any from the region and are capable of improving in bottle for some years. The white Beaujolais from the Grand Clos de Loye is also fine. Best years: 1998, '97, '96, '95, '94.

LOUIS JADOT
FRANCE, Burgundy, Beaune
🍷 *Pinot Noir*
🍷 *Chardonnay*

One of Burgundy's most respected *négociant* houses, with holdings in many of the CÔTE D'OR's best sites, Jadot has generally kept to a high quality level when many neighbouring firms have slipped. Its leading white wines are BÂTARD-MONTRACHET and CORTON-CHARLEMAGNE, and there are first-rate reds from BEAUNE Premier Cru sites such as Clos des Ursules and from CORTON, GEVREY-CHAMBERTIN and MUSIGNY. Under its brilliant winemaker, Jacques Lardière, Jadot often manages to produce a more than acceptable range of wines in difficult vintages such as 1994. The sign of a good *négociant* is the ability to produce simpler and less expensive wines of good quality, and here too Jadot excels, with excellent wines from villages such as FIXIN,

The finest sherry vineyards are located on deep, snow-white albariza chalk soil which absorbs the winter rain like a sponge; this then sustains the vines during the long summer drought.

RULLY and ST-AUBIN for short-term drinking. In 1998 the firm moved into a spacious new winery on the outskirts of Beaune. Best years: 1997, '96, '95, '94, '93, '91, '90, '89, '88, '85.

JOSEF JAMEK
AUSTRIA, Niederösterreich, Wachau, Joching
🍷 *Riesling, Grüner Veltliner, Pinot Blanc (Weissburgunder), Muscat (Gelber Muskateller)*

During the late 1950s Josef Jamek began his crusade for dry, unchaptalized wines in the WACHAU. After a period of erratic quality during the early 1990s, things have taken a decisive upturn since the arrival of his daughter Jutta, and her husband Hans Altmann. They have not made any fundamental changes, but brought new energy and ambition and the wines have taken a leap forward as a result. Top of the range are the Rieslings from the Ried Klaus of Weissenkirchen, which have a classical elegance and great aging potential. The eponymous restaurant serves Austrian cooking of the highest standard. Best years: 1998, '97, '95, '93, '90, '88, '86, '83, '79, '77.

JOSEPH JAMET
FRANCE, Northern Rhône, Côte-Rôtie AC
🍷 *Syrah*

Jean-Luc and Jean-Paul Jamet, the two brothers who run this small family estate, own vineyards that are exceptionally well located on the best slopes of the appellation. The wines remain traditionally made, with destemming a

function of each vintage, a lengthy maceration in good years, and bottling without filtration. Aging takes place in casks of various sizes, and in recent vintages the brothers have introduced a modest percentage of new barriques. However, the wine is never oaky in flavour. On the contrary, the Jamet wines used to show a certain rusticity, although the style has become more elegant in the 1990s. Thanks to the excellent vineyards, the Jamets usually produce a stylish and thoroughly drinkable wine even in difficult vintages. But it's in the great years that the full smoky splendour of Syrah comes shining through. Best years: 1996, '95, '94, '91, '90, '89, '88, '87, '85, '83.

JASPER HILL
AUSTRALIA, Victoria, Central Victoria Zone, Bendigo
🍷 *Syrah (Shiraz), Cabernet Franc*
🍷 *Riesling*

Ron Laughton produces an amiable Riesling, but why he bothers no-one knows. Simply try the majestically profound Emily's Paddock Shiraz-Cabernet Franc (only 5 per cent Cabernet Franc) with its yield of 16 hectolitres per hectare, or Georgia's Paddock Shiraz, soaring to the dizzy heights of 35 hectolitres per hectare, and you will find some of Australia's greatest Shiraz, ultimate expressions of the terroir of the Heathcote sub-region of BENDIGO. No irrigation, organic viticulture, and minimal intervention in the winery (acid adjustment is extremely rare) are the pillars of Ron Laughton's approach to winemaking. Twin vertical tastings in late 1998 were inspiring: the 1983 Emily's and Georgia's are as beautiful as any 15-year-old daughters could ever be, with their whole life in front of them. Best years: 1997, '96, '93, '91, '90, '85, '83.

JEREZ Y MANZANILLA DO
SPAIN, Andalucía
♀ *Palomino Fino, Palomino de Jerez, Pedro Ximénez, Moscatel*

Real sherry comes from Spain's south-west corner, near Cádiz. Other Spanish regions (RUEDA, CONDADO DE HUELVA and MONTILLA-MORILES) make similar wines, but nothing ever reaches true sherry's quality peaks. The best quality grapes from the finest *albariza* – chalk soil – vineyards generally go to make fino and manzanilla, the lightest sherries, fortified to between 15.5 and 17 per cent alcohol. Both have a characteristic salty-tangy flavour (even more pronounced in manzanilla) which they develop while aging under flor yeast.

To the English-speaking world, amontillado and oloroso tend simply to mean 'medium' and 'sweet', and such wines sold outside Spain are generally young, cheap and unexceptional. In fact, as made and drunk in Jerez, both are bone dry, as are most of the finer versions exported. Authentic amontillados were once finos, but were then refortified to between 16 and 18 per cent and aged till they turned tawny-brown and developed a rich, nutty flavour as well as the fino tang. Olorosos are more heavily fortified at the beginning, ending up at between 18–20 per cent, and age – without ever growing flor in contact with the air – into richly fragrant, dark, nutty-pruny wines. Cream sherry is generally a concoction of inexpensive oloroso sweetened with concentrated grape juice, and pale cream sherry is cheap fino sweetened.

All sherry has to be aged in barrel for a minimum of three years, but all the really good ones are aged for much longer. As they age, the wines pass through a 'solera system', a complicated form of pre-blending. Only one-quarter of each barrel in the solera is ever drawn off at one time for bottling. The space is filled up with similar but younger wine from another barrel and so on, down a line of four or more. The older wine is freshened by the younger, but the younger takes on the character of the older. Best producers: BARBADILLO, CABALLERO, DÍEZ-MÉRITO, DOMECQ, GONZÁLEZ BYASS, HARVEYS, LUSTAU, OSBORNE, VALDESPINO.

JERMANN
ITALY, Friuli-Venezia Giulia
♂ *Cabernet Sauvignon, Pinot Noir (Pinot Nero)*
♀ *Chardonnay, Pinot Gris (Pinot Grigio), Ribolla and others*

Probably the most successful wine in modern Friulian history has, year after year, been Silvio Jermann's Vintage Tunina. In 1977 Jermann decided that the way to make a wine of unique character, avoiding the pitfalls of passing fashion, was to blend. Although the proportions may vary, the varieties used in Vintage Tunina are the same every year and, unusually, they are all picked and vinified together: Sauvignon, Chardonnay, Ribolla, Malvasia and Picolit. The fruit must be absolutely clean and ripe, Jermann's idea being to make a wine of complex aroma, with the accent on fruits and flowers, and luscious palate: one may detect peaches, tropical fruits, spices. There is absolutely no wood.

Jermann does not actually disdain the use of wood in the making of whites, as do his legendary neighbours Mario SCHIOPETTO and Vittorio Puiatti, who scorns oak-aging even for red wines. Indeed, some of Jermann's most successful white wines have been 'educated' in oak – examples being the much sought-after, barrique-fermented Chardonnay originally called 'Where the Dreams Have No End' (now, believe it or not, called 'Was Dreams, Now It Is Just Wine') and the blended Capo Martino, aged in Slavonian and Czech *botti*. Jermann also makes a range of varietal wines, of which the Pinot Bianco is perhaps the most consistently successful, and the Moscato Rosa the most unusual. Best years: 1998, '97, '96, '95, '94, '93.

JERMANN
Although based in the Collio zone, Silvio Jermann produces only vino da tavola wines. His varietal whites include the very successful Pinot Bianco.

JOHANNISBERG
GERMANY, Rheingau

There are three Johannisbergs, the Bereich, the town and the Schloss, and it is the last that has brought fame to the other two. The Bereich covers the whole of the RHEINGAU. The town has other vineyards as well as its famous eponymous Schloss: there is the

Klaus, the Hölle, Mittelhölle and Hansenberg among others, but none has the reputation of Schloss Johannisberg. During the 1980s and '90s, the quality of the wines from the Schloss was a rollercoaster ride, more down than up. However, with the 1996 vintage, a big step in the direction of past glories was taken. Best producers: Prinz zu Hessen, JOHANNISHOF.

JOHANNISHOF
GERMANY, Rheingau, Johannisberg
♀ *Riesling*

The Eser family make the finest Riesling in JOHANNISBERG and these are wines truly worthy of the town's reputation for making the most sophisticated and subtle wines in the RHEINGAU. In 1996 the Esers took a big leap into deep water by adding 4.5ha (11 acres) of vineyards in RÜDESHEIM to their 13ha (32 acres) in Johannisberg, GEISENHEIM and Winkel. These are wines of crystalline clarity and individuality. Best years: 1998, '97, '96, '95, '94, '93, '92, '90, '89, '88, '86, '83, '79, '76, '75, '71.

KARL-HEINZ JOHNER
GERMANY, Baden, Bischoffingen
♂ *Pinot Noir (Spätburgunder) and others*
♀ *Pinot Blanc (Weissburgunder), Müller-Thurgau, Pinot Gris (Ruländer) and others*

This BADEN producer likes to break the rules – and he says he got many of his winemaking ideas from England. For many years he was the winemaker at LAMBERHURST, and in 1985 started off with 0.75ha (1.9 acres) in Bischoffingen. Since then he's increased his vineyards bit by bit and now he spends all his time there, making supple, scented Spätburgunders and firm, complex whites, all of which are vinified in barriques or *pièces*. He's also experimenting with Cabernet Sauvignon. Not surprisingly, all these ideas do not sit well with the German wine laws, and all Johner's wines are classified as Tafelwein. Best years: (reds) 1997, '96, 95, '93, '92, '90; (whites) 1998, '97, '96, '94, '93, '90.

JORDAN VINEYARD
USA, California, Sonoma County, Alexander Valley AVA
♂ *Cabernet Sauvignon, Merlot*
♀ *Chardonnay*

When efforts to buy a BORDEAUX château were rebuffed, Colorado oil explorer Tom Jordan decided to build a château-like winery in the ALEXANDER VALLEY. Developing 101ha (250 acres), Jordan has emphasized a concentrated, yet soft, accessible style of Cabernet

Sauvignon (blended with Merlot) that displays an unusual cedary and herbaceous character. Though soft and supple, Jordan Cabernet ages surprisingly well for a decade. Best years: 1996, '95, '94, '92, '91. His attempts to come up with a similarly attractive Chardonnay were delayed until he cultivated Chardonnay in the cooler RUSSIAN RIVER VALLEY. Brighter, better balanced Chardonnays began to appear in the early 1990s. Best years: 1997, '95, '94, '92.

In the 1980s, Jordan and his daughter Judy launched a sparkling wine company named 'J' that has come on strong after a slow start to take its place among CALIFORNIA's best bubbly. Before long, 'J' had acquired the winery and vineyards once belonging to Piper Sonoma. The quality of the vintage brut continues to improve with each new vintage. Best years: 1995, '94, '93, '92. With the release of impressive Pinot Noir and Pinot Gris from Judy Jordan's Russian River vineyard, 'J' is on a course to possibly becoming more highly regarded than Jordan Vineyard.

TONI JOST
GERMANY, Mittelrhein, Bacharach
♟ *Pinot Noir (Spätburgunder)*
♀ *Riesling*

Owner Peter Jost has a foot in two camps: as well as vineyards at BACHARACH and Steeg in the MITTELRHEIN he also owns some at Walluf and Martinsthal, some distance away in the RHEINGAU. The Spätburgunder comes from Walluf and, like the Jost Rieslings, sees no new wood during the winemaking process; all the casks are old and neutral. Though delicious young, the Rieslings are worth keeping for a few years. The reds should be drunk young. The Jost Rieslings from the Bacharacher Hahn site have splendidly steely and concentrated fruit from soaking up the sun on those steep slopes. Best years: 1998, '97, '96, '94, '93, '92, '90, '89, '88.

TONI JOST
The Mittelrhein's leading estate makes delicious, racy, attractively ripe Rieslings from the Bacharacher Hahn vineyard, including exotic, fruity and honeyed Auslese.

JULIÉNAS AC
FRANCE, Burgundy, Beaujolais, Beaujolais cru
♟ *Gamay*

Juliénas is rather a serious name; the school prefect rather than the tearaway among the BEAUJOLAIS crus. The flavour often reflects that too. It frequently lacks the happy-fruit style which we think of as Beaujolais' calling-card. But what it does have is enough weight and strength to develop in the bottle: Juliénas may have a little too much tannin and acid to be as immediately enjoyable as the others, but in years like 1995 and '96 there is a solid juiciness of peaches and cherry and strawberry which may not make great glugging, but which makes delicious, if slightly more 'serious' drinking. With age the wines develop a distinct spiciness. There are 586ha (1448 acres), producing about four million bottles a year. Best years: 1998, '97, '96, '95, '94, '93, '91, '85. Best producers: Descombes, DUBOEUF, Ch. de Juliénas, Juliénas co-opérative, Pelletier, Tête.

JULIUSSPITAL WEINGUT
GERMANY, Franken, Würzburg
♟ *Pinot Noir (Spätburgunder)*
♀ *Silvaner, Müller-Thurgau, Riesling*

This charitable foundation has long had a reputation for making some of FRANKEN's best wines, which is good news for the sick and poor for whose support it was established in 1576. With 115ha (284 acres) under vine it is one of the largest estates in the Franken, with vines on limestone and gypsum marl soil on some of the best slopes in the region, primarily WÜRZBURGer Stein, with its smoky, earthy Rieslings, Escherndorfer Lump, and several at IPHOFEN. The Silvaner grape, which accounts for 35 per cent of the estate's vineyards, gives powerful savoury, pithy dry wines, those from Iphofen even gain a hint of something exotic in good years. The new vine crossing, Huxelrebe, comes into its own here in wines at higher Oechsle levels: the Auslesen wines can be surprisingly rich and balanced. Best years: 1998, '97, '94, '93, '92, '90, '89.

JUMILLA DO
SPAIN, Murcia and Castilla-La Mancha
♟♀ *Mourvèdre (Monastrell), Garnacha Tintorera, Tempranillo (Cencibel), Merlot, Cabernet Sauvignon, Syrah*
♀ *Airén, Merseguera, Pedro Ximénez*

Jumilla's speciality has long been big, dark, old-fashioned, alcoholic reds for blending with weedy wines from elsewhere. About 80 per cent of the wine still goes for blending,

mainly to central Europe. Monastrell, the main grape, has huge potential that has seldom been exploited due to poor winemaking. A little white wine is made, almost always alcoholic and dull, and some rosé. Most wineries are still using antiquated equipment and methods, but some have been improving their facilities in recent years, installing cooling equipment and insulating tanks. So things are finally looking up (and more is to come). Best producers: Agapito Rico (Carchelo), Casa Castillo, Castillo de Luzón.

JURA
FRANCE

The Jura is a large and beautiful area of France running south along the Swiss border between ALSACE and Lake Geneva. Although many of the Jura wines have a unique character, vineyards are scattered and occupy only a tiny fraction of the region. The main regional AC is CÔTES DU JURA, with ARBOIS, CHÂTEAU-CHALON, l'ÉTOILE and CRÉMANT DU JURA the others. The region is much better known for its hills and rich pasture for cattle and also for being the home of Pernod. During the nineteenth century large quantities of absinthe were made here; Anis is the modern, tamed-down version.

JURANÇON AC
FRANCE, South-West
♀ *Petit Manseng, Gros Manseng, Courbu*

Historically, Jurançon in the western Pyrenees has always been known for its sweet white wine. After a period of perilous survival, the vineyards have been expanded and today it is an area that produces exquisite, late-harvested sweet wines and refreshing dry white Jurançon Sec. The wine is made mostly from the excellent Petit Manseng and the not-quite-so-good Gros Manseng and can be crisp and refreshing or lusciously sweet and spicy.

From one of the independent growers, the sweet wine can be heavenly. The growers leave the Petit Manseng grapes on the vines till late November – when they become shrivelled and thick with sugar – and then slowly ferment the juice. The wine is then left for a couple of years to age in oak barrels until it develops a lusciousness of honey, nuts and mangoes, spiced with cinnamon, cloves and ginger cut by a pure laser streak of lemon acidity. Nowadays, a greater percentage of new oak barrels is being used. Best producers: Bellegarde, Bru-Baché, CAUHAPÉ, Clos Castera, Clos Thou, CLOS UROULAT, Lapeyre, Larrédya, de Souch. Best years: 1997, '96, '95, '94, '93, '90.

URIS (STIEGELMAR)

AUSTRIA, Burgenland, Neusiedlersee, Gols
Pinot Noir, St Laurent, Zweigelt, Pinot Noir (Blauburgunder)
Chardonnay, Pinot Blanc, Welschriesling and others

One of the few Austrian growers with an international reputation, Georg Stiegelmar is based in NEUSIEDLERSEE, a region famous for its sweet wines. However, Stiegelmar produces almost entirely dry wines, which he then sells at fairly scary prices.

There is Blauburgunder and barrique-aged Chardonnay, which is made in an international style for international markets; the Gewürztraminer and Weissburgunder are also good. There is a Buschenschank (watering hole) in Gols where the wines may be tasted. Georg's multilingual son, Axel, acts as the firm's ambassador abroad. Best years: 1997, '95, '92, '91, '90.

JUVÉ Y CAMPS

SPAIN, Cataluña, Cava DO, Penedès DO
Cabernet Sauvignon, Pinot Noir
Monastrell
Macabeo, Parellada, Xarel-lo and others

Quality is very good in this most traditional family-owned PENEDÈS company, known for its CAVA fizz. The winemaker uses only free-run (unpressed) juice, both for the Cava, and the still white wine, which is made in much smaller quantities. With quality in mind, fermentation is done in small, temperature-controlled, stainless steel tanks. All the *remuage* is done by hand for the sparklers. The company is now self-sufficient in grapes. Apart from the traditional Penedès trio of Parellada, Macabeo and Xarel-lo, Juvé y Camps' vineyards are planted with Chardonnay, Cabernet Sauvignon and Pinot Noir, with which the family intends to launch a range of varietal still wines. Reserva de la Familia Extra Brut is the best in the sparkling wine range, soft, honeyed and chocolaty.

KAISERSTUHL

GERMANY, Baden

This wine region is one of BADEN's best. The name means Emperor's Throne and comes from an ancient volcano whose lower slopes provide some of the warmest vineyard land in all Germany. Storms frequently edge their way around this tephrite mass, leaving it as an island of sunshine. This is often too hot for Riesling, but ideal for the 'Burgunder' or Pinot family of grapes: Spätburgunder (Pinot Noir), Weissburgunder (Pinot Blanc), Grauburgunder (Pinot Gris) and Chardonnay.

In a good vintage 13 degrees of natural alcohol and the richness to go with it are easy to achieve. Best producers: BERCHER, Dr HEGER, K-H JOHNER, KELLER, Salwey, Stigler.

KAMPTAL

AUSTRIA, Niederösterreich

This predominantly white wine region is centred around the town of LANGENLOIS, just north of the town of Krems on the Danube. The majority of the production is light- and medium-bodied dry Grüner Veltliner for drinking young, but in the hands of the region's dynamic young wine growers Riesling, Grüner Veltliner and Weissburgunder (Pinot Blanc) are all capable of giving serious, intense dry wines with excellent aging potential. Blauburgunder (Pinot Noir) can give good wines here, but other noble red grapes struggle to ripen fully in this coolish climate. Best producers: BRÜNDL-MAYER, Dolle, L Ehn, Hiedler, Jurtschitsch, Loimer, Schloss Gobelsburg.

KANONKOP

SOUTH AFRICA, Western Cape, Stellenbosch WO
Cabernet Sauvignon, Pinotage, Merlot and others

This exclusively red wine farm is run by Johan and Paul Krige with the characterful Beyers Truter as winemaker since 1981. His wines have won many prizes both locally and internationally. Many old vines continue to yield well, including some of the first commercially planted Pinotage. Truter is one of the variety's most vociferous advocates and one of the driving forces behind the Pinotage Producers' Association, a body set up to improve the quality of the Cape's own grape. There is now plenty of competition for this farm's renowned Pinotage. Both the standard and Auction Reserve are aged in new oak.

However, the BORDEAUX-blend, Paul Sauer, is arguably the flagship wine and its ripe concentration derives much from many older vines. The varietal Cabernet Sauvignon does

KANONKOP
The Bordeaux blend Paul Sauer, named after Kanonkop's founder, is the flagship wine from this exclusively red wine estate.

not seem to achieve the same punchy layers. Truter and the Kriges also join forces at nearby Beyerskloof, where Truter makes a striking Cabernet as well as a juicy Pinotage that is very quaffable when young. The substantial quantities made necessitate buying in grapes, although the first crop from home vineyards was harvested in 1998. Best years: (Paul Sauer) 1996, '95, '94, '93, '92, '91, '90, '89; (Pinotage) 1997, '95, '94, '93, '92, '91.

KANZEM

GERMANY, Mosel-Saar-Ruwer

This oft-forgotten Saar commune has some of the best vineyards on the entire river, most notably the soaring south-east facing slope of the Altenberg, a Riesling 'Grand Cru' if there ever was one. The favoured conditions here result in wines with a less piercing acidity than normal for the area and a wonderful white peach bouquet. Best producers: von KESSELSTATT, von Othegraven, J P Reinert.

KARLSMÜHLE

GERMANY, Mosel-Saar-Ruwer, Mertesdorf
Riesling

Peter Geiben may look like he has just come in from the fields, and his Karlsmühle hotel may bear an unintentional resemblance to Fawlty Towers, but there is no arguing about the high quality of his Rieslings or their modest prices. Confusingly, he has two estates in the Ruwer Valley: Karlsmühle, most of whose wines come from his wholly-owned Lorenzhöfer site, and Patheiger, most of whose wines are from the excellent Kehrnagel and Nies'chen sites of KASEL. There are plenty of dry wines, many of which are good, as well as superb Auslese and Eiswein dessert wines. Best years: 1998, '97, '95, '94, '93, '92, '90, '89, '88.

KARTHÄUSERHOF

GERMANY, Mosel-Saar-Ruwer, Trier
Riesling

A former Carthusian monastery, but when Napoleon separated the Church from its land the current owner's ancestor moved in. The estate's considerable reputation for marvellously steely yet ripe Rieslings had sadly slumped by the 1980s, but a new generation of the family, Christof Tyrell, took charge with the 1986 vintage and is restoring the estate to its former greatness. The wines, from the Eitelsbacher Karthäuserhofberg, are now on top form, even at QbA level, and almost equal to the other great Ruwer estate, von Schubert at MAXIMIN-GRÜNHAUS. Best years: 1998, '97, '95, '94, '93, '91, '90, '89, '88.

KASEL
GERMANY, Mosel-Saar-Ruwer

This small village in the Ruwer Valley is blessed with two of the best vineyards in the entire region and a handful of producers who turn this potential into aromatic, racy Riesling wines. Those from the Kehrnagel site are slightly leaner with more piercing acidity; those from the Nies'chen are richer and more gentle. Both have a distinctive blackcurrant (berry and leaf) aroma, and can age for a decade or more. Best producers: von Beulwitz, BISCHÖFLICHE WEINGÜTER, KARLSMÜHLE, von KESSELSTATT.

KATNOOK ESTATE
AUSTRALIA, South Australia, Limestone Creek Zone, Coonawarra
♦ *Cabernet Sauvignon, Merlot*
♀ *Chardonnay, Riesling, Sauvignon Blanc*

Katnook is one part of the Wingara Wine Group, which owns large vineyards in COONA-WARRA (as well as being the largest contract grape-grower) and near MILDARA (Deakin Estate) and it also processes a great many tonnes of grapes into juice or newly fermented wine.

The Katnook Rhine Riesling is the most powerful and concentrated of its kind in the area. The Sauvignon Blanc is smoky, fruitily pungent and long-lived; the Chardonnay is similarly long-lived and herbal with melon flavours, and the Cabernet Sauvignon is often complex and outstanding, demanding a decade or more of bottle-aging. Ultra-premium, rich, Cabernet-based Odyssey was introduced in 1997 with the '91 vintage. Best years: 1997, '96, '94, '93, '91, '90, '88.

KATNOOK ESTATE
Coonawarra is generally known for its Cabernet-based red wines, but Katnook somehow manages to produce a brilliant sweet Riesling from a few remaining vines.

KELLER
GERMANY, Rheinhessen, Flörsheim-Dalheim
♦ *Pinot Noir (Spätburgunder)*
♀ *Riesling, Rieslaner, Huxelrebe, Pinot Gris (Grauburgunder), Pinot Blanc (Weissburgunder)*

In the middle of nowhere up in the hill country of RHEINHESSEN the Keller family have built up one of the region's best estates. Although their Rieslings up to Auslese level lack the sophistication of those from NACK-ENHEIM or NIERSTEIN, they are full of fruit and beautifully made. The Riesling and Rieslaner dessert wines are spectacular, and the dry Weissburgunder and Grauburgunder perhaps the best examples of these styles in the region. Best years: 1998, '97, '95, '94, '93, '92, '90, '89.

KENDALL-JACKSON
USA, California, Sonoma County, Alexandra Valley AVA
♦ *Cabernet Sauvignon, Zinfandel, Syrah, Pinot Noir*
♀ *Chardonnay, Sauvignon Blanc, Riesling*

Kendall-Jackson started in 1981 and is now one of CALIFORNIA's largest producers of barrel-fermented Chardonnay (in competition with SONOMA's CLOS DU BOIS, and NAPA's BERINGER and Robert MONDAVI). Its popular Vintners Reserve Chardonnay owes much of its crowd-pleasing style to more than a hint of sweetness adding body and instant appeal. But recently the sweetness level is less obvious.

For its other wines, notably its deluxe Grand Reserve Chardonnay, Merlot, Zinfandel and Pinot Noir, the winery is out to compete with the big boys. It has recently been fine-tuning vineyard-designated wines such as its Buckeye Vineyard Cabernet Sauvignon and Cabernet Franc, Durrell Syrah, and Camelot Vineyard Chardonnay. Best years: (Chardonnays) 1998, '97, '96, '95, '94. Jess Jackson also owns other wineries in California, including Cambria, Cardinale, Edmeades, Hartford Court, Robert Pepi, LA CREMA, Lokoya and STONESTREET. He also owns wine properties in Chile (Viña Calina), Argentina (Mariposa) and CHIANTI (Villa Arceno).

KENWOOD VINEYARDS
USA, California, Sonoma County, Sonoma Valley AVA
♦ *Cabernet Sauvignon, Zinfandel, Pinot Noir and others*
♀ *Sauvignon Blanc, Chardonnay, Chenin Blanc*

The late Martin Lee, his two sons Marty and Mike, and son-in-law John Sheela, started Kenwood in what had been a small, local winery in 1970. The family quite simply revolutionized the place. Sauvignon Blancs are polished and subtle (best years: 1998, '97, '96, '95, '91, '90, '88), as are several Chardonnays, two of them from individual vineyards called Beltane and Yulupa (best years: 1997, '96, '95, '94). The Cabernet Sauvignons tend to be tannic, especially the Jack London Vineyard and Artist Series bottlings. Kenwood

Zinfandels may be best of all, each one rich, supple, spicy – and a perfect evocation of the variety's blackberry fruit. Best years: 1997, '96, '95, '94, '93, '92, '91, '90. Gary Heck, owner of Korbel and Valley of the Moon Winery, acquired Kenwood in 1998.

HERIBERT KERPEN
GERMANY, Mosel-Saar-Ruwer, Wehlen
♀ *Riesling*

This small estate concentrates on wines from the famous WEHLENer Sonnenuhr site. While they may not have the aging potential of Rieslings from the top producers of the Middle MOSEL they could hardly be more florally charming when drunk young. Best years: 1998, '97, '95.

REICHSGRAF VON KESSELSTATT
GERMANY, Mosel-Saar-Ruwer, Trier
♀ *Riesling*

This huge MOSEL-SAAR-RUWER company has recently been slimming itself down, having fattened itself up since it was bought by Günther Reh-Gartner in 1978. It is now run by his daughter, Annegret Reh. All the winemaking is done at Schloss Marienlay, but there are four estates in all, planted with Riesling. Much of the wine is *trocken* or *halbtrocken* in style.

With so many different vineyards to choose from, it is difficult to generalize about the house style, save to say that the wines are meticulously made and designed for long life. The best can be equal to any, especially the wines from the wholly owned Josephshöf site in GRAACH. The lesser wines in the past tended to be reliable but not terribly exciting; during the '90s they have been on the upward turn. Best years: 1997, '96, '95, '94, '93, '92, '90, '89, '88.

KHAN KRUM
BULGARIA, Eastern Region
♀ *Rkatziteli, Dimiat, Muscat and others*

One of the first things you notice about Bulgarian wineries, including Khan Krum, is that their stainless steel tanks are of special shapes and sizes, unlike anything found elsewhere. Bulgaria has for a long time had the ability to make good stainless steel, and these stainless steel tanks are able to make good clean wine should grapes of the right quality be available. The Khan Krum winery is surrounded by just the sort of grapes to benefit most from clean stainless steel fermentation and storage conditions – white grapes – and some of Bulgaria's rare good whites come from here. Chardonnay is the best bet, although some Sauvignon Blanc can also achieve typical aromas and freshness. Reserve Chardonnay, with warm hints of oak, is a good buy. Drink the wines young.

KIEDRICH

GERMANY, Rheingau

This beautiful old RHEINGAU village in the hills above ELTVILLE has a Gothic church that was restored in the nineteenth century by an Englishman, John Sutton. As one would expect of a place in the heart of the Rheingau, there are good vineyards here, owned by good growers. The vineyards need a decent sunny year to produce grapes showing their full character, and in lesser years they can lack distinction. The best sites are Gräfenberg and Wasseros. Best producers: Freiherr zu Knyphausen, Robert WEIL.

KING VALLEY

AUSTRALIA, Victoria, North East Victoria Zone

The fertile soils and equable climate of the beautiful King Valley lured Italian farmers forming part of the post-World War Two emigration, who quickly established a thriving tobacco industry. However, in 1970, before the storm clouds had formed over tobacco-growing, two Australian farmers decided to plant vines; immediately and spectacularly successful, they were eagerly followed by their Italian neighbours. BROWN BROTHERS played a key role in that success, and for the next 20 years the King Valley was virtually a Brown bailiwick. Since then, plantings have increased so rapidly that the 10,000 tonnes produced in the region find purchasers, large and small, across Australia. Relatively high yields depress structure and intensity, but the varietal character in the wines is plain to see. Chardonnay, Riesling, Cabernet Sauvignon and Merlot are the most successful, and, other than Brown Brothers, there are 11 small wineries now established in the King Valley. Best producer: BROWN BROTHERS. Best years: 1998, '97, '96, '94, '92, '91, '90.

KISTLER VINEYARDS

USA, California, Sonoma County, Sonoma Valley AVA

♥ Pinot Noir

♀ Chardonnay

Once one of the best-kept secrets within CALIFORNIA, Kistler was originally located at the end of a tortuous road high in the Maya-camas Mountains overlooking SONOMA VALLEY. While retaining this original vineyard, known as Kistler Estate, the owners moved into a bigger winery in the RUSSIAN RIVER VALLEY, and developed the Vine Hill vineyard nearby. Winemaker Mark Bixler, working with the Kistler brothers, has earned a reputation for Chardonnays that at their best combine the depth of top California Chardonnay with the balance, finesse and nerve of fine white Burgundy. In addition to the Kistler hillside estate Chardonnay, other vineyard bottlings are Vine Hill, McCrea, Dutton Ranch and Durell. Best years: 1998, '97, '96, '95, '94, '93, '92, '90, '89, '87.

In the 1990s, Kistler dropped Cabernet Sauvignon production and focused attention on Pinot Noir made from Russian River Valley sites. Early vintages have yielded full flavours and balance. Best years: 1998, '97, '95.

KLEIN CONSTANTIA

SOUTH AFRICA, Western Cape, Constantia WO

♥ Cabernet Sauvignon, Merlot, Syrah (Shiraz) and others

♀ Sauvignon Blanc, Chardonnay, Riesling (Rhine/Weisser Riesling), Muscat Blanc à Petits Grains (Muscat de Frontignan/Muscadel)

This is part of the original CONSTANTIA estate that was famous throughout Europe in the eighteenth and nineteenth centuries for the dessert wine of the same name. Klein Constantia was the first producer in the twentieth century to resurrect a similar style of unfortified wine made from Muscat de Frontignan, and demand for the luscious Vin de Constance has led to further plantings. In 1980, the Jooste family rescued the farm from alien vegetation and creeping urbanization and replanted the land.

The first vintage (1986) yielded a striking Sauvignon Blanc, which owed much to winemaker Ross Gower's experience gained at CORBANS in New Zealand; it shot the estate to fame and established a reputation which has not dimmed since. If the whites generally have performed consistently in this relatively cool region, the reds have struggled with inconsistency, a shortcoming that should be rectified by the purchase of red wine vineyards in warmer STELLENBOSCH. Best years: (whites) 1998, '97, '96, '95, '93, '92, '91.

KLEIN CONSTANTIA
ESTATE WINE
Vin de Constance
Natural Sweet Wine
Grown, Made and Bottled on Klein Constantia, Constantia, Constantia
500ml 13.5% vol
Produce of South Africa. A296

KLEIN CONSTANTIA
With concentrated flavours of dried peach, apricot and honey, Vin de Constance is a reincarnation of a famous historic sweet wine from Muscat de Frontignan.

KNAPPSTEIN

AUSTRALIA, South Australia, Mount Lofty Ranges Zone, Clare Valley

♥ Cabernet Sauvignon, Merlot, Syrah (Shiraz)

♀ Riesling, Sauvignon Blanc, Chardonnay, Gewurztraminer

Knappstein has now been well and truly subsumed into owner PETALUMA's group structure; to emphasize the change 'Tim' has been dropped from the label, and Petaluma stalwart Andrew Hardy is in charge of winemaking. The best wine is the Riesling, often high-toned when young, but developing serenely over many years. An elegant, faintly herbal Cabernet-Merlot, a trendy Cabernet Franc simply labelled 'The Franc', and a dark, brooding, faintly foresty Reserve Shiraz are among many releases, some of which do incorporate a percentage of ADELAIDE HILLS fruit, sourced via Petaluma's numerous vineyards and contracts in that area. Best years: 1997, '96, '92, '91, '90, '87, '86, '84, '80, '75.

EMMERICH KNOLL

AUSTRIA, Niederösterreich, Wachau, Loiben

♀ Grüner Veltliner, Riesling, Chardonnay (Feinburgunder), Muscat (Muskateller)

Three generations of Knolls, all called Emmerich, are responsible for the unique dry Riesling and Grüner Veltliner wines which this small WACHAU estate produces. These are some of the most minerally and long-living white wines in all of Austria, tight and unyielding when young, but blossoming into idiosyncratic beauties with bottle age. The most extraordinary of these are the concentrated, spicy wines from the Schütt site of DÜRNSTEIN and the sleeker, but no less powerful wines from the Loibenberg site in Loiben. The rich dry Riesling from the Kellerberg site of Dürnstein is a new addition to the range. Best years: 1998, '97, '96, '95, '94, '93, '92, '90, '89, '88, '86.

KOEHLER-RUPRECHT

GERMANY, Pfalz, Kallstadt

♥ Pinot Noir (Spätburgunder), Cabernet Sauvignon

♀ Riesling, Pinot Blanc (Weissburgunder), Chardonnay, Pinot Gris (Grauburgunder), Scheurebe, Gewürztraminer

Bernd Philippi is the larger than life winemaking genius behind two ranges of wines. The Koehler-Ruprecht wines are made in an uncompromisingly traditional manner with wild yeast fermentations that last up to an entire year in large wooden casks. The result, particularly in the case of the Rieslings from the great Kallstadter Saumagen vineyard, is dry and dessert wines of enormous power that need several years of body-building in the bottle before they emerge as the Mr Universe of German wines. The wines sold under the Philippi name are all vinified in a non-traditional, international style. Best of these are the Spätburgunders, which must be the closest thing to Grand Cru red Burgundy produced in Germany. The 'Elysium' is an YQUEM look-alike, and the Pinot Blanc and Pinot Gris are among the best barrique-aged German whites. There is great sparkling wine, too. Best years: (reds) 1997, '96, '93, '92; (whites) 1998, '97, '96, '95, '93, '90, '89, '88.

KOLLWENTZ

AUSTRIA, Burgenland, Neusiedlersee-Hügelland, Grosshöflein

♥ *Blaufränkisch, Blauer Zweigelt, Cabernet Sauvignon*

♀ *Chardonnay, Sauvignon Blanc, Pinot Blanc (Weissburgunder), Welschriesling*

The town of Grosshöflein lacks the kind of winemaking traditions that nearby RUST enjoys, but ambitious Anton Kollwentz and his charming son Andi have more than made up for this with new ideas and winemaking skills. In Austria they are best known for their Cabernet Sauvignon, which has a genuine blackcurrant and smoke character, and is probably the best example of this grape from BURGENLAND. Steinzeiler is a successful blend of Cabernet and local grapes with rich fruit, toasty oak and good tannins. Both can age very well. The dry whites tend to be a little clinical. Best is the Sauvignon Blanc, which has a pronounced nettle and gooseberry character. There are good dessert wines, too. Best years: 1998, '97, '95, '94, '93, '90.

KOSHUSHNY

MOLDOVA, Kishinov

♥ *Cabernet Sauvignon, Merlot, Pinot Noir, Saperavi*

♀ *Aligoté, Welschriesling (Laski Rizling), Sauvignon Blanc and others*

This Moldovan winery makes more than 20 different types of wines and about 20 million litres (4,400,000 gallons) in all each year. A quarter of its wine comes from its own vineyards, which are in the Kamrat region. This is one of Moldova's best areas, some 100km (62 miles) south of the capital, Kishinev. Like many Moldovan wineries, its cellars are underground, giving ideal conditions for the slow maturation of reds – so long as they can survive the fairly rudimentary conditions in the winery upstairs during the early stages. Western investors are taking a close interest in

Kunde Estate belongs to a family of Sonoma grape growers who revived the winery in 1990 and became instant superstars. The magnificent aging cellars are dug into the hillside beneath a Chardonnay vineyard.

Moldova; providing the political and economic situation doesn't get too hairy the wines should continue to improve year by year.

ALOIS KRACHER

AUSTRIA, Burgenland, Neusiedlersee, Illmitz

♥ *Blauer Zweigelt*

♀ *Chardonnay, Welschriesling, Scheurebe, Gewürztraminer (Traminer), Muscat (Muskat Ottonel), Bouvier*

'Here, like everywhere else, the best wines come from the hills,' Kracher told me, gesturing towards the vineyards of Illmitz which lie upon rises a metre or two above reed beds and ponds at the edge of Lake Neusiedl. It might seem crazy, but his words are true, and in his hands they give some of the world's most luxurious dessert wines. The Zwischen den Seen (between the lakes) wines are vinified in old acacia barrels on their lees, while the Nouvelle Vague (new-wave) wines ferment and mature in barriques like SAUTERNES. In a great vintage like 1995, Kracher makes up to 15 different Trockenbeerenauslese wines in quantities that make his German colleagues green with envy. The Scheurebe is lusciously exotic with breathtaking acidity, the Chardonnay-Welschriesling as grand and opulent as any top Sauternes, the Traminer firm and imposing and the Muskat-Ottonel ravishingly citric. The Bouvier Beerenauslese is Kracher's cheapest dessert wine, and though less exciting has plenty of dried fruits character. 'Days of Wine and

Roses' is a savoury, dry Chardonnay-Welschriesling blend. All in all, not bad for a country boy who worked in the pharmaceutical industry until 1992! Best years: 1998, '96, '95, '94, '93, '91, '89, '81.

KREMSTAL

AUSTRIA, Niederösterreich

This small wine region straddles the river Danube around the town of Krems. The best vineyards – Stein and Senftenberg in Krems – give dry white wines with a similar combination of power and elegance to those of the WACHAU. This is not surprising, since the vineyards here are also narrow terraces on steep hillsides with stony soils. Here, too, the Grüner Veltliner and Riesling grapes dominate. The heavier soils elsewhere in the region give generous, juicy wines that are less subtle and quicker developing. Best producers: Emmerich KNOLL, Nigl, NIKOLAIHOF, Erich SALOMON.

KREYDENWEISS

FRANCE, Alsace, Alsace AC

♥ *Pinot Noir*

♀ *Riesling, Pinot Gris, Gewurztraminer, Pinot Blanc Muscat*

Based in Andlau, far from the more southerly heartland of Alsace, Marc Kreydenweiss has developed an enviable reputation as one of the region's most skilful and original winemakers, occasionally experimenting with fermentation in barriques. Although his 10ha (25 acres), which are biodynamically cultivated, only yield about 50,000 bottles each year, Krey-denweiss keeps his various terroirs separate, with intriguing bottles from no fewer than three Grands Crus: Kastelberg, Moenchberg and Wiebelsberg. His wines are not crowd-pleasers. In their youth they are lean, discreet, and show more finesse than power. An unusual wine is the Clos du Val d'Eléon, a remarkable blend of Riesling and Pinot Gris from a single vineyard. For some palates Krey-denweiss's style can be too austere and acidic, but with time the wines expand into full-flavoured and complex expressions of grape and soil. The rare late-harvest wines can be quite exceptional. Best years: 1997, '96, '95, '94, '93, '90, '89, '88, '87, '85, '83, '76.

KRIKOVA

MOLDOVA, Kishinov
♀ *Cabernet Sauvignon, Merlot*
♀ *Aligoté, Traminer, Riesling*
One of some 160 wineries in Moldova, this one has put itself ahead of its rivals in the drive for Western currency by acquiring that most impressive of Moldovan status symbols, a new bottling line. Dull though this may sound, it means it can produce the sort of wines the West wants: fresh and fruity, rather than hot-bottled and stewed to death. Even before this, the winery was attracting attention with deep, raisiny Cabernets.

KRONDORF

AUSTRALIA, South Australia, Barossa Zone, Barossa Valley
♀ *Cabernet Sauvignon, Syrah (Shiraz)*
♀ *Riesling, Chardonnay, Sauvignon Blanc*
Krondorf burst onto the scene in 1978 thanks to the combined talents of the late Ian Wilson and winemaker Grant BURGE (who now has his own winery). MILDARA took over Kron-dorf in 1986 and has sensibly followed the founders' formula. The best wines are the EDEN VALLEY Riesling, majestic at three to five years, with fleshy, lime juice fruit, the golden-hued Show Chardonnay, turning pre-cociously peachy and creamy at one to two years, and a range of Cabernet Sauvignons made from bought-in grapes. Best years: 1997, '96, '94, '91, '90, '88, '86, '85, '80, '79.

KRUG

FRANCE, Champagne, Champagne AC
♀ ♀ *Pinot Noir, Chardonnay, Pinot Meunier*
If BOLLINGER has cornered the image of high society's favourite fizz for whooping it up, Krug has always had a much more demure reputation, partly because the cheapest bottle

of Krug costs more than most companies' most expensive cuvées. The Krug Grande Cuvée knocks spots off the general run of de luxe brands. Although splendid on release, it gets much more exciting with a year or two's extra aging. The blend is made up of as many as 50 different wines from up to 25 different villages and utilizing perhaps eight different vintages, going back ten years or more. Krug also makes an excellent vintage wine, a rosé and an amazingly expensive single-vineyard Clos du Mesnil Blanc de Blancs. New owners LVMH are unlikely to muck about with the quality or style. Best years: 1989, '88, '86, '85, '83, '82, '81, '79.

KUENTZ-BAS

FRANCE, Alsace, Alsace AC
♀ *Pinot Noir*
♀ *Riesling, Pinot Gris, Gewurztraminer, Pinot Blanc, Muscat*
With purchases from contract growers as well as the production from their own 22 ha (54 acres) of vineyards, the present directors of this merchant house, Christian Bas and Jacques Weber, have built up a reputation for extremely consistent and well-made wines.

The wines can be somewhat inexpensive in their youth, but age extremely well. Although the basic range – the Cuvée Tradition made from purchased grapes – can be a touch bland and unexciting, the best wines are superb. Kuentz-Bas believes in the Sigillé system, a seal of approval attached to the neck of the bottle and awarded after a locally based wine competition. Also worth looking out for are the Grand Cru bottlings from Eichberg and Pfirsigberg, as well as the intense and costly late-harvest wines. Best years: 1998, '97, '96, '95, '94, '93, '90, '89, '88, '85, '83, '76.

KUMEU/HUAPAI

NEW ZEALAND, North Island
This attractive rural area north-west of Auck-land is home to 11 winemakers, although two (Kim Crawford and SELAKS) do not make

KUMEU RIVER
Remarkably intense Chardonnay, with pronounced barrel-fermented and malolactic-influenced flavours, is one of Kumeu River's most obvious successes.

wine from grapes grown in their region. Heavy loam and clay soils and a high risk of autumn rain for a time made this a relatively unfashionable area. Only five wineries (Bazzard Estate, Harrier Rise, Kerr Farm Vineyard, KUMEU RIVER and Rabbit Ridge) make wine from grapes grown only in the Kumeu/Huapai district. The rest import grapes from other regions, especially GIS-BORNE, HAWKE'S BAY and MARLBOROUGH. Careful site selection and viticultural tech-niques have been necessary to control excessive vigour in this often damp climate. Kumeu River Chardonnay and Harrier Rise Merlot clearly demonstrate the quality poten-tial of the Kumeu/Huapai area. Best years: 1998, '96, '94, '93, '91. Best producers: COOPERS CREEK, Harrier Rise, Kumeu River, MATUA VALLEY, NOBILO.

KUMEU RIVER

NEW ZEALAND, North Island, Kumeu
♀ *Merlot, Cabernet Franc, Cabernet Sauvignon*
♀ *Chardonnay, Sauvignon Blanc, Pinot Gris, Semillon*
Michael Brajkovich of Kumeu River was the first New Zealander to pass the British Mas-ter of Wine exam, as well as the man who introduced many of the classic Burgundian and BORDEAUX winemaking methods into New Zealand. As a result, despite the Kumeu vineyards being located north-west of Auck-land on heavy clay soils and handicapped by a humid climate, he produces some stunning wines. The Sauvignon Blanc-Semillon is good, the Chardonnay as rich and textured as any in New Zealand and the Merlot-Caber-net is deep, supple and seductively ripe. Best years: 1998, '96, '95, '94, '91, '90.

KUNDE ESTATE WINERY

USA, California, Sonoma County, Sonoma Valley AVA
♀ *Cabernet Sauvignon, Merlot, Syrah, Zinfandel*
♀ *Chardonnay, Sauvignon Blanc, Gewürztraminer, Viognier*
Highly regarded vineyard owners, the Kunde family oversees 304ha (750 acres) planted along rolling hillsides in the middle of the SONOMA VALLEY. Winemakers before prohi-bition, the family sold their grapes until easing into winemaking in the mid-1980s. With extensive aging caves, dug deep into the hill-sides, the Kunde Winery offers Chardonnay in a succulent fruit style under four guises: Sonoma Valley, Wildwood Ranch, Kinney-brook Ranch and Reserve. The two single-vineyard Chardonnays are intense and richly oaked, and the Reserve, a combination of both vineyards, can be awesome. Best years:

1998, '97, '95, '94. A sinfully perfumed, exotically flavoured Viognier is always appealing, and a rich Sauvignon Blanc (enhanced by a dash of Viognier) is also enticing. Its red wines include a round, supple Merlot, an unusual, earthy, powerful Zinfandel from Century Vines, and Cabernet Sauvignon which has yet to reveal its full potential. Best years (reds): 1997, '96, '95, '94, '92.

FRANZ KÜNSTLER

GERMANY, Rheingau, Hochheim
♥ *Pinot Noir (Spätburgunder)*
♀ *Riesling*

Founded only in 1965 by Franz Künstler, father of current owner, Gunter Künstler, this estate's rise has been meteoric. With his first vintage, 1988, Gunter Künstler proved that dry Rheingau Riesling could be a rich, harmonious wine with a decade and more of aging potential. Since then he has perfected the style, making ever more concentrated wines. Those from the great Hölle site are the most impressive, with an apricot and earth character and enormous power. His classic Spätlese can also be impressive, and his Auslese and higher Prädikat dessert wines are slow-developing masterpieces. In 1996 Künstler made a big leap forward by buying the neighbouring Geheimrat Aschrott estate, almost tripling his vineyard holdings in HOCHHEIM to 18ha (44 acres), but did not miss a stride. Best years: 1998, '97, '96, '95, '93, '92, '90.

KWV

SOUTH AFRICA, Western Cape, Stellenbosch

The KWV was formed in 1918 as a winegrowers' co-operative with the aim of controlling the sale of its members' produce to ensure they received an adequate return. A necessity in those days of over-production and unstable markets, but it wasn't long before its control and power became absolute over the majority of the grape-growers, who made up the members. This, in turn, led to an unhealthy protectionist approach, which has left many growers and co-operatives finding it difficult to cope with the free-market forces they are faced with now that South Africa is again part of the international trading scene.

KWV has recently converted to a company. It has, however, retained its well-known brand name. To mark its new status, huge investment is being made in cellar equipment and oak. The flagship Cathedral Cellar range, especially the reds, are the best wines. The standard range is more commercial, although recently has shown a more modern approach. Styles are wide-ranging, with the dessert, sherry and often well-matured PORT-styles offering superb value. Best years: (Cathedral Cellar reds) 1996, '95, '94, '93, '92.

LA CREMA

USA, California, Sonoma County, Russian River Valley AVA
♥ *Pinot Noir, Zinfandel, Syrah*
♀ *Chardonnay*

After several ownership changes, La Crema became part of the expanding KENDALL-JACKSON group in 1993. Despite its chequered history, it has continued to focus on Chardonnay and Pinot Noir grown in cool climates. It offers early-maturing wines under the CALIFORNIA appellation and limited amounts of classically structured Reserve Chardonnay and Reserve Pinot Noir. With 18ha (45 acres) of its own and access to the parent company's vineyards, La Crema produces about 100,000 cases a year. Reserve Syrah and Zinfandel are also produced. Best years: (Reserves) 1997, '95, '94, '93.

LA CREMA
La Crema's Reserve Chardonnay combines concentrated fruit character with depth and creamy texture, acquired through extended aging on the lees in French barrels.

LACKNER-TINNACHER

AUSTRIA, Steiermark, Südsteiermark, Gamlitz
♀ *Sauvignon Blanc, Chardonnay (Morillon), Pinot Blanc (Weissburgunder), Pinot Gris (Grauburgunder), Muscat (Muskateller), Welschriesling*

Fritz Tinnacher and his wife Wilma Lackner never went in for all the experimenting with barrique-aging which many of their colleagues in STEIERMARK (Styria) did during the early 1990s, and their wines are none the worse for it. Here, purity of fruit, clarity and elegance are the guiding principles and result in archetypal Styrian dry whites. Most impressive are the dry and dessert Grauburgunders. Best years: 1998, '97, '95, '93, '92, '90.

LACRYMA CHRISTI DEL VESUVIO DOC

ITALY, Campania
♥ *Piedirosso, Sciascinoso, Aglianico*
♀ *Coda di Volpe, Verdeca, Falanghina, Greco*

Variously written as Lacrima, Lachryma and Lacryma, it's the latter which appears to have settled as the correct, though somewhat un-Italian spelling of the 'Tear of Christ'. There are several versions of how the name came about. The most common is that when Lucifer was booted out of heaven he grabbed a piece of it as he fell, then let it go. It landed around the Gulf of Naples. God recognized his lost territory, cried, his tears landed on target and, as they did so, vines appeared. The stories are the best thing about the wine. The wines' usual name is just Vesuvio and the Superiore versions are 'honoured' by the name Lacryma Christi. Sweaty reds that age quickly and earthy whites, sometimes sweet or fortified, are the norm. Best producers: Caputo, De Angelis, Grotta del Sole, MASTRO-BERARDINO, Sorrentino.

LADOIX AC

FRANCE, Burgundy, Côte de Beaune
♥ *Pinot Noir*
♀ *Chardonnay*

Ladoix-Serrigny is the most northern village in the CÔTE DE BEAUNE, and one of the least known. Its best wines are usually sold as CORTON, ALOXE-CORTON or Aloxe-Corton Premier Cru and the less good ones as CÔTE DE BEAUNE-VILLAGES. Even so, wine labelled with the name Ladoix does occasionally surface and can be worth a try – there are several good growers in the village and it is likely to be reasonably priced. The output is overwhelmingly red, quite light in colour and a little lean in style, but after a few years the rough edges slip away and a rather attractive soft, savoury style emerges.

White Ladoix is very rare – they only produce 50,000 bottles each year. It's good, a light, clean Chardonnay flavour, softened to nuttiness with a little oak aging and two or three years' maturity. Best years: (reds) 1997, '96, '95, '93, '90, '89, '88, '85. Best producers: F Capitain, Chevalier Père et Fils, E Cornu, Raymond Launay, M Mallard, A & J-R Nudant, Prince de Mérode, Ravaut.

CH. LAFAURIE-PEYRAGUEY

FRANCE, Bordeaux, Sauternes AC, Premier Cru Classé
♀ *Sémillon, Sauvignon Blanc, Muscadelle*

It's fashionable to criticize the detrimental effect on quality following the takeover of a property by a large merchant, but the large Domaines Cordier company has always taken great care of its properties (they bought this one in 1913). In the 1980s and '90s their investment and commitment in this 40-ha (99-acre) Premier Cru have made Lafaurie-Peyraguey one of the most improved SAUTERNES properties. It made outstanding wines in the great vintages of 1990, '89, '88, '86 and '83 and was equally successful in 1997, '96 and '95, and also came through well in the lesser years. Lafaurie-Peyraguey has a deep apricot and pineapple syrup sweetness, a cream and nuts softness and a good, clear, lemony acidity which give it wonderful balance for long aging. Best years: 1998, '97, '96, '95, '94, '90, '89, '88, '86, '85, '83, '82, '81, '80, '79.

CH. LAFITE-ROTHSCHILD
FRANCE, Bordeaux, Haut-Médoc, Pauillac AC,
Premier Cru Classé
♥ Cabernet Sauvignon, Merlot, Cabernet Franc, Petit Verdot

This is possibly the most famous red wine in the world. This First Growth PAUILLAC of 100ha (247 acres) is frequently cited as the epitome of elegance, indulgence and expense, but it was wretchedly inconsistent in the 1960s and '70s. This has all changed in the last 20 years, with Lafite back to top form and if anything adding on extra density and structure to its legendary elegance. The 1996 is one of the most complete Lafites in recent years and the '97 is the best of the First Growths in that difficult vintage.

Since Lafite often takes 15 years to weave its subtle strands into cloth of gold, and can need 30 years or more to come finally into balance, we won't know for a while yet quite how good the 'new' Lafites are going to be. But there seems every chance that they will attain that magical marriage of the cedarwood fragrance and the blackcurrant fruit, the hallmark of the great bottles of the past. Second wine: les Carruades de Lafite-Rothschild. Best years: 1998, '97, '96, '95, '94, '90, '89, '88, '86, '85, '82, '81, '79, '76.

CH. LAFLEUR
FRANCE, Bordeaux, Pomerol AC
♥ Merlot, Cabernet Franc

This tiny estate of only 4ha (10 acres) has some of POMEROL's oldest vines, some of Pomerol's most traditional winemaking, and the potential to equal Ch. PÉTRUS for sheer power and flavour. Vintages like 1982, '85, '86, '88, '89, '90 and '96 already exhibit a massive, old-fashioned, unsubtle brute strength loaded with the fatness of oak and soaked in the sweet fruit of plums – unforgettable mouthfuls which will need years to evolve into memorable wines, but they'll get there in the end. The price, though, is as monumental as the wines. Best years: 1998, '97, '96, '95, '90, '89, '88, '86, '85, '82.

Meursault's top producer and one of Burgundy's current superstars, Dominique Lafon stands with his wife, Anne, in the Clos de la Barre vineyard.

COMTE LAFON
FRANCE, Burgundy, Côte de Beaune, Meursault AC
♥ Pinot Noir
♀ Chardonnay

The exuberant personality of Dominique Lafon seems to be reflected in his wines, which many plausibly believe to be the finest expressions of MEURSAULT you can find. They are bold and richly flavoured, almost flamboyant. The Lafons own some excellent vineyards: Clos de la Barre in Meursault, and Premiers Crus that include Genevrières, Charmes and Perrières. The estate's pride and joy is the MONTRACHET, which is produced in tiny quantities. There are three red vineyards in VOLNAY, most notably in the Premier Cru Santenots, and the quality of these wines is equally exceptional.

Of course, it isn't all to do with vineyard sites. Lafon is a brilliant, non-interventionist winemaker, leaving the barrels in the estate's exceptionally cold cellars to mature in their own sweet time. Grapes are harvested as late as possible, yields are very low and filtration unusual, even for the whites. Lafon uses a modest amount of new oak, up to 40 per cent, and such is their richness of fruit that the wines scarcely ever taste oaky. Lafon's brilliance as a winemaker is evident from the estate's MONTHÉLIE Duresses, not a particularly profound wine but always dramatic and satisfying, and thus one of the best from this underrated village. Given their concentra-

tion, it comes as no surprise that the Lafon wines, red and white, age superbly. Best years: (whites) 1997, '96, '95, '94, '93, '92, '90, '89, '88, '86, '85, '82, '78; (reds) 1997, '96, '95, '93, '92, '90, '89, '88, '87, '85, '78.

CH. LAFON-ROCHET
FRANCE, Bordeaux, Haut-Médoc, St-Estèphe AC,
4ème Cru Classé
♥ Cabernet Sauvignon, Merlot

Guy Tesserson started improving Lafon-Rochet in the 1960s and the work has since been continued by his sons, Alfred and Michel. The effort and investment is now showing in the wines. The vineyard is a good one: 45ha (111 acres) at the western end of the slopes which COS D'ESTOURNEL also occupies. The wines used to be considered hard and austere, a problem caused by the youthful nature of the vineyard and the high percentage of Cabernet Sauvignon on a part of the vineyard better suited to Merlot. The vineyard has now matured and the percentage of Merlot has been increased to over 50 per cent, resulting in wines which are more supple than in the past. The price, too, is competitive, making Lafon-Rochet one of the best value wines in the MÉDOC. Best years: 1998, '97, '96, '95, '94, '90, '89, '88, '86, '85, '83, '82, '79.

ALOIS LAGEDER
ITALY, Alto Adige, Alto Adige DOC
♥ Cabernet Sauvignon, Cabernet Franc, Merlot, Schiava, Lagrein and others
♀ Chardonnay, Pinot Blanc (Pinot Bianco), Pinot Gris (Pinot Grigio), Sauvignon Blanc and others

The current Alois Lageder, vintage 1950, is the fifth consecutive holder of that name to head this firm since 1855. It is a task which, it must be said, he has undertaken with resounding success, the winery generally being rated today as the leading producer in the ALTO ADIGE region. Lageder was among the first in the region to introduce high-density planting to *spalliera*-trained vines, organic methods of viticulture, restricted yields and crop-seeding between rows – and not just into its own 17ha (42 acres) of vineyards in various parts of the province, but increasingly into those belonging to the 150 growers from whom Lageder regularly purchases grapes. The *cantina*, too, run by Alois' brother-in-law Luis von Dellemann, is one of the most modern in Italy.

South Tyrolean producers tend to go in for a wide range of wines and Lageder is no exception. There are medium-priced varietals under the Lageder label and expensive estate and single-vineyard wines that really steal the show. These are divided into three ranges: 'Classic' varietals, 17 of them no less, including the well-known Buchholz Chardonnay and Mazon Pinot Nero Riserva; single-vineyard selections, including the partially oak-fermented and/or oak-matured Haberlehof Pinot Bianco, Benefizium Porer Pinot Grigio and Lehenhof Sauvignon; and third, the estate wines which are barrique-matured whites (Tannhammer Terlaner and Chardonnay Löwengang) and reds (Löwengang Cabernet and the flagship Cabernet Cor Römigberg). Lageder also owns the Casòn Hirschprunn estate which produces Alto Adige varietals. Best years: (Cor Römigberg) 1998, '97, '96, '95, '94, '93, '92, '91, '90, '89.

ALOIS LAGEDER
Benefizium Porer, an archetypal classy, fragrant, slightly spicy Pinot Grigio with excellent style and balance, is one of the many star wines from Lageder.

LAGO DI CALDARO DOC

ITALY, Trentino-Alto Adige

♀ *Schiava, Pinot Noir (Pinot Nero), Lagrein*

The wine from Caldaro, a lake surrounded by vines near the upper reaches of the Adige river, can be pleasant enough. Lightish red, sometimes no more than deepish pink, it is often low in alcohol, with the smoky, strawberry-yogurt flavours of the Schiava grape. Young and fresh, it's a perfect lightweight quaffer. And there's a lake-full of it (around 200,000 hectolitres a year), so even if the Germans, Austrians and Swiss, who call it Kalterersee, continue to consume it with their customary thirst, there's still plenty to go round. Only the Classico version comes from around the lake. Otherwise, vineyards stretch from north of Bolzano right down the Adige valley into TRENTINO.

The wine labelled Superiore has half a per cent more alcohol and that labelled Scelto is a whole per cent higher. German speakers call Scelto Auslese but Lago di Caldaro has nothing to do with sweet German Auslese wine. It is always dry – but the extra alcohol gives it a touch more flavour. Best producers: Brigl, Castel Ringberg, Hofstätter, LAGEDER, Karl Martini, Niedermayr, Prima e Nuova and San Michele Appiano co-operatives, Schloss Sallegg, TIEFENBRUNNER.

CH. LAGRANGE

FRANCE, Bordeaux, Haut-Médoc, St-Julien AC, 3ème Cru Classé

♀ *Cabernet Sauvignon, Merlot, Petit Verdot*

To many people, this ramshackle, lumbering estate – 113ha (279 acres) of vines at the very western borders of ST-JULIEN – didn't seem a candidate for super-stardom, but it had potentially one of the finest vineyards in the whole MÉDOC. The Japanese Suntory company bought Lagrange in 1983, and transformed the wine style in a single vintage. It is no longer an amiable, shambling wine, but instead a clear-eyed, single-minded one of tremendous fruit, from meticulous winemaking, and a fine quality that needs at least ten years to come round and show just how good the vineyard can be. Second wine: les Fiefs de Lagrange. Best years: 1998, '97, '96, '95, '94, '90, '89, '88, '86, '85.

CH. LA LAGUNE

FRANCE, Bordeaux, Haut-Médoc AC, 3ème Cru Classé

♀ *Cabernet Sauvignon, Cabernet Franc, Merlot, Petit Verdot*

La Lagune is just to the south of the village of MARGAUX, and the closest Classed Growth to the city of Bordeaux itself, making a consistently excellent red wine, rich and spicy, but full of the charry chestnut sweetness of good oak and with a deep, cherry-blackcurrant-and-plums sweetness to the fruit which, after ten years or more, is outstanding, always accessible, yet perfect for the long haul. The most recent vintages have been less substantial than usual. Best years: 1996, '95, '94, '93, '90, '89, '88, '86, '85, '83, '82, '78.

LAKE BALATON

HUNGARY, Transdanubia

The large Lake Balaton is a favourite with Hungarians as a holiday resort as much as a source of wines, but the wines used to be, and could be again, terrifically stylish and unusual. There are various wine regions clustered round its shores: Dél-Balaton to the

BALATONBOGLÁR
This winery dominates wine production around Lake Balaton. It makes a wide range of wines, including the Chapel Hill label for the export market. The Irsai Oliver is a powerful and pungent red wine.

south, and Badacsony, Balatonmellék and Balatonfüred-Csopak to the north. As well as familiar grape varieties like Sauvignon Blanc, Chardonnay, Rhine Riesling, Traminer and Rizlingszilváni (Müller-Thurgau), there are interesting native grapes, especially Kéknyelü and Szürkebarát, and it is these that could produce some splendidly fiery wines. But first of all the winemaking needs to be spruced up, and that means outside investment, something that has begun with the wines known as CHAPEL HILL made for the Balatonboglár winery by Kym Milne.

LAKE'S FOLLY

AUSTRALIA, New South Wales, Hunter Valley Zone, Hunter

♀ *Cabernet Sauvignon, Merlot, Syrah (Shiraz), Petit Verdot*
♀ *Chardonnay*

Where would the Australian wine industry be without the ebullient, abrasive, irrepressible Max Lake? In 1963 Max, already a renowned surgeon in Sydney, established a high class 'weekend' winery in the HUNTER VALLEY. He wanted to use Cabernet Sauvignon and the winemaking methods used by the great French winemakers. Everyone said it was doomed to failure but the success of his Lake's Folly 'hobby' encouraged scores of other professional men to set up their boutique wineries throughout Australia and provide a quality standard the big companies that dominate Australian wine didn't even know existed. And Lake's Folly is still a leader, with marvellously Burgundian Chardonnay, and fragrant, beautifully balanced Cabernet. Best years: 1998, '97, '96, '93, '92, '91, '89, '87, '86, '85, '83, '81.

LALANDE-DE-POMEROL AC

FRANCE, Bordeaux

♀ *Merlot, Cabernet Franc, Cabernet Sauvignon, Malbec*

Although the Lalande-de-Pomerol appellation is regarded as a POMEROL satellite, with nearly 1105ha (2730 acres) of vines, it is actually bigger than Pomerol's 785ha (1940 acres). The wines are usually full, soft, plummy and even chocolaty, very attractive to drink at only three to four years old, but aging reasonably well. They lack the mineral edge and the concentration of top Pomerols, but are nonetheless extremely attractive, full, ripe wines. They are not particularly cheap, but then nothing with the name Pomerol included in it is cheap these days. Best years: 1998, '97, '96, '95, '94, '90, '89, '88, '85, '83, '82.

Best producers: Annereaux, Belles-Graves, Bertineau-St-Vincent, la Croix-Chenevelle, la Croix-St-André, Garraud, Grand-Ormeau, Haut-Chaigneau, Sergant, Siaurac, Tournefeuille, de Viaud.

LAMBERHURST

ENGLAND, Kent

♥ *Rondo*

♀ *Müller-Thurgau, Schönburger, Seyval Blanc*

Reliability is the name of the game at this English vineyard, and anyone who interprets that to mean dullness should just try the top wines. With 23ha (57 acres) of its own vines, Lamberhurst is one of England's biggest wine estates; Huxelrebe and Bacchus grapes are also bought in from a further 40ha (100 acres) of contracted vineyard to make good, fruity, off-dry whites.

The Gore-Browne Trophy (England's most important wine award) has been twice awarded to Lamberhurst's Schönburger, and once to the Huxelrebe. The new Time Zone range has been produced to celebrate the new millennium.

LAMBRUSCO DOC

ITALY, Emilia and elsewhere

♥ ♥ ♀ *Lambrusco*

True Lambrusco wine should be red and makes an ideal cherry-flavoured match for the rich, buttery, cheesy sauces and the fat salami and sausages of its native lands, around Modena, where the best three sub-varieties of the Lambrusco grape are found. It should also be dry, which might come as a surprise to those who have a fondness for the cheaper versions, and should have a cork closure if it's DOC, which it isn't when it's cheap.

Major DOCs are Lambrusco di Sorbara, whose characteristics are a pronounced and elegant perfume and good acidity; Lambrusco Grasparossa di Castelvetro, more tannic than most, with fuller flavour and deeper colour; and Lambrusco Salamino di Santa Croce, whose wines are richer and fatter, although with enlivening good acidity.

These traditional Lambruscos are only occasionally found outside EMILIA. Cavicchioli are the most vociferous 'real' Lambrusco campaigners, with both their dry, bitter-sharp, morello-like Lambrusco Tradizione and their low-yield, white-heart cherry Vigna Del Cristo. Also good in a traditional style are Francesco Bellei, Casali, Ferrari and Stefano Spezia. For more 'normal' wines there are the wines from the giant industrial companies – Chiarli, Giacobazzi, Fini and Riunite.

It is a costly and skilled job to extract good white juice from red Lambrusco grapes, which means that white Lambrusco can't be too cheap. And if it is dirt cheap it is probably in large part from Trebbiano instead.

LAMOREAUX LANDING

USA, New York State, Finger Lakes AVA

♥ *Pinot Noir, Cabernet Franc*

♀ *Chardonnay, Riesling*

Although only established as recently as 1990, Lamoreaux Landing is already a major producer in the Finger Lakes District AVA, having over 55ha (135 acres) of vineyards, and is now one of the most important wineries in the eastern United States. The Reserve Chardonnay, aged in new oak, and the dry Riesling are wines of note. Best years: 1997, '95, '94, '93.

HELMUT LANG

AUSTRIA, Burgenland, Neusiedlersee, Illmitz

♀ *Scheurebe, Pinot Blanc (Weissburgunder), Grüner Veltiner, Welschriesling*

Helmut Lang is one of Illmitz's band of fiercely independent dessert wine producers. While his wines are a bit hit and miss, the best are very rich, succulent and clean. His highest success rate is with Scheurebe. Best years: 1998, '95, '91.

LANGENLOIS

AUSTRIA, Niederösterreich, Kamptal

This town on the river Kamp just north of Krems on the Danube is one of the most important centres of quality wine production in Austria, producing large quantities of good to outstanding dry whites from Grüner Veltliner and Riesling, along with some interesting Weissburgunder (Pinot Blanc) and Chardonnay. Good red wines are still rare, though Blauburgunder (Pinot Noir) shows potential. Best producers: BRÜNDLMAYER, Hiedler, Jurischitsch, Loimer.

LANGHE DOC

ITALY, Piedmont

♥ *Nebbiolo, Dolcetto, Freisa and others*

♀ *Favorita, Chardonnay, Arneis, Sauvignon Blanc*

In the mid-1990s the wise legislators of PIEDMONT decided that all the wines of their august region should be, at least, DOC. Hence the new denominations of LANGHE, Monferrato and Piemonte, among others, to catch those renegades who previously had been selling their wines as VINO DA TAVOLA. Varietal Nebbiolo was introduced to catch those quasi-BAROLOS which, their producers

had decided, were not suitable to suffer the aging requirements imposed by the DOCG regulations, or which were blended in some way inconsistent with the law. The new DOC also gave growers the possibility of producing varietal Chardonnay, or Arneis and Favorita outside of their previously restricted zones.

Perhaps of greatest significance, however, were the new blends, Langhe Rosso and Langhe Bianco, open to just about any grape variety provided it was 'recommended' or at least 'authorized'. In this way the legislators opened the floodgates for wines which, while limited in number today, can be expected to multiply in future as the inventive Italian genius finds its path.

LANGHORNE CREEK

AUSTRALIA, South Australia, Fleurieu Zone

The fertile, alluvial and flat river plains, coupled with the bountiful irrigation water from Lake Alexandrina and the Bremer River, have proved such an ideal combination that this is not only one of the largest, but also one of the fastest-growing, wine regions in Australia.

Yet its history goes as far back as 1850, when Frank Potts established Potts Bleasdale Vineyards, by diverting the winter floods of the Bremer River on to his vineyards, literally submerging them in late winter; these days drip irrigation does the job far more efficiently. While ORLANDO is the most obvious landholder, with almost 1000ha (2470 acres) producing grapes for its various Jacobs Creek wines, Wolf BLASS has long understood the quality of the grapes that can be grown in this surprisingly cool maritime climate. More recently Lake Breeze Wines has produced opulent, rich, trophy-winning red wines variously fashioned from Cabernet Sauvignon, Merlot and Shiraz. Best Years: 1998, '97, '96, '93, '92. Best producers: (local wineries) Bleasdale Vineyards, Bremerton Lodge, Lake Breeze Wines, Temple Bruer.

BLEASDALE

This is the oldest winery in the important Langhorne Creek region of South Australia and Verdelho is one of the original white grape varieties.

LANGUEDOC-ROUSSILLON France

THE LANGUEDOC-ROUSSILLON is a huge viticultural area that sweeps around the Mediterranean rim from the foothills of the Pyrenees on the Spanish border to the gates of the old Roman town of Nîmes. It encompasses the *départements* of the Pyrénées-Orientales, Aude, Hérault and Gard which together provide one-third of France's vineyard acreage and an average yearly production of 18 million hectolitres of wine.

How times have changed though. Twenty years ago, the Languedoc-Roussillon was still the butt of disdain for its overproduction of *gros rouge* – cheap, rough, red wine that was sold on its alcoholic strength rather than any discernible character. Now it's the symbol of a modern, liberated, high-tech wine industry for which innovation has become the byword.

So what has wrought the changes within this vast viticultural arena? First of all a consciousness that the old days of quantity rather than quality were long gone and subsequently a move to producing clean, modern, fruit-driven wines for today's contemporary market. This has meant new investment, temperature-controlled vinification, lower vineyard yields and better grape varieties and this from the smallest producer up to the regionally powerful co-operatives.

The reorganization of the vineyards has been a key element and coupled with the creation of vin de pays, a more flexible system for regulating wine production than appellation contrôlée, has been the saving grace of the Languedoc-Roussillon. These factors have permitted the planting of the international grape varieties Merlot, Cabernet Sauvignon, Chardonnay and Sauvignon Blanc and others like Syrah and Viognier providing wines that can compete on the world market. The Languedoc-Roussillon now produces 83 per cent of France's vins de pays of which a large percentage are varietal wines labelled as Vin de Pays d'Oc.

But vin de pays does not just mean good-value varietal wines but also the liberty to produce some highly individual, world-class wines from imaginative blends. Aimé Guibert of the Mas de Daumas Gassac estate has proved this over the years and he has now been joined by Laurent Vaillé of la Grange des Pères and other young producers.

In the AC regions of the Languedoc-Roussillon there has also been a positive domino effect. Producers have returned to cultivating the better hillslope sites, planted more Syrah, Grenache and Mourvèdre and, in some cases, wrought miracles with the often denigrated Cinsaut and Carignan. There are now some excellent reds with real regional character from the areas of Corbières, Costières de Nîmes, Coteaux du Languedoc, Côtes-du-Roussillon, Faugères, Minervois and St-Chinian. The whites, too, are gradually improving with the addition of Viognier, Marsanne, Roussanne and Rolle in the blends and some lively Chardonnay is being produced in the Limoux AC.

A movement to identify individual sub-regions within the ACs is also underway. Eleven sub-zones in the Coteaux du Languedoc, including Pic St-Loup, Montpeyroux and La Clape, have been designated. The Corbières has also pinpointed 11 distinct areas within its boundaries. La Livinière in Minervois has been elevated to Cru status and Tautavel now has its own identity in the Côtes du Roussillon.

Tradition in the Languedoc-Roussillon, however, still lives on with the sweet, fortified *vins doux naturels*, the whites being made from the Muscat grape and the reds from Grenache Noir. These grapes achieve very high natural sugar levels in the hot Mediterranean sun and the racy Muscat de Rivesaltes and richly complex Banyuls, France's answer to port, are two fine examples.

Nestling in the trees high up in the Gassac valley, Mas de Daumas Gassac's beautiful old stone farmhouse, or mas, is surrounded by vineyards hacked out of the natural scrub vegetation, or garrigue.

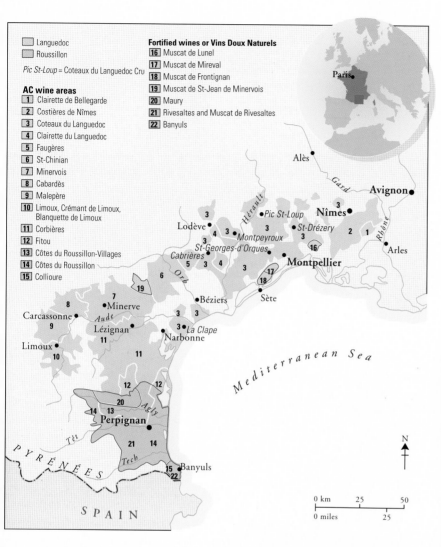

Key:
- Languedoc
- Roussillon

Pic St-Loup = Coteaux du Languedoc Cru

AC wine areas
1. Clairette de Bellegarde
2. Costières de Nîmes
3. Coteaux du Languedoc
4. Clairette du Languedoc
5. Faugères
6. St-Chinian
7. Minervois
8. Cabardès
9. Malepère
10. Limoux, Crémant de Limoux, Blanquette de Limoux
11. Corbières
12. Fitou
13. Côtes du Roussillon-Villages
14. Côtes du Roussillon
15. Collioure

Fortified wines or Vins Doux Naturels
16. Muscat de Lunel
17. Muscat de Mireval
18. Muscat de Frontignan
19. Muscat de St-Jean de Minervois
20. Maury
21. Rivesaltes and Muscat de Rivesaltes
22. Banyuls

MAS AMIEL
The best-known estate in Maury is noted for its range of traditional fortified wines which spend a year outdoors in glass bonbonnes, followed by aging in large old casks for anything up to 30 years.

DOMAINE GAUBY
Yields are very low at this top Roussillon estate, giving wines of enormous concentration. The Côtes du Roussillon, from Carignan, Grenache and Syrah, has solid tannins and ripe, berry fruit.

DOMAINE CAZES
This long-established estate makes outstanding Rivesaltes, including the quite powerful, sweet, rich Tuilé from Grenache.

MAS DE DAUMAS GASSAC
This inspirational property north of Montpellier makes wines of great power and longevity.

CH. MOURGUES DU GRÈS
François Collard is one of several young growers in the Costières de Nîmes AC aiming for quality.

REGIONAL ENTRIES
Aude, Banyuls, Blanquette de Limoux, Collioure, Corbières, Costières de Nîmes, Coteaux de Languedoc, Côtes du Roussillon, Faugères, Fitou, Gard, Hérault, Maury, Minervois, Muscat de Frontignan, Muscat de Rivesaltes, Vin de Pays d'Oc, Pyrénées-Orientales, Rivesaltes, St-Chinian.

PRODUCER ENTRIES
Dom. de l'Aigle, Dom. Alquier, Dom. Cazes, Cellier des Templiers, Clos Centeilles, des Estanilles, Fortant de France, Dom. Gauby, Dom. de l'Hortus, Mas Amiel, Dom. du Mas Blanc, Mas Bruguière, Mas de Daumas Gassac, Mas Jullien, Prieuré de St-Jean de Bébian, Dom. de la Rectorie, Sieur d'Arques, la Voulte Gasparets.

CH. DE JAU
The town of Rivesaltes is renowned for its Muscat wine and this example from the large de Jau estate is rich and honeyed with a dry finish.

DOMAINE DE L'AIGUELIÈRE
This dense and powerful Syrah wine comes from Montpeyroux, one of the 11 Crus allowed to add their name to the Coteaux du Languedoc AC.

DOMAINE ALQUIER
This is one of the best estates in Faugères. The top wine, les Bastides, is made from the oldest vines (70 per cent Syrah) and aged for up to 15 months in new oak.

LANSON

FRANCE, Champagne, Champagne AC

♀♥ *Chardonnay, Pinot Noir, Pinot Meunier*

The jewel in the crown of the vast Marne-et-Champagne group since 1991, Lanson has kept a very distinctive style. None of the six million bottles of CHAMPAGNE produced each year undergoes malolactic fermentation, so these Champagnes can be aggressive when young, and sometimes it seems that the wines are put on sale too soon. This does a disservice to the inherent quality of the Pinot-dominated Black Label Brut.

The vintage wines, including the delicious, lemony Blanc de Blancs, are a better indication of Lanson's quality. The Noble Cuvée can be very long-lived. Lanson's excellent vineyards were not included in its sale to Marne-et-Champagne. However, since the owners have access to equally good vineyards and since they regard Lanson as their top brand, quality is likely to remain high. Best years: 1993, '92, '90, '89, '88, '86, '85, '83, '82, '79.

LANSON

Noble Cuvée is Lanson's prestige vintage Champagne. Made in a dry, fairly rich, powerful style, it nonetheless has an attractive softness and fruit depth.

DOMAINE LAROCHE

FRANCE, Burgundy, Chablis AC

♀ *Chardonnay*

The urbane Michel Laroche is both an estate owner and a *négociant*, and has recently developed a large property in the LANGUEDOC. But CHABLIS remains the focus of his activities as a wine producer. His 100-ha (247-acre) portfolio of vineyards includes a wide range of Premiers Crus (Beauroy, Fourchaume and Vaillons) and Grands Crus (Les Clos, Blanchots and Bougros). In the 1980s Laroche was using a fair amount of new oak for some of these Crus, but in recent years he has moderated their use, preferring older barrels. Wines like Les Clos and Blanchots, consistently among his finest, are barrel-fermented and often aged in about 15 per cent new oak, but they have the structure and concentration to handle it without being too marked by woody flavours. In exceptional vintages, Laroche releases a kind of prestige cuvée, made from selected parcels in Blanchots and called Réserve de l'Obédiencerie. Laroche's

competence and ambition have led some critics to underrate this large domaine, but in a good vintage the wines can be as fine as most in Chablis. A new development in the Languedoc under the Domaine de la Chevalière label is rapidly proving itself to be a quality leader in the South. Best years: 1997, '96, '95, '93, '92, '90, '89, '88, '85.

CH. LAROSE-TRINTAUDON

FRANCE, Bordeaux, Haut-Médoc, Haut-Médoc AC, Cru Bourgeois

♥ *Cabernet Sauvignon, Merlot, Cabernet Franc*

This is the largest property in the MÉDOC – 172ha (425 acres) in St-Laurent, producing some 100,000 cases of wine a year. It's a real success story because this massive vineyard was planted from scratch in 1966. The aim has always been to produce large amounts of good-quality, affordable, red BORDEAUX with direct easy flavours at a decent price – and Larose-Trintaudon achieves it almost every year. Rumour has it it's the most popular red Bordeaux in the United States and the reason is simple – immediately recognizable Médoc flavours, yet without being tannic nor tough – and at a reasonable price. The wines are made to drink at about five years old, but can happily age for ten. Best years: 1996, '95, '90, '89.

CH. LASCOMBES

FRANCE, Bordeaux, Haut-Médoc, Margaux AC, 2ème Cru Classé

♥♀ *Cabernet Sauvignon, Merlot, Cabernet Franc, Petit Verdot*

This is a large and important MARGAUX Second Growth which hasn't matched the efforts of its peers for some time. This could be because the remarkable achievement of properties like Ch. LÉOVILLE-LAS-CASES and PICHON-LONGUEVILLE-COMTESSE DE LALANDE are due to the dedication of a single owner, whereas Lascombes is owned by the massive Bass-Charrington brewery group. However, the management has shown the will to improve and there has been steady investment in the vineyards and in new vinification cellars. The problem could be the relatively young age of the vines and the fine tuning that is still needed. Some improvements can be seen in recent vintages and if Lascombes can repeat the wonderfully elegant floral-vanilla bouquet found in the 1996 vintage with a little more density on the palate then it will be on the right track. The Chevalier de Lascombes rosé is good. Second wine: Ch. Ségonnes. Best years: 1998, '96, '95, '90, '89, '88, '86, '85.

CH. LATOUR

FRANCE, Bordeaux, Haut-Médoc, Pauillac AC, Premier Cru Classé

♥ *Cabernet Sauvignon, Merlot, Cabernet Franc, Petit Verdot*

In years when the rest of BORDEAUX might as well have packed up and gone home without pressing a grape, Latour stuck to it and produced good wine. All through the 1950s, '60s and '70s Latour stood for integrity, consistency and refusal to compromise in the face of considerable financial pressure. The result was that in poor years the wine was good; in merely adequate years – like 1960, '67, '74 – the wine was excellent. In great years like 1966, '70, '75, '82 and '86, Latour's personality – the sheer power of blackcurrant fruit, the temple columns of tannin daring anyone to broach a bottle before its 20th year, the full-tilt charge of cedar-dry flavours, rich, expensive, but as unconcerned with fashion and fawning as a fifteenth-generation duke – marks it as the most imperious of PAUILLAC's three First Growths. Interestingly, the 65ha (161 acre) vineyard is on the southern side of the AC, bordering ST-JULIEN. This might lead one to expect a lighter style of wine, but the vineyard, planted with 75 per cent Cabernet Sauvignon, 20 per cent Merlot, 4 per cent Cabernet Franc and 1 per cent Petit Verdot, generally gives as big and proudly impressive a wine as any in Bordeaux.

There have been some curiously unsatisfactory bottles from vintages like 1988, '85, '83 and '81, but this seems to have been due to management decisions rather than any fundamental decline in quality, and 1989 and '90 show the winemakers back on top again. The frosted-out 1991 vintage is remarkable, and the 1996 and '95 are truly great Latours with perhaps a little more suavity of texture than in the past. Second wine: les Forts de Latour. Best years: 1998, '97, '96, '95, '94, '93, '91, '90, '89, '86, '82, '79, '78, '75, '74, '70.

LOUIS LATOUR

FRANCE, Burgundy, Beaune

♥ *Pinot Noir*

♀ *Chardonnay*

Generations of Latours have directed the fortunes of this large firm of *négociants*, whose activities encompass more southerly regions such as MÂCON and the Ardèche as well as the entire CÔTE D'OR. Like so many of the older *négociant* houses of Burgundy, Louis Latour is also a major owner of vineyards, with a domaine of some 50ha (124 acres), including 17ha (42 acres) of Grand Cru vineyards in CORTON and CORTON-CHARLEMAGNE.

Latour, now run by Louis-Fabrice Latour, who has succeeded his much respected father Louis, is better known for its white wines than its red. The Grands Crus are aged in 95 per cent new oak, and Premier Crus in about 50 per cent. The firm has always followed a controversial procedure with its reds, subjecting the wine to a flash pasteurization for a few seconds. This means, say the Latours, that the wine needs fewer treatments subsequently, especially filtration, but there is little doubt that the red wines are generally less complex than the whites. Nonetheless, wines such as Romanée-St-Vivant and Corton-Grancey can be exquisite, and age surprisingly well. However, even finer is their Corton-Charlemagne, a perfect example of the blend of power and fruit that characterizes this large site. The simpler appellations tend to be rather bland. Best years: (whites) 1997, '96, '95, '93, '92, '90, '89, '88, '86, '85, '83, '79; (reds) 1997, '96, '95, '93, '90, '89, '88, '85, '78.

CH. LATOUR-À-POMEROL
FRANCE, Bordeaux, Pomerol AC
Merlot, Cabernet Franc

Luscious, almost juicy fruit, soft and ripe and very easy-to-drink wine has always been a hallmark of Latour-à-Pomerol, but the wines also have enough tannin to age well for ten years or so. Recent vintages, now directed by Christian Moueix of Ch. PÉTRUS, show a beefier, brawnier style, but still with the super-ripe softness of fruit. The vineyard covers 8ha (20 acres). Best years: 1997, '96, '95, '94, '90, '89, '88.

LAUREL GLEN VINEYARDS
USA, California, Sonoma County, Sonoma Mountain AVA
Cabernet Sauvignon, Merlot, Cabernet Franc

A philosophy student and professional musician was staying with a Zen Buddhist community only to find his true calling in an abandoned nearby vineyard. Patrick Campbell developed that land to Cabernet Sauvignon, producing his first wine in 1981. Made with a

LAUREL GLEN
Laurel Glen's Cabernet Sauvignon is a simply terrific wine, loaded with intense black cherry and dark plum fruit and aging to a perfumed, complex Bordeaux style.

strictly non-interventionist approach, Laurel Glen's Cabernets develop a sweet blackcurrant, slightly minty perfume, packaged in a supple, inviting texture. Campbell's skills have also been applied to a blend of declassified Cabernet labelled Counterpoint, to Terra Rosa, a Cabernet made from bought-in wine, and even to Reds, a low-priced wine which occasionally has been from Chile. Best years: 1997, '96, '95, '94, '93, '92, '91, '90, '89, '87.

DOMINIQUE LAURENT
FRANCE, Burgundy, Nuits-St-Georges

From modest premises, Dominique Laurent has, since the 1988 vintage, been turning out some of Burgundy's most remarkable, and costly, wines. Much has been made of his fondness for aging in '200 per cent new oak'. This simply means that after a year in new barrels, the wine is then decanted into other brand-new barrels for the remainder of its aging period before being bottled by hand without filtration. The aim of this expensive procedure is not to impart a heavily oaky taste to the wines, but to ensure a perfect and controlled aeration of the wines while they are in barrel.

More significant is Laurent's purchasing policy. He is a *négociant*, buying up small parcels of young wine from some of Burgundy's top domaines, insisting on very ripe fruit from low-yielding vines. By offering very high prices he ensures that he obtains the best and not surprisingly his wines have a cult following, partly because some of them are only made in minuscule quantities. Although some of the wines are excessively oaky, their quality is nonetheless outstanding. Since he does not disclose his sources, it is hard to define the appellation character of any wines from his range, but he does buy wines from the same producers each year, so there will be consistency from vintage to vintage. With Michel Tardieu, he runs a similar operation in the RHÔNE Valley known as Tardieu-Laurent; the first releases were in 1994. Best years: 1997, '96, '95, '94, '93, '91, '90, '89.

LAURENT-PERRIER
FRANCE, Champagne, Champagne AC
Chardonnay, Pinot Noir, Pinot Meunier

This esteemed CHAMPAGNE producer has been in the hands of the Nonancourt family since the late nineteenth century. With annual production at six million bottles, it is not surprising that quality, especially of the more basic wines in the range, can be variable, although the Brut is less green than it often used to be. Chardonnay is the dominant grape variety, even in the regular Brut. Laurent-Perrier has a fine reputation for its

full-bodied Rosé Brut, and an unusual wine in the range is the Ultra Brut, a Champagne with no *dosage*, and thus compelled to rely solely on the quality of the grapes that go into it. It's a style that takes some getting used to, but it can be one of the most pure and bracing of Champagnes. The regular vintage wines are outclassed by the superb (and very expensive) cuvées de prestige called Grand Siècle. Both the white and rosé are subtle, delicate and exquisitely balanced. Best years: 1990, '88, '85, '82, '79.

CH. LAVILLE HAUT-BRION
FRANCE, Bordeaux, Pessac-Léognan AC, Cru Classé de Graves
Sémillon, Sauvignon Blanc, Muscadelle

A GRAVES Classed Growth, Laville Haut-Brion produces exclusively white wines from a 3.7ha (9-acre) plot of land adjacent to Ch. La MISSION HAUT-BRION. Both estates, as well as HAUT-BRION across the road, are located in Bordeaux's suburbs and are owned by the American Dillon family. Unlike the majority of white wines in the PESSAC-LÉOGNAN AC, which have a heavy percentage of Sauvignon Blanc, Laville Haut-Brion places the emphasis firmly on Sémillon, which accounts for 70 per cent of the vineyard. This grape gives the wine an amazing aging potential as well as plenty of flesh and a rich, honeyed bouquet. However, the small quantity of an average 13,000 bottles a year means that there is a high price tag on the wine. Best years: 1998, '97, '96, '95, '94, '93, '92, '90, '89, '88, '85.

LAZIO
ITALY

The hub of Lazio is Rome. And Rome's is the easiest image to stamp on this longish, disparate region which, at its northern end, skirts Tuscany and UMBRIA with their enthralling scenery, their calm and cultured existence; while its southern part mingles with the laid-back, wilder, much hotter Mezzogiorno (southern Italy). A vast semi-circular ridge of hills called the Castelli Romani to the south and east of Rome is home to the most typical wines of Lazio: FRASCATI and other similar wines, for example, white Marino, Velletri, Colli Albani. They are usually dry, mostly from various combinations of tricky-to-handle Malvasia and unexciting Trebbiano, and keep both Romans and tourists well lubricated.

To find real Roman reds it is necessary to travel sunwards on the Autostrada del Sole until you hit the area where Cesanese is cultivated, turning out wines called Cesanese del Piglio, di Affile or di Olevano Romano.

Further north, Cerveteri produces decent red blends with Montepulciano plus Sangiovese and/or Cesanese. Whites stay unswervingly Trebbiano-Malvasia blends. For something different look north by the lake of Bolsena, where there's sweet, strong, red Aleatico di Gradoli. Nearby there is also EST! EST!! EST!!!, and a little bit of the ORVIETO zone overlapping from its main home in Umbria. New reds based on Cabernet and Merlot are now the region's best wines.

LEASINGHAM

AUSTRALIA, South Australia, Mount Lofty Ranges Zone, Clare Valley

♥ *Cabernet Sauvignon, Syrah (Shiraz), Malbec*

♀ *Riesling, Semillon*

Leasingham was established in 1893, initially known as Stanley, then as Stanley Leasingham. Always a source of high-quality wine for companies such as LINDEMANS, it was acquired by BRL HARDY in 1987, and has since gone from strength to strength.

Steely, minerally Riesling is by far the best white, particularly under the Classic Clare label, but it is the reds that can stop you in your tracks. Bin 61 Shiraz, Classic Clare Shiraz, Bin 56 Cabernet-Malbec and Classic Clare Cabernet Sauvignon are monumental wines, flooded with fruit, saturated with oak, and with enough tannin and extract to stop a runaway truck. They do particularly well in wine shows but in the real world need ten years or so to be broken in. Best years: 1997, '95, '94, '91, '90, '88, '86, '85.

LEASINGHAM
With a core of high-quality, old vineyards to draw on, Leasingham produces red wines of great power. The Cabernet Sauvignon-Malbec blend has been a Clare Valley speciality for decades.

LEEUWIN ESTATE

AUSTRALIA, Western Australia, South West Australia Zone, Margaret River

♥ *Cabernet Sauvignon, Pinot Noir*

♀ *Chardonnay, Riesling, Sauvignon Blanc*

Since Leeuwin's debut vintage in 1980, its Art Series Chardonnay has been one of Australia's best. Indeed, in the early days, it was the best, and even now is rarely overshadowed by rivals. Incredibly concentrated and long-lived, these nectarine-, melon- and grapefruit-flavoured wines, coupled with sophisticated but subtle barrel-fermented and occasional malolactic characters, have all the complexity and richness of a Bayeux tapestry. Prelude Chardonnay (the bits that don't make the Art Series Chardonnay), Sauvignon Blanc and Cabernet Sauvignon are fine wines also. The Riesling is beautifully made and is delightful young but ages very well. Best years: (Chardonnay) 1995, '94, '92, '90, '89, '87, '85, '83, '82, '81, '80.

DOMAINE LEFLAIVE

FRANCE, Burgundy, Côte de Beaune, Puligny-Montrachet AC

♀ *Chardonnay*

Vincent Leflaive was a much respected and much loved personality in Burgundy for many decades. He ruled over Leflaive, one of PULIGNY-MONTRACHET's great domaines, with 22ha (54 acres) of vines almost entirely within this celebrated commune. Almost half the vineyards are in Premier Cru sites, and there are also small parcels in Bienvenues-Bâtard-Montrachet, BÂTARD-MONTRACHET, Chevalier-Montrachet and Le MONTRACHET itself. Perhaps it was because of the high regard in which Vincent was held that few dared to declare publicly that by the late 1980s the wines seemed to lack concentration and elegance. In 1990 he retired, but his daughter Anne-Claude and nephew Olivier were in effect already running the estate. After Vincent's death in 1993, Anne-Claude became the sole administrator, although Olivier, who had by then developed his own successful *négociant* business, was still associated with the domaine.

Anne-Claude persuaded her team, including the domaine's respected winemaker Pierre Morey, to adopt biodynamism in the vineyards. Whether these controversial viticultural practices are responsible for the wines' swift improvement it is hard to say, but since 1995 Leflaive has regained its place among the great white Burgundy producers. The wines are definitely built for the long haul and the domaine aims for a purity and precision of flavour, even if it takes a few years for those flavours to emerge. Best years: 1997, '96, '95, '93.

OLIVIER LEFLAIVE

FRANCE, Burgundy, Côte de Beaune, Puligny-Montrachet AC

♥ *Pinot Noir*

♀ *Chardonnay*

For about a decade Olivier Leflaive combined two separate roles. He was a director of the

Since taking over Domaine Leflaive in 1993, Anne-Claude Leflaive has encouraged a move to biodynamic viticulture, with encouraging results.

revered Domaine LEFLAIVE and at the same time built up a successful *négociant* business. With the brilliant winemaker Franck Grux at his side, he was able to release each year a range of Burgundies, mostly but not exclusively white, that were as good as those of most domaines. The range was striking: from the finest Grands Crus to well-made village wines, and a generous selection of Premiers Crus from MEURSAULT, PULIGNY-MONTRACHET and CHASSAGNE-MONTRACHET. For many years Olivier Leflaive has carefully sought out good-quality grapes from villages such as RULLY and ST-AUBIN, which offer excellent value.

Leflaive does not use a great deal of new oak, and even for the superior appellations he rarely uses more than 50 per cent. He is scrupulous in his selection process after the wines are vinified, and in tricky vintages some of the wine may well be declassified. The whites are relatively fleshy and full, but certainly don't lack finesse. The 20 per cent of his production which consists of red wines is mostly sold within France. Best years: (white) 1997, '96, '95, '93, '92, '90, '89, '88, '86.

PETER LEHMANN

AUSTRALIA, South Australia, Barossa Zone, Barossa Valley

♥ *Cabernet Sauvignon, Syrah (Shiraz)*

♀ *Riesling, Chardonnay, Semillon, Chenin Blanc, Sauvignon Blanc*

Peter Lehmann is a larger-than-life figure who has stood astride his beloved BAROSSA VALLEY for 30 years. However, since his son Doug and a new winemaking team have taken charge in the 1990s, the quality has been transformed. Riesling, Semillon, Shiraz, Cabernet Sauvignon and the blended Clancy's red are the best wines among a large portfolio, particularly when (in the case of all except Clancy's) they appear under either a Cellar Reserve label, or as Stonewell Shiraz or Mentor (mainly Cabernet). The reds have a luscious depth of fruit flavour and have received real oak maturation (neither chips nor staves), and show the Barossa at its seductive best. Best years: 1997, '96, '93, '91, '90, '88, '87, '86, '83, '80.

JOSEF LEITZ
GERMANY, Rheingau, Rüdesheim
🍷 Pinot Noir (Spätburgunder)
🍷 Riesling

Virtually self-taught, Johannes Leitz rapidly established himself in the early 1990s as one of the RHEINGAU's leading young winemakers with some ravishingly elegant dry and off-dry Rieslings from the top RÜDESHEIM sites (the great Berg Schlossberg and Berg Rottland). Very low yields and extremely long fermentations result in concentrated wines that need time to show their best. Best years: (whites) 1998, '96, '94, '93, '92, '90.

LEIWEN
GERMANY, Mosel-Saar-Ruwer

Despite having the excellent Laurentiuslay site – which can produce magnificent Spätlese and Auslese wines with natural sweetness – this large wine commune in the Mittel MOSEL used to be famous for quantity rather than quality. However, during the 1990s a new generation of winemakers has set about changing this reputation. Best producers: GRANS-FASSIAN, Carl LOEWEN, Alfons Stoffel, Werner & Sohn.

JEAN LEÓN
SPAIN, Cataluña, Penedès DO
🍷 Cabernet Sauvignon, Cabernet Franc, Merlot
🍷 Chardonnay

Jean León emigrated to the USA in the 1950s, made his fortune, and returned to plant a vineyard of Cabernet Sauvignon, Cabernet Franc and Chardonnay in PENEDÈS in 1964. His Chardonnay and Cabernet Sauvignon have a good claim to be Spain's best. The Chardonnay, made in a distinctly CALIFORNIAn style, is oaky, with rich, biscuity, pineappley fruit underneath. Up until 1980, the Cabernet Sauvignon was a big, tannic red wine that sometimes needed as many as ten years before being ready. Since then, the wine has included 13 per cent Cabernet Franc and 2 per cent Merlot and the winemaking has been adapted

so that the resulting blend is softer and easier to drink in its youth. Miguel TORRES took over after León's death in 1996. Best years: (reds) 1995, '92, '91, '90, '88, '87, '85, '83, '81, '78.

LEONETTI CELLAR
USA, Washington State, Columbia Valley AVA
🍷 Merlot, Cabernet Sauvignon, Sangiovese

A leading WASHINGTON STATE producer with an international reputation for Merlot, Leonetti Cellar has been producing wine since 1978. Experiments with different oaks and new barrels each year give winemaker Gary Figgins a range of ways to craft round and supple wines needing only short aging. The superlative Merlot has a loyal following and can be exceptionally hard to acquire. His Cabernet Sauvignon is ripe and soft-textured. A tiny amount of Sangiovese is produced. Best years: 1997, '96, '94.

CH. LÉOVILLE-BARTON
FRANCE, Bordeaux, Haut-Médoc, St-Julien AC, 2ème Cru Classé
🍷 Cabernet Sauvignon, Merlot, Cabernet Franc

Anthony Barton, whose family has run this Second Growth ST-JULIEN since 1821, has resolutely refused to profiteer in spite of considerable pressure to do so, especially in the early to mid-1980s, when every Classed Growth BORDEAUX vintage was released at a substantially higher price than the last, regardless of actual worth. But he refused to raise the prices of his wines above a level he considered fair. By 1986 he was charging only half what one or two of his more ambitious neighbours thought 'reasonable'. Yet as he freely declares, he still runs a profitable business. He knows what it costs to make fine wine, he never stints on quality, and he certainly doesn't intend to make a less than satisfactory profit. Prices in the 1990s have of course moved with the market, but as a Second Growth Léoville-Barton still remains reasonably priced.

This 47-ha (116-acre) estate – with 72 per cent Cabernet Sauvignon, 20 per cent Merlot, and only 8 per cent Cabernet Franc – makes dark, dry, tannic wines, difficult to taste young and therefore frequently underestimated at the outset, but over ten to 15 years they achieve a lean yet beautifully proportioned quality, the blackcurrants and cedarwood very dry, but pungent enough to fill the room with their scent. They are a traditionalist's delight. Vintages throughout the 1980s and '90s have been successful and even the off-vintages are good. Best years: 1998, '97, '96, '95, '94, '93, '91, '90, '89, '88, '86, '85, '83, '82, '81, '78, '75.

CH. LÉOVILLE-LAS-CASES
FRANCE, Bordeaux, Haut-Médoc, St-Julien AC, 2ème Cru Classé
🍷 Cabernet Sauvignon, Merlot, Cabernet Franc, Petit Verdot

The ST-JULIEN AC wasn't accorded a First Growth in the 1855 Classification. Any re-evaluation would change all that, because in Léoville-Las-Cases, St-Julien has a property and an owner whose dedication to quality would put most First Growths to shame. Going to meet Monsieur Delon who runs Léoville-Las-Cases is rather like having an audience with your headmaster at school, but these challenging tasting sessions in his cellars give one a true understanding about the passion and commitment that is great BORDEAUX.

The 97-ha (240-acre) vineyard is the biggest of the three Léoville estates, and a neighbour of the great Ch. LATOUR. There are similarities in the wine because since 1975 Las-Cases has been making wines of dark, deep concentration. Yet there is also something sweeter and more enticing right from the start – the fumes of new oak spice linger over the glass even in the wine's most stubborn adolescent sulks, and the tannins, strong though they are, have a habit of dissolving into smiles in your mouth exactly at the moment you've decided that they are just too much. Las-Cases from a good year really needs 15 years to shine. Second wine: Clos de Marquis. Best years: 1998, '97, '96, '95, '94, '90, '89, '88, '86, '85, '83, '82, '81, '79, '78, '75.

CH. LÉOVILLE-LAS-CASES
This château is probably now making the most exciting of all St-Julien wines. It has startlingly deep, dark concentration and really needs at least 15 years of aging.

CH. LÉOVILLE-POYFERRÉ
FRANCE, Bordeaux, Haut-Médoc, St-Julien AC, 2ème Cru Classé
🍷 Cabernet Sauvignon, Merlot, Petit Verdot, Cabernet Franc

Until comparatively recently, Léoville-Poyferré was the least good of the three Léoville properties. The 1980s saw a marked improvement, however, with a string of excellent wines made under the watchful eye of Didier Cuvelier, who has gradually increased the richness of the wine without wavering from its austere style. The 1990s have followed in the same vein, with the

'95 and '96 ranking with the best from this Second Growth ST-JULIEN. The wines need eight to ten years to blossom. Second wine: Ch. Moulin-Riche. Best years: 1998, '97, '96, '95, '94, '90, '89, '88, '87, '86, '85, '83, '82.

DOMAINE LEROY, MAISON LEROY

FRANCE, Burgundy, Côte de Nuits, Vosne-Romanée AC

❦ *Pinot Noir*

♀ *Chardonnay*

The dynamic Lalou Bize-Leroy was, until 1992, in the enviable position of running a highly regarded *négociant* business, Maison Leroy, based in AUXEY-DURESSES and was at the same time a major partner and co-director in the Domaine de la ROMANÉE-CONTI (DRC). But in the early 1990s questionable commercial decisions led to her being ousted from the DRC. Another factor that precipitated her departure was her decision to purchase the Charles Noëllat estate in VOSNE-ROMANÉE, which, some argued, could be seen as a conflict of interest. Her departure left her free to develop the combined Noëllat and Leroy business as she saw fit.

Maison Leroy had always pursued a costly strategy of holding vast stocks of mature wines, gradually released as Madame Bize-Leroy saw fit. Although older vintages still remain available, she now focuses more on developing the superb vineyards of the former Noëllat estate, renamed Domaine Leroy. From the cellars in Vosne, she offers a range of wines from the greatest sites: CHAMBERTIN, MUSIGNY, RICHEBOURG, Romanée-St-Vivant, CLOS DE LA ROCHE and many more. She is an enthusiastic convert to biodynamism, and is the most fanatical of all Burgundians when it comes to controlling yields. Her yields are always extremely low – unnecessarily low, some argue – and her wines powerfully concentrated. No expense is spared, in vineyard or winery, and most of the wines are aged in new oak. This expense, not surprisingly, is passed on to her loyal customers, and her prices rival those of the DRC. She insists that given the extremely low yields she obtains from her vines, the prices

she demands are not unreasonable. Certainly, she has not lacked customers or enthusiastic reviews for her wines, which are in the starry ranks of the top tier in Burgundy. Best years: 1997, '96, '95, '94, '93, '90, '89, '88, '87, '85, '83, '80, '78.

LIBRANDI

ITALY, Calabria, Cirò DOC

❦ *Gaglioppo, Cabernet Franc, Cabernet Sauvignon*

♀ *Greco Bianco, Mantonico Bianco*

The brothers Antonio and Nicodemo Librandi have carved out their reputation by dint of an unremitting commitment to the improving quality in CIRÒ, their particular corner of CALABRIA. Working with outstanding winemakers such as Severino Garofano and, more recently, PIEDMONT's Donato Lanati; investing over a period of two decades in the best winemaking equipment and, more recently, developing new vineyards with both international and native Calabrian varieties, they have convinced the world both with their wines and with their confidence that Calabria can be Oenotria or the 'land of wine' again – although they still plough a rather lone furrow at the moment.

The classic Librandi wines are Cirò Rosso, from the native Gaglioppo grape, and Cirò Bianco, from the local version of Greco. An upmarket cru of Cirò Rosso, Duca San Felice, is perhaps their best wine, though in a market situation which seeks more recognizable flavours the Cabernet-Gaglioppo blend Gravello has had more success. The white Critone and the Rosé Terre Lontane have also won considerable praise. Best years: (reds) 1995, '93, '92, '91, '90, '88.

LIEBFRAUMILCH

GERMANY, Rheinhessen, Pfalz and Nahe

♀ *Riesling, Silvaner, Müller-Thurgau, Kerner and others*

Liebfraumilch, on the rare occasions it is well made, is the perfect beginner's wine. It is almost always sold under a brand name or a retailer's own label; it never has a grape name on the label, and it is always a Qualitätswein. It may not be *trocken* or *halbtrocken*, and the regulations are fairly vague as to what it should taste like: while 70 per cent of its grapes must be the four in the list above (in practice there is no Riesling in most Liebfraumilch – Germany's finest grape is too expensive for cheap blends), the character of the wine need only be pleasant and agreeable. The poorer, cheaper ones make you wonder just who it is who deems sulphur or oxidation to be pleasant or agreeable. Sichel's Blue Nun and Valckenberg's Madonna are good and reliable.

LIGURIA

ITALY

Flower-bedecked Liguria, 'Italy's Riviera', is a slim arc of craggy mountains, with a thin coastal strip of land, centred on Genoa. The mountains form a good barrier against the cold air from the north, and the huge mass of warm, Mediterranean water in the bay further tempers the climate, giving Liguria some of Italy's mildest winters.

Most Ligurian wine comes from the Riviera Ligure di Ponente DOC, west of Genoa. The most important grapes are light, delicate, white Vermentino; floral, peachy, white Pigato; red Ormeasco (often known as Dolcetto), which also comes, called Sciac-trà, as a deep rosé; and the succulently fruity red Rossese, particularly good from Dolceacqua. On the eastern side, the Riviera di Levante, where Colli di Luni DOC is the major wine, Vermentino is still important, but most other grapes grown here are varieties associated with neighbouring Tuscany. The exception is the tiny zone of Cinqueterre with its sought-after whites, including the sweet Sciacchetrà, not to be confused with the above-mentioned rosé.

LINDEMANS

AUSTRALIA, Victoria, North West Victoria Zone, Murray Darling

❦ *Cabernet Sauvignon, Merlot, Pinot Noir, Syrah (Shiraz)*

♀ *Chardonnay, Semillon, Sauvignon Blanc, Riesling*

Lindemans has its operational headquarters at Karadoc, where the prodigious quantities (over one million cases per year) of Bin 65 are skilfully woven together, using an extraordinary range of winemaking techniques. However, its quality feet are planted in the Limestone Coast Zone of South Australia (COONAWARRA, PADTHAWAY and Robe) and to a lesser, though historically important, degree in the HUNTER VALLEY. In a fast-changing world, the supple though undoubtedly oaky, single-vineyard St George Cabernet Sauvignon and Limestone Ridge Shiraz-Cabernet wines from Coonawarra, together with the BORDEAUX-blend Pyrus, and the similarly generously barrel-fermented and oaked Padthaway Chardonnay, keep the Lindemans flag flying high. Best years: (Limestone Coast) 1997, '96, '91, '90, '88, '86.

LINGENFELDER

GERMANY, Pfalz, Gross Karlbach

❦ *Pinot Noir (Spätburgunder), Dornfelder*

♀ *Riesling, Müller-Thurgau, Scheurebe and others*

Rainer Lingenfelder's star goes on rising higher and higher. He has not completely abjured sweeter wines, in the way of some PFALZ

MAISON LEROY

White wine from Auxey-Duresses is not generally memorable, but Maison Leroy's example is clean and well-structured, with lemon and butter aromas.

LINGENFELDER
One of the most talented winemakers in Germany, Rainer Lingenfelder turns the simple Scheurebe grape into superb wine.

roducers, but he has worked hard on his technique so that his sweeties are never heavy but always balanced with crisp acidity and fresh fruit. His dry Rieslings and Scheurebes are beautifully ripe and complex – the Scheurebes, in particular, are a revelation, with their curiously rich yet tart grapefruit and honey fruit. The Spätburgunders are his top reds, aged in used barrels from Ch. GRAND-PUY-LACOSTE in PAUILLAC – Lingenfelder does not believe in too much new oak. The Dornfelders, too, are good, with structure and character and a rich, rasping damson-skin fruit. Best years: 1998, '97, '93, '90, '89, '88.

LIRAC AC
FRANCE, Southern Rhône
Grenache, Cinsaut, Syrah, Mourvèdre
Clairette, Bourboulenc, Picpoul, Grenache Blanc and others

This excellent but underrated AC, between TAVEL and CHÂTEAUNEUF-DU-PAPE, makes wines that resemble both its more famous neighbours. There are 550ha (1359 acres) of vines producing two and a half million bottles a year, about 92 per cent of it red and rosé, though production of the white is increasing. The red has the dusty, spicy fruit of Châteauneuf-du-Pape, without achieving the intensity and power of the best examples, plus an attractive metallic streak. The rosés are breezier, more refreshing than Tavel, and can have a lovely strawberry fruit. Drink them sharpish. The reds age very well but are always delicious young. Best years: (reds) 1998, '97, '95, '94, '91, '90. Best producers: (reds) Aquéria, Assémat, Devoy, la Genestière, Maby, de la Mordorée, St-Roch, Ségriès, la Tour.

When on form, the white can be as good as white Châteauneuf-du-Pape. Clairette is the chief grape, with other local varieties like Bourboulenc and Picpoul added. You must drink it young, though, because the perfume goes and what's left is nice, soft RHÔNE white – which tastes OK, but isn't a patch on what was there before. Best producer: (whites) Maby.

LISTRAC-MÉDOC AC
FRANCE, Bordeaux, Haut-Médoc
Cabernet Sauvignon, Merlot, Cabernet Franc,

This is one of the six specific ACs inside the HAUT-MÉDOC area, but does not possess any Classed Growths. All the best Haut-Médoc vineyards are on gravel soil and mainly on ridges within sight of the Gironde estuary. Listrac, however, is set several miles inland, its 650ha (1606 acres) of vineyards fashioned on outcrops of partially gravelled heavy soil, encircled by forest. Even so, the wine can be good, although the relative lack of gravel means few of its vines have the tantalizing fragrance of top MARGAUX or ST-JULIEN wines, being nearer to ST-ESTÈPHE in style. Solid fruit, a slightly coarse tannin and an earthy flavour are the marks of most Listracs. Those properties able to invest in new oak make more attractive, balanced wines. The percentage of Merlot, better suited to the heavy soils, has also increased to provide wines with more generosity of fruit. Best years: 1998, '96, '95, '94, '90, '89, '88, '86, '85, '83, '82. Best producers: Cap-Léon-Veyrin, CLARKE, Ducluzeau, Fonréaud, Fourcas-Dupré, Fourcas-Hosten, Fourcas-Loubaney, Grand Listrac co-operative, Mayne-Lalande, Saransot-Dupré.

LIVERMORE VALLEY AVA
USA, California, Alameda County

The gravelly terrain around the town of Livermore attracted a number of French growers in the 1880s, visions of the GRAVES region of BORDEAUX dancing in their head. But it was the Irish-Italian Concannons and the German WENTES who first made the place go, and who then kept it going after Prohibition. Never a large area, the valley now has only 729ha (1800 acres) of vines. The Frenchmen who wanted to build a new Graves were not far off the mark, as Sauvignon Blanc and Sémillon probably do better here than any other grapes, and recent releases show considerable style; however, Chardonnay and Sauvignon Blanc are the most widely planted, with Cabernet Sauvignon and Petite Sirah the leading reds. In addition to Concannon and Wente, there are small wineries like Cedar Mountain, Chouinard, Retzlaff Vineyards and Fenestra Winery. Best years: 1997, '95, '94, '92, '91, '90.

LJUTOMER
SLOVENIA, Podravski Region
Laski Rizling, Furmint (Sipon), Sauvignon Blanc and others

The Ljutomer-Ormoz wine region of Slovenia is the country's best source of whites, though anyone familiar with the feeble, branded Ljutomer (or Lutomer) wines that venture abroad would be forgiven for disagreeing. Most of the wine comes from the two co-operatives, at Ljutomer and Ormoz, the latter being the bigger and better. The best wines are extraordinarily good: fresh, full Laski Rizling, balanced, rich Sipon (alias Furmint, which makes Hungary's TOKAJI), and splendid botrytis-affected dessert wines. Ormoz's Jeruzalem Sekt is remarkably classy for a Charmat-method fizz.

LOS LLANOS
SPAIN, Castilla-La Mancha, Valdepeñas DO
Tempranillo (Cencibel)
Airén

Some of the best-value, mature red wines in Spain come out of this large, sparklingly clean and well-equipped bodega. The huge barrel-maturation cellar is unparalleled in VALDEPEÑAS, where most reds are drunk young and without any wood-aging. The inexpensive red Señorío de Los Llanos Reservas and Gran Reservas, made exclusively from Cencibel, are some of the best buys in all Spain. Best years: 1996, '95, '93, '91, '90, '89.

LOCOROTONDO DOC
ITALY, Puglia
Verdeca, Bianco d'Alessano, Fiano and others

Locorotondo might not claim to be anything extraordinary but there's a tacit acceptance in and around the Salento peninsula, its homeland, that it is quite simply the white to go for. Its refreshingly light, lively, almondy, apricotty fruit makes it a delight to drink, as young as possible, either chilled or icy cold in the heat of a Puglian summer. Best producers: Borgo Canale, Locorotondo co-operative.

CARL LOEWEN
GERMANY, Mosel-Saar-Ruwer, Leiwen
Riesling

During the 1990s Karl-Josef Loewen has systematically worked to make his estate one of the best in the Mittel MOSEL. He makes the best Rieslings from the excellent Laurentiuslay site of LEIWEN. His old vines here give naturally sweet Spätlese and Auslese wines with a rich peachy fruit and an intense minerally character. The second string to his bow are the firm, tight wines from the terraces of the Thörnicher Ritsch. Lighter, but with a brilliance reminiscent of the Saar, are his Rieslings from the Maximiner Klosterlay of Detzem, which are fermented almost to dryness. Towering above all of these are his monumental Eisweins from the Klostergarten of Leiwen. Best years: 1998, '97, '96, '95, '94, '93, '92.

LOIRE France

THE LOIRE RIVER CUTS RIGHT THROUGH the heart of France, east to west. It rises in the Ardèche gorges only a mere 50km (30 miles) from the Rhône Valley and, after surging northwards, executes a graceful arc up to Orléans where it then sets off westwards for the sea. Along the way the river encompasses some of France's best-known wines – Sancerre, Anjou and Muscadet – and some of its most obscure – Jasnières, Bonnezeaux and Vin de l'Orléanais, as well as some of its most thrilling and individual wines – in particular, the sweet wines of the Layon Valley. Altogether there are about 70 different wine appellations located here, producing reds, rosés, sparkling, and the entire gamut of whites, from searingly dry to unctuously sweet.

The upper reaches of the Loire south of Nevers don't produce any wines of great consequence and there isn't much of it anyway. Sancerre and Pouilly-Fumé, regarded by many as the quintessential Sauvignon Blanc styles, are the first really important wines areas heading downstream.

The province of Touraine is a positive market garden, with vines taking their place alongside other crops, but the Sauvignon grape excels here too, and at Vouvray and Montlouis the Chenin makes good fizz and still whites ranging from sweet to very dry. A bit of Chardonnay starts to make its presence felt, and there's some pretty decent red from Cabernet and Gamay. But the Loire's best reds are made just downstream at Chinon and Bourgueil from Cabernet Franc – they are wonderful young but also capable of staying fresh for decades.

Anjou is most famous for its rosé, though there are some tasty reds (Anjou-Villages and Saumur-Champigny are the best appellations). But the best wines are white, either sweet from the Layon Valley, and to a lesser extent, the Aubance Valley, or very dry from Savennières on the north bank of the Loire and all made from the Chenin Blanc grape. The climatic feature that allows Chenin Blanc to ripen at all along the cool Loire Valley is a generally warm, early autumn, that with luck, pushes the late-ripening Chenin to a decent level of maturity and also encourages the development of the *Botrytis cinerea* or noble rot fungus in the grapes, which as in Sauternes, naturally concentrates their sweetness to a remarkable degree.

Saumur is one of France's chief centres for sparkling wine. The soils here are more chalky than in the rest of Anjou and this encourages a certain leanness in the wines, which along with cool ripening conditions, produces the sort of acid base wine that sparkling wine producers like. The soft local limestone (tuffeau) is ideal rock for excavating cellars to mature the sparkling wine. Many of the cellars began life as quarries for the honeyed-colour stone used to build the famous Loire châteaux.

Finally, at the western end of the Loire Valley, in the low flatland around Nantes, they make that uncomplicated light neutral white, Muscadet. At its best, a Muscadet *sur lie* from the Sèvre-et-Maine appellation, it does an excellent job of providing cheap light wine to accompany the superb local seafood.

The vineyards around Chaume are some of the best in the sheltered Layon Valley where Chenin Blanc produces one of the world's great sweet wines. Only the most favoured sites can produce grapes with the necessary overripeness.

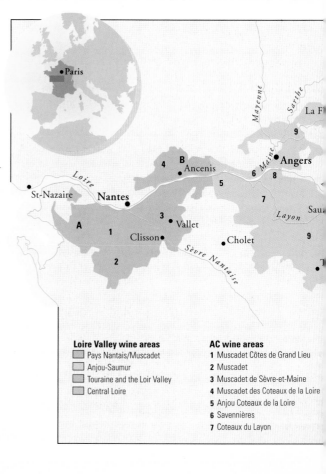

Loire Valley wine areas
- Pays Nantais/Muscadet
- Anjou-Saumur
- Touraine and the Loir Valley
- Central Loire

AC wine areas
1 Muscadet Côtes de Grand Lieu
2 Muscadet
3 Muscadet de Sèvre-et-Maine
4 Muscadet des Coteaux de la Loire
5 Anjou Coteaux de la Loire
6 Savennières
7 Coteaux du Layon

REGIONAL ENTRIES
Anjou, Anjou-Villages, Bonnezeaux, Bourgueil, Cabernet d'Anjou, Cheverny, Chinon, Coteaux du Layon, Crémant de Loire, Gros Plant du Pays Nantais, Haut-Poitou, Menetou-Salon, Montlouis, Muscadet, Vin de l'Orléanais, Pouilly-Fumé, Quarts de Chaume, Quincy, Reuilly, Rosé d'Anjou, Rosé de Loire, St-Nicolas-de-Bourgueil, St-Pourçain-sur-Sioule, Sancerre, Saumur, Saumur-Champigny, Saumur Mousseux, Savennières, Touraine, Vouvray.

PRODUCER ENTRIES
Ackerman-Laurance, Bourgeois, Clos Rougeard, Couly-Dutheil, Dagueneau, de Fesles, Huet, Mellot, Métaireau, de Villeneuve.

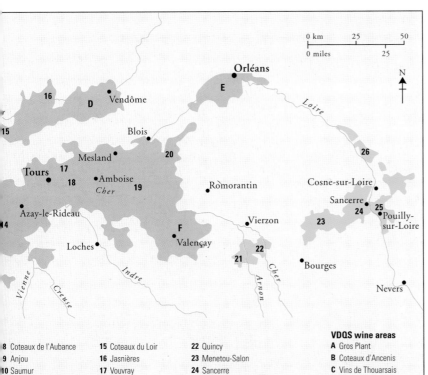

Map legend

					VDQS wine areas
8	Coteaux de l'Aubance	15	Coteaux du Loir	22	Quincy
9	Anjou	16	Jasnières	23	Menetou-Salon
10	Saumur	17	Vouvray	24	Sancerre
11	Saumur-Champigny	18	Montlouis	25	Pouilly-Fumé, Pouilly-sur-Loire
12	St-Nicolas-de-Bourgueil	19	Touraine	26	Coteaux du Giennois
13	Bourgueil	20	Cheverny, Cour-Cheverny		
14	Chinon	21	Reuilly		

VDQS wine areas

- A Gros Plant
- B Coteaux d'Ancenis
- C Vins de Thouarsais
- D Coteaux du Vendômois
- E Vins de l'Orléanais
- F Valençay

DOMAINE RICHOU
This sweet Coteaux de l'Aubance is a marvellous combination of richness and fresh, lime flavours.

CH. DE FESLES
In good years la Chapelle is a fabulously rich and long-lived Bonnezeaux.

JOSEPH RENOU
Sold under the Domaine du Petit Metris label, this is excellent intense Quarts de Chaume.

CLOS DE LA COULÉE-DE-SERRANT
Made exclusively from Chenin Blanc, this dry white has a fascinating honeyed, floral bouquet.

CLOS ROUGEARD
This unusual oak-fermented Saumur Blanc comes from old vines.

CHARLES JOGUET
From very old vines the Clos de la Dioterie shows dark red and black fruit with penetrating depth.

HUET
Le Haut Lieu is one of three excellent sites owned by this top Vouvray estate.

PAUL COTAT
The Cotat Sancerres have a concentration of fruit that few other growers achieve.

DIDIER DAGUENEAU
Dagueneau is best known for his barrel-fermented Sauvignon Blanc called Silex, which needs several years for the real style to emerge.

LOMBARDY
ITALY

Arriving at Milan airport (if it isn't fog-bound) and heading through the pollution of the city, along the factory-lined, lorry-clogged, east-west motorway, it is not easy to be enamoured of Lombardy at first impression. But deeper exploration of the region reveals plentiful compensations. In the north are magnificent alpine slopes, the north-west has the lakes of Maggiore, Como and Varese, while the east boasts tranquil Lakes Iseo and Garda. The broad Po river is Lombardy's southern boundary for most of its extent. There's just a small, gently hilly triangle known as OLTREPÒ PAVESE lying across the river in the west of the region. This is also one of Lombardy's major wine areas, with assorted grape varieties like Barbera, Bonarda, Moscato, Riesling, Pinot Grigio and Pinot Nero jostling for position, and it's the source of much of Italy's fizz.

In the far north of the region, there is a long, thin strip of alpine vineyards, the VALTELLINA, making Nebbiolo-based wine in much softer styles than in Piedmont. In the extreme east is LUGANA, with its remarkably charasterful clone of Trebbiano. But the most illustrious of Lombardy's wines come from FRANCIACORTA in the middle, with a red from a strange FRIULI-PIEDMONT grape blend, a Pinot-based white and a range of stunning sparklers. Just to the west of Franciacorta, around the delightful city of Bergamo, is the Cabernet and Pinot-based Valcalepio zone and there are various others, for example on the western shores of Garda and on the slopes above the city of Brescia at Mario Pasolini's Mompiano.

So there's no need to spend a triple fortune in one of Milan's sophisticated restaurants or *enoteche* when a single fortune at a local winery will do.

DR LOOSEN
GERMANY, Mosel-Saar-Ruwer, Bernkastel
♀ *Riesling, Müller-Thurgau (Rivaner), Pinot Blanc (Weissburgunder)*

Without in any way compromising the MOSEL's tradition for Rieslings with a naturally low alcoholic content (7.5 – 8.5 degrees) Ernst Loosen makes some of the most concentrated and complex Rieslings anywhere in the world. The definition of vineyard character is almost supernaturally clear: Dr Loosen's WEHLENer Sonnenuhr wines are the archetypal wines of this site, with tremendous elegance, peachy fruit and a very clean finish,

DR LOOSEN
Ernst Loosen's estate has portions of some of the Mosel's most famous vineyards, including the Sonnenuhr (or Sundial) in Wehlen.

while the bigger wines from the ERDENer Treppchen site have a herbal character which grows in intensity as they age and are even longer at the finish. The ÜRZIGer Würzgarten wines really live up to their name, Würzgarten meaning 'spice garden', and the wines, from vines up to 100 years old, are packed with mineral extract.

Finest of all are the Ausleses from the Erdener Prälat site, enjoying the most favoured climate in the entire region, which have a lavish exotic fruits character and enormous intensity. Even Ernst Loosen's basic Dr L Riesling is a textbook example of regional style. In 1996 Loosen took over the WOLF estate at WACHENHEIM in the PFALZ. Best years: 1998, '97, '96, '95, '94, '93, '92, '90, '89, '88, '85, '76, '75, '71.

LÓPEZ DE HEREDIA
SPAIN, La Rioja, Rioja DOC
♂ *Tempranillo, Grenache Noir (Garnacha Tinta), Carignan (Cariñena, Mazuelo), Graciano*
♂ *Grenache Noir (Garnacha Tinta), Macabeo (Viura)*
♀ *Macabeo (Viura), Malvasia*

This endearingly old-fashioned RIOJA bodega makes wines that are fine and delicious by any standards, ancient or modern. The wines ferment and pass their early months in large wooden fermentation vats, they are clarified in the age-old way with egg whites, and never see a filter. All the grapes López de Heredia uses come from the Rioja Alta, half of them from its own vineyards. Reds represent three-quarters of the production, and age for a considerable time in wood. The youngest red, Viña Cubillo, is soft, fine and lightly oaky, and the Viña Tondonia Tinto is elegant, strawberry-fruity and oaky. Whites are excellent too and will mature for many years: this is one of the few bodegas still making old-style, oaked white Rioja. Best is the delicious, spicily oaky, honey-and-vanilla-flavoured Viña Tondonia Blanco. Best years: (reds) 1995, '94, '91, '90, '89, '87, '86, '85.

LOUPIAC AC
FRANCE, Bordeaux
♀ *Sémillon, Muscadelle, Sauvignon Blanc*

This sweet wine area is directly across the river Garonne from BARSAC. But the Loupiac growers, despite using the same grapes, can't persuade noble rot to affect their vines nearly as frequently as it does in Barsac, and they do have a far higher permitted yield – 40 hectolitres per hectare as against Barsac's 25 hectolitres. Despite this, there are some good estates producing wine which is attractively sweet, if not really gooey. Drink young, though the best can age. Best years: 1998, '97, '96, '95, '90, '89, '88, '86, '85, '83. Best producers: Clos Jean, du Cros, Loupiac-Gaudiet, Mémoires, du Noble, de Ricaud.

LOUREIRO
One of the better indigenous grape varieties of north-west Portugal, the white Loureiro has traditionally been blended with Trajadura and Paderna to produce VINHO VERDE. It is now being used on its own to make fresh, lightly scented dry white wines which are typically low in alcohol and high in acidity. It is mostly planted in the cooler districts near the coast and is occasionally found north of the River Minho in Spain's GALICIA region.

CH. LA LOUVIÈRE
FRANCE, Bordeaux, Pessac-Léognan AC
♂ *Cabernet Sauvignon, Merlot*
♀ *Sauvignon Blanc, Sémillon*

If ever they get around to revising the GRAVES classification you can take a safe bet that Ch. la Louvière will find a place in the new order. For the time being, though, la Louvière remains one of PESSAC-LÉOGNAN's unclassified stars and this is largely due to the dynamic owner André Lurton who has revitalized the property over the last 35 years.

The estate is large, with 50ha (125 acres) under vine producing an average of 300,000 bottles per year. The lion's share of this is red, with 35ha (86 acres) planted with 65 per cent Cabernet Sauvignon and 35 per cent Merlot. The wines are well structured but attractively fruity, making them drinkable when young but with an aging potential of ten years or more. The Sauvignon-based whites tend to be vigorous and aromatic and also age surprisingly well. In today's heady market both red and white remain excellent value for money. Second label: (red and white) L de la Louvière. Best years: (reds) 1997, '96, '95, '94, '90, '89, '88, '86, '85; (whites) 1997, '96, '95, '94, '90, '89, '88.

LUGANA DOC

ITALY, Lombardy
♀ *Trebbiano di Lugana*

How do the growers of Lugana, at the southern tip of Lake Garda, turn out characterful, floral, appley whites when the grape is Trebbiano, king of neutrality? It is said that their Trebbiano di Lugana clone, like Trebbiano di Soave which is supposedly the same, is a version of Verdicchio – by which I mean that it has far more stuffing and flavour than the usual limp offerings from normal Trebbiano. Lugana should be drunk young – and it mainly is, by the hordes of tourists who flock to Garda's shores every summer. It can age for a year or two. Best producers: Ca' dei Frati, Premiovini, Provenza, Zenato.

LUNGAROTTI

ITALY, Umbria, Torgiano DOC
♂ *Sangiovese, Cabernet Sauvignon, Canaiolo*
♀ *Trebbiano, Malvasia, Chardonnay*

Lungarotti was one of the first wineries to reinstate the concept of quality in central Italy, way back in the 1970s. This was achieved not only with the wines, but with the establishment of an annual wine-tasting competition to establish the best wines of the land, called the Banco di Assaggio; also by the painstaking assembly of one of the finest wine museums in the world, at the Lungarotti headquarters in the village of TORGIANO, near Perugia.

Lungarotti's best wine has always been Torgiano Riserva Vigna Monticchio, a Sangiovese-based blend which is aged (voluntarily) for up to ten years, of which several are in bottle, although the DOCG regulations (which virtually only applies to this, the dominant producer) only calls for three years. Second to this is the Sangiovese-Cabernet blend called San Giorgio which undergoes equally impressive aging. A number of varietals and blends follow, the best of which is probably the Cabernet Sauvignon. After a period in the doldrums, when it seemed to be resting on its past laurels, Lungarotti, under the late founder Giorgio Lungarotti's stepdaughter Teresa Lungarotti, is moving forward once again. Best years: (Torgiano Riserva) 1995, '90, '88, '86, '85.

LUSTAU

SPAIN, Andalucía, Jerez y Manzanilla DO
♀ *Palomino Fino, Pedro Ximénez*

Emilio Lustau fills as many sherry bottles under supermarket own-labels as it sends out under its own name. General quality here is sound to good, but the quality of special bottlings rises to some delightful peaks. Lustau's wonderful almacenista sherries are unique. There remain about 50 smallish sherry-maturing businesses, or almacenistas, more often than not run by wealthy individuals with a career elsewhere – doctors, lawyers, cattle breeders. Lustau hit upon the idea of bottling almacenista wines from single casks, and selling them as small-scale specialities under the Lustau name in conjunction with that of the almacenista. These can be really exceptional, complex sherries. The bodega is now part of the Caballero group.

LÜTZKENDORF

GERMANY, Saale-Unstrut, Bad Kösen
♀ *Silvaner, Riesling, Pinot Blanc (Weissburgunder), Müller-Thurgau, Gewürztraminer (Traminer)*

The Lützkendorf family look back on more than a century of winemaking history, and Udo Lützkendorf made some remarkably good wines when director of the Naumburg state domaine during the communist period, so perhaps it should be no surprise that his son Uwe should make the best wines from the SAALE-UNSTRUT region today. Riesling from the Karsdorfer Hohe Gräte, Silvaner from the Pfortenser Köppelberg and Traminer from the Freyburger Schweigenberg are all serious dry wines with plenty of fruit and substance. Best years: 1998, '97, '95, '94, '93.

CH. LYNCH-BAGES

FRANCE, Bordeaux, Haut-Médoc, Pauillac AC, 5ème Cru Classé
♂ *Cabernet Sauvignon, Merlot, Cabernet Franc*
♀ *Sauvignon Blanc, Sémillon, Muscadelle*

Sometimes, tasting this wonderful wine with its almost succulent richness, its gentle texture and its starburst of flavours all butter and blackcurrants and mint, you may wonder why it only has a comparatively lowly position as a Fifth Growth PAUILLAC. It can only be because the chaps who devised the 1855 BORDEAUX Classification were basically puritans. They couldn't bear to admit that a wine as openheartedly lovely as Lynch-Bages could really be as important as other less generous Growths. Well, it is. Wine is about pleasure. Great wine is about great pleasure and there are few wines which will so regularly give you such great pleasure as Lynch-Bages.

The 90ha (222 acres) of vines in the middle of the AC, near the town of Pauillac, are planted in the traditional Pauillac mix, with a lot of Cabernet Sauvignon – 75 per cent – and 15 per cent Merlot and 10 per cent Cabernet Franc. This sounds like a tough wine taking a long time to mature – but that's the magic of Lynch-Bages – rich and ripe when young, beautiful at ten years old, even more beautiful at 20 years. Second wine: Ch. Haut-Bages-Avérous. A small amount of white wine, Blanc de Lynch-Bages, has been made since 1990. Best years: (reds) 1997, '96 ,'95, '94, '90, '89, '88, '87, '86, '85, '83, '82, '81, '79.

MACABEO

The most common white grape of northern Spain, and stretching south to La MANCHA, the MACABEO can make light, fresh, fairly fruity wine with a slight floral perfume when young – but it loses its freshness within a year or so. Alias the Viura, it is very important in RIOJA, where it manifests itself in a leaner, greener way. Along with Xarel-lo and Parellada, Macabeo is one of the trio of grapes that make most of Spain's CAVA fizz.

MACEDON RANGES

AUSTRALIA, Victoria, Port Phillip Zone

With an average January temperature of 17.2°C (63°F) Macedon has a cooler climate than does Reims in northern France's CHAMPAGNE region. Without question, this region is at the sharp end of cool-climate viticulture in Australia, and self-evidently does best in the warmest vintages, and struggles (not with total conviction) in the normal to cool years.

The Champagne varieties (Chardonnay and Pinot Noir) dominate the plantings and

The beautiful Macedon region is one of Australia's coolest wine regions: site selection and careful matching of site and grape variety are crucial.

also the wine styles, whether still or sparkling. Highly textured, nutty, creamy Chardonnays which have necessarily undergone a full malolactic fermentation and delicate, sappy/foresty Pinot Noirs are the leaders, although VIRGIN HILLS, Knights Granite Hills and (sometimes) Cobaw Ridge show it is possible to make convincing spicy/leafy Shiraz and Cabernet Sauvignon, or blends thereof. Best years: 1997, '95, '94, '93, '91, '90. Best producers: Bindi, Cleveland, Cobaw Ridge, Cope-Williams, Hanging Rock, Knights Granite Hills, Portree, Virgin Hills.

MÂCON AC, MÂCON SUPÉRIEUR AC, MÂCON-VILLAGES AC
FRANCE, Burgundy, Mâconnais
🍷 🍷 *Gamay, Pinot Noir*
🍷 *Chardonnay, Pinot Blanc*

Mâcon AC is the most basic appellation in the large Mâconnais region, directly north of BEAUJOLAIS, and accounts for three million of the 14 million bottles produced. The AC is increasingly used for red wines, but has been usurped by the superior Mâcon-Villages AC for whites. Whatever the colour, the flavours are rarely exciting; the red usually has a 'rooty', vegetal rasp, and the rosé lacks the fresh, breezy perfume which can make pink wine such fun. Gamay reds are normally sold as Mâcon or Mâcon Supérieur and Pinot Noir reds as BOURGOGNE AC.

Mâcon Blanc used to be a cheap, bland quaffer. Now it is a rather expensive, basic quaffer, since the magic variety Chardonnay has allowed prices to boom. Quality has rarely kept pace with prices, and it is generally worth moving up to Mâcon-Villages if you want more than simple lemony zing. Occasionally, good wines will appear from quality-conscious shippers like DUBOEUF, but in any case the wine should be drunk as young as possible.

Mâcon-Villages should be an enjoyable fruity, fresh white wine but again, because it comes from the fashionable Chardonnay grape it is often sold at far too high a price. There are 38 villages in the region entitled to the Mâcon-Villages AC, or they can add their own name, as in Mâcon-Lugny. Best villages: (in the north) Chardonnay, Igé, Lugny, St-Gengoux-de-Scissé, Uchizy; (in the south) Charnay, Prissé. The villages of Viré and Clessé and two other small ones were promoted in 1998 to their own AC, Viré-Clessé. The co-operatives, who are as strong in the Mâcon region as anywhere in France, make 75 per cent of Mâconnais wines.

Mâcon Supérieur is not a quality indicator, merely a sign that the wine has reached a minimum alcohol level one degree higher than basic Mâcon. Best years: (Mâcon-Villages) 1997, '96, '95, '94, '93. Best producers: Duboeuf; (Mâcon-Villages) Bonhomme, de la Condemine, Deux Roches, Guichard, de Guillemot-Michel, Manciat-Poncet, Olivier Merlin, Roally, Talmard, Thévenet, Tissier, Valette, Verget; co-operatives at Chardonnay, Lugny, Prissé, St-Gengoux-de-Scissé.

MACULAN
ITALY, Veneto, Breganze DOC
🍷 *Cabernet Sauvignon, Merlot*
🍷 *Chardonnay, Sauvignon Blanc, Vespaiolo and others*

It was in the late 1970s that Fausto Maculan, scion of a family whose wine roots in BREGANZE go back generations, decided to 'withdraw from the rat-race of low-price, high-volume production to concentrate on quality'. For decades in central VENETO this has meant using mainly French grapes, and Fausto, ever a keen observer of French methods, decided in 1984 to plant the newly acquired Ferrata hill to Cabernet Sauvignon, Chardonnay and Sauvignon Blanc (French clones) at 10,000 vines to the hectare. The resulting non-DOC reds and whites in the Ferrata range have been steadily improving as the vines mature, and as Fausto's quasi-obsession with the latest enological equipment has refined cellar-techniques (he is particularly proud of a slow-moving belt which allows unsound or unripe grapes to be eliminated prior to crushing).

Maculan's greatest strength, apart from Cabernet Sauvignons Ferrata, Fratta and Palazzotto and Merlot Marchesante, have always been the dessert wines, Torcolato and the outstanding botrytis-affected Acininobili, both mainly from Vespaiolo grapes. Best years: (Acininoboli) 1995, '93, '92, '91, '90, '89, '88, '87, '85, '83.

MACULAN
Acininobili is one of Italy's best dessert wines. Made from local grapes, especially Vespaiolo, the wine is intensely sweet but with good acidity.

MADEIRA DOC
PORTUGAL, Madeira
🍷 *Tinta Negra Mole*
🍷 *Sercial, Bual, Verdelho, Malvasia (Malmsey), Terrantez*

Fine Madeira can be relied upon to survive for centuries, preserving layer upon layer of complex flavour. The trouble is that not much of the island's production can be classified as 'fine' as it has mostly been made from the rather neutral, red Tinta Negra Mole grape, rather than the four traditional top-quality white grapes, Sercial, Bual (or Boal), Verdelho and Malvasia or Malmsey. Now there are incentives to replant the vineyards with these 'noble' grapes but progress is slow (having now crept up to 15 per cent of total plantings).

Good Sercial is a pale, incisive dry wine with searing (sometimes punishing) acidity. Verdelho tends to be medium-dry in style with a soft, peachy character when young, offset by high acidity. Bual is more full bodied and fairly sweet, and Malmsey, the darkest in colour, has a rich, raisiny character but due to naturally high levels of acidity is never cloying.

The best Madeiras are aged for years in old wooden casks, then stored in sun-baked attics. Lesser wines are subject to an artificial heating process known as *estufagem* which helps to simulate the effects of age. All this heating and aging before bottling means that exposure to air is unlikely to damage your bottle of Madeira once it is opened – Madeira is one wine you can enjoy, glass by glass, for months. Much the largest producer on the island is the MADEIRA WINE COMPANY which bottles a full range of wines under various labels. The next largest (and main competitor) is HENRIQUES & HENRIQUES. Good smaller producers include d'Oliveira and Artur Barros e Souza.

MADEIRA WINE COMPANY
PORTUGAL, Madeira, Madeira DOC
🍷 *Tinta Negra Mole*
🍷 *Sercial, Verdelho, Bual, Malvasia (Malmsey), Terrantez*

The Madeira Wine Company was formed from an amalgam of historic MADEIRA firms, including Blandy's, Cossart Gordon, Leacock and Miles. Of these, Blandy and Cossart Gordon are now the company's principal brands. The Madeira Wine Company has developed by leaps and bounds since the Symington family (of DOW, GRAHAM and WARRE PORT fame) moved in back in 1989. They now control the company although the Blandy family still retains an interest.

The Madeira Wine Company produces a complete range of Madeiras: from inexpensive wines destined for the French market to venerable old vintages, cask-aged in warm attics at the São Francisco lodge in Funchal for a minimum of 20 years. Highlights in the range include the 5-Year-Old wines, all of which are made from the four noble white grapes as opposed to the red Tinta Negra Mole. Ten-Year-Old wines are much improved, particularly the nervy, medium-dry Verdelho and the rich, raisiny Malmsey. Stocks of bottled vintage Madeira include Blandy's fine, concentrated 1958 Bual and Cossart's 1908 Bual, bottled in 1985 after spending 77 years in wood! Look out for the fine, aromatic wines (10-Year-Old and vintage) made from the rare Terrantez grape.

MADIRAN AC

FRANCE, South-West
♥ *Tannat, Cabernet Sauvignon, Cabernet Franc*

In the gentle Vic Bilh hills just south of Armagnac there has been a steady revival of the Madiran AC since 1953 when the vineyards had virtually died out and were down to only 6ha (15 acres).

The tannic Tannat grape is the main variety and it had become too degenerate to cultivate. But modern botanical science found a way, and now there are 1400ha (3459 acres) of vineyards, and suddenly Madiran is popping up all over the place. Alain Brumont of Ch. MONTUS and Bouscassé has led the charge. New oak has helped the wine achieve a more attractive, less tannic style, and several of the best producers are now using it. Also helpful in reducing painful tannin levels is a system of micro-oxygenation known as *microbullage* that has been developed by Patrick Ducournau of la CHAPELLE LENCLOS and is being used to good effect, both in Madiran and other regions in France. Best years: 1997, '96, '95, '94, '93, '90, '89, '88, '85. Best producers: d'Aydie, Barréjat, Berthoumieu, Bouscassé, Capmartin, la CHAPELLE LENCLOS, Crampilh, Cave de Crouseilles, Laffitte-Teston, Montus, Mouréou, Producteurs PLAIMONT.

MAGAÑA

SPAIN, Navarra, Navarra DO
♥ *Merlot, Cabernet Sauvignon, Cabernet Franc, Syrah*

The Magaña brothers sold their nursery and started Bodegas Magaña in 1973, with the intention of making top-quality red wine. With plantings of Merlot, Cabernet Sauvignon, Cabernet Franc, Malbec and Syrah, they have pioneered the use of French grape varieties in Navarra.

Magaña wines are made only from the bodega's own grapes which, because of the dry climate, yield little juice – but are of high quality. After fermentation, they are aged for up to six years before bottling. The result is often that the excellent, rich fruit of the young wine has faded by the time the wine is released for sale. Best years: 1991, '87, '82.

CH. MAGDELAINE

FRANCE, Bordeaux, St-Émilion Grand Cru AC, Premier Grand Cru Classé
♥ *Merlot, Cabernet Franc*

This is very much a wine of two personalities. In lighter years – because of its tremendously high percentage of Merlot (90 per cent) – the wine has a gushing, tender juicy fruit, easy to drink at only four to five years old, which seems to epitomize the indulgent softness of wines from ST-ÉMILION.

However, in the grand vintages, Magdelaine changes gear. Those 11ha (27 acres) of Merlot-dominated vineyard sit on the steep slopes or côtes just south-west of the town of St-Émilion adjacent to the vineyards of Ch. CANON and BELAIR – a plum position for super-ripeness. Because the property is owned by the quality-conscious company of J-P Moueix in nearby Libourne, the grapes are left to hang until the last possible moment, then an army of pickers swoops in. This means the grapes have a significantly higher ripeness than in neighbouring vineyards. Then the wine is fermented long and slow, and finally the wine is then aged in predominantly new barrels for a year and a half.

The result? Dark, firmly structured wines, yet behind the tough exterior there is luscious fruit and oaky spice and as the tannin fades, a gentle glyceriny texture takes over. Great years such as 1995, '90, '89, '86 and '85 will take 15 years to mature. Best years: 1998, '97, '96, '95, '94, '90, '89, '88, '86, '85, '83, '82, '75.

CH. MAGDELAINE
Ch. Magdelaine enjoys a classic St-Émilion location on the edge of the limestone ridge outside the town, with vineyards divided between the plateau and the slopes.

MÁLAGA DO

SPAIN, Andalucía
♀ *Pedro Ximénez (Pedro Ximén), Moscatel de Málaga*

Most bottles of Málaga contain a curious blend of wines, juices and alcohol, which can be stunningly complex, or, more often, cloyingly sweet and boring. The basic wines are made in varying degrees of sweetness out of Pedro Ximén grapes – often with the illegal addition of Lairén (Airén) – or from Moscatel de Málaga. These are then blended with a variety of sweetening, flavouring and colouring liquids: partially-fermented raisin juice, fortified grape juice, and grape juice that has been boiled down until it's thick, dark and gooey. Alcohol ranges from 15 to 23 per cent and the label will give an indication of sweetness and colour. Production has been dwindling throughout the twentieth century. The minimum two-year aging period must be done in the city of Málaga, which is cooler than the inland vineyards where the wines are actually fermented. The revered Scholtz Hermanos winery closed down in 1996, dealing the DO a near-fatal blow. Best producers: Gomara, Larios, Lopez Hermanos.

CH. MALARTIC-LAGRAVIÈRE

FRANCE, Bordeaux, Pessac-Léognan AC, Cru Classé de Graves
♥ *Cabernet Sauvignon, Cabernet Franc, Merlot*
♀ *Sauvignon Blanc*

This is one of the few PESSAC-LÉOGNAN Classed Growths whose reputation has been upheld by its white rather than its red wine (though the red is also good). It is a relatively small property, set in 19ha (47 acres) near the woods just south of Léognan. The white wine (100 per cent Sauvignon Blanc) is given new oak aging, but still has a startling nettle green fruit at first, which then softens over three to four years into a really lovely nutty wine.

The property was acquired in 1997 by the Belgian businessman, Alfred Bonnie who began an extensive programme of modernization and renovation, including a new ultra-modern, stainless steel cuverie and barrel cellars. A draconian system of selection for the red wine was introduced for the 1997 vintage with positive results. Malartic-Lagravière red, which had generally been good but not stunning, looks like it could now take on a new dimension of fruit and flavour. Only time will tell. The wine can age brilliantly. Best years: (reds) 1998, '97, '96, '95, '94, '90, '89, '88, '87, '85, '83, '82, '81, '78; (whites) 1998, '97, '96, '95, '92, '90.

MALBEC

In France Malbec only really produces exciting wine in Cahors (where it is known as Auxerrois), although it is planted in the Loire (where it is known as Cot) and in Bordeaux (where the St-Émilion growers call it Pressac). In Bordeaux and the Loire it can soften the other grapes, but in Cahors it makes deep, chewy, plum-and-tobacco-flavoured wine unlike any other in France.

In Argentina, Malbec (sometimes spelled Malbeck) is the most planted French varietal. It has adapted well, and at an altitude of 850m (2800ft) in Luján de Cuyo, Mendoza, it produces exceptional wines – deep, plummy and perfumed. Its success there has persuaded growers in Chile and Australia to take a closer look.

MALVASIA

This grape, widely planted in Italy, is found in several guises, red and white. It is said to have arrived in Italy in centuries past from the port in Greece's Peloponnese peninsula called, today, Monemvasia. The general characteristic of Malvasia is an aromatic quality somewhat diverse from, and considerably less obvious than, that of Muscat. The best sub-variety for dry white and slightly fizzy semi-sweet whites in northern Italy is the Malvasia Istriana of FRIULI, which seems to be related to EMILIA's Malvasia di Candia. The latter is also its name in FRASCATI, where its wines tend to be somewhat flabby, with a tendency to oxidation, and where the

HAUNER
On the volcanic Lipari Islands off the coast of Sicily Malvasia is used to make really tasty, apricotty-sweet wines.

Malvasia Puntinata or di Lazio is seen as the superior clone. Whether the Malvasia di Toscana is a different sub-variety is a moot point, but certainly it can lay little claim to quality in that region and is being grafted over or replaced as fast as growers can get round to it.

White Malvasia seems to do best in the islands off Sicily, where it is used to make *passito* or *liquoroso* style wines, as in the case of the the well-known Malvasia delle Lipari. Malvasia di Cagliari and Malvasia di Bosa are two Sardinian DOCs of little commercial note although, in the latter case at least, of considerable potential quality, especially in the style called *dolce naturale*. The word *liquoroso*, in this context, indicates addition of alcohol, which helps to maintain perfumes but also to promote hangovers.

There is also Malvasia Nera, which is, generally found in southern PUGLIA and, surprisingly, in Tuscany, where it can combine well with Sangiovese. There exist also a couple of obscure DOCs in PIEDMONT, both rather obscure, called Malvasia di Casorzo d'Asti and Malvasia di Castelnuovo Don Bosco producing frothing, light reds. Variants of Malvasia also grow in northern Spain and Portugal. On the island of MADEIRA it produces sweet, varietal fortified wine, often known by its English name of Malmsey.

LA MANCHA DO

SPAIN, Castilla-La Mancha
🍷🍷 *Tempranillo (Cencibel), Grenache Noir (Garnacha Tinta), Cabernet Sauvignon, Merlot, Syrah, Petit Verdot, Moravia Buena*
🍷 *Airén, Macabeo, Pardilla, Chardonnay*

This is the largest controlled appellation region in Europe and, indeed, the world, with more than 188,000ha (470,000 acres) under vine. It is much too large to mean much in terms of a wine's 'origin', despite a number of common soil and climate features. The most obvious unifying factor is one that modern producers could do without: the prevalence of the white Airén grape, which still covers 154,000ha (380,534 acres) of the vineyards and gives, at most, cleanly neutral wines when vinified in the modern way (in stainless steel under temperature controls). Most of the bottled La Mancha white wines are made in that style now, but most of the wine is distilled into alcohol, to be sold to Brazil as automobile fuel.

Airén is hardy and survives the region's lack of rain. It plays a major ecological role in preventing desertification, but impedes wine-making progress. When vineyard irrigation

was legalized in Spain there was at last an opportunity for improvement. From 1996 all new Airén plantings were banned. By 1999 about 40,000 ha (99,000 acres) were being replanted with or grafted to new recommended varieties, led by Cencibel (Tempranillo), Cabernet Sauvignon and even some Merlot. The Australian viticulturist Richard Smart, who was active in the region, had been advocating the changes.

In such a changing environment the roll-call of leading producers changes fast. Best producers: Ayuso (Estola Reserva), Vinícola de Castilla (Castillo de Alhambra and Señorío de Guadianeja), Bodegas Centro Españolas (Allozo and Rama Corta), Vinícola de Tomelloso (Añil and Torre de Gazate), Torre del Granero, Torres Filoso (Árboles de Castillejo); and the co-operatives Jesús del Perdón (Yuntero), Nuestra Señora de la Cabeza (Casa Gualda), Nuestra Señora de Manjavacas (Zagarrón), Santa Catalina (Los Galanes).

MARANGES AC

FRANCE, Burgundy, Côte de Beaune
🍷 *Pinot Noir*

In 1989 this single AC was created to represent the villages of Cheilly-lès-Maranges, Dezize-lès-Maranges and Sampigny-lès-Maranges in the southern tip of the CÔTE DE BEAUNE. The wines are rarely exciting, being rather thin and harsh, except in vintages like 1990, although they can sometimes have a pleasant strawberry perfume. In practice, most of the growers sell their wine as CÔTE DE BEAUNE-VILLAGES – a catch-all appellation applying to 16 different Côte de Beaune communes – and that is probably the best fate for most of it. Best years: 1997, '96, '95, '93, '90. Best producers: Bachelet, Chevrot, Colin-Déleger, V Girardin, B Morey.

MARCASSIN WINERY

USA, California, Sonoma County, Russian River Valley AVA
🍷 *Pinot Noir*
🍷 *Chardonnay*

Arguably the best-known winemaker in CALIFORNIA and, without question, the most famous consulting winemaker, Helen Turley has developed her 4-ha (10-acre) vineyard in the cool western sector of SONOMA COUNTY to supply Chardonnay and Pinot Noir for her own brand, Marcassin. Establishing herself years ago with stints as winemaker for the B R Cohn and Peter MICHAEL wineries, Turley is noted for her signature style of winemaking that shoots from the hip in terms of ripe fruit, oncentration, power and, for reds, lots of oak nd rich, supple tannin. Her clients are mong the most collectible names today – Colgin Cellars, Bryant Family, Pahlmeyer – nd she helped established her brother's Napa vinery, TURLEY CELLARS.

For Marcassin she has been offering Chardonnay from the Gauer Ranch's Upper Barn, Lorenzo Vineyard, Hudson Vineyard as well as from Marcassin Vineyard. Best years: 1998, '97, '96, '95, '94. Her Pinot Noir Marassin Vineyard quickly achieved cult status or its incredible depth and restrained power.

MARCHE
ITALY

The Marche stretches, long and lean, along the Adriatic coast from Romagna to ABRUZZO, its hills, sandwiched between sea and mountain, covered seemingly ubiquitously by vines. It has always seemed a particularly blessed region – not highly populated, relatively rarely on travellers' itineraries, yet enjoying a rich patrimony of agricultural wealth, artistic and architectural splendour and touristic attractions.

The VERDICCHIO DEI CASTELLI DI JESI zone put the Marche on the wine map, but ROSSO PICENO is the largest zone, followed by other little known, Trebbiano-based wines like Bianco dei Colli Maceratesi and Falerio dei Colli Ascolani. But the Castelli di Jesi area is certainly the most intensively cultivated. Verdicchio is grown elsewhere, too, especially further inland around Matelica, where it produces wines with a steely character though there are fewer quality producers. The best known Marche red is ROSSO CONERO, from a smallish area on the massif of Monte Conero, behind the port of Ancona. While for those who like oddities, there is Vernaccia di Serra petrona: a perfumed, fizzy, dark red, made dry, medium or sweet.

MARCILLAC AC
FRANCE, South-West
♣ ♀ *Fer, Gamay, Jurançon Noir*

In the Aveyron *département* the locals lap up most of what wine there is. There are just 135 ha (334 acres) of Marcillac vineyards and the Fer is the main grape variety. The red wine is strong and dry, rasping with herbs, grassy freshness and a slightly metallic zing. That may sound a bit off-putting, but it copes remarkably well with the local Roquefort cheese. There is a little rosé, too. Best producers: Domaine du Cros, Marcillac-Vallon co-operative. Best years: 1996, '95, '94.

MARGARET RIVER
AUSTRALIA, Western Australia, South West Australia Zone

This is the fastest growing of all premium regions in Australia, irresistible for tourists and investors alike. The wines are delicately balanced, coming from vines that are spared excesses of heat or cold. Its most challenging wine is Semillon, with asparagus and gooseberry flavours that successfully emulate Sauvignon Blanc, which is also successful in its own right. Chardonnay goes from strength to strength, particularly from LEEUWIN ESTATE. Cabernet Sauvignon and its blends do best of all, from the definition of CAPE MENTELLE and CULLEN WINES to the softer MOSS WOOD and VASSE FELIX. Syrah (Shiraz) and Zinfandel also flourish. Best years: 1997, '96, '95, '94, '93, '92, '90, '87, '86, '85, '82, '81. Best producers: Cape Mentelle, Cullen Wines, EVANS & TATE, Leeuwin Estate, Moss Wood, PIERRO, Vasse Felix.

MARGAUX AC
FRANCE, Bordeaux, Haut-Médoc
♣ *Cabernet Sauvignon, Cabernet Franc, Merlot, Petit Verdot*

Margaux is the most sprawling of the six specific ACs in the HAUT-MÉDOC, with the vineyards centred on the village of Margaux but also spreading through the communes of Arsac, Cantenac, Labarde and Soussans. It covers 1358ha (3356 acres), just a little more than the more compact ST-ESTÈPHE's 1245ha (3076 acres) in the north.

The key to Margaux's style is the pale gravel banks which cleave their way through the vineyards, giving little by way of nutrition, but providing perfect drainage (supplemented by artificial drainage) so that the wines are rarely heavy and should have a quite divine perfume when they mature at seven to 12 years old. The best examples of this style are Ch. BRANE-CANTENAC, la Gurgue, d'ISSAN, Labégorce-Zédé, Ch. MARGAUX, PALMER and RAUZAN-SÉGLA. A fuller, rounder but still perfumed style comes from the southern part of the AC, and is at its best from Ch. ANGLUDET, GISCOURS, Monbrison, Siran and du Tertre. Altogether there are 21 Classed Growths in the AC, as well as good unclassified properties, such as Ch. Siran, Angludet and Monbrison. Also good are Ch. Bel Air Marquis d'Aligre, Dauzac, Ferrière (since 1993), Kirwan, Malescot-St-Exupéry, PRIEURÉ-LICHINE and LASCOMBES. With a change of generation the AC now has a new dynamism and could be one of the most interesting to watch over the coming decade. Winemaking techniques are also changing the style of the wines, making it more difficult to identify the archetypal Margaux. Bottles merely labelled 'Margaux' shouldn't be taken too seriously since almost all the decent stuff sports a property's name. Best years: 1998, '96, '95, '94, '90, '89, '88, '86, '85, '83, '82, '81, '79.

CH. MARGAUX
FRANCE, Bordeaux, Haut-Médoc, Margaux AC, Premier Cru Classé
♣ *Cabernet Sauvignon, Merlot, Petit Verdot, Cabernet Franc*
♀ *Sauvignon Blanc*

After a long period of decline, Ch. Margaux fought back so successfully during the 1980s that it now lays fair claim to being the most exciting property in the whole MÉDOC. A large 78-ha (193-acre) property set back in the trees just outside the village of MARGAUX, Ch. Margaux gives a new meaning to the words perfume and fragrance in a red wine, as though an inspired *parfumeur* had somehow managed to combine a sweet essence of blackcurrants with oil from crushed violets and the haunting scent of cedarwood, then swirled them together with more earthy pleasures like vanilla, roasted nuts and plums, and spirited all these into the bottle. The surprising element is that Margaux also has a subdued power and structure as well. Second wine: Pavillon Rouge du Ch. Margaux. Best years: (reds) 1998, '97, '96, '95, '94, '93, '90, '89, '88, '86, '85, '83, '82, '81, '80, '79, '78.

There is also some white wine. The grapes don't come from the precious Margaux vineyards, but from Soussans, outside the best red wine area. There are 10ha (25 acres) of Sauvignon Blanc, which is vinified at the château, but in a separate cellar so that the red wine is not in any way affected. The result is delicious, but Pavillon Blanc must be the most expensive BORDEAUX AC by a mile. Best years: (whites) 1998, '97, '96, '95, '94, '90, '89, '88, '86, '85.

CH. MARGAUX
As well as its world-famous red wine, Ch. Margaux, one of the greatest properties of the Médoc, makes a delicious white wine called Pavillon Blanc.

MARLBOROUGH New Zealand

FLY INTO BLENHEIM AIRPORT and you begin to feel some of the excitement that the Marlborough region generates in all who visit New Zealand's largest and best-known wine region. For a start it feels like wine country. The rugged hills that adorn the well-known Cloudy Bay label, one of the world's most sought-after wines, form a semi-circle around the valley with the distant coastline completing the ring. In summer the burnt yellow and brown hills form a stark contrast to the lush, green and well-watered valley floor. Vines surround the airport and form a patchwork quilt throughout the valley. Once the valley was used to graze sheep that picked their way between the rocks in search of precious grass. High demand for Marlborough wine has boosted vineyard prices to the point where cherry orchards and crops disappear overnight to be replaced by fields of rocky brown earth studded with bare posts and puny vine cuttings.

It is hard to believe that until 1973 few people believed that grape vines could survive Marlborough's dry summers or frosty winters. Montana Wines took an enormous, but care-fully calculated risk when the company established the region's first vineyard on a scale that dwarfed any other previous vineyard development. The rest, as they say, is history.

Marlborough now has more than 40 resident winemakers with at least as many out-of-town producers making wine from grapes grown in the region. Many of these wineries do not own a wine-press. They are grape-growers who once supplied grapes to wineries but then seized the opportunity to make wine under their own label by contracting to have wine made for them. Some, like Kim Crawford, produce Marlborough wine without owning either a vineyard or a winery. The contract winemaking facility, Raupara Vintners (once called Vin Tech), is the closest thing that New Zealand has to a co-operative winery.

Marlborough's greatest assets are high sunshine hours, dry autumn weather, cool nights and free-draining alluvial soils littered with river boulders that retain heat and reflect sunshine. Without irrigation, however, much of the valley would be unable to support a viable wine industry. Although frost pro-tection measures are used at the cooler northern end of the Wairau Valley frost has been a relatively minor problem. In 1990 an autumn frost stripped the leaves off vines towards the end of vintage, forcing growers to harvest before the grapes were fully ripe – but this was an isolated incident.

Sauvignon Blanc from Marlborough has stunned the Old World with its startling, tangy intensity and this was the style that first brought the region fame worldwide. Chardonnay isn't far behind although there is a still a tendency for wine-makers to blur delicious tangy white peach and citrus flavours with an excess of oak to give an occasionally resinous result. Riesling is one of Marlborough's star wines. Occasionally dry but mostly off-dry, Marlborough Riesling offers delicious lime/citrus flavours with a seductive suggestion of honey and tropical fruit in a year when botrytis affects the crop.

Great sparkling wines are made with a classic Pinot Noir and Chardonnay blend, sometimes together with a dash of Pinot Meunier. People thought the cool conditions in Marlborough were tailor-made for Pinot Noir but it has been a slow starter, possibly because it has been a victim of over-cropping, but Cloudy Bay, Fromm and Isabel have now shown the world what the winemakers can do with this fickle variety. Cabernet Sauvignon struggles to get ripe although Merlot, in warmer years, can produce surprisingly good red. The Awatere Valley is only just over the Wither

The Richmond Ranges as viewed from a vineyard near the Wairau River is the scene depicted on the Cloudy Bay label (see facing page). Marlborough's most famous winery achieved cult status overnight with the 1985 Sauvignon Blanc.

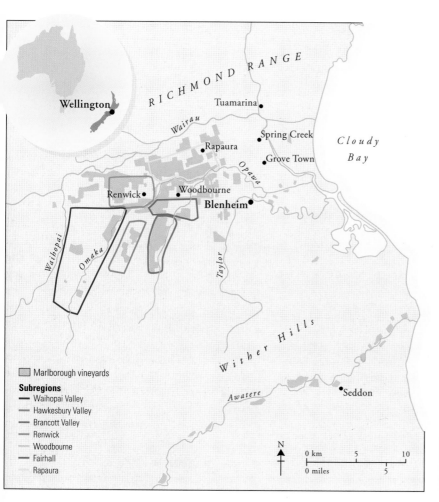

Marlborough vineyards

Subregions
- Waihopai Valley
- Hawkesbury Valley
- Brancott Valley
- Renwick
- Woodbourne
- Fairhall
- Rapaura

N

0 km   5   10

0 miles   5

Hills Range but the mesoclimate is significantly different and it seems to manage the virtually impossible – make wines with even more intensity than the main bulk of Marlborough. Though less protected from rain, the stony river terraces offer warmer conditions when it's dry and, as well as superb Sauvignon Blanc, there's been some truly classy cedary Cabernet Sauvignon.

REGIONAL ENTRY
Marlborough.

PRODUCER ENTRIES
Cloudy Bay, Corbans, Fromm Winery, Hunter's, Montana Wines, Selaks, Seresin Estate, Vavasour.

CLOUDY BAY
This is Cloudy Bay, New Zealand's most famous wine. The country's entire wine industry benefitted from Cloudy Bay's overnight star status.

STONELEIGH
Stoneleigh is a brand name used by Corbans and the Marlborough Riesling is an aromatic wine with floral and citrus fruit overtones.

JACKSON ESTATE
Unirrigated vineyards are used to produce classic Marlborough Sauvignon Blanc – intensely fruity, concentrated and ripe with a subtle herbaceous influence.

VAVASOUR
Based in the relatively new and exciting Awatere Valley, Vavasour has enjoyed spectacular success since its first wines were released in 1989. The Sauvignon Blanc is ripe and concentrated with all the gooseberry and limegrass attack you could wish for.

SERESIN ESTATE
This is a majestic Burgundian style of Chardonnay with oatmeal and hazelnuts and long, lingering richness.

HUNTER'S
Lean and elegant Chardonnays have helped keep this established Marlborough winery at the very top for more than a decade.

NAUTILUS ESTATE
This Champagne-method sparkling wine shows just how ideal Marlborough's cool climate and silty soils are to the production of quality fizz.

DEUTZ
Montana, New Zealand's largest wine company, makes austere, elegant Champagne-method sparkling wine with the help of the Champagne house, Deutz.

MARLBOROUGH

NEW ZEALAND, South Island
See also Marlborough, pages 234–235.

This remarkable viticultural area – where a flat river plain with leached silt and millions of water-rounded stones combines with a cool, yet dry summer and autumn climate – produces just the right balance between stress and encouragement for the vines. Sauvignon Blanc from Marlborough has stunned the Old World with its startling, tangy intensity. Chardonnay isn't far behind with its remarkable concentration of fruit, and recent vintages of Merlot have shown superb rich, creamy flavours. Add to that Pinot Noir (blended with Chardonnay) to produce great sparkling wine from Deutz/MONTANA, CLOUDY BAY/Pelorus and Le Brun – and you have one of the world's most thrilling vineyards. Best years: 1997, '96, '94, '91. Best producers: Cloudy Bay, FROMM, Forrest, Grove Mill, HUNTER'S, Isabel, Jackson Estate, Lawson's Dry Hills, Le Brun, Montana, Nautilus, Oyster Bay, VAVASOUR.

MARQUÉS DE CÁCERES

SPAIN, La Rioja, Rioja DOC
🍷 *Tempranillo, Graciano*
🍷 *Tempranillo, Grenache Noir (Garnacha Tinta)*
🍷 *Macabeo (Viura)*

Back in the 1970s, Marqués de Cáceres was the first RIOJA bodega to produce light, fresh, fruity whites that had never seen the inside of an oak barrel – a style which all the forward-looking Rioja bodegas have since attempted to emulate. The bodega was established in the early 1970s by Enrique Forner, a Spaniard who had long lived in France and who owned Ch. de Camensac in BORDEAUX. When he found it impossible to persuade local growers to sell him their vineyards, he set up agreements with the local growers in Cenicero.

Over 90 per cent of the red wines are made in-house, in up-to-the-minute equipment. Marqués de Cáceres reds have always been made in the fruity, not too oaky style which is now more popular with other Rioja bodegas, too. So they have never been recognizably 'Rioja' in style, more jammy than delicately wild-strawberry-oaky. The whites are all made by modern methods and are very good, fresh, herby and grassy-fruity, more reminiscent of wines made from Sauvignon Blanc grapes than of other white Riojas. The rosés are particularly fresh and fruity, but sadly as much out of fashion here as rosés are in the rest of the world. Best years: (reds) 1995, '94, '93, '92, '91, '90, '89, '87, '85, '82.

MARQUÉS DE GRIÑÓN
The Marqués de Griñón has expanded from his base in central Spain and now makes successful Riojas, including a Reserva version.

MARQUÉS DE GRIÑÓN

SPAIN, Castilla-La Mancha
🍷 *Tempranillo, Cabernet Sauvignon, Cabernet Franc, Syrah, Petit Verdot*
🍷 *Verdejo, Macabeo (Viura), Sauvignon Blanc, Chardonnay*

These mould-breaking wines are the brainchildren of a real Marquis of Griñón, Carlos Falcó, who studied winemaking at the University of California at Davis. His 1400-ha (3500-acre) Casadevacas estate lies on the edges of the Tagus Valley, 50km (30 miles) west of Toledo. Instead of the unexciting Airén – the traditional white grape planted in Spain's parched central plains – Falcó planted non-native red grapes, Cabernet Sauvignon and later Syrah and Petit Verdot. His vineyards were also, in 1975, the first ones in Europe to use drip irrigation. Chardonnay was added to the range in the early 1990s.

The Marqués de Griñón red can be utterly delicious, with richly minty Cabernet character and quite firm tannin. Since the Marqués sold a stake to the giant Berberana company and expanded his activities in other areas of Spain and in Argentina, his Toledo estate wines have used the Dominio de Valdepusa label.

The Marqués has been at work in other areas of Spain, too. The red Durius is a blend of Toro and RIBERA DEL DUERO. The white version is a blend of Verdejo, Viura and Sauvignon Blanc from RUEDA, and there are two new red RIOJAs, a young wine and a Reserva. Best years: (reds) 1997, '96, '95, '94, '93, '92, '91, '90, '89, '86, '85.

MARQUÉS DE MONISTROL

SPAIN, Cataluña, Penedès DO
🍷 *Tempranillo, Grenache Noir (Garnacha Tinta), Cabernet Sauvignon*
🍷 *Monastrell (Cava), Grenache Noir (Garnacha Tinta)*
🍷 *Xarel-lo, Macabeo, Parellada*

Owned by Arco (the new group headed by the Berberana company), this is a beautiful bodega, built around a medieval monastery and set among its own vines, in a wooded valley. The surrounding vineyard – 520ha (1285 acres) – is apparently the biggest single vineyard in CATALUÑA. All the wine comes from this vineyard, planted mainly with traditional native varieties and producing up to 1.5 million bottles of still wine each year and 2.5 million bottles of CAVA.

Among the various Cavas, Brut Selección, the youngest, is the best. It is fruity, simple and attractive and lacks the earthy flavour of its elders and theoretical betters – Brut Reserva, Gran Tradición and others. The still whites are better than the reds: Blanc de Blancs is good, simple and fruity and the fuller Blanc en Noirs (made in the red wine style) has really concentrated, appley fruit, though is a shade bitter round the edges.

MARQUÉS DE MURRIETA

SPAIN, La Rioja, Rioja DOC
🍷 *Tempranillo, Grenache Noir (Garnacha Tinta), Carignan (Cariñena, Mazuelo), Graciano*
🍷 *Grenache Noir (Garnacha Tinta), Tempranillo, Carignan (Cariñena, Mazuelo), Macabeo (Viura)*
🍷 *Macabeo (Viura), Malvasia, Grenache Blanc (Garnacha Blanca)*

Vicente Cebrian junior is steadily advancing the plan laid out by his father before his untimely death – that the Marqués de Murrieta bodega should become the leading producer of red wine not only in RIOJA but in the whole of Spain. Whether Murrieta will topple VEGA SICILIA from its pedestal of adulation is dubious, but certainly the wines are as good as ever they have been – and a good deal better than they had been in recent vintages. Sadly, however, they have shot up in price – maybe to pay for the new fermentation vats and bottling line.

The bodega's vineyards, outside the village of Ygay, have been extended to 162ha (400 acres), planted 90 per cent with Tempranillo, and will eventually cover 210ha (519 acres). Ygay is a fine spot for vineyards, right at the conjunction of the three Rioja sub-regions.

No wine here spends less than two years in oak and top Gran Reservas remain for at least 30 years in barrel. Out of a total of 11,500, the bodega buys around 500 new or nearly new barrels each year – mostly made of American oak, but some come second-hand from the top Bordeaux châteaux of YQUEM, LAFITE and PAVIE.

A decision has been made recently to release more wines under the Castillo de Ygay bel – a label previously reserved for the special Gran Reserva, made only from the best ears' wines and only released after at least wo decades of aging in barrel. Best years: reds) 1996, '95, '94, '92, '91, '90, '89, '86, 35, '70, '68, '59, '42.

MARQUÉS DE RISCAL

PAIN, País Vasco, Rioja DOC; Castilla-León, Rueda
O
Tempranillo, Graciano, Carignan (Cariñena, Mazuelo), Cabernet Sauvignon
Grenache Noir (Garnacha Tinta), Macabeo (Viura)
Macabeo (Viura), Verdejo, Sauvignon Blanc

Things have changed dramatically for the better in these family-owned bodegas in RIOJA and RUEDA since the younger generation took over the reins in 1987. The Rioja bodega, where they make their red wine, has considerably spruced up its winemaking and cleared out 75 per cent of the old barrels. They now intend to change their barrels every five to seven years and aim for a more modern, fruitier style of wine.

Having had a Cabernet Sauvignon vineyard since the 1860s, this is the Rioja bodega that has been pushing the hardest for the variety's legalization in Rioja. It has been 'tolerated' as an 'experimental' variety in the 1990s. In 1991 a new wine, Barón de Chirel – 45 per cent Cabernet, 55 per cent Tempranillo and aged in new oak – was launched, modelled on the Italian SUPER-TUSCAN blends of Sangiovese and Cabernet Sauvignon. The Riscal Reservas, however, are made mainly from Tempranillo. An important part of Barón de Chirel and the other Riscal blends is the excellent Rioja, grape red Graciano which is now being replanted throughout the region.

The white comes from Riscal's Rueda bodega, Vinos Blancos de Castilla. The simple, fresh Rueda is made mainly from Verdejo; the Sauvignon Rueda is grassy, rounded and fruity; and the Rueda Reserva Limousin from Verdejo is soft, oaky and well-balanced. Best years: (reds) 1995, '94, '92, '91, '90, '89.

MARSALA DOC

ITALY, Sicily
Catarratto, Inzolia, Damaschino and others

Although Marsala, produced on the quasi-African flatlands of the western tip of Sicily, was once as highly esteemed as sherry or MADEIRA, and can still be a great fortified wine, until recently very little of it was. After World War Two most Marsala producers

thought they could make a very nice living churning out wines sweetened or flavoured in artificial ways. While elsewhere in Italy people by the 1980s were waking up to the fact that to survive in the modern world you needed to aim for quality – or change jobs – in Marsala they seemed happy to enjoy today and let *domani* take care of itself.

When business got so bad that even they could no longer deny reality, they revised the law (in 1984), basically reducing the production area slightly and withdrawing the DOC from egg-, almond- or other flavoured Marsalas. New titles like 'Cremovo' were introduced for what had been called 'Marsala all'uovo'. During the 1980s, following the efforts of the rebel Marco DE BARTOLI along with a few other producers, Marsala began to regain its prestige. However, De Bartoli's objection to fortifying his best wines up to 18 per cent alcohol tends to disqualify them from using the Marsala DOC because they are unfortified.

Finest of the traditional Marsala styles is Marsala Vergine, an unsweetened, intense, subtly caramelly, yet dry apéritif wine made by the solera system, which also produces sherry. Marsala Superiore and Marsala Superiore Riserva tend to be sweet, and can reach interesting quality levels. Best producers: (Vergine) De Bartoli, Florio.

MARSANNAY AC

FRANCE, Burgundy, Côte de Nuits
Pinot Noir
Chardonnay, Pinot Blanc

Marsannay is north of the village of FIXIN, with some of its vineyards virtually adjoining the suburbs of Dijon. Until 1987 the village was famous only for its rosé wine which can be pleasant but a little too austere and dry but since 1987 Marsannay has been an AC in its own right for reds, whites and rosés.

The red, however, is one of the revelations of the 'new wave' in Burgundy – rarely very fleshy in texture, but with a delightful cherry and strawberry fragrance that is irresistible in good examples. There is very little white wine, but what there is isn't bad. Bruno CLAIR is the village's most ambitious grower, lavishing great care on the full range of Marsannays that he releases each year. There are no Premiers Crus in Marsannay, but top growers such as Clair bottle single-vineyard wines. Best years: 1997, '96, '95, '93, '90, '89, '88, '85. Best producers: Bart, R Bouvier, P Charlopin, Chenu, Bruno Clair, Fougeray, Huguenot, JADOT, Labouré-Roi, Naddef, Quillardet.

MARTINBOROUGH

NEW ZEALAND, North Island

Now generally known as Wairarapa, this wine region at the southern tip of the North Island sprang into prominence in the late 1980s. Debate rages as to whether it is better suited to Pinot Noir, Chardonnay, Cabernet Sauvignon, Merlot or Shiraz – let alone Sauvignon Blanc, Riesling or Gewurztraminer – as this outcrop of gravelly soil, allied to a remarkable mesoclimate in what is otherwise, frankly, a clay-ridden and rather damp area just east of Wellington, is producing superlative grapes from most of these varieties. MARTINBOROUGH VINEYARD, Palliser, Dry River and Ata Rangi are already showing how good the potential is with high-quality winemaking. Best years: 1998, '96, '94, '91, '90, '89, '86. Best producers: Ata Rangi, Benfield, Delamere, Dry River, Martinborough Vineyard, Nga Waka, Palliser.

MARTINBOROUGH VINEYARD

NEW ZEALAND, North Island, Martinborough
Pinot Noir
Chardonnay, Sauvignon Blanc, Riesling and others

Larry McKenna of Martinborough Vineyard is the man to thank for showing just how exciting the grapes from the MARTINBOROUGH region can be. His Pinot Noir and Chardonnay wines are some of New Zealand's most thrilling examples – veering between an unashamedly Burgundian style and something intensely South Pacific – and his Riesling and Sauvignon Blanc wines are way ahead of most of the competition. Despite being in charge of the winery since 1987, he has almost single-handedly established Martinborough as one of the great New World vineyard areas. It is sad news for both Martinborough Vineyards and the region in general that he's given up his role as winemaker here. Best years: 1998, '96, '94, '91, '90, '89.

MARTINBOROUGH VINEYARD
This impressive Chardonnay, with toasty, nutty notes and slightly sweet fruit, is made using the whole range of Burgundian techniques.

MARTÍNEZ BUJANDA
SPAIN, País Vasco, Rioja DOC
🍷 *Tempranillo, Carignan (Cariñena, Mazuelo), Cabernet Sauvignon*
🍷 *Grenache Noir (Garnacha Tinta)*
🍷 *Macabeo (Viura), Malvasia*

Martínez Bujanda, founded in 1890, is a hi-tech company that never stops trying to do better – even though its wines are already some of the best modern RIOJAS around.

All the grapes come from its own 250ha (618 acres) of vineyards. The Tempranillo is made by the carbonic maceration method into deliciously soft, fruity, cherry-flavoured red wine. This is sold under the Valdemar label, as are the white and the rosé. Crianza, Reserva and Gran Reserva red wines are sold under the Conde de Valdemar label, and are usually full of all the best flavours of Rioja, wild strawberry, plum and vanilla when young, developing into prune, cream and mint with age. Best years: (reds) 1996, '95, '94, '93, '92, '91, '90, '87, '86, '85.

MARTINEZ GASSIOT
PORTUGAL, Douro, Port DOC
🍷 *Tinta Roriz (Tempranillo), Tinta Barroca, Tinto Cão, Touriga Nacional, Touriga Francesa and others*
🍷 *Gouveio, Malvasia Fina, Rabigato, Viosinho and others*

The PORT shipper Martinez Gassiot often plays second fiddle to its larger sibling, COCK-BURN, and, as a result, its wines are somewhat unfairly overlooked. Martinez makes an elegant, pale 20-year-old tawny known as 'Directors' and in years like 1994, '87 and '85 the company's open, voluptuous middle-distance vintage ports compete with the best. Martinez also produces an excellent single-quinta vintage port from the Newman family's Quinta da Eira Velha which overlooks the town of Pinhão in the very heart of the DOURO Valley. Best years: (vintage ports) 1994, '87, '85, '67.

LOUIS M MARTINI
USA, California, Napa County, Napa Valley AVA
🍷 *Cabernet Sauvignon, Zinfandel, Pinot Noir, Barbera*
🍷 *Chardonnay, Gewurztraminer, Riesling, Sauvignon Blanc and others*

Since its founding in the 1930s this winery has reliably turned out reds of great early charm and remarkable staying power. For many years all were marked by distinctive Martini house aromas; in recent vintages the wines have developed more varietal character. Cabernets from Monte Rosso returned to form in the mid-1980s. Old Vine Zinfandel

At Mas Amiel, many of the wines are aged outside for a year in the traditional manner, in glass jars or bonbonnes which are exposed to all weathers to induce a measure of oxidation in the wines known as rancio.

from Monte Rosso followed in the '90s to win new friends. Pinot Noir's best showings have been 1997, '95, '94, '92, '91. The white wines have taken a marked turn for the better in recent vintages. Chardonnay from CARNEROS and RUSSIAN RIVER VALLEY grapes has been impressive for its subtle but indelible flavours and impeccably clean winemaking. Best years: 1997, '96, '95, '94.

Gewurztraminer, long a mainstay, dipped for a while, but has regained its old form as plantings in the Russian River have matured.

MARYLAND
USA

For a long while winemaking in the state of Maryland was almost a one-man operation, as the late Phillip Wagner, one of America's winemaking pioneers, spent years at his Boordy Vineyards exploring the possibilities of French-American hybrid varieties instead of native American *Vitis labrusca* grapes.

In the late 1970s others began attempting to grow the classic European grape varieties and then to make wine from them. Now there is a small but thriving wine industry towards the eastern tip of the state. Cabernet Sauvignon is the great hope, with Chardonnay and Riesling the main white varieties. Best producers: Basignani Winery, Byrd Vineyards, Catoctin Winery, Montbray Cellars, Woodhall Vineyards.

MAS AMIEL
FRANCE, Languedoc-Roussillon, Maury AC
🍷 *Grenache, Carignan*
🍷 *Muscat, Macabeo*

This 155-ha (387-acre) estate located to the west of Perpignan is the largest individual producer of the MAURY AC. The Vintage, produced from 100 per cent Grenache, is bottled soon after the harvest, without aging in oak casks, to guard a rich plum and cherry fruit character. The other cuvées – 6 Ans d'Age, 10 Ans d'Age and 15 Ans d'Age – are all aged for a year outside in glass jars exposed to both summer and winter conditions before being aged inside in large, old oak casks. This provides a complex panoply of nutty, coffee, chocolate and preserved fruit flavours. The wines are ready to drink when released.

DOMAINE DU MAS BLANC
FRANCE, Languedoc-Roussillon, Banyuls AC
🍷 *Grenache, Mourvèdre, Syrah, Counoise*
🍷 *Grenache Blanc, Muscat*

A local legend and ardent promoter of the wines of BANYULS, Doctor André Parcé died in 1998, leaving the management of this 21-ha (52-acre) family domaine in the more than capable hands of his son, Jean-Michel. The reputation of the domaine is based on a range of powerful, aromatic Banyuls but one shouldn't forget the four cuvées of dark, spicy COLLIOURE – Clos du Moulin, les Piloums,

Cosprons Levants and les Junquets – all made from varying blends of Syrah, Mourvèdre and Counoise. The Banyuls include a vintage or Rimage, Cuvée la Coume, Vieilles Vignes St-Martin and a Rimage Mise Tardive, bottled five years after vinification. The Banyuls Hors d'Age de Solera is produced using a sherry-like solera system. There is also an anecdotal amount of white Banyuls that tastes of citrus fruit and peaches. Best years: (Collioure) 1998, '97, '96, '95.

MAS BRUGUIÈRE

FRANCE, Languedoc-Roussillon, Coteaux du Languedoc–Pic St-Loup AC

♥ *Syrah, Grenache, Mourvèdre*

♀ *Roussanne*

One of the early pioneers of quality in the COTEAUX DU LANGUEDOC appellation, Guil-hem Bruguière continues to produce consistently firm, rich, spicy wines that are redolent of the local *garrigue* or scrub. The 9-ha (22-acre) domaine was replanted in the 1970s with Syrah, Grenache and Mourvèdre and in 1992 with a little white Roussanne. The Cuvée Calcadiz, (made from young vines) part-vinified by carbonic maceration, makes light and easy drinking. The Cuvée Classique is vinified in a traditional manner as is the Fût de Chêne, the top wine at the domaine, which has an addition of Mour-vèdre in the blend and is then aged for 11 months in oak barrels. The characterful and increasingly good white Coteaux du Langue-doc is soft, round and aromatic in style. Best years: (reds) 1997, '96, '95, '94.

MAS DE DAUMAS GASSAC

FRANCE, Languedoc-Roussillon, Vin de Pays de l'Hérault

♥ *Cabernet Sauvignon, Syrah, Merlot, Malbec and others*

♀ *Viognier, Chardonnay, Muscat and others*

Trail-blazing producer of world-class red and white in the HÉRAULT *département*,

MAS DE DAUMAS GASSAC
This inspirational property, north of Montpellier, makes tannic, yet rich Cabernet Sauvignon-based reds and fabulously scented whites along with rosé.

Aimé Guibert was the first to prove that great wine could be made in the unheralded vineyards of France's Midi (then associated with cheap wine), where by chance he dis-covered perfect vineyard soil on his isolated holiday property near Montpellier. With the help of BORDEAUX experts, he planted a vineyard based largely on Cabernet Sauvi-gnon, but also including Syrah, Pinot Noir, Merlot, Malbec, Chardonnay, Viog-nier, Petit Manseng, and the old Biblical variety, Neher Leschol. There are now 25ha (62 acres) of vines.

Professor Peynaud provided winemaking advice and 1978 saw the first deep, mouth-coating red of what has become known as 'the LAFITE of the Languedoc'. The style is robust now, but still impressive and exciting and the wines need several years of bottle age to give their best. His fabulously scented white is based on Viognier and is heavenly stuff, as good as most CONDRIEU from the northern RHÔNE. Best years: 1996, '95, '94, '93, '92, '91, '90, '88.

MAS JULLIEN

FRANCE, Languedoc-Roussillon, Coteaux du Languedoc AC

♥ *Grenache, Cinsaut, Syrah, Carignan, Mourvèdre*

♀ *Grenache Blanc, Chenin Blanc, Viognier, Clairette and others*

Olivier Jullien of Mas Jullien is one of the COTEAUX DU LANGUEDOC's youthful pio-neers. He was only 20 when in 1985 he created the domaine which now totals 17ha (42 acres). Working with traditional Midi grape varieties he makes some of the region's most exciting wines, but they are severely rationed. The reds include the sweet, spicy, approachable les États d'Ame and two more elegantly structured cuvées, les Depierre and les Cailloutis. The white les Vignes Oubliés is powerful and generous in style with the aroma of vanilla, honey and dried apricots. There is also a late-harvested Clairette Beudelle from 70-year-old vines. Best years: (reds) 1998, '97, '96, '95, '94.

MAS MARTINET

SPAIN, Cataluña, Priorat DO

♥ *Grenache Noir (Garnacha Tinta), Cabernet Sauvignon, Merlot, Syrah, Cariñena*

Josep-Lluís Pérez i Verdú has led an adven-turous life – there's a long trek between the young emigrant to Switzerland who worked as a barber and a taxi driver to pay for his studies to the highly trained enology profes-sor at Tarragona University that he is today.

With his family, he runs the most scientific-minded of the new PRIORAT estates. As the oldest member of the 'band' who revolution-ized the region in the late 1980s, he exerted considerable influence and lent an academic hand that was instrumental in the decision to complement traditional local grape varieties with French cultivars.

From his manicured vineyards, some rather controversially at the bottom of the val-ley instead of being on the precipitous slopes, he makes the steady and reliable Clos Martinet, plus an excellent second wine, Martinet Bru. He has also experimented with small-batch varietal reds. The family's new joint venture with singer Lluís Llach and the Porrera co-operative has already produced one smashing Garnacha-Cariñena blend, Cims de Porrera. Best years: 1996, '95, '94, '93, '91, '90.

GIUSEPPE MASCARELLO

ITALY, Piedmont, Barolo DOCG

♥ *Nebbiolo, Barbera, Dolcetto, Freisa*

Mauro Mascarello now runs this famous BAROLO estate. His riverside winery was viciously attacked by the floodwaters of 1994, but he still shows no sign of moving it up to his prime site, the superb 7-ha (17-acre) Monprivato vineyard in Castiglione Falletto. His wines have great intensity of perfume and wonderful balance despite a tendency to light colour – proof, he maintains, that they are not blended with any 'improving' grape varieties, although the wonderful primary aromas he gets in his Barolos, such a relief in a blind tast-ing after copious waftings of toasty oak, is proof enough. Monprivato is his principal Barolo and consistently one of the best in the region, but he produces good Barolo Villero and Barolo Bricco too, as well as excellent Nebbiolo d'Alba San Rocco. His dense, vibrant Dolcetto d'Alba and intense Barbera d'Alba can be phenomenal. Best years: (Mon-privato) 1996, '95, '93, '91, '90, '89, '88, '85, '82, '78, '74.

MASI

ITALY, Veneto, Valpolicella Classico DOC

♥ *Corvina, Rondinella, Molina and others*

This dynamic group run by the Boscaini fam-ily (growers here since the late eighteenth century) under the genial Sandro Boscaini, has been a leading innovator since the 1960s and this is now probably the best-known estate in VALPOLICELLA today. It was among the first to introduce single-vineyard or AMARONE with the Mazzano and Campo-longo di Torbè crus, and RECIOTO with the cru Mezzanella. During the 1960s, when the wizard of Valpolicella, Nino Franceschetti, was still with Masi, it was the first to re-establish the traditional *ripasso* fermentation method with its Campo Fiorin wine. In the 1980s Masi took the neighbouring estate of Serègo Alighieri, property of the heirs of Dante, under its wing, widening its range with Amarone Vajo Armaron and Recioto Casal dei Ronchi. Today, Masi controls production in some 160ha (395 acres) in the Verona area.

For decades Masi has been at the forefront of experiments with training systems, clones and forgotten varieties, and the upmarket oaky VINO DA TAVOLA Toar, a blend of Corvina and Rondinella together with the obscure Oseleta, Rossignola and Dindarella, is one result of this activity. Best years: (Mazzano) 1993, '90, '88, '86, '85, '83, '81, '79, '76, '74.

MASSANDRA

UKRAINE, Crimea
- Saperavi and others
- Muscat and others

The winery at Massandra, a hamlet on the CRIMEAN coast near Yalta, was built to supply the Russian Tsar's summer palace at Livadia. It survived the twentieth century rather better than the Romanovs, and today is the central winery for the coastal Crimean vineyards, taking wine from nine other wineries. It makes no wine itself, but instead matures and bottles numerous different styles. Indeed, most of the great dessert wines of the West have been imitated here and standards have often been very high. Recent table wines, including a Cabernet Sauvignon, are promising.

MASTROBERARDINO

ITALY, Campania, Aglianico DOC
- Aglianico, Piedirosso
- Fiano, Greco, Falanghina

For years Mastroberardino was held up as the leading producer not just of CAMPANIA but of all Italy's south, and it remains a potent force, even if it appears to be marking time somewhat while other producers have been catching up fast. It was traditionally a *négociant* house, buying grapes under contract year after year from the same growers, but it was canny enough to see that the growers would become producers in their turn, as indeed has happened, and some years ago Mastroberardino began buying its own vineyards. The most important one is Radici where, at altitudes of up to 700m (2300ft), it

grows the traditional Aglianico (red) and Fiano (white) grapes. TAURASI Radici DOCG, 100 per cent Aglianico, remains Mastroberardino's top red wine.

As for the white wines, Fiano Radici, Fiano Vignadora and Greco di Tufo Vignadangelo, one can't help thinking that today's versions lack the concentration and contour necessary to excel in this highly competitive and highly expensive world of wine. Perhaps the new Fiano More Maiorum, a white of real interest with, unusually for Italian whites until quite recently, a couple of years' aging before it reaches the market – will be the beginning of a new era. Best years: 1995, '90, '88.

MATANZAS CREEK WINERY

USA, California, Sonoma County, Sonoma Valley AVA
- Merlot
- Chardonnay, Sauvignon Blanc

One of SONOMA's most prestigious small wineries, Matanzas Creek made most of its reputation with boldly styled Chardonnay. Soon after the first vintage in 1977, the owners, Sandra and Bill MacIver, began toning the style down, but the wine still remains rich and solidly built. The Sauvignon Blancs are equally sturdy. For a time the Merlots were almost too dark and concentrated for their own good; only since 1984 has the style moderated enough to make the wines accessible early and graceful later, but they still pack a marvellously juicy-sweet punch. Best years: 1997, '96, '95, '94, '92, '91, '90, '88, '87, '86, '85. In some vintages, deluxe Merlot and Chardonnay, representing two to four barrels on average, are labelled Journey and have fetched shockingly high prices.

MATANZAS CREEK WINERY
The Merlot is a rich and elegant wine with a silky finish and loaded with plum and spicy oak.

MATAWHERO

NEW ZEALAND, North Island, Gisborne
- Cabernet Sauvignon, Merlot
- Gewurztraminer, Chardonnay, Chenin Blanc, Sauvignon Blanc

Matawhero wines can be great or pretty dreadful, conventional or decidedly unconventional. Denis Irwin believes in doing things naturally – though wildly might be a

better description. His use of wild, rather than cultured, yeasts, though by no means without parallel in New Zealand, is indicative of his desire to go his own untrammelled way in winemaking.

The aromatic Gewurztraminer is, and always has been, the best and most reliable wine, with an astonishing depth of velvety lychee flavour. Best years: 1998, '96, '94, '91, '89, '87, '86, '82, '78, '77.

MATUA VALLEY

NEW ZEALAND, North Island, Waimauku
- Cabernet Sauvignon, Merlot, Pinot Noir
- Chardonnay, Sauvignon Blanc, Chenin Blanc and others

Matua Valley deserves the credit for pioneering New Zealand's most spectacularly successful wine style, Sauvignon Blanc, which was fermented in an old puncheon, in a tin shed previously used for making 'sherry'. An innovative and adventurous approach to winemaking has seen the tin shed turn into a modern show-piece winery with row upon row of expensive new French barriques rather than a lonely old puncheon.

Matua's reputation has been based primarily on its reds, in particular the Cabernet Sauvignon from the Dartmoor-Smith vineyard, although the Ararimu Estate bottling can be even better – one of the best in New Zealand in a fine year like 1991. The Merlot should be equally good but rarely is. The Judd Estate Chardonnay can be superb, mixing deep, syrupy orange and apricot fruit with good spicy oak. The Sauvignon Blanc from MARLBOROUGH is one of the area's finest and snappiest under the Shingle Peak label. Best years: 1998, '96, '94, '91, '90, '89.

MAURO

SPAIN, Castilla-León, Vino de Mesa de Castilla-León
- Tempranillo (Tinot Fino), Grenache Noir (Garnacha Tinta), Syrah

Based a short distance downriver from the western boundary of the RIBERA DEL DUERO DO, Mauro is rightfully considered today as one of the 'Super-Spanish' estates outside DO regulations. Founder Mariano García, the erstwhile VEGA SICILIA winemaker, can now officially direct the operations at the small winery, which depends on its 30ha (74 acres) of vineyards around Tudela de Duero. The style of wine here is full, lush, warm, with an accessibility that is perhaps due to the use of a little old-vine Garnacha fruit in the blends.

Terreus, a single-vineyard cuvée from the estate's oldest vineyard, the 3-ha (7 ½-acre)

Pago de Cueva Baja, has added an extra dimension to the range. The extraordinary fruit from the 60-year-old vines is given Vega Sicilia-like depth and complexity by García's deft hand. Even the basic Mauro is a mouthful of rich, berryish, oak-tinged pleasure. Best years: 1997, '96, '95, '94, '91.

MAURY AC

FRANCE, Languedoc-Roussillon
🍷 *Grenache*
🍷 *Macabeo, Malvoisie*

This is a *vin doux naturel* or fortified wine produced essentially from Grenache. The AC covers approximately 1628ha (4023 acres) located on high schistous soils on the borders between the LANGUEDOC and Roussillon. Yields must not exceed 30 hectolitres per hectare, resulting in a powerful, sweet, tannic wine that is deeper coloured and more rustic in style than BANYULS, its cousin in the Roussillon. Styles also vary from the early bottled vintage, which places the emphasis on the fruit character, to the older *rancio* style where the wine has been aged for a number of years in glass demi-johns or *bonbonnes* and wooden casks, under conditions of controlled oxidation. Best producers: Cave de Maury, MAS AMIEL, Maurydoré.

MAXIMIN GRÜNHAUS

GERMANY, Mosel-Saar-Ruwer, Grünhaus
🍷 *Riesling*

Maximin Grünhaus is the name of the estate on the Ruwer, part of the MOSEL-SAAR-RUWER region, where Carl von Schubert makes some of Germany's greatest wines. This is the Ruwer estate with the best, and longest, reputation of all: the records date it back as far as 966. It was a Benedictine monastery at one time, and its three vineyards (all wholly owned) are still called Bruderberg, Herrenberg and Abtsberg (in ascending order of monastic importance and quality).

Over half the wines are *trocken* and the vineyards are almost entirely Riesling. Winemaking is traditional, and the wines have a

MAXIMIN GRÜNHAUS
From the best estate in the Ruwer Valley, the Riesling Spätlese from the Abtsberg site is intensely fruity, rich and elegant.

piercing intensity of flavour, steely in their fruit and stabbed through with keen Riesling acidity softened by perfume and honey. Best years: 1998, '97, '95, '94, '93, '92, '90, '89, '88, '85, '83, '81, '79, '76, '75, '71.

McCREA CELLARS

USA, Washington State, Columbia Valley AVA
🍷 *Syrah, Grenache*
🍷 *Chardonnay, Viognier*

Working with Chardonnay and RHÔNE varietals exclusively, Doug McCrea produces full-flavoured wines. His excellent buttery, apple-scented Chardonnay is one of the best in WASHINGTON STATE. The winery pioneered Syrah in Washington, taking it from relative obscurity to its current popularity. Aged in a blend of French and American oak, it is a most impressive red. A small amount of spicy Viognier is produced. Best years: 1998, '97, '94.

McCREA CELLARS
Made only in the best years, Washington State's top Syrah is the spiciest of its kind and aged in a blend of French and American new oak barrels.

McLAREN VALE

AUSTRALIA, South Australia, Fleurieu Zone

For a century McLaren Vale was known for massive reds, prescribed by British doctors of Queen Victoria's time for their restorative powers. The region emerged as a serious quality producer in the latter part of the 1970s and '80s, but it is for its black cherry, plum Shiraz and its faintly gamy, faintly spicy but ever fruity Grenache that McLaren Vale is most highly regarded. Indeed, in major Shiraz tastings and competitions in the late 1990s, McLaren Vale has emerged as the winner by large margins. Best years: 1997, '96, '94, '93, '91, '90, '88, '86, '85, '82, '80, '78, '75. Best producers: CHAPEL HILL, CHATEAU REYNELLA, Coriole, D'ARENBERG, Garrett, HARDY, Ingoldby, Geoff MERRILL, Norman's, SEAVIEW, WIRRA WIRRA, Woodstock.

McWILLIAM'S

AUSTRALIA, New South Wales, Big Rivers Zone, Riverina
🍷 *Syrah (Shiraz), Cabernet Sauvignon, Merlot*
🍷 *Semillon, Riesling, Chardonnay and others*

Like LINDEMANS, but perhaps to a greater degree, this is a company which has its operational heart in one place (in this case, the

RIVERINA) where it produces the bulk of its wines, but with increasingly important and strategic holdings in the HUNTER VALLEY (long held, and the provider of the ludicrously cheap Elizabeth Semillon released at five years of age, already glowing with hints of honey, butter and lightly browned toast), Coonawarra (where it owns Brand's but has bought and planted extensive additional vineyards) and Barwang, the pioneer of the HILLTOPS region in NEW SOUTH WALES, and which is poised to take McWilliam's into the US export market in a big way. And yes, it makes some marvellous fortified wines at its home base. Best years: (Hunter Semillon) 1997, '96, '95, '93, '91, '87, '86, '84, '82, '80, '79.

MÉDOC AC

FRANCE, Bordeaux
🍷 *Cabernet Sauvignon, Merlot, Cabernet Franc and others*

This appellation technically applies to the whole MÉDOC peninsula but is, in fact, only used for the villages in the northern half, starting north of the ST-ESTÈPHE AC at St-Seurin-de-Cadourne. The appellation should be called Bas-Médoc – reflecting the area's downstream position on the Gironde estuary. But *bas* means low in French – and the growers didn't want the connotation of 'low' quality, especially when their neighbours in the southern part of the peninsula could already use the more attractive title 'HAUT-MÉDOC'. The fact that the 'high' Médoc wines were superior to the 'low' ones was regarded by them as irrelevant.

The Médoc AC vineyards cover 4740ha (11,712 acres) and the AC applies only to red wines, which can be very attractive – dry but juicy, with a little grassy acidity to keep them refreshing. This easy-drinking style results from there being very little gravel in the Médoc AC, unlike in the Haut-Médoc to the south and here, in these flat, meadow-like, clay vineyards, the Merlot grape dominates instead of Cabernet Sauvignon.

Most Médoc wines are best to drink at three to five years old, but the brilliant Ch. POTENSAC takes ten years' aging with ease. About 33 per cent of production in the region is controlled by the co-operatives. Best years: 1998, '96, '95, '94, '90, '89, '88, '85, '83, '82. Best producers: la Cardonne, les Grands Chênes, Lacombe-Noaillac, Loudenne, les Ormes-Sorbet, Patache d'Aux, Plagnac, POTENSAC, Rolland de By, la Tour-de-By, la Tour-Haut-Cassan, la Tour-St-Bonnet, Vieux Ch. Landon, Vieux-Robin.

MÉDOC France, Bordeaux

Ch. Pichon-Longueville in Pauillac has seen a remarkable change of fortune since its purchase by AXA-Millésimes in 1987. The fairytale turreted château has been renovated and a state-of-the art winery built.

FROM A TOTAL VINEYARD AREA of about 15,000ha (37,000 acres) the Médoc produces a good fistful of the world's most renowned red wines – great wines like Ch. Margaux, Lafite-Rothschild, Mouton-Rothschild and Latour, whose names have resonated down through the ages. Or have they? Well, they haven't resonated for that long, because until the seventeenth century this narrow lip of land running north from the city of Bordeaux was just marshland. It was dangerous and inaccessible and although there are records of the odd wine like Lafite being made in the seventeenth century, it really wasn't until the middle of the eighteenth century that Médoc wines began to establish themselves. And for that we have to thank the Dutch engineers who arrived during the seventeenth century to drain these useless marshlands, and in doing so revealed the key to great wine in the Médoc – gravel. These deep, ancient banks of gravel are often only 10–15m (33–50ft) higher than the damp clay meadowlands in between, hardly enough to notice as you drive up the Médoc's tiny roads. But every single great wine of the Médoc is grown on gravel. Nothing beyond the merely decent can grow on the heavy clays that surround the great gravelly vineyard sites.

Between the villages of Macau in the south near Bordeaux and St-Seurin-de-Cadourne in the north there are great banks of gravel, providing warm ripening conditions and perfect drainage for the Cabernet Sauvignon grape which dominates the vineyards. This whole area is called the Haut-Médoc – the Upper Médoc – and all the best wines come from here, from one of the villages with the best gravel banks – Margaux, Listrac, Moulis, St-Julien, Pauillac and St-Estèphe – each with their own appellation. Vineyards not covered by the village appellations take the Haut-Médoc AC. There are also vineyards on the low-lying land or *palus* near the estuary, which produce generic red Bordeaux AC.

Further north the land becomes flatter, verdant with pasture and dotted with quiet villages. But the gravel's place has been taken by damp clay and hence there is a preponderance of Merlot in the vineyards. The wines become fruitier and simpler. This is the Bas-Médoc – the Low Médoc. But the appellation is plain Médoc – the growers understandably felt that 'low' sounded disparaging. So long as it's a warm vintage, this is good hunting ground for some of the few value-for-money wines of the region.

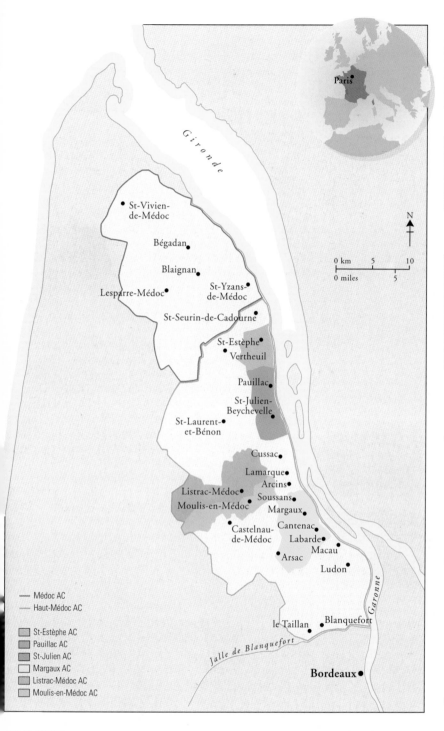

CH. LAFITE-ROTHSCHILD
Renowned for its elegant, restrained wine, this famous Premier Cru estate has seen great improvements in the last 20 years.

CH. LATOUR
Latour's great reputation is based on powerful, long-lasting classic wines. After 30 years in British hands, the property is now French-owned.

CH. LÉOVILLE-BARTON
Austere and restrained at first, this excellent traditional St-Julien wine unfolds into a purist's dream of blackcurrant and cedarwood. It has been outstanding in recent vintages.

CH. PICHON-LONGUEVILLE COMTESSE DE LALANDE
Brilliant, classic Pauillac, this is Bordeaux's leading 'Super-Second' wine.

CH. COS D'ESTOURNEL
The undoubted leader in St-Estèphe, Cos d'Estournel is renowned for its dark, tannic, oaky wines that are classically made for long aging.

CH. CHASSE-SPLEEN
The leading Cru Bourgeois estate built up a reputation in the 1980s for its tremendously consistent and marvellously ripe, concentrated wine.

CH. SOCIANDO-MALLET
A leading Haut-Médoc estate, Sociando-Mallet makes dark, tannic wines with classic red Bordeaux flavours emerging after 10–15 years.

AC ENTRIES
Haut-Médoc, Listrac-Médoc, Margaux, Médoc, Moulis, Pauillac, St-Estèphe, St-Julien.

CHÂTEAUX ENTRIES
Angludet, Batailley, Beychevelle, Brane-Cantenac, Calon-Ségur, Cantemerle, Chasse-Spleen, Cissac, Clarke, Cos d'Estournel, Ducru-Beaucaillou, Giscours, Grand-Puy-Lacoste, Gruaud-Larose, Haut-Bages-Libéral, Haut-Batailley, Haut-Marbuzet, d'Issan, Lafite-Rothschild, Lafon-Rochet, Lagrange, la Lagune, Larose-Trintaudon, Lascombes, Latour, Léoville-Barton, Léoville-Las-Cases, Léoville-Poyferré, Lynch-Bages, Margaux, Meyney, Montrose, Mouton-Rothschild, Palmer, de Pez, Pichon-Longueville, Pichon-Longueville Comtesse de Lalande, Pontet-Canet, Potensac, Poujeaux, Prieuré-Lichine, Rauzan-Ségla, St-Pierre, Sociando-Mallet, Talbot, du Tertre.

MEERLUST

SOUTH AFRICA, Western Cape, Stellenbosch WO
♟ *Cabernet Sauvignon, Merlot, Cabernet Franc, Pinot Noir*
♀ *Chardonnay*

Eight generations of the same family have run this farm, where vines have been grown for over 300 years. The current owner, Hannes Myburgh, has followed his father's fondness for BORDEAUX; the Cabernet Sauvignon-Merlot-Cabernet Franc blend, known as Rubicon, was one of the first such wines made in the Cape and is still one of the best.

Italian cellarmaster Giorgio Dalla Cia, now entering his third decade behind the press, is strictly European in his approach – none of the modern gushy fruit for him. The restraint of Meerlust's reds can thus seem confusing coming from such a warm climate and New World-orientated industry. Pinot Noir, benefiting from more new oak, has improved and the farm's first white, a full lemony-rich, toasty Chardonnay, immediately drew approving comments. Over the past few years, Dalla Cia has shown off his distilling skills with some fruity, potent grappas. Best years: (Rubicon) 1995, '94, '93, '92, '91; (Chardonnay) 1997, '96, '95.

ALPHONSE MELLOT

FRANCE, Central Loire, Sancerre AC
♟ *Pinot Noir*
♀ *Sauvignon Blanc*

The Mellots are an old winemaking family dating back to 1513. The eldest son is always called Alphonse which clearly makes baptism easy. The eighteenth-generation Alphonse is one of the most dynamic characters in the SANCERRE region. The Mellots are both growers and *négociants* but Alphonse would now prefer to concentrate on his own vineyards, in particular, his prized 50-ha (124-acre) la Moussière to the south-west of the town of Sancerre. The white unoaked Domaine de la Moussière is good value, often with exotic fruit, while the barrel-fermented Cuvée Edmond is the flagship wine. The 1997 was particularly fine with the rich, concentrated fruit gaining from the oak – a real revelation that a Sancerre could be this good.

Until recently Mellot's red Sancerre has not been treated as seriously as the white. This has changed with the arrival of the nineteenth Alphonse. The 1996 and '97 Generation XIX are impressively concentrated Pinots and certainly not typical of usually lightweight red Sancerres. These are Sancerres that will benefit from at least three years' aging. Alphonse

Mellot should not be confused with Joseph Mellot whose wines are, sadly, indifferent. Best years: (reds) 1997, '96, '95; (whites) 1998, '97, '96, '95, '90, '89.

CHARLES MELTON

AUSTRALIA, South Australia, Barossa Zone, Barossa Valley
♟ *Syrah (Shiraz), Grenache, Mourvèdre, Cabernet Sauvignon*
♀ *Grenache*

There's a bunch of young turks who have followed the lead of Peter Lehmann in reviving the BAROSSA VALLEY's reputation as a tip-top producer of super-ripe, sensually scented reds bubbling with personality and alcoholic power. Twinkly eyed Graham 'Charlie' Melton is among the pace-setters with a rich, spicy mix of locally grown Shiraz, Grenache and Mourvèdre called Nine Popes, a smashing juicy pink Rosé of Virginia as well as a fizzy fantasy of a plum-red sparkling Shiraz which sells out to a frantic public almost before it's been released. His opulently luscious Shiraz and Cabernet Sauvignon are made in the same style. Best years: (Nine Popes) 1995, '94, '93, '92, '91.

CHARLES MELTON
From this gifted winemaker, Nine Popes is quintessentially an Australian wine, yet based on France's Châteauneuf-du-Pape with ripe, plummy aromas and deep set fruit and flavour.

MENDOCINO COUNTY

USA, California

The most northerly wine county in CALIFORNIA, Mendocino is best known for its thick Redwood forests and scenic coastline. There are now 5800ha (14,000 acres) planted to vines and land is considerably cheaper here than in the long-established areas of NAPA VALLEY and SONOMA to the south. These vineyards are mostly inland in the Redwood Valley AVA, clustered around the towns of Ukiah and Talmage. This area is warm enough to do pretty well with Zinfandel, Cabernet Sauvignon and Chardonnay.

In the south near Hopland and the McDowell Valley AVA, Merlot is consistently successful. The coolest wine region is the

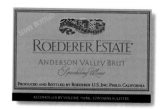

ROEDERER ESTATE
The Mendocino off-shoot of the French Champagne house Roederer is unique in California for using only grapes from its own vineyards.

ANDERSON VALLEY AVA which cries out for Gewurztraminer, Chardonnay and Pinot Noir and gets them. Delicious Gewurztraminers are already appearing, and sparkling wines from the ROEDERER ESTATE and Pacific Echo (formerly Scharffenberger) are taut, clean and refreshing, but with lovely yeast nuttiness.

MENDOZA

ARGENTINA

If you wanted to visit every winery in Mendoza and set yourself the challenging pace of say three bodegas a day, it would take you a year to complete your survey. There are 150,000ha (370,000 acres) of vineyards, with the spectacular backdrop of the massive Andes mountains and azure blue skies for company. Snow-melt waters irrigate a region that receives a risible rainfall of 1.78cm (0.7in) per year, mostly in hailstones. Temperatures in most of Mendoza are not as hot as most people seem to think: 30°C (88°F) in summer to 7°C (40°F) in winter and becoming slightly cooler as you approach the Andes.

The principal wine region, encompassing the DOs of Luján de Cuyo and Maipú, skirts around the capital city, Mendoza. Sometimes referred to as Primera Zona, this is the home land par excellence of Malbec. Unfortunately some of its best vineyards are under threat from ever-expanding urbanization. Further south there is a vast region known as San Rafael, also a DO and to the west, nestling close to the Andes, is the coolest and most promising region of all, Tupungato.

Mendoza can produce exceptional Chardonnays, deep and powerful Cabernet and the now renowned Malbec but also excellent lesser reds like Tempranillo, Barbera and Bonarda. Vintages don't really vary that much – rain-sodden 1998 is an exception – and individual wineries can get it right some years and really right in others. Best producers: La AGRÍCOLA, CATENA, Norton, TRAPICHE. Up-and-coming, good-value wineries include Balbi, Medrano and Resero.

MENETOU-SALON AC

FRANCE, Central Loire

♥ Pinot Noir

♀ Sauvignon Blanc

Menetou-Salon adjoins the larger and more famous appellation of SANCERRE. Indeed, at one point, vineyards to the south of the main road between Sancerre and Bourges are classified Sancerre AC, while those to the north are Menetou-Salon. During the 1990s Menetou-Salon has grown three-fold and there are now nearly 400ha (1000 acres) of vines, roughly in the proportion of 65 per cent white to 35 per cent red. The soil is mainly clay and limestone, with Morogues and the rather nondescript little town of Menetou-Salon as the two centres of production. During the 1990s standards have also risen as have prices (which are now on a level with much Sancerre, apart from the top cuvées) as Menetou-Salon has become very fashionable in France. And there's no better way to guarantee a price rise than that!

The whites are very dry, but soft Sauvignon wines, with a nice hint of gooseberry and blackcurrant leaves in the taste and a pleasant chalky-clean feel. So far they are not as good as the best Sancerre, but they are cheaper – and they often have a more attractive, focused fruit because, so far, they don't resort to overcropping as much as their neighbours in Sancerre. The reds quite often have a very attractive, lean but strawberry-perfumed style, and can be good and cherry-fresh. Whereas the white Menetou-Salon is a Sancerre country cousin, the reds and rosés can be better than many of Sancerre's offerings. Best years: 1998, '97, '96, '95. Best producers: (reds and whites) de Chatenoy, Jacolin, Pellé, Teiller; (whites only) Audiot, Chavet.

MÉO-CAMUZET

FRANCE, Burgundy, Côte de Nuits, Vosne-Romanée AC

♥ Pinot Noir

Until 1983 all the grapes grown at this impressive 12-ha (30-acre) estate were sold to *négociants*, but then Jean Méo, the owner, decided to make and sell his own wines. In practice, the domaine has been run for some years by his youthful son, Jean-Nicolas Méo. The renowned Henri Jayer was consultant to the domaine in the 1980s, and the wines are made in line with his non-interventionist views. There is a cold soak, complete destemming, no addition of cultivated yeasts and a prolonged aging of the wine in entirely new oak before bottling without filtration. Not surprisingly, the wines emerge as very rich, dense and long-lived. The major problem has been their high price. The estate's largest holdings are in CLOS DE VOUGEOT where it owns 3ha (7 acres); the other Grand Cru holdings are in RICHEBOURG and CORTON, and both can be immensely impressive wines. Better value, however, are the splendid Premiers Crus from VOSNE-ROMANÉE and NUITS-ST-GEORGES, which are made in the same sumptuous style. Best years: 1997, '96, '95, '93, '90, '89, '88, '87, '85.

DOMAINE MERCOURI

GREECE, Western Peloponnese, Korakohori

♥ Refosco, Mavrodaphne, Mourvèdre and others

♀ Roditis

This small, very high-quality estate based near Olympia was renovated in the late 1980s. The top wine is a fine red, from Refosco grapes originally brought from north-east Italy in the nineteenth century and blended with the great Greek variety, Mavrodaphne. There is also a light dry white, called Foloe, made from a red clone of the Roditis grape. Future wines include Mourvèdre. The reds can age for three to five years. Best years: (reds) 1997.

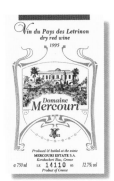

DOMAINE MERCOURI
1990 was the first vintage of the new era at this impressive estate. The Domaine Mercouri red is deep-coloured, powerful and marked by Refosco's typical acidity in the finish.

MERCUREY AC

FRANCE, Burgundy, Côte Chalonnaise

♥ Pinot Noir

♀ Chardonnay

This is easily the biggest and most important of the four main Côte Chalonnaise villages; 640ha (1580 acres) of vines produce more wine than the three other specific ACs, RULLY, GIVRY and MONTAGNY, combined.

Whereas much of the Côte Chalonnaise is in the hands of smallholders or independent proprietors, over half of Mercurey's vines are owned by merchant houses, so the wines are the most widely distributed of the region. Red wine production is over three million bottles a year. The flavour is usually a somewhat rustic imitation of the CÔTE DE BEAUNE just to the north, never very deep in colour, sometimes earthy but often with a quite attractive cherry and strawberry fruit which can take some aging. Best years: (reds) 1997, '96, '93, '90, '89, '88, '85. Best producers: Brintet, Chanzy, FAIVELEY, JADOT, Jeannin-Noltet, Juillot, Meix-Foulot, RODET, Saier, E de Suremain, Voarick.

The white wine of Mercurey has never had a very good press. It's always accused of being heavy, lifeless, cloddish, lardy – making it sound more like a pile of potato pancakes than a white Burgundy. There isn't a lot of the white, only 400,000 bottles a year, and the locals rather dismissively whisper that they only plant Chardonnay on ground unsuitable for Pinot Noir – but the wine can be as good as many far more expensive offerings from the more fashionable CÔTE D'OR to the north. It is quite full with a very attractive, buttery, nutty, even spicy taste. Drink at three to four years old – but no older. Best years: (whites) 1997, '96, '95, '92, '90, '89, '88. Best producers: Chartron & Trébuchet, FAIVELEY (Clos Rochette), Genot-Boulanger, Juillot, Olivier LEFLAIVE, Meix-Foulot, RODET (Chamirey), Suremain.

MERIDIAN VINEYARDS

USA, California, San Luis Obispo, Paso Robles AVA

♥ Cabernet Sauvignon, Merlot, Pinot Noir, Syrah,

♀ Chardonnay, Sauvignon Blanc

Established in the early 1970s as Estrella River Winery, Meridian traces its success back to the day in 1984 when it came under the direction of winemaker Chuck Ortman. After righting the property, Ortman sold it to BERINGER estate which invested in vineyards while allowing him to focus on winemaking.

Known for a deft hand with Chardonnay, Ortman proved equally adept at coaxing flavour and balance from Meridian's SANTA BARBARA Chardonnay and its Reserve Chardonnay, Edna Valley which has greater richness and complexity. Made in a delicate, refined style, the Pinot Noir is often charming and the Reserve, when offered, displays more intensity and power, while retaining lots of charm. After redeveloping its 200-ha (500-acre) PASO ROBLES vineyard in the 1990s, Meridian has improved the overall quality of the competently made Sauvignon Blanc and has expanded production of Syrah, a deep-flavoured wine that promises to do well in the future. Best years: 1998, '97, '96, '95, '94.

MERLOT

Merlot is still somewhat in the shadow of Cabernet Sauvignon, even though its plantings in Bordeaux these days outpace those of Cabernet Sauvignon. This never used to be the case. Merlot was always present in Bordeaux, but its fleshy, perfumed style never got as much acclaim as the elegant austerity of Cabernet Sauvignon. Then tastes began to change: suddenly the ability, nay the necessity, to age a wine for a decade or more before drinking it was far less important than the ability to take a wine off the shop shelf and drink it that night. And that's when the amount of Merlot in the vineyards of Bordeaux began to outstrip Cabernet Sauvignon. Producers also realized that Merlot was better adapted than Cabernet to heavy, clay soils.

Merlot will age, of course. Look at Ch. Pétrus: one of the most expensive reds in the world, made from Merlot with a handful of Cabernet Franc and which has no difficulty in lasting for 20–30 years. And Pomerols generally, now in huge demand worldwide, do not exactly fall apart in your glass – in fact, they age more gracefully than many Médocs. Merlot planted in the clay-limestone soils of St-Émilion also produces wines of great 'ageability'. But Merlot does make a rounder, softer wine, which is one reason why it has always been useful in softening the hard edges of Cabernet in the Bordeaux blend.

It is used in precisely the same way in the New World, where the craze for varietal Cabernet Sauvignon is still going strong. However, alongside it is a growing realization that Cabernet Sauvignon can be too tannic from a warm climate like California and not ripe enough from somewhere cool like New Zealand. So Bordeaux-type blends are popping up all over. But equally important are the single-varietal Merlots that are the current rage. In the USA Napa and Sonoma both make good examples. Washington State is also producing rich, well-structured Merlot as are a handful of producers north of the border in British Columbia's Okanagan Valley. Further south Chile has produced some stunning deep, plummy Merlots during the 1990s. Some of New Zealand's most delicious reds are from Merlot. Merlot was welcomed with open arms by South African winemakers in the early 1980s when vines became more readily available. But only now are the best (cooler) areas being identified. The wine has made its mark both as a varietal and in blends, mainly with Cabernet Sauvignon but Pinotage and Syrah (Shiraz) have also proved interesting partners. It's never made much impact in Australia, primarily because its juicy softness isn't needed there.

In Europe, north-east Italy has a long tradition of using Merlot for its 'jug' wine, but when yields are kept down, Merlot can be just as full of blackberry and plum and fruit-cake juiciness in Italy as it is elsewhere. It makes some of Friuli's most attractive reds, and produces reasonable quality in Alto Adige and Trentino, and over the border in Switzerland's Ticino. Further south, Tuscan growers like Ornellaia (Masseto), Frescobaldi (Lamaione), Tua Rita (Redigaffi) and Castello di Ama (Vigna l'Apparita) are making world-class Merlot.

Merlot also floods out of eastern Europe: Bulgarian, Hungarian and Greek Merlot can be attractive, and there's no reason to believe these juicy reds won't go on providing easy-drinking, quality wines.

GEOFF MERRILL

AUSTRALIA, South Australia, Fleurieu Zone, McLaren Vale
♟ Cabernet Sauvignon
♟ Grenache
♀ Semillon, Chardonnay, Sauvignon Blanc

Merrill is one of the characters of Australian wine; if he weren't a winemaker he would surely be on the comedy stage. Fortunately, his winemaking, though clearly 'showbiz' in feel, embraces the classics as well as 'end-of-pier' stuff. His Chardonnay is heavily oaked and slow maturing but worth the wait. It is lean when young and nutty and rich when mature. He also does a flowery, passion fruit and gooseberry Sauvignon Blanc to buy and gulp down with maximum speed. The Cabernet Sauvignon reflects Merrill's penchant for early picking, being zesty and crisp, with tart redcurrant flavours and low tannin but it ages to a delicious blackcurrant maturity. The Mount Hurtle Grenache, all tingling cherry and strawberry, reflects the winemaker's enthusiasm for pleasure in the bottle first and foremost. And he's made wine in Italy, under the La Veritière label. Best years: 1997, '96, '95, '94, '93, '91, '90, '88, '86, '85.

LOUIS MÉTAIREAU

FRANCE, Loire, Pays Nantais, Muscadet de Sèvre-et-Maine AC
♀ Muscadet

In an appellation which has often been careless of its reputation, Louis Métaireau has long stood out as someone special. For many years he has campaigned for real sur lie bottling, the wines being bottled where they were made rather than being transported elsewhere and then bottled, so losing the residual carbon dioxide which is an essential characteristic of sur lie. There may be other MUSCADETs as good as these but there are few better. Métaireau is actually the figurehead and organizational genius of a group of vignerons, who cultivate their own vines and make their own wine, all sold under the Métaireau name.

All of the wines are tasted blind on several occasions before they are bottled. The mark the wine receives determines under which cuvée it is sold. The top cuvée is called Number 1, followed by Cuvée LM. Grand Mouton comes from a 27-ha (67-acre) vineyard owned jointly by the group. There is also a Petit Mouton and two VIN DE PAYS Melon de Bourgogne. Forget your prejudices about Muscadet, the wines of Métaireau have elegance and finesse. Best years: 1998, '97, '96, '95, '93, '90, '89.

MEURSAULT AC

FRANCE, Burgundy, Côte de Beaune
♟ Pinot Noir
♀ Chardonnay

The wine is pale gold, glinting in the cool, bright sunlight. The powerful scent catches the aroma of spring blossoms in the courtyard and mingles tantalizingly with the sweet perfume of fresh-hewn oak casks. It is Meursault from the latest vintage, still raw and bony, but already promising the smooth-sided succulence which will make the wine cling to the memory for years to come.

Here's another wine, straw-gold but cut with green. The smell is buttery, peachy too, cream coating the fruit, with honey and hazelnuts hiding behind the richness, and the distant breakfast smells of coffee and buttered oast. Another Meursault, now perhaps two years old, already so lovely, yet still only hinting at what's to come. And one more wine weaves its magic. Deep golden, almost savoury – the rich smoke of toast and roasted almonds and a flash of cinnamon spice, the cream and melted butter of its youth now gone golden, halfway to brown – less luscious but deeper, richer. A conversation, a dream, an ideal, all in itself; Meursault-Charmes, or Meursault-Perrières maybe, the 1992 perhaps, or even the '89. White wine perfection.

Ah, if it were all like this – but Burgundy being Burgundy, for every grower striving to excel there's another with his eye on the cash register, because Meursault, at 417ha (1030 acres) is the biggest white wine village in the CÔTE D'OR, is also the most popular. The general standard of the wine is rather variable, though this is more the fault of advantage-taking producers than of inferior land. There are no Grands Crus in Meursault, but a whole cluster of Premiers Crus. The tiny hamlet of BLAGNY on the slopes south of Meursault is allowed to sell its lean but classy whites as Meursault-Blagny. Altogether, Meursault produces perhaps two million bottles of wine a year that is lovely to drink young, but better aged for five to eight years. Best years: (whites) 1996, '95, '92, '90, '89. Best producers: Ampeau, Boisson-Vadot, Bouzereau, COCHE-DURY, DROUHIN, Grivault, JADOT, Javillier, F Jobard, LAFON, LEROY, Matrot, Michelot-Buisson, Pierre Morey, Potinet-Ampeau, Prieur, Roulot.

There is a little red wine, mainly from vines grown on the VOLNAY side of the village and if it comes from the Premier Cru Les Santenots it can be sold as Volnay-Santenots. Red wine is also produced at the southern end of the village, especially around Blagny where it is good, but a little hard, and is sold under as Blagny. Best years: (reds) 1997, '96, '95, '93, '90, '89, '88, '85. Best producers: Ampeau, LAFON, Matrot.

CH. MEYNEY
FRANCE, Bordeaux, Haut-Médoc, St-Estèphe AC,
Cru Bourgeois
♥ *Cabernet Sauvignon, Merlot, Petit Verdot, Cabernet Franc*

This is one of those châteaux that has quietly but determinedly been making wines of a regular consistency and quality for a number of years. Meyney's vineyard is good – 52ha (128 acres) with 58 per cent Cabernet Sauvignon, 25 per cent Merlot, 10 per cent Petit Verdot and 7 per cent Cabernet Franc, on the same riverside plateau as the Second Growth

Ch. MONTROSE. But what has made this wine so reliably fine is the effort made by Domaines Cordier, the owners; maximizing the quality and ripeness of the fruit, and ruthlessly selecting only the best vats. The result is big, broad-flavoured wine, generally a little short on nuance but with lovely dark plummy fruit that successfully evolves over 10–15 years. Second wine: Prieur de Meyney. Best years: 1998, '96, '95, '94, '90, '89, '88, '87, '86, '85, '84, '83, '82, '81, '78, '75.

PETER MICHAEL WINERY
USA, California, Sonoma County, Knights Valley AVA
♥ *Cabernet Sauvignon, Cabernet Franc, Merlot*
♀ *Chardonnay, Sauvignon Blanc*

British-born Peter Michael expanded his country vacation home into a small vineyard and hired Helen Turley now of MARCASSIN to design his small winery and oversee his early vintages. The launch was made easy by spectacular Chardonnays which were soon joined by an estate-grown red Meritage, Les Pavots. The winery has enjoyed smooth sailing after Turley departed, and has added an intense, blockbuster Chardonnay named Mon Plaisir and an equally sensational Sauvignon Blanc. Made in tiny quantities, Cuvée Indigne and Pinot Rouge are exquisite Chardonnays securing this winery's reputation for uncompromising quality. Best years: (Chardonnay) 1998, '97, '96, '95, '94, '92; (reds) 1997, '95, '94, '92, '90.

LOUIS MICHEL & FILS
FRANCE, Burgundy, Chablis AC
♀ *Chardonnay*

The CHABLIS growers are divided between those who believe the steely character of authentic Chablis is best expressed through wines that have never been near an oak barrel, and those who argue that some aging in oak, even a proportion of new oak, can lend complexity to the wine. Louis Michel is widely regarded as the finest of the producers following the no oak approach.

The estate is fairly substantial and of its 20ha (49 acres), 2ha (5 acres) are Grand Cru (Grenouilles, Vaudésir and Les Clos) and 13ha (32 acres) are Premier Cru (Montmains being the largest holding). The wines, which age beautifully, are wonderful examples of the complexity that can be achieved without oak. Rather than imposing flavours on the wine, the Michel approach allows the specific mineral complexity of each vineyard to express itself to the full. Best years: 1997, '96, '95, '94, '93, '92, '90, '89, '88, '85, '78.

MILDARA
Though based at Mildara on the Murray River, the best Mildara wines are from vast Coonawarra vineyards.

MILDARA
AUSTRALIA, Victoria, North West Victoria Zone,
Murray Darling
♥ *Cabernet Sauvignon, Syrah (Shiraz), Merlot*
♀ *Riesling, Chardonnay, Sauvignon Blanc*

Ray King of Mildara was for long the hunter (hence the Mildara Blass group which now includes Andrew Garrett, Augustine, BAILEYS, Wolf BLASS, Dorrien Estate, Ingoldby, KRONDORF, Maglieri, Mount Helen, Mount Ida, Quelltaler, ROTHBURY ESTATE, Saltram, St Huberts, YARRA RIDGE and YELLOWGLEN) but in 1996 became the prey of brewing giant Fosters. The Mildara group is the third largest wine group in Australia behind Southcorp and BRL HARDY, but doubtless could become the biggest if Fosters really put its mind to the task.

Wine of every hue, style and price is made somewhere in the group somewhere or other in Australia, none of it bad, and a lot of it good to very good. Best years are largely meaningless because of the spread. Every year some of the labels will produce excellent wines but, correspondingly some will disappoint. Based on the Murray River, Mildara's best wines are from large COONAWARRA vineyards, including the hugely popular and fairly priced Jamieson's Run and Saltram in the BAROSSA.

MILLBROOK VINEYARDS
USA, New York State, Hudson River AVA
♥ *Cabernet Franc, Cabernet Sauvignon*

Millbrook Vineyards makes fine, delicate Cabernet Franc and good Cabernet Sauvignon from its 20-ha (50-acre) vineyard in the Hudson River AVA in north-east NEW YORK STATE. Part-owner John Dyson also owns vineyards in California, purchasing WILLIAMS SELYEM in 1998. Best years: 1997, '95, '94.

MINERVOIS AC
FRANCE, Languedoc-Roussillon
♥♀ *Carignan, Grenache, Cinsaut and others*

Minervois hasn't quite got the wild 'mountain-man' reputation of CORBIÈRES. This is partly because – until recently – the wines have been relatively light, spicy, dusty and deliciously fruity but not in any way challenging, and partly because with Corbières we all dash off into those untamed sub-Pyrenean hills and are soon lost in a timeless twilight world, but with Minervois we generally stay in the AUDE valley to the north-east of Carcassonne rooting round the co-operatives and estates within easy reach of civilization.

In fact, the high, wind-swept, herb-strewn plateau of the Minervois is exciting, and offers a potential that is beginning to be exploited. But Minervois' great strength is in the admittedly boring concept of 'organization'. Big companies like Nicolas and Chantovent have worked hard with local co-operatives to produce good-quality, juicy, quaffing wine at reasonable prices, and you can now find numerous sturdy, rough-fruited reds and juicy rosés under merchant labels that come from the revitalized co-operatives. The best wines are made by the estates: full of ripe, red fruit and pine-dust perfume for drinking young.

Minervois, like the rest of the LANGUEDOC, is evolving towards wines of greater quality. From 1999, Carignan can represent only 40 per cent of the blend. A number of small domaines are now producing richer, more complex wines from blends of Syrah, Grenache and Mourvèdre aged in oak barrels and there has generally been greater investment in the region.

Individuality within the AC has also been proclaimed with the raising of the village of La Livinière and several surrounding communes to cru status in 1998. There are 5130ha (12,676 acres) of the Minervois AC producing up to 30 million bottles a year, almost all of it red. It is best drunk young, but can age, especially if a little new oak has been used. Best producers: CLOS CENTEILLES, Clos l'Escandil, Coupe Roses, Fabas, de Gourgazaud, La Grave, Meyzonnier, Nicolas, Oupia, Piccinini, Ste-Eulalie, la Tour Boisée, Vassière, Villerambert-Julien, Violet. Best years: 1998, '96, '95, '94.

MISSION HILL
CANADA, British Columbia, Okanagan Valley VQA
♥ *Cabernet Sauvignon, Pinot Noir*
♀ *Chardonnay, Pinot Gris*

The beginnings of Mission Hill date back to 1981, when the owner, Anthony von Mandl established the first family-owned, commercial winery in the OKANAGAN VALLEY. After years of steady growth, things changed in

1992 with the arrival of winemaker, John Simes. The former Kiwi vintner and cool-climate specialist has developed a series of intense, highly flavoured varietals that have propelled Mission Hill into the upper echelon of Canada's wineries.

Best bets include a citrus-flavoured Chardonnay, a fine Merlot-Cabernet blend and more recently, Pinot Gris. The future of Mission Hill lies in a spectacular new 89-ha (220-acre) vineyard planted to Cabernet Sauvignon, Merlot, Shiraz and Viognier at the southern end of the valley, just north of the US border. Best years: 1998, '97, '95, '94.

MISSION HILL
The 1992 Grand Reserve Barrel Select Chardonnay, with its overpowering mix of heady, tropical fruit, made this winery well known overnight

CH. LA MISSION-HAUT-BRION
FRANCE, Bordeaux, Pessac-Léognan AC, Cru Classé de Graves
♥ *Cabernet Sauvignon, Merlot, Cabernet Franc*

This is one of those BORDEAUX properties which, by a show of hands and shouts of 'aye', could be promoted to First Growth one day. The wines are powerful – almost bullying and hectoring by nature – but, unlike those of its neighbour Ch. HAUT-BRION, never charming, and rarely with that lovely, ruminative flavour-memory which other blockbusters like Ch. LATOUR and PÉTRUS always have.

The strength of these wines lies in a dark-plums-and-chocolate fruit braided with an earthy dryness which rarely opens out before ten years and often needs 20 or more to achieve its memorable tangle of tobacco, cedar and herb garden perfumes. Since 1983 it has been under the same ownership and management as Ch. Haut-Brion but the two estates have kept their own identities. Surrounded by the Bordeaux suburbs, La Mission covers 21ha (52 acres) of vines which are sliced through by the Bordeaux-Arcachon main railway line. Second wine: La Chapelle de la Mission -Haut-Brion. Best years: 1998, '97, '96, '95, '94, '93, '90, '89, '88, '85, '83, '82, '81, '79, '78, '75.

MITCHELTON
AUSTRALIA, Victoria, Central Victoria Zone, Goulburn Valley
♥ *Cabernet Sauvignon, Merlot, Syrah (Shiraz)*
♀ *Riesling, Marsanne, Chardonnay, Semillon*

Now part of PETALUMA, Mitchelton is the largest producer in the GOULBURN region and one which combines a high-quality range and tasty bargain-priced selection with reasonable success. Marsanne is perhaps Mitchelton's best-known wine, but Riesling, Semillon and Chardonnay are all beautifully crafted. Reds are best in the juicy easy-drinking style, and the best examples use fruit from several different areas. Best years: 1997, '96, '94, '93, '92, '91, '90, '86.

MITTELRHEIN
GERMANY

The Mittelrhein region runs along the Rhine south of Bonn; the AHR and the MOSEL rivers flow into it, and the NAHE and the RHEINGAU regions bring it up short in the south. Tourists love the Mittelrhein, sailors hated it (the Rhine Gorge was home to the sirens of the Lorelei and – who knows? – may still be) and winemakers seem increasingly dissatisfied with life here: the area under vine has been declining since the 1960s and now stands at around 620ha (1532 acres). One reason is that the area has always been overshadowed by its more famous neighbours, the Mosel and Rheingau. The vineyards are 75 per cent Riesling, and the wines are steely and fresh; ripe and good in warm vintages, distinctly lean in cool ones, but here the demands of the Sekt industry come to the rescue. J WEGELER's good Lila brand is drawn largely from the Mittelrhein.

The vineyards, on slaty soil, are poised on the steep slopes near the Rhine and its tributaries, mostly on the east bank in the north of the region and mostly on the west bank in the south. In the past the vineyards were terraced and highly picturesque, but these days the success of Flurbereinigung (the restructuring of vineyards into more workable units), has meant that the Mittelrhein has become more a region of sloping vineyards than it used to be. They are easier to work that way, but the change does not seem sufficient to keep the growers at work. The potential for quality is high, but there are few outstanding producers. BACHARACH is the wine centre; the castles that dot the region were built not to make wine but to extract tolls from luckless travellers. Best producers: Toni JOST, Lanius-Knab, Heinrich Müller, August Perrl, Weingart.

Moët et Chandon is the giant of the Champagne region. There are over 28km (17 miles) of cellars in Épernay to house its stocks of more than 100 million bottles. Underground cellars such as these are ideal for Champagne's second fermentation in the bottle which should be as cool, as slow and as long as possible.

MOËT ET CHANDON

FRANCE, Champagne, Champagne AC

♀ ♟ *Pinot Noir, Chardonnay, Pinot Meunier*

If there is one company that rules our perception of CHAMPAGNE as a drink, it has to be Moët et Chandon, with its enormous production of more than 28 million bottles a year, and its domination of the Champagne market. People seem to be shooting the corks out of gigantic bottles of Moët at every first night, every film award, every Grand Prix victory or glossy showbiz wedding – in fact anywhere there is likely to be a photographer who is likely to get a picture of the event – and a bottle of Moët – into the newspapers. The result is that Moët is the most famous Champagne in the world yet you hardly ever see an advertisement for it – you just see lots of famous people spraying each other with it.

With all this notoriety comes inconsistency – which is a great pity, because when you get a good bottle of Moët non-vintage it is soft, creamy, a little spicy – and absolutely delightful. The vintage wine is more consistent, and usually has a good strong style to it, though Moët is one of those houses which are apt to release a vintage rather too frequently, when some might suggest the quality of the harvest left a bit to be desired. Dom Pérignon is their de luxe cuvée, famous throughout the night spots of the world. It can be one of the

greatest and most refined of Champagnes, but it must be given several years' aging, even after release. Moët Rosé is one of the few rosé Champagnes that actually tastes pink. Best years: 1992, '90, '88, '86, '85, '83, '82.

MOLISE

ITALY

A small, sparsely populated region south of ABRUZZO and north of PUGLIA on the Adriatic coast, Molise prides itself on its hard wheat, for quality pasta and long-lived bread, olive oil, honey and any number of other agricultural crops. Until the mid-1980s only one thing was missing: it suffered the ignominy of being the only region in Italy without a single DOC. Then two were awarded at once: Biferno and Pentro. Not that this seems to have inspired many producers to create elevated wines, even though the potential is there. Di Majo Norante is the longest-standing exception; Borgo di Colloredo is a recent challenger.

MONBAZILLAC AC

FRANCE, South-West

♀ *Sémillon, Sauvignon Blanc, Muscadelle*

The leading sweet wine of the BERGERAC region, and the only one which is sometimes made in the style of SAUTERNES, rather than mildly sweet in a light and unmemorable way. A lot of Monbazillac is just that – light,

vaguely sweet and entirely forgettable – largely because the botrytis or noble rot fungus, needed on the overripe grapes to concentrate sweetness, doesn't always appear here, or the growers won't take the risk of selective late harvesting to obtain grapes with noble rot. Those that do, like the owners of the sublime Ch. Tirecul-la-Gravière, produce rich, exotic wines that will happily develop over ten years or more. The price of these wines is, needless to say, higher.

A growing number of properties now make traditional rich Monbazillac but most of the eight million bottles produced each year come from the competent but unadventurous co-operative (Ch. de Monbazillac). At its best Monbazillac is full and honeyed, with a sweetness of peaches and barley sugar. Lighter versions are likely to be very pale and resemble pleasantly drinkable sweet apples with just a touch of honey. The vineyards, south of Bergerac town, run up a north-facing slope to the impressive Ch. de Monbazillac (the wine's not as exciting as the architecture). In general drink young, but a real late-harvested example can happily last 10 years. Best years: 1998, '97, '96, '95, '90, '89, '88, '86, '85, '83. Best producers: la Borderie, Bélingard Blanche de Bosredon, Grand Maison, Grand Marsalet, Hébras, Ch. de Monbazillac, Tirecul-la-Gravière, Treuil-de-Nailhac.

ROBERT MONDAVI WINERY

USA, California, Napa County, Napa Valley AVA

♥ *Cabernet Sauvignon, Pinot Noir, Merlot, Zinfandel*

♀ *Chardonnay, Sauvignon Blanc, Riesling and others*

Robert Mondavi has made his name one of the most instantly recognizable in the world of wine and has to be counted as the man who revolutionized Californian wine in the 1960s and '70s. The winery, now run by his sons Michael and Tim, makes both regular and reserve bottlings of the principal grapes, the former being lighter than the assertively rich, well-wooded reserves.

The regular Cabernet Sauvignon is pleasant, blackcurranty and easy to drink young or if aged. The Reserve is dark, rich and structured for aging. Best years: 1996, '95, '94, '93, '92, '91, '90, '88, '87, '86. Pinot Noir has emerged relatively recently, largely because of a shift in grape sources to CARNEROS and because of changes in the winemaking. Best years: 1997, '96, '95, '94, '92, '91. Mondavi coined the name Fumé Blanc to revive interest in Sauvignon Blanc, and the wine has a pleasant but unmemorable crisp Sauvignon flavour. Best years: 1998, '97, '96. Chardonnay is less successful, though the Reserve can be exciting. Best years: 1997, '96, '95, '92, '91. Mondavi offers non-Napa varietals under the Robert Mondavi-Woodbridge label and is co-owner of OPUS ONE in the Napa Valley.

Mondavi also owns Byron Winery, Vichon Mediterranean, La Famiglia di Robert Mondavi in Oakville, and has built a large production facility in MONTEREY. The company also has joint winemaking ventures with FRESCOBALDI of Italy and ERRÁZURIZ of Chile.

DOMAINE MONT D'OR

SWITZERLAND, Valais, Sion

♥ *Pinot Noir, Gamay, Syrah, Humagne Rouge, Cornalin*

♀ *Sylvaner (Johannisberger), Pinot Gris (Malvoisie), Petite Arvine, Marsanne (Ermitage)*

The 20ha (49 acres) of steep terraced vineyards have been planted for centuries, but the estate has existed in its present form for only 150 years. Its speciality is late-harvested, or Flétri, wines from the Johannisberger or Sylvaner grape which have an elegance rarely shown by the variety elsewhere. The late-harvest wines from Malvoisie, Petite Arvine and Ermitage can also be very impressive in a style reminiscent of ALSACE Vendange Tardive. Chasselas and Riesling are the main grapes for dry whites though neither scales these heights. The reds are interesting, but as good as the whites. Best years: 1997, '95, '93, '90.

MONTAGNY AC

FRANCE, Burgundy, Côte Chalonnaise

♀ *Chardonnay*

Montagny is a large white-only AC at the southern end of the Côte Chalonnaise. Until recently the wines were dull and listless – dry and rather lean. But then Montagny discovered the new barrel. Just a few months' aging in a new, or relatively new, oak barrel adds the nuttiness and soft spice which have been conspicuously lacking up until now, and Burgundy has found itself a new and much-needed, high-quality, fair-price appellation.

If you see a wine labelled Montagny Premier Cru don't be fooled into thinking it comes from a superior vineyard site. Somehow the Montagny growers wangled it that any white wine which reaches 11.5 degrees of alcohol – half a degree more than usual – can call itself Premier Cru. Recently a more usual definition of Premier Cru was adopted, but as no fewer than 53 sites have been given this status, the words on the label remain fairly meaningless. Best years: 1997, '96, '95, '92, '90, '89. Best producers: BUXY co-operative, Davenay, Louis LATOUR, Olivier LEFLAIVE, B Michel, Steinmaier, Alain Roy, Vachet.

MONTANA WINES

NEW ZEALAND, North Island, Auckland

♥ *Cabernet Sauvignon, Merlot, Pinot Noir*

♀ *Gewurztraminer, Riesling, Sauvignon Blanc, Chardonnay*

Montana produces nearly half of New Zealand's total wine output, under a range of 150 labels or so, and its philosophy has always been to make New Zealand's best wines at every price level. It has sustained an impressive export growth and is clearly New Zealand's largest wine exporter. Grape quality is ensured through owning a high level of their own vineyards. Over 1000ha (2471 acres) of vineyards in HAWKE'S BAY, GISBORNE and MARLBOROUGH are owned and managed by Montana – more than twice the holdings of any other winery. As further consolidation Montana expects to invest NZ$15 million per year for the next five years in vineyards, winery facilities and maturing stocks.

The company's desire to make top-quality, CHAMPAGNE-method sparkling wine saw Montana enter into an arrangement with Champagne DEUTZ IN 1987 to produce the mellow, complex Deutz Marlborough Cuvée, the elegant age-worthy Deutz Blanc de Blancs and the recently released, full-flavoured Deutz Pinot Noir Cuvée. These are some of the New World's most consistent bubblies

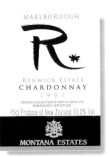

MONTANA WINES
The Renwick Estate Chardonnay, using Marlborough grapes, has fine, spicy oak with good fruit flavour and depth.

and are Champage in all but name. They show how brilliantly suited New Zealand is to sparkling wine production.

After a slow start Montana has become a producer of very serious single-estate Chardonnay from each of the country's three major regions; Marlborough, Hawke's Bay and Gisborne. They were the first to plant grapes in Marlborough and the first to produce Sauvignon Blanc on a grand scale. Marlborough Sauvignon Blanc is a remarkably reliable wine with aggressive gooseberry and herbaceous flavours.

In order to increase their red winemaking capability Montana has a joint venture with the French wine company Cordier, to refine red wine quality at their flagship McDonald Winery in Hawke's Bay. After persevering for too long with Cabernet Sauvignon in Marlborough and riding a roller-coaster between barely ripe and under-ripe reds Montana has now replaced many of their Marlborough Cabernet Sauvignon vines and has expanded their red grape vineyards in the more reliable Hawke's Bay region. Best years: Marlborough: (reds) 1998, '96, '94, '91; (whites) 1999, '97, '96, '94, '91. Hawke's Bay: (reds) 1998, '96, '95, '94, '91; (whites) 1999, '98, '96, '95, '94, '91.

MONTECARLO DOC

ITALY, Tuscany

♥ *Sangiovese and others*

♀ *Trebbiano Toscano, Sémillon, Pinot Gris (Pinot Grigio), Pinot Blanc (Pinot Bianco), Vermentino, Sauvignon Blanc and Roussanne*

This wine comes from a small, hilly area in northern Tuscany near the town of Lucca. Whites vary between the nutty and appley and depressingly neutral. Considering the variety of grapes they're allowed one would think the producers ought to do better. Reds are reminiscent of lightish, dusty CHIANTI. Drink the whites young, the reds from current vintages. Best producer: del Buonamico; also Fuso Carmignano, Michi, del Teso, La Torre, Wandanna.

MONTECILLO

SPAIN, La Rioja, Rioja DOC
🍷🍷 *Tempranillo, Grenache Noir (Garnacha Tinta),*
Carignan (Cariñena, Mazuelo)
🍷 *Macabeo (Viura)*

Montecillo, owned by the sherry company OSBORNE, possesses no vineyards of its own, but its stringent selection of bought-in grapes shows in the excellent quality of its wines. Eighty-five per cent of the production is red and owes its rich, fruity style to long bottle aging, rather than excessive periods in wood. The youngest reds, Viña Cumbrero Tinto, have rich, savoury, strawberry-raspberry fruit, and the Gran Reservas, called Viña Monty – quite tannic when first sold – have wonderful, rich, savoury wild strawberry flavours. Montecillo Especial is made from the pick of the red grapes in the best years. The white Viña Cumbrero Blanco, with a grassy-gooseberry flavour, epitomizes modern RIOJA at its best. Best years: 1995, '94, '91, '89, '87, '85.

MONTEFALCO DOC, MONTEFALCO SAGRANTINO DOCG

ITALY, Umbria
🍷 *Sangiovese, Trebbiano Toscano, Sagrantino and others*

Montefalco is arguably UMBRIA's most interesting wine, as the international community is gradually coming to recognize. Set right in the middle of this land-locked region, between Assisi and Spoleto, it is marked out from other Sangiovese-and-white-grape-based reds from central Italy by the addition of up to ten per cent of Sagrantino. This gives it a real boost of dark cherries, plums, prunes and licorice richness and an enlivening swipe of acidity.

Even better is Montefalco Sagrantino where, with nothing else to dilute its character, the flavours of 100 per cent Sagrantino surge out with a glorious punch. This wine ought to be an obligatory experience, though it's not easy to find. Sagrantino grapes can be semi-dried in *passito* styles, yielding an explosively concentrated *abboccato* version. Drink Montefalco at two to five years and Sagrantino with three years or more of aging. Best producers: Adanti, Antonelli, Caprai.

MONTEPULCIANO

Let's get the confusion sorted out. Montepulciano, the red grape, grows widely in south-eastern Italy, from the MARCHE right down to PUGLIA. Montepulciano is also the name of a town in Tuscany in western Italy, which gave its name to a Sangiovese-based wine called VINO NOBILE DI MONTEPULCIANO. Whether the similarity is coincidental is a moot point (might the grape possibly have originated from the Tuscan town?), but it is important to note that there is no vinous connection between the two.

Montepulciano, the grape, is most widely planted in, and ideally suited to, the conditions in ABRUZZO and, to a lesser extent, the Marche, and only occasionally is it used unblended elsewhere. It is high-yielding and, even when not restrained too much, produces a deep-coloured, rich wine, dominated by brambly fruit, with pepper and a touch of spice. When its yield is held properly in check – not an easy task on the traditional *tendone* method – it can be a delicious monster, filling your mouth with a surge of concentrated ripe fruit which is prevented from getting out of control by its peppery-spicy dry finish. Making wine that is almost always good and occasionally outstanding, this is one of Italy's great grapes.

Other Montepulciano-based red wines include ROSSO CONERO (Marche); Biferno, Pentro (MOLISE); San Severo (Puglia); and Cerveteri, Cori, Velletri (LAZIO); with Rosso Piceno (Marche) containing a substantial minority of the grape.

MONTEPULCIANO D'ABRUZZO DOC

ITALY, Abruzzo
🍷🍷 *Montepulciano, Sangiovese*

Vast swathes of ABRUZZO are planted with the Montepulciano grape; in theory, at least, Montepulciano d'Abruzzo comes from the entire length of the region and stretches inland from the Adriatic coast until the Apennines rise too high for grapes to ripen.

The wine is rarely less than respectable, sometimes wonderfully concentrated with loads of character, and can be long lived. The only complaint could be that it is sometimes a little rustic for drinking without food. Red Montepulciano, brambly, peppery, spicy, is naturally deep in colour. Yet there is also a superb rosé version, called Cerasuolo (or sometimes Rubino), made by giving the grape juice the merest contact with its dark-coloured skins. Best years: 1997, '95, '94, '93, '90, '88, '87, '86, '85, '83, '82, '81, '80, '79, '77. Worthy producers range from the quality-fanatic Valentini and the idiosyncratic Emidio Pepe through to the very good Barone Cornacchia, Filomusi Guelfi, Illuminati, Masciarelli, Montori, Nicodemi, Cantina Tollo, UMANI RONCHI, La Valentina, Ciccio Zaccagnini.

MONTEREY COUNTY

USA, California

The semi-arid Salinas Valley acts as a wind-funnel for the cold Pacific Ocean air. To the north lettuces and other vegetables still grow in profusion, but moving south, the winds become gentler and warmer, and vineyards take over. White varieties – Chardonnay, Riesling and Pinot Blanc – have proved most successful. Up in the hills and areas away from the valley floor we're beginning to see some excellent whites, as well as reds, from Pinot Noir (in the cooler north), Merlot and Cabernet Sauvignon from Carmel Valley. Important AVAs include Arroyo Seco, CHALONE and Carmel Valley. Best producers: BERNARDUS, Boyer, CHALONE VINEYARD, Durney, Jekel, J Lohr, Mirassou, Monterey Vineyard, Morgan, Paraiso Springs, Smith & Hook, Robert Talbott, Ventana.

MONTES

CHILE, Curicó Valley
🍷 *Cabernet Sauvignon, Merlot, Malbec*
🍷 *Sauvignon Blanc, Chardonnay*

One of Chile's most frustrating underachievers, Aurelio Montes has made a bid to be taken more seriously as a winemaker of great stature with the launch of his super-premium red 'M'. It'll take time before we know if he has succeeded because his reds nearly all take years to open up. All the Montes wines, including the Montes Alpha range, need bottle age, in some cases a great deal, before they can appear approachable. This is a fate that will befall his 'M' range as well. Older Montes wines really impress (but where can one find them?), whereas younger wines appear dense, packed, tight, over-oaked and simply too muscular. Nevertheless, the Sauvignon Blanc is good and improving and has just the right degree of aroma and finesse to impress, and a deep-coloured Malbec, with bold, black fruit perfume, is by far the juiciest of his reds.

MONTES
The Montes Alpha Cabernet Sauvignon r-- top wine from this Chilean producer and up to ten years of aging.

MONTEVERTINE
Though based in the heart of Chianti Classico, Montevertine is most famous for its super-Tuscan, Le Pergole Torte from 100 per cent Sangiovese.

MONTEVERTINE

ITALY, Tuscany, Chianti Classico DOCG
🍷 *Sangiovese, Canaiolo*
🍷 *Malvasia, Trebbiano*

Sergio Manetti's estate in the hills of Radda is firmly established as part of the legend of modern CHIANTI CLASSICO – even if he ceased years ago to classify his wines as DOC. The wines are all based on Sangiovese or other Tuscan varieties and the revised DOC legislation means they would all now qualify for the DOC; but in the 1970s it was their 'atypicity' which got them disqualified and which raised Sergio's ire to such extent as to make him break with all officialdom.

The flagship wine, Le Pergole Torte, was and is made from 100 per cent Sangiovese, which then, absurdly, it was not allowed to be, and it was refined in barrique, which gave it, according to the official tasters, a style which lacked the roughness and rusticity of the so-called 'typical' Chiantis of that time.

Today Montevertine, after years of basking in international glory, is going through a slightly lean period, the restrained style of the wine having difficulty finding favour in an age when voluptuousness of fruit and unobtrusiveness of structure are so highly prized. But with vineyards of the quality of those of Montevertine there is no reason why they should not make their way back to the top again. Best years: 1998, '97, '96, '95, '90, '88, '85, '81.

MONTHÉLIE AC

FRANCE, Burgundy, Côte de Beaune
🍷 *Pinot Noir*
🍷 *Chardonnay*

Monthélie is an attractive village looking down on MEURSAULT from the north. Its steep streets and huddled houses give some clue to the wine's character, which is generally of the strong, herby, but satisfying type. Monthélie

wines were historically sold as VOLNAY, the next village to the north-east. That was fine for as long as the appellation laws allowed it, but when Monthélie had to stand on its own two feet and trade under its own name, it languished in the shadows while barrels of Volnay reached ever higher prices – bad luck on the growers, but good news for us.

Most of Monthélie's 150ha (371 acres) of vines, many of them old, have an excellent south-east to south exposure, and the wines have a lovely chewy, cherry-skin fruit and a slight piney rasp which make good value drinking. A few rows of Chardonnay vines produce a little white Monthélie. Best years: 1997, '96, '95, '93, '92, '90, '89, '88, '85. Best producers: Deschamps, Paul Garaudet, LAFON, Olivier LEFLAIVE, LEROY, Monthélie-Douhairet-Porcheret, Parent, Potinet-Ampeau, Roulot, E de Suremain, Thévenin-Monthélie.

MONTILLA-MORILES DO

SPAIN, Andalucía
🍷 *Pedro Ximénez, Airén (Lairén), Moscatel and others*

Montilla resembles sherry in style. It is made in the same way as sherry from fruit grown on the chalky *albariza* soils as found in JEREZ but from Pedro Ximénez rather than Palomino and less grape spirit is needed to fortify it because the grapes become riper and sweeter and produce more alcohol of their own. The wines exported – as a cheap alternative to sherry – are lighter in alcohol and go by the names Dry, Medium and Sweet (or Cream).

Moriles is a little village in the region, reputed to make lighter, more elegant wines than Montilla itself, but in practice these wines are rarely seen outside the immediate area, except blended with Montilla wines. In the Spanish market some outstanding Montilla-Moriles can be found at very modest prices – particularly the amontillado and Pedro Ximénez styles. Best producers: Tor Albalá, Alvear, Pérez Barquero, Gracia Hermanos, Robles.

DOMAINE HUBERT DE MONTILLE

FRANCE, Burgundy, Côte de Beaune, Volnay AC
🍷 *Pinot Noir*
🍷 *Chardonnay*

Hubert de Montille has long led a double life: as a Dijon lawyer and winemaker in VOLNAY, where his estate is based, although he has important holdings among Premiers Crus in POMMARD too: Épenots, Pezerolles and Rugiens. The Premiers Crus in Volnay are Taillepieds, Mitans and Champans.

Whereas most Burgundian winemakers routinely chaptalize their wines to ensure they have between 12.5 and 13 degrees of alcohol, Hubert de Montille is a firm believer in keeping the alcoholic level to about 12 degrees, except, of course, when the vintage produces exceptionally ripe grapes. Nonetheless, his wines age very well; indeed, they demand bottle-aging and can taste dour and almost rustic in their youth. With low alcohol, cautious use of new wood and no filtration, these wines are always expressive of their terroir. Hubert de Montille is now semi-retired and the vinification is undertaken by his children, but the practices he established are likely to continue. A small quantity of PULIGNY-MONTRACHET has been made since 1993. Best years: 1997, '96, '95, '94, '93, '90, '89, '88, '85, '78.

HUBERT DE MONTILLE
The Pommard les Pezerolles is full-bodied, powerful and firmly tannic but between ten and 20 years it reveals its true glory.

MONTLOUIS AC

FRANCE, Loire, Touraine
🍷 *Chenin Blanc*

Montlouis is VOUVRAY's southern neighbour, just across the river Loire. But despite sharing the same grape (Chenin Blanc); the same type of soil (chalk, limestone, gravel and clay); and the same styles of wine (dry, medium and sweet whites, and CHAMPAGNE-method fizz, Montlouis Mousseux) Montlouis doesn't share its fame, and you can sense the growers' resentment and frustration.

Yet the style is a little different – the dry wines leaner and the sweet wines developing quite an attractive flavour of nuts and honey, but rarely subduing the high Chenin acidity. Only the sparkling wines (80 per cent of the more than four million bottles produced annually) match Vouvray with their green appley fruit sometimes touched by honey. The still wines need aging for five or maybe ten years, particularly the sweet (*moelleux*) Montlouis, but sparkling Montlouis should be drunk young. Best years: 1997, '96, '95, '94, '93, '90, '89, '88, '86, '85, '83, '79, '78, '76, '70. Best producers: Berger, Chaput, Chidaine, Delétang, Levasseur, Moyer, Taille aux Loups.

DOMAINE JACQUES PRIEUR
This domaine is one of the best whose wines are made and sold through the négociant Antonin Rodet, who has an excellent range of wines from throughout Burgundy.

LE MONTRACHET AC, CHEVALIER-MONTRACHET AC

FRANCE, Burgundy, Côte de Beaune, Grands Crus
♀ *Chardonnay*

Those who love white Burgundy dream of Montrachet. There have been more adjectives expended on this than on any other wine in the world. Tasted in its infancy, it flows pale from the barrel and stings your mouth with a piercing richness far beyond youthful flavours of fruit. Later on it can be so thick in the glass it seems like syrup, and so coarse and bloated in the mouth it's almost shocking and needs ten years to sort itself out. At ten years old and more the sheer concentration of the wine is unchanged. But all the coarseness is gone, and there seems to be a richness which owes nothing to sugar, everything to the ripest of fruits, the most tantalizing of scents, and the most fragrant of drifting woodsmoke wrapped in triple-thick cream.

Le Montrachet comes from a 7.5ha (18½ acre) vineyard, 4ha (10 acres) in PULIGNY-MONTRACHET and 3.5ha (8½ acres) in CHASSAGNE-MONTRACHET. The land is nothing to look at – poor, stony – but there's a thick vein of limestone just below the surface, the drainage is exceptional, and the perfect south to south-east exposure soaks up the sun from dawn to dusk. If you stand among the vines of Montrachet at sunset, a dip in the hills to the west is still allowing the sun's rays to warm these grapes while all the great surrounding vineyards are in shadow.

Another Grand Cru, Chevalier-Montrachet, lies immediately above it on the slope. The higher elevation yields a slightly leaner wine that is less explosive in its youth, but good examples will become ever more fascinating over 20 years or more. Best years: 1997, '96, '95, '93, '92, '90, '89, '88, '86, '85, '83, '82, '78, '71, '70. Best producers: Bouchard Père et Fils (since 1995), Colin, DROUHIN (Laguiche), LAFON, Domaine LEFLAIVE, RAMONET, Domaine de la ROMANÉE-CONTI, Thénard.

MONTRAVEL AC, CÔTES DE MONTRAVEL AC, HAUT-MONTRAVEL AC

FRANCE, South-West
♀ *Sémillon, Sauvignon Blanc, Muscadelle*

These are white wines from the western fringe of the BERGERAC region. Basic Montravel is usually dry, while Côtes de Montravel and Haut-Montravel – from hillside vineyards – are sweeter, and can be exotically fragrant and delicately rich. The Montravel wines, falling uneasily between proper sweet and proper dry, are not much in fashion and so production – already low at 300,000 bottles a year – is unlikely to increase. Red wines use the Bergerac AC. Best producers: Dauzin la Vergne, de Gouyat, de Krevel, Puy-Servain, le Raz, de Roque Peyre. Best years: 1997, '96, '95.

CH. MONTROSE

FRANCE, Bordeaux, Haut-Médoc, St-Estèphe AC, 2ème Cru Classé
♠ *Cabernet Sauvignon, Merlot, Cabernet Franc*

This leading ST-ESTÈPHE property of 68ha (168 acres) used to be famous for its dark, brooding, Cabernet Sauvignon-dominated style that only slowly revealed its blackcurrant and pencil-shavings scent. Twenty years was regarded as reasonable time to wait before broaching a bottle, and around 30 years to drink it at its prime. Then vintages of the late 1970s and early '80s underwent a sea change, becoming lighter, softer, less substantial, ready to drink at a mere ten years old. Thankfully, since 1988 this trend has been reversed, Montrose finding its former intensity coupled with extra richness and ripeness. The 1989 and '90 were stupendous and vintages of the 1990s have been equally rich and profound. The wines look set to age well, too. Welcome back to the top table. Best years: 1997, '96, '95, '94, '93, '90, '89, '88, '86, '85, '82, '81, '79, '76.

CH. MONTUS

FRANCE, South-West, Madiran AC
♠ *Tannat, Cabernet Sauvignon, Cabernet Franc*
♀ *Courbu, Gros Manseng, Petit Manseng, Arrufiac*

Alain Brumont has been largely responsible for the resurgence in quality in MADIRAN. A strong advocate of the Tannat grape, harvested at optimum ripeness, and the use of new oak barriques, he has introduced a richer, more refined style to these robust wines. At the 160-ha (395-acre) domaine he produces wines under two labels: Bouscassé from vineyards on clay-limestone soils located in the Gers *département* and Montus from vineyards in the Hautes-Pyrénées *département* on gravelly soils. Among the range of wines the top of the line Bouscassé Vieilles Vignes, from vines over 50 years' old, and Montus Prestige, from vines of an average of 25 years, are both made from 100 per cent Tannat and aged for 16 months in new oak casks.

The white Pacherenc du Vic Bilh is produced in dry and sweet styles. There are three cuvées of sweet: Vendémiaire, Brumaire and Frimaire with the Petit Manseng grapes picked progressively later and more raisined or *passerillé* in respectively October, November and December. Best years: (reds) 1997, '96, '95, '94, '90, '89.

MÓR

HUNGARY, Northern Transdanubia
♀ *Ezerjó, Muscat Ottonel, Traminer (Tramini), Müller-Thurgau (Rizlingszilváni)*

The Rizlingszilváni is none other than our old friend the Müller-Thurgau, grown in this white wine region in the north of Hungary, between the Danube and Lake Balaton. Traminer here is called Tramini, but the grape is the same. A lot of the soil is volcanic loess, which suits it, and also suits the most acidic grape variety, the Ezerjó, which is a Hungarian speciality. There is increasing evidence of good, perfumed but dry blends of Traminer and Ezerjó finding their way on to the export market.

MORAVENKA

CZECH REPUBLIC, Moravia
♀ *Pinot Gris (Ruländer), Riesling (Rhine Riesling), Müller-Thurgau and others*

The Znovin-Satov winery in Moravia turns out quite solid, quite well-made wines which are exported under the Moravenka label. The grape varieties are the classic German ones, since the climate here is fairly cool and white wine varieties rule the roost. The wines are rather more old-fashioned than some now appearing from this country (such as wine made from Rebula grape, the local name for Ribolla). The Moravenka wines can be a little lacking in acidity and are made to drink young.

MORELLINO DI SCANSANO DOC

ITALY, Tuscany
♠ *Sangiovese*

Scansano is a commune in that part of coastal Tuscany called the Maremma, Morellino being a local clone of Sangiovese. The name means 'little Morello' (cherry) and the aromas are reputed to put one in mind of that fruit. Morellino di Scansano, in its simple form, is indeed an easy-drinking, fruity red with appreciably less astringency than is often displayed by Sangiovese from central Tuscany. Until recently the denomination was cloaked in obscurity, but two recent stars, Fattoria le Pupille and Moris Farms, have demonstrated that Morellino can be a wine of fleshy yet concentrated fruit, with ripe tannins – exactly the sort of thing that appeals to pundits these days and we can expect to hear a lot more about this wine in the future. Best years: 1998, '97, '96, '95, '94, '93, '91, '90, '88, '85.

MOREY-ST-DENIS AC

FRANCE, Burgundy, Côte de Nuits

🍷 Pinot Noir

🍾 Chardonnay, Aligoté

After decades of being treated as Cinderella – squashed between CHAMBOLLE-MUSIGNY to the south and GEVREY-CHAMBERTIN to the north – Morey-St-Denis has recently been flexing its muscles, and now commands a price for its wine equal to its more famous neighbours. Certainly the vineyards deserve it. There are five Grands Crus (BONNES-MARES, Clos des Lambrays, CLOS DE LA ROCHE, Clos de Tart and Clos St-Denis) as well as some very good Premiers Crus, but the entire extent of the village's vineyards is only 133ha (329 acres) – neighbouring Gevrey-Chambertin, for instance, has 500ha (1235 acres) – and so the *négociants* have paid less heed to Morey, simply because there was less wine to go round. Nowadays most basic village Morey wine does come from *négociants*.

However there is better Morey, in particular from the Premier Cru and Grand Cru vineyards and usually from single growers. These wines generally have a good strawberry or redcurrant fruit, sometimes a little meaty and gaining an attractive chocolate and licorice depth. Best years: (reds) 1997, '96, '95, '93, '92, '91, '90, '89, '88, '85, '83, '80, '78. Best producers: Amiot, Castagnier-Vadey, CLAIR, DUJAC, FAIVELEY, Georges Lignier, Hubert Lignier, Moillard-Grivot, Perrot-Minot, Ponsot, Jean Raphet, ROUMIER, ROUSSEAU.

DOMAINE PONSOT

Back on form after an erratic patch in the 1980s, this domaine makes some sublime, old-fashioned wines from top vineyard sites in Morey-St-Denis.

Believe it or not, there is actually a white Morey-St Denis. In the Monts Luisants vineyard to the north of the village, Ponsot produced about 3000 bottles from a weird white mutation of Pinot Noir. These vines no longer exist, and nowadays Ponsot's wine is made from Chardonnay and Aligoté. It's a strange wine, showing an almost overpowering, honeyed nutty weight, which is impressive if somewhat overbearing. Bruno Clair and Dujac also make white Morey. Best years: (whites) 1996, '95, '93, '92, '90, '89, '88.

MORGON AC

FRANCE, Burgundy, Beaujolais, Beaujolais cru

🍷 Gamay

Although MOULIN-À-VENT is the BEAUJOLAIS cru that is supposed to come closest to maturity to a fine CÔTE D'OR Burgundy, Morgon could easily lay claim to that reputation. Indeed, there is even a French verb *morgonner* to describe how the local wine begins to lose its fresh, plummy fruit after two to three years and evolves into something chocolaty, cocoa-ish and strongly perfumed with cherries or even kirsch. Sounds good? It is. But only the best wines are like this, usually from a single grower, and from the slopes around Mont du Py. You may see Le Py, Les Chaumes or Le Clachet marked as vineyard names, and snap a bottle up if you do. Most Morgon is less special, but it still manages a soft, cherry, easy-drinking fruit. Best years: 1998, '97, '96, '95, '94, '93, '91, '85. Best producers: Aucoeur, Georges Brun, la Chanaise, Charvet, Descombes, Desvignes, DUBOEUF, Janodet, Lapierre, Longuepierre, Paquet, Savoye.

MORNINGTON PENINSULA

AUSTRALIA, Victoria, Port Phillip Zone

This is a super-trendy, fast-growing region near Melbourne where many of the 39 wineries make high-quality wine on a doll's house scale. The 1998 acquisition of a controlling interest in STONIER'S by PETALUMA has given the region an added dimension to its previous reputation as a playground for the wealthy dilettante. Land prices are high and consequently the price-quality ratio can get a bit stretched. Even so, for marvellously piercing fruit quality in Chardonnay, Riesling, Pinot Noir and Cabernet, the Peninsula has a lot to offer. The climate is ideal and the potential is excellent. Best years: 1998, '97, '94, '93, '92, '91, '88, '87, '86, '84. Best producers: DROMANA ESTATE, Elgee Park, King's Creek, Massoni, Merricks, Moorooduc Estate, PARINGA ESTATE, STONIER'S, Tuck's Ridge.

MORRIS

Morris is probably the greatest fortified wine producer in Australia. The Old Premium Tokay is remarkably luscious and has real complexity.

MORRIS

AUSTRALIA, Victoria, North East Victoria Zone, Rutherglen

🍷 Cabernet Sauvignon, Syrah (Shiraz), Durif

🍾 Muscat, Muscadelle (Tokay), Chardonnay, Semillon

Until his retirement in 1992 when he handed over the reins to his son David, Mick Morris was the most important producer of fortified wine in North-East Victoria and part of the ORLANDO group since 1970. He made his raisiny, fortified Muscat and aromatic Tokay much as he always had in a winery as antiquated as any in the hemisphere.

The Old Premium range sits at the top of the quality tree and they are absolute bargains, given the age and quality of these wines, as are the Mick Morris range at the bottom, the latter selling for a song in Australia – and inducing more than a song at the end of a dinner party. Why is it that the Muscat is always blamed for the hangover? Maybe because it's so rich and scented and delicious you can never resist another glass.

DENIS MORTET

FRANCE, Burgundy, Côte de Nuits, Gevrey-Chambertin AC

🍷 Pinot Noir

After Denis Mortet's father retired in 1991, this domaine was divided between Denis and his brother Thierry. Both make very good wines, but Denis's are more dramatic and have attracted greater attention. The core of his 10-ha (25-acre) estate is a range of single-vineyard GEVREY-CHAMBERTIN wines from village sites of outstanding quality with very old vines: Motrot, En Vellé and En Champs. There are also Premiers Crus such as Lavaux as well as small parcels in CLOS VOUGEOT, CHAMBERTIN and CHAMBOLLE-MUSIGNY.

Yields are kept low, the grapes are selected at the winery and destemmed before fermentation on the indigenous yeasts. Mortet uses a lot of new oak, up to 80 per cent, even 100 per cent, arguing that his wines have sufficient concentration and power to absorb the wood. It is hard to disagree. In fact there isn't a barrel in his cellar that is more than two years old. The wines are very dense and tannic in their youth and need patience. But those who cellar the wines will be rewarded with some of the most flamboyant expressions of the Côte de Nuits, oozing plum and blackberry fruit, with a firm underpinning of vanilla and licorice. Denis Mortet has acquired something of a cult following, and prices are, needless to say, high. Best years: 1997, '96, '95, '94, '93.

MORTON ESTATE
NEW ZEALAND, North Island, Waikato
♂ *Cabernet Sauvignon, Pinot Noir, Merlot*
♀ *Chardonnay, Sauvignon Blanc, Gewürztraminer, Riesling*

Morton Estate built its reputation on Chardonnay with a range based on a top-of-the-line blockbuster Black Label and stylish, great value White Label – both from HAWKE'S BAY grapes grown in the company's Riverview vineyard. Hawke's Bay Sauvignon Blanc was another notable Morton style although their MARLBOROUGH Sauvignon Blanc is more highly regarded today.

Since the mid-1990s the winery has begun to make top-flight reds, particularly with a full-flavoured, ripe and rich Black Label Merlot/Cabernet and perhaps the best Hawke's Bay Pinot Noir. CHAMPAGNE-method fizz is another strength – look for the vintage Black Label. Best years: (Hawke's Bay) 1998, '96, '95, '94, '91.

MORTON ESTATE
Morton's best wines include the robust, complex Black Label Chardonnay made from grapes from the cool Riverview vineyards in Hawke's Bay.

GEORG MOSBACHER
GERMANY, Pfalz
♀ *Riesling*

This small estate makes some of the best Riesling and Scheurebe wines from the famous vineyards of FORST. They are always packed with peachy and citrus fruit, but absolutely pure and clean. Top of the range is the Riesling Erstes Gewächs from the Forster Ungeheuer site, a complex and sophisticated dry wine with an intense mineral character. However, even the estate's Kabinett wines are full of fruit and beautifully balanced. They too can age five years and more without any trouble. The estate is now run by Sabine Mosbacher-Düringer and her husband Jürgen Düringer. Best years: 1998, '97, '96, '94, '93, '92, '90, '89, '88, '86.

MOSCATO
In Italy there are three distinct sub-varieties of the MUSCAT or Moscato grape variety making quality white wines in various regions; plus the extraordinary Moscato Rosa. In PIEDMONT the dominant type is Moscato Bianco or Moscato di Canelli, the latter named after a town in the heart of the ASTI zone from which rivers of ordinary, and increasing amounts of extraordinary, semi-sparkling wine hails. Moscato Bianco is also fairly widespread in the major islands: Sardinia's Moscato di Cagliari, Moscato di Sorso-Sennori and Moscato di Sardegna as well as Sicily's Moscato di Noto and Moscato di Siracusa are all DOCs for Moscato Bianco.

In ALTO ADIGE, TRENTINO and the Colli Euganei sector of VENETO the sub-variety is Moscato Giallo (Orange Muscat), known to the German-speaking South Tyroleans as Goldmuskateller. The wines in Colli Euganei, best exemplified by Vignalta, may be referred to as Fior d'Arancio. In the island of Pantelleria, off the tip of Sicily, they make luscious sweet wines from Zibibbo, the local name for Muscat of Alexandria.

The wine of Moscato Rosa, or Rosenmuskateller as it is known in Südtirol (Alto Adige), is potentially a mind-blowing experience, the pale-pink liquid throwing off aromas for all the world like roses at their height of redolence. The palate, for its part, is generally sweet, though occasionally it's dry. Best producer in Alto Adige today is Franz Haas, with Graf Kuenburg, Heinrich Plattner, Laimburg and TIEFENBRUNNER in pursuit. JERMANN makes a good one in Friuli, AVIGNONESI does likewise in Tuscany.

MOSCATO D'ASTI DOCG, MOSCATO DI STREVI DOC, LOAZZOLO DOC
ITALY, Piedmont
♀ *Muscat (Moscato Bianco)*

Moscato d'Asti is the upmarket version of ASTI. Moscato Bianco vines seem to cover practically every hillside not already covered by Barbera in PIEDMONT's heartland, from Mango in the west to Strevi in the east, and even though the market for Asti, the inexpensive sparkling stuff which may be helped along with sugar, is declining, demand for Moscato, the much less sparkling version (maximum 1.7 atmospheres pressure), is going up by leaps and bounds as the wine world discovers the joys of this delightfully aromatic, lightweight (maximum 5.5 per cent alcohol), sweet but not cloying apéritif or dessert wine.

Production of Moscato d'Asti, and especially of Asti, is dominated by large-scale private and co-operative producers, some of which are capable of wines of real quality. Best producers: (smallscale) Bera, Ca d'Gal, Caudrina, Degiorgis, Il Falchetto, Cascina Fonda/Secondino Barbero, Icardi, Marenco, La Morandina, Perrone, Cascina Pian d'Or, Saracco, Scagliola, La Spinetta, Vignaioli di Santo Stefano; (largescale) Banfi, Cinzano, Contratto, Fontanafredda, Gancia, Martini & Rosso; (co-operatives) Araldica Vini Piemontesi, Viticoltori dell'Acquese.

White Muscat is also used in Piedmont to produce a marvellously grapy *passito* wine which may go under the name of Loazzolo DOC or, if from Strevi, just a brand name such as Casarito.

MOSCATO DI PANTELLERIA DOC
ITALY, Sicily
♀ *Muscat (Zibibbo)*

Pantelleria is a small island off the south-west coast of Sicily, lying nearer to Tunisia in north Africa than to Sicily itself. It is rocky, with one green part covered by pine scent, small towns, weird round-domed houses called *dammusi*, terraces mostly growing capers and the wind. There's always wind, be it from south (unbearably hot), north (shiveringly cold, even in an African August), east or west. Hence Pantelleria's name, 'Island of the Winds'. The vines are Muscat of Alexandria, locally called Zibibbo and low-trained to withstand the buffeting

The most typical Pantellerian Moscato wine is *passito*, the grapes being dried out of doors as quickly as the sun's strength allows and at its best, like DE BARTOLI's Bukkuram, has been called liquid sunshine, grape, raisin, oak, toffee flavours, all combining to a terrific luscious whole. There are numerous other styles too, some rarely seen, of which the *naturale* (non-*passito*) stands out. Murana leads the Pantelleria-based producers; Florio Morsi di Luce and Donnafugata the other Sicily-based ones.

MOSEL Germany

MANY OF EUROPE'S GREAT WINE REGIONS have evolved along the banks of rivers. Ease of transport of the finished product may have been one practical reason, but there are other, still more fundamental advantages that come from having an expanse of water at your feet. It mitigates the extremes of climate, which in chilly northern spots like Germany's Mosel-Saar-Ruwer region is no small point; and it reflects the sun's rays back onto the vines, giving the heat-hungry grapes a much-needed boost. Up here they need all the heat and sun they can get, because the Mosel-Saar-Ruwer is at the northerly edge of vine-growing in the northern hemisphere and it is at this point, on the margin of where the grapes will ripen, that the greatest wines can be made.

'Can' is the operative word. Not all Mosel-Saar-Ruwer wine is great; some is very poor indeed. And how are you to tell the difference? Well, not by looking for the word 'Mosel' on the label, that's for sure. The river Mosel runs for 500km (310 miles) from its source in France's Vosges mountains (where it is called the Moselle), through Luxembourg (it's

still the Moselle) and across the German border, where it becomes the Mosel. The Saar and the Ruwer rivers flow into it either side of the city of Trier; and together they join the Rhine at Koblenz. And one would hardly expect over 485km (300 miles) of river, and 12,215ha (30,185 acres) of German vineyards, to produce a consistent quality of wine.

The remarkable thing about the wine of the Mosel-Saar-Ruwer, however, is that its style is so homogeneous. There is a lightness and a delicacy that marks it out from the wine of the Rhine; a combination of fragility and intensity that reaches its long-lived peak in the estate-bottled Rieslings from the Saar and Ruwer valleys and the Middle or Mittel Mosel, with the stretch from Piesport to Erden at the heart of the latter. For this is the key to choosing fine Mosel-Saar-Ruwer: look for the name of the region's finest grape, the Riesling, and look for the names of the best growers, most of whom are listed on page 257. Vintages vary enormously, but an off-vintage from a top grower can still be a better bet than a good vintage from a poor producer.

Good growers are usually helped by having good vineyards. Site is all-important here; instead of heading straight for Koblenz, the Mosel finds itself constantly deflected by sheer walls of rock that rise high and vine-clad above the water, so it meanders back and forth, in the process revealing umpteen ideal, south-facing suntrap slopes; these are where the Riesling is king, and where the best Mosel wines come from. Lesser wines are made from Müller-Thurgau, Elbling or Kerner among other varieties. Their quality is not a patch on that of the Riesling, and at best their wines are clean and attractive.

The best parts of the Mosel-Saar-Ruwer are the Saar and the Ruwer valleys and the Mittel Mosel. Here the slopes are steepest, the soil is slate, dark and heat-absorbing, dry and instantly draining, and there is a whiff of smoke to Riesling made from grapes grown on this slate. Elsewhere in the Mosel the soil may be sandstone, marl or limestone in the Upper Mosel or Obermosel, or mixed with clay in the Lower Mosel, between Zell and Koblenz, and the slopes are usually gentler. The Saar shares the steep slopes and slate soil of the Mittel Mosel, but it is appreciably colder. If a Riesling from the Mittel Mosel has the steeliness of acidity and the ripeness of honey, the Saar in an off-vintage can have considerably more steel than honey; but in good years it triumphs. The same is true of the Ruwer: a tiny area this, but boasting a great concentration of quality.

The amphitheatre of the Goldtröpfchen vineyard high above the village of Piesport is one of the greatest sites in the Mittel Mosel, producing Rieslings with baroque fruit aromas and a firm structure.

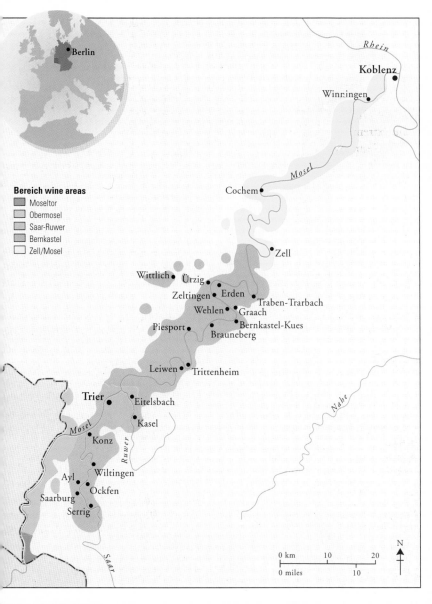

Bereich wine areas
- Moseltor
- Obermosel
- Saar-Ruwer
- Bernkastel
- Zell/Mosel

ZILLIKEN
This small estate makes classic, piercing minerally Saar Rieslings. A fashionable speciality is Eiswein from the Saarburger Rausch site.

JOH. JOS. PRÜM
This legendary Mosel estate has vines in top sites such as the famous Sonnenuhr in Wehlen.

REINHOLD HAART
Theo Haart's Rieslings from the Piesporter Goldtröpfchen site are explosively fruity yet crisp wines.

DR LOOSEN
Ernst Loosen is one of Germany's leading organic winemakers. The Prälat wines combine aromatic richness with monumental concentration.

EGON MÜLLER-SCHARZHOF
If you want the ultimate in sweet Riesling try the wines from this estate but be prepared for crazy prices.

FRITZ HAAG
For more than 30 years Wilhelm Haag has made the finest Rieslings from the great Brauneberg vineyards.

WILLI SCHAEFER
This very small estate makes the best and most minerally wines from Graach.

REGIONAL ENTRIES
Ayl, Bernkastel, Brauneberg, Erden, Graach, Kanzem, Kasel, Leiwen, Ockfen, Piesport, Saarburg, Serrig, Trier, Trittenheim, Ürzig, Wehlen, Wiltingen, Winningen, Zeltingen.

PRODUCER ENTRIES
Bischöfliche Weingüter, Christoffel, Friedrich-Wilhelm-Gymnasium, Grans-Fassian, Haag, Haart, Heymann-Löwenstein, von Hövel, Karlsmühle, Karthäuserhof, Kerpen, von Kesselstatt, Loewen, Loosen, Maximin Grünhaus, Müller-Scharzhof, Pauly-Bergweiler, J J Prüm, S A Prüm, Richter, Schaefer, Schloss Lieser, Schloss Saarstein, Selbach-Oster, Thanisch, Wagner, Wegeler, Zilliken.

KARTHÄUSERHOF
This top Ruwer estate has gone from strength to strength since the mid-1980s and makes wines of concentration and character.

CARL LOEWEN
Karl-Josef Loewen is the rising star of the Mittel Mosel, making rich yet beautifully crafted Rieslings in the naturally sweet style.

HEYMANN-LÖWENSTEIN
Reinhold Löwenstein makes some of the Mosel's few exciting dry Rieslings as well as some magnificent dessert wines.

LENZ MOSER

AUSTRIA, Niederösterreich

♥ *Zweigelt, Pinot Noir (Blauburgunder), Cabernet Sauvignon, Merlot*

♀ *Grüner Veltliner, Pinot Blanc (Weissburgunder), Riesling (Rhine Riesling), Bouvier*

Probably the most famous name in Austrian wine, this is a merchant house as well as a grower – and the name behind wines which are at least reliably good, and at best very good. It has three arms: the wines it buys from small growers, many of whom are in BUR-GENLAND; the Klosterkeller Siegendorf in Burgenland, which it rents; and the vines in the WEINVIERTEL, which it rents from the Knights of Malta. The Weinviertel wines are mostly red, and often among Austria's best, especially the Cabernet-Merlot blends, which are ripe, classically structured and capable of aging. The Zweigelt is generally pretty good, especially when it is made dry and appetizing, and the Blauburgunder is promising, but is not yet a challenge to Burgundy. Best years: (reds) 1997, '93, '92; (whites) 1998, '97, '95.

MOSS WOOD

AUSTRALIA, Western Australia, South West Australia Zone, Margaret River

♥ *Cabernet Sauvignon, Pinot Noir*

♀ *Semillon, Chardonnay*

Moss Wood's finely structured, softly fleshy yet long-lived Cabernet Sauvignon is rightly revered, and peaks at seven to ten years. The Semillons, one oak-matured, the other not, are no less delicious, honeyed rather than grassy, with a long finish and capable of considerable aging. The Chardonnay can be dazzling in its peachy, butterscotch opulence, and one or two superb Pinot Noirs have emerged. Best years: 1996, '95, '93, '92, '91, '90, '87, '86, '85, '83, '80.

MOULIN-À-VENT AC

FRANCE, Burgundy, Beaujolais, Beaujolais cru

♥ *Gamay*

Moulin-à-Vent would like to be a big, burly, world-famous Burgundy like CHAMBERTIN. But sadly it is in the wrong place – a good 240km (150 miles) too far south – and it grows the wrong grape – the Gamay, rather than the much more vaunted Pinot Noir. It is in fact one of the ten crus of the BEAUJOLAIS region. Undaunted by that fact, it keeps on trying, and the wine does in fact do a pretty good job of impersonating a fairly full, chocolaty Burgundy – slightly short on perfume, but good and rich, if you leave it for six to ten years to mature.

Moulin-à-Vent means 'windmill' in French and that's what the wine is named after – an old building standing in 643ha (1590 acres) of vines between Romanèche-Thorins and CHÉNAS. DUBOEUF and other producers are using new oak barrels experimentally and the first wines released are delicious. Best years: 1998, '96, '96, '95, '94, '93, '91, '90, '85. Best producers: Brugne, Champagnon, G Charvet, Duboeuf (single domaines), Ch. des Jacques, Janodet, Ch. du Moulin-à-Vent, Siffert, la Tour de Bief.

MOULIS AC

FRANCE, Bordeaux, Haut-Médoc

♥ *Cabernet Sauvignon, Cabernet Franc, Merlot and others*

This is the smallest of the six communal ACs within the HAUT-MÉDOC area, with only 550ha (1359 acres) of vines. Moulis had no properties included in the famous 1855 Classification of BORDEAUX wines, but much of the wine is excellent, yet rarely over-priced. The best vineyards are on a gravel plateau centred on the village of Grand-Poujeaux.

These wines are beautifully balanced, surprisingly soft behind their early tannin, and delicious to drink at five to six years old, though good examples should age for ten to 20 years. New oak is being increasingly used to age the wines. Best years: 1998, '96, '95, '94, '90, '89, '88, '86, '85, '83, '82. Best producers: Anthonic, Biston-Brillette, Brillette, CHASSE-SPLEEN, Duplessis, Dutruch-Grand- Poujeaux, Gressier-Grand-Poujeaux, Maucaillou, Moulin-à-Vent, POUJEAUX.

MOUNT BENSON AND ROBE

AUSTRALIA, South Australia, Limestone Coast Zone

It says more about parish pump politics than commonsense that these two small, adjacent and physically very similar regions should have decided to go their own way in seeking GI status. Situated, as they are, so close to the coast (and the Southern Ocean) the climate is strongly maritime-influenced, to the extent that the risk of frost seems improbable, but nonetheless poses one of the climatic threats.

There are alternating patches of terra rossa and more sandy soils which should (and generally do) play a determining role in the choice of grape varieties. Southcorp is by far the largest vineyard owner, and has placed its money on Shiraz, Cabernet Sauvignon, Chardonnay and Merlot (in that order). The only resident wineries are Cape Jaffa Wines and Mount Benson Winery. Best years: too early to tell.

MOUNT LANGI GHIRAN

AUSTRALIA, Victoria, Western Victoria Zone, Grampians

♥ *Syrah (Shiraz), Cabernet Sauvignon, Cabernet Franc, Merlot*

♀ *Riesling*

If ever you wish to discover the taste of pepper and spice in Shiraz – and a top RHÔNE Valley wine is not to hand – take a bottle of Mount Langi Ghiran and drink it with a thick piece of rare, char-grilled rump steak. These red wines (the Cabernet Sauvignon is structurally similar but less reliably impressive) are the vinous equivalent of that steak: layers of velvety flavour and great complexity, yet broodingly, impressively dry. The Riesling is surprisingly good, perfumed, yet dry and touched with petrol and lime. Best years: 1997, '96, '94, '93, '92, '91, '90, '88, '86, '84.

MOUNT MARY

AUSTRALIA, Victoria, Port Phillip Zone, Yarra Valley

♥ *Cabernet Sauvignon, Pinot Noir, Cabernet Franc and others*

♀ *Chardonnay, Sauvignon Blanc, Semillon, Muscadelle*

For many this is the leading YARRA VALLEY winery, its tiny production eagerly sought by a fanatically loyal band of followers, and its Cabernets (in fact, BORDEAUX blends) are among the finest in Australia, with fragrant varietal red berry, cigar box and leafy aromas and a silky smooth, remarkably persistent flavour. They seem to reach their peak in five years, but in fact go on improving for ten or more. The Pinot Noir is nearly as good, and has an even more surprising capacity to improve with age. The white wines are simply not in the same Olympian class. Best years: 1997, '94, '92, '91, '90, '88, '84, '80.

MOUNTADAM

AUSTRALIA, South Australia, Barossa Zone, Eden Valley

♥ *Cabernet Sauvignon, Pinot Noir, Merlot*

♀ *Chardonnay*

The superbly designed Mountadam winery, perched high in the hills above the EDEN VAL-LEY, takes its grapes from the low-yielding estate vineyards. Wind and drought are constant foes but the concentration of flavour is more than enough recompense. The Chardonnay is complex and long-flavoured; the Pinot Noir, stylish and deep; the Cabernet Sauvignon similarly stylish and dark-fruited; and a complex, lees-aged sparkling is a worthy addition. Eden Ridge and David Wynn are excellent labels for non-estate grapes. Best years: (Chardonnay) 1997, '96, '94, '93, '91, '90.

MOURVÈDRE

One of the best red grapes of the South of France, this plays a starring role in Bandol and is increasingly being used to add a little extra something to the wines of the Languedoc-Roussillon – that something being buckets of plummy, spicy fruit, a wild-herby perfume and a more solid tannic structure for aging the wine. But Bandol is underrated outside the Midi and so is Mourvèdre; a pity, because its wine is full of blackcurrants, herbs and spice with good tannic backbone. The better producers in Châteauneuf-du-Pape have, however, noted its qualities and Mourvèdre is a key component in wines like Ch. de Beaucastel.

In the New World, it had long been known as Mataro and after being dismissed for years as a junk grape, California and Australia are beginning to make exciting brawny wines from it, often blended with Syrah and Grenache in Australia. The name comes from that of the port city of Murviedro, north of Valencia, and indeed this is originally a south-eastern Spanish variety. The local name is Monastrell. Valencia and Murcia have the world's largest surface devoted to this variety: about 50,000ha (123,550 acres) of vines.

CH. MOUTON-ROTHSCHILD

FRANCE, Bordeaux, Haut-Médoc, Pauillac AC, Premier Cru Classé
♥ ♀ *Cabernet Sauvignon, Cabernet Franc, Merlot, Petit Verdot*
♀ *Sémillon, Sauvignon Blanc, Muscadelle*

Baron Philippe de Rothschild died in 1988 and so ended a remarkable era in BORDEAUX's history. For 65 years he had managed the estate, raising it from a run-down Second Growth to one of the most famous wines in the world, achieving promotion to First Growth status in 1973 – the only promotion ever effected within the traditional 1855 Classification. He did this by unremitting commitment to quality. But you can't rely on quality alone if you're determined to force the Bordeaux establishment into admitting you into

the top class. So he did it by flair, imagination and brilliant marketing.

The Mouton-Rothschild he created is a 75-ha (185-acre) estate planted with 80 per cent Cabernet Sauvignon, 10 per cent Cabernet Franc, 8 per cent Merlot and 2 per cent Petit Verdot on the northern side of Pauillac, but south of Ch. LAFITE-ROTHSCHILD. The high proportion of Cabernet Sauvignon and the perfectly situated gravel banks of the vineyard give a wine which, in most years, is astonishingly exotic and heavy. It manages to transform the cedarwood, cigarbox, pencil-shavings spectrum of dry, restrained fragrances into a steamy, intoxicating swirl of head-turning richness, backed up by a deep, chewy, pure blackcurrant fruit. Mouton is tannic when young, often taking 15–20 years to open up fully, but the richness is always there behind the tough exterior. Each year Mouton commissions a different artist to design the label, and most of the modern greats like Chagall, Miró, Picasso and Warhol have had a go. Best years: 1998, '97, '96, '95, '90, '89, '88, '86, '85, '82, '81, '75, '70.

A tiny amount of white Bordeaux, Aile d'Argent, is produced from 4ha (10 acres) of the vineyard.

Mouton-Cadet started out as a sort of 'younger brother' of Mouton-Rothschild and is now the world's most widely sold red Bordeaux. It is a correct but uninspiring Bordeaux AC, whose grapes are sourced from all over the Bordeaux region. That goes for the white and rosé versions, too.

MOVIA

SLOVENIA, Primorski Region, Dobrovo
♥ *Merlot*
♀ *Chardonnay, Pinot Blanc, Pinot Gris and others*

Movia is the brand name adopted by Mirko and Ales Kristancic, who have 10ha (26 acres) of vineyards in Slovenia, including some across the Italian border. The Kristancics were the first private producers to start bottling in their area; now they make stainless steel-fermented Pinot full of freshness and subtlety and spice, and barrique-aged Merlot and Chardonnay. They also make a good dessert wine by drying the otherwise dull white Rebula grape.

MUDGEE

AUSTRALIA, New South Wales, Central Ranges Zone

'A nest in the hills', the Aborigines called it, giving us the name Mudgee. And indeed it is a nest, with hills surrounding all sides, and many of the vineyards running off the flat bottom of

the nest into those hills. The region is warm but generally slightly cooler than the HUNTER VALLEY thanks to the altitude (around 500m/1640ft) and the cool nights. Not surprisingly, the reds – notably Shiraz and Cabernet Sauvignon – are better than the whites, though there is some rich, buttery Chardonnay and fair to good Semillon. The reds are deep coloured, robust and taste of dark chocolate, plum and blackcurrant when young, but after seven to ten years show strong similarities with Hunter Valley reds. And it is to the big Hunter wineries that much of the wine goes for blending and sale. Best years: 1996, '95, '94, '91, '88, '85, '84, '81, '79, '78. Best producers: Botobolar, Craigmoor, HUNTINGTON, Miramar, Montrose, Thistle Hill.

MUGA

SPAIN, La Rioja, Rioja DOC
♥ *Tempranillo, Grenache Noir (Garnacha Tinta), Carignan (Cariñena, Mazuelo) and others*
♀ *Macabeo (Viura), Grenache Noir (Garnacha Tinta), Tempranillo*
♀ *Macabeo (Viura)*

If you visit Isaac Muga's bodega by prior appointment, you will no doubt arrive to find him busily beating egg whites. It's not that he's obsessed with meringues, simply that Muga wines stick to tradition and are still clarified with beaten egg whites, about six per cask, hand-beaten. Red wine production here has changed little since the bodega's foundation in 1932. The reds are still fermented in huge wooden vats, then filtered off through bundles of vine prunings for aging in oak casks. The results of these artisanal methods are very good. Muga Crianza has soft, rich but elegant strawberry fruit, the Reserva, Prado Enea, is rich with strawberry-minty flavours.

Whites and rosés were best avoided, but in the late 1980s, new, modern pressing equipment was installed and the bodega began to buy grapes more selectively. Though still fermented in big wooden vats, the whites are now delicious, extraordinarily perfumed and grassy-flavoured. The rosés are pleasantly fresh and fragrant, too. A modern, highly concentrated red (Torre Muga) and a barrique-fermented white are recent additions. Best years: (reds) 1995, '94, '90, '89, '87, '85, '82, '81, '78, '75.

JACQUES-FRÉDÉRIC MUGNIER

FRANCE, Burgundy, Côte de Nuits, Chambolle-Musigny AC
♥ *Pinot Noir*

Although Jacques-Frédéric Mugnier rarely seems to be satisfied with his own wines, most tasters and wine drinkers are more than pleased by what they find. Mugnier is a former engineer who could not resist the temptation to vinify himself the grapes from the domaine's exceptional vineyards in CHAMBOLLE-MUSIGNY Les Amoureuses, BONNES-MARES and MUSIGNY. Until 1985 the wines had been made by the estate manager. Apart from the partially replanted Bonnes-Mares, the average vine age is high and yields are low.

A high proportion of new oak is used, but the wines usually have the body and structure to sustain it. Mugnier aims for a delicate, almost racy style, wines that are accessible young but capable of aging well in bottle. FAIVELEY's well-known NUITS-ST-GEORGES Premier Cru vineyard, the Clos de la Maréchale, is, in fact, leased from the Mugniers, but in 2002 it will revert to the owners and will make an important contribution to the Mugnier portfolio. Best years: 1997, '96, '94, '93, '92, '90, '89, '88.

MULDERBOSCH

SOUTH AFRICA, Western Cape, Stellenbosch WO
♥ Merlot, Cabernet Sauvignon, Cabernet Franc, Malbec
♀ Sauvignon Blanc, Chardonnay, Chenin Blanc

The partnership established between previous and founding owner, Dr Larry Jacobs, and winemaker, Mike Dobrovic in the early 1990s soon convinced wine lovers that there were many more sites in STELLENBOSCH than previously supposed which could produce top-notch Sauvignon Blanc. The sleek, gooseberry-infused Sauvignon has remained a medal-bedecked cult wine ever since. Consistent Chardonnay, oak-brushed Chenin Blanc (called Steen-op-Hout) and a barrel-fermented Sauvignon also benefit from Dobrovic's thoughtful inspiration; as does the lone red, the gentle, BORDEAUX-style blend called Faithful Hound. The new, corporate owners have sensibly avoided change for change's sake. Best years: (reds) 1996, '95, '94, '93; (whites) 1998, '97, '96, '95, '94.

MULDERBOSCH
Faithful Hound, a Bordeaux-style blend, takes its name from a vineyard planted next to a hut where an abandoned dog lived out its last years in expectation of his master's return.

MÜLLER-CATOIR
One of the best estates in Germany today, this Pfalz producer makes sensational, full-bodied dessert wines from Rieslaner.

MÜLLER-CATOIR

GERMANY, Pfalz, Neustadt-Haardt
♥ Pinot Noir (Spätburgunder)
♀ Riesling, Scheurebe, Pinot Gris (Grauburgunder), Rieslaner and others

This PFALZ producer makes explosively powerful, dry whites – and while Müller-Catoir Rieslings are excellent, packed with fruit and endowed with a remarkable intensity and vibrancy, it is other, supposedly lesser varieties that really display the skills of winemaker Hans-Günter Schwarz. The Scheurebe is heavenly stuff, grapefruit coated in honey; his Grauburgunder is top-notch, and his Rieslaner (Riesling x Silvaner) dessert wines are sensational and very long living.

He believes in minimal handling of his wines, which means no malolactic fermentation and as little racking and fining as possible, to allow the qualities of the individual vineyard and year to shine through. But what shines through most is the richness of the fruit and the heady perfumes. The vineyards are in Haardt, Gimmeldingen and Neustadt, among other places. Best years: 1998, '97, '96, '95, '94, '93, '92, '90, '89, '88.

EGON MÜLLER-SCHARZHOF

GERMANY, Mosel-Saar-Ruwer, Wiltingen
♀ Riesling and others

This is one of Germany's top estates and is run by Egon Müller IV. He favours a conservative style in his wines and still vinifies everything in wood, which is very rare these days in the MOSEL-SAAR-RUWER. Rigorous selection is the rule here, first of grapes then of wines. Müller's truly amazing Beerenauslese and Trockenbeerenauslese are the most expensive young wines in the world. Best years: 1998, '97, '96, '95, '94, '93, '91, '90, '89, '88, '83, '79, '76, '75, '71.

MÜLLER-THURGAU

This aromatic white grape, also known as Rivaner, is probably a cross between Riesling and Sylvaner, and covers vast amounts of land in Germany, where it is the most widely planted grape variety. Although a crucial factor in the lighter flowery styles of

LIEBFRAUMILCH and similar blends, it can produce quite exciting wines in the colder areas of FRANKEN, BADEN and the PFALZ. However, its ability to produce high yields has caused it to be planted on some of the better vineyard sites in the MOSEL, devaluing the reputation of the whole region. Austria and the Czech and Slovak Republics have extensive plantations and with skilled growers it shows the pleasant potpourri of grapy freshness, spice and flowers that is Müller-Thurgau's strong point. New Zealand makes good use of its extensive, but declining plantations to make a succession of off-dry, gently floral styles. In both England and Luxembourg it is widely planted and capable of pleasant, reasonably floral wines.

G H MUMM

FRANCE, Champagne, Champagne AC
♀♥ Chardonnay, Pinot Noir, Pinot Meunier

Of German origin, Mumm was sold by the Seagram group in 1999 to a US investment firm. It has for some time been one of the most inconsistent of the leading CHAMPAGNE houses. The once lovely Mumm de Cramant, a Blanc de Blancs from outstanding vineyards, now seems much duller than it used to be. With 150ha (371 acres) of vines located in Grand Cru sites, Mumm should be producing first-class Champagne, but rarely does. Nor has it ever been clear why it launched two prestige cuvées, Grand Cordon and René Lalou (the latter is now being phased out). However, changes in the winemaking team in the late 1990s should lead to improvements in quality, but at present the non-vintage Cordon Rouge remains a rich but ungainly and short mouthful of Champagne. Best years: 1990, '89, '88, '85, '82.

MUMM NAPA VALLEY

USA, California, Napa County, Napa Valley AVA
♀♥ Chardonnay, Pinot Noir, Pinot Meunier

One of the younger of the CHAMPAGNE-North American collaborations (in this case G H MUMM and Seagram), Mumm Napa made its first wines in 1983, then began substantial production in 1985.

Winemaker Greg Fowler pays tribute to the light, undemanding Mumm style, but in fact frequently produces a more successful non-vintage wine than does Mumm itself. The single-vineyard Winery Lake Cuvée gains character from the high quality of its CARNEROS fruit, but needs some aging to show its paces. DVX, the new prestige cuvée, is in top form now after a lacklustre beginning. Best years: 1995, '94, '92.

MURCIA

SPAIN

Murcia is the little-known region south of VALENCIA. It is surrounded by fabulously rich orchard land, but the vineyard regions further inland have little rainfall and summer temperatures can be suffocating. The soil is extremely poor. But this suits the late-ripening Monastrell (Mourvèdre) grape, of which there are more than 50,000ha (123,500 acres): it makes for very low yields, great concentration and potentially great quality. Unfortunately, production facilities are mostly huge and basic and there are few temperature-controlled vats and aging cellars in any of the three DOs in the region: Jumilla, Yecla and Bullas. Best producers: Agapito Rico, Casa Castillo, Castillo de Luzón.

MURFATLAR

ROMANIA, Dobrogea

On the Black Sea coast of Romania, Murfatlar has long been recognized as a quality wine region. It has its own denomination and one look at the immaculately kept vineyards gives you an idea why. Winemaking is still influenced by domestic market requirements, and you can find some interesting, not to say bizarre, Pinot Noir wines with more than a hint of residual sugar. There is also wine aimed at international markets, though, and Pinot Gris and Chardonnay deliver rich, varietal fruit. Some oak-aged Chardonnay can be excellent value and one of Murfatlar's specialties is its late-harvested, Botrytis-affected Chardonnay. Cabernet Sauvignon and Merlot are potential sources of ripe, soft reds. Sparkling wines are being made too. Vie Vin is probably the most consistent producer, and it looks set to begin a slow conversion to private ownership that will surely improve its quality.

MURPHY-GOODE WINERY

USA, California, Sonoma County, Alexander Valley AVA

🍷 *Cabernet Sauvignon, Merlot, Pinot Noir, Zinfandel*

♀ *Chardonnay, Pinot Blanc, Sauvignon Blanc*

A partnership of two excellent grape-growing families with over 120ha (300 acres) of vineyards in the heart of the ALEXANDER VALLEY and over 40ha (100 acres) in the RUSSIAN RIVER VALLEY, the late-developing Murphy-Goode Winery has emerged at last as nothing short of a superstar.

Its barrel-fermented Sauvignon Blancs, named Fumé Blanc Reserve and Fumé II La Deuce, may well be CALIFORNIA's two finest examples of the grape. Similarly intense and improving with each vintage are two Chardon-

Aging in small old oak barrels is an essential step in making Australia's glorious fortified wines from the Muscat and Muscadelle (called Tokay locally) varieties.

nays, Island Block from Alexander Valley, and J & M Vineyard from Russian River Valley. Best years: 1998, '97, '96, '95. Among its reds, Murphy-Goode offers a rich, big-bodied Merlot, a ripe, but balanced Zinfandel, and Cabernet Sauvignon, Brenda Block, with concentrated black-cherry fruit, great depth, and excellent aging ability of eight to ten years or longer. Best years: (reds) 1997, '95, '94, '93, '92.

MUSCADELLE

This grape has nothing to do with either Muscat or MUSCADET, even though it has an aromatic muskiness that might lead one to think it was related to the former. In BORDEAUX it is grown in small quantities to add a pleasant, honeyed aroma to the rather neutral dry ENTRE-DEUX-MERS whites, and spice to SAUTERNES. It is believed to be the same grape as CALIFORNIA's little-planted Sauvignon Vert.

Where Muscadelle triumphs is in North-East Victoria in Australia at RUTHERGLEN and Glenrowan, where it goes under the name of Tokay. Elsewhere in the country, it may be used for table wines; here, it makes glorious, fortified wines which start off life in cask a pale golden yellow-brown, and finish it (still in cask) a dark burnt sienna with an olive green rim, and with a flavour and aroma described with various degrees of likelihood as fish oil or cough sweets, but most accurately as cold tea leaf and dried rose petals, intensely sweet in flavour but with a haunting, cleansing finish.

MUSCADET AC

FRANCE, Loire, Pays Nantais

♀ *Melon de Bourgogne (Muscadet)*

Muscadet is now so popular that its name has become a kind of generic term for cheap, dry French white, but in reality it can only come from a legally defined area at the mouth of the river Loire. The Melon de Bourgogne grape migrated from Burgundy in the seventeenth century and, en route, changed its name to Muscadet. It became very popular with growers all over the Nantes area and they simply called their wine after the grape. There is an enormous amount planted (13,000ha/ 32,100 acres) and whether we really need this much is debatable. The answer is almost certainly not and this has created big problems in the region because of the low prices many of the growers receive from the merchants.

Muscadet is the basic appellation and can come from anywhere within the delimited area. In practice only wine from less good vineyards, mostly closer to the sea, carries the plain Muscadet AC. This is usually pretty bland wine, but does have one thing in its favour – the maximum alcoholic strength of 12.3 degrees. This legal maximum at least preserves a modicum of freshness in the wine. Coteaux de la Loire Muscadet, a little fuller than straight Muscadet, comes from a large area between Nantes and Angers but only accounts for 5 per cent of total production. The newest AC, the Côtes de Grand Lieu, covers the best vineyards around the large Lac de Grandlieu, southwest of Nantes. However, the largest production of top wine still comes from the extensive Muscadet de Sèvre-et-Maine AC. This is the AC used by most quality-conscious estates.

A lot of Muscadet can be dry and acid with a pretty neutral taste (that is, when it isn't wrecked by profligate use of sulphur) but a good Sèvre-et-Maine example should have a creamy softness with just enough prickle to make your tongue tingle. Look for the term *mise en bouteille sur lie*, indicating the traditional method of bottling the wine directly off its sediment or lees. This preserves some of the carbon dioxide in the wine and emphasizes a soft lees creaminess on the palate. Always drink straight Muscadet very young. Top *sur lie* Muscadets can age for several years, becoming quite full and nutty and finally gaining a passing resemblance to a reasonable Burgundy. Best years: (Sèvre-et-Maine) 1998, '97, '96, '95. Best producers: Michel Bahuaud (estate wines), Bossard, Chasseloir, Chéreau-Carré, Chéreau-Dimerie, Donatien-Bahuaud, Dorices, Marquis de Goulaine, Luneau-Papin, MÉTAIREAU, Sauvion, Touche-Tourmaline.

MUSCAT

There are some 200 varieties of the Muscat grape in one big, happy, grapy family, though thankfully only four are important for winemaking. Even so, those four can reach the extremes of wine styles: for a light, 7 per cent alcohol sparkling wine to drink on a hot day in the garden, try Asti Spumante. For a thick, dark brown, treacly fortified to sip on a winter's evening, try a fortified Muscat from Victoria in Australia. In between there are the elegant, dry Alsace Muscats and the lightly fortified Muscat de Beaumes-de-Venise. Yet all these wines share the essential Muscat flavour, because whether it is light or massive, dry, sweet or fortified, that clean, grapy flavour is always there.

The aristocrat of the family is the Muscat Blanc à Petits Grains. Its numerous aliases include Gelber Muscatel, Muskateller (in Austria), Muscat de Frontignan, Muscat Blanc (in California), Brown Muscat and Muscat Canelli; it also has a pink sibling, Muscat Rosé à Petits Grains, and it is not unusual to find the two in the same vineyard. The Muscat Blanc à Petits Grains used to be, and is becoming again, the principal Muscat in Alsace, where its refinement shows well. The slightly less perfumed but hardier Muscat Ottonel (a crossbreed created in 1852) supplanted it, but the Petits Grains is on the increase again as growers begin to realize its greater quality. Further south, in the Rhône Valley, it makes sublimely grapy fizz, in the form of Clairette de Die Tradition, and the peachy, apples-and-honey, rose-scented Muscat de Beaumes-de-Venise as well as being the main grape in Languedoc's Muscat de Frontignan.

In California, as Muscat Blanc, the grape makes mostly sweetly grapy, perfumed wines, plus a few fortifieds, but Petits Grains reaches its fortified apogee in Australia's North-East Victoria, at Glenrowan and Rutherglen, producing glowing, mahogany-coloured wines of extraordinary lusciousness and intensity. It may be called White, Red or Brown Frontignac or Frontignan, or even Brown Muscat: the grape, and the taste, are the same. Elsewhere in Australia it may be made into light, dry wines or any other style along the way; and Australia does not confine itself just to the Petits Grains variety.

The Muscat of Alexandria, otherwise known as Muscat d'Alexandrie, Moscatel, Muscatel or Zibibbo, among many synonyms, shares the perfume and grapy freshness of the Petits Grains variety, but with a streak of coarseness that tends to make its wines a little heavier, a little clumsier. In Australia it is known as Muscat Gordo Blanco, and is by far the largest single Muscat variety, contributing little to quality.

Spain's principal Muscat is the Alexandrian variety, used to make aromatic, raisiny wines. In Penedès Miguel Torres grows some Petits Grains to blend into his Viña Esmeralda. Muscat of Alexandria dominates in Portugal, too, and on the Setúbal peninsula it makes very sweet, grapy-raisiny wines, usually fortified.

In South Africa, Muscat Blanc was one of the grapes behind the historically famous Constantia dessert wine; it is the sole variety used in Klein Constantia's Vin de Constance, a modern reconstruction of that celebrated wine. The grape's more common usage, under the synonym Muscadel, is in the delicious fortified dessert wines, both white and red, which are the specialities of the warmer, inland regions. Muscat d'Alexandrie, also known as Hanepoot in the Cape, is more prolific but considered less fine than Muscat Blanc. In Tunisia, Muscat makes some of the best wines in North Africa.

Back in France, Muscat d'Alexandrie is widely planted in the South, particularly for the rather raisiny, marmalady fortified wines around Rivesaltes in Roussillon (Muscat à Petits Grains is the minor partner here).

MUSCAT DE BEAUMES-DE-VENISE AC

FRANCE, Southern Rhône
♀ Muscat Blanc à Petits Grains

This is the most delicious manifestation of sweet Muscat in France, and consequently the most expensive. But that's fair enough because the wine is a beauty and in a period in the late 1970s when sweet wines looked to be in terminal decline, the phenomenal success of Muscat de Beaumes-de-Venise as a sophisticated pudding wine sparked a new interest and the world's attention has now turned their way once more.

Beaumes-de-Venise is an attractive village huddled up against the crags of the Dentelles de Montmirail. If you ask the locals they'd probably be prouder of their gutsy red CÔTES-DU-RHÔNE-VILLAGES, but they've been making Muscat wine there since the Middle Ages. It's what is called a *vin doux naturel* – a fortified wine where the fermentation is arrested by the addition of a slug of high-strength spirit. This preserves the flavour of the unfermented grape juice and accounts for the wine's sweet, grapy taste

Muscat de Beaumes-de-Venise is rich, often very rich, full of the flavour of peach and grapes, orange peel, apples and honey, and with a wisp of the scent of roses left hanging in the air. But the secret is that the wine has a fruit acidity and a bright fresh feel to it which satisfies your thirst as well as stimulates your after-dinner wit. It can age, but is best drunk young to get all that lovely grapy perfume. Best producers: Beaumes-de-Venise co-operative, Castaud-Maurin, Coyeux, Durban, JABOULET, Vidal-Fleury.

MUSCAT DE FRONTIGNAN AC, MUSCAT DE LUNEL AC, MUSCAT DE MIREVAL AC, MUSCAT DE ST-JEAN DE MINERVOIS AC

FRANCE, Languedoc-Roussillon
♀ Muscat Blanc à Petits Grains

Muscat de Frontignan is the leading Muscat *vin doux naturel* on the Mediterranean coast and comes from Frontignan, a small town south-west of Montpellier in the HÉRAULT. It is supposed to be made 100 per cent from Muscat Blanc à Petits Grains, but there is probably an increasing amount of the coarser Muscat of Alexandria being used in the wine. This would go some way to explaining why much of the wine, though sweet and quite impressive, has a slightly cloying taste, like cooked marmalade, militating against the fresh grapy sweetness. The grapes are harvested as ripe as possible, partially fermented and then 'muted' by the addition of high-strength spirit. This stops the fermentation and leaves a substantial amount of the grape sweetness still in the wines. Varying between bright gold and a deep orange gold, Muscat de Frontignan is good, but not quite top class. Mireval is a less well known, inland neighbour of Frontignan and the wines, while still sweet and ripe, can have a little more acid freshness, and quite an alcoholic kick as well.

Although the little town of Lunel, northeast of Montpellier, boastfully gives itself the title of 'la Cité de Muscat' (the city of Muscat), few people who don't actually live there would agree. Muscat de Lunel is not well-known but the fairly small amounts made aren't bad with a very good raisiny flavour and less of the flat marmalady character than the better-known ones exhibit. Muscat de St-Jean-de-Minervois comes from the north-east corner of the MINERVOIS region and the wines are pleasantly sweet but not that concentrated.

Best producers: (Frontignan) Frontignan co-operative, la Peyrade, Robiscau; (Lunel): Belle-Côte, Lunel co-operative; (Mireval): la Capelle, Mas des Pigeonniers, Moulinas; (St-Jean-de-Minervois) Barroubio, St-Jean-de-Minervois co-operative, Siglé.

MUSCAT DE RIVESALTES AC
FRANCE, Languedoc-Roussillon
♀ *Muscat of Alexandria, Muscat Blanc à Petits Grains*

Rivesaltes, a small town just north of Perpignan, makes good CÔTES DU ROUSSILLON wines but its reputation is based on *vins doux naturels* – the traditional fortified wines of the South of France. The best of these is Muscat de Rivesaltes, made primarily from the Muscat of Alexandria grape; usually a big, rather thick, deep-coloured wine, not as aromatic as the best Muscats, and with a sweetness veering between raisins, honey and cooked orange marmalade. Modern producers like CAZES and de Jau are now producing more perfumed wines. Best producers: Cave de Baixas (Ch. les Pins), Casenove, Cazes, de Chênes, Forca Real, de Jau, Laporte, Mas Crémat, Mas Rous, Piquemal, Sarda-Malet.

MUSIGNY AC
FRANCE, Burgundy, Côte de Nuits, Grand Cru
♥ Pinot Noir
♀ Chardonnay

This extremely fine 10.7-ha (26-acre) Grand Cru vineyard gave its name to the village of CHAMBOLLE-MUSIGNY. Located on the slopes directly above CLOS DE VOUGEOT, it has the ability to produce red wines of such fragrance and delicacy of texture, that they have memorably been described as being 'of silk and lace', the perfume being 'a damp garden, a rose and a violet covered in morning dew'. In the hands of a few winemakers Musigny can truly be exceptional. Although very expensive, the wines show great power and finesse. The de VOGÜÉ estate owns two-thirds of the Grand Cru and also makes a tiny amount of white. Best years: 1997, '96, '95, '93, '92, '90, '89, '88, '85. Best producers: DROUHIN, JADOT, LEROY, J-F MUGNIER, ROUMIER, de VOGÜÉ.

NACKENHEIM
GERMANY, Rheinhessen

This village just north of NIERSTEIN is famous as the setting for Karl Zuckmayer's play 'The Jolly Vineyard' and for its Rothenberg vineyard from where some of the greatest Rieslings made anywhere on the Rhine originate. The red colour of the Rothenberg's slate soil, from which it gets its name, is so intense it can be seen from miles away. Best producers: GUNDERLOCH, HEYL ZU HERRNSHEIM.

NAHE
GERMANY

It can be easy to overlook the Nahe. It does not have an easily encapsulated character, unlike some German wine regions. It's relatively small at 4590ha (11,342 acres) and many of its vineyards are scattered rather than being neatly grouped. In addition, until 1935, its wines were sold as Rhine wines, or were sent to the RHEINGAU or MOSEL for blending.

Like any wine region, the quality of its output varies, and is not helped by the amount of the acceptable but unexciting Müller-Thurgau in its vineyards. But its top wines – made from Riesling – can be sublime. They have the nerve of the Saar wines combined with some of the body of a Rheingau, though they are seldom as weighty: they have finesse, delicacy and excitement built in. But these wines come from only a 8-km (5-mile) stretch of the steepest parts of the north bank of the river Nahe south of BAD KREUZNACH. The Rotenfels cliff at Bad Münster sends the river hurtling south-east, and here, in a 2-ha (5-acre) patch of land at its foot, are grown some of the Nahe's finest wines, in the Traiser Bastei vineyard.

In the Lower Nahe, from Bad Kreuznach north to the Rhine at Bingen, the wines, and the vineyards, sober down a little. There are good wines, often very good, but it's just that short stretch of river south of Bad Kreuznach that makes the best of the Nahe stand out from the rest of the region, and puts it into the league of Germany's greats. Elsewhere, away from the steepest bits, the vineyards may be as flat as the RHEINHESSEN, and the wines are soft and gentle. Further south the vineyards are more fragmented. Good wines are made here, but there are no famous names.

CH. NAIRAC
FRANCE, Bordeaux, Barsac AC, 2ème Cru Classé
♀ *Sémillon, Sauvignon Blanc, Muscadelle*

An established star in BARSAC, which by dint of enormous effort and considerable investment, produces a wine sometimes on a level with the SAUTERNES First Growths – not as intensely perfumed, not as exotically rich, but proudly concentrated, with a fine lanolin richness and buttery honey, and with spice from aging in new oak barrels. Annual production is rarely more than 15,000 bottles – sometimes less – from this 16-ha (40-acre) property. The influence of aging in new oak casks, adding spice and even a little tough tannin, make the wines a good candidate for aging for 10–15 years. Best years: 1998, '97, '96, '95, '90, '89, '88, '86, '83, '82, '81, '80.

NAOUSSA AO
GREECE, Macedonia
♥ *Xynomavro*

The small area of Naoussa is on the mainland, west of Thessaloniki and centred on the south-eastern slopes of Mount Velia. It produces one of Greece's better wines, a red made from the native Xynomavro grape that has plenty of spice and fruit – *mavro* means 'black' in Greek. The vineyards here are fairly high, around 350m (1150ft). Best producers: Boutari, Chateau Pegasos, Tsantalis, Vaeni. Best years: 1997, '93, '92, '90.

BOUTARI
Boutari is one of the most reliable producers of full-bodied, spicy red Naoussa wines from the local Xynomavro grape that can age well.

NAPA USA, California

TRADITIONALLY SYNONYMOUS with quality California wine, Napa County draws its wine identity, which is its only distinction these days, from its major AVA, Napa Valley, flanked on the west by the Mayacamas Mountains and on the east by the Coast Range. Most of its 300 or so wineries line the valley or overlook it from slopes and mountain perches. Over 20 major sub-areas with their own recognizable mesoclimates have now been recognized, either along the valley floor or at high elevations. The most southerly and coolest AVA is Carneros, noted for Pinot Noir and Chardonnay used for both still and sparkling wines. In the mid-valley areas of Rutherford, Oakville and Yountville, Cabernet Sauvignon justifiably dominates, and its vinous hallmarks are dusty, dried sage and

The bulk of grape-growing in the Napa Valley takes place on the valley floor and on the gentle slopes adjoining the floor and there is little land left that can now be converted into new space for grapes.

extra-ripe blackcurrant notes. Softer and more supple Cabernets and Merlots originate in the Stags Leap District AVA to the south-east and Spring Mountain to the west. In the northeast hills of the Howell Mountain AVA, Zinfandel and Cabernet develop really exciting depth and perfume. Diamond Mountain and Mount Veeder are AVAs along the Mayacamas mountain range to the west, and are best known for Cabernet Sauvignon while Atlas Peak, in the hills north-east of Stags Leap AVA, is best known for its Sangiovese.

DUNN VINEYARDS
Randy Dunn's Howell Mountain Cabernet is a massive wine, with ripe fruit and supreme balance that can easily age for a decade and often much longer.

JOSEPH PHELPS
Ripe, big and oaky, Insignia is one of California's top Meritage wines and is usually based on Cabernet Sauvignon with some Merlot and Cabernet Franc.

NEWTON
Newton's latest release, a massive reserve-style Chardonnay which is unfiltered and unrefined, has been widely acclaimed.

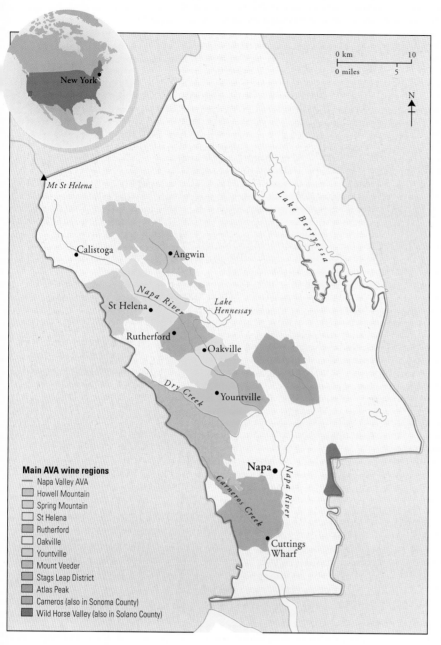

DIAMOND CREEK
Three Cabernet Sauvignon wines are made at this hillside winery, each from a vineyard planted on different soils and at different gradients. Red Rock is the most approachable of the three with vivid Cabernet fruit.

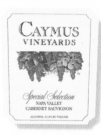

CAYMUS VINEYARDS
A Cabernet Sauvignon star for over 20 years, Caymus emphasizes a deep, ripe intense and generally well-oaked tannic style and the Special Selection can be outstanding.

STAG'S LEAP WINE CELLARS
From a winery reputed for its Cabernets, Cask 23 Cabernet Sauvignon is only made in the best years and has remarkably complex, enticing perfume and flavour.

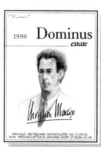

DOMINUS ESTATE
Christian Moueix of Ch. Pétrus fame has created a top Pomerol lookalike in the Napa Valley. Concentrated, with tremendous ripe fruit and lavish oak, the wine has enjoyed a string of outstanding vintages during the 1990s.

JADE MOUNTAIN
This big, ripe, gamy Syrah is one of several Rhône-style wines made by Jade Mountain.

HARLAN ESTATE
Using rigorous grape selection, skilled winemaking and new French oak, this Bordeaux-style red achieved critical fame overnight.

Main AVA wine regions
- Napa Valley AVA
- Howell Mountain
- Spring Mountain
- St Helena
- Rutherford
- Oakville
- Yountville
- Mount Veeder
- Stags Leap District
- Atlas Peak
- Carneros (also in Sonoma County)
- Wild Horse Valley (also in Solano County)

REGIONAL ENTRIES
Atlas Peak, Carneros, Howell Mountain, Napa Valley, Rutherford District, Spring Mountain District, Stags Leap District.

PRODUCER ENTRIES
Acacia Winery, Atlas Peak Vineyards, Beaulieu Vineyard, Beringer Vineyards, Cakebread Cellars, Caymus Vineyards, Chateau Montelena, Clos du Val, Clos Pegase, Cuvaison, Dalle Valle, Diamond Creek Vineyards, Domaine Carneros, Domaine Chandon, Dominus Estate, Duckhorn Vineyards, Dunn Vineyards, Far Niente Winery, Franciscan Vineyards, Frog's Leap Winery, Grgich Hills Cellar, Heitz Cellars, The Hess Collection, Louis M Martini, Robert Mondavi Winery, Mumm Napa Valley, Newton Vineyards, Niebaum Coppola Winery, Opus One, Pahlmeyer Winery, Paradigm Winery, Joseph Phelps, Pine Ridge Winery, Saintsbury, Schramsberg Vineyards, Shafer Winery, Silver Oak Cellars, Silverado Vineyards, Spottswoode, Staglin Family Vineyards, Stag's Leap Wine Cellars, Sterling Vineyards, Sutter Home Winery, Swanson Vineyards, Turley Cellars, Viader Vineyards, Villa Mt. Eden, ZD Wines.

NAPA VALLEY AVA

USA, California, Napa County
See also Napa, pages 264–265.

The Napa Valley looks the way a wine region should: a mixture of flat land and hills, a river, plenty of good architecture in its wineries, and rows of vines everywhere. By 1998 the sprawling valley had more than 14,165ha (35,000 acres) of vines and about 20 major sub-areas already identified, compared to barely 4047ha (10,000 acres) in the mid-1960s. The Napa Valley was built in two great, giddy waves of enthusiasm, the first in the 1880s and '90s, the second in the 1970s and '80s, when the number of wineries began to swell from a mere dozen to the 380-odd today. In spite of phylloxera, Prohibition, the Great Depression and a second round of phylloxera in the 1990s, winemaking here has had impressive continuity. Of the great winery names of the nineteenth century, BERINGER, BEAULIEU VINEYARD and Charles Krug are still in use.

Napa's adaptation to Cabernet Sauvignon has been just as steady. By the beginning of the twentieth century, Beaulieu and Inglenook were growing and making it as a varietal. The same vineyards at RUTHERFORD still contribute to BV's Georges de Latour Reserve but, like most of its neighbours, this famous vineyard was replanted in the 1990s. In the monumental replanting process, quality-minded winemakers seized the opportunity to relocate Cabernet Sauvignon and Merlot to more suitable sites and Merlot is now usually found in cooler pockets in the CARNEROS or spots immediately north of Napa city itself.

More sweeping changes occurred with Chardonnay; most Napa Chardonnay has been shifted to Carneros and other cool adjacent areas. Phylloxera also forced a few hillside vineyards to replant, but most stuck to Cabernet Sauvignon and other red varieties. Indeed, the hillsides and various other well-drained outcrops such as the benchlands in the western edge of the Oakville and RUTHERFORD AVAs are, generally, better for reds. Somewhat diminished in importance, Sauvignon Blanc still offers a decent wine in a soft-focused way.

As it emerged from the throes of replanting, the Napa Valley is much better aligned viticulturally not only with improved rootstocks but also with a greater overall emphasis on matching grape variety to site for improved quality. Best years: (Cabernet Sauvignon and Merlot) 1997, '95, '94, '93, '92, '91, '90, '87, '86, '85, '84. The list below only begins to cover the cream of the crop. Best producers: ATLAS PEAK, Araujo, BEAULIEU, BERINGER, Burgess, Cafaro, Cain, CAKEBREAD, CAYMUS, Chappellet, CHATEAU MONTELENA, CLOS PEGASE, CLOS DU VAL, Colgin, CUVAISON, DALLA VALLE, DIAMOND CREEK, DOMAINE CHANDON, DOMINUS, DUCKHORN, Etude Wines, FAR NIENTE, Flora Springs, Forman, FRANCISCAN, FROG'S LEAP, Grace Family, GRGICH HILLS, HEITZ, HESS COLLECTION, Charles Krug, Lewis Cellars, Markham, Louis M MARTINI, Mayacamas, Merryvale, MONDAVI, MUMM NAPA VALLEY, NEWTON, OPUS ONE, PAHLMEYER, PARADIGM, Joseph PHELPS, St Clement, St Supery, SAINTSBURY, SCHRAMSBERG, SILVER OAK, SILVERADO, SPOTTSWOODE, STERLING, Stony Hill, SUTTER HOME, SWANSON, Trefethen, TURLEY, VILLA MT EDEN, Whitehall Lane, ZD.

NAVARRA DO

SPAIN, Navarra
♥ ♥ *Grenache Noir (Garnacha Tinta), Tempranillo, Carignan (Cariñena, Mazuelo), Cabernet Sauvignon, Merlot and others*
♀ *Macabeo (Viura), Grenache Blanc (Garnacha Blanca), Malvasía, Chardonnay, Moscatel de Grano Menudo (Muscat Blanc à Petits Grains)*

Though containing a slice of the RIOJA DOC, the Navarra region's increasing fame comes from its eponymous DO, which is a shining example to the rest of Spain. Through an ambitious research and education programme, the Navarra authorities and producers have raised the quality of their wine to rival that from neighbouring Rioja and PENEDÈS. Such a revival only echoes history, for in the eleventh century the powerful kingdom of Navarra included both BORDEAUX and Rioja, thus uniting three very prestigious wine regions. But, in the late 1800s, the phylloxera plague hit Navarra just as badly as it did Bordeaux and Rioja.

Although Garnacha has been Navarra's principal red grape in recent decades, almost all replanting is now with Tempranillo and already some top Tempranillo wines are rivalling those from Rioja. Other newcomers are Cabernet and Merlot – which can both be very successful blended with Tempranillo – and Chardonnay which blends well with Viura. Chardonnay must be harvested promptly, as overripe grapes can lead to very fat, alcoholic wines. Best years: 1996, '95, '94, '93, '90, '89. Best producers: Camilo Castilla, Julian CHIVITE, GUELBENZU, MAGAÑA, Vicente Mulumbres, Alvaro Marino, Castillo de Monjardin, Vinícola Navarra, Nekeas co-operative, OCHOA, Palacio de la Vega, Piedemonte co-operative, Señorío de Sarría, Príncipe de Viana.

NEBBIOLO

This Italian red grape, even with the most modern winemaking techniques, still makes pretty insular wines. That is to say that they're not international in style: they're not drinkable young, they're not soft and fruity and they don't taste like red Bordeaux. Italophiles and other lovers of distinctive wines will regard all this as an advantage.

Nebbiolo is based in Piedmont, with some found in Lombardy's Valtellina, where its name is Chiavennasca, and it is the grape behind Piedmont's two great red wines, Barolo and Barbaresco. To be sure, Barolo is not a wine to drink young. It's too tannic, too acidic and not fruity enough – but that's the chrysalis from which emerge flavours of violets, truffles, raspberries, licorice, prunes, chocolate and goodness knows what else – with time. Nebbiolo reaches its greatest heights in the south of Piedmont, around Alba. In the north the wines get less intense, more violetty but often more chocolaty, too, and apart from Carema, these northern wines may be blended with less tannic red grapes such as Bonarda and Vespolina. Nebbiolo has to be grown on south-facing slopes, but it still ripens late, sometimes even as late as November. There is plenty of fog by then, and fog in Italian is *nebbia*, hence the grape's name. In the provinces of Novara and Vercelli, in the north of Piedmont, Nebbiolo is also called Spanna.

NEBBIOLO D'ALBA DOC

ITALY, Piedmont
♥ *Nebbiolo*

Nebbiolo d'Alba is ideal if you feel like a taste of Nebbiolo but don't feel the occasion merits the power and cost of a classic wine. It is grown in lands adjacent to BAROLO and BARBARESCO but doesn't have their long aging requirement: one year is enough. Until recently, conventional wisdom had it that Nebbiolo d'Alba was a poor man's Barolo, but Matteo Correggia has disproved that theory, his version being quite capable of taking on and beating most Barolos. Most, however, remain in the lighter mode, the compensation being that they are both much more approachable and much less expensive.

NEETHLINGSHOF

SOUTH AFRICA, Western Cape, Stellenbosch WO
� *Cabernet Sauvignon, Merlot, Syrah (Shiraz), Pinotage and others*
♀ *Chardonnay, Sauvignon Blanc, Gewurztraminer, Riesling (Rhine/Weisser Riesling) and others*

International financier Hans-Joachim Schreiber was one of the first major-league foreigners to invest in the Cape back in 1985. He is a man who thinks big; not content with purchasing Neethlingshof, he also bought the then unknown farm on the opposite side of the valley, Stellenzicht. He has subsequently added three other farms in different parts of the STELLENBOSCH area to his impressive portfolio. The vineyards on all these properties have undergone a complete re-vamp and have been planted with premium, virus-free varieties. Modern cellar facilities were carefully incorporated around the old, historic building and the 1814 Manor House was also restored. Winemaker Schalk van der Westhuizen, who was born on the farm, has been a steadying influence in a cellar where many of his colleagues have filled the post more temporarily. His and the farm's pride and joy is the consistent Weisser Riesling Noble Late Harvest with its rich botrytis character and steely clean acid. Sauvignon Blanc and Gewurztraminer are more individual whites. The reds are led by Lord Neethling Reserve, a serious Cabernet Sauvignon-Merlot-Shiraz blend, and a sound, straight Cabernet Sauvignon. Best years: (Weisser Riesling Noble Late Harvest) 1998, '97, '96, '95, '94, '93, '92, '91, '90.

NELSON

NEW ZEALAND, South Island

Nelson, on the north-western tip of the South Island, is in the shadow of the large and glamorous MARLBOROUGH region. Vineyard area is a relatively humble 160ha (395 acres), shared between 14 mostly small wineries. Chardonnay is the most widely planted and most prestigious grape variety, with NEUDORF producing what is occasionally the country's best example. Sauvignon Blanc ranks second and although Nelson makes very creditable Sauvignon wine it lacks the prestige of Marlborough Sauvignon Blanc and struggles to command a similar price, despite higher production costs on the smaller and often more labour-intensive vineyards. Nelson makes

creditable Riesling in a range of mostly dry styles with strong lime flavours and a botrytis influence when the vintage allows. Stylish Pinot Noir is made by Neudorf, Ruby Bay, Greenhough and specialist Pomona Ridge. Best years: 1998, '96, '94, '91. Best producers: Greenhough, Neudorf, Seifried Estate, Spencer Hill Estate.

NEMEA AO

GREECE, Peloponnese
♥ *Aghiorghitiko*

Hercules killed the Nemean lion and was possibly glad of a drink afterwards; and wine from Nemea, in the Peloponnese near Corinth, *has* been around for 2500 years. The Aghiorghitiko (St-George) grape, grown in vineyards between 250 and 800m (820 and 2620ft), is native to Greece and produces a big, rich wine known locally as the 'Blood of Hercules'. It can be long-lived, but like all Greek wines, so much depends on the skill of the individual winemaker. Only an example whose burly, rugged power has not been diminished by oxidation and lazy winemaking will age properly. Drink young or with short aging. Best years: 1997, '94, '92, '90. Best producers: Boutari, Achaia, Andrew P. Cambas, Kourtakis, SEMELI, Skouras, STROFILIA.

NERO D'AVOLA

This is Sicily's most important native red grape, a variety of tremendous potential but with one major defect. The potential consists in its ability to deliver wines big in colour and fruit, with firm but not excessive tannins and lots of stuffing, capable of fairly long aging as in the case of REGALEALI/CONTE TASCA D'ALMERITA's Rosso del Conte. The defect – high fixed (tartaric) acidity – could also be regarded as a merit, since loss of acidity would seem in these torrid, drought-prone climes to be a danger. The problem is that in all but the ripest of vintages that acidity is just too high, which generally means blending with a variety of low acid content, like Frappato. New blends with Syrah seem to be working well.

NEUCHÂTEL

SWITZERLAND
♥ ♀ *Pinot Noir*
♀ *Chasselas, Chardonnay*

One of the French-speaking Swiss cantons, Neuchâtel has vineyards that stretch in a long strip along the shore of Lake Neuchâtel, with the Jura mountains protecting their backs. The wines can be some of Switzerland's best, with some character getting into the Pinot

Noir; the Chasselas is light and bone dry, often with a slight prickle. The Oeil de Perdrix Pinot Noir rosé is particularly delicate and attractive. There are three small individual appellations: Schloss Vaumarcus, Hôpital Poutalès and Domaine de Champrevèyres. Best producers: Ch. d'Auvernier, de Montmollin, Porret.

NEUDORF

NEW ZEALAND, South Island, Nelson
♥ *Pinot Noir*
♀ *Chardonnay, Sauvignon Blanc Riesling*

Winemaker/owner Tim Finn has made some of the most exciting and stylish Chardonnays to come from New Zealand to date, textured and complex with masses of grilled hazelnut, butter and peach flavours matching the best in Australia, yet with that unmistakable South Island New Zealand intensity of fruit. Neudorf Riesling is one of the few New Zealand examples to capture a steely, mineral character which adds extra depth to classic apple/lime flavours. The Pinot Noir, too, can stand out from the crowd with its strawberry fruit and ethereal perfume, although NELSON has a very temperamental climate and late summer rainfall is always a threat down here. Best years: 1998, '96, '94, '91, '90, '89.

NEUSIEDLERSEE, NEUSIEDLERSEE-HÜGELLAND

AUSTRIA, Burgenland

Lake Neusiedl lies, reedy and pleasure-boat-filled, in the north of Austria's BURGENLAND, almost on the border with Hungary. Thanks to the lake, which gives the right amount of morning humidity followed by dry sunshine, fine, sweet botrytis-affected wines are produced in remarkable quantities almost every year. The eastern side, the district called Neusiedlersee, produces the most. Here in the south, in an area called Seewinkel around Illmitz, the effect of the lake is enhanced by umpteen tiny lakes, and botrytis will attack just about anything. In the north, around Gols and Mönchhof, red and dry white wines are made as well. The western side, Neusiedlersee-Hügelland, is more varied, in that sweet wines are mostly made in a narrow strip near the lake, with the town of RUST an important centre, and they tend to be less opulent and sweet. Elsewhere, dry, ripe whites and soft, velvety reds are produced. Best years: (sweet wines) 1998, '96, '95, '94, '93, '91. Best producers: FEILER-ARTLINGER, Gernot HEINRICH, JURIS, Anton KOLLWENTZ, Alois KRACHER, NITTNAUS, Peter Schandl, Heidi Schröck, TRIEBAUMER, Robert WENZEL.

NEW SOUTH WALES Australia

FOR THE FIRST 170 OR SO years of viticulture and winemaking in New South Wales, the wine map was dominated by the Hunter Valley, albeit with a sideways glance at the vast sprawl of bulk production in the Riverina. But since the early part of the 1990s, the small, premium quality regions hugging the western side of the Great Dividing Range have assumed rapidly growing importance. The long-term resident was Mudgee, but it has now been joined by Orange, at a significantly higher elevation, Cowra, a distinctly warm region, Hilltops, dominated by McWilliam's with its Barwang property, the Canberra District, which has recently seen the arrival of BRL Hardy, and finally, well into the foothills of the Australian Alps, Tumbarumba. Of these Mudgee, Cowra and the Hilltops already stand as major producers in terms of volume, and as significant contributors to the pool of Australian premium wine. Orange, Canberra District and Tumbarumba have great quality potential, although site selection (particularly to guard against spring frosts) is essential.

The Hunter Valley remains an enigma, yet it is sharing in the near-hysterical growth of the latter part of the 1990s. Max Lake of Lake's Folly once said that the only thing wrong with Coonawarra (in the remote south-east corner of South

In the Lower Hunter Valley the smoky blue Brokenback Range makes a dramatic backdrop to the vineyards along Broke Road near Pokolbin. These vineyards, belonging to Tyrrell's, are some of the best in the Hunter Valley.

Australia) is that it is so far from Sydney. It might equally well be said that the only thing right with the Hunter Valley is that it is only 145km (90 miles) from Sydney, Australia's most populated area.

Australian winemakers – including some in the Hunter Valley itself – have been quoted as saying that, with the level of knowledge we now have about climate, soil and the grape vines' various needs, no-one in their right mind would ever plant a vineyard in the Hunter Valley. It's far too hot and humid during the growing season for quality grapes, the spring is generally a period of drought while the autumn vintage is regularly devastated by rainstorms. Much of the soil is impenetrable 'pug' clay. But somehow the Hunter has produced some of Australia's greatest wines; and as tourism has flourished so has the Hunter duly blossomed.

In the brave new world of Geographic Indications, the five most important zones in New South Wales are Hunter Valley, Central Ranges, Big Rivers and Southern New South Wales.

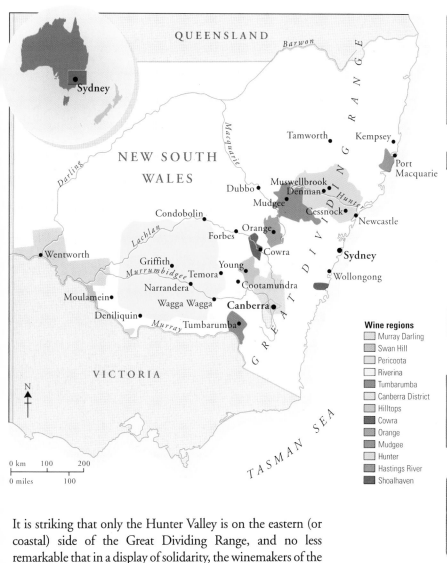

HUNTINGTON ESTATE
Huntington Estate is one of the leading wineries in the rediscovered Mudgee region where Cabernet Sauvignon makes the best wines, usually as a varietal wine.

ROSEMOUNT ESTATE
Complex, weighty Roxburgh Chardonnay is one of the top wines from this model Hunter Valley winery.

TYRRELL'S
Vat 1 Semillon is a true Hunter Valley classic, taking on great honeyed richness with age.

DE BORTOLI
Noble One is brilliant noble-rot Semillon that can equal any of the world's great sweet wines.

BROKENWOOD
The best wine from this high-profile Hunter Valley winery is the Graveyard Vineyard Shiraz.

LAKE'S FOLLY
The austere Chardonnay from this revered winery is designed for long aging and can reach Burgundian peaks of elegance and intensity.

LINDEMANS
This large historic Hunter Valley winery is now part of Southcorp and a recent programme of investment should help restore quality.

Wine regions
- Murray Darling
- Swan Hill
- Pericoota
- Riverina
- Tumbarumba
- Canberra District
- Hilltops
- Cowra
- Orange
- Mudgee
- Hunter
- Hastings River
- Shoalhaven

It is striking that only the Hunter Valley is on the eastern (or coastal) side of the Great Dividing Range, and no less remarkable that in a display of solidarity, the winemakers of the regions traditionally known as the Lower Hunter and Upper Hunter have agreed that their region will simply be known as the Hunter, with a host of sub-regions yet to come.

It is only when you travel west out into the hinterland that you come to the Riverina (also known as the Murrumbidgee Irrigation Area or as Griffith). Here, the high-yielding vineyards are irrigated through the growing season, and every grape variety known is propagated here, chiefly feeding the bulk market. But even here the quality message is hitting home. Several companies are bottling premium lines and even trying their hand at Estate labels, and one of the world's greatest sweet wines – De Bortoli's Noble One – comes from Riverina fruit.

REGIONAL ENTRIES
Canberra District, Cowra, Hastings River, Hilltops, Hunter Valley, Mudgee, Orange, Riverina.

PRODUCER ENTRIES
Brokenwood, De Bortoli, Huntington Estate, Lake's Folly, McWilliam's, Rosemount Estate, Rothbury Estate, Tyrrell's, Wyndham Estate.

NEW YORK STATE USA

NEW YORK STATE IS HOME TO the oldest continuously operating winery in the USA, Brotherhood Winery established in 1839. Native and hybrid American varieties were originally planted in the Atlantic Northeast of the United States in what is now the Hudson River AVA. By the end of the nineteenth century, there were more than 8094ha (20,000 acres) of vineyards in New York State.

Most of this huge increase in planting took place in the Finger Lakes region. Early viticulturists believed that severe winter temperature swings (perhaps 50 degrees or more in a single day) made it impossible to grow *Vitis vinifera* grapes successfully here. Table and juice grapes were planted instead and it wasn't until the 1950s that vinifera grapes were cultivated by Dr Konstantin Frank, whose experience in Europe and the Ukraine had convinced him that these varieties could survive such harsh winters. Vinifera varieties are now replacing many French and American hybrids as vineyards are dug up and replanted.

There are nearly 100 wineries and more than 12,140ha (30,000 acres) of vine in the six New York State AVAs which are split between four distinct regions. The western portion of the state falls within the Lake Erie AVA (including parts of Pennsylvania and Ohio). The Finger Lakes AVA is named after the series of deep lakes that form the fingers of a hand below Lake Ontario. Steep slopes on the edges of these deep lakes provide a moderating climate against severe winter cold. The relatively new Cayuga Lake AVA is lower in altitude and is a deeper lake creating a unique mesoclimate suitable for vinifera grapes. Riesling and Chardonnay are the trump cards here. The historic Hudson River AVA on steep hillsides along the river's edge is about 65km (40 miles) north of New York City. Most of the wines here are from French hybrids, especially Seyval Blanc and Baco Noir, although Pinot Noir and Chardonnay have been planted.

Finally, on the eastern edges of the state there are two AVAs on Long Island, the most exciting area and a cool region with a long growing season that gives great concentration of fruit in a good year. The Hamptons AVA is a tiny vineyard area along the south fork of Long Island bordering the Atlantic Ocean. The weather can cause havoc here and several good vintages have been ruined by hurricanes, an

The Finger Lakes region, here at Seneca Lake, one of the best sites in the AVA, relies on the critical effects of water in tempering a climate that would otherwise be far too harsh for conventional wine grape-growing.

FOX RUN
The strength here at this Finger Lakes winery is the Chardonnay Reserve with layers of buttery, toasty flavours.

BEDELL CELLARS
Kip Bedell' s wines include a Merlot Reserve which is now considered one of Long Island's top red wines. With layers of dark, concentrated black cherry and berry fruit, the wine is capable of extended aging.

HARGRAVE VINEYARD
The pioneering name in Long Island's fine wines in the early 1970s, Hargrave makes substantial, rich Merlot with wonderfully round, yet dry fruit and cedarwood scent.

LAMOREAUX LANDING
Bold, oaky Chardonnay has helped make this Finger Lakes winery one of the most important on the East Coast.

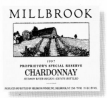

MILLBROOK VINEYARDS
From the Hudson River Valley, Millbrook makes a range of stylish wines including ripe, oaky Chardonnay.

PALMER VINEYARDS
Established in 1982, Palmer was among the first to offer eye-catching Merlot from Long Island.

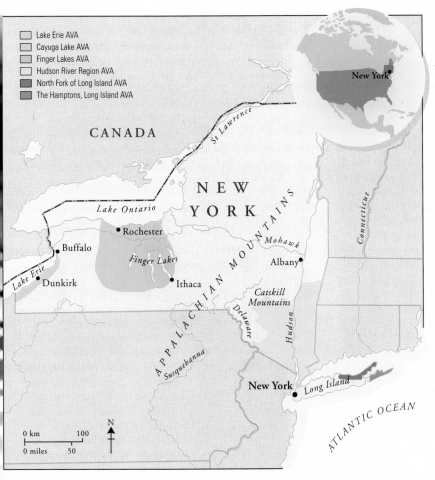

obstacle few other premium wine regions in the world have to face. The North Fork of Long Island AVA is a rapidly expanding area with a maritime climate where the growing season is long enough to ripen Bordeaux varietals and provide excellent concentration of fruit in a good year and many world-class wines are being made.

Native American and hybrid varieties, especially Concord which makes excellent grape juice but pretty duff wine, continue to dominate the East Coast vineyards but vinifera vines are on the increase. Chardonnay, Riesling, Gewurztraminer and Pinot Blanc are the white vinifera varietals that have succeeded best in most of the New York AVAs. Sauvignon Blanc, especially, is suited to the Long Island climate. For reds, Merlot ripens early and does well in the both the Finger Lakes and Long Island regions. Cabernet Sauvignon and Cabernet Franc just about reach maturity in Long Island's long growing season but usually retain a grassy, though attractive, character.

PRODUCER ENTRIES
Glenora Wine Cellars, Hargrave Vineyard, Lamoreaux Landing, Millbrook Vineyards, Palmer Vineyards.

NEWTON VINEYARDS

USA, California, Napa County, Napa Valley AVA

♏ *Merlot, Cabernet Sauvignon*

♀ *Chardonnay, Viognier*

Su Hua Newton's breathtaking wine estate, with its striking Chinese-style architecture and gardens, is built on the hillside overlooking the NAPA VALLEY, west of St Helena. Its main vineyards are carved onto steep slopes, with cellars tunnelled into them. The Cabernet and Merlot are two of CALIFORNIA's most successful examples, showing a distinct BORDEAUX style with their ripe, black-cherry and plum fruit. Best years: 1997, '96, '95, '94, '93, '92, '91, '90, '89, '87, '85. Newton's Claret is on a par with the finest Meritage wines around. The Chardonnays improve with every vintage and the top release is now an unfiltered, unfined wine that owes a good deal to the best wines of MEURSAULT. Lush Viognier is next in the pipeline. Best years: 1998, '97, '96, '95, '94, '93, '92. Second label, Newtonian, is also good.

NGATARAWA

NEW ZEALAND, North Island, Hawke's Bay

♏ *Cabernet Sauvignon, Merlot, Cabernet Franc*

♀ *Chardonnay, Sauvignon Blanc, Riesling (Rhine Riesling)*

One of HAWKE'S BAY's longest-established wineries, the Ngatarawa estate vineyards were created in 1981 by winemaker-partner Alwyn Corban on a sheep station in Henderson owned by the other partner, the Glazebrook family. The viticulture is organic.

Using Hawke's Bay fruit, the Special Selection wines are bottled under the Glazebrook label, including a fine Chardonnay and a Cabernet-Merlot blend, to be enjoyed at their best within five years. The Glazebrook botrytized, late-harvest Rhine Riesling, which comes from a specially reserved vineyard block by the winery, can be outstanding. Wines under the Stables label are less exciting. Best years: 1998, '96, '95, '94, '91, '90.

NGATARAWA

Ngatarawa's Special Selections are sold under the Glazebrook label. The Chardonnay is complex, ripe and exotically flavoured.

NIAGARA PENINSULA

CANADA, Ontario

Situated on the 43rd parallel, the Niagara Peninsula is a narrow finger of land sandwiched between the Niagara Escarpment and Lake Ontario and is the most important wine region of southern Ontario. In terms of sunshine hours and rainfall, the Peninsula enjoys a climate similar to Burgundy's in France and the thermal influence of both Lake Erie and Ontario is a significant aid to viticulture. The vineyards begin just east of Hamilton and stretch along the south shore of Lake Ontario, all the way to Niagara Falls. Some of the best sites lie 30–50m (90–150ft) above the plain on the sloping benchland that runs along the escarpment. The most successful vinifera varieties are led by Riesling, Chardonnay and Pinot Noir. Best years: 1998, '97, '95. Best producers: CAVE SPRING CELLARS, CHATEAU DES CHARMES, HENRY OF PELHAM, INNISKILLIN WINES, Marynissen Estates, Thirty Bench Winery.

NIEBAUM COPPOLA WINERY

USA, California, Napa County, Rutherford AVA

♏ *Cabernet Sauvignon, Cabernet Franc, Merlot, Zinfandel*

♀ *Chardonnay*

Movie director Francis Ford Coppola entered the wine world by buying the historic Gustav Niebaum (Inglenook's founder) estate and surrounding RUTHERFORD vineyards which are some of NAPA's oldest. A decade later he added the Inglenook winery and tourist centre. His pride and joy is a red Meritage, Rubicon, a blend of Cabernet Sauvignon, Merlot and Cabernet Franc, that in its early vintages tended towards the powerful and rustic, but has since been reined in to display greater harmony and youthful appeal. It can still be aged for a decade. Best years: 1996, '95, '94, '92, '91, '90, '87. There is also Zinfandel Edizione Pennino and a variety of mid-priced wines under the Coppola Family label, including Merlot, Cabernet Franc, Chardonnay and two blends, Rosso and Bianco.

NIEDERHAUSEN

GERMANY, Nahe

This is the most important quality wine commune in the NAHE. Here, on steep slopes with extremely stony volcanic soils, the Riesling grape gives some of the most intensely minerally wines in the entire world. The top vineyard is the Hermannshöhle, which was rated first among all the Nahe vineyard sites in the Royal Prussian classification of the region of 1901. Almost as good are the Hermannsberg, Kertz and Rosenberg sites. Best producers: H DÖNNHOF, Mathern, Gutsverwaltung Niederhausen, Sitzius.

NIEDERÖSTERREICH

AUSTRIA

The state of Niederösterreich or Lower Austria has a clutch of wine regions, notably the KAMPTAL, KREMSTAL and WACHAU, which have firmly established reputations for distinctive and high-quality, dry white wines. At the other extreme is the large, but comparatively unknown WEINVIERTEL region, much of whose production is sold in bulk for blending or as a base wine for cheap Sekt. As yet, the name Niederösterreich does not appear on wine labels as a legally defined designation, but plans are afoot to change this.

NIEPOORT

PORTUGAL, Douro, Douro DOC, Port DOC

♏ *Tinta Roriz (Tempranillo), Tinta Barroca, Tinta Cão, Touriga Naçional, Touriga Francesa and others*

♀ *Gouveio, Viosinho, Rabigato, Malvasía Fina and others*

This small but very high-quality PORT company was founded in 1842 and is still family run by Rolf Niepoort and his son Dirk. Niepoort has earned a reputation for tawny ports, particularly the elegant, aromatic colheita wines (tawnies from a single year), which mature for many years in barrel before being bottled and sold. Garrafeira ports are another speciality, wood-aged for five years, then transferred to glass demijohns for perhaps another 20 years, and finally into bottles. The vintage ports should not be overlooked for they are very long-lived. The company also produces a single-quinta vintage from Quinta do Passadouro deep in the Pinhão Valley. Late Bottled Vintages (bottled without filtration) are also extremely good and will develop well in bottle. Niepoort also produces an extremely good, solid DOURO red and one of the few really drinkable white Douro wines under the Redoma label. Best years: (vintage ports) 1994, '92, '91, '87, '82, '70, '63.

NIERSTEIN

GERMANY, Rheinhessen

This is a very famous wine town in the RHEINHESSEN – so famous, indeed, that one third of the Rheinhessen basks in its reflected glory: this is the size of the Bereich Nierstein, which extends over the north-east of the region. Then there is Nierstein Gutes Domtal, a Grosslage covering 15 villages west of Nierstein itself, and including only one vineyard

Pfaffenkappe, which is technically part of Nierstein. Traps for the unwary, indeed: wines sold under the Bereich or Grosslage names are unlikely to be more than basic, and will probably contain mainly Müller-Thurgau.

The name of Nierstein has been so devalued that it is sometimes hard to believe that it can be a source of seriously good wine. However, the town does boast a string of steep vineyards with red slate soil, which can give richly fruity, intensely minerally Rieslings as great as any in Germany, and the quality banner is carried by such estates as GUNDERLOCH, HEYL ZU HERRNSHEIM and ST-ANTONY.

NIKOLAIHOF

AUSTRIA, Niederösterreich, Wachau
♀ *Riesling, Grüner Veltliner and others*

Nikolaihof is one of the best wine estates in the WACHAU, and its owner Nikolais Saahs and his wife boast splendid, classically structured Rieslings and Grüner Veltliners that are several notches higher than the general run. The house (and chapel) are marvellous, and the courtyard is one of the most sympatico places anywhere to taste a glass of wine. Look out particularly for the Cuvée Elisabeth blend, named after the Saahs' eldest daughter. Their most famous wine, however, is the Riesling from the Steiner Hund vineyard: firm when young, it ages magnificently. Best years: 1997, '95, '94, '92, '91, '90, '86.

NITRA

SLOVAKIA, Nitra
♥ *Frankovka and others*
♀ *Pinot Blanc, Irsay Oliver and others*

The Nitra winery is situated in south-east Slovakia. The vines are mostly grown at between 125 and 250m (410 and 820ft) above sea level, on south-west-facing hillsides, and the process of restitution of previously nationalized property means that most have been returned to private hands. Wines here are being made under Western supervision to produce crisp, aromatic, light whites and light, fruity reds that can only get better as Western expertise spreads to the vineyards. Drink the wines young.

HANS & ANITA NITTNAUS

AUSTRIA, Burgenland, Neusiedlersee, Gols
♥ *Blaufränkisch, Blauer Zweigelt, Cabernet Sauvignon*
♀ *Sauvignon Blanc, Chardonnay, Welchriesling, Neuburger*

Hans Nittnaus makes no bones about the fact that white wine is something of a sideline for him, although his Sauvignon Blanc can have good gooseberry fruit and his Pannobile Weiss is a satisfyingly full, barrique-aged blend of Chardonnay, Neuburger and Sauvignon Blanc. The real thing for him is red wine, and here he does not hold back on the tannins or the oak. Once the result used to be brutally hard monsters, but in recent years he has moderated both to great advantage. Best and most powerful is the Comondor, a rich plum and blackcurrant blend of Blaufränkisch and Cabernet, followed by the somewhat suppler, faster-maturing Pannobile Rot. Best years: 1998, '97, '94, '93, '92.

NOBILO

NEW ZEALAND, North Island, Huapai
♥ *Cabernet Sauvignon, Merlot, Pinotage, Pinot Noir*
♀ *Chardonnay, Sauvignon Blanc, Gewurztraminer, Riesling*

Nobilo was at the forefront of the quality end of the New Zealand wine industry for decades. The initial impetus came from a 1966 partnership with the English company Gilbeys, of gin fame, but now the family (complete with the towering presence of Nick Nobilo) are back in control. A range of totally or partially barrel-fermented and matured Chardonnays, sometimes showing rich, toasty oak and fruit, lead the way alongside the MARLBOROUGH and HAWKE'S BAY Cabernet Sauvignon, and the stylish Marlborough Sauvignon Blanc, Riesling and Gewurztraminer. In 1998 Nobilo bought SELAKS, a successful mid-sized family winemaker with wineries in AUCKLAND and Marlborough. The Australian giant BRL HARDY subsequently purchased 25 per cent of the enlarged company which gained stock exchange listing in 1998. Best years: (Marlborough) 1996, '94, '91; (Hawke's Bay) 1998, '96, '95, '94, '91.

NORTON

ARGENTINA, Mendoza, Luján de Cuyo
♥ *Cabernet Sauvignon, Malbec, Merlot, Bonarda*
♀ *Chardonnay, Torrontés*

Austrian millionaire Swarowski has ploughed a staggering fortune into Norton, based in Luján de Cuyo. Not only has he bought first-class vineyards around the winery (just the right area for high-quality Malbec), he has established a high-tech winery to rival any. With single-minded perfectionist Michael Halstrich (Swarowski's step-son) in charge, expect to see major wines emerge from here. Some good wines are already available, especially Norton Privada, a BORDEAUX-style red. The range is wide, from reasonably delicate Torrontés to barrique-fermented Chardonnay, plus some chewy and amiable Bonarda. Best years: 1999, '97, '96, '94.

QUINTA DO NOVAL

PORTUGAL, Douro, Douro DOC, Port DOC
♥ *Tinta Roriz (Tempranillo), Tinta Barroca, Tinto Cão, Touriga Nacional, Touriga Francesa and others*
♀ *Gouveio, Viosinho, Rabigato, Malvasía Fina and others*

Quinta do Noval, one of the finest properties in the DOURO, is also the name of a PORT shipper. It belonged to the Van Zeller family until 1993, when it was sold to the French insurance group AXA, who also have substantial wine interests in BORDEAUX. Noval is the first major port shipper to move lock, stock and barrel from Vila Nova de Gaia (the traditional home of the port business) to the Douro Valley where it has built an impressive, air-conditioned storage facility.

Noval produces a complete range of ports, all of which are of a high standard. But their most prestigious wine is their 'Naçional' vintage port, made entirely from low-yielding, ungrafted vines planted on the Noval estate. The wines are some of the most concentrated of all vintage ports, with a deep, opaque colour when young and an almost overpowering intensity of fruit. The 1931 Naçional is legendary, not just for its superb quality, but because it holds the record as the most expensive bottle of port ever sold.

Noval has recently begun to produce its own unfortified DOURO wine under the Corucho brand label. The company also works closely with Quinta do Roriz and produces both port and Douro wine from the property. Best years: (vintage ports) 1994, '91, '85, '70, '66, '63.

NUITS-ST-GEORGES AC

FRANCE, Burgundy, Côte de Nuits
♥ *Pinot Noir*
♀ *Chardonnay, Pinot Blanc, Pinot Noir (sic)*

Nuits-St-Georges is one of the few relatively reliable 'village' names in Burgundy. The appellation, which includes the village of Prémeaux, is big, with 375ha (927 acres) of

NORTON
From one of Argentina's top wineries, the complex, classy Privada is a full-bodied Bordeaux blend with a gorgeous silky texture and a hint of perfume.

vines. Though it has no Grands Crus, there are 38 Premiers Crus (more than any other AC); many of them are extremely good. The wine can be rather slow to open out, often needing at least five years, but then it gains a lovely dry, plumskins chewiness which ages to a delicious deep figs-and-pruneskins fruit, chocolaty, smoky and rather decayed. Best years: (reds) 1997, '96, '95, '93, '91, '90, '89, '88, '85, '83, '81, '78. Best producers: l'Arlot, Chauvenet, CHEVILLON, Chopin-Groffier, Confuron, Dubois, FAIVELEY, GOUGES, GRIVOT, LEROY, MÉO-CAMUZET, Michelot, Moillard, Mongeard-Mugneret, Rion.

There are also minuscule amounts of a strange but delicious white Nuits-St-Georges, believe it or not. The few precious bottles made by Domaine Henri Gouges are the most famous whites made in the Côte de Nuits, where the red Pinot Noir is so completely dominant that Monsieur Gouges doesn't even grow Chardonnay and Pinot Blanc but a strange white mutation of Pinot Noir. Annual production is never more than 2500 bottles and often considerably less. L'Arlot, Rion and Chevillon also make small quantities of white wine, but none to match Gouges for power and complexity. Best years: (whites) 1996, '95, '93, '92, '90, '89, '88, '86, '85.

NYETIMBER

ENGLAND, West Sussex
♀ ♟ *Chardonnay, Pinot Noir, Pinot Meunier*

This estate, originally named in the eleventh-century Domesday Book, was rescued by two expatriate Chicagoans, Stuart and Sandy Moss, who not only restored the rundown buildings and barns, but, against the advice of the Ministry of Agriculture, planted vines (mostly Chardonnay) on well-drained green-sand over chalk. There are now over 20ha (50 acres) of vines. First production of the Champagne-method sparkling wine was an exciting Chardonnay Blanc de Blancs in 1992. Subsequent vintages include Pinot Noir and Meunier in the blend.

VIN DE PAYS D'OC

FRANCE, Languedoc-Roussillon
♟ ♟ *Merlot, Cabernet Sauvignon, Syrah, Grenache, Carignan and others*
♀ *Chardonnay, Sauvignon Blanc, Viognier, Grenache Blanc, Marsanne and others*

Covering the huge area of the LANGUEDOC-ROUSSILLON, the Vin de Pays d'Oc has become the symbol of the Midi's new liberated, modern, high-tech image. It has also ballooned into a formidable commercial success and now represents 33 per cent of all French VINS DE PAYS. The achievement is due in large part to the decision to produce New World-style reds and whites, using internationally successful varieties such as Merlot, Cabernet Sauvignon, Syrah, Chardonnay, Sauvignon Blanc and Viognier. These essentially varietal wines represent around 80 per cent of the production. Other grape varieties include Pinot Noir and the southern varieties such as Grenache, Mourvèdre, Cinsaut and Carignan for reds and rosés and Marsanne, Roussanne and Rolle for the whites.

Heavyweight local producers like FORTANT DE FRANCE and Val d'Orbieu have given impetus to the movement and have been complemented by the arrival of outside investors and talented winemakers from Australia, England and Switzerland. Best producers: de l'AIGLE, de la Baume, Clovallon, Fortant de France, Grand Crès, la Grange de Quatre Sous, Henry, Herrick, J Lurton, d'Ormesson, Pierres Plantées, Ryman, Terre Mégère, Val d'Orbieu, Virginie.

OCHOA

SPAIN, Navarra, Navarra DO
♟ *Tempranillo, Cabernet Sauvignon, Merlot, Grenache Noir (Garnacha Tinta)*
♟ *Grenache Noir (Garnacha Tinta), Cabernet Sauvignon*
♀ *Macabeo (Viura), Ugni Blanc, Moscatel de Grano Menudo (Muscat Blanc à Petits Grains)*

Bodegas Ochoa, using techniques such as stainless steel fermentation and maceration of grape skins before fermentation for both whites and rosés, is the perfect demonstration of the vastly improving face of NAVARRA wine.

The white is ultra-modern, fresh, clean and lemony-minty, and the rosé soft, attractive and dominated by almondy, creamy flavour. There are wines made from 100 per cent Tempranillo, Merlot and Cabernet Sauvignon, all with over a year's aging in oak barrels, the Tempranillo, savoury and herby; the Cabernet Sauvignon, blackcurranty, herbaceous, ripe and gluggable; the Merlot intensely floral and

jammy. The Reserva and Gran Reserva wines are blends of all three varieties. Already excellent, these wines will almost certainly improve even further. Best years: 1996, '95, '94, '93, '91, '90, '89.

OCKFEN

GERMANY, Mosel-Saar-Ruwer

This Saar village boasts a good few top producers, such as the State Domaine, ZILLIKEN and Heinz Wagner, but like most of the Saar, it needs a good warm year if the wines are not to be a bit green or raw. In such good years, however, they are immensely long-lived and packed with piercing fruit. Bockstein is the top vineyard site, planted mostly with Riesling and producing very stylish wines.

OKANAGAN VALLEY

CANADA, British Columbia

The bulk of British Columbia's 132 vineyards covering 1117ha (2761 acres) are situated in the Okanagan Valley. A spectacular semi-arid region, the valley runs some 120km (75 miles) along the shores of Lake Okanagan from the town of Vernon in the north, to Penticton in the south. From here it heads south all the way to the WASHINGTON STATE border. Over 40 wineries produce a wide range of still and sparkling wines made from Chardonnay, Pinot Blanc, Pinot Gris, Gewurztraminer, Pinot Noir, Merlot, Gamay and Cabernet Sauvignon. Best producers: BURROWING OWL, INNISKILLIN Okanagan, MISSION HILL, QUAILS' GATE, SUMAC RIDGE. Best years: 1998, '95, '94.

OLTREPÒ PAVESE DOC

ITALY, Lombardy
♟ *Barbera, Bonarda, Pinot Noir (Pinot Nero)*
♟ *Pinot Noir (Pinot Nero)*
♀ *Cortese, Muscat (Moscato), Pinot Gris (Pinot Grigio), Pinot Noir (Pinot Nero), Welschriesling (Riesling Italico), Riesling (Riesling Renano)*

The Oltrepò (over the Po) Pavese (in Pavia province) is one of just two patches of LOMBARDY lying south of the lumbering Po river, which almost bisects Italy. Its soft, rolling hills bring blessed relief from the humidity and fog of the Po valley. Many of the wines in the Oltrepò Pavese DOC are single varietal and for drinking young, mainly in the bars and restaurants of nearby Milan.

Given a choice from all these varieties, the best and most typical are Bonarda, Barbera or white Moscato, or the straight Oltrepò Pavese Rosso (Bonarda with Barbera, Uva Rara, Ughetta). If from one of three sub-zones, the

Rosso glories in the additional names of Bar-bacarlo, Buttafuoco or Sangue di Giuda. With all these, varietals and blends, reds and whites, there is a strong tendency for the wines to be a bit fizzy; that's how they like them there. Hardly surprisingly in this land where bubble is king, there's plenty of Spumante, best from Pinot-type grapes, and even more bulk Spumante, trucked out to feed the voracious sparkling wine houses of Turin. Monsupello (for fizz), Fugazza and Tenuta Mazzolino lead a long list of good producers.

OMAR KHAYYAM

INDIA, Maharashtra

♟ *Pinot Noir and others*

♀ *Ugni Blanc, Chardonnay, Pinot Meunier, Thompson Seedless*

Indian mega-millionaire Sham Chougule started producing India's first CHAMPAGNE-method sparkling wine back in the 1980s, with technical assistance from Champagne's Piper-Heidsieck. The vineyards are about 750m (2460ft) up, near the Sahyadri moun-tains, but they need plenty of irrigation – to produce just one litre of fizz requires about 100 litres of water per day. After a promising start the wine now bears little resemblance to its prototype and has become rather clumsy, and inelegant. There are other blends as well: Marquise de Pompadour, with extra dosage, a demi-sec version and a still dry white. The still red needs work yet.

WILLI OPITZ

AUSTRIA, Burgenland, Neusiedlersee, Illmitz

♟ *Pinot Noir (Blauburgunder)*

♀ *Pinot Blanc (Weissburgunder), Welschriesling, Gewürztraminer and others*

Opitz is an eccentric Austrian grower from Illmitz in NEUSIEDLERSEE; as one would expect from this part of the country near Lake Neusiedl, he specializes in sweet wines. There

are dry wines as well, and good reds, but even Grüner Veltliner gets turned into Auslese or Beerenauslese, and grapes (red and white) that are unaffected by noble rot are liable to become Schilfwein, or 'reed' wine. You'd be hard put to find much about Schilfwein in the Austrian rule book, because it is Opitz's own idea: it involves drying ripe grapes on reeds to concen-trate their sugar before fermentation. The principle is similar to that of the region's Stroh-wein, or 'straw' wine, but the quality is higher. Best years: 1998, '95, '94, '93, '92, '91, '89.

OPPENHEIM

GERMANY, Rheinhessen

The town of Oppenheim is in the Rhein Terrasse area of the RHEINHESSEN, the stretch of river bank that produces wines with more concentration and finesse than those from the neighbouring areas. Good, refined wines come from the Sackträger vineyard site; Kreuz, part of which is in the village of Dienheim, is also distinguished. What is less exciting is the Grosslage of Krötenbrunnen, which covers about 1800ha (4448 acres). It is largely either flat or very nearly flat, and is used mostly for simple QbA wines of little interest and gener-ally a rather earthy taste. Best producers (in Oppenheim itself): Carl Koch Erben, Louis Guntrum, Kühling-Gillot, Staatsweingut mit Weinbaudomäne (a research institute with umpteen new crossings in its vineyards).

OPUS ONE

USA, California, Napa County, Napa Valley AVA

♟ *Cabernet Sauvignon, Cabernet Franc, Merlot and others*

In 1969 the MONDAVI family and Baron Philippe de Rothschild (of Ch. MOUTON-ROTHSCHILD fame) joined together to see if a red BORDEAUX-style wine could be made that was neither purely CALIFORNIAN nor imita-tion Bordeaux, but a synthesis of the two. In most years this ultra-expensive wine could be legally identified as a varietal Cabernet Sau-vignon, but it never has been, in order to preserve the freedom to blend in Merlot, Petit Verdot or Cabernet Franc. The early vintages were supple and oaky; more recent ones have perhaps been more tannic, but in general Opus One does a very good job in creating a laudable and attractive cultural hybrid that still bears witness to the warmer climate of the NAPA VALLEY, yet captures some of the clear-eyed, cedary, cool-fruited classicism of a fine PAUILLAC. At first, Opus One was priced insanely, but now with so many similarly priced competitors, the wine, which has only

OPUS ONE
This is a consistent, high-quality Bordeaux-style blend from the Napa Valley. Concentrated and with loads of tannin, the wine acquires delicacy and finesse with age.

got better, doesn't seem quite so expensive. But it is. Best years: 1996, '95, '94, '93, '92, '91, '90, '88, '87, '86, '85, '84, '80.

ORANGE

AUSTRALIA, New South Wales, Central Ranges Zone

Initially known as the Central Highlands, this important fruit region has diversified into wine in a big way, with a mix of small producers and a huge, single 500-ha (1235-acre) vineyard development at Molong for Southcorp. Most of the grapes are sold to outsiders (notably ROSEMOUNT ESTATE and Reynolds Yarraman). Altitude (between 600 and 900m/1970 and 2950ft) and cold nights are the key to the ele-gant yet flavoursome Chardonnays, the dry, warm autumns to the dark berry/briary/herba-ceous Cabernet family – and a lovely Malbec-based rosé from Bloodwood. Best (local) producers: Bloodwood, Brangayne of Orange, Canobolas-Smith, Highland Heritage Estate. Best years: 1998, '97, '96, '92, '90.

DOMAINE DE L'ORATOIRE ST-MARTIN

FRANCE, Southern Rhône, Côtes-du-Rhône-Villages AC

♟ *Grenache, Syrah, Mourvèdre*

♀ *Marsanne, Roussanne, Clairette, Viognier*

In 1936 Frédéric Alary became the first grower in Cairanne to bottle his own wines. Today his descendants, the brothers Frédéric and François, are determined to keep this domaine in the forefront of southern RHÔNE estates. Although all the 25ha (62 acres) of vineyards lie within Cairanne, not all are bottled with the Villages appellation. The basic Cairanne wine, called Réserve, is made from much older vines as well as an invigorating percentage of Mourvèdre. The Cuvée Prestige has even more Mourvèdre and is intended for medium-term aging. The only wine aged in barriques is the Cuvée Haut-Coustias. The most intriguing white is the Haut-Coustias, which is pure Marsanne, fermented and aged in barrels. Best years: 1997, '95, '94, '93, 90, '89.

WILLI OPITZ
Schilfwein, made from grapes dried on reeds from the shores of the nearby Lake Neusiedl, is one of Opitz's more unusual wines. The sweet white wine is remarkably intense.

OREGON USA

TO A STUNNING DEGREE, Oregon's young wine industry has put its eggs in one basket, that of Pinot Noir from the Willamette Valley, and one must search diligently to find out about Oregon Riesling and Cabernet Sauvignon as well as the other wine regions, the Umpqua and Rogue Valleys.

Though there were faint glimmerings before and after America's Prohibition in the 1920s, successful winemaking in Oregon really dates from 1972 to 1973, when the first few expatriates from California came to the Willamette Valley thinking they had found the new Burgundy. Richard Erath of Erath Vineyards and David Lett of Eyrie both planted vineyards near the town of Dundee, while William Fuller of Tualatin sought out the rolling hills a little further north near Forest Grove. By 1980, everyone had decided that Pinot Noir was the path to fame. Apart from some producers of Champagne-method sparkling wines, not one of the wineries within the adjacent counties of Washington and Yamhill has tried to make its primary reputation on another wine.

And have they found a new Burgundy in the distant Pacific Northwest? Well, what they do seem to have done is discover an area that does virtually mirror the bad side of Burgundy – poor weather at flowering, unreliable summer sunshine and heat, strong likelihood of vintage-time rain and the rest. What they have not done is to find somewhere that mirrors the Burgundian conditions that produce the greatest Burgundian wines. Too many of the Pinot Noirs have been almost self-consciously light in colour and texture, thereby aping a Burgundian myth – that all their red wines are delicate and fragrant. Many of the best modern Burgundies are in fact robust, richly textured and sensuous in a positively full-blooded way. These are the styles that Oregon should try to emulate – and indeed producers, like Rex Hill and Domaine Drouhin, do just that with conspicuous success.

And there is another side to Oregon. Before the Willamette pioneers had begun to operate, Richard Sommer, who had different visions, had set up Hillcrest Vineyard in the Umpqua Valley west of Roseburg. His choice was less immediately rewarded by the public clamour that attended the state's first dozen vintages of Pinot Noir from the more northerly Willamette Valley. The Umpqua may have come along more slowly, but it has still come along. Oregon's other wine regions are smaller still, and even more recent. The smaller, warmer Rogue Valley has half a dozen small wineries, and only approximately 225ha (550 acres) of vineyards. A district called Hood River, flanking the Columbia River east of Portland, is smaller and newer still, with three small wineries sharing about 16ha (40 acres) of vines. And in the north-east corner Walla Walla, shared with Washington State, produces powerful, warm-climate wines.

Though the winemakers and critics talk about Pinot Noir and Pinot Noir, there are only 1175ha (2900 acres) planted out of a vineyard total of 2875ha (7100 acres). Among white wines, Chardonnay, Riesling and Gewurztraminer all have their aficionados. The first Pinot Gris wines – Eyrie, Ponzi and Adelsheim have made the most impressive examples so far – are challenging Chardonnay for pride of place. If all of this sounds small, it is. All of Oregon has but one-sixth the vineyard acreage of the Napa Valley alone, and its largest winery would not come in Napa's top 20. Oregon's founding winemakers were, for the most part, under-capitalized yet idealistic refugees from California. They set strict labelling

The Dundee Hills, an important sub-region of the Willamette Valley, is noted for its steep hillsides and red volcanic soils. Many of Oregon's leading producers for both Pinot Noir and sparkling wine are based here.

THE EYRIE VINEYARDS
David Lett's experiments with Pinot Gris and Pinot Noir have set the style for Oregon wine.

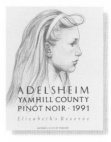

ADELSHEIM VINEYARD
With an increasing reputation for Pinot Noir, Adelsheim's Elizabeth Reserve is one of the best Pinot Noir wines made in Oregon.

REX HILL
Like many Oregon wineries, Pinot Noir is the main focus here and is sometimes very, very good with fine balance and rich, intense black cherry fruit.

AMITY VINEYARDS
Myron Redford was one of the pioneers in Oregon back in the mid-1970s. The dry, spicy Gewurztraminer is outstanding.

WILLAKENZIE
Pinot Noir is the focus at this exciting new, all gravity-fed winery in the Willamette Valley. Pierre Leon is one of the Reserve style wines.

laws in place and also made smallness a prime virtue. Since the late 1980s several overseas wine companies, in particular, Burgundy's Robert Drouhin (Domaine Drouhin) and Champagne's Laurent-Perrier, have begun to invest in the Willamette Valley, spurred on by the state's reputation for Pinot Noir and by the relatively low cost of vineyard land.

REGIONAL ENTRY
Willamette Valley.

PRODUCER ENTRIES
Adelsheim Vineyard, Archery Summit Winery, Argyle, Beaux Frères, Cameron Winery, Domaine Drouhin, The Eyrie Vineyards, Ponzi Vineyards, Rex Hill Vineyards, WillaKenzie Estate, Ken Wright Cellars.

KEN WRIGHT CELLARS
Ken Wright has fostered single-vineyard bottlings of Pinot Noir, including one from the Guadalupe Vineyard.

DOMAINE DROUHIN
The beautifully scented Pinot Noir Laurène is capable of surpassing many of Drouhin's top Burgundies.

ARGYLE
Oregon's cool climate is perfect for growing high-acid Pinot Noir and Chardonnay needed for quality Champagne-method sparkling wine as made by Argyle.

ORLANDO

The Flaxman's Eden Valley Traminer, from cool vineyards planted high in the Barossa Ranges, is a fragrant and delightful wine.

ORLANDO

AUSTRALIA, South Australia, Barossa Zone, Barossa Valley

♟ *Cabernet Sauvignon, Syrah (Shiraz), Malbec*
♀ *Riesling, Chardonnay, Semillon, Gewurztraminer*

Orlando is responsible for some of the most valuable and well-known wine names in Australia. Coolabah boxed wines and Jacobs Creek bottled wines underpin the range here. In 1993 Jacobs Creek became the biggest brand of bottled wine in Britain – edging out GALLO and Piat d'Or, and trouncing old codgers such as Blue Nun, Mateus and Mouton-Cadet. And why the success? The wine is totally consistent – consistently attractive and easy to drink, consistently reasonable in price. The basic red – loosely based on the BORDEAUX varieties from a number of different sources – and the basic white – a pleasant, soft, off-dry Semillon-Chardonnay blend – have now been supplemented by a pleasant-flavoured, pleasant-priced Chardonnay, a rather good spicy, limy Riesling and a Grenache. The Gramps range sits in the mid-upper price bracket, while a notch higher are St Helga Rhine Riesling, St Hugo Cabernet Sauvignon and St Hilary Chardonnay, and finally the luxury Flaxman's Traminer, Steingarten Rhine Riesling, Lawson's Shiraz and Jacaranda Ridge Cabernet Sauvignon. By and large these wines do not need keeping, and have generous fruit, soft acid and (with the reds) low tannin. Best years: 1996, '94, '93, '92, '91, '90, '88, '87, '86.

VIN DE L'ORLÉANAIS VDQS

FRANCE, Central Loire

♟ 🍷 *Pinot Noir, Pinot Meunier, Cabernet Sauvignon*
♀ *Chardonnay (Auvernat Blanc), Pinot Blanc*

Orléans is the vinegar capital of France. Situated on the northernmost point of the LOIRE's long arc across France, and perilously close to the point where grapes just won't ripen at all, it looks to be a very sound location for such an enterprise. Most of the wine is Gris Meunier d'Orléans, a very pale rosé of distinctly

fragile constitution. There are also whites made from Pinot Blanc and Chardonnay and, astonishingly, the Clos de St-Fiacre somehow manages to produce a deliciously drinkable Chardonnay. Drink the whites and rosés as young as possible. Best producers: Clos St-Fiacre, Legroux.

TENUTA DELL'ORNELLAIA

ITALY, Tuscany, Bolgheri DOC

♟ *Cabernet Sauvignon, Cabernet Franc, Merlot*

This is the estate of Lodovico ANTINORI, brother of Piero, cousin of Marchese Niccolò Incisa della Rocchetta, and like the latter's world-famous Tenuta San Guido (see SASSICAIA) it is situated in the coastal hills of the province of Livorno. The original wine, called simply Ornellaia, is a blend mainly of Cabernet Sauvignon with Merlot, and a little Cabernet Franc. The first release from the architecturally idiosyncratic winery was in 1985, but it was the superb 1990 that confirmed it as one of the benchmarks of Italian winemaking. Since that time Ornellaia has almost been overtaken as the winery's sexiest product by the varietal Merlot Masseto, for an allocation of which wine merchants worldwide are prepared to grovel in the dirt (not to mention buy a load of other wines which they don't want). There is also a Sauvignon, Poggio alle Gazze, one of Italy's – certainly central Italy's – most convincing; and a second red wine, Le Volte, made mainly from Sangiovese. Best years: 1997, '96, '94, '93, '91, '90, '88.

ORVIETO DOC

ITALY, Lazio and Umbria

♀ *Trebbiano Toscano (Procanico), Verdello, Grechetto and others*

Orvieto in south-west UMBRIA is a curious but beguiling town atop a mass of hill that rises so sheer from the surrounding countryside one might wonder how anybody ever manages to get to the top. Orvieto used to be seen mainly as a medium-dry wine with a hint of crystallized sultanas and honey in its make-up. There is still a little *abboccato* around, more *amabile* and even on occasions some quite delectable honeyed sweet Orvieto, made by grapes affected by noble rot. ANTINORI's Muffato della Sala is the best known and Barberani's Calcaia, Decugnano dei Barbi's Pourriture Noble and Palazzone's Muffa Nobile are also excellent. Usually, though, Orvieto is dry.

Trebbiano (locally called Procanico) at the head of the list of grape varieties isn't good

news. But Grechetto is the saviour, giving a much-needed dollop of nuttiness and green fruits to the wine. With the right vineyard site in the central, Classico area, low yields and proper attention Orvieto really can pull something out of the bag. A few cru wines may age well but generally it's made for drinking young. Best producers: Barberani, Bigi, Decugnano dei Barbi, Il Palazzone, Castello della Sala, Tenuta di Salviano, Vaselli.

OSBORNE

SPAIN, Andalucía, Jerez y Manzanilla DO

♀ *Palomino Fino, Pedro Ximénez*

Osborne, the biggest drinks company in Spain, has the potential to make fino sherry of very high quality, based as it is in the seaside town of Puerto de Santa María (in 40 delightful whitewashed bodegas in the old town centre). Flor grows thicker here than in JEREZ, so that resultant sherries can be finer and tangier. Osborne's raw materials are good, too: two-thirds of the grapes come from its own top-quality *albariza* vineyard. Fino Quinta is light and creamy, relatively young, but pleasant. Amontillado Coquinero and rich Bailén Oloroso are properly nutty and dry.

OVENS VALLEY

AUSTRALIA, Victoria, North East Victoria Zone

The splitting of North East Victoria into four regions makes eminent sense: RUTHERGLEN and Glenrowan on the warm plains producing (*inter alia*) the gorgeous fortified wines, and the major valleys of the King River and Ovens River, respectively, running away from the plains up into the mountains, producing steadily more elegant, lighter table wines as the altitude increases.

The Ovens Valley took in some famous goldfields in the nineteenth century and viticulture got away to a flying start; indeed, the 660-ha (1630-acre) high point of 1891 is still to be exceeded. By far the most distinguished resident winery is GIACONDA, with some support from Boyntons of Bright and Sorrenberg. Most of the region's grapes, however, are sold to outsiders, including ORLANDO and BROWN BROTHERS. Best years: 1998, '97, '95, '93, '91, '90.

OVERGAAUW

SOUTH AFRICA, Western Cape, Stellenbosch WO

♟ *Cabernet Sauvignon, Merlot, Cabernet Franc, Tinta Barocca and others*

♀ *Chardonnay, Sauvignon Blanc, Sylvaner*

It's easy to overlook this low-profile producer but if the course is set to 'steady as you go' and the wines are gently undramatic, that in no way indicates a lack of progress nor innovation. Proprietor, Braam van Velden, bottled South Africa's first varietal Merlot and first Touriga Naçional vintage port-style. His Sylvaner remains unique in the Cape, while an imaginative Pinotage/Cabernet Franc blend has resulted in a friendly, fruity combination. Van Velden's father was one of the first to experiment with small oak barrels. These are now common-place in the cellar, where winemaker, Chris Joubert, uses them sensitively on the slow-developing Cabernet, the BORDEAUX-blend Tria Corda and increasingly elegant Chardonnay. Best years: (reds) 1997, '96, '95, '94, '93, '92, '91.

PAARL WO

SOUTH AFRICA, Western Cape

Paarl is possibly one of the most confusing of the Cape's wine regions. When regional boundaries were drawn up in the early 1970s, it was along political lines rather than anything to do with climate or soil and this has meant a lack of obvious identity in the wines. On the more positive side, the diversity of soil and climate allows for success with many different styles; anything from Cap Classique (CHAMPAGNE-method) sparkling wine to sherry styles. As the Paarl vineyards account for nearly 19 per cent of South Africa's entire area under vine, there is room for all of these.

Wineries, too, span all sizes: the KWV with its 22-ha (54-acre) quasi-industrial complex, one of the world's largest wineries, makes stark contrast with tiny 3500-case Welgemeend. Smaller designated areas within Paarl, but at opposite ends of the Berg Valley, are Franschhoek, where the Huguenots eventually settled in the seventeenth century and passed on their winemaking skills to the Dutch, and Wellington. Best producers: (Paarl) BACKSBERG, Boschendal, FAIRVIEW, GLEN CARLOU, Plaisir de Merle, Veenwouden, Villiera, Welgemeend; (Franschhoek) Cabrière, La Motte, L'Ormarins; (Wellington) Claridge.

VEENWOUDEN

Paarl is basically a warm area and the red Bordeaux varieties do well here. Veenwouden specializes in red wines, especially classic Merlot.

PACHERENC DU VIC BILH AC

FRANCE, South-West

♀ *Gros Manseng, Petit Manseng, Ruffiac and Courbu*

Pacherenc is local dialect for *piquets en rang* or 'posts in a line', and Vic Bilh are the local hills. So the name literally translates as 'posts in a line from the Vic Bilh hills' – a reference to the local habit of training vines very high on tall posts. Whatever the explanation it still does not do much for one's thirst. But actually the wine, sometimes medium-dry or sweet but usually dry, can have an exciting flavour of pears and apricots – especially if bottled straight off its lees. The production is tiny, but overall quality is very good. Most of the top MADIRAN estates produce excellent Pacherenc du Vic Bilh. The sweeter versions can be aged a little and the dry is for drinking young. Best producers: Aydie, Berthoumieu, Brumont, Capmartin, Crampilh, Damiens, Lafitte-Teston, Producteuers PLAIMONT. Best years: 1997, '96, '95.

PADTHAWAY

AUSTRALIA, South Australia, Limestone Coast Zone

SEPPELT was the first company to grow grapes here, in 1963, armed with a government soil study; LINDEMANS and BRL HARDY followed in 1968, and then WYNNS. The soil is terra rossa over limestone, making it effectively a replica of nearby COONAWARRA. The climate is marginally warmer than Coonawarra's, but that hasn't prevented it rapidly achieving the status of one of Australia's most exciting and most reliable wine areas. Chardonnay can be absolutely stunning and is never worse than good, and Rieslings, either tangy with lime acidity or lusciously botrytized, are also exceptional. Best years: 1998, '97, '96, '94, '91, '90, '88. Best producers: BRL Hardy, Lindemans, Padthaway Estate, SEPPELT, Wynns.

PAHLMEYER WINERY

USA, California, Napa County, Napa Valley AVA

♟ *Cabernet Sauvignon, Merlot*

♀ *Chardonnay*

Unlike many of his NAPA VALLEY colleagues, former trial attorney Jayson Pahlmeyer makes his wines in a no-frills winery which frees capital to invest in grapes, equipment and winemaking expertise. After a few decent vintage featuring a red Meritage from the five BORDEAUX varieties, Pahlmeyer enlisted the services of famed consultant Helen Turley (see MARCASSIN). With her arrival the Estate Red has exhibited layers of enticing flavours and an ability to age for eight to ten years. A splendid, multi-layered, unctious Merlot

joined the roster in the late 1990s. Best years: (reds) 1996, '95, '94, '93, '92. Chardonnay in a massive, unfined and unfiltered style, ranks among the Napa's richest and acquires harmony and complexity with three to four years of aging. Best years: 1997, '96, '95, '94. With the 1998 acquisition of vineyard land in the RUSSIAN RIVER VALLEY, Pahlmeyer is moving towards producing Pinot Noir.

PAÍS VASCO

SPAIN

Were it not for the 12,000ha (29,700 acres) of RIOJA DOC land in the Alavesa sub-region, which administratively belong to the autonomous Basque community, Spain's Basque Country (País Vasco in Castilian, Euskadi or Euskal Herria in Basque) wouldn't count for much in the wine world. But Rioja Alavesa, with powerful financial and technical assistance from the regional government, channelled through the Laguardia enological station, has made great strides recently. Dozens of small growers have been encouraged to become wine producers as well. Some of them (ARTADI, Fernando Remírez de Ganuza, Primicia, Luis Cañas, Herencia Lasanta, Luis Ángel Casado, Solagüen, Luberri, San Pedro) have come to join the older, élite bodegas in the area such as MARQUÉS DE RISCAL, PALACIO, CONTINO, REMELLURI or CAMPILLO. With its pale, chalky soils under the protection of the Sierra Cantabria mountains, Alavesa's terroir is much like Rioja Alta, and so are the wines.

Further north, right on the Bay of Biscay, there remain a few dozen hectares of vineyards making pale, spritzy wines that are the Basque answer to VINHO VERDE, and can actually be very attractive when the harvest is truly ripe in hot years. They occupy two DOs – the newer Bizkaiko Txakolina and the more renowned GETARIAKO TXAKOLINA, where the native Hondarribi Zuri white is prevalent.

BODEGAS PALACIO

SPAIN, País Vasco, Rioja DOC

♟♀ *Tempranillo*

♀ *Macabeo (Viura)*

Jean Gervais, who revolutionized this sleepy bodega in the late 1980s, sold it to the RIBERA DEL DUERO winery, Viña Mayor, in 1998. Gervais introduced new Allier and Nevers oak barrels to Palacio. That, plus advice from Michel Rolland, a well-known Pomerol enologist, have given some of the company's younger wines a distinctly French character. The Cosme Palacio red is plummy and soft, with good, savoury oak flavour, whereas the traditional Glorioso Crianza and Reserva wines are jammier, though still full of rich, plum-pudding fruit. The Glorioso Gran Reserva is even better, rich and plummy with a fine, wild strawberry overtone. Best years: 1996, '95, '94, '91, '89.

ÁLVARO PALACIOS

SPAIN, Cataluña, Priorat DO
♥ *Grenache Noir (Garnacha Tinta), Cariñena, Cabernet Sauvignon, Syrah, Merlot,*
♀ *Grenache Blanc (Garnacha Blanca)*

The scion of an old RIOJA Baja family was ready, by his mid-20s, for an adventure somewhere else. He had already trained with Christian Moueix of Ch. PÉTRUS in BORDEAUX, he had been in the oak barrel trade and he was obsessed with making world-class wine. He was the youngest member of the group that revolutionized the PRIORAT region, and a dozen years later he is the best known of the group. In his futuristic winery he produces a top, modern Priorat blend, Finca Dofí, and, from bought-in grapes, Les Terrasses which is outstanding value. But his star wine comes from the best 5ha (12 acres) of his 35ha (86 acres) of vineyards: the 50-year-old L'Ermita. A powerful wine, it shares the spotlight with Peter Sisseck's PINGUS as the new Spain's leading cult wine. Best years: 1997, '96, '95, '94, '91, '90.

PALETTE AC

FRANCE, Provence
♥ ♀ *Grenache, Mourvèdre, Cinsaut, Syrah and others*
♀ *Clairette, Grenache Blanc, Ugni Blanc and others*

Pine needles and resin are what you taste in the wines of Palette – a tiny AC hidden away in the pine forests just east of Aix-en-Provence. Not that the local winemakers actually employ these to make the wine, but the slopes on which the 25ha (62 acres) of vines grow are covered in pines and herbs. The rosé is herby and rather dry, and the red: well, herby again, and tough, needing several years' bottle age to even hint at a softer side.

But the appellation can be proud of one achievement. Given the basic neutral bunch of southern white grapes, Ch. SIMONE, the only producer of white Palette, has managed to squeeze more flavour out of this motley crew than any other AC. Its success must be due to the appellation's limestone soil and the two years' sojourn in oak barrels. The wines are again better with four or five years' bottle age. Best producers: Ch. Crémade, Ch. Simone. Best years (reds) 1995; (whites) 1996, '95.

PALMELA DOC

PORTUGAL, Terras do Sado
♥ *Periquita, Alfrocheiro, Espadeiro*
♀ *Fernão Pires, Arinto, Rabo de Ovelha and others*

The sandy plain surrounding the hill-top town of Palmela is ideally suited to the red Periquita grape (sometimes called Castelão Francês in Portugal). Local winemakers José Maria da FONSECA and J P VINHOS and talented interloper BRIGHT BROS produce many wines but Periquita is the mainstay for some distinctive raspberryish reds which gain in complexity with age. Caves ALIANÇA also makes a good red, 'Palmela Particular'. Best producers: Caves Aliança, Bright Bros, José Maria da Fonseca, Pegos Claros, João Pires. Best years: 1997, '95, '94, '92, '91.

CH. PALMER

FRANCE, Bordeaux, Haut-Médoc, Margaux AC, 3ème Cru Classé
♥ *Cabernet Sauvignon, Merlot, Cabernet Franc, Petit Verdot*

Of all the properties that could justifiably feel underrated by the 1855 BORDEAUX Classification, Ch. Palmer has traditionally the best case. Palmer's reputation is based, above all, on its perfume. It is as though every black and red fruit in the land has thrown in its ripest flavours: blackcurrant, blackberry, plum, loganberry.

But Palmer can go further. Sometimes there's a rich, almost fat core to the wine; and curling through the fruit and the ripeness are trails of other fragrances – roses, violets, cedar and cigars, all in abundance. Sometimes. There was a period in the 1960s and '70s when Palmer held aloft the banner of brilliance for the MARGAUX AC virtually single-handed. However, as properties like Ch. MARGAUX itself and RAUZAN-SÉGLA soared to new heights during the 1980s and '90s, Palmer became lighter, less substantial, its fabled perfume now struggling without the original core of sweetness. There were still some notable successes in the 1980s, like '89, but in the 1990s Palmer disappointingly failed to find top gear – good, but unmemorable.

Named after a British major-general who fought in the Napoleonic Wars, it is a 45-ha (111-acre) site on excellent gravel right next to Ch. Margaux. The wine's irresistible plump fruit is caused by the very high proportion of Merlot (40 per cent) with only 55 per cent Cabernet Sauvignon, 3 per cent Cabernet Franc and 2 per cent Petit Verdot. Second wine: Réserve-du-Général. Best years: 1998, '97, '96, '95, '90, '89, '88, '86, '85, '83, '82, '79, '78, '75, '70.

PALMER VINEYARDS
The Cabernet Franc wine from Palmer Vineyards is one of Long Island's best and a recent success for this winery.

PALMER VINEYARDS

USA, New York State, North Fork of Long Island AVA
♥ *Cabernet Franc, Merlot, Cabernet Sauvignon*
♀ *Chardonnay*

High-tech winemaking in an old country estate, Palmer Vineyards gained a reputation in the 1980s for Merlot and Cabernet Sauvignon, to which it has added a good Cabernet Franc. The star turn, however, is the barrel-fermented Chardonnay. Best years (reds): 1997, '96, '95, '94, '93.

PALOMAS

BRAZIL, Rio Grande do Sul
♥ *Merlot, Cabernet Sauvignon, Pinot Noir*
♀ *Chenin Blanc, Chardonnay, Ugni Blanc*

Turbulence in Brazil's financial sector has placed RIO GRANDE DO SUL in a new light as a wine-producing area. Winemaking in Brazil was never going to be easy, the conditions can make for expensive grape production and low aromatic content. The near collapse of Brazil's currency has meant that wine imports into Brazil have become prohibitively expensive, and internal production costs have come down in relative terms. This has put the Palomas winery in a better position than ever to supply both domestic and export markets. Stainless steel technology has resulted in reasonably good aromas and flavours from white grapes, particularly Chenin Blanc and Chardonnay. The reds are well rounded on the palate, even if aromatically they are not as intense as cooler climate rivals.

CH. PAPE CLÉMENT

FRANCE, Bordeaux, Pessac-Léognan AC, Cru Classé de Graves
♥ *Cabernet Sauvignon, Merlot*
♀ *Sauvignon Blanc, Sémillon, Muscadelle*

This famous GRAVES Classed Growth was languishing in the doldrums until a new broom in the form of manager Bernard Pujol arrived in

1985. A certain amount of fine tuning, investment in stainless steel tanks, a system of temperature control and new oak barrels and as a result since 1986 the estate has become one of the established stars of BORDEAUX. Like Ch. HAUT-BRION down the road the 30-ha (74-acre) vineyard is located on Pessac's fine, gravelly soils in the suburbs of Bordeaux, and planted to 60 per cent Cabernet Sauvignon and 40 per cent Merlot. The wines are deep-coloured, rich and powerful but elegantly aromatic and should be kept for ten years or more. In recent years Pape Clément has also produced a very fine but unclassified white wine from a further 3.5ha (8.6 acres). The wine is barrel-fermented in new oak casks and is rich and full bodied with the aroma and flavour of citrus fruits, vanilla and just a hint of musk. Second wine: (reds) Clémentin. Best years: (reds) 1997, '96, '95, '94, '93, '90, '89, '88, '86, '85, '75; (whites) 1997, '96, '95, '94.

PARADIGM WINERY
USA, California, Napa County, Oakville District AVA
 Cabernet Sauvignon, Merlot, Zinfandel
In the early 1990s several small wineries popped up in the Oakville District which is justly prized for its Cabernet Sauvignon. One of those small gems was Paradigm, owned by long-time NAPA VALLEY residents, Ren and Marilyn Harris. Before taking the wine-making plunge, they sold their grapes from their established 5-ha (12-acre) vineyard in the heart of Oakville. Building a winery within view of FAR NIENTE, Martha's Vineyard, and MONDAVI's To Kalon Vineyard, Paradigm has been turning out highly distinctive Cabernet Sauvignon made in a powerful style with the structure and balance that are hallmarks of their consulting winemaker, Heidi Peterson Barrett. An intensely fruity, full-bodied, but balanced Merlot is usually made, but in tiny quantities. From several rows of Zinfandel, Paradigm produces a barrel or two of delicious Zinfandel filled with blackberry fruit and spices. Best years: 1997, '96, '95, '94, '93, '92.

PARELLADA
Parellada – the most aromatic of the three major white grapes in PENEDÈS – is exclusive to CATALUÑA. Apart from Penedès, it is very important in TARRAGONA DO, but also grows in the province of Lleida (including the new COSTERS DEL SEGRE DO) and in CONCA DE BARBERÁ DO. It makes light, fresh, fruity wines with a floral aroma, good, fresh acidity, and, unlike most Spanish whites, is fairly low in alcohol, usually somewhere between

These vast vineyards belong to Meridian Vineyards, an important producer in the warm Paso Robles region of California's Central Coast which is fast gaining a reputation for the quality of its red grapes.

9 and 11 per cent. Maybe this is why it has not been more widely grown in Spain. These wines are not for long keeping – they are best in the spring after the harvest, and usually begin to taste dull by the following year. To preserve the grape's aromas Parellada tends to be grown in the coolest spots, often up in the hills; and it is late to ripen – always the last of the whites to be picked. Parellada is also the most characterful constituent of the Catalan CAVA sparkling wines and it is also successfully blended with Chardonnay or Sauvignon Blanc.

FESS PARKER WINERY
USA, California, Santa Barbara County, Santa Maria Valley AVA
 Cabernet Sauvignon, Cabernet Franc, Pinot Noir, Syrah
 Chardonnay, Riesling, Viognier
In the early 1980s, retired actor Fess Parker (who played Davey Crockett and Daniel Boone in the 1950s) developed vineyards on his ranch in SANTA BARBARA COUNTY. Run by Fess and his son, Ely, the winery attracts thousands of visitors hoping to get a glimpse of the former actor. A superb slightly sweet Riesling and a standard CALIFORNIA-style Chardonnay were the key wines initially, but Parker has been flying the RHÔNE wine banner of late with remarkably strong showings. His Reserve Syrah is loaded with ripe berry and peppery-smoky character, and the winery

is making good progress with Viognier and inexpensive Rhône red and white blends. Best years: 1998, '97, '96, '95. Both the Reserve Chardonnay and Reserve Pinot Noir have been coming along nicely to capture all the right stuff from their Santa Maria Valley sources. Best years: 1997, '96, '95, '94.

PASO ROBLES AVA
USA, California, San Luis Obispo County
One of the older districts in the Central Coast, Paso Robles made its way from the 1880s into the 1970s with sturdy, rustic Zinfandels. In spite of its proximity to the sea, the region is among the warmest of the coastal valleys in summer because hills keep out the cool sea air, but the altitude does cool it down at night. As well as Zinfandel it has full-flavoured Cabernet Sauvignon and some good Chenin Blanc and Sauvignon Blanc. Chardonnays so far are affable though quick to age. Nebbiolo and Syrah are recent welcome additions, large commercial plantings of Merlot less so. Encouraged by the presence and also by the viticultural experiments of the Perrin family (owners of Ch. BEAUCASTEL), many growers here have developed new plantings of Syrah, Mourvèdre and related RHÔNE varieties. Best producers: Adelaida Cellars, Creston Vineyards, Eberle, Justin, Martin Bros, MERIDIAN, Peachy Canyon, Tablas Creek, Wild Horse. Best years: (reds) 1998, '97, '95, '94, '92, '91, '90.

LUÍS PATO

PORTUGAL, Beira Litoral, Bairrada DOC
♥ ♟ *Baga, Touriga Nacional, Cabernet Sauvignon*
♀ *Fernão Pires (Maria Gomes), Bical, Cerceal, Cercealinho*

Luís Pato is one of Portugal's star winemakers. A combination of astute marketing and good winemaking has given Pato a high profile on the home market and, consequently, some of his wines command high prices. He began making wine in 1980 when he inherited the family estate from his late father, João. After a decade or more of trial and error, Pato has finally worked out a philosophy based on the French concept of 'terroir'. He reserves the sandier soils for dry whites and some lighter reds like Quinta do Ribeirinho and the heavier clay soils for full-bodied reds. His most impressive wines are solid, tannic, but rich reds from individual plots of old, low-yielding vines: Vinha Barrosa and Vinha Pan. He also has 1ha (2 acres) of ungrafted vines which yields a tiny quantity of intensely rich red wine Luís Pato has christened 'Pé Franco'. Pato's eclectic range of wines includes a deliciously creamy sparkling rosé made from the local Baga grape. *Pato* means 'duck' in Portuguese and this has inevitably become his trademark. Best years: 1997, '95, '92, '91, '88.

PATRIMONIO AC

FRANCE, Corsica
♥ ♟ *Nielluccio, Grenache*
♀ *Vermentino, Muscat*

Patrimonio was Corsica's first AC and is located on the south-west side of the island's finger-shaped cape. There are 440ha (1087 acres) of vines, mainly Nielluccio for the reds and rosés and Vermentino for the whites. The best producers have invested in modern winemaking equipment and produce fresh, fruity reds and rosés and aromatic white wines for drinking young. Patrimonio also

forms part of the delimited zone for Muscat du Cap Corse, a fragrantly sweet *vin doux naturel*. Best producers: Antoine Arena, Catarelli, Gentile, Leccia, Orenga de Gaffory. Best years: (reds) 1997, '96, '95, '94.

PAUILLAC AC

FRANCE, Bordeaux, Haut-Médoc
♟ *Cabernet Sauvignon, Merlot, Cabernet Franc and others*

If there is a king of red wine grapes it probably has to be Cabernet Sauvignon. In every corner of the world where there is enough sun to ripen the fruit, it has spread to make dark, dense, rather tough but wonderfully flavoured wines. Yet its heartland remains the single village of Pauillac in the HAUT-MÉDOC region of BORDEAUX. Throughout the New World – and in much of southern France, Spain and Italy too – if you ask ambitious winemakers what model they take for Cabernet Sauvignon they will no doubt say Ch. LATOUR, LAFITE-ROTHSCHILD or MOUTON-ROTHSCHILD. These are the three Pauillac First Growth properties, each of which, in its different way, is an ultimate expression of Cabernet Sauvignon.

There are 1185ha (2928 acres) of vines in the AC, on deep gravel banks to the north, west and south of the town of Pauillac. This makes Pauillac AC the third biggest commune in the Haut-Médoc. Sleepily huddled at the muddy edge of the Gironde estuary – with a faded promenade, boats idling, a few listless fishermen chatting on the quay, the local restaurant specializing in herrings – you'd never guess that for many this town is the Mecca of the red wine world.

Apart from the three First Growths, there are 15 other Classed Growth estates, including the world-famous Ch. PICHON-LONGUEVILLE-COMTESSE DE LALANDE and LYNCH-BAGES. The wines go from terse, fretful and austere to blooming with friendly fruit, but the uniting characteristic of blackcurrant fruit and cedar or pencil-shavings perfume – the tell-tale signs of Cabernet Sauvignon – is never far distant.

Few Pauillacs are ready young and the Classed Growths often need 20 years. Best years: 1998, '96, '95, '94, '90, '89, '88, '86, '85, '83, '82, '81, '79, '78. Best producers: d'Armailhac, BATAILLEY, Clerc-Milon, Duhart-Milon, Fonbadet, Grand-Puy-Ducasse, GRAND-PUY-LACOSTE, HAUT-BAGES-LIBÉRAL, HAUT-BATAILLEY, Lafite-Rothschild, Latour, Lynch-Bages, Mouton-Rothschild, Pibran, PICHON-LONGUEVILLE, Pichon-Longueville-Comtesse de Lalande, PONTET-CANET.

DR PAULY-BERGWEILER

GERMANY, Mosel-Saar-Ruwer, Bernkastel-Kues
♟ *Pinot Noir (Spätburgunder)*
♀ *Riesling and others*

This state-of-the-art MOSEL estate belongs to Dr Peter Pauly, whose wife owns the estate of Weingut Peter Nicolay. The winemaking is designed to produce clear, clean flavours in the wines, and is one of the most modern on the Mosel.

The estate has vines in some of the best vineyard sites in the Mosel, like WEHLENer Sonnenuhr, BRAUNEBERGer-Juffer Sonnenuhr and GRAACHer Himmelreich. The vast majority of the vineyards are planted with Riesling. Spätburgunder, which only accounts for about 3 per cent of the total vineyard holdings, is planted in the Graacher Domprobst vineyard; the quality is good, and the wines have plenty of attractive varietal character. Best years: 1997, '95, '94, '93, '90, '89.

CH. PAVIE

FRANCE, Bordeaux, St-Émilion Grand Cru AC, Premier Grand Cru Classé
♟ *Merlot, Cabernet Franc, Cabernet Sauvignon*

The second largest of the ST-ÉMILION Premiers Grands Crus (after Ch. FIGEAC) at 37.5 ha (93 acres) enjoys a superb site on steep, south-facing slopes just to the south-east of the town of St-Émilion. Being biggest was obviously a bit more than Pavie could cope with in the 1960s and '70s because none of the wines was outstanding; even the potentially strongest vintages had a soft, simple, buttered-brazil kind of flavour – very attractive but somewhat one-dimensional.

After 1979 things bucked up dramatically, and Pavie became one of the most improved properties in St-Émilion. The attractive fruit was still there, but the wines were far more concentrated and, while drinkable young, happily improved for a decade or more to something very good indeed. Vintages in the early 1990s, however, suffered a dramatic drop in quality, but Pavie's purchase in 1998 by Gérard Perse, followed by a radical reduction in yields and heavy investment, should see it returning rapidly to top form. Best years: 1998, '96, '95, '90, '89, '88, '86, '85, '83, '82, '81.

PÉCHARMANT AC

FRANCE, South-West
♟ *Merlot, Cabernet Sauvignon, Cabernet Franc, Malbec*

These are lovely red wines from a small enclave in the BERGERAC region. The soil is relatively chalky, giving wines that are usually quite light in body but with a delicious, full, piercing flavour of blackcurrants and a most attractive grassy acidity. They are rarely very tannic but are, in general, so well-balanced that good vintages can easily age ten years and end up indistinguishable from a good St-Émilion. Best years: 1998, '97, '96, '95, '94, '90, '89, '88, '86, '85, '83. Best producers: Bertranoux, Champarel, Clos Peyrelevade, Haut-Pécharmant, Puy de Grave, Tiregand.

PEDRO XIMÉNEZ

The stronghold of the PX, as this white grape is generally known, is the heart of Spain's Andalucía. Given enough sun, it produces incredibly sweet grapes, sometimes dried almost to raisins before use, and the wines occasionally produced are sensationally rich and viscous. Montilla-Moriles uses PX for its sherry-style wines, even the fino style; it's also the major grape of Málaga, and elsewhere in Spain, especially in Extremadura and the Canaries, it makes table wines, which in recent years have become fresh though bland. Its use in fortified wines is duplicated in California, South America and South Africa.

PEMBERTON

AUSTRALIA, Western Australia, South West Australia Zone

This is another Australian Geographic Indication which emerged only after bitter in-fighting over its name, the Warren Valley being the most favoured of the alternatives. The Pemberton GI neatly fills in the space between Margaret River (to the north-west) and Great Southern (to the south-east). Established with enormous enthusiasm for its perceived potential to produce high-quality Chardonnay and Pinot Noir, the barometer has swung more towards sparkling wine use. There are two soil types in the region: the first, and most suitable, are lateritic gravelly sands and loams of moderate fertility, and which produce the best wines. The second are the far more fertile Karri loams which lead to vigorous growth, excessive yields and flavour dilution. Best producers: Chestnut Grove, Picardy, Salitage, Smithbrook.

PEÑAFLOR

ARGENTINA, Mendoza

🍷 *Cabernet Sauvignon, Malbec, Syrah*

🍷 *Chardonnay, Sauvignon Blanc and others*

Bodegas Peñaflor is a bit of a mystery. It seems to have everything, beautifully kept vineyards in the most enviable locations, especially one known as El Chiche on the road to Tupungato, a gigantic winery with technology to match and first-class human resources. So why doesn't it make Argentina's best wine? One reason used to be that the owners, the Pulenta family, had fingers in so many pies that they took their eye off the ball when it came to wine. No longer. Another Pulenta (from Miami this time) has bought the winery, including the upmarket Trapiche label and intends to concentrate on quality. Since 1997 there has been a massive turnaround. Even in the difficult '98 vintage, good, juicy reds were made from Peñaflor's considerable vineyard resources, and the whites, especially Chardonnay and Sauvignon Blanc were the best yet.

PEÑALBA LÓPEZ

SPAIN, Castilla-León, Ribera del Duero DO

🍷 *Tempranillo (Tinto Fino), Cabernet Sauvignon, Merlot*

🍷 *Viura, Albillo*

When Ribera del Duero was not even an official wine district name, Vega Sicilia and the Ribera Duero (Protos) co-operative were already proving in the western part of the region (in the Valladolid province) that there was an alternative to cheap rosés sold in bulk. To the east, in Burgos province, there was nothing much of that sort. But at least the Torremilanos bodega at Aranda de Duero held the fort for a number of years with its light oak-aged reds, similar to traditional Riojas. The estate, with its 170ha (420 acres) of vineyards, was acquired by the Peñalba López family in the early 1970s. Quality has been progressively upgraded, and the Torremilanos cuvées have been joined by a more powerful and concentrated wine, Torre Albéniz, which is aged in French oak. A little non-DO white is also made here. Best years: 1995, '94, '91, '90.

PENEDÈS DO

SPAIN, Cataluña

🍷🍷 *Grenache Noir (Garnacha Tinta), Carignan (Cariñena), Tempranillo (Ull de Llebre), Monastrell (Mourvèdre), Cabernet Sauvignon and others*

🍷 *Parellada, Macabeo, Xarel-lo, Chardonnay, Riesling, Gewürztraminer, Sauvignon Blanc and others*

Winemaking technology in the Penedès region is way ahead of the rest of Cataluña, and ahead of most of Spain, largely because of the wealth and technical expertise generated by the booming Cava industry. Although many of the grapes for making Cava come from elsewhere, the vast majority of the Cava companies are based in Penedès and many of them make still wines as well. The bodegas that specialize in still wines include the famous Torres, the trailblazer for modern Spanish wine. Co-operatives are as strong here as in the rest of Spain, but so also are the Cava companies who own one-fifth of the vineyards.

White wines predominate, and 90 per cent of these are made principally from the three local grapes, Xarel-lo, Macabeo and (best for quality) Parellada. They can be fresh, lightly aromatic and pleasantly lemony-fruity, but are never great wines. Chardonnay has been permitted in Penedès DO wines since 1986, and is now being used more widely to improve local blends. The reds made from local varieties tend to be thin, but the finest Penedès reds are made partially or entirely from the Cabernet Sauvignon grape, by Torres, Jean León and a growing group of smaller producers. Tempranillo also can produce some fairly rich flavours here. Best years: 1996, '93, '91, '88. Best producers: Albet i Noya, Can Feixes, Can Ráfols dels Caus, Cavas Hill, Juvé y Camps, Jean Léon, Marqués de Montistrol, Masía Bach, Albert Milá i Mallofré, Puig y Roca, Torres, Vallformosa, Jané Ventura.

PENFOLDS

AUSTRALIA, South Australia, Barossa Zone, Barossa Valley

🍷 *Cabernet Sauvignon, Syrah (Shiraz), Merlot, Grenache and others*

🍷 *Riesling, Chardonnay, Semillon and others*

For many, Penfolds and Grange, Australia's most famous red wine, are synonymous, but the modern Penfolds is actually more important for its budget-priced wines than for creating what was once called Australia's only First Growth. Through a series of acquisitions Penfolds, along with Lindemans, Wynns, Seaview and many others all under the umbrella name of Southcorp Wines, now dominates Australian wine production, and is the leader in full-flavoured reds at a fair price. However, it has excellent whites too; a

PENFOLDS

Koonunga Hill Shiraz-Cabernet, with its ripe, spicy aroma and soft attractive fruit, proves that at Penfolds quality can go hand in hand with quantity.

series of ADELAIDE HILLS-sourced Semillon and Chardonnay are first rate. A top white called Yaltarna, rather pointlessly called the 'White Grange', is Chardonnay but presumably could be a finely tuned blend in the future.

Grange is still the flagship red. The secret lies in 50- to 100-year-old, low-yielding Shiraz vines picked at peak ripeness, and in the skilled use of new American oak: a heady profusion of blackberry, cherry and vanilla aromas and flavours is supported by a structure of exceptional strength and complexity. Cabernet Sauvignon Bin 707, St Henri Claret, Magill Estate, The Clare Estate and Cabernet/Shiraz Bin 389 are the other top-ranking reds, with ripe fruit and lavish use of new or near-new oak as cornerstones. But even down the range with wines like Bins 28 and 128, Koonunga Hill and Rawsons Retreat, the same broad-fruited, packed-with-flavour style is evident, and these reds have probably done more than any other wines to turn the rest of the world on to Aussie red. Best years: 1997, '96, '94, '93, '92, '91, '90, '88, '86, '84, '83, '82, '80, '78, '76, '71.

PENLEY ESTATE

AUSTRALIA, South Australia, Limestone Coast Zone, Coonawarra
🍷 *Syrah (Shiraz), Cabernet Sauvignon*
🍾 *Chardonnay*

Kym Tolley comes from the famous PENFOLD family, born with both wine and a silver spoon in his mouth. Penley Estate generated more publicity prior to producing or releasing its first wine than any other Australian winery, but after a few uncertain steps, the wine has well and truly lived up to the propaganda. Satin-smooth Cabernet Sauvignon, with highly skilled use of French and American oak, can show COONAWARRA at or near its best. Best years: 1997, '96, '94, '93, '91, '90.

HERMANOS PÉREZ PASCUAS-VIÑA PEDROSA

SPAIN, Castilla-León, Ribera del Duero DO
🍷🍾 *Tempranillo (Tinto Fino), Cabernet Sauvignon, Merlot*

The immaculate Perez Pascuas winery, in the village of Pedrosa de Duero, has modern stainless steel tanks for fermentation, the latest in filtration and bottling equipment and ranks of new oak barrels for aging. Most of the grapes (Tinto Fino, supplemented by some Cabernet Sauvignon and Merlot) come from the family vineyards in one of the highest and coolest parts of the RIBERA DEL DUERO region. Viña Pedrosa is the brand name for the wines. There is a

RIBERA DEL DUERO
Denominación de Origen
Nº 019015

Viña Pedrosa
TINTO

Elaborado con uvas "Tinto del País"
y embotellado en la propiedad por:
Bodegas Hnos. Pérez Pascuas
PEDROSA DE DUERO (Burgos) ESPAÑA
PRODUCT OF SPAIN

75 cl.   *Reserva*   12,5% Vol.

HERMANOS PÉREZ PASCUAS
This small family winery in Ribera del Duero makes delicious, elegant reds. The Viña Pedrosa Reserva is a single-vineyard wine from very old vines.

lovely, burstingly fruity Tinto Joven (young, unoak-aged red). The Crianzas and Reservas have wonderful raspberry fragrance, sweet oak flavour and enough tannin to age well. The Perez Pascuas Reserva Especial, from the estate's oldest vineyard, had its debut in 1990. Best years: 1996, '94, '91, '90, '89.

PERIQUITA

This productive, early-ripening red grape variety is grown all over southern Portugal. It is particularly important in the ALENTEJO and RIBATEJO, where its ebullient loganberry and mulberry fruitiness, allied to a fair acidity and a tobaccoey, cedary perfume as the wine ages, produces some of Portugal's most attractive reds. So far there is little sign of it being planted elsewhere in the world, which is a pity.

PERNAND-VERGELESSES AC

FRANCE, Burgundy, Côte de Beaune
🍷 *Pinot Noir*
🍾 *Chardonnay, Aligoté*

Pernand-Vergelesses is another of those off-the-beaten-track Burgundy villages which nevertheless has a considerable slice of luck; the great hill of CORTON comes round from the east, and at its western end a decent-sized chunk of it lies inside the Pernand-Vergelesses boundary. Red Corton from these vines lacks the richness of the wines of ALOXE-CORTON from the south- and east-facing slopes and takes longer to mature into a finely balanced, savoury-rich wine. Pernand-Vergelesses red is generally softer, lighter, very attractive young with nice raspberry pastille fruit and a slight earthiness, though good to age for six to ten years. The 143ha (353 acres) of vineyards produce about 85 per cent red wine and, apart from le Corton, the best vineyards are Île des Hautes Vergelesses and les Basses Vergelesses, both Premiers Crus. And whereas Aloxe-Corton is often overpriced, Pernand-Vergelesses can

be a bargain. Best years: (reds) 1997, '96, '95, '93, '90, '89, '88, '85. Best producers: (reds) Besancenot-Mathouillet, CHANDON DE BRIAILLES, Cornu, Denis, Dubreuil-Fontaine, JADOT, Laleure-Piot, Rapet, Rollin.

Although a sizeable part of the white Grand Cru CORTON-CHARLEMAGNE lies within the parish boundaries, no-one ever links poor old Pernand with the heady heights of Corton-Charlemagne because the name Pernand-Vergelesses never appears on the label (Grand Cru vineyards don't have to use their village name), yet much of the best white Corton-Charlemagne comes from this western end. Most of the 50,000 bottles of white Pernand are made from Chardonnay, and although they're a bit lean and earthy to start with, they fatten up beautifully after two to four years in bottle. But there are also some very old plantings of Aligoté, and the wine is super – dry, deep, snappy, almost peppery and scoured with lemon peel. Best years: (whites) 1997, '96, '95, '92, '90, '89, '88, '86, '85. Best producers: (whites) Chandon de Briailles, Dubreuil-Fontaine, Germain, Guyon, Jadot, Laleure-Piot, Pavelot, Rapet, Rollin.

PERRIER-JOUËT

FRANCE, Champagne, Champagne AC
🍾🍷 *Chardonnay, Pinot Noir, Pinot Meunier*

This medium-sized CHAMPAGNE house, sold by Seagram in 1999 to a US investment firm, and producing about three million bottles annually, has long been a triumph of imaginative marketing which has not always been matched by the quality of the wines. Recent releases of the non-vintage, in particular, have shown a slide towards mediocrity that is deeply worrying. Great reputations take a long time to build, but can be lost in no time at all. At its best, Perrier-Jouët is made in an understated style, emphasizing lightness and delicacy rather than power and richness. In addition to the non-vintage Brut, there's a premium non-vintage range called Blason de France. Most celebrated of all is the prestige cuvée La Belle Époque, in its distinctive enamelled bottle. Here, too, elegance is prized over richness and body and quality has remained pretty good. Best years: 1992, '90, '89, '88, '85, '83, '82, '79, '78, '76.

PERTH HILLS

AUSTRALIA, Western Australia, Central Western Australia Zone

This little-recognized wine region, 30km (19 miles) east of Perth, is centred around the very pretty Bickley Valley. The climate is warm y any standards. The most promising grape varieties are Chardonnay, Semillon, Shiraz (Syrah) and Cabernet Sauvignon. Best years: 1997, '96, '95, '94, '93. Best producers: Chittering Estate, Darlington, Hainault, Plesse Brook.

PERVINI

ITALY, Puglia, Primitivo di Manduria DOC
Primitivo, Negroamaro, Montepulciano and others
Negroamaro, Primitivo
Chardonnay

The ancient town of Manduria, once occupied by Hannibal, is home to this dynamic winery in the heart of the Primitivo homeland. For decades Pervini was a major player in the bulk-wine business but in the 1990s, it decided to add a range of fine wines, and has steadily built up an impressive network of grower-suppliers not just in Primitivo country, but in the Negroamaro lands farther south in the Salento peninsula. These fascinating wines, combining power with elegance, include Primitivo di Manduria DOC Archidamo and the Primitivo-Negroamaro blend Bizantino. A parallel blend, Felline, has been remarkably successful, too. Best years: 1998, '97, '96, '94.

PESSAC-LÉOGNAN AC

FRANCE, Bordeaux
Cabernet Sauvignon, Cabernet Franc, Merlot and others
Sémillon, Sauvignon Blanc, Muscadelle
See also Graves and Pessac-Leognan, pages 190–191.

The 1987 revision of the AC system in the GRAVES area south of Bordeaux saw the creation of the new Pessac-Léognan AC by hiving off the area immediately to the south of the city – centred on the villages of Pessac and Léognan, but also including the communes of Talence, Cadaujac, Villenave d'Ornon and Martillac as well as four others. This is the area of Graves which includes all the Classed Growths, and has the highest proportion of the classic gravelly soil which gives the Graves its name.

The quality of the reds from this area has long been recognized. Although Cabernet is the main grape, as in the Médoc, a lot of emphasis is placed on Merlot, and the resulting wines can be softer than Médoc equivalents. The top half-dozen properties (such as Ch. HAUT-BRION, la MISSION-HAUT-BRION, Domaine de CHEVALIER and PAPE CLÉMENT) are superb, the others of a very high standard. They can be a little reserved in youth and need seven or eight years before extending a subtle, earthy bouquet of dark fruits and tobacco with

a firm minerally nuance. As for the whites, cool fermentation, controlled yeast selection and the use of new oak barrels for fermentation and aging of the wines, has made this one of the most exciting areas of France for top-class whites. Best years: (reds) 1998, '96, '95, '94, '90, '89, '88, '86, '85, '83, '82, '81, '79, '78; (whites) 1998, '96, '95, '94, '93, '90, '89, '88, '86. Best producers: (reds) les Carmes Haut-Brion, Domaine de Chevalier, de FIEUZAL, HAUT-BAILLY, Haut-Brion, Larrivet-Haut-Brion, la LOUVIÈRE, MALARTIC-LAGRAVIÈRE, la Mission-Haut-Brion, Pape Clément, Rochemorin, SMITH-HAUT-LAFITTE, la Tour-Haut-Brion, la TOUR-MARTILLAC; (whites) Carbonnieux, Domaine de Chevalier, Couhins-Lurton, de Fieuzal, Haut-Brion, Laville-Haut-Brion, la Louvière, Malartic-Lagravière, Pape Clément, de Rochemorin, Smith-Haut-Lafitte, la Tour-Martillac.

PETALUMA

AUSTRALIA, South Australia, Mount Lofty Ranges, Adelaide Hills
Cabernet Sauvignon, Merlot, Pinot Noir
Chardonnay, Riesling

Petaluma is the brainchild of the legendary Brian Croser, whose winemaking techniques have had the most influence on Australia's emergence as a leading wine nation.

Interestingly, Petaluma has taken many years to evolve its own wine style to the high level Croser demands, but recent vintages, in which he has finally been able to use exactly the grapes he wants, in particular ADELAIDE HILLS fruit for his Chardonnay and COONAWARRA Cabernet and Merlot grapes for his red, have been stunningly good. Croser CHAMPAGNE-method sparkling wine continues to improve but still has a rather austere style. The CLARE VALLEY Riesling is at the fuller end of the Australian spectrum and requires long aging. Other wines are made under the Sharefarmers and Bridgewater Mill labels. Petaluma has acquired a number of significant producers and brands since being listed on the Stock Exchange, including Mitchelton, KNAPPSTEIN, Smithbrook and Stoniers. In typical Australian form, it is a company on the march. Best years: 1997, '96, '94, '93, '92, '91, '90, '88.

CH. PETIT-VILLAGE

FRANCE, Bordeaux, Pomerol AC
Merlot, Cabernet Franc, Cabernet Sauvignon

This is not the wine to get in a blind tasting because, although this property produces one of the top POMEROL wines, the style is much

sterner and less sumptuous than that of its neighbours. This may partly be because the manager (it is owned by the insurance company AXA) is Jean-Michel Cazes, who owns Ch. LYNCH-BAGES in PAUILLAC and who perhaps brings a little of his Médocain instinct to bear on this Pomerol property.

However, the soil also plays a part. There was a time when half this 11-ha (27-acre) vineyard was planted with Cabernet Sauvignon, reflecting its gravel content, though now it is 82 per cent Merlot, 9 per cent Cabernet Franc and 9 per cent Cabernet Sauvignon. Some years, like 1985 and '90, are luscious and rich, but in general it is worth aging Petit-Village for eight to ten years, even for 10–15 years in vintages like 1989, '88 and '83. Vintages in the late 1990s have more weight and texture in the true Pomerol style. Best years: 1997, '96, '95, '94, '93, '90, '89, '88, '85, '83, '82, '81, '79, '78, '75.

CH. PETIT VILLAGE

Located at the highest point of Pomerol's gravel ridge, this château makes very concentrated wines with great depth of fruit.

CH. PÉTRUS

FRANCE, Bordeaux, Pomerol AC
Merlot, Cabernet Franc

Ch. Pétrus is a small, 11.5-ha (28-acre) estate with charmingly unimpressive buildings in an area that, 40 years ago, used to merit merely a paragraph or two in 'other Bordeaux wines' sections. Yet Pétrus is now one of the most expensive red wines in the world. Its AC is POMEROL, so recently acclaimed that it still has no 'classification' of quality. If it did, Pétrus would stand proud and magnificent at the very head, and for two reasons.

First, the vineyard, which is situated on an oval of imperceptibly higher land which is virtually solid clay, shot through with nuggets of iron. Only Merlot can flourish in this soil, and Pétrus is at least 95 per cent Merlot. These vines are remarkably old, often up to 70 years of age, which is rare in Pomerol and ST-ÉMILION because the great frost of 1956 destroyed most of the vines and caused wholesale replanting. The owner of Pétrus simply waited patiently for several years while the old vines got their strength back. The result is a concentration of intensely pure fruit.

The second factor in Pétrus' quality is the caring genius of its co-owners, the Moueix family. They ensure that only totally ripe grapes are picked (they only harvest in the afternoon to avoid dew diluting the juice); any portion of the wine which doesn't exude Pétrus quality is rejected and the whole crop is then aged in new oak barrels. The result is a wine of powerful, viscous intensity, a celestial syrup of ripe blackcurrants, blackberries, mulberries, plums and cream, overlaid with mint and tobacco scents and the perilously earthy excitement of fresh-dug truffles. Best years: 1998, '97, '96, '95, '94, '93, '90, '89, '88, '86, '85, '82, '79, '75, '71.

CH. DE PEZ
FRANCE, Bordeaux, Haut-Médoc, St-Estèphe AC, Cru Bourgeois
♂ *Merlot, Cabernet Sauvignon, Cabernet Franc, Petit Verdot*

Sturdy fruit, slow to evolve, but mouthfilling and satisfying, with a little hint of cedarwood and a good deal of blackcurrant to ride with their earthy taste – that's ST-ESTÈPHE's forte. De Pez – for long regarded as St-Estèphe's leading non-classified Growth, but now at least equalled by Ch. MEYNEY, Phélan-Ségur and HAUT-MARBUZET – adds a leathery, plummy dimension in good vintages. The 23-ha (57-acre) vineyard, well-placed inland from the Third Growth Ch. Calon-Ségur, has 43 per cent Cabernet Sauvignon, 46 per cent Merlot, 8 per cent Cabernet Franc and 3 per cent Petit Verdot; this goes a long way to explain why the wines have such a generosity of fruit and depth of flavour. The estate is now owned by the highly regarded CHAMPAGNE house Louis ROEDERER. Best years: 1997, '96, '95, '94, '90, '89, '88, '86, '85, '83, '82.

ROMAN PFAFFL
AUSTRIA, Niederösterreich, Weinviertel, Stetten
♂ *Blauer Zweigelt, Cabernet Sauvignon*
♀ *Grüner Veltliner, Riesling, Chardonnay, Sauvignon Blanc*

In very few years Roman Pfaffl has built up his estate at Stetten not only in terms of vineyard area (now 20ha/50 acres), but also in reputation. His rather pretentiously named Excellent, a blend of Cabernet and Zweigelt, is one of Austria's best reds, not least because Pfaffl long ago mastered the art of moderating the tannins without sacrificing body or

A few German winemakers still use large oak barrels, such as this one in the cellars of Dr Bürklin-Wolf at Wachenheim, for making and storing wine.

flavour. However, his best wines are his range of dry Grüner Veltliner, which are peppery and racy with excellent aging potential. Since 1995 a fine dry Riesling has been made, too. Best years: 1998, '97, '95, '94, '93, '92.

PFALZ
GERMANY

At 23,800ha (58,800 acres), this is Germany's second-biggest wine region, but tops them all for climate. It's the driest and sunniest part of the country, with the vineyards stretching in a north-south strip between the Haardt mountains and the Rhine. Mountains, river and vineyards all continue southwards after they cross the French border; the mountains change their name to the Vosges, and the vineyards become those of ALSACE.

Pfalz wines, however, are not that similar to those of Alsace. They are more flowery and less vinous; and traditionally they used to be a lot fatter and sweeter. But the region has undergone a revolution in the last few years, and while in the decades immediately after World War Two it was known for the Rhine's most luscious wines, wines that could turn flabby in too warm a year, now they have slimmed down, spruced up and become elegant, well structured and, at their best, distinctly refined.

The biggest revolution of all is taking place in the south of the region. This, even more than the rest of the Pfalz, is a land of part-time farmers who sell their wine to the

co-operatives. These co-operatives themselves have improved their standards (though a lot of this wine still goes into the likes of LIEBFRAUMILCH) and there are a number of growers making wines that could cause the famous names of the north a few headaches.

The best wines of the Pfalz are not always Riesling. As in Alsace, Pinot Blanc and Pinot Gris do well – here called Weissburgunder and Ruländer – and there is some outstanding Scheurebe, especially at the higher Prädikat levels. Good reds are made from Pinot Noir (Spätburgunder) and Dornfelder. The best vineyard sites, and the top producers, are clustered in a handful of villages in the middle of the northern Bereich, the Mittelhaardt/Deutsche Weinstrasse. RUPPERTSBERG, DEIDESHEIM, FORST and WACHENHEIM are the best villages here, though the best wines, as always, are not sold under the Bereich name; there is only one other Bereich in the Pfalz, and that is the Südliche Weinstrasse; in all there are 25 Grosslagen.

PFEFFINGEN
GERMANY, Pfalz, Bad Dürkheim
♀ *Riesling, Scheurebe, Silvaner and others*

This fine PFALZ estate is well known in Germany and in the USA, but much less so in Britain, to Britain's disadvantage. The wines are rich and well-structured, and the estate specializes in wines of higher Prädikat level: Auslese and upwards, making these almost every year. Its Scheurebes are particularly noteworthy. The dry wines are elegant and age well. The Ungsteiner Herrenberg site is one of the best. Best years: 1997, '96, '95, '92, '90, '89.

JOSEPH PHELPS
USA, California, Napa County, Napa Valley AVA
♂ *Cabernet Sauvignon, Zinfandel, Syrah, Merlot*
♂ *Grenache*
♀ *Chardonnay, Sauvignon Blanc, Gewurztraminer, Viognier and others*

Joseph Phelps came to the NAPA VALLEY to build a winery for someone else, decided winemaking was more fun than construction, and built a place of his own in time to make a 1973 Johannisberg Riesling that happened to catch the public fancy. Since then the emphasis has shifted away from Riesling in favour of Cabernet Sauvignon and Chardonnay.

Most famous was the dark, iron-hard Eisele Vineyard Cabernet Sauvignon made until 1991; the Napa Valley Cabernet is less tannic, but will age. Insignia is usually based on Cabernet Sauvignon: ripe, big, oaky and since 1990, it has been a marvellous complex, supple red, and outstanding in most vintages. Best years: 1996, '95, '94, '93, '92, '91, '90, '87, '85. Others of note include a much improved Syrah, splendid Viognier, and zesty RHÔNE-style Grenache rosé. The Chardonnays are a typical marriage of fruit and wood flavours, but the best Chardonnay named Ovation offers enticing ripe fruit and great flavour concentration. Best years: 1998, '97, '95, '94, '92, '91, '90. Phelps' other expertise is in the production of rich, botrytis-affected whites that can be some of CALIFORNIA's best.

PIAVE DOC

ITALY, Veneto

🍷 *Cabernet, Merlot, Pinot Noir (Pinot Nero), Raboso*
🍷 *Pinot Blanc (Pinot Bianco), Pinot Gris (Pinot Grigio), Tocai, Verduzzo*

The Piave Valley, north of Venice, is broad alluvial plain and there is no shortage of wine that is just as dismal as this uninspiring terrain would lead you to expect. But Italy is always full of surprises and there is plenty of lively enough wine to raise a few eyebrows. The most exciting wine of Piave's eight varietals is Raboso. An indigenous grape that hasn't spread far afield can usually be relied on to give a worthwhile taste, and red Raboso, all earthy, herby fruit and tannic clout, is no exception. Drink the whites young, Raboso up to eight years, the other reds up to four. Best years: 1997, '95, '94, '93. Best producers: Collalto, Rechsteiner, Castello di Roncade.

CH. DE PIBARNON

FRANCE, Provence, Bandol AC

🍷🍷 *Mourvèdre, Cinsaut, Grenache*
🍷 *Clairette, Bourboulenc and others*

Comte Henri de St-Victor and his son Eric have turned Pibarnon into one of the best estates in BANDOL. The 45-ha (111-acre) vineyard is planted mainly with Mourvèdre on magnificent, rocky, terraced slopes that overlook the Mediterranean sea. The red Bandol is a classic. Produced from 95 per cent Mourvèdre, it is vinified in a traditional way with the grapes fermented and macerated over a period of three weeks and the wine then aged in large oak *foudres* for 18 months. This results in a compelling flavour of sweet red-berry fruits, leather, spice and mint and firm but fine tannic texture that necessitates at least five to six years' bottle age.

There is also a solid rosé made from equal amounts of Mourvèdre and Cinsaut and an average to good white made essentially from Clairette and Bourboulenc. Best years: (reds) 1997, '96, '95, '93, '90, '89.

F X PICHLER

AUSTRIA, Niederösterreich, Wachau, Loiben

🍷 *Grüner Veltliner, Riesling, Muscat (Muskateller), Sauvignon Blanc*

'F X', as Austrian wine enthusiasts nickname him, is the nation's most famous producer of dry white wines. If you experience one of his incredibly concentrated Smaragd wines from either Grüner Veltliner or Riesling you will see that there are good reasons for all the fuss. If there is a large 'M' – for 'Monumental' – or the vineyard designation Dürnsteiner Kellerberg on the label then you have hit the jackpot.

The Rieslings are peachy and citric and the Grüner Veltliners packed with herb and exotic flavours. Dry white wine does not get any richer or more intense than this, and most of Pichler's wines age very well. His Muskateller is a remarkable wine too, one of the most elegant in Austria, but also rare. Best years: 1998, '97, '95, '94, '93, '92, '90, '88, '86.

RUDI PICHLER

AUSTRIA, Niederösterreich, Wachau, Wösendorf

🍷 *Grüner Veltliner, Riesling*

The best grower in the village of Wösendorf, Rudi Pichler makes big, succulent, just off-dry Grüner Veltliners and Rieslings which are easy to enjoy. Best of the bunch is the peachy-minerally Riesling from the Achleiten vineyard of Weissenkirchen. Best years: 1998, '97, '95, '94, '93.

CH. PICHON-LONGUEVILLE

FRANCE, Bordeaux, Haut-Médoc, Pauillac AC, 2ème Cru Classé

🍷 *Cabernet Sauvignon, Merlot, Petit Verdot*

Somehow Ch. Pichon-Longueville (formerly known as Pichon-Baron) got left behind in the rush. Its PAUILLAC neighbour, Ch. PICHON-LONGUEVILLE-COMTESSE DE LALANDE, and its ST-JULIEN neighbours, Ch. LÉOVILLE-LAS-CASES and LÉOVILLE-BARTON, leapt at the chance offered by the string of fine vintages from 1978. These châteaux established a leadership at the top of BORDEAUX's Second Growths which now seriously challenges the First Growths for sheer quality and equals several of them for consistency.

What about Pichon-Longueville? Its 50ha (124 acres) of vineyards are regarded as superb and its mixture of 75 per cent Cabernet Sauvignon and 25 per cent Merlot is ideal for making great Pauillac. Yet it needed the arrival of Jean-Michel Cazes of LYNCH-BAGES in 1987, supported by his brilliant winemaker and a large investment by the new owners, the giant AXA company, to bring all this to

fruition. The 1988, '89 and particularly the '90 are stupendous wines, easily the equal of the First Growths, with an intensity of dark, sweet fruit yet structured for a very long life. Subsequent vintages have been more difficult but Pichon-Longueville is now up there alongside the rest of the 'Super Seconds'. Best years: 1998, '97, '96, '95, '94, '90, '89, '88, '86, '82.

CH. PICHON-LONGUEVILLE
Since 1987 this château has had a remarkable change of fortune. Recent vintages have been of First Growth standard, with firm tannic structure and rich, dark fruit.

CH. PICHON-LONGUEVILLE-COMTESSE DE LALANDE

FRANCE, Bordeaux, Haut-Médoc, Pauillac AC, 2ème Cru Classé

🍷 *Cabernet Sauvignon, Merlot, Cabernet Franc, Petit Verdot*

Of all the top-notch wines in the HAUT-MÉDOC, none has been so consistently exciting or beguiling as Pichon-Longueville-Comtesse de Lalande. The vineyard is on excellent land on the edge of the PAUILLAC AC that runs alongside the vines of Ch. LATOUR and LÉOVILLE-LAS-CASES in ST-JULIEN. In fact, some of the vines are actually in St-Julien; this, combined with the highest proportion of Merlot in Pauillac (35 per cent of the blend) and some old, low-yielding Petit Verdot, may account for the sumptuous, fleshy richness of the wine, and its burst of blackcurrant, walnut and vanilla perfume.

But the real cause of Pichon-Longueville-Comtesse de Lalande's sensual triumph over the usually austere Pauillac community is the inspired, messianic figure of Mme de Lencquesaing. She took over the property in 1978 and still runs the show and for almost a decade led the château upwards in a wave of passion and involvement while the winemaker quietly interpreted her vision with brilliant wine after brilliant wine. This success story has run on through into the 1990s. Don't be deceived by the lush caress of the rich fruit – there's lots of tannin and acid lurking, and good examples, though wonderful at six to seven years old, will usually last for 20 years or more. Second wine: Réserve de la Comtesse. Best years: 1998, '97, '96, '95, '94, '93, '90, '89, '88, '87, '86, '85, '83, '82, '81, '80, '79, '78, '75.

PIEMONTE (Piedmont) Italy

TUCKED AWAY UP IN THE north-west corner of Italy, up against the mighty Alps, the Piedmont region has neither coastline nor any city of the fame of Rome or Venice to attract the crowds; yet for many wine lovers a visit to the region is as de rigueur as a pilgrimage for a devout Catholic. For Piedmont is the home of Nebbiolo, Italy's most mystical grape variety, the merits of which are more hotly contested than any other, and of Nebbiolo's most prestigious wines, Barolo and Barbaresco.

The alpine foothills in north and west Piedmont often have too harsh a climate for vines, and grapes can ripen only where river valleys bring air movement and so extra sunshine. The Dora Baltea, flowing south through Ivrea, carves out the Nebbiolo zone of Carema and the area of white Erbaluce di Caluso and sweet Caluso Passito. The river Sesia

brings viticulture to the Novara and Vercelli hills, south of Lake Maggiore, in the zone of Gattinara and Ghemme.

It is the south of Piedmont, though, that harbours most of the region's wines. South-east of Turin the landscape becomes characterized by angular hills with perfectly straight rows of vines stretching horizontally across the slopes. This is the heart of Nebbiolo country, with the wine zones of Barolo and Barbaresco on either side of, and that of Roero just across the Tanaro river from, the little town of Alba, also famous for its fabulous white truffles. There, as elsewhere in the region, the late-ripening Nebbiolo is planted on the sunniest, south-facing slopes, leaving other slopes for less fussy varieties or for other grapes – Dolcetto, Barbera, perhaps Chardonnay. A hilltop vineyard site, called a *bricco* in dialect, is particularly prized.

Other indigenous grape varieties can be found here too, most of them only in tiny amounts and some on their way back from virtual extinction. These include Freisa and Grignolino, Pelaverga and Rouchet. All these red varieties, despite their wide differences, have a common core of austerity (especially when their wines are still young) that makes them typically Piedmontese.

White wines take very much second place in the region afer reds. Apart from fashionable Gavi in the south-eastern corner, made from the Cortese grape, it was only in the 1980s that interest was shown again in the native varieties, Arneis and Favorita, as well as in imported Chardonnay. Yet the strangest thing about south Piedmont is that just next door to what are probably the harshest, most mouth-attacking reds from anywhere in Italy are the lightest, most delicate mouthfuls of grapiness you could ever hope to find – lightly sparkling Moscato d'Asti and its fully sparkling counterpart, called simply Asti.

Since 1994 Piedmont has had a regional denomination: Piemonte DOC. This is an umbrella DOC covering a wide range of grape varieties – Pinot Bianco, Pinot Grigio, Cortese, Chardonnay and Moscato for whites and Pinot Nero, Barbera, Bonarda, Grignolino and Brachetto for reds. The idea is that it acts as a catch-all for quality wines which might fail for one reason or another to be classified under a local DOC: Piedmont's wine legislators apparently think that vino da tavola, even in its trendily elevated guise, is beneath any wine produced in their region. In recent years the great Piedmont wines have become targets for collectors the world over, causing

The small village of Castiglione Falletto viewed over vineyards at Perno. Together with the village of Barolo itself, Castiglione Falletto forms the heart of the Barolo zone and includes some prime vineyards such as Monprivato.

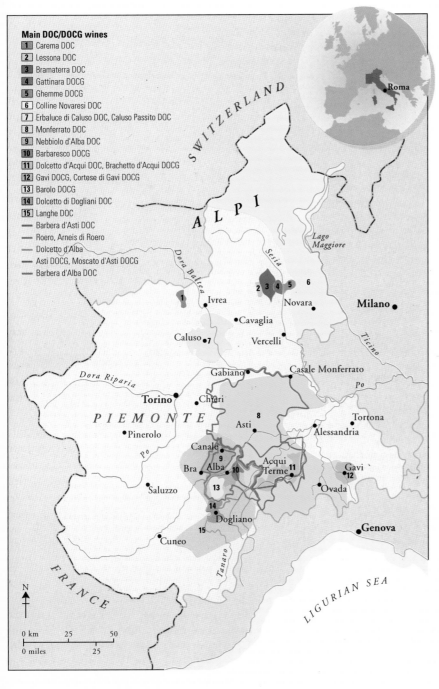

Main DOC/DOCG wines

1. Carema DOC
2. Lessona DOC
3. Bramaterra DOC
4. Gattinara DOCG
5. Ghemme DOCG
6. Colline Novaresi DOC
7. Erbaluce di Caluso DOC, Caluso Passito DOC
8. Monferrato DOC
9. Nebbiolo d'Alba DOC
10. Barbaresco DOCG
11. Dolcetto d'Acqui DOC, Brachetto d'Acqui DOCG
12. Gavi DOCG, Cortese di Gavi DOCG
13. Barolo DOCG
14. Dolcetto di Dogliani DOC
15. Langhe DOC
— Barbera d'Asti DOC
— Roero, Arneis di Roero
— Dolcetto d'Alba
— Asti DOCG, Moscato d'Asti DOCG
— Barbera d'Alba DOC

ROBERTO VOERZIO
Cerequio is one of several outsanding single-vineyard Barolos from this talented Barolo producer, one of the best of the younger generation.

GIACOMO CONTERNO
The winery owned by Giovanni Conterno is famed for its monumental Riserva Monfortino, traditional Barolo at its best.

GAJA
Angelo Gaja's traditional strength has always been in his single-vineyard Barbarescos, including the modern classic Sorì Tildìn.

BRAIDA
The late Giacomo Bologna achieved fame through this single-vineyard, barrique-aged Barbera.

BAVA
This ripe, melony white wine is an example of the recently established Monferrato white blend which can include various white grapes as well as Barbera.

prices to rocket alarmingly. As long as quality is maintained or improved, however, there seems nothing can be done. It's the old, old story of supply (in this case tiny) and demand (mushrooming).

REGIONAL ENTRIES

Asti, Barbaresco, Barbera d'Alba, Barolo, Brachetto d'Acqui, Carema, Erbaluce di Caluso, Gattinara, Gavi, Langhe, Moscato d'Asti, Nebbiolo d'Alba, Roero.

PRODUCER ENTRIES

Altare, Antinori, Braida, Aldo Conterno, Giacomo Conterno, Fontanafredda, Gaja, Giacosa, Mascarello, Produttori del Barbaresco, Prunotto, Sandrone.

ELIO ALTARE
This oak-aged Nebbiolo wine is one of several modern Piedmontese wines from this new wave producer.

PIEROPAN

ITALY, Veneto, Soave Classico DOC

♀ *Garganega, Trebbiano di Soave, Riesling Italico, Sauvignon Blanc*

No producer in Italy has been more faithful and courageous than the house of Pieropan, which for three generations kept the flag of quality flying through those years when the industrialists of Verona were churning out vast quantities of SOAVE rubbish and quietly continued to turn out, year after year, wines of which it was often said: 'Too good to be Soave'. With outstanding vineyards at La Rocca, behind the famous castle, and at Calvarino, Leonildo Pieropan and his wife Teresita, now joined by their sons, make an excellent regular Soave Classico, as well as the two single-vineyard versions, Calvarino and La Rocca, the definitive wines of the zone.

With intelligent modifications, Pieropan not only continues to fly the traditionalist flag but matches, quality for quality, the young turks who have risen like chest-beating Tarzans during the past ten to 20 years, claiming the 'new Soave' as their territory. Pieropan is more than a match for them, for although he does not resort to using Chardonnay or Sauvignon (for his dry wines), or use barriques in the making of anything but sweet wines, his Soaves not only perform well in professional tastings but also have several times proved their ability to age amazingly well into their second decade. Although he does not use barriques, he has recently taken to fermenting his cru La Rocca in *tonneaux* (500-litre barrels), after which it spends a year in *botte grande* (2000-litre vats).

But if the dry wines are good, Pieropan's sweet wines can on occasion be exceptional. The classic example is Recioto di Soave le Colombare, from Garganega grapes dried conventionally on *graticci* (racks) until the February after the harvest. It is a model of

PIEROPAN
This wine, made from dried grapes in the millennia-old tradition of Verona, is an unusual example of a non-cloying sweet white with refreshing acidity.

restraint and balance, perhaps not the type of wine that wins blind tastings, rather the type of which you actually want to drink more than one glass. There is also a Passito della Rocca, from Sauvignon Blanc, Riesling Italico and Trebbiano di Soave grapes which are dried for slightly less time on *graticci*, then fermented and aged in barrique; plus, two or three times a decade, when conditions are right, a mind-blowing late-harvest (*vendemmia tardiva*) wine from Garganega grapes left to dry on the vine until mid-December in order to develop about 40 per cent noble rot. Best years: (Recioto) 1994, '93, '91, '90, '88.

PIERRO

AUSTRALIA, Western Australia, South West Australia Zone, Margaret River

♂ *Cabernet Sauvignon, Cabernet Franc, Merlot, Pinot Noir and others*

♀ *Chardonnay, Semillon, Sauvignon Blanc*

Dr Michael Peterkin has an iconoclastic attitude to winemaking, and dislikes convenient pigeon-hole descriptions of his winemaking practices and philosophy. Towering Chardonnay, very complex and rich, usually high in alcohol, is his benchmark wine and one of the most exciting in Australia; his potent Cabernets (an impressive five varietal BORDEAUX-style blend) is equally powerful and long-lived. The Semillon-Sauvignon Blanc blend is a fruity, crisp style for early drinking. The second label is Fire Gully. Best years: (Chardonnay) 1996, '95, '94, '93, '92.

PIESPORT

GERMANY, Mosel-Saar-Ruwer

This village, in one of the steepest parts of the MOSEL, has been much devalued by having its name included in the Piesporter Michelsberg Grosslage, one of the main generic wines in Germany, churning out vast amounts of wines that are soft, light and insipid. Yet Piesport's own wines are a delight – elegant, relatively light and very stylish. Rieslings from the famous, steep Goldtröpfchen vineyard site are powerful and concentrated with intense blackcurrant and peach aromas. Best producers: GRANS-FASSIAN, Reinhold HAART, von KESSELSTATT.

PIEVE SANTA RESTITUTA

ITALY, Tuscany, Brunello di Montalcino DOCG

♂ *Sangiovese, Cabernet Sauvignon*

♀ *Malvasia, Trebbiano*

This superbly sited BRUNELLO DI MONT-ALCINO estate attracted the attention of

Angelo GAJA, who now owns the company. Single-vineyard bottlings of Brunello Rennina and Sugarille are very expensive, but benefit from a vigorous selection. Somewhat austere and overwhelming when young, they will repay keeping for 15 years or more, when their deep, earthy notes and concentrated red and black fruits emerge. The winemaker is one of Italy's best, Attilio Pagli, and his SUPER-TUSCAN Sangiovese-Cabernet Sauvignon blend, Promis, is a fine example of the genre. He also makes an outstanding, fabulously rich VIN SANTO called Dols. Best years: (Brunello) 1993, '91, '90; (Vin Santo) 1990, '88.

LE PIN
This concentrated and elegant Pomerol, made entirely from Merlot, was first produced as recently as 1979; it now fetches huge prices at auction.

CH. LE PIN

FRANCE, Bordeaux, Pomerol AC

♂ *Merlot*

Here's a success story if ever there was one. The first vintage of Le Pin was produced by owner Jacques Thienpont in 1979 (before that the wine had been sold in bulk to merchants) and now it's one of the most expensive wines in the world, prices at auction frequently outstripping those for Ch. PÉTRUS. The '82, only the fourth vintage, became so insanely popular that it was selling for £1000/US$1600 a bottle. The reasons for this sensation are twofold: scarcity and style of wine. There are barely 2ha (5 acres) of vineyard, superbly located close to those of Ch. TROTANOY and VIEUX-CHÂTEAU-CERTAN (also owned by the Thienponts), which produce an average 8500 bottles a year from lowly yields of some 35 hectolitres per hectare.

The wine, made entirely from Merlot and lavishly aged in 100 per cent new oak barrels for 18 months, is rich, lush and velvety with an almost Burgundian aroma of ripe cherries and raspberries. It's a magical experience but you have to dig deep in the pocket for the privilege of tasting it. It is best with five to ten years' age, though it will age comfortably for 20 years. Best years: 1997, '96, '95, '94, '90, '89, '88, '86, '85, '83, '82, '81.

PINE RIDGE

Pine Ridge's popular dry Chenin Blanc Yountville Cuvée has crisp, bright flavours that become floral and honeyed with a little age.

PINE RIDGE WINERY

USA, California, Napa County, Stags Leap District AVA

♦ *Cabernet Sauvignon, Merlot*

♀ *Chardonnay, Chenin Blanc*

Founded in the 1970s, this STAGS LEAP DISTRICT winery produces most of its sizeable output from grapes sourced in other NAPA VALLEY AVAs. However, its reputation was founded on its soft, supple, tantalizing Cabernet Sauvignon from Stags Leap, and its Chardonnay (one of several offered) remains one of the finest from the Stags Leap District. It is being surpassed of late by a poised, delicious apple fruit and layered CARNEROS Chardonnay. Best years: (Chardonnays) 1997, '96, '95, '94.

Its RUTHERFORD Cabernet Sauvignon captures cassis and dusty regional flavours, albeit in a tight, lean style. Both the limited volume HOWELL MOUNTAIN Cabernet Sauvignon and Andrus Reserve (a massive red BORDEAUX-style blend) are huge, muscular wines built to age a decade or longer. Managing partner Gary Andrus is a strong believer in CARNEROS Merlot, and his current vintages showcase the region's bright red cherry side and layered flavours. Best years: (reds) 1997, '96, '95, '94, '92. The popular, sweet-edged Chenin Blanc sells out quickly.

Part owners, the Andrus family also run the new and already highly rated OREGON winery, ARCHERY SUMMIT.

DOMINIO DE PINGUS

SPAIN, Castilla-León, Ribera del Duero DO

♦ *Tempranillo (Tinto Fino), Petit Verdot*

Danish winemaker Peter Sisseck, a consultant in RIBERA DEL DUERO, has created his own tiny winery in a converted shed in Quintanilla de Onésimo – very modest facilities for a venture that has made such a huge impression. From two small vineyards in La Horra and Valbuena de Duero (old, gobelet-pruned

Tinto Fino vines and a little experimental Petit Verdot) totalling 4.5ha (11 acres), he has produced one of the world's best and most expensive new wines, Pingus. Bunch-by-bunch selection in the vineyard, grape-by-grape destemming by hand at the winery, fermentation in oak vats, malolactic fermentation in new French oak barrels, and aging on lees without any racking for one year or more show the enormous effort that goes into the wine.

Pingus is a great, dark, concentrated red of undeniable world class. There's also a second wine for export markets called Flor de Pingus, which is made from bought-in grapes and is scented and delicious. Best years: 1996, '95.

PINOT BLANC

Pinot Blanc is a chorus member rather than a solo artiste in the white grape hierarchy of France. This grape is not the same as Chardonnay, even though the two can taste similar when the wine is young and unoaked.

In Italy, however, exciting things are achieved with Pinot Blanc, or Pinot Bianco. In ALTO ADIGE and FRIULI-VENEZIA GIULIA it can outshine Chardonnay, it plays a major role in what is arguably Tuscany's finest white, QUERCIABELLA's Batàr, and it is even found as far south as PUGLIA, though in those hot conditions it tends to ripen too soon to develop complexity. In the FRANCIACORTA zone in Lombardy it plays a vital role in Italy's best sparkling wines.

When picked early Pinot Blanc is neutral and quite acid – the perfect base material for sparkling wine, and in France, where its heartland is ALSACE, it makes most of the local fizz, CRÉMANT D'ALSACE. With the similar-tasting Auxerrois, it is taking over the 'workhorse' role for Alsace wines from Sylvaner and Chasselas, but as a varietal. Pinot Blanc produces round, fat, apple-creamy wine, positively rich in a warm year. It is also used as part of the blend with Chardonnay in several Burgundian appellations.

In Austria and Germany it's known as Weissburgunder or Klevner; it's also found in Slovakia and Slovenia, and many other eastern and central European areas, as well as in CALIFORNIA and OREGON, with both states experiencing a revival of interest in the varietal. British Columbia's OKANAGAN VALLEY boasts more than 25 producers of cool-climate citrus-flavoured Pinot Blanc that can be stainless steel or barrel fermented. It hasn't made much impact on Australia or South Africa.

PINOT GRIS

The grapes can be anything from greyish blue to brownish pink and they are often mistaken for Pinot Noir. Another of the world's more amenable grape varieties, Pinot Gris will amiably produce whatever is required of it, from crisp, refreshing whites to intense, luscious dessert wines. Even when the wine is dry and light it should have a lick of honey and spice; this increases, often becoming earthier and even a little mushroomy, as the sweetness increases. Pinot Gris is nicely susceptible to noble rot, becoming smoky, raisiny and fat.

The best dry examples come from Alsace, where its official name is Tokay-Pinot Gris; Germany, particularly Baden and the Pfalz (as Ruländer or Grauburgunder); Styria (Steiermark) and Burgenland in Austria; north-eastern Italy (as Pinot Grigio); eastern Europe; and Oregon, where it has the edge on Chardonnay. The southerly reaches of Canada's Okanagan Valley turns out a small amount of rich, ripe, fruity Pinot Gris.

Superb dessert versions come from Alsace (Vendange Tardive or the even sweeter Sélection de Grains Nobles), Germany, Austria's Burgenland and Murfatlar in Romania. As winemaking in eastern Europe improves, expect some goodies, both sweet and dry, from there.

PINOT MEUNIER

The red Pinot Meunier (or plain Meunier as it is sometimes called) is the most widely planted grape in the CHAMPAGNE region and makes up more than a third of the blend in much non-vintage Champagne, even though it is the least well regarded of the three permitted varieties (Pinot Noir and Chardonnay are the other two). Elsewhere in France, it is to be found in the LOIRE Valley where it is used in the fragile rosé, Gris Meunier d'Orléans.

In other parts of the world (from Australia through California to Canada) it is usually grown as a crucial component of the sparkling wine blend and occasionally for rosé and red wines.

PINOT NOIR

This is the most capricious, ungracious, unforgiving, fascinating grape of them all – and the one that everybody wants to grow. In Burgundy, where it's been established for a millennium or so, they still have endless problems with it, so it's not surprising that in places like Oregon, with hardly more than 20 years experience of Pinot Noir, they are only just discovering the problems.

What are the problems? For a start it's difficult to grow. It buds early and ripens early, which makes it suitable for cold climates. But its tight bunches are seriously prone to rot, it reacts to overcropping by producing wine little better than rosé, and yet because its fruit sets very irregularly, it is often pruned for extra quantity. So when it does set, you're going to overcrop, which means the juice will be pale.

Then the wines are difficult to make. The Burgundians produce the most exciting flavours by living dangerously and fermenting as hot as they dare – but if they go just a bit too far they get stewed flavours instead of the silky, ripe, vegetal strawberry and gamy tastes that are the ideal. Yet play safe and all you'll get is safe, fruity wine of no particular distinction.

The Pinot Noir that all the world wants to ape is that of the Côte d'Or, where it can produce the most startling, fascinating flavours. Can, but does not always – in fact does not probably more often than it does. Elsewhere in France, Pinot Noir makes light perfumed reds or tasty, strawberryish rosés in Savoie, Jura, the Loire – especially Sancerre – and Alsace, but its major role outside Burgundy is in Champagne. In this even cooler climate it gives pale wines which still have enough body to round out the leaner Chardonnay. It provides much of the colour in rosé Champagne, but for white Champagne it is pressed straight away and vinified like a white wine, the juice being barely coloured. This classic formula for sparkling wines, Pinot Noir, Pinot Meunier and Chardonnay, is the basis of much Champagne-method fizz around the world, including California and Australia.

In Italy only a few producers seem to have come near to cracking Pinot Noir's code as a still red: Ca' del Bosco and Bellavista in Lombardy's Franciacorta, and La Stoppa in Colli Piacentini are almost there, as are Fontodi in Tuscany; but closest of all are the growers in the Adige valley: Franz Haas, Ochsenreiter of Haderburg, and especially Hofstatter. In Germany it is most at home in Baden and the Pfalz, and the newish German fashion for dry, well-structured reds is helping its development no end; the same goes for Austria. In Germany it is called Spätburgunder, and in Austria Blauburgunder.

Tim Hamilton-Russell, a pioneering Pinot Noir producer in South Africa, has always maintained the country needs to be 200km (125 miles) further south to produce great Pinot Noir. Hamilton-Russell and Bouchard-Finlayson are the most consistent producers and much Pinot Noir is now successfully used here in fizz.

The real leader in the southern hemisphere is New Zealand, whose sunny but cool climate (especially in Martinborough in the North Island and between Central Otago, Canterbury and Marlborough in the South Island) seems well suited to the variety. The quality of Australian Pinot Noir has improved in leaps and bounds, the Yarra Valley leading the way, followed by Gippsland, Geelong, Mornington Peninsula, Adelaide Hills and Tasmania. Plum, cherry, spice and tobacco are the key characters. Early Canadian results from Ontario and British Columbia are promising. Pinot Noirs from Chile have been increasingly good – scented and soft – and Rio Grande in Argentina looks promising.

So far the best Pinot Noir outside Burgundy is in California. About 25 per cent of the Pinot Noir here is used for sparkling wine; for red wines the most promising areas are Carneros, the Russian River Valley, parts of Monterey and Santa Barbara Counties.

Some years ago Oregon was being hyped as the US Côte d'Or, but when a couple of poor vintages meant that the wines failed to live up to the hype they were just as extravagantly damned. However, Oregon was chosen for Pinot Noir because it is a marginal region, and the process is a gradual one. The best wines are ripe and vegetal with a touch of silkiness. The promise is still there, and hopes have been given a boost by the performance of Domaine Drouhin.

PINOTAGE

This red grape, South Africa's speciality, is a cross between Pinot Noir and Cinsaut. It was developed in South Africa in 1925, but only introduced widely into Cape vineyards in the 1950s; it is rarely grown elsewhere (New Zealand and Zimbabwe have a little).

Pinotage produces a wine with a quite distinctive flavour, likened to fresh bananas and marshmallows crossed with the sweet/sour flavours of plum and redcurrant when young. Age brings a more mellow plummy character. The abrasive, estery styles of old are being taken over by wines with cleaner, more intense fruit. Successful both in a fresh, juicy style, as well as more structured with new oak, it has attracted international attention as a novelty and is now very fashionable. On the home front, winemakers have mixed feelings about its future, although members of the Pinotage Producers' Association are active and enthusiastic promoters of the grape.

PIPERS BROOK VINEYARDS

AUSTRALIA, Tasmania

🍷 *Cabernet Sauvignon, Pinot Noir*

🍷 *Riesling, Chardonnay, Gewurztraminer, Pinot Gris*

In 1972 Andrew Pirie identified the cool Pipers Brook region of northern TASMANIA as most likely to produce wines of European style. And indeed, he has produced some of the most refined wines in Australia despite a continual battle against what, for Australia, is a very marginal climate for ripening grapes. In vintages such as 1991 and '98 the red wines come into their own, with an added dimension of fruit and a perfumed, Burgundian style that is lacking in cooler years – when his aromatic whites often excel.

An unlisted public company, Pipers Brook has been decidedly aggressive in its expansion activities, first acquiring the important Rebecca Vineyard on the Tamar River, and then buying neighbours, Heemskerk and Rochecombe, making it by far the biggest wine company in Tasmania. Best years: (Chardonnay) 1998, '94, '92, '91, '88, '86, '84.

PIRINEOS

SPAIN, Aragón, Somontano DO

🍷 *Moristel, Tempranillo, Merlot, Cabernet Sauvignon, Parraleta*

🍷 *Tempranillo, Macabeo, Moristel, Grenache Noir (Garnacha Tinta)*

🍷 *Macabeo, Chardonnay*

In the 1990s, when the rich newcomers (VIÑAS DEL VERO, then ENATE) set up shop near Barbastro in SOMONTANO, ARAGÓN'S coolest wine region, the old Somontano del Sobrarbe co-operative might have given up all hope of competing and reverted to bulk wines and cheap bottlings. Instead, it metamorphosed itself into a private winery, with its members holding part of the shares, changed its name to Bodega Pirineos and embarked on an ambitious investment programme.

In contrast with the newcomers, who largely rely on new plantings of foreign grape varieties, Pirineos has large, well-established tracts of the native Macabeo and Moristel grape varieties and even a little of the almost extinct, powerful, musky Parraleta. It makes light young reds from Moristel, a delightful late-harvest (*vendimia tardía*) dry Macabeo and increasingly ambitious oak-aged blends of Moristel, Tempranillo and the French varieties, under the Montesierra label. Merlot here is particularly impressive. Prices are modest and quality exciting for a winery producing more than 200,000 cases every year. Best years: 1997, '96, '95, '94, '91.

ROBERT PLAGEOLES

FRANCE, South-West, Gaillac AC

🍷 *Duras, Gamay, Syrah, Fer Servadou and others*
🍾 *Mauzac, Ondenc, Loin de l'Oeil, Muscadelle and others*

Robert Plageoles, assisted by his son Bernard, is a tireless defender of the local grape varieties of his native Gaillac region. As well as Ondenc and Loin de l'Oeil he has preserved and replanted seven different strains of Mauzac – Vert, Roux, Jaune, Côte de Melon, Rose, Gris, Noir – at his 20-ha (49-acre) estate. These grapes are harvested at various stages of maturity and vinified in different ways to produce a dry Mauzac Vert, sweet Mauzac Roux, the sparkling, demi-sec Gaillac Nature, which is made by the *méthode rurale*, and a sherry-like Vin de Voile, aged under a film of flor for seven years in 600-litre oak barrels. Recent vintages of the Vin de

VIN D'AUTAN DE ROBERT PLAGEOLES & FILS 1996

A nul autre comparable, je suis le vin du vent et de l'esprit

ROBERT PLAGEOLES
The Gaillac Vin d'Autan is a deliciously aromatic sweet wine made from Ondenc, a perfumed white grape, one of several local varieties resurrected from near-extinction by Robert Plageoles.

Voile include the 1992, '87 and '83. There is also a sweet Ondenc made from the first selection of late-harvested grapes and the Vin d'Autan from the second selection when the grapes are truly raisined or *passerillé*. The wines are both original and extremely good.

PRODUCTEURS PLAIMONT

FRANCE, South-West

🍷 *Tannat, Cabernet Sauvignon, Cabernet Franc, Fer Servadou and others*
🍾 *Colombard, Ugni Blanc, Gros Manseng, Petit Manseng, Courbu and others*

This grouping of three Gascon co-operatives (Plaisance, Aignan and St-Mont) is the largest, most reliable, and most go-ahead producer of Vin de Pays des CÔTES DE GASCOGNE and CÔTES DE ST-MONT AC. It accounts for 2500ha (6177 acres) of vineyard and produces an average 18 million bottles of wine a year. Investment through the 1980s and '90s in stainless steel tanks, temperature control and new bottling equipment has provided the means to produce clean, modern wines using regional grape varieties.

The whites, including the Côtes de Gascogne Colombelle, are generally crisp and fruity. The reds, in particular the Côtes de St-Mont Ch. St-Go and de Sabazan, are well structured with quite rounded fruit benefiting from some oak aging and can age for upwards of five years. The co-operative also produces an average 200,000 bottles a year of MADIRAN, including the Cuvée Collection, a powerful but refined wine matured in oak barriques and capable of aging for five years' or more. There is also a small amount of sweet PACHERENC DU VIC BILH, notably the Cuvée St-Albert.

PLANTAGENET

AUSTRALIA, Western Australia, South West Australia Zone, Great Southern

🍷 *Syrah (Shiraz), Cabernet Sauvignon, Pinot Noir*
🍾 *Riesling, Chardonnay, Chenin Blanc*

The senior winery in the Mount Barker sub-region of the GREAT SOUTHERN region, Plantagenet makes around 35,000 cases a year on its own account but also provides a foster home for many other producers in the region by supplying winemaking facilities.

The quality of Plantagenet's wine is usually very good and sometimes great: an intense, lime-and-passionfruit Riesling, a stylish, spicy oak, melon-accented Chardonnay, a riotously spicy, peppery Shiraz and a wonderfully supple and complex, cherried Cabernet Sauvignon lead the way – and all made in an

PLANTAGENET
This Western Australian winery is known for its superb wines from a wide range of varieties, including stylish Chardonnay.

unglamorous apple-packing shed. The reds in general benefit from a little aging. Best years: 1996, '95, '94, '93, '91, '90, '88, '86, '85.

PLOVDIV

BULGARIA, Southern Region

🍷 *Cabernet Sauvignon, Merlot, Pamid, Mavrud and others*
🍾 *Red Misket, Rkatsiteli and others*

Plovdiv is one area in Bulgaria where the grapes are generally allowed to mature fully on the vine and not picked when they are still unripe. The result is red wines, in particular, that can exhibit the scent and depth generally so singularly lacking from Bulgaria. Cabernet Sauvignon is the top red wine here, but the native Mavrud also provides a fleshy mouthful, structured and with good length. Good-quality stainless steel in the winery protects the fruit, and the slow but steady incorporation of new wood is producing some very polished red wines.

PODRAVSKI

SLOVENIA

This district in the north-east of Slovenia, adjoining Austria's STEIERMARK, can be translated as the Drava Valley, and is the home of the country's best whites. The trouble is, they tend not to get exported, and the wines from the LJUTOMER-Ormoz sub-region that do get abroad are not much of an advertisement for Podravski. But as well as Ljutomer-Ormoz there are other sub-regions here: Prekmurje, Padgone-Kapela, Maribor, the snappily named Central Tract of Slovenske Gorice and the Hilly Tract Haloze. Names apart, the white grapes of the Pinot family do well, as does Welschriesling (Laski Rizling), but this is only to be drunk on the spot. There's good, rich Traminer (alias Traminec), occasional Rumeni Muskat or Yellow Muscat (elegant, with great finesse) and excellent late-harvest wines. Best producers: BRKO, Jurij Hlupic, LJUTOMER winery, Ormoz winery, Protner, Radgonske Gorice winery.

IL POGGIONE
ITALY, Tuscany, Brunello di Montalcino DOCG
♟ *Sangiovese, Cabernet Sauvignon*

BRUNELLO DI MONTALCINO is touted as Italy's longest-lasting red wine, and while most producers today, for all the megabucks they command for their bottles, would be incapable of demonstrating this thesis, Il Poggione still can. Pierluigi Talenti has been winemaker since 1958 at this large and historic estate – owned for some 200 years by the de Franceschis of Florence – which includes 86ha (213 acres) of vineyard. Talenti may be old and frail now, and the estate is certainly traditional, but it is not short of new ideas, having recently added to the range of Rosso and Brunello di Montalcino a SUPER-TUSCAN called San Leopoldo (75 per cent Sangiovese, 25 per cent Cabernets Sauvignon and Franc) which brings to the restrained house style an exciting extra burst of berry fruit. Best years: 1997, '95, '93, '91, '90, '88, '86, '85, '82.

POL ROGER
FRANCE, Champagne, Champagne AC
♟ ♀ *Pinot Noir, Chardonnay, Pinot Meunier*

If you look closely at the label of Pol Roger non-vintage CHAMPAGNE, you'll see it is bordered in black as a mark of respect for Sir Winston Churchill when he died. This may sound far-fetched, but Pol Roger is the most anglophile of Champagne houses, and the current head, Christian de Billy, would probably take it as a great compliment if you mistook him for an Englishman. Churchill was a voracious consumer of Pol Roger, and it was Pol Roger he was thinking of when he said, in the dark days of World War Two, 'In victory we deserve it, in defeat we need it.'

In 1984 Pol Roger launched a Cuvée Sir Winston Churchill, which, in a period when many special de luxe Champagnes are proving overpriced disappointments, is a delicious, refined drink worthy of the name. However, most of the production is of the non-vintage White Foil, which is gentle, light and reasonably consistent. There is also a Vintage Champagne which regularly equals the best of its year, a Rosé, a delicate Vintage Chardonnay, and a Vintage Reserve Special. Best years: 1990, '89, '85, '82, '79.

POLIZIANO
ITALY, Tuscany, Vino Nobile di Montepulciano DOCG
♟ *Sangiovese, Canaiolo, Cabernet Sauvignon, Merlot*
♀ *Trebbiano, Malvasia, Chardonnay, Gewurztraminer and others*

This estate of 120ha (297 acres) of vineyard was purchased by the Carletti family in 1961, but it was not until the 1980s, when the present owner Federico Carletti came on board, that it began the journey which has taken it to the highest level in VINO NOBILE DI MONTEPULCIANO particularly, and Tuscany generally. Carletti is a viticulturist by training, and more than most who give lip-service to the theory that 'great wine is born in the vineyard', he backs the idea in practice, supported by one of Tuscany's great consultant agronomist/enologists, Carlo Ferrini.

'For the time being', he says, he does not believe in blending Sangiovese with the French red varieties (Cabernets Sauvignon and Franc), which he vinifies separately for the excellent SUPER-TUSCAN Le Stanze, first made in 1983. He is also strict about not making the Vino Nobile crus Vigna Asinone and Vigna Caggiole, nor the 100 per cent Sangiovese super-Tuscan Elegia, in years of medium quality, preferring rather to ensure the quality of his basic Vino Nobile.

The style of Poliziano's Vino Nobile is deep and vibrant of colour, rich and concentrated of fruit, firm of tannic backbone but with that soft cherry-berry fruit overlaying the tannins, seemingly powerful but more thanks to concentration than to alcohol (Ferrini tries to keep the wines around 13 degrees, when from other producers it can easily climb to 14 degrees or more in good years), and ultimately quite elegant. Best years: 1997, '95, '93, '90, '88, '85.

POLIZIANO
From a blend of Cabernet Sauvignon and Cabernet Franc, Le Stanze is one of Tuscany's top Bordeaux-style wines and is packed with rich blackcurrant fruit.

ERICH & WALTER POLZ
AUSTRIA, Steiermark, Südsteiermark, Spielfeld
♀ *Sauvignon Blanc, Chardonnay (Morillon), Pinot Blanc (Weissburgunder), Pinot Gris (Grauburgunder) and others*

Brothers Erich and Walter Polz are perhaps the most consistent wine producers in all of STEIERMARK (Styria). Year in, year out, every wine from the light dry Welschriesling up to the powerful, intensely aromatic Sauvignon Blanc from the Hochgrassnitzberg site is a model of modern winemaking. Using a combination of stainless steel and large wooden casks, some of which are new, Erich Polz vinifies whites with the vibrant fruit and herbal aromas and crisp flavours that are the region's hallmark. Only the Morillon (Styrian for Chardonnay) from the Obegg site is given the full new oak treatment, giving a big, buttery wine. Best years: 1997, '95, '94, '93, '92, '90.

POMEROL AC
FRANCE, Bordeaux
♟ *Merlot, Cabernet Franc, Cabernet Sauvignon*
See also St-Émilion & Pomerol, pages 326–327.

From being a virtually unknown AC, Pomerol is possibly now the most famous of the Bordeaux regions, at least in the USA. Home to Ch. PÉTRUS, and the tiny, exorbitantly priced Ch. le PIN, it has become one of the most expensive of the Bordeaux ACs across the board. You can't tell why Pomerol is so special just by looking at the landscape – and a mere country lane divides it from the vines of ST-ÉMILION.

The unique quality lies in that soil – 784ha (1960 acres) of deep, close-packed cloddish clay, interspersed with iron, a little gravel, a little sand, but ultimately it is the clay that makes Pomerol great. The only grape that relishes clay is the Merlot. Most properties have over 80 per cent and the result is superb, inimitable wine – richer than any dry red wine should be, sometimes buttery, sometimes creamy with honeyed spices too; often plummy, but there's blackcurrant there as well, raisins, chocolate, roasted nuts and the disturbing perfume of truffles, with mint to freshen it up. No wonder it's expensive. And if all that sounds as though the wines won't age – they will, brilliantly. Best years: 1998, '96, '95, '94, '93, '90, '89, '88, '87, '86, '85, '83, '82, '81, '79, '78. Best producers: Beauregard, Bon-Pasteur, Certan-de-May, Clinet, Clos du Clocher, CLOS RENÉ, la Conseillante, l'Eglise-Clinet, l'Évangile, la Fleur-Pétrus, le Gay, GAZIN, la Grave-à-Pomerol, LAFLEUR, LATOUR-À-POMEROL, PETIT-VILLAGE, Pétrus, le Pin, de Sales, TROTANOY, VIEUX-CHÂTEAU-CERTAN.

POMINO DOC
ITALY, Tuscany
♟ *Sangiovese, Canaiolo, Cabernet Sauvignon and others*
♀ *Pinot Blanc (Pinot Bianco), Chardonnay, Trebbiano Toscano and others*

Pomino, within the CHIANTI RUFINA zone, was first mentioned in the Bando, a document of 1716 defining the boundaries of the four most illustrious wines of the time. Over 90 per cent of production comes from one large estate owned by the Marchesi de FRESCOBALDI. Frescobaldi's plummy Pomino Rosso owes much of its character to the admixture of Cabernet, while Pomino Bianco is a soft, full, carefully thought-out blend. Best years: 1997, '95, '94, '93, '90, '88, '85. The only challenge to Frescobaldi comes from the Fattoria di Petrognano, whose wines are made at Fattoria SELVAPIANA, and are therefore very good.

POMMARD AC

FRANCE, Burgundy, Côte de Beaune
♦ *Pinot Noir*

The problem with Pommard is quality control. Its easily pronounceable name made the wine very sought-after in export markets, and until the 1970s much so-called Pommard was fraudulent. Today the problem is inconsistency. Quite often you find bottles at distressingly high prices which are coarse and rough with sullen, scentless flavours; and good BOURGOGNE Rouge from the same producers in Pommard can be actually better than their Pommard. Good Pommard should have full, round, beefy flavours, a bit jammy when young but becoming plummy, chocolaty and a little meaty with age. But fruit has to be at the core of the flavour. When it's good, Pommard ages well, often for ten years or more, retaining a thick core of fruit while gradually shedding its tannin.

There are no Grands Crus in the 340ha (840 acres) of vines but les Rugiens Bas, les Épenots and les Arvelets (all Premiers Crus) are the best vineyard sites. Best years: 1997, '96, '95, '93, '90, '89, '88, '87, '85, '80, '78. Best producers: Comte ARMAND, J-M Boillot, de Courcel, Gaunoux, Lejeune, LEROY, Monnier, de MONTILLE, A Mussy, Parent, Ch. de Pommard, Pothier-Rieusset, POUSSE D'OR.

POMMERY

FRANCE, Champagne, Champagne AC
♀♦ *Chardonnay, Pinot Noir, Pinot Meunier*

Pommery is a house rich in history. Madame Pommery was one of the celebrated CHAMPAGNE widows, and ran the business for three decades, developing the crucial English market, which has always retained a fondness for Pommery Champagnes. Indeed, the fantastical Pommery mansion is supposed to be a homage to the English country house, but students of architecture would find the references baffling. Her descendant, Prince Alain de Polignac, is the present winemaker, but since 1991 Pommery has been owned by the

The Pommard appellation has no less than 28 Premier Cru vineyards. On the Beaune side of the village les Grands Epenots is one of the best ones.

luxury products group LVMH, who also own KRUG and MOËT ET CHANDON.

The style is light and elegant and does not always show well in the form of non-vintage Brut Royal. But the vintage Brut can be delicious, and there is an ethereal delicacy to the prestige Cuvée Louise, which, dominated by Chardonnay, is slow to evolve in bottle. Even in very tricky years such as 1987, Prince Alain managed to make a very fine wine. Good though the Pommery Champagnes undoubtedly are, given that the house owns 275ha (680 acres) of Grand Cru vineyards, it is surprising that the regular cuvées are not even better, although the new Brut cuvée called Apanage is of high quality. Best years: 1991, '90, '89, '88, '87, '85, '83, '82, '81, '79, '76.

CH. PONTET-CANET

FRANCE, Bordeaux, Haut-Médoc, Pauillac AC, 5ème Cru Classé
♦ *Cabernet Sauvignon, Merlot, Cabernet Franc*

Pontet-Canet was, until the mid-1970s, one of the most popular and widely available of the HAUT-MÉDOC Classed Growths. The 75-ha (185-acre) vineyard next door to Ch. MOUTON-ROTHSCHILD regularly produced the largest amount of wine of any of the Classed Growths, and no wine was château-bottled until 1972. Since 1979 Pontet-Canet has been owned by the Tesserons of Ch. LAFON-ROCHET, and we are now seeing a return to the big, chewy, blackcurrant and

sweet-oak style that is typical of the great PAUILLAC wines. Recent vintages show an impressive ripeness and concentration. Best years: 1997, '96, '95, '94, '93, '90, '89, '88, '86, '85, '83, '82.

PONZI VINEYARDS

USA, Oregon, Willamette Valley AVA
♦ *Pinot Noir*
♀ *Pinot Gris, Chardonnay*

The first vineyard at Ponzi was planted in 1970 and the winery soon gained a reputation for Pinot Gris and Pinot Noir. Dick Ponzi was an early advocate of the use of new oak for his Pinot Noir Reserve, which is a bright and boldly flavoured wine. Chardonnay production has generally fallen, but Ponzi still make two versions. The first is labelled Willamette Valley and is from older OREGON clones. The other, Clonal Selection, is from newly planted Dijon clones. Best years: (reds) 1998, '97, '96, '94, '93; (whites) 1998.

PORT DOC

PORTUGAL, Douro
♦ *Touriga Naçional, Touriga Francesa, Tinta Roriz (Tempranillo) and others*
♀ *Gouveio, Viosinho, Rabigato, Malvasia Fina and others*

The world regards PORT as a global wine style, but Portugal is the originator and the master. Named after Portugal's second city, Porto (Oporto in English), the port wine region (Vinho do Porto) starts out on the steep slopes of the DOURO Valley and its tributaries some 70km (43 miles) inland. The hillsides have been carved over the centuries into narrow step-like terraces, each of which support a row or two of vines. Mechanization is difficult and many of the finest vineyards are still cultivated by man and mule. Few places in the world are quite so challenging for growing grapes.

Many of the larger port shippers have built modern, well-equipped wineries in the Douro but a large amount of port is still produced in the traditional manner, the grapes being trodden by foot on small private farms known as quintas. Most of the quality ports leave the Douro Valley in the spring following the vintage, and travel by tanker to the lodges (or above ground cellars) to age in the cooler maritime environment of Vila Nova de Gaia, on the opposite bank of the river Douro from Oporto.

Ports may be either red or white and fall into two categories: wood-matured or bottle-matured. Wood-matured ports range from the youngest, most basic ruby through premium ruby (sometimes misleadingly called

Vintage Character) to the finest, oldest, most delicate tawnies. All are aged in wooden vats and casks, possibly for only a few months for a component of a young ruby blend but 20 years or more is not uncommon for a fine tawny. Colheita ports, cask-aged tawnies from a single year, also fall into this category.

The finest of the bottle-matured ports is known as vintage, which is only 'declared' by the shippers after a truly exceptional harvest. It spends a mere two years in wood before being bottled (without any treatment or filtration), where it will age for another 15 or 20 years before being ready to drink. During this time the wine throws a 'crust' or sediment in bottle and therefore requires decanting. The best wines from great vintages like 1994, '77, '66 and '63 will continue to develop well in bottle for half a century or more. In good in-between years, many shippers bottle vintage ports from single estates or quintas. These wines tend to be slightly earlier maturings although some independent quintas (Quinta do VESUVIO, Quinta de la ROSA, Quinta do CRASTO) have become shippers in their own right. Best years: (vintage ports) 1997, '94, '92, '91, '85, '83, '80, '77, '70, '66, '63.

A good, relatively inexpensive alternative to vintage port is crusted or crusting port. It is usually made from a blend of wines from two or three good years, aged for a short period in cask and then bottled, like vintage port, without filtration. Then there is also the unfiltered style of late bottled vintage (LBV) port, which is aged for four to six years in cask before bottling. Both will develop in bottle over the medium term and need decanting. Most LBV is made in large quantities and filtered before bottling. Although considerably better than a basic ruby it is a poor substitute for vintage port or traditional, unfiltered LBV. White port (made from white grapes) tends to be fairly dull unless it is given extended aging in wood, which gives the wine an incisive 'nutty' character. Best producers: DOW, FERREIRA (tawnies), FONSECA, GRAHAM, NIEPOORT, RAMOS PINTO (tawnies), TAYLOR, WARRE.

POSAVSKI
SLOVENIA

This is the name of Slovenia's Sava valley district, in the south-east of the country, where it borders Croatia. Between half and two-thirds of the wine is red, with the local favourite being a light, acidic, bilberry- and blueberry-tasting number called Cvicek. It's a blend of various grapes (such as Portugalka and Zametna Crnina), all of which are tradi-tionally grown all muddled up in the vineyards, and is surprisingly attractive. Otherwise there are light, fresh whites for drinking young. Best producers: Istvenic, Krsko, Martincic, Pleterje monastery, Plut.

CH. POTENSAC
FRANCE, Bordeaux, Médoc AC, Cru Bourgeois
♀ *Cabernet Sauvignon, Merlot, Cabernet Franc*

What a pleasure to be able to give an unreserved thumbs-up to a BORDEAUX wine. Thumbs-up for quality, thumbs-up for consistency – and thumbs-up for value.

There are two keys to Potensac's success. First, there is a ridge of gravel here. These are rare in the northern MÉDOC AC but are crucial to allow a well-drained vineyard capable of making fine wine. Second, the 50-ha (124-acre) estate is owned and run by Michel Delon, the genius of ST-JULIEN's great Second Growth Ch. LÉOVILLE-LAS-CASES.

Of all the proprietors in the lowly Médoc AC, Michel Delon is the one who succeeds in drawing out a richness, a concentration and a complexity of blackcurrant, vanilla and spice flavour in his wine which, during the 1980s and '90s, has regularly surpassed many Classed Growths for quality. Potensac can be drunk at four to five years old, but fine vintages will improve for at least ten. Best years: 1997, '96, '95, '94, '93, '90, '89, '88, '86, '85, '83, '82, '81, '79, '78.

CH. POTENSAC
Potensac's success is based on quality, consistency and value for money. The wine has delicious blackcurrant fruit and considerable depth.

POUILLY-FUISSÉ AC
FRANCE, Burgundy, Mâconnais
♀ *Chardonnay*

Pouilly-Fuissé is a dry white wine from the vineyards of five villages – Pouilly, Fuissé (yes, you did see a comma, they're two different villages), Vergisson, Chaintré and Solutré – that has become faddish and expensive because of insatiable demand from the American market. The vineyards are beautiful – clustered under the startling rock outcrop of Solutré. Many are ideally situated to produce fine wine, but the overbearing importance of the Chaintré co-operative, and the cynical disregard for quality by many of the merchants who buy three-quarters of the wine, has meant that most growers can get a good living by simply milking their vineyards of every last grape.

Luckily, 2 or 3 per cent of the AC is in the hands of committed growers who care passionately about the quality of Pouilly-Fuissé. They restrict their yields, use only ripe grapes, employ wooden barrels to ferment and mature their wines, and the result is wine of character and individuality – buttery, nutty, the fruit full of peach and melon and banana, and all this enriched with the spice of cloves and cinnamon and a generous splash of honey. These wines can be wonderful at two years old, but often last up to ten. Best years: 1997, '96, '95, '92, '90, '89, '88, '86, '85. Best producers: Corsin, Denogent, B & J-M Drouin, C & T Drouin, Ferret, Forest, Ch. FUISSÉ (Vincent), Guffens-Heynen, Lassarat, Léger-Plumet, Luquet, Noblet, Valette.

POUILLY-FUMÉ AC
FRANCE, Central Loire
♀ *Sauvignon Blanc*

'Fumé' means 'smoky', and there's no doubt that a good Pouilly-Fumé has a strong pungent smell. The old-time wine writers used to say it had a whiff of gunflint (*pierre à fusil*) about it. In fact, the smokiness is more that fabulous, fresh yet acrid aroma of roasting coffee. The only grape allowed is Sauvignon Blanc, which is famous for its gooseberry, grassy-green, even asparagus flavours, and what gives the extra smokiness and elderflower and lychee perfume in Pouilly is that many of its vineyards – covering 1250ha (3090 acres) on slopes near the town of Pouilly-sur-Loire – are planted on a particularly flinty soil called silex.

Increasingly, producers are making several cuvées, especially in good years such as 1997 and '96. Often there will be a 'basic' cuvée, then a more concentrated one made from a particular vineyard or old vines. The prestige cuvées are priced accordingly. Best years: 1997, '96, '95, '90, '89. Best producers: Didier DAGUENEAU (his 'silex' is superb), Serge Dagueneau, Ch. de Favray, Landrat-Guyollot, de Ladoucette, Jean Pabiot, Robert Pabiot, Redde, Saget, Seguin, Tracy.

POUILLY-LOCHÉ AC, POUILLY-VINZELLES AC
FRANCE, Burgundy, Mâconnais
♀ *Chardonnay*

Loché and Vinzelles are two perfectly decent Mâconnais villages with the vines on the flatter land just to the east of Fuissé. Funnily enough, the growers of Vinzelles tried to organize their own AC in 1922 – long before POUILLY-FUISSÉ – but as Pouilly-Fuissé's Midas touch turned every bottling run into a money-minting extravaganza, it seemed obvious that adding Pouilly to their own names might prove profitable. That's the angle. So does it work? Yes, Pouilly-Vinzelles and Pouilly-Loché are more expensive than equivalent wines like MÂCON-Lugny. And no, the quality of the wine – largely processed by the Loché co-operative, but sold as Pouilly-Vinzelles regardless of which village it came from – is not a patch on a good Pouilly-Fuissé – it's really just Mâcon-Blanc-Villages with a fancy name. Best years: 1997, '96, '95, '92. Best producers: Caves des Grands Crus Blancs, St-Philibert.

CH. POUJEAUX

FRANCE, Bordeaux, Haut-Médoc, Moulis AC, Cru Bourgeois

🍷 *Cabernet Sauvignon, Merlot, Cabernet Franc, Petit Verdot*

Poujeaux is one of the properties whose wine-making standards have helped to nudge the MOULIS AC into the limelight. It's a big property of some 50ha (125 acres) and is beautifully located on the gravel banks around the village of Grand-Poujeaux. Although its reputation is for dry, long-lived wines, vintages in the 1980s and '90s have been richer, more supple, with a delicious chunky fruit, new-oak sweetness and a slight scent of tobacco. This more accurately reflects the very high percentage of Merlot in the vineyard – 40 per cent, with 50 per cent Cabernet Sauvignon, 5 per cent Cabernet Franc and 5 per cent Petit Verdot. The consistency of the wines at this estate and their long aging potential – 20–30 years for good vintages – make Poujeaux a Classed Growth in all but name. Best years: 1997, '96, '95, '94, '93, '90, '89, '88, '86, '85, '83, '82, '81, '78.

DOMAINE DE LA POUSSE D'OR

FRANCE, Burgundy, Côte de Beaune, Volnay AC

🍷 *Pinot Noir*

The renown of this 13-ha (32-acre) estate was established by the late Gérard Potel, who had a knack of producing stylish, zesty wines even in vintages such as 1984, when other growers looked at their vines and despaired.

The domaine's best-known wines emanate from sites within VOLNAY – Clos de la Bousse d'Or and Caillerets – but there is also a fine POMMARD Les Jarolières, and one of the finest

wines from SANTENAY, the Clos Tavannes. These were never powerfully extracted wines: instead, the focus was on elegance and purity of fruit. Potel was never a formulaic wine-maker, but aligned his practices to the nature of the fruit delivered to him by each vintage. Sometimes he would destem all the grapes; in other years he would retain some of the stems. He was a firm believer in *saignier*, the practice of bleeding the tanks of juice in years when dilution was a problem; he claimed to have been a pioneer of the technique in 1973. Sadly, the estate was sold in 1997, and Gérard Potel died suddenly on the day the sale was ratified, so the future of the domaine, in terms of quality and style, has to be somewhat uncertain. Best years: 1996, '95, '94, '93, '91, '90, '89, '88, '87, '85, '80, '78.

CH. PRADEAUX

FRANCE, Provence, Bandol AC

🍷🍷 *Mourvèdre, Cinsaut, Grenache*

In every sense of the word this is a traditional domaine which continues to produce one of the great BANDOLs. Owner Cyrille Portalis cultivates the 19-ha (47-acre) vineyard along organic lines. At the harvest the grapes are lightly crushed but not destemmed and the resulting wine then spends three or four years aging in large wooden barrels called *foudres*. This makes for a powerful, tightly textured red wine with enormous aging potential. Twenty years is not a problem for this essentially Mourvèdre-based wine. The rosé is made from Cinsaut and Mourvèdre. Second wine: l'Enclos de Pradeaux. Best years: (reds) 1996, '95, '93, '92, '91, '90.

CH. PRADEAUX
This is a big, deep-hued red wine from mainly Mourvèdre which is aged for three to five years in wood to soften Mourvèdre's tannin.

FRANZ PRAGER

AUSTRIA, Niederösterreich, Wachau, Weissenkirchen

🍷 *Riesling, Grüner Veltliner, Chardonnay (Feinburgunder), Sauvignon Blanc*

Franz Prager was one of the dry wine pioneers in the WACHAU from the late 1950s. Since the end of the 1980s, when his daughter Ilse and

son-in-law Toni Bodenstein took over the estate, it has gone from strength to strength. Bodenstein, who is also a director of one of Austria's largest banks, is obsessed with vineyard character, and every year his Riesling from the Steinriegel, Achleiten and Klaus sites of Weissenkirchen are strikingly different from one another. The Steinriegel is always the sleekest and most open, the Achleiten shows seductive apricot fruit and lots of minerals, the Klaus concentrated and severe with great aging potential. The best Grüner Veltliner is a succulent wine from the Achleiten, the site from which Bodenstein's magnificent Riesling Trockenbeerenauslese also originates. Quantities are tiny, but the quality is sensational. Best years: 1998, '97, '95, '94, '93, '92, '91, '90, '86, '81, '79.

PREMIÈRES CÔTES DE BLAYE AC

FRANCE, Bordeaux

🍷 *Merlot, Cabernet Sauvignon, Cabernet Franc, Malbec*

🍷 *Sémillon, Sauvignon Blanc, Muscadelle*

Premières Côtes de Blaye is the supposedly superior AC for reds and whites from the Blayais, a wine area of 4400ha (10,872 acres) on the opposite side of the Gironde to Lamarque in the HAUT-MÉDOC. (Technically, AC Blaye or Blayais is also allowed in this area, but virtually all the red wines are sold as Premières Côtes de Blaye.) There are definite signs of improvement in this region. Until now the problems have been a lack of that acid bite and tannic grip which make red BORDEAUX special. The wines have been smudgy, sludgy things, jammy and sweet to taste and earthy of texture. The AC for whites permits only three grape varieties, as against seven for CÔTES DE BLAYE. The wines can be dry, medium or even sweet, but in practice only a tiny amount of white wine is produced. Premières Côtes de Blaye white accounts for only 170ha (420 acres), but can, like the excellent Ch. Haut-Bertinerie, be very good.

Although vines were planted here long before they were in the MÉDOC, any wine fame the Premières Côtes de Blaye once had is long gone, and Blaye itself, a rather attractive little town, is best known for its great seventeenth-century citadel and the car ferry to Lamarque across the Gironde. However, a new generation – one-third of the growers are now under 35 – with the assistance of a technical adviser, is now producing red wines with more zip and fruit. Investment in wine-making equipment and new oak barrels along with better vineyard management have been largely instrumental in the lift in quality. Best years: 1998, '96, '95, '94, '93, '90, '89, '88. Best producers: Bel Air La Royère, Charron, Haut-Bertinerie, Haut-Grelot, Haut-Sociando, Jonqueyres, Rolande Lagarde, Loumède, Monconseil Gazin, Marcillac co-operative (Duchesse de Tutiac), Mondésir Gazin, Peybonhomme, Ségonzac, des Tourtes.

PREMIÈRES CÔTES DE BORDEAUX AC

FRANCE, Bordeaux

Merlot, Cabernet Sauvignon, Cabernet Franc
Sémillon, Sauvignon Blanc, Muscadelle

The Premières Côtes de Bordeaux region has some of the most captivating scenery in BORDEAUX. This lovely hilly AC stretches for 60km (38 miles) down the right bank of the Garonne river. Time and again as you breast a hill you find yourself at the top of steep slopes running down to the Garonne, with an unparalleled view across the river to the famous properties of GRAVES and SAUTERNES on the opposite bank.

The Premières Côtes de Bordeaux used to be thought of as sweet white territory, especially since three communes here – CADILLAC, LOUPIAC and STE-CROIX-DU-MONT – do specialize in 'Sauternes look-alike' sweeties. But as the fashion for sweet wines faded during the 1970s, more and more growers turned to red wine with a good deal of success. Since the 1980s plantings of white varieties have dropped by over 20 per cent to about 456ha (1127 acres). Most of this white wine, however, only qualifies for the Bordeaux Sec AC, since the Premières Côtes AC requires a minimum of four grams of sugar per litre of wine. This isn't a lot, but it is too much for growers who are trying to make fashionable dry whites. As well, the best sweet wines tend to qualify for the Cadillac AC. The result is that red wines forge ahead. There are now 2868ha (7087 acres) of red vineyards.

In the north, near Bordeaux, a certain amount of clairet – light red, halfway to rosé – is made for quick and easy drinking. However, as the vineyards mature, a very attractive juicy fruit quality has become evident in the reds, and – with investment in better equipment, including some oak barrels for aging – the future is already looking bright for the area, particularly as the wines represent excellent value for money in today's high-flying market. Reds and rosés are usually delicious at two to three years old, but should last for five to six; the whites, especially the dry ones, won't last that long. Best years: (reds)

1998, '96, '95, '94, '90, '89, '88. Best producers: (reds) Brethous, Carsin, Chelivette, Constantin, Grand Mouëys, Joachet, Juge, Lamotte de Haux, du Peyrat, de Pic, Puy-Bardens, Reynon, Le Sens, Suan.

CH. PRIEURÉ-LICHINE

FRANCE, Bordeaux, Haut-Médoc, Margaux AC, 4ème Cru Classé
Cabernet Sauvignon, Merlot, Cabernet Franc, Petit Verdot

If you're short of something to do on Christmas Day, no problem. Nothing on this Easter? Here's what to do. And also on New Year's Day, Ash Wednesday, Labour Day, May Day, Hallowe'en, or any other day you care to mention. You go to visit Ch. Prieuré-Lichine in BORDEAUX, because this property is open 365 days a year. But then Prieuré-Lichine has never been an ordinary château.

Alexis Lichine, who was probably the greatest promoter and apostle of French wines in the second half of the twentieth century, owned and ruled the property until his death in 1989. This extraordinary man can be credited with virtually single-handedly creating the American market for high-quality, estate-bottled wines from France. This zeal to press the flesh and pop the top of a bottle in persuasive mood is what kept his property – 69ha (170 acres) spread all over Cantenac and MARGAUX – open all year round.

The wine has a gentle, perfumed style but does not lack tannin and recent vintages look to be on the up, especially since the involvement of consultant enologist, Michel Rolland. Best years: 1998, '96, '95, '94, '93, '90, '89, '88, '86, '85, '83, '82, '78.

CH. PRIEURÉ-LICHINE
This is reliable, gently perfumed red Bordeaux with fine, soft tannin for aging for ten to 15 years. Since the mid-1990s there has been a marked improvement in quality.

PRIEURÉ DE ST-JEAN DE BÉBIAN

FRANCE, Languedoc-Roussillon, Coteaux du Languedoc AC
Grenache, Syrah, Mourvèdre and others
Grenache Blanc, Clairette, Roussanne and others

During the 1970s and '80s Alain Roux made this a ground-breaking domaine, planting Syrah, Grenache and Mourvèdre and turning

out rich, spicy, powerful, if slightly rustic wines. The quality faded in the early 1990s but has again been on the upward turn since new owners, former wine writer Chantal Lecouty and her husband, purchased the domaine in 1994. The grapes are now partially destemmed and the wine aged in barriques and 600-litre casks in order to produce a more refined tannic structure. There is also a barrel-fermented white COTEAUX DU LANGUEDOC. Second wine: la Chapelle de Bébian. Best years: (reds) 1997, '96, '95, '94.

PRIMITIVO

Pundits seems satisfied that the Italian red grape Primitivo, so named because it is an early ripener, is identical to Zinfandel, both hailing from former Yugoslavia where it still exists under the name Mali Plavac.

Today Primitivo thrives in the sunbaked flatland around Manduria (east of Taranto in PUGLIA's Salento peninsula), turning out its richest, most concentrated grapes on low trained *alberello* bushes – those that remain, that is, after the EU in its total absence of wisdom got through paying fortunes for having these high-quality vineyards ripped out. No grape beats Primitivo for grape sugar, which when fermented means high alcohol levels, and indeed Primitivo di Manduria wine can achieve some frighteningly high levels of alcohol. Most of the grapes are used to bump up the weedier offerings of elsewhere in Italy and Europe (mainly France). Those that are used for Primitivo di Manduria proper make, traditionally, a dark purple, dry, slightly or fully sweet, occasionally fortified, gutsy beast of 14 per cent minimum alcohol. But one producer, Pervini, is turning out blended wines of real elegance, under names like Felline or Bizantino, the other grapes being Negroamaro and Montepulciano.

Primitivo is also the grape behind the reds of Gioia del Colle, a zone inland and upland from Manduria.

PRIMORSKI

SLOVENIA

Translated into English as the Littoral wine-growing district, this is the part of Slovenia that borders the FRIULI region of Italy, and makes wines which, not surprisingly, can resemble north-eastern Italian wines from the COLLIO zone in their freshness and lightness. There's good Sauvignon Blanc and Merlot in Primorski, but the most popular wine locally is Refosk (in some places called Teran), made from the red grape that over the border in

In the mountainous, isolated region of Priorat, a remote area of Cataluña, vineyards are planted in deep, slate soil on precipitous slopes. Vineyard yields here are some of the lowest in Spain.

Italy is called Refosco. It's lean, with razor-like acidity and cherry-like fruit, and is opaquely black. The Malvasia can be good and apricotty; the Chardonnay is fair but seldom matches up to those from elsewhere in the world. Best producers: Dobrovo, Lisjak, MOVIA, Sezana, Ivan Stojan, VIPAVA.

PRIORAT DO

SPAIN, Cataluña

Grenache Noir (Garnacha Tinta), Garnacha Peluda, Cariñena, Cabernet Sauvignon, Merlot, Syrah

Garnacha Blanca, Macabeo, Pedro Ximénez, Cariñena Tinta

Situated in the south of CATALUÑA, this is one of the loveliest and wildest regions of Spain, with scrubby, craggy mountains and narrow, winding roads. Traditionally Garnacha Tinta and Garnacha Peluda predominated, but Cariñena now accounts for a third to a half of most blends. Tiny yields mean Priorat (Priorato in Spanish) produces extremely concentrated, dark, intense wines. They are also inevitably alcoholic: the minimum legal strength for table wines is 13.5 per cent. Most of the wines lately have been 'young' reds, sold at between three and four years old, but Priorat also makes some excellent *rancio*-styled wines and *generosos* – dry to sweet, penetratingly flavourful, nutty, raisiny wines, wood-aged for a minimum of five years. White wines are very scarce.

However, alongside such tradition, a revolution is taking place. A group of new producers moved into the village of Gratallops during the 1980s, planted French varieties to make blends with the native Garnacha and Cariñena, introduced modern winemaking techniques and new French oak barrels, and created a new style of Priorat which astonished the world's critics and emptied their wallets. So far, tradition and revolution seem to be good for each other. Best years: 1996, '95, '94, '93, '92. Best producers: Clos Mogador, Clos i Terrasses, COSTERS DEL SIURANA, Joset Maria Fuentes, MAS MARTINET, Alvaro PALACIOS, Pasanau Germans, Rottlan Torra, Scala Dei, Vall-Llach.

PRODUTTORI DEL BARBARESCO

ITALY, Piedmont, Barbaresco DOCG

Nebbiolo

No co-operative in Italy enjoys such a reputation for quality and consistency as does this one. Founded – or refounded – in 1958 (the origins actually go back over 100 years), they work by committee ably led by Celestino Vacca, aided by his son Aldo, once of GAJA.

They process only the Nebbiolo grapes of their 60-odd members, controlling around 100ha (247 acres), mostly in BARBARESCO: around one quarter of all Barbaresco production. Vinification and maturation are along traditional lines. Their crus include some of the zone's best (Asili, Moccagatta, Montefico, Montestefano, Ovello, Pajè, Pora, Rabajà and Rio Sordo). There is also good-value basic Barbaresco and Langhe Nebbiolo. Best years: 1997, '96, '95, '93, '90, '89, '88, '85.

PROSECCO DI CONEGLIANO-VALDOBBIADENE DOC

ITALY, Veneto

Prosecco, Verdiso

Sparkling Prosecco is one of those wines the locals – such as the few Italians who live in Venice – take for granted, a little like brown ale in Newcastle. Generally, it's a simple, yeasty little number, made in a sizeable zone in eastern VENETO at the western and eastern edges of which are the towns of Valdobbiadene and Conegliano. The wine may take the name of just one of them, an option that most producers thankfully use.

At the Valdobbiadene end is a sub-zone called Cartizze, credited with producing the finest wines and so granted its own sub-denomination, Superiore di Cartizze. Prosecco di Conegliano-Valdobbiadene can be a still wine, but is usually frizzante or spumante, as Prosecco is one of those grapes that tend to produce fizz, sometimes whether you want it or not. The wine is made sparkling by a second fermentation in tank, not in the bottle as in CHAMPAGNE. All three styles of Prosecco can be dry or sweet. So there is plenty to keep label printers happy and to confuse potential customers.

When in Venice, Prosecco, with its soft, floral, appley, milky flavours will taste great. Back home it won't taste as good – you can't export atmosphere – but it will still be a refreshing glass of simple, soft wine with bubbles. Drink young. Best producers: Adami, Bisol, Canevel, Carpenè Malvolti (the best-known name), Le Case Bianche, Le Cotture, Nino Franco, Gregorio Gatto, Le Groppe, Merotto, Mionetto, Ruggeri, Zardetto.

PROTOS

SPAIN, Castilla-León, Ribera del Duero DO

Tempranillo (Tinto Fino)

Tempranillo (Tinto Fino), Grenache Noir (Garnacha Tinta), Valenciano and others

Housed in cellars under the castle hill of Peñafiel, this was the region's best-known co-operative before it became a private winery, whose shareholders are the former co-operative members. The name change also portended other improvements through the 1990s, as more consistently fruity and clean wines were produced from the large (400-ha/988-acre) vineyard holdings. The price remains, thankfully, a notch below that of other RIBERA DEL DUERO wines. The Gran Reserva was consistently a very good wine through all the upheaval. Best years: 1995, '94, '91, '89, '86.

J J PRÜM

GERMANY, Mosel-Saar-Ruwer, Wehlen
♀ *Riesling*

The Prüm estate, one of the biggest and probably the most famous of the Mittel MOSEL producers, was divided in 1911. J J Prüm is now the best known of several Prüms on the Mosel, making some of the region's finest Rieslings. The wines are of excellent quality, sometimes unapproachable in youth but remarkably long-lived and rewarding to those who can be bothered to age them. The estate owns a large part of the WEHLENer Sonnenuhr vineyard as well as parts of GRAACHer Himmelreich and BERNKASTELer Lay. Best years: 1997, '96, '94, '93, '90, '89, '88, '86, '85, '83, '79, '76, '75, '71.

S A PRÜM

GERMANY, Mosel-Saar-Ruwer, Wehlen
♀ *Riesling*

This chunk of the original Prüm estate in the MOSEL, divided in 1911, is owned by Renate Willkomm and the wines are made by Raimond Prüm. Not surprisingly, it shares some vineyard sites in common with J J PRÜM, notably the WEHLENer Sonnenuhr, and GRAACHer Himmelreich and Domprobst. J J Prüm has the greater reputation but S A Prüm should not be overlooked: the wines are made with great care, with no Süssreserve, and with extensive cask-aging. The QbA wines these days are sold under the estate name alone, with vineyard names only being used for the higher quality designations, a practice that is becoming quite common among the best estates (German). Best years: 1997, '95, '94, '93, '90, '89, '88.

PRUNOTTO

ITALY, Piedmont, Barolo DOCG
♟ *Nebbiolo, Barbera, Dolcetto*
♀ *Arneis, Moscato Bianco*

Following Alfredo Prunotto's retirement in 1956, Bepe Colla became the winemaker at this high-class *commerciante* establishment (buying grapes on long-term contracts from top growers). One of the quality leaders and trend-setters of the Albese region, he pioneered the concept of the single-vineyard cru, way back in the early 1960s. Meanwhile he continued to believe in blended BAROLO and BARBARESCO and maintained that great Nebbiolo and barrique do not go together.

ANTINORI, of Tuscan fame, bought the company in 1989 and not surprisingly, is modernizing practices. In 1995, after the end of Colla's consultancy, Prunotto began using

PRUNOTTO
The Cannubi Barolo Cru is a perfumed, velvety Barolo with superb fruit and excellent in its well-balanced smoothiness.

French-oak 5-hectolitre *fusti* for the aging of some Barolo and Barbaresco, as well as shortening maceration time and, perhaps most important of all, purchasing new vineyards.

Despite these changes, Prunotto still remains one of the pillars of classic Piedmont reds. The Barolo crus Bussia and Cannubi and the Barbaresco Montestefano have all been delicious recently, as have BARBERA D'ALBA Pian Romualdo, which really shows how exciting Barbera can be given the chance, and the NEBBIOLO D'ALBA Occhetti di Monteu. Best years: (Barolo) 1993, '90, '89, '88, '86, '85, '82, '79, '78, '74, '71.

PUGLIA

ITALY

Puglia, the heel of the Italian boot, is an elongated region whose northern limit is on the same latitude as Rome and whose southern limit parallels the island of Corfu in Greece. Winewise, it divides into three parts. The first is in the north, a virtual extension of ABRUZZO and MOLISE, where Montepulciano dominates in DOCs San Severo and Cacc'e Mmitte di Lucera; there is nothing here to get excited about. In the centre, around the Murge plateau, there are a cluster of DOCs of which CASTEL DEL MONTE is the least obscure.

It is from the south, however – the Salento peninsula – that the most interesting wines come. The heat of the low-lying flatlands is mitigated by sea-breezes from either side, and there is a long tradition of planting the dominant Primitivo and Negroamaro grapes to the high-quality, if labour-intensive, free-standing, bush-training system called *alberello*. Wines include Primitivo di Manduria DOC and Primitivo del Salento IGT, plus a host of Negroamaro-based wines headed, in popularity terms, by SALICE SALENTINO and including BRINDISI, Copertino, Leverano, Alezio and Squinzano. The red dessert wine, Aleatico di Puglia DOC, is mostly produced south of Bari; so, too, is the key white wine of Puglia, LOCOROTONDO DOC.

PULIGNY-MONTRACHET AC

FRANCE, Burgundy, Côte de Beaune
♀ *Chardonnay*

If you feel a thirst coming on in PULIGNY-MONTRACHET, making a beeline for the Café du Centre won't do you much good. Although the sign is still there, the café has been closed for years. In fact all the cafés and bars in Puligny are shut. It's a strange feeling. Puligny-Montrachet – the home of what most people reckon is the greatest dry white in the world – and yet you can't get a drink there for love or money. The reason is probably to be found in the fact that this dull little village has been declining in population for years as the mighty merchants of neighbouring Beaune buy up the land to guarantee their supplies of wine, and families whose forebears have worked the vineyards for generations must shuffle off townwards in search of work.

But the mediocrity of the village cannot dim the brilliance of its best vineyards. The pinnacle is the Grand Cru le MONTRACHET, an ordinary-looking 7.5-ha (18½ acre) vineyard which manages to produce such a wine that the French author Alexandre Dumas said it should only be drunk 'on one's knees with head uncovered'.

There are three other Grands Crus, almost as good, and ten Premiers Crus, which are still among the most exciting wines in Burgundy. These take up all the best slopes above the village, and although the flatter land is allowed the Puligny-Montrachet AC, the result is less thrilling. Good vintages really need five years to show what all the fuss is about, while the Premiers Crus and Grands Crus wines may need ten years and can last for 20 or more. Best years: 1997, '96, '95, '93, '92, '90, '89, '88, '86, '85, '83, '82, '79, '78. Best producers: Boillot, CARILLON, Chartron & Trébuchet, Clerc, DROUHIN, JADOT, Labouré-Roi, LATOUR, Domaine LEFLAIVE, Olivier LEFLAIVE, Ch. de Puligny-Montrachet, RAMONET, RODET, Sauzet, Gérard Thomas.

PYRENEES

AUSTRALIA, Victoria, Western Victoria Zone

The Australian Pyrenees are but a faint echo of their European counterpart, with eucalyptus trees thickly carpeting gentle slopes. The region got off to an erratic start. In 1962 Chateau Remy was founded to produce brandy from Trebbiano, without evident success – the Trebbiano has now been replaced by Chardonnay and Pinot Noir, which now make reasonably good CHAMPAGNE-method sparkling wine – in a region more suited to the production of very robust reds. Luckily DAL-WHINNIE, Redbank, Summerfield, TALTARNI and others do produce stunning Shiraz and Cabernet as well as surprisingly fresh and tasty Chardonnay and Sauvignon Blanc. Best years: 1998,'97, '96, '94, '92, '91, '89, '88, '86, '84, '82, '79. Best producers: Dalwhinnie, Mount Avoca, Redbank, Taltarni.

PYRÉNÉES-ORIENTALES
FRANCE, Languedoc-Roussillon

The Pyrénées-Orientales is the torrid, gale-scoured, southernmost French *département*, climbing up to the Spanish border in a succession of thin-aired high passes which start on the sheer cliffs above the Mediterranean, and end shrouded in clouds near Andorra. Annual wine production is usually about 55 million bottles, over half of which are VINS DE PAYS. The ACs are, first, the *vins doux naturels* – sweet, fortified wines, of which RIVESALTES and BANYULS are the best known; the dark red COLLIOURE from near the Spanish border; and CÔTES DU ROUSSILLON and CÔTES DU ROUSSILLON-VILLAGES, whose reds and rosés are some of the south's best cheap wines. The extreme climate is much better suited to red than white, but there is some quite attractive Côtes du Roussillon white from Macabeo and Grenache Blanc, occasionally improved by the introduction of grape varieties like Rolle, Viognier, Roussanne or Marsanne. The one white wine glory of the Pyrénées-Orientales – the rich and gooey MUSCAT DE RIVESALTES – is nearer a burnished gold in colour.

Unlike other southern vins de pays, there is little experimental vine planting, but a few estates, like La Barrera and Mas Chichet, are making exciting use of Merlot and Cabernet Sauvignon and the ever-present Chardonnay pops up here too, giving attractive, quick-maturing wines, sometimes made with a little oak. The Vin de Pays des Pyrénées-Orientales designation covers the *département*, though there are five zonal vins de pays, of which 'Catalan' is the most important. Best years: 1996, '95, '94. Best producers: (Vin de Pays des Pyrénées-Orientales) Vignerons Catalans, CAZES, Mas Chichet.

QUAILS' GATE
CANADA, British Columbia, Okanagan Valley VQA
♦ *Pinot Noir, Syrah (Shiraz)*
♀ *Chardonnay, Gewurztraminer, Chenin Blanc, Riesling*

Quails' Gate was first developed in the early 1900s when the Stewart family opened the OKANAGAN VALLEY's first nursery business to serve local orchard owners. By the mid-1950s they were growing grapes and in 1990, they opened the doors to Quails' Gate Estate Winery. In 1993 Australian winemaker Jeff Martin put Quails' Gate on the map with his fruit-driven, limited-release varietals led by Chenin Blanc, Gewurztraminer, Riesling and a range of highly regarded Chardonnay and Pinot Noir offerings. The winery has also developed a cult following for its Old Vines Foch, a Shiraz-style, blockbuster, hybrid red. The recent departure of Martin has opened the door for another Australian winemaker, Peter Draper, from MOUNT MARY in the YARRA VALLEY, to join the firm. Best years: 1998, '95, '94.

QUAILS' GATE
This Okanagan Valley's Pinot Noir is made in a big, full-bodied alcoholic style and has slightly minty, cooked fruit flavours.

QUARTS DE CHAUME AC
FRANCE, Loire, Anjou-Saumur, Grand Cru
♀ *Chenin Blanc*

Sample a young Quarts de Chaume, and you'd never know that you were experiencing one of the world's greatest sweet wines in its infancy. Whereas most dessert wines at least taste rich right from the start, Quarts de Chaume can be rather nuttily dull, vaguely sweet in a crisp apple kind of way and acidic – above all, acidic. This is thanks to the Chenin grape – the most fiercely, raspingly acidic of all France's great grapes, frequently used to make dry whites so strangled with their own sourness they never recover. But on the gentle slopes protected by a low horseshoe of hills around the village of Chaume, the Chenin finds one of its best mesoclimates.

The vineyards slope south to the little Layon river, and if the sun shines, the grapes ripen more than any others in the LOIRE Valley. And as the mists of autumn begin to twine and curl off the river, the magic noble rot fungus concentrates the richness to as great a degree as in SAUTERNES. Pickers have to go through the vineyard several times so as to select only the grapes affected by noble rot and this contributes to Quarts de Chaume having the lowest maximum yield of any AC in France – 22 hectolitres per hectare; in many years they don't even achieve that. The winter often closes in as the pickers toil through the vineyard for a last time, and in the following few months the wine ferments quietly until the spring.

The result is all fruit and no oak influence. And it lasts for as long as any sweet wine in the world – thanks to Chenin's acidity. It may seem dull for its first few years, but after ten years the pale gold becomes tinged with orange, the apple sweetness blends with apricot and peach… and in the full sunset glow of 20 years' maturity, honey fills out the perfume of the peach – with a bitter twist of nut kernel roughness and the dark, fascinating intensity of quince jelly. The wine may then stay in this happy state for another 20 years. Production of this classic is less than 80,000 bottles a year, and the price is now fairly high, which, frankly, is how it should be. Best years: 1997, '96, '95, '94, '93, '90, '89, '88, '85, '83, '81, '79, '78, '76, '70, '69, '66, '59, '47. Best producers: Baumard, Bellerive, Pierre-Bise, Joseph Renou, Suronde.

QUEENSLAND
AUSTRALIA

The vine fever that swept across Australia in the second half of the 1990s has extended into Queensland. Until 1996 or thereabouts, the only significant region here was the high-altitude GRANITE BELT. Yet 25 years previously, its wine was sold in bulk with safety-first instructions that it be drunk immediately. Now the map extends to a group of wineries around Kingaroy, north-east of Brisbane, which includes what is now Queensland's largest winery, Barambah Ridge. Other groups are found around Toowoomba, and yet another around the tourist mecca of Mount Tamborine – appropriately enough, because 90 per cent of all Queensland wine is sold to tourists. The best producers in Queensland are those of the Granite Belt region.

QUERCIABELLA
ITALY, Tuscany, Chianti Classico DOCG
♦ *Sangiovese, Cabernet Sauvignon, Merlot and others*
♀ *Chardonnay, Pinot Blanc (Pinot Bianco)*

In the unlikely event of there ever being a BORDEAUX-like classification of the great estates of Tuscany, Querciabella would surely be in the running for Premier Cru status. Founded in the early 1970s by Giuseppe Castiglione, whose way of spending his fortune was on his jewel in the hills of Greve, Querciabella has arrived at a point where one expects at least near perfection from every bottle produced. The CHIANTI CLASSICO may not be pure Sangiovese – there's about 10 per cent of Cabernet Sauvignon and Merlot in it – but it is exquisitely crafted by resident enologist Guido de Santi, a man soft of speech and a million miles removed from the type of self-promoting loud-mouth that seems to be springing up in the region as Tuscan wines attract more international acclaim.

The top red is an illustrious SUPER-TUSCAN, Camartina, a rich and grandly elegant blend of 75 per cent Sangiovese and 25 per cent Cabernet Sauvignon and aged in new barriques. Perhaps the most surprising wine, however, is the super-Tuscan white Batàr. This is a barrique-aged blend of half Pinot Bianco-half Chardonnay of astonishing complexity and concentration, at times just a bit too much in terms of richness and oak. But am I complaining? Best years: (Camartina) 1994, '93, '91, '90, '88.

QUILCEDA CREEK VINTNERS
USA, Washington State, Columbia Valley AVA
♟ *Cabernet Sauvignon*

Begun in 1979, Quilceda Creek is a boutique winery devoted to producing only fine WASHINGTON Cabernet Sauvignon. The winemaking team of Alex and Paul Golitzen makes compelling wines, including Reserve versions, which now enjoy a cult following – from grapes sourced from several Washington vineyards. They are deeply coloured, with pure varietal character, very full body and require time to show their potential. They also age gracefully for well over a decade. Best years: 1998, '96, '95, '94.

QUINCY AC
FRANCE, Central Loire
♀ *Sauvignon Blanc*

Sometimes Quincy seems to pack more unmistakable Sauvignon flavour into its bottles than any other French wine. We're supposed to find flavours of gooseberry, asparagus and nettles in SANCERRE and POUILLY-FUMÉ – but these Sauvignon wines have become so popular, and the vineyards so burdened with overproduction as a consequence, that we rarely do. Yet Quincy, from vineyards clustered along the left bank of the river Cher, just west of Bourges, always reeks

of gooseberry and asparagus and nettles and, if you really want a nostril-full of unashamed Sauvignon, this intensely flavoured dry white is worth seeking out. You can age it for a year or two, but it won't improve during this period, it will merely become slightly less outrageous. Best years: 1998, '97, '96, '95. Best producers: Ballandors, Jaumier, Mardon, MELLOT, Portier, Rouze, Sorbe.

QUINTARELLI
ITALY, Veneto, Valpolicella DOC
♟ *Corvina, Rondinella, Molinara, Cabernet Franc, Cabernet Sauvignon and others*
♀ *Garganega, Trebbiano Toscano, Sauvignon Blanc and others*

The Quintarellis have been working their vineyard at Monte Cà Paletta since 1924, and third-generation Giuseppe Quintarelli still stands as a living monument to the splendour of traditional VALPOLICELLA. He is the ultimate believer in letting nature do her own thing, allowing each individual wine to make itself according to its own biochemical lights, tending to each drying berry, each gently bubbling barrel, each humble demijohn with the loving care a father would bestow upon his children. One realizes in his presence, as he draws samples from this and that barrel, that it is this attention to every detail that constitutes the difference between the great and the good in artisanal winemaking.

Undoubtedly Quintarelli's wines can be great in terms of wealth of extract and complexity of aroma (dried fruits, herbs, spices, tar, leather), and if they have to spend seven to ten years in barrel to achieve this, so be it. But being a traditionalist does not mean that he does not experiment – he makes Valpolicella Classico, Recioto and the outstanding Amarone. He was the first, he maintains, to bring Cabernet into the Valpolicella blend, and he still makes *passito* wines from Cabernet Franc (the much sought-after wine called Alzero) as well as from Nebbiolo. His *passito* whites, from Garganega, Tocai and the local Saorin, sometimes with a high percentage of grapes which have developed noble rot in the drying process, are equally amazing. Best years: (Amarone) 1991, '90, '88, '86, '85, '83.

QUIVIRA VINEYARDS
USA, California, Sonoma County, Dry Creek Valley AVA
♟ *Zinfandel, Grenache, Syrah*
♀ *Sauvignon Blanc*

Founded in 1981 by Henry Wendt, Quivira started off with a real bang by producing a

series of bright, deliciously fruity Zinfandels in an early-drinking style that has since become the norm. However, the 30-ha (75-acre) estate vineyard located in the western edge of DRY CREEK VALLEY also supplies rich, melony Sauvignon Blanc which the winery makes in two styles, a charming, snappy fruit-driven regular version and an oak-aged, richer-flavoured Reserve. Best years: 1998, '97, '95. Quivira's signature wine may ultimately be the Dry Creek Cuvée, a RHÔNE-inspired red blend of Grenache, Mourvèdre and Syrah. It can be drunk on release, but becomes more Rhône-like with three to four years of aging. Best years: (reds) 1997, '96, '95, '94, '92, '91, '90.

QUPÉ WINERY
USA, California, Santa Barbara County, Santa Maria Valley AVA
♟ *Syrah, Mourvèdre*
♀ *Chardonnay, Marsanne, Roussanne, Viognier*

Winemaker Bob Lindquist shares a winery and an iconoclastic outlook with Jim Clendenen of AU BON CLIMAT. One of the pioneers of Syrah and other RHÔNE-style wines in CALIFORNIA, Lindquist is no slouch when it comes to Chardonnay. Favouring ripe apple fruit and plenty of toasty oak, he offers a lovely Santa Maria Chardonnay, a Reserve wine from Bien Nacido Vineyards that comes together after three to four years of aging. Other Qupé whites are Marsanne in full-bodied nutty style, Viognier with effusive fruit intensity, and a lovely dry blend of Chardonnay and Viognier called Bien Nacido Cuvée. Best years: (whites) 1998, '97, '96, '95, '94, '93.

Always among the top-ranked Syrah producers in California, Qupé is concentrating on a fruity Central Coast Syrah, a deep, broadly flavoured Bien Nacido, and a Reserve Syrah that improves with five to six years of bottle age. Los Olivos Cuvée is a rich blend of Syrah and Mourvèdre. Best years: (reds) 1997, '96, '95, '94, '92.

QUPÉ
From the famous Bien Nacido vineyard, Qupé's opulent Syrah is a thrilling Rhône-like wine but with even riper blackcurrant and berry fruit.

Built in 1918, the old bodega at the Raimat winery was Spain's first building in reinforced concrete; it was designed by Rúbio Bellver, a student of the famous Catalan architect, Antoni Gaudí.

A RAFANELLI

USA, California, Sonoma County, Dry Creek Valley AVA

♟ *Cabernet Sauvignon, Zinfandel*

Occupying a superbly located site along the upper hillsides of DRY CREEK VALLEY, the Rafanelli family's 30-ha (75-acre) vineyard was established decades ago. Having become winemakers, they insist on including wines from the oldest, non-irrigated, low-yielding parcels. Starting out in the 1970s, Rafanelli set a high standard for Dry Creek Zinfandel – deep, lush, black-cherry, black-berry fruit, enormous flavours, and yet soft and easy to drink when young. The quality and style have been maintained, despite an ever-increasing demand. Cut from the same cloth, Rafanelli Cabernet Sauvignon shows slightly more tannin and has the structure needed to see it through a decade of aging. Best years: 1997, '96, '95, '94, '92, '91, '90, '87, '85.

RAIMAT

SPAIN, Cataluña, Costers del Segre DO

♟ *Cabernet Sauvignon, Tempranillo, Merlot, Pinot Noir*

♟ *Tempranillo, Chardonnay, Grenache Noir (Garnacha Tinta), Macabeo*

♀ *Chardonnay, Parellada, Macabeo, Xarel-lo*

Several of Spain's most affordable top-quality wines, both sparkling and still, come from this remarkable estate in the near-desert country of Lleida (Lérida in Spanish) province. It belongs to the Raventós family of the giant CODORNÍU group, who bought it in a run-down condition in 1914. The vines that now grow on over one-third of Raimat's 3000ha (7413 acres) could not survive without irrigation – and somehow the company has managed to circumvent both national and EU regulations that ban the irrigation of vines (irrigation was banned in Spain until 1999). These are no ordinary Spanish vineyards. On advice from the California universities of Davis and Fresno, the vines are trained along wire trellises and much more densely planted than the traditional vineyards of Spain.

Raimat and its Codorníu parent were the force behind the granting of a DO to several patches of land in Lleida, now collectively known as COSTERS DEL SEGRE. None of the region's other wines was really up to much, but Raimat's wines have been consistently good to excellent. There's sparkling Raimat Chardonnay as well as a fruity, rounded and honeyed still Chardonnay; fruity, richly flavoured and heavily oaked Raimat Cabernet Sauvignon and Raimat Tempranillo; there is also a blend of Cabernet Sauvignon and Merlot sold under the brand name Abadia.

Recent additions to the range are three top-notch, single-vineyard Cabernet Sauvignons, a barrel-fermented Chardonnay – rich and toasty with a creamy pineapple fruit – an authentically savoury, fruity Pinot Noir and an oaky Merlot. Best years: (reds) 1996, '95, '94, '92, '91, '90.

DOMAINE RAMONET

FRANCE, Burgundy, Côte de Beaune, Chassagne-Montrachet AC

♟ *Pinot Noir*

♀ *Chardonnay*

It is hard to challenge those who assert that Ramonet is the outstanding estate in the village of CHASSAGNE-MONTRACHET. As well as a fine cluster of Premiers Crus from the village (Ruchottes, les Vergers, Morgeot, Chaumées and Caillerets), the family are the proud owners of choice parcels within MONTRACHET, BÂTARD-MONTRACHET and Bienvenues-Bâtard-Montrachet. The wines are invariably characterized by their depth of flavour, complexity and capacity for long aging, although there seem to be no secrets in the winery. Nor is there a heavy dependence on new oak. But the Ramonets are adamant about such matters as planting vines that bear only small berries and about low yields.

The only problem with Ramonet wines is finding them. In general, wine lovers have a better chance of encountering them on the wine lists of leading restaurants than on the lists of wine merchants, however distinguished. Less expensive options are the regular Chassagne-Montrachet and the ST-AUBIN. The clamour is directed at the white wines, but Jean-Claude and Noël Ramonet also make very fine reds, especially from Chassagne's Clos St-Jean. Best years: (whites) 1997, '96, '95, '93, '92, '90, '89, '88, '86, '85, '83, '82, '79.

RAMOS PINTO

PORTUGAL, Douro, Port DOC

♟ *Tinta Roriz(Tempranillo), Tinta Barroca, Tinto Cão, Touriga Nacional, Touriga Francesa and others*

♀ *Gouveio, Viosinho, Rabigato, Malvasia Fina and others*

Family owned until it was bought by the CHAMPAGNE house of ROEDERER in 1990, Ramos Pinto has always been a company with foresight. In the late nineteenth century it was one of the first PORT shippers to build a brand name in the lucrative Brazilian market and more recently it was a pioneer in the remote DOURO Superior, planting a vineyard on a relatively flat site at Quinta de Ervamoira. Ervamoira is now the source of a deliciously rich 10-Year-Old Tawny, with Quinta do Bom Retiro downstream providing the basis for a supremely refined 20-Year-Old. Vintage ports, on the other hand, have tended to be fairly light and forward, so aged tawnies are the pride of the Ramos Pinto range. In line with its forward thinking, Ramos Pinto has expended much time and effort on its unfortified Douro wines. Duas Quintas (a blend of wine from Ervamoira and Bom Retiro – hence the name) is one of the leading Douro reds. Best years: (vintage ports) 1994, '91, '85, '83, '82.

CASTELLO DEI RAMPOLLA
ITALY, Tuscany, Chianti Classico DOCG
♦ *Sangiovese, Cabernet Sauvignon*
♀ *Chardonnay, Traminer, Sauvignon Blanc*

The late Alceo di Napoli, undoubtedly one of the great personalities of CHIANTI CLASSICO since World War Two, was a fervent believer in Cabernet Sauvignon in Tuscany, considering Sangiovese to be a poor second cousin. By the time he died in 1991, he had planted about half his 40ha (99 acres) of vines to his favourite grape, for use in his great SUPER-TUSCAN, Sammarco, as well as for blending with his Chianti Classico Riserva, and was planning a new Cabernet cru. He left behind some of the most superb vineyards in Tuscany – located in the golden shell of Panzano, they are visible from afar as you drive over the crest from the direction of San Donato – as well as a family mess, which was finally resolved with the second son, Luca, taking command.

With Giacomo Tachis continuing as consultant, however, it wasn't too long before Rampolla was back on top form, Sammarco, as always, receiving maximum plaudits from the pundits. Recently, however, Alceo's dream has come to fruition in the form of a new wine called La Vigna di Alceo (Alceo's vineyard), putting even Sammarco in the shade. Best years: 1998, '97, '96, '95, '90.

CASTELLO DEI RAMPOLLA
More Cabernet-influenced than the non-Riserva version, this is rich, complex Chianti of great depth, refinement and aging potential.

RANDERSACKER
GERMANY, Franken

Just south-east of WÜRZBURG, this is arguably the leading wine commune of FRANKEN, due to a string of top vineyards – Pfülben, Son-

nenstuhl, Teufelskeller and part of the Marsberg – and a hardly less impressive string of small growers. Mainly medium-bodied dry Rieslings and dry Silvaners, these are elegant wines in the Franken context. Best producers: Martin Goebel, Robert Schmitt, Schmitt's Kinder, Josef Störrlein.

KENT RASMUSSEN WINERY
USA, California, Napa County, Carneros AVA
♦ *Pinot Noir, Syrah, Merlot*
♀ *Chardonnay*

The absolute antithesis of most CALIFORNIA winemaker-proprietors, Kent Rasmussen strives to maintain a low profile and to keep his winery small-scale. Using only the barest winemaking necessities, he has always followed a hands-off, traditional approach to Pinot Noir, which is now becoming common practice, and to Chardonnay, which is still unusual. Old Pinot vines owned by Kent's father provide the richness and complex aromas that define his Pinots. Best years: 1997, '96, '95, '94, '92, '91, '90, '89, '88. Blended from a dozen or more small batches, Rasmussen's Chardonnays have uncanny depth. Best years: 1997, '95, '94, '93, '91, '90.

DOMAINE RASPAIL-AY
FRANCE, Southern Rhône, Gigondas AC
♦ *Grenache, Syrah, Mourvèdre, Cinsaut*

François Ay gives the impression that he doesn't greatly care what you think about his wines. He knows the wines, which all originate from his vineyards on sloping clay and limestone soils, are among the best of the GIGONDAS appellation, which is to say they are deep, rich and full-bodied. The vines are on average 30 years old, and Syrah and Mourvèdre contribute to the Grenache-dominated blend. The wines are aged in large casks, and Ay is opposed to the use of barriques for Gigondas. Treatments are minimal: indigenous yeasts ferment the wine, and fining and filtration are avoided whenever possible. The result is a ripe, harmonious wine, packed with fruit. In top years this Gigondas can take seven or eight years to reach its peak. Best years: 1997, '95, '94, '91, '90, '89, '88, '86, '85.

RASTEAU AC
FRANCE, Southern Rhône
♦♀ *Grenache, Syrah, Cinsaut, Mourvèdre*
♀ *Clairette, Roussanne, Bourboulenc*

Rasteau, east of Cairanne and north-east of CHÂTEAUNEUF-DU-PAPE, is an important village entitled to the CÔTES DU RHÔNE-VILLAGES AC. Its reds are usually fairly

old-fashioned, taking several years to soften and rarely having the fresh burst of spice and raspberry which makes some of the other 'Villages' so attractive when young.

Even more old-fashioned is the speciality of Rasteau – a *vin doux naturel* made from very ripe Grenache grapes which are fermented for three to four days only. Then pure alcohol is added to kill the yeasts and stop fermentation. The remaining sugar-rich juice gives a sweet, raisins-and-grape-skins flavour to the wine. It is usually red – or rather a deep tawny after some aging – but there is also a 'white', which is made by draining the juice off the skins at the start of fermentation. If it is left in barrel for several years it is then called *rancio* and tastes a bit like raspberry jam, raisins and tired toffee all mixed up and can be curiously exquisite as an apéritif, if you go for that sort of thing. Best years: 1997, '95, '94, '93, '90. Best producers: (Côtes du Rhône-Villages AC) Bressy-Masson, Cave des Vignerons, Meffre, Rabasse-Charavin, Domaine de la SOUMADE; (Rasteau AC) Bressy-Masson, Cave des Vignerons, St Gayan, Domaine de la Soumade.

RAUENTHAL
GERMANY, Rheingau

This ought to be one of the most famous wine villages in Germany, since it has as many good vineyards – Baiken, Gehrn, Nonnenberg, Rothenberg and Wulfen – as any other wine commune in the country. However, few of the winemakers here manage to capture the uniquely spicy, piquant character that Riesling from these vineyards should have. A glowing exception is the Georg BREUER estate of RÜDESHEIM.

CH. RAUZAN-SÉGLA
FRANCE, Bordeaux, Haut-Médoc, Margaux AC, 2ème Cru Classé
♦ *Cabernet Sauvignon, Merlot, Cabernet Franc, Petit Verdot*

A new broom, in the shape of Monsieur Jacques Théo, arrived at Rauzan-Ségla in 1983; rejecting half the crop as inadequate, he telephoned BORDEAUX's most famous wine doctor, Professor Peynaud, for advice and then set about producing one of the finest 1983s in the whole MARGAUX AC. He then produced a superb '85 and a marvellous '86 and wines in '88, '89 and '90 are some of the best in all Bordeaux. The good work has continued in the 1990s with a further change of ownership – the property was bought in 1994 by French perfume and fashion company Chanel – and the implementation of a massive programme of investment. The wines are marked by a rich blackcurrant fruit, almost tarry, thick tannins and weight, excellent woody spice and real concentration. Don't buy any of the wines of the 1970s, but since 1983 Rauzan-Ségla has been a worthy Second Growth. The second wine is called Ségla. Best years: 1998, '97, '96, '95, '94, '90, '89, '88, '86, '85, '83.

JEAN-MARIE RAVENEAU

FRANCE, Burgundy, Chablis AC
♀ *Chardonnay*

Jean-Marie Raveneau's 7.5-ha (18 ½-acre) estate, which produces about 50,000 bottles each year, is so blessed with good sites that it produces no generic CHABLIS at all. Its Grands Crus are Les Clos and Blanchots, and the Premiers Crus are Montée de Tonnerre, Chapelots, Butteaux, Vaillons and Montmains. Although all the wines are aged for 12 months in barrels of various sizes, including the small Chablisien *feuillettes*, they are fermented in tanks, where they remain for six months before the oak-aging process begins. Raveneau is very careful not to allow any woody flavours to penetrate the wine. These are highly traditional wines, which are more austere and hence less enjoyable in their youth than those from many other growers. But they age as well as any wines from Chablis, and a bottle of Les Clos at ten years or more, with its magical blend of fruit and minerals, can be a memorable glass of wine. Best years: 1997, '96, '95, '94, '93, '92, '90, '89, '88, '86, '85.

CH. RAYAS

FRANCE, Southern Rhône, Châteauneuf-du-Pape AC
♦ *Grenache, Syrah*
♀ *Grenache Blanc, Clairette, Chardonnay*

Rayas became celebrated for the eccentricities of its owner as well as for the splendour of its wines. Jacques Reynaud was intensely shy, reluctant to receive visitors and even more reluctant to show them round. Reynaud died in 1997 and the estate is now run by his nephew Emmanuel.

The wine became famous for its power and concentration. Made almost entirely from old Grenache vines, the excellence of Rayas was usually attributed to the very low yields from the vineyards. More sceptical observers pointed out that the low yields were a consequence of the unhealthy condition of the vineyards, in which many vines were missing. Whatever the real reason, Rayas could indeed be exceptional, although some vintages could also be deeply disappointing and hardly worth

Two of the specialities of the Valpolicella region are Recioto and Amarone, wines made from grapes dried for several months after the harvest.

the very high prices Reynaud demanded for them. The second wine, Pignan, only sporadically available, was often better value. The estate also produced a superb CÔTES-DU-RHÔNE called Fonsalette, which came in two forms, of which the most alluring was pure Syrah. Some of the whites from Rayas and Fonsalette have been rich and flamboyant; others seemed to tire fast. No doubt it will be the task of Emmanuel Reynaud to ensure that buying a bottle here is less of a lottery than it has been in the past. Best years: (reds) 1996, '95, '94, '93, '90, '89, '88, '85, '83, '81, '79, '78.

REBHOLZ

GERMANY, Pfalz, Siebeldingen
♦ *Pinot Noir (Spätburgunder)*
♀ *Riesling, Pinot Blanc (Weissburgunder), Pinot Gris (Grauburgunder), Chardonnay, Gewürztraminer, Muscat (Muskateller)*

Whether red or white, dry or sweet, the Rebholz wines are certainly no charmers in their youth, but give them a couple of years in bottle and they'll blossom into classic PFALZ wines of great individuality.

While most Pfalz wines taste heavier and more alcoholic than they actually are, the Rebholz wines always taste lighter than their often considerable alcoholic content would suggest. The barrique-aged Pinot Noir and Chardonnay which Hans-Jörg Rebholz sells under the 'HJR' label are among the best wines in these styles made in Germany, with real depth. Best years: (reds) 1997, '96, '93, '90; (whites) 1998, '96, '94, '93, '92, '90.

JOAQUÍN REBOLLEDO

SPAIN, Galicia, Valdeorras DO
♦ *Mencía, Merlot*
♀ *Godello*

Joaquín Rebolledo is a lawyer and a grape-grower who has found the time to make, in very small quantities, some of GALICIA's best wines. He is also an innovator who has planted, under the VALDEORRAS DO's apparently tolerant eye, a number of foreign grape varieties that are not officially allowed. His oak-aged red wine, therefore, is a Merlot varietal, and it can be lush and full in good warm years – not always the case in this wet, humid region of Spain. He also makes a convincing, fruity unoaked Mencía red and a confident Godello white. Best years: 1997, '96, '90.

RECIOTO DELLA VALPOLICELLA DOC

ITALY, Veneto
♦ *Corvina, Rondinella, Molinara and others*

Ears in Italian are *orecchie*, in Veronese dialect, *recie*. And Recioto, a wine whose origins go back at least two thousand years, was once supposedly made solely from the 'ears' of the grape bunches – those top parts most exposed to the sun, which ripen more fully. More probably in the past, as in the present, only the most conscientious growers chose this time-consuming path, most others using the whole bunch. Recioto is basically a *passito* wine, the grapes drying for four months or more, in a well-ventilated room, before fermenting. The fermentation stops naturally before all the sugars turn to alcohol, or it is stopped by human design so that the wine, dark and strong, remains sweet.

Recioto is a far cry from ordinary VALPOLICELLA – one could be excused for not recognizing it as a version of the same wine. But tasting its luscious, intense, bitter cherries, plums, smoke and meat stock flavours, then concentrating on the essential flavours of a top-notch Valpolicella, the common origin becomes clear. Sweet Recioto is not often seen, the trend these days heavily favouring the fermented-out, relatively dry version called AMARONE. There is a sparkling version too, which can be highly enjoyable. Recioto shows best after the meal, like PORT (without the headache). Neighbouring SOAVE also makes its own version of Recioto from white grapes. Best producers: Accordini, ALLEGRINI, Bertani, Bussola, DAL FORNO, MASI, Montresor, QUINTARELLI, Le Ragose, Serègo Alighieri, Speri, Viviani. Best years: 1997, '95, '93, '90, '88, '86, '85, '83.

DOMAINE DE LA RECTORIE

FRANCE, Languedoc-Roussillon, Banyuls AC
🍷 *Grenache, Carignan, Syrah*
🍸 *Grenache Blanc, Grenache Gris*

Since bottling their first wine in 1984 Marc and Thierry Parcé have become the undisputed specialists of vintage BANYULS and COLLIOURE. The secret of their success is the work they put into maintaining the low-yielding 22-ha (54-acre) vineyard which comprises some 30 parcels of vines, all of which are harvested and vinified separately. Among the vintage Banyuls the Cuvée Parcé Frères is full of youthful fruit while the Cuvée Léon Parcé, aged for 18 months in barriques, is richer and more structured in style. There are also a number of longer-aged traditional Banyuls, the Cuvée Docteur Camou having a typical *rancio* character. The three cuvées of Collioure – Col del Bast, le Seris and Coume Pascole – are made from varying blends of Grenache, Carignan and Syrah and aged in *foudres* and barriques. Best years: (reds) 1998, '97, '96, '95, '94, '93.

REFOSCO

When good, wine from the Italian red grape Refosco, or, to give the best sub-variety its full name, Refosco dal Peduncolo Rosso, is deeply coloured with a tangy, tarry, grassy, summer-pudding flavour and a streak of wild-fruit acidity. But it can also be lean and dull. The grape is stalwartly Friulian, the best examples being found in COLLIO and COLLI ORIENTALI. A sub-variety called Refosco Nostrano crops up in small amounts in the Carso zone, by Trieste, where it is called Terrano. Best producers: Dorigo, Marco Felluga, Livon, Meroi, Ronchi di Cialla, Ronchi di Manzano, Venica & Venica, Volpe Pasini, Zamò e Zamò. The best producer in Terrano is Edi Kante.

REGALEALI/CONTE TASCA D'ALMERITA

ITALY, Sicily
🍷 *Nero d'Avola, Perricone*
🍷 *Nerello Mascalese, Nero d'Avola*
🍸 *Inzolia, Catarratto, Grecanico*

Regaleali, bang in the uplands of central Sicily, must be one of the last bastions of old-style Sicilian aristocracy. Run by the venerable Count Tasca d'Almerita and his family, this huge estate has 240ha (593 acres) of vineyards. Both red and white wines have been acclaimed as the best in Sicily, though all are classified as VINO DA TAVOLAS. The altitude of the site helps, and the fact that it is kept from over-heating by breezes and night-time mists.

REGALEALI/CONTE TASCA D'ALMERITA
Some of Sicily's most admired wines come from this estate, including the white Nozze d'Oro which is based on a local variety called Inzolia.

The relatively simple Regaleali red and white are always highly reliable. The top red is Rosso del Conte, all punchy plums, coffee and tobacco flavours from selected late-picked Nero d'Avola grapes. The 1980 is still going strong and more recent vintages, benefiting from updated winemaking, are increasingly impressive. There is also a special white, Nozze d'Oro from the Sicilian Inzolia grape. The first vintage was 1985 and its lemony, leafy, herby taste – like a non-sweetened and non-spirity vermouth – meant it was snapped up fast, and continues to be so. In recent years international grapes, especially Chardonnay and Cabernet Sauvignon, have been planted and the resulting varietal wines are of great concentration and intensity. Best years: 1995, '94, '93, '92, '90, '89.

RÉGNIÉ AC

FRANCE, Beaujolais, Beaujolais Cru
🍷 *Gamay*

'Lucky' is what the village of Régnié and its neighbour Durette were when their combined vineyards were confirmed as the tenth BEAUJOLAIS cru in 1988. What distinguishes each 'patch' of land or cru in Beaujolais is that the wines have consistently been of a higher standard than the general run. For this reason the wines can sport their own specific AC.

The other nine crus without doubt deserve their position, but Régnié is less convincing. The soil has a high proportion of sand whereas granite typifies the best areas. The vineyards are just west of MORGON and BROUILLY, and the light, attractive wine is much closer to Brouilly in style. It does not seem to age for more than three years after bottling. In poor years the wines definitely do not rate as cru status, and even in great years like 1991 there were some unattractive attempts. Best years: 1998, '97, '96, '95, '94, '93, '91. Best producers: Beaujeu, Cinquin, Crêt des Bruyères, DUBOEUF, Laforest, Magrin, Rampon, Trichard.

ALENTEJO-REGUENGOS DOC

PORTUGAL, Alentejo
🍷 *Tempranillo (Aragonez), Moreto, Periquita, Trincadeira*
🍸 *Mantuedo, Perrum, Rabo de Ovelha, Roupeiro*

The agricultural town of Reguengos de Monsaraz has become one of the principal wine centres in the ALENTEJO. This is largely due to two heavyweight producers: the huge ESPORÃO estate and José Maria da FONSECA which owns the historic José de Sousa winery located in the town. With over 3000 hours of sunshine a year, the area lends itself to grape growing. Soils tend to be schistous (similar in places to the DOURO), but on the rolling plains vineyards are extensive and relatively easy to cultivate. The only drawback is drought, but with drip irrigation being installed local winemakers are succeeding with commercial quantities of ripe, warm country red. Despite the heat, Esporão also produces some attractive dry whites. In 1999 Reguengos became a sub-DOC of the new Alentejo DOC. Best years: 1997, '95, '94, '92.

REMELLURI

SPAIN, País Vasco, Rioja DOC
🍷 *Tempranillo, Macabeo (Viura)*

Based in the RIOJA Alavesa, La Granja Nuestra Señora de Remelluri was the first of the modern wave of Rioja producers. The winemaker is now Telmo Rodríguez, who studied enology at Bordeaux University (he prefers to use French oak rather than the more normal American oak), and he has dramatically improved quality. Remelluri is not a wine to rush to drink, as the flavour from the organically cultivated chalk and clay hillside vineyards takes time to develop. Best years: 1995, '94, '93, '91, '90, '89, '87, '85.

RETSINA

GREECE

This Greek wine has links to antiquity. Airtight pottery sealed with a mixture of clay and resin kept the wine fresh, but also imparted a slight taste of resin to the wine. It was this flavour which, erroneously, was believed to give the wine its keeping quality. This led to the practice of adding bits of pine resin to the grape must prior to fermentation, and removing it at the first racking, as a (supposed) preservative; but the taste caught on. Today the once-massive production is falling, but white and pink retsinas (mainly from the Savatiano grape) are still found. The Limnos winery has an interesting Muscat retsina. Best commercial producers: Boutari, Cambas, Kourtakis, Tsantalis.

REUILLY AC

FRANCE, Central Loire

🍷 Pinot Noir, Pinot Gris

🍾 Sauvignon Blanc

Reuilly lies west of Bourges in the featureless agricultural land which is typical of central France. There is a little rather pallid red from Pinot Noir, but the speciality here is rosé. The best ones are from Pinot Gris, very pale pink, quite soft but with a lovely, fresh, slightly grapy fruit. Sauvignon Blanc is used for the white wine, and the very high limestone element in the soil makes good Reuilly extremely dry, but with an attractive nettles and gooseberry nip to the fruit. Drink all Reuilly wines young. Best years: 1998, '97, '96, '95. Best producers: Beurdin, Cordier, Lafond, Malbète, Martin, Sorbe.

DOMAINE HENRI BEURDIN
Pinot Noir is the grape used for red wines in the Central Loire. This example has floral and cherry character and becomes more complex with a little age.

REX HILL VINEYARDS

USA, Oregon, Willamette Valley AVA

🍷 Pinot Noir

🍾 Chardonnay, Pinot Gris, Sauvignon Blanc

Rex Hill vineyards makes fine Pinot Gris and Pinot Noir. The Pinot Noir Reserve is a big, full-bodied wine with rich, intense black cherry fruit that ages gracefully. Winemaker Lynn Penner-Ash has a skilled hand and selects fruit from over 100ha (250 acres) of vineyards managed by the winery. Best years: (reds) 1996, '95 '94; (whites) 1998, '97.

TEÓFILO REYES

SPAIN, Castilla-León, Ribera del Duero DO

🍷 Tempranillo (Tinto Fino)

The longtime consulting enologist with Alejandro FERNÁNDEZ at Pesquera received a welcome gift from his sons when he had long retired as a chemistry teacher in secondary school and was past the age of 70: a small bodega, ready to let him make some wine under his own name, in Peñafiel, where he had started his winemaking career in the 1950s at the RIBERA DEL DUERO (PROTOS) co-operative. The Reyes style is of great

concentration but perhaps a little more finesse than at Pesquera. The first vintage, 1994, was a huge hit in the USA, where his name became instantly better known than in the region where he had worked for almost 50 years. The winery only owned 3ha (7.5 acres) of vineyards at the start, but another 60ha (148 acres) were soon planted. In the meantime, it had to rely on grapes it bought from growers Teófilo Reyes had known for decades. This is, no doubt, one of the best new wineries in Ribera. Best years: 1996, '95, '94.

RHEINGAU

GERMANY

This is not Germany's largest wine region – at 3249ha (8028 acres) it is dwarfed by the RHEINHESSEN, and even the NAHE can outdo it – but it competes with the MOSEL for the greatest fame. Partly it's because the Rheingau village of HOCHHEIM has had its name mangled and abbreviated in the English language as 'hock,' the term for all Rhine wine, and partly it is because of the concentration of high-profile aristocratic estates in the region. It is also, of course, because of the quality of its wine, because Rheingau Riesling from a top vineyard is outstanding – a combination of power, concentration, elegance and breed that will improve in bottle for years. The whole region comes under a single Bereich named, confusingly, after the Rheingau's most famous village, JOHANNISBERG.

Inevitably, the wines of the Rheingau are not all of a style. Those of the western stretch of the river, from Lorch to RÜDESHEIM, are lighter and often have a touch of slatiness, and Assmannshausen is famous throughout Germany for its Pinot Noir (Spätburgunder) reds. Those from the eastern end, from Wiesbaden along the river Main to Hochheim and beyond, are earthier but frequently attractively ripe. It is the central stretch, between

WEINGUT JOHANNISHOF
This top estate from Johannisberg, the Rheingau's leading wine village, makes super-elegant, top-quality Rieslings.

Rüdesheim and Wiesbaden, that produces the epitome of Rheingau Riesling. The river here is broad, more than half a mile across, and this not only helps to stabilize the temperature but reflects the sun back on to the grapes. Many of the big estates here have been resting on their laurels for years, but the most helpful sign recently has been the (admittedly still unofficial) classification of the top vineyards.

RHEINHESSEN

GERMANY

This is the largest of the German wine regions, but often the least distinguished; these gentle, rolling vineyards hemmed in by the Rhine on two sides have become unshakeably associated with LIEBFRAUMILCH and its cousins on the blended wine shelf, NIERSTEINer Gutes Domtal and Bereich Nierstein. It's a shame, because although there is a lot of land planted with vines here that could never produce anything of character, and although the name of Nierstein, one of the region's most famous villages, has been so utterly devalued, there are some excellent estates here, and even in the hinterland there are growers beginning to distinguish themselves by their drive for quality.

The best area of the Rheinhessen, though, is the 'Rhein Terrasse'. This is a stretch of nine villages along the banks of the Rhine: from north to south these are Bodenheim, NACKENHEIM, Nierstein, OPPENHEIM, Dienheim, Guntersblum, Ludwigshöhe, Alsheim and Mettenheim. The vineyards here are on steeper slopes descending to the Rhine. As with any wine area, it should not be supposed that quality is uniformly high, but Rieslings from good growers in Nierstein and Nackenheim, in particular, can be absolutely delicious, full, perfumed, and balanced. As always, it's a question of seeking out the good growers.

But many Rheinhessen vineyards are nowhere near the Rhine at all. There are smaller rivers weaving their way through this flattish countryside, to be sure, but even the best parts of the Rheinhessen are not the places to look for Rheingau-style austerity and power. The Riesling is a minority grape variety overall (although it dominates the best sites), coming in sixth after Bacchus and generally found on the heavier marl. The Silvaner wines can be among the Rheinhessen's better offerings, particularly if they are vinified dry.

There are three Bereiche, namely Nierstein, Bingen and Wonnegau, and a total of 24 Grosslagen – the most famous, and most abused, is Gutes Domtal.

RHEIN (Rhine) Germany

THE RHINE IS THE QUINTESSENTIAL RIVER of German wine. It rises in the Swiss Alps and ambles westwards, more or less along the Swiss border, before crossing into Germany at Basel, and no sooner is it there than the vineyards start. The river heads northwards, keeping company (though not always closely) with the vineyards of Baden, the Pfalz, Rheinhessen; and here it plunges back into the vines, with the best sites of the Rheingau depending heavily on its proximity. The vines of the Mittelrhein go with it as far north as they dare, and to the north of them is the tiny region of the Ahr, but then the river is on its own. On its journey the Rhine travels from one extreme of German wine to the other; from the substantial, ripe reds and whites of Baden to the steely Rieslings of the Mittelrhein; it also demonstrates just how much German wine is totally unlike the stereotype of wine that is sweetish, white and grapy.

Down in the south, the wines of Baden are predominantly dry. They can afford to be: this is Germany's warmest wine region, and if the wines resemble any others it is the well-built dry wines of Alsace, just over the Rhine to the west. A little further downstream, in the Pfalz, the wines, particularly in the south, are changing rapidly. The Pfalz used to be a warm, gently hilly region of fat, soft wines which in a hot year veered into blowsiness; now they're elegant, sharp-suited and a whole lot drier. In many cases they overshadow the Rheinhessen wines. Rheinhessen wines are generally rather soft, perhaps slightly earthy and without the nerve or depth of a good Rheingau.

The Rheingau is the land of aristocratic estates and aristocratic wines. The wines have fire and concentration and a marvellous, tense balance of acidity; and just across the river, in the Nahe, there are wines of complexity that often combine the fullness of the Rheingau with the steeliness of the Mosel. Going north again, the small region of Mittelrhein yields lean but tangy wines that are mostly Riesling and regrettably unfashionable. In the Ahr most of the wines are pale red, but there is as yet little incentive to improve quality.

In the Rheingau the Charta organization has been at the forefront of popularizing a drier style of German wine. It is one of several groups that have sprung up in the last few

This view of the Rhine looks from the great sweep of vines in the Hipping vineyard south to the village of Nierstein. This stretch of vineyards rising directly from the river is the heart of the Rheinfront along Rheinhessen's eastern border.

years. Voluntary groupings of like-minded growers, they impose strict conditions of quality on their members, and the indication on a label that a producer belongs to one should be a reassuring sign for consumers. Charta has an embossed double-window symbol, and its name, on its bottles. Other groups include the Deutsches Eck in the Mosel and, my favourite, the VDP (Verband Deutscher Prädikats- und Qualitätsweingüter).

H DÖNNHOFF
Helmut Dönnhoff produces the finest Rieslings from the famous Nahe vineyards of Niederhausen, Schlossböckelheim and Oberhausen.

SCHLOSS REINHARTSHAUSEN
This large estate with first class vineyards has had an excellent track record since 1989 and it is now one of the Rheingau's most important producers.

WEINGUT GUNDERLOCH
The great Rothenberg site, which soars above the Rhine at Nackenheim, gives some of richest and sweetest Rieslings made on the entire Rhine.

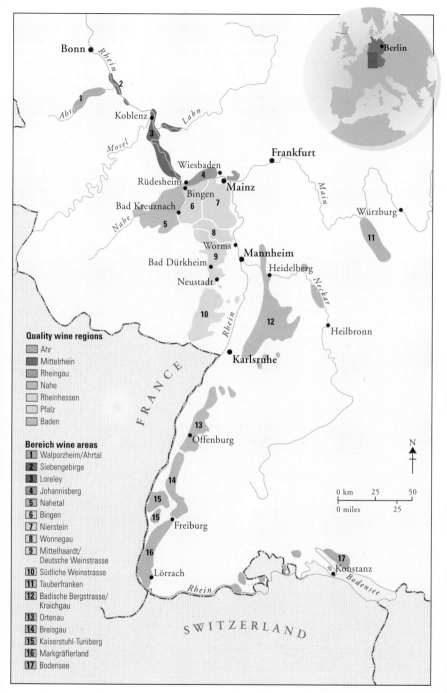

Quality wine regions
- Ahr
- Mittelrhein
- Rheingau
- Nahe
- Rheinhessen
- Pfalz
- Baden

Bereich wine areas
1. Walporzheim/Ahrtal
2. Siebengebirge
3. Loreley
4. Johannisberg
5. Nahetal
6. Bingen
7. Nierstein
8. Wonnegau
9. Mittelhaardt/ Deutsche Weinstrasse
10. Südliche Weinstrasse
11. Tauberfranken
12. Badische Bergstrasse/ Kraichgau
13. Ortenau
14. Breisgau
15. Kaiserstuhl-Tuniberg
16. Markgräflerland
17. Bodensee

ROBERT WEIL
The top wines from this Rheingau estate are classic concentrated and very rich Rieslings from the Kiedricher Gräfenberg site.

DR HEGER
At Ihringen in the Kaiserstuhl region, Joachim Heger makes some of the best dry Weissburgunder and Grauburgunder wines in Baden.

DR BÜRKLIN-WOLF
Today Bürklin-Wolf once again stands in the first rank of Pfalz estates. The village of Forst has long been regarded as the best in the Pfalz.

MÜLLER-CATOIR
From little-known Pfalz vineyards Müller-Catoir produce wines of a piercing fruit flavour and powerful structure from a long list of varieties.

SCHLOSSGUT DIEL
Sensational Riesling Eiswein, and among the best in Germany, is the top wine from this well-known Nahe estate.

REGIONAL ENTRIES
Ahr, Bad Kreuznach, Baden, Deidesheim, Durbach, Eltville, Erbach, Forst, Geisenheim, Hattenheim, Hessische Bergstrasse, Hochheim, Ihringen, Johannisberg, Kaiserstuhl, Kiedrich, Liebfraumilch, Mittelrhein, Nackenheim, Nahe, Niederhausen, Nierstein, Oppenheim, Pfalz, Rauenthal, Rheingau, Rheinhessen, Rüdesheim, Ruppertsberg, Schlossböckelheim.

PRODUCER ENTRIES
von Bassermann-Jordan, Bercher, Bergdolt, Biffar, Breuer, von Buhl, Bürklin-Wolf, Crusius, Schlossgut Diel, Dönnhoff, Emrich-Schönleber, Gunderloch, Heger, Heyl zu Herrnsheim, Huber, Johannishof, Johner, Jost, Keller, Koehler-Ruprecht, Künstler, Leitz, Lingenfelder, Mosbacher, Müller-Catoir, Pfeffingen, Rebholz, Sankt Antony, Schloss Reinhartshausen, Schloss Schönborn, Schloss Vollrads, Weil, Wegeler, Werner'sches Weingut, Wolf.

FRANZ KÜNSTLER
Since taking over the estate in 1988, Gunter Künstler has been one of the leading producers of Rheingau Riesling.

RHÔNE France

IT'S ONE OF THOSE TRICK QUESTIONS: 'What is the most northerly wine grown in the Rhône Valley?' Tricky indeed. It isn't even in France – it's in the Valais high up in the Swiss Alps. We always forget that the Rhône starts out as a Swiss river, ambling through Lake Geneva before hurtling southwards into France and out into the Mediterranean.

Well, as far as the AC Côtes du Rhône is concerned, we are in France. This appellation starts below Vienne, just south of Lyon, but nowhere near Switzerland, and finishes just south of Avignon. Below this the river sprawls out and fragments into marshlands which soon become the wild Camargue swamps. 'Côtes du Rhône' does, after all, mean 'Rhône slopes', or at least 'Rhône banks', and south of Avignon, there isn't much of either. But between Avignon in the south and Vienne in the north there's enough excitement to show the Rhône as one of France's greatest, most diverse wine regions.

This central section of the valley splits naturally into two parts. The north doesn't produce much wine, but the little that does appear is of a remarkable individuality. On the vertigo-inducing slopes of Côte-Rôtie at Ampuis, the Syrah grape produces sensuously fragrant, long-lasting reds, while at Tain-l'Hermitage the great hill of Hermitage produces what they used to call France's 'manliest' wine. St-Joseph and Crozes-Hermitage also make excellent reds, while Cornas, a few miles south, makes a marvellous monster red too. The white Viognier grape yields perfumed, pungent wine at Condrieu and the tiny AC, Château-Grillet.

There is a gap as the valley widens and flattens, and the slopes give way to vast expanses of land, rising a little into the hills both east and west but, in general, flat, with vines sweltering under the sun. Most of these vineyards are either Côtes du Rhône or Côtes du Rhône-Villages, reds, whites and rosés, but there are also various specific ACs. Red Gigondas is to the east, huddled under the jagged fangs of the Dentelles de Montmirail hills on ridges of thin, stony soil which descend into the valley floor. This is also the home of luscious, golden Muscat de Beaumes-de-Venise. South-west are Lirac and Tavel. But the best-known wine name of all is south of Orange – Châteauneuf-du-Pape, which has long been one of the most celebrated wines of France.

The steeply terraced vineyards on the famous hill of Hermitage overlook the town of Tain l'Hermitage and the Rhône far below. The steep granite hill has excellent exposure to the sun and is possibly the oldest vineyard in France.

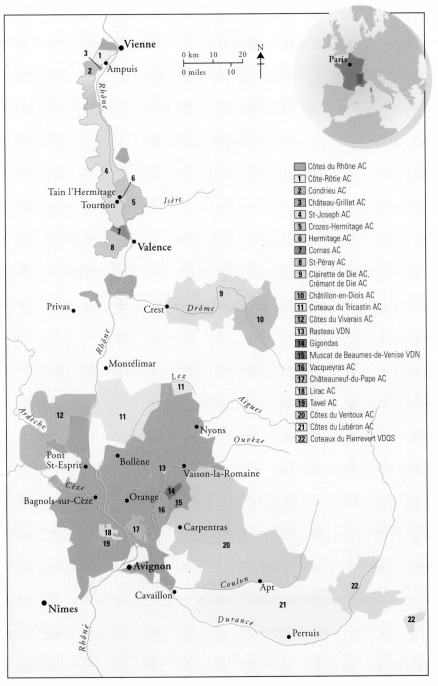

Côtes du Rhône AC
1 Côte-Rôtie AC
2 Condrieu AC
3 Château-Grillet AC
4 St-Joseph AC
5 Crozes-Hermitage AC
6 Hermitage AC
7 Cornas AC
8 St-Péray AC
9 Clairette de Die AC,
   Crémant de Die AC
10 Châtillon-en-Diois AC
11 Coteaux du Tricastin AC
12 Côtes du Vivarais AC
13 Rasteau VDN
14 Gigondas
15 Muscat de Beaumes-de-Venise VDN
16 Vacqueyras AC
17 Châteauneuf-du-Pape AC
18 Lirac AC
19 Tavel AC
20 Côtes du Ventoux AC
21 Côtes du Lubéron AC
22 Coteaux du Pierrevert VDQS

GUIGAL
The brilliant Marcel Guigal is especially famous for his various Côte-Rôtie wines.

M CHAPOUTIER
This négociant company specializes in wines from the northern Rhône, as well as Châteauneuf-du-Pape.

GEORGES VERNAY
The leading Condrieu estate produces excellent wines, including opulent, rich Coteau de Vernon.

AUGUSTE CLAPE
The top estate in Cornas is very traditional, making dense tannic wines with rich roasted fruit.

JEAN-LOUIS CHAVE
This red Hermitage is one of the world's great wines, a thick, complex expression of the Syrah grape at its best.

DOMAINE DE L'ORATOIRE ST-MARTIN
This estate based in Cairanne makes exciting Côtes du Rhône.

CLOS DES PAPES
Viticulture and vinification are meticulous here. The Grenache-based red wine has about 20 per cent Mourvèdre in the blend.

CH. DE BEAUCASTEL
The exquisite white Vieilles Vignes is a powerful white Châteauneuf-du-Pape made from 100 per cent Roussanne.

REGIONAL ENTRIES
Château-Grillet, Châteauneuf-du-Pape, Clairette de Die, Condrieu, Cornas, Côte-Rôtie, Coteaux du Tricastin, Côtes du Lubéron, Côtes du Rhône, Côtes du Rhône-Villages, Côtes du Ventoux, Côtes du Vivarais, Crozes-Hermitage, Gigondas, Hermitage, Lirac, Muscat de Beaumes-de-Venise, Rasteau, St-Joseph, St-Péray, Tavel, Vacqueyras.

PRODUCER ENTRIES
de Beaucastel, Bonneau, Burgaud, Chapoutier, Chave, Clape, Clos des Papes, Clos du Mont-Olivet, Colombo, Cuilleron, Delas, Dom. les Goubert, Graillot, Guigal, Jaboulet, Jamet, Dom. de l'Oratoire St-Martin, Dom. Raspail-Ay, Rayas, Rostaing, Dom. de St-Gayan, Dom. la Soumade, Vernay, Verset, Dom. de Vieux Télégraphe.

RÍAS BAIXAS DO

SPAIN, Galicia

♥ *Caiño Tinto, Sousón, Mencía and others*
♀ *Albariño, Loureira Blanca, Treixadura and others*

Rías Baixas' reputation rests on the low-yielding Albariño grape, but not all the whites here are made from this quality grape. Rías Baixas is split into three sub-regions: Val do Salnés (on the west coast and with a reputation for varietal Albariño wines), O Rosal (the last tip of west coast before Portugal) and Condado do Tea (further inland along the Miño). Individual vineyards are tiny by comparison with other Spanish regions – the RIOJA bodega, La RIOJA ALTA, owns the largest single vineyard in the entire region, 25ha (62 acres), from which come the grapes for its Lagar de Cervera Albariño. Rías Baixas wines will never be cheap, but the best ones are among Spain's most deliciously fragrant whites. Drink young or occasionally with short aging. Best producers: Adegas Galegas, Agro de Bazán, Lusco do Miño, Martín Códax, Palacio de Fefiñanes, Salnesur, Santiago Ruiz, TERRAS GAUDA.

RIBATEJO DOC

PORTUGAL

♥ *Cabernet Sauvignon, Camarate, Merlot, Periquita, Pinot Noir, Syrah, Tinta Miuda, Trincadeira Preta*
♀ *Arinto, Chardonnay, Esgana Cão and others*

The Ribatejo extends from the broad Tejo estuary near Lisbon upstream as far as the towns of Tomar and Chamusca, both of which are sub-DOCs of the new Ribatejo DOC. The Ribatejo Vinho Regional is now called Ribatejano.

The river has a moderating effect on the climate. Vineyards on the fertile plain produce large amounts of fairly ordinary red and white for drinking young. Away from the Tejo, the dry hills tend to produce fuller flavoured wines. White wines predominate but reds from producers like Quinta de Casal Branco (Falcoaria) and Quinta da Lagoalva are gaining a good reputation. The Ribatejo is almost unique in Portugal in having commercial quantities of foreign grape varieties (Cabernet Sauvignon, Merlot, Chardonnay and Sauvignon Blanc). Best producers: Quinta de Casal Branco, Fiúza BRIGHT, Horta de Nazare, Quinta de Lagoalva.

RIBEIRO DO

SPAIN, Galicia

♥ *Caiño, Garnacha Tintorera, Ferrón and others*
♀ *Treixadura, Palomino, Torrontés and others*

Stainless steel has become commonplace in new bodegas throughout this enchanting region of hills and little valleys, winemaking techniques have improved immensely and there has been a return to the good, native grapes of the region, Loureira, Treixadura, Torrontés, Godello and, to a lesser extent, Albariño. Even so, Palomino, a neutral import from the south of Spain, is still the most widely grown grape. The quality drive is being led by small, private producers – particularly Alanís, Emilio Rojo, Vilerma, Viña Mein.

RIBERA DEL DUERO DO

SPAIN, Castilla-León

♥ ▮ *Tempranillo (Tinto Fino), Grenache Noir (Garnacha Tinta), Cabernet Sauvignon, Merlot, Malbec*

Ribera del Duero reds, at best richly aromatic, well balanced and very fine, have become something of a cult. And like all cult items, the best have become extremely expensive. VEGA SICILIA, Ribera del Duero's oldest and still its most prestigious estate, has been renowned since the nineteenth century for its powerful, complex, lengthily wood-aged wines, made partly from the French grapes Cabernet Sauvignon, Merlot and Malbec, and partly from the local Tinto Fino (Tempranillo). But it took the discovery of Alejandro FERNÁNDEZ's bodega by the American critic Robert Parker – followed by a wealth of publicity for his excellent Pesquera wines – for the outside world to recognize the potential of this region.

Ribera del Duero means 'the banks of the Duero' (which flows on to become the DOURO, Portugal's port river). The gentle, often pine-covered hills around the valley lie 700–800m (2300–2625ft) above sea level, near the upper limits for vines, and this helps explain the wines' intense flavours. The town of Roa is fast becoming the region's new winemaking centre. Most of the grapes are Tinto Fino (Tempranillo), but other bodegas have followed Vega Sicilia and planted Cabernet and Merlot. They make an excellent blend with Tempranillo, and ideally suited to oak-aging. Ribera del Duero makes mostly reds and some rosés. White wines are not included in the DO. Best years: 1996, '95, '94, '91, '90, '89, '86, '85, '82. Best producers: Ismael ARROYO, Fernández, PEÑALBA LÓPEZ, PÉREZ PASCUAS, Dominio de PINGUS, PROTOS, Téofilo REYES, Vega Sicilia.

RICHEBOURG AC

FRANCE, Burgundy, Côte de Nuits, Grand Cru

♥ *Pinot Noir*

What a name! Richebourg has resonances of tremendous opulence, of sumptuous velvet and silk-smooth flesh, of scents dark and musky, of dishes based on fatted calves and cream served to corpulent prelates and princes. This 8-ha (20-acre) Grand Cru, one of Burgundy's most famous and most expensive, at the northern end of the village of VOSNE-ROMANÉE, does produce a rich, fleshy wine, its bouquet all flowers and sweet, ripe fruit and its flavour an intensity of spice and perfumed plums which fattens into chocolate and figs and cream as it ages. Most domaine-bottlings are exceptional. Best years: 1997, '96, '95, '93, '91, '90, '89, '88, '87, '85, '83, '80, '78. Best producers: GRIVOT, Anne Gros, Jean Gros, Jayer, LEROY, MÉO-CAMUZET, Domaine de la ROMANÉE-CONTI.

MAX FERD RICHTER

GERMANY, Mosel-Saar-Ruwer, Mülheim

♀ *Riesling and others*

This MOSEL grower makes wines with great individuality and even the most basic Riesling is an excellent example of the grape – and good value too. There are vines in such superb vineyards as WEHLENer Sonnenuhr, GRAACHer Himmelreich, Graacher Domprobst and BRAUNEBERGer Juffer. Mülheimer Helenenkloster is where Richter attempts to make an Eiswein every year. Or nearly every year: wild boar ate the whole crop in 1991, but then Germans have always maintained that Riesling goes with wild boar. There is good Riesling-based Sekt too. Best years: 1998, '97, '95, '94, '93, '92, '90, '89, '88, '85.

RIDGE VINEYARDS

USA, California, Santa Clara County, Santa Cruz Mountains AVA

♥ *Cabernet Sauvignon, Zinfandel, Petite Sirah*
♀ *Chardonnay*

Ridge is one of CALIFORNIA's most outstandingly original wineries, started by a group of scientists from nearby Stanford University who hankered after the sylvan lifestyle. The current winemaker, Paul Draper, pursues a positively nineteenth-century, low-tech winemaking style (though backed by impressive technology, just in case) and the results are quite unlike those of any other West Coast winery. The main releases are Cabernet Sauvignon – the remarkable Monte Bello and Zinfandels from various parts of California. These wines are now lighter than they used to be, the tannins less evident, but they still easily have enough stuffing to put together a series of shocking, intense, unexpected flavours, both when the wines are young and after long aging. There is also a little Petite Sirah and Chardonnay. Best years: (Monte Bello Cabernet) 1996, '95, '94, '93, '92, '91, '90, '84, '81, '77, '75, '70, '69.

RIESLING

Riesling may not be the world's most popular white wine grape, but there are many who would say it is the best, capable of surpassing in quality even the ubiquitous Chardonnay. It is not, however, so easy to understand. Riesling is a demanding grape. Its wine can be greenly acidic, but with age (and great, classic Riesling must have bottle age) it mellows, the acidity providing the backbone for honeyed fruit that often develops a nose and flavour described as 'petrolly', and tasting a million times more delicious than it sounds.

But it is also the victim of many a misconception. For a start, many of the cheap and nasty wines from eastern Europe that incorporate Riesling or Rizling in their titles are not from the Riesling grape at all. Riesling is not automatically sweetish: the cheap sugar-water that pours out of German wine factories has done an efficient job in blackening the name of even the finest German wines, but is virtually never made from Riesling grapes. Fashionable taste in Germany and Austria is for dry Rieslings, and the Rieslings of Alsace and Italy's Alto Adige (Südtirol) have long been vinified dry. But when the Riesling does make sweet wines from grapes affected by noble rot, they are dessert wines to remember: racily acidic, richly honeyed and complex, and generally needing years to show at their best. The Beerenauslesen, Trockenbeerenauslesen and Eiswein of Germany and Austria and the dessert Rieslings of Australia, New Zealand and California and the Riesling Icewine of Canada can be exceptional.

The Riesling by which all other Riesling is measured comes from Germany, and in particular from the Rhine and Mosel. In the Mosel it is light and delicate; in the Rheinhessen softer, in the Rheingau bigger and well-structured, in the Rheinpfalz broader but still firm. It is Germany's second most widely planted grape behind the Müller-Thurgau, accounting for just over 20 per cent of the vineyard area.

Hot climates produce Riesling that is fat and blowsy, sometimes keeping a reasonably simple fruit, but often ending up tasting like diesel fuel. In Australia all the best Rieslings come from regions blessed with cold nights, which yield wines that have a fresh, limy streak of acidity and, frequently, a delightful floral perfume. In the USA, cool-climate Washington State, Oregon and New York State are all making a name for the grape. New Zealand's Rieslings tend to be most exciting when botrytis-affected and sweet.

The name Riesling immediately evokes bewilderment in South Africa. The grape most people know by the name Cape Riesling is in fact the ordinary French variety, Crouchen Blanc. There is far less of the true and altogether more noble German Riesling, known as Rhine or Weisser Riesling. Confusion over name and style does little to promote consumer enthusiasm, although the climate is too warm except at Constantia to capture the grape's light, scintillating character. Best examples are in the botrytis-affected, dessert styles.

In Europe, Rieslings to rival those of the Rhine and Mosel come from Austria's Wachau and Kamptal-Donauland regions in Niederösterreich, and often have higher alcohol than their German equivalents. Alsace Rieslings are also fuller and higher in alcohol, particularly when grown on one of the Grand Cru sites. In Italy's German-speaking Südtirol or Alto Adige the wines are often very light, steely-fresh and bone dry for drinking young. Jermann, in Friuli, makes a good varietal called Afix. No-one in Italy, however, is getting anywhere near the quality levels attained further north.

A distinction should be made, though, between the grape variously called Welsch Riesling, Laski Rizling, Olasz Rizling or, in Italy, Riesling Italico, and the true Riesling. The former is not Riesling at all. Synonyms for the true Riesling include Riesling Renano (in Italy), Rhine Riesling (in Austria and Australia) and Johannisberg or White Riesling (in the USA).

CH. RIEUSSEC

FRANCE, Bordeaux, Sauternes AC, Premier Cru Classé
♀ *Sémillon, Sauvignon Blanc, Muscadelle*

Apart from the peerless Ch. D'YQUEM, Rieussec is often the richest SAUTERNES. The 75ha (185 acres) of vineyards, on high ground just inside the commune of Fargues, lie alongside Yquem and, since the property was bought in 1984 by the Rothschilds of Ch. LAFITE-ROTHSCHILD, one wondered if they were going to try to challenge the pre-eminence of Yquem. Fermentation in barrel was reintroduced from 1995, adding extra glycerol and complexity to the marvellous trio of 1997, '96 and '95 and greater intensity to wines that are already super rich, but not only affordable to the super-rich – which is more than one can say for Yquem. Crème de Tête is a remarkable, very rare special selection and there is a dry wine called 'R' which is pretty dull. Second wine: Clos Labère. Best years: 1998, '97, '96, '95, '90, '89, '88, '86, '85, '83, '81, '79, '76, '75.

RIO GRANDE DO SUL

BRAZIL

The beautiful, green, rolling landscape of Rio Grande do Sul is the site of Brazil's wine industry. Near the border with Uruguay, it is as close to winemaking country as Brazil can manage. The fight against predators, fungal as well as creepy crawly, is a constant one, so winemaking can be relatively expensive. There are two main sub-regions, Serra Gaucha and the more recently established Frontera, near the Uruguayan border, growing varieties such as Cabernet Sauvignon, Chardonnay, Trebbiano, Cabernet Franc, Merlot and Petite Sirah. MOËT ET CHANDON, Provifin (a Moët subsidiary making large quantities of sparkling wine), Martini & Rossi and Pedro DOMECQ are the major producers.

RIO NEGRO

ARGENTINA

A handful of brave winemakers are ploughing a lonely furrow in the cool-climate, fruit-growing Rio Negro Valley at the northern end of Patagonia, on the same latitude as New Zealand's South Island and almost as isolated. Time will tell if wine wins over the current lucrative crops of plums, pears and cherries. Humberto Canale is the largest quality producer, and FABRE MONTMAYOU (bottled as Infinitus) and WEINERT also have interests here. Malbec, Merlot, Pinot Noir, Sauvignon Blanc, Chardonnay and Torrontés are all grown with considerable success. Canale has massively modernized its plant to tremendous effect. Others are sure to follow.

LA RIOJA Spain

The Marqués de Riscal bodega was a pioneering firm in Rioja in the 1860s – this is their fermentation cellar built in 1883 – and in Rueda in the 1970s and is still up there in Rioja's top rank making classic pungent red wines.

JUST BECAUSE YOU SEE A SIGN by the roadside welcoming you to La Rioja, there's no reason to believe that you've arrived in the Rioja DOC, even if the car window does give you an uninterrupted vista of vines. La Rioja, the autonomous region, has quite different boundaries from Rioja, the Denominación de Origen Calificada. Not all the vines that grow in the autonomous region are entitled to the name Rioja. And the Rioja DOC stretches way out into Navarra, where vines yield priority to asparagus, artichokes and spicy red peppers, all flourishing in the fertile soil, while an important part of the DOC (Rioja Alavesa) lies inside the boundaries of the Basque country (País Vasco) and there are some western patches in Castilla-León.

There is a certain logic to the Rioja DOC region taken as a whole. Named after the Rio or River Oja, a tributary of the River Ebro, the region is centred on the Ebro Valley and, for much of its length, is bounded to the north and south by dramatic chains of mountains, particularly the Sierra de Cantabria. (Take a half-hour drive south of Logroño, the wine capital of the region, through cornfields and vineyards, and you'll suddenly find yourself amid rough-hewn mountains of spectacular beauty, dotted with half-deserted villages.) But when you get down to the three official sub-regions of Rioja – Rioja Alta, Rioja Alavesa and Rioja Baja – it soon becomes evident that the characteristics of the three regions are less clear-cut than sometimes suggested and many Riojas are a blend of wines from two or more of these regions.

The Rioja Baja (to the south-east and mostly in Navarra), accounts for 39 per cent of the Rioja DOC. Enjoying a Mediterranean climate, it is indeed as hot and dry here as books say, and much of its silt or clay soil on the flat valley floor is too fertile for good-quality grapes. The resulting wines are fatter and more alcoholic – generally from the Garnacha Tinta, which survives better than the Tempranillo in these hot conditions. But the borders between the Rioja Alavesa (which accounts for just 18 per cent of the total Rioja vineyard area) and the Rioja Alta were drawn simply along the edges of the Basque province of Alava.

The most aromatic Tempranillo red wines come from grapes grown on the yellow calcareous clay which occurs all over the Rioja Alavesa and extends well into the Alta region; Tempranillo flourishes here in the limestone, producing

REMELLURI

The wines from this organic estate have considerable extract and structure as well as fruit and will age well.

LA RIOJA ALTA

One of the very best of the old-established Rioja producers, La Rioja Alta makes almost entirely Reservas and Gran Reservas.

CVNE

From a new, ultra-modern winery, CVNE's top wine, Imperial Gran Reserva, is long-lived and impressive.

ARTADI

The Artadi brand name is used by the up-and-coming Cosecheros Alaveses co-operative. Pagos Viejos is made from very old vines.

MARQUÉS DE RISCAL

The exotic Barón de Chirel wine is made only in selected years and predominantly from Cabernet Sauvignon.

BODEGAS RODA

This company applies Catalan winemaking skills to two old-vine Rioja wines, called Roda I and Roda II, with exciting results.

grapes with high acidity and a good concentration of flavours. Much more of the Alta soil is very similar to the silt and clay of the Baja and consequently grows Garnacha. But, unlike the Baja, both the Alta and the Alavesa regions have climates in which the hot, Mediterranean weather is moderated by cooler breezes from the Atlantic Ocean.

REGIONAL ENTRY
Rioja.

PRODUCER ENTRIES
AGE, Allende, Artadi, Barón de Ley, Bilbainas, Campillo, Campo Viejo, Contino, CVNE, Domecq, Faustino Martínez, López de Heredia, Marqués de Cáceres, Marqués de Murrieta, Marqués de Riscal, Martínez Bujanda, Montecillo, Muga, Bodegas Palacio, Remelluri, La Rioja Alta, Riojanas, Roda, San Vicente.

BODEGAS BRETÓN

The single-vineyard Dominio de Conté shows the demanding Rioja traditions of long barrel-aging from low-yielding old vines at their best.

BODEGAS PALACIO

Benefiting from the advice of Michel Rolland, the Pomerol winemaker, Palacio's top wine, Cosme Palacio quickly became a cult wine in Spain.

MARTÍNEZ BUJANDA

This is a rich and intense, buttery, barrel-fermented white entirely from the Viura grape and the first single-vineyard white in modern Rioja.

RIOJA DOC

SPAIN, La Rioja, Navarra, País Vasco, Castilla-León

▮ ▯ *Tempranillo, Grenache Noir (Garnacha Tinta), Carignan (Cariñena, Mazuelo), Graciano*

▯ *Macabeo (Viura), Garnacha Blanca, Malvasía de Rioja*

See also Rioja, pages 314–315

In the 1970s, when Rioja first became popular outside Spain, people learned to expect oaky-flavoured reds smelling and tasting of vanilla – partly because there were a lot of new oak barrels in use, and partly because flavour merchants were doing a roaring trade in bottles of dark, gooey oak essence. All that changed in the 1980s, as the regulations tightened and those serried ranks of once-new barrels, oaky taste long gone, had now become flavourless containers. Red Riojas today are almost always less vanilla-oaky, sometimes more positively fruity, and only 40 per cent of Riojas are oak-aged. But some of the best bodegas are turning to expensive new oak again, following a worldwide change in fashion – and they can afford it, because Rioja prices soared at the end of the 1980s and again at the end of the 1990s. In 1991, Rioja became the first region to be granted Spain's new superior quality status, Denominación de Origen Calificada (DOC).

Traditional white Riojas were also oak-aged, but this style became unpopular during the 1980s. However, many bodegas now make barrel-fermented creamy whites. Though more than three-quarters of the grapes are produced by small-scale growers, the big Rioja firms bottle and sell most of the wines. The two major grapes for red Rioja are Tempranillo, with an elegant, plummy character that develops well with age in barrel and bottle into wild strawberry and savoury flavours, and Garnacha Tinta, whose fat, jammy-fruit flavours fade fast. Of the minor grapes, Graciano has recently become more popular because its flavour is excellent. Cabernet Sauvignon is also creeping into the vineyards under the pretext of experimentation. It can make fine wine and must have a strong chance of becoming officially accepted in the Rioja grape mix. Best years: 1995, '94, '91, '90, '89, '87, '85, '82, '81. Best producers: (reds) ALLENDE, Amézola de la Mora, Artadi, BARON DE LEY, Beronia, Bretón, CAMPILLO, CAMPO VIEJO (Marqués de Villamagna), CONTINO, El Coto, CVNE, LÓPEZ DE HEREDIA, MARQUÉS DE CÁCERES, MARQUÉS DE MURRIETA, MARQUÉS DE RISCAL, MARTÍNEZ BUJANDA, MONTECILLO, MUGA, Navajas, Palacios Remondo, Rémélluri, Remirez de Ganuza,

La RIOJA ALTA, RIOJANAS, RODA, Señorio de SAN VICENTE, Sierra Cantabria; (whites) CVNE, López de Heredia, Marqués de Cáceres, Marqués de Murrieta, Martínez Bujanda, Navajas, La Rioja Alta, Riojanas.

LA RIOJA ALTA

SPAIN, La Rioja, Rioja DOC

▮ *Tempranillo, Grenache Noir (Garnacha Tinta), Graciano and others*

▯ *Macabeo (Viura), Malvasía de Rioja*

Although La Rioja Alta only makes a tiny per cent of RIOJA's total production, it sells almost one-fifth of all the Reserva and Gran Reserva wine made in the region. In the past few years, it has made massive investments and wood-aging is still one of the major hallmarks of this traditional bodega. Viña Alberdi, a Crianza, and the Reserva Viña Arana contain about 70 per cent Tempranillo and are rather light, elegant wines. The other Reserva, Viña Ardanza, is a fuller, richer wine, with about 60 per cent Tempranillo and a higher proportion of Garnacha Tinta. Gran Reservas labelled with the numbers 904 and 890 are produced only in the best years, and, for Reserva 890, the wine has to be truly exceptional.

The only white wine is the very good Viña Ardanza Reserva Blanco, not as aggressively oaky as MARQUÉS DE MURRIETA's white, though along similar lines – but, so far, it is made only in tiny quantities. To be able to offer enough good white wine to its clients, La Rioja Alta is also the owner of a GALICIAn bodega, in the RÍAS BAIXAS DO. Best years: (reds) 1996, '95, '94, '91, '90, '89, '85, '83, '82, '81, '78.

BODEGAS RIOJANAS

SPAIN, La Rioja, Rioja DOC

▮ *Tempranillo, Carignan (Cariñena, Mazuelo), Graciano, Cabernet Sauvignon*

▯ *Tempranillo, Grenache Noir (Garnacha Tinta)*

▯ *Macabeo (Viura), Malvasía de Rioja*

The Artacho family, owners of Bodegas Riojanas for decades, sold half their shares in the early 1970s to the Banco de Santander in order to finance massive improvements. These were completed in 1990, making this one of the most modern wineries in RIOJA.

Reds are the bodega's main business, and the best are the Reservas and Gran Reservas, which are consistently fine even before the improvements take effect. Both are sold under two brand names: Viña Albina, soft, plummy, elegant and principally Tempranillo, and Monte Real, a bigger, darker, more tannic wine with complex wild strawberry and cedar flavours, also predominantly

BODEGAS RIOJANAS
The richer and more concentrated wines from this winery, one of the most modern in the Rioja region, are sold under the Monte Real label.

Tempranillo but with some Mazuelo and Garnacha. The younger reds, the basic, fruity traditional Canchales (made by carbonic maceration) and Puerta Vieja Crianza, are both made entirely from Tempranillo. Monte Real Blanco Crianza, peachy and oaky, is one of Rioja's best whites. Best years: (reds) 1995, '94, '91, '90, '89, '87, '83, '82, '78, '73, '64.

RIOS DO MINHO VINHO REGIONAL

PORTUGAL, Minho

▮ *Azal Tinto, Borracal, Vinhão, Cabernet Sauvignon, Merlot and others*

▯ *Alvarinho, Avesso, Azal Branco, Loureiro, Paderna, Trajadura, Chardonnay, Riesling and others*

Named after the rivers that surge down from the mountains in the Minho province of north-west Portugal, Rios do Minho corresponds to the VINHO VERDE DOC. The name was changed to Minho in 1999. The grapes are similar too, but the Vinho Regional category permits foreign varieties as well, including Chardonnay, Riesling, Cabernet Sauvignon and Merlot. So far there are few wines bottled under the Minho designation as most producers prefer to stick with the traditional strictures of Vinho Verde. One exception is the Quinta de Covela estate near the DOURO, which is successfully blending indigenous and international grapes.

RIVERA

ITALY, Puglia, Castel del Monte DOC

▮ *Nero di Troia, Montepulciano, Aglianico, Uva di Troia, Montepulciano and others*

▯ *Bombino Nero*

▯ *Bombino Bianco, Pampanuta, Chardonnay, Sauvignon Blanc, Pinot Blanc (Pinot Bianco)*

One of southern Italy's most dynamic producers, Rivera is situated in the Murge uplands of central Puglia, in the area called Rivera. The local CASTEL DEL MONTE DOC is named after the extraordinary octagonal castle of Frederick II of Swabia. Rivera, owned by the de Corato family, started experimenting with on-traditional varieties like Sauvignon Blanc, Chardonnay, Pinot Bianco and Aglianico as far back as the 1950s while aiming simultaneously to get the best out of local grapes like Bombino and Montepulciano. Today, Rivera's greatest wine is probably still the full rich, red Il Falcone, made from Uva di Troia and Montepulciano grapes. But hard on its heels is the Aglianico Rosso under the Terre al Monte label, a range that also includes the three French white varietals mentioned above, plus an Aglianico Rosato – rosé, after all, is Puglia's traditional wine; Rivera's 'classic' Castel del Monte rosé is produced from the local Bombino Nero grape. Best years: (Il Falcone) 1997, '96, '94, '93, '92, '91, '85.

RIVERINA
AUSTRALIA, New South Wales, Big Rivers Zone
Also called the Murrumbidgee Irrigation Area (MIA), this isolated area is one of the engine-rooms of the Australian wine industry. The hot, dry summers mean total reliance on irrigation: Semillon, Trebbiano, Chardonnay and Syrah (Shiraz) dominate and yields are abundant. Three-quarters of the grapes are white and mainly used in boxed wine, but the outstanding DE BORTOLI Botrytis Semillon and similar wines made by LINDEMANS, McWILLIAMS and ORLANDO are good. McWilliams do well with Riesling and Cabernet-Merlot. Best producers: De Bortoli, McWilliams, Miranda, Riverina Wines, Wilton Estate.

RIVERLAND
AUSTRALIA, South Australia, Lower Murray Zone
The Riverland produces around a third of the Australian grape harvest. Most ends up in wine boxes, but magic can occur at Berri, Renmano, Kingston Estate and at Angove's. The most important of Australia's vast irrigated vineyard areas stretches along the serpentine loops of the Murray River and many of the country's most successful brands of wine have a base of Riverland fruit. White wines from Chenin Blanc, Chardonnay, Colombard and Riesling are the region's forte, but there are good, though unsubtle, juicy reds as well.

RIVESALTES AC
FRANCE, Languedoc-Roussillon
♟♟ *Grenache*
♀ *Grenache Blanc, Macabeo, Malvoisie*
The fame of Rivesaltes, a small town just north of Perpignan, lies in its being the home of some of France's best *vins doux naturels*. The most

famous and best of these are deep and gold, from the Muscat grape (see MUSCAT DE RIVESALTES AC). Red and rosé Rivesaltes AC are made from Grenache, and white from Grenache Blanc, Macabeo and Malvoisie. If stored for several years in barrel to produce a maderized *rancio* style the wines acquire an attractive barley sugar, burnt toffee taste in addition to Grenache's original plummy grapiness. The Rivesaltes AC covers 90 communes in the PYRÉNÉES-ORIENTALES *département* and nine in the AUDE, and about five million bottles of Rivesaltes VDN are produced a year. There is also a growing interest in table wines, and some decent whites and fruity 'Nouveau' style reds are made. Best producers: Cave de Baixas, Casenove, Cazes, Forca Real, GAUBY, Mas Christine, Sarda-Malet, Vignerons Catalans.

ROBERTSON WO
SOUTH AFRICA, Western Cape
What do vines, horses and roses have in common? A love of limestone soils, which, although uncommon elsewhere in the Cape, abound in this hot inland area, where all three thrive. About 200km (125 miles) from Cape Town, Robertson is separated from mainstream PAARL and STELLENBOSCH by imposing mountain ranges. It also marks the start of the country's dry interior and irrigation is the norm. The dominant plantings of Colombard and Chenin Blanc give evidence of the area's standing as a distilling region.

Today it is also well known for sound, reasonably priced Chardonnay. In pursuit of a regional blend, serendipity decreed the matching of Chardonnay and Colombard; this has resulted in some good wines. Many of the Cape's excellent fortified Muscadels and Jerepigos also come from here. Red varieties have hardly had a look in until recently, but producers such as Graham Beck, Robertson Winery and Van Loveren are showing that Cabernet, Merlot and Shiraz have exciting potential. Best producers: Bon Courage, Graham Beck, DE WETSHOF, Robertson Winery, Springfield, Van Loveren, Zandvliet.

ROCCA DELLE MACÌE
ITALY, Tuscany, Chianti Classico DOCG
♟ *Sangiovese, Canaiolo, Cabernet Sauvignon, Merlot and others*
♀ *Trebbiano Toscano, Malvasia del Chianti, Chardonnay, Pinot Gris (Pinot Grigio)*
Rocca delle Macìe is not renowned for wines of quality and outstanding personality (although the winery may not agree), rather for value for money. And one gets it – because

this large estate, with 300ha (741 acres) of vineyard, produces some five million bottles annually (including wines bought in in bulk) which are widely distributed in Italy and 40 countries abroad, and in a relatively short period Rocca della Macie has become one of the bestselling brands in Tuscany.

But don't forget that price is only one of the factors in the formula of 'value-for-money' – nor indeed are Rocca's by any means the cheapest wines around; just reasonable. The basic CHIANTI CLASSICO never fails to deliver drinkability combined with typicity; the Riserva delivers that bit extra, as it should. The newer Chianti Classico Tenuta Sant' Alfonso is more concentrated and complex, and the Riserva di Fizzano represents the peak of Rocca's DOCG Chiantis, though in a recent tasting it was found to be suffering just a touch from that slightly stewed, old-fashioned character that the other Rocca wines seem to have overcome. The SUPER-TUSCAN Ser Gioveto, with its coffee and spice and fruit that's real nice, delivers a lot of quality for not too much money. Best years: (Ser Gioveto) 1995, '93, '91, '90.

ROCCA DELLA MACÌE
The oak-aged Ser Gioveto from 100 per cent Sangiovese is full of accessible, plummy fruit and is the top wine from this large estate.

J ROCHIOLI VINEYARDS
USA, California, Sonoma County, Russian River Valley AVA
♟ *Pinot Noir, Zinfandel*
♀ *Chardonnay, Gewürztraminer, Sauvignon Blanc*
For years one of the best-kept secrets among winemakers was the high-quality grapes grown by the Rochioli family on their 45-ha (110-acre) vineyard in the RUSSIAN RIVER VALLEY. Planted in the 1930s, this vineyard features Pinot Noir, Chardonnay, Sauvignon Blanc and Gewürztraminer. Now they also produce their own wine and they have earned high praise for the powerful, perfumed character of their varietals. The Reserve Sauvignon Blanc ranks among the New World's finest. Intensely ripe Zinfandel from the neighbouring Sodini Vineyard is often rated near the top. But the wise money is on the estate-grown

Pinot Noir, and Rochioli regularly offers three versions – Russian River Valley, Reserve and West End Vineyard. Each displays luxuriant black cherry fruit, layers of subtle flavours and delightfully smooth texture. Give the Reserve at least five years to reveal its more subtle beauty. Occasionally, the winery offers Pinot Noir from a special parcel. Best years: 1997, '96, '95, '94, '92, '91. Rochioli also sells Pinot Noir grapes to top names such as Gary Farrell, WILLIAMS-SELYEM and Davis Bynum.

RODA

SPAIN, La Rioja, Rioja DOC

🍷 Tempranillo, Grenache Noir (Garnacha Tinta), Mazuelo

Roda is an acronym for the Barcelona family, Rotllan-Daurella, which has launched one of the most impressive new bodegas in RIOJA. Roda's winery is in the heart of the historic Railway Station section of Haro, surrounded by the great classic bodegas. Some 60ha (148 acres) of vineyards were planted in the late 1980s and '90s in top Rioja Alta sites, but the grapes will be sold to other producers until the vineyards are more than 15 years old. In the meantime, some very old plots have been leased near Haro, and their fruit goes into some of the densest, most aromatic new Riojas. They are made in utterly traditional style, including fermentation in oak vats, but new French oak is used. The top Roda I cuvée is mostly Tempranillo, while Roda II contains one-quarter Garnacha and is ready sooner. Best years: 1995, '94, '92.

ANTONIN RODET

FRANCE, Burgundy, Côte Chalonnaise, Mercurey

🍷 Pinot Noir

🍷 Chardonnay

Rodet is a large *négociant* house based in Mercurey, and indeed wines from both the Ch. de Mercurey and the Ch. de Rully are usually excellent examples of these two Chalonnaise appellations. But in recent years Rodet has bought other domaines, which operate with varying degrees of independence, although still overseen by the parent company. The best known of these is the MEURSAULT estate of Jacques Prieur, which Rodet acquired in 1988. The following year it bought half of the Ch. de Mercey, with 65ha (161 acres) of vineyards in Mercurey and the HAUTES-CÔTES DE BEAUNE. Domaine Jacques Prieur has a most enviable portfolio of vineyards, with holdings in MONTRACHET and MUSIGNY for a start. But everyone agreed that in the 1980s the estate was performing poorly, and its wines

lagged far behind the standards expected from such a well-endowed domaine. Rodet has been doing its best to turn things around, and has had a fair degree of success, although there are still some lacklustre wines. Finally, in 1996 Rodet bought the Perdrix domaine in Prémeaux, adjoining NUITS-ST-GEORGES, an estate with Premier Cru sites in Nuits as well as vineyards in VOSNE-ROMANÉE, including the ÉCHÉZEAUX Grand Cru. The best wines from the Rodet estates are labelled Cave Privée. Rodet is still, with FAIVELEY, the major player in the Côte Chalonnaise, and its wines from these villages are inexpensive and very well made. Best years: (reds) 1997, '96, '95, '93, '92, '90, '89, '88.

ANTONIN RODET

Some of the best Côte Chalonnaise wines come from Rodet's estate, Ch. de Rully. The label features the distinctive slate turrets of the château.

ROEDERER ESTATE

USA, California, Mendocino County, Anderson Valley AVA

🍷 Chardonnay, Pinot Noir, Pinot Meunier

After a long and exhaustive search, this CALIFORNIA outpost of the CHAMPAGNE house of ROEDERER developed 140ha (346 acres) in the cool western corner of the ANDERSON VALLEY. This site was chosen for its climatic similarity (meaning dicey and cool) to Champagne, and indeed the harvest is late and the yields are low. Chardonnay and Pinot Noir predominate here as they do in Champagne, but there is also some Pinot Meunier. Maintaining the same emphasis on owning and controlling grape sources as the parent company, Roederer Estate succeeded from the start with its Brut, a crisp bubbly full of complex yeasty character, yet more austere than the California competition. Introduced in 1994 as a limited edition prestige wine, L'Ermitage offers a creamy complexity and refinement and is an extraordinary rich bubbly by any standard. It would take well to aging, but is too attractive to often be given that opportunity. A tiny amount of Brut Rosé and a L'Ermitage Rosé, both gorgeous, decadent bubblies, are now available. Best years: (L'Ermitage) 1994, '92, '91.

LOUIS ROEDERER

FRANCE, Champagne, Champagne AC

🍷 Pinot Noir, Chardonnay, Pinot Meunier

This company has the reputation of having the best winemaker in CHAMPAGNE. Obviously the word's got around, because the chief problem with Roederer is to try to find a bottle which is mature enough for you to experience its full splendour. But despite that, the quality is consistently good, and the green edges which afflict so much over-young Champagne are soothed and softened here by the cool creaminess of the yeast and the evidence of reserve wines used in the blends.

As well as the excellent non-vintage and pale rosé, it also makes a big, exciting Vintage, a rare but delicious vintage Blanc de Blancs, and the famous Roederer Cristal, a de luxe cuvée which comes in a clear bottle originally designed for the Russian Tsar. Louis Roederer makes the best non-dry Champagnes on the market, too. They need aging to show their class, but can be rich and honeyed and not at all cloying – unlike most sweet Champagnes, which are feeble stuff. Best years: 1993, '90, '89, '88, '86, '85.

ROERO DOC, ROERO ARNEIS DOC

ITALY, Piedmont

🍷 Nebbiolo

🍷 Arneis

This is a zone of hills similar in shape (if rather more abrupt) to those of BAROLO and BARBARESCO, just across the river Tanaro, but divided between soils that resemble those of the famous neighbours – on which are grown the red Nebbiolo and Barbera – and lighter, sandier soils on which growers today tend to plant the white Arneis and Favorita. The Nebbiolo wines are classified simply as Roero DOC, the Barberas as BARBERA D'ALBA, the Arneis as Roero Arneis DOC and Favorita falls under the LANGHE DOC.

There is, to be sure, a certain overlap of styles, so alongside the fuller reds which are in the process of being developed (top producers are Correggia and Malvirà) there are a number of much lighter ones which accentuate the aromatic and youthful-fruity character of Nebbiolo. Now that the Roero has been 'discovered' it seems to have been designated Alba's prime area for experimentation with alternative – i.e. international – grape varieties: Syrah and Viognier as well as Cabernet and Merlot, Chardonnay and Sauvignon, are all being attempted here. But Roero is best known today, and rightly, for its whites, especially the fairly recently resurrected

Aubert de Villaine in the cellar at Domaine de la Romanée-Conti, the largest owner of Vosne-Romanée's Grands Crus. The wines are fabulously scented and rich in texture – and generally Burgundy's most expensive.

Arneis, whose nutty, peachy, pear and apples aromas make it unique among Italian whites. Best producers: Almondo, Ascheri, Luigi Bertini, Correggia, Deltetto, Malabaila, Malvirà, Negro, Rabino, Vietti.

LA ROMANÉE AC, ROMANÉE-CONTI AC, ROMANÉE-ST-VIVANT AC

FRANCE, Burgundy, Côte de Nuits, Grands Crus

♥ *Pinot Noir*

These are three of the six Grands Crus in the Burgundy village of VOSNE-ROMANÉE. La Romanée is the smallest AC in France, covering a touch over 0.8ha (2 acres), but this tiny little scrap of magic dirt doesn't produce wines of the class of the other Vosne Grands Crus. While the wines made by its neighbour Domaine de la ROMANÉE-CONTI are all rich flavours and exciting perfumes, La Romanée, wholly owned by the Comte Liger-Belair, is strangely lean and glum. For many years the wine has been cellared and distributed by BOUCHARD PÈRE ET FILS, and the change of ownership in the mid-1990s should signal a step up in quality for La Romanée from the 1995 vintage onwards. Best years: 1996, '95, '93, '91, '90, '89, '88, '87, '85, '80, '78.

Romanée-Conti is the pinnacle of red Burgundy for many extremely wealthy Burgundy lovers. The latest release, from

1996, is priced at £650 (US$1040) a bottle and you must still fight off competition to buy a single bottle. The wine has a remarkable, satiny texture, its bouquet shimmering with the fragrance of sweet-briar and its palate an orgy of wonderful scents and exotic opulence which has been known to strike wine-writers dumb. But not many of us can comment on that, because Romanée-Conti, wholly owned by the Domaine de la Romanée-Conti, is only 1.8ha (4.4 acres) and only produces 7000 bottles in a good year. Best years: 1996, '95, '93, '91, '90, '89, '85, '82.

Of Vosne's great Grands Crus, Romanée-St-Vivant is the one which has proved most troublesome to love of late. The wine doesn't seem so rich as it used to, and there is even a rather gruff, rough edge which isn't easy to interpret. Perhaps it is simply that this 9.5-ha (23-acre) vineyard, crunched up to the houses of Vosne-Romanée below the RICHEBOURG Grand Cru, is no longer having to pander to the instant gratification market and at ten to 15 years these wines will show the keenly balanced perfume and brilliance of which the vineyard is capable. I hope so. Even so, they are rarely as long-lived as those from Romanée-Conti. Best years: 1996, '95, 93, '92, '91, '90, '89, '88, '87, '85, '84, '78. Best producers: Arnoux, LATOUR, LEROY, Thomas-Moillard, Domaine de la Romanée-Conti.

DOMAINE DE LA ROMANÉE-CONTI

FRANCE, Burgundy, Côte de Nuits, Vosne-Romanée AC

♥ *Pinot Noir*

♀ *Chardonnay*

The Domaine de la Romanée-Conti (or DRC as it is known to intimates) is unique in Burgundy, since every one of its wines is a Grand Cru. As an estate it is a twentieth-century creation, having been shaped by the grandfather of the present owner Aubert de Villaine, who took in as partners the Leroy family. The estate's policy was to sell off lesser vineyards in exchange for outstanding ones. The partnership between the two families persisted until an almighty row broke out in 1992, which led to the ousting of Lalou Bize-Leroy, who left in order to develop further her own Domaine LEROY. Her place at DRC was taken by Henri Roch.

Aubert de Villaine insists there are no secrets to DRC's eminence. The vineyards are top quality and are cultivated pretty much along organic principles; yields are low, though not fanatically so, and the grapes are picked as late as possible to ensure optimal ripeness. Vinification is traditional, with no cold soak, and a fairly high fermentation temperature. The wine is aged in new oak for up to 18 months and bottled without fining or filtration. Of the six VOSNE Grands Crus, the finest are usually RICHEBOURG, La TÂCHE, and Romanée-Conti itself, although the other three, ÉCHÉZEAUX, Grands-Échézeaux and Romanée-St-Vivant can also be superb. In addition the DRC produces small quantitites of incredibly expensive MONTRACHET.

The question is always asked: are the DRC wines worth the very high prices demanded for them? The answer has to be no: there are other wines in each vintage that can usually rival the DRC range in intensity and quality. Twenty years ago that was not the case, and the DRC wines were unmatched for their splendour and longevity and no other estate had a comparable track record. Today there are other domaines practising the kind of perfectionism in vineyard and winery that once made the DRC unique. Quality hasn't slipped at the domaine, and if anything, the wines are better than ever. But quality has risen elsewhere too. Nonetheless, the DRC wines are of rare beauty and in the eyes of many, the most perfect imaginable expression of Pinot Noir in all its subtlety and complexity. In top vintages, the wines last for decades, and these great Grands Crus can also succeed in vintages written-off by other domaines. Best years: 1996, '95, '94, '93, '91, '90, '89, '88, '87, '85, '83, '80, '78.

RONGOPAI

NEW ZEALAND, North Island, Waikato

🍷 *Cabernet Sauvignon, Pinot Noir, Malbec, Merlot*

🍷 *Riesling, Chardonnay, Müller-Thurgau, Sauvignon Blanc*

One of the smaller (5500 cases) and newer wineries, Rongopai has made a disproportionate impact since the release of its first wines in 1986. All the wines are very distinctive (and appropriately expensive), especially the botrytized sweet whites; a concentrated Müller-Thurgau which almost succeeds in throwing off its humble beginnings as a vine of no great distinction, and an intense lime and apricot Riesling Auslese, which proclaims its classic birth and breeding. The '97 Botrytis Selection achieved a New Zealand record for wine when it was offered for sale at NZ\$100 for a 375ml bottle. Best years: 1998, '96, '94, '93, '91, '90.

LA ROSA

CHILE, Rapel Valley

🍷 *Cabernet Sauvignon, Merlot and others*

🍷 *Sauvignon Blanc, Chardonnay*

Founded in 1824 by Don Gregorio Ossa with a cutting brought over from France, La Rosa is clearly no newcomer to Chilean winemaking. Situated in the Cachapoal Valley, La Rosa made substantial investments in 1990, including new vineyards, and since then, aided by roving wine consultant, Ignacio Recabarren, the wines have become better and better. The unoaked varietals include a weighty, complex Chardonnay and a pungent Merlot, as well as an unoaked Cabernet-Merlot blend and oaked Reserves and Gran Reservas. From 1998 the wines have been sold under La Palmería label. Best years: 1998, '97, '96.

QUINTA DE LA ROSA

PORTUGAL, Douro, Port DOC, Douro DOC

🍷 *Tinta Roriz (Tempranillo), Tinta Barroca, Tinto Cão, Touriga Nacional, Touriga Francesa and others*

🍷 *Gouveio, Viosinho, Rabigato, Malvasia Fina and others*

Unhitching themselves from a mainstream PORT shipper, the Bergqvist family have quickly established La Rosa as one of the leading independent quintas in the DOURO. It makes a full range of ports, from a good midweight vintage, through LBV, 10-Year-Old Tawny, a robust premium ruby known as 'Finest Reserve', to basic ruby and tawny and a wood-aged, dry white port. Unlike the port shippers, La Rosa works on a similar basis to a French château, declaring a vintage port in all but the worst years. At the time of writing, 1993 is the only year to have been bypassed

since its first vintage port in 1988. Although port comes first, with the help of winemaker David Baverstock (of ESPORÃO), La Rosa also makes a firm, fragrant Douro red. Best years: (vintage ports) 1995, '94, '92, '91.

ROSÉ D'ANJOU AC

FRANCE, Anjou-Saumur

🍷 *Cabernet Franc, Cabernet Sauvignon, Malbec (Côt), Gamay, Grolleau, Pineau d'Aunis*

Varying from off-dry to reasonably sweet, most Rosé d'Anjou is made by the local co-operatives and *négociants* and to a price. Most individual producers prefer to make ROSÉ DE LOIRE or CABERNET D'ANJOU instead. Although it remains the most important AC in Anjou, it is now difficult to sell and production is gradually declining. Best producers: Angeli, de Tigné.

ROSÉ DE LOIRE AC

FRANCE, Anjou-Saumur and Touraine

🍷 *Cabernet Franc, Cabernet Sauvignon, Gamay, Grolleau, Pineau d'Aunis, Pinot Noir*

This is a catch-all appellation covering ANJOU, SAUMUR and TOURAINE. It can be made from a range of grapes but Cabernet must make up a minimum of 30 per cent. These rosés are generally dry and can be very attractive young, with lovely red fruit aromas and flavours and enough acidity to make them refreshing. Drink within a year. Best producers: Daviau, Ogereau, Passavant, Pierre-Bise.

ROSÉ DES RICEYS AC

FRANCE, Champagne

🍷 *Pinot Noir*

This is a real oddball still rosé, from les Riceys in the very south of the CHAMPAGNE region, and made only in the ripest years. The wine is a strange sort of dark golden pink, and tastes full and rather nutty. Only about 7500 bottles are made a year and it's expensive. Although usually drunk young, it can age surprisingly well. Best years: 1997, '96, '95, '93, '90, '89, '88. Best producers: Bonnet, Morel.

ROSEMOUNT ESTATE

AUSTRALIA, New South Wales, Hunter Valley Zone, Hunter

🍷 *Syrah (Shiraz), Cabernet Sauvignon, Pinot Noir*

🍷 *Chardonnay, Semillon, Riesling, Sauvignon Blanc*

Rosemount first challenged Australia, and then took on the world, with a small but very talented winemaking and management team, and with success following success. Its vineyard holdings now include prime land in the Upper HUNTER VALLEY, MUDGEE, COONAWARRA,

McLAREN VALE and the ADELAIDE HILLS, while its grape purchasing tentacles extend into every worthwhile nook and cranny of South Eastern Australia. All of this has meant a proliferation of labels, yet these are so well disciplined that they seem to fall into place with a strangely compelling simplicity and logic. As volume increases and stainless steel keeps appearing at its wineries, the question has to be – will quality maintain its present high level? Roxburgh Chardonnay (Upper Hunter), Mountain Blue Shiraz-Cabernet (Mudgee), Balmoral Syrah (McLaren Vale) and Show Reserve Cabernet Sauvignon (Coonawarra) are the flagships, and a mighty armada following behind, with the Diamond Label range at its core. Best years: 1997, '96, '94, '93, '91, '90, '89.

ROSEMOUNT ESTATE
Balmoral Syrah is a monumental concentration of plum, spice, fruit and American vanilla oak and is fast becoming one of Australia's best Shiraz wines.

ROSETTE AC

FRANCE, South-West

🍷 *Sémillon, Sauvignon Blanc, Muscadelle*

Hurry, hurry, hurry! Rosette is fading fast. Well, don't give yourself a hernia in the rush, because Rosette isn't that splendid, but this tiny AC for semi-sweet wines from the hills just north and west of BERGERAC is now down to 20,000 bottles a year. And each year local pundits predict that this is the year the AC will die out completely. In recent years it has been kept alive by the efforts of two producers, François Eckert of Ch. Combrillac and Nicolas Eckert of Ch. la Cardinolle. The wine can be lightly sweet in a rather whimsical way – as befits an AC which is rapidly becoming an afterthought. Best years: 1997, '96, '95, '94, '90, '89. Best producers: Ch. la Cardinolle, Ch. Combrillac, Puypezat.

ROSSESE DI DOLCEACQUA DOC

ITALY, Liguria

🍷 *Rossese*

Right by the French border in the far west of Italy's rocky and riotously colourful Riviera of Flowers, Rossese di Dolceacqua continues to turn out small quantities of its own, much sought-after, gulpably round, fragrant wine, although it is contained within the new Riviera Ligure di Ponente zone, which also harvests the Rossese grape. Rossese di Dolceacqua is a delight when young and just as good, and much softer, after a couple of years. Most of it comes from tiny, artisanal producers. Best producers: Cane, Guglielmi, Lupi, Maccario, Castello di Perinaldo.

ROSSO CONERO DOC

ITALY, Marche

♥ *Montepulciano, Sangiovese*

Rosso Conero is the MARCHE's best red wine, primarily because it is made almost entirely from the gutsy Montepulciano grape and the general level is pretty reliable, although a few bottles taste as if the grapes had been crushed by a steamroller. This area near the Adriatic coast is towards the northern limit of where the Montepulciano grape will thrive, so its almost voluptuous brambly fruit gets a sharper edginess along with its pepper and spice. The name of the DOC comes from a particular type of cherry tree (called Conero by the Greeks) that grows on the stony white soil of its peaks. Best producers: Dittajuti, Marchetti, Mecella, Moncaro, Moroder, Garofoli, Le Terrazze, Umani Ronchi, La Vite. Best years: 1998, '97, '95, '94, '93, '90, '88.

ROSSO DI MONTALCINO DOC

ITALY, Tuscany

♥ *Sangiovese*

BRUNELLO DI MONTALCINO is a big, serious, slow-maturing wine that needs years of aging before it can be sold. In other words, the high price aside, it is a wine that one wouldn't want to drink every day. Plus the fact that producers would expire of cash flow strangulation if they only had their big wine to sell.

Hence Rosso di Montalcino, which is basically a less intense, fresher version of Brunello that can be sold after only one year. But what it loses in mature complexity, Rosso often gains in youthful excitement. It is affordable too. Any recent vintage is worth a gamble, because even in poor vintages responsible growers will sell what would otherwise have been Brunello as Rosso. Some Rossos today are, however, made along Brunello lines except for the aging, and these deserve greater attention – an example is Caparzo's La Caduta. Best producers: Argiano, BANFI, Casanova di Neri, Cerbaiona, Ciacci Piccolomini, Col d'Orcia, Costanti, Fuligni, Lisini, Agostina Pieri, Il POGGIONE, Primo Pacenti, Siro Pacenti, San Filippo, Talenti, Val di Suga.

ROSSO DI MONTEPULCIANO DOC

ITALY, Tuscany

♥ *Sangiovese, Canaiolo, Malvasia and others*

This wine was conceived on the same lines as ROSSO DI MONTALCINO, which it followed in time, but has been much less of a success in its own right. For one thing, VINO NOBILE producers do not have to wait four years for their principal wine to be saleable. For another, Vino Nobile is rather nearer in style to the second wine, creating a certain confusion in the minds of producers and consumers alike. The upshot is that no-one has taken on the Rosso di Montepulciano DOC with the enthusiasm that has greeted its colleague from that other hill town of the province of Siena, and it has yet to establish a recognizable style. Best producers: La Braccesca (ANTINORI), Le Casalte, del Cerro, Fassati, Valdipiatta.

ROSSO PICENO DOC

ITALY, Marche

♥ *Sangiovese, Montepulciano, Trebbiano, Passerina*

This wine is made here and there in most of the southern half of the MARCHE as a fruitier and less interesting version of ROSSO CONERO, with the corresponding fluctuations in quality one might expect from such a basic beverage. But the Superiore version, from a restricted zone near the ABRUZZO border, is distinctly better. For once the word 'Superiore' does not just imply slightly higher alcohol, but rather a more traditional and suitable terroir in the spirit of 'Classico'. Best years: 1998 ,'97, '95, '94, '93, '90, '88. Best producers: Boccadigabbia, Cocci Grifoni, La Vite, Villa Pigna, Villamagna.

RENÉ ROSTAING

FRANCE, Northern Rhône, Côte-Rôtie AC

♥ *Syrah*

♀ *Viognier*

By profession René Rostaing is an estate agent, but he now spends more time tending his own property, as in 1990 and '93 he acquired more land from his relatives, bringing his holdings in this prestigious appellation to almost 7ha (17 acres) as well as a further 1ha (2½ acres) in CONDRIEU. The diversity of his sites permits him to make four cuvées of CÔTE-RÔTIE: a regular bottling, La Landonne, La Viaillière and Côte Blonde, which is usually his finest wine. The vines on the Côte Blonde are 80 years old, so yields are minimal. In difficult vintages, such as 1992 and '93, not all four wines are made. The wines, aged in fairly young wood including 15 per cent new barriques, are elegant and

Rostaing believes they are best enjoyed relatively young, though they do age effortlessly. The Condrieu is delicious. Best years: 1997, '96, '95, '94, '93, '91, '90, '89, '88, '85, '82.

ROTHBURY ESTATE

AUSTRALIA, New South Wales, Hunter Valley Zone, Hunter

♥ *Syrah (Shiraz), Cabernet Sauvignon, Pinot Noir*

♀ *Chardonnay, Semillon*

The king is dead, and neither queen, prince or princess to follow him. Following its acrimonious acquisition by Fosters, Len Evans has left Rothbury for good, but is busily creating a new, multi-faceted empire in the HUNTER VALLEY. Rothbury meanwhile is making some effort to redefine and reposition itself and its products, with modest success. The imposing winery is still there, and the Fosters Group now owns one of the largest direct mail wine businesses in the world, into which the Rothbury Estate Society direct mail club naturally fits. Soulless stuff, perhaps, but properly handled, keeps shareholders happy. Best years: (Semillon) 1996, '95, '93, '91, '90, '86, '84, '79.

DOMAINE GEORGES ROUMIER

FRANCE, Burgundy, Côte de Nuits, Chambolle-Musigny AC

♥ *Pinot Noir*

♀ *Chardonnay*

Although this well-known estate is based in CHAMBOLLE-MUSIGNY, its holdings are quite dispersed. There are Grands Crus in GEVREY-CHAMBERTIN, a monopole Premier Cru in MOREY-ST-DENIS called Clos de la Bussière, and vines in CLOS VOUGEOT and CORTON-CHARLEMAGNE. But Chambolle remains Roumier's heartland, and their BONNES-MARES and MUSIGNY are as exquisite as any. Yields are invariably low, which partly accounts for the wines' intensity.

The domaine has enjoyed a high profile under the energetic Christophe Roumier. The winemaking is a blend of traditional and innovative techniques: there is a cold soak before fermentation, maceration at relatively high temperatures, and aging in a moderate proportion of new oak. The wines fetch deservedly high prices but Christophe Roumier is so adept at teasing out the best that any vineyard has to offer that even his basic BOURGOGNE Rouge is often superior to other growers' Premiers Crus, and Clos de la Bussière is always good value. Best years: 1997, '96, '95, '93, '91, '90, '89, '88, '87, '85, '83, '78, '72.

ROUSSANNE

This is the better of the two major white grapes of France's northern RHÔNE Valley (Marsanne is the other). Both may be added, in small quantities, to the red wines of HERMITAGE as well as making whites in their own right. Roussanne makes fine, delicate wines which, however, are often too delicate to stand up on their own; without the body-building addition of Marsanne they fade rapidly. It is also one of the improving white varieties being planted in the LANGUEDOC-ROUSSILLON, where there are now some interesting examples made with barrel fermentation and oak aging. It is increasingly being planted in the southern Rhône, and a truly outstanding (if costly) example is the Vieilles Vignes from CHÂTEAUNEUF-DU-PAPE's Ch. de BEAUCASTEL.

DOMAINE ARMAND ROUSSEAU

FRANCE, Burgundy, Côte de Nuits, Gevrey-Chambertin AC
♥ Pinot Noir

With its impressive holdings in Grand Cru vineyards – including CHAMBERTIN itself – this domaine has long been one of the standard bearers of the Côte de Nuits. The diffident, courteous Charles Rousseau has been in charge here for 40 years and has maintained high standards. From time to time, however, there have been lapses and odd disappointments, especially in the early 1980s. In general, though, these are rich, well-structured wines that can age extremely well. Despite the impressive array of Grands Crus – Charmes-Chambertin, CLOS DE LA ROCHE, Mazis-Chambertin, Ruchottes-Chambertin, and the splendid Clos de Bèze – insiders often opt for the Premier Cru GEVREY-CHAMBERTIN Clos St-Jacques, which many authorities and growers consider close to Grand Cru quality. Rousseau has very old vines in the Clos, which no doubt contribute to the wine's intensity. He is wary of using new oak indiscriminately, and usually only the most powerful of the Grands Crus – Chambertin and Clos de Bèze – are given the

100 per cent new oak treatment. As Charles's son Eric gradually takes the reins here, it will be interesting to see what, if any, changes are introduced. Best years: 1997, '96, '95, '93, '91, '90, '89, '88, '87, '85.

RÜDESHEIM

GERMANY, Rheingau

This RHEINGAU town should not be confused with that of the same name in the NAHE. It has some of the steepest vineyards in the Rheingau, particularly those west of the town. A few years ago they were intricately terraced, but Flurbereinigung, the radical restructuring of vineyards to make them more economic and easier to work, has done away with the terraces. The best vineyard sites include the Berg Schlossberg and Berg Rottland. The wines are big, ripe and powerful, making up in concentration what they lack in subtlety. Best producers: Georg BREUER, Josef LEITZ, SCHLOSS SCHÖNBORN, J WEGELER.

RUEDA DO

SPAIN, Castilla-León
♀ Verdejo, Palomino, Macabeo (Viura), Sauvignon Blanc

Rueda is capable of making some of Spain's best whites for two reasons. First, the predominant grape variety, the Verdejo, has more character and flavour than most Spanish white grapes, making fresh, fruity, nutty wines with lots of body. Second, the Verdejo's potential is maximized here because of the altitude – between 700 and 800m (2300 and 2625ft) above sea level – and consequent big temperature drops on summer nights, which enable the grapes to retain their aromas. Rueda was once famous for its sherry-style wines but the light, fresh whites are now far more important here.

The full, fresh Rueda Superior by MARQUÉS DE RISCAL is the benchmark wine for this new style. Indeed it was this RIOJA bodega which created the new style, from scratch, after opening its Rueda subsidiary in the 1970s. Marqués de Riscal also introduced the Sauvignon Blanc grape and made the first modern barrel-fermented Verdejo. All these developments relaunched a moribund region and helped the other top producers: Castilla la Vieja (Palacio de Bornos), ÁLVAREZ Y DÍEZ (Mantel Blanco), Antaño (Viña Mocén), Belondrade y Lurton, Ángel Lorenzo Cachazo (Martivellí), Félix Lorenzo Cachazo (Carrasviñas), Cerrosol (Doña Beatriz), Hermanos Lurton, Javier Sanz (Villa Narcisa), Ángel Rodriguez Vidal (Martinsancho), Viñedos de Nieva (Blanco Nieva), Viños Sanz.

RUFFINO

ITALY, Tuscany, Chianti Rufina DOCG
♥ Sangiovese, Cabernet Sauvignon, Merlot, Canaiolo
♥ Sangiovese
♀ Chardonnay, Trebbiano Toscano, Malvasia and others

The Folonari family – owners of Ruffino since 1913 – are fond of saying that Sangiovese is a grape capable of every style of wine, from the light, easy and early-drinking to the big, concentrated and long-maturing. This they demonstrate by producing not just millions of bottles of what is arguably the world's most famous CHIANTI but with various crus at different levels of quality. Top CHIANTI CLASSICO is their Riserva Ducale and its superior version, Riserva Ducale Oro. On a similar level is the VINO NOBILE DI MONTEPULCIANO Lodola Nuova, while BRUNELLO DI MONTALCINO Greppone Mazzi can be put on a par with 'Oro', though retaining a structure and a character typical of good Brunello.

Varietal Sangiovese is not the aim at Ruffino. Nearest to it comes the SUPER-TUSCAN Romitorio di Santedame which is 40 per cent Sangiovese with the balance made up of the Colorino, one of Tuscany's more obscure but, when vinified correctly, most exciting grapes. This is a wine full of the wild cherry and blackberry aromas of the Tuscan hills with firm acidity and ripe tannins at a level capable of allowing improvement and aging for years.

Il Pareto is a tremendously full, complex (berry fruit, raisin, dark chocolate and coffee, toast and spice, long sweet finish) wine designed successfully to impress at international level. But perhaps the most famous of Ruffino's crus is Cabreo Il Borgo, 70 per cent Sangiovese with 30 per cent Cabernet Sauvignon, and much hailed since its first appearance in 1983: in good years, this wine has tremendous concentration and richness of fruit and is perhaps more muscular than subtle, but very modern, and endowed with considerable aging potential. The twin white, Cabreo la Pietra, a barriqued Chardonnay complete with *bâtonnage*, is equally impressive for concentration and wealth of fruit, although it hasn't yet developed a memorable personality. Its non-oaked partner, Libaio (85 per cent Chardonnay with a drop of Pinot Gris) perhaps works a little better, making as it does less claim to complexity. Best years: 1997, '95, '93, '90, '88.

RUINART
FRANCE, Champagne, Champagne AC
Chardonnay, Pinot Noir, Pinot Meunier

Age isn't everything, but Ruinart is the oldest surviving CHAMPAGNE house, having been founded in 1729. Today it is part of the giant LVMH group, but has managed to maintain its own identity; nor has production risen significantly: a manageable two million bottles are produced each year.

'R' de Ruinart is the standard range, and comes in both non-vintage and vintage versions. Although Pinot dominates all the 'R' wines, it's a close thing, and Chardonnay makes up a generous proportion of the blend. Quality here is very consistent, and the vintage 'R' is a fine biscuity mouthful. Ruinart's pride and joy, however, is the Dom Ruinart Champagne, exceptional in both its manifestations: Blanc de Blancs and Rosé. What makes the Blanc de Blancs unusual is that much of the fruit comes not from the prestigious Côte des Blancs but from the Montagne de Reims, which may account for the richness of the wine. In 1998 Ruinart launched L'Exclusive, blending a number of different vintages in an expensively packaged magnum. Best years: 1993, '92, '90, '88, '86, '85, '83, '82, '81, '79, '75.

RULLY AC
FRANCE, Burgundy, Côte Chalonnaise
Pinot Noir
Chardonnay

This is an example of a little-known wine village hauling itself up by the bootstraps. Rully is the northernmost of the individual Côte Chalonnaise ACs (though Bouzeron, with its special AC for Aligoté, is further north still), and in reputation is more of a white wine village than a red. In fact the amounts of red and white wine produced are roughly equal and Rully is one of the few areas in Burgundy where there is room for expansion, with some very promising steep slopes facing east to south-east, recently planted and coming into full production.

The vines of Rully, covering 300ha (740 acres), once provided thin light base wine for the village's thriving fizz industry, which meant the village had no real reputation for its still wines. This all changed in the 1970s and '80s as the prices of both red and white Burgundy from the CÔTE D'OR, just a few miles to the north, began to go crazy – not only was there a lot of new planting in Rully, but the bubbly-makers began to bring in their base wines from elsewhere, leaving Rully's own vineyards to capitalize on a sudden demand for good-quality, reasonably priced Burgundy. Red Rully is light, with a pleasant strawberry and cherry perfume. There could be a bit more body in the wines, but at two to four years they can be very refreshing. You may see Premier Cru on some labels but such epithets have little importance here, and several of the best vineyards are not Premiers Crus. Best years: (reds) 1997, '96, '95, '93. Best producers: (reds) Cogny, Delorme, Durevil-Janthial, Duvernay, la Folie, Jacqueson, JADOT, RODET.

Rully has always made fairly light whites, due to its limestone-dominated soil, but in recent vintages the wines have become fuller, rather nutty, their appley acidity jazzed up by an attractive hint of honey. As some growers also begin to use oak barrels, we should start to see an increasing amount of exciting wine, at a price nearer to a MÂCON Blanc-Villages than a MEURSAULT. Some wines sport the name of a vineyard – probably one of the 19 Premiers Crus, but, as is usual in the Côte Chalonnaise, the term Premier Cru doesn't mean a lot. Best years: (whites) 1997, '96, '95. Best producers: (whites) Belleville, Brelière, Delorme, Dureuil-Janthial, Duvernay, FAIVELEY, la Folie, Jacqueson, Jadot, Rodet.

RUPPERTSBERG
GERMANY, Pfalz
This little village lies to the south of DEIDESHEIM in the PFALZ; it marks the southern end of the Mittelhaardt, the stretch of the Pfalz making the region's greatest

VON BASSERMANN-JORDAN
The Ruppertsberg wines are known for their floral charm and delicate fruit and the Reiterpfad site is one of the best in the village.

wines. Most of the vineyards here are flat or gently sloping, but the soil is good. The pedigree of the wines is good, too, with growers like von BASSERMANN-JORDAN, von BUHL, BÜRKLIN-WOLF, Dr Kern and J WEGELER having vines in sites like Reiterpfad, Hoheburg, Gaisböhl and Spiess.

RUSSE
BULGARIA, Northern Region
Cabernet Sauvignon, Merlot and others
Sauvignon Blanc, Riesling, Muskat Ottonel, and others

As the name suggests, this sprawling winery was built, on the northernmost border, to cater for one major client to the north: Russia, or rather, the former Soviet Union. With a vast acreage fanning out around it, Russe produces a large array of wines. Stainless steel technology allows for some more than passable Sauvignon Blanc. Red wines, especially Cabernet Sauvignon, tend to be upright and firm, thanks to rock-steady acidic structures. One of the largest wineries to face privatization in Bulgaria, Russe looks set to take Bulgarian winemaking into the twenty-first century with a degree of assurance, albeit it will be some time before the vineyards pass into private hands.

RUSSIAN RIVER VALLEY AVA
USA, California, Sonoma County
Until the American wine boom caught hold in the early 1970s, conventional wisdom in SONOMA COUNTY had it that Russian River, in northern Sonoma, was too cold and too foggy for grapes, a view formulated mostly by aging Italians with a penchant for ultra-ripe Zinfandel. Later arrivals tested other varieties, and found that Riesling and Gewürztraminer did well, Chardonnay and Pinot Noir even better. These four command most of the 4047ha (10,000 acres) of vineyards, though Zinfandel and Merlot do surprisingly well.

Two sub-AVAs fall within the Russian River Valley, wholly or in part. At its western edge, the compact Sonoma-Green Valley is home to about 400ha (1000 acres) of vineyard, mostly Chardonnay and Pinot Noir. In the east it encompasses much of the similarly sized Chalk Hill AVA, mostly Chardonnay and Sauvignon Blanc. Best producers: Davis Bynum, De Loach, DEHLINGER, Gary Farrell, Foppiano, Hanna, Hop Kiln, IRON HORSE, KISTLER, Martinelli, Rabbit Ridge, ROCHIOLI, Rodney Strong, SONOMA-CUTRER, Joseph Swan, WILLIAMS-SELYEM. Best years: 1998, '97, '95, '94, '92, '91, '90.

RUSSIZ SUPERIORE

ITALY, Friuli-Venezia Giulia, Collio DOC

♟ *Cabernet Sauvignon, Cabernet Franc, Merlot*

♀ *Pinot Blanc (Pinot Bianco), Pinot Gris (Pinot Grigio), Sauvignon Blanc and others*

This winery is in FRIULI, best known for its part in Italy's white wine revolution, although Russiz is also making rapid strides with reds. An excellent example is the barrique-aged Rosso degli Orzoni, a Cabernet Sauvignon blend with some Cabernet Franc and Merlot. It began life in the mid-1980s with something of that monolinear character from which COLLIO reds have suffered, but as the vineyards mature and the techniques refine the wine is becoming fuller.

The Felluga family acquired this ancient estate dating back to the thirteenth century in the 1960s and they make their top range of wines here, including good varietal Cabernet Franc and Merlot wines. There are also, more predictably, some first-class Collio whites in the form of Pinot Bianco, Pinot Grigio, Sauvignon and Tocai Friulano. They also control the separate winery of Marco Felluga, at Gradisca d'Isonzo, which produces a worthy rival to Rosso degli Orzoni called Carantan. Committed to experimentation in the vineyards and advised by viticultural consultant Attilio Scienza, Russiz Superiore is one of the most dynamic producers in Friuli. Best years: 1998, '97, '96, '95, '93, '89.

RUST

AUSTRIA, Burgenland, Neusiedlersee-Hügelland

It would be hard for the town of Rust, in the NEUSIEDLERSEE-HÜGELLAND on the western shore of Lake Neusiedl, to be any prettier. It has painted baroque houses, it has Buschenschanken (watering holes) galore, it has mellow old churches and it even has storks. Unfortunately all these delights attract the tourists, and Rust in summer has coaches lined up like cows at a milking parlour. Good news for the tills at the Buschenschanken, but not a lot of fun for the serious wine taster.

FEILER-ARTINGER
Feiler-Artinger is best known for its stunning Ausbruch dessert wines, the most elegant examples of this local wine style.

Even so, Rust has plenty of good winemakers, producing some of Austria's best sweet wines. These come from vineyards running in a narrow strip near the lake, which is broad and shallow and offers a perfect mesoclimate for the development of the noble rot fungus. Dry reds and whites come from other Rust vineyards further back from the lake, but Rust's own speciality is Ausbruch, a sweet wine made by adding non-botrytized must to nobly rotten must. The best examples are closer to SAUTERNES in style than Germanic sweet wines, with less fruit flavour but greater complexity and power. Best growers: FEILER-ARTINGER, Hans Holler, Bruno Landauer, Peter Schandl, Heidi Schröck, Ernst TRIEBAUMER, Robert WENZEL.

RUSTENBERG

SOUTH AFRICA, Western Cape, Stellenbosch WO

♟ *Cabernet Sauvignon, Merlot and others*

♀ *Chardonnay, Sauvignon Blanc and others*

It takes guts – and a deep pocket – to drop out of the market for three vintages, but this is what owner Simon Barlow did when problems arose with some wines of the early 1990s. In the meantime, the farm has undergone a complete revamp, from vineyards to a new cellar skilfully inserted into the skeleton of the old dairy. All the new buildings have certainly not destroyed the ambience of this magnificent old farm and national monument. New varieties, many reflecting the worldwide interest in RHÔNE grapes, are being introduced and a nursery has been established to propagate the farm's own vines.

To complement all this activity, the farm has now bounced back with some fine wines. Starting level is the competitive Brampton label, which includes fruit from Simon Barlow's farm on the Helderberg; this range concentrates on varietal fruit. The premium, classically styled Rustenberg wines include the individual Five Soldiers Chardonnay and the flagship wine called Peter Barlow, a 100 per cent Cabernet. Beautifully oaked and balanced, these are wines with excellent aging potential; they will also assure this dedicated producer a flying start into the twenty-first century. Best years: 1997, '96, '95, '91, '90, '89.

RUTHERFORD AVA

USA, California, Napa County

With the Oakville District as its southern boundary and St Helena to the north, Rutherford lies in the middle section of the NAPA VALLEY. Made famous decades ago by Cabernet Sauvignon grown by BEAULIEU and

Inglenook (now NIEBAUM-COPPOLA), Rutherford's terroir was said to contribute a dried herb, earthy character called 'Rutherford dust'. Most of the historic vineyard sites and many of the new cult producers are found along the western foothills. Vineyard redevelopment in the 1990s left no doubt that Cabernet Sauvignon is the preferred variety, with a smattering of Merlot and a patch or two of Chardonnay still to be found. Total plantings are holding steady at 2020ha (5000 acres). Best years (reds): 1998, '97, '95, '94, '93, '92, '91, '90. Best producers: Beaulieu, CAYMUS, Flora Springs, Freemark Abbey, HEITZ, Livingston, PINE RIDGE, Niebaum-Coppola, STAGLIN FAMILY.

RUTHERGLEN AND GLENROWAN

AUSTRALIA, Victoria, North East Victoria Zone

Steeped in history – just drive through the main street of Glenrowan or visit MORRIS, BAILEYS or Fairfield, or read about Ned Kelly and his last stand – these regions (they are being split like Siamese twins under the Geographic Indications scalpel) produce Australia's most remarkable wines: the fortified Tokays (read Muscadelle) and Muscats (read Muscat à Petits Grains, or at least the brown clone thereof).

Wrinkled, raisined and incredibly sweet grapes are harvested very late in the season, and barely allowed to ferment before alcohol is added, the fermentation stopped, and the long period of barrel aging commenced – still aided by storage towards the ceiling of the corrugated iron wineries, borrowing directly from the Madeira 'cooking' approach. Suitably monumental and long-lived reds are also made, most notably from Shiraz. Best years: 1996, '94, '92, '91, '90. Best producers: (Rutherglen) All Saints, Bullers Calliope, Campbells, CHAMBERS Rosewood, Morris; (Glenrowan) BAILEYS, Mount Prior, Pfeiffer, St Leonards, Stanton & Killeen.

SAALE-UNSTRUT

GERMANY

The Saale and the Unstrut are both rivers, and together they make up one of the wine regions of the former East Germany. There are only 506ha (1250 acres) under vine and these are Germany's most northerly vineyards. Frost can be a serious problem, and this, together with low rainfall, poor vine clones and gaps in the vineyards where replanting has not been possible, makes for low average yields of 34 hectolitres per hectare, compared with around 100 hectolitres per hectare in the former West Germany. The soil is generally chalky and the wines light with plenty of acidity. Nearly the whole production is divided between the State Domaine at Naumburg and the larger Freyburg co-operative, with 500 members. There are already a few private growers. The other large producer in the region, the Rotkäppchen Sektkellerei at Freyburg, imports the base wine for its fizz from abroad. Best producer: LÜTZKENDORF.

SAARBURG
GERMANY, Mosel-Saar-Ruwer
The most important town on the stretch of the Saar valley where vines are still grown is dominated by its ruined medieval castle (which houses a good restaurant). Less well-known than this and the cable car that pulls in the tourists are the excellent vineyards, most notably the Saarburger Rausch. Best producers: Dr WAGNER, ZILLIKEN.

SACHSEN
GERMANY
If the vineyards of Sachsen somehow survived economic crises, the Nazis, the destruction of central Dresden in 1945 and half a century of Communism, then it was because of the patriotism of the people of Saxony who remembered their country's great past. Until Saxony was cut down to size at the Vienna Congress in 1815 it was a great European power with a thriving wine industry. The best vineyards, on steep terraces above the river Elbe, have been replanted with good vine material during the 1990s and are starting to yield good wines. Best are the dry Riesling, Grauburgunder and Traminer, all of which can have astonishing power along with the crisp acidity you would expect from a region north of the 51° latitude. Best producers: Schloss Proschwitz, Klaus ZIMMERLING.

CH. ST-AMAND
FRANCE, Bordeaux, Sauternes AC, Cru Bourgeois
♀ *Sémillon, Sauvignon Blanc*
This is one of the few non-Classed Growth properties that manages to produce big, rich, classic SAUTERNES – and which doesn't charge the earth. The 22-ha (54-acre) estate is in the commune of Preignac – right next to the little river Ciron, whose autumn mists have so much to do with the formation of the noble rot fungus on the grapes. Recent vintages have been less consistent. The second wine is Ch. la Chartreuse. Best years: 1998, '97, '96, '94, '90, '89, '88, '86, '83, '81, '80.

JEAN-MICHEL PATISSIER
The northernmost Beaujolais cru produces juicy, soft-fruited wines such as this example which lasts well for two to three years.

ST-AMOUR AC
FRANCE, Burgundy, Beaujolais, Beaujolais cru
♥ *Gamay*
What a lovely name – the 'Love Saint'. Obviously this BEAUJOLAIS cru has missed its vocation: it ought to be a honeymoon retreat. The calf-eyed couples would certainly find it quiet: there isn't even a village inn. So perhaps the inhabitants are better off making a particularly juicy, soft-fruited Beaujolais, ready to drink within the year, but lasting well for two or three. The village lies just inside the Saône-et-Loire *département* (all the other Beaujolais crus are in the RHÔNE *département*) and so is theoretically in the Mâconnais. Indeed any white wine from its 304ha (751 acres) of vineyards can legally be called ST-VÉRAN. There is no co-operative at St-Amour, and several *négociant* offerings are better than average. Best years: 1998, '97, '96, '95. Best producers: Billards, DUBOEUF, Raymond Durand, Domaine du Paradis, Patissier, Poitevin, Revillon, Saillant, Ch. de St-Amour.

ST-AUBIN AC
FRANCE, Burgundy, Côte de Beaune
♥ *Pinot Noir*
♀ *Chardonnay*
St-Aubin is not actually on the CÔTE D'OR's Golden Slope but in its own cleft, just up the hill from PULIGNY-MONTRACHET, which means that prices are comparatively low, and despite recent replanting there are lots of old vineyards producing quite big, chewy-fruited reds. There is a fair bit of old Gamay – which can't be used for the St-Aubin AC, but which makes the Gamay-Pinot Noir blend, BOURGOGNE PASSE-TOUT-GRAINS particularly tasty here. In fact most of the 120ha (297 acres) of vineyards are on good east- to south-east-facing slopes, and two-thirds of them are classified Premiers Crus. Les Frionnes and les Murgers des Dents de Chien are two of the best. Best years: (reds) 1997, '96, '95, '93, '90. Best producers: J-C Bachelet, Patrick Clerget, Colin, Lamy-Pillot, Prudhon, Roux, Gérard Thomas.

It's a great pity that perhaps only one-third of the vineyards are planted with white grapes because the lean, racy fruit combined with a delicious toasty, biscuity perfume from a little oak aging makes these wines as good as many CHASSAGNE-MONTRACHETs or MEURSAULTs. They're delicious young, but are better after five years' aging. Perhaps St-Aubin is in fact the patron saint of the white Burgundy lover with limited means, because these delicious wines are never over-priced. Best years: (whites) 1997, '96, '95, '92, '90. Best producers: Patrick Clerget, Colin, Girardin, JADOT, Jaffelin, Lamy-Pillot, Albert Morey, Prudhon, Roux, Gérard Thomas.

ST-CHINIAN AC
FRANCE, Languedoc-Roussillon
♥ *Carignan, Grenache, Cinsaut and others*
Along with FAUGÈRES, this was the first of the red wines of the HÉRAULT *département* to break away from the pack and start making a name for itself back in the 1980s. In the hill villages set back from the coast, the rocky slopes can produce strong, spicy reds with a fair amount of fruit and far more personality than the run of the Hérault mill – particularly when carbonic maceration has been employed at least partially.

About 16 million bottles of St-Chinian are produced annually from around 2760ha (6820 acres) of vines in the hills above Béziers. Carignan is the main grape, but increasingly Grenache, Syrah and Mourvèdre are being planted. The wines can be drunk very young but age happily for two to three years. Though they have a good, strong taste, they are usually a little lighter-bodied than neighbouring Faugères, and as yet not quite so consistent. Best years: 1998, '96, '95. Best producers: Borie la Vitarèle, Canet-Valette, Cazal-Viel, Clos Bagatelle, Coujan, Maurel Fonsalade, des Jougla, Mas Champart; and the Berlou, Roquebrun and St-Chinian co-operatives.

ST CLEMENT
USA, California, Napa County, Napa Valley AVA
♥ *Cabernet Sauvignon, Merlot*
♀ *Chardonnay*
Always a consistent producer of high-quality Chardonnay, most notably the Abbot's Vineyard bottling, this Napa winery has become known recently for fruity Merlot as well as luscious, concentrated Cabernet Sauvignon, including the White Cottage Ranch Vineyard and the Meritage blend, Oroppas. Best years: 1996, '95, '94, '93, '92, '91, '90,

ST-ÉMILION & POMEROL France, Bordeaux

THE RIGHT BANK OF THE DORDOGNE RIVER in Bordeaux is dominated by the Merlot grape, and the greatest right bank wines are those of St-Émilion and Pomerol. Indeed, the hill-top citadel of St-Émilion, huddled into clefts of rock above the vineyards and looking out over the valley, is the most ancient wine region in Bordeaux. Over 1800 years ago the Romans were planting the steep south-facing slopes just out-side the town, and several leading properties, like Ch. la Gaffelière and Ch. Ausone (named after the Roman poet Ausonius to whom the vineyards once belonged), can trace their records as far back as the second century.

The finest St-Émilion vineyards with most of the famous names and all but two of the Premiers Grands Crus Classés lie on the steep sites round the town, on the *côtes* or 'slopes'. But there is also an enclave to the west of the town, towards Libourne, called the *graves* where two of St-Émilion's greatest estates – Ch. Cheval Blanc and Ch. Figeac – are situated. The *graves* refers to a gravel ridge, which is more suited to Cabernet Sauvignon than other parts of St-Émilion, on a plateau which is otherwise noted for its heavy clay soil.

The clay soil comes into its own in Pomerol, which begins right next to Cheval Blanc and continues westward to the outskirts of Libourne, and means that Merlot is the dominant grape here. There are no fancy buildings here, no signs of affluence and renown, just an almost monotonous stretch of vineyards, yet one of the world's most expensive red wines – Ch. Pétrus – is made in a tiny, inconspicuous building in the heart of Pomerol. Here, on the highest part of the Pomerol plateau, the soils are 90 per cent clay mixed with gravel, and the compact blue clay limits vigour in the vine, regulates water supply and dictates that almost 100 per cent Merlot is used. The resulting wine with an unctuous richness of fruit, exotic aromas and a firm but fine structure is echoed by numerous other modest-looking, mainly family-owned properties crammed into the tiny area. None is as great as Pétrus, not even the micro-property le Pin whose wines have

Below the beautiful town of St-Émilion, the Roman town at the centre of Bordeaux's most historic region, is a labyrinthine network of ancient cellars used by some of the châteaux for aging their wines.

from time to time outstripped Pétrus in price, but many Pomerols give more than just a suggestion of the power and succulence which make Pétrus so dazzling.

CH. CHEVAL BLANC
This is the leading St-Émilion estate and likely to remain so for the foreseeable future, fully justifying its ranking as an 'A' category Premier Grand Cru Classé.

CH. FIGEAC
This is one of the better Premiers Grands Crus Classés and like Cheval Blanc Figeac uses a high proportion of Cabernet in the blend.

CH. ANGÉLUS
Excellent wines in the 1980s, an energetic owner and talented winemaker brought well-deserved promotion for this estate to Premier Grand Cru Classé in 1996.

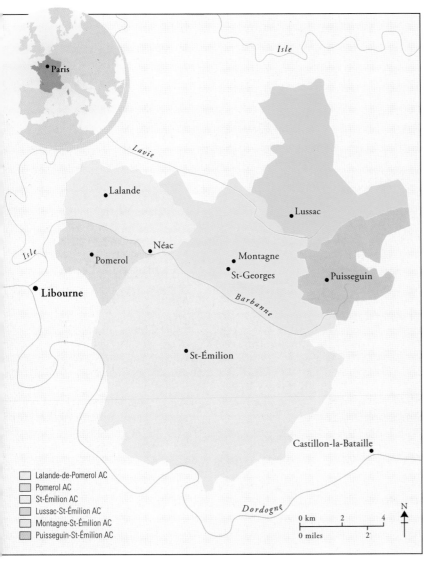

Lalande-de-Pomerol AC
Pomerol AC
St-Émilion AC
Lussac-St-Émilion AC
Montagne-St-Émilion AC
Puisseguin-St-Émilion AC

CH. DE VALANDRAUD
This tiny estate has only existed since 1991 yet the immensely rich and concentrated wine has already become one of the most expensive in Bordeaux.

LA MONDOTTE
Newly launched in 1996, this is a remarkable micro-cuvée from a vineyard belonging to Ch. Canon-la-Gaffelière.

CH. DE BARBE-BLANCHE
The Cuvée Henri IV is a good example of a lighter St-Émilion wine from one of its satellite appellations.

CH. GAZIN
Situated next door to the legendary Ch. Pétrus, Ch. Gazin is now one of the most improved Pomerol properties and vintages in the mid-1990s show real potential.

CH. LAFLEUR
Using some of Pomerol's most traditional winemaking, this tiny estate makes wines that seriously rival those from Ch. Pétrus for sheer power, tannic structure and hedonistic richness and concentration.

CH. DES ANNEREAUX
This is one of the better estates from Pomerol's neighbour, Lalande-de-Pomerol and in top years, the wine is very Pomerol-like – plump and plummy with a certain opulence.

Both Pomerol and St-Émilion have 'satellite' appellations which employ hyphenated versions of the more famous names. Though they are never as good as the top Pomerols and St-Émilions, Lalande-de-Pomerol, in particular, produces many lush, soft reds that certainly equal Pomerol's lesser lights. North of St-Émilion a group of small appellations (Lussac, Puisseguin, St-Georges and Montagne) all produce sturdy but attractively fruity reds. It's difficult to gauge quite how exciting the vineyards could be because these appellations are dominated by co-operatives which, good though they are, don't push individuality to the limit.

AC ENTRIES
Lalande-de-Pomerol, St-Émilion, St-Émilion Grand Cru Classé, St-Émilion Premier Grand Cru Classé, St-Émilion Satellites.

CHÂTEAUX ENTRIES
Angélus, l'Arrosée, Ausone, Balestard-la-Tonnelle, Beau-Séjour Bécot, Belair, Canon, Cheval Blanc, Clos René, l'Evangile, Figeac, Gazin, Lafleur, Latour-à-Pomerol, Magdelaine, Pavie, Petit-Village, Pétrus, le Pin, Trotanoy, Vieux-Château-Certan.

ST-ÉMILION AC, ST-ÉMILION GRAND CRU AC

FRANCE, Bordeaux

🍷 *Merlot, Cabernet Franc, Cabernet Sauvignon, Malbec (Pressac)*

See also St-Émilion & Pomerol, pages 326–327.

If William the Conqueror had decided to take some BORDEAUX wines to England with him when he laid low poor old Harold at the Battle of Hastings in 1066, there's a good chance his triumphant tipple would have been St-Émilion, because the Brits have been drinking it very happily for over 800 years. And it became so popular so quickly because the one thing that marks the flavour of St-Émilion is a gorgeous softness, a buttery, toffeeish sweetness and a fruit whose flavour owes more to the dark, chewy richness of raisins in a fruit cake, than to the leaner, more demanding tastes of the wines of the GRAVES and MÉDOC.

The St-Émilion ACs are centred on the Roman town of St-Émilion on the right bank of the Dordogne, east of Bordeaux. The vines cover 5400ha (13,350acres) in eight different communes, although the best vineyards lie within the boundaries of the St-Émilion commune itself. It is a region of smallholdings, with over 1000 different properties, the smallest being Ch. le Couvent actually in the town of St-Émilion. Consequently, the co-operative (the Union des Producteurs) is of great importance, and vinifies over 20 per cent of the entire St-Émilion crop to a consistently high standard.

St-Émilion AC is the region's basic AC, accounting for roughly 45 per cent of the production, much of this handled by the co-operative. St-Émilion Grand Cru AC is St-Émilion's top quality AC. Geographically, it has the same delimitations as St-Émilion AC, but a lower yield and higher minimum degree of alcohol are demanded as well as a supplementary tasting examination before a wine will be granted the AC certificate. It includes St-Émilion's classified wines. Undoubtedly, with its more qualitative approach, the best wines fall into this AC, including the unclassified but highly priced micro-crus, like de Valandraud and La Mondotte, that made an appearance in the 1990s.

Best years: 1998, '97, '96, '95, '94, '90, '89, '88, '86, '85. Best producers: (Grand Cru AC – unclassified) Bellefont-Belcier, Destieux, Faugères, Fleur-Cardinale, Fombrauge, la Gomerie, La Mondotte, Moubousquet, Moulin St-Georges, Pipeau, Rol Valentin, Tertre-Rôteboeuf, Teyssier, de Valandraud.

CH. PAVIE-MACQUIN
Great strides were made at this estate in the late 1980s. The vineyard is run on biodynamic lines and the wine is now delicious and sumptuous.

ST-EMILION GRAND CRU CLASSÉ

FRANCE, Bordeaux, St-Émilion Grand Cru AC

🍷 *Merlot, Cabernet Franc, Cabernet Sauvignon*

This is the first category of ST-ÉMILION's two-tier system of classification. The St-Émilionnais were late in devising an order of grading for their châteaux, introducing the first classification in 1955, exactly 100 years after the famous 1855 classification of the MÉDOC. Châteaux are nominated for two categories, St-Émilion Grand Cru Classé and St-Émilion Premier Grand Cru Classé. But there is an original aspect to the arrangement, which is that the classification is reviewed every ten years. Hence, there were new classifications in 1969, 1985 (following postponement) and most recently in 1996, when 55 châteaux were attributed with the title St-Émilion Grand Cru Classé. Obviously, with such a large number of properties, styles of wine and even quality vary considerably but the best ones can age for ten to 15 years. Best producers: l'ARROSÉE, BALESTARD-LA-TONNELLE, Canon-la-Gaffelière, Clos de l'Oratoire, Dassault, la Dominique, Grand-Mayne, Grand-Pontet, Larcis-Ducasse, Larmande, Pavie-Decesse, Pavie-Macquin, Soutard, la Tour Figeac, Troplong-Mondot. Best years: 1998, '97, '96, '95, '94, '90, '89, '88, '86, '85, '83, '82.

ST-ÉMILION PREMIER GRAND CRU CLASSÉ

FRANCE, Bordeaux, St-Émilion Grand Cru AC

🍷 *Merlot, Cabernet Franc, Cabernet Sauvignon*

The elite category of the ST-ÉMILION classification, the Premiers Grands Crus Classés are further divided into two grades – 'A' and 'B' – with only the much more expensive Cheval Blanc and Ausone in grade 'A'. There are 11 'B' châteaux, with ANGÉLUS and FIGEAC the outstanding names. Since the inauguration of the classification in 1955 Angélus is the only château to be added to the original list of 12, receiving promotion in 1996. BEAU-SÉJOUR

Bécot was demoted in 1985 and then re-elected again in 1996. Most of the wines drink superbly with ten to 15 years' aging but much depends on the vintage and château. AUSONE and CHEVAL BLANC occasionally last half a century or more. Best producers: ANGÉLUS, Ausone, Beau-Séjour Bécot, Beauséjour-Duffau-Lagarosse, BELAIR, CANON, Cheval Blanc, Clos Fourtet, FIGEAC, la Gaffelière, MAGDELAINE, PAVIE, Trottevieille. Best years: 1998, '97, '96, '95, '94, '90, '89, '88, '86, '85, '83, '82.

ST-ÉMILION SATELLITES: LUSSAC-ST-ÉMILION AC, MONTAGNE-ST-ÉMILION AC, PUISSEGUIN-ST-ÉMILION AC, ST-GEORGES-ST-ÉMILION AC

FRANCE, Bordeaux

🍷 *Merlot, Cabernet Franc, Cabernet Sauvignon, Malbec*

There are four satellite ST-ÉMILION ACs, totalling 3860ha (9540 acres), lying a few miles north of the town of St-Émilion in gently hilly countryside. The wine can be tasty, if a little solid, and is normally drunk within four years of the vintage. Some of the best may keep up to ten years. There is an important co-operative at Puisseguin producing a large percentage of the wines of Lussac and Puisseguin. Best years: 1998, '96, '95, '94, '90, '89, '88. Best producers: (Lussac) Barbe-Blanche, Bel-Air, Courlat, de la Grenière, Lyonnat, Villadière; (Montagne) Calon, Faizeau, des Moines, Montaiguillon, Négrit, Plaisance, Roc de Calon, Roudier, Vieux Château St-André; (Puisseguin) Bel-Air, Durand-Laplagne, Guibeau, des Laurets, Producteurs Réunis, Soleil, Vieux-Château-Guibeau; (St-Georges), Calon, Macquin St-Georges, St-André Corbin, Ch. St-Georges, Tour-du-Pas-St-Georges.

ST-ESTÈPHE AC

FRANCE, Bordeaux, Haut-Médoc

🍷 *Cabernet Sauvignon, Cabernet Franc, Merlot and others*

The wines of St-Estèphe are frequently accorded only grudging praise. Yet, in its old-fashioned, tweeds-and-plus-fours way, St-Estèphe is the most reliable and the least over-priced of the HAUT-MÉDOC's specific ACs. It is a large AC at 1245ha (3080 acres), but the most recently established of the great Haut-Médoc areas, partly because the gravel soil which gives all the finest wines in PAUILLAC, ST-JULIEN and MARGAUX is much less prevalent here – clay clogs your shoes as you wander these vineyards. It also has a cooler climate than the other main villages and the vines may ripen a week later than those in Margaux. This means that most of the properties have a fairly high proportion of the earlier-ripening Merlot, though Cabernet Sauvignon is still the leading grape. St-Estèphe has only five Classed Growths, due partly to the clay soils, and partly to the late development of the area – many vineyards were not fully established by 1855. Several non-classified properties consistently make fine wine of Classed Growth quality.

St-Estèphe wines are not the most likeable wines straight off. They have high tannin levels, and a definite earthy scratch in their texture. Give them time, however, and those sought-after flavours of blackcurrant and cedarwood do peek out – but rarely with the brazen beauty of a Pauillac or a St-Julien. There is some evidence of a softer style of winemaking, but although this is fine for the lesser properties, for the leading châteaux the end result is a bit half-hearted and St-Estèphe's best efforts are still in the brawny mould, demanding ten to 20 years of aging. Best years: 1998, '96, '95, '94, '90, '89, '88, '86, '85, '83, '82, '79, '78, '76, '75. Best producers: Andron-Blanquet, CALON-SÉGUR, COS D'ESTOURNEL, Cos Labory, HAUT-MARBUZET, LAFON-ROCHET, Lilian-Ladouys, Marbuzet, MEYNEY, MONTROSE, les Ormes-de-Pez, de PEZ, Phélan-Ségur.

ST FRANCIS WINERY
USA, California, Sonoma County, Sonoma Valley AVA
♟ *Cabernet Sauvignon, Merlot, Zinfandel*
♀ *Chardonnay*

In the 1980s St Francis quickly moved out of the shadow cast by its neighbour CHATEAU ST JEAN on the strength and individuality of its Merlot. Today it has evolved into a 100,000-case-a-year winery offering a modest range of high-quality wines. Aged in both American and French oak barrels, Merlot, so soft, supple, and fruity, remains its calling card. The Sonoma Valley Reserve is ripe, supple yet more powerful and intense than most. After acquiring vineyards in the 1990s, the winery has dramatically improved its Cabernet Sauvignons, and the incredible Cabernet Reserve is full of cassis fruit and deep, rich flavours. New vineyards are responsible for the wonderful, intense Old Vine Zinfandel, which is occasionally bested by the winery's special Pagani Ranch Zinfandel, a powerful, thick, velvety wine. Best years: (reds) 1997, '96, '95, '94, '92, '91, '90. Chardonnays should not be ignored, with the Reserve

usually having plenty of depth and oak to rise far above the ordinary. Best years: 1998, '97, '95, '94, '93, '92.

DOMAINE DE ST-GAYAN
FRANCE, Southern Rhône, Gigondas AC
♟ *Grenache, Syrah, Mourvèdre*

The Meffre family have inhabited this region since the fifteenth century, and St-Gayan remains very much a family business, with Jean-Pierre Meffre and his wife Martine representing the current generation. The high quality of the wines probably originates with the very old vines, up to a century old, which are planted on one-third of the estate's 16ha (40 acres). Yields are low, and the wines are aged initially in tanks and then large casks. St-Gayan is not a blockbuster GIGONDAS but an elegant, soft-textured wine that can be drunk fairly young. With age it shows intriguing leathery, earthy aromas. There is also a CÔTES DU RHONE-Villages-Rasteau. Best years: 1997, '96, '95, '94, '90, '89, '88, '85, '82.

ST HALLETT
AUSTRALIA, South Australia, Barossa Zone, Barossa Valley
♟ *Syrah (Shiraz), Cabernet Sauvignon, Merlot, Grenache*
♀ *Chardonnay, Semillon, Sauvignon Blanc, Riesling*

This winery is a highly disciplined producer of four excellent table wines, headed by the stellar Old Block Shiraz, made from vines all older than 60 years (some over 100 years). This is the velvet fist in the velvet glove, so smooth and seductive is it, recently with a touch of vanilla American oak. As its fame spreads, BAROSSA growers get in touch and say they've got some gnarled old Shiraz vines too and does St Hallett want the fruit for Old Block? Varietal brand-extension has seen the introduction of Blackwell Shiraz and Faith Shiraz below Old Block. The Riesling is good, as is the Poachers Blend Dry White. Best years: 1996, '94, '93, '92, '91, '90, '88, '86.

ST HALLETT
One of the Barossa Valley's best red wines is Old Block Shiraz from St Hallett. Full of ripe tannins, the wine is made from very old vines.

ST-JOSEPH AC
FRANCE, Northern Rhône
♟ *Syrah*
♀ *Marsanne, Roussanne*

If ever the Syrah grape wished to show the smiling side of its nature in the northern RHÔNE, it would have to be at St-Joseph. Most of the wines are an absolute riot of rich, mouthfilling fruit with an irresistible black-currant richness. The St-Joseph AC used to be limited to the granite slopes of half-a-dozen right-bank villages centred on Mauves, just south of HERMITAGE, and all the best wine still comes from there. But, inexplicably, the AC was extended in 1969 to take in another 20 communes on flat land north of Tournon and Hermitage. Their wine isn't anything like as good, although it's still a jolly nice drink. St-Joseph is brilliant at only one to two years old; it can age for up to ten from the area around Mauves, but you'll gradually lose that wonderful fruit, so drink it before five years old. Best years: (reds) 1998, '97, '96, '95, '94, '92, '91, '90. Best producers: CHAPOUTIER, CHAVE, Chèze, Courbis, Coursodon, CUILLERON, Gaillard, Gonon, GRAILLOT, Gripa, Grippat, JABOULET, St-Désirat co-operative, Tardieu-Laurent, Trollat.

At their best, St-Joseph whites have an astonishing flavour halfway between the peach and apricot headiness of a CONDRIEU and the buttery richness of a good MEURSAULT. At worst, with bad winemaking, they are flat, hollow wines with no fruit or acidity. Somewhere in between, with up-to-date winemaking, is a pleasant, flowery, apple-scented wine for drinking without too much ceremony at a year old or so. The old-style wines are made from low-yielding vines around Tournon and Mauves, matured in old oak and capable of lasting 20 years. They are rich, heavy, scented with sandalwood, woodsmoke and peaches, and tasting of toast and brazil nuts draped in butter caramel – with a strong acidity gnawing at a central kernel of fruit that is as dry-yet-rich as preserved apricots. That's when they are well made. Unfortunately there are quite a few stale, oxidized examples on offer. Best years: (whites) 1998, '97, '96, '95. Best producers: Chèze, Coursodon, Cuilleron, Gonon, Gripa, Grippat, Trollat.

ST-JULIEN AC
FRANCE, Bordeaux, Haut-Médoc
♟ *Cabernet Sauvignon, Cabernet Franc, Merlot and others*

If someone said to me, 'show me the perfect red Bordeaux, the quintessence of restrained cedarwood perfume and lean but mouth-watering blackcurrant fruit' – St-Julien is where I would look. Of all the HAUT-MÉDOC ACs St-Julien has the perfect balance between substance and delicacy, between opulence and austerity, between the necessary brashness of youth and the lean-limbed genius of maturity. Although the great PAUILLACs are the models for winemakers across the world, if it were the perfect Bordeaux they sought to emulate, St-Julien should be their target.

There's not very much of it: at 900ha (2224 acres) it is the smallest of the four main Haut-Médoc communal appellations, but almost all of it is vineyard land of the highest class, on gravelly outcrops near the Gironde estuary, and 85 per cent of the land is taken up by 11 Classed Growths. The Second Growths, Ch. LÉOVILLE-LAS-CASES, DUCRU-BEAUCAILLOU and LÉOVILLE-BARTON are the leaders, and not far behind are GRUAUD-LAROSE, LÉOVILLE-POYFERRÉ, LAGRANGE and TALBOT. Also making excellent wine are Branaire-Ducru, BEYCHEVELLE, Gloria, Hortevie, ST-PIERRE and Langoa-Barton. Best years: 1998, '97, '96, '95, '94, '93, '90, '89, '88, '86, '85, '83, '82, '81, '79, '78.

CH. TALBOT
A superb Fourth Growth St-Julien, Ch. Talbot has a reputation for consistency. The wine is chunky, soft-centred but capable of aging extremely well for ten to 20 years.

ST-NICOLAS-DE-BOURGUEIL AC

FRANCE, Loire, Touraine
♟♀ *Cabernet Franc, Cabernet Sauvignon*

This enclave inside the BOURGUEIL area produces two million bottles of red and rosé wine annually. Cabernet Franc is usually the sole grape sometimes with some Cabernet Sauvignon. St-Nicolas has a higher proportion of gravel soils than Bourgueil, otherwise there is little to distinguish between them. It probably owes its existence to a forceful mayor of the village in the 1930s, who insisted that his village deserved an AC of its own. Almost all the wine is red and the best has the piercing raspberry and blackcurrant flavours of neighbouring Bourgueil and CHINON. But they are prone to be a little tannic and have an earthy background which is pleasant enough if the fruit is

there. Drinkable at two to three years, they will last seven to ten years from warm vintages. Best years: 1997, '96, '95, '93, '89, '88, '86, '85. Best producers: Yannick Amirault, Audebert, P Jamet, Lorieux, J P Mabileau, Joël Taluau, Vallée.

ST-PÉRAY AC

FRANCE, Northern Rhône
♀ *Marsanne, Roussanne*

A century ago St-Péray was the producer of France's most famous fizz – after CHAMPAGNE, of course. Sparkling wine is supposed to be lively, vivacious, witty stuff – but this is the hot RHÔNE Valley, and it seems extremely unlikely that the remaining 62ha (153 acres) of vineyards can produce the light, acid wine favoured by fizz-makers. Well, they can't. The Marsanne and Roussanne grapes make big round wines which undergo the Champagne method and turn out as – big round wines with fizz in them. Most of it goes no further than the local bars and restaurants. There is a little still white, usually dry and stolid, but occasionally more exciting. The wine can have a lovely golden feel of nuts and honey and fruit brushed with the spice of apricots and quince, with a flicker of orange peel at the end. This is Marsanne at its best, but it's rare. Best years: 1998, '97, '96, '95, '94. Best producers: Chaboud, CLAPE, DELAS, Gripa, Marcel Juge, Lionnet, Thiers, Voge.

CH. ST-PIERRE

FRANCE, Bordeaux, Haut-Médoc, St-Julien AC
♟ *Cabernet Sauvignon, Merlot, Cabernet Franc*

After a century of anonymity, Ch. St-Pierre (previously St-Pierre-Sevaistre) has stepped forward to claim its place in the sun. It used to be undervalued, and in years like 1979, '81, '82 and '83 you got superb quality at half the price of the better-known ST-JULIENs. It isn't a big property, only 17ha (42 acres), but the vines, close to BEYCHEVELLE, are well sited and old. The wine often lacks the startling beauty of the best St-Julien, but makes up for this with a lush feel and full, almost honeyed flavour – plums and blackberries and soft vanilla backed up by unassertive but effective tannins. It is often ready quite young. Top vintages can easily improve for 20 years. Best years: 1998, '97, '96, '95, '94, '93, '90, '89, '88, '86, '85, '83, '82, '81, '79.

ST-POURÇAIN-SUR-SIOULE VDQS

FRANCE, Upper Loire
♟♟ *Gamay, Pinot Noir*
♀ *Tressallier, Chardonnay, Sauvignon Blanc*

If you've ever had the misfortune to sample Vichy-St-Yorre, you'll begin to understand

the gastronomic distress inflicted upon health-fad tourists taking the waters at Vichy. And you'll agree that after a couple of days spent glugging Vichy water – overpoweringly salty and minerally – even the feeblest brew would be welcomed with open arms. Well, feebleness isn't the problem at St-Pourçain-sur-Sioule, a small VDQS north of Vichy. It's just that most of the wines, the whites in particular, have a very strange smokiness to them, rather like wet hay trying to catch fire. Presumably this is due to the local Tressallier grape. The reds and rosés can have quite a pleasant fruit to them when young. Best years: 1997, '96, '95. The whites are light and generally sharp and rather acidic. About 30 per cent of the production is white, 15 per cent rosé and 55 per cent is red. The well-equipped Union des Vignerons de St-Pourçain accounts for about 60 per cent of production. Best producers: Bellevue, Nebout, Union des Vignerons.

ST-ROMAIN AC

FRANCE, Burgundy, Côte de Beaune
♟ *Pinot Noir*
♀ *Chardonnay*

St-Romain is better known for barrels than wine, since François Frères, barrel-makers to the Domaine de la ROMANÉE-CONTI and other top estates, are based here. Actually there isn't much room for vines, since St-Romain is at the rocky head of a little side valley running up through AUXEY-DURESSES from MEURSAULT, and the difficult growing conditions mean there are more trees than vines around. Part of the problem is altitude: up here the grapes ripen fully only in the warmest years. Only 140ha (346 acres) out of a possible 2000 (4942) are cultivated, and the poor geological situation results in its being the only CÔTE DE BEAUNE AC without any Premiers Crus. In fact, but for kind officialdom and a certain historical reputation for quality, St-Romain would have had to be happy with the lowly HAUTES-CÔTES DE BEAUNE AC.

The reds often have a slightly unnerving earthiness which can verge on the resinous, but they also have a firm, bitter-sweet cherrystone fruit and can age very well for five to seven years. Best years: (reds) 1997, '96, '95, '93, '90. Best producers: Bazenet, H & G Buisson, A Gras, P Taupenot, Thévenin-Monthélie. The white tastes more like a CHABLIS than a Meursault, although Meursault is only a few miles away. The wine is flinty dry, hinting at ripeness but held back by a rather herby, stony personality which can be quite refreshing.

It will probably age well for a good five years or more. Best years: (whites) 1997, '96, '95, '92, '90. Best producers: Bazenet, Buisson, DROUHIN, J Germain, A Gras, Olivier LEFLAIVE, Taupenot, Thévenin-Monthélie.

ST-VÉRAN AC
FRANCE, Burgundy, Mâconnais
♀ *Chardonnay*

Until 1971 the Mâconnais had one star white AC – POUILLY-FUISSÉ – and then merely a welter of MÂCON-VILLAGES; in the south, there was also a certain amount of BEAUJOLAIS Blanc shared with the Beaujolais communes of Leynes, St-Vérand (yes, there is a 'd') and ST-AMOUR. It was clear, however, that these three villages – and five others tightly grouped round the Pouilly-Fuissé AC – were far better than the general run, more closely resembling the classier examples of Pouilly-Fuissé than the normally anonymous glut of Mâcon-Villages. So in 1971 they were given their own AC – St-Véran – and it immediately came to be thought of as a Pouilly-Fuissé understudy. Often, however, it is much more than that, because while the best Pouilly-Fuissés are superb, the majority veer between adequate and disgraceful – whereas the overall quality of St-Véran is good and the price fair.

Oak is very rarely used, revealing the gentle Mâconnais Chardonnay at its clearest and best – very fresh but with a richness combining bananas, apples, pineapples, peaches and even musky grapes, softened with a yeasty creaminess. The wines don't gain a great deal from aging more than a year. Best years: 1997, '96. Best producers: G Chagny, Corsin, Deux Roches, DUBOEUF, B & J-M Drouin, Duperron, Grégoire, Guerrin, Lassarat, E Loron, Lycée Agricole de Davayé, J-L Tissier, J-J Vincent; and the Prissé co-operative.

STE-CROIX-DU-MONT AC
FRANCE, Bordeaux
♀ *Sémillon, Sauvignon Blanc, Muscadelle*

Historically, this is the best of the three sweet wine ACs (LOUPIAC and CADILLAC are the others) that gaze jealously across at SAUTERNES and BARSAC from the other – wrong – side of the Garonne river. The views are magnificent as the vines tumble down what look to be perfectly sited, south-west-facing slopes. But to make great sweet wine, sunshine and a great view aren't enough; you must have the clammy, humid autumn days that encourage the noble rot fungus to shrivel your grapes and concentrate their sugar. The little river Ciron running through Sauternes creates these conditions,

The Cosimo Taurino estate is one of the leading producers in Salice Salentino. Here Francesco Taurino is tying up Chardonnay vines.

but the wide Garonne is far less likely to waft morning mists towards Ste-Croix-du-Mont. Even so, the vines do occasionally produce splendidly rich wines, but more often the wine is mildly sweet – very good as an apéritif or with hors d'oeuvres, but not really luscious enough for the end of a meal. Best years: 1998, '97, '96, '95, '90, '89, '88, '86, '85, '83. Best producers: Crabitan-Bellevue, Loubens, Lousteau-Vieil, du Mont, la Rame.

SAINTSBURY
USA, California, Napa County, Napa Valley AVA
🍷 *Pinot Noir*
♀ *Chardonnay*

Saintsbury was the first CARNEROS winery to find a way of regularly producing high-quality Pinot Noir – something most American wineries are still finding difficult. Garnet is a light, fragrant style, while the straight and Reserve Pinot Noirs are also cherry-perfumed but fuller and more structured. The Chardonnays are delicious, cleverly balancing good fruit with toasty oak. The Reserve is lush and ripe and packed with toasty spice. Best years: 1997, '95, '94, '93, '92.

DUCA DI SALAPARUTA/CORVO
ITALY, Sicily, Vino da Tavola
🍷 *Nerello Mascalese, Perricone, Nero d'Avola*
♀ *Inzolia, Trebbiano, Catarratto*

Corvo is the trading name of the Casa Vinicola Duca di Salaparuta, whose giant-size, state-of-

the-art winery near Sicily's northern coast transforms grapes culled from every corner of the island. The standard red and white have for decades constituted a reliable if unexciting choice on the wine lists of more second-rate Italian restaurants around the world than one could possibly imagine. The winery has decided, though, to nail its banners to the mast with four other higher quality wines. White Colomba Platino has a high proportion of aromatic Inzolia, making it more fragrant than the ordinary white. The reds, Duca Enrico and Terre d'Agala, are based on Nero d'Avola. Aged in barriques, these two serious reds need four to five years to soften their tannins. A similarly oaked Inzolia white, Bianca di Valguarnera, completes a fine foursome. Best years: (Duca Enrico) 1993, '92, '90.

SALICE SALENTINO DOC
ITALY, Puglia
🍷 *Negroamaro, Malvasia Nera, Aleatico*
♀ *Chardonnay, Pinot Blanc (Pinot Bianco), Sauvignon Blanc*

The best known wine of that southern tip of PUGLIA, the Salentino peninsula, is the deep-coloured, richly fruity red from the commune of Salice Salentino. It is made principally from the Negroamaro variety which, centuries ago, made the crossing from Greece, where it still thrives as Xynomavro. Generally its 'black bitterness' is attenuated by a dose of soft, aromatic Malvasia Nera and the wine needs several years to settle down before it comes good. Several other local DOCs (Copertino, Alezio, Brindisi, Leverano, Lizzano, Nardò and Squinzano) are similar in style, some of them including Montepulciano in the blend.

The Salice Salentino DOC extends to an excellent rosé, from the same grapes, and to a rare but potentially lip-smacking aromatic sweet red from the Aleatico grape. The whites are distinctly less interesting. Best years: 1998, '97, '96, '95, '94, '93, '91, '90. Best producers: Candido, de Castris, TAURINO, Vallone. Some of the best wines fall outside the DOC: Cappello di Prete and Duca di Aragona (Candido), Donna Lisa Riserva (de Castris), Notarpanaro and Patriglione (Taurino) and Graticciaia (Vallone).

ERICH SALOMON
AUSTRIA, Niederösterreich, Kremstal, Stein
♀ *Grüner Veltliner, Riesling, Pinot Blanc (Weissburgunder), Gewürztraminer (Traminer)*

Erich Salomon's creation, the Kloster Und, is a rarity in Austria: a vinothèque converted from a former monastery where visitors can eat, drink and be merry on his and other growers' wines. Salomon's own wines are elegant and medium-bodied and among the best in the region, and include Grüner Veltliners and Rieslings of immense character and style. He has some vines in the Steiner Hund vineyard, as well as in Ried Kogl, and Steiner Pfaffenberg. His remarkable dry Traminer is the best example in Austria. Best years: 1998, '97, '95, '94, '93, '92, '91, '90, '86.

SALON

FRANCE, Champagne, Champagne AC
♀ *Chardonnay*

Salon is truly unique: a CHAMPAGNE produced from a single grape variety from a single village, Mesnil, and from a single vintage. Moreover the wine is made in a most uncompromising way, aging for many years on its lees before disgorgement and release. Thus, when many Champagne houses were releasing their 1989s or '90s, Salon was reluctantly allowing its 1983 out of the cellars.

In some years no wine is produced at all, and the grapes, which come from very old vines, are offered to the neighbouring house of Delamotte which, like Salon, is part of the LAURENT-PERRIER group. The style is monumental, austere, powerful and penetrating. This is indeed one of the few Champagnes that really can be enjoyed with a meal. Moreover, it has such richness and breadth that it is possible to consume Salon in a non-dosé (unsweetened) version, as is sometimes done at the winery when unreleased vintages are pulled from the cellar and disgorged. Production is minimal – about 50,000 bottles in any declared vintage – and prices very high, but you do get a lot of flavour for your money. Best years: 1990, '88, '85, '83, '82, '79, '76, '73, '71, '69, '66, '64, '61.

SALON
Few Champagnes can match Salon for depth and power. The fine fruit richness becomes increasingly apparent with age.

SALTA

ARGENTINA

The Cafayate Valley in the province of Salta is Argentina's most northerly and remote wine area. Set in the most beautiful, crisp and clean mountain countryside imaginable, with vineyards being planted at up to 1830m (6000ft),

it is a natural home for the scented, delicate Torrontés. Malbec from here is sensuous, supple and fragrant. Enormous investments are being made in new vineyards, to complement what Pernot Ricard has already committed at Bodegas ETCHART. Salta, though still in a rather rudimentary state, could become a crucial part of the Andean wine scene, offering scent and sensuality rather than power. There are three main producers: Etchart, Michel Torino and an independent member of the Etchart family.

SAMOS AO

GREECE

This mountainous island has its own appellation for Muscat wines. Grown on steep, terraced slopes in vineyards ranging from 150m to 800m (500ft to 2600ft) the Muscat Blanc à Petits Grains grape (local name Moschato Samou) produces sweet wines, primarily a luscious and well-priced fortified Samos Muscat, as well as the deep gold, honeyed Samos Nectar, made from sun-dried grapes and aged in oak, and a dry wine known as Samena. Best producer: Union de Co-operatives Vinicoles de Samos.

SAN FELICE

ITALY, Tuscany, Chianti Classico DOCG
♟ *Sangiovese, Cabernet Sauvignon, Colorino*
♟ *Canaiolo*
♀ *Chardonnay, Vermentino, Sauvignon Blanc and others*

This large estate (with vineyards in Castelnuovo Berardenga in CHIANTI CLASSICO and at Campogiovanni in BRUNELLO DI MONTALCINO) was one of the first to bring quality production to Chianti Classico. From the late 1960s until his death in 1994, Enzo Morganti inspired the transformation of the Castelnuovo estate from the traditional 'promiscuous culture' (vines mixed in with olive and fruit trees, sometimes vegetables) to specialized viticulture, creating in the process one of the first major SUPER-TUSCAN wines (Vigorello – a blend of 80 per cent Sangiovese and Cabernet Sauvignon) and two very fine Chianti Classicos, Poggio Rosso and Il Grigio. Perhaps his most important contribution, however, was his experimental vineyard for purposes of clonal selection, not only for Sangiovese but for lesser Tuscan varieties and international varieties. Best years: 1998, '97, '96, '95, '93, '90.

SAN LUIS OBISPO COUNTY

USA, California

This county includes an historic, warm AVA, PASO ROBLES (2830ha/7000 acres), in its northern interior, and an ocean-cooled, rela-

tively new one, Edna Valley, in its south western corner. Historically, Paso Robles is Zinfandel country, and the onc heady, rustic style has given way to something slightly more polished. Cabernet Sauvignon i tasty here, but Syrah looks highly promising especially from Alban, QUPÉ and MERIDIAN With 608ha (1500 acres) of vineyards, th Edna Valley has a fine record for Chardonnay Best producers: Alban, Claiborne & Churchill, Corbett Canyon, Creston Vine yards, Eberle, EDNA VALLEY VINEYARD, Justin Martin Brothers, Meridian, Morgan, Talley.

SAN PEDRO, SANTA HELENA

CHILE, Lontué Valley
♟ *Cabernet Sauvignon, Merlot*
♀ *Sauvignon Blanc, Riesling, Chardonnay*

San Pedro is one of the oldest and largest Chilean wineries and is now emerging from a dull patch thanks to a take-over by Chile's largest brewery, a new winery and consultancy from the flying winemaker Jacques Lurton. The best wines are sold under the Castillo de Molina label (Sauvignon Blanc, an oak-aged Chardonnay and two Cabernet Sauvignons, one oak-aged. The Gatos label covers the cheaper range.

The nearby winery of Santa Helena has been under the same ownership since the 1970s. Santa Helena has three labels, in ascending order: Gran Viño; Siglo de Oro for Sauvignon, Cabernet, Merlot and a lightly oaked Chardonnay; and Seleccion del Directorio for a Cabernet, aged in American oak, and Chardonnay, fermented in French barriques. The quality is not great as yet and the wines need more fruit flavours.

SAN PEDRO
The revival in quality at the large San Pedro winery is shown in the Castillo de Molina range of wines, both white and red.

SEÑORÍO DE SAN VICENTE

SPAIN, La Rioja, Rioja DOC
♟ *Tempranillo Peludo*

For the past century, the Eguren family has been making the best wines in the Sonsierra area of the RIOJA Alta sub-region – the only part of Rioja Alta on the left bank of the Ebro river. The imposing Sierra de Cantabria mountains give their name to the family's traditional bodega in San Vicente de la Sonsierra, where wines of exceptional value are made. In 1991 a separate bodega was created to vinify the grapes from the family's best vineyard, 18ha (44½ acres) of poor, pale, chalky soils planted to the unique Tempranillo Peludo ('hairy' Tempranillo) clone, a Sonsierra speciality which gives low yields but great finesse. The San Vicente cuvée is one of the most elegant and silkiest of the new-age Riojas. Some 5000 cases are made annually by Marcos Eguren, the enologist in the family. Best years: 1995, '94, '91.

SANCERRE AC

FRANCE, Central Loire

♥ ♟ *Pinot Noir*

♟ *Sauvignon Blanc*

The omni-thirsty Henry IV of France is on record as saying that if all his subjects were to drink Sancerre there'd be no more religious wars. Louis XVI said much the same thing a short while before the French Revolution proved otherwise. And then, in the 1970s, some Paris journalists (always on the lookout for a new fad wine) noticed the high mound of Sancerre rising above the Loire, tasted the wines from its steep chalk and flint vineyards, and tore back to Paris with the news – Sancerre was the super-freshest, ultra-modernest white wine in France. Sancerre-mania broke out – first with the white, which can indeed be a wonderful, refreshing drink, tasting of nettles, asparagus and gooseberries, and a whiff of brewing coffee, and then with the far less exciting reds and rosés. This is excellent news for the growers, but Sancerre is now the expense-account white and consequently is rarely a bargain.

But even so, a Sancerre from a village like Bué, Chavignol, Verdigny or Ménétréol, made by a good grower in a vintage which wasn't too hot, and drunk before it is two years old, can be one of the most deliciously refreshing French whites. The top wines can last for five years or so. Over the last three or four years a group of young producers has emerged, who have inspired a greater emphasis on quality. Now the overall level is higher in Sancerre than in neighbouring POUILLY-FUMÉ. Best years: (whites) 1998, '97, '96, '95. Best producers: Bailly-Reverdy, BOURGEOIS, Cotat, Crochet, André Dezat, Gitton, Laloue, Serge Laporte, Alphonse MELLOT, Merlin-Charrier, Migeon, Paul Milléroux, Henri Natter, Vincent Pinard, Pascal and Nicolas Reverdy, Reverdy-Cadet, Jean-Max Roger, Vacheron, André Vatan.

Pre-phylloxera Sancerre was largely a red wine area. In modern times the emphasis has been on Sauvignon, with Pinot Noir often relegated to the least good sites. Now there is increased emphasis on the reds and, although quality is still very variable, growers like Alphonse Mellot, Nicolas Reverdy and the Vacherons are making concentrated, serious reds especially in years like 1996 and '97. There are two styles of reds: light, charming quaffers and a few more concentrated examples that benefit from three or four years' aging. The rosé is usually very dry, sometimes with a hint of fruit. Best years: (reds) 1997, '96, '95. Best producers: (reds) Bailly-Reverdy, André Dezat, Alphonse MELLOT, Pascal and Nicolas Reverdy, Jean-Max Roger, Vacheron.

LUCIANO SANDRONE

ITALY, Piedmont, Barolo DOCG

♥ *Nebbiolo, Barbera, Dolcetto*

Sandrone learned the art of making great BAROLO as winemaker at Marchesi di Barolo. He began producing wine from his own grapes in the late 1970s, and increasing fame induced him in the late 1990s to set up on his own. Today, his cru Cannubi Boschis and blend Le Vigne, wines at their best miraculously combining power and concentration with elegance, are almost impossible to obtain even at high prices. Generally associated with the Barolo modernists, Sandrone uses French oak *tonneaux* for aging his Barolo and barriques for his Barbera d'Alba. The unoaked Dolcetto is another impressive mouthful of sheer fruit. Best years: 1998, '97, '96, '95, '93, '90.

SANFORD WINERY

USA, California, Santa Barbara County, Santa Ynez Valley AVA

♥ *Pinot Noir*

♟ *Chardonnay, Sauvignon Blanc*

Richard Sanford has one of the longest track records for winemaking in SANTA BARBARA COUNTY. Balanced, richly varietal yet green-streaked Pinot Noirs are his mainstay, primarily from the Santa Maria Valley AVA and the tip-top Benedict vineyard in Santa Ynez Valley. There is also a good new 'Signature' series of Pinot Noir. Best years: 1998, '97, '96, '95, '94, '93, '92, '91, '90. The Chardonnays are huge, a remarkable balance of fruit and toast, and his Sauvignon Blancs, oaked or unoaked, are far better than most examples from CALIFORNIA. Best years: 1998, '97, '96, '95, '94, '93, '92, '91.

SANGIOVESE

Almost certainly of Tuscan origin, Italy's most-planted grape variety (100,000ha/ 247,100 acres) is by far the most important one in central Italy. Indeed, it is planted in at least 16 of Italy's 20 regions, not to mention in several other countries, notably California and Argentina. Along with Barbera, Sangiovese is undisputedly the nearest Italy gets to an 'international' grape variety.

Sub-varieties and clones abound, even within small areas, sometimes graced with exotic or parochial names like San Zoveto (the first recorded name, in the year 1600), Sangioveto (central Tuscany and Elba), Brunello (Montalcino, though for fear of Californian rip-offs the name no longer applies to a grape but only to a wine), Prugnolo Gentile (Montepulciano) and Romagnolo (Romagna), all of which have greater marketing than ampelographical significance. The fundamental distinction is between Sangiovese Grosso and Sangiovese Piccolo, the adjectives mainly referring to berry size. The Grosso is generally considered superior, and is more diffuse. But the reality is that over a period of time within a given area it becomes difficult, if not impossible, to distinguish between them. Perhaps the main point to remember is that Sangiovese is a highly adaptable variety, capable of changing radically, even morphologically in terms of leaf shape, bunch character and berry size, according to its immediate environment – much more so than Merlot or Cabernet Sauvignon varieties.

In California, Sangiovese was a late arrival, despite the number of immigrant Italian wine families. In the 1990s Sangiovese began slowly but has mounted a bit of a charge as growers in Napa and Sonoma led the way in planting it. Winemakers are trying out various styles of wine, from simple and tart to super-Tuscan versions blended with Cabernet Sauvignon and aged in small oak barrels.

Argentina's Sangiovese was brought to the country by waves of Italian immigrants and ripens fully here to produce an attractive fruity wine.

SANKT ANTONY
GERMANY, Rheinhessen, Nierstein
♀ *Riesling, Silvaner, Weissburgunder*

The MAN truck company should count itself lucky to have Dr Alex Michalsky running its wine estate in NIERSTEIN, for he not only makes the best wines in town, but also some of the best dry Rieslings in all Germany. Full of ripe peach and berry flavours and mineral extract from the red slate soil, they have a rich texture and generous natural alcohol which makes them closer to top Alsace wines than the lean, acidic style most wine drinkers associate with German Riesling. The top sites are the Oelberg and Pettenthal, with the Orbel closing fast as the vines there gain in age. Best years: 1998, '96, '94, '93, '92, '91, '90, '89.

SANT'ANTIMO DOC
ITALY, Tuscany
♂ *Cabernet Sauvignon, Merlot, Pinot Noir (Pinot Nero)*
♀ *Chardonnay, Sauvignon, Pinot Gris (Pinot Grigio)*

This recent DOC (1996) is named after the sublime basilica of Sant'Antimo in the BRUNELLO DI MONTALCINO hinterlands and was devised as a catch-all DOC for VINO DA TAVOLA wines from the south-east corner of the Montalcino area that are not 100 per cent Sangiovese. Apart from various varietal wines, the DOC covers a blended white and a blended red, which may be from any combination of indigenous Tuscan and international varieties, VIN SANTO (including Occhio di Pernice) and joy of joys, a juicy Novello. Best producers: too early to tell.

SANTA BARBARA COUNTY
USA, California

This coastal county north of Los Angeles is where many Hollywood stars and politicians retire, usually to large ranches. It is also where some of CALIFORNIA's most distinctive Pinot Noir and Chardonnay grapes now grow. Vineyard development did not begin in

SANFORD
One of Santa Barbara's pioneers, Richard Sanford put the region on the map with a series of big, powerful, yet velvety textured Pinot Noirs.

earnest until the late 1960s, and today there are 4450ha (11,000 acres) of vineyards. Both of Santa Barbara's AVAs – Santa Ynez Valley and Santa Maria Valley – are sufficiently cooled by ocean breezes and fog to do justice also to Riesling and Gewürztraminer.

Santa Maria Valley is one of California's coolest wine areas. It is also one of California's only true east-west valleys, and was dragged into prominence by Byron Vineyards and later by AU BON CLIMAT, QUPÉ and Cambria. Pinot Noir is the rising star, especially from the Bien Nacido vineyard, and Qupé excels with Syrah. Other best producers: BABCOCK, Cambria, FIRESTONE, Foxen, Gainey, Lane TANNER, Andrew Murray, Il Podere dell'Olivos, Rancho Sisquoc, SANFORD, Whitcraft and Zaca Mesa.

SANTA CAROLINA
CHILE, Maipo Valley
♂ *Cabernet Sauvignon, Merlot*
♀ *Sauvignon Blanc, Chardonnay*

Santa Carolina was founded in 1875 by Luis Pereira Cotapos, who wanted to celebrate his wife's name in the finest way he knew how – by naming a bodega after her. He turned to Germain Bachelet, a Frenchman, for advice and so solid were the foundations they laid that not only is the firm still in business, but the Santa Carolina bodega has been declared a national monument!

Modern investment has meant that the winery has kept pace with the times. Grapes come from Maipo, San Fernando and, more recently, CASABLANCA (especially high-quality Sauvignon Blanc and Chardonnay). The Gran Reserva Merlot and Cabernet are the best reds and drink well with two to four years' aging. The whites include a good Sauvignon Blanc and Chardonnay Reservas and an excellent botrytized Semillon-Sauvignon Blanc. Drink the dry whites soon after release. VIÑA CASABLANCA is a sister winery.

SANTA RITA
CHILE, Maipo Valley
♂ *Cabernet Sauvignon*
♀ *Sauvignon Blanc, Chardonnay, Riesling and others*

Santa Rita was the first Chilean winery to make a real impression on the export market in the 1980s with its succulent, juicy reds. The 120 range (named after 120 patriots who hid from the Spanish in Santa Rita's cellars) was such good value that it couldn't fail to impress. Inexplicably, Santa Rita turned to making wines in a tougher, leaner style, but it now looks as though fruit is on the way back. Santa Rita owns vineyards in the

Maipo Valley, 40km (25 miles) south of Santiago, and three other valleys, CASABLANCA, Rapel and Maule. The Maipo successes include the much-improved Casa Real Cabernet Sauvignon which has all the spicy, blackcurrant-soaked fruit that used to prove so seductive in the past. The Casablanca stars are a dark, juicy Pinot Noir under the 120 label, and a Merlot and Chardonnay under the Medalla Real label. The arrival of winemaker, Andres Ilabaca from CANEPA should see quality continue to improve. Best years: 1998, '97, '96.

SANTENAY AC
FRANCE, Burgundy, Côte de Beaune
♂ *Pinot Noir*
♀ *Chardonnay*

You can almost taste the CÔTE DE BEAUNE winding down in the red wines of Santenay, yet the village (really a little town) is an important one, and there are good wines. The vineyards to the north-east, well angled towards the morning sun, give the best wines – rarely heavy and sometimes a little stony and dry, but reasonably fruity and reasonably priced. Occasionally a full, rather savoury style appears from a Premier Cru vineyard like les Gravières, on the border with CHASSAGNE-MONTRACHET, and it is worth aging Santenay for at least four to six years in the hope that the wine will open out. Best years: (reds) 1997, '96, '95, '93, '90. Best producers: A Belland, J Belland, Bourgeot, CLAIR, Colin, Fleurot-Larose, Girardin, Louis Lequin, Mestre, B Morey, POUSSE D'OR, Prieur-Brunet, Roux.

Most Santenay white is drunk locally, since the village has a casino and a spa to boost demand. The wine isn't bad but often has that rather earthy lack of definition which affects a lot of the red. The best results come from the les Gravières Premier Cru. Best years: (whites) 1997, '96, '95, '92. Best producers: Bourgeot, Jaffelin, Jessiaume, Louis Lequin, Maufoux, Prieur-Brunet.

SANTORINI AO
GREECE

This small, volcanic Aegean island produces high-quality dry whites, both oaked and unoaked, mainly from the Assyrtiko grape (which is wonderful for retaining its acidity in hot climates). Additionally there is Vissanto, a wine of great antiquity, originally the communion wine of the Greek Orthodox Church, made from sun-dried grapes. Best years: 1997, 94. Best producers: Boutari, Gaia Thalassitis, Sigalas.

CAVES SÃO JOÃO

PORTUGAL, Beira Litoral, Bairrada DOC, Dão DOC

♟ *Bairrada: Baga, Periquita, Moreto; Dão: Touriga Nacional, Jaen, Bastardo*

♀ *Bairrada: Fernão Pires (Maria Gomes), Bical; Dão: Arinto, Dona Branca, Barcelo, Encruzado*

Wines from this resolutely traditional family firm have long been among the best in both BAIRRADA and DÃO. The Frei João Bairrada and Porta dos Cavaleiros Dão reds are both rich and complex, the Reservas (with cork labels) particularly so, and develop impressively with age. Even the white wines have real character and age well in bottle. Much of the wine is bought in from local growers and co-operatives and aged in neat, cobwebby cellars in the heart of the Bairrada region at São João de Anadia. Selection is paramount. It is perhaps paradoxical for such a traditional firm that São João's latest venture has been to plant Cabernet Sauvignon on the family's own estate at Quinta do Poço do Lobo.

Although not entitled to the Bairrada DOC, Caves São João has managed to produce a very passable BORDEAUX-style red from maritime central Portugal. Best years: 1997, '95, '94, '92, '91, '90, '85, '83.

SARDEGNA (SARDINIA)

ITALY

Traditional Sardinian wines are big, fat and strong: some dry, and a goodly number sweet and sticky. But there are also plenty of light, fresh wines, red, white and rosé, from all over the island, mostly from the co-operatives. This huge, hilly island was ruled by the Spanish for many years and grapes of Spanish origin dominate production. The major red grape, Cannonau, is none other than Spain's Garnacha. Native grapes include Nuragus and Vernaccia. Best producers: ARGIOLAS, Santadi co-operative, SELLA & MOSCA.

SASSICAIA

ITALY, Tuscany, Bolgheri Sassicaia DOC

♟ *Cabernet Sauvignon, Cabernet Franc*

Sassicaia, from the Tenuta San Guido estate at BOLGHERI near the Tuscan coast, started the Cabernet Sauvignon craze in Tuscany. The first commercial release, in 1968, astounded everyone with its wonderfully seductive, fruit-dominated, blackcurrant and mint flavours. The archetypal SUPER-TUSCAN, it was also the first of the big-gun VINO DA TAVOLAs to be absorbed into the DOC system when it was awarded its very own sub-zone status in 1994, under the simultaneously created Bolgheri DOC.

Devised by the BORDEAUX-loving Marchese Mario Incisa della Rochetta, father of the present incumbent Niccolò, Sassicaia was conceived along cru classé lines, with the help of Bordeaux's Professor Émile Peynaud and Italy's most renowned enologist, Giacomo Tachis of ANTINORI. Aged for 18 months to two years in French barriques and another year at least in bottle before release, the blend is Cabernet Sauvignon with a touch of Cabernet Franc. Older vintages have demonstrated that Sassicaia ages well and from a good vintage it continues to blossom for 20 years or more. Some say the greatest year ever was 1985, but 1997, '95, '93, '90, '88, '84, '83, '78, '75 and '68 are all memorable.

SAUMUR AC

FRANCE, Loire, Anjou-Saumur

♟♟ *Cabernet Franc, Cabernet Sauvignon, Pineau d'Aunis*

♀ *Chenin Blanc, Chardonnay, Sauvignon Blanc*

You only have to taste the basic still white wine of Saumur to realize why most of it is rapidly transformed into fizz – it is thin, harsh stuff, often showing off the Chenin Blanc grape at its graceless worst. Now change is in the air, in line with the improvements being made with Chenin Blanc elsewhere in the LOIRE Valley. Producers like Jean-Pierre Chevallier (Ch. de VILLENEUVE), Philippe Vatan (Ch. du Hureau), the Foucault brothers at CLOS ROUGEARD and Thierry Germain, as well as the St Cyr-en-Bourg co-operative, are showing how complex properly ripe and well made dry Chenin wine can be. Fortunately, the important local *négociant*, ACKERMAN-LAURANCE, has also realized that there is no longer any future in poor quality wines.

The Saumur region is also a fairly important producer of rather sharp reds, mainly from Cabernet Franc and lighter than those from the SAUMUR-CHAMPIGNY AC. There is a little reasonable dry to off-dry Cabernet rosé. There is also a little sweet white Coteaux de Saumur. Best years: 1998, '97, '96, '95. Best producers: Clos Rougeard (Foucault), Yves Drouineau, Fourrier, Ch. du Hureau, Pérols, Roches Neuves, St-Cyr-en-Bourg co-operative, Patrick Vadé, de VILLENEUVE.

SAUMUR-CHAMPIGNY AC

FRANCE, Loire, Anjou-Saumur

♟ *Cabernet Franc, Cabernet Sauvignon, Pineau d'Aunis*

The vineyards for the best red wine in the SAUMUR region are found on a chalk and lime-

stone plateau above the river Loire. Cabernet Franc is the dominant grape, and in hot years the wine can be superb, with a piercing scent of blackcurrants and raspberries easily overpowering the earthy finish. There are two styles of Saumur-Champigny: one is a light, early quaffer while the other, one of the best reds in the Loire, is more concentrated and may have had some wood aging. An increasing number of producers make several cuvées of differing weight and concentration. Technically it is permissible to use Pineau d'Aunis in the blend but this is now very rare. Best years: 1998, '97, '96, '95, '93, '90, '89. Best producers: Chaintre, Duveau, Filliatreau (especially the Vieilles Vignes cuvée), CLOS ROUGEARD (Foucault), Thierry Germain, Ch. du Hureau, Legrand, Neau, Roches Neuves, St-Cyr-en-Bourg co-operative, Sanzay, Val Brun, Ch. de VILLENEUVE.

CLOS ROUGEARD

Les Poyeux is a single-vineyard wine from Cabernet Franc and with an emerging bouquet of floral, herbal notes, berried fruit and some oak.

SAUMUR MOUSSEUX AC

FRANCE, Loire, Anjou-Saumur

♀♟ *Chenin Blanc, Chardonnay, Cabernet Franc, Grolleau, Sauvignon Blanc, Cabernet Sauvignon, Cot, Gamay, Pineau d'Aunis, Pinot Noir*

For many years SAUMUR Mousseux – made by the CHAMPAGNE method since 1811 – was regarded as the natural cheap alternative to Champagne. However, the Chenin base wine doesn't have the ability of Champagne's Chardonnay or Pinot Noir to start harsh and dry yet fill out, after a few years, to something gentle and honeyed. Nor does it pick up the creamy, toasty flavours of the yeast cells which lie in the bottle during the second fermentation, and which are a mark of true Champagne. So you could only use it as a substitute for 'cheap' Champagne (classy Champagne taste-alikes are CRÉMANT DE BOURGOGNE or CRÉMANT D'ALSACE). Efforts are now being made to produce a rather more charming wine, and the addition of Chardonnay and Cabernet Franc (red but pressed as white) does make for softer, more interesting results. Best producers: Bouvet-Ladubay, GRATIEN & Meyer, Caves de Grenelle, Nerleux, St-Cyr-en-Bourg co-operative.

SAUTERNES France, Bordeaux

IT SEEMS STRANGE TO THINK that not long ago the names Sauternes and Barsac had come to suggest sweet gooey wines without much character, to be passed off on anyone who doesn't like dry wines. This implies that they are easy and cheap to produce, and incapable of achieving any memorable personality. Nothing could be further from the truth – these are the best sweet wines in the world. The production of fine sweet white wine is an exhausting, risk-laden and extremely time-consuming and expensive affair, requiring nerves of steel, a huge bank balance, and just the right mix of grape varieties, vineyard sites and quite idiosyncratic local climatic conditions. It so happens that Bordeaux has half a dozen localities where, to a greater or lesser extent, the vineyards and the climate get the balance right.

Greatest of these areas are Barsac and Sauternes. Just north of the town of Langon, the little river Ciron sidles up from the south to join the larger river Garonne. On the Ciron's east bank lie the vineyards of Sauternes and on its west bank those of Barsac. Adjoining Barsac to the north is Cérons, whose speciality is a light sweet white, but increasingly Cérons vineyards are now producing reds and dry whites (which are not allowed the Cérons AC). On the opposite bank of the Garonne river are the areas of Cadillac, Loupiac and Ste-Croix-du-Mont whose speciality is also sweet white wine, but whose vineyards rarely produce anything with the concentration of a good Sauternes.

Sauternes and Barsac produce the most exciting sweet wines because their vineyards enjoy humid conditions ideal for the onset of 'noble rot' or *pourriture noble* which is caused by the fungus *Botrytis cinerea* which settles on the skins of the grapes, feeding off the water inside. This dramatically reduces the amount of juice, but what is left is extra concentrated in sugar and flavour. Noble rot occurs only in the autumn months, and needs a mixture of humidity and warmth to take root. On warm autumn days, fogs rise off the river in the mornings, only to be driven away later in the day by the sun's heat – the perfect combination. Cérons and the ACs on the Garonne's right bank get these conditions to a much lesser

Distinguished as a Premier Cru Classé in the famous 1855 Bordeaux Classification, Ch. d'Yquem is still recognized as the world's greatest sweet wine. Its richness and astonishingly exotic flavour mean it is constantly in demand.

degree than they do in Sauternes and Barsac. Noble rot usually strikes late in the autumn, if at all, so the possibility of storms are an ever-present threat for the growers, since a couple of days' heavy rain can dilute the juice and bloat the grapes. In some years the whole crop can be ruined this way.

Another complication is that noble rot does not strike consistently. On one bunch, some grapes may be totally rotted, some may be partially affected and some untouched. So the pickers have to go through the vines time after time snipping off only the most affected bunches, or sometimes only the most rotted single grapes on a bunch! Needless to say, anything so labour-intensive is very expensive, and takes a lot of time, sometimes dragging on for more than two

CH. DE FARGUES

This small property making fine, rich wine is owned by the Lur-Saluces family of Yquem fame and run with similar perfectionist zeal.

CH. LAFAURIE-PEYRAGUEY

From a property now returned to cracking form, this is wonderfully balanced, beautifully rich Sauternes, usually scented with new oak to great effect.

CH. COUTET

Barsac's largest Cru Classé property makes sweet wines that are aromatic and complex with added concentration in recent vintages.

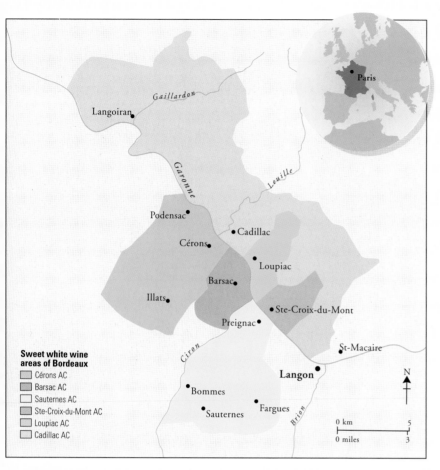

Sweet white wine areas of Bordeaux
- Cérons AC
- Barsac AC
- Sauternes AC
- Ste-Croix-du-Mont AC
- Loupiac AC
- Cadillac AC

CH. LA TOUR BLANCHE
Thanks to dynamic direction and a generous investment in new oak for both fermentation and aging, this wine now has the rich unctuousness of great Sauternes.

CH. DOISY-VÉDRINES
From the commune of Barsac, this rich, intensely fruity wine is one of the most reliable Sauternes, and usually good value, too.

CH. NAIRAC
The influence of fermentation and aging in new oak casks produces a concentrated oaky style of Sauternes.

CH. RAYNE-VIGNEAU
Huge investments here have brought impressive results and this great Sauternes property, enjoying probably the finest soil and mesoclimate after d'Yquem, is once more on the rise.

months – and only the top châteaux, whose wines command the very top prices, can afford to do this.

When you realize that a single vine may produce as little as one glass of wine, as against the bottle or more that a producer of dry wine could expect, it becomes painfully obvious that we've been underestimating – and underpricing – these great wines for far too long.

AC ENTRIES
Barsac, Cadillac, Loupiac, Ste-Croix-du-Mont, Sauternes.

CHÂTEAUX ENTRIES
Bastor-Lamontagne, Broustet, Climens, Coutet, Doisy-Daëne, Doisy-Védrines, de Fargues, Gilette, Guiraud, Lafaurie-Peyraguey, Nairac, Rieussec, St-Amand, Suduiraut, la Tour Blanche, d'Yquem.

CH. RABAUD-PROMIS
At last, vintages since the mid-1980s have shown a long-awaited return to First Growth quality and the wines are rich and opulent but with fine balancing acidity.

CH. SUDUIRAUT
Often regarded as a close runner-up to Yquem, new ownership should ensure the rivalry is maintained.

CH. GILETTE
This remarkable property ages its wines in concrete tanks for 20–30 years before releasing them.

CH. CLIMENS
The leading estate in Barsac, using rigorous selection to keep yields low, makes rich, elegant wines with a light, lemony acidity ensuring wonderful freshness.

CH. RIEUSSEC
Situated on a hill adjacent to Ch. d'Yquem, Rieussec has a reputation for producing the richest, most succulent wine of Sauternes.

SAUTERNES AC

FRANCE, Bordeaux

♀ *Sémillon, Sauvignon Blanc, Muscadelle*

See also Sauternes, pages 336–337

What marks out this small enclave of vineyards on the left bank of the Garonne is the particular susceptibility of its grapes to go rotten before they are picked in the autumn.

That doesn't sound very encouraging so I'll explain. If you ripen a grape fully during a good summer, it will have enough sugar to convert to a lot of alcohol during fermentation, but the wine will be dry. For a really sweet wine you need to have so much sugar in the grapes that the yeasts ferment out as much as they can, yet you are still left with masses of unfermented sugar to provide rich concentration. That's where the 'rot' comes in. There is a particular sort of rot (called 'noble') which attacks grapes and, instead of ruining the flavour, eats into the skin, then sucks out the water in the grape, leaving behind most of the sugar, which then gets more and more concentrated, and may end up twice as strong as in a normally ripe grape with perhaps 25 degrees of potential alcohol in the sugar. Since yeast can't convert more than about 14–15 degrees to alcohol, all the rest remains as sweetness. The result is a wine of high alcoholic strength and deep, mouth-coating richness, full of flavours like pineapples, peaches, syrup and spice.

In some vintages the 'rot' doesn't develop, and then it is not possible to make intensely sweet wine, although it may still be sold as Sauternes, and can be a pleasant, adequately sweet drink, especially from a château that uses modern methods of cryo-extraction to concentrate the sugar. It is always expensive, though, because the permitted yield is extremely low at 25 hectolitres per hectare – less than half that of a HAUT-MÉDOC red – and because production is labour intensive, the grapes being selectively picked. Sometimes pickers make up to seven or eight passages or *tris* through the vines. The top wines are also fermented and aged in new oak barrels. Good vintages should age for five to ten years and often twice as long. Best years: 1998, '97, '96, '95, '90, '89, '88, '86, '83, '81, '80, '76, '75, '71, '70. Best producers: Cru Barrejats, BASTOR-LAMONTAGNE, Clos Haut-Peyraguey, DOISY-DAËNE, DOISY-VÉDRINES, de FARGUES, GILETTE, GUIRAUD, les Justices, Lafaurie-Peyraguey, Lamothe-Guignard, de Malle, Rabaud-Promis, Rayne-Vigneau, RIEUSSEC, ST-AMAND, Sigalas-Rabaud, SUDUIRAUT, La TOUR BLANCHE, YQUEM.

SAUVIGNON BLANC

This is a grape that wears its heart on its sleeve. Its wine is sharp, green and tangy, reeking of newly mown grass, gooseberries and crushed nettles and blackcurrant leaves, clear, clean and refreshing. It seldom has any great complexity, whether it is sweet or dry, oaked or unoaked. That description is of classic Sancerre or Pouilly-Fumé from France's Loire Valley, the benchmark areas for Sauvignon wine – until New Zealand came along.

It is also grown by the mile in Bordeaux, but has never been so popular, for the simple reason that instead of tasting of fresh gooseberries it was liable in the past to taste of old socks. But the spread of cold fermentation worked wonders, and the average Bordeaux Blanc Sec, made entirely or mostly from Sauvignon Blanc, while lacking the pungency of the Loire wines, is at least these days likely to be clean and fresh, even if dull. In the northern Graves area of Pessac-Léognan where white wines are made from a majority of Sauvignon Blanc, fermentation and aging in new oak barrels has provided a rich, citrus, tropical fruit and vanilla slant to the variety.

Sauvignon Blanc plays a big part in the blend for Sauternes and Barsac. It is susceptible to noble rot, though less so than Sémillon, and freshens up the wine no end, adding crucial zip. It is often similarly employed in the New World but most Sauvignon Blanc, however, is made dry. Regional characteristics come through strongly, with California producing wines that are melony or sweetly grassy, sometimes asparagus-like in flavour. North Coast vineyards and the northern Napa Valley produce the most melony wines while the southern Napa wines are grassier and those from Sonoma even grassier still. It was Robert Mondavi who coined the now-popular New World synonym for Sauvignon Blanc: his dry Fumé Blanc is aged in new oak and shows a distinctly rounder character, more vanilla and less grass.

This second style has spread rapidly, but the distinction between the two names, since it is nowhere legally defined, has become muddled. A wine from California or Australia labelled Fumé Blanc may be slightly sweet, be blended with other grape varieties, or indeed not be Sauvignon Blanc at all.

In Australia Sauvignon Blanc tends to be broad, generous and tropical-fruit-flavoured, sometimes gooseberryish and often aged in oak. It seldom approaches the pungency of the New Zealand examples – because these have really shown the world what can be done with the grape, particularly in the Marlborough region of South Island. Cloudy Bay may be the cult wine but it is by no means the only one: New Zealand Sauvignon Blancs may be brilliantly gooseberryish or tropically fruity; they are often highly aromatic, generally full in texture, strong in acid and quite unmistakable.

South Africa has had Sauvignon Blanc since the 1920s but only since the early 1980s has the cool region of Constantia proved that Sauvignon world-beaters could be produced in South Africa. Styles vary from the overtly New World, with ripe tropical character, to the more aggressive flinty keenness of the Loire. The majority of wines are unwooded.

The occasional good example emerging from eastern Europe, especially Hungary and Drama in Northern Greece, shows that these countries, too, could do good things with the grape. Austria produces clean, acidic versions, particularly from Steiermark, under the pseudonym of Muscat-Sylvaner. Sauvignon has been present in Italy for well over 100 years, but it is only recently that producers, mainly in Friuli and Alto Adige, have begun making high-class wine. Recently, too, the grape has begun to spread south, penetrating as far as Puglia and Sicily. Sauvignon Blanc is playing a growing role in Spain, mostly in Rueda and Cataluña, where it usually produces freshly aromatic wines.

DOMAINE DES BAUMARD
As part owners of the Clos du Papillon, the Baumard family produce fine Savennières, combining accessibility with elegance and a typical ability to age.

SAVENNIÈRES AC

FRANCE, Anjou-Saumur
♀ *Chenin Blanc*

Savennières is often hailed as the crowning dry wine glory of the Chenin grape – and there are two vineyards designated Grand Cru which further enhance this theory. But as frequently happens with Chenin, the wine is so rough and unfriendly when young, and the maturation period is so painfully slow – often lasting ten years or more – that it is difficult to embrace Savennières' undoubted quality in an entirely whole-hearted way.

The AC's 80ha (198 acres) are on perilously steep slopes on the north bank of the Loire, opposite the little river Layon, and annual production veers between 70,000 and 170,000 bottles – the wide variation is caused by a particularly capricious mesoclimate. Because Savennières used traditionally to be a sweet wine, the AC laws only allow a very low yield of 30 hectolitres per hectare, and demand a very high minimum alcohol of 12 degrees. This results in much wine having to be declassified to Anjou AC in cooler years.

Young Savennières is gum-judderingly dry – the sensation is of feeling, rather than tasting, as the steely, ice-bright wine sweeps over your palate. But the wines do get there in the end. Even if it takes a decade or two, honey begins to soften the steel, and the creaminess of nuts soothes the gaunt herb-harsh dryness. But even at the peak of maturity, there'll still be an acid freshness.

The two Grand Cru vineyards have their own ACs. They are Savennières-la-Coulée-de-Serrant, a 7-ha (17-acre) plot which makes the subtlest and most refined wine; and another vineyard twice the size, Savennières-la-Roche-aux-Moines, whose wines are lighter, but also extremely good. Best years: 1998, '97, '96, '95, '93, '90, '89, '88, '85, '83, '82, '78, '76, '71, '70, '69, '66. Best producers: Baumard, Bizolière, Chamboureau, Clos de la Coulée-de-Serrant, Clos de Varennes (Bernard Germain), Closel, d'Épiré, Madame Laroche, Ch. de Pierre-Bise, Soulez.

SAVIGNY-LÈS-BEAUNE AC

FRANCE, Burgundy, Côte de Beaune
♀ *Pinot Noir*
♀ *Chardonnay, Pinot Blanc*

Although Savigny-lès-Beaune is off the main 'Côte', in the side valley through which the Autoroute du Soleil now leaps, its parish boundaries are far flung, spreading right down to BEAUNE, and across to ALOXE-CORTON. The vines follow the cleft in the hills, facing both north-east and south to south-east. This less than perfect aspect does show in the wines, which are usually fairly light with a rough minerally streak, but there can also be a very pleasant strawberry fruit. The richest Premiers Crus tend to be Marconnets and Narbautons; the most elegant include Lavières and Vergelesses.

Savigny whites aren't terribly impressive when young, but manage to show a bit of dry, nutty class after three or four years. Best years: (reds) 1997, '96, '95, '93, '90, '89, '88; (whites) 1996, '95, '92, '90, '88, '86. Best producers: Bize, Camus-Bruchon, CHANDON DE BRAILLES, Bruno CLAIR, Écard, Fougeray, Girard-Vollot, Guillemot, LEROY, Maréchal, Pavelot, TOLLOT-BEAUT, Villamont.

VIN DE SAVOIE AC

FRANCE, Savoie
♀ *Mondeuse, Gamay, Pinot Noir*
♀ *Altesse, Jacquère, Chardonnay, Roussanne and others*

Apart from CRÉPY and SEYSSEL, which have their own ACs, most Savoie wines are simply labelled Vin de Savoie AC, sometimes with the name of a village. The best of these are Abymes, Apremont, Arbin, Chignin, Cruet and Montmélian. The vines here have to contend with holiday chalets, ski-lifts and fairly intense agriculture – so they tend to spring up all over the region, wherever there's a south-facing slope not yet nabbed for a ski run. There are 1700ha (4200 acres) of vineyards altogether, producing about 16 million bottles a year, most of it white wine. You can age the wines for a year or two, especially those with some Chardonnay in them, but then they lose their thrilling snap of tangy fruit.

There is some good sparkling wine made, but most of that comes under its own appellation at Seyssel, although Ayze, south-east of Geneva, also has a reputation for it – and its own AC within the Vin de Savoie. The best reds are made from the Mondeuse grape; plummy, chewy wines capable of aging. Best years: 1998, '97, '96, '95. Best producers: Belluard, Boniface, Cavaillé, Cave de Chau-

tagne, Monin, Monterminod, Neyroud, Perret, Perrier, Quénard, de Ripaille, Rocailles, Tiollier, le Vigneron Savoyard.

SAXENBURG

SOUTH AFRICA, Western Cape, Stellenbosch WO
♀ *Cabernet Sauvignon, Shiraz, Pinotage, Merlot and others*
♀ *Chenin Blanc, Chardonnay, Sauvignon Blanc and others*

After a few false starts in its modern renaissance, this Kuils River property finally found top gear with the 1991 vintage. Its success is in no small part due to the symbiotic partnership between the philosophical owner, Swiss businessman Adrian Buhrer, and his decidedly non-mainstream Afrikaaner winemaker, Nico van der Merwe. They make a successful pair in both hemispheres; van der Merwe is also in charge of winemaking at Buhrer's other property, Ch. Capion, neighbour to MAS DE DAUMAS GASSAC in the LANGUEDOC. Red wines are the STELLENBOSCH property's real forte, with a warm, densely fruited Shiraz the accepted leader. Cabernet Sauvignon, some from bought-in grapes, is also striking. Chardonnay and Sauvignon Blanc are generally impressive. Most intriguing members of the range are the Grand Vin Blanc and Grand Vin Rouge blends, each a happy marriage of Ch. Capion and Saxenburg wines. Best years: 1995, '94, '93, '92, '91.

WILLI SCHAEFER

GERMANY, Mosel-Saar-Ruwer, Graach
♀ *Riesling*

If the village of Graach long lacked the cachet of its neighbours WEHLEN and BERNKASTEL, then it was because it was not home to any important estates. Although Willi Schaefer hardly has more than 2.5ha (6 acres) of vines the quality of his wines during the 1990s has been enough to make his estate important within the region. These are almost immortal wines that still taste fresh at 20 and more years of age, but can also give pleasure when drunk for their youthful vivacity and piercing acidity. Best are the spectacular Auslese and Beerenauslese wines from the Graacher Domprobst site, which are among the greatest wines in the region. Best years: 1998, '97, '96, '95, '94, '93, '92, '90, '89, '88, '85, '83, '79, '76, '75, '71.

SCHEUREBE

Scheurebe is a white crossing of Sylvaner with Riesling found in Germany and Austria, where it produces some good, rich Prädikat wines. The dry wines, though, especially in the hands of a lesser winemaker, can be a bit dodgy: 'catty' can be the kindest way of describing some of them. It's generally assertive and lacks subtlety, but some good producers are making some serious, and seriously enjoyable, wines packed with honey and the fruit of pink grapefruit. Low yields and very good winemaking seem to be the key. It's good at higher Prädikat levels, as well.

MARIO SCHIOPETTO
ITALY, Friuli-Venezia Giulia, Collio DOC
♟ *Merlot, Cabernet Franc, Cabernet Sauvignon*
♀ *Tocai Friulano, Pinot Blanc (Pinot Bianco), Pinot Gris (Pinot Grigio), Chardonnay and others*

Mario Schiopetto is admired as the father of modern Friulian viniculture, and hence of modern Italian white wine. He began in the 1960s in his modest plot in Capriva del Friuli, where he remains to this day, lord of one of the most remarkable wineries in Italy. His precarious health never seems to have compromised his steely purpose to achieve high-quality, intensely concentrated wines and today he is helped by his children.

There is a wide range of COLLIO wines, including outstanding Sauvignon Blanc and Pinot Bianco (cru Amrità, Sanskrit for deathless) as well as excellent Pinot Grigio, Malvasia and Riesling among whites, Merlot and Cabernet franc among reds. Merlot and the Cabernets are also blended for the vino da tavola, Rivarossa. But the real speciality is Tocai Friulano. Best years: 1998, 97, '96, '95.

SCHLOSS LIESER
GERMANY, Mosel-Saar-Ruwer, Lieser
♀ *Riesling*

Lieser and its excellent Niederberg-Helden vineyard were virtually unknown until Thomas Haag, the son of Willhelm Haag from BRAUNEBERG's famous Fritz HAAG estate, took over this estate in 1992. Within a remarkably short space of time it joined the first rank of Middle MOSEL producers with good dry, Auslese and higher Prädikat dessert wines with great purity of flavour. Best years: 1998, '96, '95, '94, '93.

SCHLOSS REINHARTSHAUSEN
GERMANY, Rheingau, Erbach
♟ ♟ *Pinot Noir (Spätburgunder)*
♀ *Riesling, Pinot Blanc (Weissburgunder), Chardonnay and others*

The most aristocratic estate of an aristocratic region, Schloss Reinhartshausen belonged to the Prince of Prussia and is now owned by a

SCHLOSS REINHARTSHAUSEN
The organic Weissburgunder and Chardonnay blend comes from vines in the Erbacher Rheinhell site on an island in the middle of the Rhine.

consortium of Frankfurt businessmen. The winery is in the village of ERBACH, with vines in the vineyard sites of Marcobrunn, Schlossberg, Rheinhell and others, and at other top RHEINGAU villages. The wines are rich and quite full, though often made dry. The estate is known for its experiments with Chardonnay, and there is a good Weissburgunder-Chardonnay blend as well as pretty passable fizz, made using the CHAMPAGNE method. Best years: 1998, '97, '96, '95, '94, '93, '92, '90, '89.

SCHLOSS SAARSTEIN
GERMANY, Mosel-Saar-Ruwer, Serrig
♀ *Riesling, Müller-Thurgau, Kerner*

This Saar property, run by Christian Ebert, places an emphasis on QbA and Kabinett wines: Ebert makes Spätlese and Auslese in the best years, and they can be terrifically powerful and concentrated. There is also the occasional Eiswein. But this is after all the Saar and there's no shortage of acidity: when young the wines can be pretty lean. There is also a vineyard called Schloss Saarsteiner. Best years: 1997, '95, '94, '93, '92, '90, '89, '88, '86, '85.

SCHLOSS SCHÖNBORN
GERMANY, Rheingau, Hattenheim
♟ *Pinot Noir (Spätburgunder)*
♀ *Riesling*

These seem to be love 'em or hate 'em wines. Some people find them heavy, others swear they're refined – though the enormous variety of vineyards (in some of the RHEINGAU's top villages) may have something to do with this. The 1980s undoubtedly saw an improvement in winemaking – the wines are now drier and fermented and matured, as often as not, in traditional wooden casks; there are also some remarkable reds. Best years: 1998, '96, '94, '93, '92, '90, '89.

SCHLOSS VOLLRADS
GERMANY, Rheingau, Winkel
♀ *Riesling*

Since the great prophet of dry German Riesling, Erwin Count Matuschka-Greiffenclau, commited suicide in the summer of 1997 the

future of this famous estate has hung in the balance. For the time being it will be administered by his bank, advised by a group of top RHEINGAU winemakers. They have their work cut out to improve quality, though, for the wines during the 1990s were often shockingly bad. Best years: 1990, '89, '86, '83.

SCHLOSSBÖCKELHEIM
GERMANY, Nahe

The village of Schlossböckelheim is home to the State Domaine of Niederhausen-Schlossböckelheim. The village's best vineyard sites are the famous Kupfergrube, planted over the workings of an old copper mine, and Felsenberg; these are vineyards with ideal exposure to the sun. The Grosslage name is Burgweg. Best producers: CRUSIUS, DÖNNHOF, Hehner-Kilz, the Nahe State Domaine.

SCHLUMBERGER
FRANCE, Alsace, Alsace AC
♟ *Pinot Noir*
♀ *Gewurztraminer, Pinot Gris, Riesling, Pinot Blanc, Muscat, Sylvaner*

Looming above the town of Guebwiller are the mighty flanks of the steep vineyards that contain the Grands Crus of Kitterlé, Kessler, Saering and Spiegel, where Schlumberger is easily the most important producer. Indeed, with 140ha (346 acres) of vineyards under cultivation, this is the largest estate in ALSACE.

The Schlumberger style is always broad and rich, and often better suited to Gewurztraminer, Pinot Gris and Pinot Blanc than to Riesling, though the Saering Rieslings can be very fine. The Schlumberger family have acquired an intimate knowledge of the vineyards and their characteristics, and these wines illustrate as well as any in Alsace the true diversity of terroirs that make the region so fascinating. The full-blown sumptuous style of these wines may not be to everyone's taste, but they are an impressive expression of Alsace at its most lush. Although they come across as low in acidity, they age extremely well. The Vendange Tardive and Sélection de Grains Nobles from Gewurztraminer and Pinot Gris are impressive and surprisingly elegant, but extremely expensive. Best years: 1997, '96, '95, '94, '93, '92, '90, '89, '88, '85, '83, '76.

SCHRAMSBERG VINEYARDS
USA, California, Napa County, Napa Valley AVA
♟ ♀ *Chardonnay, Pinot Noir, Flora*

Starting in 1965, the late Jack Davies at Schramsberg jerked CALIFORNIA sparkling wine out of a long drift towards a drab regional character of its own, turning it back to the classic standards of CHAMPAGNE. Where others were using a purely Californian mixture of grapes, Davies returned to the more traditional varieties of Chardonnay and Pinot Noir and used techniques culled from French sources. There is a Reserve, Brut and Blanc de Noirs, all of them strongly marked by the flavours of yeast and toast; the Brut Rosé is a traditional dry rosé; the dessert-sweet Cremant uses a Californian white grape called Flora as its base. The prestige cuvée is named J Schram and, in some vintages, it can dazzle, and in most is very good. Best years: 1995, '94, '92, '90.

SEAVIEW

AUSTRALIA, South Australia, Fleurieu Zone, McLaren Vale

♀ *Cabernet Sauvignon, Syrah (Shiraz), Pinot Noir*

♀ *Riesling, Chardonnay, Semillon*

The Seaview name (owned by PENFOLDS) is one of the best known in Australia: the Riesling, Chardonnay, Cabernet Sauvignon and Seaview sparkling wines have all been best-sellers at one time or another. The Cabernet Sauvignon is often very good, given its modest price, showing restrained black-currant fruit and sweet vanilla oak, while Seaview's sparkling wines have recently improved dramatically. The Cabernet Sauvignon and Chardonnay are made primarily from McLAREN VALE grapes; the other wines are blends of grapes from unspecified (and varied) origins. The super premium Edwards and Chaffey label adorns wines of typically outstanding quality. Best years: 1997, '96, '93, '91, '90, '88, '86, '84, '82, '76, '72.

SEIFRIED ESTATE

NEW ZEALAND, South Island, Nelson

♀ *Pinot Noir, Cabernet Sauvignon*

♀ *Riesling, Gewürztraminer, Sauvignon Blanc, Chardonnay*

Hermann Seifried had made wine in Europe and South Africa and had worked for the New Zealand Apple and Pear Board before he was out of his twenties, and since setting up the Seifried Estate he has produced technically flawless whites, especially from the German varieties. The lime-flavoured Rhine Riesling and spicy lychee Gewürztraminer are especially good, while the Beerenauslese Rhine Riesling outstanding. His Sauvignon Blanc, made from MARLBOROUGH grapes, is also good and tangy. The Redwood Valley label is often used in export markets. Best years: 1998, '96, '94, '91, '90, '89.

Together with Montana, the Selak family, seen here at their winery at Kumeu near Auckland, were responsible for bringing New Zealand Sauvignon Blanc to the world's attention in the 1980s.

SELAKS

NEW ZEALAND, North Island, Kumeu

♀ *Cabernet Sauvignon, Merlot, Pinot Noir*

♀ *Sauvignon Blanc, Semillon, Chardonnay, Riesling and others*

The Selaks winery, with an annual production of over 50,000 cases, makes a substantial number of wines, including a CHAMPAGNE-method fizz which is particularly good. But none go close to matching the quality of the Sauvignon Blanc, its piercing fruit flavour balanced by a hint of residual sugar, or the more complex, yet less stridently fruity, barrel-fermented Sauvignon Blanc/Semillon blend. In 1998 Selaks was bought by NOBILO. Best years: 1998, '97.

SELBACH-OSTER

GERMANY, Mosel-Saar-Ruwer, Zeltingen-Rachtig

♀ *Riesling*

This estate is the source of some benchmark MOSEL Riesling – nervy, racy and maturing to flavours of honey and petrol. Some of the vines are over a hundred years old and ungrafted, which makes them quite genuinely pre-phylloxera, and the wines are matured in traditional oak casks. The vineyards, at BERNKASTEL, WEHLEN, GRAACH and ZELTINGEN-Rachtig, are top-notch. Best years: 1998, '97, '96, '95, '94, '93, '92, '90, '89, '88, '85.

SELLA & MOSCA

ITALY, Sardinia, Alghero

♀ *Sangiovese, Grenache Noir (Cannonau), Cabernet Sauvignon, Merlot, Carignan (Carignano) and others*

♀ *Sangiovese, Cabernet Sauvignon, Grenache Noir (Cannonau), Carignan (Carignano)*

♀ *Vermentino, Torbato, Trebbiano Toscano, Sauvignon Blanc and others*

For decades this large company has been the leading private player in the Sardinian wine field, turning out wines at ever-increasing levels of quality. On the native side are the whites Terre Bianche, from the Torbato grape which is virtually exclusive to Sella & Mosca, and La Cala, from the island's most widespread and versatile grape, Vermentino; also the red Cannonau di Sardegna, a clean, gutsy red. On the international side are a Sauvignon called Le Arenarie, which is surprisingly fresh and varietal for its provenance, and a highly praised Cabernet Sauvignon, Marchese di Villa-marina. The Cannonau/Cabernet blend, Tanca Farrà, is a long-standing favourite with followers of Sella & Mosca.

Their most idiosyncratic wine, however, is the sweet, red dessert Anghelu Ruju, made from Cannonau grapes which, after picking, are left outside to dry on cane mats for some three weeks. There being plenty of heat left in the sun at that period, the already rich grapes concentrate their sugars to such an extent that the wine can approach 18 per cent alcohol with plenty of natural sweetness remaining. The wine is then matured five years in large oak barrels before release. Best years: 1997, '94, '93, '92, '90, '87.

FATTORIA SELVAPIANA
ITALY, Tuscany, Chianti Rufina DOCG
♟ *Sangiovese, Cabernet Sauvignon, Merlot*
♟ *Pinot Blanc (Pinot Bianco), Trebbiano, Malvasia*

Apart from FRESCOBALDI, Selvapiana is alone among the estates of the Rufina district, east of Florence, in that it is regularly included by pundits as among the finest of Tuscany. Owned by one of the great gentlemen of Chianti, Francesco Giuntini, and run by Federico Masseti with the very active consultancy of enologist Franco Bernabei, its wines always have a richness and ripeness of fruit to cover that inbuilt Rufina structure which other Rufina wines achieve only sporadically.

The top wine, the 100 per cent Sangiovese Bucerchiale, is only produced in good to great years, when the grapes are not needed to boost the perennial CHIANTI RUFINA which must meet minimum standards. The recently introduced Riserva Fornace, which includes 10 per cent or so Cabernet Sauvignon in the blend, while very well made, does not have quite the terroir character of the others – but after all, the other wines have had decades, if not centuries, to find their true path. Another newish venture is the promising red POMINO Petrognano, the only challenger in the Pomino DOC zone to Frescobaldi.

On the other side of the coin, since World War Two Selvapiana has held back some bottles of the best vintages. You can still buy wines there going back to 1947 – and they're still good! Selvapiana VIN SANTO, too, is a classic, and so is the olive oil, if you like your oil seriously green and spicy. Best years: 1997, '95, '94, '93, '90, '85, '70, '68, '47.

SEMELI/KTIMA KOKOTOS
GREECE, Attica, Stamata
♟ *Agiorgitiko, Cabernet Sauvignon*
♟ *Savatiano*

This estate is the brainchild of an Englishwoman, Anne Kokotos, who in 1979 persuaded her hotelier husband to plant their estate with vines, and to arrange contracts with other local producers. The top wine, Chateau Semeli, is based on Cabernet Sauvignon and aged for two years in barriques. Other good wines include a white, rosé and stunning red Nemea. Best years: (reds) 1997, '93, '90.

SÉMILLON

Sémillon is grown all over the place but only in two places does it really have star status and in one of these, Bordeaux in South-West France, it needs a little help from its friends. Sauternes and Barsac were the regions to give it fame in the first place. But with a couple of exceptions in Bordeaux – the dry Ch. Rahoul in Graves and the sweet Ch. Doisy-Daëne in Barsac, both of which are more or less 100 per cent Sémillon, virtually all France's best Sémillon-based wines are blended with Sauvignon Blanc. They complement each other perfectly, the weighty, smooth, waxy Sémillon needing that 20 per cent or so of Sauvignon Blanc to liven it up. The great dry whites of Graves are also based on this formula.

Sémillon's thin skin and susceptibility to rot make it invaluable in Sauternes. This is one of the few places in the world where rotten grapes are essential – providing that it is the right sort of rot, *Botrytis cinerea*, occurring only at the right time, once the grapes are ripe. Then the fungus shrivels and concentrates the grapes, sucking the water out and leaving behind it a concentrated, thick, sugary goo, the base material for some of the most complex dessert wines in the world. Sémillon is also used for dessert wines in California and Australia, where they tend to be chunkier and more intensely sweet (though high-quality), for drinking young.

The other spot where Sémillon hits the heights is Australia, in particular the Hunter Valley. The traditional way of making Sémillon here is to bottle it young and green and lemony, and then not touch it for perhaps five to ten years. What emerged then was one of the great white wines of the world, at least as good and sometimes better than fine, mature Chardonnay, all restrained mellowness, creamy texture and a unique flavour of nutty biscuits and lime. Elsewhere in Australia the grape reappears with Sauvignon Blanc.

SEPPELT
AUSTRALIA, Victoria, Western Victoria Zone, Grampians
♟ *Syrah (Shiraz), Pinot Noir, Cabernet Sauvignon*
♟ *Chardonnay, Riesling, Semillon*

Another member of the Southcorp family, Australia's largest wine company, Seppelt's portfolio offers still, sparkling and fortified wines. Seppelt has led the way in Australia in creating good CHAMPAGNE-method fizz, all made from Pinot Noir and Chardonnay: Drumborg (from very cool vineyards in the far south of Victoria) and Salinger are its leading labels, both of high quality, while Great Western, Queen Adelaide and Fleur de Lys are all remarkably good value for money. Seppelt's other fizzy speciality is sparkling Shiraz – deep mulberry red and foaming full of fun – a brilliant madcap wine.

In still wines Seppelt makes some of Australia's best Shiraz from GRAMPIAN fruit, and a variety of fine Chardonnay and Semillon from vineyards in both cool and warm areas. But it may be the Seppelt fortified wines from the historic Seppeltfield winery in the Barossa Valley that show the higher class. Disregarding whether or not the names 'sherry' and 'port' should be allowed, the Seppelt efforts at recreating these classic European styles are frequently magnificent, as are their entirely Australian-inspired Liqueur Muscats.

SERESIN ESTATE
NEW ZEALAND, South Island, Marlborough
♟ *Pinot Noir*
♟ *Sauvignon Blanc, Chardonnay, Riesling, Pinot Gris*

This quality-focused winery was established in Marlborough by London-based film director Michael Seresin and immediately made its mark with its first vintage in 1996. One of the reasons for the intensely focused fruit flavours may be that Seresin is one of the few MARLBOROUGH wineries that can boast true 'domaine' status, all the wines being made from grapes grown in their own vineyards. A new state-of-the-art winery and talented winemaker, Brian Bicknell, ensure that nothing has been left to chance.

Seresin makes one of Marlborough's best and most complex Sauvignon Blancs with the help of some oak fermentation, although the oak influence is slight. Two rich and complex Chardonnays, the region's best Pinot Gris and a knockout Riesling complete the range of white wines. A stylish Pinot Noir is also one of the best from Marlborough. All the wines, apart from the Sauvignon Blanc, have good aging prospects. Best years: 1998, '97, '96.

SERRIG

GERMANY, Mosel-Saar-Ruwer

This is the last wine commune as you travel up the Saar from its confluence with the MOSEL just above Trier and it makes the most extreme of all Saar wines. Serrig's Rieslings have precisely the piercing steeliness for which the Saar is famous and in a great vintage the wines can shine with an astonishing brilliance, even though you may have to wait five to ten years for the beauty to shine through. The downside of this is that in a poor year they are very lean and tart. Best producers: Bert Simon, SCHLOSS SAARSTEIN.

SETÚBAL DOC

PORTUGAL, Terras do Sado Vinho Regional

Muscat (Moscatel de Setúbal), Moscatel Roxo, Tamarez, Arinto, Fernão Pires

The fishing port of Setúbal lends its name to an unctuous fortified wine made mainly from different types of Moscatel grown on the surrounding hills. The wine is called Moscatel de Setúbal when made from at least 85 per cent Moscatel, and Setúbal when it's not. Prolonged maceration on the grape skins for up to six months following partial fermentation and fortification powerfully accentuates the aroma and grapy richness.

Setúbal varies in style according to age. Younger wines (bottled after spending around five years in wood) are orange-brown in colour with a spicy-raisiny character. Older wines (with 20 or more years in wood) are darker with butterscotch and molasses flavours. J M da FONSECA maintain stocks of old wines in wood, some of which date back to the nineteenth century. Wines from the 1955 and the '38 vintages are outstanding. Deep in the cellars there are also wines dating from the time when casks of Setúbal were shipped (like MADEIRA) across the equator and back. These are bottled as Torna Viagem (return journey). Fonseca also makes a small quantity of wine from the rare Moscatel Roxo (red Muscat).

JOSÉ MARIA DA FONSECA

This company is by far the largest and most important producer of rich, raisiny fortified Moscatel wine from Setúbal.

SEYSSEL MOUSSEUX AC

FRANCE, Savoie

Molette, Altesse (Roussette)

Seyssel is the best known of the Savoie wine villages, mainly because it is the headquarters of the region's sparkling wine industry – and we used to see quite a bit of sparkling Seyssel. Now this really was featherlight, water-white fizz and made a fabulous summer Sunday gulper. But the vineyards of Seyssel are extremely limited – less than 80ha (198 acres) of chalky limestone slopes on the banks of the Rhône. However, the ambitions of the local growers were distinctly beady-eyed and as sales grew and grew, the use of local grapes dropped and dropped. Finally we were left with heavy, sickly fizz of no style whatsoever – a disgrace to the Seyssel tradition.

Luckily, good sense has now prevailed and real Seyssel Mousseux AC – the lovely sharp peppery bite of the Molette and Altesse grapes smoothed out with a creamy yeast – is tasting even better than in its previous heyday over a generation ago. The wines are often released with a vintage date and are worth seeking out. There is a little still white Seyssel AC, from the Altesse grape: very light and slightly floral. Best producers: Mollex (La Tacconière), Varichon & Clerc.

SEYVAL BLANC

This white grape, being a hybrid, is banned by the EU for quality wines, which in bureaucratic terms means wines of AC level or the equivalent. It is grown in France and in New York State, but has so far produced its finest wines in England, where its resistance to disease and ability to continue ripening in a damp autumn means it crops reliably in an unreliable climate. It consistently produces some of England's best wines, light, flowery, nettly and crisp when young, but capable of developing a full, nutty, Burgundian depth with age. Seyval Blanc is also the base for much of England's best fizz.

SHAFER VINEYARDS

USA, California, Napa County, Stags Leap District AVA

Cabernet Sauvignon, Merlot, Sangiovese

Chardonnay

Not your typical Mom & Pop winery, Shafer moved steadily towards New World fame under the guidance of a father-and-son team, John and Doug Shafer. From their 32-ha (80-acre) hillside vineyards tucked away within a unique warm pocket in the STAGS LEAP DISTRICT, they craft unusually intense,

SHAFER

Remarkable red wines, including unusually fruity Cabernets, are the hallmark of this rising star, one of the best of the newer Napa Valley wineries.

black-fruit-driven Cabernet Sauvignon and Reserve-style Hillside Select Cabernet. Though the Hillside Select is built to evolve with five to seven years of aging, it too displays the black-cherry flavour and soft and supple tannin that is characteristic of the region. Merlot is also allowed to showcase lush fruit and seductive softness. After several trial vintages, the Shafers have come up with Firebreak, their version of a SUPER-TUSCAN that has plenty of charm to accompany the pert, bright Sangiovese fruit. Best years: (reds) 1997, '96, '95, '94, '93, '92, '91.

Searching for a better place to grow Chardonnay, the Shafers settled on a site in CARNEROS which they later named Red Shoulder Ranch. It has yielded highly concentrated, succulent Chardonnays with the complexity needed to raise them to the high level of the reds. Best years: 1998, '97, '96, '95.

SHAW & SMITH

AUSTRALIA, South Australia, Mount Lofty Ranges Zone, Adelaide Hills

Sauvignon Blanc, Chardonnay

Michael Hill-Smith MW (Australia's first Master of Wine) and his cousin, peripatetic winemaker Martin Shaw, have founded a vibrant, internationally focused business making satisfyingly powerful Sauvignon Blanc, elegant (sometimes effete) unoaked Chardonnay, and an utterly convincing, complex pear, citrus, nut and cream-influenced Reserve Chardonnay. Best years: 1997, '96, '94, '93, '92.

SHAW & SMITH

This Adelaide Hills winery makes wines of great definition and flavour, including tangy, fresh Sauvignon Blanc for drinking as young as possible.

SICILIA & SOUTHERN ITALY

ON A FIRST VISIT TO SICILY (Sicilia in Italian) the island can seem harsh and barren. Travelling through the interior seems to take forever, with not a sign of habitation, just an endless succession of mountainous rocks. The lack of enchantment will not last long, however. Those craggy lumps soon stop looking bleak and start to appear austerely magnificent. And when finally one discovers the island's proudly maintained villages, vivid colours and flowers are everywhere and in the countryside the stunning straw-coloured swathes of wheat (Sicily was once called the bread-basket of Europe) make a vivid contrast with the vistas of olive trees with their silver-grey leaves glistening under the burning sun.

The Sicilians haven't worried too much in the past about bringing their wines into the DOC net. Many of the island's most important wines, such as Corvo, Regaleali and Terre di Ginestra, have made their names on their own merits, and producers have been able to adapt their techniques and grape blends freely with experience. Even some of the DOCs that do exist are so obscure as to be practically unobtainable.

Despite generally accepted wine lore that cooler climates are better for white wines, hotter zones for reds, Sicily's greatest success has been with its light, crisp whites from indigenous grapes such as Catarratto or Inzolia, which suit its climate perfectly. They're found mainly in the west of the island. Reds have taken longer to find their feet, not because the local varieties such as Nero d'Avola, Nerello Mascalese, Frappato and Perricone, are inferior but because there was a reluctance to take up modern winemaking techniques quite as enthusiastically. Part of this was the esteem given by some to wines that are *marsalesi* (Marsala-like) and therefore what would today be dismissed as oxidized and faulty. But the past few years have seen some amazing developments, particularly with Nero d'Avola, Sicily's best and most original grape.

Marsala is one of Italy's most famous wines, and, theoretically, one of the world's great fortified wines, but, despite an upturn in its fortunes, there's still a lot produced that is nowhere near great now. The real dessert-wine gems come instead from the islands off Sicily: Moscato di Pantelleria from Pantelleria to the south-west towards Tunisia, and Malvasia delle Lipari from the Aeolian (or Lipari) archipelago to the north-east. They are gems not just because they are (when properly made) delicately sweet and delicious but because they are the true heritage of Sicily, especially the *passito* versions, the most typical.

'Mezzogiorno' is the general if unofficial name applying to Italy's South, as 'Midi' applies to France's South, and they mean the same thing: midday (i.e. the land of the overhead sun at noon). This is a huge area which has suffered over the centuries in a variety of ways – politically and economically. Winewise the Mezzogiorno has been a producer of enormous volumes of full-bodied bulk blenders for sale at low, low prices to other parts of Italy and Europe, notably France and Germany. It is only relatively recently – within the last 20 years or so – that the Mezzogiorno has begun to follow the Midi's lead and sell some of the millions of hectolitres in bottle. The potential is for a massive market in value-for-money reds and whites, although, while a good beginning has been made in some quarters, a lot of work remains to be done to catch up with the Midi. The real ace – or aces – in the hand of the South are its traditional grape varieties, some of which have real personality and quality. In addition the international varieties have proved that they can achieve real quality not to say excellence in southern Italy.

The potential for quality in southern Italy has been shown by recent progress with fresh, dry whites, especially from Pinot Bianco, seen here on the Rivera estate in Puglia, and Chardonnay, as well as with the more famous red wines.

Campania
Puglia
Basilicata
Calabria
Sicilia

LIBRANDI
Chocolaty, black cherry-fruited Gravello, from a blend of Gaglioppo and Cabernet Sauvignon, is one of the leading wines from this exciting Calabrian producer.

DR COSIMO TAURINO
Patriglione is an increasingly famous, wonderfully harmonious and complex Brindisi red made from late-picked 90 per cent Negroamaro and Malvasia Nera.

REGALEALI
The estate of Conte Tasca d'Almerita makes some of Italy's most admired wines, including elegant Cabernet Sauvignon.

D'ANGELO
Basilicata's leading winery makes this richly aromatic, barrique-aged Aglianico wine called Canneto.

MASTROBERARDINO
Fiano di Avellino is among the leading white wines produced by this famous family firm which has long flown the flag for southern Italy.

Main DOC/DOCG wines

1 Falerno del Massico DOC
2 Solopaca DOC
3 Greco di Tufo DOC
4 Taurasi DOCG
5 Fiano di Avellino DOC
6 Lacryma Christi del Vesuvio DOC Vesuvio DOC
7 Ischia DOC
8 Capri DOC
9 Aleatico di Puglia DOC
10 San Severo DOC
11 Cacc'e Mmitte di Lucera DOC

12 Moscato di Trani DOC
13 Castel del Monte DOC
14 Gravina DOC
15 Gioia del Colle DOC
16 Locorotondo DOC
17 Martina Franca DOC
18 Brindisi DOC
19 Primitivo di Manduria DOC
20 Salice Salentino DOC
21 Squinzano DOC
22 Copertino DOC
23 Leverano DOC

24 Alezio DOC
25 Aglianico del Vulture DOC
26 Cirò DOC
27 Donnici DOC
28 Savuto DOC
29 Greco di Bianco DOC
30 Faro DOC
31 Malvasia delle Lipari DOC
32 Etna DOC
33 Alcamo, Bianco d'Alcamo DOC
34 Marsala DOC
35 Moscato di Pantelleria DOC

REGIONAL ENTRIES
Aglianico del Vulture, Alcamo, Basilicata, Calabria, Campania, Castel del Monte, Cirò, Etna, Falerno del Massico, Fiano di Avellino, Lacryma Christi del Vesuvio, Locorotondo, Marsala, Moscato di Pantelleria, Puglia, Salice Salentino, Taurasi.

PRODUCER ENTRIES
Argiolas, De Bartoli, Librandi, Mastroberardino, Pervini, Regaleali, Rivera, Duca di Salaparuta, Sella & Mosca, Taurino.

DE BARTOLI
At his Vecchio Samperi winery Marco de Bartoli makes dry, intense fortified wines released as 10-, 20- and 30-year-old versions.

SIEUR D'ARQUES

FRANCE, Languedoc-Roussillon, Limoux AC
♀ *Mauzac, Chardonnay, Chenin Blanc, Sauvignon Blanc*

This dynamic co-operative accounts for some 2000ha (4942 acres) of vineyard and around 90 per cent of the production in the Limoux area west of Carcassonne. It pioneered the cultivation of Chardonnay in the South of France and has had all members' vineyards surveyed and classified into four climatic zones. A range of barrel-fermented Limoux Chardonnays, labelled Toques et Clochers, are produced from each of the four zones: Océanique, Méditerranéen, Haute Vallée and Terroir d'Autan. The Caves du Sieur d'Arques also produces 90 per cent of all sparkling BLANQUETTE DE LIMOUX and CRÉMANT DE LIMOUX as well as small quantities of *méthode ancestrale*, a sparkling wine made by bottling the wine before the primary fermentation has been completed. Most wines are ready to drink on release.

SILVER OAK CELLARS

USA, California, Napa County, Napa Valley AVA
♀ *Cabernet Sauvignon*

Only Cabernet Sauvignon is made here by veteran winemaker, Justin Meyer, but each year he bottles two distinct versions. His style of winemaking favours a lengthy aging regime – three years in cask and one in bottle – for ultra-softness and suppleness. Both Cabernets – ALEXANDER VALLEY and NAPA VALLEY – are aged in American oak. Both manage to be approachable when young but capable of sustained aging, even in the weaker years. The Alexander Valley Cabernet reverberates with irresistible berry fruit and velvety oak spice, the other is more in line with the depth and force of Napa Valley. Though its production ceased after 1991, a special Bonny's Vineyard bottling was supremely attractive and intensely flavoured. The Napa bottling is good, but more tannic and angular than the Alexander version. Best years: 1996, '95, '94, '93, '92, '91, '90, '88, '87, '86, '85, '84, '83, '78.

SILVERADO VINEYARDS

USA, California, Napa County, Stags Leap District AVA
♀ *Cabernet Sauvignon, Merlot, Sangiovese*
♀ *Chardonnay, Sauvignon Blanc*

Too much has been made of the fact that this winery is owned by the Disney family (Walt Disney's wife and daughter), because it diminishes the goals and accomplishments of what is certainly a class act. The winery's impressive 142ha (350 acres) of vineyards are spread out over five sites (three in STAGS LEAP, one in CARNEROS, and the last in a remote corner of the NAPA VALLEY). Among the first winery to master the juicy-fruity, 'come-hither' style of Merlot now so popular, Silverado has also succeeded with inviting, supple Cabernet and a tasty Sauvignon Blanc. The limited edition, judiciously oaked, massive Reserve Cabernet is worth aging for up to a decade. To follow a work in progress, Sangiovese, sometimes blended with Cabernet or Zinfandel, sometimes bottled straight, is the wine on the verge of a breakthrough. Best years: (reds) 1997, '96, '95, '94, '92, '91, '90.

SIMI WINERY

USA, California, Sonoma County, Alexander Valley AVA
♀ *Cabernet Sauvignon, Pinot Noir*
♀ *Chardonnay, Sauvignon Blanc*

Simi is a historic winery dating from pre-Prohibition times, but its greatest winemaking flowering began with the arrival of winemaker and now president Zelma Long from MONDAVI in 1979. She took charge of its winemaking and its vineyard development programmes, and before too long the winery was offering Chardonnays that are impeccable in their balance of reserved fruit and toasty oak. Today Simi offers Chardonnay from CARNEROS and a Reserve from Goldfield Vineyard. It has added a brilliant white Meritage, Sendal, redolent with delicious flavours in a big, juicy style, and its Chenin Blanc with a wisp of sweetness is fresh, light, and likeable. Best years: (whites) 1998, '97, '96, '95, '94.

For a long time red wines proved more of a problem for Simi, but with new and improved vineyards in the ALEXANDER VALLEY, Simi now offers Cabernet in both a classically structured Reserve wine that ages well for a decade and a ripe, fruity style from SONOMA COUNTY. Carneros Pinot Noir with typical cherry, strawberry fruitiness and a mouth-filling, big-flavoured Shiraz have improved Simi's red wine range. Best years: (reds) 1997, '95, '94, '93, '92, '91.

SIMI
Sendal is Simi's Bordeaux-style blend of Sauvignon Blanc and Semillon and is a richly fruity but well-balanced wine.

CH. SIMONE

FRANCE, Provence, Palette AC
♀♀ *Grenache, Mourvèdre, Cinsaut, Syrah and others*
♀ *Clairette, Grenache Blanc, Ugni Blanc, Muscat*

This extraordinary domaine is to all intents and purposes the AC PALETTE, the 17ha (42 acres) of vineyard representing 80 per cent of the area under vine. René Rougier and his son Jean-François have not been swung by fashions, remaining loyal to local grape varieties and traditional methods of vinification. The white is made essentially from Clairette, fermented and aged in barrel. It is rich, full, dry, complex and balanced but needs at least four to five years and can age for ten years or more. The rosé is a fairly robust wine, best drunk with a little age and with food. The old-style red, with its leather and prune flavours and sometimes delicate constitution, is made from 13 varieties and undergoes a long aging in old wood. Best years: (reds) 1996, '95, '93; (whites) 1996, '95, '94, '93, '92.

CH. SIMONE
A special mesoclimate near Aix-en-Provence, some very old vines and traditional winemaking all combine to make these robust wines. Even the rosé is designed to age.

SION

SWITZERLAND, Valais

Sion is the centre of the Valais wine industry and also of industry generally in this beautiful part of the Upper RHÔNE Valley. Chasselas (known here as Fendant) dominates the vineyards, followed by Pinot Noir and Gamay for the light red Dôle, but more exciting grape varieties, ranging from the traditional Petite Arvine and Sylvaner (here called Johannisberg) to Syrah and Chardonnay, produce more interesting wines. Best producers: Robert Gilliard, Domaine du MONT D'OR.

SLIVEN

BULGARIA, Southern Region
♀ *Cabernet Sauvignon, Merlot and others*
♀ *Rkatsiteli, Red Misket, Muscat Ottonel and others*

Smaller and less cumbersome than some of its rivals, the Sliven winery has been able to adapt more rapidly to the demand for fruitier wines. Although Cabernet Sauvignon is still the workhorse, giving slightly more supple, aromatic fruit than it did in years gone by, Chardonnay is also a worthy contender. It was Emil Razlogov, a visionary administrator, who set about rescuing the Bulgarian wine industry from certain collapse by targeting British supermarkets in the belief that if British consumers bought good-value Bulgarian wine, then the rest of Europe, not to say the world, would perhaps follow. By harnessing wineries like Sliven, his plan was given a reasonable chance of working. The next thing is to spread out from the narrow base of Chardonnays and Cabernets, and results so far with Merlot and Pinot Noir are encouraging.

CH. SMITH-HAUT-LAFITTE

FRANCE, Bordeaux, Pessac-Léognan AC, Cru Classé de Graves
♦ *Cabernet Sauvignon, Merlot, Cabernet Franc*
♀ *Sauvignon Blanc*

The property is one of the region's biggest at 55ha (136 acres), producing about 230,000 bottles of red and 58,000 bottles of white a year. The vineyard is planted for the reds with 55 per cent Cabernet Sauvignon, 35 per cent Merlot and 10 per cent Cabernet Franc. The soil is good and gravelly on a swell of ground to the north of Martillac. The property has undergone a revolution since the arrival of new owners, Daniel and Florence Cathiard, in 1990 who restored the vineyards and modernized winemaking facilities. Only the red wine is classified but until the 1990s it was rather lean and uninteresting. A reduction in yields, careful tending of the vineyard, severe selection and aging in new oak barrels, 50 per cent of which are from the estate's own cooper, has resulted in wine of an additional concentration, structure and elegance. From the 1994 vintage it can be ranked with the best in the PESSAC-LÉOGNAN AC. Best years: (reds) 1998, '97, '96, '95, '94, '90, '89, '88, '86, '85, '83.

The whites too have undergone a change and have been in the forefront of BORDEAUX's white wine revolution. Using barrel fermentation and maturation in new oak, today the château stands as a shining example to others in the region of what investment and commitment can do to a wine. So far only 9ha (22 acres) of land are planted with white grapes, which are all Sauvignon. Interestingly, the white is not classified since there were no white grapes at all when the Graves Classification was decided in 1959, but it surely deserves classification today. Second wine (red and white): les Hauts de Smith. Best years: (whites) 1998, '97, '96, '95, '94, '93.

Ch. Smith-Haut-Lafitte's vines are superbly located in a single block on a gravel hillock – the gravel soils provide excellent natural drainage and the pebbles retain heat which helps to ripen the grapes.

SMITH WOODHOUSE

PORTUGAL, Douro, Port DOC
♦ *Tinta Roriz (Tempranillo) , Tinta Barroca, Tinto Cão, Touriga Naçional, Touriga Francesa and others*
♀ *Gouveio, Viosinho, Rabigato, Malvasia Fina and others*

One of six PORT firms belonging to the Symington family (the others are DOW, GRAHAM, WARRE, Quarles Harris and Gould Campbell) Smith Woodhouse is often rather unfairly thought of as a second-tier shipper. The fact is that in years like 1977, '83 and '85 Smith Woodhouse vintage ports frequently match the very best.

Unlike Dow and Graham, Smith Woodhouse is not attached to any particular quinta (although the company does own a small property in the Torto Valley). Smith Woodhouse wines therefore tend to be a finely tuned exercise in blending. It is true that much of the company's output is inexpensive standard tawny, but Smith Woodhouse is also the source of some excellent value-for-money port. The company has created a niche for itself with its unfiltered LBV, which is only released when the wine is ready to drink, having spent four to six years in barrel followed by between six and ten years in bottle. The result is a very acceptable poor man's vintage port. Best years: (vintage ports) 1994, '91, '85, '83, '77.

SOAVE DOC, SOAVE CLASSICO DOC, RECIOTO DI SOAVE DOCG

ITALY, Veneto
♀ *Garganega, Trebbiano di Soave, Chardonnay*

There can't be many wine drinkers in the world who haven't drunk Soave at some stage, as over 65 million bottles are produced a year. Yet the area of Soave, east of Verona and bordering the VALPOLICELLA zone, is not enormous. The only way to achieve this high figure is to exploit the vines for all they are worth – in other words, to extract large yields. This is not difficult, especially on the flat land or *pianura*, where the vines for most ordinary Soave are planted. Only the small Classico zone behind the villages of Soave and Monteforte d'Alpone is hilly – and in this region you need sloping vineyards for high-quality fruit. This is why so much Soave is innocuous swill with little more than an almondy hint and a slightly bitter finish. Not only innocuous, but also monothematic, not surprisingly given that 80 per cent of production is controlled by the local co-operative and bottled for various companies under different in labels or sold in bulk to them.

The most important development in Soave recently has been the elevation of the *passito* version, called Recioto as in Valpolicella, to the status of DOCG. Soave Recioto is a sweet wine with a difference – there is nothing cloying about it, given its firm acidity and unrelenting freshness. Soave growers who have dedicated themselves to quality in recent years include ANSELMI (who introduced the international taste in Soave with Chardonnay and the use of barriques), Cantina del Castello (a Recioto specialist, with no fewer than three types: oaked, unoaked and sparkling/bottle-fermented non-disgorged), Coffele, la Cappuccina, Gini, Inama, PIEROPAN, Portinari, Prà and Suavia. Even the big producers like C S Soave, Bertani, Bolla, Masi, Montresor and Pasqua are coming up with cru Soaves from particular vineyards which are streets ahead of the norm. But, remember, if you want Soave with flavour the grapes must come from the Classico zone. Best years: 1998, '97, '96, '95.

CH. SOCIANDO-MALLET

FRANCE, Bordeaux, Haut-Médoc, Haut-Médoc AC, Cru Bourgeois

🍷 *Cabernet Sauvignon, Merlot, Cabernet Franc*

This established star holds lonely vigil over the last really decent gravel outcrop of the HAUT-MÉDOC at St-Seurin-de-Cadourne. The château is presided over by the beady-eyed, furiously passionate owner, Monsieur Gautreau, and the results are impressive – dark, brooding, tannic, dry, but with every sign of great, classic red BORDEAUX flavours to come if you could hang on for ten to 15 years.

So hats off to Monsieur Gautreau for his dedication and for believing in his wine, which now easily attains Classed Growth quality – it achieves Classed Growth prices too. Up to 100 per cent of the oak barrels used to mature the wine are new; this is an unusually high percentage and really very rare for a non-Classed Growth. The second wine is la Demoiselle de Sociando-Mallet. Best years: 1997, '96, '95, '94, '93, '90, '89, '88, '86, '85, '83, '82, '78, '76, '75.

SOGRAPE

PORTUGAL, Bairrada DOC, Dão DOC, Douro DOC, Vinho Verde DOC, Alentejo Vinho Regional

🍷 *Alentejo: Aragonês (Tempranillo), Trincadeira, Moreto and Periquita; Bairrada: Baga; Dão: Touriga Naçional, Bastardo, Jaen and others; Douro: Tinta Roriz, Touriga Francesa, Touriga Naçional and others Mateus Rosé: Baga and others*

🍷 *Bairrada: Maria Gomes, Bical, Rabo de Ovelha and others; Dão: Encruzado, Bical (Borrado das Moscas) and others; Douro: Viosinho, Malvasia, Gouveio and others; Vinho Verde: Alvarinho, Loureiro, Padernã and others*

This huge company (the largest wine producer in Portugal) is still in private hands by

SOGRAPE
Though still partly family run, Ferreira, an important producer of port and Douro table wines, has been owned by Sogrape since the late 1980s.

the Guedes family. It was established on the back of the ubiquitous Mateus Rosé, which developed into one of the world's most successful wine brands. Originally made in the DOURO (at a winery close to the palace depicted on the label), Mateus is now mostly produced at a high-tech winery in the BAIRRADA region. Even though the Portuguese don't actually drink it themselves, Mateus still accounts for the lion's share of Sogrape's sales.

Since the early 1980s Sogrape has been very active in other areas of Portugal and the company has built up a huge portfolio of wines. It now owns both FERREIRA and Offley PORT shippers and produces unfortified red and white Douro wines under the Vila Regia and Sogrape Reserva labels. The latter is always a good buy. Sogrape has also bought land in the VINHO VERDE region, where it produces four different wines: the fresh, fruity, off-dry Gazela, Chello, an authentically dry Vinho Verde, the crisp Quinta de Azevedo and an aromatic Alvarinho named Morgadio da Torre.

Sogrape has also developed new styles of wine in Bairrada (the white Quinta de Pedralvites is exemplary), but it is in the DÃO region where the company has really made the running with a brand new winery for Grao Vasco, the best-selling brand of peppery red and crisp dry white Dão. Sogrape has expanded its range of Dão wines to include some impressive oak-aged reds and whites: Duque de Viseu and Quinta dos Carvalhais (based on Touriga Nacional). The best reds in particular can age for five years or more.

No longer confined exclusively to northern Portugal, Sogrape has made a successful foray into the ALENTEJO, where a supple, fleshy red wine, Vinha do Monte, captures the warmth of the southern sun. Sogrape also has interests in Argentina, where it recently purchased an estate.

FELIX SOLÍS

SPAIN, Castilla-La Mancha, Valdepeñas DO

🍷🍷 *Tempranillo (Cencibel), Airén, Cabernet Sauvignon*

🍷 *Airén, Chardonnay, Riesling, Macabeo*

Felix Solís is by far the biggest wine company in VALDEPEÑAS and, according to the brothers who own it, the largest in the whole of Castilla-La Mancha. It makes – at the top of the range – some of the very best wines of Valdepeñas and some of the best-value wine in Spain. In this predominantly white wine area, Solís has planted its own 700ha (1730 acres) of vineyards with red Cencibel (Tempranillo), plus the inevitable experimental plantations of Cabernet Sauvignon and a few foreign white-grape vines. The Viña Albali Reservas tend to be more impressive than the Gran Reservas, with a lovely oaky nose and good, meaty fruit. Until recently, whites have not been its strong point, but the latest whites are also delicious, particularly the aromatic Viña Albali Early Harvest Blanco. Best years: 1996, '95, '93.

SOMONTANO DO

SPAIN, Aragón

🍷🍷 *Moristel, Tempranillo, Grenache Noir (Garnacha Tinta), Parraleta, Cabernet Sauvignon, Merlot, Pinot Noir*

🍷 *Macabeo, Grenache Blanc (Garnacha Blanca), Alcañón, Chardonnay, Gewürztraminer*

Somontano means 'under the mountain', and that is just where this enchantingly pretty region is, isolated from other DO areas up in the green foothills of the central Pyrenees. Its altitude keeps the temperature bearable, while the mountains protect it from cold winter winds. There have recently been plantations of Cabernet Sauvignon, Chardonnay, Tempranillo, Merlot, Pinot Noir and Gewürztraminer, which now form the backbone of new-age Somontano wines. Chenin Blanc and Riesling, also planted in the 1980s, were subsequently excluded from DO recognition and had to be grafted with other

BODEGAS PIRINEOS
This unoaked red wine from the local Moristel grape is one of several successful wines from this enterprising company which used to be the former local co-operative.

varieties – mostly the successful Merlot. Three modern, highly innovative bodegas now make 95 per cent of the wine in the region. The largest one is VIÑAS DEL VERO, followed by Bodega PIRINEOS (the former Somontano co-op, which became a corporation in 1993) and ENATE (Viñedos y Crianzas del Alto Aragón). Best years: 1996, '95, '94.

SONOMA COUNTY
USA, California

Unlike the compact and easy-to-access NAPA VALLEY wine region, Sonoma is a big, sprawling area that includes dozens of mesoclimates and soil types. The climates range from the warm areas in the northern ALEXANDER VALLEY to the cool, often foggy and chilly regions in the southwest corner of the RUSSIAN RIVER VALLEY and Green Valley.

Historically, its pioneering producers sent their wines to Napa wineries for blending and bottling, and in all honesty, Sonoma was identified with cheap jug wines until the wine boom finally occurred here. The wine boom demonstrated just why the big companies were so keen on Sonoma fruit – the wines had a succulence and gentle power quite unlike those of neighbouring areas like Napa. After playing second fiddle for years to Napa Valley, Sonoma County began to come alive in the 1970s when it was home to 24 wineries. It has grown to over 200 producers today. With room available for further vineyard expansion, its current 17,000ha (42,000 acres) of vines already surpasses plantings in Napa. It is now the leader in Chardonnay and Pinot Noir acreage, and makes some of the best of each. Fortunate to have numerous pre-Prohibition vineyards still in production, Sonoma also enjoys a well-deserved reputation for Zinfandel.

Among Sonoma's AVAs, the warm DRY CREEK VALLEY is practically synonymous with intensely fruity Zinfandel, and there is also some lively, succulent Sauvignon Blanc from Dry Creek AVA. The neighbouring Alexander Valley, after some uninspiring early vintages, is now on track for big-bodied, lush, and lightly tannic Cabernet Sauvignon and large-scale Merlot.

Sharing the CARNEROS District with Napa, Sonoma County also has the RUSSIAN RIVER VALLEY as a prime region for concentrated, balanced Chardonnay. Improving steadily since the mid-1980s, Russian River Valley Pinot Noir has come along to challenge the New World's best regions and growers in Burgundy have also taken note of the velvety smooth, black-cherry-fruited Pinots from better sites within this AVA. Other AVAs are SONOMA

SONOMA-CUTRER

The Les Pierres, from a single vineyard in the Sonoma Valley, is the most complex and richest of the three Chardonnays made by Sonoma-Cutrer.

VALLEY, Knights Valley, Chalk Hill, Green Valley, and Sonoma Coast. Even though it lacks real precision an AVA status Sonoma County is often used on labels by producers who own vineyards in several of these AVAs. Sonoma's best-known wineries are the two big players in the Chardonnay category – KENDALL-JACKSON and GALLO – but it is also home to many outstanding small wineries such as KISTLER, MATANZAS CREEK, LAUREL GLEN VINEYARDS, Peter MICHAEL, MARCASSIN, Marimar TORRES and others.

SONOMA-CUTRER
USA, California, Sonoma County, Russian River Valley AVA
♀ *Chardonnay*

Sonoma-Cutrer was established in 1981 to do just one thing: make Chardonnays of distinction from individual vineyards. Chardonnay Les Pierres, from the SONOMA VALLEY, leads with depth and age-worthiness and Chardonnay Cutrer Vineyard challenges it. Chardonnay Russian River Ranches is blended from grapes from four or five vineyards in the RUSSIAN RIVER VALLEY owned by Sonoma-Cutrer and doesn't get anywhere near the other two wines for quality. Best years: 1997, '96, '95, '94, '93, '92, '91, '90, '88, '87, '86.

SONOMA MOUNTAIN AVA
USA, California, Sonoma Valley

Falling within the SONOMA VALLEY AVA, Sonoma Mountain includes both the east- and west-facing slopes above the fog line along the mountains west of Glen Ellen. This small, quite warm mountainside AVA produces intense but fruit-filled Cabernet Sauvignon and Zinfandel and includes several pre-1920 Zinfandel vineyards. Pioneered by Louis MARTINI at his Monte Rosso Vineyard, Sonoma Mountain was later chosen by owner CHALONE as the best site for CARMENET. Other leading producers today are LAUREL GLEN and BENZIGER. Best years: 1997, '96, '95, '94, '92, '91, 90.

SONOMA VALLEY AVA
USA, California, Sonoma County

Sonoma Valley has one of the longest and the most romantic histories of any wine district in CALIFORNIA. Franciscan missionaries planted vines almost as soon as they arrived in 1825. Mariano Vallejo took over the vineyard when the Mexican government secularized the town a few years later, and – after the revolt that made California part of the United States – he stayed on as a winemaker.

Long and narrow, the valley runs exactly parallel to the NAPA VALLEY, which lies to the east. While Napa grows steadily warmer south to north, Sonoma hits its warmest spot more or less at its mid-point. In the south it overlaps the CARNEROS AVA, allowing some vineyards to use either name. In the east is a sub-appellation, SONOMA MOUNTAIN, known for Cabernet Sauvignon. In general, Sonoma fruit produces reds and whites that are softer and more approachable than Napa wines, but often of similarly high quality.

Sebastiani Vineyards is the largest winery; Glen Ellen is of similar size, and CHATEAU ST JEAN and KENWOOD are substantial. Other smaller firms include ARROWOOD, B R COHN (wonderful Cabernet), Gundlach-Bundschu (great Gewürztraminer, Cabernet Sauvignon and Chardonnay), HANZELL, Haywood (splendid, slightly rustic Zinfandel), KUNDE, Ravenswood (rich Zinfandel and Cabernet), Richardson (good Pinot Noir) and ST FRANCIS. Best years: (reds) 1998, '97, '95, '94, '93, '92, 90; (whites) 1997, '96, '95, '94, '93.

DOMAINE LA SOUMADE
FRANCE, Southern Rhône, Rasteau AC
♥ *Grenache, Syrah*

André Roméro is not a grower who makes many concessions to those touting the virtues of lighter, slimmer wines from the southern RHÔNE. His 24ha (59 acres) are well situated and the grapes routinely reach high ripeness levels, which are translated into alcohol levels of 14 degrees or more. Roméro expects his clients to keep his wines for a few years for their tannins to harmonize. As well as the regular Côtes du Rhône-Villages, there is, in some years, a Cuvée Prestige and a Cuvée Confiance from his oldest vines, which are 93-year-old Grenache. Roméro is also a leading producer of Rasteau's speciality: the *vin doux naturel*. This is made from Grenache and Syrah, and the fermentation is arrested by adding grape spirit. The result is a powerful sweet fortified red reminiscent of a MAURY from the Roussillon. Best years: 1997, '95, '94, '90, '89.

SOUTH AUSTRALIA Australia

SOUTH AUSTRALIA IS not only the engine-room but also the
standard bearer for Australian wine. Thanks to the massive
irrigated Riverland plantings that spread relentlessly along
the banks of the Murray River, the state generally provides
over half of Australia's wine. But thanks to many of
Australia's most famous wine companies producing some of
the country's most thrilling flavours, in the regions of Clare,
Barossa, McLaren Vale and Coonawarra, for many people
South Australia wine *is* Australian wine.

All the biggest Australian wine companies are either based
in South Australia, or have substantial operations there.
Lindemans may have its main winery at Karadoc in north-
western Victoria, but its principal vineyards are in
Coonawarra and Padthaway. Seppelt may have a major
presence at Great Western in Victoria, but its most visible
asset is at the end of the palm-tree-lined approach to the
historic Seppeltsfield Winery in Barossa, and some of its
most valuable vineyards are in Padthaway. Penfolds, Hardys
and Orlando are South Australian through and through, as
are Wolf Blass, Yalumba and the other major names within
the Penfolds and BRL Hardy conglomerates.

The focal point of this activity is the Barossa Valley, an
easy hour's drive north of Adelaide, where almost all
Australia's major players have operations. However, they
largely use cheaper, high-yield fruit from the Riverland, and
at one time it looked as though Barossa, one of Australia's
first and best grape-growing regions, might merely become
a processing centre for grapes from elsewhere. But there is a
new pride in the region and its history these days; new vineyards have been established and old ones revitalized. It
remains, in particular, a producer of ultra-typical, full-bodied Australian red wines, with voluptuously sweet and rich
fruit reaching its zenith in Penfolds Grange.

The contrast comes in the East Barossa Ranges. The
climate here is very much cooler: Riesling performs superbly
in the windswept Eden Valley. The red wines are tighter, yet
still generously proportioned in the hands of a maker such
as Stephen Henschke. Going south to the Adelaide Hills, the
climate becomes cooler still. Sauvignon Blanc, Chardonnay
and Pinot Noir thrive as the numerous small vineyards vie
for space with Adelaide's inhabitants intent on a home in the
Hills. North of the Barossa is the Clare Valley, theoretically
too warm for vines yet a regular producer of toasty Riesling
and structured Shiraz and Cabernet Sauvignon.

McLaren Vale lies south of Adelaide, past the virtually
suburban vineyards of Adelaide Metropolitan. Here the
wineries, most of them small and sitting cheek by jowl
among ominously encroaching housing, are producing a

*The Hill of Grace vineyard north of Keyneton in the Eden Valley is one of
Australia's most famous Shiraz vineyards. Owned by Henschke the Shiraz vines
are over 100 years old and very low-yielding.*

surprising range of white and red wines united by the
generosity of their flavour. Glowing, buttercup-yellow
Chardonnay fills the mouth with peaches and cream and
Sauvignon Blanc with gooseberries and passionfruit – yet
traditionally McLaren Vale is famous for dark-chocolate-
flavoured reds and concentrated, pungent 'vintage ports'.

Finally, there are the vast open expanses of the Limestone
Coast Zone, visually boring, but of ever increasing importance. Coonawarra and Padthaway need no herald, but the
emerging regions of Wrattonbully, Robe, Mount Benson
and Bordertown point the way for the future. Limestone-
laced soils, plentiful underground water, and a moderately
cool climate all contribute to the making of elegant,
premium wines from the classic core of grape varieties, led
by the cassis, blackberry and mulberry Cabernet Sauvignon
of Coonawarra. During the years ahead plantings in these
new regions are bound to increase significantly.

CHATEAU REYNELLA

This historic winery has been given a new lease of life under new owners, the giant BRL Hardy company. The Basket Pressed range covers three varietal reds, including Cabernet Sauvignon.

HENSCHKE

Hill of Grace, a stunning wine with dark, exotic flavours, comes from a single plot of low-yielding Shiraz, first planted in the 1860s (see photo facing page).

PENFOLDS

The thrillingly rich Penfolds Grange is generally considered to be Australia's best red wine and only really shows its magnificence after at least ten years of bottle aging.

WYNNS

The name of Wynns is synonymous with the Coonawarra region. The powerful, long-lived John Riddoch Cabernet Sauvignon is made in top years only.

Wine regions

1. Clare Valley
2. Riverland
3. Adelaide Plains
4. Barossa Valley
5. Eden Valley
6. Adelaide Hills
7. McLaren Vale
8. Langhorne Creek
9. South Fleurieu
10. Padthaway
11. Wrattonbully
12. Coonawarra
13. Mount Benson
14. Robe

REGIONAL ENTRIES

Adelaide Hills, Barossa Valley, Clare Valley, Coonawarra, Eden Valley, Langhorne Creek, McLaren Vale, Mount Benson & Robe, Padthaway, Riverland, Wrattonbully.

PRODUCER ENTRIES

Tim Adams, Basedow, Wolf Blass, Bowen Estate, Brand's Laira, Grant Burge, Leo Buring, Chapel Hill, Chateau Reynella, Clarendon Hills, d'Arenberg, Grosset, Hardys, Henschke, Hollick, Katnook Estate, Tim Knappstein, Krondorf, Leasingham, Peter Lehmann, Charles Melton, Geoff Merrill, Mountadam, Orlando, Penfolds, Penley Estate, Petaluma, St Hallett, Seaview, Seppelt, Shaw & Smith, Geoff Weaver, Wendouree, Wirra Wirra, Wynns, Yalumba.

MITCHELL

Much of Australia's finest Riesling comes from the Clare Valley. This is benchmark Riesling with limy-citrus aromas and crisp piercing acidity.

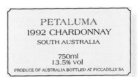

PETALUMA

Made by the talented Brian Croser, Petaluma's Chardonnay from the cooler Adelaide Hills is recognized as one of Australia's best.

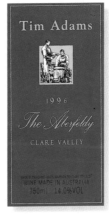

TIM ADAMS

Wines with exceptional depth of flavour are the hallmark here. The peppery Aberfeldy Shiraz is a remarkable wine from 90-year-old vines growing near Wendouree in the Clare Valley.

SPITZ

AUSTRIA, Niederösterreich, Wachau

Spitz is the last important wine commune as you travel west through the WACHAU up the Danube. The climate is cooler here than further east due to the vineyards' proximity to the Jauerling Mountain and the way in which the massive cliffs at DÜRNSTEIN block the flow of warm 'Panonian' air streams from the Hungarian plain. However, some of the most exciting and aromatic late-harvested Wachau wines can be produced here. Best producers: Franz HIRTZBERGER, Josef HÖGL, Lagler, Freie Weingärtner WACHAU.

SPOTTSWOODE

USA, California, Napa County, Napa Valley AVA
🍷 *Cabernet Sauvignon, Merlot, Cabernet Franc*
🍷 *Sauvignon Blanc, Semillon*

In the 1970s, after purchasing a majestic Victorian home in St Helena, the Novak family revived its adjacent pre-Prohibition 102-ha (40-acre) vineyard. The Novaks planted BORDEAUX varieties, first red then white. In 1982, with Tony Soter at the helm, Spottswoode began an enviable record for sturdy, spot-on Cabernet Sauvignon. Today, with a completely replanted vineyard and Soter now a consultant, the Novaks, mother Mary and daughter Beth, maintain high standards. Spottswoode's recent Cabernets are more supple and inviting in their youth, but destined to age well for at least a decade. Best years: 1997, '96, '95 '94, '93, '92, '91 '90, '89, '87. Partially barrel-fermented and enhanced by a generous splash of Semillon, the Sauvignon Blancs are an enticing mouthful of melon fruit and lovely figs, balanced by a touch of oak. Best years: 1998, '97, '96, '95, '94.

SPRING MOUNTAIN DISTRICT AVA

USA, California, Napa County

Spring Mountain District begins west of St Helena at the foothills above 122m (400ft) and continues on up to the top of the ridge separating NAPA VALLEY from SONOMA COUNTY. Although its pioneering winery, Stony Hill, is a Chardonnay specialist with an interest in Riesling and Gewürztraminer, Spring Mountain is best suited today to red varieties such as Cabernet Sauvignon, Merlot, Petite Sirah and Syrah. These reds dominate the 1214ha (3000 acres) presently planted to vines. Best producers: Barnett, Cain Five, Keenan, NEWTON, Spring Mountain Vineyards, Phillip Togni. Best years: (reds) 1998, '97, '95, '94, '92, '91, '90.

The dramatic rocky peak of Stag's Leap in the hills on the eastern side of the Napa Valley, has given its name to the picturesque Stags Leap District, which has built up a reputation for distinctive Cabernet Sauvignon.

STAGLIN FAMILY VINEYARDS

USA, California, Napa County, Rutherford AVA
🍷 *Cabernet Sauvignon, Sangiovese*
🍷 *Chardonnay*

In 1985 Garen and Shari Staglin purchased a prime 19-ha (47-acre) vineyard in the western edge of RUTHERFORD. Developed by BEAULIEU, this vineyard was a key component in many vintages of Beaulieu Private Reserve Cabernet Sauvignon. However, it had become phylloxera-infested. The Staglins systematically replanted the vineyard, and Staglin Cabernet began on a high level in 1989. With each vintage, even more of the cassis, dried sage and incredible depth characteristic of the Rutherford mesoclimate is captured. Not to be overlooked is a highly concentrated, splendid Sangiovese labelled Stagliano. Best years: (reds) 1997, '96, '95 '94, '92. Replanting disrupted Staglin's Chardonnay production, but it resumed in 1997 with bright fruit, fine balance, and a streamlined personality. Best years: 1998, '97.

STAGS LEAP DISTRICT AVA

USA, California, Napa County, Napa Valley AVA

Cabernet Sauvignon has been the focus in this small but beautiful sub-AVA in the southeastern NAPA VALLEY ever since its vineyards were replanted in the early 1970s. CLOS DU VAL and STAG'S LEAP WINE CELLARS soon produced impressive Cabernet Sauvignons, and other wineries have since followed suit.

The district threads its way east from the Napa River up increasingly steep slopes to the foot of a towering basaltic palisade. The combination of shading hills, alluvial soils, west-facing exposure and morning fogs can yield Cabernets and Merlots with berryish flavours and softer tannins than those from the Valley floor, which lies to the west. There is also estimable Zinfandel (Clos du Val) and above-average Chardonnay (S Anderson). Best producers: Chimney Rock, Clos du Val, PINE RIDGE, SHAFER VINEYARDS, SILVERADO VINEYARDS, Robert Sinskey, STAG'S LEAP WINE CELLARS, Stelzner. Best years: 1998, '97, '95, '94, '93, '92, '91, '90, '87.

STAG'S LEAP WINE CELLARS
Recent vintages at this winery have been back on top form. The SLV Cabernet Reserve, from estate vineyards, is full, velvety and well-structured.

STAG'S LEAP WINE CELLARS

USA, California, Napa County, Stags Leap District AVA

♥ *Cabernet Sauvignon, Merlot, Petite Sirah*

♀ *Chardonnay, Sauvignon Blanc*

As an upstart winery back in 1976, Stag's Leap put CALIFORNIA on the international wine map when its Cabernet Sauvignon bested BORDEAUX's biggest names in the now-famous Paris tasting. No flash in the pan, Stag's Leap has gone on to develop an impressive record for its Cabernet Sauvignons. The deluxe limited edition is the Cask 23 Cabernet, a supple, ultra-voluptuous wine made only in exceptional vintages. Not far behind is the SLV Reserve, a sturdy, classically sculpted, yet supple Cabernet from the original parcel of the Stag's Leap Vineyard. Made in slightly larger volume is the Fay Vineyard Cabernet Sauvignon, and this is complemented by the Napa Valley Cabernet Sauvignon. Best years: (Cabernets) 1997, '96, '95, '94, '93, '92, '91, '90, '87, '85, '84.

Recently, owner Warren Winiarski has applied his talents to Chardonnay and his Reserve is one of NAPA's most complete, complex and layered versions on the market. Best years: 1998, '97, '95, '94. Even his Petite Sirah rises above its pedigree to display some complexity and considerable intrigue.

STAPLE VINEYARDS

ENGLAND, Kent

♀ *Müller-Thurgau, Huxelrebe*

This vineyard, with just under 3ha (7 acres) of vines, produces a good, smoky, grapefruity Huxelrebe under the Staple St James label as well as a sharply focused but full-bodied Müller-Thurgau. The joy of Staple St James is the intense fruit in a bone-dry style, but there are some medium-dry ones as well. Drink the wines young, or several years' age.

STEELE WINES

USA, California, Lake County

♥ *Pinot Noir, Syrah, Zinfandel*

♀ *Chardonnay, Pinot Blanc*

Veteran winemaker Jed Steele was the mastermind behind the KENDALL-JACKSON popular style of Chardonnay that made the winery king of Chardonnay in the 1990s. Starting his own winery after a long dispute with Mr Jackson, Steele returned to his favourite wine, Zinfandel, and Zinfandel fans are happy he did.

Now ensconced in Lake County, he offers a range of Zinfandel from some of the oldest vineyards in MENDOCINO and Lake County. He has recently turned his many talents to Chardonnay from several vineyard sources such as Sangiacomo, Durrell and DuPratt, and offers Pinot Noir from Sangiacomo's CARNEROS vineyard, from Bien Nacido Vineyard in Santa Maria Valley and from other growers. Balancing ripe fruit and oak, Steele's Chardonnays and Pinot Noirs develop nicely with three to four years of aging. Best years: 1998, '97, '96, '95. Shooting Star is a second label offering lower-priced wines. Steele has encouraged Lake County growers to develop Syrah and plans to make Syrah part of his primary roster in the future.

STEIERMARK

AUSTRIA

This region, called Styria in English, is divided into three areas: Weststeiermark, Südsteiermark and Süd-Oststeiermark. Steiermark has the distinction of being Austria's favourite wine region: its lean, austere style of wine proved a perfect antidote to the scandal-tainted sweet wines of the 1980s, and fashion has stayed with Styria ever since, inexorably raising the prices.

Of the three areas, Südsteiermark is the smallest but has the most vineyards (1902ha/4670 acres). It also has the best-quality wine, particularly from Chardonnay (here called Morillon), Sauvignon Blanc, Pinot Blanc and Gelber Muskateller. Weststeiermark's speciality is a light, acidic rosé wine called Schilcher, made from the local Blauer Wildbacher grape and produced by almost every grower in the region. Drink it young and fresh. Try it if you find yourself in the region, but don't bother bringing it home. Most of the wine from the Süd-Oststeiermark is sold in the local taverns. Best producers: GROSS, LACKNER-TINNACKER, POLZ, TEMENT, Winkler-Hermaden.

STELLENBOSCH WO

SOUTH AFRICA, Western Cape

See also Stellenbosch, pages 354–355

East of Cape Town, this wine region is the most important in South Africa. Nearly half of all the Cape's Cabernet Sauvignon, Merlot and Shiraz are planted in the Stellenbosch region and many of the country's finest red wines come from here. Some very fine whites are also made – selected sites, such as those at THELEMA and MULDERBOSCH, consistently turn out Sauvignon Blanc of international standing. There are plenty of excellent Chardonnays too, although the winemaker's influence still often overrides that of the vineyard. Stellenbosch is the base for industry giants STELLENBOSCH FARMERS' WINERY and Distillers Corporation. It is also home to South Africa's only university offering Viticulture and Enology, Elsenburg Agricultural College, where many winemakers train, and to the Viticultural and Enological Research Station. Best producers: L'Avenir, Avontuur, Beyerskloof, Blaauwklippen, Bredell, Cordoba, Delheim, Eikendal, Neil ELLIS, GRANGEHURST, Hartenberg, Jordan, Kaapzicht, KANONKOP, Le Bonheur, Longridge, Louisvale, MEERLUST, Morgenhof, Mulderbosch, NEETHLINGSHOF, OVERGAAUW, Rust-en-Vrede, RUSTENBERG, SAXENBURG, Simonsig, Stellenzicht, Thelema, Uiterwyk, Vergelegen, Vriesenhof, WARWICK.

STELLENBOSCH FARMERS' WINERY (SFW)

SOUTH AFRICA, Western Cape

♥ *Cabernet Sauvignon, Pinotage, Merlot, Shiraz and others*

♀ *Chenin Blanc, Sauvignon Blanc, Cruchen Blanc (South African/Cape Riesling), Chardonnay and others*

This is South Africa's largest wine merchant-producer (founded by American William Charles Winshaw in 1935). It should be, and has the resources to be, South Africa's equivalent to Australia's PENFOLDS but regrettably, nowadays, lacks the vision of the Aussie giant. In 1961 it launched South Africa's first bottled Pinotage and the semi-sweet white Lieberstein which started the county's unfortified wine revolution. Many of those early brands, now decidedly old-fashioned, are still among the industry's bestsellers.

Two PAARL wineries are also part of the SFW, but run separately. The Nederburg range is commercial but also produces a Reserve range of premium varietals, Cabernet Sauvignon, Chardonnay and Sauvignon Blanc. The high point is the dessert wine; the pioneering botrytized Edelkeur is now being strongly challenged by Private Bin Rhine Rieslings and a more SAUTERNES-style Semillon Noble Late Harvest. All are sold only through the annual Nederburg Wine Auction, the industry's premier social event.

Plaisir de Merle is SFW's flagship winery on the Paarl slopes of the Simonsberg. It is notable for a creamy, soft Cabernet Sauvignon from new-clone vines. Winemaker Neil Bester has spent some time at Ch. MARGAUX working with its technical director, Paul Pontallier. Best years: (Plaisir de Merle Cabernet Sauvignon) 1996, '95, '94, '93.

STELLENBOSCH South Africa

THE PICTURESQUE WINE REGION OF STELLENBOSCH can be likened to a vast amphitheatre, the towering mountains represent the curve of seats, the vine-clad slopes and valley the stage and False Bay its backdrop. No wonder it struck Simon van der Stel, after whom the town is named, as an ideal spot for farming and settlement. That was in 1679; in the intervening 320 years, the area has established itself as the hub of South Africa's wine industry and producer of many of the country's finest red wines. The town itself boasts many national monuments, thousands of oak trees (introduced by van der Stel) and an ever-increasing number of restaurants, never sufficient it seems to cope with residents, a university population and flocks of tourists.

As might be expected of a region covering more than 15,500ha (38,300 acres), there are many different climates and soils, one to suit each of the major grape varieties currently available and probably all the new ones starting to make an appearance. This diversity and versatility is partly due to the fact that the region's boundaries were originally drawn up along all-inclusive political rather than climatic lines. But the most famous wines traditionally from Stellenbosch were Cabernet Sauvignon – and they still are.

The historic Vergelegen estate at Somerset West lies on the western foothills of the Hottentots Holland mountains and benefits as much from the cooling breezes from Walker Bay as from those from nearby False Bay.

Stellenbosch boasts the greatest concentration of wineries of any region in the Cape and was the first region in South Africa to develop a wine route for tourists. The burgeoning number of wineries has encouraged producers in smaller, more homogenous areas within the region to recognize they have a certain similarity of style. These are gradually being demarcated as wards, where criteria for inclusion features, *inter alia*, topography and mesoclimate. There is, however, no restriction on grape varieties planted, viticultural nor winemaking practices. It is becoming noticeable that varieties that do particularly well within a ward are being promoted by the producers. Bottelary is known for red wines, Shiraz in particular but also Merlot and Cabernet Sauvignon. Stylistically, the red wines of Simonsberg-Stellenbosch are big and muscular, while those of the Helderberg, not yet legally a ward, but a continuous stretch of mountain close to the cooling influence of False Bay with its maritime breezes, are united by finer-honed tannins and breed.

VERGELEGEN
The stylish barrel-fermented Chardonnay Reserve is one of the leading wines from this stunning estate with its new, state-of-the-art octagonal winery built on top of a hill.

KANONKOP
Kanonkop has long produced South Africa's best-known Pinotage wine from mostly old bush vines. The Estate wine is vividly coloured with intense fruit and some new oak.

Stellenbosch Wards
— Stellenbosch WO wine area
▢ Bottelary
▢ Devon Valley
▢ Papegaaiberg
▢ Simonsberg-Stellenbosch
▢ Jonkershoek Valley

CLOS MALVERNE
The Pinotage grape, South Africa's own local variety, can produce powerful, flavoursome, opulently plummy wines, some of them world-class. Clos Malverne has sumptuous fruit but just enough structure to age.

REGIONAL ENTRY
Stellenbosch.

PRODUCER ENTRIES
The Bergkelder, Neil Ellis, Grangehurst, Kanonkop, Meerlust, Mulderbosch, Neethlingshof, Overgaauw, Rustenberg, Saxenburg, Stellenbosch Farmers' Winery, Thelema, Warwick Farm.

SAXENBURG
The headily scented, burly Private Collection Shiraz with good tannin is the top wine at this renowned red wine estate.

THELEMA
From vineyards located high up in the Simonsberg range, Gyles Webb makes first-rate Chardonnay with fine spicy, toasty oak and ripe peachy, lemony fruit.

PLAISIR DE MERLE
The Stellenbosch Farmers' Winery acquired this Paarl winery in the 1960s and the red wines are beginning to win considerable acclaim.

MEERLUST
Rubicon was one of the Cape's first Bordeaux-style reds and continues to be among South Africa's top two or three wines of this style.

STERLING VINEYARDS

USA, California, Napa County, Napa Valley AVA

♟ *Cabernet Sauvignon, Pinot Noir, Merlot*

♀ *Chardonnay, Sauvignon Blanc and others*

Sterling has had three owners since its founding in 1969, which has caused it to look a bit rudderless at times. But the new winemaking team of Rob Hunter and Greg Fowler of MUMM NAPA is beginning to improve quality and consistency. The NAPA VALLEY Chardonnays have settled into a rich, balanced, subtle and age-worthy style, and the Diamond Mountain Chardonnay is not far behind. Best years: 1997, '96, '95, '93, '91. Sauvignon Blancs, once understated and iron-hard, have become suppler. The Cabernet-based Reserve remains dark and forbiddingly built. Three Palms (a single-vineyard red based on Merlot) more closely resembles the rather lean regular Cabernet. Best years: 1997, '95, '94, '92, '91, '90, '87, '86, '85. Just starting to make waves is a Pinot Noir from the Winery Lake Vineyard, a famous CARNEROS property. Even so, consistency is still elusive, particularly with the Cabernets and Merlots.

STONECROFT

NEW ZEALAND, North Island, Hawke's Bay

♟ *Cabernet Sauvignon, Merlot, Syrah*

♀ *Chardonnay, Gewurztraminer, Sauvignon Blanc*

Dr Alan Limmer, an analytical chemist, is an enthusiastic promoter of the Gimblett district of HAWKE'S BAY. Deep gravel beds provide free drainage and accelerate the ripening process by reflecting the sun's rays and retaining heat in the large river stones that litter the vineyard. Stonecroft pioneered quality Syrah in New Zealand and its lead has encouraged others, particularly in Hawke's Bay and on WAIHEKE ISLAND. The winery makes intensely floral Gewurztraminer, a weighty Chardonnay with strong tropical fruit and a ripe, concentrated Sauvignon Blanc that is a far cry from the MARLBOROUGH wines. Reds age magnificently while the whites, particularly Gewurztraminer and Chardonnay, also improve with bottle age. Best years: 1998, '96, '94, '91.

STONESTREET WINERY

USA, California, Sonoma County, Alexander Valley AVA

♟ *Cabernet Sauvignon, Merlot, Pinot Noir*

♀ *Chardonnay, Sauvignon Blanc*

Owned by KENDALL-JACKSON and now in a large, new winery in the ALEXANDER VALLEY, Stonestreet's best wines are BORDEAUX-style reds, led by Legacy. However, both Cabernet Sauvignon and an intense, ripe cherry Merlot are now displaying some needed restraint. Still, because these wines are made from choice hillside vineyards, they are built to survive the test of time and at least five years is needed for the Merlot, and closer to ten for the others. Best years: 1997, '96, '95, '94, '93, '92. Stonestreet also makes a full-bodied RUSSIAN RIVER VALLEY Pinot Noir and a CARNEROS Chardonnay. On a tiny scale, the winery makes an amazing, concentrated Sauvignon Blanc and an over-the-top Chardonnay, both from the former Gauer Ranch, an outstanding mountain vineyard in the Alexander Valley owned by Kendall-Jackson.

STONIER'S

AUSTRALIA, Victoria, Port Phillip Zone, Mornington Peninsula

♟ *Pinot Noir, Cabernet Sauvignon, Cabernet Franc*

♀ *Chardonnay, Sauvignon Blanc*

In a move that surprised some, PETALUMA acquired 70 per cent of Stonier's in 1998. The chief attraction was the quality of its Chardonnay and Pinot Noir, particularly the Reserve wine. At 18,000 cases a year, it's also the largest winery on the Peninsula. The Chardonnay is always creamy textured with melon, fig and cashew flavours, and is slightly less susceptible to vintage variation than the Pinot Noir, though the Reserve often has attractive flavours of strawberry, plum, cherry and violet. Best years: 1998, '97, '94, '92, '91, '90.

STONYRIDGE

NEW ZEALAND, North Island, Waiheke Island

♟ *Cabernet Sauvignon, Merlot, Cabernet Franc, Malbec, Petit Verdot, Syrah*

Owner Stephen White believes the vinous world starts at BORDEAUX and finishes at WAIHEKE ISLAND – well, almost. The wine comes in two guises: Larose (named after the roses at the ends of the rows of vines) and Airfield (there is one close by) for the second label. The Larose is a very successful Bordeaux style, concentrated and deep and proven to age well. Best years: 1998, '96, '94, '93, '91, '89, '87.

STROFILIA

GREECE, Attica, Anavissos

♟♀ *Agiorgitiko, Cabernet Sauvignon*

♀ *Savatiano, Rhoditis, Assyrtiko and others*

This interesting estate was started in 1981 by two engineers who were convinced that the land lying between Athens and Cape Sounion could produce fine wine. In addition to an excellent basic range of red, rosé and white under the Strofilia label, there is a wonderful Nafssika white. The Strofilia wine bar in central Athens showcases all the best Greek wines. Best years: (reds) 1997, '95.

CH. SUDUIRAUT

Although the wine is delicious at only a few years old, the richness and excitement increases enormously after a decade or so.

CH. SUDUIRAUT

FRANCE, Bordeaux, Sauternes AC, Premier Cru Classé

♀ *Sémillon, Sauvignon Blanc*

Although d'YQUEM is universally acclaimed as the greatest sweet wine in SAUTERNES, its neighbour to the north, Suduiraut, has often been suggested for the role of runner-up. Suduiraut has a fresher, more perfumed quality than the other chief contender, Yquem's neighbour to the east, Ch. RIEUSSEC – and if Rieussec is sometimes more blatantly sumptuous, Suduiraut can counter this with a viscous ripeness that coats your mouth as if the whole were wrapped in melted butter and cream. Add to this a delicious fruit, like pineapples and peaches soaked in syrup, and you can get some idea of the expansive, lusciousness of which Suduiraut is capable.

Strangely, although Suduiraut made excellent Sauternes in the two difficult vintages of 1979 and '82, its form in the 70s and most of the '80s was unconvincing. Recently, though, it has been back on top form with some superb vintages. The owners, insurance company AXA, have invested heavily in the large 90-ha (222-acre) estate, which usually produces about 132,000 bottles a year. Best years: 1998, '97, '96, '95, '90, '89, '88, '86, '82, '79, '76.

SUHINDOL

BULGARIA, Northern Region

♟ *Cabernet Sauvignon, Merlot, Gamza and others*

♀ *Dimiat and others*

The Suhindol winery perfected the creamy, curranty style of Cabernet Sauvignon now synonymous with Bulgaria. Its transition from state co-operative to quasi-private concern has been reasonably seamless. The use of stainless steel and temperature-controlled fermentation has enabled the winemakers to concentrate on clean, supple wines. In recent years it has not been easy to obtain totally mature fruit at harvest times because growers have become wary of losing their harvest to rot, bad weather and even piracy in the vineyards. Nevertheless, Suhindol still provides the yardstick for Bulgarian Cabernet Sauvignon. Gamza is a native red grape variety that also delivers wines with subtle, damson-like flavours and a firm, earthy structure. Better-looking bottles and prettier labels are adding to the modern feel that is slowly overtaking this winery. Having recently bought several other wineries, it is now one of Bulgaria's largest producers, making 30 million bottles a year.

SUMAC RIDGE
CANADA, British Columbia, Okanagan Valley VQA
❧ *Cabernet Sauvignon, Merlot*
♀ *Gewurztraminer, Pinot Blanc*

Sumac Ridge and its founder and managing partner Harry McWatters are at the heart of the British Columbia wine industry. McWatters opened the doors of Sumac Ridge in 1980. He later played a key role in building the British Columbia Wine Institute and establishing Canada's national Vintners Quality Alliance (VQA) wine laws. Sumac's diverse range of mostly varietal wines is led by one of the valley's finest Gewurztraminers, a fine Pinot Blanc, and one of the country's best CHAMPAGNE-method sparklers – Stellar's Jay Brut. A vineyard acquisition in the southern part of the OKANAGAN VALLEY is expanding the production of red wine, including both blended (Meritage) and varietal wines from Cabernet Sauvignon, Cabernet Franc, Merlot and Pinot Noir. Best years: 1998, '97, '95, '94.

SUNBURY
AUSTRALIA, Victoria, Port Phillip Zone
Two of VICTORIA's most historic wineries can be found in this region, only 20 minutes' drive north of Tullamarine Airport. Goona Warra was built in 1863, and Craiglee the following year, each by wealthy citizens of their time. After a hiatus in the first half of this century, viticultural life has returned to Sunbury, and Craiglee is producing one of Australia's best cool-climate Shiraz wines – harking back to its famous 1872 vintage, which a number of lucky connoisseurs have been able to taste over the past 20 years after a cache was unearthed at the winery. The key to the modern Shiraz is the intensity of the black cherry, spice and licorice flavours enveloped in a skein of fine tannin. Best years: 1998, '97, '94, '92, '91, '90. Best producers: Craiglee, Goona Warra, Wildwood.

SUPER-TUSCAN
ITALY, Tuscany
The super-Tuscan phenomenon started life as a high-class VINO DA TAVOLA revolt against prevailing restrictive DOC laws, in particular in

CHIANTI CLASSICO; today, the laws are in the process of being altered to bring most examples back into the DOC fold, under denominations such as the revised Chianti Classico, SANT'ANTIMO or even the new regional DOC for TOSCANA. Basically there are three types of super-Tuscan: 100 per cent Sangiovese; 100 per cent French red grapes such as Cabernet, Merlot, Syrah or Pinot Noir, separately or as a blend; and Italian grape (read Sangiovese) and French (usually Cabernet or Merlot) blended. The wines will be barrique-aged and will be at Riserva quality level at least, although that description cannot be used on the label. Prototypes are usually considered to be MONTEVERTINE's Le Pergole Torte of the first type; of the second, SASSICAIA; of the third, ANTINORI's Tignanello or Solaia.

The law is determined that the strays will be brought back into the fold and already a vino da tavola that does not satisfy the admittedly flexible laws of IGT has no right to state a grape variety, a provenance or a vintage on the label. The first two one could do without, but the year is more crucial – there's a world of difference, for example, between a wine of 1996 and '97.

SUTTER HOME WINERY
USA, California, Napa County, Napa Valley AVA
❧ *Cabernet Sauvignon, Zinfandel*
❦ *Zinfandel*
♀ *Chardonnay, Sauvignon Blanc, Chenin Blanc*

Though its home is the NAPA VALLEY, Sutter Home made its mark with grapes from outside. Known in the 1970s for its robust Amador County Zinfandels, this winery experimented with a sweetish White Zinfandel in 1975 and struck it rich. The mass market sucked up every drop the winery was able to bottle, and White Zinfandel sales soared to four million cases. Profits have enabled the Trinchero family, the savvy owners, to purchase other wineries such as Montevina and to develop vineyards north of Sacramento for successful low-priced wines, led by a bland but reasonably pleasant Chardonnay. Its Reserve Amador Zinfandel still packs a wallop. New signature wines (Zinfandel, Chardonnay and Sauvignon Blanc) are sure to please bargain hunters. Most of the wines are ready to drink on release.

SWAN DISTRICT
AUSTRALIA, Western Australia, Greater Perth Zone
The Swan District boasts the oldest Australian winery in continuous production: Olive Farm, started in 1829. It is mainly a white wine

region, with Chenin Blanc the most important decent variety, followed by Verdelho, Chardonnay, Muscadelle, Shiraz (Syrah) and Cabernet Sauvignon. Best years: 1998, '97, '95, '94, '93, '91. Best producers: Jane Brook, HOUGHTON, Lamont, Olive Farm, Westfield.

SWANSON VINEYARDS
USA, California, Napa County, Rutherford District AVA
❧ *Cabernet Sauvignon, Merlot, Sangiovese, Syrah*
♀ *Chardonnay, Semillon*

After systematically developing over 61ha (150 acres) of vineyards in the Oakville area, Swanson began on a high note and has not lost a beat since. Its regular Chardonnay is bright and balanced, and the Reserve displays loads of new oak complexity. An occasional Late Harvest Semillon enjoys a strong following. Best years: 1998, '97, '96, '95, '94. The Cabernet Sauvignon is solid and the Merlot captures more intense berry fruit and complexity than most. Swanson has earned high marks for its velvety, cherry-fruity, poised Sangiovese and a massive, peppery Syrah. Best years: (reds) 1997, '96, '95, '94, '92.

SWANSON VINEYARDS *Sangiovese is the new darling of California, but Swanson was in the forefront and has settled on a California style midway between a Chianti and a super-Tuscan.*

SYLVANER
This grape may not be exciting (it is generally rather acidic and appley), but it certainly gets around. It is found all over Central Europe, where it is often spelled Silvaner. It is particularly common in Germany's FRANKEN but is losing ground all over the country to other varieties. In France it is planted only in ALSACE, and even there it is giving way to Pinot Blanc, which has the same advantages as Sylvaner (producing big yields on uninspired vineyard land) but with the added attraction of good creamy flavours.

SYRAH

Syrah, the great red grape of the northern Rhône in France, leapt from relative obscurity in the 1980s to worldwide fame during the '90s – but it largely achieved this using an entirely different name, Shiraz. This was because, though it makes such stupendous wines as Hermitage and Côte Rôtie in the Rhone Valley, the name of the grape is never on the label. It was Australia's rapid ascent to global popularity during the '90s that catapulted Shiraz into pole position as the quality alternative to Cabernet Sauvignon, because in Australia it is the name of the grape variety on the label in capital letters that is important, rather than the vineyard region. Why the Australians call the Syrah Shiraz isn't clear – although the Iranian city of Shiraz is thought to have been the birthplace of the grape as long ago as 600BC – but the grape is the same, and it makes many of the most thrilling, enthralling and unique wines to come out of Australia. And since, during the 1990s, the New World dictated terms more than the old, the name Shiraz spread round the world faster than the name Syrah. Still, the original wines to make the grape famous are from France, so let's go back there.

In the northern Rhône ACs of Hermitage, Côte-Rôtie, Cornas, St-Joseph and, in milder form, Crozes-Hermitage, it makes dark, concentrated wine, thick with tannin and hot with jammy fruit and pepper and tar that, between five and ten years after its birth, undergoes a transformation. The tar and pepper subside into a smoky, leathery perfume, while the tannins drop away to reveal a wonderful sweet fruit – blackberries, blackcurrants, raspberries, violets and plums – the black chewiness of dark treacle and licorice, the slightly bitter edge of pine. Further south in the Rhône Valley, and in the Languedoc, Syrah is used to add a dark juicy fruit and a floral perfume to many more mundane reds. It is showing powerful form in Spain, and both Italy and Greece have succeeded with it, as, amazingly, has Switzerland!

The most famous – or infamous – Australian example of Shiraz was from New South Wales' Hunter Valley, where a tarry 'sweaty saddle' pong was thought of as true varietal style. Nowadays far more exciting examples are made elsewhere – in particular in South Australia, where Clare, Barossa and McLaren Vale produce wines of enormous power but heady, giddy sweetness as well. Victoria and Western Australia also do fine versions and even New Zealand has a couple of examples.

South Africa's love affair with Cabernet Sauvignon hindered Shiraz's development there, but recent examples have shown good, quite rich style. California, too, was late getting going with Shiraz/Syrah, largely because the other Rhône grapes were preferred in the nineteenth century. Countries such as Mexico, Chile and Argentina are ideally suited to Shiraz and we'll see some exciting flavours from them in the coming years.

LA TÂCHE AC

FRANCE, Burgundy, Côte de Nuits, Grand Cru
🍷 *Pinot Noir*

Along with Romanée-Conti, la Tâche is at the very peak of VOSNE-ROMANÉE's Grands Crus, and similarly owned by Domaine de la ROMANÉE-CONTI. But there's a lot more la Tâche – 6.1ha (15 acres) as against 1.8ha (4.4 acres) – and annual production is generally around 24,000 bottles. The vineyard's position is superb, just yards south of Romanée-Conti, fractionally more southeast, at the perfect altitude of between 250 and 300m (800–1000ft). The wine is not only a sensation for the palate, but also for the brain and the heart, because this is the most sensuous and emotional of all Burgundy's great reds. Best years: 1996, '95, '93, '91, '90, '89, '88, '87, '85, '83, '80, '79, '78, '71.

TAITTINGER

FRANCE, Champagne, Champagne AC
🍾 🥂 *Pinot Noir, Chardonnay, Pinot Meunier*

This is one of the few large independent CHAMPAGNE houses. For many years it was infuriating that the top-of-the-line Comtes de Champagne Blanc de Blancs was one of the most memorable wines produced in Champagne, while the non-vintage Brut – the affordable one – was dull, lifeless and extremely short on fun. Well, there's been a change of direction. The non-vintage is now soft, honeyed, much better balanced between fresh acidity and spice, and showing a relatively high percentage of Chardonnay. The marketing men have found a way to create yet another ultra de-luxe, called Vintage Collection, each vintage in a specially commissioned modern art bottle. The wines are certainly good, but not cheap. Those more interested in Champagne than packaging should stick to the delicious Comtes de Champagne. Best years: 1991, '90, '89, '88, '86, '85, '82, '79.

CH. TALBOT

FRANCE, Bordeaux, St-Julien AC, 4ème Cru Classé
🍷 *Cabernet Sauvignon, Merlot, Cabernet Franc, Petit Verdot*

Talbot is a superb BORDEAUX Fourth Growth which probably should be upgraded to a Second. It's a very big estate – 101ha (250 acres) – occupying a single chunk of land bang in the middle of the ST-JULIEN AC. The wine is big, soft-centred but sturdy, capable of aging extremely well for ten to 20 years, going from rather rich, almost sweet beginnings to a maturity of plums, blackcurrants and cigarbox scent – yet never to quite the same extent as its neighbour GRUAUD-LAROSE, but then Gruaud-Larose is a Second Growth. A small amount of white Bordeaux, Cailloux Blanc de Talbot, is also produced from mainly Sauvignon Blanc. The second wine is Connétable Talbot. Best years: 1998, '97, '96, '95, '94, '90, '89, '88, '86, '85, '83, '82, '81, '79, '78.

TALTARNI

AUSTRALIA, Victoria, Western Victoria Zone, Pyrenees
🍷 *Cabernet Sauvignon, Merlot, Syrah (Shiraz), Malbec*
🍾 *Sauvignon Blanc, Riesling*

After 26 years in the job, Taltarni's only winemaker, Frenchman Dominique Portet, has retired. He leaves a legacy of some of Australia's most formidable red wines, hewn in a bold form from Syrah, Cabernet Sauvignon and Merlot, replete with plum pudding fruit and masses of tannin. Crisp, tangy Sauvignon Blanc is a total, but very enjoyable contrast. With such a strong base, the new owners should have no trouble excelling. Best years: 1996, '94, '93, '92, '91, '90, '88, '86, '84, '82.

LANE TANNER

USA, California, Santa Barbara County, Santa Maria Valley AVA
🍷 *Pinot Noir, Syrah*

Lane Tanner worked her way up the ranks from cellar rat to winemaker before starting out on her own. Her speciality is Pinot Noir, made by traditional cellar procedures of minimum handling. Early vintages from Sierra Madre Vineyard and Bien Nacido Vineyard, captured the individuality of each site with elegance and subtlety. Today she focuses on Pinot from both Bien Nacido Vineyard and from SANTA BARBARA COUNTY. Her signature style continues to be lush, silky Pinots that age well and show their best after five to seven years. Best years: 1998, '97, '96, '95. Recent experiments with Syrah show a subtle hand with that grape as well.

TARNAVE
ROMANIA, Transylvania

♥ *Oporto*

♀ *Fetească, Riesling, Muscat Ottonel and others*

Tarnave, in the north of the country with its mixed population of Romanians and Hungarians, is almost entirely given over to white wines. The vineyards are quite high, at about 400m (1300ft), and it's cool enough to get a bit of freshness into the wines, though whether this survives the winemaking process is another matter. The Jidvei winery is a great deal better than some in Romania, but standards are still erratic. A really young Fetească is probably a good bet, as is a young Sauvignon Blanc or Muscat-Riesling blend, but once the wines are a couple of years old, or if they are sweetish, they may well be getting coarse. Some dessert wines are made, generally from late-harvested rather than botrytized grapes.

TARRAGONA DO, TERRA ALTA DO
SPAIN, Cataluña

♥ ♀ *Grenache Noir (Garnacha Tinta), Carignan (Cariñena), Samsó, Cabernet Sauvignon, Merlot, Syrah, Tempranillo (Ull de Llebre)*

♀ *Macabeo, Xarel-lo, Parellada, Chardonnay, Grenache Blanc (Garnacha Blanca), Moscatel de Alejandría (Muscat of Alexandria)*

Adjoining the reborn PRIORAT DO, the two southernmost Catalan DOs are trying to catch a ray of the spotlight now shining on their neighbour. The DO was essentially awarded to Tarragona to upgrade its longstanding trade in alcoholic bulk wines with southern France and, later, it became an important supplier of base wines for CAVA. Terra Alta, a wild, hilly area, was for a long time mainly white wine country, centred on the Garnacha Blanca grape, and home of the De Muller vineyard which made the Vatican's communion wine.

First, producers in the favoured Falset subregion of Tarragona, the one closest to Priorat (and with thin soils over granite bedrock that approach Priorat's slate for quality), took their clue from the Priorat newcomers and began producing big, fruity, deep red wines in similar fashion. Cabernet Sauvignon, Merlot and Syrah were extensively planted. The Capçanes cooperative, now probably Spain's best, led the charge with a dazzling array of wines. In turn, the smaller family bodegas in Terra Alta awoke from their slumber and began turning out some of the more interesting, markedly Mediterranean whites in Spain. Fast improvement in winemaking was apparent, yet much remains to be done, particularly by the predominant cooperatives. Best years: 1996, '95, '94. Best producers: (Tarragona) Josep Anguera Beyme, Capafons-Ossó, Capçanes co-operative, De Muller, Emilio Miró Salvat; (Terra Alta) Xavier Clua, De Muller, Bàrbara Forés, Gandesa cooperative, Vidal i Vidal, Viños Piñol.

TARRAWARRA
AUSTRALIA, Victoria, Port Phillip Zone, Yarra Valley

♥ *Pinot Noir*

♀ *Chardonnay*

Local wits call TarraWarra Disneyland; certainly until DOMAINE CHANDON came along it was the YARRA VALLEY's only answer to the NAPA VALLEY. Multi-millionaire owners Marc and Eva Besen have spared no expense on the winery, where winemaker David Wollan has fashioned a complex, rich, slow-maturing Chardonnay. His dense, dark plum Pinot Noir is equally slow to mature. Best years: 1997, '96, '95, '94, '92, '90, '89, '88.

TASMANIA
AUSTRALIA

Cool-climate Tasmania supplied the grape vines which established both the Victorian and South Australian wine industries; wine was sold on a commercial scale in Tasmania before those states' vines were even planted, but vine-growing declined by 1860, then ceased until 1956. Now vines are grown in a number of areas – except for the mountains in the west – but as yet results with different grapes are confusing. What is certain is the outstanding potential for high-acidity base wine for CHAMPAGNE-method sparkling wine. PIPERS BROOK's new fizz Pirie is exceptional, the racily biting Jansz sparkling wine started in collaboration with ROEDERER is now owned outright by YALUMBA, and various vineyards have been planted solely to supply sparkling base wine. However, delightful still Pinot Noir can be produced, especially on the East Coast, Chardonnay is often good, and Riesling and Gewurztraminer are a delight.

TAURASI DOCG
ITALY, Campania

♥ *Aglianico, Piedirosso, Barbera*

Taurasi comes from well-drained, cool, hilly country well inland of Vesuvius, and was promoted from DOC in 1993. It is often held up as the great red wine of southern Italy that exemplifies the glories of the Aglianico grape. Yet it can be disappointing, and consecutive vintages can have remarkably different characters, too. Most Taurasi is sold at three years old, four if a Reserva; so don't worry, just tuck the bottle away somewhere for a few years because Taurasi really needs to age. Or if you lack the patience, try leading producer MASTROBERARDINO's more stylish, single-vineyard, Radici, or Caggiono's Salae Domini. Best years: 1995, '94, '93, '90, '88, '86, '85, '83, '82, '81. Other good producers: Feudi di San Gregorio, Struzziero.

COSIMO TAURINO
ITALY, Puglia, Salice Salentino DOC

♥ *Negroamaro, Malvasia Nera*

♥ *Negroamaro*

♀ *Chardonnay*

Of the several producers of the Salentino peninsula who have emerged nationally and internationally over the past few years, most of them under the winemaking tutelage of Dr Severino Garofano, Taurino is the one which has enjoyed the highest profile. The principal wines are red, indeed almost black, and the main grape is Negroamaro, which needs several years of aging before emerging, butterfly-like, from its chrysalis, aided in the case of the principal red wines by Malvasia Nera. The range of wines is typical of the Salento area, ranging from the rich, late-picked, Brindisi red called Patriglione, a dark and brooding wine full of coffee, dark chocolate and raisiny fruit tones, to the relatively light, summery *rosato* – a must for any producer down here – called Scaloti, via the elegant red Notarpanaro and the standard-bearer Salice Salentino Rosso. Best years: (reds) 1995, '94, '93, '90, '88.

COSIMO TAURINO
Some of the best warm, aromatic reds from southern Italy include a consistently good Salice Salentino Rosso Riserva from Taurino.

TAVEL AC

FRANCE, Southern Rhône

🍷 *Grenache Noir, Cinsaut, Clairette and others*

The Tavel AC applies only to one colour of wine – pink. It is a big wine and boasts a hefty degree of alcohol as well as a big, strong, dry taste. But if rosé is supposed to be bright, cheerful and refreshing Tavel misses the mark because it just takes itself too seriously; it's also generally too old by the time it reaches the shops. One year old is fine, but examples at nearer three years old have lost their pretty pink bloom and gone orange at the edges.

The Tavel vineyards, west of Orange, are fairly extensive at 950ha (2347 acres). Grenache Noir is the dominant grape and gives ripe juicy flavours to the young wine. Unfortunately, as is often the case in the South of France, the use of Cinsaut prevents the taste from getting really fleshy and exciting. Altogether nine grapes are allowed, but Grenache and Cinsaut are the important ones. The best producers allow the grapes to soak with the juice for a few hours before fermentation to add colour as well as perfume and flavour, but too frequently Tavel is very pale orange-pink and decidedly short on perfume and freshness. Best producers: Aquéria, Genestière, Maby, Mejan-Taulier, Trinquevedel, Vieux Moulin.

TAYLOR, FLADGATE & YEATMAN

PORTUGAL, Douro, Port DOC

🍷 *Tinto Roriz (Tempranillo), Tinto Barroca, Touriga Naçional, Touriga Francesa and others*

🍷 *Gouveio, Viosinho, Rabigato, Malvasia Fina and others*

Taylor, Fladgate and Yeatman (to use its full title) has established itself as something of a 'first growth' among PORT shippers. Its vintage ports frequently reach the highest prices at auction and are famous for their richness, perfume and longevity. Taylor's owns a number of fine properties in the DOURO including Quinta de Terra Feita and the stately Quinta de Vargellas, both of which provide the backbone for the vintage ports. The wine from Vargellas has a fragrance all of its own and is bottled as a single-quinta vintage port in good interim years; (Vargellas) 1995, '91, '88, '87, '82, '78, '67, '64, '61. A recent innovation has been to bottle wine from the old Vargellas vines separately under the Vinha Velha (Old Vineyard) label.

Taylor's rather pukka image extends to the remainder of its wines, including a ripe LBV (filtered, unfortunately, but still fairly good) and First Estate, an upmarket premium ruby. Aged tawnies can also be extremely good, particularly the Over-40-Year-Old Tawny – one of the few wines in this sub-category to combine both freshness and the complexity of age. Taylor's White Port (which can make a long drink with tonic) is called Chip Dry. Best years: (vintage ports) 1994, '92, '85, '83, '80, '77, '70, '66, '63, '55, '48, '45, '27.

TE MATA

NEW ZEALAND, North Island, Hawke's Bay

🍷 *Cabernet Sauvignon, Merlot and others*

🍷 *Sauvignon Blanc, Chardonnay*

This happens to be New Zealand's oldest winery, but the story really starts in 1980 with the first Te Mata Cabernet Sauvignon, a remarkably good BORDEAUX look-alike. In 1982 came Awatea Cabernet Sauvignon and Coleraine Cabernet Merlot. In weight and style these are between a top Australian and a good Bordeaux, and better than many of either. Rich and powerful yet almost Burgundian, Elston Chardonnay is regularly one of New Zealand's best. Experiments with Shiraz are interesting, though Cape Crest and Castle Hill Sauvignon are generally a bit short of zip. Best years: 1998, '96, '94, '91, '90, '89, '83, '82.

E & M TEMENT

AUSTRIA, Steiermark, Südsteiermark, Ehrenhausen

🍷 *Sauvignon Blanc, Chardonnay (Morillon), Pinot Gris (Grauburgunder), Muscat (Gelber Muskateller), Gewürztraminer (Roter Traminer), Welschriesling*

Manfred Tement's cellar may look chaotic, but his wines are STEIERMARK's most dramatic and concentrated. Even weedy Welschriesling is capable of giving an exciting wine in his hands. However, it is for other things that wine lovers in Austria and, more recently, the USA idolize him. The serious wines are divided into two ranges: Steierische Klassik, which is made without any new oak, and the vineyard-designated wines which are made in a mix of new and used barrels. Best of all are explosively intense Sauvignon Blanc and the powerful, toasty Morillon both from the Zieregg site both fermented and aged in new oak. Best years: 1998, '97, '95, '94, '93, '92, '90.

DOMAINE TEMPIER

FRANCE, Provence, Bandol AC

🍷 *Mourvèdre, Cinsaut, Grenache and others*

🍷 *Ugni Blanc, Clairette, Bourboulenc*

Owned by the Peyraud family since 1834, Tempier has been consistently one of the best BANDOL estates for a number of years. The 28ha (69 acres) of vines are planted in tiny parcels spread through three communes, enabling Jean-Marie and François Peyraud to make a number of different cuvées. These have varying amounts of Mourvèdre in the blend, but rarely less than 60 per cent. The standard wine is the Bandol Classique, followed by the Cuvée Speciale and then the individual vineyard sites: la Migoua, la Tourtine and the 100 per cent Mourvèdre Cabassaou from 40-year-old vines. These wines have a rising crescendo of power, volume and structure and need a minimum four to five years' age and probably eight years for the Cabassaou. The rosé is one of Provence's best. The white represents only 4 per cent of the production. Best years: (reds) 1998, '97, '96, '95, '93, '90, '89.

TEMPRANILLO

Spain's best native red grape is grown widely over the northern and central parts of the country. It goes by different names in different regions: Tempranillo in Rioja and Navarra, but Tinta Fino or Tinta del País in Ribera del Duero, Tinto de Toro in Toro, Cencibel in La Mancha and Valdepeñas, and Ull de Llebre or Ojo de Liebre (hare's eye) in Cataluña.

Tempranillo performs best in the cooler regions: Ribera del Duero, the Rioja Alavesa and Alta, and the higher parts of Penedès. Here, it can make elegant wines with good colour and balancing acidity, and wild strawberry and spicy, tobaccoey flavours. It is enhanced by blending – usually with Garnacha, Graciano and Mazuelo in Rioja, and Cabernet Sauvignon in Navarra, Penedès and other parts of Spain. It can be made into lovely young, fruity wines, yet is suitable for aging in oak barrels.

In Portugal as Tinta Roriz it is the most planted red variety in the Douro, where it is used both for port and unfortified wine. It is also increasingly important in the Alentejo, where it acknowledges its Spanish origins with the title Aragonez.

The variety hasn't travelled to many countries but Argentina (especially Mendoza) has quite a bit and makes a soft juicy red, and California has a little.

TEROLDEGO ROTALIANO

The Italian red grape Teroldego is planted virtually exclusively on the gravelly soil of the Campo Rotaliano plain in TRENTINO between Mezzocorona and Lavis. Teroldego is called the 'Prince' of Trentino red wines, prized for its elegance, complexity and harmony. Overcropped, as it too often is, it can be very ordinary, at best a pleasant wine for early drinking. But in the hands of a quality producer it can reach impressive heights of breeding and concentration, capable of considerable aging. The only DOC is the varietal Teroldego Rotaliano, which may be red, rosé or Superiore, the latter qualifying as Riserva after two years of aging. Nowadays the undisputed top producer of Teroldego is Elisabetta Foradori of Mezzolombardo. Other best producers: (all north of Trento) Barone de Cles, Dorigati, Lavis co-operative, Conti Martini, Giuseppe Sebastiani.

TERRAS GAUDA

SPAIN, Galicia, Rías Baixas DO
Albariño, Loureiro, Caíño Branco

The Albariño grape gives, in good warm vintages, immensely glyceriny, potent, dizzyingly aromatic wines. But don't count on this being the rule as warm vintages aren't too common in GALICIA. One of the most consistently dazzling and mouthcoating Albariño wines, Terras Gauda is not a varietal but a blend with the interesting Loureiro and Caíño Branco varieties, which add a perceptible element of complexity. The winery opted for this style, a tradition in the O Rosal sub-region of RÍAS BAIXAS (on the Portuguese border at Tui), and made the (very good) varietal Albariño, Abadía de San Campío, its second wine. There is a rare, but less convincing, barrel-fermented Terras Gauda Black Label. The bodega owns 70ha (173 acres) of vineyards, which in the area is huge, and makes a sizeable amount of wine (up to 50,000 cases a year). Drink young or with short aging.

TERRAS DO SADO VINHO REGIONAL

PORTUGAL, Terras do Sado
Periquita, Aragonez (Tempranillo), Cabernet Sauvignon, Touriga Naçional, Trincadeira and others
Fernão Pires, Arinto, Chardonnay, Muscat of Alexandria (Moscatel de Setúbal) and others

Apart from the long-established SETÚBAL DOC for Moscatel wines, the Setúbal Peninsula (now officially called Terras do Sado), to the south of Lisbon, contains two smaller wine regions: Arrabida IPR and PALMELA IPR. These regions produce some of the best red wines in Portugal thanks mainly to three innovative wine producers: José Maria da FONSECA, BRIGHT BROS and J P VINHOS. Most of the vineyards are concentrated in the north of the region on the limestone slopes of the Serra da Arrabida and the sandy soils along the northern side of the Sado estuary. Good wines are produced around Pegoes, which has a well-run co-operative. The warm maritime climate is well suited to viticulture and a number of different grape varieties flourish in the area, particularly the red Periquita. Most wines are for drinking young.

CH. DU TERTRE

FRANCE, Bordeaux, Haut-Médoc, Margaux AC, 5ème Cru Classé
Cabernet Sauvignon, Cabernet Franc, Merlot

At last du Tertre is beginning to gain recognition – which it really does deserve because stuck out in the wilds of Arsac, on the edge of the MARGAUX AC, it's not exactly going to benefit from any passing trade. But this 48-ha (119-acre) vineyard is well situated atop a knoll (*tertre* means 'knoll') on the highest ground in the AC, with extremely gravelly soil.

The mixture of 80 per cent Cabernet Sauvignon, 10 per cent Cabernet Franc and 10 per cent Merlot could be expected to produce hard, difficult, slow-maturing wine, but in fact du Tertre shows wonderful fruit, with strawberries, blackcurrants and mulberries apparent right from the start. There is tannin too, certainly, but also a glyceriny ripeness coating your mouth and a marvellous cedar, strawberry and blackcurrant scent building up after a few years. It's usually delicious at five to six years old, but will happily age 10–15 years. Hopefully du Tertre's new ownership (1998) will provide the necessary impetus for further improvement. Best years: 1998, '96, '95, '94, '90, '89, '88, '86, '85, '83, '82, '80, '79, '78.

TEXAS

USA

Vineyards came to Texas during the wine boom of the 1970s, as they did to most parts of the USA. Their success has been something of a surprise to many who cast glances across the mostly parched landscapes – seemingly fit only for cowboy movies – and thought, 'No, never'. Never say 'never' when it comes to Texas. There is no place like Texas to hide 2024ha (5000 acres) of anything. The High Plains (Lubbock and surrounds) has 800ha (2000 acres) of vineyards; an area called Trans-Pecos (centred on Midland) has 490ha (1200 acres), largely because of a University of Texas-Cordier joint venture called Domaine Cordier; the Hill Country (north and west of Austin) has 280ha (700 acres). The rest are scattered through the state. All together they yield about 300,000 cases a year, a figure that will nearly double when the vines are mature. In 1998 the state had 28 wineries. The oldest of them, Llano Estacado, has had the most impressive track record, especially for its Chardonnays. Fall Creek has made several of the worthiest reds to date, particularly from Carnelian grapes. Oberhellman, Pheasant Ridge and Slaughter-Leftwich are others to keep in mind, but, to be honest, Texas wines are still a fair amount of sizzle, and not an awful lot of steak.

THAMES VALLEY

ENGLAND, Berkshire, Twyford
Pinot Noir
Schönburger, Reichensteiner, Würzer and others

This is an English vineyard with an Australian winemaker, John Worontschak, coaxing almost unheard-of flavours out of English grapes. There are 8ha (20 acres) of vines, planted with 18 different grape varieties (the viticulturalist, Jon Leighton, although English born, comes from Australia, too) and not surprisingly, there's a fair bit of Aussie experimentation. Straightforward whites are fruity and refreshing. Thames Valley Fumé is an oak-aged white of quite remarkable quality, made from Madeleine Angevine, Schönburger, Ortega and Regner, and there's an excellent botrytized sweet wine made mostly from Ehrenfelser and Scheurebe. The influence of Worontschak (who is also a flying winemaker in Brazil and China among other places) and Leighton on English wine has so far been dramatic. Best years: 1995, '94, '93, '92, '90, '89, plus '91 for the Fumé.

DR H THANISCH

GERMANY, Mosel-Saar-Ruwer, Bernkastel
Riesling

This estate was one of the original owners of the BERNKASTELer Doctor vineyard and still has a chunk of it; 'still', because in 1988 the original Thanisch estate was split up. The better part bears the VDP eagle on its labels; the other part confusingly uses the Thanisch name but the wines are made by the Müller-Burggraef family at Reil. Standards have swung wildly in recent years: there are vines in many of the Mosel's top vineyard sites, and when on form, the wines are classic. Best years: 1996, '92, '90, '89, '88.

THELEMA

SOUTH AFRICA, Western Cape, Stellenbosch WO

🍷 *Cabernet Sauvignon, Merlot and others*

🍷 *Chardonnay, Sauvignon Blanc and others*

From the first vintage in 1987, this former fruit farm has shown that South Africa can make world-class wine. The priority here is always quality fruit; these high mountain vineyards have won as many awards as the wines. The owner/winemaker Gyles Webb brings a very international perspective to wine: he has travelled to most of the world's major wine regions and tastes widely. He also calls on the viticultural expertise of Californian, Phil Freese. Both Cabernet Sauvignon and Merlot are truly ripe and well-structured with a distinctive hint of mint. Barrel-fermented Chardonnay has juicy yet firm, nutty, limy complexity; the Sauvignon Blanc bursts with vigour and fruit, while the Riesling is delicate and dryish. Best years: 1998, '97, '96, '95, '94, '93, '92, '91.

THERMENREGION

AUSTRIA, Niederösterreich

This area used to be called Gumpoldskirchen und Vöslau (after its two famous wine villages) but Gumpoldskirchen's sweetish whites went out of fashion following Austria's diethylene glycol scandal in the 1980s, and the new wine law paid tribute to the local thermal spas. Today Thermenregion produces far more dry wines than sweet, though Gumpoldskirchen still produces traditional wines. In the north of the region there is a lot of Rotgipfler and Zierfandler, both white, plus other varieties; in the south there is more red, generally fairly light, cherryish wine from Blauer Portugieser. Best producer: Stadlmann.

THREE CHOIRS

ENGLAND, Gloucestershire

🍷 *Reichensteiner, Seyval Blanc, Huxelrebe and others*

Along with THAMES VALLEY, Three Choirs is one of the leaders in the new wave of quality English wine. Tom Day has 25ha (62 acres) of vines between the three cathedral cities of Gloucester, Hereford and Worcester, where the Three Choirs music festival takes place every summer. The wine ranges from a CHAMPAGNE-method fizz from Seyval Blanc through to a mainly Huxelrebe and Reichensteiner New Release – available to coincide with each year's BEAUJOLAIS Nouveau – to late-harvest wines from Huxelrebe when the vintage permits. Best years: 1997, '95, '94, '93.

TICINO

SWITZERLAND

Merlot was introduced into this Italian-speaking Swiss canton in the late nineteenth century, and has flourished ever since. It can make juicy, attractive wines which generally sell at what for Switzerland are reasonable prices; the letters VITI on the label are held to be a guarantee of quality. However, poor examples can be green and vegetal. Other grapes, generally a mixture of Italian varieties, are blended into the Nostrano, a cheaper everyday wine. Best producers: Cantina di Beride, Delea, Daniel Huber, Cantina di Ronco, Tamborini, Valsangiacomo fu Vittore, ZÜNDEL.

TIEFENBRUNNER-SCHLOSS TURMHOF

ITALY, Alto Adige, Alto Adige DOC

🍷🍷 *Cabernet Sauvignon, Cabernet Franc, Lagrein and others*

🍷 *Gewürztraminer (Traminer Aromatico), Chardonnay, Pinot Gris (Pinot Grigio) and others*

Herbert Tiefenbrunner is probably the longest-serving *cantiniere* in Italy (he would prefer the word *Kellermeister*; indeed, he would prefer not to be in Italy), having celebrated his 50th anniversary in that role in 1993; and while, bit by bit, he is yielding ground to his son Christof, he can still be found wearing his cellarmaster's blue apron whenever you turn up for a tasting.

The house of Tiefenbrunner, having a thriving in-house tourist trade in the form of busloads of Austrians and Germans, offers a vast range of wines covering every South Tyrolean possibility – red, white and pink wines from Germanic, French and local varieties, from its own and from bought-in grapes. Somehow it manages to keep track of it all, turning out excellent Cabernet and Pinot Nero (Linticlarus), Lagrein (Castel Turmhof), two excellent Chardonnays (Linticlarus and Turmhof), Pinots Grigio and Bianco, Sauvignon, Riesling, Goldmuskateller and, most importantly, a steely, elegantly perfumed Müller-Thurgau called Feldmarschall.

TOCAI FRIULANO

ITALY

The Italian white grape Tocai is the vine of the white 'jug wine' of the plains of FRIULI in north-east Italy. It is also one of Friuli's prized native varieties and when pruned hard the resulting wine has enough stuffing to allow its alluring, broad, nut-cream, oily, appley, slightly figgy character to emerge. It flourishes throughout Friuli and in central and eastern VENETO. A few Californians are trying to prove Tocai has a bright future in their vineyards. It is not the same variety as Tokay-Pinot Gris found in ALSACE.

TOKAJI

HUNGARY

🍷 *Furmint, Hárslevelü, Muskat Ottonel (Muskotály)*

This potentially wonderful, and historic wine, drunk by Russia's Tsars, comes from a small hilly area of north-east Hungary. To make Tokaji aszú, those grapes affected by botrytis (or *aszú*) are separated from the rest, and collected in a wooden tub, or *putton*; their free-run juice is called *essencia*, and makes the finest Tokaji of all. The grapes are then mashed to a pulp and added to a 140-litre cask, or *gönc*, of dry wine. The result can, accordingly, be described as 2, 3, 4 or 5 Puttonyos, depending on how much pulp was added. There is also Szamorodni, which is Tokaji from which the *aszú* grapes were not separated out; it can be sweet (*édes*) or dry (*száraz*). A recent wave of Western investment, notably from Spain and France, is beginning to precipitate a new range of more modern styles and higher quality. Best years vary according to style; Tojaji should be sold ready to drink. Best producers: Ch. Megyer, Ch. Pajzos, Disnókö, Royal Tokaji Wine Company.

DOMAINE TOLLOT-BEAUT & FILS

FRANCE, Burgundy, Côte de Beaune, Chorey-lès-Beaune AC

🍷 *Pinot Noir*

🍷 *Chardonnay*

This family-owned estate became well known in the USA before World War Two, and has also enjoyed a firm following in Britain. Most of the vineyards are fairly modest – in ALOXE-CORTON, CHOREY and SAVIGNY – but there are also impressive holdings in BEAUNE (Clos du Roi and Grèves) and CORTON, both red and white. The wines are not quite in the first rank, but they are very well made, nicely balanced, stylishly oaked and very reasonably priced. The wines often taste better from the cask than after bottling, which suggests that they are excessively filtered. The Cortons are particularly good value, combining high quality with modest prices; and at the other end of the price scale, the Premier Cru Savigny Champ Chevrey is worth seeking out. Best years: 1997, '96, '95, '93, '91, '90, '89, '88, '87, '85.

TORGIANO DOCG, DOC

ITALY, Umbria
(DOCG) Sangiovese, Canaiolo and others; (DOC) Sangiovese, Canaiolo, Cabernet Sauvignon, Pinot Noir (Pinot Nero) and others
Trebbiano Toscano, Grechetto, Chardonnay, Pinot Gris (Pinot Grigio), Riesling Italico

This famous UMBRIAN DOC is effectively dominated by one producer, LUNGAROTTI. The Rosso Riserva wine was elevated to DOCG status in 1990, with a requirement that it be aged for at least three years, although Lungarotti gives its Vigna Monticchio nearer to ten. In 1990 the Torgiano DOC was revised to include various wines: Rosso, Cabernet Sauvignon, Pinot Nero, Rosato, Bianco, Chardonnay, Pinot Grigio, Riesling Italico and Spumante. The principal wine is the Rosso, best known under the Lungarotti brand name of Rubesco. Best years: (Torgiano Rosso) 1995, '93, '91, '90.

TORO DO

SPAIN, Castilla-León
Tempranillo (Tinta de Toro), Grenache Noir (Garnacha Tinta)
Verdejo, Malvasía

Toro became a DO in 1987 and for years it had one winemaking star, originally known as Bodegas Porto, now as Bodegas Fariña. Fariña's reds are big and fairly alcoholic, but well made, fruity and oaky – and reasonably cheap. General standards in Toro are on the up, however. The flat Toro country is lower, hotter and drier than nearby RIBERA DEL DUERO and yields are very low indeed. The reds tend to be darker, more tannic, more alcoholic, lower in acidity and distinctly less fine (but also vastly cheaper). Vega Saúco and Frutos Villar are two more up-and-coming producers. Best years: 1997, '96, '95, '94, '91.

TORO ALBALÁ

SPAIN, Andalucía, Montilla-Moriles DO
Pedro Ximénez

Anyone still believing that MONTILLA-MORILES is just a poor man's JEREZ should taste the sweet fortified wines made by Antonio Sánchez in the idiosyncratic bodega built on the premises of an old power station in the 1920s (hence one of its brands, Eléctrico). These are not just sherry wannabes.

Pedro Ximénez is the native Montilla-Moriles grape variety, and really performs best in this region. Toro Albalá was the pioneer of vintage Pedro Ximénez wines of tremendous depth, viscosity and coffee-like warmth, such as the Gran Reserva 1972. In addition, the wines offer uncommon value. Sánchez only owns 3ha (7 ½ acres) of vineyards, at Aguilar de la Frontera, on the Jerez-like *albariza* soils, and, in addition, he buys grapes from his neighbours. His best dry wine is the old Amontillado, made by the solera method.

TORRES

SPAIN, Cataluña, Penedès DO
Tempranillo, Grenache Noir (Garnacha Tinta), Carignan (Cariñena), Cabernet Sauvignon and others
Grenache Noir (Garnacha Tinta), Carignan (Cariñena)
Parellada, Gewürztraminer, Sauvignon Blanc, Xarel-lo, Macabeo, Chardonnay and others

Spain's most influential winemaker must be Miguel Torres of PENEDÈS. Since his return from studying wine in France in 1971, he has worked magic on the family wines, as well as masterminding vineyards in CALIFORNIA and Chile. And his reward for all this hard work? Bodegas Torres is now Spain's largest independent wine company with 600ha (1483 acres) of vines, mostly Parellada and Tempranillo, but also including French varieties, planted close together on wires in a quite un-Spanish way. About half the grapes (mostly the local Catalan varieties) are bought from local growers. Viña Sol is unusually flavourful for Parellada, Viña Esmeralda is a spicy, off-dry blend of Muscat d'Alsace and Gewürztraminer, Waltraud is a floral, fragrant Riesling, and Fransola is a rich, grassy, oaky Parellada and Sauvignon Blanc blend. His top white wine achievement has been the lovely, rich and complex, barrel-fermented Chardonnay from the company's Milmanda vineyard in neighbouring CONCA DE BARBERÀ.

Red wines include two full-bodied ones from Garnacha and Cariñena, Tres Torres and Gran Sangredetoro, Coronas (Tempranillo), soft, oaky, blackcurrant Gran Coronas (Caber-

net and Tempranillo) and Viña Magdala (Pinot Noir and Tempranillo), perhaps the least successful of Torres's innovative combinations. A single-vineyard wine, Mas La Plana (formerly Gran Coronas Black Label), is made from Cabernet Sauvignon. In its youth, it is ripe and blackcurranty, backed up with good but not overdone oak aging, and ages well. The Grans Muralles vineyard outside Penedès, with only old Catalan varieties, and new vineyards in PRIORAT are the latest initiatives. Best years: (reds) 1996, '93, '91, '88, '85, '78.

MARIMAR TORRES

USA, California, Sonoma County, Sonoma-Green Valley AVA
Pinot Noir
Chardonnay

Part of the TORRES wine dynasty of Spain, Marimar selected a cool vineyard site in the far west of SONOMA COUNTY. Adhering to the European concept of viticulture (vines packed tightly together for stress and low yields) she has planted 20ha (50 acres) of vines. Concentrated, but closed-in when young, her Chardonnays blossom with age, and need two to three years' aging. Along with typical cherry fruit and spice, her Pinot Noirs are becoming more complex with each vintage, showing a chalky, mineral side that adds charm and intrigue. Best years: 1998, '97, '96, '95.

MIGUEL TORRES

CHILE, Curicó Valley
Cabernet Sauvignon
Sauvignon Blanc, Riesling, Gewürztraminer, Chardonnay

Miguel TORRES' place in the firmament of great winemakers would have been assured had he never stepped out of Spain – but seduced by Chile's near-perfect viticultural conditions and its lack of phylloxera he then set about transforming winemaking there. When he arrived in 1979, winemaking was as it had been more or less for a hundred years, sleepy and slapdash. He led the way with technical innovation and it did not take long before all of Chile had copied him, followed now by Argentina. His fame is well-founded, although his wines in Chile no longer command the high ground. His new Manso de Velasco premium Cabernet, made from very old vines, is a step towards righting what could have been interpreted as complacency. His Cabernet Sauvignon rosé is still a summer delight. Santa Digna whites are recovering their balance and fruit after a dull patch. Best years: (Manso) 1996, '95, '94.

TOSCANA (Tuscany) Italy

FOR MANY PEOPLE CENTRAL TUSCANY represents Italy. Steep rolling hills in all shades of green, tall cypresses, delicate olive trees, sturdy vines and the occasional pretty stone house all combine to form a captivating scene. Wine is central to the culture – the vine has been cultivated here for nearly 3000 years and Tuscan wines today include some of Italy's best. The atmosphere in Tuscany is a heady mix of respect for wine traditions, regard for quality and enthusiasm for innovation.

Central to Tuscany – and not just geographically – is Chianti. Not all that long ago it typified the pits of Italian wine: cheap, acidic and sold in a wicker-covered flask aptly called a *fiasco*. Now the *fiaschi* are gone, yields have plummeted, white grapes have all but gone from the blend and a new commitment to investment has massively improved producers' understanding of the Sangiovese grape. High-calibre Chianti is now abundant, mainly in the Classico zone but also in others, principally Rufina, a small area east of Florence. And prices have soared.

Most Chianti producers are deeply wedded to Sangiovese, some using nothing else for their Chianti and many making a separate super-Tuscan solely from the grape. There are also numerous Sangiovese/Cabernet Sauvignon super-Tuscans and a few based primarily on Cabernet Sauvignon and, increasingly, Merlot, grapes that have also infiltrated into a number of Chiantis. Almost all these wines are barrique-aged.

This evocative Tuscan scene of vines interspersed with olives and the occasional cypress grove is of La Rancia vineyard near Castelnuovo Berardenga which belongs to a leading Chianti Classico producer, Fattoria di Felsina.

But Tuscany is far more than just Chianti. Brunello di Montalcino and Vino Nobile di Montalcino to the south, and Carmignano to the west, with their 'younger brother' wines Rosso di Montalcino, Rosso di Montepulciano and Barco Reale respectively all show Sangiovese at its classiest and Morello di Scansano from the south-west emphasizes its chewy fruit. A fast-developing area for high-quality reds is the coastal zone, from Pisa to Grosseto. In the northern section, mainly in the province of Livorno, French varieties thrive in the communes of Bolgheri and Suvereto-Val di Cornia. Farther south, the boom is on in areas like Scansano and Massa Marittima, mainly based on Sangiovese, which there comes that bit riper and plummier than from the higher vineyards of central Tuscany.

Striking whites come mainly from the native Vernaccia and imported Chardonnay and Viognier, sometimes barrique-aged. In the coastal areas there is an increasingly impressive resurgence of whites based on Vermentino, often associated with Sardinia and Liguria. The traditional Trebbiano and Malvasia are rapidly giving way to higher-quality varieties, except in the case of Vin Santo.

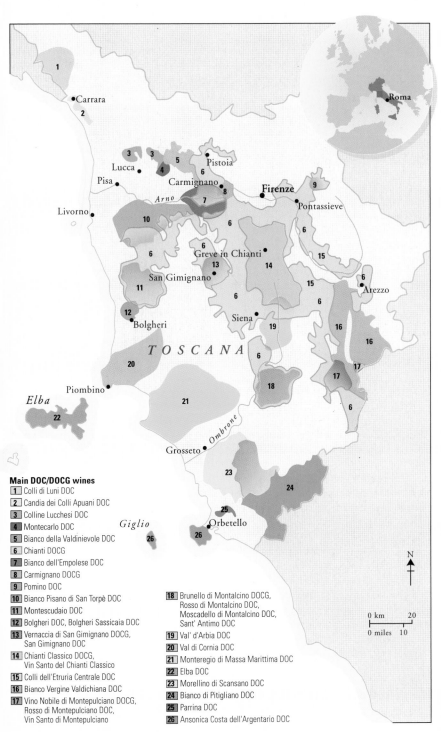

SASSICAIA
Since the first release of the 1968 vintage, this wine has consistently proved itself to be one of the world's great Cabernets. It was recently granted a special DOC under the Bolgheri appellation.

FONTODI
The Flaccianello della Piave super-Tuscan is from a single vineyard of old vines and has shown the world what the Sangiovese grape can achieve on its own.

CASTELLO DI AMA
From this model Chianti Classico estate L'Apparita is the greatest of Tuscany's burgeoning, high-quality Merlots. It commands a phenomenal price and is almost impossible to obtain.

CAPEZZANA
This increasingly fine wine is another Tuscan mould-breaking red from Capezzana in the Carmignano zone.

RIECINE
This tiny, high-altitdue estate in Gaiole has long made outstanding Chianti Classico and Reserva.

BIONDI-SANTI
This estate helped forge the international reputation of Brunello di Montalcino.

AVIGNONESI
Long years in small barrels have made this wine one of the most sought-after Vin Santos, the traditional dessert wines of Tuscany.

Main DOC/DOCG wines

1. Colli di Luni DOC
2. Candia dei Colli Apuani DOC
3. Colline Lucchesi DOC
4. Montecarlo DOC
5. Bianco della Valdinievole DOC
6. Chianti DOCG
7. Bianco dell'Empolese DOC
8. Carmignano DOCG
9. Pomino DOC
10. Bianco Pisano di San Torpè DOC
11. Montescudaio DOC
12. Bolgheri DOC, Bolgheri Sassicaia DOC
13. Vernaccia di San Gimignano DOCG, San Gimignano DOC
14. Chianti Classico DOCG, Vin Santo del Chianti Classico
15. Colli dell'Etruria Centrale DOC
16. Bianco Vergine Valdichiana DOC
17. Vino Nobile di Montepulciano DOCG, Rosso di Montepulciano DOC, Vin Santo di Montepulciano
18. Brunello di Montalcino DOCG, Rosso di Montalcino DOC, Moscadello di Montalcino DOC, Sant' Antimo DOC
19. Val' d'Arbia DOC
20. Val di Cornia DOC
21. Monteregio di Massa Marittima DOC
22. Elba DOC
23. Morellino di Scansano DOC
24. Bianco di Pitigliano DOC
25. Parrina DOC
26. Ansonica Costa dell'Argentario DOC

REGIONAL ENTRIES
Bolgheri, Brunello di Montalcino, Carmignano, Chianti, Chianti Classico, Chianti Rufina, Montecarlo, Morellino di Scansano, Pomino, Rosso di Montalcino, Rosso di Montepulciano, Sant'Antimo, Sassicaia, Super-Tuscan, Vernaccia di San Gimignano, Vin Santo, Vino Nobile di Montepulciano.

PRODUCER ENTRIES
Castello di Ama, Antinori, Avignonesi, Badia a Coltibuono, Castello Banfi, Biondi-Santi, Boscarelli, Castello di Brolio, Castelgiocondo, Felsina, Castello di Fonterutoli, Fontodi, Frescobaldi, Isole e Olena, Montevertine, Ornellaia, Pieve di S. Restituta, Il Poggione, Poliziano, Querciabella, Castello dei Rampolla, Rocco delle Marche, Ruffino, San Felice, Selvapiana, Vecchie Terre di Montefili, Castello di Volpaia.

CH. LA TOUR BLANCHE

FRANCE, Bordeaux, Sauternes AC, Premier Cru Classé

♀ *Sémillon, Sauvignon Blanc, Muscadelle*

In the 1855 classification of BORDEAUX wines la Tour Blanche was classified first of the First Growths just behind Ch. d'YQUEM but until the mid-1980s it hardly justified this status. Now, thanks to dynamic direction and a generous investment in new oak barrels for fermentation and aging, the wines are again among the best in the AC, rich and unctuous with a generous but elegant underpin of oak. The 34-ha (84-acre) estate, which is owned by the French Ministry of Agriculture, is planted with 77 per cent Sémillon, 20 per cent Sauvignon Blanc and 3 per cent Muscadelle, the latter adding a little exotic fruitiness to the blend. Best years: 1998, '97, '96, '95, '94, '90, '89, '88, '86.

CH. TOUR DES GENDRES

FRANCE, South-West, Bergerac AC

❗♀ *Merlot, Cabernet Sauvignon, Cabernet Franc*

♀ *Sémillon, Sauvignon Blanc, Muscadelle*

This is now the benchmark domaine in the BERGERAC AC. Owner Luc de Conti vinifies with as much sophistication as is found in the BORDEAUX Crus Classés. The 40-ha (100-acre) domaine is split evenly between red and white wines. The white Cuvée des Conti is almost pure Sémillon with a dash of Muscadelle, vinified in vat and aged on lees, while the Moulin des Dames is a blend of 60 per cent Sémillon, 25 per cent Sauvignon Blanc and 25 per cent Muscadelle, fermented and aged in 70 per cent new oak barrels.

The top of the range red, Moulin des Dames, comes from a 6-ha (15-acre) *clos* and is made from a majority of Cabernet Franc, with the malolactic fermentation conducted in barrel and the wine aged for 18 months in 60 per cent new oak barrels. The Côtes de Bergerac la Gloire de Mon Père is from mainly Merlot. The wines are best drunk with between three and four years' age. Best years: (reds) 1997, '96, '95, '94.

TOURAINE AC

FRANCE, Loire

❗♀ *Gamay, Cabernet Franc, Cabernet Sauvignon and others*

♀ *Sauvignon Blanc, Chenin Blanc*

Touraine is the most interesting of the LOIRE's wine regions. All the best wines have their own specific appellations – the red wine ACs are CHINON, BOURGUEIL and ST-NICO-LAS-DE-BOURGUEIL; the chief white ACs are VOUVRAY, MONTLOUIS and Jasnières. However, there is still a large amount of wine made, red, white and rosé, which merely qualifies for the Touraine AC, a fairly general appellation covering 97km (60 miles) of the Loire Valley to the east and west of Tours, the region's capital.

The red grapes used reflect Touraine's position on the Loire, between the wine cultures of BORDEAUX and Burgundy. The Loire grapes Grolleau and Pineau d'Aunis are used for rosé only, whereas the Bordeaux grapes Cabernet Sauvignon, Cabernet Franc and Malbec (here known as Cot), the Pinot Noir from Burgundy and the Gamay from BEAU-JOLAIS are used for rosés and reds. Although most of the reds are from Gamay and in hot years can be juicy, rough-fruited wines, the best are often made from Cot, especially if the vigneron has old vines. Touraine Tradition is a blend of Cabernet, Cot and Gamay. In the Touraine-Amboise AC, this is called Cuvée François I.

Fairly good white wines come from the Chenin (often called Pineau de la Loire here), but the best are from Sauvignon. Dry, tangy, with a light apple-and-gooseberry fruit and a flicker of nettly acidity, Sauvignon de Touraine can be a good Sancerre substitute at half the price.

There are three villages which can add their names to Touraine AC on the label. Touraine-Amboise is a surprisingly good red from Cabernet or Cot, made in an area of high chalk cliffs on the south bank of the river. Gamay can be used if it is blended with the other two varieties.

Touraine Azay-le-Rideau is pink or white – the rosé, based on the Grolleau, is adequate and can be raspingly dry or slightly sweet; the whites, dry and off-dry, are fair in quality. Touraine-Mesland, to the west of Blois, produces reds from Gamay which can be Touraine's best wines from this grape. The rosé is fair.

Touraine whites should be drunk young, in the year following the vintage, though Chenin Blanc can last longer. Best years: 1998, '97, '96, '95. Best producers: d'Artois (Mesland), Barbou, Baron Briare, Aimé Boucher, Bougrier, Brossillon (Mesland), la Chapelle de Cray, Charmoise, Clos Roche Blanche, Chenonceau, Corbillières, Joël Delaunay, Delétang, Denay (Amboise), Dutertre (Amboise), Gibault, Girault-Artois (Mesland), Octavie, Oisly & Thésée co-operative, de Pocy (Amboise).

TOURIGA NAÇIONAL

This has long been one of Portugal's leading red grapes, having found its way into most of the finest ports as it contributes deep colour and tannin to the blend. As a result of Portugal's long overdue viticultural sort-out in the 1980s, Touriga Naçional is being increasingly revered for unfortified red wines, not only in the Douro, but also in Dão, Estremadura and Terras do Sado. Aside from port, its full potential can be seen in a growing number of varietal wines like the impressive Touriga Naçional from Quinta dos Roques in Dão. The wines tend to be solid, foursquare, but multi-textured if softened by some new oak aging. The only problem is that it is difficult to grow and can therefore be properly described as a winemaker's rather than a viticulturalist's grape. Indeed, even inside Portugal there are hundreds of different strains, yielding wines that range from pale and insipid to dense, damsony and perfumed with violets.

Surprisingly, few other countries so far have taken much note of this grape, but Australia, with its fortified wine tradition, is making some progress.

TRAISENTAL

AUSTRIA, Niederösterreich

With only 700ha (1730 acres) of vineyards this is the newest of Austria's wine regions. If it were not for the excellent Neumayer estate in Inzersdorf it might have taken a lot longer for the region to gain a profile. Its complex dry Grüner Veltliners and rich peachy dry Rieslings prove that this region has a future.

TRAPICHE

ARGENTINA, Mendoza

❗ *Cabernet Sauvignon, Malbec, Syrah and others*

♀ *Chardonnay, Sauvignon Blanc*

Trapiche continues to produce enjoyable Chardonnay, unoaked and oaked, some good snappy Sauvignon Blanc, some fairly rich Malbec and some interesting Syrah. Although Trapiche is simply a trademark produced by the giant PEÑAFLOR company, it has no excuse not to occupy a top-quality position, thanks to having access to grapes harvested from some of MENDOZA's best vineyards. So Trapiche, despite good results recently, has to be seen as an underperformer in a market moving forward at a hectic pace. Best years: 1999, '97.

TRÁS-OS-MONTES VINHO REGIONAL

PORTUGAL

♥ *Touriga Nacional, Touriga Francesa, Tinta Roriz (Tempranillo), Tinta Barroca, Tinto Cão, Tinta Amarela and others*

♀ *Gouveio, Viosinho, Rabigato, Malvasia Fina, Donzelinho*

This remote wine region covers the entire north-east corner of Portugal. It is bounded on one side by mountains (hence the name meaning 'behind the mountains') and on the other by Spain. Soils are poor, mostly based on either granite or schist, and the climate becomes progressively more arid nearer Spain. There is a sub-division called Terras Durienses, which covers some of the southern part of the region. The range of grape varieties is similar to the Douro's but also includes foreign grapes such as Cabernet Sauvignon and Sauvignon Blanc. The wine is rarely found outside the region apart from a distinctive, young, cherryish red from Caves ALIANÇA called Terra Boa and the red Reserva and Quinta dos Bons Ares from RAMOS PINTO which include foreign grapes in the blends. Valle Pradinhos is probably the best known wine estate.

TREBBIANO

This white grape takes neutrality to extremes. From its base in central Italy it has spread so far that wherever you are in Italy you are never far from a Trebbiano vine; only the border regions of Piedmont, VALLE D'AOSTA and FRIULI-VENEZIA GIULIA escape its insidious influence. But while it tastes of very little, it yields huge quantities – and these days, when quality matters, that is a millstone.

There are numerous different sub-varieties, Trebbiano Toscano being the most common and least distinguished, followed by Trebbiano di Romagna. Trebbiano di Lugana or Trebbiano di Soave, on the other hand, does have plenty of character. Perhaps Trebbiano's greatest attribute is its ability to retain acidity at high productivity levels which, together with its neutrality, make it a good stretcher for both white and red wines in the very noble cause of reaching supermarket price-points.

In France there's plenty of Trebbiano, under the name of Ugni Blanc, but it has no more character there. This is fine for distilling Cognac and Armagnac, but there's VIN DE PAYS wine to be dealt with as well from these regions: generally it's light and fresh and sometimes oaked, but some CÔTES DE GASCOGNE is fruity and snappy. In Australia it used to be planted in places like the HUNTER VALLEY to provide acidity for reds, but now it mostly fills wine boxes in which the actual flavour comes from the Muscat Gordo Blanco grape.

TRENTINO

ITALY

Trentino is essentially the province of Trento, the southern half of the Trentino-Alto Adige region, whose northern half, ALTO ADIGE, fiercely retains its Austrian character. Viticulturally and culturally, the province splits at the city of Trento. To its north, the wines are almost indistinguishable from Alto Adige's; white wines are in the ascendant (except for TEROLDEGO ROTALIANO) and the feel of the place is Austrian. To the south, the atmosphere is irrefutably Italian; the Adige river valley gradually widens out and the climate becomes less sub-Alpine. The wines are softer and broader, and full reds are more important, while the overcropping found all over the region cannot be so easily disguised. Wine classifications do not reflect this division, unfortunately.

The Trentino DOC covers a wide range of red (Cabernets Franc and Sauvignon, Lagrein, Marzemino, Merlot and Pinot Noir/Pinot Nero) and white varietals (Chardonnay, Orange Muscat, Müller-Thurgau, Nosiola, Pinot Blanc/Pinot Bianco, Pinot Gris/Pinot Grigio, Welschriesling/ Riesling Italico, Riesling/Riesling Renano and Gewürztraminer/ Traminer Aromatico) and stretches along the river valley the entire length of the province, as do the Casteller and Valdadige DOCs. Other Trentino specialities include the rare blend Sorni, some elegant VIN SANTO and some excellent CHAMPAGNE-method sparkling wine. Best producers: (Trentino DOC) Bossi Fedrigotti, Nilo Bolognani, Cerconi, de Tarczal, Ferrari, Foradori, Letrari, Maso Cantanghel, Castel Noarna, San Leonardo, Vallarom.

DOMAINE DE TREVALLON

FRANCE, Provence, Vin de Pays des Bouches-du-Rhône

♥ *Cabernet Sauvignon, Syrah*

♀ *Marsanne, Roussanne*

Excluded from les BAUX-DE-PROVENCE AC since the 1994 vintage for having too much

Cabernet Sauvignon in its 20-ha (50-acre) vineyard, Domaine de Trévallon is still the revelation of Provence. Eloi Dürrbach's tradition-busting blend of Cabernet Sauvignon and Syrah aged in oak casks or *foudres* provides a rich palette of flavours combining blackberry, blackcurrant and plum with the laurel and thyme of the surrounding *garrigue*. The wines are best drunk with a minimum of five years' aging but improve with longer keeping. A tiny amount of intense, elegant white is produced from a blend of Roussanne and Marsanne fermented and aged in new oak barrels. Best years: (reds) 1998, '97, '96, '95, '94, '93, '92, '90, '89.

ERNST TRIEBAUMER

AUSTRIA, Burgenland, Neusiedlersee-Hügelland, Rust

♥ *Blaufränkisch, Cabernet Sauvignon, Merlot*

♀ *Chardonnay, Sauvignon Blanc, Gewürztraminer (Traminer), Muscat (Gelber Muskateller), Welschriesling*

Known as ET to his loyal Austrian followers, Triebaumer makes the best wines from indigenous Blaufränkisch grapes from his holdings in the Marienthal site of RUST. Old vines and an obsession with extracting everything the grape has to give result in very deep-coloured, powerful wines with an intense blackberry-mulberry character and substantial tannins. His other Blaufränkisch wines are also impressive, but mature more quickly. His Cabernet-Merlot is another power pack. Drink these on release or after a few years' bottle aging. The dry whites are crisp and fresh rather than exciting, but the AUSBRUCH dessert wines from various grape varieties not only have loads of alcohol but also stacks of flavour. Best years: (reds) 1997, '94, '93, '92, '90; (whites) 1998, '97, '95, '94, '91.

TRIER

GERMANY, Mosel-Saar-Ruwer

Trier is a beautiful city and, in fact, the oldest in Germany – it was the capital of the Roman Empire in the fourth century. It hugs the Mosel river just west of its confluence with the Ruwer, and its wines come under the heading of Ruwer. The wines seem fragile and light and often have a mouthwatering green fruit like the flesh of a cooking apple, but they are surprisingly long lived; in lesser years they remain tart and lean. Best producers: BISCHÖFLICHE WEINGÜTER, FRIEDRICH-WILHELM-GYMNASIUM, von KESSELSTATT.

F E TRIMBACH

FRANCE, Alsace, Alsace AC

♀ *Riesling, Pinot Gris, Gewurztraminer, Pinot Blanc, Muscat, Sylvaner*

Decades ago, it would seem, the Trimbach family decided on the style of the wine they were going to make, and have stuck to that resolution ever since. Despite the fact that Trimbach produces close to a million bottles each year, the style has remained utterly consistent and the quality exemplary.

No wine typifies the assertive, minerally Trimbach style more vividly than the Riesling from Clos St-Hune, an enclave within the Rosacker Grand Cru. It is hard to disagree with those who claim that this is ALSACE's finest Riesling and even in poor vintages it can be compellingly good, though it is often unapproachable in its youth. But the range is excellent across the board. Riesling is always exceptional, both the bone-dry generic bottling and the steely, long-lived Cuvée Frédéric Émile, which is essentially the Grand Cru Osterberg by another name. Pinot Gris is usually a safer bet here than Gewurztraminer, although the Gewurztraminer Cuvée de Seigneurs de Ribeaupierre is often first-rate. Vendange Tardive and Sélection de Grains Nobles wines from Pinot Gris can be sensational in years such as 1997. Best years: 1998, '97, '96, '95, '94, '93, '90, '89, '88, '85, '83, '76.

TRINCADEIRA

Planted in the DOURO for PORT (where it is known as Tinta Amarela) and the ALENTEJO, Trincadeira is emerging as one of Portugal's best red grape varieties. In the north it has an alarming tendency to rot as soon as there is any rain or humidity but on the searing plains of the deep south it produces big, ripe, spicy wines which sometimes have a passing resemblance to Syrah. A number of innovative producers in the Alentejo (ESPORÃO and João Portugal Ramos) are now making varietal wines.

TRINITY HILL

NEW ZEALAND, North Island, Hawke's Bay

♥ *Cabernet Sauvignon, Cabernet Franc, Merlot, Syrah*

♀ *Chardonnay, Riesling, Sauvignon Blanc*

Talented ex-winemaker of MORTON ESTATE, John Hancock, is one of three partners in this

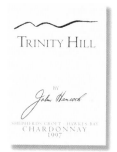

TRINITY HILL
Trinity Hill is a new trailblazer in Hawke's Bay with star winemaker John Hancock in charge. Shepherd's Croft is a new vineyard on well-drained gravel soils.

exciting new HAWKE'S BAY winery. Hancock is a passionate fan of the Gimblett Road district of Hawke's Bay, where Trinity Hill has established its vineyards. A stylish and moderately complex Cabernet Franc-Merlot-Shiraz blend is made from grapes purchased from growers in the Shepherd's Croft vineyard in Hawke's Bay, while a steely, dry Riesling is produced from MARTINBOROUGH grapes. Gimblett Road is the winery's top label featuring an elegant, nutty Chardonnay and three ripe, concentrated reds: Cabernet Sauvignon, Cabernet Sauvignon-Merlot and Syrah. Gimblett road wines are hot prospects for long term aging while the others should be enjoyed within a few years of release. Best years: 1998, '97.

TRITTENHEIM

GERMANY, Mosel-Saar-Ruwer

This important Mittel MOSEL commune has a string of excellent vineyard sites – Apotheke, Altärchen, Felsenkopf and Leiterchen – which produce very elegant Rieslings. For some years there were few exciting wines though, because of the high-yield policy pursued by most of the local growers. However, during the late 1990s this has changed significantly for the better. Best producers: Ernst Clüsserath, Clüsserath-Weiler, Milz.

CH. TROTANOY

FRANCE, Bordeaux, Pomerol AC

♥ *Merlot, Cabernet Franc*

Trotanoy puts itself up as Ch. PÉTRUS' main challenger for the title 'King of Pomerol' but, except in vintages like 1978 (when Pétrus was inexplicably disappointing) and '62 (when Trotanoy was an enormous, broad-flavoured wine, smacking of chocolate and hazelnuts, brown sugar and blackberry jam), it has to be content with the role of crown prince.

The wine is tremendous stuff, though, and another example (along with Ch. Pétrus, LAFLEUR, LATOUR-À-POMEROL and a gaggle of others) of the brilliant touch of Jean-Pierre Moueix and his son Christian. The Jean-

Pierre Moueix company owns this 8-ha (19-acre) property to the west of Pétrus on slightly more gravelly soil, and though the plantings of 90 per cent Merlot and 10 per cent Cabernet Franc do give a rich, massively impressive, Pétrus-like wine, they are also likely to have a tempering of leather and tobacco scents, and just lack the magic mingling of sweetness, spice and perfume which makes Pétrus so memorable. Best years: 1998 '97, '96, '95, '94, '93, '90, '89, '88, '85, '83 '82, '81, '79, '78, '76, '75.

CAVE VINICOLE DE TURCKHEIM

FRANCE, Alsace, Alsace AC

♥ *Pinot Noir*

♀ *Riesling, Pinot Gris, Gewurztraminer, Pinot Blanc, Muscat, Sylvaner*

Unlike most regions of France, ALSACE is studded with good-quality wine co-operatives, and none has performed more consistently over the years than Turckheim. It's not just a question of good management and good winemaking: the growers attached to this co-operative have vineyards in some outstanding sites, including the Brand, Sommerberg and Hengst Grands Crus. But all co-operatives survive by their bread-and-butter wines and by and large even the generic bottlings at Turckheim are soundly made and attractive, although the special bottlings, notably the Grands Crus, show much more complexity. Turckheim also succeeds with varieties such as Pinot Noir and Sylvaner, which can often be dull in Alsace. The range is completed with attractive rosé and CRÉMANT D'ALSACE. Best years: 1998, '97, '96, '95, '94, '93, '90, '89, '88, '85.

TURLEY CELLARS

USA, California, Napa County, Napa Valley AVA

♥ *Petite Sirah, Zinfandel*

♀ *Sauvignon Blanc*

After many successful years with FROG'S LEAP, co-founder Larry Turley started his own brand and his former partner Larry Williams continued with Frog's Leap at another site. Assisted during the first two vintages by his famous sister, winemaker Helen Turley, Larry

TURLEY
Larry Turley's obsession is with Zinfandel and Petite Sirah from very old vines. The wines are incredibly powerful, with loads of fruit and ripe tannin.

pursued his interest in making Zinfandel and Petite Sirah from several old, low-yielding, head-pruned vineyards. Small amounts of Sauvignon Blanc are made from the adjacent vineyard. In recent vintages, he has made Zinfandels from six individual vineyards and as many as four single-vineyard Petite Sirahs. Made in small-case lots, Turley's red wines are highly concentrated, with intense fruit and unusually high alcohol levels. Though likely to be consumed young by their avid fans, the Zinfandels develop some harmony with four to five years of aging. Turley experimented with Zinfandels from old vineyards in Contra Costa County and Lodi and liked the results well enough to add Zinfandels from these appellations to his ever-expanding roster. Best years: 1997, '96, '95, '94.

TYRRELL'S

AUSTRALIA, New South Wales, Hunter Valley Zone, Hunter

♦ *Syrah (Shiraz), Pinot Noir, Cabernet Sauvignon*
♀ *Semillon, Chardonnay*

The foghorn bellow of Murray Tyrrell railing at the authorities, the weather, ignorant wine writers and the other annoyances of life have earned him the sobriquet 'Mouth of the Hunter'. But he has driven his family operation to national prominence. From prime lower HUNTER vineyards, his astonishingly rich 1971 Vat 47 Chardonnay was the first of its kind and is still one of the most highly regarded Chardonnays. His Vat 1 Semillons can be every bit as good, if not better, and he has periodically made extraordinary Pinot Noir. However, Shiraz remains the principal red grape. Recent vintages have been rather more mainstream, less likely to amaze or shock, but very tasty. Best years: 1998, '96, '95, '94, '93, '92, '91, '90, '87, '86, '85.

UMANI RONCHI

ITALY, Marche, Rosso Conero DOC

♦ *Montepulciano, Sangiovese, Cabernet Sauvignon, Merlot*
♀ *Verdicchio, Bianchelle e Trebbiano, Chardonnay, Sauvignon Blanc*

This is a fairly large establishment, which has been improving year after year since being acquired in 1970 by the Bernetti family from Gino Umani Ronchi, becoming in the process one of the two or three leading producers in the MARCHE. Both the red and white wines are made to a high standard, each in their own winery. Among the reds are the two ROSSO CONERO crus, Cùmaro and San Lorenzo, the former of higher prestige than

UMANI RONCHI
Pélago is a promising new powerful red vino da tavola from a blend of Cabernet Sauvignon, Montepulciano and Merlot.

the latter, though its thunder has to some appreciable extent now been stolen by the much lauded blend called Pélago. On the white side, VERDICCHIO DEI CASTELLI DE JESI not surprisingly reigns supreme, the two crus, Plenio Riserva and Casal di Serra, vying with each other for top honours. Among other whites are a Verdicchio-Chardonnay blend called Osimo and a Sauvignon Blanc called Tajano, plus a dessert wine, Maximo. Best years: 1998, '97, '95, '94.

UMATHUM

AUSTRIA, Burgenland, Neusiedlersee, Frauenkirchen

♦ *Blaufränkisch, Blauer Zweigelt, St Laurent, Cabernet Sauvignon, Merlot, Pinot Noir (Blauburgunder)*
♀ *Sauvignon Blanc, Welschriesling, Pinot Gris (Grauburgunder)*

It is not by chance that Josef Umathum's 1992 St Laurent wine beat all the Burgundy Grands Crus to win the International Wine Challenge Pinot Noir Trophy. The wine, from St Laurent, a mutation of Pinot Noir, is so Burgundian in style that even an expert would be fooled. His winery, with its new vaulted barrique cellar, could also be in Burgundy and looks a bit lost among the flat vineyards of Frauenkirchen. That does not matter because Umathum makes a string of superb reds, most notably the powerful, tannic Blaufränkisch-Cabernet blend from the Ried Hallebühl site, that needs five years to reveal its considerable spicy depths. The Zweigelt-Merlot blend from the Ried Haideboden site is more supple, but hardly less impressive. The relatively new Blauburgunder has become Austria's best Pinot Noir wine. Best years: 1997, '95, '94, '93, '92, '90.

UMBRIA

ITALY

'The green heart of Italy' is what the publicity posters call the region of Umbria. And it is Italy's geographical heart, midway between Florence and Rome, and it is green. It is also predominantly hilly – often inducing a feeling of remoteness – and with a treasure trove of Etruscan remains. Perugia, its capital,

is a town of only 150,000 inhabitants, its hill-top walled medieval centre neatly concealing the urban sprawl below. The hilliness of Umbria is reflected in the names of some of its wines: Colli del Trasimeno (meaning the Hills of Trasimeno, from around Lake Trasimeno), Colli Altotiberini (in the north, along the course of the upper river Tevere or Tiber which flows through the region on its way to Rome) and Colli Perugini (south of Perugia). These light red and white wines are not the ones to write home about, though. Far more impressive are TORGIANO, a tiny area just south of Perugia; MONTEFALCO, with its brilliant red Sagrantino grape, between Assisi and Spoleto in mid-Umbria; and ORVIETO in the south-west of the region on the border of Lazio. Orvieto is one of Italy's best known whites and has more than its fair share of quality-conscious producers.

ÜRZIG

GERMANY, Mosel-Saar-Ruwer

The village of Ürzig faces ERDEN across the Mosel, each village vying with the other for the steepest slopes; Erden's best vineyards are on the same side of the river as Ürzig's, all of them squeezed between mountains and water. The soil at Ürzig is a mixture of red slate and red sandstone, and the name of the Einzellage Würzgarten, which means 'spice garden', gives a clue as to the style of the wine: rich, racy and aromatic, concentrated and characterful. Best producers: J J CHRISTOFFEL, Dr LOOSEN, Mönchhof (Robert Eymael).

UTIEL-REQUENA DO

SPAIN, Valencia

♦♀ *Bobal, Tempranillo, Grenache Noir (Garnacha Tinta), Cabernet Sauvignon, Merlot*
♀ *Macabeo, Merseguera, Planta Nova, Chardonnay*

Utiel-Requena – remote, high country west of Valencia city – is the source of some of Spain's best rosé. It is made principally from the Bobal grape, and with modern methods is now often light, fresh and fragrant. There are also good reds with a strong, herby character in which there is now an ever greater proportion of Tempranillo, and the emergence of some high-quality, fairly-priced, creamy RIOJA look-alikes is encouraging. Like other VALENCIA DOs, Utiel-Requena also makes strong, dark red tinto *doble pasta*, made with a double dose of colour and tannin-rich skins. Whites can be fresh, but are never very characterful. Best years: 1996, '94, '93, '92. Best producers: Vicente Gandía Pla, Schenk, Torre Oria.

The Valais vineyards high above the Rhône Valley are some of the most spectacular in the world. The vines seem to climb up every available mountainside in the search for sun and shelter.

VACQUEYRAS AC

FRANCE, Southern Rhône

🍷 🍷 *Grenache, Syrah, Cinsaut, Mourvèdre*

🍷 *Clairette, Grenache Blanc, Bourboulenc, Roussanne*

Vacqueyras was the most important and consistently successful of the southern Rhône's CÔTES DU RHÔNE-VILLAGES communes, where Grenache is the chief red grape variety, and was promoted to its own AC in 1989. The village itself is rather a large one, liable to be raucous with visitors in summer and silent as a tomb in winter, and lies on the flat land just south of GIGONDAS.

However, the terraced vineyards of Vacqueyras sweep up towards the jagged, dramatic-looking Dentelles de Montmirail and produce red wines of a lovely dark colour, a round, warm, spicy bouquet and a fruit that happily mixes plums and raspberries with the wind-dried dust of the South. Lovely at two to three years, good producers' reds from good vintages will age well for ten years or more. The whites and rosés still lag far behind the reds in terms of quality. Best years: 1998, '97, '95, '94, '93, '91, '90, '89, '88. Best producers: Clos des Cazaux, la Fourmone, la Garrigue, JABOULET, Lambertins, la Monadière, Montmirail, Palleroudias, Pascal, Roques, Sang des Cailloux, des Tours, Vacqueyras co-operative, Vieux Clocher.

VALAIS

SWITZERLAND

🍷 *Pinot Noir, Gamay and others*

🍷 *Chasselas (Fendant), Sylvaner, Riesling and others*

From a wine perspective, this is by far the most interesting and innovative of the Swiss cantons; it's also the most famous. The vineyards are terraced high on the Alpine slopes and since they are possibly the driest in Switzerland, irrigation is necessary. Chasselas (here called Fendant) is the most planted grape variety and it makes light, dry whites, sometimes with a touch of *pétillance*. DÔLE, a blend of Pinot Noir and Gamay, is the Valais red speciality. But tucked away in odd corners are other vines: Malvoisie (or Pinot Gris), Marsanne (here called Ermitage), Amigne, Arvine, Humagne (white and red), Païen and Rèze as well as international interlopers like Chardonnay and Syrah. Best producers: Charles Favre, Maurice Gay, Robert Gilliard, Caves IMESCH, MONT D'OR, Alphonse Orsat, Louis Vuignier.

VALDEORRAS DO

SPAIN, Galicia

🍷 *Garnacha Tintorera (Alicante), Mencía, Grau Negro and others*

🍷 *Palomino, Godello, Doña Blanca*

The Valdeorras vineyard area has declined to 1500ha (3700 acres), but quality is better, since almost half are now planted with the outstanding native Godello grape, which almost became extinct in the 1970s. The red Mencía is also making a comeback. The land is barren and mountainous, and the inhabitants have little alternative to growing vines. The return has been scant, scarcely enough to prevent a drift away by the next generation anxious to find more rewarding ways of making a living. Production is dominated by two co-operatives, Barco de Valdeorras and La Rua, both of which have upgraded their winemaking equipment recently, and are able to make good wines – as long as they can get good grapes from their members. But the strong Godello revival has been spearheaded by three private bodegas: Godeval, La Tapada and Joaquín Rebolledo.

VALDEPEÑAS DO

SPAIN, Castilla-La Mancha

🍷 🍷 *Tempranillo (Cencibel), Grenache Noir (Garnacha Tinta), Cabernet Sauvignon, Airén*

🍷 *Airén, Macabeo*

Though some of Spain's best red wine bargains come from this hot, dry undulating country in the south of the great central plains, much of the region's output is very poor. One of the main problems is the large proportion of dull, white Airén grapes that goes into the blends, red, white and rosé. More Cencibel (Tempranillo), the region's best grape has been planted recently, along with some Cabernet Sauvignon.

The most common style of Valdepeñas is Clarete, a pale red made with a legal minimum of 20 per cent Cencibel, otherwise with white grapes, and very popular in Spain. These wines can easily shoot up to a headache-inducing 15 per cent of alcohol (though the best are now kept at around 12.5 per cent), but colour and flavourwise this is feeble stuff. The best reds contain only red grapes. Producers to look out for are Los LLANOS and Félix SOLÍS (under the brand name Viña Albali). Luis Megía (Marqués de Gastañaga) is also quite good for younger wine, as are all the reds from Casa de la Viña. Some rosés and whites are now made by modern methods, and are simple, fresh and fruity, rather like the whites of La MANCHA. Best years: 1996, '95, '93, '92, '87.

VALDESPINO

SPAIN, Andalucía, Jerez y Manzanilla DO

🍷 *Palomino Fino, Pedro Ximénez*

This old-fashioned, family-owned sherry company makes wines of very fine quality in limited quantities. Its Inocente bodega, in an old monastery with paved patio and beautiful gardens, is one of the oldest in JEREZ. Most unusually nowadays, Valdespino still ferments most of its wines in wooden casks (rather than stainless steel) and blends from myriad individual wines. The best-known wine is the lovely, classic Fino Inocente. Other wines include Tio Diego, a good, subtle amontillado (in such demand in Spain that it often runs out); a richly flavourful, amontillado-style Palo Cortado Cardenal; dark, dry, immensely concentrated Amontillado Coliseo; dry, nutty-tangy Don Tomás Amontillado; complex, malty, raisiny Don Gonzalo Old Dry Oloroso; and, for the sweet-toothed, a dense, demerara-and-raisin flavoured Pedro Ximénez Solera Superior. It also makes brandy and excellent sherry vinegar.

VALDIVIESO

CHILE, Curicó Valley

🍷 *Cabernet Sauvignon, Merlot, Cabernet Franc, Malbec*

🍷 *Chardonnay*

When Valdivieso's premium Caballo Loco first came out in 1997 it caused quite a stir, and rightly so. Here was a non-vintage Chilean blend that really did pack in modern, New World fruit with Old World class. Californian Paul Hobbs (who also helps CATENA in Argentina) provides the know-how to make top-notch Chardonnay (especially the Reserve Chardonnay). Vineyards in Lontué and Curicó supply Cabernet Sauvignon, Merlot, Cabernet Franc and Malbec. The Reserva wines use oak but do not represent a superior selection. Sparkling wine is made by both the CHAMPAGNE and *charmat* methods and overseen by Raphael Brisbois, who used to work at Piper-Heidsieck in Champagne and also consults for OMAR KHAYYAM. Wines are sold in the USA under the Stonelake label. Best years: 1999, '98.

VALENCIA

SPAIN

Save for small pockets of quality and the great, unfairly ignored treasure of its sweet Muscat wines, the Valencia region has been for a long time the realm of huge, industrial wineries producing bulk wines. There are only three DOs in a region where vineyards cover 102,000ha (252,000 acres) – Spain's second largest after La MANCHA. The VALENCIA DO is disparate, with four sub-zones, from the inland, mountainous Valentino to the hills right above the city of Valencia. The UTIEL-REQUENA DO, much further inland on the central plateau, adjoins the lesser known Manchuela area of Castilla-La Mancha, with which it shares the

undistinguished Bobal red grape. The ALICANTE DO would hold the most promise, were it not for the prevalence of dull co-operatives (with one exception: Bocopa at Petrer).

VALENCIA DO

SPAIN, Valencia

🍷 *Mourvèdre, (Monastrell), Forcayat, Grenache Noir (Garnacha Tinta), Garnacha Tintorera, Tempranillo, Cabernet Sauvignon, Merlot*

🍷 *Merseguera, Malvasía, Planta Fina, Chardonnay and others*

Down in the south-east, this is one of Spain's big exporting wine regions. Much of the wine is made in co-operatives, but it is the five modern, private companies, Vinival, Schenk, Vicente Gandia Pla, Valsangiacomo and Egli, that do most of the foreign trade. Valencian wines are reasonably cheap and can be good value if well made. They can never be great wines, however, because the raw materials are boring grape varieties. Most of the wines are white, and mainly made from the unimpressive Merseguera grape, with some reds and rosés made largely from Garnacha Tinta and Garnacha Tintorera, and from the Monastrell in the south of the region. Moscatel de Valencia is perhaps the region's most exciting drink; a lusciously sweet, grapy combination of Moscatel juice and wine alcohol. Minimum legal alcohol levels were recently reduced to a sensible 11 per cent. Best producers: Vincente Gandía Pla, Schenk (Las Monteros), Cherubino, Valsangiacomo (Marqués de Caro).

VALENTINI

ITALY, Abruzzo, Montepulciano d'Abruzzo DOC

🍷🍷 *Montepulciano*

🍷 *Trebbiano d'Abruzzo*

Eduardo Valentini is a gentleman farmer with a large estate planted to a variety of crops under the shadow of the Apennines' highest peak, Gran Sasso. The vineyards comprise 120ha (297 acres) of vines – Montepulciano and Trebbiano d'Abruzzo, as is the norm in this region –

VALENTINI

Eduardo Valentini uses only his best grapes for his own wines. The stunning Trebbiano d'Abruzzo is a lustrous, gold-green colour with exotic flavours.

on the ubiquitous and much-reviled, for its tendency to overproduce, training system called *tendone*. So far no surprises. But Valentini is an almost fanatical perfectionist, making wine to sell under his label from only 5 per cent of the total crop (he sells the other grapes to a local co-operative), and since he never knows until vintage time where the 5 per cent will come from the whole lot get looked after as if they were in the vineyard of Ch. LATOUR.

The secret of Valentini's hugely successful red MONTEPULCIANO D'ABRUZZO and white Trebbiano d'Abruzzo (he also makes a pink Cerasuolo) is, therefore, in the fruit quality – although he would maintain, no doubt with some truth, that the secret is also in the wine-making methods, which are as artisanal and non-interventionist as possible. Valentini's wines have to be drunk – not just tasted – to be understood, but one should not get the idea that they are in any way typical of Montepulciano and, especially, of Trebbiano d'Abruzzo. They are, instead, individual creations. Best years: 1995, '93, '92, '90, '88, '85, '77.

VALLE D'AOSTA DOC

ITALY, Valle d'Aosta

🍷 *Gamay, Nebbiolo, Petit Rouge, Pinot Noir (Pinot Nero), Vien de Nus*

🍷 *Nebbiolo, Petit Rouge*

🍷 *Blanc de Morgex, Muscat (Moscato), Müller-Thurgau, Pinot Gris (Pinot Grigio), Pinot Noir (Pinot Nero)*

The long Aosta Valley, down-river from the ski resort of Courmayeur, has been divided into a string of sub-denominations, comprising numerous wine styles, all belonging to the Valle d'Aosta DOC. From west to east these are Blanc de Morgex et de La Salle (white, from Blanc de Morgex grapes); Enfer d'Arvier, Torrette (both red, from Petit Rouge); Nus (white and *passito* from Pinot Grigio, but this local sub-variety is often called Malvoisie); Nus Rosso (red, from Vien de Nus); Chambave (white and *passito* from Moscato); Chambave Rosso (red, from Petit Rouge); Arnad-Montjovet and Donnaz (both red, from Nebbiolo).

There are also varietal sub-denominations, for Gamay (red), Müller-Thurgau (white) and Pinot Nero (red and also white, if the grape juice is quickly removed from the dark skins). To make it even more confusing, labels may be in either Italian or French and some styles only exist in minute quantities. Excellent producers do not abound, but there is a remarkably good wine school, the Institut Agricole Régional, whose top wine, from a wide range, is a Cabernet-Merlot blend called Vin du Prévot.

VALLE CENTRAL (Central Valley) Chile

IN 1990 CHILE SOLD $50 MILLION of wine on the export markets of the world. By 1998 this figure had soared to half a billion dollars. The powerhouse behind this dramatic rise is the Valle Central, or Central Valley. Extending southwards from the capital, Santiago, the Valle Central widens and undulates as it dips into the deeper river valleys that criss-cross it east to west as they drain the Andes into the Pacific Ocean. Rivers like the Lontué, Rapel and Maipo flow down from the majestic Andes and wash silt and volcanic debris through their dramatic valleys. The mineral-rich deposits left behind, the by-product of the tumultuous growth of the Andes, have created slopes and valleys with excellent viticultural, potential. The only problem is that although the Pacific Ocean provides ambient humidity, there isn't enough rainfall to sustain widespread farming. Over a thousand years ago the Incas devised a sophisticated irrigation system for harnessing the water in the rivers, and gave rise to an agriculture now dedicated to viticulture.

Viticulture came to Chile with Spanish colonization and soon Chile was supplying wine to much of Spanish America. Immigrants brought vines with them and eventually French varietals began to show their liking for the conditions. Development continued slowly until the mid-1970s, when

The Central Valley climate is strongly influenced by the Andes mountains that tower above the flat valley floor. The combination of cool nights and hot days in the vineyards during the growing season enhances grape acidity and flavour.

Miguel Torres arrived from Spain with the first stainless steel technology on the continent. It wasn't long before most other bodegas copied him, and the modern Chilean wine revolution was underway. There has been no stopping it since. Chile is now the third-leading exporter of wine to the USA, after France and Italy. New vineyards have been planted in just about every suitable spot. Good-value Cabernet Sauvignon, with attractive blackcurrant, green pepper and fresh mint aromas led to nicely focused, aromatic Sauvignon Blanc. Deep, luscious and friendly Merlots followed. Then, we were introduced to the concept of Carmenère, an ancient Bordeaux grape variety that performs brilliantly in Chilean conditions.

The latest development is super-premium reds, blends to die for. This generally involves an outside investor – like Bruno Prats and Paul Pontallier of Bordeaux who have a project outside Santiago, Ch. Mouton-Rothschild with Concha y Toro or Robert Mondavi with Errázuriz. The prices are always high – sometimes silly, especially when the wines end up tasting more international than Chilean.

Central Valley sub-regions
- Maipo Valley
- Rapel Valley
  (Cachapoal Valley and Colchagua Valley)
- Curicó Valley
  (Teno Valley and Lontué Valley)
- Maule Valley
  (Claro Valley, Loncomilla Valley and Tutuvén Valley)

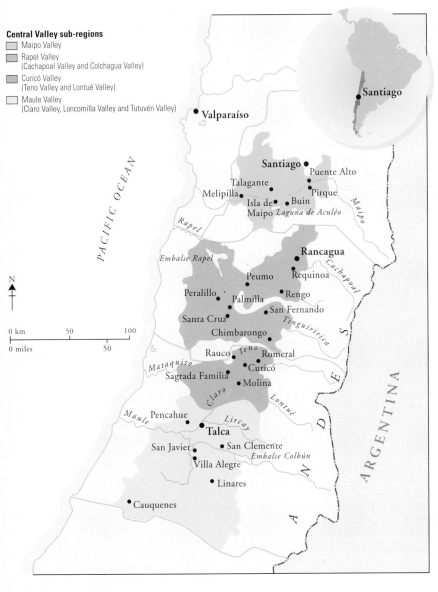

LA ROSA
This winery is one of the rising stars of the Cachapoal Valley, making unoaked varietal wines, including full-flavoured and rich Chardonnay.

SANTA RITA
The much improved Casa Real Cabernet Sauvignon is one of the highlights from this large, old Chilean winery.

CONCHA Y TORO
The Don Melchor Cabernet Sauvignon shows a depth and richness that should be the watchword in Chilean reds.

CONO SUR
The name of this winery has become synonymous with good Chilean Pinot Noir.

CARMEN
A subsidiary of the larger Santa Rita winery, Carmen makes well-focused wines, especially the reds from the Medella Real or Gold Label range.

PRODUCER ENTRIES
Canepa, Carmen, Casa Lapostolle, Concha y Toro, Cono Sur, Cousiño Macul, Montes, La Rosa, Santa Carolina, Santa Rita, Miguel Torres, Valdivieso.

VALDIVIESO
This rising star in Chile makes succulent juicy reds from many varieties including Malbec. This is a seriously fruity wine, brimming with fresh berry flavours.

MONT GRAS
This wonderfully equipped new winery in the Colchagua Valley is building a reputation for red wines. The Reserva Merlot is oaky but shows good fruit intensity.

CASA LAPOSTOLLE
The intense, structured Merlot Cuvée Alexandre offers sweet-damson proof that this grape is Chile's trump card.

VALPOLICELLA DOC

ITALY, Veneto

🍷 *Corvina, Rondinella, Molinara and others*
See also Recioto della Valpolicella

It really is a sad state of affairs when such a fine wine – for so it is – becomes so debased. Originally grapes for Valpolicella were grown on the hillsides of a series of parallel valleys north-west of Verona near Lake Garda. As time went by plantings gradually spread onto less hilly and even unashamedly flat country-side. But demand continued apace and the temptation became ever stronger to squeeze as much production as possible from the grapes. So Valpolicella became an over-extended area with the vines giving a far too generous yield. The original Valpolicella zone was given the Classico tag, but the coin-cidence of the Valpolicella name was enough to bring even Classico crashing in terms of price and, consequently, of quality.

Nonetheless, it is a mistake to think that good Valpolicella comes only from the Classico zone, and that everything from the extended zone is rubbish. On the contrary, there are some outstanding wines from the eastern sector (DAL FORNO, arguably the greatest contemporary producer, is in Illasi; Bertani, high-priests of traditional AMARONE DELLA VALPOLICELLA, is in Valpantena). The overproduced stuff comes not from the east *per se*, but from the plains where the vines yield more.

Young Valpolicella, made for drinking with a year or so of aging, can be lovely: light and fresh, fully packed with its typical bitter morello cherries flavour. But much Valpolicella is sold at two or three years old, often already tired as it is too insubstantial to age properly. It is better to find a Ripasso wine, the most traditional style of Valpolicella, strengthened by a re-fermentation on flavour-soaked lees of the *passito* wines. It picks up richness, weight and structure and its bitter cherries flavour gets augmented by chocolate – altogether a much more serious proposition. It is not easy to distinguish from the label which wines are made in this style, but the designation Valpolicella (Classico) Superiore can be a pretty reasonable clue.

Best years: 1998, '97, '95, '94, '93, '91, '90, '88. Good producers are becoming rapidly more numerous and include: Accordini, ALLEGRINI, Bertani, Brigaldara, Brunelli, Tommaso Bussola, Corte Sant'Alda, Dal Forno, MASI, Montresor, Pasque, QUINTARELLI, Le Ragose, Le Salette, San Rustico, Speri, Tedeschi, Tommasi, Viviani.

VALTELLINA DOC, VALTELLINA SUPERIORE DOCG

ITALY, Lombardy

🍷 *Nebbiolo (Chiavennasca), Pinot Noir (Pinot Nero), Merlot and others*

Valtellina is an Alpine wine, produced in a narrow strip along the south-facing, steep-sided valley of the Adda river, which flows west across LOMBARDY, just below the Swiss border. It is only the air movement caused by the river and the heat trap of the valley that enable the grapes to reach ripeness. When they do, in the hands of a skilled wine-maker, Valtellina is one of the most elegant and refined incarnations of Nebbiolo, locally called Chiavennasca. The predominant flavour is violetty with some raspberry and walnuts, quite soft, although Nebbiolo's characteristic tannin is still around.

Valtellina Superiore is a cut above the nor-mal version, still all made from Nebbiolo, but with a lower vineyard yield. It is also pro-duced in one or more of four sub-districts: Sassella, Grumello, Inferno and Valgella. Sas-sella is the best, but choosing a good producer such as La Castellina, Negri, Pelizzatti, Sertoli Salis, Rainoldi or Triacca is more important. Eight years is the usual limit for aging. Best years: 1998, '97, '96, '95, '93, '90, '88.

Sfursat or Sforzato wines, are lightly *passito*, enough to get the alcohol up to 14.5 per cent, although the wine remains dry, like AMARONE DELLA VALPOLICELLA. Some think Sfursat is the best type of Valtellina. It's just a question of whether you prefer the big and butch to the subtle and elegant.

LOS VASCOS

CHILE, Colchagua Valley

🍷 *Cabernet Sauvignon*
🍷 *Sauvignon Blanc, Chardonnay*

In 1988 the Eyzaguirre family (Basque immi-grants – hence the name of the winery) sold a 51 per cent stake of Los Vascos to BORDEAUX's Ch. LAFITE-ROTHSCHILD. The marriage of two winemaking styles has led, via a substan-tial investment programme, to red wines with deep, aromatic qualities, tending more to blackcurrant than to capsicum. If the wines

made at Los Vascos have not lit up the firmament with the highest praise it might be due to the fact that not all the available poten-tial has been fully harnessed. In particular, relatively few new barrels were used, and whites were inclined to be overcropped and lacking in zip. Since 1995 the red wines have improved enormously, benefiting from more active involvement from Lafite's winemaker. Best years: 1999, '97, '96, '95.

VASSE FELIX

AUSTRALIA, Western Australia, South West Australia Zone, Margaret River

🍷 *Cabernet Sauvignon, Syrah (Shiraz)*
🍷 *Riesling, Chardonnay*

Although such outstanding wineries as MOSS WOOD, LEEUWIN ESTATE and CAPE MENTELLE were founded in the MARGARET RIVER region before Vasse Felix was in 1969, this winery took everybody's palates by storm with the piercing blackcurrant and black cherry fruit of its Cabernet Sauvignon that still managed to remain almost austere.

In 1987 the wealthy Holmes à Court fam-ily bought Vasse Felix and since then a new winemaking team has pushed up the fruit and oak flavour in the reds, and introduced com-plexity to the whites, by a huge degree – especially in the flagship Heytesbury range. A brand new winery was in use for the 1999 vintage. Best years: 1998, '97, '96, '95, '94, '93, '91, '90, '88, '86, '84, '83, '79.

VASSE FELIX
Already famous for its red wines, Vasse Felix has made great strides recently with the whites. The delicious, barrel-fermented Semillon has spicy, ripe fruit aromas.

VAUD

SWITZERLAND

🍷 *Gamay, Pinot Noir*
🍷 *Chasselas (Dorin) and others*

Most of the vineyards along Lake Geneva's northern shore are in the Vaud canton, with the region of CHABLAIS being famous for its tangy Chasselas. Lavaux is probably the best region and includes the village of DÉZALEY, Vaud's top appellation. Other regions are La Côte, Côte de l'Orbe-Bonvillars and Vully.

LOS VASCOS
Jointly owned by Bordeaux's Ch. Lafite-Rothschild, Los Vascos is best at Bordeaux-style Cabernet Sauvignon. Even the label is modelled on that of Lafite.

Nearly all the wine is white, and nearly all from the Chasselas grape, here called Dorin; Salvagnin is the name of the red, from either Gamay or Pinot Noir or a blend of the two. Best producers: Badoux, Louis Bovard, Conne, Delarze, Dubois Fils, Grognuz, Massy, Obrist, Pinget, J & P Testuz.

VAVASOUR

NEW ZEALAND, South Island, Marlborough

♥ *Pinot Noir*

♀ *Sauvignon Blanc, Chardonnay, Riesling*

Established in 1986 Vavasour is a high-profile newcomer, situated in MARLBOROUGH's high-quality and drier Awatere Valley. Vavasour started out making high-quality, BORDEAUX-style blends with intense, blackcurrant fruit and cedar perfume and barely a hint of green acid. A series of cool vintages in the early 1990s encouraged Vavasour to remove their Cabernet Franc vines and to plant Pinot Noir. Powerful, high-flavoured Sauvignon Blanc and Chardonnay are also impressive. Dashwood is the second label. Best years: (Pinot Noir) 1999, '98, '97.

VAVASOUR
Ripe Sauvignon Blanc with all the gooseberry and limegrass attack you could wish for is just one of several outstanding wines from this relatively new winery in Marlborough's Awatere sub-region.

VECCHIE TERRE DI MONTEFILI

ITALY, Tuscany, Chianti Classico DOCG

♥ *Sangiovese, Cabernet Sauvignon*

♀ *Chardonnay, Sauvignon Blanc, Gewürztraminer (Traminer)*

The Accuti family have built this small high-altitude estate at Greve into a Tuscan star. Even more admired than the wonderfully perfumed CHIANTI CLASSICO, are the SUPER-TUSCANS Anfiteatro (Sangiovese), and Bruno di Roca (Cabernet Sauvignon and Sangiovese). Barrique-aged Vigna Regis is a blend of Chardonnay, Sauvignon Blanc and Traminer. Best years: 1998, '97, '95, '93.

Spain's most expensive red wines, rich, fragrant, complex and very slow to mature, come from the Vega Sicilia bodega in the Ribera del Duero region. This estate was the first in Spain to grow French grape varieties.

VEGA SICILIA

SPAIN, Castilla-León, Ribera del Duero DO

♥ *Tempranillo (Tinto Fino), Cabernet Sauvignon, Merlot, Malbec*

Even the King of Spain is on strict allocation for Vega Sicilia, Spain's most expensive wine. The large estate has been famed since the nineteenth century for its rich, fragrant, complex and long-lasting wines. Prices have always been extremely high, vying with those for top BORDEAUX.

Vega Sicilia was the first of a growing number of RIBERA DEL DUERO bodegas making extensive use of the Bordeaux grape varieties. Apart from the extraordinary richness of the grapes, one of Vega Sicilia's main hallmarks has been unusually long wood-aging. Depending on the vintage, the top red, Vega Sicilia Unico, would spend up to ten years in large wooden vats and oak barrels – new and old, American and French. If these wines were still richly alive and complex after treatment that would kill most other great wines, how much greater would they be if given more time in bottle and less in wood?

So from the 1982 vintage, the aging process was reduced to only five to six years in wood (including only a few months in new oak). Now at least half of the pre-release aging is spent in the bottle. Valbuena is the label for a five-year-old wine from a specified vintage and the Alión label, from a separate winery, is for modern, 100 per cent Tempranillo reds, aged for 18 months in new French oak. Best years: (Unico) 1987, '86, '85, '82, '81, '79, '76, '75, '74, '73, '70, '68, '62; (Valbuena and Alión) 1996, '95, '94, '91, '90, '89.

VELICH

AUSTRIA, Burgenland, Neusiedlersee, Apetlon

♀ *Chardonnay, Neuburger, Muscat (Muskat Ottonel), Gewürztraminer (Traminer), Welschriesling*

Roland Velich leads a double life of wine-grower by day and casino croupier by night. That does not stop him from making by far the best Austrian Chardonnay. Unlike its rivals, his Tiglat Chardonnay is neither too alcoholic nor too heavily oaked, nor does it have the caricature butter and caramel flavours so often found in Austrian Chardonnay. Instead, the old vines planted on stony soil give the wine a waxy-nutty character and great elegance. The slightly less refined Chardonnays from Darscho and Illmitzer Weg vineyards are almost as good. The spectacularly concentrated Welschriesling Trockenbeerenauslese is Velich's best sweet wine. Best years: (dry whites) 1997, '95, '94, '93, '92; (sweet whites) 1998, '96, '95, '91.

VENETO Italy

THERE IS NO SHORTAGE OF WINE in the Veneto, Italy's third-largest wine-producing region and number one in respect of DOC wines. The province of Verona alone produces more than enough to satisfy the entire region. Some of the best-known and mostly widely available Italian wine names come from there: Soave, Valpolicella and Bardolino. But a passing acquaintance with those three wines plus a random dip into the wines of the more easterly Piave and Lison-Pramaggiore zones or the central Colli Berici and Colli Euganei, and one could be excused for thinking that the good folk of the Veneto are far more concerned about how much wine they are making than how good it is. While reasonable enough, the average Veneto wine can hardly be described as exciting. Too many of the vineyards are on its extensive plains and too many DOCs provide for over-abundant yields, resulting in wines that, even when well enough made, lack real flavour. The bigger problem is that many of them are *not* well made. The Merlot that grows on the Veneto plains in vast profusion gives cheap, simple wines that must rate as just about the lightest reds that Mer-

lot produces anywhere in the world. And the bulk producers of Soave and Valpolicella, including some very well-known companies, should be ashamed by the appalling quality of their ordinary blends. But then the DOC authorities should be ashamed of themselves for allowing such debasing and perversion of traditionally fine wine names as Soave and Valpolicella in the name of politics and profit.

The Veneto, however, doesn't lack potential once wine-making is in the hands of quality-conscious producers, who make the most of any nearby hills and prune vines ruthlessly to keep yields down (and thereby ensuring better quality). Soave Classico and Valpolicella Classico (the Classico zones cover the better hill sites), each with a number of estates committed to quality, produce an increasing amount of first class wines, which bear no resemblance to cheap commercial offerings. Real Soave Classico is a full, broad white, beautifully balanced and developing a delightful richness of nuts and honeysuckle with age. Real Valpolicella Classico, especially one dominated by the excellent Corvina grape, manages to provide cherry-rich fruit, as well as a delightful bitter-sour twist. And the remarkable red Amarone and Recioto wines of Valpolicella – rich, yet bitter – and the sublime Recioto di Soave are among Italy's finest wines. Breganze does produce an eclectic range of high-quality dry and sweet wines. Even the rarely seen Colli Berici and Colli Euganei, areas with a number of single-varietal wine styles (Cabernet, Merlot, Pinot Bianco, Tocai, the exotically named Fior d'Arancia), have glorious hilly terrain, which so far only a very few producers fully exploit.

The Veneto wines of Lake Garda are young, cherry-fresh red Bardolino and white Bianco di Custoza. The hilly, southern part of the Bardolino zone overlaps that of Bianco di Custoza. This has two advantages. Bianco di Custoza usually comes from only the slopes best suited for white wine, and Bardolino only from slopes better for red; and producers are used to making white wines, hence they make a marvellous crisp, fresh, pale rosé, Bardolino Chiaretto.

There is no doubt about the wine to drink in Venice. Although nearby Piave has eight wines from different grape varieties to choose from (red Raboso is especially invigorating), and next-door Lison-Pramaggiore has even more, Venice is the place for Prosecco. Lorryloads of bottles of this light, fruity fizzy stuff, from the grape of the same name, trundle down from north of Treviso to keep both Venetians and tourists happily lubricated.

The best vineyards in the Valpolicella DOC are situated on the steep slopes of the various valleys. Some of the most famous wines come from the valley of Fumane in the Classico zone.

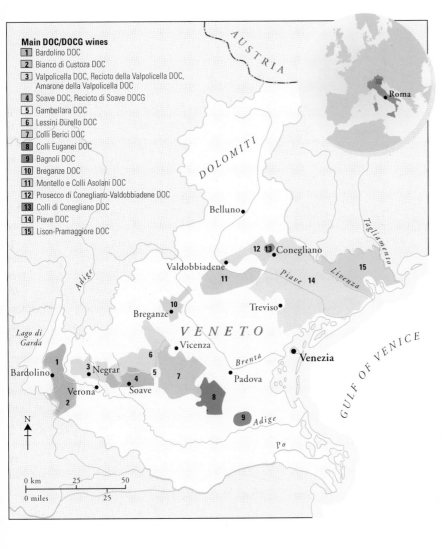

Main DOC/DOCG wines

1. Bardolino DOC
2. Bianco di Custoza DOC
3. Valpolicella DOC, Recioto della Valpolicella DOC, Amarone della Valpolicella DOC
4. Soave DOC, Recioto di Soave DOCG
5. Gambellara DOC
6. Lessini Durello DOC
7. Colli Berici DOC
8. Colli Euganei DOC
9. Bagnoli DOC
10. Breganze DOC
11. Montello e Colli Asolani DOC
12. Prosecco di Conegliano-Valdobbiadene DOC
13. Colli di Conegliano DOC
14. Piave DOC
15. Lison-Pramaggiore DOC

VIGNALTA

The Vignalta estate makes Cabernet with vibrant herbal and blackcurrant fruit way above the quality of most of the other wines from the Colli Euganei zone.

PIEROPAN

Pieropan's Soave Classico from La Rocca vineyard is one of the benchmark wines from the DOC. Slightly steely and austere at first, it develops richness and flavour with time.

ALLEGRINI

This high-profile producer in Valpolicella Classico is concentrating increasingly on quality. La Poja, an elegant oak-aged wine made solely from Corvina, Valpolicella's best quality grape, has shown the potential of the Valpolicella DOC.

REGIONAL ENTRIES

Amarone della Valpolicella, Bardolino, Bianco di Custoza, Breganze, Colli Berici, Piave, Prosecco di Conegliano-Valdobbiadene, Recioto della Valpolicella, Soave, Valpolicella.

PRODUCER ENTRIES

Allegrini, Anselmi, Dal Forno, GIV, Masi, Pieropan, Quintarelli.

MACULAN

Fausto Maculan is one of the leading Francophiles of Italy's wine renaissance and makes a wide range of wines based on French grape varieties.

GUISEPPE QUINTARELLI

These distinctive handwritten labels herald some of the most remarkable wines in Valpolicella. This is complex, powerful and benchmark Amarone.

ANSELMI

Roberto Anselmi showed the world that Soave can have personality when carefully made. The Recioti I Capitelli is a gently honeyed wine with a rich, smooth texture.

ROMANO DAL FORNO

Dal Forno's Amarone della Valpolicella from the Monte Lodoletta vineyard is a voluptuous wine of massive structure, deep ruby colour and spicy bouquet.

VERDEJO

The Verdejo is one of Spain's few characterful white grapes, capable of making crisp, fruity white wines that are full in body without being too high in alcohol, and slightly nutty in flavour. Sadly, there is not much planted – only just over 7000ha (17,300 acres) in the whole of Spain.

Verdejo's main habitat is RUEDA on the river Duero, over towards the north-eastern tip of the Portuguese border. There must be a minimum 75 per cent Verdejo in the top-category wines, Rueda Superior, but a small addition of Sauvignon Blanc often adds greatly to the perfume and fruit. It is also used in Rueda to make the traditional fortified, sherry-style wines, aged in wooden barrels under flor, which scarcely ever leave the area now. The rest of Spain's Verdejo grows in areas near Rueda, such as TORO and CIGALES.

VERDICCHIO

Home for the white Verdicchio grape is the MARCHE in central Italy. It has been there since the fourteenth century and has not, as far as we know, spread further afield, unless rumours that the stylish Trebbiano di Lugana is a form of Verdicchio are true.

Verdicchio's name derives from the word *verde* (Italian for 'green') as the grapes, even when ripe, remain strongly greenish in colour. The wine, too, has in youth a greenish tinge to its pale straw colour. Verdicchio produces one of the most refreshing white wines, with high natural acidity which keeps it crisp. This acidity also makes Verdicchio a natural for sparkling wine. The grape is also amenable to unconventional treatments such as late-picking or aging in large oak casks, and certain producers like Bucci have shown that it can improve with a few years of bottle age and hold its own for a surprisingly long time. Its yield may not be reliable but it is hardy. For all these reasons there is a school of thought today that considers Verdicchio one of the best of Italian white natives.

VERDICCHIO DEI CASTELLI DI JESI DOC, VERDICCHIO DI MATELICA DOC

ITALY, Marche

♀ *Verdicchio, Trebbiano Toscano, Malvasia*

Castelli di Jesi (named after the river Esino and nothing to do with Jesus) is a sizeable wine region inland from the port of Ancona, specializing in whites from the Verdicchio grape. In the post-World War Two period, when times were hard and the producers

GAROFOLI
The Macrina vineyard produces Verdicchio with fresh, flowery aromas and ripe fruit flavours that become increasingly refined with several years' aging.

needed a different image to bring recognition to their wine, they resorted to the amphora bottle, partly to emphasize the Greek influence on these parts in ancient days. The marketing trick worked too well, because today an amphora-shaped bottle immediately suggests the cheap and cheerful Verdicchio associated with days when quantity, not quality, was the criterion. So it is difficult to persuade consumers that Verdicchio, the grape, is one of Italy's finest and that the Castelli di Jesi DOC is capable of offering some very serious white wine, with, at its best, tremendous concentration and richness of mouth-feel and the ability to age, in the right conditions, for several years. The number of top producers seems to grow every year. Best producers: Brunori (San Nicolò), Bucci (Villa Bucci Riserva), Casalfarneto (Gran Casale), Colonnara (Cuprese), Coroncino (Gaiospino), Fazi-Battaglia (Le Moie), Garofoli (Macrina), Mancinelli (S. Maria del Fiore), Moncaro (Ca Ruptae), Sartarelli (Tralivio), Tavignano (Selezione Misco), UMANI RONCHI (Casal di Serra), Vallerosa-Bonci (San Michele), La Vite (Coste del Molino, Palio di San Floriano), Zaccagnini Fratelli (Salmagina). All these wines, though varying in style, have a dry nuttiness and a rich-sharp salty edge that the old wines lacked. Sparkling Verdicchio (especially from Le Terrazze) is one of Italy's most tasty fizzes.

Verdicchio di Matelica, from a smaller region further inland towards the Apennines, at a somewhat higher altitude, produces wines that tend to have a more acid bite. Best producers: Belisario, Bisci-Castiglioni, Mecella, La Monacesca.

VERDUZZO

This Italian grape makes some pretty lively dry whites but is more famous for its sweet wines. Best suited to COLLI ORIENTALI in

FRIULI, as it spreads west it makes wines that are drier and more bitingly fresh. Sweet Verduzzo is richly honeyed – runny honey – and floral, with a meadow full of flowers and an enlivening backbone of acidity. It can be aged, but it is really best young and fresh.

VERMENTINO

The best dry white wines of Sardinia generally come from the Vermentino grape. Light, dry, perfumed and nutty, the best of these tend to be from the north of the island, where in Gallura Vermentino now has its own DOCG. It is also found along the Tyrrhenian coast from LIGURIA's Ponente down to Tuscany's Maremma. In PROVENCE it is known as Rolle. It is important in Corsica (where its name is Malvoisie de Corse) and is now permitted and is on the increase in LANGUEDOC-ROUSSILLON.

VERNACCIA

The word Vernaccia means something along the lines of 'belonging to here', which goes some way to explaining why there are at least three grape varieties in Italy called Vernaccia (four if you reckon Alto Adige's Vernatsch or Schiava to be a variation on the theme), none bearing any relation to any of the others.

Vernaccia number one is an ancient white variety from Tuscany and grown mainly around the famous hill town of San Gimignano. Here, it makes wines that are white, dry and anything from lean to rich. The word Vernaccia on its own almost always refers to the wine from San Gimignano.

Vernaccia number two is also a white grape but this time from the central west of Sardinia, just north of Oristano. The outstanding, oxidized, almost sherry-like wines can be strong and dry or fortified (dry or sweet).

Vernaccia number three is a red grape variety and comes from the central-southern Marche, around Serrapetrona. The wines it makes here are usually sparkling and can be dry, semi-sweet or sweet.

VERNACCIA DI SAN GIMIGNANO DOCG

ITALY, Tuscany

♀ *Vernaccia di San Gimignano, Chardonnay*

San Gimignano, the 'town of towers', is on the itinerary of nearly every tourist in Tuscany. With so many visitors tramping up and down the steep streets, it wouldn't have been at all surprising if Vernaccia di San Gimignano had degenerated to a tourist gimmick of no intrinsic quality. Yet very few of San Gimignano's wine producers have fallen into this profitable but short-sighted trap.

Traditionally, the wines of San Gimignano were golden in colour, rich, broad and often oxidized. The modern wave of winemaking brought in pale, tight, lean, crisp and restrained wines, which kept the characterful Vernaccia grape held so tightly in check that it had a real struggle to stamp its personality on the wine. Now some estates are slackening the reins, resulting in salty, creamy, nutty, tangy wine, with, in the hands of masters like Teruzzi & Puthod, a buttery richness that lasts a good three years or so. In 1993 it was made DOCG and Chardonnay is now allowed in the blend (up to 10 per cent). Best producers: Ambra delle Torri, Casale-Falchini, Cesani, Montenidoli, Panizzi, Pietrafitta, Pietraserena, San Quirico, Guicciardini Strozzi, Teruzzi & Puthod.

GEORGES VERNAY

FRANCE, Northern Rhône, Condrieu AC

♀ *Viognier*

The genial but elderly Georges Vernay is without doubt the leading father figure of the CONDRIEU appellation, although these days he lets his son Luc make the wine, while Georges makes himself useful in the busy tasting room. With 6ha (15 acres) of vineyards in Condrieu, Vernay is a major player, and he also produces CÔTE-RÔTIE and ST-JOSEPH. There are a number of different cuvées of Condrieu. The regular bottling is aged for six months, while the other cuvées are aged for 12 months before bottling. Coteau de Vernon is a single vineyard, as is the Chaillées de l'Enfer, which is often the most impressive wine. Vernay

believes in bottling relatively late to keep the aromas fresh, although conventional wisdom would favour the opposite approach. Wines from young vines are usually bottled separately as VIN DE PAYS, ensuring that only the best wines are released under the precious Condrieu appellation. Vernay produces about 25,000 bottles a year, of which 6000 are Coteau de Vernon. Best years: 1998, '97, '96, '95, '94.

NOËL VERSET

FRANCE, Northern Rhône, Cornas AC

♀ *Syrah*

Noël Verset, now in his eighties, has been taking things easy in recent years, and some of his vines have been sold to other growers such as Thierry Allemand. What remains, however, includes some of the oldest and lowest yielding parcels in CORNAS. The winemaking is a no-frills exercise, with the wines aged in large casks for about 18 months and bottled without filtration. They can be tannic but are also long-lived, a living reminder of how the strapping wines of Cornas used to taste. Best years: 1998, '97, '96, '95, '94, '91, '90, '89, '88, '85.

QUINTA DO VESÚVIO

PORTUGAL, Douro, Port DOC

♀ *Touriga Nacional, Touriga Francesa, Tinta Roriz (Tempranillo), Tinta Barroca, Tinto Cão and others*

♀ *Gouveio, Viosinho, Rabigato, Malvasia Fina, Donzelinho*

One of the largest and most stately properties in the DOURO, Quinta do Vesúvio belonged to the FERREIRA family until it was bought by the Symington family (owners of DOW, GRAHAM and WARRE) in 1989. Quinta do Vesúvio is now a PORT wine producer in its own right and, in all but the poorest years, the property bottles a single-quinta vintage port. Packed with ripe minty fruit, Vesúvio's vintage ports appeal particularly to North American consumers who enjoy drinking their ports young. Best years: 1995, '94, '92, '91.

VEUVE CLICQUOT

FRANCE, Champagne, Champagne AC

♀ ♀ *Pinot Noir, Chardonnay, Pinot Meunier*

Widows have featured prominently in the affairs of the CHAMPAGNE houses, but when someone talks of 'The Widow' in Champagne, they are sure to be talking of the Widow Clicquot or Veuve Clicquot. Not only was she Champagne's dominant figure at the beginning of the nineteenth century, but she invented the winemaking process of *remuage* – the last stage in the process needed to obtain clear Champagne.

VEUVE CLICQUOT
Veuve Clicquot's prestige cuvée is called la Grande Dame after the original widow. With real refinement, it is fairly rich and full-bodied.

Modern Veuve Clicquot Champagne can, but doesn't always, live up to the Widow Clicquot's original high standards. The non-vintage Champagne is full, toasty, slightly honeyed and quite weighty for a sparkling wine and is only marred by inconsistency. There is also a vintage which resembles the non-vintage but is even fuller, and a prestige cuvée, la Grande Dame, which usually manages to be exquisite and impressive at the same time. Best years: 1991, '90, '89, '88, '85, '82, '79.

VIADER VINEYARDS

USA, California, Napa County, Howell Mountain AVA

♀ *Cabernet Sauvignon, Cabernet Franc, Merlot*

Born in Argentina, Delia Viader enjoyed the NAPA VALLEY lifestyle so much she joined in by developing a vineyard along the steep, rocky slopes of HOWELL MOUNTAIN. Doing everything first-class, she enlisted the services of vineyard developer David Abreu and winemaking consultant Tony Soter to oversee the production of her estate red.

Made from two-thirds Cabernet Sauvignon and one-third Cabernet Franc, Viader red quickly established an engaging, supple style that yet maintained its mountain-grown, long-lived personality. The Cabernet Franc reins in the Cabernet Sauvignon and adds subtle flavour nuances to the wine. On average, her 6-ha (15-acre) vineyard yields enough fruit to produce 4000 cases per year of this one wine. Best years: 1997, '96, '95, '94, '93, '92, '91, '90, '89.

GEORGES VERNAY
Condrieu les Chaillées de l'Enfer is a rare and supremely scented wine from Condrieu's best slopes.

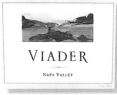

VIADER VINEYARDS
This powerful and elegant red wine is the only one made by this small Howell Mountain winery. The wine has a rich flavour and will keep for up to 15 years.

VICTORIA Australia

IN 1890 VICTORIA'S VINEYARDS produced well over half of Australia's wine, yet by 1960 there were only four wineries in the state outside North-East Victoria: Chateau Tahbilk, Osicka's, Best's and Seppelt Great Western. Today, there are almost 300 licensed winemakers. From being on its knees, Victoria is now bursting with new wineries and new regions. Tomorrow, who knows?

There are 19 wine regions in Victoria, most of them grouped within a radius of 200km (125 miles) from Melbourne. The outposts are the distinctly chilly Drumborg near Portland in the far west, the bountifully mass-producing Murray Valley extending beyond Mildura in the furthest north-west corner, and Rutherglen and Milawa in the north-east. In between, virtually every kind of wine style and climate is covered, though most of Victoria's most famous wines are from relatively small wineries, in relatively cool areas.

Indeed, Victoria is the state of the small winery. True, it is home to Lindemans' vast Karadoc winery (the company's operational headquarters) and to Mildara, both adjacent to Mildura in the extensive Murray Darling region; but, apart from these, most of the wineries, even those owned by the large national groups, are small- to medium-sized operations.

The small wineries are primarily red wine producers, though there is exciting Chardonnay, Sauvignon, Riesling and

Located only a few kilometres from the sea, Stonier's Winery is the leading producer in the cool-climate, windy Mornington Peninsula region and not surprisingly, Chardonnay and Pinot Noir are the main specialities here.

Gewurztraminer, and even Marsanne in small quantities. Red wine production is focused on the Grampians (formerly known as Great Western)-Pyrenees-Bendigo-Goulburn Valley belt of Central Victoria. Here you find dark, blood-red Shiraz, sometimes spicy, sometimes with a distinctly minty character. Cabernet Sauvignon is similarly intense and concentrated, once again with mint running into dark berry and blackcurrant flavours. The wines have weight and power, ranging from the almost silky smoothness of those produced by Best's or Seppelt through to the rasping tannin and astringency of the young reds of producers such as Taltarni and Chateau Tahbilk.

Nearer Melbourne, Yarra Valley, the Mornington Peninsula and Geelong are all very cool districts, with a maritime climate. A total of 90 wineries here produce elegant, crispy fruit wines, with Chardonnay, Pinot Noir and the Cabernet family the centre of attention. While Australia still has to convince the sceptics about the intrinsic merits of its best Pinot Noir, it is from these regions that the best Pinots come.

Gippsland is a rambling, flat region with cool but very dry growing conditions. Cooler still is the Central Victorian

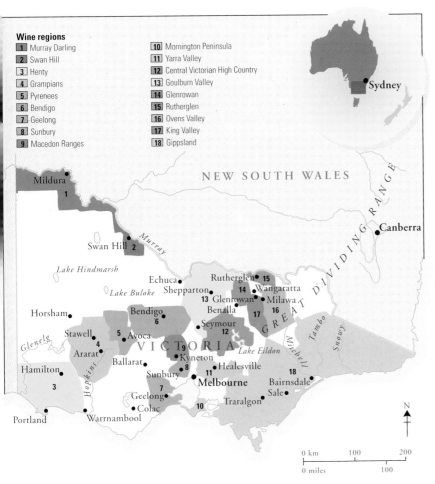

Wine regions

1. Murray Darling
2. Swan Hill
3. Henty
4. Grampians
5. Pyrenees
6. Bendigo
7. Geelong
8. Sunbury
9. Macedon Ranges
10. Mornington Peninsula
11. Yarra Valley
12. Central Victorian High Country
13. Goulburn Valley
14. Glenrowan
15. Rutherglen
16. Ovens Valley
17. King Valley
18. Gippsland

CHAMBERS
Bill Chambers is one of the characters of the Australian wine industry. His speciality is remarkably powerful liqueur Muscat and Tokay.

JASPER HILL
Highly regarded and eagerly sought after, these Shiraz wines have immense richness and structure.

GIACONDA
Beautifully balanced and packed with fruit sweetness, this wine nevertheless clearly has Burgundy as its role model.

MORRIS
This historic winery makes some of the most magnificent Australian fortifieds. The Old Premium Muscat has intense sultana and date sweetness but divine aroma.

MOUNT LANGI GHIRAN
With deep colour and intense pepper/spice aromas Langi Shiraz is one of the top Shiraz wines in Australia.

MOUNT MARY
This classic Yarra estate takes Bordeaux as its role model. Cabernets Quintet is based on all five red Bordeaux varieties.

BANNOCKBURN
The experience of several vintages spent at Domaine Dujac in the Côte de Nuits is reflected in Gary Farr's Meursault-like Chardonnay.

High Country where grapes actually struggle to ripen. The North-East, centred on Rutherglen, Glenrowan and Milawa, produces Australia's distinctive fortified Muscats and Tokays. It is also the home of some massive red wines: Morris's Durif and Shiraz from Campbells and Baileys still produce echoes of the past. But these days the most interesting wines are more likely to be those from the slopes of the King and Ovens valleys, which produce much of Brown Brothers' white table wines and which, in the future, will provide the grapes for Orlando's sparkling wine.

Two of Australia's top sparkling wine producers are based in the Central Victoria region: Seppelt at Great Western and Yellowglen near Ballarat.

REGIONAL ENTRIES
Bendigo, Central Victoria High Country, Geelong, Gippsland, Goulburn Valley, Grampians, King Valley, Macedon Ranges, Mornington Peninsula, Ovens Valley, Pyrenees, Rutherglen and Glenrowan, Sunbury, Yarra Valley.

PRODUCER ENTRIES
Baileys, Bannockburn, Bass Phillip, Best's, Brown Brothers, Chambers, Chateau Tahbilk, Coldstream Hills, Dalwhinnie, Delatite, Domaine Chandon, Dromana Estate, Giaconda, Jasper Hill, Lindemans, Mildara, Mitchelton, Morris, Mount Langi Ghiran, Mount Mary, Seppelt, Stonier's, Taltarni, TarraWarra, Virgin Hills, Yarra Burn, Yarra Ridge, Yarra Yering, Yellowglen, Yeringberg.

CH. LA VIEILLE CURE

FRANCE, Bordeaux, Fronsac AC
♥ *Merlot, Cabernet Franc*

La Vieille Cure is symbolic of the progress that has been made in FRONSAC over the last 15 years. In 1986 the 18-ha (44-acre) estate, which is located on clay-limestone slopes overlooking the river Isle, had new American owners, and a programme of restoration and investment was launched. The vineyard was in part replanted, the equipment updated, new vinification cellars built and aging in oak barrels introduced. Above all, the winemaking was adapted to produce riper, rounder wines and avoid the rustic tannins typical of Fronsac at the time. Now the wines are not only richly textured, oaky and finely but firmly structured, but a commercial success too. Best years: 1998, '97, '96, '94, '90, '89.

CH. VIEUX-CHÂTEAU-CERTAN

FRANCE, Bordeaux, Pomerol AC
♥ *Merlot, Cabernet Franc, Cabernet Sauvignon,*

Traditionally the position of runner-up to Ch. PÉTRUS in POMEROL has always been occupied by Vieux-Château-Certan, but le PIN and TROTANOY now dispute the title. But whereas they often seem to ape Pétrus, Vieux-Château-Certan goes out of its way to be different. It is owned by the Thienpont (not Moueix) family and, although it is only a few hundred yards down the road, its soil is different, mixing sand and gravel with its clay. But most importantly it has only 60 per cent Merlot as against Pétrus' 95 per cent. The rest of the 13-ha (34-acre) vineyard is 30 per cent Cabernet Franc and 10 per cent Cabernet Sauvignon, and it is this unusually strong presence of Cabernet for Pomerol which makes Vieux-Château-Certan drier, leaner, less sumptuous. The slow-maturing wine gradually builds up over 15–20 years into an exciting 'MÉDOC' blend of blackcurrant and cedarwood perfume just set off by the brown sugar and roasted nuts of Pomerol. Best years: 1998, '96, '95, '94, '93, '90, '89, '88, '87, '86, '85, '83, '82, '81, '75.

VIEUX-CHÂTEAU-CERTAN
This is a slow-developing and tannic red wine. Recent vintages, while still long-lived, reveal more of a rich, very ripe fruit from the outset.

DOMAINE DU VIEUX TÉLÉGRAPHE

FRANCE, Southern Rhône, Châteauneuf-du-Pape AC
♥ *Grenache, Syrah, Cinsaut, Vaccarèse, Counoise, Mourvèdre*
♀ *Clairette, Grenache Blanc, Bourboulenc, Roussanne*

The Brunier family have been managing this extremely well run and consistent estate since 1898. Most of the 70ha (173 acres) of vineyards lie in the eastern part of the CHÂTEAUNEUF-DU-PAPE AC, where the grapes ripen earlier than elsewhere. Many of the vines are over 60 years old, which accounts for the wine's consistent richness. The winery, unlike many in the region, is modern and well equipped, and this is reflected in the wines, which are full of fruit, not unduly tannic, and accessible young, though they do age well. In the 1990s the proportion of Mourvèdre has been increasing, giving the red wine more backbone. In 1994 the luxury Cuvée Hippolyte was introduced. The white Châteauneuf includes a portion of barrel-fermented Roussanne and can be delicious. Annual production is quite high, at about 220,000 bottles. The Bruniers also own another Châteauneuf estate, Domaine la Roquette. Best years: 1998, '97, '95, '94, '93, '90, '89, '88, '85, '81, '80, '79, '78.

VILLA MARIA

NEW ZEALAND, North Island, South Auckland
♥ *Cabernet Sauvignon, Merlot, Syrah*
♀ *Chardonnay, Gewurztraminer, Sauvignon Blanc, Riesling and others*

George Fistonich, the founder and co-owner of the Villa Maria-Vidal-Esk Valley group, has always been a doughty street-fighter, several times knocked down by economic disasters yet always struggling back to his feet. The results are now plain to see. Villa Maria, Vidal and Esk Valley make some of the best and most fairly priced commercial wines in all New Zealand. The Recent Reserve Bin wines from Villa Maria have also been outstandingly good. What other New Zealand wine company can claim to make some of the country's best Sauvignon Blanc, Chardonnay, Riesling, BORDEAUX-style reds and botrytis-affected sweet wines? Best years: (Marlborough) 1998, '97, '96, '94, '91; (Hawke's Bay) 1998, '96, '95, '94, '91, '89.

VILLA MT EDEN

USA, California, Napa County, Oakville AVA
♥ *Cabernet Sauvignon, Merlot, Syrah, Zinfandel*
♀ *Chardonnay, Pinot Blanc*

Acquired by Stimson Lane (owners of CHATEAU STE MICHELLE among others) in 1986 after its founders ran out of gas, Villa Mt Eden has been redesigned into a large but efficient brand. Guided by winemaker Mike McGrath and consultant Jed Steele, the winery splits most of its production into two lines, Cellar Select varietal wines, which deliver plenty of flavour for the money, and Grand Reserve wines, hand-crafted to compete with the best. The impressive Reserve line includes a blockbuster Old Vine Zinfandel, concentrated Chardonnay and impressive Pinot Blanc from the Bien Nacido vineyards in Santa Maria, and outstanding Pinot Noir. Both winemakers lend their names and creativity to two superb, limited production Signature Series wines, Cabernet Sauvignon and Chardonnay. Best years: (reds) 1997, '96, '95, '94, '93, '92; (whites) 1998, '97, '96, '95, '94.

VILLANY

HUNGARY, Southern Transdanubia

Right down in the south of Hungary, the Villany region makes grassy yet reasonably ripe reds, of which the best are from Cabernet and Merlot: the Kékoportó is a much leaner, peppery and plummy proposition, yet with low acidity for drinking young. The climate is warm and sunny and unless the prices get silly we can expect to see a lot more goodies from here. Until privatization all the wines came from the state monopoly, Hungarovin; good new names have yet to emerge.

CH. DE VILLENEUVE

FRANCE, Loire, Anjou-Saumur, Saumur AC
♥ *Cabernet Franc*
♀ *Chenin Blanc*

During the 1990s, Jean-Pierre Chevallier established Villeneuve as a leading SAUMUR estate. His success comes from his work in the vineyard and he is a passionate believer in the quality of Chenin Blanc. In 1994, a year of widespread rot, Chevallier's grapes remained remarkably healthy and he was able to leave picking them until they were properly ripe, unlike his neighbours who had to rush out to save what remained of their harvest before it was overwhelmed by rot.

There are three reds – the estate SAUMUR-CHAMPIGNY, the Vieilles Vignes which has some barrel aging and le Grand Clos, which is aged in newer oak for about 18 months. Both these big wines need aging to show their best. Even the Villeneuve 'basic' cuvée is more concentrated than many other Saumur-Champignys.

Chevallier is equally successful with his dry Saumur whites, made entirely from

Chenin Blanc. The straight Saumur is wonderfully floral, often with some rich exotic fruit and crisp acidity in the finish. Les Cormiers, from old, single-vineyard vines, is fermented and aged in new oak. This needs to age and is one of the best examples of how complex ambitiously made Chenin Blanc can be. Best years: 1998, '97, '96, '95, '94, '93.

VIN DE PAYS

FRANCE

There's no doubt about it. The 'New World' is alive and well in France. But it isn't living in the famous regions of BORDEAUX or Burgundy, CHAMPAGNE or CHÂTEAUNEUF-DU-PAPE. It's living in the forgotten byways and backwaters of French wine regions that until recently had never made decent wine.

Until 20 years ago all the most famous French wines had come from various renowned ACs, hallowed by time and tradition. But the 1980s brought the wines of Australia, California, New Zealand and Chile rushing to the front of the world stage and enthused a whole generation of winemakers with the idea that anyone with passion, commitment, some decent grape varieties and some money to invest in good equipment could make great wine. As for the French idea of a sacred terroir, there was no such thing in Australia or New Zealand. There were simply places where you could grow good grapes and places where you couldn't. And in most of France it was exactly the same. Most French vineyards had been condemned for generations simply to produce basic table wine, usually from mediocre grape varieties, because they fell outside the AC boundaries.

Then came the lead set by the Californians, Australians and New Zealanders in taking the great French grapes and creating 'varietal' wines – wines that were first and foremost dependent on the actual grape variety for the flavour. Previously no-one outside the ACs had had the confidence to strike out for quality. Now it became clear that the names of the producer and the grape variety were sufficient to sell wine at a decent price and of an exciting quality.

Of course, this being France and the EU, there has to be some kind of legal framework. And this is provided by the vin de pays category of wines. 'Country wines', the direct translation, implies that these are the traditional wines of the country districts of France which have been enjoyed for centuries by the locals. The reality is a little different and the vast majority are impressively modern.

DOMAINE DE LA BAUME
The French outpost of the Australian giant, BRL Hardy, is situated just outside Béziers and makes chiefly varietal wines, very much New World in style to emphasize fruit and varietal aroma.

The name vin de pays was conceived as a category of French wine only in 1968, with improvements made to the concept in 1973. Until then, in many parts of the country – especially the far south – there was a serious problem of overproduction of very mediocre wine and no incentives available to the grower to improve quality since all the wines were consigned to the anonymity of the blending vats of various shippers and merchants. The aim was to encourage quality, and to provide a specific guarantee of geographical origin for the wines. In this the vin de pays system follows the example set by the two top quality tiers in French wines. In effect, vins de pays became the third tier of quality control, following similar guidelines based on geographical origin, yield of grapes per hectare, minimum alcohol level and choice of grape varieties, though the controls are looser and generally a wider choice of grape varieties is permitted, including those not 'native' to the region.

There are three geographical categories, each one becoming more specific. Vins de pays régionaux cover a whole region, encompassing several *départements*. There are only four of these and any wine made in the region concerned may qualify. The most important is Vin de Pays d'OC, which accounts for 33 per cent of all vin de pays and which is France's principal source of 'varietal' wines. Vins de pays départementaux cover the wines of a whole *département*. There are approximately 40 of these. Vins de pays de zone is the most specific category, and relates only to the wines of a specific community or locality. There are about 100 of these but many are unknown outside their region.

Overall, the LANGUEDOC-ROUSSILLON is the leading vin de pays producer, accounting for 83 per cent of the production. Yield is higher than for ACs since the vins de pays can as yet rarely command high prices, and alcoholic strength is generally lower. The grape varieties are specified to eliminate the worst sorts, but the crucial element here is that excellent varieties excluded from a region's ACs but capable of producing high-quality wine are included. Consequently, for example, we are seeing excellent white Chardonnay and Sauvignon Blanc and red Merlot and Cabernet Sauvignon from the Languedoc-Roussillon – varieties which had previously been virtually unknown there. These varieties, along with Syrah, Grenache and Cinsaut, now represent nearly 50 per cent of plantings in the Languedoc-Roussillon, with other noble varieties like Pinot Noir and Viognier also to be found. Increasingly, vins de pays are labelled with the grape variety – and these are now the source of some of France's best-value flavours. Lower yields and better winemaking has also enabled less fashionable grape varieties, like Carignan, to make a comeback in a minor way as a 'varietal' wine. Whereas vins de pays are generally regarded as good value, some producers have pushed the bounds with lower yields and aging in new oak barrels to produce higher quality but more expensive wines. The pioneer of this up-market style is Aimé Guibert of MAS DE DAUMAS GASSAC.

VIN SANTO

ITALY, Tuscany, Umbria and Trentino-Alto Adige
♀ *Malvasia, Trebbiano, Grechetto, Nosiola*

The 'Holy Wine' is called Vino Santo in Trentino, where the grapes were traditionally left to dry until Holy Week, just before Easter; Vin Santo elsewhere. Unlike most *passito* wines, the grapes for Vin Santo are usually dried hanging in bunches in airy barns; only occasionally flat on straw mats. After crushing, the juice is put into very small barrels (50 litres is most traditional), called *caratelli*, together with the mother yeast or *madre*, left in after the previous wine's racking, and it ferments very slowly over a couple of years. Indeed, the wine stays sealed in the *caratelli* long past the period of fermentation; three to six years is not unusual. The white juice deepens to gold. The barrel is then opened, the wine tasted, and if deemed good enough goes into the blend for bottling. In each barrel, a little *madre* is left behind for next time.

There is, however, little consistency of style between producers. Making Vin Santo is such an artisanal process that everyone's ideas on how to make it differ. It may be dry, sweet or anything in between. Modern producers have for the most part eschewed the oxidized style that might remind one of sweet sherry and look instead for vibrant if raisiny fruit. The best Vin Santo comes from AVIGNONESI which uses Grechetto as well as the Malvasia-

Trebbiano blend more usual in Tuscany, and keep it for eight years in *caratelli*. Other good Tuscan examples are Cacchiano, Fattoria di FELSINA, ISOLE E OLENA, PIEVE SANTA RESTITUTA, POLIZIANO, San Giusto a Rentennano, SELVAPIANA and Villa di Capezzana. Umbria's star is from Adanti (made from Grechetto) and Trentino's (made from Nosiola) comes from Pisoni. Beware of versions declaring themselves to be *liquoroso* – they are fortified and usually pretty nasty.

Vin Santo, in Tuscany, is seen as a post-prandial or as a mid-afternoon pick-me-up, and can be taken with *cantuccini*, those hard, sweet biscuits baked with almonds, often rather ingloriously dunked into the wine.

VIÑA CASABLANCA

CHILE, Casablanca Valley
♥ Cabernet Sauvignon, Merlot
♀ Sauvignon Blanc, Chardonnay

The Santa Carolina winery invested in this winery in the CASABLANCA VALLEY with the aim of bolstering its range with more aromatic white wines. The measure of its success is that winemaker Ignacio Recabarren has been honoured with many prizes since he took up the challenge at Casablanca. Sauvignon Blanc from this valley has helped to redefine Chilean white wine production. Chardonnay made here is vibrant if not tropically pungent. Merlot and Cabernet from the Santa Isabel Estate are thrilling in their piercing blackcurrant fruit. Some of the best reds made here are from fruit harvested in other valleys, further south. Good examples are White Label Cabernet (from San Fernando) and El Bosque Cabernet Sauvignon (Maipo). Best years: 1998, '97, '96.

VIÑAS DEL VERO

SPAIN, Aragón, Somontano DO
♥ Tempranillo, Merlot, Cabernet Sauvignon, Moristel, Pinot Noir
♥ Tempranillo, Moristel, Cabernet Sauvignon
♀ Chardonnay, Macabeo, Gewürztraminer

With strong backing from the Aragón regional government, Viñas del Vero was created from scratch in the late 1980s as a giant bodega with important vineyard holdings (550ha/1360 acres) destined to exploit the cool SOMONTANO region's potential and make quality wine at all price levels. With the able enologist Pedro Aibar deftly controlling a sizeable annual production of 500,000 cases in his high-tech winery, that goal was reached by the late 1990s, when everything from unoaked young Tempranillo to the top wines

was uniformly good. Fine vintages in 1994, '95 and '96 helped the top reds reach their full potential, especially the outstanding Gran Vos, a Merlot-Cabernet blend with a dollop of Pinot Noir. The top white, Clarión, is an age-worthy, partly barrel-fermented blend whose components are doggedly kept a secret by Aibar. Best years: 1996, '95, '94.

VINHO VERDE DOC

PORTUGAL, Minho and Douro Litoral
♥ Azal Tinto, Borracal, Espadeiro, Vinhão and others
♀ Loureiro, Trajadura, Paderna, Azal Branco, Avesso, Alvarinho

Portugal's largest DOC region, Vinho Verde is one of the country's most distinctive wines. It translates as 'green wine' but Vinho Verde may be either red or white. The 'green' refers to the need to drink the wines young as opposed to the designation Vinho Maduro ('mature wine'). Few Vinhos Verdes have a vintage date on their labels as it is assumed that the wines will be from the most recent harvest.

The relatively cool, damp maritime climate of north-west Portugal conspires with high yields to produce grapes that are naturally low in sugar and high in acid. Most wines therefore have natural alcohol levels of no more than 10 per cent and many white Vinhos Verdes are slightly sweetened for export to balance the rasping acidity. Red wines are best kept for the local food. Nearly all Vinhos Verdes have a slight *pétillance* which results from carbon dioxide being injected into the wine before bottling. At its best it is a crisp, dry white to drink ice cold on a hot summer's day, but there are still far too many cheap, over-sulphured wines on the market. A number of single estates (quintas) are now producing varietal Vinhos Verdes from Loureiro or Alvarinho grapes and these wines have a much fuller flavour than is the norm in this part of Portugal. Best producers: Aveleda, Quinta da Franqueira, Paço de Teixeiro, Palácio de Brejoeira, Casa de Sezim, SOGRAPE (Gazela), Quinta de Tamariz.

J P VINHOS

PORTUGAL, Setúbal DOC, Terras do Sado Vinho Regional, Alentejo Vinho Regional, Estremadura Vinho Regional
♥ Terras do Sado: Periquita, Cabernet Sauvignon, Merlot and others; Alentejo: Periquita, Aragonez (Tempranillo), Alfrocheiro, Trincadeira, Moreto; Estremadura: Tinta Miuda
♀ Setúbal: Moscatel de Setúbal; Terras do Sado: Arinto, Fernão Pires, Moscatel de Setúbal, Chardonnay and others

J P Vinhos (alias João Pires) is the brainchild of entrepreneur António Avillez. He was aided early on by Australian winemaker Peter Bright, who developed an eclectic range of wines from different parts of the country. Bright has now left to run his own venture (see BRIGHT BROS) but still acts as a consultant. J P's mainstay in the João Pires brand is an aromatic off-dry white based on the local Muscat grape. Other wines in the J P range include the red and white J P Barrel Selection, Quinta da Bacalhoa (a BORDEAUX-style blend of Cabernet and Merlot) and Tinto da Anfora, a rich, leathery ALENTEJO red. There is also a barrel-fermented Chardonnay, Cova de Ursa, and an attractive, spicy varietal from the ESTREMADURA grape, Tinta Miuda. Best years: 1997, '95, '94, '92.

VINO NOBILE DI MONTEPULCIANO DOCG

ITALY, Tuscany
♥ Sangiovese (Prugnolo Gentile), Canaiolo, Malvasia and others

Vino Nobile, unlike its rival BRUNELLO DI MONTALCINO, is a wine with a centuries-old tradition of quality, but it has had its ups and downs. At present it is well on the way to coming out of a very deep depression lasting most of the middle part of the twentieth century, when it descended to the level of ordinary CHIANTI, itself at a pretty low ebb. During the 1990s there have been energetic efforts to raise quality and today there are several wineries equal with the best of Tuscany.

The vineyards are located at 250 to 600m (820 to 1970ft) on the sides of a massive hill, atop which sits the narrow, cobbled, steeply sloping streets of Montepulciano itself. Exposures are excellent, the climate more benign than in Chianti to the north.

The principal grape variety is Sangiovese, here called Prugnolo Gentile, supported by Canaiolo, with the optional addition of other grapes such as Cabernet, Merlot and others. The wine must be aged for two years before release, three years for Riserva. This puts its image somewhere between Chianti Classico and Brunello di Montalcino, and the truth is that Vino Nobile has not yet decided exactly who it is. But there are some excellent producers and every year Vino Nobile's identity becomes clearer. Best producers: AVIGNONESI, Bindella, BOSCARELLI, Canneto, Le Casalte, Fattoria del Cerro, Contucci, Dei, Fassati, Il Macchione, POLIZIANO, Redi, Salcheto, Trerose, Valdipiatta. Best years: 1998, '97, '95, '93, '90, '88, '85.

VINO DA TAVOLA
ITALY

In Tuscany the first vini da tavola were born of the desperate need to do something to restore the fortunes of Tuscan viticulture. The CHIANTI laws were simply too restrictive, insisting on practices including the addition of the white grape, Trebbiano, to the Chianti blend that made the production of serious red wine a virtual impossibility; the only way for talented and innovative winemakers to express their frustration with the DOC laws was for them to produce their wines as humble vini da tavola.

Although SASSICAIA was the very first SUPER-TUSCAN, as these vini da tavola came to be called, it was really ANTINORI'S Sangiovese-Cabernet blend called Tignanello that provided the inspiration for the many others that have followed in its wake. There is now widespread use of new and small oak barrels, non-Tuscan grape varieties, notably Cabernet Sauvignon and Chardonnay, as well as wines made only of Sangiovese and blends of Sangiovese with Cabernet Sauvignon. The super-Tuscans are also recognized by their stylish presentation, with designer labels and prices to match.

The same spirit of experimentation now prevails all over Italy. There are examples of Chardonnay in Puglia and Cabernet Sauvignon in Piedmont and so on. Many of these wines will eventually come within the confines of the law. New legislation means an end is in sight to the confusion caused by a myriad of fantasy names. Further regional DOCs, a new IGT category – equivalent to French VIN DE PAYS – improved Chianti Classico regulations and the like will slowly swallow them all up.

VINOS DE MADRID DO
SPAIN, Madrid
♥♀ *Garnacha, Tinto Fino (Tempranillo)*
♀ *Malvar, Airén, Albillo*

With five centuries of winemaking behind them, perhaps it's surprising Madrid's wine producers gained their DO only as recently as 1990. The DO covers three areas, all to the south of the capital, with 13,000ha (32,000 acres) of vineyards. Arganda, the eastern one, produces most of the DO's white wines, as well as the best reds – made from Tinto Fino as opposed to the Garnacha used in the other two areas, Navalcarnero and the more promising, mountainous San Martín de Valdeiglesias. Quality remains average throughout the DO. Best producers: Ricardo Benito, Jesús Diaz, Jeromín.

VIOGNIER

You may well wonder why Viognier is one of France's leading grape varieties when there are less than 1000ha (2500 acres) planted in the whole of the country and only small amounts in the rest of the world, mainly in California and Australia. Ah, but never mind the quantity, taste the wine – if you can find any. The vine is an incredibly poor yielder, producing less than any other mainstream dry white variety, and the two tiny Rhône vineyards – Château-Grillet and Condrieu – which make 100 per cent Viognier wines are some of the rarest and most sought-after labels in the world. It has one of the most memorable flavours of any white grape because it manages to blend the rich, musky scent of an overripe apricot with the breeze-blown perfume of springtime orchard flowers. Autumn and spring in one glass. Taste the wine and you'll swear it's sweet but it isn't. It's strange but also very special.

Viognier also occurs in Côte-Rôtie, just north of Condrieu, where it can be blended with Syrah to make one of France's greatest red wines. Can be, but few growers have more than 5 per cent of Viognier today. It is also planted in the Ardèche, southern Rhône and Languedoc-Roussillon, where it is having a certain success as a 'varietal' wine and to add elegance and aroma to blends. California now has a rapidly growing number of exciting producers and Australia, South America and South Africa are getting in on the act too.

VIPAVA
SLOVENIA, Primorski Region
♥ *Merlot, Cabernet Sauvignon and others*
♀ *Laski Rizling, Pinot Blanc, Chardonnay and others*

Slovenia's Vipava winery takes its grapes from the area of the same name, a sub-region of Primorski adjoining north-east Italy. The wines from the Vipava winery, not surprisingly, are nearest to those of FRIULI in style: there are light, crisp whites and juicy reds. The whites are made in stainless steel, which shows in the form of clean, fresh fruit; the reds are made in old wooden vats, and at the last count there were two barriques in the winery. Well, they're a luxury in these parts.

VIRGIN HILLS
AUSTRALIA, Victoria, Port Phillip Zone, Macedon Ranges
♥ *Cabernet Sauvignon, Syrah (Shiraz), Malbec, Merlot*

Virgin Hills is one of the few Australian wineries content to produce just one wine, a Cabernet Sauvignon-dominated blend which is the epitome of elegance, fine and supple, yet long-lived. The winery was established by the flamboyant restaurateur Tom Lazar, who chose a high-altitude, ultra-cool growing area with no viticultural history (hence the name), but who made a great wine with his first vintage in 1973. Under the 15-year ownership of Maral Gilbert, the wine became organic (not just the vineyards), made without the use of sulphur dioxide. It is now owned by Vincorp, a listed company. Best years: 1998, '97, '94, '93, '91, '90.

VIRGINIA
USA

The eastern state of Virginia is, vinously speaking, small but growing. There are more than four dozen cellars, and lean but full-flavoured Chardonnays head the list, with Barboursville Vineyards, Prince Michael and Meredyth Vineyards the labels to watch out for. Cabernet Sauvignon and other BORDEAUX varieties are the best hopes for reds. Horton Vineyards appears to be showing the way.

COMTE GEORGES DE VOGÜE
FRANCE, Burgundy, Côte de Nuits, Chambolle-Musigny AC
♥ *Pinot Noir*
♀ *Chardonnay*

One of the oldest estates in Burgundy, de Vogüé is celebrated for its MUSIGNY Vieilles Vignes, which at its best can be one of the most sumptuous and breathtakingly elegant wines in all of Burgundy. Those unable to afford its astronomic price should settle for one of the 'lesser' wines: the BONNES-MARES or exquisite CHAMBOLLE-MUSIGNY les Amoureuses. De Vogüé has substantial holdings in all these vineyards – including 70 per cent of Musigny itself – so these wines are produced in generous quantities.

It is no secret that in the 1980s the wines slipped well below the standards established by the domaine in the '40s and '50s. However, since the arrival of the taciturn François Millet as winemaker in the late '80s there has been a marked improvement. The 1990 Musigny was magnificent and subsequent vintages have shown this was no fluke. The wines are once again quintessential elegant Chambolle, yet they never lack depth or concentration. The estate also produces the most costly white wine of the CÔTE DE NUITS, from a parcel planted in Musigny. After recent replantings, the wine was declassified to BOURGOGNE Blanc and although a marvel of richness and complexity it will not be released as Musigny until the quality is once again impeccable. Best years: 1997, '96, '95, '94, '93, '91, '90, '89.

VOLNAY AC
FRANCE, Burgundy, Côte de Beaune
♥ *Pinot Noir*

Until the eighteenth century, Volnay produced Burgundy's Nouveau wine, much the same way as BEAUJOLAIS does now. The wine was extremely pale and was snapped up for high prices. The soil has a fair bit of chalk and limestone, particularly in the higher vineyards – normally the cue for planting white vines, but there isn't a white vine in Volnay's 215ha (531 acres) of vineyards.

There are, in fact, two main styles of Volnay. One is light, perfumed in a delicious cherry and strawberry way, sometimes even lifted by a floral scent. However, there are also some wines of tremendous, juicy, plummy power, particularly from the lower vineyards like Champans and Santenots (which is actually in MEURSAULT but is called Volnay-Santenots). Volnay is drinkable at three to four years old, but unless the wine is very light this is usually a pity, because lovely flavours can develop between seven and ten years. Best years: 1997, '96, '95, '93, '90, '89, '88. Best producers: R Ampeau, d'ANGERVILLE, J-M Boillot, R & P Bouley, Yvon Clerget, Lafarge, LAFON, MONTILLE, Potinet-Ampeau, POUSSE D'OR, Vaudoisey-Mutin.

CASTELLO DI VOLPAIA
ITALY, Tuscany, Chianti Classico DOCG
♥ *Sangiovese, Merlot, Cabernet Sauvignon, Pinot Noir (Pinot Nero), Syrah and others*
♀ *Trebbiano Toscano, Malvasia, Chardonnay, Sauvignon Blanc and others*

Volpaia, a beautifully preserved Tuscan hamlet perched high up in the hills of CHIANTI CLASSICO in the commune of Radda, is entirely devoted to the production of wine, olive oil and other fine products. Winewise, proprietors Carlo Mascheroni and Giovanella

CASTELLO DI VOLPAIA
Coltassala is a top-quality super-Tuscan from Sangiovese with a drop of Mammolo. The bouquet has a classic trace of ripe blackcurrants and vanilla.

Stianti have, in the 20-odd years of their tenancy, stuck to the road of elegance and perfume rather than power and opulence. It is to some extent a way consistent with the position of their vineyards – at between 450 and 600m (1500–200ft) some of the highest in Chianti – and with the nature of their soil, which has a marked sandy component.

The top wines are the stylish SUPER-TUSCANs Coltassala and Balifico. The former is a barrique-aged, mainly Sangiovese wine whose intense cherry-fruit and floral aromas are joined by hints of vanilla. Balifico is a blend of Sangiovese topped up with Cabernets Sauvignon and Franc, combining gentle soft-fruit aromas (strawberry, loganberry) with the same fine-grained tannins that grace the Coltassala. The Chianti Classicos, *normale* and Riserva, have less of the concentration and intensity of the super-Tuscans but they share the tendency towards gracefulness, while achieving relatively early drinkability. Best years: 1998, '97, '95, '94, '93, '91, '88, '87, '86.

VOSNE-ROMANÉE AC
FRANCE, Burgundy, Côte de Nuits
♥ *Pinot Noir*

They call it the greatest village in Burgundy – simply because it has an incomparable clutch of five Grands Crus at its heart. There are 240ha (593 acres) of vineyards of which just under 27ha (66 acres) are the Grands Crus themselves, but this figure rises to 66ha (163 acres) if the ÉCHÉZEAUX and Grands-Échézeaux Grands Crus (technically belonging to the village of Flagey-Échézeaux) are included in the total, as normally happens.

However, a village's reputation is not just made on its Grands Crus. There are 48ha (120 acres) of Premiers Crus which match other villages' Grands Crus in quality. Best of these are Malconsorts and Suchots. And the fact that all of Vosne-Romanée's other AC land is on the slopes to the west of the N74 road, rather than slipping across to the inferior plains beyond, also helps to keep the wine quality high.

The mix of exciting, red-fruit ripeness with a delicious tangle of spices and smoke that finally ages to the deep, decaying pleasures of prunes, brown sugar and chocolate, moist autumn dampness and well-hung game – all these make Vosne-Romanée red one of the world's really exciting experiences. In good years the wines should have at least six years' age – 10–15 would be even better. Lighter years still need five to eight years. Best years: 1997, '96, '95, '93, '91, '90, '89, '88, '87, '85. Best producers: Robert Arnoux, J Cacheux, Cathiard, R ENGEL, Grivot, Anne Gros, Jayer, F Lamarche, LEROY, MÉO-CAMUZET, Mongeard-Mugneret, Mugneret-Gibourg, Rion, Domaine de la ROMANÉE-CONTI, Sirugue, Thomas-Moillard.

VOUGEOT AC
FRANCE, Burgundy, Côte de Nuits
♥ *Pinot Noir*
♀ *Chardonnay*

Most people are accustomed to seeing CLOS DE VOUGEOT rather than plain Vougeot on a label. But there are 17ha (42 acres) of Vougeot vines outside the famous walled Clos, producing annually about 70,000 bottles of wine, divided six to one in red's favour. It's not bad stuff – full and slightly solid to start but gaining a really good chocolaty richness with a few years age – and it's a lot cheaper than Clos de Vougeot – but then, what isn't? Premiers Crus Clos de la Perrière and les Petits Vougeots are best. Best years: 1997, '96, '95, '93, '92, '91, '90, '89, '88. Best producers: Bertagna, Chopin-Groffier, C Clerget, Héritier Guyot.

CH. LA VOULTE-GASPARETS
FRANCE, Languedoc-Roussillon, Corbières AC
♥ *Carignan, Grenache, Syrah*
♀ *Grenache Blanc, Rolle, Macabeo*

The leading light in CORBIÈRES, la Voulte Gasparets produces two top wines from hillside vineyards on the 46-ha (114-acre) estate. The Cuvée Reservée and Romain Puc are both made from 60 per cent Carignan, 30 per cent Grenache and 10 per cent Syrah, but whereas the vines for the Cuvée Reservée average 20 to 40 years, those for Romain Puc average 45 to 90 years and are much lower yielding, giving the wine an extra edge of concentration and intensity. Romain Puc is also aged for longer in barriques, 10 per cent of which are renewed yearly. These wines require four to five years of aging in bottle whereas the generic Corbières, made from young vines, can be drunk early. There is also a crisp, fruity white Corbières for drinking young.

VOUVRAY AC
FRANCE, Touraine
♀ *Chenin Blanc*

Chenin's excruciatingly high acidity is both the main problem with young Vouvray, and also the reason why the best ones last 50 years. The grapes in this decidedly one-grape town grow in 1742ha (4304 acres) of picturesque vineyards east of Tours, on a limestone and chalk clay soil – which yields intensely flavoured juice, but in cool years creates even more acidity. Unripe grapes traditionally go to make Vouvray Mousseux AC, produced by the CHAMPAGNE method and usually of a high standard. The best sparkling Vouvray is the semi-sparkling *pétillant* but sadly it remains a little known local speciality.

However, the still wines are more exciting. They can be dry – in which case they'll start out bitingly sharp, but round out beautifully into a dry buttermilk and nuts flavour after about ten years. And they can be sweet *(moelleux)* with occasional noble rot, producing wines of peach and honey-soft sweetness but ever-present acidity. Vouvray's greatest role is as a medium-dry *(demi-sec)* wine. Cheap Vouvray has spoilt our appreciation of this style, but when it is properly made from a single domaine, it will slowly, perhaps over 20 years, build up an exciting, smoky peach, pears and quince fullness. Best years: 1998, '97, '96, '95, '93, '92, '90, '89, '88, '85, '83, '82, '78, '76, '59, '47. Best producers: Bidaudières, Bourillon-Dorléans, Brédif, Champalou, Pascal Delaleu, P Foreau, Fouquet (Dom. des Aubuisières) Freslier, Gaudrelle, HUET, F Mabille, Rohart.

WACHAU
AUSTRIA, Niederösterreich

This is Austria's top region for dry white wines, of which the best are from the Rhine Riesling grape. There is good Grüner Veltliner too, but the Riesling is sublime: classically structured, and maturing to refined honey and petrol flavours. There are steep, often terraced slopes here, yielding wines with great breed and race. Best producers: ALZINGER, F HIRTZBERGER, HÖGL, Emmerich KNOLL, Jamek, NIKOLAI-HOF, F X PICHLER, Rudi PICHLER, F PRAGER, Freie Weingärtner WACHAU.

FREIE WEINGÄRTNER WACHAU
AUSTRIA, Wachau, Dürnstein
♂ *Pinot Noir (Blauburgunder), St Laurent*
♀ *Grüner Veltliner, Riesling, Pinot Blanc, Müller-Thurgau, Muscat (Gelber Muskateller), Chardonnay*

This co-operative winery regularly produces some of the Wachau's best white wines, even though it takes the grapes from fully 565ha (1340 acres) of vineyards. Of course, with production on this scale there are bound to be some simpler wines, but everything sold under the main label depicting the baroque 'Kellerschlössl' is good to first class.

Top of the range are the Smaragd wines from the region's top sites: the Rieslings from the Singerriedel and Tausendeimerberg of Spitz, and the Rieslings and Grüner Veltliners from the Achleiten of Weissenkirchen, the Kellerberg of Dürnstein and the Loibenberg of Loiben. These are powerful, concentrated dry wines which can age magnificently. Best years: 1998, '97, '96, '95, '93, '91, '90.

FREIE WEINGÄRTNER WACHAU
The Achleiten site at Weissenkirchen produces intensely fruity, dry Riesling that is some of the best from the Wachau region.

DR HEINZ WAGNER
GERMANY, Mosel-Saar-Ruwer, Saarburg
♀ *Riesling*

Heinz Wagner is one of very few growers who have mastered the art of making harmonious dry Saar wines, and as a result these are almost permanantly sold out. Thankfully for us his classic style Rieslings with natural sweetness are even better and not in such hot demand. The best of these come from the SAARBURGer Rausch, which gives firm, intensely minerally wines, and the OCKFENer Bockstein, whose wines are packed with peach and currant aromas. There is excellent sparkling Riesling too. Best years: 1997, '95, '94, '93, '92, '90, '89, '88, '86, '85, '83.

WAIHEKE ISLAND
NEW ZEALAND, North Island

Goldwater established the first vineyard on this small island in AUCKLAND Harbour and made the first Waiheke wine in 1982. Now there are more than 20 winemakers on this fashionable island. Waiheke boasts a hotter, drier climate than Auckland and mostly free-draining clay/loam soils of moderate to low fertility. Cabernet Sauvignon represents nearly one-third of Waiheke's production although it is always blended with at least one partner, usually more.

Although the island is regarded as probably New Zealand's best BORDEAUX-style red wine region there is growing interest in Chardonnay, possibly in response to market demand rather than the island's ability to make great white wine. Syrah is growing in popularity, with the first small release from STONYRIDGE suggesting that the variety has a future there. Best years: 1998, '96, '94, '93, '91, '89, '87. Best producers: Goldwater, Stonyridge, Twin Bays, Waiheke Vineyards (Te Motu).

WARRE
PORTUGAL, Douro, Port DOC
♂ *Touriga Naçional, Touriga Francesa, Tinta Roriz (Tempranillo), Tinta Barroca, Tinto Cão, Tinta Amarela and others*
♀ *Gouveio, Viosinho, Rabigato, Malvasia Fina, Donzelinho*

Warre is the oldest British PORT shipper, having been founded in 1670. Although the family still retain a link with the company it is owned (along with DOW and GRAHAM) by the Symingtons. Its style of port is usually somewhere between the dry austerity of Dow and the richness of Graham. Warre's vintage ports, based on the company's Quinta de Cavadinha vineyard, combine perfumed opulence with the substance and structure to last. Wine from Cavadinha is also bottled as a single-quinta vintage port in good interim years and, like SMITH WOODHOUSE, which belongs to the Symington family, Warre produces an unfiltered, bottle-matured LBV. One of Warre's greatest triumphs is Warrior, a rich, dense premium ruby port which is consistently the among the very best in its class. Best years: (vintage ports) 1994, '91, '85, '83, '80, '77, '70, '66, '63.

WARWICK FARM
SOUTH AFRICA, Western Cape, Stellenbosch WO
♂ *Cabernet Sauvignon, Merlot, Cabernet Franc, Pinotage*
♀ *Chardonnay*

Until recently this farm, run by the dynamic Norma Ratcliffe, was best known for its BORDEAUX-style reds, especially the Cabernet-based Warwick Trilogy, and a successful Cabernet Franc – this variety has performed much better for Norma Ratcliffe than for many other Cape producers. In earlier years the tannins were a bit overdone, but they are now softer and the wines riper but without loss of inherent elegance. Pinotage, from old untrellised vines, and Chardonnay are recent additions to the range. Best years: (reds) 1996, '95, '94, '93, '92, '91.

WASHINGTON STATE USA

WASHINGTON STATE IS DIVIDED neatly into two by the high, ever-snowy Cascade Range, as is Oregon, its neighbour to the south. On the west is the cool, often rainy Puget Sound basin, where sun is at a premium and on the east is the dry, generally sunny Columbia River basin where irrigation is an absolute necessity. Washington's grape growers and wine-makers have almost exactly reversed the Oregon experience. While their southern neighbours have their vines in the cool west and lean heavily to grape varieties developed in Burgundy, Washingtonians grow the great majority of their vines in the warm east and – except for the ubiquitous Chardonnay – they favour vine types native to Bordeaux, most particularly Semillon for whites and Cabernet Sauvignon and Merlot for reds.

A pair of Washington wineries began to make varietal table wines from vinifera grapes in the late 1960s but the real blossoming did not come until the 1970s. Even faster growth came in the 1980s when the roster of cellars climbed near its current number of 106, and wine grape plantings totalled nearly 9510ha (23,500 acres).

Washington had the ill fortune, in the short term at least, of winning its first great public acclaim with Riesling, just as the variety was beginning its unaccountable but continuing decline as a favourite with wine drinkers. The state is only now starting to win recognition for its red wines from Merlot and Cabernet Sauvignon, and has only a few vintages of Semillon and Sauvignon Blanc to its credit as alternatives to its still-admirable Rieslings. Washington Chardonnays match up favourably with California's when the wines are young and each passing year shows that they are capable of aging at least as well as their southern counterparts.

Producers in Washington have begun the process of carving their state into various growing regions. The foremost one is the semi-arid Yakima Valley, a long, straight slice from the eastern foothills of the Cascades down to the Yakima River's confluence with the Columbia River near an urban centre called Tri-Cities (Pasco, Kennewick and Richland).

The Yakima Valley is a prosperous agricultural region and densely planted with vineyards. Mechanical harvesting, here at Covey Run, one of the Yakima's largest producers, is the only practical way of harvesting such large quantities of grapes.

The Yakima Valley holds a little more than half of Washington's vineyards, along with far larger plantings of dozens of other crops. The Walla Walla Valley east of the Columbia River is the other specific growing region. These AVAs and all other grape-growing regions in eastern Washington fall within the umbrella Columbia Valley AVA, which also includes a big slice of land in northern Oregon. Most eastern Washington vineyards not in the Yakima or Walla Walla Valleys lie near the Columbia River between Vantage and the Tri-Cities or along the Snake River east of Tri-Cities. No one region in Washington has established itself yet as notably more adapted to any one grape variety than its neighbours.

LEONETTI CELLAR
This small winery based in the Walla Walla Valley makes outstanding Merlot and Cabernet Sauvignon. The wines are immense with concentrated fruit.

CHATEAU STE MICHELLE
The international acclaim achieved by this pioneering winery making an enormous range of wines has created a market for Washington State wines.

THE HOGUE CELLARS
This long-established winery continues to turn out really splendid, ripe brambly Cabernet Sauvignon with abundant and delicious fruit.

ANDREW WILL WINERY
First made in 1994, Sorella is one of the top wines here. A Bordeaux blend, the wine balances ripe berry fruit and oak with an elegant texture.

L'ECOLE No 41
Rich, oaky Semillon is one of the most popular wines from this consistent performer.

KIONA
A family operation in sagebrush country, Kiona has a growing reputation for its marvellous fruit. The Late-Harvest White Riesling has clean, pure fruit flavours and heady perfume.

Many of the state's most important wineries (for example Chateau Ste Michelle, Columbia Cellars and Arbor Crest) are in or near the cities of Seattle and Spokane, well placed to serve their local markets. In western Washington there are just a handful of vineyards, including Salishan Vineyards just across the Columbia River from Portland in Oregon and Mount Baker Vineyards near the border with Canada.

REGIONAL ENTRY
Yakima Valley.

PRODUCER ENTRIES
Andrew Will Winery, Chateau Ste Michelle, Chinook Wines, Columbia Winery, DeLille Cellars, Hedge Cellars, The Hogue Cellars, Leonetti Cellar, McCrea Cellars, Quilceda Creek Vintners, Woodward Canyon Winery.

MCCREA CELLARS
Doug McCrea's interest in Rhône grape varieties includes a small planting of white Viognier.

QUILCEDA CREEK VINTNERS
This tiny winery has built a cult following in Washington because of its big, rich Cabernet Sauvignon that ages gracefully for well over a decade.

WOODWARD CANYON WINERY
Big, barrel-fermented Chardonnay with layers of new oak is the trademark of this renowned winery. The Celilo Vineyard blend is the best wine.

COVEY RUN
The cold late-autumn weather in eastern Washington frequently allows for the production of Icewine from grapes frozen on the vine. This is one of the best ones.

GEOFF WEAVER

AUSTRALIA, South Australia, Mounty Lofty Ranges Zone, Adelaide Hills

♥ Cabernet Sauvignon, Merlot

♀ Riesling, Sauvignon Blanc, Chardonnay

Former BRL HARDY's chief winemaker, Geoff Weaver produces consistently elegant, long-lived Riesling and superb Chardonnay from his small, high-quality vineyard high in the ADELAIDE HILLS. The Sauvignon Blanc is equally good when young, but does not improve with age as do the other wines. Geoff Weaver is also an artist and arguably has the most beautiful labels in Australia.

GEOFF WEAVER
This accomplished winemaker produces intensely fruity Sauvignon Blanc, jammed with intense varietal character and lovely fruit sweetness.

J WEGELER ERBEN

GERMANY, Rheingau, Mosel-Saar-Ruwer and Pfalz

♀ Riesling and others

Deinhard is one of the largest wine companies in Germany, and until 1997 it was owned by the Wegeler family. When they sold Deinhard, they kept their estates in the RHEINGAU, MOSEL and PFALZ. They are a member of Charta (a voluntary group of leading estates whose aim is to revive the reputation of Rheingau Riesling) and are keen on drier wines (although never for their own sake – balance is all). They are trying to wean those markets that still like their wines sweet – Japan for example – on to *halbtrocken* styles. Wegeler have also taken the plunge and eradicated vineyard names from all but their very top Einzellage wines – names like WEHLENer Sonnenuhr or BERNKASTELer Doctor. All other wines are now sold under the village name and the grape name, which is virtually always Riesling. And they've launched Geheimrat J, a de luxe cuvée Riesling Spätlese *trocken*. Best years: 1998, '97, '95, '94, '93, '90, '89.

WEHLEN

GERMANY, Mosel-Saar-Ruwer

This is the village that offers the best view of the Sonnenuhr vineyard (together with the eponymous sundial), since the village is directly across the river from its most famous Einzellage. The vineyard is part of the sheer wall of slate that towers over the Mosel river from BERNKASTEL to ERDEN and just beyond.

The site imparts steely intensity and fire to the wines – archetypal Mosel, archetypal Riesling. Wehlen's fame, in fact, rests on this one vineyard. It has others, on the same side of the river as the town, and Nonnenberg is good – but nothing can compete with Wehlener Sonnenuhr. Best producers: Heribert KERPEN, Dr LOOSEN, J J PRÜM, S A PRÜM, PAULY-BERGWEILER, St Nikolaus Hospital, Studert-Prüm, WEGELER.

ROBERT WEIL

GERMANY, Rheingau, Kiedrich

♥ Pinot Noir (Spätburgunder)

♀ Riesling

Renamed Robert Weil from Dr Weil after its purchase by the Japanese drinks giant Suntory a decade ago, this estate has since soared to the pinnacle of the RHEINGAU. Huge investments in the most modern cellars in the region are only one of the reasons for this; director Wilhelm Weil's fanaticism is at least as important. This is most apparent in the Auslese and higher Prädikat wines, which are among the finest Riesling dessert wines in Germany. Prices may be high, but these wines have a pristine clarity, great concentration and enormous aging potential. The only vineyard designation used is the KIEDRICHer Gräfenberg, one of the Rheingau's undisputed 'Grands Crus'. The best bottlings from this site get the additional 'Gold Cap' designation and are sold through auction. All other wines are sold under just the estate name. Best years: 1998, '96, '95, '94, '93, '92, '90, '83, '76, '71.

DOMAINE WEINBACH

FRANCE, Alsace, Alsace AC

♥ Pinot Noir

♀ Riesling, Gewurztraminer, Pinot Gris, Pinot Blanc, Muscat, Sylvaner

There's a lot to be said for matriarchy if the Weinbach estate in Kaysersberg is typical of it. Mme Colette Faller plus daughters run this impeccable estate. Visitors are ushered into a drawing-room, and one of the Fallers will enter from time to time bearing a bottle for tasting, beginning with classic Rieslings and Pinot Gris and culminating, perhaps, with a celestial Sélection de Grains Nobles. The cuvées, such as Cuvée Théo, are often named after family members. Fortunately everything's good, and most of the wines are superb, lean, classic, and long-lived. Grapes are picked as late as possible and many of the most elegant come from the Grand Cru Schlossberg vineyard. The Cuvée Ste Cathérine is usually picked on or around 25 November: St Catherine's Day. These are

DOMAINE WEINBACH
This excellent Alsace estate is run by Madame Faller; the Cuvée Théo Gewurztraminer and Riesling wines are named in honour of her late husband.

expensive wines but they are hand-crafted and of the highest quality. Best years: 1997, '96, '95, '94, '92, '90, '89, '88, '87, '85, '83.

WEINERT

ARGENTINA, Mendoza

♥ Cabernet Sauvignon, Merlot, Malbec

Although some good concentration is achieved through modest cropping, much of Weinert's output is hampered by financial difficulties that have slowed inward investment. Weinert's considerable reputation was based on deep, powerful but somewhat oxidized reds that seem strangely out of step with the modern Argentina. I am still waiting to see whether Nicolás CATENA's involvement and the efforts of a new young Austrian winemaker will lift this faded star back into the front line. Best years: (reds) 1999, '97.

WEINVIERTEL

AUSTRIA, Niederösterreich

With 18,000ha (44,480 acres) of vineyards this is easily Austria's largest wine region, and most of the wine made is light, crisp Grüner Veltliner for quaffing. Only in a few corners, such as the Mailberg Valley close to the border with the Czech Republic, Falkenstein and around Korneuburg, close to Vienna, do the wines rise to greater things. Best producers: Graf Hardegg, Jauk, PFAFFL, Zull.

WEISSENKIRCHEN

AUSTRIA, Niederösterreich, Wachau

This important and beautiful old wine town lies at the centre of the WACHAU and includes some of the region's finest vineyards, the Achleiten, Klaus and Steinriegl. Best producers:, Jäger, Rudi PICHLER, Franz PRAGER, Freie Weingärtner WACHAU.

WELSCHRIESLING

This is a grape of Italy and eastern Europe, and has nothing whatever to do with the far superior Rhine Riesling. Welschriesling can also be

Famous for its great Rieslings, the steep Sonnenuhr vineyard at Wehlen in the Mittel Mosel is named after its prominent sundial, built in 1842 for the vineyard workers.

called Laski Rizling, Olasz Rizling, Italian Riesling or Riesling Italico. Watch out for it, and when it comes from eastern Europe, avoid it if seeking quality. At best, drink it as a basic apéritif. In Italy matters are a little better, with good refreshing acidity tweaking up its soft, gentle flavours. It mainly appears in the north-east, especially in FRIULI and the VENETO. In Austria Welschriesling is actually fashionable, and usually made either very dry or very sweet.

WENDOUREE

AUSTRALIA, South Australia, Mount Lofty Ranges Zone, Clare Valley

🍷 *Syrah (Shiraz), Cabernet Sauvignon, Mourvedre, Malbec*

♀ *Muscat of Alexandria*

Wendouree must rank at the very top of the vinous national treasures of Australia. The stone winery was constructed by A P Birks in 1895, and much of the second-hand equipment he obtained for the winery is still in use. Then there are the 100-year-old vines planted in a truly unique pocket of the CLARE VALLEY, with a magic combination of climate and soil. And for the past 20 years there has been the fierce guardianship of Tony and Lita Brady, and the winemaking skills of Stephen George. If you want the most profound and timeless red wines, which need 25 years before they

begin to unfold, and with another 50 years' life thereafter, forget the concentrated and full-bodied wines from CLARENDON HILLS and all the new pretenders and come to Wendouree, where patient, exhaustive pursuit of ultimate quality has been going on without any fanfare for 100 years. There is also excellent medium-sweet Muscat. Best years: 1996, '95, '93, '91, '90, '88, '86, '83, '82, '78, '76.

WENTE VINEYARDS

USA, California, Alameda County, Livermore Valley AVA

🍷 *Pinot Noir*

♀ *Chardonnay, Sauvignon Blanc, Riesling*

Wente was founded in 1883 by two brothers who believed the LIVERMORE VALLEY had great potential for white wines: the gravelly soils reminded them of the GRAVES region. A little empire was built on the strength of their whites, with Sauvignon Blanc and Semillon the quality leaders. Today, Wente controls most vineyards in Livermore and owns 267ha (660 acres) in MONTEREY, where it pioneered grape-growing. Its prestige wines are labelled Wente Vineyards and include Monterey Pinot Noir and Chardonnay. CHAMPAGNE-method sparkling wines are also made, but Sauvignon Blanc remains its bread-and-butter wine. Best years: (whites) 1998, '97, '95.

ROBERT WENZEL

AUSTRIA, Burgenland, Neusiedlersee-Hügelland, Rust

🍷 *Blaufränkisch*

♀ *Chardonnay, Müller-Thurgau, Ruländer, Muskateller, Furmint*

AUSBRUCH is an Austrian speciality, made nowhere else, and Robert Wenzel makes the most traditional Ausbruch in RUST, which is effectively to say the best in Austria; his dry wines are pretty stylish too, with bags of character. He was the first grower in Rust to replant Furmint, which was always traditional here (it is the principal grape variety in the great sweet wines of TOKAJI in Hungary, which is not far away).

The Ausbruch wine spends a long time in cask and the results are totally different to a Trockenbeerenauslesen: less grapy and with a touch of tangy *rancio*. The grapes are similarly botrytized, but fresh grapes or must are added to help the fermentation along. Best years: (Ausbruch) 1998, '95, '93, '92, '91, '90.

ROBERT WENZEL
Robert Wenzel is one of the masters of Ausbruch dessert wines, an Austrian speciality. He often uses the traditional late-ripening Furmint grape, which is particularly susceptible to the botrytis or noble rot fungus.

DOMDECHANT WERNER'SCHES WEINGUT

GERMANY, Rheingau, Hochheim

🍷 *Pinot Noir (Spätburgunder)*

♀ *Riesling*

Traditional techniques and well-sited vineyards combine here to produce full-flavoured, long-lived wines. All the vineyards are in HOCHHEIM – Domdechaney, Kirchenstück, Hölle, Stielweg, Stein and Reichestal; even in less good years these wines are reliably classy. The Werner family bought the estate from the Duke of York in 1780; in the next generation Dr Franz Werner was the Dean (Domdechant) of Mainz who saved the cathedral from the rampaging French army. The family is now called Werner Michel but it is still in charge of the estate. Best years: 1996, '94, '92, '90, '89, '88, '86.

WESTERN AUSTRALIA Australia

IT'S THE SHEER VASTNESS of Western Australia that hits you first. That and the emptiness. If you approach Perth, the one centre of population, from the north or the east, you can gaze from the plane window in vain for any signs of life. Any township, any road or railway, any river even, or lake – and the searing orange soils glare back at you, offering nothing and no-one. Since the state covers well over a third of Australia's landmass, yet boasts a population of a mere 1.7 million, you begin to understand how isolated the few inhabitants must feel. The export markets of Asia are closer to Perth than the domestic markets of the rest of Australia to the east. Yet Western Australia can lay fair claim to being one of the originators of vineyards in Australia. Though New South Wales, where the first fleet arrived in 1788, was the first to plant vines, Western Australia wasn't far behind – and was way ahead of South Australia and Victoria. Olive Farm had planted vines in 1829 on the banks of the Swan River just outside Perth, and since it is still going today, counts as the oldest operating winery in Australia. And it must have been reasonably decent stuff they made in the Swan Valley, because towards the end of the nineteenth century the valley had more wineries than any other Australian region. And until the 1970s there was only one wine that regularly found its way out of the local market – Houghton's White Burgundy – now renamed Houghton's Supreme and still selling worldwide – all the rest was drunk locally.

Of course, it may have been the heat. The Swan has the hottest climate of any serious Australian wine region, having summer temperatures that can soar to 45°C (113°F), low humidity and virtually no summer rain at all. If this sounds like a place where you should be making port and sherry-style wines – you're right. And yet, remarkably, many of the most successful Swan wines are white. This is probably because of the happy chance of grape varieties. Chenin is the leading variety, and prides itself on retaining acidity, whatever the heat.

Even so, despite the continual success of large companies like Houghton and Sandalford – who both, by the way, source much of their fruit from elsewhere – the winds of fashion are blowing most of our attention way to the south – to the Margaret River and Great Southern regions. The conditions couldn't be more different from the Swan District – cool, temperate, often compared to Bordeaux or Burgundy rather than to the baking Douro Valley of Portugal. And the wines are totally different too.

The Margaret River area was established by a variety of local medics and one or two Perth bigwigs in the late 1960s and 1970s after a visiting expert had noted remarkable similarities between its climate and that of Bordeaux. Indeed, it

has less frost risk, more summer sunshine and less risk of vintage rain than Bordeaux – it's like Bordeaux in a really nice, warm year. With this in mind, Cabernet and Merlot regularly produce stunning results, but so too do Shiraz, Pinot Noir, Chardonnay, Sauvignon Blanc, Semillon and Riesling – and even Zinfandel. A dog's dinner, then? Not at all. Just another of these remarkable Australian regions that seem to be able to take the grapes of anywhere from northerly Germany to southern Italy – and achieve brilliant results with them all.

Being even more isolated than the Margaret River in Australia's most isolated wine-growing state, the Great Southern region has made haphazard progress, but there's no doubting that this relatively cool remote region can produce smashing wine – and again it manages to excel with such wildly different varieties as Cabernet, Shiraz, Pinot, Chardonnay, Sauvignon and Riesling. All it lacks is a ready market. Luckily, at the moment, Australia's export boom provides that.

Harvesting Zinfandel at Cape Mentelle in the Margaret River. Associated mainly with California, Zinfandel is planted commercially in only a few regions in Australia which is a pity as Cape Mentelle's example has lots of chewy fruit.

Wine regions
- Swan District
- Perth Hills
- Geographe
- Margaret River
- Blackwood Valley
- Pemberton
- Great Southern

REGIONAL ENTRIES
Geographe, Great Southern, Margaret River, Pemberton, Perth Hills, Swan District.

PRODUCER ENTRIES·
Alkoomi, Cape Mentelle, Capel Vale, Cullen Wines, Devil's Lair, Evans & Tate, Goundrey Wines, Houghton, Howard Park, Leeuwin Estate, Moss Wood, Pierro, Plantagenet, Vasse Felix.

LEEUWIN ESTATE
Many rate this premium Chardonnay from the Art Series as the finest in the whole of Australia. Very oaky when young, the wine becomes complex and full-bodied with impressive richness.

CAPE MENTELLE
This leading Margaret River winery, co-owned by founder David Hohnen and the Champagne house Veuve Clicquot, makes tangy Semillon/Sauvignon Blanc.

HOWARD PARK
Expensive but superb, long-lived wines come from this dynamic winery on the south coast near Denmark.

CULLEN WINES
This is one of the original and best Margaret River wineries. The Cabernet/Merlot blend is deep, well-structured and scented and even better now that the Reserve version is no longer being made.

MOSS WOOD
Cabernet Sauvignon is the wine upon which Margaret River's reputation was founded. This wine is silky smooth, rich but structured.

EVANS & TATE
Chardonnay is one of the Margaret River's most successful wine styles. This restrained but complex example from Evans & Tate is best at five to ten years old.

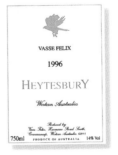

FRANKLAND ESTATE
Riesling vies with Cabernet Sauvignon as the most important wine from the vast Great Southern region. This estate makes a consistently good example.

VASSE FELIX
The Heytesbury range (oaky, buttery Chardonnay and a delicious red Bordeaux blend) are the flagship wines from this dynamic Margaret River winery.

WIEN

AUSTRIA

Vienna, or Wien, is proud of its claim to have more hectares of vines than any other capital city; but we are not talking about the city centre here. Vienna's vineyards are mostly on the outskirts, in the semi-rural villages that get choked with tourists every summer: Grinzing, Stammersdorf and Nussdorf are the main centres, and in Grinzing the tourists must outnumber the locals by several to one. The traditional wine of Vienna is Gemischter Satz, a blend of whatever varieties were mixed up in the vineyard; these days the vines are separated according to variety and Vienna's best are the Grüner Veltliner, Rhine Riesling, Weissburgunder (Pinot Blanc), Chardonnay, Welschriesling, Gewürztraminer and Neuburger (Aut hill). Riesling from the steep, south-facing slopes of the Nussberg rises well above these everyday levels, as do the wines of Fritz WIENINGER, Peter Bernreiter and Franz Mayer.

FRITZ WIENINGER

AUSTRIA, Wien

🍷 Pinot Noir (Blauburgunder), Cabernet, Merlot, Blauer Portugieser

🍷 Chardonnay, Grüner Veltliner, Riesling

Fritz Wieninger may be something of a playboy, but he is also Vienna's best winemaker, and he also runs one of its best Heurigen in the suburb of Stammersdorf close to his vines on the slopes of the Bisamberg. His top wines, such as the barrique-fermented Grand Select Chardonnay, a big mouthful of butter and pear, and the Pinot Noir, which in a good vintage has intense cherry aromas and plenty of soft tannins, have been influenced by his experiences in CALIFORNIA. However, the Rieslings and Grüner Veltliners are not quite as good as those made by Fritz's father during the 1970s and '80s. Best years: 1998, '97, '95, '93, '92, '90, '88.

WILLAKENZIE ESTATE

USA, Oregon, Yamhill County, Willamette Valley AVA

🍷 Pinot Noir, Gamay

🍷 Chardonnay, Pinot Gris, Pinot Blanc

WillaKenzie Estate is a modern, gravity-flow winery, built in 1995. The vineyards (170 ha/420 acres) are densely planted with traditional varietal clones and newer, early-ripening ones. Fine Pinot Noir is vinified by winemaker Laurent Monthelieu. The Pinot Gris is viscous and intense and the Pinot Blanc is rich and impressive. Best years: (Pinot Noir) 1998, '96; (Pinot Gris and Pinot Blanc) 1998.

PONZI VINEYARDS
Dick Ponzi was one of the first in Oregon to make Pinot Gris, now the local speciality after Pinot Noir. This wine has a delicate creamy character and gently spicy, ripe fruit perfume.

WILLAMETTE VALLEY AVA

USA, Oregon

By far the most developed of OREGON's wine regions, the Willamette Valley grew more swiftly than its competitors because early acclaim for Pinot Noir grown here brought a continuous supply of new hopefuls to augment the small handful of pioneers.

The valley is a long one, beginning south of Eugene and extending all the way north to Portland, where the Willamette empties into the Columbia River. Low, forested hills form its west boundary; the rock-ribbed, snow-capped Cascade Mountains limit it on the east. Rain is both a salvation and a curse. It helps keep the climate cool, but sometimes drowns both the flowering vines and the harvest. Hail is not unknown, nor are spring frosts. All this makes Willamette winemakers believe they have found America's CÔTE D'OR, though Oregon's soils do not much resemble Burgundy's and it is the bad, not good, climatic conditions that are more similar. Even so, the resemblances are enough to have caused Robert DROUHIN of Burgundy to buy land and plant vines here with considerable success (see DOMAINE DROUHIN).

Washington County, west and south-west of Portland, is home to Montinore, Oak Knoll Winery, PONZI VINEYARDS, Shafer Vineyard Cellars (consistent Chardonnay, but not to be confused with NAPA VALLEY's SHAFER VINEYARDS). The more heavily planted Yamhill County flanks Washington County to the south. Wineries include ARCHERY SUMMIT, WILLAKENZIE ESTATE, DOMAINE DROUHIN, St-Innocent, Ken WRIGHT, Domaine Serene, Eola Hills, The EYRIE VINEYARDS, Erath, ADELSHEIM VINEYARD, Amity Vineyards, BEAUX FRÈRES, CAMERON WINERY, Cristom, Elk Cove Vineyards, REX HILL VINEYARDS, Sokol-Blosser Winery, Panther Creek and Yamhill Valley Vineyards. From here, vineyards and wineries tail off all the way to Eugene, 190km (120 miles) south of Portland, and include good Pinot Noir from Bethel Heights and Tyee

Wine Cellars. To hear people talk, Pinot Noir is the main game – almost the only one. Most of the state's 809ha (2000 acres) of this variety grow in the Willamette. Chardonnay and Riesling dominated at the start, and still do in acreage. Pinot Gris is up and coming.

CHAMPAGNE-method sparkling wines could prove best of all Willamette's wine styles. The Champagne house LAURENT-PERRIER is developing vineyards here. The best bubbly to date comes from ARGYLE, partly owned by the talented Australian winemaker Brian Croser of PETALUMA.

WILLIAMS SELYEM WINERY

USA, California, Sonoma County, Russian River Valley AVA

🍷 Pinot Noir, Zinfandel

🍷 Chardonnay

Founders Ed Williams and Burt Selyem took a threadbare, low-budget operation and converted it into one of CALIFORNIA's top names. Emphasizing cool-climate, oak-aged blockbuster Pinot Noir, their non-interventionist winemaking style developed a cult following, especially for the single-vineyard Pinots from Rochioli, Allen and Olivet Lane vineyards.

After moving to a larger facility in 1990, they added Zinfandel and Chardonnay, and both were well-received by fans of big, upfront wines. With annual production averaging only 2500 cases, the winery had such a faithful fan club that it was selling Pinot Noir for the price of $100 a bottle (tops for California Pinot Noir). However, the physical toil persuaded the partners to sell the winery which, after a heated bidding war, was acquired in 1998 by John Dyson, who owns NEW YORK STATE's MILLBROOK WINERY. Let's hope not too much changes because under the previous owners, the Pinot Noirs were often more than capable of seven to ten years' aging before displaying their sumptuous best. Best years: 1998, '97, '96, '95, '94, '93, '92, '91.

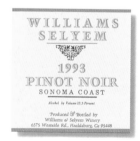

WILLIAMS SELYEM
Pinot Noir was the only wine made here until 1990 and it is still very, very good. Made in a traditional style, the wine is big, uninhibited and very fruity.

WILTINGEN

GERMANY, Mosel-Saar-Ruwer

This town is the heart of the Saar region and has the Saar's most famous vineyard (the great Scharzhofberg) and one of Germany's top estates, making some of the world's greatest dessert wines (Egon MÜLLER-SCHARZHOF).

The Saar is a cool, even chilly region, where in most years the wines will be lean and acidic, mellowing after a few years to be sure, but without the ripeness and richness that can make wines great. But when the weather obliges with a long warm autumn with plenty of sun, then everything changes. Then the wines have a knife-edge excitement which few can match – and even in the Saar, few can match the Müller-Scharzhof wines. This estate produces Wiltingen's, and the Saar's, best wines, especially from the steep slopes of the Scharzhofberg vineyard. Other great wines come from Hohe Domkirche, von HÖVEL, von KESSELSTATT and Bischöfliches Priesterseminar Trier. The Kabinett wines can be drunk young but everything will benefit from bottle age; the Auslese need ten years to reach their peak.

WINNINGEN

GERMANY, Mosel-Saar-Ruwer

The last major wine commune before the Mosel flows into the Rhine at Koblenz has the best vineyards in the 'Terrassen-Mosel', as this lower part of the MOSEL Valley is called. As the name suggests, the vines cling to narrow terraces along the steep, rocky, valley sides, and in Winningen's excellent Röttgen and Uhlen sites the terraces are literally like steps climbing up to heaven. Best producers: HEYMANN-LÖWENSTEIN, von Heddesdorf.

WIRRA WIRRA

Australia, South Australia, Fleurieu Zone, McLaren Vale

🍷 *Cabernet Sauvignon, Merlot, Shiraz, Mourvèdre*

🍷 *Riesling, Semillon, Sauvignon Blanc*

The modern day Wirra Wirra winery was not established until 1969, but the viticultural and winemaking links of the family of proprietor Greg Trott – a wonderfully eccentric and much-loved figure, usually called 'Trottie' – go back to the nineteenth century.

Trottie has recently been joined by Dr Tony Jordan (ex-DOMAINE CHANDON), and one can expect much of this already impressive winery. Its best white wines are tropical gooseberry Sauvignon Blanc and sculpted Chardonnay, but its stellar acts are the super-premium, chocolaty RSW Shiraz and The Angelus Cabernet Sauvignon, whose blackcurrant,

WIRRA WIRRA

The delicious Angelus Cabernet Sauvignon was one of the first Cabernet wines to draw attention to the McLaren Vale region.

berry, cedary aroma and impressive depth of fruit are partly due to an addition of COONAWARRA grapes. Best years: 1997, '96, '94, '92, '91, '90.

WIRSCHING

GERMANY, Franken, Iphofen

🍷 *Sylvaner (Silvaner), Riesling, Müller-Thurgau, Pinot Blanc (Weissburgunder)*

This large, family estate has 63ha (156 acres) of vineyards in the Steigerwald area of FRANKEN, including substantial holdings in top sites like the Julius-Echter-Berg and Kronenberg. While the dry Spätleses are among the finest wines in Franken, lower down the price scale there are some simple, rustic wines. Best years: 1998, '97, '94, '93, '92, '90, '88, '85, '83.

J L WOLF

GERMANY, Pfalz, Deidesheim

🍷 *Pinot Noir (Spätburgunder)*

🍷 *Riesling, Pinot Gris (Grauburgunder)*

For years this estate, based in one of the most beautiful of many imposing PFALZ villas, made mediocre wines in spite of having old vines in many of the region's top sites. When Ernst Loosen from the Dr LOOSEN estate in the MOSEL arrived for the 1996 vintage, things changed dramatically. The concentrated Rieslings from 1996, followed by the '97 and '98, have put Wolf straight in the first rank of Pfalz estates, even if some leading Pfalz winemakers complain that the wines taste too much like Mosels! Best years: 1998, '97, '96.

WOODWARD CANYON WINERY

USA, Washington State, Walla Walla AVA

🍷 *Cabernet Sauvignon, Merlot*

🍷 *Chardonnay*

Chardonnay has been the banner varietal for this renowned WASHINGTON winery since it began in 1981. The Chardonnay Reserve is an excellent, oaked, toasty wine. Cabernet Sauvignon and Merlot that spend lots of time in new oak are becoming the emphasis here as the focus shifts from Chardonnay to popular red varieties. Best years: 1998, '96, '94.

WOOTTON

ENGLAND, Somerset

🍷 *Müller-Thurgau, Schönburger, Seyval Blanc, Auxerrois*

Look for good snappy dry wines from this Somerset vineyard. Owner Colin Gillespie has 2.4ha (6 acres) of vines, most of which are coming up to their quarter-century, and he is becoming increasingly involved in making sensational, perfumed eau de vie from Seyval Blanc and Müller-Thurgau, which is then aged in oak barrels for nine months. Gillespie bemoans the lack of a main road past his front door to bring wine-buying visitors, so do him a favour and make a detour. Wines are pleasant young but will keep.

WRATTONBULLY

AUSTRALIA, South Australia, Limestone Coast Zone

Every country is entitled to a practical joke, and this is Australia's. Instead of taking the name Koppamurra (first choice), Naracoorte Ranges (second choice), Joanna (third choice) or one or two others, and at the end of interminable wrangling, this important grape-growing region has, at least for the time being, christened itself Rat and Bully – sorry, Wrattonbully – under the GI legislation. With over 1000ha (2470 acres) of vines and annual production of over 10,000 tonnes of grapes it deserves better. Koppamurra Wines is the long-term resident winery, Heathfield Ridge Wines a newly constructed, large, grape-purchasing winery serving part of the needs of the many major Australian companies drawing grapes from this region – notably BRL HARDY, MILDARA Blass and YALUMBA. Situated just south of PADTHAWAY, Wrattonbully is equally at home producing generous yields of Sauvignon Blanc, Chardonnay and Riesling on the one hand and Cabernet Sauvignon, Shiraz and Merlot on the other. Whether it will ever aspire to greatness remains to be seen. Best years: 1998, '97, '96, '94, '91, '90.

KEN WRIGHT CELLARS

USA, Oregon, Yamhill County, Willamette Valley AVA

🍷 *Pinot Noir*

🍷 *Chardonnay, Pinot Blanc*

Ken Wright specializes in single-vineyard Pinot Noirs. The collection of wines includes Carter, Canary Hill, Shea, Quadalupe, McCrone and Elton Vineyards. Ripe fruit and lots of new wood make these wines impressive at an early age. His Chardonnay 'Celilo Vineyard' (from WASHINGTON fruit) is excellent. A small amount of Pinot Blanc is also made. Best years: 1998, '96, '94.

WÜRTTEMBERG

GERMANY

🍷 🍷 *Trollinger, Pinot Meunier (Schwarzriesling), Lemberger and others*

🍷 *Riesling, Kerner, Müller-Thurgau and others*

Red wines are Württemberg's speciality. Just over half its 11,224ha (27,735 acres) of vines are planted with red varieties, of which the Trollinger is far and away the most popular. In spite of the region's warm climate the red wines are seldom very dark in colour, seldom tannic and frequently sweetish; one reason for their lightness is the large yields obtained by the growers. But the locals like them like this, and since it's the locals who drink them… And although the climate is warm in the summer, it is cold in the winter and so vineyard site selection is as important here as anywhere else in Germany.

The main white grape, the Riesling, can sometimes lack the startling acidity of other German regions because malolactic fermentation, which has the effect of softening the taste of the wine, is traditional here. Württemberg's other speciality is rosé, here called Schillerwein. This is a mix of red and white grapes; a rosé made just with red grapes, in the more usual way, may be called Weissherbst.

There are three Bereichs: Remstal Stuttgart in the south, which encompasses the car-making centre of Stuttgart; Württembergisch Unterland in the centre, which takes in most of the vineyards; and tiny Kocher-Jagst-Tauber in the north, specializing in white wines. Best producers: Graf Adelmann, Ernst Dautel, Graf Neipperg, Wöhrwag.

WÜRZBURG

GERMANY, Franken

The cultural, political and viticultural centre of FRANKEN, Würzburg is one of Europe's great wine cities. It is worth visiting for the historical monuments alone, which include Balthasar Neumann's Baroque palace, the Residenz. However, the three large wine estates owned by charitable foundations – the Bürgerspital, the JULIUSSPITAL and the Staatliche Hofkeller – are also good reasons to make the pilgrimage. Best producers: Bürgerspital, JULIUSSPITAL, Staatlicher Hofkeller.

WYNDHAM ESTATE

AUSTRALIA, New South Wales, Hunter Valley Zone, Hunter

🍷 *Cabernet Sauvignon, Syrah (Shiraz), Merlot, Malbec*

🍷 *Chardonnay, Semillon, Riesling and others*

Just before the company was bought by Pernod-Ricard's ORLANDO group in 1990,

Although semi-arid, the Yakima Valley has produced some of Washington State's most distinctive wines. Kiona Vineyards is located in a barren subregion called Red Mountain where little grows except for sagebrush.

Wyndham had set up a vast viticultural trust to provide it with the equivalent of 1,600,000 cases of wine per year from vineyards all over Australia. If one includes the associate brands of Richmond Grove and Hunter Estate, there must have been more than 50 different (at least one assumes they were different) wines. Wyndham quality has been poor for a number of years, but new, more imaginative winemaking from Orlando's top guys is starting to improve things.

WYNNS

AUSTRALIA, South Australia, Limestone Coast Zone, Coonawarra

🍷 *Cabernet Sauvignon, Syrah (Shiraz), Pinot Noir*

🍷 *Riesling, Chardonnay and others*

Wynns is not only the largest COONAWARRA producer but arguably the best. Aromatic, limy Riesling sells for a song, yet performs like a thoroughbred in the cellar, building complexity for five years at least. Chardonnay is becoming more subtle and complex with each successive vintage. The spicy, cherry Shiraz is widely held to be the best-value red in Australia; the Cabernet Sauvignons provide enormous flavour at six years, peaking at 12 to 15 years. Top of the line John Riddoch Cabernet is stupendous, packed with concentrated fruit and capable of aging a generation. The top Shiraz is called Michael and is incredibly oaky. Wynns is part of the Southcorp group, Australia's largest wine company. Best years: (premium reds) 1996, '94, '93, '91, '90, '88, '86, '84, '82, '80, '76, '66, '62, '55.

XAREL-LO

This low-quality white Spanish grape is the curse of CAVA, though few producers would admit it. Most Catalan Cava (and that means most Spanish Cava) is made from a blend of Xarel-lo with the somewhat higher-quality Macabeo and even better Parellada. While none of these three is capable of retaining its fruitiness and freshness throughout the lengthy aging periods to which much Cava is subjected, Xarel-lo takes on a particularly unfortunate earthy flavour within a very short time. Some of the best Penedès producers wisely choose to leave it out of their blends. When scrupulously made as still wine, young Xarel-lo wine can show an attractive gooseberries and cream character, though it can easily become over-alcoholic and coarse, or just bland. It is exclusive to Cataluña, but it grows there in such profusion that it ranks as Spain's sixth most-planted white grape variety. In Alella it is the principal grape and is known as Paisá Blanca.

YAKIMA VALLEY AVA

USA, Washington State

The Yakima Valley is a curious place, a sort of linear oasis that is also one of America's great food baskets. Nothing looks easy here, nor is. Hard in the lee of the Cascade Mountains, the valley gets so little rain that any unirrigated land resembles desert. The Yakima's summer climate is hot, with more than a few days of 37°C (100°F) temperatures. In winter, the thermometer can stay below −17°C (0°F) for days on end.

Yet, amid the apples and apricots and beans and hops are vines that regularly yield the United States's most consistently underrated wines, especially Sauvignon Blanc, Semillon, Cabernet and Merlot. These, plus Chardonnay, Chenin Blanc, Riesling, a red called Lemberger and even some Grenache, are the most successful.

Wineries to explore include Covey Run, CHATEAU STE MICHELLE (the biggest producer and particularly good at tangy whites), Columbia Crest (everything is cheap; most are good) and Staton Hills Vineyard & Winery. There are another dozen or so wineries in the valley, including Chinook, HOGUE CELLARS, Hyatt, Kiona and Wineglass Cellars. Several other Washington wineries use Yakima Valley grapes, including ANDREW WILL, Chaleur Estate, QUILCEDA CREEK, Silver Lake and Paul Thomas.

YALUMBA

AUSTRALIA, South Australia, Barossa Zone, Barossa Valley

♥ Cabernet Sauvignon, Syrah (Shiraz), Pinot Noir
♀ Riesling, Chardonnay, Semillon

Owned by the Hill-Smith family, Yalumba is one of the most successful of Australia's independent wine companies and manages to operate on several levels, all with considerable success. In particular, it has managed to have a smash hit with its sparkling wine portfolio, led by huge-selling, enjoyable Angas Brut, but followed by some extremely classy wines higher up the range. Oxford Landing is also developing a good reputation as a keenly-priced range of varietal wines, while Family Selection and Signature Collection embody a rather more traditional but high-quality approach.

Yalumba also operates three separate estates – Hill-Smith Estate, Pewsey Vale and Heggies – all producing good, single-vineyard wines from the northern end of the ADELAIDE HILLS with particular emphasis on slow-maturing wines from Riesling, Semillon and Chardonnay. Best years: (Signature reds) 1998, '97, '95, '94, '93, '92, '91, '90.

YARRA BURN

AUSTRALIA, Victoria, Port Phillip Zone, Yarra Valley

♥ Pinot Noir, Syrah (Shiraz)
♀ Sauvignon Blanc, Semillon, Chardonnay

Acquired by BRL HARDY in the mid-1990s, Yarra Burn is the focal point for that company's wines in the YARRA VALLEY. Much of the very large vineyard resources (Hardy also acquired two of the largest independent vineyards in the Yarra Valley) go to making

Hardy's top-end sparkling wines and (in varying proportions) its Eileen Hardy Chardonnay. Bastard Hill Chardonnay and Pinot Noir are the best two Yarra Burn wines (yes, the name is real, coming from the terrifying degree of slope of the up-and-down vineyards) and after a run of poor vintages, one expects great things of the 1998 and '97 wines. Best years: 1998, '97, '94, '92, '91, '90.

YARRA RIDGE

AUSTRALIA, Victoria, Port Phillip Zone, Yarra Valley

♥ Pinot Noir, Cabernet Sauvignon, Merlot
♀ Chardonnay, Sauvignon Blanc

Founded by lawyer Louis Bialkower in 1983, Yarra Ridge enjoyed a meteoric rise in production and reputation, then was first partially and then wholly acquired by MILDARA Blass. Yarra Ridge made its reputation with a trail-blazing, tangy, tropical gooseberry Sauvignon Blanc, but as volume grew rapidly, it lost its edge and indeed moved outside the YARRA VALLEY for its grape sources. The loss of quality fruit particularly shows in disappointing Pinot Noir, but cunningly oaked Chardonnay is still a reasonable drink. Best years: 1997, '96, '94, '92, '91, '90.

YARRA VALLEY

AUSTRALIA, Victoria, Port Phillip Zone

If Australia's table wines were world-renowned at the end of the nineteenth century, it was Yarra Valley vines that provided the grapes for her greatest triumphs. Yet for the first half of the twentieth century, this beautiful valley on the outskirts of Melbourne was used for grazing cattle and at the end of the 1960s there were just 1.2ha (3 acres) of vines planted. By 1996 there were over 1300ha (3212 acres) of vineyards, a figure still on the rise, with 43 wineries and millions of dollars of foreign investment pointing up the fabulous potential of Yarra Valley vineyards.

As it is slightly cooler than BORDEAUX, yet warmer than Burgundy, and with a much more regular rainfall pattern than either of these two regions which provides essentially dry summers and autumns, it is Pinot Noir and Chardonnay that have shown the most exciting flavours so far. Cabernet Sauvignon, especially blended with the earlier-ripening Cabernet Franc, Merlot and Malbec can be good, if sometimes a little grassy. Yarra Valley Shiraz is interesting, Sauvignon Blanc good, and the occasional botrytis-affected sweet wines can be luscious.

However, not surprisingly considering the success of the two CHAMPAGNE grapes (Pinot Noir and Chardonnay) here, it is as a provider of sparkling wines that the Yarra Valley's most regular triumph has so far been seen – Green Point Vineyards (DOMAINE CHANDON), founded in 1985, is already making some of Australia's best fizz. Best years: 1998, '97, '94, '93, '92, '91, '90, '88, '86, '85. Best producers: DE BORTOLI, COLDSTREAM HILLS, DIAMOND VALLEY, Green Point (Domaine Chandon), Lillydale Vineyards, MOUNT MARY, Oakridge, St Hubert's, Seville Estate, TARRA WARRA, YARRA RIDGE, YARRA YERING, YERINGBERG.

YARRA YERING

AUSTRALIA, Victoria, Port Phillip Zone, Yarra Valley

♥ Cabernet Sauvignon, Syrah (Shiraz), Pinot Noir and others
♀ Chardonnay, Semillon, Viognier

Bailey Carrodus makes the richest, deepest, most complex and (for many years) least understood reds in the YARRA VALLEY, hiding their laurels under the enigmatic labels Dry Red Wine No 1 (a BORDEAUX blend) and Dry Red Wine No 2 (a RHÔNE-style wine based on Shiraz but including some white Viognier). Carrodus believes that great wine is made in the vineyard, and practises benign neglect (except for a generous purchase of new oak barrels each year) in his winemaking, allowing vintage variation full play.

The result is red wines crammed full of personality, which make the blood race despite sometimes upsetting the purists. They may not always fit into a mainstream style based solely on varietal flavours – but so what? You don't buy Yarra Yering in a spirit of complacent certainty but rather in a lather of uncertain anticipation.

His latest mould-breakers are a delicious, idiosyncratic Pinot Noir and a Chardonnay strongly reminiscent of old-fashioned PULIGNY-MONTRACHET. Yarra Yering also releases some peppery Shiraz under the Underhill label and a few cases of frighteningly expensive Merlot. Best years: 1995, '94, '93, '92, '91, '90, '86, '82.

YARRA YERING
Bailey Carrodus uses unusual winemaking methods to create extraordinary wines from his exceptional vineyards. Dry Red Wine No 2 is a delicious, perfumed Shiraz blend with ripe, sweet, berried fruit.

YELLOWGLEN

AUSTRALIA, Victoria, Western Victoria Zone, Ballarat

❧ *Pinot Noir*

♀ *Semillon, Colombard, Trebbiano, Chardonnay*

Yellowglen specializes in sparkling wine, but the wine in the bottle isn't as important as the company's phenomenal marketing success. No-one had heard of it in January 1982; in March Dominique Landragin left SEPPELT and joined Ian Home in partnership and within two years they had created a national brand. MILDARA then bought the company, and its profits are now significantly helped by Yellowglen's success. Quality has even become predictable, but predictability is no bad thing in a fizz. Best years: (Cuvée Victoria) 1996, '94, '91, '88.

YERINGBERG

AUSTRALIA, Victoria, Port Phillip Zone, Yarra Valley

❧ *Pinot Noir, Cabernet Sauvignon, Merlot, Malbec*

♀ *Chardonnay, Marsanne, Roussanne*

From Guillaume, Baron de Pury, formerly of Neuchâtel in Switzerland and cousin of the first Governor of Victoria, Charles la Trobe, the ownership of Yeringberg has passed in direct succession to his grandson, Guill de Pury. The once-large vineyards are now reduced to a token 3ha (7.4 acres), and de Pury makes a little wine for his health's sake in the unbelievably well-preserved wooden winery, built in 1885. The wines rival those of YARRA YERING for depth and richness. Best years: 1997, '94, '92, '91, '90, '88, '87, '86, '85.

YERINGBERG
This small but important Yarra Valley producer, one of Australia's oldest, produces Chardonnay in a lean, almost austere style.

CH. D'YQUEM

FRANCE, Bordeaux, Sauternes AC, Grand Premier Cru

♀ *Sémillon, Sauvignon Blanc*

Many people would rate Ch. d'Yquem as the greatest wine in BORDEAUX and maybe even the greatest wine in France. Certainly, if we're talking about total commitment to quality and a no-compromise approach to winemaking, you simply cannot fault Yquem – the supreme example of the majestic sweet wines of SAUTERNES. In 1855, when Bordeaux was busy classifying wine, Yquem was accorded a sort of 'first of firsts' position as against the other famous First Growths like Ch. MARGAUX, LATOUR, and, of course, several other top Sauternes. Ch. d'Yquem's title was Premier Cru Supérieur or Great First Growth. It was the only wine accorded the title, and this shows that Yquem was regarded as supreme all those years ago – and its position hasn't changed since then.

The vineyard is large – 102ha (252 acres), planted with Sémillon (80 per cent) and Sauvignon Blanc (20 per cent) – but production is tiny, an average of 95,000 bottles per year. Only fully noble-rotted grapes are picked – often berry by berry. This means that the pickers may have to go through the vineyard as many as eleven times, selecting the grapes by hand; it's a slow process and can also mean that the vintage doesn't finish until the freezing winter days of December. There is no sacrifice that is too much for Yquem.

Noble rot concentrates the juice but radically reduces the volume produced. Although the Sauternes AC allows a yield of 25 hectolitres per hectare – which is already very low – at Yquem the yield is more like 8 hectolitres. This works out at a glass of wine per vine (a great red wine estate might easily produce a bottle of wine per vine). This precious liquid gold is then fermented in new oak barrels and left to mature for three-and-a-half years, before bottling and eventual release.

If the wine isn't outstanding, it simply isn't released as Yquem. In 1964, '72, '74 and '92 the entire crop was declassified and in 1978, 85 per cent of the wine was refused the château label. The result is a frantically expensive wine, which is nonetheless in constant demand, because for sheer richness, for exotic flavours of vanilla, pineapple, melons, peaches and coconut, enveloped in a caramel richness so viscous and lush your mouth feels coated with succulence for an eternity after swallowing the wine; for all that, and for its ability to age a decade, a generation, or a century even, when the wine will be deep, dark brown, barely glinting with gold, and will taste of orange chocolate, butterscotch, barley sugar and caramel… no wine in the world can touch Yquem. The takeover in 1999 by LVMH after 406 years of ownership by the Lur-Salices family should not affect its supreme quality. In certain years a bone dry white Bordeaux (called 'Ygrec') is made from equal amounts of Sémillon and Sauvignon Blanc. Best years: 1991, '90, '89, '88, '86, '83, '81, '80, '79, '76, '75, '71, '67, '62, '59, '55, '53, '49, '47, '45, '43, '37, '29, '28, '21.

ZD WINES

USA, California, Napa County, Napa Valley AVA

❧ *Cabernet Sauvignon, Merlot, Pinot Noir*

♀ *Chardonnay*

Founded in 1969, this family-owned winery has at times been a leader, and at all other times has kept pace with the competition. Its lush, barrel-fermented Chardonnay (combining fruit from the NAPA VALLEY and SANTA BARBARA), with a hint of tropical fruit, has always been rich and responds well to three to four years of aging. Best years: 1998, '97, '96, '95, '94.

With the acquisition of vineyards in the CARNEROS region, Pinot Noir has lost its rough edges and recent vintages display pretty black cherry fruit, satiny-smooth texture, and fine aging ability. Also benefiting from the inclusion of Carneros-grown fruit, the winery's Merlot is packed with berry-spicy fruit. Made in a firm, classically structured style, the Reserve Cabernet from the winery's RUTHERFORD vineyard is one to age for a decade and has been a dramatic addition to the roster. Best years: (reds) 1997, '96, '95, '94, '93.

ZELTINGEN

GERMANY, Mosel-Saar-Ruwer

This is a Mittel MOSEL town between ÜRZIG and GRAACH, but without quite the fame of either. Sonnenuhr and Schlossberg are its best known vineyards. Its growers claim, with some reason, that Zeltingen's Sonnenuhr vineyard is every bit as good as nearby WEHLEN's. Zeltingen Sonnenuhr can have great elegance and the site seems particularly good for sweet wines. The Schlossberg vineyard is good at putting muscle into dry wines. Zeltingen can muster a good list of top growers. Best producers: MOLITOR, J J PRÜM, SELBACH-OSTER.

ZERBINA

ITALY, Emilia-Romagna, Albana di Romagna DOCG

❧ *Sangiovese, Cabernet Sauvignon, Merlot*

♀ *Trebbiano di Romagna, Albana di Romagna, Sauvignon Blanc*

Of all the Italian wine regions which promise greater things in the future, Romagna, and specifically the lower slopes of the Apennines between Bologna and Cesena, probably ranks as number one. And by common consent, the top estate is Zerbina, owned by Cristina Giminiani, abetted by one of Italy's great consultant enologists, Vittorio Fiore.

Her wines are at such a high general level, indeed, as to make it difficult to choose between them. There's the Sangiovese di Romagna Superiore Pietramora Riserva,

ZERBINA

This estate near Faenza has rapidly ascended to become Romagna's leading producer. Scacco Matto is a wonderful passito wine from the local Albana grape.

which single-handedly puts the lie to the myth that Sangiovese from Romagna is nothing but bulk table wine, as does the barriqued Sangiovese di Romagna Torre di Ceparano. The Cru Marzieno is also Sangiovese, but this time blended with Cabernet Sauvignon. Then there is the wonderful dessert wine Scacco Matto which, again almost single-handedly, justifies the DOCG status of this all-too-often ordinary wine. If Zerbina can reach these heights in much maligned Romagna, why not others? And, in fact, some producers in the COLLI BOLOGNESI zone are at last beginning to make waves. Best years: 1997, '95, '93, '90.

ZILLIKEN (FORMEISTER GELTZ)

GERMANY, Mosel-Saar-Ruwer, Saarburg
♀ *Riesling*

This old-established estate at SAARBURG is soaring to even greater heights under its current owner, Hans-Joachim Zilliken. The vineyards are in some of the best spots on the Saar and winemaking is traditional, using only old oak casks, giving elegant, racy wines that are often lean in youth. Those from the Rausch vineyard, with its notable weathered grey slate and diabase soil, are often particularly long-lived. There are also vines in the Bockstein vineyard at OCKFEN. The estate makes a speciality of Eiswein, producing one most years, which is unusual because it can only be harvested if temperatures reach −8°C (19°F) or lower. Best years: 1997, '95, '94, '93, '91, '90, '89, '88, '85, '83.

ZIMMERLING

GERMANY, Sachsen, Pillnitz
♀ *Riesling, Pinot Gris (Grauburgunder), Gewürztraminer*

Using only axes and ropes to help him, Klaus Zimmerling began clearing ancient vineyard terraces at the southern edge of the city of Dresden in 1987. From these primitive beginings has grown a 4-ha (10-acre) estate

which makes the finest wines in former East Germany. Zimmerling's rich and intense dry Riesling, Grauburgunder and Traminer all come from the slopes of the Königlicher Weinberg, vineyards established during the early eighteenth century when August the Strong, Elector of Saxony, was one of Europe's most powerful rulers. Best years: 1998, '97, '95, '93, '92.

ZIND-HUMBRECHT

France, Alsace, Alsace AC
♟ *Pinot Noir*
♀ *Riesling, Gewurztraminer, Pinot Gris, Pinot Blanc, Muscat, Sylvaner*

There are many connoisseurs convinced that this estate is the source of the very finest ALSACE wines. They are certainly among the richest and most powerful. Léonard Humbrecht, who established the reputation of the 30-ha (74-acre) estate, is now semi-retired, and his son Olivier (the first French Master of Wine) now runs the property. The estate has vines in four Grands Crus – Rangen, Hengst, Goldert and Brand – but also produces a whole range of single-vineyard bottlings from individual sites the Humbrechts consider outstanding. These include Clos Windsbuhl for Riesling and Clos Jebsal for Pinot Gris. The Humbrechts are fanatical about low yields that will permit a full expression of the estate's varied terroirs, and this allows them to produce Vendange Tardive and Sélection de Grains

Nobles wines even in vintages such as 1991 and '92 that were not especially good for late-harvested wines. In terms of concentration and richness, these wines are beyond compare, but the very ripe grapes often result in residual sugar remaining in the wines, which may not be to everyone's taste. Best years: 1998, '97, '96, '95, '94, '93, '92, '90, '89, '88, '87, '85, '83.

ZÖBINGEN

AUSTRIA, Niederösterreich, Kamptal

This village, close to the wine centre of LAN-GENLOIS, has one of Austria's greatest Riesling vineyards, the steep, terraced Heiligenstein. It produces wines with less opulence and more elegance than those from the top sites in the nearby WACHAU, and with astonishing aging potential. Best producers: BRÜNDLMAYER, Ehn, Hiedler, Jurtschitsch, Loimer.

CHRISTIAN ZÜNDEL

SWITZERLAND, Ticino, Beride
♟ *Cabernet Sauvignon, Merlot*

Although German speaking and with vineyards in the Italian-speaking province of Ticino, Zündel has an uncompromisingly French approach to winemaking. That may seem eccentric, but his Orizzonte (Horizon), Cabernet-Merlot blend is the region's most impressive red wine. Its big blackberry and plum fruit is well supported by spicy oak and it has enough tannin to need three or four years in bottle to give its best. Best years: (Orizzonte) 1997, '95.

ZINFANDEL

Zinfandel may be the Primitivo grape of southern Italy, but it has followed the example of many of its compatriots and made good in the New World. Grown and made by a mere handful of producers in South Africa, nevertheless, they produce some interesting examples, especially when well-oaked. A little Zinfandel is found in Australia, Mexico and Chile, but it is unshakably associated with California, where at times it seems cursed by its very versatility. It makes excellent sweetish 'blush' or rosé wines, mostly labelled White Zinfandel, fruity reds made using the Beaujolais method of carbonic maceration, headily alcoholic reds with enough tannin to cure leather,

and – last but not least – fortified wines styled after ruby or vintage-character ports. It can be cheap and cheerful or it can appear as pricy, classy, single-vineyard bottlings from top winemakers. Some is even made properly sweet, but this style is very much in the minority.

Except for the big burly styles found in Amador County, Sonoma County seems to have an edge over the rest of California, especially in the Sonoma Valley and Dry Creek Valley AVAs and other fairly cool areas. But good vineyards are pretty well scattered, and the largest plantings are in the Lodi AVA in San Joaquin County. Excellent vineyards exist, too, in parts of San Luis Obispo, notably around Paso Robles. After a long period of being unfashionable, there is now renewed interest in full-blooded red Zinfandels as the craze for Cabernet wines wanes.

VINTAGES French Wines

Vintage guides are only relevant to wines which have personality and individuality – to the top five or ten per cent of any one country's wine. Any mark given to a vintage is a broad generalization to steer you towards the best bottles – there are brilliant wines made in difficult years and disappointing wines in brilliant years. The highest marks are for vintages where the ripeness of the grapes is best balanced by the acidity of the juice – and, for red wines, the proper amount of tannin, giving wines which have the potential to age.

HOW TO READ THE CHART

Numerals (1–10) represent an overall rating for each year

▲ = not ready   ● = just ready   ★ = at peak   ▼ = past its best   ○ = not generally declared

	98	97	96	95	94	93	92	91	90	89
BORDEAUX										

The following ratings apply only to the top châteaux in each area. Vintages can vary a lot within the large Bordeaux region – a great year in Sauternes is not necessarily the same for the Médoc.

	98	97	96	95	94	93	92	91	90	89
Margaux	7 ▲	6 ▲	8 ▲	8 ▲	7 ▲	6 ●	4 ★	4 ★	10 ●	8 ●
St-Julien	7 ▲	6 ▲	9 ▲	8 ▲	7 ▲	6 ●	4 ★	4 ●	10 ●	9 ●
Pauillac/St-Estèphe	7 ▲	6 ▲	9 ▲	8 ▲	7 ▲	6 ●	4 ★	4 ●	10 ●	9 ●
Listrac/Moulis	7 ▲	6 ▲	8 ▲	7 ▲	6 ▲	5 ●	4 ★	4 ●	9 ●	8 ●
Graves/Pessac-Léognan (reds)	8 ▲	6 ▲	8 ▲	7 ▲	6 ▲	6 ●	4 ★	4 ●	8 ●	8 ●
Graves/Pessac-Léognan (whites)	9 ▲	5 ▲	8 ▲	8 ▲	8 ●	6 ●	4 ★	4 ★	9 ★	8 ★
St-Émilion	8 ▲	7 ▲	7 ▲	9 ▲	7 ▲	6 ●	4 ★	2 ★	10 ●	9 ●
Pomerol	8 ▲	7 ▲	7 ▲	9 ▲	8 ▲	6 ●	4 ★	2 ★	10 ●	9 ●
Barsac, Sauternes	7 ▲	9 ▲	9 ▲	7 ▲	5 ▲	4 ●	3 ★	3 ★	10 ●	9 ●

BURGUNDY

Red Burgundy is desperately unreliable so the vintage has been rated according to what can be expected from a decent domaine. White Burgundy is generally more reliable and top examples are some of the longest-living white wines in the world.

	98	97	96	95	94	93	92	91	90	89
Chablis	7 ▲	10 ▲	9 ▲	8 ●	6 ●	7 ●	7 ★	6 ▲	9 ★	8 ★
Côte de Nuits	7 ▲	8 ▲	9 ▲	8 ▲	5 ▲	8 ▲	6 ●	6 ▲	10 ▲	8 ★
Côte de Beaune (reds)	8 ▲	8 ▲	9 ▲	8 ▲	5 ●	8 ●	6 ★	7 ★	10 ▲	8 ★
Côte de Beaune (whites)	8 ▲	9 ▲	9 ▲	9 ▲	6 ●	7 ●	9 ★	6 ★	9 ★	8 ★
Côte Chalonnaise (reds)	7 ▲	7 ▲	8 ▲	8 ●	5 ●	7 ●	6 ▼	7 ▼	9 ★	8 ▼
Côte Chalonnaise (whites)	7 ▲	8 ▲	8 ▲	8 ●	6 ★	6 ★	8 ★	6 ★	8 ▼	9 ▼
Mâconnais (whites)	7 ▲	8 ▲	8 ▲	8 ●	7 ★	7 ★	8 ★	6 ▼	7 ▼	8 ★
Beaujolais Crus	8 ▲	7 ▲	8 ●	8 ●	5 ▲	7 ★	5 ▼	9 ★	6 ▼	8 ▼

	98	97	96	95	94	93	92	91	90	89

LOIRE

With so many different climates to be found in the vineyards of the Loire any vintage assessment is a broad generalization. In general Loire wines should be drunk young within a year of two of the harvest but the best wines in fine vintages will age well, in particular the Cabernet Franc reds and the sweet Chenin whites.

	98	97	96	95	94	93	92	91	90	89
Bourgueil, Chinon and Saumur-Champigny	8 ●	9 ●	10 ●	8 ●	4 ★	6 ●	5 ★	4 ★	9 ●	10 ●
Vouvray (whites)	6 ▲	9 ▲	9 ▲	9 ▲	8 ▲	6 ●	5 ●	4 ★	9 ▲	10 ▲
Anjou and Vouvray (sweet whites)	7 ▲	9 ▲	9 ▲	9 ▲	8 ▲	6 ●	5 ●	4 ★	9 ▲	10 ▲
Sancerre (reds)	7 ▲	8 ●	8 ●	7 ●	6 ★	6 ★	5 ★	7 ★	9 ★	8 ▼
Sancerre (whites)	8 ●	9 ●	9 ●	8 ●	6 ●	6 ●	5 ▲	7 ●	9 ★	8 ▼

RHÔNE

The Rhône Valley suffers fewer really difficult vintages than cooler parts of France, though rain can still be a problem as can rot. The Syrah-based reds of the northern Rhône take to aging well. Southern Rhône reds can age but mature sooner. White wines, especially those from the South, should be drunk young; the exceptions are white Hermitage and Château-Grillet.

	98	97	96	95	94	93	92	91	90	89
Côte-Rôtie	7 ▲	6 ▲	8 ▲	9 ▲	6 ▲	4 ★	6 ●	9 ●	8 ●	9 ●
Condrieu	8 ●	7 ●	9 ●	8 ★	8 ▼	5 ▼	7 ▼	9 ▼	8 ▼	9 ▼
Hermitage (reds)	7 ▲	6 ▲	8 ▲	9 ▲	6 ▲	3 ★	6 ●	8 ●	10 ●	9 ●
Hermitage (whites)	8 ▲	6 ▲	8 ▲	9 ▲	7 ▲	6 ●	6 ●	7 ●	10 ●	9 ●
Crozes-Hermitage (whites)	8 ▲	7 ▲	8 ▲	8 ●	7 ●	4 ★	6 ★	8 ★	9 ●	7 ★
Cornas	8 ▲	7 ▲	7 ▲	8 ▲	8 ▲	4 ★	6 ●	8 ●	9 ●	8 ●
St-Joseph (whites)	8 ▲	7 ▲	7 ▲	8 ●	7 ●	3 ★	6 ★	8 ★	9 ●	8 ★
Châteauneuf-du-Pape (reds)	9 ▲	7 ▲	6 ▲	9 ▲	7 ●	7 ●	5 ★	5 ★	10 ●	9 ●
Châteauneuf-du-Pape (whites)	8 ▲	7 ●	7 ●	8 ●	7 ★	6 ★	8 ▼	7 ▼	8 ▼	8 ▼

ALSACE

Simple Alsace wines are best drunk within two to four years of the harvest. Wines from the best Grands Crus and *lieux-dits* can be kept longer, as can the late-picked Vendange Tardive wines and the botrytized Sélections de Grains Nobles.

	98	97	96	95	94	93	92	91	90	89
Alsace Grand Cru	8 ▲	10 ▲	7 ▲	8 ▲	5 ●	6 ●	7 ●	5 ★	10 ●	9 ★
Vendange Tardive	8 ▲	9 ▲	7 ▲	8 ▲	9 ●	5 ●	5 ●	4 ★	9 ●	10 ●

CHAMPAGNE

Most Champagne is non-vintage and in this cold, northerly region it is blending (of different vintages and vineyards) that produces the most consistently elegant and ripe wine. Vintage wines are usually only 'declared' in the best years, several years after the harvest. A few Champagne houses will make vintage Champagne virtually every year.

	98	97	96	95	94	93	92	91	90	89
Vintage Champagne	8 ▲	7 ▲	9 ▲	7 ▲	5 ○	5 ▲	5 ●	6 ○	9 ●	8 ★

VINTAGES Rest of the World

HOW TO READ THE CHART

Numerals (1–10) represent an overall rating for each year

▲ = not ready   ● = just ready   ★ = at peak   ▼ = past its best   ○ = not generally declared

	98	97	96	95	94	93	92	91	90	89
ITALY										

Though vintages are of considerable importance for the best Italian wines, winemaking methods of individual producers differ so widely within the same DOCs that these ratings are only approximate.

	98	97	96	95	94	93	92	91	90	89
Barolo/Barbaresco	9 ▲	10 ▲	9 ▲	8 ▲	6 ▲	7 ●	4 ★	5 ●	10 ●	10 ●
Chianti Classico	7 ▲	10 ▲	8 ▲	9 ▲	7 ●	8 ●	5 ★	6 ★	10 ★	5 ★
Brunello di Montalcino/ Vino Nobile di Montepulciano	9 ▲	10 ▲	8 ▲	9 ▲	8 ▲	8 ●	5 ★	7 ★	10 ●	6 ★
Recioto della Valpolicella/ Ripasso della Valpolicella	7 ▲	10 ▲	7 ▲	10 ●	7 ★	8 ●	5★	5 ★	10 ★	6 ★
Amarone della Valpolicella	7 ▲	10 ▲	7 ▲	10 ▲	7 ●	8 ●	5★	5 ★	10 ●	6 ●

GERMANY

Since 1988 German vintages have been at least good, often very good or outstanding and fine Rieslings have been made in most regions. Germany's cool climate means there can be substantial variation between vintages in both style and quality but at the top estates improved viticulture and rigorous selection means poor Riesling vintages are a thing of the past.

	98	97	96	95	94	93	92	91	90	89
Mosel-Saar-Ruwer (QbA, Kabinett, Spätlese)	8 ▲	9 ▲	7 ▲	9 ▲	8 ●	9 ●	7 ★	6 ●	10 ▲	7 ★
Mosel (Auslese, Beerenauslese, Trockenbeerenauslese)	7 ▲	9 ▲	8 ▲	9 ▲	9 ▲	9 ▲	7 ●	6 ●	10 ▲	8 ●
Rhine (QbA, Kabinett, Spätlese)	8 ▲	9 ▲	8 ▲	7 ▲	7 ●	8 ●	9 ●	6 ●	10 ●	7 ★
Rhine (Auslese, Beerenauslese, Trockenbeerenauslese)	7 ▲	9 ▲	8 ▲	7 ▲	9 ▲	8 ▲	8 ●	6 ●	9 ●	9 ★

SPAIN (red wines)

A relatively even climate makes for less exaggerated vintage differences than in northern Europe. Many Spanish wines have traditionally been released when ready to drink, although this is changing slowly and an increasing number are now released early and need further bottle aging.

	98	97	96	95	94	93	92	91	90	89
Navarra	6 ▲	7 ▲	9 ▲	8 ●	8 ●	7 ●	7 ★	7 ★	8 ★	8 ★
Penedès	7 ▲	7 ▲	8 ▲	7 ▲	8 ●	7 ●	6 ●	8 ★	8 ★	6 ★
Ribera del Duero	7 ▲	6 ▲	9 ▲	8 ●	9 ●	4 ★	6 ●	8 ●	9 ●	6 ★
Rioja	6 ▲	7 ▲	8 ●	8 ●	9 ●	5 ★	6 ★	7 ●	7 ★	8 ★

	98	97	96	95	94	93	92	91	90	89

PORTUGAL (red wines)

Port is one of the great vintage wines though a vintage is only declared in exceptional years.

	98	97	96	95	94	93	92	91	90	89
Alentejo	7 ▲	8 ▲	6 ●	8 ●	7 ●	5 ★	6 ★	7 ★	9 ★	8 ★
Dão	7 ▲	8 ▲	8 ●	7 ●	7 ●	4 ★	7 ★	7 ★	6 ★	6 ★
Douro	7 ▲	8 ▲	7 ●	8 ●	9 ●	3 ●	8 ●	7 ●	7 ★	7 ★
Port	6 ▲	9 ▲	7 ○	8 ○	10 ▲	2 ○	9 ▲	8 ▲	6 ○	6 ○

USA

There are major weather variations in both California and the Pacific Northwest and vintage ratings are bound to be general.

	98	97	96	95	94	93	92	91	90	89
Napa Cabernet	8 ▲	8 ▲	7 ▲	8 ▲	9 ▲	7 ●	8 ●	9 ●	8 ★	5 ★
Sonoma Chardonnay	7 ▲	7 ▲	6 ●	8 ●	8 ●	7 ★	7 ★	9 ★	8 ▼	7 ▼
Carneros Pinot Noir	9 ▲	8 ▲	8 ●	8 ●	9 ●	7 ★	8 ★	9 ★	8 ★	8 ▼
Santa Barbara Pinot Noir	8 ▲	9 ▲	8 ●	8 ●	9 ●	7 ★	8 ★	9 ★	9 ★	8 ▼
Oregon Pinot Noir	6 ▲	6 ▲	7 ▲	5 ●	10 ●	6 ★	9 ★	8 ★	9 ★	8 ▼
Washington State Cabernet Sauvignon	9 ▲	8 ▲	9 ▲	8 ▲	9 ▲	7 ★	9 ●	8 ●	7 ★	9 ★

AUSTRALIA

In most instances in Australia the skill of the winemaker is more important than the vintage.

	98	97	96	95	94	93	92	91	90	89
Coonawarra Cabernet	9 ▲	7 ▲	8 ▲	5 ●	8 ▲	7 ●	7 ★	9 ★	10 ★	5 ▼
Hunter Semillon (unoaked)	9 ▲	7 ▲	8 ▲	8 ▲	7 ▲	7 ●	5 ●	9 ▲	6 ★	8 ●
Barossa Shiraz	10 ▲	8 ▲	9 ▲	8 ●	9 ●	7 ●	6 ★	8 ★	8 ★	5 ★
Padthaway Chardonnay	8 ●	9 ●	9 ★	8 ★	8 ★	7 ▼	6 ▼	8 ▼	10 ▼	6 ▼
Margaret River Cabernet Sauvignon	6 ▲	9 ▲	10 ▲	8 ▲	8 ●	9 ●	6 ●	9 ★	8 ★	8 ★

NEW ZEALAND

As winemaking expertise improves more New Zealand wines are showing some capacity for aging.

	98	97	96	95	94	93	92	91	90	89
Marlborough Sauvignon	7 ●	9 ★	9 ★	4 ▼	10 ★	7 ▼	6 ▼	10 ★	6 ▼	9 ▼
Hawke's Bay Cabernet	9 ▲	8 ●	8 ●	7 ★	8 ★	5 ★	5 ★	9 ★	7 ★	9 ★

SOUTH AFRICA

Most of South Africa's ageworthy red wines come from the Stellenbosch area. Most whites are for drinking young.

	98	97	96	95	94	93	92	91	90	89
Cape Cabernet Sauvignon	8 ▲	9 ▲	5 ●	9 ●	8 ●	6 ★	8 ★	8 ★	7 ★	8 ★
Cape Chardonnay	7 ●	9 ●	7 ★	7 ★	6 ▼	8 ▼	9 ▼	9 ▼	6 ▼	8 ▼

GLOSSARY

Acidity Naturally present in grapes; gives red wine an appetizing 'grip' and whites a refreshing tang. Too much can make a wine seem sharp but too little and it will be flabby.

Aging Essential for fine wines and for softening many everyday reds. May take place in vat, barrel or bottle, and may last for months or years. It has a mellowing effect on a wine but too long in storage, though, and the wine may lose its fruit.

Alcoholic content Alcoholic strength, sometimes expressed in degrees, equivalent to the percentage of alcohol in the total volume.

Alcoholic fermentation Biochemical process whereby yeasts, natural or added, convert the grape sugars into alcohol and carbon dioxide, transforming grape juice into wine. It normally stops when all the sugar has been converted or when the alcohol level reaches about 15 per cent.

American Viticultural Area (AVA) American appellation system introduced in the 1980s. AVA status requires that 85 per cent of grapes in a wine come from a specified region. It does not guarantee any standard of quality.

Appellation d'Origine Contrôlée (AC or AOC) Official designation in France guaranteeing a wine by geographical origin, grape variety and production method. When used loosely in a general wine context it means any legally defined wine area.

Assemblage Final blending of fine wines, especially Bordeaux wines and Champagne.

Auslese German and Austrian quality wine category for wines made from grapes 'selected' for higher sugar levels. The wines will be generally sweet.

Barrel aging Time spent maturing in wood, normally oak, during which the wines take on flavours from the wood.

Barrel fermentation Oak barrels may be used for fermentation instead of stainless steel to give a rich, oaky flavour to the wine.

Barrique The *barrique bordelaise* is the traditional Bordeaux oak barrel of 225 litres (50 gallons) capacity, used for aging and sometimes for fermenting wine.

Beerenauslese German and Austrian quality wine category for wines made from berries 'individually selected' for higher sweetness. The wines are sweet to very sweet.

Bereich German for region or district within a wine region.

Bin number Australian system used by wine companies to identify batches of wine.

Blanc de blancs White wine, especially Champagne, made only from white grapes. Blanc de Noirs is white wine from black grapes.

Blending The art of mixing together wines of different origin, styles or age, often to balance out acidity, weight etc.

Bodega Spanish winery or wine firm.

Botrytis *Botrytis cinerea* fungus which, in warm autumn weather, attacks white grapes, shrivels them and concentrates the sugars to produce quality sweet wines, as in Sauternes. Also called 'noble rot'.

Brut Term for 'dry', usually seen on Champagne labels and sparkling wines in the New World. In Champagne the term 'Extra Dry' is, in fact, slightly sweeter.

Canopy management Adjustments to alter the exposure of a vine's fruit and leaves to the sun, to improve quality, increase yield and help to control disease. Simpler measures include leaf trimming, early fruit culling and more general pruning.

Carbonic maceration Winemaking method traditional to Beaujolais and now widely used in warm wine regions all over the world. Bunches of grapes, uncrushed, are fermented whole in closed containers to give well-coloured, fruity wine for early drinking.

Cava Spanish Champagne-method fizz.

Cask Wooden (usually oak) barrel used for aging and storing wine. Known in France as *foudres*, Germany as *fuders* and Italy as *botti*.

Chai Bordeaux term for the building in which wine is stored.

Champagne method Traditional way of making sparkling wine by inducing a second fermentation in the bottle in which the wine will be sold.

Chaptalization Addition of sugar during fermentation to raise a wine's alcoholic strength. More necessary in cool climates where lack of sun produces insufficient natural sugar in the grape.

Château A wine-producing estate. Applied to all sizes of property, especially in Bordeaux.

Claret English term for red Bordeaux wine.

Clarification Term covering any winemaking process (such as filtering or fining) that involves the removal of solid matter either from the must or the wine.

Classico Italian heartland of a zone from where its best wines come.

Climat French term meaning a specifically defined area of a vineyard, often very small.

Clone Propagating vines by taking cuttings produces clones of the original plant. Vine nurseries now enable growers to order specific clones to suit conditions in their vineyards. Through this clonal selection it is possible to control yield, flavour and general quality.

Clos Term for a vineyard that is (or was) wall-enclosed; traditional to Burgundy.

Cold fermentation Long, slow fermentation at low temperature to extract maximum freshness from the grapes. Crucial for whites in hot climates.

Corked/corky Wine fault derived from a cork that has become contaminated, usually with Trichloranisole or TCA, and nothing to do with pieces of cork in the wine. The mouldy, stale smell is unmistakable.

Commune A French village and its surrounding area or parish.

Cosecha Spanish for 'vintage'.

Côtes/Coteaux French for 'slopes'. Hillside vineyards generally produce better wine than low-lying ones.

Crémant Champagne-method sparkling wine from French regions other than Champagne, e.g. Crémant de Bourgogne.

Crianza Spanish term used to describe both the process of aging a wine and the youngest official category of matured wine. A Crianza wine is aged in barrel, tank and/or bottle for at least two years.

Cross, Crossing Grape bred from two *Vitis vinifera* varieties.

Cru French for 'growth'. Used to describe a wine from a single vineyard.

Cru Bourgeois In Bordeaux, a quality rating immediately below Cru Classé.

Cru Classé Literally 'Classed Growth', indicating that a vineyard is included in the top-quality rating system of its region.

Cuve close Less expensive method of making sparkling wine where the second fermentation takes place in closed tanks, not in bottle as in the Champagne method.

Cuvée Contents of a *cuve* or vat. The term usually indicates a blend, which may mean different grape varieties or simply putting together the best barrels of wine.

Demi-sec Confusingly, it means medium tending to sweet, rather than medium-dry.

Denominacón de Origen (DO) The main quality classification for Spanish wine. Rules specify each region's boundaries, grape varieties, vine-growing and winemaking methods.

Denominaçao de Origem Controlada (DOC) Portugal's top quality classification. Rules specify each region's boundaries, grapes, vine-growing and winemaking methods.

Denominacíon de Origen Calificada (DOC) New Spanish quality wine category, one step up from DO. So far only the Rioja DO has been promoted to DOC.

Denominazione di Origine Controllata (DOC) Italian quality wine classification for wines of controlled origin, grape types and style.

Denominazione di Origine Controllata e Garantita (DOCG) Top Italian quality wine classification meant to be one notch above DOC.

Domaine Estate, especially in Burgundy.

Einzellage German for an individual vineyard site, which is generally farmed by several growers. The name is generally preceded by that of the village, e.g. Wehlener Sonnenuhr is the Sonnenuhr vineyard in the village of Wehlen.

Eiswein Rare German and Austrian wine made from grapes harvested and pressed while still frozen, thus concentrating the sweetness. Known as icewine in Canada.

Élevage French term covering all wine-making stages between fermentation and bottling.

Embotellado de/en Origen Spanish term for estate-bottled.

Engarrafado na Origem Portuguese term for estate-bottled.

Enologist Wine scientist or technician.

Espumoso Spanish for 'sparkling'.

Estate-bottled Wine made from grapes grown on the estate's vineyards and then bottled where it has been made. In France, this is indicated on the label as *mis en bouteilles* followed by *au domaine, au château*.

Fermentation See Alcoholic fermentation, Malolactic fermentation.

Filtering Removal of yeasts, solids and any impurities from a wine before bottling.

Fining Method of clarifying wine by adding coagulants, traditionally egg-whites, to the surface. As these fall through the wine they collect impurities.

Flor Special film of yeast that grows on the surface of certain wines when in barrel, especially sherry. Protects the wine from air, and imparts a unique taste.

Flying winemaker Term coined in the late 1980s to describe enologists, many of them Australian-trained, brought in to improve quality in many of the world's under-performing wine regions.

Fortified wine Wine which has high-alcohol grape spirit added, usually before the initial alcoholic fermentation is completed, thereby preserving sweetness.

Frizzante Italian term for lightly sparkling wine.

Garrafeira Portuguese term for high-quality wine with at least half a per cent of alcohol higher than the required minimum, that has had at least three years' aging for reds, and at least one year for whites.

Geographical Indication (GI) Australian term to indicate the origin of a wine.

Gran Reserva Top quality, mature Spanish wine from an especially good vintage, with at least five years' aging (cask and bottle) for reds, and four for whites.

Grand Cru 'Great growth'; the top quality classification in Burgundy, used less precisely in Alsace, Bordeaux and Champagne.

Grand vin Term used in Bordeaux to indicate a producer's top wine. Usually bears a château name.

Hectolitres 100 litres; 22 imperial gallons or 133 standard 75-cl bottles.

Hybrid Grape bred from an American vine species and European *Vitis vinifera*.

Indicaçao de Proveniência Regulamentada (IPR) Official Portuguese category for wine regions aspiring to DOC status.

Indicazione Geografica Tipica (IGT) A quality level for Italian wines (roughly equivalent to French vin de pays) in between vino da tavola and DOC.

Kabinett Lowest level of German QmP wines.

Late harvest Late-harvested grapes contain more sugar and concentrated flavours; the term is often used for sweetish New World wines.

Lees Coarse sediment – dried yeasts etc – thrown by wine in a cask and left behind after racking. Some wines stay on the lees for as long as possible to take on extra flavour.

Liquoroso Italian term for wines high in alcohol, often – but not always – fortified.

Malolactic fermentation Secondary fermentation whereby sharp, appley malic acid is converted into mild lactic acid and carbon dioxide; occurs after alcoholic fermentation. It is encouraged in red wines, softening them and reducing their acidity, but often prevented in whites to preserve a fresh taste, especially in wines made in warm regions, where natural acidity will be lower.

Maturation The beneficial aging of wine.

Meritage American, primarily Californian, term for red or white wines made from Bordeaux grape varieties.

Mousseux French term for sparkling wine.

Must The mixture of grape juice, skins, pips and pulp produced after crushing (but prior to completion of fermentation), which will eventually become wine.

Négociant French term for merchant or shipper who buys in wine from growers, then matures, maybe blends and bottles it for sale.

Noble rot See Botrytis.

Nouveau, novello French and Italian terms for new wine. Wine for drinking very young, from November in year of vintage.

Oak Traditional wood for wine casks. During aging or fermenting it gives flavours, such as vanilla and tannin, to the wines. The newer the wood, the greater its impact. French oak is often preferred for aging fine wine. American oak is cheaper but can give strong vanilla overtones.

Oechsle German scale for measuring must weight; in effect, it indicates the level of sweetness in the juice. Each quality category has a minimum required Oechsle degree.

Oxidation Over-exposure of wine to air, causing bacterial decay and loss of fruit and flavour. Often characterized by a rather sherry-like aroma.

Passito Italian term for dried or semi-dried grapes, or strong, sweet wine made from them.

Pétillant French for semi-sparkling wine.

Phylloxera Vine aphid (*Phylloxera vastatrix*) which devastated viticulture worldwide in the late 1800s. Since then, the vulnerable European *Vitis vinifera* has been grafted on to phylloxera-resistant American rootstocks. Phylloxera has never reached Chile and parts of Australia, so vines there are ungrafted and can live up to twice as long.

Prädikat The grade, based on must weight, that defines top-quality wine in Germany and Austria. The grades are, in ascending order of ripeness in the grapes, and therefore sweetness: Kabinett, Spätlese, Auslese, Beerenauslese, Eiswein, Ausbruch (for Austria only) and Trockenbeerenauslese.

Premier Cru 'First growth'; the top quality classification in Bordeaux, but second to Grand Cru in Burgundy. Also used in other parts of France, not always with the same precision.

Prohibition 18th Amendment to the US

Constitution, passed in 1920, banning alcoholic beverages; the measure ruined most wineries, but some survived making grape juice, communion and medicinal wines. Repealed in 1933.

Qualitätswein bestimmter Anbaugebiete German wine classification (abbreviated to QbA) for 'quality wine from designated regions' – the middle level, for fairly ordinary wines, though some good experimental wines can also be QbA.

Qualitätswein mit Prädikat German wine classification (abbreviated to QmP) for 'quality wine with distinction' (the top level), which is further subdivided into the various categories of Prädikat.

Quinta Portuguese farm or wine estate.

Racking Gradual clarification of a quality wine as part of the maturation process. The wine is transferred from one barrel to another, leaving the lees or sediment behind. Racking also produces aeration necessary for the aging process, softens tannins and helps develop further flavours.

Rancio Style of wine that is deliberately oxidized; either naturally strong or fortified, it is aged in the sun in glass bottles, earthenware jars or wooden barrels.

Récoltant French for 'grower'. They may make their own wine or sell the grapes to a merchant.

Reserva In Spain, quality wine from a good vintage with at least three years' aging (cask and bottle) for reds, and two for whites. In Portugal it designates wine that has an alcohol level at least half a per cent higher than the minimum for the region.

Réserve The term should indicate the wine has been aged longer in oak but many New World producers use it freely on their wine labels to indicate different wine styles or a special selection rather than a better wine. It has no legal meaning. Other similar terms are Private Reserve and Special Selection.

Ripasso Valpolicella wine refermented on the lees of Amarone della Valpolicella to give extra richness.

Riserva Italian term meaning wines aged for a specific number of years according to DOC(G) laws.

Rootstock The root stump of the vine on to which the fruiting branches are grafted. Most rootstocks are from phylloxera-resistant American vines.

Rosado, rosato Spanish (or Portuguese) and Italian for pink wine or rosé.

Sec French for 'dry'. When applied to

Champagne, it actually means medium-dry.

Second wine Wine from a designated vineyard which is sold separately from the main production, under a different name. Usually lighter and quicker-maturing than the main wine.

Sekt German term for sparkling wine.

Solera Blending system used for sherry and some other fortified wines. When mature wine is run off a cask for bottling, only a quarter or so of the volume is taken, and the space is filled with similar but younger wine from another cask, which in turn is topped up from an even younger cask, and so on.

Spätlese German quality wine category for wines made from 'late-picked' grapes.

Spumante Italian for sparkling wine.

Sugar Naturally present in grapes. Transformed during fermentation into alcohol and carbon dioxide.

Sulphur Sulphur is commonly used during vinification as a disinfectant for equipment; with fresh grapes and wine as an anti-oxidant; and added as sulphur dioxide to the must to arrest or delay fermentation.

Supérieur French term for wines with a higher alcohol content than the basic AC.

Superiore Italian term for wines with higher alcohol, maybe more aging too.

Super-Tuscan English term for high-quality non-DOC Tuscan wine.

Sur lie French for 'on the lees', meaning wine bottled direct from the fermentation vat or cask to gain extra flavour from the lees. Common with quality Muscadet, white Burgundy, similar barrel-aged whites and, increasingly, commercial bulk wines.

Tafelwein German for 'table wine', the most basic quality designation.

Tannin Harsh, bitter element in red wine, derived from grape skins, pips, stems and from aging in oak barrels; softens with time and is essential for a wine's long-term aging.

Terroir A French term used to denote the combination of soil, climate and exposure to the sun – that is, the natural physical environment of the vine.

Trocken German for 'dry'. Applied to new-style German wines made dry in an effort to make them better matches for food.

Trockenbeerenauslese German quality wine category for wines made from noble-rotted single grapes – the highest level of sweetness.

Varietal The character of wine derived from the grape; also wine made from, and named after, a single or dominant grape

variety and usually containing at least 75 per cent of that variety. The minimum percentage varies slightly between countries and, in the USA, between states.

Vendange tardive French for 'late harvest'; grapes are left on the vine after the normal harvest time to concentrate the flavours and sugars.

Vieilles vignes Wine from mature vines.

Vin Délimité de Qualité Supérieure Second category of French quality control for wines, below AC, abbreviated to VDQS.

Vin de paille Wine made by drying the grapes on straw (*paille*) before fermentation. This concentrates the sugar in the grapes: the resulting wines are sweet but slightly nutty. Mostly from the Jura region of France.

Vin de pays French for 'country wine'. Although it is the third and bottom category for quality in the official classification of French wines, it includes some first-class wines which don't follow local AC rules.

Vin doux naturel (VDN) French sweet wine fortified with grape spirit. Mostly from Languedoc-Roussillon.

Viña Spanish for 'vineyard'. Often loosely used in names of wines not actually from a vineyard of that name.

Vinification The process of turning grapes into wine.

Vino da tavola Italian for 'table wine'. Quality may be basic or exceptional.

Vino tipico New Italian category for vino da tavola with some regional characteristics.

Vintage The year's grape harvest, also used to describe the wine of a single year.

Viticulture Vine-growing and vineyard management.

Vitis vinifera The species of vine, native to Europe and Central Asia, responsible for most of the world's quality wine, as opposed to other species such as the native American *Vitis labrusca*, which is still used in the eastern USA to make grape juice and sweetish wines but which is more suited to juice and jelly manufacture.

Wine of Origin (WO) South African equivalent of Appellation Contrôlée.

Yeast Organism which, in the wine process, causes grape juice to ferment. In the New World it is common to start fermentation with cultured yeasts, rather than rely on the natural yeasts present in the winery, known as ambient yeasts.

Yield The amount of fruit, and ultimately wine, produced from a vineyard, generally ranging between 40 and 100 hectolitres per hectare.

INDEX

Numbers in **bold** refer to main entries. Numbers in *italic* refer to photograph and label captions.

Acknowledgments

The publishers would like to thank the following for their help: Rachael Clifford, Kevin Judd of Cloudy Bay; Rebecca Khan, Claire Langford, David Moore, Nadja Radulovic, Phillip Williamson.
Photographs of Oz Clarke by Stephen Bartholomew 6, 27, 28. Photographs of bottles by Steve Marwood 14, 15, 18, 19. All other photographs supplied by Cephas Picture Library. All photographs by Mick Rock except: Jerry Alexander 352; Nigel Blythe 8 (left), 286, 308; Andy Christodolo 4, 9, 198, 218, 229, 370, 376; Bruce Fleming 106, 128, 137, 264; Bruce Jenkins 6 (right); Kevin Judd 2–3, 3, 5, 6 (left), 48, 185, 234, 392; Herbert Lehmann 305; Steven Morris 10 (left), 372, 380; R & K Muschenetz, 44, 46, 396; Alain Proust 5, 28, 54–55, 186, 354; Ted Stefanski 212.